Sommario

Nomenclatura delle località citate e carta della regione
Alphabetisches Ortsverzeichnis und Übersichtskarte

Inhaltsverzeichnis

MAJOR ROADS AND PRINCIPAL SHIPPING ROUTES

Motorway and access roads

Road number A 4. T 35. N 2

Mileage 20

PRINCIPALES ROUTES ET LIAISONS MARITIMES

Autoroute et accès

N° de route A 4. T 35. N 2

Distance en miles 20

PRINCIPALI STRADE E ITINERARI MARITTIMI

Autostrada e accessi

Numero di strada A 4. T 35. N 2

Distanza in miglia 20

HAUPTVERKEHRSSTRAßEN UND SCHIFFSVERBINDUNGEN

Autobahn mit Anschlußstelle

Straßennummer A 4. T 35. N 2

Entfernung in Meilen 20

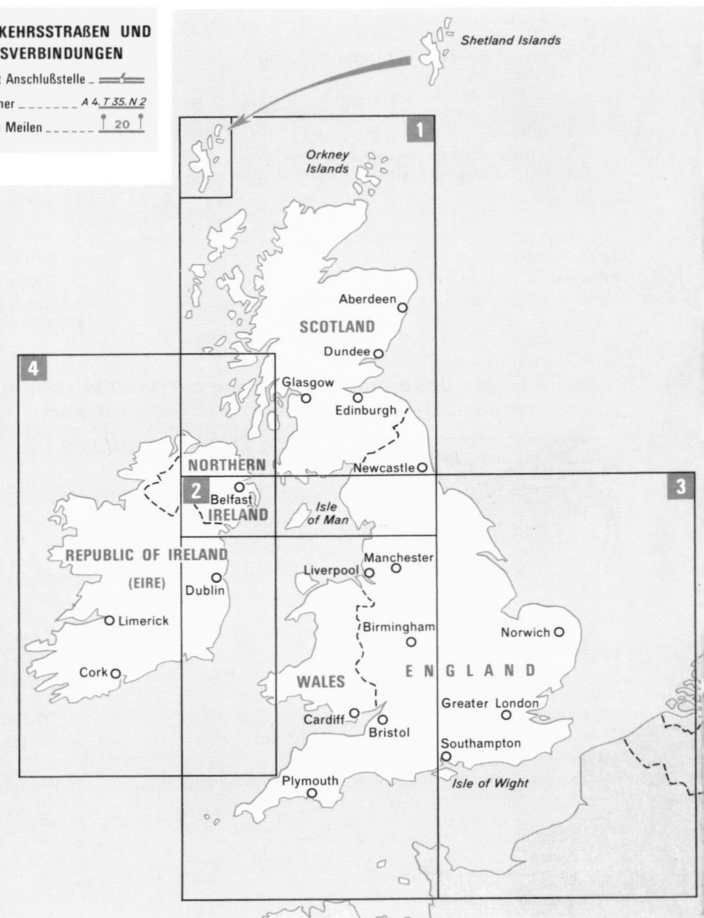

GREAT BRITAIN : the maps and town plans in the Great Britain Section of this Guide are based upon the Ordnance Survey of Great Britain with the permission of the Controller of Her Majesty's Stationery Office. Crown Copyright reserved.

NORTHERN IRELAND : the maps and town plans in the Northern Ireland Section of this Guide are based upon the Ordnance Survey of Northern Ireland with the sanction of the Controller of H.M. Stationery Office.

REPUBLIC OF IRELAND : the maps and town plans in the Republic of Ireland Section of this Guide are based upon the Ordnance Survey of Ireland by permission of the Government of the Republic, Permit number 2909.

SHETLAND ISLANDS

Unst
Yell
Whalsay
Mainland
Lerwick
Kirkwall
Aberdeen

ORKNEY ISLANDS

Westray
Sanday
Rousay
Stronsay
Mainland
Stromness
Kirkwall
Lerwick
Aberdeen
Hoy

Thurso
A 836
A 882
Wick
A 9
Loch Shin
Brora
Stornoway
Lewis
NORTH MINCH
Tarbert
Ullapool
A 835
Garve
North Uist
Lochmaddy
Uig
Skye
Portree
Elgin
Banff
Fraserburgh
Nairn
Keith
A 98
Inverness
A 96
Kyle of Lochalsh
A 82
Loch Ness
A 95
South Uist
Lochboisdale
Sea of the Hebrides
Armadale
A 87
Spey
Rhum
Mallaig
Invergarry
Kingussie
ABERDEEN
Lerwick
Kirkwall
Castlebay
A 86
Dee
A 830
Fort William
Stonehaven
A 9
A 92
Coll
SCOTLAND
Tiree
Mull
Loch Tay
Craignure
Oban
A 85
A 82
DUNDEE
A 849
Perth
A 85
Lochearnhead
St. Andrews
A 816
A 83
A 84
A 9
A 91
Tarbet
Colonsay
Stirling
Lochgilphead
Kirkcaldy
Dunfermline
Falkirk
Greenock
Port Askaig
Jura
Skelmorlie
GLASGOW
Tarbert
M 8
EDINBURGH
Rothesay
Largs
Motherwell
Islay
Millport
Berwick upon Tweed
Port Ellen
A 7
A 83
Ardrossan
A 70
Peebles
A 699
Brodick
A 74
Galashiels
Arran
A 77
A 72
NORTH CHANNEL
Ayr
Abington
Hawick
A 698
Campbeltown
Douglas
A 713
A 1
A 702
A 701
A 68
Coleraine
A 2
A 77
New Galloway
Dumfries
Bergen
Stavanger
Oslo
Kristiansand
Esbjerg
A 26
Waterfoot
A 74
A 7
A 75
Cairnryan
A 69
Tynemouth
Ballymena
A 6
Larne
Stranraer
A 75
CARLISLE
NEWCASTLE
A 8
SUNDERLAND
Liverpool
Douglas
A 596
Penrith
Lough Neagh
Workington
A 66
Bangor
Ballygawley
BELFAST
Whitehaven
A 595
Keswick
A 66
Darlington
M 1
A 3
Strangford Lough
M 6
Armagh
Banbridge
ENGLAND
A 25
Monaghan
Isle of Man
Kendal
A 1
N 2
Newcastle
Ardrossan
Belfast
Dublin
Douglas
A 65
A 2
Barrow in Furness
Liverpool
Dundalk
Heysham
Lancaster
A 1
M 1

2
BELFAST
Ardrossan
Bangor
Armagh
Banbridge
Monaghan
Newcastle
Dundalk
Kells
Drogheda
River Boyne
DUBLIN
Naas
Bray
Wicklow
Carlow
Arklow
Enniscorthy
Wexford
Rosslare
Isle of Man
Douglas
IRISH SEA
ST GEORGE'S CHANNEL
le Havre
Workington
Whitehaven
Penrith
Keswick
Kendal
Darlington
ENGL
Barrow in Furness
Heysham
Lancaster
Wharfe
Harrogate
BLACKPOOL
PRESTON
BRADFORD
LEED
Burnley
Halifax
Southport
BOLTON
Wakefie
LIVERPOOL
MANCHESTER
Birkenhead
Stockport
SHEFFIE
Warrington
Chester
Mold
Wrexham
Holyhead
Colwyn Bay
Caernarfon
Matlock
STOKE
ON TRENT
DERBY
Shrewsbury
Dolgellau
Welshpool
WOLVERHAMPTON
Dudley
BIRMINGHAM
COVENTRY
Aberystwyth
Ludlow
Warwick
Llandrindod Wells
Severn
Worcester
Stratford on Avon
WALES
Wye
Fishguard
Hereford
Carmarthen
Brecon
Ross
Gloucester
Cheltenham
Milford Haven
Merthyr Tydfil
THAMES
Swindon
SWANSEA
Newport
Cork
CARDIFF
BRISTOL
Bath
Bristol Channel
Ilfracombe
Minehead
Wells
Taunton
Salisbury
Yeovil
Avon
Bude
EXETER
Honiton
Dorchester
BOURNEMOUTH
Exmouth
Weymouth
Newquay
Torquay
PLYMOUTH
Penzance
Falmouth
ENGLIS
St. Malo
Roscoff
Isles of Scilly
Alderney
Cherbourg
Guernsey
Sark
St.Peter-Port
Jersey
St.Hélier
St.Malo

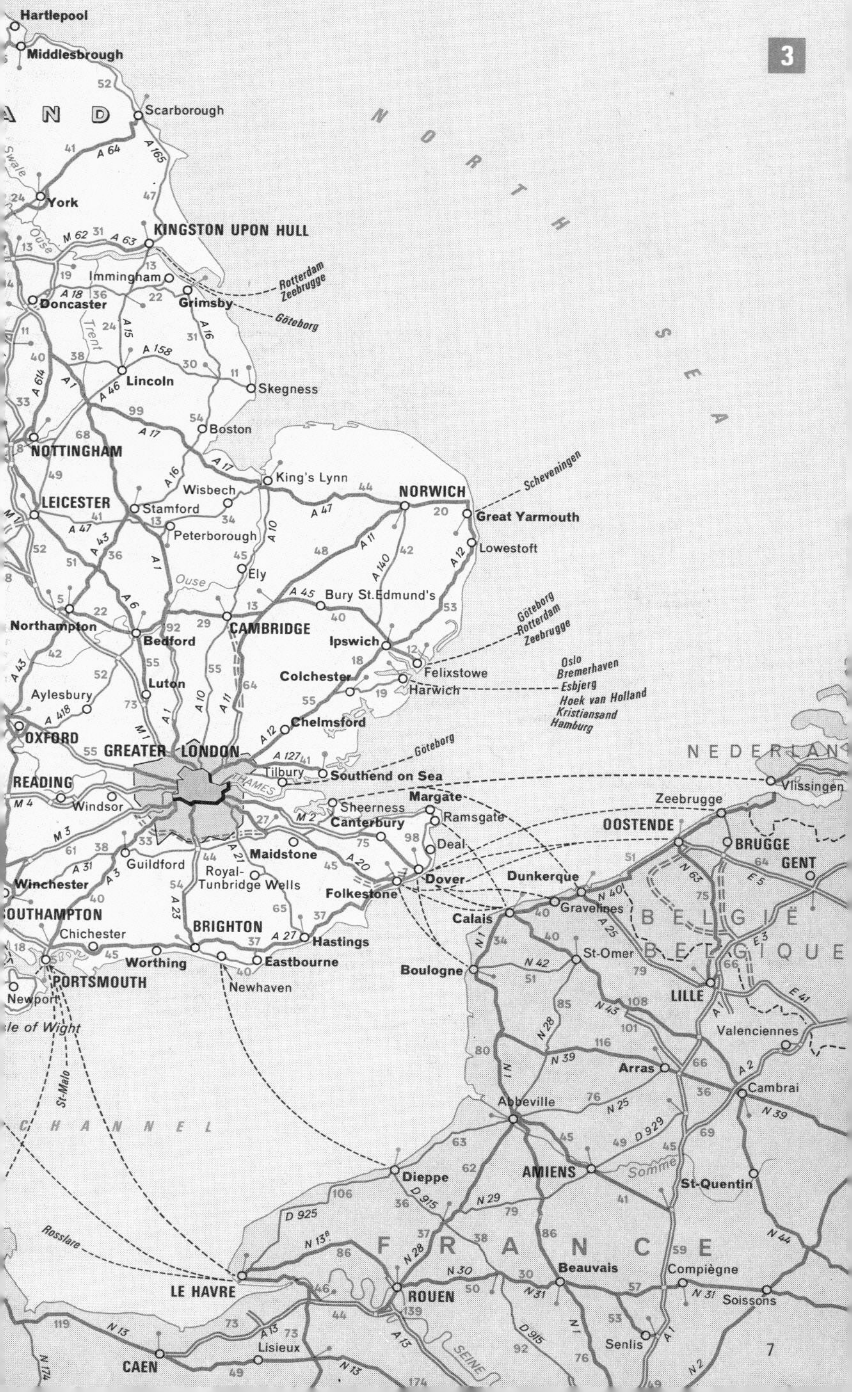

NORTH SEA

CHANNEL

NEDERLAND

BELGIË BELGIQUE

FRANCE

Hartlepool
Middlesbrough
Scarborough
York
KINGSTON UPON HULL
Immingham
Grimsby
Doncaster
Lincoln
Skegness
Boston
NOTTINGHAM
King's Lynn
Wisbech
LEICESTER
Stamford
Peterborough
NORWICH
Great Yarmouth
Lowestoft
Ely
Bury St. Edmund's
Northampton
Bedford
CAMBRIDGE
Ipswich
Felixstowe
Harwich
Colchester
Luton
Aylesbury
OXFORD
Chelmsford
GREATER LONDON
Tilbury
Southend on Sea
READING
Windsor
Sheerness
Margate
Ramsgate
Canterbury
Deal
Maidstone
Guildford
Royal-Tunbridge Wells
Dover
Folkestone
Winchester
SOUTHAMPTON
Chichester
BRIGHTON
Hastings
Worthing
Eastbourne
Newhaven
PORTSMOUTH
Newport
Isle of Wight

Swale
Ouse
Trent
Thames

Rotterdam
Zeebrugge
Göteborg
Scheveningen
Oslo
Bremerhaven
Esbjerg
Hoek van Holland
Kristiansand
Hamburg
St-Malo
Rosslare

Vlissingen
Zeebrugge
OOSTENDE
BRUGGE
GENT
Dunkerque
Gravelines
Calais
St-Omer
Boulogne
LILLE
Valenciennes
Arras
Cambrai
Abbeville
Dieppe
AMIENS
St-Quentin
Somme
LE HAVRE
ROUEN
Beauvais
Compiègne
Soissons
Senlis
CAEN
Lisieux
Seine

4
ATLANTIC OCEAN
NORTH CHANNEL
IRISH SEA
ST GEORGE'S CHANNEL
CELTIC SEA
NORTHERN IRELAND
EIRE
Oban
Mull
Colonsay
Jura
Lochgilphead
Port Askaig
Tarbert
Islay
A 83
Campbeltown
Coleraine
Waterfoot
Londonderry
Letterkenny
Ballymena
Larne
Cairnryan
Stranraer
Liverpool
Douglas
Donegal
Omagh
Lough Neagh
Bangor
BELFAST
Ballygawley
Enniskillen
Strangford Lough
Sligo
Armagh
Banbridge
Ballina
Monaghan
Newcastle
L. Allen
Boyle
Cavan
Dundalk
Westport
L. Mask
Edgeworthstown
Kells
Drogheda
Roscommon
Clifden
L. Corrib
L. Ree
Mullingar
River Boyne
Athlone
Galway
DUBLIN
Ballinasloe
Tullamore
Liverpool
Holyhead
Douglas
Naas
Bray
Lisdoonvarna
River Shannon
Roscrea
Ennis
Wicklow
Kilkee
Carlow
Thurles
Arklow
LIMERICK
Kilkenny
Cashel
R. Barrow
Enniscorthy
Tralee
Cahir
Dingle
Wexford
Carrick on Suir
Killarney
Fermoy
Waterford
Rosslare
R. Blackwater
Lismore
Youghal
CORK
Cobh
Glengarriff
Bantry
Fishguard
Milford Haven
Swansea
le Havre

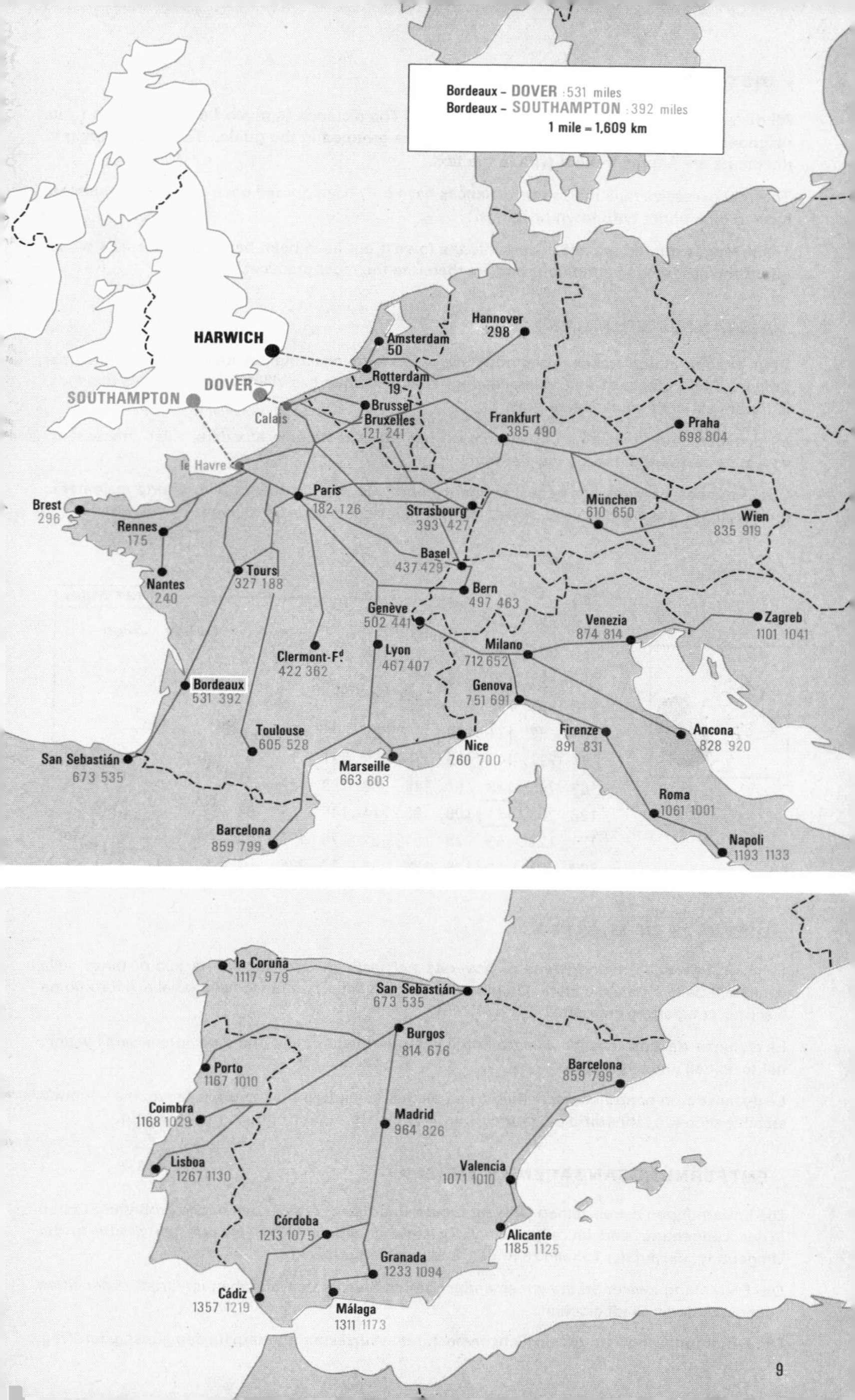
Bordeaux - DOVER : 531 miles
Bordeaux - SOUTHAMPTON : 392 miles
1 mile = 1,609 km
HARWICH
DOVER
SOUTHAMPTON
Calais
le Havre
Amsterdam 50
Rotterdam 19
Hannover 298
Brussel Bruxelles 121 241
Frankfurt 385 490
Praha 698 804
Paris 182 126
Strasbourg 393 427
München 610 650
Wien 835 919
Brest 296
Rennes 175
Nantes 240
Tours 327 188
Basel 437 429
Bern 497 463
Genève 502 441
Venezia 874 814
Zagreb 1101 1041
Clermont-Fd 422 362
Lyon 467 407
Milano 712 652
Bordeaux 531 392
Genova 751 691
Toulouse 605 528
Firenze 891 831
Ancona 828 920
San Sebastián 673 535
Nice 760 700
Marseille 663 603
Roma 1061 1001
Barcelona 859 799
Napoli 1193 1133
la Coruña 1117 979
San Sebastián 673 535
Burgos 814 676
Porto 1167 1010
Barcelona 859 799
Coimbra 1168 1029
Madrid 964 826
Lisboa 1267 1130
Valencia 1071 1010
Córdoba 1213 1075
Alicante 1185 1125
Granada 1233 1094
Cádiz 1357 1219
Málaga 1311 1173

DISTANCES

All distances in this edition are quoted in miles. The distance is given from each town to its neighbours and to the capital of each region as grouped in the guide. Towns appearing in the charts are printed in bold type in the text.

To avoid excessive repetition some distances have only been quoted once — you may therefore have to look under both town headings.

The mileages quoted are not necessarily the lowest but have been based on the roads which afford the best driving conditions and are therefore the most practical.

DISTANCES EN MILES

Pour chaque région traitée, vous trouverez au texte de chacune des localités sa distance par rapport à la capitale et aux villes environnantes. Lorsque ces villes sont celles des tableaux, leur nom est écrit en caractère gras.

La distance d'une localité à une autre n'est pas toujours répétée aux deux villes intéressées : voyez au texte de l'une ou de l'autre.

Ces distances ne sont pas nécessairement comptées par la route la plus courte mais par la plus pratique, c'est-à-dire celle offrant les meilleures conditions de roulage.

	Belfast	Cork	Dublin	Dundalk	Galway	Killarney	Limerick	Londonderry	Omagh	Sligo	Tullamore
Cork	253										
Dublin	103	161									
Dundalk	52	201	51								
Galway	195	119	132	155							
Killarney	270	55	190	218	126						
Limerick	201	62	121	149	57	69					
Londonderry	71	277	145	96	176	290	221				
Omagh	69	245	113	64	146	258	189	32			
Sligo	128	203	131	106	88	214	145	88	68		
Tullamore	131	122	59	79	81	139	70	155	123	94	
Waterford	200	77	99	148	134	116	77	236	204	175	81

131 Miles

Dublin - Sligo

DISTANZE IN MIGLIA

Per ciascuna delle regioni trattate, troverete nel testo di ogni località la sua distanza dalla capitale e dalle città circostanti. Quando queste città sono comprese nelle tabelle, il loro nome è scritto in carattere grassetto.

La distanza da una località all'altra non è sempre ripetuta nelle due città interessate : vedere nel testo dell'una o dell'altra.

Le distanze non sono necessariamente calcolate seguendo il percorso più breve, ma vengono stabilite secondo l'itinerario più pratico, che offre cioè le migliori condizioni di viaggio.

ENTFERNUNGSANGABEN IN MEILEN

Die Entfernungen der einzelnen Orte zur Landeshauptstadt und zu den nächstgrößeren Städten in der Umgebung sind im allgemeinen Ortstext angegeben. Die Namen der Städte in der Umgebung, die auf der Tabelle zu finden sind, sind fettgedruckt.

Die Entfernung zweier Städte voneinander können Sie aus den Angaben im Ortstext der einen oder der anderen Stadt ersehen.

Die Entfernungsangaben gelten nicht immer für den kürzesten, sondern für den günstigsten Weg.

DISTANCES BETWEEN MAJOR TOWNS

DISTANCES ENTRE PRINCIPALES VILLES

DISTANZE TRA LE PRINCIPALI CITTÀ

ENTFERNUNGEN ZWISCHEN DEN GRÖSSEREN STÄDTEN

	Aberdeen	Ayr	Birmingham	Blackpool	Brighton	Bristol	Cambridge	Cardiff	Carlisle	Coventry	Dover	Dumfries	Dundee	Edinburgh	Glasgow	Inverness	Ipswich	Kingston upon Hull	Leeds	Leicester	Liverpool	London	Manchester	Middlesbrough	Newcastle	Norwich	Nottingham	Oban	Oxford	Plymouth	Portsmouth	Sheffield	Southampton	Stoke on Trent	Swansea
Ayr	175																																		
Birmingham	422	290																																	
Blackpool	321	189	126																																
Brighton	587	455	170	291																															
Bristol	502	370	84	206	150																														
Cambridge	461	353	110	213	111	164																													
Cardiff	523	391	105	227	182	43	196																												
Carlisle	226	94	196	95	361	276	259	297																											
Coventry	440	308	23	144	148	91	88	118	214																										
Dover	615	483	198	319	81	202	128	234	389	176																									
Dumfries	205	59	231	130	396	311	294	332	35	249	424																								
Dundee	64	115	362	261	527	442	393	463	166	380	555	145																							
Edinburgh	124	77	294	193	443	374	337	395	98	312	471	77	56																						
Glasgow	141	34	292	191	457	373	355	394	96	310	486	75	81	43																					
Inverness	106	199	457	356	622	537	496	558	261	475	650	240	130	159	168																				
Ipswich	514	406	163	266	132	198	53	230	312	141	129	347	446	390	408	549																			
Kingston upon Hull	359	251	138	140	229	219	130	240	157	139	258	192	291	235	253	394	162																		
Leeds	328	220	113	84	243	194	143	215	126	114	271	161	260	204	222	363	196	60																	
Leicester	417	309	41	143	153	117	68	146	215	26	181	250	349	293	311	452	121	86	93																
Liverpool	353	221	99	57	264	179	199	200	127	117	292	162	293	225	223	388	252	126	70	116															
London	537	405	120	241	54	125	60	157	311	98	75	346	477	393	408	572	73	180	193	103	214														
Manchester	346	214	86	50	251	166	171	187	120	104	279	155	286	218	216	381	224	98	42	103	36	201													
Middlesbrough	269	186	170	121	300	251	194	272	94	171	328	127	201	145	188	304	247	85	61	150	148	250	120												
Newcastle	232	147	202	136	332	283	226	304	58	203	360	88	164	108	149	267	279	124	93	182	180	282	152	39											
Norwich	491	383	158	249	174	222	61	254	289	143	171	324	423	367	385	526	42	141	173	117	242	112	207	224	256										
Nottingham	391	283	50	135	182	143	87	164	189	55	210	224	323	267	285	426	140	87	67	24	110	132	69	124	156	123									
Oban	175	124	385	284	550	466	448	487	189	403	579	168	115	122	93	114	501	346	315	404	316	501	309	281	242	478	378								
Oxford	487	355	63	191	99	69	78	101	261	50	151	296	427	359	357	522	129	183	158	68	164	58	151	215	247	136	97	450							
Plymouth	615	483	197	319	213	120	282	156	389	204	320	424	555	487	485	650	316	332	307	230	292	243	279	364	396	340	256	578	187						
Portsmouth	570	438	146	274	49	97	134	138	344	133	130	379	510	442	441	605	161	266	241	151	247	77	234	298	330	192	180	534	82	170					
Sheffield	367	266	88	102	218	169	120	190	172	89	246	207	299	243	268	402	173	68	34	68	79	168	40	100	132	149	42	361	133	282	216				
Southampton	555	423	131	259	63	76	130	117	329	118	144	364	495	427	426	590	158	251	226	136	232	84	219	283	315	188	165	519	67	148	20	201			
Stoke on Trent	381	249	45	85	210	125	150	146	155	63	238	190	321	253	251	416	203	143	87	57	58	160	38	165	197	174	50	344	110	238	193	60	178		
Swansea	548	416	130	252	221	82	244	41	322	153	273	357	488	420	418	583	269	265	240	171	225	196	212	297	329	293	189	511	140	195	177	215	156	171	
Wick	229	308	580	479	745	660	619	681	384	598	773	363	253	282	277	123	672	517	486	575	511	675	504	427	390	649	549	223	645	773	728	525	713	539	706

Example Exemple
Esempio Beispiel
Edinburgh – Southampton
427 Miles

Dear Reader

The Michelin Guide, created for the motorist, offers a wide range of information including a selection of hotels and restaurants.

In order to get the most benefit from our guide please read the explanatory chapters that follow and pay particular attention to the symbols and characters, which in bold or light type, in red or black, have different meanings.

This book is not a list of all hotels and restaurants. We have made a choice amongst establishments of all classes in order to provide a service for all motorists.

We wish you a pleasant journey, and on your return please write to us at:

Michelin Tyre Co Ltd.

Tourism Department

81 Fulham Road, LONDON SW3 6RD

Your opinions, whether praising or criticising, are welcomed and will be examined on the spot by our inspectors in order to make our Guide even better.

Thank you in advance.

Choosing your hotel or restaurant

We have classified the hotels and restaurants with the travelling motorist in mind. In each category they have been listed in order of preference.

CLASS, STANDARD OF COMFORT

Luxury
Top class
Very comfortable
Comfortable
Good average
Plain but adequate
Other recommended accommodation, at moderate prices

without rest.	The hotel has no restaurant
with rm	The restaurant has bedrooms

HOTEL FACILITIES

Hotels in categories , , , usually have every comfort and exchange facilities; details are not repeated under each hotel.

In other categories, the listed facilities are usually to be found only in some of the rooms; these hotels generally have a bathroom or a shower for general use.

Postal code	LL35 0SB
Telephone number	64622
Number of rooms	**30 rm**
Lift (elevator)	
Television in room	TV
Private bathroom with toilet, private bathroom without toilet	wc
Private shower with toilet, private shower without toilet	wc
External phone in room	
Bedrooms accessible to the physically handicapped	
Tennis	
Outdoor or indoor swimming pool	
Golf course and number of holes	18
Fishing available to hotel guests. A charge may be made	
Garden	
Private park	park
Garage available (usually charged for)	
Car park	P
Equipped conference hall (minimum seating 25)	
Period during which a seasonal hotel is open	*May-October*
Probably open for the season — precise dates not available	*season*

Where no dates or season are shown, the establishments in bold type are open all the year round

Choosing your hotel or restaurant

AMENITY

A stay in certain hotels in this guide will, without doubt, be particularly pleasant or restful.

Such a quality may derive from the hotel's fortunate setting, its decor, welcoming atmosphere and service.

Such establishments are distinguished in the guide by the symbols shown below.

Pleasant hotels

Pleasant restaurants

« Park » — Particularly attractive feature

Very quiet or quiet, secluded hotel

Quiet hotel

sea — Exceptional view

Interesting or extensive view

The establishments shown in red e.g. with rm, or in a very quiet situation are indicated on the maps preceding each geographical area.

We do not claim to have indicated all the pleasant, very quiet or quiet, secluded hotels which exist.

Our enquiries continue. You can help us by letting us know your opinions and discoveries.

Choosing your hotel or restaurant

CUISINE

The stars for good cooking

We indicate by ✿ or ✿✿, establishments where the standard of cooking, whether particular to the country or foreign, deserves to be brought especially to the attention of our readers.

In the text of these establishments we show some of the culinary specialities, to a maximum of three, that we recommend you to try.

An especially good restaurant in its class — ✿

This symbol indicates restaurants particularly worthy of break in your journey. Beware of comparing the star of a luxury establishment with that of a more simple one. In either case an effort is made to serve you a meal of quality in relation to the price charged.

Excellent cooking, worth a detour — ✿✿

First class products and preparations... Do not expect meals of this quality to be cheap.

Your opinions and suggestions concerning restaurants that we recommend will be extremely welcome, so do not hesitate to let us know of them. Thank you in advance.

For our part, our enquiries continue.

The red « M »

Whilst appreciating the quality of the cooking in restaurants with a star, you may, however, wish to find some serving a perhaps less elaborate but nonetheless always carefully prepared meal.

Certain restaurants seem to us to answer this requirement. We bring them to your attention by marking them with a red « M » in the text of the guide.

Alcoholic beverages-conditions of sale

Licensed premises, where alcoholic drinks may be bought and consumed (public houses or pubs, hotels and restaurants), may remain open at the discretion of the landlord but may only sell drink within legally prescribed hours.

Children under 14 are not allowed in the bar of licensed premises during the prescribed hours but this prohibition does not extend to a separate restaurant or to any other part of the premises.

The sale or consumption of intoxicating liquor by persons under 18 is prohibited in the bar of licensed premises but persons over 16 may buy and consume alcoholic drink with a meal in a separate restaurant.

N.B.: Unlicensed hotels and restaurants are not permitted to serve alcoholic beverages, including beer, even accompanying meals.

Licensing hours during which alcoholic beverages may be sold: see opening pages of each region.

Choosing your hotel or restaurant

PRICES

Valid for late 1977 the rates shown may be revised if the cost of living changes to any great extent. **In any event they should be regarded as basic charges.**

Your recommendation is self-evident if you always walk into a hotel, guide in hand.

Hotels and restaurants whose names appear in bold type have supplied us with their charges in detail and undertaken to abide by them, wherever possible, if the traveller is in possession of this year's guide.

Where no mention **s.**, **t.** or **st.** is shown, prices are subject to the addition of service charge, V.A.T., or both (V.A.T. does not apply in the Channel Islands).
If you think you have been overcharged, let us know. Where no rates are shown it is best to enquire about terms in advance.

Meals

Prices are given in £ sterling.

M 4.50/6.00	**Set meals** – Lowest price 4.50, and highest price 6.00 for set meals – including cover charge, where applicable - served at normal hours (12.30 to 2.30 pm and 7 to 9 pm).
s.	Service only included.
t.	V.A.T. only included.
st.	Service and V.A.T. included (net prices).
M 6.00/8.00	See page 15.
M a la carte 6.00/8.50	**A la carte meals** – The first figure is for a plain meal and includes light entrée, main dish of the day with vegetables and dessert. The second figure is for a fuller meal and includes hors-d'œuvre, a main dish, cheese or dessert. These prices include a cover charge where applicable.
1.20	Price of 1/2 bottle or carafe of ordinary wine.
1.30	Charge for breakfast (i.e. not included in the room rate).
rm 10.00/16.00	**Rooms** – Lowest price 10.00 for a comfortable single and highest price 16.00 for the best double room (including bathroom when applicable).
rm 12.00/17.50	Breakfast is included in the price of the room.
P 15.00/18.50	**Full-Board** – Lowest and highest price per person, per day in the high season.

A FEW USEFUL DETAILS

Meals

Ask for menus including set meals and a la carte menus with the prices clearly marked if they are not produced automatically.

Hotels

Breakfast is generally included in the price of the room, even if it is not required.

Full-board

Full-board comprises: bedroom, breakfast and two meals. Terms usually only apply to a stay of three days or longer.

High season rates usually operate between June and September. It is always advisable to agree terms in advance with a hotelier.

Reservations

Hotels: Reserving in advance, when possible, is advised. Ask the hotelier to provide you, in his letter of confirmation, with all terms and conditions applicable to your reservation.

In seaside resorts especially, reservations usually begin and end on Saturdays.

Certain hoteliers require the payment of a deposit. This constitutes a mutual guarantee of good faith. Deposits, except in special cases, may amount to 10 % of the estimated hotel account.

Restaurants: it is strongly recommended always to book your table well ahead in order to avoid the disappointment of a refusal.

Animals

It is forbidden to bring domestic animals (dogs, cats...) into Great Britain and Ireland.

Seeing a town and its surroundings

TOWNS

986 ㉞	Section number on Michelin map 986
pop. 1.057	Population (last published census figures)
✉ York	Post office serving the town
☎ 0225 Bath	STD dialling code (name of exchange indicated only when different from name of the town)
BX A	Reference letters locating a position on a town plan
☀, <	Panoramic view, viewpoint
⛳18	Golf course and number of holes (visitors unrestricted)
✈	Airport
⛴	Shipping line (passengers and cars)
🚤	Shipping line (passengers only) *see list of companies at the end of the Guide*
🚗 ☎ 218	Place with a motorail connection; further information from telephone number listed
i	Tourist Information Office

SIGHTS

Star-rating

★★★	Worth a journey
★★	Worth a detour
★	Interesting
AC	Admission charge

Tourist sights and where to find them

See	Sights in town
Envir.	On the outskirts
Exc.	In the surrounding area
N, S, E, W	The sight lies north, south, east, west
A 22	Go by road A 22, indicated by the same symbol on the Guide map
2 m.	Mileage
h, mn	Walking time there and back (h: hours; mn: minutes)

Standard Time

In winter standard time throughout the British Isles is Greenwich Mean Time (G.M.T.). In summer British clocks are advanced by one hour to give British Summer Time (B.S.T.). The actual dates are announced annually but always occur over weekends in March and October.

Town Plans

CONVENTIONAL SIGNS

Streets

Some streets are only shown by their beginning
Through route or by-pass – Dual carriageway . . . .
Motorway and interchange number . . . .
One-way street – under construction . . . .
No entry, unsuitable for traffic or subject to restrictions . . . .
Railway crossing : Level crossing, road crossing rail, rail crossing road . . . .
Gateway – Street passing under arch – Tunnel . . . .
Shopping street – Public car park . . . .

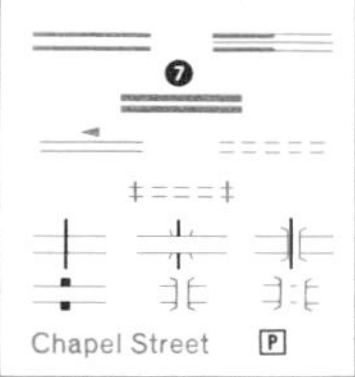

Sights - Hotels

Place of interest and its main entrance } Reference letter on the town plan . . .
Cathedral or church . . . . }
Reference letter locating hotels and restaurants on the town plan . . . .

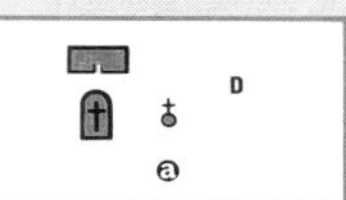

Various signs

Cathedral - Church - Hospital – Poste restante, telegraph, telephone . . . .
Public buildings located by letters :
County Council Offices – Town Hall . . . .
Police (in large towns police headquarters) – Museum . . . .
Theatre – University, Colleges . . . .
Tourist Information Office . . . .
Cemetery – Open woodland, park . . . .
Lighthouse – Sports ground, stadium . . . .
Golf course (visitors unrestricted) – (with restrictions for visitors) . . . .
Racecourse – Panorama – View . . . .
Landing stage : Passenger and car transport – Airport . . . .

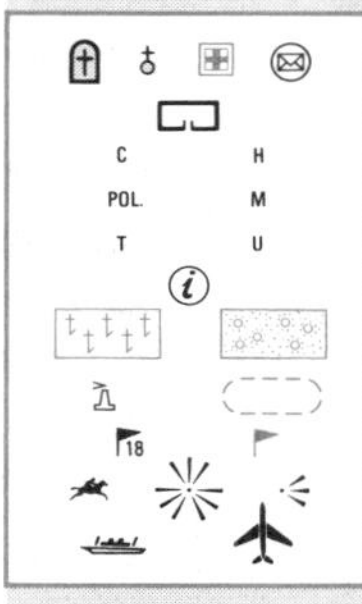

London - Special signs

Borough – Area . . . .
Borough boundary – Area boundary . . . .
Underground station. . . . .

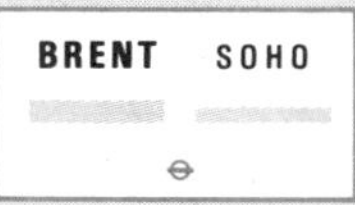

For your car

In the text of many towns are to be found the names of garages or motor agents with a breakdown service.
For your tyres refer to the pages bordered in blue.

Travelling by car

The major motoring organisations in Great Britain are the Automobile Association and the Royal Automobile Club. Each provides services in varying degrees for non-resident members of affiliated clubs.

AUTOMOBILE ASSOCIATION
Fanum House
BASINGSTOKE, Hants., RG21 2EA
☏ (0256) 20123

ROYAL AUTOMOBILE CLUB
83-85 Pall Mall
LONDON SW1Y 5HW
☏ (01) 930 4343

Ami Lecteur

Ce guide, conçu pour le voyage, vous propose une multitude de renseignements et en particulier un choix d'hôtels et de restaurants.

Pour tirer le meilleur parti de nos informations lisez attentivement les pages explicatives. Un même symbole, un même caractère en rouge ou en noir, en gras ou en maigre n'ont pas tout à fait la même signification.

Sachez aussi que cet ouvrage n'est pas un répertoire de tous les hôtels et restaurants. Nos listes sont le résultat de sélections effectuées parmi toutes les classes d'établissements afin de mieux rendre service à tous les automobilistes.

Bonne route et dès votre retour, écrivez-nous.

Services de Tourisme Michelin

46, avenue de Breteuil

75341 PARIS CEDEX 07

Vos louanges comme vos critiques seront examinées sur place par les Attachés de nos Services de Tourisme afin que ce guide soit encore meilleur dans l'avenir.

Merci d'avance!

Le choix d'un hôtel, d'un restaurant

Notre classement est établi à l'usage des automobilistes de passage. Dans chaque catégorie les établissements sont classés par ordre de préférence.

CLASSE ET CONFORT

🏨	Grand luxe	XXXXX
	Luxe	XXXX
	Très confortable	XXX
	De bon confort	XX
	Assez confortable	X
	Simple mais convenable	
	Autre ressource hôtelière conseillée, à prix modérés	

without rest. L'hôtel n'a pas de restaurant
with rm Le restaurant possède des chambres

L'INSTALLATION

Les hôtels des catégories , , , possèdent tout le confort et assurent en général le change, les symboles de détail n'apparaissent donc pas au texte de ces hôtels.

Dans les autres catégories, les éléments de confort indiqués n'existent le plus souvent que dans certaines chambres.
Ces établissements disposent de douches et de salles de bains communes.

Code postal de l'établissement	LL35 0SB
Numéro de téléphone	64622
Nombre de chambres	**30 rm**
Ascenseur	
Télévision dans la chambre	TV
Bain et wc privés, bain privé sans wc	wc
Douche et wc privés, douche privée sans wc	wc
Téléphone dans la chambre communiquant avec l'extérieur	
Chambres accessibles aux handicapés physiques	
Tennis	
Piscine: de plein air ou couverte	
Golf et nombre de trous	18
Pêche ouverte aux clients de l'hôtel (éventuellement payant)	
Jardin	
Parc	park
Garage (généralement payant)	
Parc à voitures	P
L'hôtel dispose d'une ou plusieurs salles de conférences (25 places minimum)	
Période d'ouverture d'un hôtel saisonnier	*May-October*
Ouverture probable en saison mais dates non précisées	*season*

Les établissements indiqués en caractères gras, dont le nom n'est suivi d'aucune mention, sont ouverts toute l'année.

Le choix d'un hôtel, d'un restaurant

L'AGRÉMENT

Certains établissements sélectionnés dans ce guide sont tels que le séjour y est particulièrement agréable ou reposant.

Cela peut tenir à leur environnement extérieur, à leur décoration, à leur situation, à l'accueil et au service qui y sont proposés.

Ils se distinguent dans le guide par les symboles indiqués ci-dessous.

[hôtel] ... [hôtel]	Hôtels agréables
XXXXX ... X	Restaurants agréables
« Park »	Élément particulièrement agréable
[symbole]	Hôtel très tranquille ou isolé et tranquille
[symbole]	Hôtel tranquille
< sea	Vue exceptionnelle
<	Vue intéressante ou étendue

Les établissements signalés en rouge, ex : [hôtel], XX with rm ou très tranquilles [symbole] ont été repérés sur les cartes placées au début de chacune des régions traitées dans ce guide.

Nous ne prétendons pas avoir signalé tous les hôtels agréables, ni tous ceux qui sont tranquilles, ou isolés et tranquilles.

Nos enquêtes continuent. Vous pouvez les faciliter en nous faisant connaître vos observations et vos découvertes.

Le choix d'un hôtel, d'un restaurant

LA TABLE

Les étoiles de bonne table

Nous marquons par ✿ ou ✿✿ les établissements dont la qualité de la table nous a paru mériter d'être signalée spécialement à l'attention de nos lecteurs, qu'il s'agisse de cuisines propres au pays ou étrangères.

Au texte de ces établissements nous indiquons quelques spécialités culinaires, trois au maximum, que nous vous conseillons d'essayer.

Une bonne table dans sa catégorie

✿

Ce symbole marque une bonne étape sur votre itinéraire. Ne comparez pas l'étoile d'un établissement de luxe avec celle d'une petite maison, mais dans un cas comme dans l'autre un effort est fait pour vous servir une cuisine de qualité en rapport avec les prix demandés.

Une table excellente, mérite un détour

✿✿

Produits et préparations de choix... Attendez-vous à une dépense en conséquence.

Vos avis et suggestions au sujet des tables que nous recommandons seront les bienvenus, ne manquez pas de nous en faire part. Merci d'avance.

De notre côté nos enquêtes continuent.

Le « M » rouge

Tout en appréciant les tables à « étoiles » on peut souhaiter trouver sur sa route un repas plus simple mais toujours de préparation soignée. Certaines maisons nous ont paru répondre à cette préoccupation.

Un « M » rouge les signale à votre attention dans le texte de ce guide.

La vente de boissons alcoolisées

Les lieux autorisés à la vente des boissons alcoolisées pour la consommation sur place (Public houses – pubs – hôtels, restaurants) peuvent être ouverts et fermés à la convenance de leurs gérants mais la vente de ces boissons n'y est permise que durant certaines périodes de temps fixées par la loi. Les enfants de moins de 14 ans n'ont pas accès au bar d'établissements possédant licence, durant les heures permises, mais cette interdiction ne s'applique pas au restaurant si celui-ci est séparé ou à toute autre partie de l'établissement.

Toute personne âgée de moins de 18 ans ne peut acheter ou consommer des boissons alcoolisées au bar d'un établissement possédant licence durant les heures permises, mais toute personne âgée de plus de 16 ans peut acheter ou consommer ces mêmes boissons à l'occasion d'un repas au restaurant, si séparé du bar.

NOTA : Les hôtels ou restaurants sans licence (unlicensed) ne peuvent servir aucune boisson alcoolisée, y compris bière, même à l'occasion d'un repas.

Heures de vente permises. Se reporter au début de la nomenclature de chacune des régions traitées dans ce guide.

Le choix d'un hôtel, d'un restaurant

LES PRIX

Les prix que nous indiquons dans ce guide ont été établis en fin d'année 1977. Ils sont susceptibles d'être augmentés ou modifiés si le coût de la vie subit des variations importantes. **Ils doivent, en tout cas, être considérés comme des prix de base.**

Entrez à l'hôtel ou au restaurant le guide à la main, vous montrerez ainsi qu'il vous conduit là en confiance.

Les hôtels et restaurants figurent en caractères gras lorsque les hôteliers nous ont donné tous leurs prix et se sont engagés à les appliquer aux touristes de passage porteurs de notre guide.

Lorsque les mentions **s.**, **t.**, ou **st.** ne figurent pas, les prix indiqués peuvent être majorés d'un pourcentage pour le service, la T.V.A. ou les deux. (La T.V.A. n'est pas appliquée dans les Channel Islands).

Prévenez-nous de toute majoration paraissant injustifiée.
Si aucun prix n'est indiqué, nous vous conseillons de demander les conditions.

Repas

Les prix sont indiqués en livres sterling (1 £ = 100 pence).

M 4.50/6.00	**Prix fixe** – Minimum 4.50 et maximum 6.00 des repas servis aux heures normales (12 h 30 à 14 h 30 et 19 h à 21 h) y compris le couvert éventuellement.
s.	Service compris.
t.	T.V.A. comprise.
st.	Service et T.V.A. compris (prix nets).
M 6.00/8.00	Voir page 23.
M a la carte 6.00/8.50	**Repas à la carte** – Le 1er prix correspond à un repas simple mais soigné, comprenant: petite entrée, plat du jour garni, dessert. Le 2e prix concerne un repas plus complet, comprenant: hors-d'œuvre, plat principal, fromage ou dessert. Ces prix s'entendent couvert compris s'il y a lieu.
1.20	Prix de la 1/2 bouteille ou carafe de vin ordinaire.
1.30	Prix du petit déjeuner, s'il n'est pas compris dans celui de la chambre.
rm 10.00/16.00	**Chambre** – Prix minimum 10.00 d'une chambre pour une personne et prix maximum 16.00 de la plus belle chambre (y compris salle de bains s'il y a lieu) occupée par deux personnes.
rm 12.00/17.50	Le prix du petit déjeuner est inclus dans le prix de la chambre.
P 15.00/18.50	**Pension** – Prix minimum et maximum de la pension complète par personne et par jour en haute saison.

QUELQUES PRÉCISIONS UTILES

Au restaurant

Réclamez les menus à prix fixes et la carte chiffrée s'ils ne vous sont pas présentés spontanément.

A l'hôtel

Le prix du petit déjeuner est généralement inclus dans le prix de la chambre, même s'il n'est pas consommé.

Pension

La pension complète comprend : la chambre, le petit déjeuner et deux repas. Les prix de pension sont donnés à titre indicatif et sont généralement applicables à partir de trois jours mais il est indispensable de s'entendre à l'avance avec l'hôtelier pour conclure un arrangement définitif.

Les prix haute saison sont habituellement pratiqués de juin à septembre.

Réservations

Hôtels : Chaque fois que possible, la réservation préalable est souhaitable. Demandez à l'hôtelier de vous fournir dans sa lettre d'accord toutes précisions utiles sur la réservation et les conditions de séjour. Dans les stations balnéaires en particulier, les réservations s'appliquent généralement à des séjours partant d'un samedi à l'autre.

A toute demande écrite il est conseillé de joindre un coupon-réponse international.

Certains hôteliers demandent parfois le versement d'arrhes. Il s'agit d'un dépôt-garantie qui engage l'hôtelier comme le client. Sauf accord spécial le montant des arrhes peut être fixé à 10 % du montant total estimé.

Restaurants : il est vivement recommandé de réserver sa table aussi longtemps que possible à l'avance, de façon à éviter le désagrément d'un refus.

Animaux

L'introduction d'animaux domestiques (chiens, chats...) est interdite en Grande Bretagne et en Irlande.

Pour visiter une ville et ses environs

LES VILLES

986 ㉞	Numéro de la carte Michelin et numéro du pli
pop. 1,057	Population totale (dernier recensement officiel publié)
York	Bureau de poste desservant la localité
0225 Bath	Indicatif téléphonique interurbain suivi, si nécessaire, de la localité de rattachement
BX **A**	Lettres repérant un emplacement sur le plan
	Panorama, point de vue
18	Golf et nombre de trous (accès permis à tous visiteurs)
	Aéroport
	Transports maritimes (passagers et voitures)
	Transports maritimes (passagers seulement) *Voir liste des compagnies en fin de guide*
218	Localités desservies par train-auto – Renseignements au numéro de téléphone indiqué
i	Office de Tourisme

LES CURIOSITÉS

Intérêt

***	Vaut le voyage
**	Mérite un détour
*	Intéressante
AC	Entrée payante

Situation des curiosités

See	Dans la ville
Envir.	Aux environs proches de la ville
Exc.	Excursions dans la région
N, S, E, W	La curiosité est située: au Nord, au Sud, à l'Est, à l'Ouest
A 22	On y va par la route A 22, repérée par le même signe sur le plan du Guide
2 m.	Distance en miles
h, mn	Temps de parcours à pied, aller et retour (h: heures, mn: minutes)

Heure légale

En hiver durant une période de temps fixée chaque année et s'étendant d'octobre à mars, les visiteurs devront tenir compte de l'heure officielle, égale à l'heure G.M.T. (une heure de retard sur l'heure française).

Les plans

SIGNES CONVENTIONNELS

Voirie

Certaines rues ne sont qu'amorcées

Rue de traversée ou de contournement – à chaussées séparées . . . .

Autoroute et numéro d'échangeur . . . .

Rue à sens unique – en construction . . . .

Rue interdite, impraticable ou à circulation réglementée . . . .

Passage de la rue : à niveau, au-dessus, au-dessous de la voie ferrée . . . .

Porte – Passage sous voûte – Tunnel . . . .

Rue commerçante – Parc de stationnement public . . . .

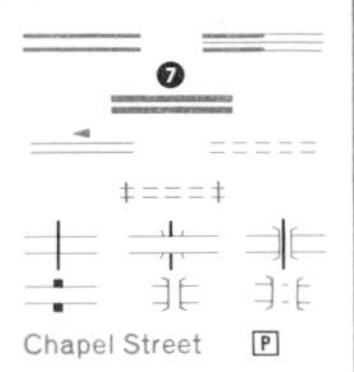

Curiosités - Hôtels

Monument intéressant et entrée principale . } Lettre les repérant sur le plan . . .

Cathédrale ou église . . . . }

Lettre repérant les hôtels et les restaurants sur le plan . . . .

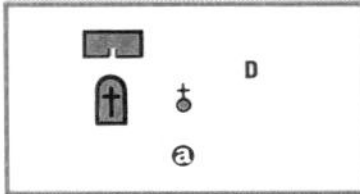

Signes divers

Cathédrale – Eglise – Hôpital – Poste restante, télégraphe, téléphone . . . . . .

Edifices publics repérés par des lettres :

Bureau de l'Administration du comté – Hôtel de ville . . . .

Police (dans les grandes villes, commissariat central) – Musée . . . .

Théâtre – Université, grande école . . . .

Office de Tourisme . . . .

Cimetière – Espace boisé, parc . . . .

Phare – Stade . . . .

Golf (accès permis à tous visiteurs) – (réservé) . . . .

Hippodrome – Panorama – Vue . . . .

Embarcadère : Transport de passagers et voitures – Aéroport . . . .

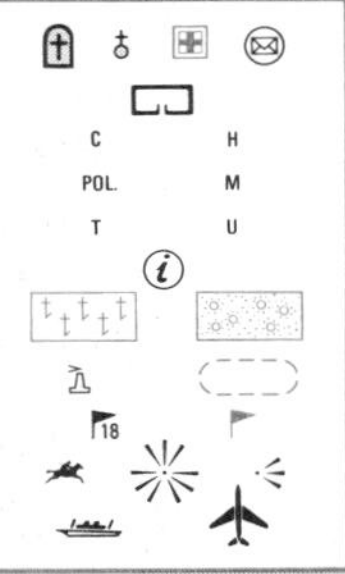

Londres - Signes particuliers

Nom d'arrondissement (borough) – de quartier (area) . . . .

Limite de « borough » – d'« area » . . . .

Station de métro . . . .

Pour votre voiture

Au texte de la plupart des localités figure une liste des garagistes ou concessionnaires automobiles pouvant, éventuellement, vous aider en cas de panne.
Pour vos pneus, consultez les pages bordées de bleu.

Voyages en voiture

Les principales organisations de secours automobile dans le pays sont l'Automobile Association et le Royal Automobile Club, toutes deux offrant certains de leurs services aux membres de clubs affiliés.

AUTOMOBILE ASSOCIATION
Fanum House
BASINGSTOKE, Hants., RG21 2EA
℡ (0256) 20123

ROYAL AUTOMOBILE CLUB
83-85 Pall Mall
LONDON SW1Y 5HW
℡ (01) 930 4343

Amici Lettori

La Guida Michelin, concepita per i viaggi, vi offre un notevole numero di informazioni ed in particolare una scelta di alberghi e ristoranti.

Al fine di trarre dalle nostre informazioni il miglior vantaggio, vi consigliamo di leggere le pagine esplicative che seguono, prestando una particolare attenzione ai simboli ed ai caratteri che, in grassetto o in magro, in nero o in rosso, hanno un significato diverso.

Questa guida non è un repertorio di tutti gli alberghi e ristoranti. Rappresenta bensì il risultato di una selezione effettuata fra le varie classi di esercizi per facilitare la scelta a tutti gli automobilisti.

Buon viaggio, ed al vostro ritorno scriveteci.

Michelin Tyre Co Ltd.

Tourism Department

81 Fulham Road, GB-LONDON SW3 6RD

I vostri giudizi, sia lodi che critiche, saranno esaminati sul posto dagli incaricati dei nostri Servizi Turismo per rendere questa guida ancora migliore.

Grazie anticipate.

La scelta di un albergo, di un ristorante

La nostra classificazione è stabilita ad uso dell'automobilista di passaggio. In ogni categoria, gli esercizi vengono citati in ordine di preferenza.

CLASSE E CONFORT

Albergo		Ristorante
	Gran lusso	XXXXX
	Lusso	XXXX
	Molto confortevole	XXX
	Di buon confort	XX
	Abbastanza confortevole	X
	Semplice ma conveniente	
	Altra risorsa, consigliata per prezzi contenuti	

without rest. — L'albergo non ha ristorante
with rm — Il ristorante dispone di camere

INSTALLAZIONI

I , , offrono ogni confort ed effettuano generalmente il cambio di valute; per questi alberghi non specifichiamo quindi il dettaglio delle installazioni.

Nelle altre categorie, gli elementi di confort indicati esistono, il più delle volte, soltanto in alcune camere ; questi alberghi dispongono tuttavia di docce e bagni comuni.

Codice postale dell'esercizio	LL35 0SB
Numero di telefono	64622
Numero di camere	**30 rm**
Ascensore	
Televisione in camera	TV
Bagno e wc privati, bagno privato senza wc	wc
Doccia e wc privati, doccia privata senza wc	wc
Telefono in camera comunicante con l'esterno	
Camere d'agevole accesso per i minorati fisici	
Tennis	
Piscina: all'aperto, coperta	
Golf e numero di buche	18
Pesca aperta ai clienti dell'albergo (eventualmente a pagamento)	
Giardino	
Parco	park
Garage (generalmente a pagamento)	
Parcheggio per auto	P
L'albergo dispone di una o più sale per conferenze (minimo 25 posti)	
Periodo di apertura di un albergo stagionale	*May-October*
Apertura in stagione, ma periodo non precisato	*season*

Gli esercizi in carattere grassetto senza tali indicazioni sono aperti tutto l'anno.

La scelta di un albergo, di un ristorante

AMENITÀ

Il soggiorno in alcuni alberghi si rivela talvolta particolarmente ameno o riposante.

Ciò può dipendere dalle caratteristiche dell'edificio, dalle decorazioni non comuni, dalla sua posizione, dall'accoglienza e dal servizio offerti.

Questi esercizi sono cosí contraddistinti:

...	Alberghi ameni
XXXXX ... X	Ristoranti ameni
« Park »	Un particolare ameno
	Albergo molto tranquillo o isolato e tranquillo
	Albergo tranquillo
≤ sea	Vista eccezionale
≤	Vista interessante o estesa

Gli esercizi indicati in rosso es.: , XX with rm, o molto tranquilli sono riportati sulle carte che precedono ciascuna delle regioni trattate nella guida.

Non abbiamo la pretesa di aver segnalato tutti gli alberghi ameni, nè tutti quelli molto tranquilli o isolati e tranquilli.

Le nostre ricerche continuano. Le potrete agevolare facendoci conoscere le vostre osservazioni e le vostre scoperte.

La scelta di un albergo, di un ristorante

LA TAVOLA

Le stelle di ottima tavola

Abbiamo contraddistinto con ✿ o ✿✿ quegli esercizi che, a nostro parere, meritano di essere segnalati alla vostra attenzione per la qualità della cucina, che puó essere tipicamente nazionale o d'importazione.

Nel testo di questi esercizi indichiamo alcune specialità culinarie, non più di tre, che vi consigliamo di provare.

✿

Un' ottima tavola nella sua categoria.

La stella indica una tappa gastronomica sul vostro itinerario. Non mettete a confronto la stella di un esercizio di lusso con quella di un piccolo esercizio, ma in entrambi i casi vi verranno serviti piatti di qualità, proporzionati al prezzo.

✿✿

Tavola eccellente : merita una deviazione.

Prodotti e menu scelti... Aspettatevi una spesa in proporzione.

Ci saranno molto graditi i pareri ed i suggerimenti che vorrete segnalarci, in relazione alle vostre esperienze negli esercizi da noi raccomandati.

Da parte nostra le ricerche continuano.

La « M » rossa

Pur apprezzando le tavole a « stella », si desidera alle volte consumare un pasto più semplice ma sempre accuratamente preparato.

Alcuni esercizi ci son parsi rispondenti a tale esigenza e sono contraddistinti nella guida da una « M » in rosso.

La vendita delle bevande alcooliche

I locali autorizzati alla vendita di bevande alcooliche da consumarsi sul posto (Public houses – pubs – alberghi, ristoranti) aprono e chiudono secondo l'orario che i loro gestori preferiscono ma la vendita di queste bevande non vi è consentita che durante certi periodi di tempo fissati dalla legge. I ragazzi inferiori ai 14 anni non possono accedere al bar di esercizi con licenza durante le ore permesse, ma tale divieto non viene applicato al ristorante a condizione che sia separato o completamente a parte dal bar.

I giovani inferiori ai 18 anni non possono acquistare o consumare bevande alcooliche al bar di un esercizio con licenza durante le ore permesse, ma se superano i 16 anni possono acquistare o consumare le suddette bevande durante i pasti in un ristorante con bar separato.

N. B. : Gli alberghi o ristoranti senza licenza (unlicensed) non possono servire nessuna bevanda alcoolica, compresa la birra, nemmeno durante i pasti.

Orari di vendita autorizzati. Vedere all'inizio della nomenclatura di ciascuna delle regioni trattate in questa Guida.

La scelta di un albergo, di un ristorante

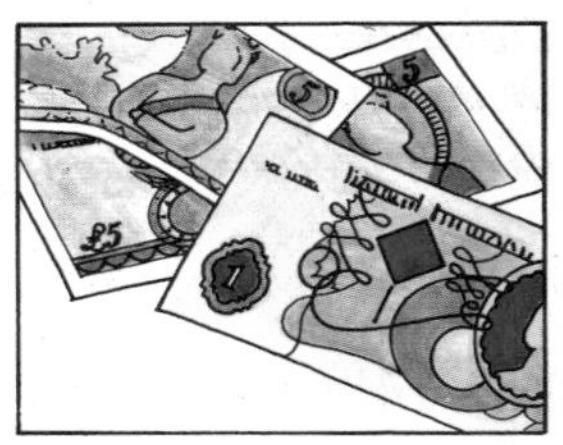

I PREZZI

Questi prezzi, redatti alla fine dell'anno 1977, possono venire modificati qualora il costo della vita subisca notevoli variazioni. **Essi debbono comunque essere considerati come prezzi base.**

Entrate nell'albergo con la Guida alla mano, dimostrando in tal modo la fiducia in chi vi ha indirizzato.

Gli alberghi e ristoranti figurano in carattere grassetto quando gli albergatori ci hanno comunicato tutti i loro prezzi e si sono impegnati ad applicarli ai turisti di passaggio in possesso della nostra pubblicazione.

Quando non figurano le lettere **s.**, **t.**, o **st.** i prezzi indicati possono essere maggiorati per il servizio o per l'I.V.A. o per entrambi. (L'I.V.A. non viene applicata nelle Channel Islands).

Segnalateci le maggiorazioni che vi sembrino ingiustificate. Quando i prezzi non sono indicati vi consigliamo di chiedere preventivamente le condizioni.

Pasti

I prezzi sono indicati in lire sterline (1 £ = 100 pence).

M 4.50/6.50	**Prezzo fisso** – Minimo 4.50 e massimo 6.50, per pasti serviti ad ore normali (dalle 12.30 alle 14.30 e dalle 19 alle 21) compreso il coperto se del caso.
s.	Servizio compreso.
t.	I.V.A. compresa.
st.	Servizio ed I.V.A. compresi (prezzi netti).
M 6.00/8.00	Vedere p 31.
M a la carte 6.00/8.50	**Alla carta** – Il 1° prezzo corrisponde ad un pasto semplice comprendente: primo piatto, piatto del giorno con contorno, dessert. Il 2° prezzo corrisponde ad un pasto più completo comprendente: antipasto, piatto principale, formaggio e dessert. Questi prezzi comprendono, se del caso, il coperto.
🍶 1.20	Prezzo della mezza bottiglia o di una caraffa di vino.
☕ 1.30	Prezzo della prima colazione se non è compreso nel prezzo della camera.
rm 10.00/16.00	**Camere** – Prezzo minimo 10.00 per una camera singola e prezzo massimo 16.00 per la camera più bella (compreso il bagno se c'è) per due persone.
rm ☕ 12.00/17.50	Il prezzo della prima colazione è compreso nel prezzo della camera.
P 15.00/18.50	**Pensione** – Prezzo minimo e massimo della pensione completa per persona e per giorno in alta stagione.

QUALCHE CHIARIMENTO UTILE

Al ristorante

Chiedete i menu a prezzo fisso e la carta coi relativi prezzi se non vi vengono spontaneamente presentati.

All'albergo

Il prezzo della prima colazione, anche se non viene consumata, è generalmente compreso nel prezzo della camera.

La Pensione

Comprende la camera, la prima colazione e due pasti. I prezzi di pensione sono dati a titolo indicativo e sono generalmente applicabili a partire da 3 giorni di permanenza: è comunque indispensabile prendere accordi preventivi con l'albergatore per stabilire le condizioni definitive.

I prezzi di alta stagione vengono generalmente praticati da giugno a settembre.

Le prenotazioni

Alberghi : appena possibile, la prenotazione è consigliabile; chiedete all'albergatore di fornirvi, nella sua lettera di conferma, ogni dettaglio sulla prenotazione e sulle condizioni di soggiorno. Nelle stazioni balneari in particolar modo, le prenotazioni si applicano generalmente a soggiorni che vanno da un sabato all' altro.

Si consiglia di allegare sempre alle richieste scritte di prenotazione un tagliando risposta internazionale.

Alle volte alcuni albergatori chiedono il versamento di una caparra. E' un deposito-garanzia che impegna tanto l'albergatore che il cliente. Salvo accordi speciali, l'ammontare della caparra può venire fissato nella misura del 10 % dell'ammontare totale previsto.

Ristoranti : è sempre consigliabile prenotare con un certo anticipo per evitare uno spiacevole rifiuto all'ultimo momento.

Animali

Non possono accedere in Gran Bretagna e Irlanda animali domestici (cani, gatti...)

Per visitare
una città
ed i suoi dintorni

LE CITTÀ

986 ㉞	Numero della carta Michelin e numero della piega
pop. 1,057	Popolazione totale (ultimo censimento ufficiale pubblicato)
✉ York	Sede dell'ufficio postale
✆ 0225 Bath	Prefisso telefonico interurbano (nome del centralino indicato solo quando differisce dal nome della località)
BX **A**	Lettere indicanti l'ubicazione sulla pianta
☼. <	Panorama, punto di vista
⛳ 18	Golf e numero di buche (accesso consentito a tutti)
✈	Aeroporto
⛴	Trasporti marittimi (passeggeri ed autovetture)
⛴	Trasporti marittimi (solo passeggeri) *Vedere la lista delle compagnie alla fine della Guida*
🚗 ✆ 218	Località con servizio auto su treno. Informarsi al numero di telefono indicato
i	Ufficio informazioni turistiche

LE CURIOSITÀ

Grado d'interesse

★★★	Vale il viaggio
★★	Merita una deviazione
★	Interessante
AC	Entrata a pagamento

Situazione delle curiosità

See	Nella città
Envir.	Nei dintorni della città
Exc.	Nella regione
N, S, E, W	La curiosità è situata: a Nord, a Sud, a Est, a Ovest.
A 22	Ci si va per la strada A 22 indicata con lo stesso segno sulla pianta
2 m.	Distanza in miglia
h, mn	Tempo per percorsi a piedi, andata e ritorno (h: ore, mn: minuti)

Ora legale

In inverno, per un periodo che va da ottobre a marzo ed è determinato di anno in anno, viene applicata l'ora ufficiale, uguale all'ora solare del meridiano di Greenwich (G.M.T.). I visitatori dovranno considerare 1 ora di ritardo sull'ora normale italiana.

Le Piante

SEGNI CONVENZIONALI

Viabilità

Per certe strade noi indichiamo solamente l'inizio

Via di attraversamento o di circonvallazione – a doppia carreggiata . . . .

Autostrada e numero di svincolo . . . .

Via a senso unico – in costruzione . . . .

Via vietata, impraticabile o a circolazione regolamentata . . . .

La via passa : a livello, al disopra, al disotto della ferrovia . . . .

Porta – Sottopassaggio – Galleria . . . .

Via commerciale – Parcheggio pubblico . . . .

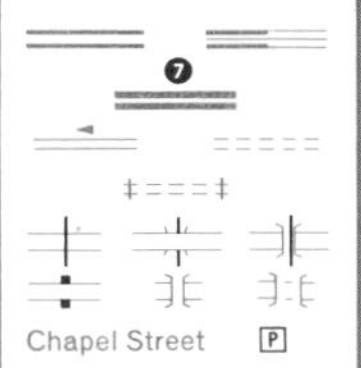

Curiosità - Alberghi

Monumento interessante ed entrata principale } Lettera di riferimento sulla pianta .
Cattedrale o chiesa . . . . }

Lettera di riferimento degli alberghi e ristoranti sulla pianta . . . .

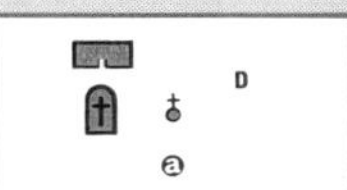
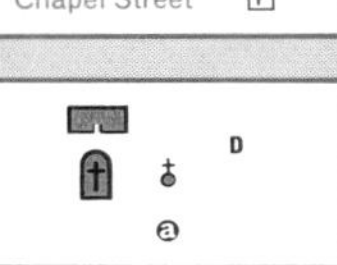

Simboli vari

Cattedrale – Chiesa – Ospedale – Fermo posta, telegrafo, telefono . . . .

Edifici pubblici indicati con lettere :

Sede dell' Amministrazione di Contea – Municipio . . . .

Polizia (Questura, nelle grandi città) – Museo . . . .

Teatro – Università, grande scuola . . . .

Ufficio informazioni turistiche . . . .

Cimitero – Zona alberata, parco . . . .

Faro – Stadio . . . .

Golf (accesso consentito a tutti) – riservato . . . .

Ippodromo – Panorama – Vista . . . .

Imbarcadero : Trasporto passeggeri ed autovetture – Aeroporto . . . .

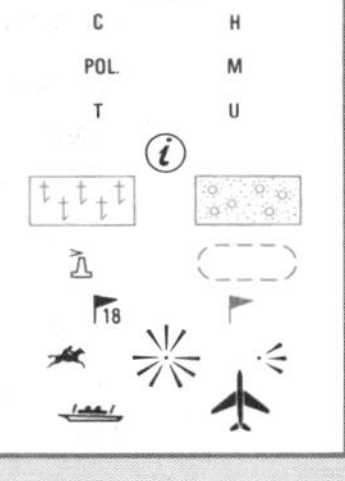

Londra - Segni particolari

Nome del distretto amministrativo (borough) – del quartiere (area). . . . .

Limite del « borough » – di « area » . . . .

Stazione della Metropolitana . . . .

Per la vostra automobile

Nel testo di molte località abbiamo elencato gli indirizzi di garage o concessionari in grado di effettuare il traino o le riparazioni.
Per i vostri pneumatici, consultate le pagine bordate di blu.

Viaggi in automobile

Le principali organizzazioni di soccorso automobilistico sono l'Automobile Association ed il Royal Automobile Club : entrambe offrono alcuni loro servizi ai membri dei club affiliati

AUTOMOBILE ASSOCIATION
Fanum House
BASINGSTOKE, Hants., RG21 2EA
℡ (0256) 20123

ROYAL AUTOMOBILE CLUB
83-85 Pall Mall
LONDON SW1Y 5HW
℡ (01) 930 4343

Lieber Leser

Der Michelin-Führer bietet Ihnen viele nützliche Hinweise für die Reise und eine umfangreiche Auswahl an Hotels und Restaurants.

Damit Sie die Vielfalt der gegebenen Auskünfte voll ausnützen können, bitten wir Sie, die Erläuterungen auf den folgenden Seiten aufmerksam durchzulesen und dabei besonders auf die Erklärungen der verwendeten Zeichen zu achten : diese haben, fett oder dünn gedruckt, in schwarz oder in rot immer eine andere Bedeutung.

Wie auch die anderen Roten Michelin-Führer ist er kein vollständiges Verzeichnis aller Hotels und Restaurants. Um den Ansprüchen aller Reisenden gerecht zu werden, empfehlen wir Häuser jeder Kategorie, wobei wir uns jedoch jeweils auf eine Auswahl beschränken mußten.

Wir wünschen Ihnen eine gute Fahrt. Bitte teilen Sie uns nach Ihrer Rückkehr Ihre Eindrücke mit.

Michelin Tyre Co Ltd.
Tourism Department
81 Fulham Road, GB - LONDON SW3 6RD

Ihre Hinweise, Ihr Lob und Ihre Kritik werden von unseren Inspektoren an Ort und Stelle überprüft ; sie helfen uns, die Angaben im Michelin-Führer noch besser, noch exakter zu machen.

Besten Dank im voraus.

Wahl eines Hotels, eines Restaurants

Unsere Auswahl ist für Durchreisende gedacht. In jeder Kategorie drückt die Reihenfolge der Betriebe eine weitere Rangordnung aus.

KLASSENEINTEILUNG UND KOMFORT

Großer Luxus
Luxus
Sehr komfortabel
Mit gutem Komfort
Bürgerlich
Einfach, ordentlich
Preiswerte, empfehlenswerte Gasthäuser und Pensionen

without rest.	Hotel ohne Restaurant
with rm	Restaurant vermietet auch Zimmer

EINRICHTUNG

Für die , , geben wir keine Einzelheiten über die Einrichtung (wc wc) an, da diese Hotels im allgemeinen jeden Komfort besitzen. Außerdem besteht die Möglichkeit, Geld zu wechseln.

In den Häusern der übrigen Kategorien sind die genannten Einrichtungen oft nur in einem Teil der Zimmer vorhanden. Diese Häuser verfügen meist über ein Etagenbad oder eine Etagendusche.

Angabe des Postbezirks (hinter der Hoteladresse)	LL35 0SB
Telefonnummer	64622
Anzahl der Zimmer	**30 rm**
Fahrstuhl	
Fernsehen im Zimmer	TV
Privatbad mit wc, Privatbad ohne wc	wc
Privatdusche mit wc, Privatdusche ohne wc	wc
Zimmertelefon mit Außenverbindung	
Für Körperbehinderte leicht zugängliche Zimmer	
Tennis	
Freibad, Hallenbad	
Golfplatz mit Lochzahl	18
Angelmöglichkeit für Hotelgäste, evtl. gegen Gebühr	
Garten	
Park	park
Garage (wird meist berechnet)	
Parkplatz	P
Konferenzraum (für mind. 25 Personen)	
Öffnungszeit eines Saisonhotels	*May-October*
Unbestimmte Öffnungszeit eines Saisonhotels	*season*

Die fettgedruckten Häuser, hinter deren Namen keine Zeitangabe steht, sind ganzjährig geöffnet.

Wahl eines Hotels, eines Restaurants

ANNEHMLICHKEITEN

In manchen Hotels ist der Aufenthalt wegen der schönen, ruhigen Lage, der nicht alltäglichen Einrichtung und Atmosphäre und dem gebotenen Service besonders angenehm und erholsam.

Solche Häuser und ihre besonderen Annehmlichkeiten sind im Führer durch folgende Symbole gekennzeichnet:

	Angenehme Hotels Angenehme Restaurants
« Park »	Besondere Annehmlichkeit
	Sehr ruhiges, oder abgelegenes und ruhiges Hotel Ruhiges Hotel
< sea <	Reizvolle Aussicht Interessante oder weite Sicht

Auf den Übersichtskarten in der Einleitung zu den einzelnen Landesteilen sind die Orte, in denen sich mindestens ein angenehmes Haus mit rotem symbol (z. B. , XX with rm) oder ein sehr ruhiges Haus ( ) befindet, eingezeichnet.

Wir wissen, daß diese Auswahl noch nicht vollständig ist, sind aber laufend bemüht, weitere solche Häuser für Sie zu entdecken; dabei sind uns Ihre Erfahrungen und Hinweise eine wertvolle Hilfe.

Wahl eines Hotels, eines Restaurants

KÜCHE

Die Sterne für gute Küche

Mit ✿ oder ✿✿ kennzeichnen wir die Häuser mit landesüblicher oder ausländischer Küche, deren Qualität wir der Aufmerksamkeit der Leser besonders empfehlen möchten.

Im Text der einzelnen Häuser geben wir einige – höchstens drei – kulinarische Spezialitäten an, die Sie versuchen sollten.

Eine gute Küche : verdient Ihre besondere Beachtung

✿

Der Stern bedeutet eine angenehme Unterbrechung Ihrer Reise. Vergleichen Sie aber bitte nicht den Stern eines teuren Luxusrestaurants mit dem Stern eines kleinen oder mittleren Hauses, wo man Ihnen zu einem annehmbaren Preis eine ebenfalls vorzügliche Mahlzeit reicht.

Eine hervorragende Küche : verdient einen Umweg

✿✿

Ausgesuchte Spezialitäten, erstklassige Zubereitung... Angemessene Preise.

Teilen Sie uns bitte Ihre Ansicht und Ihre Vorschläge bezüglich der von uns ausgezeichneten Küchen mit.

Wir danken Ihnen dafür im voraus.

Das rote « M »

Wir glauben, daß neben den Häusern mit Stern auch solche Adressen Sie interessieren werden, die einfache aber sorgfältig zubereitete Mahlzeiten anbieten.
Auf solche Häuser weisen wir im Text durch das rote « M » hin.

Ausschank alkoholischer Getränke

Betriebe mit Ausschanklizenz für alkoholische Getränke (Public houses – pubs –, Hotels und Restaurants) können zwar ihre Öffnungs-und Schließungszeiten selbst bestimmen, der Ausschank alkoholischer Getränke jedoch ist nur während gesetzlich festgelegten Zeiten erlaubt. Kindern unter 14 Jahren ist der Zutritt zu den lizensierten Hotelbars während der Ausschankzeiten untersagt. Dies gilt jedoch weder für das Hotel-Restaurant, wenn dieses von der Bar abgetrennt ist, noch für den übrigen Hotelteil.

Jugendliche unter 18 Jahren dürfen in der Bar eines lizensierten Betriebes während der Ausschankzeiten alkoholische Getränke weder kaufen noch konsumieren. Dagegen ist es Jugendlichen ab 16 Jahren erlaubt, zu einer Mahlzeit in einem Restaurant alkoholische Getränke zu trinken, vorausgesetzt, das Restaurant ist von der Bar abgetrennt.

Zur Beachtung : Hotels und Restaurants ohne Ausschanklizenz (unlicensed) dürfen alkoholische Getränke und Bier auch zu den Mahlzeiten nicht ausschenken.

Ausschankzeiten : Übersichtstabellen in der Einleitung zu den einzelnen Landesteilen.

Wahl eines Hotels, eines Restaurants

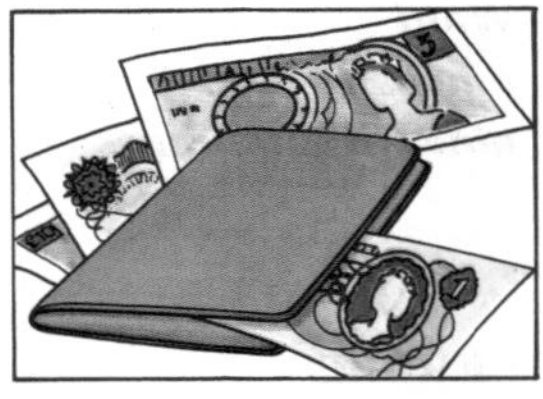

PREISE

Die in diesem Führer genannten Preise wurden uns Ende 1977 angegeben. Sie können sich 1978 erhöhen, wenn die allgemeinen Lebenshaltungskosten steigen. **Sie können aber in diesem Fall als Richtpreise angesehen werden.**

Halten Sie beim Betreten des Hotels den Führer in der Hand. Sie zeigen damit, daß Sie aufgrund unserer Empfehlung gekommen sind.

Die Namen der Hotels und Restaurants, die ihre Preise genannt haben, sind fett gedruckt. Gleichzeitig haben sich diese Häuser verpflichtet, die angegebenen Preise den Benutzern des Michelin-Führers zu berechnen.

Wenn die Buchstaben **s.**, **t.**, oder **st.** nicht hinter den angegebenen Preisen aufgeführt sind, können sich diese um den Zuschlag für Bedienung und/oder MWST erhöhen. (Keine MWST auf den Channel Islands).

Verständigen Sie uns von jeder Preiserhöhung, die unbegründet erscheint. Wenn kein Preis angegeben ist, raten wir Ihnen, sich beim Hotelier nach den Bedingungen zu erkundigen.

Mahlzeiten

Die Preise sind in Pfund Sterling angegeben (1 £ = 100 pence).

M 4.50/6.50	**Feste Menupreise** – Mindest- 4.50 und Höchstpreis 6.50 (inklusive Couvert) für die Mahlzeiten, die zu den normalen Tischzeiten serviert werden (12.30 - 14.30 und 19 - 21 Uhr).
s.	Bedienung inbegriffen
t.	MWST inbegriffen.
st.	Bedienung und MWST inbegriffen (Inklusivpreise).
M 6.00/8.00	Siehe Seite 39.
M a la carte 6.00/8.50	**Mahlzeiten « à la carte »** – Der 1. Preis entspricht einer einfachen aber sorgfältig zubereiteten Mahlzeit, bestehend aus kleiner Vorspeise, Tagesgericht mit Beilage und Nachtisch. Der 2. Preis entspricht einer reichlicheren Mahlzeit mit Vorspeise Hauptgericht, Käse oder Nachtisch (« couvert » ist in den Preisen enthalten).
1.20	Preis für 1/2 Flasche oder eine Karaffe Tafelwein.
1.30	Frühstückspreis, wenn dieser im Übernachtungspreis nicht enthalten ist.
rm 10.00/16.00	**Zimmer** – Mindestpreis 10.00 für ein Einzelzimmer und Höchst preis 16.00 für das schönste Doppelzimmer (mit Bad).
rm 12.00/17.50	Übernachtung mit Frühstück.
P 15.00/18.50	**Pension** – Mindest- und Höchstpreis für Vollpension pro Person und Tag in der Hochsaison.

NÜTZLICHE HINWEISE

Im Restaurant

Verlangen Sie die Karte der Tagesmenus zu Festpreisen und die Speisekarte, wenn sie Ihnen nicht von selbst vorgelegt werden.

Im Hotel

Im allgemeinen ist das Frühstück (auch wenn es nicht eingenommen wird) im Zimmerpreis enthalten.

Pension

Die Vollpension umfaßt Zimmer, Frühstück und zwei Mahlzeiten. Die angegebenen Vollpensionspreise sind Richtpreise und gelten im allgemeinen bei einem Aufenthalt ab 3 Tagen. Es empfiehlt sich jedoch, sich zuvor mit dem Hotelier über den endgültigen Pensionspreis zu einigen.

Hochsaisonpreise werden im allgemeinen von Juni bis September berechnet.

Zimmerreservierung

Hotels : Es ist ratsam, wenn irgend möglich, die Zimmer reservieren zu lassen. Bitten Sie den Hotelier, daß er Ihnen in seinem Bestätigungsschreiben alle seine Bedingungen mitteilt.

Besonders in Seebädern wird Vollpension im allgemeinen nur wochenweise, von Samstag zu Samstag gewährt.

Bei schriftlichen Zimmerbestellungen empfiehlt es sich, einen Freiumschlag oder einen internationalen Antwortschein beizufügen.

Einige Hoteliers verlangen eine Anzahlung (etwa 10 % wenn nichts anderes vereinbart wird) auf den voraussichtlichen Endpreis. Sie ist als Garantie für beide Seiten anzusehen.

Restaurant : Es empfiehlt sich, Tische immer und so früh wie möglich vorzubestellen.

Tiere

Das Mitführen von Haustieren (Hunde, Katzen u. dgl.) bei der Einreise in Großbritannien und Irland ist untersagt.

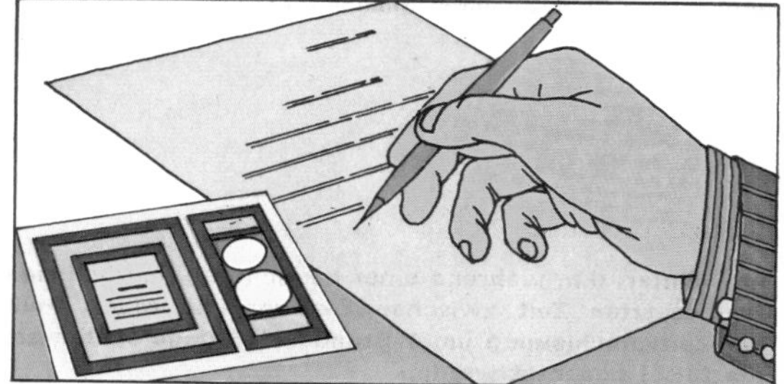

Besichtigung einer Stadt und ihrer Umgebung

STÄDTE

986 ㉞	Nummer der Faltseite auf der Michelin-Karte 986
pop. 1,057	Einwohnerzahl (nach der letzten offiziellen Volkszählung)
✉ York	Zuständiges Postamt
✆ 0225 Bath	Zuständiges Fernsprechamt
BX **A**	Markierung auf dem Stadtplan
☼, ≺	Rundblick, Aussichtspunkt
⛳18	Öffentlicher Golfplatz mit Lochzahl
✈	Flughafen
⛴	Personen- und Autofähre
⛴	Personenfähre *Liste der Schiffahrtsgesellschaften am Ende des Führers*
🚘 ✆ 218	Ladestelle für Autoreisezüge - Nähere Auskünfte unter der angegebenen Telefonnummer
i	Verkehrsverein (Informationsstelle)

HAUPTSEHENSWÜRDIGKEITEN

★★★	Eine Reise wert
★★	Verdient einen Umweg
★	Sehenswert
AC	Eintritt (gegen Gebühr)

Lage

See	In der Stadt
Envir.	In der Umgebung der Stadt
Exc.	Ausflugsziele
N, S, E, W	In N = Norden, S = Süden, E = Osten, W = Westen der Stadt
A 22	Zu erreichen über die Straße A 22
2 m.	Entfernung in Meilen
h. mn.	Zeitangabe für nicht im Wagen zurücklegbare Strecken, hin und zurück (h = Stunden, mn = Minuten)

Winterzeit

Im Winter, d.h. während einer bestimmten, jährlich neu festgesetzten Zeit zwischen Oktober und März, muß die Zeitverschiebung um 1 Stunde (1 Stunde später als die MEZ) beachtet werden.

Stadtpläne

ZEICHENERKLÄRUNG

Straßen

Nebenstraßen sind nur angedeutet

Durchfahrts- oder Umgehungsstraße – Straße mit getrennten Fahrbahnen. . . . . .

Autobahn und Nummer der Anschlußstelle . . . .

Einbahnstraße – Straße im Bau . . . .

Straße für Kfz gesperrt, nicht befahrbar oder mit Verkehrsbeschränkungen . . . . .

Bahnübergänge : schienengleich, Überführung, Unterführung . . . .

Tor – Passage – Tunnel . . . .

Einkaufsstraße – Öffentlicher Parkplatz, Parkhaus . . . .

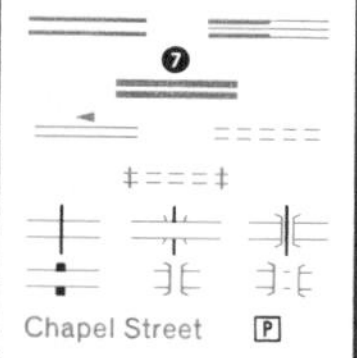

Sehenswürdigkeiten - Hotels

Sehenswertes Gebäude mit Haupteingang . } Referenzbuchstabe auf dem Plan . .
Kathedrale – Kirche . . . . }

Markierung der Hotels und Restaurants auf dem Plan . . . .

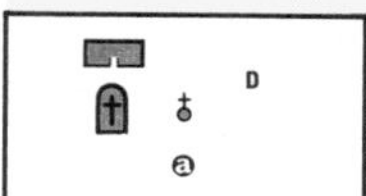

Sonstige Zeichen

Kathedrale – Kirche – Krankenhaus – Postlagernde Sendungen, Telegraph, Telefon. .

Öffentliche Gebäude, durch Buchstaben gekennzeichnet :

Sitz der Grafschaftsverwaltung – Rathaus. . . . .

Polizei (in größeren Städten Polizeipräsidium) – Museum . . . .

Theater – Universität, Hochschule . . . .

Verkehrsverein (Informationsstelle) . . . .

Friedhof – Grünfläche mit Baumbestand, Park . . . .

Leuchtturm – Sportplatz . . . .

Öffentlicher Golf – Golf (Zutritt bedingt erlaubt) . . . .

Pferderennbahn – Rundblick – Aussicht . . . .

Anlegestelle : Personen- und Autofähre – Flughafen . . . .

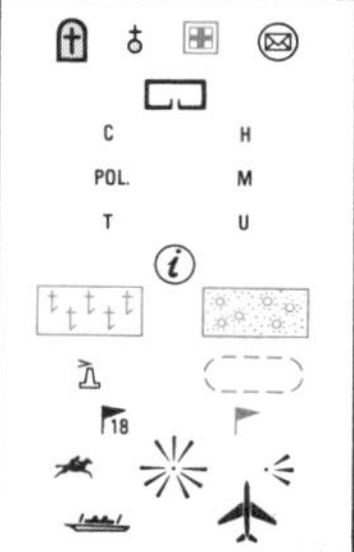

London - Besondere Symbole

Name des Verwaltungsbezirks (borough) – des Stadtteils (area) . . . .

Grenze des „ borough " – des „ area ". . . . .

U–Bahnhof . . . .

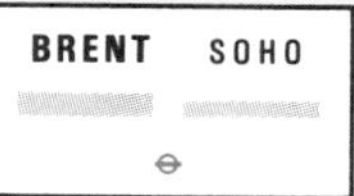

Für Ihren Wagen

Bei den meisten Orten geben wir die Adressen der Kfz- Vertragswerkstätten mit Abschlepp- bzw. Reparaturdienst an.
Hinweise für Ihre Reifen finden Sie auf den blau umrandeten Seiten.

Reisen mit Ihrem Wagen

Die wichtigsten Automobilclubs des Landes sind die Automobile Association und der Royal Automobile Club, die den Mitgliedern der der FIA angeschlossenen Automobilclubs Pannenhilfe leisten und einige ihrer Dienstleistungen anbieten.

AUTOMOBILE ASSOCIATION
Fanum House
BASINGSTOKE, Hants., RG21 2EA
☎ (0256) 20123

ROYAL AUTOMOBILE CLUB
83-85 Pall Mall
LONDON SW1Y 5HW
☎ (01) 930 4343

MOTORWAY SERVICE AREAS

RIFORNIMENTO SULLE AUTOSTRADE

RAVITAILLEMENT SUR AUTOROUTES

TANKEN UND RASTEN AN DER AUTOBAHN

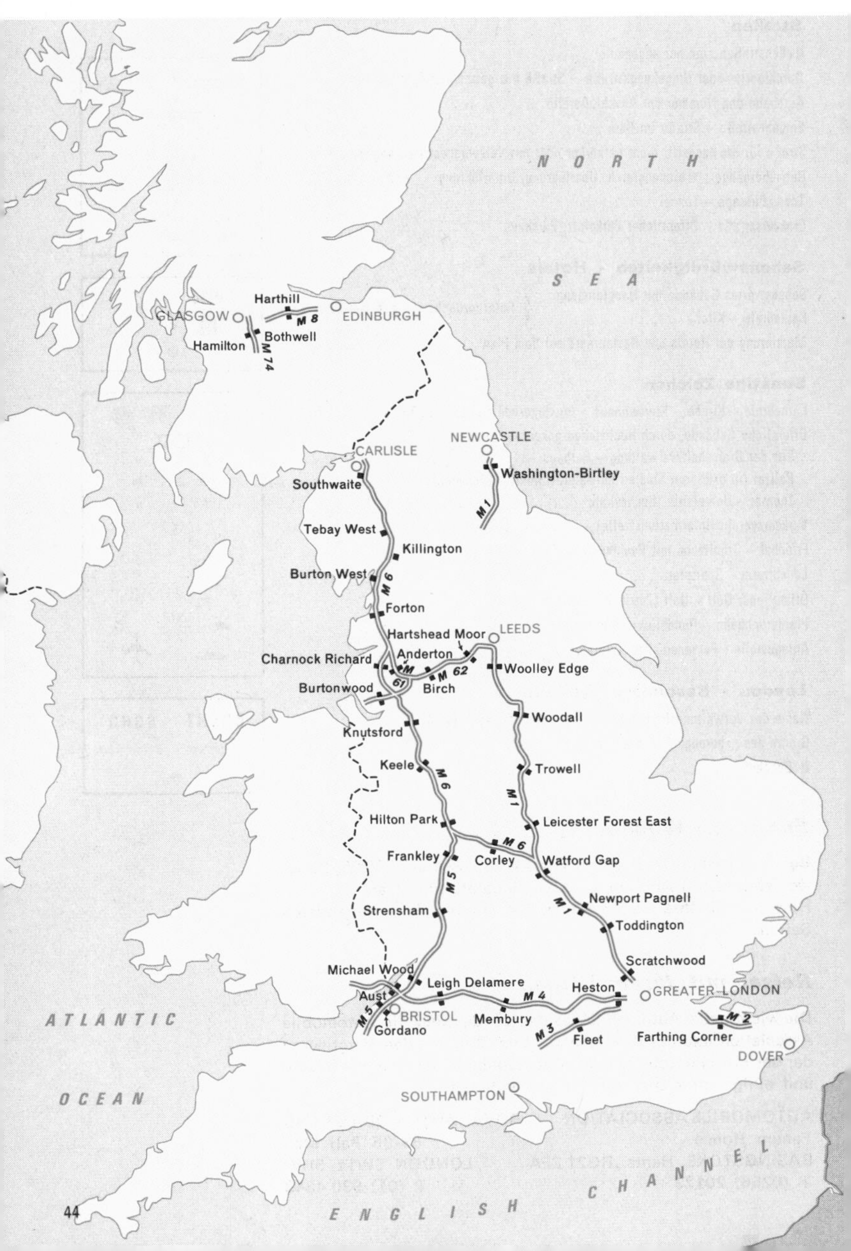

MOTORWAY HOTELS
Hotels included in the Guide on, or near the interchanges of Motorways and A (M) class roads. See appropriate town for details.

ALBERGHI AUTOSTRADALI
I sottoindicati alberghi, selezionati nella guida, si trovano lungo le autostrade o lungo le strade principali, in prossimità degli svincoli. Per ogni dettaglio vedere la località interessata.

HOTELS D'AUTOROUTE
Les hôtels ci-dessous, sélectionnés dans le guide se trouvent sur les autoroutes ou les routes principales, à proximité des échangeurs. Pour tous détails, voir le nom de la ville.

AUTOBAHN-RASTHÄUSER
Die unten aufgeführten Hotels befinden sich an Autobahnen, Hauptverkehrsstraßen oder in der Nähe von Autobahnauffahrten. Nähere Einzelheiten unter dem Ortstext.

Location	Hotel	Town	Details see page
M 1			
Scratchwood Service Area	TraveLodge	Hendon (L.B. of Barnet)	269
Junction 6 – NE: 1 m. on A 405	Noke	St. Albans	361
Junction 8 – W: ½ m. on A 4147	Post House	Hemel Hempstead	188
Junction 11 – E: ¼ m. on A 505	Luton Crest Motel	Luton	296
Junction 11 – E: ¾ m. on A 505	Luton Eurocrest	Luton	296
Newport Pagnell Service Area 3	TraveLodge	Newport Pagnell	312
Junction 18 – E: ¼ m. on A 428	Post House	Rugby (at Crick)	358
Junction 21/21A – NE: 2 ½ m. on A 46	Post House	Leicester (at Braunstone)	212
Junction 25 – W: ¼ m. on A 52	Post House	Nottingham (at Sandiacre)	329
Junction 25 – S: ½ m. on B 6002	Novotel	Nottingham (at Long Eaton)	327
Junction 40 – E: 1 m. on A 638	Post House	Wakefield	409
A 1 (M)			
Junction A 1, A 638 – N: 2 ½ m. on A 1	TraveLodge	Wentbridge (at Barnsdale Bar)	414
A 1 (M) via A 66 (M) – E: 2 m. on A 66	Europa Lodge	Darlington	151
Junction A 1 (M) and A 1000	Clock Motel	Welwyn	414
M 2			
Junction 1 – W: ¼ m. on A 2	Inn on the Lake	Shorne	375
M 3			
Junction 3 – N: 1 m. on A 30	Cricketers'	Bagshot	69
Junction 6 – SW: 1 ½ m. at junction A 30 and A 339	Hampshire Moat House	Basingstoke	72
M 4			
Junction 3 – N: 1 ½ m. off A 312	Arlington	Heathrow Airport (L.B. of Hillingdon)	276
Junction 4 – S: ½ m. on B 379	Post House	Heathrow Airport	276
Junction 4 – N: ½ m. on B 379	Holiday Inn	Heathrow Airport	275
Junction 5 – NW: ¼ m. on A 4	Holiday Inn	Slough	378
Junction 5 – SE: ½ m. on A 4	Heathrow Ambassador	Slough (at Colnbrook)	378
Junction 9A – NE: ½ m. on Shoppenhangers Rd	Maidenhead Eurocrest	Maidenhead	298
Junction 11 – N: ½ m. on A 33	Post House	Reading	351
Junction 15 – N: 2 m. on A 345	Post House	Swindon	396
Junction 19 – SW: 2 ½ m. by M 32 on A 4174	Bristol Eurocrest	Bristol (at Hambrook)	111
Junction 24 – E: 1 ½ m. on A 48	New Inn Motel	Newport (Gwent) (at Langstone)	320
Junction 24 – S: ½ m. on A 48	Gateway Motel	Newport (Gwent)	320

Location	Hotel	Town	Details see page
M 5			
Junction 1 – W: 1 m. on A 41	Europa Lodge	Birmingham (at West Bromwich)	83
Junction 5 – SW: 1 m. on A 38	Château Impney	Droitwich	157
Junction 11 – E: 1 m. on A 40	Golden Valley	Cheltenham	130
Junction 14 – N: 3 ½ m. on A 38 by B 4509	Newport Towers Motel	Berkeley (at Newport)	79
Junction 14 – SW: 1 ½ m. on A 38 by B 4509	Park	Falfield	167
M 6			
Junction 2 – S: 1 ½ m. on A 46	Coventry Eurocrest	Coventry (at Walsgrave-on-Sowe)	143
Junction 3 – S: 1 m. on A 444	Novotel	Coventry (at Longford)	143
Junction 7 – N: ¼ m. on A 34	Post House	Birmingham (at Great Barr)	83
Junction 14 – SE: ½ m. on A 5013	Tillington Hall	Stafford	384
Junction 15 – N: ¼ m. on A 519	Post House	Newcastle-under-Lyme	314
Junction 15 – S: ¾ m. on A 519	Clayton Lodge	Newcastle-under-Lyme	314
Charnock Richard Service Area	TraveLodge	Charnock Richard	129
Junction 27 – E: ¼ m. on B 5239	Casinelli's Almond Brook Motor Inn	Standish	385
Junction 38 and 39 – N: 1 m. of junction 38	Tebay Mountain Lodge Motel	Tebay	397
Junction 31 – W: ¼ m. on A 59	Tickled Trout	Preston (at Samlesbury)	349
Junction 44 – N: ¼ m. on A 7	Carlisle Crest Motel	Carlisle (at Kingstown)	125
M 20			
Junction 1 – E: ½ m. on A 20	Great Danes	Maidstone (at Hollingbourne)	299
Junction 3 – S: ½ m. on A 229	Veglios	Maidstone (at Sandling)	299
Junction with A 20 – NW: ½ m. on A 20	with rm Moat	Wrotham	434
M 23			
Junction with A 23 – S: ½ m. on A 23	Crawley Forest	Crawley (at Pease Pottage)	149
M 25			
Junction with A 217 – N: 3 ¼ m. on A 217	Pickard Motor	Burgh Heath	115
M 32 (this hotel also under M 4)			
Junction 1 – W: ½ m. on A 4174	Bristol Eurocrest	Bristol (at Hambrook)	111
M 40			
Junction 2 – E: 1 ¾ m. on A 40	Bellhouse	Beaconsfield	76
Junction 7 – NW: ½ m. on A 40	Belfry	Milton Common	309
M 56			
Junction 5 – on Airport Approach Road	Excelsior	Manchester (at Airport)	301
Junction 11 – N: ¼ m. on A 56	Lord Daresbury	Daresbury	150
Junction 12 – SE: ¼ m. off A 557	Runcorn Eurocrest	Runcorn	359
M 57			
Junction with A 580 – E: ½ m. on A 580	Liverpool Crest Motel	Liverpool (at Knowsley)	217
M 61			
Junction 5 – NE: 1 m. on A 58	Bolton Crest	Bolton	94
M 62			
Junction 24 – S: ¼ m. on A 629	Pennine President	Huddersfield	195
Junction 26 – N: 1 m. on M 606	Novotel	Bradford	100
Junction 30 – N: 1 m. on A 639	Leeds Crest Motel	Leeds (at Oulton)	207
M 63			
Junction 9 – by approach Rd	Post House	Manchester (at Northenden)	301

TOWNS INCLUDED IN THE GUIDE

To keep the full, distinctive flavour of the separate kingdoms, principality, province, republic and islands which go to make up the British Isles, the Guide has been divided into sections each preceded by a separate map.

The maps show the towns and places with establishments included in the Guide, and those particularly selected for their general attractiveness, quiet atmosphere and good food.

A map of Great Britain and the Republic of Ireland at the beginning of the Guide shows major roads and main passenger and car ferry routes.

LES VILLES CITÉES

Chaque royaume ou Etat composant les Iles Britanniques garde sa personnalité propre ; aussi sont-ils présentés en faisant précéder la nomenclature de chacun d'eux par une carte.

Cette carte signale les localités retenues et, pour chacune d'elles l'existence éventuelle d'établissements recommandés pour leur agrément, leur calme ou leur bonne cuisine.

Une carte générale de la Grande-Bretagne et de la République d'Irlande figure en outre au début de ce Guide et donne les principales voies de communications terrestres et maritimes.

LE CITTÀ COMPRESE NELLA GUIDA

Ogni Reame o Stato che compone le Isole Britanniche mantiene la sua propria personalità; perciò abbiamo ritenuto opportuno presentarli facendo precedere una carta geografica alla nomenclatura di ciascuno di essi.

Questa carta segnala le località selezionate e, per ognuna di esse, l'eventuale esistenza di esercizi particolarmente raccomandabili per la loro amenità, la loro tranquillità o la loro buona cucina.

Inoltre, una carta generale della Gran Bretagna e della Repubblica d'Irlanda figura all'inizio della Guida ed indica le principali vie di comunicazione terrestri e marittime.

DIE IM MICHELIN-FÜHRER ERWÄHNTEN ORTE

Jedes einzelne der Länder, die unter dem Begriff « Britische Inseln » zusammengefaßt sind, hat seinen eigenen Charakter; wir haben dem Rechnung getragen, indem wir dem Ortsverzeichnis jedes « Landes » eine Übersichtskarte vorangestellt haben.

Auf dieser Karte finden Sie alle im Führer erwähnten Orte, Orte mit besonders angenehmen oder ruhig gelegenen Häusern, sowie solche mit besonders guter Küche.

Eine Gesamtkarte Großbritanniens und der Republik Irland mit den wichtigsten Verkehrsverbindungen (Land- und Seewege) finden Sie in der Einleitung.

England and Wales

COUNTY ABBREVIATIONS

ABBREVIAZIONI DELLE CONTEE

ABRÉVIATIONS DES COMTÉS

ABKÜRZUNGEN DER GRAFSCHAFTEN

ENGLAND

Avon	Avon
Bedfordshire	Beds.
Berkshire	Berks.
Buckinghamshire	Bucks.
Cambridgeshire	Cambs.
Cheshire	Cheshire
Cleveland	Cleveland
Cornwall	Cornwall
Cumbria	Cumbria
Derbyshire	Derbs.
Devon	Devon
Dorset	Dorset
Durham	Durham
East Sussex	East Sussex
Essex	Essex
Gloucestershire	Glos.
Greater Manchester	Greater Manchester
Hampshire	Hants.
Hereford and Worcester	Heref. and Worc.
Hertfordshire	Herts.
Isle of Wight	I. O. W.
Kent	Kent
Lancashire	Lancs.
Leicestershire	Leics.
Lincolnshire	Lincs.
Merseyside	Merseyside
Middlesex	Middx.
Norfolk	Norfolk
Northamptonshire	Northants.
North Humberside	North Humberside
Northumberland	Northumb.
North Yorkshire	North Yorks.
Nottinghamshire	Notts.
Oxfordshire	Oxon.
Salop	Salop
Somerset	Somerset
South Humberside	South Humberside
South Yorkshire	South Yorks.
Staffordshire	Staffs.
Suffolk	Suffolk
Surrey	Surrey
Tyne and Wear	Tyne and Wear
Warwickshire	Warw.
West Midlands	West Midlands
West Sussex	West Sussex
West Yorkshire	West Yorks.
Wiltshire	Wilts.

WALES

Clwyd	Clwyd
Dyfed	Dyfed
Gwent	Gwent
Gwynedd	Gwynedd
Mid Glamorgan	Mid Glam.
Powys	Powys
South Glamorgan	South Glam.
West Glamorgan	West Glam.

LICENSING HOURS - WHEN DRINKING ALCOHOLIC BEVERAGES IS PERMITTED IN PUBS AND BARS AND OTHER ON-LICENSED PREMISES (The General Rule).

HEURES PERMISES POUR LA CONSOMMATION DES BOISSONS ALCOOLISÉES (Règle Générale).

ORARI CONSENTITI PER LA CONSUMAZIONE DI BEVANDE ALCOOLICHE (Regola Generale).

AUSSCHANKZEITEN FÜR ALKOHOLISCHE GETRÄNKE (Allgemeine Regelung).

	from de	to à	from de	to à	Possible extension to Extension possible jusqu'à	
Weekdays (other than Good Friday and Christmas Day) **Jours de semaine** (autres que Vendredi-Saint et Jour de Noël)	11.00	15.00	17.30	22.30	23.00	**Giorni della settimana** (esclusi Venerdì Santo e Natale) **Wochentags** (außer Karfreitag und Weihnachten)
Sundays, Good Friday, Christmas Day **Dimanches, Vendredi-Saint, Jour de Noël**	12.00	14.00	19.00	22.30		**Domeniche, Venerdì Santo, Natale** **Sonntags, Karfreitag und Weihnachten**
	dalle von	alle bis	dalle von	alle bis	Estensione possibile fino alle Verlängerung möglich bis	

Wines and beverages may be taken with meals until 15.00 hours in on-licensed premises.

RESIDENTS : There are no time restrictions in licensed hotels for residents and their private friends.

SUNDAYS IN WALES: as in England in Clwyd, Gwent, Powys, Mid/South Glamorgan and parts of Dyfed, Gwynedd and West Glamorgan. Full day closure in parts of Dyfed, Gwynedd and West Glamorgan.

Boissons au cours des repas: jusqu'à 15 h dans les lieux autorisés.

RÉSIDENTS : aucune restriction dans l'hôtel de résidence si celui-ci possède une licence, y compris pour leurs amis privés.

DIMANCHE au PAYS DE GALLES : mêmes horaires qu'en Angleterre pour les comtés de Clwyd, Gwent, Powys, Mid/South Glamorgan et une partie des comtés de Dyfed, Gwynedd and West Glamorgan. Fermeture totale dans les autres parties du Dyfed, Gwynedd and West Glamorgan.

Bevande durante i pasti : fino alle 15 nei locali autorizzati.

RESIDENTI : nessuna restrizione nell'albergo di residenza se ha la licenza, anche per gli amici privati.

DOMENICA nel GALLES : stessi orari dell' Inghilterra per le contee di Clwyd, Gwent, Powys, Mid/South Glamorgan e una parte delle contee di Dyfed, Gwynedd and West Glamorgan. Chiusura totale nelle altre parti del Dyfed, Gwynedd and West Glamorgan.

Getränke zu den Mahlzeiten : bis 15 Uhr in den lizensierten Betrieben.

HOTELGÄSTE : Keine Beschränkung für den Gast und dessen persönliche Freunde im Hotel selbst, sofern dieses lizensiert ist.

SONNTAGSREGELUNG in WALES : gleiche Regelung wie in England für die Grafschaften Clwyd, Gwent, Powys, Mittel/Süd Glamorgan sowie für einen Teil der Grafschaften Dyfed, Gwynedd und West Glamorgan. In den übrigen Teilen dieser Grafschaften sind die Ausschank-betriebe geschlossen.

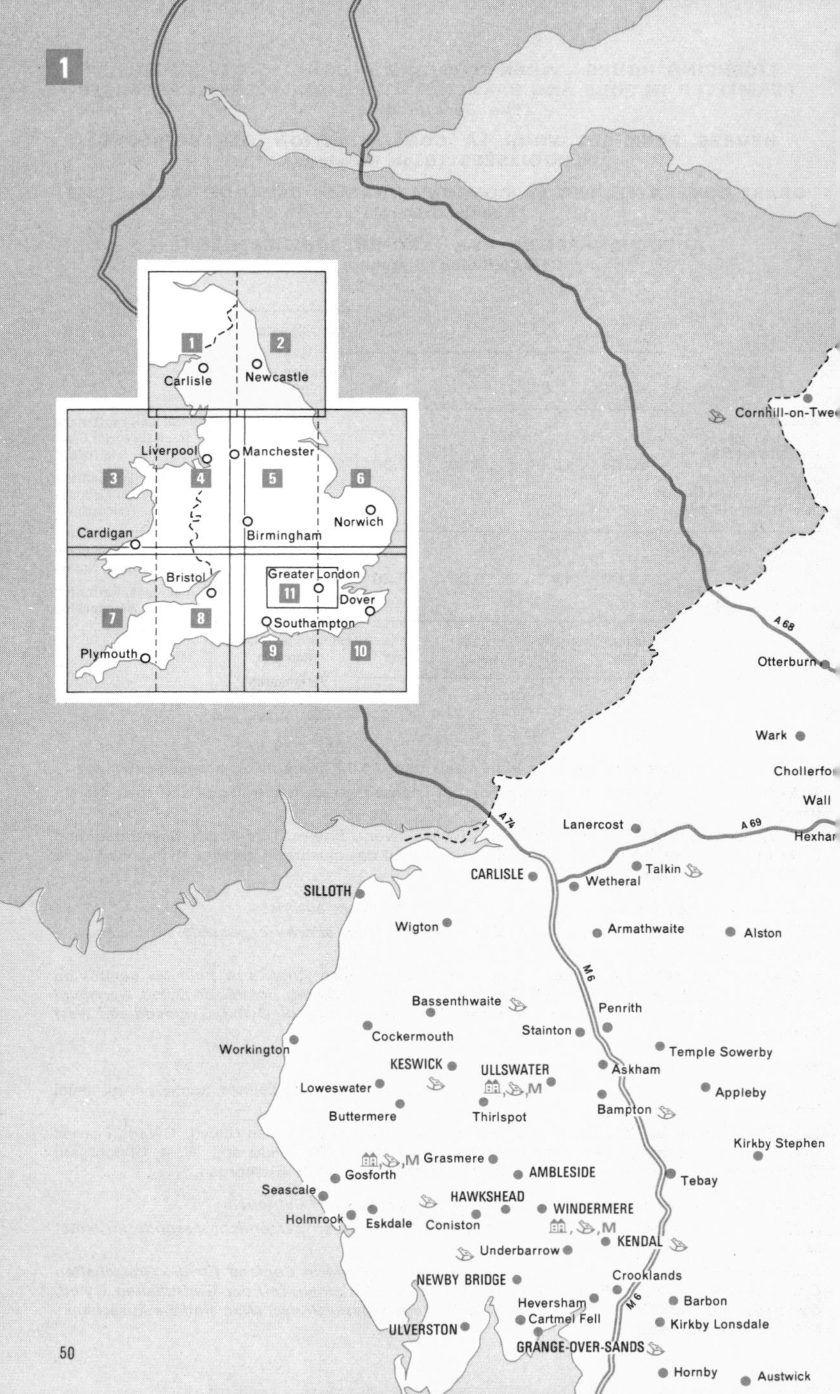
1
1
2
Carlisle
Newcastle
Liverpool
Manchester
3
4
5
6
Norwich
Cardigan
Birmingham
Bristol
Greater London
11
Dover
7
8
Southampton
Plymouth
9
10
Cornhill-on-Twe
A 68
Otterburn
Wark
Chollerfo
Wall
A 74
Lanercost
A 69
Hexhar
Talkin
CARLISLE
Wetheral
SILLOTH
Wigton
Armathwaite
Alston
M6
Bassenthwaite
Penrith
Cockermouth
Stainton
Workington
Temple Sowerby
KESWICK
ULLSWATER
Askham
Loweswater
M
Appleby
Buttermere
Thirlspot
Bampton
Kirkby Stephen
M
Grasmere
Gosforth
AMBLESIDE
Tebay
Seascale
HAWKSHEAD
WINDERMERE
Holmrook
Eskdale
Coniston
M
KENDAL
Underbarrow
Crooklands
NEWBY BRIDGE
Heversham
M6
Barbon
Cartmel Fell
Kirkby Lonsdale
ULVERSTON
GRANGE-OVER-SANDS
Hornby
Austwick

Place with at least :

one hotel or restaurant	● Durham
one pleasant hotel	🏨 , ✕ with rm.
one quiet, secluded hotel	⛐
one restaurant with	✿, ✿✿, M
See this town for establishments located in its vicinity	RICHMOND

Localité offrant au moins :

une ressource hôtelière	● Durham
un hôtel agréable	🏨 , ✕ with rm.
un hôtel très tranquille, isolé	⛐
une bonne table à	✿, ✿✿, M
Localité groupant dans le texte les ressources de ses environs	RICHMOND

La località possiede come minimo :

una risorsa alberghiera	● Durham
un albergo ameno	🏨 , ✕ with rm.
un albergo molto tranquillo, isolato	⛐
un'ottima tavola con	✿, ✿✿, M
La località raggruppa nel suo testo le risorse dei dintorni	RICHMOND

Ort mit mindestens :

einem Hotel oder Restaurant	● Durham
einem angenehmen Hotel	🏨 , ✕ with rm.
einem sehr ruhigen und abgelegenen Hotel	⛐
einem Restaurant mit	✿, ✿✿, M
Ort mit Angaben über Hotels und Restaurants in seiner Umgebung	RICHMOND

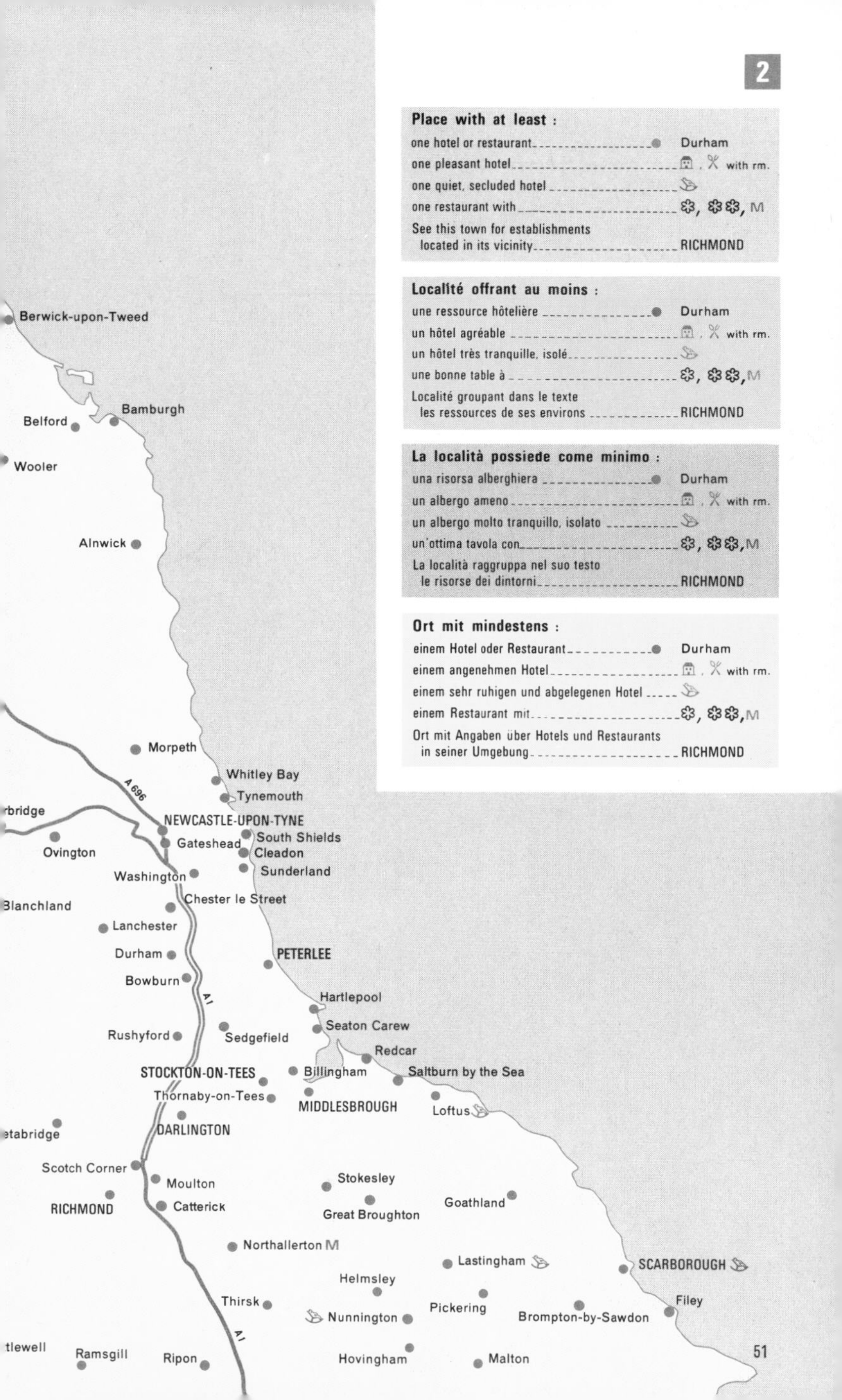

Berwick-upon-Tweed
Belford
Bamburgh
Wooler
Alnwick
Morpeth
A 696
Whitley Bay
Tynemouth
rbridge
NEWCASTLE-UPON-TYNE
Ovington
Gateshead
South Shields
Cleadon
Sunderland
Washington
Blanchland
Chester le Street
Lanchester
Durham
PETERLEE
Bowburn
A1
Hartlepool
Rushyford
Sedgefield
Seaton Carew
Redcar
STOCKTON-ON-TEES
Billingham
Saltburn by the Sea
Thornaby-on-Tees
MIDDLESBROUGH
Loftus
etabridge
DARLINGTON
Scotch Corner
Moulton
Stokesley
RICHMOND
Catterick
Great Broughton
Goathland
Northallerton M
Lastingham
SCARBOROUGH
Helmsley
Thirsk
Nunnington
Pickering
Filey
Brompton-by-Sawdon
A1
tlewell
Ramsgill
Ripon
Hovingham
Malton

3

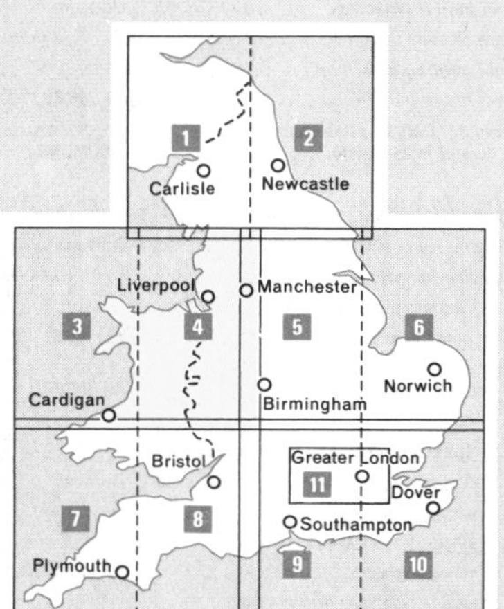
1
2
Carlisle
Newcastle
Liverpool
Manchester
3
4
5
6
Norwich
Cardigan
Birmingham
Bristol
Greater London
11
Dover
7
8
Southampton
Plymouth
9
10

Amlwch
Benllech
Trearddur Bay
A5
Beaumaris
Rhosneigr
MENAI BRIDGE
CAERNARFON
Pontlyfni
Nefyn
Criccieth
Portmeirion
ABERSOCH
HARLECH
Barmou
Fairbou
Aberdove
ABERYSTWYTH

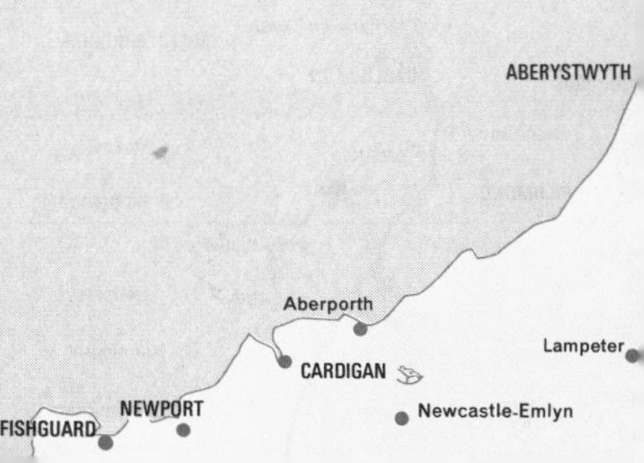
Aberporth
Lampeter
CARDIGAN
NEWPORT
FISHGUARD
Newcastle-Emlyn

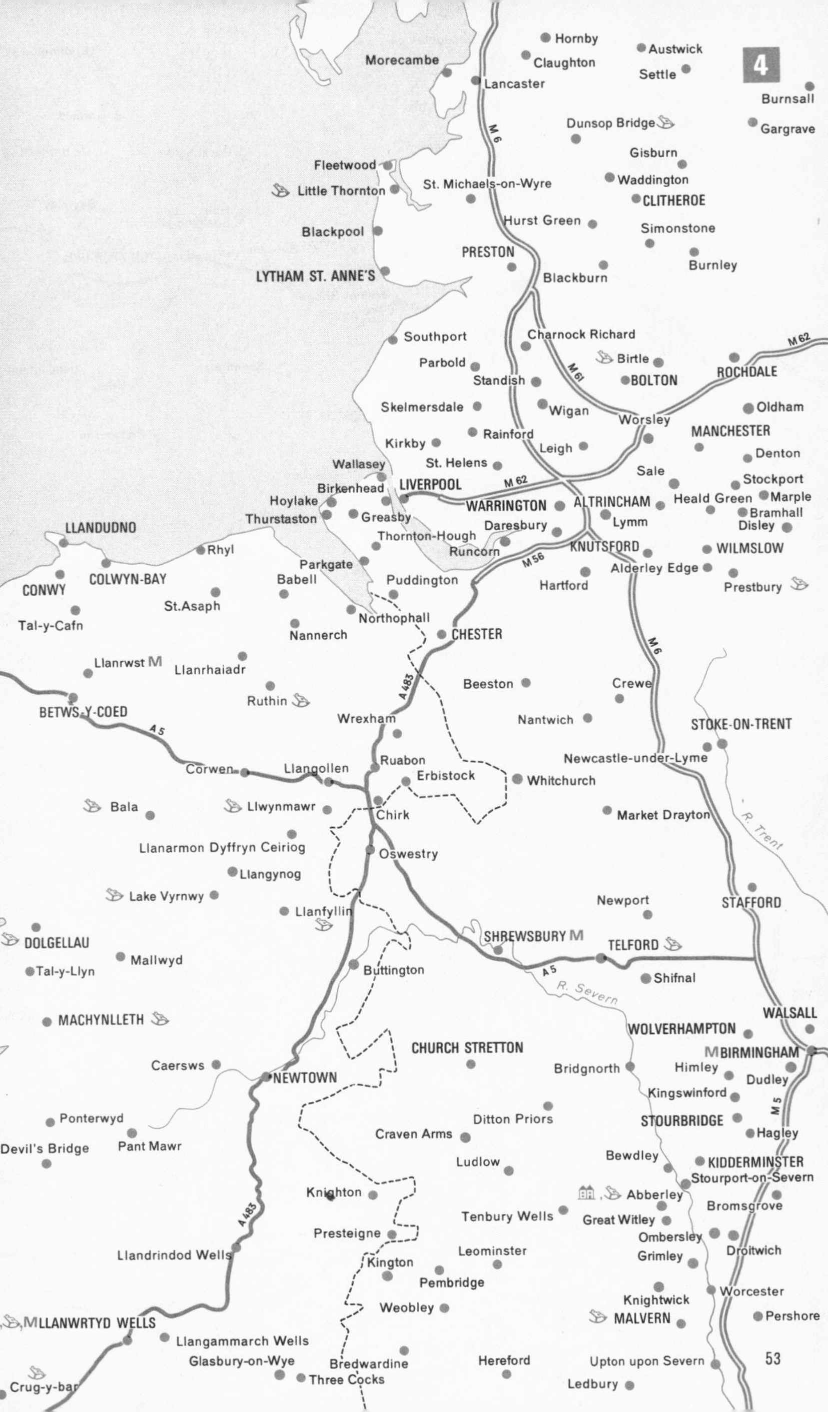

4
Morecambe
Hornby
Claughton
Austwick
Settle
Lancaster
Burnsall
Gargrave
M 6
Dunsop Bridge
Gisburn
Fleetwood
Little Thornton
St. Michaels-on-Wyre
Waddington
CLITHEROE
Blackpool
Hurst Green
Simonstone
PRESTON
Burnley
LYTHAM ST. ANNE'S
Blackburn
Southport
Charnock Richard
M 62
Parbold
Birtle
Standish
M 61
BOLTON
ROCHDALE
Skelmersdale
Wigan
Oldham
Worsley
Rainford
MANCHESTER
Kirkby
Leigh
Denton
Wallasey
St. Helens
Sale
Stockport
Birkenhead
LIVERPOOL
M 62
Heald Green
Marple
Hoylake
WARRINGTON
ALTRINCHAM
Bramhall
Thurstaston
Greasby
Lymm
Disley
LLANDUDNO
Thornton-Hough
Daresbury
Rhyl
Runcorn
KNUTSFORD
WILMSLOW
Parkgate
M 56
Alderley Edge
CONWY
COLWYN-BAY
Babell
Puddington
Hartford
Prestbury
St.Asaph
Tal-y-Cafn
Northophall
Nannerch
CHESTER
Llanrwst
Llanrhaiadr
M 6
Beeston
Crewe
A 483
Ruthin
BETWS-Y-COED
Wrexham
Nantwich
STOKE-ON-TRENT
A 5
Newcastle-under-Lyme
Ruabon
Corwen
Llangollen
Erbistock
Whitchurch
Bala
Llwynmawr
Chirk
Market Drayton
R. Trent
Llanarmon Dyffryn Ceiriog
Oswestry
Llangynog
Lake Vyrnwy
Newport
STAFFORD
Llanfyllin
DOLGELLAU
SHREWSBURY
TELFORD
Mallwyd
Buttington
A 5
Shifnal
Tal-y-Llyn
R. Severn
MACHYNLLETH
WALSALL
WOLVERHAMPTON
CHURCH STRETTON
BIRMINGHAM
Caersws
Bridgnorth
Himley
Dudley
NEWTOWN
Kingswinford
M 5
Ponterwyd
Ditton Priors
STOURBRIDGE
Devil's Bridge
Pant Mawr
Craven Arms
Hagley
Bewdley
KIDDERMINSTER
Ludlow
Stourport-on-Severn
Knighton
Abberley
A 483
Tenbury Wells
Bromsgrove
Great Witley
Presteigne
Ombersley
Droitwich
Llandrindod Wells
Leominster
Grimley
Kington
Pembridge
Worcester
Knightwick
Weobley
LLANWRTYD WELLS
MALVERN
Pershore
Llangammarch Wells
Glasbury-on-Wye
Bredwardine
Hereford
Upton upon Severn
Three Cocks
Ledbury
Crug-y-bar

5
Ripon
Ramsgill
Boroughbridge
Malton
Bridlington
Threshfield
Low Laithe
South Stainley
Burnsall
Knaresborough
Driffield
Skipton
Bolton Abbey
HARROGATE
YORK
Ilkley
Pool in W.
WETHERBY
Pocklington
Hornsea
Burley-in-W.
Harewood
Steeton
Bramhope
Holme upon
Spalding Moor
Beverley
Bingley
A1
Aldbrou
LEEDS
Selby
BRADFORD
Howden
Monk Fryston
A 63
KINGSTON-UPON-HULL
Halifax
Whitley Bridge
Wakefield
M 62
ROCHDALE
HUDDERSFIELD
WENTBRIDGE
Scunthorpe
Immingham
Brigg
Oldham
Holmbridge
BARNSLEY
DONCASTER
Crane Moor
Redbourne
Denton
M 18
Stockport
Bawtry
SHEFFIELD
Blyth
Barnby Moor
Disley
Hope
Castleton
Hathersage
Dronfield
Prestbury
Froggatt Edge
Barlborough
Baslow
Buxton
Bakewell
CHESTERFIELD
Tuxford
R. Trent
LINCOLN
Rowsley
Ollerton
Horncast
Longnor
Higham
Woodhall Spa
Matlock Bath
Farnsfield
M 1
STOKE-ON-TRENT
Thorpe
Southwell
Newark-on-Trent
M 6
Sleaford
A 17
Alton
NOTTINGHAM
DERBY
Grantham
Uttoxeter
Sudbury
Shardlow
Castle Donington
Tutbury
STAFFORD
Grimsthorpe
Burton upon Trent
Newton Solney
Hoton
Loughborough
Melton Mowbray
Bourne
Spald
RUGELEY
Ashby de la Zouch
Measham
Market Deeping
Langham
Lichfield
Cossington
Newtown Linford
Rothley
Oakham
STAMFORD
WOLVERHAMPTON
LEICESTER
WALSALL
Uppingham
PETERBOROU
BIRMINGHAM
Dudley
Coleshill
NUNEATON
Cottingham
Rowley Regis
M 6
MARKET HARBOROUGH
Corby
Oundle
Lutterworth
Hagley
Husbands Bosworth
SOLIHULL
Kettering
COVENTRY
Belbroughton
Knowle
RUGBY
Keyston
Hockley Heath
Kenilworth
Huntingd
M 5
Bromsgrove
Princethorpe
Catworth
Wellingborough
Brampton
Henley-in-Arden
REDDITCH
Royal Leamington Spa
Warwick
Buckden
Droitwich
NORTHAMPTON
Castle Ashby
Barford
Southam
St.Neots
Alcester
Kislingbury
Wellesbourne Hastings
Wilmcote
Horton
A 428
Stratford-on-Avon
Olney
Pershore
TOWCESTER
BEDFORD
Stoke Goldington
EVESHAM
Cow Honeybourne
Shipston-on-Stour
Stony Stratford
Newport Pagnell
CHIPPING CAMPDEN
BANBURY
Wicken

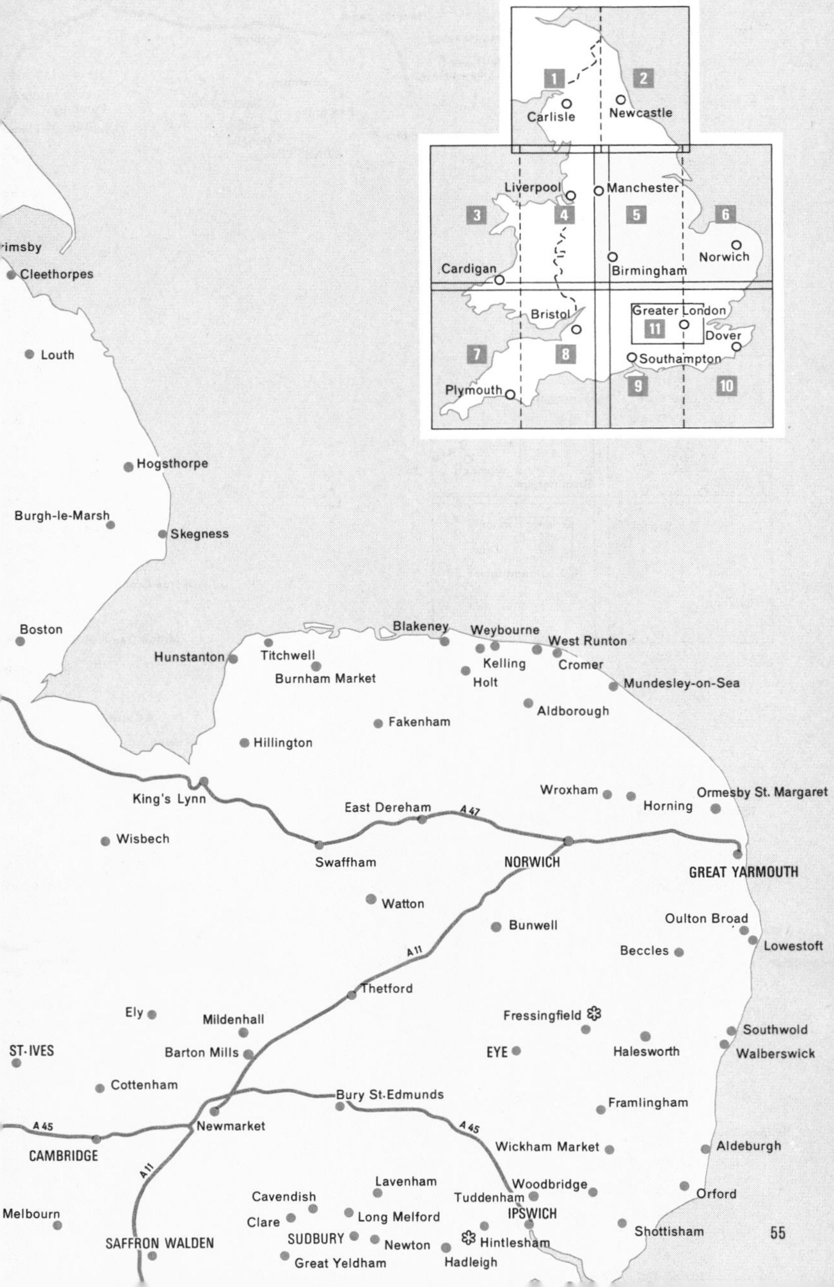

1
2
Carlisle
Newcastle
Liverpool
Manchester
3
4
5
6
Norwich
Cardigan
Birmingham
Greater London
Bristol
11
Dover
7
8
Southampton
Plymouth
9
10
rimsby
Cleethorpes
Louth
Hogsthorpe
Burgh-le-Marsh
Skegness
Boston
Hunstanton
Titchwell
Burnham Market
Blakeney
Weybourne
Kelling
Holt
West Runton
Cromer
Mundesley-on-Sea
Aldborough
Fakenham
Hillington
King's Lynn
East Dereham
A 47
Wroxham
Horning
Ormesby St. Margaret
Wisbech
Swaffham
NORWICH
GREAT YARMOUTH
Watton
Bunwell
Oulton Broad
Lowestoft
Beccles
A 11
Thetford
Ely
Mildenhall
Fressingfield
Southwold
Walberswick
ST·IVES
Barton Mills
EYE
Halesworth
Cottenham
Bury St·Edmunds
Framlingham
A 45
Newmarket
A 45
CAMBRIDGE
Wickham Market
Aldeburgh
A 11
Lavenham
Woodbridge
Orford
Cavendish
Tuddenham
Melbourn
Clare
Long Melford
IPSWICH
Shottisham
SAFFRON WALDEN
SUDBURY
Newton
Hintlesham
Great Yeldham
Hadleigh

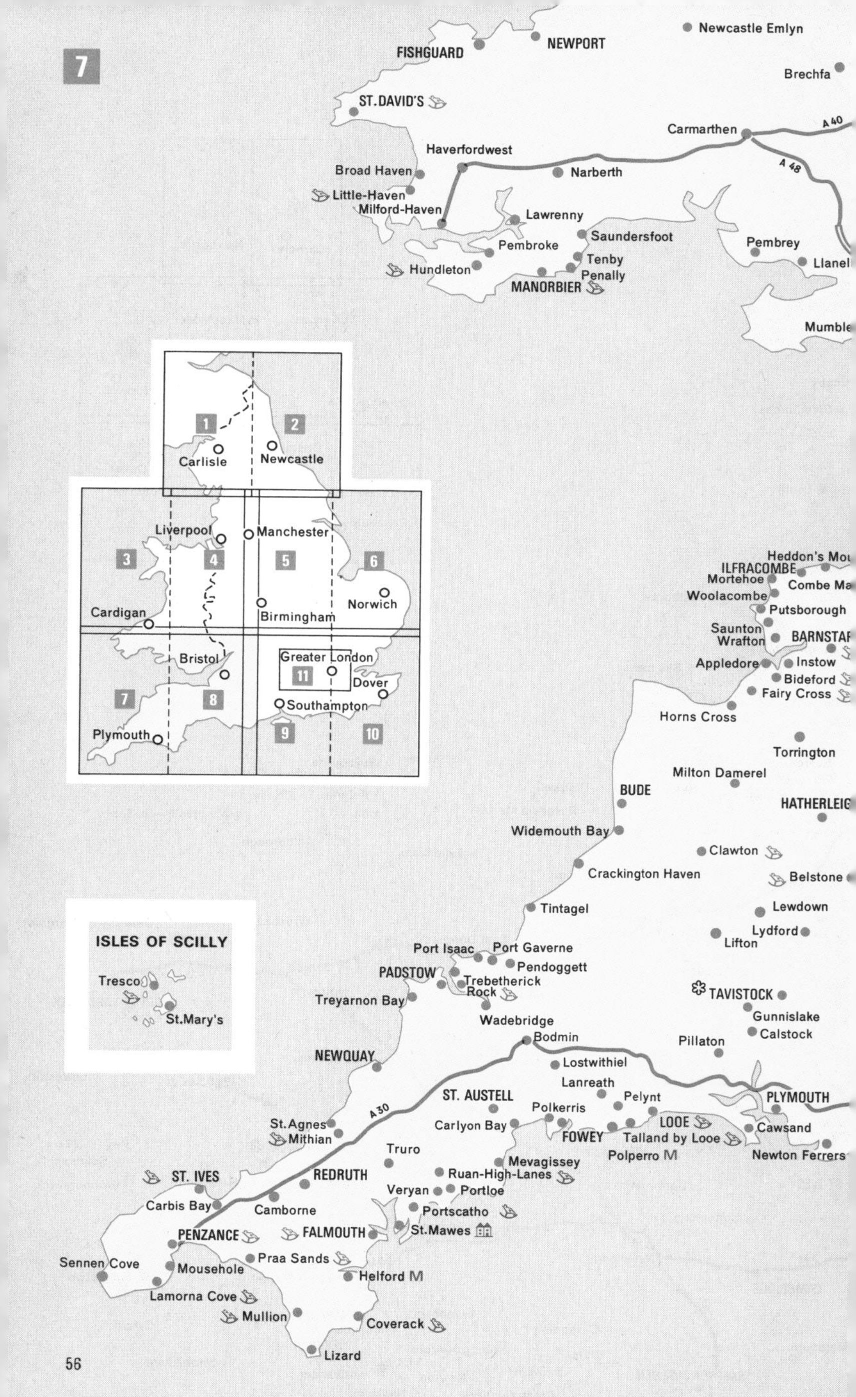

7

FISHGUARD
NEWPORT
Newcastle Emlyn
Brechfa
ST. DAVID'S
Carmarthen
A 40
Haverfordwest
A 48
Broad Haven
Narberth
Little-Haven
Milford-Haven
Lawrenny
Saundersfoot
Pembrey
Pembroke
Tenby
Llanel
Hundleton
Penally
MANORBIER
Mumble

1
2
Carlisle
Newcastle
Liverpool
Manchester
3
4
5
6
Cardigan
Birmingham
Norwich
Bristol
Greater London
11
Dover
7
8
Southampton
Plymouth
9
10

Heddon's Mou
ILFRACOMBE
Mortehoe
Combe Ma
Woolacombe
Putsborough
Saunton
Wrafton
BARNSTAP
Appledore
Instow
Bideford
Fairy Cross
Horns Cross
Torrington
Milton Damerel
BUDE
HATHERLEIG
Widemouth Bay
Clawton
Crackington Haven
Belstone
Tintagel
Lewdown
Lydford
Lifton

ISLES OF SCILLY
Tresco
St.Mary's

Port Isaac
Port Gaverne
Pendoggett
PADSTOW
Trebetherick
Rock
TAVISTOCK
Treyarnon Bay
Gunnislake
Wadebridge
Calstock
Bodmin
Pillaton
NEWQUAY
Lostwithiel
Lanreath
ST. AUSTELL
Pelynt
PLYMOUTH
Polkerris
St. Agnes
LOOE
Cawsand
Carlyon Bay
Mithian
FOWEY
Talland by Looe
A 30
Polperro
Newton Ferrers
Truro
Mevagissey
ST. IVES
REDRUTH
Ruan-High-Lanes
Veryan
Portloe
Carbis Bay
Camborne
Portscatho
PENZANCE
FALMOUTH
St.Mawes
Praa Sands
Sennen Cove
Mousehole
Helford
Lamorna Cove
Mullion
Coverack
Lizard

A 40
Llandovery
Llangadog
Glasbury-on-Wye
Three Cocks
Hereford
Upton upon Severn
Ledbury
Tewkesbury
8
Brecon
ROSS-ON-WYE
CHELTENHAM
Llangynidr
Crickhowell
GLOUCESTER
ABERGAVENNY
Symond's Yat
Newnham
Painswick
MONMOUTH
Coleford
M 5
Frampton on Severn
Merthyr Tydfil
STROUD
Aberdare
Llandogo
Lydney
BERKELEY
Usk
Tintern
Stone
Neath
Blackwood
Chepstow
Falfield
Wotton under Edge
Caerleon
Thornbury
TETBURY M
Port Talbot
MALMESBURY
Alveston
NEWPORT
Dunkirk
Sutton Benger
A 48
Chipping Sodbury
M 4
CARDIFF
Castle Combe
Chippenham
PORTHCAWL
BRISTOL
Keynsham
Cowbridge
PENARTH
Calne
Clevedon
Llantwit Major
Barry
BATH M
Lacock
Shaw
Devizes
Weston-super-Mare
Stanton Wick
Blagdon
Axbridge
Farrington Gurney
Priddy
Emborough
Lynmouth
Wedmore
Frome
Minehead
Wells
Porlock Weir
Watchet
Dunster
Holford
Shepton Mallet
Bilbrook
Williton
M Glastonbury
Upton Noble
Corton
Exford
Bridgwater
Street
Evercreech
Winsford
Castle Cary
Hindon
Somerton
Mere
Brushford
Long Sutton
Wincanton
Milton on Stour
M 5
TAUNTON M
Martock
Shaftesbury
Wellington
South Petherton
YEOVIL
SHERBORNE
Ilminster
Seavington St. Mary
TIVERTON
Sturminster Newton
Donyatt
with rm. , M
Crewkerne
Bickleigh
Chardstock
Weston
Hawkchurch
Milton Abbas
Wimborne Minster
Wilmington
Broadwindsor
Tedburn St. Mary
Gittisham
Piddletrenthide
A 30
Ottery St. Mary
COLYTON
Charmouth
Drewsteignton
EXETER
Bridport
Newton Poppleford
POOLE
A 35
Seaton
LYME REGIS
Chideock
Wareham
Dorchester
SIDMOUTH
Wool
Branscombe
West Lulworth
Budleigh Salterton
Lustleigh
Exmouth
Weymouth
Bovey Tracey
Dawlish
A 38
Portland
Two Bridges
Kingsteignton
Teignmouth
Buckland in the Moor
Shaldon
Ashburton
Newton Abbot
Buckfastleigh
TORQUAY
Staverton
South Brent
Paignton
TOTNES
A 38
Harbertonford
BRIXHAM
MODBURY
DARTMOUTH
KINGSBRIDGE
Torcross
SALCOMBE
East Prawle

9
CHIPPING CAMPDEN
BANBURY
BRACKLEY
Wicken
Woburn Sands
Steppingley
Flitton
Letchworth
BROADWAY
Blockley
Moreton-in-Marsh
Buckingham
Woburn
HITCHIN
Winchcombe
STOW-ON-THE-WOLD
Chipping Norton
Middleton Stoney
Bicester
Whitchurch
Linslade
STEVENAG
M 5
CHELTENHAM
Kingham
Chadlington
Dunstable
Luton
Bourton-on-the Water
Chesterton
Mentmore
Charlbury
Codicote
Shipton-under-Wychwood
Woodstock
Weston-on-the-Green
Ivinghoe
Harpenden
Welw
Northleach
Burford
Minster Lovell
Painswick
Fossebridge
South Leigh
Bibury
M 1
CIRENCESTER
Clanfield
Fairford
Lechlade
TETBURY
Faringdon
Cricklade
M 40
Wantage
MALMESBURY
SWINDON
GREATE
M 4
11
Sutton Benger
Chippenham
Ramsbury
M 4
Calne
Kintbury
MALBOROUGH
Hungerford
Lacock
Hamstead Marshall
Devizes
M 3
Andover
Amesbury
Elstead
Godalming
Corton
Middle Wallop
Newdiga
Alton
A 33
Churt
Chiddingfold
Cranleigh
Stockbridge
Hindhead
Alfold Crossw
Barford-St. Martin
Alresford
HASLEMERE
Winchester
Horsham
SALISBURY
Rake
Brook
West Meon
Billingshur
Shaftesbury
Ampfield
Pulborough
Midhurst
West Chiltingto
ROMSEY
Chandler's Ford
Fittleworth
Thakeha
M 27
Bramshaw
ASHINGTON
Cadnam
Stoney Cross
Southampton
M 27
A 27
Ibsley
A 31
Horton
Lyndhurst
Burley
RINGWOOD
BEAULIEU
Ferndown
Brockenhurst
New Milton
Barton
LYMINGTON
Christchurch
POOLE
Milford on Sea
Mudeford
Bournemouth
Yarmouth
Wareham
Freshwater Bay
Studland
Totland Bay
Swanage
Botley
Amberley
Storrington
Small Dole
Wickham
STEYNING
Waterlooville
ARUNDEL
M 27
Fareham
A 27
CHICHESTER
WORTHING
Climping
Portsmouth
East Preston
Rustington
Lee-on-the-Solent
Hayling Island
Middleton-on-Sea
Bognor Regis
West Wittering
Cowes
Whippingham
Ryde
Selsey
Carisbrooke
Newport
Bembridge
Sandown
ISLE OF
WIGHT
Shanklin
Bonchurch
58
Niton
Ventnor

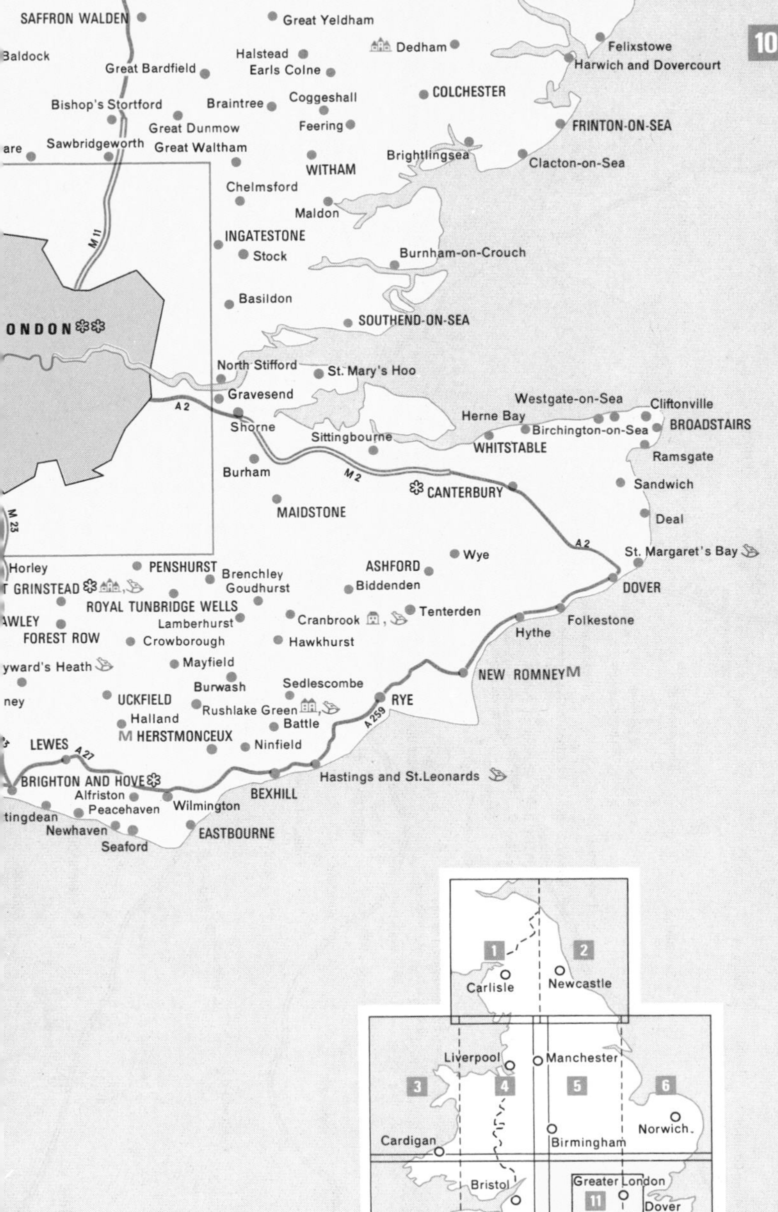
10
SAFFRON WALDEN
Great Yeldham
Dedham
Felixstowe
Harwich and Dovercourt
Baldock
Halstead
Great Bardfield
Earls Colne
COLCHESTER
Bishop's Stortford
Braintree
Coggeshall
FRINTON-ON-SEA
Great Dunmow
Feering
are
Sawbridgeworth
Great Waltham
Brightlingsea
Clacton-on-Sea
WITHAM
Chelmsford
Maldon
M 11
INGATESTONE
Stock
Burnham-on-Crouch
Basildon
ONDON
SOUTHEND-ON-SEA
North Stifford
St. Mary's Hoo
Gravesend
A 2
Westgate-on-Sea
Cliftonville
Herne Bay
Shorne
Birchington-on-Sea
BROADSTAIRS
Sittingbourne
WHITSTABLE
Ramsgate
Burham
M 2
CANTERBURY
Sandwich
MAIDSTONE
Deal
M 23
A 2
Wye
St. Margaret's Bay
Horley
PENSHURST
Brenchley
ASHFORD
T GRINSTEAD
Goudhurst
Biddenden
DOVER
ROYAL TUNBRIDGE WELLS
AWLEY
Lamberhurst
Cranbrook
Tenterden
Folkestone
FOREST ROW
Crowborough
Hawkhurst
Hythe
yward's Heath
Mayfield
NEW ROMNEY
Burwash
Sedlescombe
ney
UCKFIELD
Rushlake Green
RYE
Halland
Battle
A 259
HERSTMONCEUX
LEWES
A 27
Ninfield
BRIGHTON AND HOVE
Hastings and St.Leonards
Alfriston
BEXHILL
Wilmington
Peacehaven
tingdean
Newhaven
EASTBOURNE
Seaford
1
2
Carlisle
Newcastle
Liverpool
Manchester
3
4
5
6
Norwich
Cardigan
Birmingham
Greater London
Bristol
11
Dover
7
8
Southampton
9
10
Plymouth

11
60
Horton-cum-Studley
AYLESBURY
Aston Clinton
Tring
Redbourn
Welwyn Garden City
Hertingfordbury
HARLOW
Oxford
Milton Common
Thame
Owlswick
St.Albans
Hatfield
Hemel Hempstead
M 1
South Mimms
Radlett
Epping
Saunderton
Chipperfield
ABINGDON
Aston Rowant
M 40
Amersham
Chenies
Little Chalfont
Watford
Borehamwood
M 11
Abridge
Watlington
Penn Street
Rickmansworth
Brentwood
Fingest
High Wycombe
Chalfont.St-Giles
Chigwell
BENSON
Buckhurst Hill
Wallingford
BEACONSFIELD
Chalfont St. Peter
Bourne End
Gerrards Cross
Fawley
MARLOW
Stoke Poges
Cookham
New Denham
A 5
GREATER
Bulphan
Henley-on-Thames
Hurley-on-Thames
Iver Heath
A 11
Knowl Hill
Maidenhead
Burnham
SLOUGH
Bray-on-Thames
M 4
A 4
Thames
Purfleet
Pangbourne
Thames
Sonning-on-Thames
WINDSOR
Datchet
A 2
Yattendon
Winkfield
Reading
M 4
A 316
Staines
Englefield Green
LONDON
M
Egham
Sunbury
Newbury
Ascot
SHEPPERTON
Swanley
East Molesey
Swallowfield
Walton-on-Thames
Crowthorne
Bagshot
Silchester
Weybridge
Esher
A 23
Halstead
Camberley
Epsom
Cobham
Heckfield
Blackwater
Woking
Banstead
Wrotham
Burgh Heath
Ripley
Chipstead
Fleet
Ockham
Wrotham Heath
M 3
FARNBOROUGH
Limpsfield
BASINGSTOKE
East Horsley
GODSTONE
Westerham
SEVENOAKS
Plaxtol
ODIHAM
Redhill
Oxted
GUILDFORD
Bletchingley
FARNHAM
Gomshall
DORKING
23

ENGLAND and WALES

Towns

ABBERLEY Heref. and Worc. – pop. 558 – ✉ Worcester – ☎ 029 921 Great Witley.
London 137 – Birmingham 27 – Worcester 13.

- **The Elms**, WR6 6AT, W: 2 m. on A 443 ☎ 666, ≤, park – wc wc Ⓟ.
  M 6.50/7.50 **t.** 1.50 – 1.60 – **17 rm** 13.70/23.40 **st.** – P 22.50/24.50 **st.**

ABBOT'S SALFORD Warw. – see Evesham (Heref. and Worc.).

ABERDARE Mid Glam. 986 ㉛ – pop. 37,775 – ☎ 0685.
18 ☎ 3188.
London 179 – Cardiff 24 – Swansea 27.

- Boot, Victoria Sq., CF44 7GB, ☎ 2192 – Ⓟ
  19 rm.

ABERDOVEY Gwynedd 986 ㉗㉛ – pop. 927 – ☎ 065 472.
See: Afon Dovey's mouth (site**). **Envir.:** Llanegryn (church*) N: 8 m – Dolgoch Falls* NE: 10 m.
i Snowdonia National Park and Wales Tourist Board Centre, The Wharf ☎ 321 (Easter-September).
London 230 – Dolgellau 25 – Shrewsbury 66.

- **Trefeddian**, LL35 0SB, W: 1 m. on A 493 ☎ 213, ≤ golf course and sea, – wc Ⓟ
  22 March-23 October – **M** 4.60/4.80 **st.** 1.50 – **47 rm** (dinner included) 11.60/31.40 **st.** – P 12.30/16.40 **st.**

ABERGAVENNY Gwent 986 ㉛ – pop. 9,401 – ☎ 0873.
Envir.: Llanthony Priory* N: 10 m.
18 Llanfoist, ☎ 3171, S: 1 ¾ m.
i Brecon Beacons National Park and Wales Tourist Board Centre, 2 Lower Monk St. ☎ 3254 (Easter-September).
London 163 – Gloucester 43 – Newport 19 – Swansea 49.

- **Angel** (T.H.F.), 15 Cross St., NP7 5EN, ☎ 2613 – wc Ⓟ
  M a la carte 3.95/5.35 **st.** 1.50 – **31 rm** 9.00/17.00 **st.**
- Park, 36 Hereford Rd, NP7 5RA, ☎ 3715 – Ⓟ
  7 rm.
- XX **Lamb and Flag** with rm, NW: 1 ½ m. on A 40 ☎ 4255 – wc Ⓟ
  M *(closed Sunday dinner)* a la carte 3.55/5.50 1.50 – **3 rm** 7.00/11.00.

at Clytha SE: 7 m. on A 40 – ✉ Abergavenny – ☎ 087 385 Gobion:

- X **Clytha Arms,** NP7 9BW, ☎ 206 – Ⓟ
  closed Tuesday – **M** a la carte 4.80/9.00 **s.** 1.75.

MORRIS Brecon Rd ☎ 2126
PEUGEOT Penpergwm, Gobion ☎ 087 385 (Gobion) 287
RENAULT Monmouth Rd ☎ 2323

ABERGWESYN Powys – see Llanwrtyd Wells.

ABERMULE Powys – see Newtown.

ABERPORTH Dyfed – pop. 1,618 – ☎ 0239.
See: Site*. **Envir.:** Llangranog (cliffs*) NE: 4 m.
London 249 – Carmarthen 29 – Fishguard 26.

- **Morlan Motel,** SA43 2EN, ☎ 810611 – wc Ⓟ
  M approx. 3.00 **t.** 1.30 – 1.25 – **16 rm** 7.00/10.00 **t.**
- **Highcliffe,** SA43 2DA, ☎ 810534 – wc Ⓟ
  M (dinner only) a la carte 3.75/5.15 **t.** 1.00 – **12 rm** 9.20/16.40 **t.**

ABERSOCH Gwynedd 986 ㉖ – pop. 800 – ✆ 075 881.
Envir.: Llanengan (church* : twin aisles rood screen) W : 2 m. – Hell's Mouth* W : 3 m. – Aberdaron (site*) W : 10 m. – Braich y Pwll (<** from 2nd car park) W: 12 m.

Pwllheli, ✆ 0758 (Pwllheli) 2520, NE: 7 m. – Pwllheli, ✆ 2622.

London 265 – Caernarfon 28 – Shrewsbury 101.

Harbour, LL53 7HR, ✆ 2406 – wc wc P
Easter-25 September – **M** *(closed Sunday)* (dinner only) a la carte 4.00/6.90 – **21 rm** 9.00/22.00.

Craig-y-Môr, Lôn Pont Morgan, LL53 7AD, ✆ 2666, <, – wc P
Easter-September – **M** (dinner only) 3.50/4.50 1.80 – **7 rm** 15.00.

Llysfor, Lôn Garmon, LL53 7AL, ✉ Pwllheli ✆ 2248, – P
Easter-September – **8 rm** 5.00/10.00 **st.**

Bronheulog with rm, Lôn Garmon, LL53 7UL, W: 1 ½ m. ✉ Pwllheli ✆ 2177, – P
March-October – **M** *(closed Sunday)* (dinner only) a la carte 3.90/6.00 **st.** 1.70 – **6 rm** 6.50/13.00 **st.**

at Bwlchtocyn S: 2 m. – ✉ Pwllheli – ✆ 075 881 Abersoch:

Porth Tocyn , LL53 7BU, ✆ 2966, < sea and coast, , heated, – wc P
closed November and December – **M** approx. 6.75 – **18 rm** 10.00/22.00 – P 16.50/17.50.

ABERYSTWYTH Dyfed 986 ㉛ – pop. 10,688 – ✆ 0970.
See: <* from the National Library. **Envir.:** Devil's Bridge (Nature Trail: Mynach Falls and Devil's Bridge**) SE: 12 m. – Vale of Rheidol* SE: 6 m.

Brynmoe, ✆ 2691 N : ½ m.

i Tourist Information Centre, Promenade ✆ 7111.

London 238 – Chester 98 – Fishguard 58 – Shrewsbury 74.

Belle Vue Royal (Crest), Marine Ter., SY23 2BA, ✆ 7558, < – wc P.
M 3.75/4.70 **s.** 1.55 – **49 rm** 8.00/15.70 **s.**

Four Seasons, 50-54 Portland St., SY23 2DX, ✆ 2236 – wc P
closed 24 December-2 January – **M** 2.75/4.00 **st.** – **17 rm** 5.95/15.15 **st.** – P 11.45/15.10 **st.**

The Groves, 44-46 North Par., SY23 2NF, ✆ 617 623
closed 24 December-2 January – **17 rm** 5.25/11.25 **t.**

at Chancery S : 4 m. on A 487 – ✉ ✆ 0970 Aberystwyth :

Conrah Country , SY23 4DF, ✆ 617941, <, « 18C country house », , park – wc wc P.
M 3.50/4.50 1.20 – **25 rm** 7.00/16.00.

AUSTIN-MG-JAGUAR-ROVER-TRIUMPH Park Av. ✆ 4881
FORD North Parade ✆ 4171
SIMCA, FIAT Llanfarian ✆ 2311
VAUXHALL Pier St. ✆ 2747

ABINGDON Oxon. 986 ㉛㉟ – pop. 18,610 – ✆ 0235.
i 8 Market Pl. ✆ 22711.

London 64 – **Oxford 6** – Reading 25.

Upper Reaches (T.H.F.), Thames St., OX14 3TA, ✆ 22311, – TV wc P.
M a la carte 4.75/6.70 **st.** 1.50 – **21 rm** 11.50/17.50 **st.**

at Frilford W: 4 m. on A 415 – ✉ Abingdon – ✆ 0865 Frilford Heath:

Noah's Ark, OX13 5NZ, S : ½ m. on A 338 ✆ 391470, Italian rest., – P
closed Sunday dinner and Monday – **M** a la carte 5.00/7.45 **t.** 1.25.

AUSTIN-DAIMLER-JAGUAR-MG-ROVER-TRIUMPH-WOLSELEY Drayton Rd ✆ 4334
RENAULT North Par. ✆ 2227
VAUXHALL The Vineyard ✆ 20176

ABINGER COMMON Surrey – see Dorking.

ABRIDGE Essex – pop. 2,900 (inc. Lambourne) – ✆ 01 London.
London 15 – Chelmsford 19.

Roding, Market Pl., RM4 1UA, ✆ 849 3030
closed Sunday and 1 week at Christmas – **M** a la carte 5.40/17.50 **s.**

VW, AUDI-NSU Market Pl. ✆ 037 881 (Theydon Bois) 2722

ACKLAM Cleveland – see Middlesbrough.

AIGBURTH Merseyside – see Liverpool.

ALBRIGHTON Salop – see Shrewsbury.

ALCESTER Warw. 986 ㉛ – pop. 19,122 – ✆ 078 971.
London 104 – **Birmingham 20** – Stratford-on-Avon 8 – Worcester 18.

Cherrytrees Garden, Stratford Rd, E: 1 ½ m. on A 422 ✆ 2505 – TV wc wc P
22 rm.

MORRIS Evesham Rd ✆ 2209

ALDBOROUGH Norfolk – pop. 404 – ✉ Norwich – ☎ 026 376 Hanworth.
London 129 – Cromer 11 – Norwich 17.

XX **Old Red Lion,** The Green, NR11 7AA, ☎ 451 – P
closed Monday except Bank Holidays – **M** 3.50/6.00 🍾 1.30.

ALDBROUGH North Humberside – pop. 930 – ✉ Hull – ☎ 040 17.
London 192 – Kingston-upon-Hull 12.

XX **George and Dragon** with rm, 1 High St., HU11 4RP, ☎ 230, – TV wc ☎ P
M a la carte 3.50/8.05 **t.** 🍾 1.25 – **6 rm** ☕ 8.75/15.15 **st.**

ALDEBURGH Suffolk 986 ㉜ – pop. 2,791 – ☎ 072 885.
London 97 – Ipswich 24 – Norwich 41.

Brudenell (T.H.F.), The Parade, IP15 5BU, ☎ 2071, ← – TV wc ☎ P
M 3.95/4.20 **st.** 🍾 1.50 – **45 rm** ☕ 10.50/16.00 **st.**

Wentworth, Wentworth Rd, IP15 5BB, ☎ 2312, ← – wc P
closed mid December-mid January – **M** 4.00/4.50 **t.** – **34 rm** ☕ 10.80/21.60 **t.** – P 15.00/16.80 **t.**

X **Granville** with rm, 243-247 High St., IP15 5DN, ☎ 2708
closed 24 to 29 December – **M** a la carte 3.65/5.75 **t.** 🍾 1.00 – **9 rm** ☕ 7.50/15.00 **t.** – P 12.00/13.50 **t.**

CHRYSLER High St. ☎ 2721

ALDERLEY EDGE Cheshire 986 ⑤ and ㉗ – pop. 4,470 – ☎ 0625.
Envir. : Capesthorne Hall* (18C) *AC*, S : 4 ½ m.
London 187 – Chester 34 – Manchester 14 – Stoke-on-Trent 25.

De Trafford Arms, Congleton Rd, SK9 7AA, on A 34 ☎ 583881 – wc ☎ P
M (bar lunch) 2.50/3.00 **st.** 🍾 1.20 – **30 rm** ☕ 9.00/12.50 **st.** – P 18.50/28.00 **st.**

Edge, Macclesfield Rd ☎ 3033, – wc ☎ P – **27 rm.**

AUSTIN-JAGUAR-LAND ROVER-MORRIS-TRIUMPH London Rd ☎ 582218
OPEL-VAUXHALL Knutsford Rd ☎ 2691
VOLVO 77 London Rd ☎ 3912

ALDFORD Cheshire – see Chester.

ALFOLD CROSSWAYS Surrey – pop. 1,122 – ✉ Cranleigh – ☎ 0403 Loxwood.
London 43 – Guildford 10 – Horsham 10.

XX **Chez Jean,** Horsham Rd, GU6 8JE, on A 281 ☎ 752357, French rest. – P
closed Sunday dinner and Monday – **M** a la carte 5.25/7.10 **t.** 🍾 1.70.

ALFRISTON East Sussex – pop. 763 – ✉ Polegate – ☎ 0323.
London 66 – Eastbourne 9 – Lewes 10 – Newhaven 8.

Star Inn (T.H.F.), High St., BN26 5TA, ☎ 870495 – TV wc ☎ P
M a la carte 4.75/6.70 **st.** 🍾 1.50 – **34 rm** ☕ 11.50/19.00 **st.** – P 15.25/18.00 **st.**

Dean's Place, Seaford Rd, BN26 5TW, ☎ 870248, « Garden », heated – wc P
closed 27 December-9 February – **M** approx. 2.85 **st.** 🍾 1.10 – ☕ 0.50 – **45 rm** 6.30/11.50 **st.** – P 8.75/10.60 **st.**

X **Moonrakers,** High St., BN26 5TD, ☎ 870472
closed Monday from October to April, Sunday, first 2 weeks May and October, 25 December-1 January – **M** (dinner only) 4.95/5.45 **t.** 🍾 1.25.

ALLESLEY West Midlands – see Coventry.

ALLESTREE Derbs. – see Derby.

ALL STRETTON Salop – see Church Stretton.

ALNWICK Northumb. 986 ⑮ – pop. 7,120 – ☎ 0665.
See : Castle** (Norman) *AC*. **Envir.** : Warkworth (castle* 12C) *AC*, SE : 7 m. – Rothbury (Cragside gardens* : rhododendrons) *AC*, SW : 12 m.
9 Swansfield Park, Alnwick.
i The Shambles, Northumberland Hall ☎ 3120 (summer only).
London 320 – Edinburgh 86 – Newcastle-upon-Tyne 34.

White Swan (Swallow), Bondgate Within, NE66 1TD, ☎ 2109 – wc ☎ P.
40 rm.

Hotspur, Bondgate Without, NE66 1PR, ☎ 2924 – wc ☎ P
M *(closed Sunday from October to March and 25-26 December)* 4.00/6.00 **t.** 🍾 1.50 – ☕ 1.50 – **28 rm** 6.50/13.00 **t.**

AUSTIN-MORRIS-ROVER-TRIUMPH South Rd ☎ 2638
FORD ☎ 2294
PEUGEOT Powburn ☎ 066 578 (Powburn) 214

ALRESFORD Hants. 986 ㉟ – pop. 3,684 – ☎ 096 273.

Envir. : Marwell Zoological park** *AC*, SW : 12 m.

Cheriton Rd ☎ 3153, S : 1 m.

London 61 – Southampton 19 – Winchester 8.

Bell, West St., SO24 9AT, ☎ 2429 – Ⓟ
M 2.00/3.00 **t.** 1.25 – **6 rm** 6.50/12.50 **t.** – P 10.50/12.50 **t.**

O'Rorkes, 34 Pound Hill, SO24 9BW, ☎ 2293 – Ⓟ
closed Sunday, last week July, first week August and 4 days at Christmas – **M** (dinner only) a la carte 6.00/7.00 **t.**

AUSTIN-MORRIS-ROVER-TRIUMPH 47 West St. ☎ 2601
SAAB The Dene Ropley ☎ 096 277 (Ropley) 2307
VOLVO Broad St. ☎ 3444

ALSTON Cumbria 986 ⑲ – pop. 1,916 (inc. Garrigill) – ☎ 049 83.

Envir. : High Force** (waterfalls) *AC*, SE : 16 m.

☎ 228, N : 2 m.

i Railway Station ☎ 696.

London 309 – Carlisle 28 – Newcastle-upon-Tyne 45.

Lowbyer Manor, Hexham Rd, CA9 3JX, ☎ 230, – wc Ⓟ
15 May-15 November – **M** (dinner only and bar lunch in summer) 6.20/7.00 2.50 – **12 rm** 8.40/16.00.

Hillcrest, Townfoot, CA9 3LN, ☎ 251, – Ⓟ
M (bar lunch in winter) approx. 3.00 1.25 – **12 rm** 5.00/10.00.

Michelin n'accroche pas de panonceau aux hôtels et restaurants qu'il signale.

ALTON Hants. 986 ㊱ – pop. 12,705 – ☎ 0420.

Old Odiham Rd ☎ 82042, N : 2 m.

London 53 – Reading 24 – Southampton 29 – Winchester 18.

Swan (Anchor), High St., GU34 1AT, ☎ 83777, Group Telex 27120 – wc Ⓟ
M approx. 3.15 **t.** 1.00 – 1.00 – **24 rm** 9.60/17.05.

ASTON-MARTIN, PEUGEOT Station Approach ☎ 82222
AUSTIN-LAND ROVER-MORRIS-MG-ROVER-TRIUMPH-WOLSELEY Butts Rd ☎ 84141
CHRYSLER, MORRIS Four Marks ☎ 62354
FORD Ackender Rd ☎ 83993

ALTON Staffs. – pop. 1,195 – ✉ Stoke-on-Trent – ☎ 0538 Oakamoor.

See : Alton Towers (gardens**) *AC*.

London 157 – Derby 21 – Stafford 20 – Stoke-on-Trent 13.

Wild Duck Inn with rm, New Road, ST10 4AF, ☎ 702218 – Ⓟ
closed Sunday dinner and Monday – **M** a la carte 4.10/8.05 **st.** – **4 rm** 5.45/10.90 **st.**

ALTRINCHAM Greater Manchester 986 ⑤ and ㉗ – pop. 40,787 – ☎ 061 Manchester.

Envir. : Tatton Hall* (Georgian) and gardens** *AC*, S : 6 m.

Stockport Rd, Timperley ☎ 928 0761 – Dunham Forest ☎ 928 2605, W : 1 m.
Hale Mount, Hale Barns ☎ 980 4468.

London 191 – Chester 30 – Liverpool 30 – Manchester 8.

George and Dragon, 22 Manchester Rd, WA14 4PH, on A 56 ☎ 928 9933 – TV wc Ⓟ
M *(closed Sunday)* 3.50/4.00 **st.** 2.00 – **48 rm** 11.50/13.50 **st.**

Cresta Court (Interchange), Church St., WA14 4DP, on A 56 ☎ 928 8017 – TV wc Ⓟ.
M (grill rest. only) a la carte 2.05/3.90 **st.** 1.40 – **134 rm** 11.00/15.00 **st.**

Pelican, West Timperley, WA14 5NH, N : 2 m. on A 56 ☎ 962 7414 – TV wc Ⓟ
M (buffet lunch) (lunch only Friday-Sunday) 3.50/4.00 – **50 rm** 11.75/14.00 **st.**

Bollin, 58 Manchester Rd, WA14 4PJ, ☎ 928 2390 – Ⓟ
10 rm 4.60/9.00 **st.**

Portofino, The Downs, WA14 2QG, ☎ 928 1511, Italian rest. – Ⓟ
closed Saturday lunch and Sunday – **M** a la carte 3.65/6.35 **t.** 1.50.

La Grenouille, 20-22 Ashley Rd ☎ 928 7699, Bistro
M a la carte 3.80/5.25 **t.** 1.50.

at Hale SE : 1 m on B 5163 – ✉ Altrincham – ☎ 061 Manchester :

Ashley, Ashley Rd ☎ 928 3794 – TV wc Ⓟ.
M 2.75/3.50 **t.** – **49 rm** 12.00/16.00 **t.** – P 16.75 **t.**

at Hale Barns SE : 2 m. on A 538 – ✉ Altrincham – ☎ 061 Manchester :

Borsalino, 14 The Square, WA15 8ST, ☎ 980 5331, French Bistro
closed Sunday, Monday, Christmas Day, 1 January and Bank Holidays – **M** (dinner only) a la carte 4.10/5.70 1.20.

at Bowdon SW: **1** m. – ✉ Altrincham – ☎ **061** Manchester:

- **Bowdon,** Langham Rd, WA14 2HT, ☎ 928 7121 – TV ⌂wc ☎ **P**.
  M approx. 3.00 **st.** 1.50 – **44 rm** 6.20/14.25 **st.**
- **Alpine,** Park Rd, WA14 3JE, ☎ 928 6191 – TV ⌂wc ☎ **P**
  M a la carte 2.75/4.90 1.25 – **15 rm** 7.00/12.50.

AUSTIN 18 Old Market Pl. ☎ 928 2662
DAIMLER-JAGUAR-ROVER-TRIUMPH Victoria Rd ☎ 928 7124
DATSUN Manchester Rd ☎ 973 3021
FORD 44 Hale Rd Bridge ☎ 928 2275
HONDA, SAAB Bancroft Rd, Hale ☎ 980 8004
PEUGEOT Atlantic St. ☎ 928 3265

ALVESTON Avon – pop. **2,776** – ✉ Bristol – ☎ **0454 Thornbury.**

London 127 – Bristol 11 – Gloucester 23 – Swindon 42.

- **Post House** (T.H.F.), Thornbury Rd, BS12 2LL, on A 38 ☎ 412521, heated – TV ⌂wc ☎ & **P**.
  M 3.60/4.10 **st.** 1.50 – 2.00 – **75 rm** 13.00/18.00 **st.**
- **Alveston House,** BS12 2LJ, on A 38 ☎ 415050, – TV ⌂wc ⌂wc ☎ **P**
  M a la carte 4.20/5.75 1.60 – **14 rm** 10.00/17.50.

AUSTIN-MORRIS-MG-WOLSELEY ☎ 2207

AMBERLEY West Sussex – pop. **510** – ✉ Arundel – ☎ **079 881 Bury.**

London 58 – Brighton 23 – Chichester 12 – Worthing 14.

- **La Capanna,** Houghton Bridge, BN18 9LR, SW: ¾ m. on B 2139 ☎ 790, Italian rest. – **P**
  closed Sunday, Christmas and 1 January – **M** (dinner only) a la carte 3.50/4.70 1.65.

AMBLESIDE Cumbria 986 ⑲ – pop. **2,657** – ☎ **096 63.**

Envir.: Tarn Hows** (lake) SW: **6** m. – Langdale Valley** W: **7** m.

i The Old Court House, Church St. ☎ 2582 (summer only).

London 277 – Carlisle 47 – Kendal 14.

- **Elder Grove,** Lake Rd, LA22 0DB, ☎ 2504 – ⌂wc **P**
  mid March-mid November – **M** *(closed Monday)* (dinner only) 4.95 **t.** – **11 rm** 8.10/16.20 **t.**
- **Kirkstone Foot**, Kirkstone Pass Rd, LA22 9EH, NE: ¼ m. ☎ 2232, – ⌂wc **P**
  22 March-October – **M** (set dinner only) 4.00/4.50 **st.** 1.20 – **20 rm** 8.50/14.00 **st.**
- **Vale View,** Lake Rd, LA22 0BH, ☎ 3192 – ⌂wc **P**
  11 March-3 November – **M** (bar lunch) approx. 3.50 **st.** – **20 rm** 7.00/14.50 **st.**
- John O'Gaunt, Rothay Rd ☎ 3310 – **P** – **10 rm.**
- **Compston House,** Compston Rd, LA22 9DJ, ☎ 2305
  closed first week July, November and Christmas – **9 rm** 4.35/8.65 **t.**

at Waterhead S : **1** m. on A **591** – ✉ ☎ **096 63** Ambleside :

- **Ambleside Park**, Borrans Rd, LA22 0EW, ☎ 2571, ←, – ⌂wc ⌂wc ☎ **P**
  Easter-November – **M** approx. 4.50 – **30 rm** 7.00/18.00 – P 16.50.
- **Waterhead** (Interchange), LA22 0ER, ☎ 2566, ←, – ⌂wc ☎ **P**
  M a la carte 4.70/6.90 **st.** 1.30 – **27 rm** 11.60/17.00 **st.** – P 17.00/19.70 **st.**
- **Wateredge,** Barrans Rd, LA22 0EP, ☎ 2232, ←, – ⌂wc ⌂wc **P**
  closed November and February – **M** *(closed Monday)* (dinner only, buffet lunch Easter-October) 5.70 **t.** – **20 rm** 7.70/15.40 **t.** – P 16.50 **t.**

at Rothay Bridge S : ½ m. on A **593** – ✉ ☎ **096 63** Ambleside :

- **Rothay Manor** with rm, LA22 0EH, ☎ 3605, ←, – ⌂wc ☎ **P**
  closed January and February – **M** (cold lunch) 7.00/7.50 **t.** 1.30 – **12 rm** 10.50/23.00 **t.**

at Skelwith Bridge W : **2** ½ m. on A **593** – ✉ ☎ **096 63** Ambleside :

- **Skelwith Bridge,** LA22 9NJ, ☎ 2115, ←, – ⌂wc **P**
  closed January – **M** *(closed December and January)* (dinner only and Sunday lunch) 4.00/6.00 **st.** 0.95 – **26 rm** 7.00/16.00 **st.**

at Elterwater W : **4** ½ m. off B **5343** – ✉ Ambleside – ☎ **096 67** Langdale :

- **Britannia Inn**, LA22 9HP, ☎ 210, ← – **P**
  March-October – **M** (bar lunch) approx. 4.25 **t.** 1.65 – **10 rm** 6.50/13.00 **t.** – P 12.00 **t.**

at Chapel Stile W : **5** m. on B **5343** – ✉ Chapel Stile – ☎ **096 67** Langdale :

- **Langdales**, LA22 9JF, ☎ 253, ←, – ⌂wc **P**
  M approx. 5.00 **t.** 1.10 – **21 rm** 8.50/20.00 **t.** – P 15.00 **t.**

at Rydal NW: **1** ½ m. on A **591** – ✉ ☎ **096 63** Ambleside:

- **Rydal Lodge,** LA22 9LR, ☎ 3208,
  mid March-October – **8 rm** 5.25/10.50 **st.**

AMERSHAM (Old Town) Bucks. 986 ④ – pop. 17,254 – ☎ 024 03.
London 29 – Aylesbury 16 – **Oxford 33.**

- **Crown** (T.H.F.), High St., HP7 0DH, ☎ 21541 – TV ⇔wc ☎ P
  M a la carte 4.50/6.10 **st.** 1.50 – **17 rm** 8.50/18.00 **st.**
- XX **Mill Stream,** 49 London Rd, HP7 9DA, on A 413 ☎ 3700, Dancing (weekends) – P
  closed Sunday dinner, Monday, 25 and 26 December – **M** a la carte 4.65/7.50 **st.** 1.40.

AUSTIN-DAIMLER-JAGUAR-MORRIS-ROVER-TRIUMPH London Rd ☎ 5911
CHRYSLER-SIMCA 4/8 White Lion Rd ☎ 024 04 (Little Chalfont) 4666
PEUGEOT Hill Av. ☎ 3041
RENAULT The Broadway ☎ 4656

AMESBURY Wilts. 986 ㉟ – pop. 5,684 – ☎ 098 02.
Envir. : Stonehenge (Megalithic Monument)*** *AC*, W: 2 m.
i Redworth House ☎ 3255.
London 88 – **Bristol 52** – **Southampton 31** – Taunton 61.

- **Antrobus Arms,** Church St., SP4 7EY, ☎ 3163, – ⇔wc P
  M 2.50/3.50 **st.** 1.10 – **16 rm** 9.50/21.75 **st.**

AUSTIN-MORRIS-MG Salisbury St. ☎ 2525

AMLWCH Gwynedd 986 ㉓ and ㉗ – pop. 3,682 – ☎ 0407.
18 ☎ 830213, W : ½ m.
London 266 – Caernarfon 26 – Chester 79 – Holyhead 21.

- **Trecastell,** Bull Bay, LL68 9SA, ☎ 830651, ←, – P
  M (bar lunch) 3.00/4.25 1.30 – **17 rm** 5.00/10.00.

AMPFIELD Hants. – pop. 1,460 – ✉ Romsey – ☎ 042 15 Chandler's Ford.
London 79 – Bournemouth 31 – Salisbury 19 – **Southampton 11** – Winchester 7.

- **Potters Heron Motor,** SO5 9ZF, on A 31 ☎ 66611 – TV ⇔wc ☎ ♿ P.
  M a la carte 3.85/4.50 **t.** 1.80 – **42 rm** 13.20/20.50 **t.**

ANDOVER Hants. 986 ㉟ – pop. 25,881 – ☎ 0264.
London 74 – Bath 53 – Salisbury 17 – Winchester 11.

- **White Hart** (Anchor), Bridge St., SP10 1BH, ☎ 2266, Group Telex 27120 – TV P
  M 2.00/2.50 **t.** 1.00 – **19 rm** 9.20/18.70 **st.**

ALFA-ROMEO, FIAT Salisbury Rd ☎ 61166
AUSTIN-MG-ROVER-TRIUMPH-WOLSELEY 278 Weyhill Rd ☎ 4222
FORD West St. ☎ 3525
MORRIS-MG-WOLSELEY 94 Charlton Rd ☎ 3603
VAUXHALL Newbury Rd ☎ 4233

APPERLEY BRIDGE West Yorks. – see Bradford.

APPLEBY Cumbria 986 ⑲ – pop. 1,949 – ☎ 0930.
18 ☎ 51432, S: 2 m.
i Moot Hall ☎ 51177 (summer only).
London 284 – **Carlisle 37** – Kendal 24 – **Middlesbrough 58.**

- **Appleby Manor** ⑤, Roman Rd, CA16 6JD, NE: ½ m. off A 66 ☎ 51571, ←, – ⇔wc P
  M a la carte 4.60/6.25 **st.** 2.25 – **24 rm** 10.00/18.00 **st.**
- **Tufton Arms,** Market Sq., CA16 6XA, ☎ 51593, – ⇔wc P
  M 5.00/5.50 1.25 – **28 rm** 8.40/17.00 **st.**
- **Royal Oak Inn,** Bongate, CA16 6UN, ☎ 51463
  M 2.30/4.10 **s.** – **8 rm** 5.50/11.00 **s.**
- **Courtfield,** Bongate, CA16 6UP, ☎ 51394, – P
  M 4.00/5.50 **t.** 1.20 – **15 rm** 5.00/12.00 **t.** – P 11.50/13.50 **t.**

AUSTIN-MG-WOLSELEY The Sands ☎ 51133
CHRYSLER Appleby ☎ 460

APPLEDORE Devon – pop. 2,172 – ✉ ☎ 023 72 Bideford.
London 235 – Bideford 4 – Exeter 47 – **Plymouth 62.**

- **Seagate,** The Quay, EX39 1QS, ☎ 2589 – P
  mid April-October – **M** 2.75/3.85 1.45 – **10 rm** 5.50/11.00.

ARDSLEY South Yorks. – see Barnsley.

ARMATHWAITE Cumbria – pop. 150 – ✉ Carlisle – ☎ 069 92.
London 304 – Carlisle 10 – Penrith 12.

- **Duke's Head,** CA4 9PB, ☎ 226 – P
  M (dinner only) approx. 4.00 1.40 – **8 rm** 4.75/8.50.
- **Red Lion,** CA4 9PY, ☎ 204, ←, – P
  M 3.00/4.00 – **10 rm** 4.75/10.00 – P 8.75/10.05.

ARMITAGE Staffs. – see Rugeley.

ARUNDEL West Sussex 986 ㉖ – pop. 2,434 – ☎ 0903.

See : Castle* (keep 12C, ≤* 119 steps, State apartments*) *AC* – St. Nicholas' Church (chancel or Fitzalan chapel* 14C). **Envir. :** Bignor (Roman Villa: mosaics** *AC*) NW: 7 m.

i 61 High St. ☎ 882419 and 882268.

London 58 – **Brighton 21** – **Southampton 41** – Worthing 9.

- Norfolk Arms, 22 High St., BN18 9AB, ☎ 882101 – wc ☎ P
  M a la carte 3.05/5.15 1.50 – **19 rm.**
- **Golden Goose Motel,** BN18 9JL, E: ½ m. on A 27 ☎ 882588 – TV wc wc P
  M a la carte 3.20/4.50 **t.** 1.50 – **9 rm** 7.00/11.50 **t.**
- Bridge, Queen St., BN18 9JG, ☎ 882242, – P – **17 rm.**

at Walberton W: 3 m. on B 2132 by A 27 – ✉ Arundel – ☎ 0243 Chichester :

- **Avisford Park**, BN18 0LS, ☎ 551215, heated, , park – TV wc ☎ P.
  M approx. 4.25 **t.** 1.75 – 0.75 – **48 rm** 16.50/23.00 **st.**

AUSTIN Queen St. ☎ 882594
PEUGEOT Fontwell ☎ 024 365 (Slindon) 289

ASCOT Berks. 986 ⑧ – pop. 7,500 (inc. Sunninghill) – ☎ 0990.

London 36 – Reading 15.

- **Berystede** (T.H.F.), Bagshot Rd, Sunninghill, SL5 9JA, S: 1 ½ m. on A 330 ☎ 23311, Telex 847707, , , park – TV P.
  M 3.75/4.25 **st.** 1.50 – 2.00 – **106 rm** 16.00/21.50 **st.**
- **Royal Foresters,** London Rd, SL5 8DR, W: 1 ½ m. on A 329 ☎ 034 47 (Winkfield Row) 4747 – TV wc ☎ P
  M (grill rest. only) 2.35/4.50 **t.** 1.65 – **33 rm** 10.50/13.50 **t.**

AUSTIN-MG-WOLSELEY Ascot Motor Works ☎ 20324
DATSUN Station Approach ☎ 24791
PEUGEOT 71/75 High St. ☎ 21481
VAUXHALL Lyndhurst Rd, Station Approach ☎ 22257

ASHBURTON Devon 986 ㊴ – pop. 3,518 – ☎ 0364.

Envir. : Buckfast Abbey (the Sacrament Chapel*) SW: 2 ½ m.

i Dartmoor National Park, Pear Tree Cross (summer only).

London 220 – Exeter 20 – **Plymouth 23.**

- **Holne Chase**, TQ13 7NS, NW: 2 ½ m. on B 3357 ☎ 036 43 (Poundsgate) 280, ≤, , park, – wc wc P
  M approx. 4.35 **t.** 1.15 – **11 rm** 9.80/23.70 **t.**
- **Dartmoor Motel,** TQ13 7JW, on B 3357 ☎ 52232 – wc wc P
  M a la carte 3.60/4.85 **t.** 1.05 – 1.75 – **19 rm** 8.50/14.00 **st.** – P 12.50 **t.**
- **Tugela House,** 68-70 East St., TQ13 7AX, ☎ 52206
  10 rm 4.50/9.00 **t.**

ASHBY DE LA ZOUCH Leics. 986 ㉗ – pop. 8,311 – ☎ 053 04.

London 119 – **Birmingham 29** – **Leicester 18** – **Nottingham 22.**

- **Royal** (Crest), Station Rd, LE6 5GP, ☎ 2833, – wc P.
  M 2.70/4.35 **s.** 1.55 – **30 rm** 8.80/16.10 **s.**
- **Fallen Knight,** 16 Kilwardby St., LE6 5FR, ☎ 2230 – P
  M a la carte 3.35/5.40 **s.** 1.50.

DAF, MAZDA Tamworth Rd ☎ 2108
MORRIS-MG-WOLSELEY Bath St. ☎ 2770

ASHFORD Kent 986 ㊱ – pop. 35,615 – ☎ 0233.

Envir. : Hothfield (St. Margaret's Church : memorial tomb* 17C) NW : 3 m. – Lenham (St. Mary's Church: woodwork*) NW: 9 ½ m.

18 Sandyhurst Lane ☎ 20180, N: 1 ½ m.

London 56 – Canterbury 14 – **Dover 23** – Hastings 29 – Maidstone 19.

- **George,** 68 High St., TN24 8TB, ☎ 25512 – P
  M 1.95/4.50 **t.** 1.45 – **14 rm** 7.50/14.00 **t.**
- **Old Cottage,** 20 North St., TN24 8JR, ☎ 20347
  M a la carte 3.30/5.10 0.85.

at Kennington NE: 2 m. on A 28 – ✉ ☎ 0233 Ashford :

- **Spearpoint** (Rest. du Vert Galant) with rm, Canterbury Rd, TN24 9QR, ☎ 21833, , park, French rest. – TV wc P.
  M a la carte 4.70/6.30 1.30 – **10 rm** 8.50/14.50.

at Charing NW: 6 m. on A 252 by A 20 – ✉ Ashford – ☎ 023 371 Charing :

- **Luigi,** Charing Hill, TN27 0NG, ☎ 2286, ≤, Italian rest. – P
  closed Sunday, 25-26 December and 1 January – **M** a la carte 3.50/5.60 1.10.

P.T.O. →

at Stalisfield Green NW: 8 m. off A 20 – ✉ Faversham – ☎ 079 589 Eastling:

✗ **Plough Inn,** ME13 0HY, ☎ 256 – Ⓟ
closed Sunday dinner and Monday – **M** (dinner only and Sunday lunch) a la carte 3.20/5.05 **t.** 🍷 1.50.

AUSTIN-JAGUAR-MG-ROVER-TRIUMPH-WOLSELEY Chart Rd ☎ 20624
DAF Hamstreet ☎ 023 373 (Hamstreet) 2207
FORD Beaver Rd ☎ 25111
MORRIS-MG-WOLSELEY 20-46 New St. ☎ 20334
RENAULT Maidstone Rd ☎ 34177
VAUXHALL Faversham Rd ☎ 23173

ASHINGTON West Sussex – pop. 1,470 – ✉ Pulborough – ☎ 0903.
London 50 – Brighton 20 – Worthing 9.

Mill House 🐦, Mill Lane, RH20 3BZ, ☎ 892426, 🌳 – Ⓟ
M (dinner only) 4.00 **st.** – **12 rm** ☕ 7.00/14.00 **st.** – P 11.00 **st.**

at Washington S : 1 ¾ m. on A 24 – ✉ Storrington – ☎ 0903 Ashington :

✗✗ **Old Smithy,** Old London Rd, RH20 3BN, ☎ 892271
closed Sunday and Christmas – **M** (dinner only) a la carte 4.35/8.05 **t.** 🍷 2.25.

ASKHAM Cumbria – pop. 392 – ✉ Penrith – ☎ 093 12 Hackthorpe.
London 287 – Carlisle 27 – Kendal 28.

Queen's Head Inn, CA10 2PF, ☎ 225 – Ⓟ
Easter-October – **M** *(closed Sunday dinner to non-residents)* (bar lunch) approx. 5.00 🍷 1.80 – **8 rm** ☕ 7.20/12.50.

ASTON CLINTON Bucks. – pop. 2,473 – ✉ ☎ 0296 Aylesbury.
London 42 – Aylesbury 4 – Oxford 26.

✗✗✗ ❀ **Bell Inn** with rm, HP22 5HP, ☎ 630252, « Tasteful decor and furnishings », 🌳 – 📺 🛁wc ☎ Ⓟ. 🏃
M a la carte 12.00/16.60 **s.** 🍷 1.75 – ☕ 4.00 – **20 rm** 15.50/25.00 **s.**
Spec. Bell Inn smokies, Game and meats in season, Fresh fruit sorbets.

ASTON ROWANT Oxon. – pop. 704 – ✉ Lewknor – ☎ 0844 Kingston Blount.
London 43 – Aylesbury 15 – Oxford 16 – Reading 18.

Lambert Arms, OX9 5SB, junction A 40 and B 4009 ☎ 51496, 🌳 – 📺 🛁wc ☎ Ⓟ
M a la carte 5.45/6.95 🍷 2.50 – ☕ 2.00 – **9 rm** 12.00/16.00.

ASTWOOD BANK Heref. and Worc. – see Redditch.

AUSTWICK North Yorks. – pop. 509 – ✉ Lancaster (Lancs.) – ☎ 046 85 Clapham.
London 237 – Kendal 26 – Lancaster 23 – Leeds 47.

Traddock 🐦, LA2 8BY, ☎ 224, 🌳 – 🚿wc Ⓟ
April-October – **12 rm** ☕ 5.25/12.00 **st.**

AVEBURY Wilts. 986 ㉟ – pop. 537 – ☎ 067 23.
See : Stone circles**.
London 91 – Bristol 41 – Swindon 11.

Hotels see : Marlborough W: 6 m.
Swindon NE: **11** m.

AXBRIDGE Somerset 986 ㉟ – pop. 1,097 – ☎ 0934.
Envir. : Cheddar (Gorge*** – Gough's Caves** *AC*) E: 3 m.
London 142 – Bristol 17 – Taunton 31 – Weston-super-Mare 10.

✗ **Oak House** with rm, The Square, BS26 2AP, ☎ 732444, Telex 449748 – 🛁wc
closed 8 days after Christmas – **M** *(closed Sunday dinner to non-residents)* a la carte 2.85/5.75 **t.** 🍷 1.55 – **12 rm** ☕ 6.00/13.00 **t.**

AYLESBURY Bucks. 986 ㉜ – pop. 40,569 – ☎ 0296.
Envir. : Waddesdon Manor (Rothschild Collection***) *AC*, NW : 5 ½ m. – Ascott House** (Rothschild Collection**) and gardens* *AC*, NE: 8 ½ m. – Stewkley (St.Michael's Church* 12C) NE: 12 m.
⛳9 New Rd, Weston Turville ☎ 4084, SE: 2 ½ m.
i County Hall, Walton St. ☎ 5000 ext 308.
London 46 – Birmingham 72 – Northampton 37 – Oxford 22.

Bell (T.H.F.), Market Sq., HP20 1TX, ☎ 82141 – 📺 🛁wc 🚿wc ☎
M a la carte 4.50/6.10 **st.** 🍷 1.50 – **19 rm** ☕ 8.50/17.00 **st.**

King's Head (Crest), Market Sq., HP20 1TA, ☎ 5158 – Ⓟ
M 3.25/4.40 **s.** 🍷 1.55 – **15 rm** ☕ 8.00/13.20 **s.**

at Stoke Mandeville S : 3 ¼ m. by A 413 on A 4010 – ✉ Aylesbury – ☎ 029 661 Stoke Mandeville :

Belmore, Princes Risborough Rd, HP22 5UT, ☎ 2258, heated, – TV wc ☎ Ⓟ *(closed first 2 weekends in August)* – **M** (dinner only) (residents only) 2.70/3.20 1.10 – 1.10 – **14 rm** 9.90/13.00.

at Hartwell SW : 2 m. on A 418 – ✉ Aylesbury – ☎ 029 674 Stone :

Bugle Horn (Embassy), HP17 8QP, ☎ 209, – Ⓟ.

AUSTIN-DAIMLER-JAGUAR-MG-ROVER-TRIUMPH-WOLSELEY Buckingham Rd ☎ 84071
CHRYSLER-SIMCA 159 Tring Rd ☎ 4565
DAF, PEUGEOT 159 Tring Rd ☎ 84050
DATSUN 13/19 Buckingham St. ☎ 4226
FORD 54/56 Walton St. ☎ 4604
MORRIS-MG-WOLSELEY Bicester Rd ☎ 81641
RENAULT Little Kimble ☎ 029 66 (Stoke Mandeville) 2239
TOYOTA, VAUXHALL 143 Cambridge St. ☎ 82321
VOLVO Stocklake ☎ 5344
VW, AUDI-NSU Bicester Rd ☎ 3434

BABBACOMBE Devon – see Torquay.

BABELL Clwyd – pop. 225 – ☎ 035 282 Caerwys.
London 217 – Birkenhead 29 – Chester 21.

XX **Black Lion,** CH8 8PZ, ☎ 239 – Ⓟ
closed Sunday, Monday, mid 2 weeks August and first week November – **M** (bar lunch) a la carte 5.85/7.45 **t.**

BACKFORD CROSS Cheshire – see Chester.

BAGINTON Warw. – see Coventry.

BAGSHOT Surrey – pop. 21,074 – ☎ 0276.
London 37 – Reading 17 – **Southampton 49.**

Pennyhill Park, College Ride, GU19 5ET, off A 30 ☎ 71774, ←, , , park – TV Ⓟ.
M 3.65/6.00 **s.** 1.85 – 1.45 – **17 rm** 14.00/25.00 **s.**

Cricketers' (T.H.F.), London Rd, GU19 5HR, N : ½ m. on A 30 ☎ 73196, – TV wc ☎ Ⓟ
M a la carte 4.50/6.10 **st.** 1.50 – **26 rm** 8.50/17.50 **st.**

BAKEWELL Derbs. 986 ㉗ – pop. 4,249 – ☎ 062 981.
Envir. : Haddon Hall** (14C-16C) *AC*, SE : 3 m. – Chatsworth*** : site**, house*** (Renaissance) garden*** *AC*, NE : 2 ½ m. – Eyam (Celtic Cross* 8C) N : 5 m. **Exc. :** Dovedale** (valley) SW : 13 m.
Station Rd ☎ 2307.
i Peak District National Park, Old Market Hall ☎ 3227.
London 160 – Derby 26 – **Manchester 37** – **Nottingham 33** – **Sheffield 17.**

Rutland Arms, The Square, DE4 1BE, ☎ 2812 – wc Ⓟ
M a la carte 4.25/5.90 **st.** 1.95 – 1.80 – **22 rm** 8.90/13.50 **st.**

VAUXHALL Haddon Rd ☎ 2765

BALA Gwynedd 986 ㉗ – pop. 1,578 – ☎ 067 82.
See : Site*.
Penlan ☎ 344.
i Snowdonia National Park and Tourist Information Centre, High St. ☎ 367 (Easter-September).
London 216 – Chester 46 – Dolgellau 18 – Shrewsbury 52.

White Lion Royal, High St., LL23 7AE, ☎ 314 – wc ☎ Ⓟ
M 2.95/3.45 **t.** – **23 rm** 7.95/12.00 **t.**

Bala Lakeside Motel , SW : 1 ¼ m. on B 4403 by B 4391 ☎ 344, ←, , – wc Ⓟ
closed Christmas week and February – **M** a la carte 3.50/5.10 **s.** – **12 rm** 9.00/15.00 **s.**

Plas Teg, Tegid St., LL23 7EN, ☎ 268, – Ⓟ
closed Christmas – **8 rm** 4.50/9.00 **s.**

FORD High St. ☎ 067 84 (Llanuwchllyn) 660

BALDOCK Herts. 986 ㉜ – pop. 6,272 – ☎ 0462.
Envir.: Ashwell (St. Mary's Church* 14C : Medieval graffiti) NE : 4 ½ m.
London 42 – Bedford 20 – **Cambridge 21** – Luton 15.

Butterfield House, 4 Hitchin St., SG7 6AE, ☎ 892701, – TV wc ☎ Ⓟ
M 2.85/3.25 **s.** 1.15 – 0.70 – **11 rm** 6.50/11.50 **s.**

XX **Ye Olde George and Dragon,** 2 Church St., SG7 6AF, ☎ 892207
M a la carte 2.95/5.65 **t.** 1.30.

PEUGEOT 74 Icknield Way ☎ 893511

BAMBURGH Northumb. 986 ⑮ – pop. 458 – ✆ 066 84.
See : Castle** (12C-18C) *AC*.
18 ✆ 378.
London 337 – Edinburgh 77 – Newcastle-upon-Tyne 51.

- **Lord Crewe Arms,** Front St., NE69 7BL, ✆ 243 – wc P
mid March-mid November – **M** 4.50/4.75 **st.** 1.30 – **26 rm** 8.00/18.50 **st.** – P 14.25/15.25 **st.**

BAMFORD Greater Manchester – see Rochdale.

BAMPTON Cumbria – pop. 337 – ✉ Penrith – ✆ 093 13.
London 284 – Carlisle 30 – Kendal 25.

- Haweswater, CA10 2RP, SW : 4 m. ✆ 235, ≤ Haweswater reservoir, – P
M approx. 3.30 **t.** 0.90 – **16 rm.**

BANBURY Oxon. 986 ㉛ – pop. 29,387 – ✆ 0295.
Envir. : Upton House (pictures***, porcelain**) *AC,* NW : 7 m. – East Adderbury (St. Mary's Church : corbels*) SE : 3 ½ m. – Broughton Castle (great hall*, white room : 1599 plaster ceiling**) and St. Mary's Church (memorial tombs*) *AC,* SW : 3 ½ m. – Wroxton (thatched cottages*) NW : 3 m. – Farnborough Hall (interior plasterwork*) *AC,* NW : 6 m.
i 8 Horse Fair ✆ 52535 ext 250 – Bodycote House, Bodycote ✆ 52535.
London 76 – Birmingham 40 – Coventry 25 – Oxford 23.

- **Whately Hall** (T.H.F.), Horsefair, by Banbury Cross, OX16 0AN, ✆ 3451, Telex 837149, « Part 17C Hall », – TV P.
M 4.00/4.50 **st.** 1.60 – **75 rm** 9.00/21.00 **st.**
- **Manor,** 27 Oxford Rd, OX16 9AH, ✆ 59361, Telex 837450 – TV P.
M approx.3.50 **t.** 1.65 – 1.40 – **30 rm** 11.00/18.00 **t.**
- **White Lion,** High St., OX16 8JW, ✆ 4358 – TV P
M a la carte 2.50/4.15 **t.** 1.80 – **10 rm** 11.00/18.00 **st.**
- **Lismore,** 61 Oxford Rd, OX16 9AJ, ✆ 2105, – P
closed Christmas week – **8 rm** 6.00/12.00 **st.**

at Wroxton NW : 3 m. on A 422 by A 41 – ✉ Wroxton – ✆ 029 573 Wroxton St. Mary :

- XX **Wroxton** with rm, OX15 6PZ, ✆ 482, – wc wc P
closed 25 and 26 December – **M** a la carte 3.85/5.70 1.05 – **12 rm** 6.75/13.50.

AUSTIN-DAIMLER-JAGUAR-MORRIS-MG-ROVER-TRIUMPH-WOLSELEY Southam Rd ✆ 51551
BMW, SAAB 21/27 Broad St. ✆ 50910
CHRYSLER-SIMCA Middleton Rd ✆ 53511
FORD Warwick Rd ✆ 4311
RENAULT 15/16 Southam Rd ✆ 50141
VAUXHALL Marlborough Pl. ✆ 3551
VOLVO Main Rd, Middleton Cheney ✆ 710689
VW, AUDI-NSU Broad St. ✆ 51251

BANGOR Gwynedd 986 ㉗ – pop. 14,558 – ✆ 0248.
18 ✆ 53098, E : off A 5.
London 247 – Birkenhead 68 – Holyhead 23 – Shrewsbury 83.

- **Ty-Uchaf,** Tal-y-Bont, LL57 3UR, SE : 2 m. on A 55 ✆ 4673 – P
closed December and January – **13 rm** 4.25/8.50 **st.**

BANSTEAD Surrey 986 ⑧ – pop. 45,052 – ✆ 073 73 Burgh Heath.
London 17 – Brighton 39.

- XX **Red Coach,** 51 Nork Way, SM7 1PE, off A 2022 ✆ 57188 – P
closed Sunday, Monday and Bank Holidays – **M** a la carte 4.45/7.25 **t.** 2.10.

CHRYSLER-SIMCA 24 High St. ✆ 51414
CITROEN 91/99 High St. ✆ 2376

BARBON Cumbria – pop. 221 – ✆ 046 836.
London 262 – Kendal 13 – Lancaster 20 – Leeds 61.

- XX **Barbon Inn** with rm, LA6 2LJ, ✆ 233, « 17C country inn », – P
closed 25 and 26 December – **M** 4.50/6.00 1.30 – **9 rm** 7.60/15.00.

BARFORD Warw. – pop. 1,108 – ✉ Warwick – ✆ 0926.
London 99 – Birmingham 22 – Coventry 13 – Stratford-on-Avon 7.

- **Glebe,** Church St., CV35 8BS, ✆ 624218, – wc P
M *(closed Sunday)* (bar lunch) (residents only) 3.00/4.50 1.65 – **11 rm** 7.00/13.50.

BARFORD ST. MARTIN Wilts. – pop. 637 – ✉ ✆ 072 274 Wilton.
London 97 – Salisbury 6 – Shaftesbury 15.

- X **Chez Maurice,** SP3 4AB, on A 30 ✆ 2240, French rest. – P
closed Sunday dinner, Christmas Day dinner and 26 December – **M** a la carte 4.55/6.80 **t.** 1.60.

BAR HILL Cambs. – see Cambridge.

BARLBOROUGH Derbs. – pop. 1,778 – ✉ ☎ 0246 Chesterfield.
Envir. : Hardwick Hall** 16C (tapestries and embroideries**) *AC*, S : 10 m. – Worksop (Priory Church : Norman nave*) NE : 7 m.
London 154 – Derby 31 – **Nottingham 27** – **Sheffield 11.**

✕ **Royal Oak Inn,** High St., S43 4ET, ☎ 810425 – Ⓟ
M a la carte 4.20/6.30 **t.** 🍷 2.00.

BARMOUTH Gwynedd 986 ㉗ – pop. 2,106 – ☎ 0341.
See : Site** – Panorama walk**.
i Barmouth Publicity Department, Tourist Information Centre, The Promenade ☎ 280787 (Easter-September).
London 231 – Chester 74 – Dolgellau 10 – Shrewsbury 67.

🏨 **Cors y Gedol,** High St., LL42 1DS, ☎ 280402 – lift wc Ⓟ
M (residents only from October to March) 2.75/3.05 **t.** 🍷 1.50 – **25 rm** 6.00/13.00 **t.** – P 11.20 **t.**

DAIMLER-JAGUAR-ROVER-TRIUMPH Park Rd ☎ 280449

BARNARD CASTLE Durham 986 ⑲ – pop. 5,228 – ☎ 083 33.
See : Bowes Museum** *AC* – Castle* (ruins 12C-14C). **Envir.** : High Force** (waterfalls) *AC*. NW : 14 m. – Raby Castle* (14C) *AC*, NE : 6 m.
18 Harmire Rd ☎ 2237.
i 43 Galgate ☎ 3481.
London 258 – **Carlisle 63** – **Leeds 68** – **Middlesbrough 31** – **Newcastle-upon-Tyne 39.**

Hotels see : Darlington E : 16 ½ m.

AUSTIN-MG-WOLSELEY Prospect Pl. ☎ 2152
MORRIS-MG-WOLSELEY 19 Galgate ☎ 2129
VAUXHALL Newgate ☎ 3504

BARNBY MOOR Notts. – pop. 280 – ✉ ☎ 0777 Retford.
London 151 – **Leeds 44** – Lincoln 27 – **Nottingham 31.**

🏨 **Ye Olde Bell** (T.H.F.), DN22 8QS, ☎ 5121, Telex 56446, garden – wc ☎ Ⓟ.
M a la carte 4.60/5.75 **st.** 🍷 1.50 – **59 rm** 9.00/18.00 **st.**

BARNSDALE BAR West Yorks. – see Wentbridge.

BARNSLEY South Yorks. 986 ⑫ and ㉓ - pop. 75,395 – ☎ 0226.
18 Staincross ☎ 022 678 (Darton) 2856, N : 4 m.
London 177 – **Leeds 21** – **Manchester 36** – **Sheffield 15.**

🏨 **Queen's** (Anchor), Regent St., S70 2HQ, ☎ 84192, Group Telex 27120 – TV wc ☎.
M approx. 2.70 **t.** 🍷 1.00 – **31 rm** 11.55/16.50 **t.**

🏨 **Royal** (Anchor), Church St., S70 2AD, ☎ 203658, Group Telex 27120
M approx. 2.75 **t.** 🍷 1.00 – **17 rm** 8.25/13.50 **st.**

at Ardsley E : 2 ½ m. on A 635 – ✉ ☎ 0226 Barnsley :

🏨 **Ardsley House,** Doncaster Rd, S71 5EH, ☎ 89401, garden – TV Ⓟ.
M 4.00/4.50 **st.** 🍷 1.30 – 1.50 – **16 rm** 12.50/17.50 **st.**

AUSTIN-MG-WOLSELEY 12A Regent St. ☎ 5561
CHRYSLER-SIMCA, FIAT Stairfoot ☎ 6675
DAF Genn Lane ☎ 84138
DAIMLER-JAGUAR-MORRIS-MG-WOLSELEY 101 Old Mill Lane ☎ 6746
FIAT Peel St. ☎ 89346
FORD Dodworth Rd ☎ 5741
PEUGEOT The Cross, Silkstone ☎ 798636
RENAULT Doncaster Rd ☎ 5915
VW, AUDI-NSU Huddersfield Rd ☎ 3855

BARNSTAPLE Devon 986 ㉟ – pop. 17,317 – ☎ 0271.
Envir. : Swymbridge (church : carved woodwork* 15C) SE : 4 ½ m.
London 222 – Exeter 40 – Taunton 51.

🏨 **Imperial** (T.H.F.), Taw Vale Par., EX32 8NB, ☎ 5861 – lift TV Ⓟ.
M a la carte 4.80/6.25 **st.** 🍷 1.50 – **56 rm** 9.50/22.50 **st.** – P 15.25/18.00 **st.**

🏨 Barnstaple Motel, Braunton Rd, EX31 1LE, NW : 1 m. on A 361 ☎ 5016, pool – wc Ⓟ.
60 rm.

🏨 Royal and Fortescue, Boutport St., EX31 1HG, ☎ 2289 – lift wc Ⓟ.
54 rm.

🏨 **Roborough House** 🐦, Pilton, EX31 4JQ, NE : 1 ¼ m. off A 39 ☎ 72354, ←, garden – wc wc Ⓟ
M 3.10/3.50 **t.** 🍷 1.20 – 0.75 – **11 rm** 8.60/14.50 **t.**

XX **Lynwood House,** Exeter Rd, EX32 9DZ, on A 377 ☎ 3695 – P
closed Saturday lunch and Sunday dinner – **M** (buffet Sunday lunch) a la carte 4.40/6.70 **s.** 1.75.

XX **Sherry's,** 54 Boutport St., EX31 1SH, ☎ 5499
closed Sunday and Bank Holidays – **M** a la carte 4.35/6.55 **t.** 1.45.

at Bishop's Tawton S: 3 m. on A 377 – ✉ ☎ **0271 Barnstaple:**

Downrew House, EX32 0DY, SE: 1 ½ m. ☎ 2497, « Country house », heated, – P
mid March-October – **M** *(open February-November) (closed Sunday)* (dinner only) 5.50/6.15 1.20 – **9 rm** (dinner included) 12.50/25.00.

AUSTIN-MG-WOLSELEY Bear St. ☎ 3038
BMW, OPEL Abbey Rd Pitton ☎ 4070
CHRYSLER-SIMCA Newport Rd ☎ 5363
DAF, POLSKI 8 Boutport St. ☎ 3329
DAIMLER-JAGUAR-ROVER-TRIUMPH Boutport St. ☎ 73232
FIAT, TOYOTA, VOLVO Pottington Industrial Estate ☎ 71551
FORD Taw Vale ☎ 4173
MORRIS-MG-WOLSELEY The Square ☎ 2264
OPEL 42 Boutport St. ☎ 4366
RENAULT Bear St. ☎ 2375
VAUXHALL Pilton Bridge ☎ 2433

BARRY South Glam. 986 ㉟ – **pop. 41,681** – ☎ **0446.**

Port Rd, The Colcot ☎ 5061.

Vale of Glamorgan Borough Council, Woodlands Rd ☎ 3342 (Easter-September).

London 167 – Cardiff 10 – Swansea 39.

Mount Sorrel, Porthkerry Rd, CF6 8XY, ☎ 740069 – TV wc wc ☎ P
M 2.50/4.00 1.20 – **36 rm** 9.20/14.60 **t.**

Water's Edge, The Knap, CF6 8YY, ☎ 733392, ← – TV wc ☎ P
M approx. 2.75 1.00 – 1.75 – **38 rm** 8.00/10.00.

International, Port Rd, Rhoose, CF6 9BT, W: 2 m. by A 4226 to Llantwit Major ☎ 710787 – TV wc ☎ P
M a la carte 2.15/4.90 **s.** 1.50 – 1.20 – **30 rm** 9.50/12.00 **st.**

AUSTIN-MG-WOLSELEY Brook St. ☎ 4365
MORRIS-MG-ROVER-TRIUMPH-WOLSELEY Broad St. ☎ 2633

BARTON MILLS Suffolk – **pop. 765** – ✉ **Bury St. Edmunds** – ☎ **0638 Mildenhall.**

London 72 – Bury St.Edmund's 12 – Cambridge 21 – Norwich 40.

Bull Inn, IP28 6AP, on A 11 ☎ 713230 – wc wc ☎ P
19 rm.

BARTON-ON-SEA Hants. – **pop. 4,294** – ☎ **0425 New Milton.**

Marine Drive ☎ 615308.

London 108 – Bournemouth 11 – Lymington 8 – Southampton 23.

Red House (Interchange), Barton Court Av., BH25 7HJ, ☎ 610119, – wc P
M approx. 3.50 **t.** 1.25 – **43 rm** 8.75/14.25 **st.** – P 15.50/16.50 **st.**

BASILDON Essex – **pop. 129,330** – ☎ **0268.**

Kingswood ☎ 3297.

London 30 – Chelmsford 17 – Southend-on-Sea 13.

Essex Centre (Centre), Cranes Farm Rd, SS14 3DG, NW: 2 ¼ m. off A 176 ☎ 3955, Telex 995141 – TV wc ☎ P.
M (Carvery rest.) approx. 3.95 **s.** 1.25 – 1.50 – **120 rm** 10.75/14.50 **s.**

AUSTIN-MG-ROVER-TRIUMPH-WOLSELEY Southern Hay ☎ 22661
CHRYSLER-SIMCA Great Oakes ☎ 21241
DATSUN, OPEL Nethermayne ☎ 22261
FORD Cherrydown ☎ 23451
VAUXHALL High Rd, Laindon ☎ 42481

BASINGSTOKE Hants. 986 ㉟ ㊱ – **pop. 52,587** – ☎ **0256.**

London 55 – Reading 17 – Southampton 31 – Winchester 18.

Plan opposite

Hampshire House, Grove Rd, RG21 3EE, SW: 1 m. junction A 339 and A 30 ☎ 68181 – TV P. Z **e**
M 3.75/4.00 **t.** 1.75 – 1.75 – **84 rm** 12.60/17.50 **st.**

Mercury Motor Inn, Aldermaston Roundabout, RG24 9NV, N: 2 m. junction A 339 and A 340 ☎ 20212, Telex 628064 – TV wc ☎ P. Z **a**
M (grill rest. only) a la carte approx. 3.80 **st.** 1.35 – 1.50 – **82 rm** 13.00/17.50 **st.**

Red Lion (Anchor), 24 London St., RG21 1NY, ☎ 28525, Group Telex 27120 – TV wc wc ☎ P Y **c**
M approx. 3.25 **t.** 1.00 – **42 rm** 9.75/18.70.

at Oakley W: 5 m. on B 3400 – Z – ✉ ☎ **0256 Basingstoke:**

Beach Arms Motor Inn, RG23 7EA, on B 3400 ☎ 780210 – TV wc ☎ P
M 3.50/10.00 1.20 – **16 rm** 9.50/14.00.

BASINGSTOKE

London Street .... Y 19
Upper Church Street .... Y 24
Winchester Street .... Y 27

Aldermaston Road .... Z 2
Beaconsfield Road .... Y 3
Buckland Avenue .... Z 5
Chequers Road .... Y 6
Church Street .... Y 7
Churchill Way East .... Z 9
Churchill Way West .... Z 10
Council Road .... Y 12
Cross Street .... Y 13
Fairfield Road .... Y 14
Houndwills Road .... Z 17
New Street .... Y 20
Reading Road .... Z 22
Victoria Street .... Y 25
Wote Street .... Y 28

By spring 1979 this guide will be out of date. Get the new edition.

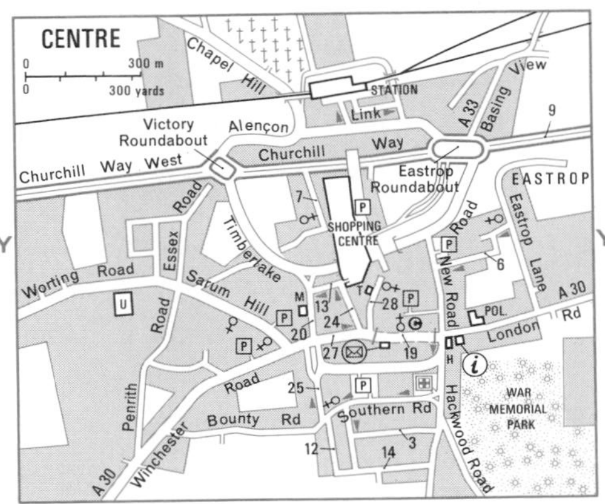

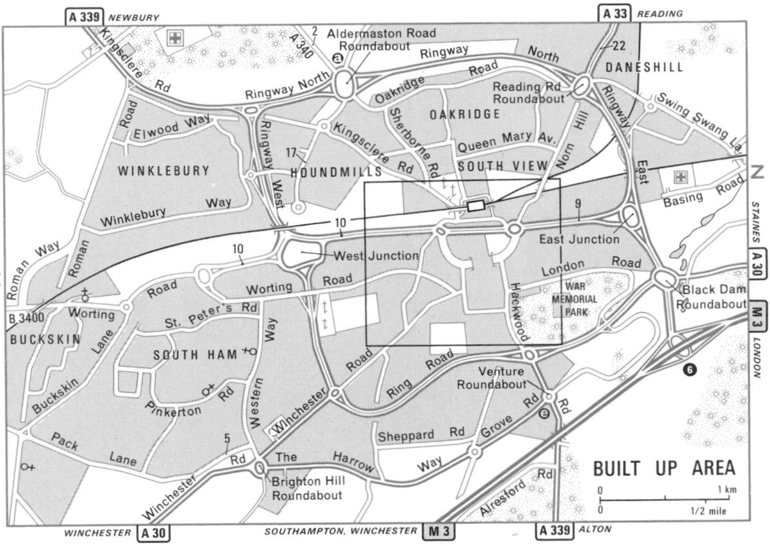

AUSTIN-DAIMLER-MG-WOLSELEY Houndmills ☏ 65991
BMW South Warnborough ☏ 045 824 (Long Sutton) 249
CHRYSLER-SIMCA Reading Rd ☏ 65454
DAF Turgis Green ☏ 267
FIAT, LANCIA London Rd ☏ 3896
FORD Lower Wote St. ☏ 3561
JAGUAR-MORRIS-MG-WOLSELEY New Loop Rd ☏ 24561
OPEL, VAUXHALL West Ham ☏ 62551
RENAULT 1/3 Winchester Rd ☏ 23211
ROVER-TRIUMPH London Rd ☏ 24444
SAAB Church St. ☏ 64822
VOLVO London Rd ☏ 3661

BASLOW Derbs. 986 ㉗ – pop. **1,166** (inc. Bubnell) – ✉ Bakewell – ☎ 024 688.
London 161 – Derby 27 – Manchester 35 – Sheffield 13.

Cavendish, DE14 1SP, on A 619 ☏ 2311, ≤, ⇖, ⚘ – TV ⊟wc ☎ ♿ Ⓟ
M 2.95/4.00 🍷 1.25 – ☕ 2.00 – **13 rm** 12.00/15.00.

Dieser Führer ist kein vollständiges Hotel- und Restaurantverzeichnis. Um den Ansprüchen aller Touristen gerecht zu werden, haben wir uns auf eine Auswahl in jeder Kategorie beschränkt.

BASSENTHWAITE Cumbria – pop. 518 – ✆ 059 681 Bassenthwaite Lake.
London 299 – Carlisle 24 – Keswick 7.

Armathwaite Hall, CA12 4RE, W : 1 ½ m. on B 5291 ✉ Keswick ✆ 551, ≤, « Stately home in extensive grounds », park – wc
M 4.50/5.50 **t.** 2.00 – **27 rm** 11.00/22.00 **t.** – P 18.25/19.75 **t.**

Castle Inn, CA12 4RG, W : 1 m. at junction A 591 and B 5291 ✉ Keswick ✆ 401, ≤, heated, – wc
closed November – **M** *(closed Christmas)* approx. 4.60 **st.** 1.60 – **20 rm** 13.00/19.50 **st.** – P 16.45/17.50 **st.**

Overwater Hall, CA5 1HH, NE : 2¼ m. on Uldale Rd ✉ Ireby, ✆ 232, ≤, park – wc
closed February – **M** *(closed lunch to non-residents)* 4.50/6.00 **s.** – **13 rm** 9.00/14.50 **s.**

Pheasant Inn, CA13 9YE, SW : 3 ¾ m. by B 5291 on A 66 ✉ Cockermouth ✆ 234, « 16C inn », – wc
closed Christmas Day – **M** 3.70/4.00 **st.** – **20 rm.**

BATH Avon 986 ㉟ – pop. 84,670 – ✆ 0225.

See : The Georgian City*** : Royal Crescent*** (Nº 1 Georgian House* *AC*) V – Circus** V – Prior Park* (Palladian Mansion ≤*) *AC* Z – Lansdown Crescent (≤*) Y – Camden Crescent (≤*) V – Pulteney Bridge (≤*) X – Assembly Rooms V **M**² (chandeliers* 18C : Ballroom and Great Octagon), Museum of Costume** – Abbey Church* 16C X **B** – Roman baths* (Pump Room) *AC* X **D** – Holbourne Museum* *AC* V **M**¹.

Envir. : Claverton Manor (American Museum**) *AC*, E : 2 ½ m. Z – Corsham Court** (Elizabethan) *AC*, NE : 10 m. by A 4 Y – Bradford-on-Avon (St. Lawrence's Church* : Saxon, Tithe Barn* 14C) SE: 9 m. by A 4 Y and A 363 – Tropical Bird Gardens* *AC*, SE : 10 m. by A 4 Y and A 363 in Rode Manor gardens. **Exc. :** Longleat House** (Elizabethan) *AC* and Lion Reserve** *AC*, S : 20 m. via Frome by B 3110 Z.

18 Sham Castle ✆ 25182, SE : 1 ½ m. Y – 18 Lansdown ✆ 25007, NW : 3 m. by Lansdown Rd Y.

i 8 Abbey Churchyard ✆ 62831 and 60521.

London 119 – Bristol 13 – Southampton 63 – Taunton 49.

Plan opposite

Francis (T.H.F.), Queen Sq., BA1 2HH, ✆ 24257, Telex 449162 – TV. X **o**
M approx. 4.20 **st.** 1.60 – 2.00 – **66 rm** 14.00/21.00 **st.**

Beaufort (Myddleton), Walcot St., BA1 5BJ, ✆ 20311, Telex 449519 – TV. V **i**
M a la carte 4.90/8.30 **st.** 1.25 – 1.05 – **100 rm** 15.25/20.70 **st.**

The Priory, Weston Rd, BA1 2XT, ✆ 21887, ≤, heated, – TV Y **c**
closed 23 December-13 January – **M** (dinner only) 6.00/8.50 **s.** 1.50 – 1.50 – **15 rm** 15.00/32.00 **s.**

Lansdown Grove (Interchange), Lansdown Rd, BA1 5EH, ✆ 315891, – wc Y **o**
M approx. 4.00 1.40 – 1.75 – **43 rm** 9.00/17.20.

Redcar, 27 Henrietta St., BA2 6LR, ✆ 65432 – TV wc V **a**
M 2.75/3.00 **t.** 1.40 – **35 rm** 10.00/17.50 **t.**

Pratt's, South Par., BA2 4AB, ✆ 60441 – wc. X **r**
M 3.25/6.00 **st.** 1.25 – **50 rm** 9.50/21.00 **st.**

Royal York (Norfolk Cap.), George St., BA1 2DY, ✆ 61541, Group Telex 23241 – wc. V **z**
M a la carte 3.50/6.05 **st.** – **56 rm** 9.95/21.05 **st.**

Royal Crescent, 15-16 Royal Crescent, BA1 2LS, ✆ 24803, ≤, – wc V **c**
closed 25 December-1 January – **M** approx. 4.60 **st.** 1.50 – **33 rm** 10.35/20.70 **st.** – P 15.50/16.65 **st.**

St. Monica's, 53-54 Gt. Pulteney St. ,BA2 4DN, ✆ 4092 – wc V **r**
M (bar lunch) – **23 rm.**

Fernley, 1 North Par., BA1 1LG, ✆ 61603 – wc X **e**
M (bar lunch) 3.30/3.75 **st.** 1.50 – **46 rm** 8.75/17.00 **st.** – P 13.45/15.20 **st.**

North Parade without rest., 10 North Par., BA2 4AL, ✆ 60007 X **n**
closed December and January – **17 rm** 5.65/11.35 **t.**

Ashley Villa, 26 Newbridge Rd, BA1 3JZ, ✆ 21683, – TV Y **i**
16 rm 7.00/14.00 **st.**

Villa Magdala, Henrietta Rd, BA2 6LX, ✆ 25836, – TV wc V **e**
Easter-October – **6 rm** 11.00/20.00 **t.**

Tasburgh, Warminster Rd, Bathampton, BA2 6SH, NE : 1 ½ m. on A 36 ✆ 25096, – Y **n**
12 rm.

Apsley House, Newbridge Hill, BA1 3PT, ✆ 21368, – Y **e**
11 rm 5.50/10.00 **t.**

BATH

Street	Square	No.
Gay Street	V	18
Green Street	VX	21
Milsom Street	V	29
New Bond Street	X	31
Avon Street	X	2
Barton Street	X	3
Beckford Road	V	4
Belvedere	V	5
Broad Quay	X	7
Charles Street	X	9
Charlotte Street	X	10
Cheap Street	X	12
Churchill Bridge	X	13
Claverton Street	X	14
Cleveland Place	V	15
Corn Street	X	16
Darlington Street	V	17
George Street	V	19
High Street	X	22
Lower Borough Walls	X	24
Manvers Street	X	27
Midland Bridge Road	X	28
Monmouth Place	X	30
New King Street	X	32
Paragon	V	34
Pierrepont Street	X	35
Queen Square	VX	37
Rossiter Road	X	38
St. James' Parade	X	39
Southgate	X	40
Sydney Place	V	41
Union Street	X	44
Upper Borough Walls	X	45
Westgate Buildings	X	47

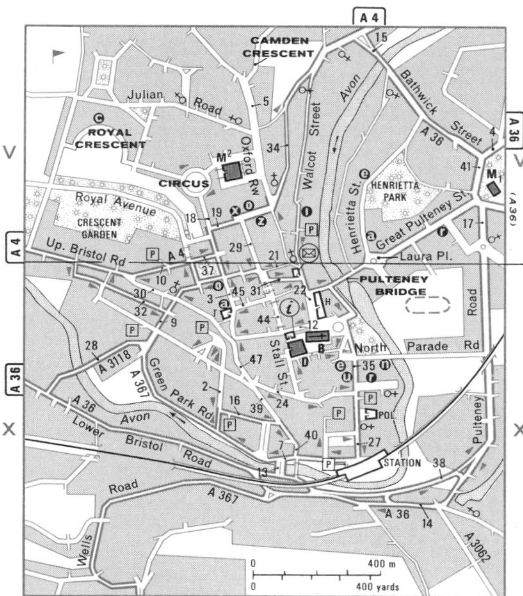

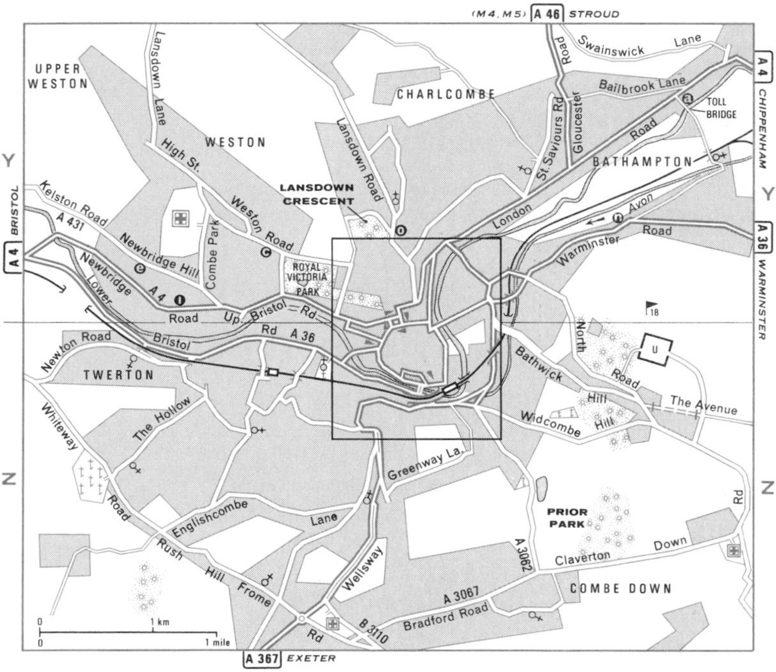

(M4, M5) A 46 STROUD

UPPER WESTON
Lansdown Lane
CHARLCOMBE
Swainswick Lane
Road
Bailbrook Lane
TOLL BRIDGE
A 4 CHIPPENHAM
WESTON
High St.
Lansdown Road
St. Saviours Rd
Gloucester Road
BATHAMPTON
LANSDOWN CRESCENT
Weston Road
London
Avon
Warminster Road
A 36 WARMINSTER
BRISTOL A 4
Kelston Road
A 431
Newbridge Hill
Combe Park
ROYAL VICTORIA PARK
Newbridge Lower
A 4
Road
Up. Bristol Rd
Rd A 36
Newton Road
Bristol
TWERTON
North Road
Bathwick Hill
The Avenue
Widcombe Hill
Whiteway
The Hollow
Greenway La.
Road
Englishcombe Lane
PRIOR PARK
Rush Hill
Wellsway
A 3062
Claverton Down Rd
Frome Rd
A 3067
B 3110
Bradford Road
COMBE DOWN
0 1 km
0 1 mile
A 367 EXETER
Y
Z

XXX **Popjoy's,** Beau Nash House, Sawclose, BA1 1EY, ☎ 60494 — X a
closed Sunday and 3 days at Christmas – **M** (dinner only) a la carte 5.70/7.70 🍾 1.60.

XX ✿ **The Hole in the Wall,** 16 George St., BA1 2EN, ☎ 25242, « Converted Georgian kitchens and coal hole » — V x
closed Sunday and Christmas – **M** a la carte 5.50/9.05
Spec. Baked Stilton creams, Escalope of pork chandelle with prawns and cream, Iced fresh lime soufflé.

XX **Old Mill** with rm, Toll Bridge Rd, BA1 7DE, NE: 2 m. off A 4 ☎ 858476, ≤, ⚓, 🌳 – 🚿wc 🅟 — Y a
M a la carte 4.25/5.15 🍾 1.80 – **12 rm** ☕ 6.50/13.00.

X **Laden Table,** 7 Edgar Buildings, George St., BA1 2EE, ☎ 64356 — V o
closed Sunday, Monday, 2 weeks at Christmas, 2 weeks summer and Bank Holidays – **M** approx. 5.95 **t.**

X **Ainslie's,** 12 Pierrepont St., BA1 1LA, ☎ 27645, Bistro — X u
closed Monday, 25-26 December and 1 January – **M** (dinner only) a la carte 4.00/5.90 **t.** 🍾 1.50.

at Lower Limpley Stoke S: 5 ¾ m. by A 36 on B 3108 – Z – ✉ Bath – ☎ 022 122 Limpley Stoke :

🏨 **Cliffe** 🐦, BA3 6HY, ☎ 3226, ≤, 🏊 heated, 🌳 – 📺 🛁wc ☎ 🅟
March-20 November – **M** (bar lunch) 5.35/6.75 **st.** 🍾 2.10 – ☕ 1.90 – **10 rm** 9.50/28.50 **st.**

XX **Tearle's,** The Bridge, BA3 6EU, ☎ 3150 – 🅟
closed Sunday dinner, Monday and 3 weeks at Christmas – **M** (dinner only and Sunday lunch) a la carte 4.80/8.10 **t.** 🍾 1.25.

ALFA-ROMEO Wellsway ☎ 29187
AUSTIN-DAIMLER-JAGUAR-MG-ROVER-TRIUMPH-WOLSELEY Newbridge Rd ☎ 26143
BMW Bathwick Hill ☎ 66286
CITROEN Prior Park Rd ☎ 29552
DAF, MAZDA, Dorchester St. ☎ 66229
DATSUN Lower Bristol Rd ☎ 25864
FORD 5/10 James St. West ☎ 61636
PEUGEOT 50/52 Wellsway ☎ 27408
RENAULT Margarets Buildings, Circus Pl. ☎ 27328
SAAB London Rd ☎ 22823
VAUXHALL Midsomer Norton ☎ 413260
VAUXHALL Upper Bristol Rd ☎ 22131
VOLVO Bathwick Hill ☎ 65814

BATTLE East Sussex 986 ㊱ – pop. 4,987 – ☎ 042 46.

See: Abbey* (11C-14C) *AC.*

i The Watch Oak ☎ 3371.

London 57 – Brighton 31 – Folkestone 43 – Maidstone 29.

🏨 **George** (T.H.F.), 23 High St., TN33 0EA, ☎ 2844 – 🛁wc 🅟
M approx. 3.00 **st.** 🍾 1.50 – **17 rm** ☕ 6.50/12.50 **st.**

AUSTIN-MG Battle Hill ☎ 2286
MORRIS-MG-WOLSELEY 32 High St. ☎ 2425

BAWTRY South Yorks. 986 ㉘ – pop. 1,497 – ☎ 0302 Doncaster.

Envir.: Gainsborough (Old Hall** 15C) *AC,* SE: 12 m.

⛳18 Austerfield, ☎ 710 850, NE: 2 m. off A 614.

London 158 – Leeds 39 – Lincoln 32 – Nottingham 36 – Sheffield 22.

🏨 **Crown** (Anchor), High St., DN10 6JW, ☎ 710341, Group Telex 27120, 🌳 – 📺 🛁wc ☎ 🅟. 🏛
M approx. 3.20 **t.** 🍾 1.00 – **40 rm** ☕ 12.95/17.90.

XX **Dower House,** Market Pl., DN10 6JL, ☎ 710497
closed Sunday, Christmas Day and 1 January – **M** a la carte 3.80/5.75.

BAYCLIFF Cumbria – see Ulverston.

BEACONSFIELD Bucks. 986 ④ – pop. 11,875 – ☎ 049 46.

London 26 – Aylesbury 19 – Oxford 32.

🏨 **Bellhouse** (De Vere), Oxford Rd, HP9 2XE, E: 1 ¾ m. on A 40 ☎ 028 13 (Gerrard's Cross) 87211, 🌳 – 🛗 📺 🅟. 🏛
M a la carte approx. 5.00 **st.** 🍾 1.45 – **125 rm** ☕ 15.50/23.75 **st.**

🏨 **Beaconsfield Crest Motel** (Crest), Aylesbury End, HP9 1LW, ☎ 71211 – 📺 🛁wc ☎ 🅟. 🏛
M (bar lunch) approx. 3.75 **s.** 🍾 1.55 – ☕ 1.60 – **40 rm** 10.95/15.50 **s.**

at Beaconsfield New Town N: ¾ m. on B 474 – ✉ ☎ 049 46 Beaconsfield :

XX **Jasmine,** 15a Penn Rd, HP9 2PT, ☎ 5335, Chinese rest.
M a la carte 4.15/5.00 🍾 1.35.

AUSTIN-MORRIS-MG-WOLSELEY Penn Rd ☎ 5272
DAIMLER-JAGUAR-ROVER-TRIUMPH, JENSEN 55 Station Rd ☎ 2141
FIAT 15 Gregories Rd ☎ 5538
VAUXHALL Knotty Green ☎ 3730

☞ *Utilizzate, per lunghe percorrenze, le carte stradali Michelin in scala 1/1 000 000.*

BEAULIEU Hants. 986 ㉟ – pop. 1,083 – ✉ Brockenhurst – ☎ 0590.
See : Beaulieu Abbey* (ruins 13C) : Palace House* 14C, National Motor Museum**, Buckler's Hard Maritime Museum *AC*.
i John Montagu Building ☎ 612345.
London 102 – Bournemouth 24 – **Southampton 13** – Winchester 23.

- **Montagu Arms,** Palace Lane, SO4 7ZL, ☎ 612324, – TV P
  M a la carte 5.35/9.20 1.75 – **21 rm** 9.75/22.00.

at Bucklers Hard S : 2 ¼ m. – ✉ Brockenhurst – ☎ 059 063 Bucklers Hard :

- **Master Builder's House** , SO4 7XB, ☎ 253, ←, – wc ☎ ♿ P.
  M a la carte 3.45/5.00 **t.** 1.30 – **23 rm** 9.00/15.00 **t.**

BEAUMARIS Gwynedd 986 ㉗ – pop. 2,102 – ☎ 0248.
See : Castle* (13 C) *AC*.
9 ☎ 810231, NW : 1 m.
London 253 – Birkenhead 74 – Holyhead 25.

- Bulkeley Arms, 19 Castle St., LL58 8AW, ☎ 810415, ← – wc P.
  42 rm.
- **Bishopsgate House,** 54 Castle St., LL58 8AB, ☎ 810302 – P
  February-October – **M** *(closed Saturday lunch)* approx. 3.00 **st.** – **12 rm** 5.00/10.00 **st.**
- **Hobson's Choice,** 13 Castle St. ☎ 810323
  closed Sunday, Monday lunch, 25 and 26 December – **M** (buffet lunch) a la carte 4.60/5.55 **t.** 1.35.

ROVER-TRIUMPH Castle St. ☎ 810355

carte	Dans les hôtels et restaurants cités avec des menus à prix fixes, il est généralement possible de se faire servir également à la carte.

BECCLES Suffolk 986 ㉜ – pop. 8,015 – ☎ 0502.
London 113 – Great Yarmouth 15 – **Ipswich 40** – **Norwich 18.**

- **Waveney House,** Puddingmoor, NR34 9PL, ☎ 712270 – TV wc ☎ P
  M *(closed Sunday dinner to non-residents)* approx. 3.45 **t.** 1.50 – **13 rm** 11.90/21.40 **t.**

FORD VAUXHALL Station Rd ☎ 712268 MORRIS-MG-WOLSELEY Beccles Rd, Barnby ☎ 050 276 (Barnby) 204

BEDDGELERT Gwynedd 986 ㉗ – pop. 671 – ☎ 076 686.
Envir. : NE : Llyn Dinas valley** – Llyn Gwynant valley*. **Exc. :** Blaenau Ffestiniog (site : slate quarries*) E : **14** m. by Penrhyndeudraeth.
London 249 – Caernarfon 13 – Chester 73.

- **Royal Goat,** LL55 4YE, ☎ 224 – wc ☎ P
  M 3.50/5.00 0.90 – **29 rm** 7.50/17.00 **s.** – P 13.00/15.00 **s.**
- Tanronen, LL55 4YB, ☎ 347 – P
  9 rm.

BEDFORD Beds. 986 ㉜ – pop. 74,000 – ☎ 0234.
See : Embankment* – Cecil Higgins Art Gallery (porcelain* 18C). **Envir. :** Elstow (Abbey Church* 11C, Moot Hall : John Bunyan Museum *AC*) S : 1 ¼ m. – Ampthill (Houghton House : site*, ←*) S : 5 m. – Old Warden (St. Leonard's Church : woodwork*; Aeroplane Museum, near Biggleswade Aerodrome : the Shuttleworth collection* *AC*) SE : 7 ½ m.
18 Green Lane ☎ 54010, N : 2 m. on A 6 – 18 Mowsbury, Cleat Hill ☎ 771042, N : 3 m.
i Town Hall, St. Paul's Sq. ☎ 67422 ext 250.
London 59 – **Cambridge 29** – Colchester 73 – **Leicester 51** – Lincoln 95 – Luton 20 – **Oxford 52** – Southend-on-Sea 83.

- **County,** St. Mary's St., MK42 0AR, ☎ 55131, Telex 825243, ← – TV P.
  M approx. 4.00 2.00 – **80 rm** 11.50/17.00.
- **Swan,** High St., MK40 1RW, ☎ 46565 – wc ☎ P.
  M 2.95/3.50 **s.** 1.75 – **90 rm** 8.50/15.75 **s.**
- De Parys, 41 de Parys Av., MK40 2UA, ☎ 52121, – wc ♿ P.
  53 rm.
- **Embankment** (Crest), The Embankment, MK40 3PD, ☎ 61332 – wc P.
  M *(closed Sunday dinner)* 2.85/4.10 **s.** 1.45 – **21 rm** 8.00/13.35 **s.**

at Wilshamstead (Wilstead) S : 5 m. by A 6 – ✉ ☎ 0234 Bedford :

- **Old Manor House,** Cotton End Rd, MK45 3BT, ☎ 740262 – P
  closed Christmas week – **9 rm** 5.50/11.00.

P.T.O. ⟶

at ***Houghton Conquest*** S: 6 ½ m. by A 6 – ✉ ☎ 0234 Bedford:

XX **Knife and Cleaver,** MK45 3LA, ☎ 740387 – Ⓟ
closed Monday dinner, Saturday lunch and Sunday – **M** a la carte approx. 5.10 **st.** 🍷 1.55.

at ***Turvey*** W: 7 m. on A 428 – ✉ Bedford – ☎ 023 064 Turvey:

🏠 **Laws,** MK43 8DB, ☎ 213, 🌳 – Ⓟ
closed 25 and 26 December – **M** *(closed Sunday dinner, Easter Sunday and Monday and August Bank Holidays)* a la carte 3.60/5.10 **st.** 🍷 1.30 – **8 rm** ☕ 7.50/15.00 **st.**

at ***Clapham*** NW: 2 m. on A 6 – ✉ ☎ 0234 Bedford:

🏨 **Woodlands Manor,** Green Lane, MK41 6ET, ☎ 63281, 🏊 heated, 🌳 – 📺 🛁wc 🚿wc ☎ Ⓟ. 🐕
M a la carte 4.65/6.40 🍷 1.45 – **9 rm** ☕ 12.00/16.00.

at ***Milton Ernest*** NW: 5 m. on A 6 – ✉ Bedford – ☎ 023 02 Oakley:

XX **Milton Ernest Hall** 🔇 with rm, MK44 1RF, ☎ 4111, ≤, « Victorian gothic country house », 🎣, 🌳, park – 🛁wc Ⓟ
closed 2 weeks January and 1 week August/September – **M** *(closed Sunday dinner, Monday and Bank Holidays)* a la carte 3.85/5.50 🍷 1.30 – **6 rm** ☕ 9.00/18.00.

at ***Bletsoe*** NW: 6 ½ m. on A 6 – ✉ ☎ 0234 Bedford:

XX **Falcon Inn,** Rushden Rd, MK44 1QN, ☎ 781222 – Ⓟ
closed Saturday lunch, Sunday dinner and 25-26 December – **M** a la carte 3.85/5.95 **s.** 🍷 1.40.

MICHELIN Branch, Kingfisher Wharf, London Rd, MK42 0PE, ☎ 51541.

AUSTIN-MG-WOLSELEY Station Rd, Oakley ☎ 023 02 (Oakley) 3118
AUDI-NSU, MERCEDES-BENZ, ROLLS ROYCE, VAUXHALL Barker's Lane ☎ 50011
AUSTIN-DAIMLER-JAGUAR-MG-ROVER-TRIUMPH-WOLSELEY 120 Goldington Rd ☎ 55221
BMW, ROLLS ROYCE, BENTLEY Shuttleworth Rd Goldington ☎ 60412
CHRYSLER-SIMCA 1 The Kingsway ☎ 58581
CITROEN Kempston ☎ 854423
DAF, VOLVO Windsor Rd ☎ 45454
DAIMLER-JAGUAR-ROVER-TRIUMPH 6 Kingsway ☎ 50781
DATSUN 180 Goldington Rd ☎ 60121
FORD 8/10 The Broadway ☎ 58391
MORRIS-MG-WOLSELEY Bromham Rd ☎ 63299
PEUGEOT Kingsway ☎ 212636
RENAULT 87 High St., Clapham ☎ 54257
VW, AUDI-NSU 20 Grove Pl. ☎ 51431

BEESTON Cheshire – pop. 221 – ✉ Tarporley – ☎ 0829 Bunbury.
London 186 – Chester 15 – **Liverpool 40** – Shrewsbury 32.

XXX Wild Boar Inn 🔇 with rm, CV6 9NW, on A 49 ☎ 260309, Telex 61455, 🌳 – 📺 🛁wc ☎ ♿ Ⓟ
closed 3 days over Christmas – **M** *(closed Sunday dinner)* – **30 rm.**

BELBROUGHTON Heref. and Worc. – pop. 2,421 – ✉ Stourbridge – ☎ 0562.
London 123 – **Birmingham 14** – Kidderminster 6.

XX **Talbot,** Hartle Rd, DY9 9TG, ☎ 730249 – Ⓟ
closed Sunday dinner, Monday, 4 days January and 3 weeks August/September – **M** (buffet lunch except Sunday) a la carte 3.60/5.80 **t.** 🍷 1.50.

BELFORD Northumb. 986 ⑮ – pop. 960 – ☎ 066 83.
London 335 – **Edinburgh 71** – **Newcastle-upon-Tyne 49.**

🏠 Blue Bell (Swallow), Market Sq., NE70 7NE, ☎ 203, Group Telex 53168, 🌳 – 🛁wc 🚗 Ⓟ
13 rm.

BELSTEAD Suffolk – see Ipswich.

BELSTONE Devon – pop. 282 – ✉ Okehampton – ☎ 083 784 Sticklepath.
London 221 – Exeter 20 – **Plymouth 34** – Torquay 30.

🏡 **Skaigh House** 🔇, EX20 1RD, ☎ 243, ≤, 🏊, 🌳, park – Ⓟ
14 March-October – **M** (dinner only) 4.25/4.75 🍷 1.00 – **10 rm** ☕ 7.60/19.00 **s.**

BEMBRIDGE I.O.W. 986 ㊵ – see Wight (Isle of).

Oltre ai ristoranti indicati con
XXXXX ... X,
si può trovare un buon ristorante
anche in molti alberghi.

BENLLECH Gwynedd – pop. 2,554 – ☎ 024 874 Tynygongl.
London 258 – Caernarfon 17 – Chester 70 – Holyhead 22.

- **Bay Court,** Beach Rd, LL74 8SW, ☎ 2573 – wc Ⓟ
  M (dinner only) approx. 4.20 **s.** – **21 rm** 9.00/12.00 **s.**
- **Glanrafon,** LL74 8TF, on A 5025 ☎ 2364 – wc Ⓟ.
  M (bar lunch) 3.50/4.50 1.50 – **24 rm** 6.50/15.00 – P 11.00/12.50.
- **Rhostrefor,** LL74 8SR, on A 5025 ☎ 2347, ←, – Ⓟ
  Easter-October – **M** (residents only in summer) approx. 2.00 **s.** – **10 rm** 6.00/12.00 **s.** – P 9.50 **s.**
- **Hafod Wyn,** LL74 8SD, W: ¾ m. on B 5110 ☎ 2357 – wc Ⓟ
  11 rm (dinner included) 7.50/15.00.

BENSON Oxon. – pop. 4,603 – ☎ 0491 Wallingford.
Envir. : Dorchester-on-Thames (Abbey Church* 14C) NW: 3 ½ m.
London 52 – Oxford 13 – Reading 14 – Swindon 35.

- **White Hart,** 1 Castle Sq., OX9 6SD, ☎ 35244, – Ⓟ
  M 2.00/3.00 **t.** 1.10 – **10 rm** 6.60/12.00 **t.**

at Roke E: 2 m. off B 4009 – ✉ Dorchester – ☎ 0491 Wallingford:

- XX **Home Sweet Home Inn,** OX9 6JD, ☎ 38249, – Ⓟ
  closed Sunday dinner and Monday – **M** 4.25/7.00 **t.** 2.00.

BERKELEY Glos. – pop. 1,449 – ☎ 045 381.
See : Castle** (12C) *AC.*
London 134 – Bristol 20 – Gloucester 16 – Swindon 49.

- **Berkeley Arms,** 4 Canonbury St., GL13 9BG, ☎ 291 – wc Ⓟ
  M a la carte 3.60/5.50 **st.** 1.00 – **13 rm** 6.50/10.50 – P 12.00/14.00 **st.**

at Newport SE: 2 m. on A 38 – ✉ ☎ 045 381 Berkeley:

- **Newport Towers Motel,** GL13 9PX, on A 38 ☎ 575, – TV wc ☎ Ⓟ.
  M 2.75/3.50 **s.** 1.00 – **60 rm** 10.00/15.00 **s.** – P 12.00/15.00 **s.**

BERKSWELL West Midlands – see Coventry.

BERRYNARBOR Devon – see Ilfracombe.

BERRY POMEROY Devon – see Totnes.

BERWICK-UPON-TWEED Northumb. 986 ⑮ – pop. 11,647 – ☎ 0289.
See : City Walls* 16C. **Envir.** : Norham Castle* (12C) SW: 7 m.
18 Goswick ☎ 028 287 (Ancroft) 256, SE: 5 m.
i Castlegate Car Park ☎ 7187 (summer only).
London 349 – Edinburgh 57 – Newcastle-upon-Tyne 63.

- **Turret House,** Etal Rd, TD15 2EG, S: ¾ m. off A 1 on B 6354 ☎ 7344, – wc ☎ Ⓟ
  closed February – **M** *(closed Tuesday dinner)* (residents only) (bar lunch) approx. 5.00 **t.** 1.00 – **11 rm** 11.50/21.00 – P 13.00/15.50.
- **King's Arms** (Interchange), Hide Hill, TD15 1EJ, ☎ 7454, – TV wc ☎ Ⓟ.
  M 4.00/5.00 **s.** 1.30 – **37 rm** 11.00/21.00 **s.**
- **Castle,** Castlegate, TD15 1LF, ☎ 6471 – Ⓟ
  M 4.00/5.00 **s.** 1.30 – **15 rm** 7.50/14.00 **s.** – P 14.00/15.50 **s.**

AUSTIN-MG-ROVER-TRIUMPH-WOLSELEY Golden Sq. ☎ 7371
FORD Castle Garage ☎ 7459
MORRIS-MG-WOLSELEY 55 Hide Hill ☎ 7561
VAUXHALL 12 Silver St. ☎ 7436
VOLVO Tweed St. ☎ 7537
VW, AUDI-NSU Spittal ☎ 7214

BETHESDA Gwynedd 986 ㉗ – pop. 4,163 – ☎ 0248.
See : Slate quarries*. **Envir.** : Nant Ffrancon Pass** SE : 4 m.
London 241 – Chester 60 – Holyhead 29 – Shrewsbury 77.

- **Snowdonia Park Motel,** Ty'n Maes, Nant Ffrancon, LL57 3LX, S: 2 m. on A 5 ☎ 600548 – TV wc wc Ⓟ
  closed 4 days at Christmas – **M** (dinner only) a la carte 2.80/4.50 **st.** 1.75 – 1.60 – **30 rm** 7.50/15.00 **t.**

RENAULT Bangor Rd ☎ 600451

BETWS-Y-COED Gwynedd 986 ㉗ – pop 729 – ☎ 069 02.
Envir. : Nant Ffrancon Pass** NW : 12 m. – Fairy Glen and Conway Falls* *AC*, SE : 2 m. – Swallow Falls* *AC*, NW : 2 m. – Nanty Gwyrd valley* W : by Capel Curig.
ℹ Wales Tourist Office (Waterloo Hotel Complex) ☎ 426.
London 226 – Holyhead 44 – Shrewsbury 62.

- **Waterloo,** LL24 0AR, on A 5 ☎ 411 – wc ☎ P.
M (buffet lunch) a la carte 3.45/5.60 1.40 – **30 rm** 9.50/15.50.
- **Henllys,** LL24 0AL, ☎ 534, « Converted courthouse and jail », – P
closed 15 January-15 March – **8 rm** 4.00/10.00 **st.**

at Penmachno S : 4 ½ m. by A 5 on B 4406 – ✉ Betws-y-Coed – ☎ 069 03 Penmachno :

- **Eagles,** LL42 0UG, ☎ 203 – P
closed February – **M** (bar lunch) approx. 3.50 1.25 – **8 rm** 6.00/9.50.

BEVERLEY North Humberside 986 ㉔ – pop. 17,132 – ✉ ☎ 0482 Kingston-upon-Hull.
See : Minster** 13C-15C – St. Mary's Church* 14C-15C.
18 Ante Mill ☎ 881390.
ℹ The Hall, Lairgate ☎ 882255.
London 188 – Kingston-upon-Hull 8 – Leeds 52 – York 29.

- **Beverley Arms** (T.H.F.), North Bar Within, HU17 8DD, ☎ 885241 – TV wc ☎ P
M a la carte 5.00/6.30 **st.** 1.50 – **61 rm** 11.00/17.00 **st.**

AUSTIN-JAGUAR-MG-ROVER-TRIUMPH 20 Norwood ☎ 886222
FORD Wednesday Market ☎ 80211
VAUXHALL Swinemoor Lane ☎ 882207

BEWDLEY Heref. and Worc. 986 ㉛ – pop. 7,237 – ☎ 0299.
London 140 – Birmingham 20 – Worcester 16.

- **Black Boy,** Kidderminster Rd, DY12 1AG, ☎ 402119 – P
M approx. 3.85 **st.** 1.80 – **20 rm** 7.95/14.95 **st.** – P 14.75/20.65 **st.**

RENAULT Severn Bridge ☎ 403016

BEXHILL East Sussex 986 ㊱ – pop. 32,892 – ☎ 0424.
18 Cooden Beach ☎ 042 43 (Cooden) 2040.
ℹ De La Warr Pavilion, Marina ☎ 212023.
London 66 – Brighton 32 – Folkestone 42.

- **Granville,** Sea Rd, TN40 1EE, ☎ 215437 – ☎
M 3.10/3.50 **st.** 2.50 – **50 rm** 7.50/15.50 **st.** – P 13.45/15.00 **st.**

at Cooden W : 2 m. on B 2182 – ✉ Bexhill – ☎ 042 43 Cooden :

- Cooden Beach, Sea Rd, TN39 4TX, ☎ 2281, <, heated, – TV P.
38 rm.

AUSTIN-MG-WOLSELEY 21 Station Rd ☎ 210098
CHRYSLER-SIMCA, TOYOTA 25 Bell Hill ☎ 215252
CITROEN, PEUGEOT Ninfield Rd ☎ 0424 (Ninfield) 892177
DAF London Rd ☎ 213577
DAIMLER-JAGUAR-ROVER-TRIUMPH 57-69 London Rd ☎ 212000
FORD Terminus Rd ☎ 1111
LANCIA Cooden Beach ☎ 2224
MORRIS-MG-WOLSELEY 68 Sackville Rd ☎ 212255
RENAULT London Rd ☎ 210485

BIBURY Glos. 986 ㉛ – pop. 599 – ✉ Cirencester – ☎ 028 574.
See : Arlington Row* 17C.
London 86 – Gloucester 26 – Oxford 30.

- **Swan,** GL7 5NN, ☎ 204, « Garden and Trout Stream », – wc ☎ P
M 4.75/7.50 **t.** 1.50 – **26 rm** 9.00/20.00 **t.**

BICESTER Oxon. 986 ㉛ – pop. 12,355 – ☎ 086 92.
London 61 – Birmingham 55 – Northampton 31 – Oxford 14.

- **Kings Arms** (Embassy), Market Sq., OX6 7AN, ☎ 2015 – P
closed Christmas – **M** approx. 2.80 **st.** 1.45 – **14 rm** 7.60/11.15 **st.**

BICKLEIGH Devon – pop. 230 – ✉ Tiverton – ☎ 088 45.
London 195 – Exeter 9 – Taunton 28.

- **Fisherman's Cot,** EX16 8RW, on A 396 ☎ 237, <, – TV wc ☎ P
M (bar lunch) a la carte approx. 4.10 **t.** 1.45 – **8 rm** 6.00/14.00 **st.**

BIDDENDEN Kent 986 ㊱ – pop. 2,154 – ✉ Ashford – ☎ 0580.
London 51 – Folkestone 29 – Hastings 25 – Maidstone 13.

- **Ye Maydes,** 13-15 High St., TN27 8AL, ☎ 291306
closed Sunday dinner and Monday – **M** a la carte 4.00/6.10 **t.** 1.45.

BIDEFORD Devon 986 ㉟ – pop. 11,802 – ☎ 023 72.
Envir. : Clovelly (site**) W : 11 m.
Torrington ☎ 2792.
The Quay ☎ 77676 (summer only).
London 231 – Exeter 43 – **Plymouth 58** – Taunton 60.

Durrant House, Heywood Rd, EX39 3QB, Northam N : 1 m. on A 386 ☎ 2361, heated – TV P.
M approx. 4.50 1.70 – **58 rm** 12.00/21.50.

Yeoldon House (Interchange), Durrant Lane, EX39 2RL, Northam N : 1 m. on A 386 ☎ 4400, Taw estuary, – TV wc P
closed Christmas – **M** (bar lunch) 4.00/5.00 **st.** 1.50 – **10 rm** 13.30/19.60.

AUSTIN-MG-ROVER-TRIUMPH-WOLSELEY Kingsley Rd ☎ 2546
CHRYSLER-SIMCA Bridgeland St. ☎ 2016
MORRIS-MG-WOLSELEY Kingsley Rd ☎ 3304
SAAB Meddon St. ☎ 2467
VAUXHALL Handy Cross ☎ 2282

BILBROOK Somerset – pop. 100 – ✉ Minehead – ☎ 098 44 Washford.
London 181 – Minehead 5 – Taunton 19.

Dragon House with rm, TA24 6HQ, ☎ 215, « Part 18C house with gardens » – wc P
closed Christmas and 1 January – **M** a la carte 4.90/7.80 1.30 – **10 rm** 7.50/17.00.

BILLINGHAM Cleveland – pop. 8,656 – ✉ ☎ 0642 Stockton-on-Tees.
Sandy Lane ☎ 554494, W : boundary Billingham.
London 255 – **Middlesbrough 3** – Sunderland 26.

Billingham Arms (Thistle), Town Sq., TS23 2LH, ☎ 552104 – TV wc wc P.
64 rm.

MORRIS-MG-WOLSELEY ☎ 553959
PEUGEOT New Town Centre ☎ 551883
RENAULT ☎ 553071

BILLINGSHURST West Sussex 986 ㊱ – pop. 4,421 – ☎ 040 381.
London 44 – **Brighton 30** – Guildford 20 – **Portsmouth 40.**

Great Groomes, Pulborough Rd, RH14 9EU, S : ½ m. on A 29 ☎ 2571 – P
closed Saturday lunch, Sunday and Monday – **M** a la carte 3.20/6.00 **t.** 1.60.

XVth Century, 42 High St., RH14 9NY, ☎ 2652
closed Sunday, Monday and 25-26 December – **M** (dinner only) a la carte 4.55/6.30 **st.** 1.40.

AUSTIN-JAGUAR-MORRIS-MG-ROVER-TRIUMPH 62 High St. ☎ 2022
CHRYSLER-SIMCA Five Oaks ☎ 2075
MERCEDES-BENZ, PORSCHE High St. ☎ 3341

BINGLEY West Yorks. – pop. 26,475 – ✉ Bradford – ☎ 097 66.
St. Ives, ☎ 2506 – Beckfoot ☎ 3212, near Cottingley Bridge.
London 204 – Bradford 6 – Skipton 13.

Bankfield (Embassy), Bradford Rd, BD16 1TV, ☎ 7123, – TV P.
closed Christmas – **M** approx. 2.75 **st.** 1.45 – **74 rm** 10.15/15.40 **st.**

LANCIA Park Rd ☎ 3556

BIRCHINGTON-ON-SEA Kent – pop. 7,923 – ☎ 0843 Thanet.
See : In Quex Park : Powell-Cotton Museum* of African and Asian natural history and ethnology *AC.*
London 70 – Maidstone 38 – Margate 4.

Bungalow (T.H.F.) Lyall Rd, CT7 9HX, ☎ 41276, heated, – TV wc P.
M approx. 3.00 **st.** 1.50 – **26 rm** 7.00/14.50 **st.**

AUSTIN-MG 214 Canterbury Rd ☎ 41241

BIRKENHEAD Merseyside 986 ⑤ and ㉗ – pop. 137,852 – ☎ 051 Liverpool.
Arrowe Park Woodchurch ☎ 677 1527 – 93 Bidston Rd ☎ 652 5797.
Central Wirral Area Library, Borough Rd ☎ 652 6106.
London 222 – **Liverpool 2.**

Bowler Hat, 1 Talbot Rd, Oxton, L43 2HH, ☎ 652 4931, – TV P.
M 4.00/4.50 1.55 – 1.95 – **27 rm** 8.50/19.00.

AUSTIN-MG-ROVER-TRIUMPH Park Rd North ☎ 647 9445
CHRYSLER-SIMCA Woodchurch Rd, Prenton ☎ 608 2205
DAF, PEUGEOT 222 New Chester Rd ☎ 645 5891 and 644 9333
FORD Hind St. ☎ 647 9851
MORRIS-MG-WOLSELEY 15 Upton Rd ☎ 647 2453
RENAULT 790 Borough Rd ☎ 709 9944
VAUXHALL 6 Woodchurch Rd ☎ 652 2366

BIRMINGHAM West Midlands 986 ⑫ and ㉛ – pop. 1,014,670 – ☏ 021.

See : Museum and Art Gallery** JZ **M¹** – Museum of Science and Industry* JY **M²** – Cathedral (stained glass windows* 19C) KYZ **E**.

18 Alcester Rd South, King's Heath ☏ 444 3584, S : 6 ½ m. by A 435 FX – 18 Church Rd ☏ 454 1736, S : 1 m. FX – 18 Eachelhurst Rd, Walmley ☏ 351 1014, NE : 7 ½ m. DT – 9 Elmdon Lane, Marston Green ☏ 779 2449, E : 7 m. by East Meadway HV – 9 Vicarage Rd, Harborne ☏ 427 1204, SW : 5 m. EX – 9 Warley Park, Bearwood ☏ 429 2440, W : 5 m. BU.

✈ Birmingham Airport : ☏ 743 4272, E : 6 ½ m. by A 45 DU – **Terminal :** Station St.

i Council House, Victoria Sq. ☏ 235 3411/3412.

London 120 – Bristol 84 – Liverpool 99 – Manchester 86 – Nottingham 50.

Town plans: Birmingham pp. 2-7
Except where otherwise stated see pp. 6 and 7

- **Albany** (T.H.F.), P.O. Box 149, Smallbrook Queensway, B5 4EW, ☏ 643 8171, Telex 337031, ≤, ▭ – 🛗 TV. 🧑‍🏫 — JKZ **a**
M 4.25/4.75 **t.** 🍾 1.60 – ▭ 2.00 – **253 rm** 17.50/23.00 **st.**
- Midland, 128 New St., B2 4JT, ☏ 643 2601, Telex 338419 – 🛗 TV ♿. 🧑‍🏫 — KZ **r**
117 rm.
- **Plough and Harrow** (Crest), 135 Hagley Rd, Edgbaston, B16 8LS, W : 1 ½ m. on A 456 ☏ 454 4111, Telex 677147 – 🛗 TV ♿ **P**. 🧑‍🏫 — p. 4 EX **a**
M a la carte 4.50/9.35 **s.** 🍾 1.60 – ▭ 1.80 – **44 rm** 19.25/23.00 **s.**
- **Holiday Inn,** A.T.V. Centre, Holliday St., B1 1HH, ☏ 643 2766, Telex 337272, ≤, ▭ – 🛗 TV ♿ **P**. 🧑‍🏫 — JZ **z**
M 5.00/12.50 🍾 1.75 – ▭ 2.20 – **298 rm** 16.00/20.00.
- **Grand** (Gd Met.), Colmore Row, B3 2DA, ☏ 236 7951, Telex 338174 – 🛗 TV **P**. 🧑‍🏫 — JKY **c**
M a la carte 3.25/5.95 **st.** – **154 rm** ▭ 14.50/20.00 **st.**
- Strathallan (Thistle), 225 Hagley Rd, Edgbaston, B16 9RY, W : 2 m. on A 456 ☏ 455 9777, Telex 336680 – 🛗 TV **P**. 🧑‍🏫 — p. 4 EX **i**
165 rm.
- **Royal Angus,** St. Chad's Queensway, B4 6HY, ☏ 236 4211, Telex 336889 – 🛗 TV. 🧑‍🏫 — KY **s**
M 3.30/5.00 **st.** – ▭ 1.75 – **140 rm** 12.00/18.00 **s.** – P 22.50/25.00 **st.**
- **Birmingham Centre** (Centre), New St., B2 4RX, ☏ 643 2747, Telex 338331 – 🛗 TV 🛁wc ☎. 🧑‍🏫 — KZ **u**
M (Carvery rest.) approx. 2.95 **s.** 🍾 1.25 – ▭ 1.50 – **200 rm** 10.75/14.50 **s.**
- Apollo Motor, 243-247 Hagley Rd, B16 9RS, W : 2 ¼ m. on A 456 ☏ 455 0271 – TV 🛁wc ☎ ♿ **P**. 🧑‍🏫 – **60 rm.** — p. 4 EX **o**
- **Norfolk,** 259-267 Hagley Rd, Edgbaston, B16 9NA, W : 2 ¼ m. on A 456 ☏ 454 8071, Telex 339715, 🌳 – 🛗 🛁wc 🚿wc ☎ ♿ **P**. 🧑‍🏫 — p. 4 EX **u**
M approx. 2.70 **st.** – **200 rm** ▭ 7.05/16.20 **st.**
- **Cobden,** 166-174 Hagley Rd, Edgbaston, B16 9N2, W : 2 m. on A 456, ☏ 454 6621, Telex 339715, 🌳 – 🛗 TV 🛁wc 🚿wc ☎ **P**. 🧑‍🏫 — p. 4 EX **n**
M approx. 2.70 **st.** – **175 rm** ▭ 7.05/16.20 **st.**
- Links, 313 Hagley Rd, B16 9LQ, W : 2 ½ m. on A 456 ✉ Edgbaston ☏ 455 0535, 🌳 – 🛁wc **P** — p. 4 EX **c**
20 rm.
- **Berrow Court** 🐌, Berrow Drive, off Westfield Rd, B15 3UD, W : 2 ¾ m. off A 456 ☏ 454 1488, 🌳 – **P** — p. 4 EX **e**
M (dinner only) approx. 2.75 – **15 rm** ▭ 6.50/10.50.
- **Hagley Court** without rest., 229 Hagley Rd, Edgbaston, B16 9RP, W : 2 m. on A 456 ☏ 454 6514 – **P** — p. 4 EX **s**
21 rm ▭ 6.90/14.00 **st.**
- **Heath Lodge,** Coleshill Rd, Marston Green, B37 7HT, ☏ 779 2218 – **P** — p. 5 HV **a**
11 rm ▭ 9.50/12.80 **st.**
- **Dormy,** 304-306 Hagley Rd, B17 8DJ, ☏ 429 4455 – **P** — p. 4 EX **r**
28 rm ▭ 5.00/9.00.
- **Wentworth,** 103 Wentworth Rd, B17 9SU, ☏ 427 2839 – 🚿 **P** — p. 4 EX **x**
22 rm ▭ 4.50/9.50.
- **Kerry House,** 946 Warwick Rd, Acocks Green, B27 6QG, ☏ 707 0316 – **P** — p. 5 GX **a**
20 rm ▭ 7.00/9.75 **st.**
- **Norwood,** 87 Bunbury Rd, Northfield, B31 2ET, ☏ 475 3262 – **P** — p. 3 by A 38 CU
15 rm ▭ 5.35/9.50 **st.**
- XXX Rajdoot, 12-22 Albert St., B4 7UD, ☏ 643 8805, Indian rest. — KZ **c**
- XX **Lorenzo,** 3 Park St., B5 5JD, ☏ 643 0541, Italian rest. — KZ **o**
closed Sunday, Christmas and Bank Holidays – **M** a la carte 3.40/6.20 🍾 1.20.
- XX **Burlington,** Burlington Pass., New St., B2 4JY, ☏ 643 3081 — KZ **v**
closed Sunday and Bank Holidays – **M** a la carte 2.35/5.50 🍾 1.10.
- XX **La Capanna,** 43 Hurst St., B5 4BN, ☏ 622 2287, Italian rest. — KZ **n**
closed Sunday and Bank Holidays – **M** a la carte 4.15/5.30 🍾 1.05.

Pinocchio, 8 Chad Sq., off Harborne Rd, B15 3TQ, W: 2 ¾ m. off A 456 ☎ 454 8672, Italian rest. p. 4 EX **v**
closed Sunday and Bank Holidays – **M** a la carte 2.40/6.10 **t.**

Danish Food Centre, 10 Stephenson Pl., B2 4PY, ☎ 643 2837, Smorrebrod KZ **i**
closed Sunday and Bank Holidays – **M** a la carte 3.45/6.25 **st.** 1.75.

Except where otherwise stated see pp. 2 and 3

at Streetly **N: 7 m. on A 452 – ✉ Sutton Coldfield – ☎ 021 Birmingham:**

Parson and Clerk (Ansells) without rest., Chester Rd North, B73 6SP, S: 1 ½ m. on A 452 ☎ 353 1747 – wc Ⓟ CT **s**
31 rm 10.30/13.75 **st.**

at Walmley **NE: 6 m. off B 4148 – ✉ Sutton Coldfield – ☎ 021 Birmingham:**

Penns Hall (Embassy), Penns Lane, B76 8LH, ☎ 351 3111, – Ⓟ. DT **v**
closed Christmas – **M** approx. 3.40 1.65 – 1.20 – **67 rm** 12.25/16.75.

at Sutton Coldfield **NE: 8 m. by A 38 – ✉ Sutton Coldfield – ☎ 021 Birmingham:**

Belfry, Lichfield Rd, Wishaw, B76 9PR, E: 3 m. on A 446 ☎ 0675 (Curdworth) 70301, <, 18, , park – Ⓟ. E: 3 m. on A 446 DT
M 2.00/9.00 **st.** 1.70 – **59 rm.**

Moor Hall (Interchange), Moor Hall Drive, B75 6LN, NE: 1 m. off A 453 ☎ 308 3751, – wc Ⓟ. DT **r**
closed 1 week after Christmas – **M** 3.95/4.30 **st.** 1.05 – **55 rm** 13.25/19.75 **st.** – P 19.10/20.10 **st.**

Stanbridge, 138 Birmingham Rd, B72 1LY, ☎ 354 3007, – Ⓟ DT **a**
closed 2 weeks Spring Bank Holidays and 2 weeks at Christmas – **9 rm** 6.25/10.35 **st.**

La Gondola, Mere Green Precinct, 304 Lichfield Rd, B74 2UW, N: 2 m. on A 5127 ☎ 308 6782, Italian rest. DT **o**
M a la carte 3.20/6.85.

at Sheldon **SE: 6 m. on A 45 – ✉ ☎ 021 Birmingham:**

Wheatsheaf (Ansells), 2225 Coventry Rd, B26 3EH, ☎ 743 2021 – wc Ⓟ p. 5 HX **a**
M *(closed Sunday dinner)* approx. 3.25 **st.** – **76 rm** 13.00/16.00 **st.**

at Birmingham Airport **SE: 7 m. on A 45 – DU – ✉ ☎ 021 Birmingham :**

Excelsior (T.H.F.), Coventry Rd, Elmdon, B26 3QW, ☎ 743 8141, Telex 338005 – Ⓟ.
M 3.85/4.25 **st.** 1.65 – 2.00 – **141 rm** 14.50/20.00 **st.**

at Kings Heath **S: 3 ½ m. on A 435 by A 41 – ✉ ☎ 021 Birmingham:**

Giovanni's, Poplar Rd off High St., B14 7AA, ☎ 443 2391 p. 4 FX **a**
closed Sunday dinner, Monday, 25-26 December and last 2 weeks February – **M** a la carte 4.20/6.70 **t.** 1.50.

at National Exhibition Centre **E: 9 ½ m. on A 45 – DU – ✉ ☎ 021 Birmingham:**

Metropole, Blackfirs Lane, Bickenhill, B40 1PP, ☎ 780 4242, Telex 336129, < – Ⓟ.
M a la carte 5.60/8.80 **t.** 2.50 – 2.75 – **498 rm** 28.00/32.00.

Warwick, Blackfirs Lane, Bickenhill, B40 1PP, ☎ 780 4242, Telex 336129 – wc Ⓟ
M approx. 6.60 **s.** 1.15 – 2.75 – **200 rm** 20.00.

Arden Motel, Coventry Rd, Bickenhill, B92 0EH, S: ½ m. on A 45 ✉ Solihull ☎ 067 55 (Hampton-in-Arden) 2912 – wc Ⓟ
M approx. 3.00 **st.** 0.95 – 1.50 – **24 rm** 10.00/13.00 **st.**

at Smethwick **W: 3 ½ m. off A 456 – ✉ Warley – ☎ 021 Birmingham:**

La Copper Kettle, 151 Milcote Rd, Bearwood, B56 5BN, ☎ 429 7920, French rest.
closed Sunday and Bank Holidays – **M** a la carte 3.70/5.60 **st.** 1.50. p. 4 EV **a**

at West Bromwich **NW: 6 m. on A 41 – ✉ West Bromwich – ☎ 021 Birmingham :**

Europa Lodge (County), B70 6RS, SE: 1 m. off A 41, ☎ 553 6111, Telex 336232 – wc Ⓟ. BU **c**
M approx. 3.75 **st.** 1.10 – **133 rm** 12.50/16.50 **st.**

Manor House (Ansells), Hall Green Rd, B71 2EA, N: 2 m. off A 41 ☎ 588 2035, « 13C timbered manor house » – Ⓟ. BT **a**

at Great Barr **NW: 6 m. on A 34 – ✉ Great Barr – ☎ 021 Birmingham:**

Post House (T.H.F.), Chapel Lane, B43 7BG, ☎ 357 7444, Telex 338497, heated, – wc Ⓟ. CT **x**
M 2.95/4.00 **st.** 1.50 – 2.00 – **204 rm** 13.00/18.00 **st.**

Barr, Pear Tree Drive, Newton Rd, B43 6HS, W: 1 m. off A 4041 ☎ 357 1141, – wc Ⓟ. CT **z**
M 3.50/3.75 **st.** 1.50 – **90 rm** 10.00/12.50 **st.** – P 15.00/17.00 **st.**

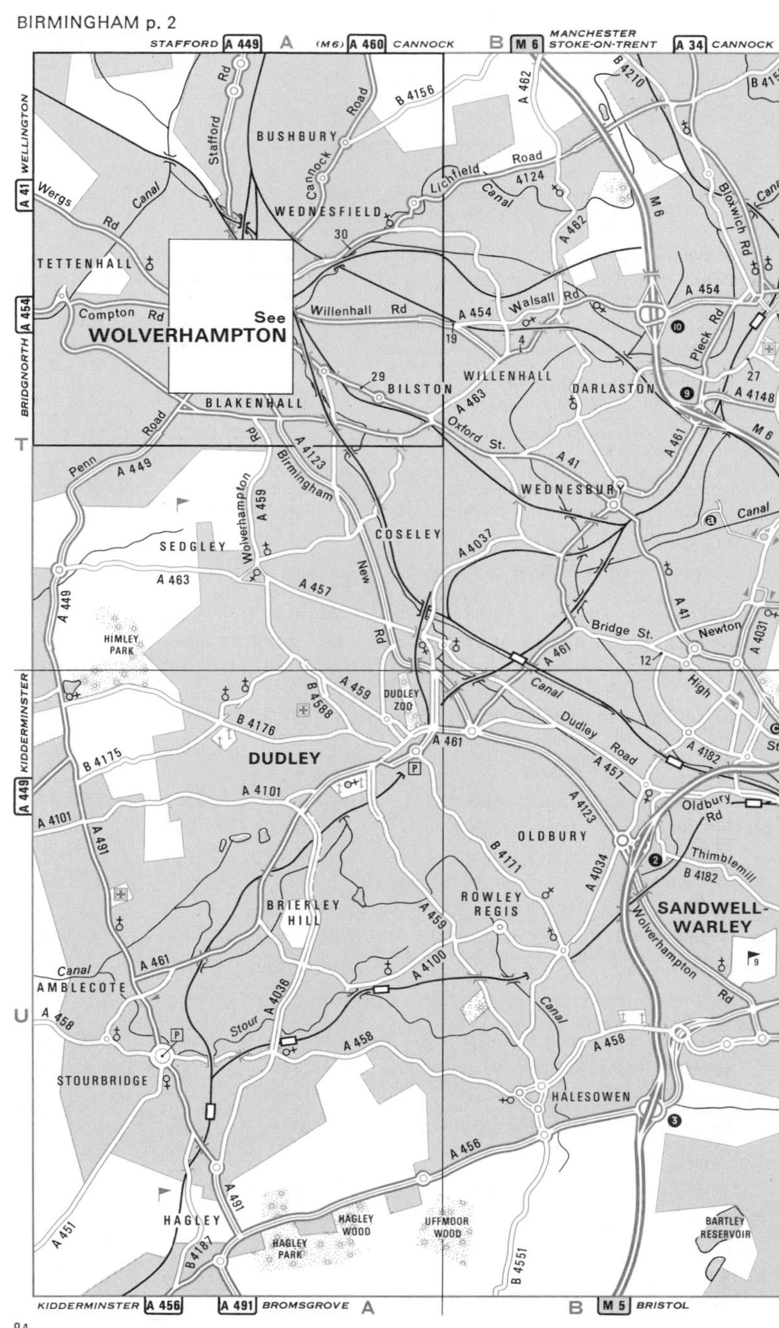
STAFFORD A 449
A
(M6) A 460 CANNOCK
B
M 6 MANCHESTER STOKE-ON-TRENT
A 34 CANNOCK
A 41 WELLINGTON
A 454 BRIDGNORTH
A 449 KIDDERMINSTER
T
U
KIDDERMINSTER A 456
A 491 BROMSGROVE
A
B
M 5 BRISTOL
BUSHBURY
WEDNESFIELD
TETTENHALL
See WOLVERHAMPTON
BLAKENHALL
BILSTON
WILLENHALL
DARLASTON
WEDNESBURY
COSELEY
SEDGLEY
HIMLEY PARK
DUDLEY ZOO
DUDLEY
OLDBURY
ROWLEY REGIS
BRIERLEY HILL
SANDWELL-WARLEY
AMBLECOTE
STOURBRIDGE
HALESOWEN
HAGLEY
HAGLEY WOOD
HAGLEY PARK
UFFMOOR WOOD
BARTLEY RESERVOIR
Stafford Rd
Cannock Road
B 4156
A 462
B 4210
Lichfield Road
Canal 4124
Wergs Rd
Canal
Compton Rd
Willenhall Rd
A 454
Walsall Rd
M 6
Bloxwich Rd
Pleck Rd
A 4148
A 463
Oxford St.
A 41
A 461
Penn Road
A 449
Wolverhampton Rd
A 459
Birmingham A 4123
A 4037
A 463
A 457
New Rd
Bridge St.
Newton
A 4031
High
Canal
Dudley Road
A 4182
St
B 4588
B 4176
B 4175
A 4101
A 491
Oldbury Rd
Thimblemill
B 4182
A 4123
A 4034
B 4171
A 459
A 4100
Canal
Wolverhampton Rd
A 461
A 458
Stour
A 4036
A 458
A 456
A 451
B 4187
A 491
B 4551
30
19
4
29
27
12

BIRMINGHAM AND WOLVERHAMPTON

ENLARGED AREA

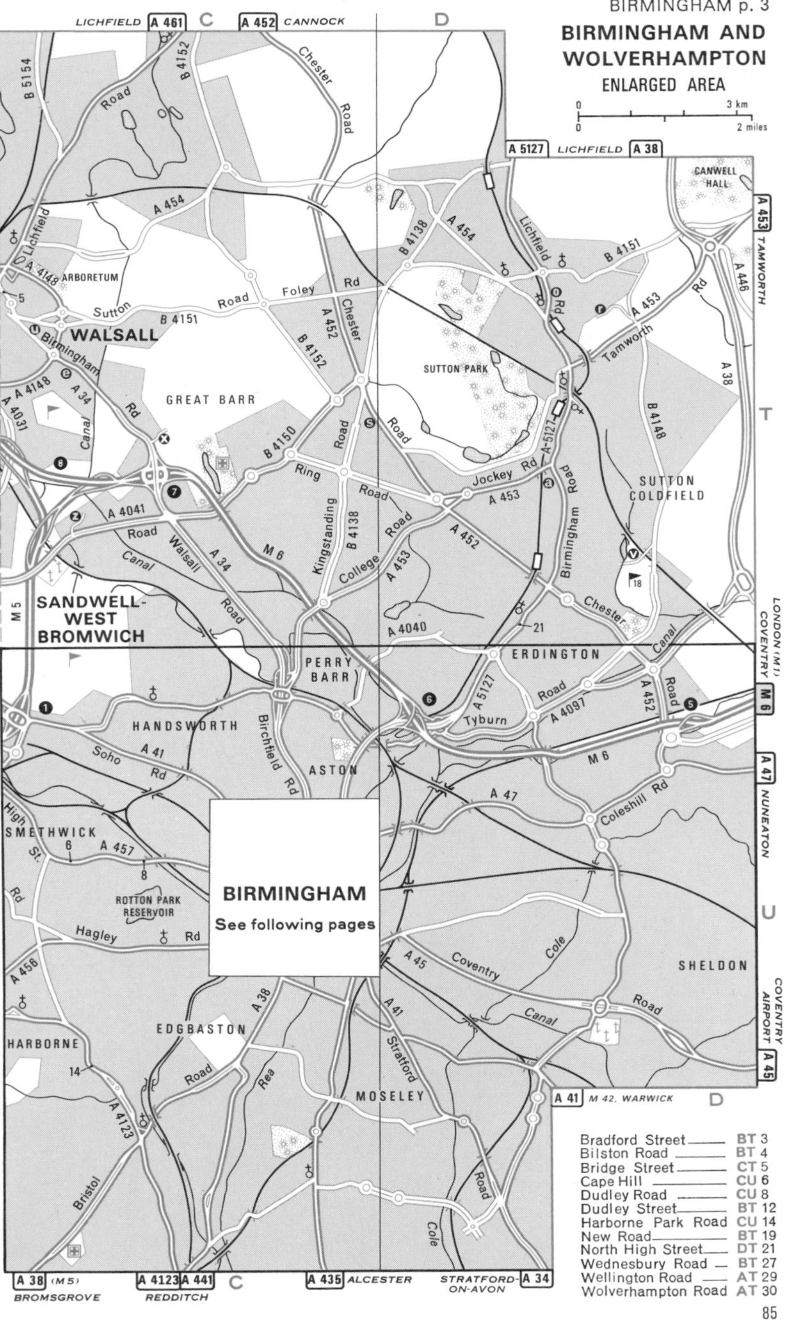

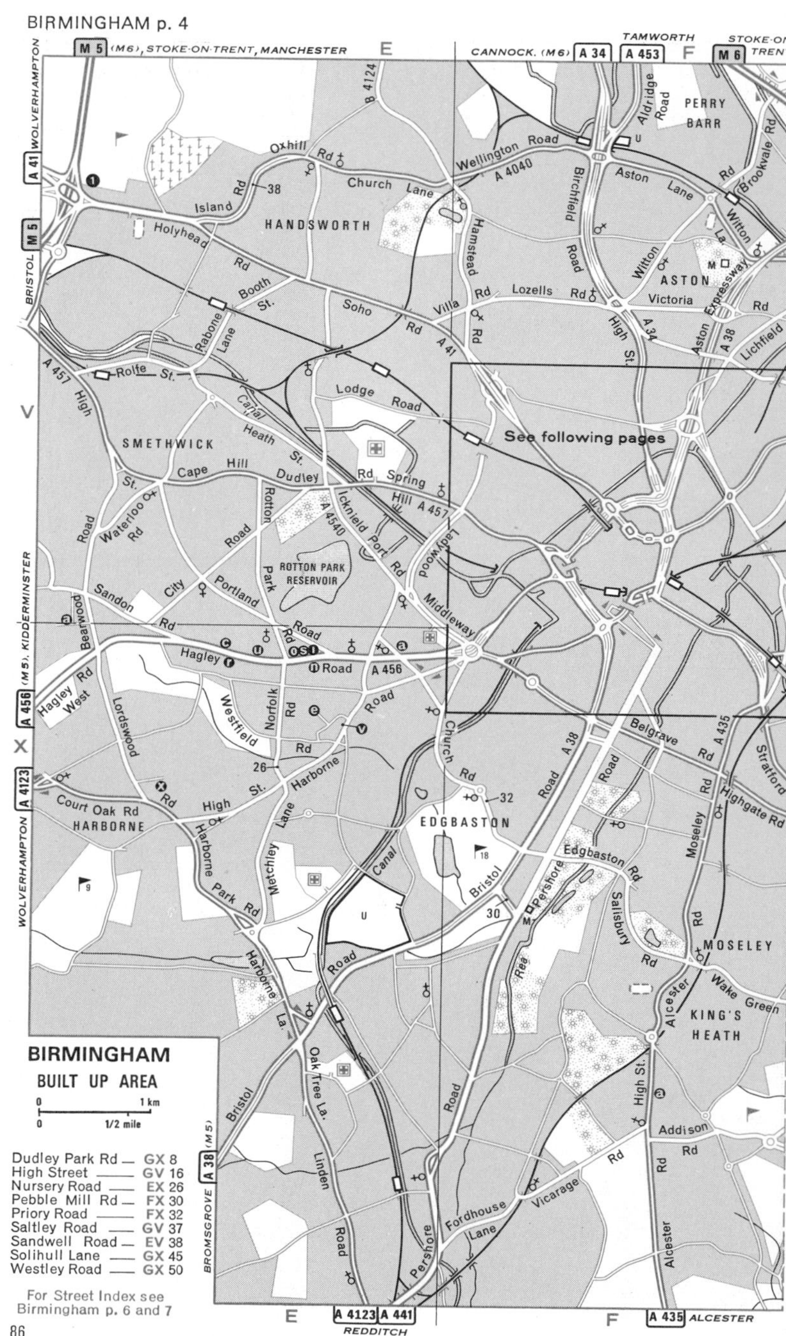

BIRMINGHAM
BUILT UP AREA

0 — 1 km
0 — 1/2 mile

Dudley Park Rd	GX	8
High Street	GV	16
Nursery Road	EX	26
Pebble Mill Rd	FX	30
Priory Road	FX	32
Saltley Road	GV	37
Sandwell Road	EV	38
Solihull Lane	GX	45
Westley Road	GX	50

For Street Index see Birmingham p. 6 and 7

A 38 LICHFIELD
CANNOCK A 452
A 4097 (A38-A446)
LONDON (M1) COVENTRY M 6
A 47 NUNEATON
A 45 COVENTRY AIRPORT
WARWICK M 42 A 41
A 34 STRATFORD-ON-AVON
ERDINGTON
GRAVELLY-HILL-JUNCTION
CASTLE BROMWICH
SALTLEY
YARDLEY
SHELDON

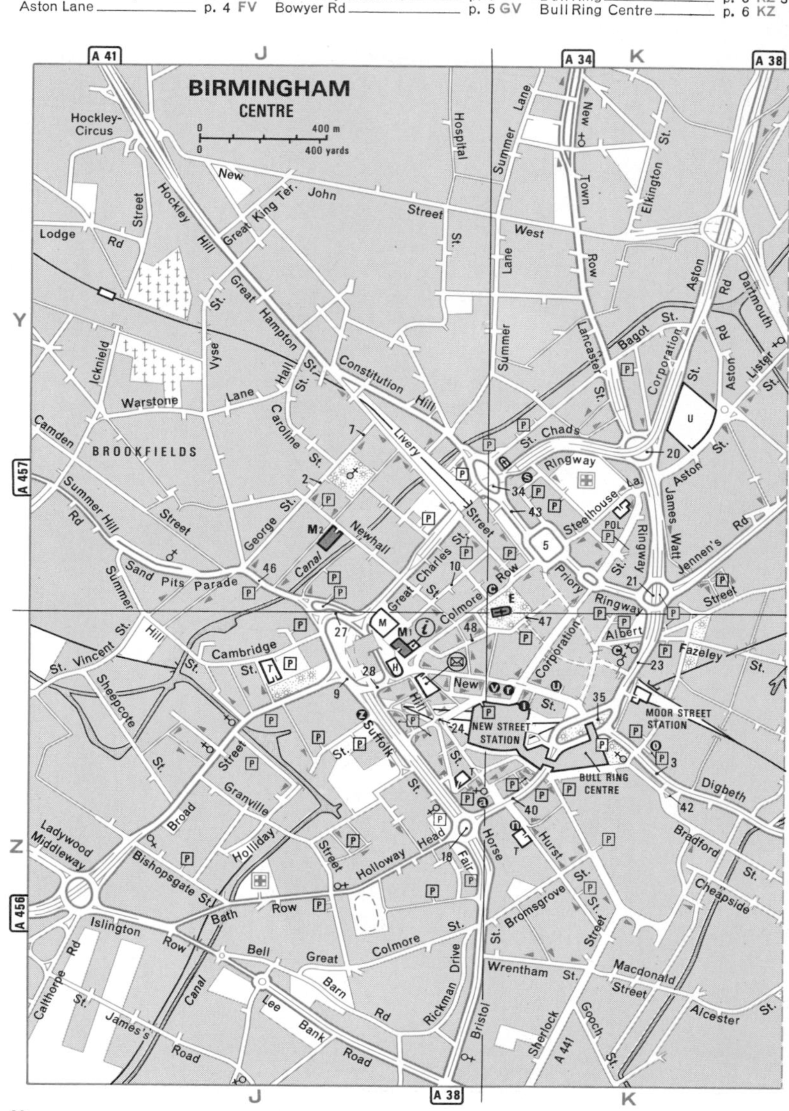
BIRMINGHAM
CENTRE
400 m
400 yards
A 41
J
A 34
K
A 38
Y
Z
A 457
A 456
Hockley-Circus
New John Street
Great King Ter.
Hospital St.
Summer Lane
New Town Row
Elkington St.
West
Lodge Rd
Street
Hockley Hill
Great Hampton St.
Vyse St.
Icknield
Warstone Lane
Hall St.
Constitution Hill
Lancaster St.
Bagot St.
Corporation St.
Aston Rd
Dartmouth
Lister St.
Camden
BROOKFIELDS
Caroline St.
Livery Street
St. Chads
Ringway
Aston St.
Summer Hill Rd
Street
George St.
Newhall
Great Charles St.
Steelhouse La.
POL
James Watt
Jennen's Rd
Sand Pits Parade
Summer Hill St.
Canal
Colmore Row
Priory
Ringway
Albert
Fazeley St.
St. Vincent St.
Cambridge St.
New St.
Corporation
MOOR STREET STATION
NEW STREET STATION
BULL RING CENTRE
Sheepcote St.
Suffolk St.
Hill St.
Digbeth
Broad Street
Granville
Ladywood Middleway
Holliday
Holloway Head
Horse Fair
Hurst St.
Bradford St.
Bishopsgate St.
Bath Row
Bromsgrove St.
Cheapside
Islington Row
Bell
Great Colmore St.
Calthorpe Rd
St. James's Road
Lee Bank Road
Barn Rd
Rickman Drive
Bristol St.
Wrentham St.
Macdonald Street
Alcester St.
Sherlock
A 441
Gooch St.
U
E
M
M1
M2
2
3
5
7
9
10
18
20
21
23
24
27
28
34
35
40
42
43
46
47
48

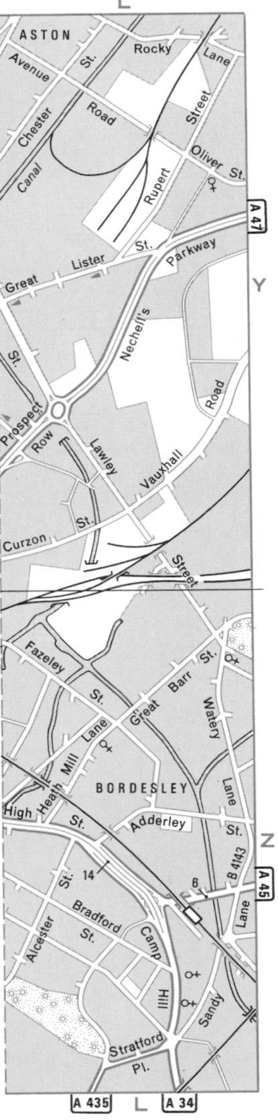
L
ASTON
Avenue
Rocky
Lane
St.
Road
Street
Chester
Canal
Oliver St.
Rupert
A 47
Great
Lister
St.
Parkway
Y
Nechell's
St.
Road
Prospect
Row
Lawley
Vauxhall
St.
Curzon
Street
Fazeley
St.
Barr
St.
Great
Watery
Lane
Mill
Heath
High
St.
BORDESLEY
Lane
St.
Adderley
Z
B 4143
A 45
14
6
St.
Bradford
St.
Camp
Lane
Alcester
St.
Hill
Sandy
Stratford
Pl.
A 435
L
A 34

ASTON-MARTIN, TRIUMPH 1-3 Woodthorpe Rd ☎ 444 2715
AUDI-NSU Barnes Hill ☎ 427 6201
AUSTIN-DAIMLER-MG-WOLSELEY 71 Aston Rd North ☎ 359 2011
AUSTIN-MG-WOLSELEY 1014/1018 Kingsbury Rd ☎ 747 2065
AUSTIN-MG-WOLSELEY 479 Bristol Rd ☎ 472 1331
AUSTIN-MORRIS-MG-WOLSELEY 415 Stratford Rd, Sparkhill ☎ 772 5897
AUSTIN-MORRIS-MG-WOLSELEY 361/365 Moseley Rd ☎ 440 1131
AUSTIN-MG-WOLSELEY Hagley Rd West, Quinton ☎ 422 7171
AUSTIN-MG-WOLSELEY 283 Broad St. ☎ 643 5111
AUSTIN-MG-WOLSELEY Alcester Rd, Moseley ☎ 449 6115
CHRYSLER-SIMCA 10 Church Lane ☎ 554 2182
CHRYSLER-SIMCA Newport Rd ☎ 747 4712
CHRYSLER-SIMCA Coventry Rd ☎ 772 4388
CHRYSLER-SIMCA 4 Birmingham Rd ☎ 357 4049
CHRYSLER-SIMCA 90/94 Charlotte St. ☎ 236 4382
CHRYSLER-SIMCA 103 Goosemoor Lane, Erdington ☎ 373 4360
CHRYSLER-SIMCA 15 Newton Rd ☎ 357 1131
DAF Bromford Lane ☎ 327 1030
DAF 9/11 Watford Rd ☎ 458 3408
DAF Hagley Rd, Hasbury ☎ 550 6416
DATSUN 504/508 College Rd ☎ 373 2542
DATSUN Newall St. ☎ 236 7548
DATSUN 120/126 Alcester Rd ☎ 449 4751
DATSUN, PEUGEOT 110/124 Victoria Rd ☎ 327 3591
DATSUN, VAUXHALL Summer Lane ☎ 359 4848
FIAT Roebuck Lane, West Bromwich ☎ 553 1116
FIAT 979 Stratford Rd, Hall Green ☎ 777 6181
FIAT 71 Sutton New Rd, Erdington ☎ 350 1301

FORD 156/182 Bristol St. ☎ 622 2777
FORD Long Acre ☎ 327 4791
FORD Wolverhampton Rd, Warley ☎ 429 7111
FORD Kingsbury Rd ☎ 373 8121
FORD 264 Oxhill Rd ☎ 554 3539
JAGUAR-ROVER-TRIUMPH 1507 Coventry Rd ☎ 706 5441
JAGUAR-MORRIS-MG-PRINCESS-ROVER-TRIUMPH, ROLLS ROYCE Manor Lane, Halesowen ☎ 550 7611
JENSEN, SAAB, TOYOTA Hamstead Rd ☎ 554 6311
MERCEDES-BENZ, PEUGEOT 240 Broad St. ☎ 643 9045
MORRIS-MG-WOLSELEY 40 Cherrywood Rd ☎ 772 3394
MORRIS-MG-WOLSELEY Warwick Rd, Tyseley ☎ 706 4331
MORRIS-MG-WOLSELEY 193/194 Broad St. ☎ 643 4971
MORRIS-MG-WOLSELEY Aston Hall Rd ☎ 328 0833
MORRIS-MG-WOLSELEY 884 Warwick Rd ☎ 706 8271
PEUGEOT 2119 Coventry Rd, Sheldon ☎ 742 5533
PEUGEOT Fordhouse Lane, Stircflley ☎ 459 1611
RENAULT Chester Rd North ☎ 5196
RENAULT Old Walsall Rd, Great Barr ☎ 357 5411
SAAB 138 Soho Hill, Handsworth ☎ 554 6311
TOYOTA 490 College Rd ☎ 350 4212
VAUXHALL 18 Stewart St. ☎ 454 4351
VAUXHALL 16 Ryland St. Fiveways ☎ 454 8111
VAUXHALL, OPEL 870 Stratford Rd ☎ 777 3361
VAUXHALL 364 Chester Rd, Castle Bromwich ☎ 747 4601
VAUXHALL Newton Rd ☎ 357 2912
VAUXHALL Charles Henry St. ☎ 622 3031
VAUXHALL 203/217 Lozells Rd ☎ 523 9231
VAUXHALL 291 Shaftmoor Lane ☎ 777 1074
VOLVO Bristol St. ☎ 622 4491
VW, AUDI-NSU Digbeth ☎ 643 7341

BIRTLE Greater Manchester – pop. 1,989 (inc. Ashworth) – ✉ Bury – ☎ 061 Manchester.
London 217 – Bolton 10 – **Manchester 11.**

XX **La Normandie** with rm, Elbut Lane, BL9 6UT, N : 1 m. off B 6222, ☎ 764 3869, French rest. – TV wc wc ☎ P
closed first 3 weeks July and Christmas Day – **M** *(closed Sunday)* (dinner only) a la carte 4.40/6.45 **s.** 1.30 – **17 rm** 10.75/15.25 **s.**

BISHAM Bucks. – see Marlow.

BISHOP'S CLEEVE Glos. – see Cheltenham.

BISHOP'S HULL Somerset – see Taunton.

BISHOP'S LYDEARD Somerset – see Taunton.

BISHOP'S STORTFORD Herts. 986 ㉜ – pop. 22,121 – ☎ 0279.
✈ Stansted Airport : ☎ 502380, NE : 3 ½ m.
London 34 – Cambridge 27 – Chelmsford 19 – Colchester 33.

Foxley, Foxley Drive, Stansted Rd, CM23 2DS, N : ¾ m. on A 11 ☎ 53977, – wc P
M a la carte 3.00/6.75 **t.** 1.50 – **12 rm** 10.50/15.50 **st.**

Dane House, Hadham Rd, CM23 2QD, W : ¾ m. on A 120 ☎ 52289, – wc P
closed 1 to 9 January – **M** approx. 3.50 **t.** 0.90 – **12 rm** 8.00/15.00 **st.**

Brook House, 29 Northgate End, CM23 2LD, ☎ 57892, – P
M 2.50/4.00 **s.** 1.60 – **17 rm** 6.75/10.00 **st.**

AUSTIN-DAIMLER-JAGUAR-MG-ROVER-TRIUMPH 123 South St. ☎ 52266
CHRYSLER-SIMCA Dunmow Rd ☎ 54335
DATSUN London Rd ☎ 54181
FIAT London Rd, Spelbrook ☎ 55424
FORD London Rd ☎ 52214

MORRIS-MG-WOLSELEY, PEUGEOT 26 Northgate End ☎ 53494
RENAULT Northgate End ☎ 53127
VAUXHALL The Causeway ☎ 52304
VW, AUDI-NSU Dane St. ☎ 54680

BISHOP'S TAWTON Devon – see Barnstaple.

BISHOPTHORPE North Yorks. – see York.

BLACKBURN Lancs. 986 ㉓ – pop. 101,816 – ☎ 0254.

Beardwood Brow, ☎ 51122 – *i* Town Hall, Library St. ☎ 53277.

London 228 – Leeds 47 – Liverpool 39 – Manchester 24 – Preston 11.

Saxon Inn Motor, Preston New Rd, Yew Tree Drive, BB2 7BE, NW: 2 m. at junction A 677 and A 6119 ☎ 64441, Telex 63271 – TV P.
M 2.55/3.00 **s.** 1.80 – 1.55 – **98 rm** 10.00/13.00 **s.**

AUSTIN-DAIMLER-JAGUAR-MG-ROVER-TRIUMPH Park Rd ☎ 662721
CHRYSLER-SIMCA King St. ☎ 52981
DATSUN Lower Darwen ☎ 53894
FIAT, RENAULT 52/56 King St. ☎ 667 782
FORD Montague St. ☎ 57021
MERCEDES-BENZ Harwood Rd, Rishton, Great Harwood ☎ 884202
MORRIS-MG-WOLSELEY Simmons St. ☎ 52121
MORRIS-MG-WOLSELEY Accrington Rd ☎ 57333
PEUGEOT Roe Lee Garage, Whalley New Rd ☎ 52781
RENAULT Gt. Harwood ☎ 886590
VAUXHALL Quarry St., Eanam ☎ 51191
VW, AUDI-NSU 854 Whalley New Rd ☎ 48091

BLACKPOOL Lancs. 986 ㉓ – pop. 151,860 – ☎ 0253.

See : Illuminations (late September and early October) – Tower* (*) *AC* AY A.**

Devonshire Rd ☎ 51017, N: 1 ½ m. from main station BY – Stanley Park ☎ 33960, E: 1 ½ m. BY.

Blackpool Airport : ☎ 43061, S: 2 ½ m. BZ.

i Central Promenade ☎ 21623.

London 241 – Leeds 84 – Liverpool 57 – Manchester 50 – Middlesbrough 121.

Plan on next page

Imperial, North Promenade, FY1 2HB, ☎ 23971, <, – TV P. – **152 rm.** AY c

Savoy, Queens Promenade, FY2 9SJ, ☎ 52561 – wc wc P. AY a
M 3.20/5.00 **st.** – **141 rm** 8.50/16.00 **st.**

Clifton, Talbot Sq., FY1 1ND, ☎ 21481 – wc . AY i
M approx. 3.70 0.90 – **85 rm** 10.70/21.25 – P 16.00/16.25.

Gables, Balmoral Rd, FY4 1HP, ☎ 45432 – TV wc AZ r
M (buffet lunch) a la carte 2.00/4.00 **s.** – **72 rm** 6.50/12.00 **s.**

Warwick, 603-609 New South Promenade, FY4 1NG, ☎ 42192, – wc P. BZ u
closed 1 to 20 November – **M** (dinner only) 2.75/3.50 **st.** – **77 rm** 7.00/15.00 **st.**

Queens, South Promenade, FY4 1AY, ☎ 42015, – wc P AZ c
M 2.25/2.60 **st.** 2.00 – **80 rm** 6.50/13.00 **st.** – P 9.40/10.25 **st.**

Stuart, Clifton Drive, South Shore, FY4 1NT, ☎ 45485 – P AZ a
M *(from November to April: closed to non-residents Thursday, Saturday, Sunday dinner; from May to October: closed to non-residents except Sunday lunch)* (dinner only and Sunday lunch) 2.50/3.75 **s.** 1.15 – **26 rm** 4.50/9.50.

Mimosa, 24a Lonsdale Rd, FY1 6EE, ☎ 41906 – TV wc P BZ c
15 rm 8.00/10.50.

Sunray, 42 Knowle Av., off Queen's Prom., FY2 9TQ, ☎ 51937 – P BY c
May-October – **7 rm** 4.45/9.75 **s.**

Deneley, 15 King Edward Av., FY2 9TA, ☎ 52757 – P AY e
7 rm 4.35/8.65 **t.**

Manxonia, 248 Queens Prom., Bispham, FY2 9HA, ☎ 51118 – P BY a
mid May - November – **20 rm** 3.95/7.40 **s.**

Trattoria da Vinci, 27-29 King St., FY1 3EJ, ☎ 21602, Italian rest. AY r
closed Sunday – **M** (dinner only) a la carte 3.50/5.90 **t.** 1.35.

ALFA-ROMEO Alfred St. ☎ 28401
AUSTIN-MG-WOLSELEY Cherry Tree Rd ☎ 67811
CHRYSLER-SIMCA Squires Gate Lane ☎ 45544
CITROEN 145/147 Dickson Rd ☎ 21469
DAF, SAAB 181 Waterloo Rd ☎ 41081
DAIMLER-JAGUAR-ROVER-TRIUMPH 159 Devonshire Rd ☎ 34301
DATSUN 234 Talbot Rd ☎ 26688
FORD Whitegate Drive ☎ 63333
MERCEDES-BENZ Buchanan St. ☎ 22257
MORRIS-MG-WOLSELEY 307 Whitegate Drive, Marton ☎ 63873
PEUGEOT 79/83 Breck Rd, Poulton-le-Fylde ☎ 882571
TOYOTA Devonshire Rd, Bispham ☎ 51870
VW, AUDI-NSU Rigby Rd ☎ 21417

BLACKWATER Hants. – pop. 6,231 (inc. Hawley) – ✉ Camberley (Surrey) – ☎ 0252 Yateley.

London 42 – Basingstoke 17 – Camberley 4 – Reading 15.

Ely, Hertford Bridge Flats,, GU17 9LS, W: 2 m. on A 30 ☎ 873163 – P
M a la carte 4.05/6.45 **t.** 1.75.

BLACKWOOD Gwent – pop. 6,488 – ☎ 0495.

Maesycwmmer, Hengoed ☎ 225590.

London 158 – Cardiff 15 – Newport 13.

Maes Manor , Maes Rudded, N: 1 ¼ m. off A 4048 by Rocks Inn, NP2 0AG, ☎ 224551, , park – TV wc P
M a la carte 3.95/5.50 **s.** 1.20 – 1.45 – **26 rm** 10.00/18.00 **st.**

AUSTIN-DAIMLER-JAGUAR-MORRIS-MG 5/6 Pentwyn Rd ☎ 223388

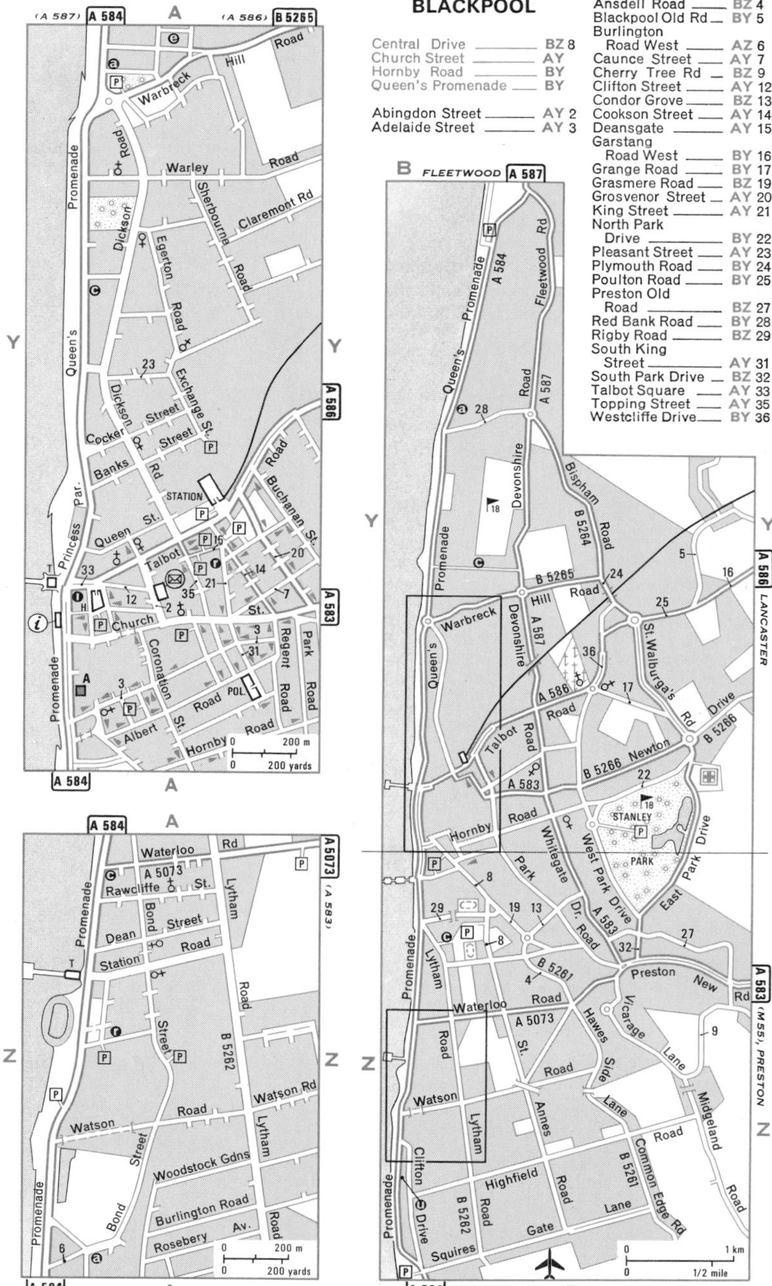
BLACKPOOL
Central Drive BZ 8
Church Street AY
Hornby Road BY
Queen's Promenade BY
Abingdon Street AY 2
Adelaide Street AY 3
Ansdell Road BZ 4
Blackpool Old Rd BY 5
Burlington Road West AZ 6
Caunce Street AY 7
Cherry Tree Rd BZ 9
Clifton Street AY 12
Condor Grove BZ 13
Cookson Street AY 14
Deansgate AY 15
Garstang Road West BY 16
Grange Road BY 17
Grasmere Road BZ 19
Grosvenor Street AY 20
King Street AY 21
North Park Drive BY 22
Pleasant Street AY 23
Plymouth Road BY 24
Poulton Road BY 25
Preston Old Road BZ 27
Red Bank Road BY 28
Rigby Road BZ 29
South King Street AY 31
South Park Drive BZ 32
Talbot Square AY 33
Topping Street AY 35
Westcliffe Drive BY 36
FLEETWOOD A 587
LANCASTER
(M 55), PRESTON
ST-ANNES
STANLEY PARK

BLAGDON Avon – pop. 1,238 – ✉ Bristol – ☎ 0761.
London 138 – Bath 19 – **Bristol 17** – Taunton 39.

- **Mendip** ⛰, Street End, BS18 6TS, ☏ 62688, ← – TV Ⓟ.
  M 4.90/7.90 – **37 rm** 11.00/16.00.

BLAKENEY Norfolk 986 ㉘ – pop. 677 – ✉ Holt – ☎ 026 374 Cley.
London 127 – King's Lynn 37 – **Norwich 28.**

- **Blakeney,** The Quay, NR25 7NE, ☏ 797, ▣, – wc ☎ Ⓟ
  M 2.50/3.25 1.20 – **53 rm** 6.20/27.00 **st.**
- **Manor,** The Quay, NR25 7ND, ☏ 376, – wc Ⓟ
  closed 2 weeks mid November – **M** (Monday to Saturday buffet lunch only) approx. 3.50 1.30 – **22 rm** 7.50/9.50 – P 12.20/14.20.

BLANCHLAND Northumb. – pop. 167 – ✉ Consett (Durham) – ☎ 043 475.
London 293 – **Middlesbrough 49** – **Newcastle-upon-Tyne 25.**

- Lord Crewe Arms (Swallow), DH8 9SP, ☏ 251, « 12C inn », – wc ☎ – **14 rm.**

BLENHEIM Oxon. 986 ㉛ – pop. 114.
See : Blenheim Palace*** 18C (park and gardens ***) *AC*.
London 65 – **Oxford 8** – Stratford-on-Avon 30.

Hotels and restaurants see : ***Oxford*** SE : 8 m.
Woodstock NE : 1 m.

BLETCHINGLEY Surrey – pop. 3,107 – ✉ Redhill – ☎ 088 384 Godstone.
London 25 – **Brighton 34.**

- XX **Ye Olde Whyte Harte** with rm, High St., RH14 4PB, ☏ 3231, – wc Ⓟ
  M a la carte 4.20/6.65 1.20 – **9 rm** 10.00/15.00.

BLETSOE Beds. – see Bedford.

BLOCKLEY Glos. – pop. 1,853 – ✉ Moreton-in-Marsh – ☎ 038 676.
London 89 – **Birmingham 40** – Gloucester 29 – **Oxford 33.**

- XX **Lower Brook House** ⛰ with rm, Lower St., GL56 9DS, ☏ 286, – wc Ⓟ
  closed 25 December-26 January – **M** *(closed Sunday dinner and Monday lunch)* 3.50/6.50 **t.** 1.50 – **6 rm** 8.25/18.50 **t.**

BLOFIELD Norfolk – see Norwich.

BLUNDELLSANDS Merseyside – see Liverpool.

BLUNSDON Wilts. – see Swindon.

BLYTH Notts. – pop. 1,131 – ✉ Worksop – ☎ 090 976.
London 154 – **Leeds 41** – Lincoln 29 – **Nottingham 31** – **Sheffield 21.**

- **Fourways,** High St., S81 8EW, ☏ 235 – Ⓟ
  M 2.70/4.50 1.50 – **9 rm** 8.00/12.00.

BODIAM East Sussex – see Robertsbridge.

BODMIN Cornwall 986 ㊳ – pop. 9,207 – ☎ 0208.
London 273 – Exeter 63 – Penzance 47 – **Plymouth 30.**

- **Westberry,** Rhind St., PL31 2EL, ☏ 2772 – wc ☎ Ⓟ
  M (bar lunch) 3.50/5.00 **s.** 1.35 – **24 rm** 6.50/14.00 **s.**

BOGNOR REGIS West Sussex 986 ㊱ ㊵ – pop. 34,452 – ☎ 024 33.
i Belmont St. ☏ 23140.
London 65 – **Brighton 31** – **Portsmouth 25** – **Southampton 37.**

- Royal, The Esplanade, PO21 1SZ, ☏ 4665, ← – ☎
  40 rm.
- **Clarehaven,** Wessex Av., PO21 2QW, ☏ 23265 – wc Ⓟ
  April-October – **M** *(open all year except Sunday dinner)* 3.00/4.25 **st.** 1.10 – **35 rm** 7.15/19.20 **st.** – P 11.90/14.85 **st.**
- XX **Blackbird's,** 11 Bedford St., PO21 1SB, ☏ 3835
  closed Sunday and Monday – **M** a la carte 3.70/6.70 **t.** 1.40.

AUSTIN-MG-ROVER-TRIUMPH 65 Aldwick Rd ☏ 4041
MORRIS-MG-WOLSELEY Lennox St. ☏ 4641
PEUGEOT 131 Elmer Rd, Middleton-on-Sea ☏ 024 369 (Middledon-on-Sea) 2432
VAUXHALL High St. ☏ 5515
VW, AUDI-NSU 126 Felpham Way ☏ 024 369 (Middleton-on-Sea) 3185

BOLHAM Devon – see Tiverton.

BOLNEY West Sussex – pop. **1,120** – ✆ **044 482.**
London 41 – **Brighton 13** – Haywards Heath 6.

XX **Bolney Stage,** London Rd, RH17 5RL, on A 23 ✆ 312 – Ⓟ
M 5.25/7.10 **t.** 🍷 2.10.

BOLTON Greater Manchester **986** ⑤ and ㉓ – pop. **154,199** – ✆ 0204.
Envir. : Hall I'Th'Wood* (16C) AC, N : 1 ½ m.
18 ✆ 42336 – 18 Off Junction Rd, Deane ✆ 61944, W : 4 m. – 18 Longworth Lane, Bromley Cross ✆ 53321, N : 3 m. – 9 Longsight Park, Harwood Bolton N : 2 m.
i Town Hall, ✆ 22311 ext 211/485.
London 214 – Burnley 19 – **Liverpool 32** – **Manchester 11** – Preston 23.

Bolton Crest (Crest), Beaumont Rd, BL3 4TA, W : 2 ½ m. on A 58 ✆ 651511 – TV wc ☎ Ⓟ.
M 3.15/4.40 **s.** 🍷 1.55 – ☕ 1.60 – **100 rm** 10.95/15.50 **s.**

Pack Horse, 1 Nelson Sq., BL1 1DP, ✆ 27261 – lift TV wc ☎.
M approx. 3.40 **st.** – **87 rm** ☕ 8.60/13.70 **st.**

at Bromley Cross N : 4 m. by A 676 – ✉ ✆ 0204 Bolton :

Last Drop Village, Hospital Rd, BL7 9PZ, ✆ 591131, Telex 635322, « Converted farm », – TV wc ☎ Ⓟ.
M a la carte 4.65/6.70 **s.** – **46 rm** ☕ 15.50/22.50 **s.**

AUDI-NSU, PEUGEOT Blackburn Rd ✆ 31464
AUSTIN-DAIMLER-JAGUAR-MORRIS-MG-ROVER-TRIUMPH Blackburn Rd ✆ 387011
AUSTIN-MORRIS-MG-ROVER-TRIUMPH-WOLSELEY Manchester Rd ✆ 32241
AUSTIN-MORRIS-MG-ROVER-TRIUMPH-WOLSELEY Manchester Rd ✆ 22577
CHRYSLER-SIMCA, LANCIA Bradshawgate ✆ 31323
DAF Thynne St. ✆ 25090
DATSUN, PEUGEOT Moor Lane ✆ 33941
FORD 54/56 Higher Bridge St. ✆ 24474
FORD, OPEL Manchester Rd ✆ 26566
RENAULT 154-160 Crook St. ✆ 24686
TOYOTA Radcliffe Rd ✆ 382234
VW, AUDI-NSU St. Helens Rd ✆ 62131

BOLTON ABBEY North Yorks. **986** ㉓ – pop. **136** – ✉ **Skipton** – ✆ **075 671.**
See : Bolton Priory* (ruins) and woods (the Strid* and nature trails in upper Wharfedale.
London 215 – Harrogate 17 – **Leeds 22** – Skipton 6.

Devonshire Arms, Bolton Bridge, BD23 6AJ, ✆ 265, ≤, – ☎ Ⓟ
M approx. 6.70 **st.** 🍷 2.25 – ☕ 2.50 – **10 rm** 9.70/21.00 **st.**

BONCHURCH I.O.W. – see Wight (Isle of).

BONTDDU Gwynedd – see Dolgellau.

BOREHAM STREET East Sussex – see Herstmonceux.

BOREHAMWOOD Herts. **986** ④ – pop. **1,858** – ✆ **01 London.**
London 15 – Luton 21.

Thatched Barn (Thistle), Barnet by-Pass, WD6 5PE, W : 1 ½ m. at junction A 1 and A 5135 ✆ 953 1622, heated – TV wc ☎ Ⓟ. – **60 rm.**

XX **Grosvenor** with rm, 148 Shenley Rd, WD6 1EQ, ✆ 953 3175 – Ⓟ
M a la carte 2.55/6.25 **t.** 🍷 1.30 – **18 rm** ☕ 8.00/14.00 **t.**

XX Signor Baffi, 195 Shenley Rd, WD6 1AW, ✆ 953 8404, Italian rest.

BOROUGHBRIDGE North Yorks. – **986** ㉓ – pop. **1,864** – ✆ **090 12.**
London 216 – **Leeds 26** – **Middlesbrough 35** – York 17.

Three Arrows (Embassy), Horsefair, YO5 9LL, ✆ 2245, park – wc Ⓟ
closed Christmas – **M** approx. 3.20 🍷 1.50 – **19 rm** ☕ 7.15/13.50 **st.**

AUSTIN-MORRIS-MG-WOLSELEY ✆ 2327

BORROWDALE Cumbria – see Keswick.

BOSTON Lincs. **986** ㉘ – pop. **26,025** – ✆ **0205.**
See : St. Botolph's Church** 14C.
9 Horncastle Rd ✆ 62306, N : 2 m. on A 16.
London 122 – Lincoln 35 – **Nottingham 55.**

New England (Anchor), Wide Bargate, PE21 6SH, ✆ 65255, Group Telex 27120 – TV wc ☎ Ⓟ
M approx. 2.75 **t.** 🍷 1.00 – **11 rm** ☕ 8.80/16.50 **st.**

ALFA-ROMEO, JENSEN, PEUGEOT, MERCEDES-BENZ 6 Horncastle Rd ✆ 64708
AUSTIN-DAIMLER-MORRIS-MG-ROVER-TRIUMPH-WOLSELEY Wide Bargate ✆ 66677
CHRYSLER-SIMCA Main Ridge ✆ 63867
CITROEN London Rd ✆ 722233
FORD 57 High St. ✆ 63991
JAGUAR-MORRIS-MG-ROVER-TRIUMPH-WOLSELEY Leverton ✆ 226
MORRIS-MG-WOLSELEY Sutterton ✆ 249
RENAULT Steaford Rd ✆ 61901
TOYOTA Tawney St. ✆ 68626
VAUXHALL Bargate End ✆ 63851
VW, AUDI-NSU 200/2 London Rd ✆ 63293

BOTLEY Hants. 986 ㉟ – pop. 2,163 – ✉ Hedge End, Southampton – ☎ 048 92.
London 83 – Portsmouth 17 – Southampton 6 – Winchester 11.

Botleigh Grange, SO3 2GA, W: 1 m. on B 3035 by A 334 ☎ 2212, ≤, park – wc ☎ ⓟ – **32 rm.**

AUSTIN-DAIMLER-JAGUAR-MG-ROVER-TRIUMPH Southampton Rd ☎ 5111
SAAB Shamblehurst Lane ☎ 3434

BOURNE Lincs. 986 ㉘ – pop. 6,465 – ☎ 077 82.
London 101 – Leicester 42 – Lincoln 35 – Nottingham 42.

Angel, North St., PE10 9AE, ☎ 2346 – ⓟ
M 3.50/5.00 **t.** – **10 rm** 7.00/11.00 **st.**

Golden Dragon, 11 South St., PE10 9LY, ☎ 3466, Chinese rest.

AUSTIN-MORRIS ☎ 2852
CHRYSLER-SIMCA Abbey Rd ☎ 2675
MORRIS-MG-WOLSELEY North St. ☎ 2129

BOURNE END Bucks. – ☎ 062 85.
London 31 – Maidenhead 4 – Oxford 31 – Reading 16.

Piccolo Mondo, The Parade, SL8 5SS, ☎ 22100, Italian rest.
M a la carte 4.00/6.05 **t.** 1.10.

BOURNEMOUTH Dorset 986 ㊴ – pop. 153,869 – ☎ 0202.
See: Central Gardens (Upper and Lower)* CDZ.
Meyrick Park ☎ 20871 CZ – Queen's Park ☎ 36198, NE: 2 m. CX – Francis Av., ☎ 020 16 (Northbourne) 2633, N: 4 m. off A 348 AX.
Hurn Airport: ☎ 020 15 (Christchurch) 6311, N: 5 m. by Hurn Rd DX.
Tourism Department, Westover Rd ☎ 291715.
London 113 – Bristol 78 – Southampton 31.

Plans on following pages

Carlton, Meyrick Rd, East Cliff, BH1 3DN, ☎ 22011, Telex 41244, ≤, heated, – ⓟ. EZ a
M approx. 6.00 **st.** 1.60 (see also **La Causerie**) – **110 rm** 16.50/33.00 **st.** – P 25.00/32.00 **st.**

Royal Bath (De Vere), Bath Rd, BH1 2EW, ☎ 25555, Telex 41375, ≤, heated, – ⓟ. DZ a
M approx. 6.75 **st.** 1.45 (see also The Buttery) – **125 rm** 15.75/31.50 **st.**

Palace Court, Westover Rd, BH1 3BZ, ☎ 27681 – ⓟ. DZ c
M approx. 5.75 **s.** 1.50 – **107 rm** 15.00/20.00 – P 18.50/22.00.

Savoy (Myddleton), West Hill Rd, West Cliff, BH2 5EJ, ☎ 20347, ≤, heated, – ⓟ. CZ x
M 5.25/5.50 1.30 – **93 rm** 11.00/28.75 – P 18.50/21.00.

Highcliff (Interchange), St. Michael's Rd, West Cliff, BH2 5DU, ☎ 27702, Telex 417153, ≤, heated, – ⓟ. CZ z
M approx. 4.50 **st.** 1.50 – **98 rm** 12.50/28.00 **st.** – P 17.00/20.50 **st.**

Round House, The Lansdowne, BH1 2PR, ☎ 23262, Telex 41232 – ⓟ. DZ r
M approx. 3.50 **s.** 1.25 – **102 rm** 11.00/22.00 **s.** – P 18.40/22.15 **st.**

Marsham Court (De Vere), Russell Cotes Rd, East Cliff, BH1 3AB, ☎ 22111, heated – ⓟ. DZ e
M approx. 5.00 **st.** 1.45 – **88 rm** 11.20/29.50 **st.**

East Cliff Court, East Overcliff Drive, BH1 3AN, ☎ 24545, ≤, heated – ⓟ. EZ u
M 5.00/5.20 **st.** 1.60 – **69 rm.**

Adelphi, 30 Manor Rd, East Cliff, BH1 3JD, ☎ 26546, – wc ☎ ⓟ CY e
M approx. 3.25 **st.** 1.50 – **60 rm** 8.00/24.00 **st.** – P 12.00/16.00 **st.**

Cliff End, Manor Rd, East Cliff, BH1 3EX, ☎ 39711, Telex 41141, heated, – wc ☎ ⓟ CY v
M approx. 3.50 **st.** 1.35 – **40 rm** 7.00/16.00 **s.** – P 12.00/15.00 **s.**

Hazelwood, 43 Christchurch Rd, BH1 3NZ, ☎ 21367, Telex 41447, – wc ☎ ⓟ CY o
M 3.00/3.95 1.20 – **58 rm** 7.00/16.00 – P 12.50/14.00.

Norfolk, Richmond Hill, BH2 6EN, ☎ 21521, – wc ☎ ⓟ CZ c
M approx. 3.75 **st.** 0.90 – **64 rm** 10.80/23.85 **st.** – P 12.50/13.60 **st.**

Pavilion (Interchange), Bath Rd, BH1 2NS, ☎ 291266, – wc ☎ ⓟ DZ n
M 4.00/4.75 **st.** – **46 rm** 10.95/23.90 **st.** – P 13.95/15.95 **st.**

Heathlands, Grove Rd, East Cliff, BH1 3AY, ☎ 23336, heated – wc ☎ ⓟ. EZ c
M 3.00/3.50 **st.** 1.40 – **120 rm** 9.00/26.50 **st.**

Anglo-Swiss, 16 Gervis Rd, East Cliff, BH1 3EQ, ☎ 24794, heated, – wc ☎ ⓟ EZ e
M approx. 3.50 **st.** 1.40 – **71 rm** 6.50/16.00 **st.** – P 9.00/12.00 **st.**

Miramar, 19 Grove Rd, East Overcliff, BH1 3AL, ☎ 26581, ≤, – wc ☎ ⓟ DZ u
M 3.50/3.75 **s.** 1.50 – **42 rm** 10.50/24.00 **s.** – P 13.00/16.00 **s.**

P.T.O. →

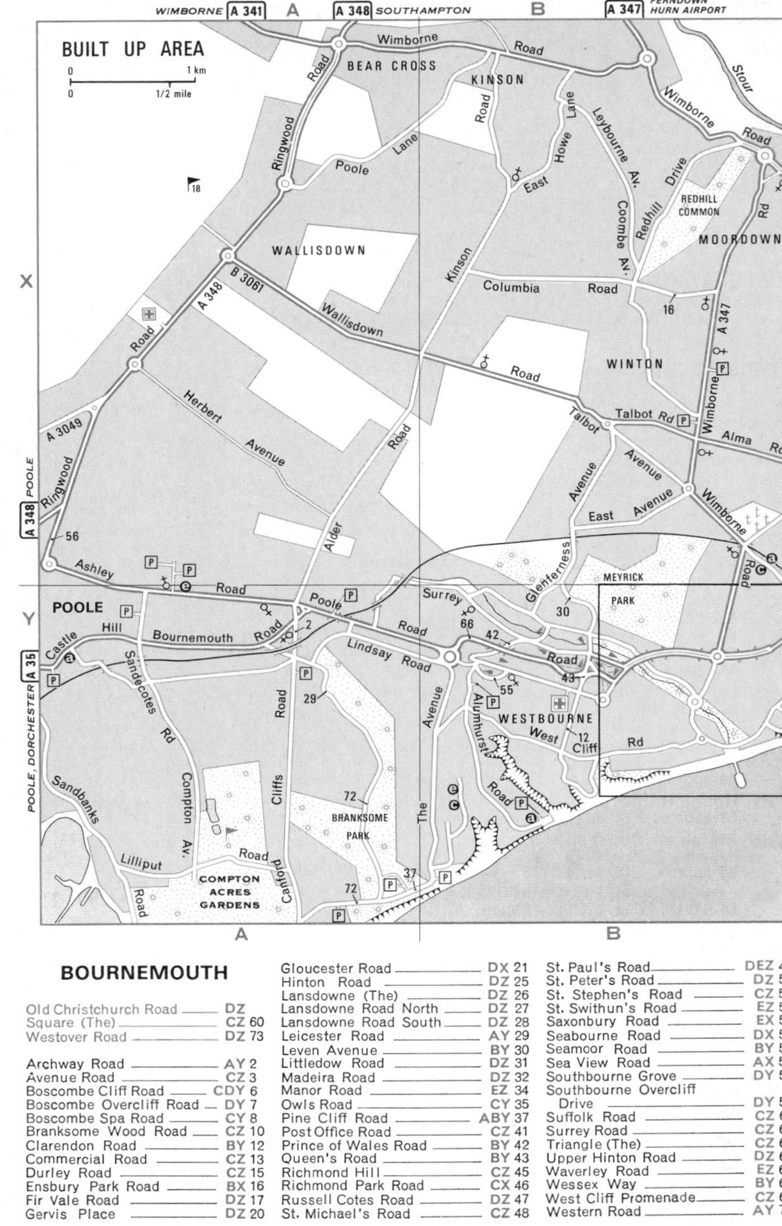

BOURNEMOUTH

Old Christchurch Road DZ
Square (The) CZ 60
Westover Road DZ 73

Archway Road AY 2
Avenue Road CZ 3
Boscombe Cliff Road CDY 6
Boscombe Overcliff Road DY 7
Boscombe Spa Road CY 8
Branksome Wood Road CZ 10
Clarendon Road BY 12
Commercial Road CZ 13
Durley Road CZ 15
Ensbury Park Road BX 16
Fir Vale Road DZ 17
Gervis Place DZ 20

Gloucester Road DX 21
Hinton Road DZ 25
Lansdowne (The) DZ 26
Lansdowne Road North DZ 27
Lansdowne Road South DZ 28
Leicester Road AY 29
Leven Avenue BY 30
Littledow Road DZ 31
Madeira Road DZ 32
Manor Road EZ 34
Owls Road CY 35
Pine Cliff Road ABY 37
Post Office Road CZ 41
Prince of Wales Road BY 42
Queen's Road BY 43
Richmond Hill CZ 45
Richmond Park Road CX 46
Russell Cotes Road DZ 47
St. Michael's Road CZ 48

St. Paul's Road DEZ 4
St. Peter's Road DZ 5
St. Stephen's Road CZ 5
St. Swithun's Road EZ 5
Saxonbury Road EX 5
Seabourne Road DX 5
Seamoor Road BY 5
Sea View Road AX 5
Southbourne Grove DY 5
Southbourne Overcliff Drive DY 5
Suffolk Road CZ 6
Surrey Road CZ 6
Triangle (The) CZ 6
Upper Hinton Road DZ 6
Waverley Road EZ 6
Wessex Way BY 6
West Cliff Promenade CZ 6
Western Road AY 7

Plans de villes : *Les noms des principales voies commerçantes sont inscrits en rouge au début des légendes rues.*

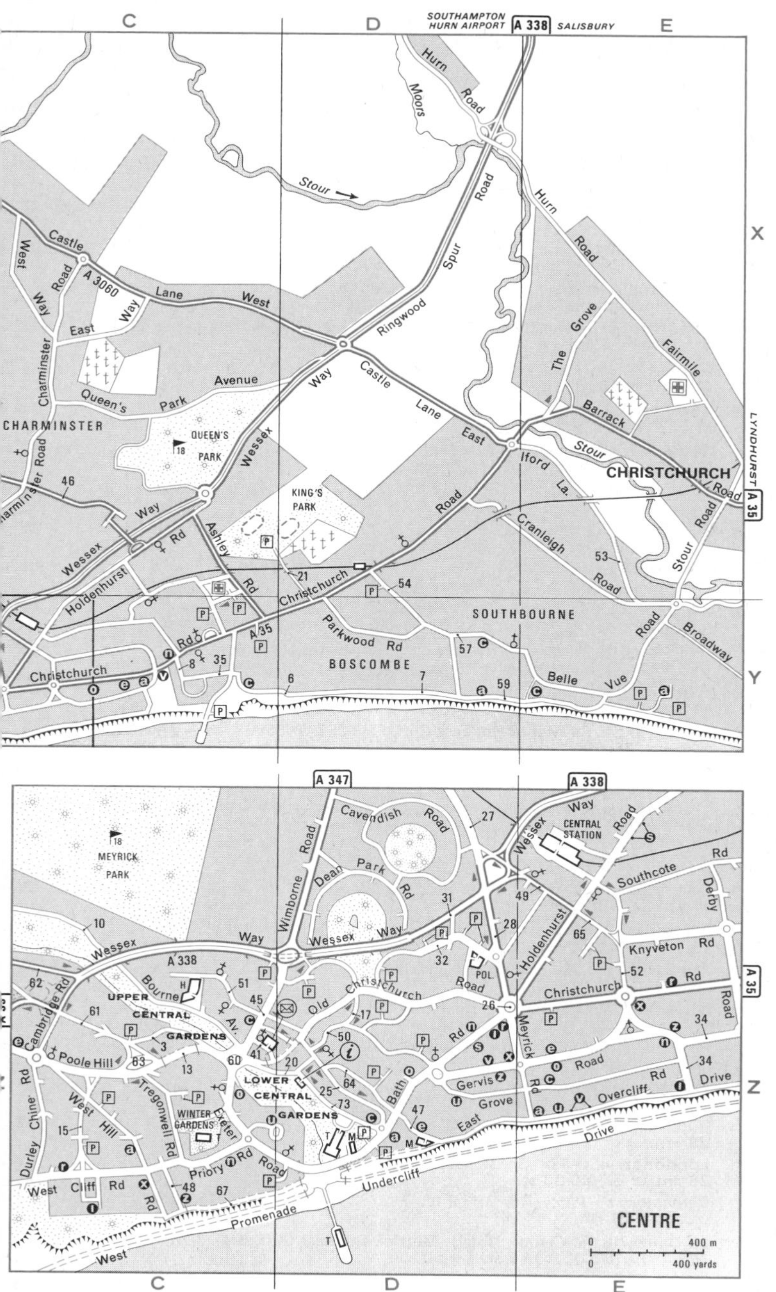
SOUTHAMPTON
HURN AIRPORT
A 338
SALISBURY
C
D
E
X
Y
Z
Hurn Road
Moors
Stour
Hurn Road
Spur Road
Ringwood
Castle Lane West
A 3060
West Way
East Way
Charminster Road
Queen's Park Avenue
CHARMINSTER
QUEEN'S PARK
18
Wessex Way
KING'S PARK
Castle Lane East
The Grove
Fairmile
Barrack Road
Stour
CHRISTCHURCH
Road
LYNDHURST
A 35
Iford La.
Cranleigh Road
Stour Road
Ashley Rd
Holdenhurst Rd
Christchurch Road
A 35
Parkwood Rd
SOUTHBOURNE
Broadway
BOSCOMBE
Belle Vue Road
46
21
53
54
57
35
8
6
7
59
A 347
A 338
Cavendish Road
Wimborne Road
Dean Park Rd
MEYRICK PARK
18
Wessex Way
A 338
CENTRAL STATION
Southcote Rd
Derby Road
Knyveton Rd
Christchurch Rd
Holdenhurst Road
POL.
Old Christchurch Road
UPPER CENTRAL GARDENS
Bourne Av.
Cambridge Rd
Poole Hill
Tregonwell Rd
West Hill Rd
Durley Chine Rd
WINTER GARDENS
Exeter Road
LOWER CENTRAL GARDENS
Bath Rd
Meyrick Rd
Gervis Rd
Grove Road
East Overcliff Drive
Priory Rd
West Cliff Rd
Undercliff Drive
Promenade
West
CENTRE
0
400 m
400 yards
10
62
61
3
63
13
60
41
20
25
64
73
15
48
67
51
45
50
17
32
31
28
49
27
26
65
52
34
47

Durlston Court, Gervis Rd, East Cliff, BH1 3DD, ☎ 291488, heated, – wc & P DZ z
M 3.50/4.50 **st.** 1.40 – **62 rm** 13.00/36.00 **st.**

Hotel Cecil, Parsonage Rd, Bath Hill, BH1 2HJ, ☎ 293336, Telex 418261 – wc wc P DZ o
M approx. 3.50 **st.** 1.50 – **27 rm** 9.50/18.00 **st.**

Cliffeside, East Overcliff Drive, BH1 3AQ, ☎ 25724, ← – wc P. EZ v
M 3.50/3.75 **s.** 1.00 – **61 rm** 7.75/23.00 **s.** – P 13.25/15.00 **s.**

Chesterwood, East Overcliff Drive, BH1 3AR, ☎ 28057, ←, heated – wc P EZ
M 3.90/4.50 **st.** – **55 rm** 8.00/17.20 **st.** – P 14.00/16.60 **st.**

Burley Court, 29 Bath Rd, BH1 2NP, ☎ 22824, – wc & P DZ
M approx. 3.75 **s.** 1.00 – **50 rm** 6.50/14.00 **s.** – P 9.25/14.75 **s.**

East Anglia, 6 Poole Rd, BH2 5QX, ☎ 765163, heated – wc P. CZ e
M approx. 3.50 **s.** – **69 rm** 8.00/20.00 **s.** – P 15.00 **s.**

Suncliff, East Overcliff Drive, BH1 3AG, ☎ 291711, – wc P EZ v
M approx. 3.75 **st.** 1.25 – **79 rm** 7.50/20.00 **st.**

Embassy, Meyrick Rd, East Cliff, BH1 3DW, ☎ 20751, heated – wc P DZ x
M approx. 3.00 **s.** 1.75 – **59 rm** 6.00/20.00 **s.** – P 8.50/13.50 **s.**

Angus, Bath Rd, BH1 2NN, ☎ 26420 – wc P DZ s
M 3.00/3.75 **t.** 1.20 – 1.50 – **50 rm** 10.60/21.60 **t.** – P 13.10/13.80 **t.**

Hinton Firs, 9 Manor Rd, East Cliff, BH1 3HB, ☎ 25409, heated – wc P EZ n
M approx. 2.50 **st.** 1.00 – **58 rm** 8.65/19.80 **st.**

Albany, Warren Edge Rd, Southbourne, BH6 4AU, ☎ 48151 – wc P EY a
17 rm.

Sun Court, 32 West Hill Rd, BH2 5PH, ☎ 21343 – wc wc P CZ a
M approx. 3.50 **s.** 1.20 – **36 rm** 5.50/13.00 **s.**

Whitehall, Exeter Park Rd, BH2 5AX, ☎ 24682 – wc P CZ u
M approx. 2.30 **st.** 1.20 – **46 rm** 5.00/11.50 **st.** – P 8.00/13.00 **st.**

St. George, West Cliff Gdns, BH2 5HL, ☎ 26038, ←, – wc CZ
April-October – **M** approx. 3.50 **st.** 1.30 – **23 rm** 7.50/18.00 **st.** – P 9.00/15.00 **st.**

Cliff Court, 15 West Cliff Rd, BH2 5EX, ☎ 25994 – wc P CZ
M (dinner only) (residents only) – **42 rm.**

Winterbourne, Priory Rd, BH2 5DJ, ☎ 24927, heated, – wc P CZ r
M approx. 3.20 **s.** 1.00 – **46 rm** 8.50/16.00 **s.**

Manor House, 34 Manor Rd, East Cliff, BH1 3EZ, ☎ 36669, – wc P CY a
season – **25 rm.**

Wood Lodge, 10 Manor Rd, East Cliff, BH1 3EY, ☎ 20891, – wc wc & P EZ
Easter-mid October – **M** 2.25/2.50 1.25 – **17 rm** 6.50/14.50 – P 7.50/9.50.

Tudor Grange, 31 Gervis Rd, BH1 3EE, ☎ 291472, – P EZ
March-October – **M** *(closed to non-residents)* (dinner only) 2.40/2.90 **t.** 1.40
12 rm 8.00/16.00 **t.**

Bursledon, Gervis Rd, East Cliff, BH1 3DF, ☎ 24622 – wc P – **23 rm.** DZ

Sandy Beach, Overcliff Drive, Southbourne, BH6 3QB, ☎ 424385, ← – wc P DY
17 rm 7.00/14.00.

Mariners, 22 Clifton Rd, Southbourne, BH6 3PA, ☎ 40851 EY
15 rm 5.00/9.00.

Alumcliff, 121 Alumhurst Rd, Alumchine, BH4 8HS, ☎ 764777, ← – wc wc P BY
16 rm 7.00/16.00 **s.**

Moorings, 66 Lansdowne Rd North, BH1 1RS, ☎ 22705 – P BX
18 rm 5.50/11.00.

Fourways, 21 Christchurch Rd, BH1 3NS, ☎ 20012 – P EZ
20 rm 5.00/12.00.

Europa, 75 Lansdowne Rd, BH1 1RN, ☎ 22978 – wc P BX
20 rm 6.00/14.00 **s.**

Britannia, Christchurch Rd, BH1 3PE, ☎ 26700 – wc P EZ
28 rm.

Londoner, 430-432 Christchurch Rd, BH1 4AY, ☎ 39877 CY
26 rm 3.50/6.00 **st.**

Carnanton, 5a Percy Rd, BH5 1JF, ☎ 37838 – P CY
season – **21 rm.**

XXXX **La Causerie** (at Carlton Hotel), Meyrick Rd, East Cliff, BH1 3DN, ☎ 22011 – P EZ
M a la carte 5.00/10.50 **st.** 1.60.

XXX **The Buttery** (at Royal Bath Hotel), Bath Rd, BH1 2EW, ☎ 25555 – P DZ
M a la carte 4.50/10.00 **st.** 1.85.

XX **La Taverna,** Westover Rd, BH1 3BZ, ☎ 27681, Italian rest. DZ **c**
closed Sunday – **M** a la carte 4.80/7.25 🍷 1.50.

XX **Opus One,** 31 Southbourne Grove, BH6 3QT, ☎ 421240 DY **c**
closed Sunday and 25-26 December – **M** (dinner only) a la carte 4.45/5.65 🍷 1.50.

XX Trattoria San Marco, 148 Holdenhurst Rd, BH8 8AS, ☎ 21132, Italian rest. EZ **s**

XX **South Western** (Dorchester Room), Holdenhurst Rd, opposite Central Station, BH8 8AS, ☎ 21801 EZ **s**
M a la carte 4.00/8.45 **s.** 🍷 1.45.

X **Crust,** Omnibus Station, Exeter Rd, BH2 5AE, ☎ 21430 CZ **o**
closed 25 and 26 December – **M** a la carte 3.05/5.25 **t.** 🍷 1.60.

AUSTIN-MG-WOLSELEY 216/218 Tuckton Rd ☎ 49234
BENTLEY, ROLLS ROYCE 26 Oxford Rd ☎ 25748
BMW Exeter Rd ☎ 24433
CHRYSLER 14 Carbery Row ☎ 43243
CHRYSLER-SIMCA 35 Holdenhurst Rd ☎ 26566
DAF Columbia Rd ☎ 56561
DAIMLER-JAGUAR-MG-MORRIS-ROVER-TRIUMPH 16/18 Poole Rd ☎ 766031
DAIMLER-JAGUAR 38 Poole Hill ☎ 25405
DATSUN 318/320 Holdenhurst Rd ☎ 33304
FORD 9 Palmerston Rd ☎ 34262
FORD Poole Rd ☎ 20731
JENSEN, VOLVO 33 R. L. Stephenson Av. ☎ 763344
MORRIS-MG-WOLSELEY 235 Castle Lane West, Redhill ☎ 50201
PEUGEOT 25/27 Palmerston Rd, Boscombe ☎ 37206
RENAULT 1114 Christchurch Rd, Pokesdown ☎ 49241
VAUXHALL 521 Christchurch Rd ☎ 37286
VAUXHALL Castle Lane West ☎ 56434
VAUXHALL 984 Christchurch Rd ☎ 43201
VAUXHALL Poole Rd ☎ 763361
VW, AUDI-NSU 723 Wimborne Rd ☎ 516222

BOURTON-ON-THE-WATER Glos. 986 ㉛ – pop. 2,251 – ✆ 0451.

London 91 – **Birmingham 47** – Gloucester 24 – **Oxford 36.**

🏨 Old Manse, Victoria St., GL54 2EY, ☎ 20642, 🌳 – 🛁wc ☎ Ⓟ
M a la carte 7.00/12.75 **st.** – **9 rm.**

🏨 **Old New Inn,** High St., GL54 2AF, ☎ 20467, « Bourton model village », 🌳 – 🚗 Ⓟ
M approx. 3.70 **t.** 🍷 1.30 – **24 rm** ☕ 6.60/14.50 **st.**

🏨 **Chester House,** Victoria St., GL54 2BU, ☎ 20286 – TV 🛁wc Ⓟ
March-October – **M** (grill rest.) a la carte approx. 3.10 **t.** – **16 rm** ☕ 9.50/16.00 **t.**

🏠 **Brookside,** Riverside, GL54 2BS, ☎ 20371, 🌳 – 🛁wc 🚿wc Ⓟ
M 3.10/4.00 **st.** 🍷 1.20 – **10 rm** ☕ 5.50/11.55 **st.** – P 7.90/10.45 **st.**

X **Rose Tree,** Riverside, GL54 2BX, ☎ 20635
M a la carte 4.60/7.20 **t.** 🍷 1.50.

CHRYSLER-SIMCA ☎ 20366

BOVEY TRACEY Devon 986 ㊴ – pop. 3,834 – ✉ Newton Abbot – ✆ 0626.

i Information Centre, Lower Car Park ☎ 832047 (summer only).

London 214 – Exeter 14 – **Plymouth 32.**

🏨 **Prestbury Country House** 🐌, Brimley Lane, TQ13 9JS, ☎ 833246, ≤, « Country house atmosphere », 🌳 – 🛁wc Ⓟ
March-October – **M** 3.75/4.25 **s.** 🍷 1.35 – **10 rm** ☕ 8.50/20.00 **s.** – P 14.00/15.00 **s.**

🏨 **Coombe Cross,** 🐌, TQ13 9EY, ☎ 832476, 🌳 – 🛁wc Ⓟ
closed 25 December-12 February – **M** (buffet lunch) 3.75/4.30 **st.** 🍷 2.00 – **20 rm** ☕ 7.00/16.50 **st.** – P 12.75/14.50 **st.**

🏨 **Dolphin,** Station Rd, TQ13 9AL, ☎ 832413 – Ⓟ
closed 25 and 26 December – **M** a la carte 2.95/3.85 **t.** 🍷 1.35 – **9 rm** ☕ 5.75/11.50 **t.**

BOWBURN Durham – ✉ ✆ 0385 Coxhoe.

London 265 – Durham 3 – **Middlesbrough 20.**

🏨 **Bowburn Hall,** DH6 5NT, E: 1 m. off A 177 ☎ 770311, 🌳 – TV 🛁wc ☎ Ⓟ
M 4.00/5.50 🍷 1.60 – **19 rm** ☕ 9.50/14.00.

BOWDON Cheshire – see Altrincham.

BOWNESS-ON-WINDERMERE Cumbria 986 ⑲ – see Windermere.

BRACKLEY Northants. 986 ㉛ ㉜ – pop. 4,615 – ✆ 0280.

London 72 – Northampton 20 – **Oxford 25.**

🏨 **Old Crown,** Market Pl., NN13 5AB, ☎ 702210 – 🚗 Ⓟ. 🏷
M 2.45/3.25 **t.** 🍷 1.85 – **15 rm** ☕ 8.00/12.50 **t.**

at Whitfield NE: 2 ½ m. off A 43 – ✉ Brackley – ✆ 028 05 Syresham :

🏨 **Sun,** NN13 5TG, ☎ 232 – 🛁wc Ⓟ
M a la carte 3.20/4.95 🍷 1.50 – **11 rm** ☕ 5.00/12.00.

at Brackley Hatch NE: 5 ¼ m. on A 43 – ✉ Brackley – ✆ 028 05 Syresham:

XX **Green Man Inn** with rm, NN13 5TX, ☎ 209 – 🛁wc Ⓟ
M a la carte 4.10/5.35 **st.** – **7 rm** ☕ 8.00/13.50 **t.**

DATSUN 71 High St. ☎ 702227

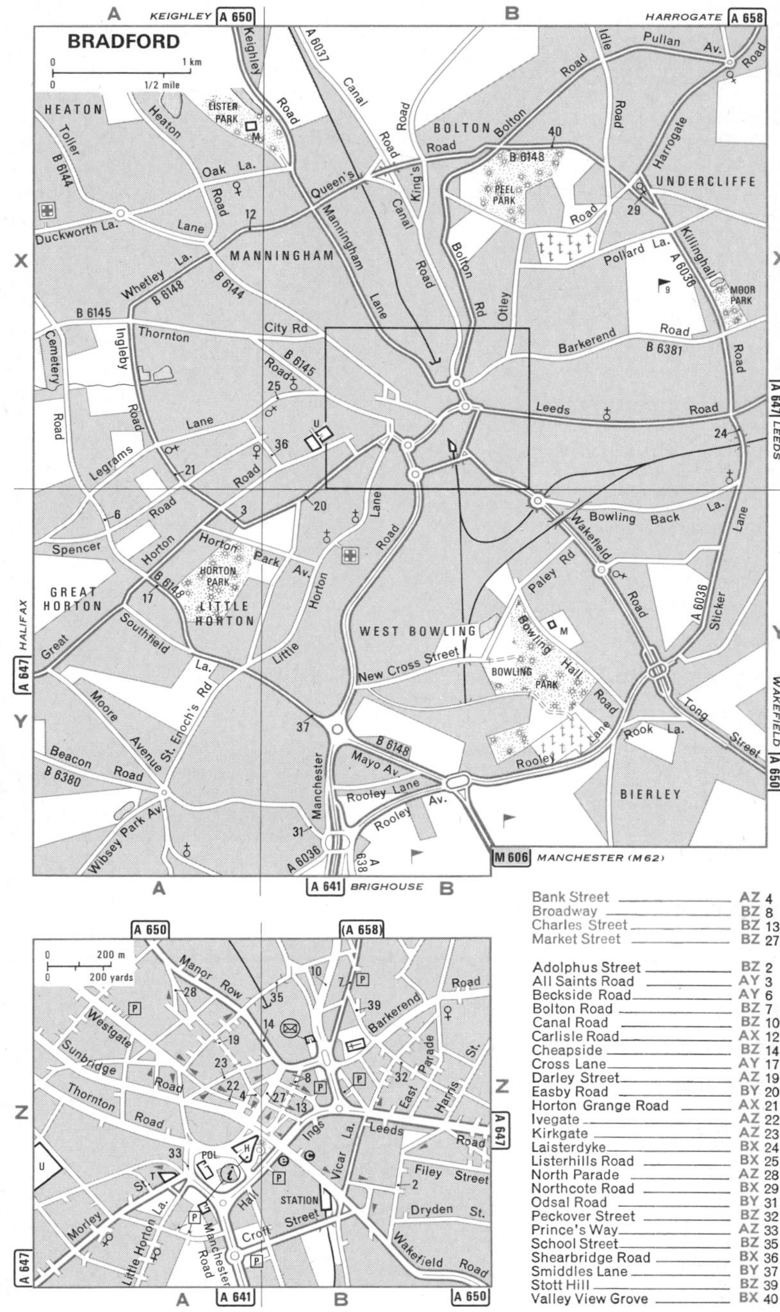

Bank Street	AZ	4
Broadway	BZ	8
Charles Street	BZ	13
Market Street	BZ	27
Adolphus Street	BZ	2
All Saints Road	AY	3
Beckside Road	AY	6
Bolton Road	BZ	7
Canal Road	BZ	10
Carlisle Road	AX	12
Cheapside	BZ	14
Cross Lane	AY	17
Darley Street	AZ	19
Easby Road	BY	20
Horton Grange Road	AX	21
Ivegate	AZ	22
Kirkgate	AZ	23
Laisterdyke	BX	24
Listerhills Road	BX	25
North Parade	AZ	28
Northcote Road	BX	29
Odsal Road	BY	31
Peckover Street	BZ	32
Prince's Way	AZ	33
School Street	BZ	35
Shearbridge Road	BX	36
Smiddles Lane	BY	37
Stott Hill	BZ	39
Valley View Grove	BX	40

BRADFORD West Yorks. 986 ⑫ and ㉓ – pop. 294,177 – ☎ 0274.
Envir.: Haworth (Brontë Parsonage Museum*) *AC,* W: 10 m. by B 6144 AX.
18 Chellow Grange, Haworth Rd ☎ 427671, NW: 3 m. by B 6144 AX – 18 Hawksworth, Guiseley ☎ 0943 (Guiseley) 73817, N: 8 m. by A 6037 BX – 9 Scarr Hall, Pollard Lane ☎ 68313 BX – 9 South View Rd ☎ 681023, SE: 4 m. on plan of Leeds BX.
Leeds and Bradford Airport: ☎ 0532 (Rawdon) 503431, NE: 6 m. by A 658 BX – **Terminal:** Chester St., Bus Station, Bradford.
i Central Library, Princes Way ☎ 33081 – Information office, City Hall ☎ 29577 ext 425.
London 198 – Leeds 9 – Manchester 37 – Middlesbrough 70 – Sheffield 38.

Plan of Bradford opposite
Plan of Enlarged Area: see Leeds

Norfolk Gardens (Stakis), Hall Ings, BD1 5SH, ☎ 34733, Telex 517573 – TV. **123 rm.** BZ e

Victoria (T.H.F.), Bridge St., BD1 1JX, ☎ 28706 – TV wc P. **M** a la carte 4.75/6.75 **st.** 1.50 – **59 rm** 11.00/18.50 **st.** BZ c

Baron, Highfield Rd, Idle, BD10 8QT, N: 2 ½ m. ☎ 611914, Telex 517229, – TV wc P **M** a la carte 3.80/5.80 1.50 – **60 rm** 14.00/18.50. on plan of Leeds AV i

Novotel, Merrydale Rd, BD4 6SA, SE: 3 m. off M 606 ☎ 683683, Telex 517312, heated – TV wc P. **M** (grill rest. only) approx. 4.00 **st.** 1.70 – 1.90 – **130 rm** 13.80/17.00 **st.** – P 13.50 **st.** on plan of Leeds AX a

at Apperley Bridge NE: 4 ½ m. on A 658 – ✉ Bradford – ☎ 0532 Rawdon:

Stansfield Arms, BD10 0NP, ☎ 502659 – P *closed Sunday* – **M** (grill rest.) a la carte 2.40/3.65 **t.** 1.10. on plan of Leeds BV n

at Thornton W: 2 ¾ m. on B 6145 – ✉ ☎ 0274 Bradford:

The Cottage, 869 Thornton Rd, BD13 3NW, ☎ 832752 – P *closed Saturday lunch and Tuesday* – **M** a la carte 3.95/5.75 **t.** 2.40. on plan of Leeds AV a

ALFA-ROMEO, BMW Oak Lane ☎ 495521
AUSTIN-MG-WOLSELEY Station Rd ☎ 882480
AUSTIN-MG-WOLSELEY Nelson St. ☎ 22271
CHRYSLER-SIMCA 150 Manningham Lane ☎ 27181
CHRYSLER-SIMCA Leeds Rd ☎ 663391
CITROEN Whetley Hill ☎ 495543
DAIMLER-JAGUAR-MORRIS-MG-WOLSELEY Canal Rd ☎ 33488
DAF 341 Leeds Rd ☎ 26812
DATSUN 88 Thornton Rd ☎ 27302
DATSUN Queens Rd ☎ 20376
FIAT Keighley Rd, Frizinghall ☎ 41337
FORD 44 Bowland St ☎ 25131
FORD 146/148 Tong St. ☎ 681601
MERCEDES-BENZ Thornton Rd ☎ 498103
MORRIS-MG-WOLSELEY Gt. Horton Rd ☎ 71749
MORRIS-MG-WOLSELEY St. Enoch's Rd ☎ 678272
OPEL 230 Manningham Lane ☎ 491432
PEUGEOT Thornton Rd ☎ 493933
RENAULT Frizinghall Rd ☎ 495711
ROVER-TRIUMPH Frizinghall Rd ☎ 42404
ROVER-TRIUMPH 38 Manningham Lane ☎ 32444
SAAB Gain Lane ☎ 632741
VAUXHALL Sticker Lane ☎ 662482
VAUXHALL Thornton Rd ☎ 34201
VOLVO 226/228 Manningham Lane ☎ 491301
VW, AUDI-NSU Ingleby Rd ☎ 491414

BRAINTREE Essex 986 ㉜ – pop. 24,856 (inc. Bocking) – ☎ 0376.
18 Kings Lane, ☎ 24117, N: 1 ½ m.
London 45 – Cambridge 38 – Chelmsford 12 – Colchester 15.

White Hart (T.H.F.), Bocking End, CM7 6AB, ☎ 21401 – TV wc P **M** a la carte 3.95/5.35 **st.** 1.50 – **35 rm** 9.50/16.00 **st.**

Old Court, 31 Bradford St., CM7 6AS, ☎ 21444, – P **M** a la carte 3.15/5.15 **t.** 1.35 – **12 rm** 7.00/10.00 **t.**

AUSTIN-MORRIS-MG Bradfordstreet ☎ 25701
CHRYSLER 253 Coggeshall Rd ☎ 25480
DAF, OPEL South St. ☎ 21313
FORD Coggeshall Rd ☎ 21202
RENAULT Railway St. ☎ 21819
ROVER-TRIUMPH Rayne Rd ☎ 24444
VAUXHALL 277/281 Rayne Rd ☎ 21456

BRAITHWAITE Cumbria – see Keswick.

BRAMBER West Sussex – see Steyning.

BRAMHALL Greater Manchester – pop. 39,619 – ☎ 061 Manchester.
London 194 – Liverpool 44 – Manchester 10 – Stoke-on-Trent 33.

Pownall Arms, Bramhall Lane South, SK7 2EB, on A 5102 ☎ 439 8116, Telex 666691 – TV wc P. **M** 3.45/3.80 **st.** 1.95 – 1.95 – **40 rm** 10.70/16.65 **st.**

BRAMHOPE West Yorks. – pop. 3,115 – ✉ Leeds – ☎ 0532 Arthington.
London 201 – Harrogate 11 – Leeds 7.5.

Post House (T.H.F.), Otley Rd, LS16 9JJ, ☎ 842911, ← – TV wc P. **M** 2.95/4.00 **st.** 1.50 – 2.00 – **120 rm** 13.50/19.00 **st.**

BMW Bramhope ☎ 2239
ROVER-TRIUMPH Breary Lane ☎ 2696

BRAMPTON Cambs. – pop. 4,494 – ✉ ☎ 0480 Huntingdon.
London 67 – Bedford 19 – Huntingdon 2.

Brampton, PE18 8NH, W : 1 ½ m. at junction A 1 and A 604 ☎ 810434 – TV wc ☎ P
M a la carte 2.55/4.15 **t.** 1.40 – **17 rm** 11.50/16.50 **t.**

CITROEN ☎ 53132

BRAMSHAW Hants. – pop. 694 – ✉ Lyndhurst – ☎ 042 127 Cadnam.
London 93 – Salisbury 13 – Southampton 11 – Winchester 21.

Bramble Hill, Bramble Hill, SO4 7JG, W: ½ m. ☎ 3165, « Former hunting lodge », park – P
Easter-October – **M** (dinner only and Sunday lunch) 3.25/3.75 **t.** 1.45 – **16 rm** 8.50/17.00 **t.**

BRANDON Warw. – see Coventry.

BRANSCOMBE Devon – pop. 477 – ✉ Seaton – ☎ 029 780.
London 167 – Exeter 20 – Lyme Regis 11.

Masons Arms, EX12 3DJ, ☎ 300, – wc P
closed 1 to 21 November – **M** (bar lunch) approx. 5.00 **t.** 1.25 – **20 rm** 7.00/18.40 **s.**

BRANSTON Lincs. – see Lincoln.

Per usare bene le piante di città, vedere i segni convenzionali a p. 35.

BRAUNSTONE Leics. – see Leicester.

BRAY-ON-THAMES Berks. – pop. 5,888 – ✉ ☎ 0628 Maidenhead.
London 34 – Reading 13.

Monkey Island, SL6 2EE, SE: 1 m. off Monkey Island Lane ☎ 23400, « Island on river Thames », – TV wc ☎ P.
M approx. 5.00 **st.** 1.85 – **24 rm** 14.00/24.00 **st.**

XXXX ✿✿ **Waterside Inn,** Ferry Rd, SL6 2AT, ☎ 20691, ←, « Thames-side setting », – P
closed Sunday dinner from October to Easter, Monday and 2 to 15 January –
M a la carte 10.10/13.40 **st.** 3.00
Spec. Mousseline de volaille au Roquefort, Gratin de crabe Jacqueline, Côte d'agneau Germaine.

XX **Hind's Head,** High St. ☎ 26151 – P
M a la carte 5.35/8.00.

BRECHFA Dyfed – pop. 175 – ✉ Carmarthen – ☎ 026 789.
London 223 – Carmarthen 11 – Swansea 30.

XX **Ty Mawr** with rm, ☎ 332, – wc P
closed first 2 weeks October – **M** *(closed Sunday to non-residents)* a la carte 3.30/4.40 **st** 1.35 – **5 rm** 7.50/15.00 **st.**

BRECON Powys 986 ㉛ – pop. 6,304 – ☎ 0874.
See : Cathedral* 13C. **Envir. :** Road* from Brecon to Hirwaun – Road* from Brecon to Merthyr Tydfil – Craig-y-Nos (Dan Yr Ogolf Caves* *AC*) SW: 18 m.
18 Penoyre House, Cradoc ☎ 2528, N : 2 m. – 9 Llanfaes, ☎ 2004, ½ m. on A 40.
i Brecon Beacons National Park, 7 Glamorgan St. ☎ 2763 (summer only) — Tourist Information Centre, Market Car Park ☎ 2485 (July-August only).
London 183 – Cardiff 41 – Gloucester 62 – Swansea 44.

Castle of Brecon, The Avenue, LD3 9DB, ☎ 2551, – wc P. – **18 rm.**

AUSTIN-MG-ROVER, VAUXHALL 41 The Watton ☎ 2223
CHRYSLER-SIMCA The Watton ☎ 2266
FORD Struet St. ☎ 2401
MORRIS-MG-WOLSELEY Ship St. ☎ 2166

BREDWARDINE Heref. and Worc. – pop. 172 – ✉ Hereford – ☎ 098 17 Moccas.
London 150 – Hereford 12 – Newport 51.

Red Lion, HR3 6BU, ☎ 303, – wc P
M (bar lunch) 4.00/6.00 1.00 – **10 rm** 7.00/14.50.

BRENCHLEY Kent – pop. 2,509 – ✉ Tonbridge – ☎ 089 272.
London 42 – Maidstone 14 – Royal Tunbridge Wells 7.

X **Rose and Crown,** TN12 7NQ, ☎ 2107 – P
closed Monday – **M** a la carte 1.75/4.00 **st.** 1.50.

AUSTIN-MORRIS-MG ☎ 2275

BRENTWOOD Essex 986 ㊱ – pop. 58,277 – ☎ 0277.
King George's Park ☎ 218714.
London 22 – Chelmsford 11 – Southend-on-Sea 21.

Brentwood Moat House, London Rd, CM14 4NR, SW : 1 ¼ m. on A 1023 ☎ 225252, Telex 995182, – TV P.
M a la carte 4.45/6.20 **t.** 1.50 – 1.80 – **25 rm** 15.00/19.25 **st.**

Post House (T.H.F.), Brook St., CM14 5NF, W: 1 ½ m. on A 1023 ☎ 210888, Telex 995379, heated – TV wc P
M a la carte 3.60/3.85 **st.** 1.50 – 2.00 – **119 rm** 13.00/18.00 **st.**

Lion and Lamb, High St., CM14 4RH, ☎ 216427 – P
9 rm.

Headley Arms, Warley Rd, CM14 0AR, S: 1½ m. ☎ 216104 – P
closed Sunday and Bank Holidays – **M** a la carte approx. 5.20 **t.** 1.90.

ALFA ROMEO, FIAT, JENSEN 2 Brook St. ☎ 216161
AUSTIN-MORRIS-MG-WOLSELEY 110 Shenfield Rd, Shenfield ☎ 222424
FORD Brook St. ☎ 215544
ROVER-TRIUMPH-WOLSELEY Kings Rd ☎ 221401
RENAULT 121/5 Kings Rd ☎ 225546
VAUXHALL Brook St. ☎ 227290
VW, AUDI-NSU Shenfield ☎ 218686

BRERETON Staffs. – see Rugeley.

BRIDGNORTH Salop 986 ㉛ – pop. 10,491 – ☎ 074 62.
Envir. : Claverley (Parish church : wall paintings* 13C-15C) E: 5 m. – Much Wenlock (Wenlock priory* (ruins 11C) *AC*, NW : 7 ½ m.
Stanley Lane ☎ 3315, N: 1 m.
London 146 – Birmingham 26 – Shrewsbury 20 – Worcester 29.

Falcon, St. John's St., Low Town, WV15 6AG, ☎ 3134 – wc P
14 rm.

Rib Room, Northgate, WV16 4ER, ☎ 3640
closed Sunday and Bank Holidays – **M** a la carte 3.35/5.65 **t.** 1.60.

Bambers, 65 St. Mary's St., WV1 1JB, ☎ 3139
closed Sunday, September and Bank Holidays – **M** (dinner only) a la carte 3.50/4.00 **t.** 1.50.

AUSTIN-MG-WOLSELEY Hollybush Rd ☎ 3402
AUSTIN-MORRIS-MG-ROVER-TRIUMPH-WOLSELEY 52 West Castle St. ☎ 2207
CHRYSLER-SIMCA Salop St. ☎ 2581
MORRIS-MG-WOLSELEY Northgate ☎ 3332

BRIDGWATER Somerset 986 ㉟ – pop 26,642 – ☎ 0278.
Envir. : Burnham-on-Sea (St. Andrew's Church: Gibbon's sculptures*) N: 9 m.
Enmore Park ☎ (027 867) 244, W: 3 m.
London 160 – Bristol 39 – Taunton 11.

Royal Clarence, High St., Cornhill, TA6 3AT, ☎ 55196, « Tastefully decorated interior » – TV wc wc P.
M a la carte 2.90/5.15 1.05 – **28 rm** 6.70/12.15.

Bristol, 16 High St., TA6 3BJ, ☎ 58197 – wc
10 rm.

AUSTIN-MG-ROVER-TRIUMPH-WOLSELEY 52 Eastover ☎ 2218
BMW Cannington ☎ 0278 (Combwich) 2233
DAF, VOLVO Bristol Rd ☎ 55333
FIAT 38 St. John St. ☎ 3312
FORD 37 Frian St. ☎ 51332
MORRIS-MG-WOLSELEY Market St. ☎ 2125
RENAULT Cannington ☎ 652228
VAUXHALL Monmouth St. ☎ 56301

BRIDLINGTON North Humberside 986 ㉔ – pop. 26,776 – ☎ 0262.
See : Priory Church* 12C-15C. **Envir. :** Burton Agnes Hall* (Elizabethan) *AC*, SW: 6 m.
Belvedere ☎ 72092, 1 m. Bridlington Station.
i Garrison St. ☎ 3474 (summer only).
London 236 – Kingston-upon-Hull 29 – York 41.

Expanse, North Marine Drive, YO15 2LS, ☎ 75347, ← – wc P
M a la carte approx. 4.00 **st.** – **45 rm** 8.00/17.20 **st.** – P 12.00/13.50 **st.**

Monarch, South Marine Drive, YO15 3JJ, ☎ 74447, ← – wc P
M approx. 2.75 **st.** – **41 rm** 8.30/23.20 **st.**

AUSTIN-MG-WOLSELEY Flamborough Rd ☎ 72226
CHRYSLER-SIMCA, VAUXHALL, VOLVO Hilderthorpe Rd ☎ 78141
DATSUN Quay Rd ☎ 78238
FIAT, VAUXHALL Promenade ☎ 3414
FORD Hamilton Rd ☎ 5336
JAGUAR-MORRIS-MG-ROVER-TRIUMPH-WOLSELEY 7 Prospect St. ☎ 72267
TOYOTA 52 Quay Rd ☎ 2022

BRIDPORT Dorset 986 ㊴ – pop. 6,369 – ☎ 0308.

West Bay ☎ 22597, S : 1 ½ m.

London 150 – Exeter 38 – Taunton 33 – Weymouth 19.

Roundham House, Roundham Gdns, West Bay Rd, DT6 4BD, ☎ 22753, – Ⓟ
closed November and December – **8 rm** 8.00/16.00 **st.**

BRIGG South Humberside 986 ㉔ – pop. 4,795 – ☎ 0652.

Envir.: Barton-upon-Humber (St. Mary's Church* 12C, Old Peter's Church* 10C-11C) N : 10 m.

London 167 – Kingston-upon-Hull 13 – Leeds 62 – Lincoln 24 – Sheffield 53.

Angel, Market Pl., DN20 8LD, ☎ 53118 – Ⓟ
M 1.75/2.50 **st.** 0.85 – **13 rm** 6.50/11.40 **st.** – P 14.00 **st.**

AUSTIN-MG-ROVER-TRIUMPH-WOLSELEY Bigby Rd ☎ 2066
DAF Greetwell ☎ 4665
FORD Market Pl. ☎ 2396
MORRIS-MG-WOLSELEY Bridge St. ☎ 2066

BRIGHTLINGSEA Essex 986 ㉜ – pop. 6,515 – ☎ 020 630.

London 65 – Chelmsford 32 – Colchester 10.

Jacobe's Hall, 44 High St. CO7 0AQ, ☎ 2113 – Ⓟ
M a la carte 2.70/3.55 1.45.

BRIGHTON AND HOVE East Sussex 986 ㊱ – pop. 234,437 (inc. Hove) – ☎ 0273.

See: Royal Pavilion* (interior**) *AC* CZ **B** – Aquarium* *AC* CZ **A** – Booth Museum (bird collection)* BV **M** – Preston Manor (Chinese collection*) BV **D** – The Lanes CZ. **Envir. :** Stanmer Park (site*) N : 3 ½ m. by A 27 CV – Clayton (church of St. John the Baptist : frescoes* 14 C) N : 6 m.

Roedean ☎ 63989 CV – **Hollingbury Park ☎ 552010** BV – **N : by Dyke Rd** BV **☎ 079 156 (Poynings) 296** – **Dyke Rd ☎ 556482** BV.

Marlborough House, 54 Old Steine ☎ 23755 – Sea Front, Kings Rd ☎ 26450 (summer only).

at Hove : Town Hall, Church Rd ☎ 775400.

London 54 – Portsmouth 49 – Southampton 63.

Plans on following pages

Grand (De Vere), 97-103 King's Rd, BN1 2FW, ☎ 26301, Telex 877410, ← – TV. BZ **s**
M approx. 5.50 **st.** 1.45 – **165 rm** 17.00/30.00 **st.**

Royal Crescent, 100 Marine Par., BN2 1AX, ☎ 66311, ← – TV CV **c**
M approx. 4.25 **st.** 1.85 – 1.75 – **66 rm** 11.50/21.00 **st.** – P 18.50/35.00 **st.**

Wheeler's Sheridan, 64 King's Rd, BN1 1NA, ☎ 23221, ← – TV BZ **e**
closed 25 and 26 December – **M** (see **Wheeler's Sheridan Tavern**) – **34 rm** 15.00/30.00 **t.**

Old Ship (Interchange), King's Rd, BN1 1NR, ☎ 29001, Telex 877101, ← – TV Ⓟ. CZ **n**
M approx. 4.00 **st.** 1.00 – **148 rm** 16.50/29.20 **st.** – P approx. 22.40 **st.**

Touring, 216 Preston Rd, BN1 6UU, on A 23 ☎ 507853 – wc Ⓟ BV **a**
M (grill rest. only) approx. 2.50 **t.** 1.20 – 0.85 – **25 rm** 7.80/17.50 **st.**

Curzon (T.H.F.), Cavendish Pl., BN1 2HW, ☎ 25788 – wc Ⓟ BZ **v**
M 2.95/3.10 **st.** 1.50 – **46 rm** 9.00/18.00 **st.** – P 13.50/17.00 **st.**

Regency without rest., 28 Regency Sq., BN1 2FH, ☎ 202690 – wc BZ **n**
closed December and January – **14 rm** 8.00/13.00 **st.**

Marina, 8 Charlotte St., BN2 1AG, ☎ 65349 CV **n**
11 rm 4.00/8.00 **st.**

Downlands, 19 Charlotte St., BN2 1AG, ☎ 61203 CV **n**
10 rm 3.25/9.00 **st.**

Ellesmere, 8 New Steine, BN2 1PB, ☎ 67812 CZ **r**
March-November – **14 rm** 4.60/11.50 **t.**

Hamilton House, 27 Lower Rock Gdns, Marine Par., BN2 1PG, ☎ 682667 CZ **u**
10 rm 4.00/7.00 **s.**

Aston, 3 Lower Rock Gdns, Marine Par., BN2 1PG, ☎ 681957 CZ **c**
13 rm 4.35/12.00 **st.**

XXX ✿ **Le Français,** 1 Paston Pl., Kemptown, BN2 1HA, ☎ 680716, French rest. CV **a**
closed 25 and 26 December – **M** (dinner only) a la carte 5.75/8.10 **t.** 1.85
Spec. Loup de mer au fenouil flambé au Pernod, Gigot d'agneau à la Beaumanière, Côte de bœuf à la moëlle.

XXX **Wheeler's Sheridan Tavern,** 64 King's Rd, BN1 1NA, ☎ 28372, Seafood BZ **e**
closed 25 and 26 December – **M** a la carte 3.65/9.45 **t.**

XX **English's Oyster Bar,** 29-31 East St., BN1 1HL, ☎ 27980, Seafood CZ **a**
closed Sunday from March to November and 25-26 December – **M** a la carte 3.85/8.95 **st.** 1.75.

XX **The French Connection,** 11 Little East St., BN1 1HT, ☎ 24454 CZ **o**
closed Sunday and Bank Holidays – **M** (dinner only) a la carte 5.30/7.65 1.75

BRIGHTON AND HOVE

Street	Grid	Street	Grid	Street	Grid	Street	Grid	Street	Grid	Street	Grid
North Street	CZ	Adelaide Crescent	AY 2	Chatham Place	BX 7	Gloucester Road	CY 14	Old Steine	CZ 22	Terminus Road	BCX 33
Queen's Road	BCY	Brunswick Place	AY 4	Denmark Road	BY 8	Grand Junction Road	CZ 15	Pavillon Parade	CZ 23	Upper North Street	BY 34
West Street	BZ	Brunswick Square	AYZ 5	East Street	CZ 9	Hove Street	AV 17	Richmond Place	CY 27	Victoria Road	AV 36
Western Road	ABY	Carlton Terrace	AV6	Eastern Road	CV 10	Market Place	CX 19	Richmond Terrace	CX 28	Warren Road	CV 37
				Gladstone Terrace	CX 12	Market Street	CZ 20	St.George's Place	CY 30	Waterloo Place	CX 39
				Gloucester Place	CY 13	Marlborough Place	CY 21	St.Peter's Place	CX 31	Wellington Road	AV 40

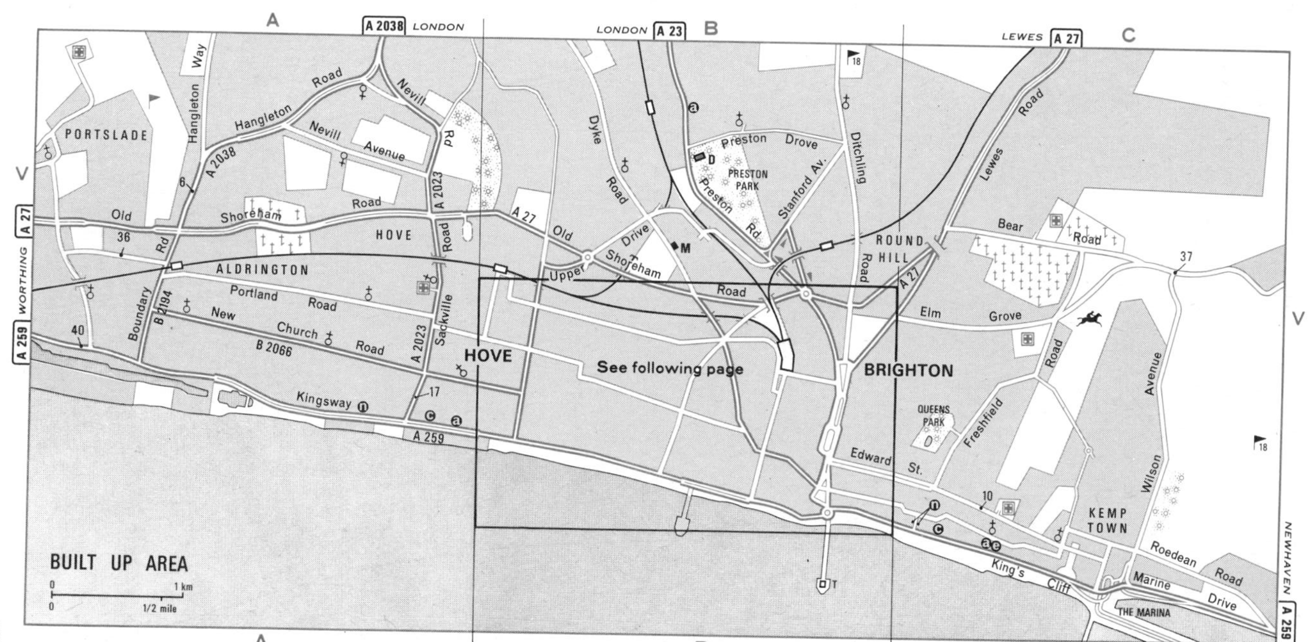

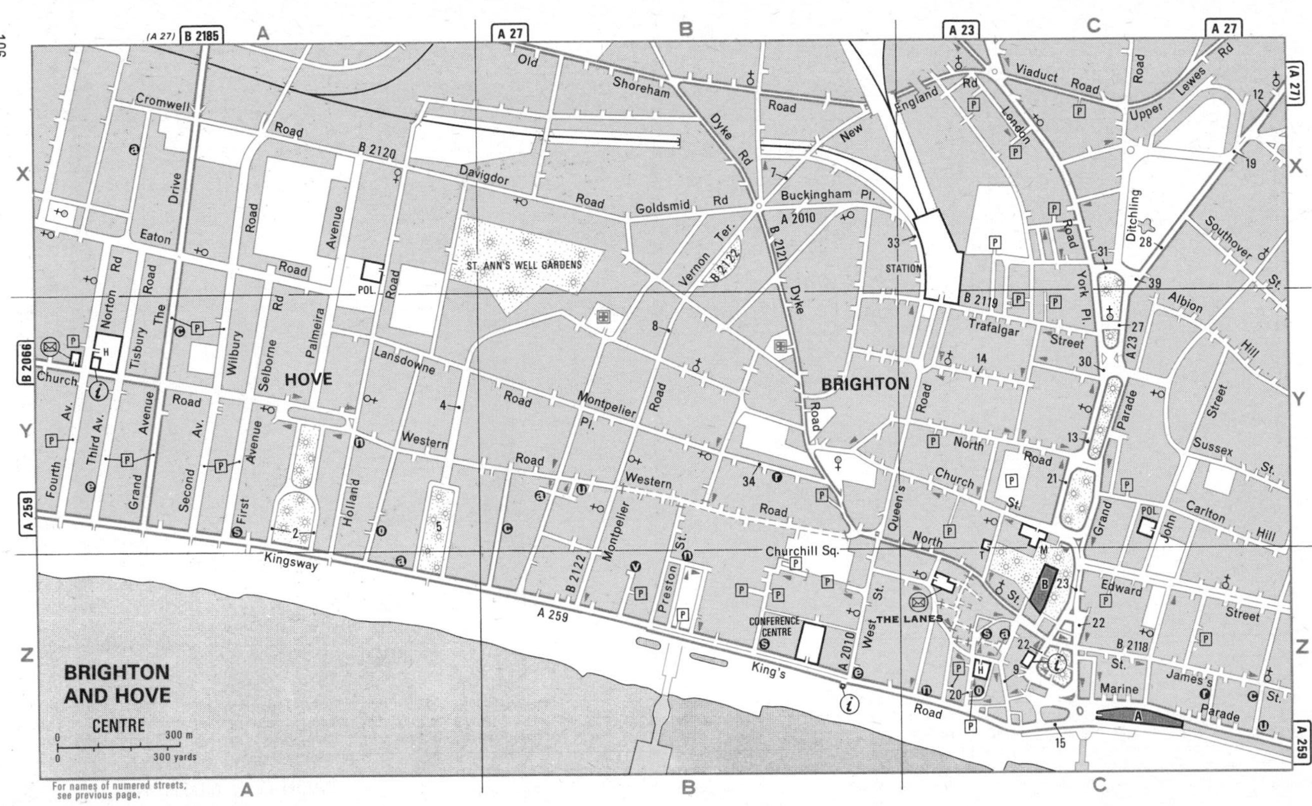

BRIGHTON
AND HOVE
CENTRE
0 300 m
0 300 yards
For names of numbered streets, see previous page.
BRIGHTON
HOVE
THE LANES
CONFERENCE CENTRE
STATION
ST. ANN'S WELL GARDENS
POL.
A 27
(A 27)
A 23
A 259
B 2185
B 2066
B 2119
B 2120
B 2121
B 2122
B 2118
A 2010
Old Shoreham Road
Dyke Rd
New England Rd
Viaduct Road
Upper Lewes Rd
London Road
Ditchling Road
Southover St.
Albion Hill
Street
Sussex St.
Carlton Hill
John St.
Edward Street
St. James's St.
Marine Parade
Grand Parade
York Pl.
Trafalgar Street
Buckingham Pl.
Vernon Ter.
Goldsmid Rd
Davigdor Road
Cromwell Road
Eaton Road
The Drive
Norton Rd
Tisbury Road
The Road
Wilbury Road
Selborne Rd
Palmeira Avenue
Lansdowne Road
Montpelier Pl.
Montpelier Road
Western Road
North Road
Church St.
North St.
Queen's Road
Dyke Road
Churchill Sq.
West St.
Preston St.
Holland Road
First Avenue
Second Av.
Grand Avenue
Third Av.
Fourth Av.
Church Road
Kingsway
King's Road
A
B
C
X
Y
Z

XX **Wheeler's,** 17 Market St., BN1 1HH, ☎ 25135, Seafood — CZ s
M a la carte 4.35/11.00 **t.** 1.10.

XX **Bannister's,** 77 St. George's Rd, Kemptown ☎ 687382 — CV e
closed Sunday, Monday and Bank Holidays – **M** (dinner only) a la carte 5.65/9.75 1.50.

X **Dolce Vito,** 106 a Western Rd, BN1 2AA, ☎ 737200, Italian rest. — BY u
closed Tuesday – **M** a la carte 4.25/6.20 **t.** 1.60.

X **Tureen,** 31 Upper North St., BN1 3FG, ☎ 28939, Bistro — BY r
closed Sunday, Monday and Bank Holidays – **M** a la carte 1.90/4.10 **t.** 1.20.

X Foggs, 5 Little Western St. ☎ 735907. — BY a

at Hove – ✉ Hove – ☎ 0273 Brighton:

Dudley (T.H.F.), Lansdowne Pl., BN3 1HQ, ☎ 736266, Telex 87537 – TV P. — AY o
M 4.00/4.40 **st.** 1.50 – 2.00 – **78 rm** 14.00/22.00 **st.** – P 17.50/21.00 **st.**

New Courtlands, 19-27 The Drive, BN3 3JE, ☎ 731055, Telex 87323, – TV P — AY c
M 4.25/4.50 **t.** 2.10 – **62 rm** 9.50/24.00 **st.** – P 16.00/20.00 **st.**

Sackville (Interchange), 189 Kingsway, BN3 4GU, ☎ 736292, ← – . — AV n
M 4.50/5.00 **st.** 1.00 – **48 rm** 13.00/25.00 **st.** – P 18.00/19.50 **st.**

Sherlock without rest., 28-29 Brunswick Terr., BN3 1HJ, ☎ 70784 – TV wc — AZ a
46 rm.

St. Catherine's Lodge, Kingsway, BN3 2RZ, ☎ 778181, – wc . — AV a
M 4.75/6.25 1.00 – **55 rm** 7.50/16.00.

Langfords, 8-16 Third Av., BN3 2PX, ☎ 738222, – wc . — AY e
M a la carte 3.15/4.30 **st.** 1.65 – **70 rm** 8.65/20.55 **st.** – P 12.95/16.20 **st.**

Imperial, 2-10 First Av., BN3 2GU, ☎ 731121, Telex 87653 – wc P. — AY s
M approx. 2.95 **s.** 1.60 – 1.00 – **76 rm** 6.75/12.00 **s.**

Albany, St. Catherine's Terr., ☎ 773807 – TV — AV c
9 rm 4.25/12.00 **st.**

XXX **Eaton,** 13 Eaton Gdns, BN3 3PJ, ☎ 738921 — AX a
closed Sunday dinner, Good Friday and Christmas Day – **M** a la carte 5.20/7.00 **t.** 3.25.

X **Lawrence,** 40 Waterloo St., BN3 1AY, ☎ 772922 — BY c
closed Sunday and 26 December – **M** (dinner only) a la carte 3.90/4.35 **t.** 1.00.

X **Vogue,** 57 Holland Rd, BN2 1JE, ☎ 775066, French rest. — AY n
closed Sunday, Monday, 2 weeks March and 3 weeks September – **M** a la carte 4.00/6.45 1.50.

MICHELIN Branch, English Close, Old Shoreham Rd, Hove, BN3 7EE, ☎ 778792.

ALFA ROMEO, BMW North Rd ☎ 684921
AUSTIN-MG-WOLSELEY 1a Lewes Rd ☎ 64131
AUSTIN-MG 154 Old Shoreham Rd at Hove ☎ 26264
CHRYSLER-SIMCA 270/272 Old Shoreham Rd ☎ 737555
DAF, MAZDA 42/43 George St. ☎ 681766
DAIMLER-JAGUAR-ROVER-TRIUMPH, JENSEN, ROLLS ROYCE Russell Sq. ☎ 21222
DATSUN 21/29 Preston Rd ☎ 685985
FIAT 24 Bedford Pl. ☎ 731118
FIAT Edward St. ☎ 63322
FORD 90/96 Preston Rd ☎ 506331
MERCEDES-BENZ Victoria Rd ☎ 414911
MORRIS-MG 117 Holland Rd at Hove ☎ 778421
MORRIS-MG-WOLSELEY 100 Lewes Rd ☎ 63244
MORRIS-MG-WOLSELEY 233 Preston Rd ☎ 553021
MORRIS-MG-WOLSELEY Longridge Av., Saltdean ☎ 31061
OPEL 100 Old Shoreham Rd ☎ 416242
PEUGEOT 7 Church Pl. ☎ 684022
PEUGEOT, TOYOTA Woodingdean ☎ 37777
RENAULT Stephenson Rd ☎ 692111
SAAB 10 Medina Pl. ☎ 71707
VW, AUDI-NSU, PEUGEOT 62/66 Station Rd, Portslade ☎ 413833

Do not mix up :

Comfort of hotels : ... , ,
Comfort of restaurants : XXXXX X
Quality of the cuisine : ✿✿✿, ✿✿, ✿, **M**

BRIMSCOMBE Glos. – see Stroud.

BRISTOL Avon 986 ㉟ – pop. 426,657 – ☎ 0272.

See: St. Mary Redcliffe Church** 13C-15C DZ **B** – Cathedral* (the Chapter House** 12C) DZ **A** – Bristol Museum and Art Gallery* CZ **M** – Bristol Zoo* *AC* AY – Clifton Suspension Bridge ≤* AY.

Envir. : Cheddar (Cheddar Gorge*** and Gough's Caves** *AC*) SW: 20 ½ m. by A 38 AY.

18 Long Ashton ☎ 027 580 (Long Ashton) 2229, S: 3 m. by A 370 AY.

Lulsgate Airport: ☎ 027 587 (Lulsgate) 4441/7, SW: 7 m. by A 38 AY. **Terminal:** Marlborough Street Bus Station.

to Newcastle ☎ 291001 ext 364.

i Colston House, Colston St. ☎ 293891.

London 125 – Birmingham 84.

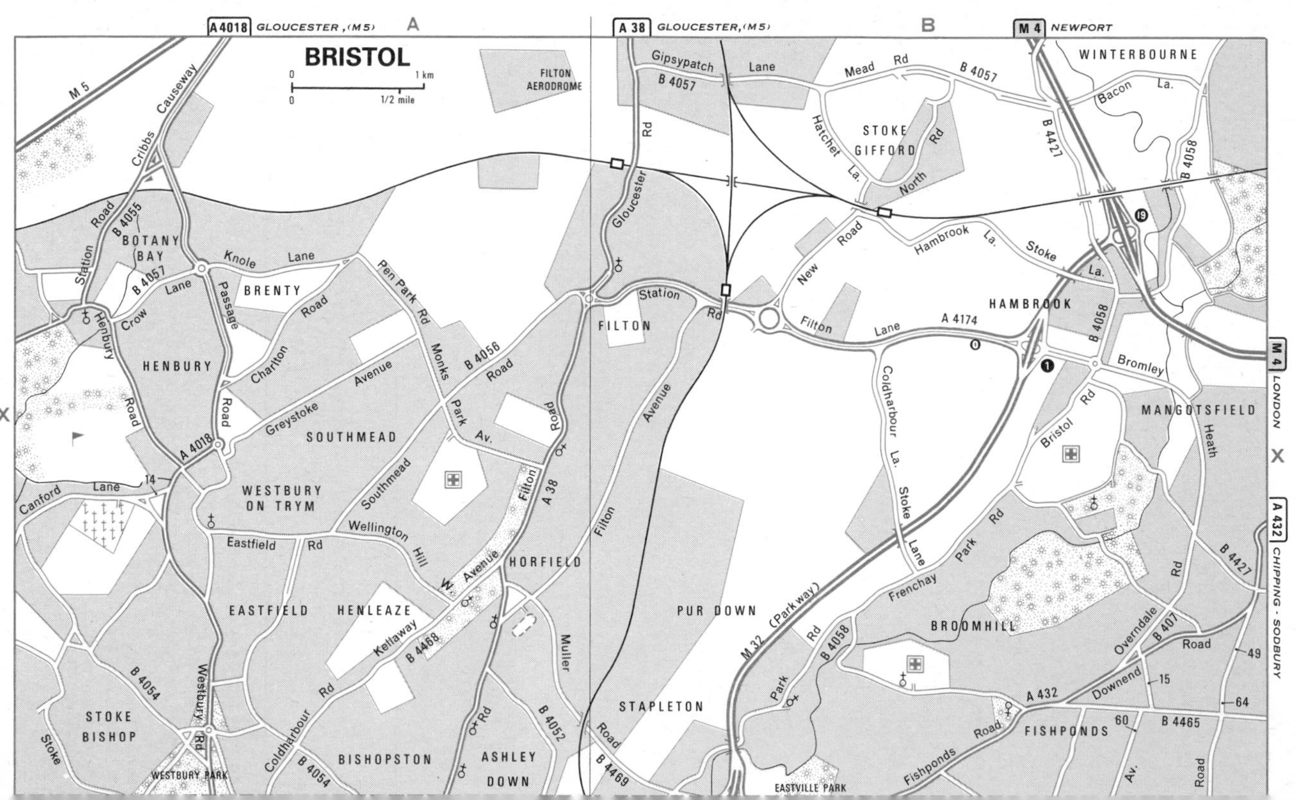

A 4018 GLOUCESTER, (M5)
A
A 38 GLOUCESTER, (M5)
B
M 4 NEWPORT
M 4 LONDON
A 432 CHIPPING - SODBURY
BRISTOL
0 1 km
0 1/2 mile
M 5
Cribbs Causeway
FILTON AERODROME
Gipsypatch Lane
B 4057
Mead Rd
WINTERBOURNE
Bacon La.
STOKE GIFFORD
Hatchet La.
North Rd
B 4427
B 4058
Gloucester Rd
Station Road
B 4055
BOTANY BAY
B 4057
Knole Lane
BRENTY
Passage Road
Pen Park Rd
Crow Lane
Henbury Road
HENBURY
Charlton Road
Greystoke Avenue
Monks Park Av.
B 4056 Road
SOUTHMEAD
A 4018
Canford Lane
14
WESTBURY ON TRYM
Southmead
Wellington Hill W.
Eastfield Rd
Filton
A 38
Road
FILTON
Station Rd
Filton Avenue
New Road
Hambrook La.
Stoke La.
HAMBROOK
Filton Lane
A 4174
Coldharbour La.
Stoke Lane
Bromley
MANGOTSFIELD
Heath
Bristol Rd
Frenchay Park Rd
HORFIELD
Avenue
EASTFIELD
HENLEAZE
Kellaway
B 4468
Muller
PUR DOWN
M 32 (Parkway)
B 4058
Park Rd
BROOMHILL
Overndale Road
B 407
B 4427
Rd
49
Downend
15
A 432
64
B 4465
60
FISHPONDS
Fishponds Road
Av.
Road
STAPLETON
Road
B 4469
B 4052
ASHLEY DOWN
Rd
BISHOPSTON
B 4054
Coldharbour Rd
Westbury Rd
B 4054
STOKE BISHOP
Stoke
WESTBURY PARK
EASTVILLE PARK

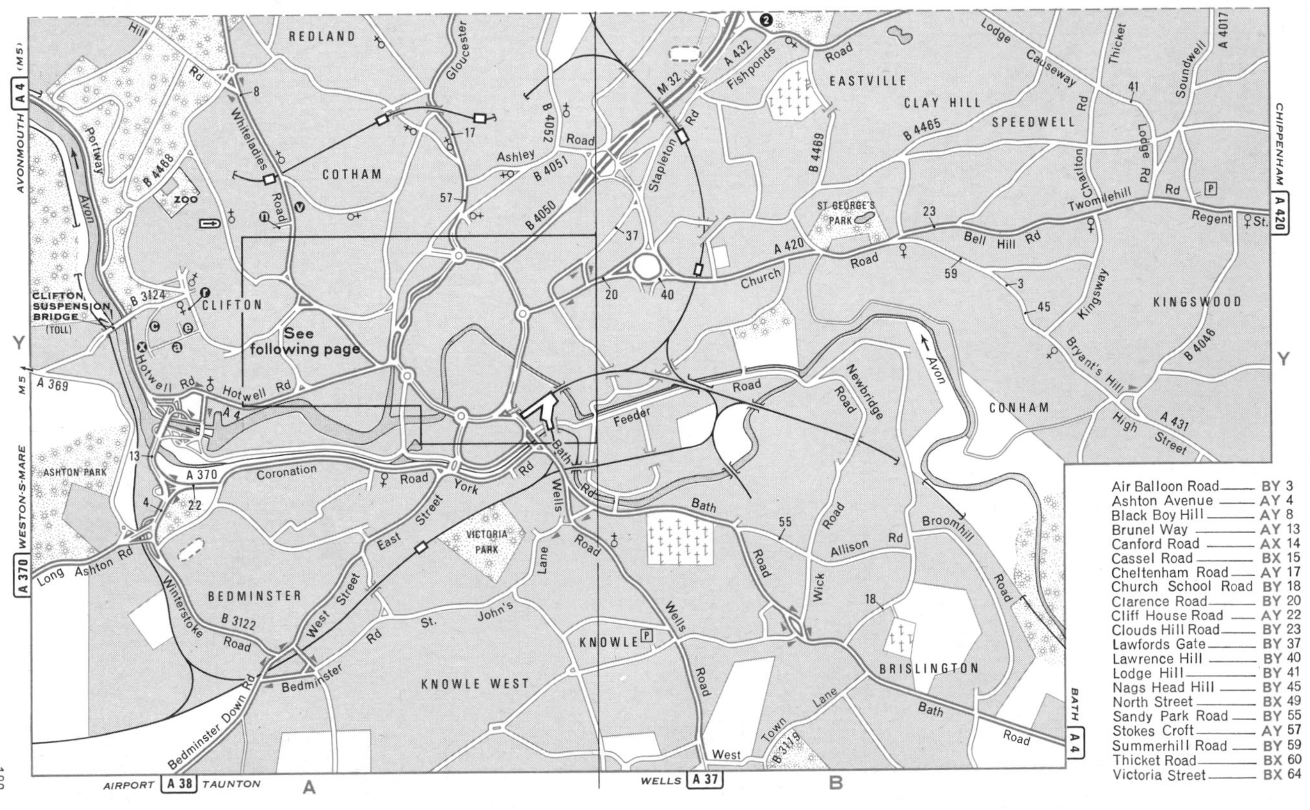
CHIPPENHAM A 420
AVONMOUTH A 4 (M5)
M5
A 369
WESTON-S-MARE A 370
AIRPORT A 38 TAUNTON
WELLS A 37
BATH A 4
Y
A
B
REDLAND
COTHAM
CLIFTON
EASTVILLE
CLAY HILL
SPEEDWELL
KINGSWOOD
CONHAM
ST GEORGE'S PARK
VICTORIA PARK
ASHTON PARK
BEDMINSTER
KNOWLE
KNOWLE WEST
BRISLINGTON
ZOO
CLIFTON SUSPENSION BRIDGE (TOLL)
See following page
Avon
Portway
Hotwell Rd
Whiteladies Road
Gloucester Road
Ashley Road
Stapleton Rd
Fishponds Road
Lodge Causeway
Lodge Rd
Thicket
Soundwell
Twomilehill Rd
Charlton
Regent St.
Bell Hill Rd
Church Road
Kingsway
Bryant's Hill
High Street
Newbridge Road
Feeder Road
Bath Rd
Wells Road
Broomhill Road
Allison Rd
Wick Road
Town Lane
West Town Lane
York Rd
Coronation Road
East Street
West Street
St. John's Rd
Long Ashton Rd
Winterstoke Road
Bedminster Down Rd
Bedminster
Lane
M 32
A 432
A 420
A 4
A 370
A 431
A 4017
B 4468
B 3124
B 4052
B 4051
B 4050
B 4469
B 4465
B 4046
B 3122
B 3119
Air Balloon Road — BY 3
Ashton Avenue — AY 4
Black Boy Hill — AY 8
Brunel Way — AY 13
Canford Road — AX 14
Cassel Road — BX 15
Cheltenham Road — AY 17
Church School Road — BY 18
Clarence Road — BY 20
Cliff House Road — AY 22
Clouds Hill Road — BY 23
Lawfords Gate — BY 37
Lawrence Hill — BY 40
Lodge Hill — BY 41
Nags Head Hill — BY 45
North Street — BX 49
Sandy Park Road — BY 55
Stokes Croft — AY 57
Summerhill Road — BY 59
Thicket Road — BX 60
Victoria Street — BX 64

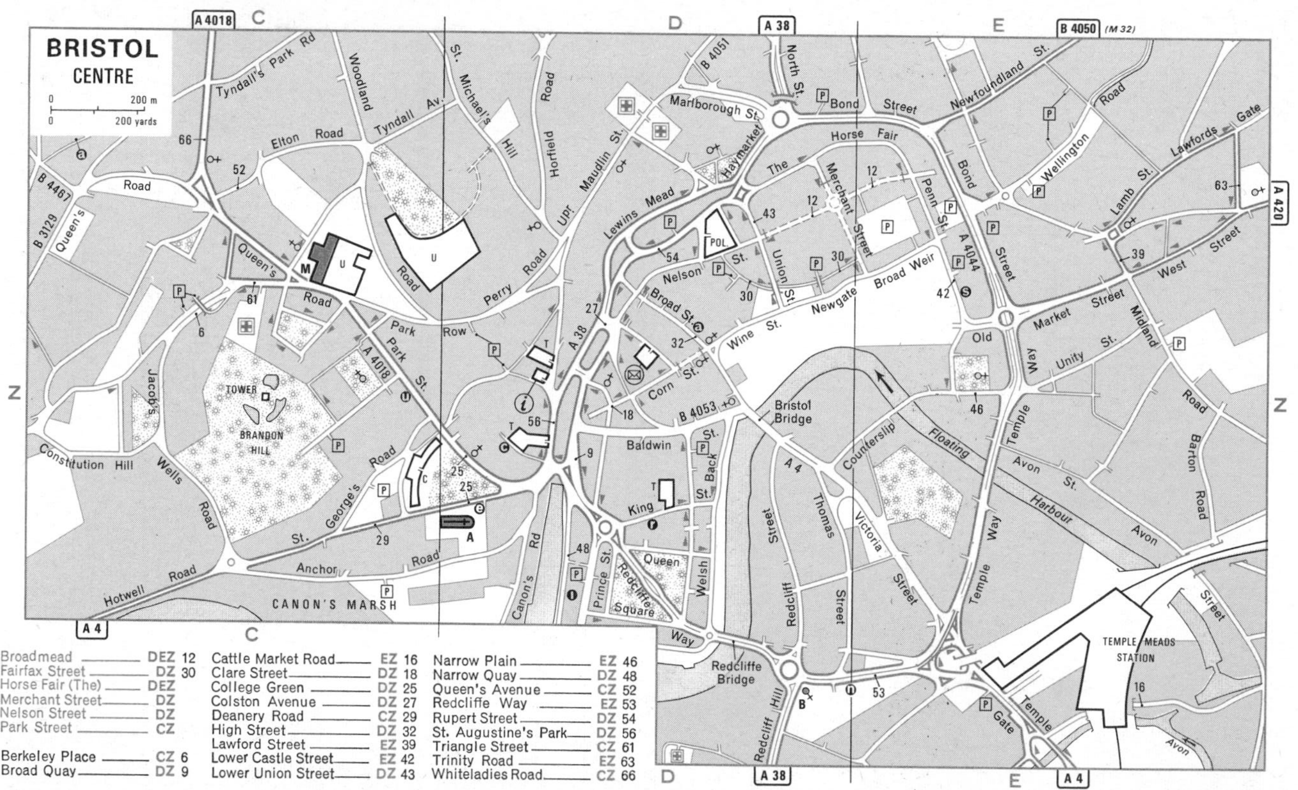

Street	Grid	No.
Broadmead	DEZ	12
Fairfax Street	DZ	30
Horse Fair (The)	DEZ	
Merchant Street	DZ	
Nelson Street	DZ	
Park Street	CZ	
Berkeley Place	CZ	6
Broad Quay	DZ	9
Cattle Market Road	EZ	16
Clare Street	DZ	18
College Green	DZ	25
Colston Avenue	DZ	27
Deanery Road	CZ	29
High Street	DZ	32
Lawford Street	EZ	39
Lower Castle Street	EZ	42
Lower Union Street	DZ	43
Narrow Plain	EZ	46
Narrow Quay	DZ	48
Queen's Avenue	CZ	52
Redcliffe Way	EZ	53
Rupert Street	DZ	54
St. Augustine's Park	DZ	56
Triangle Street	CZ	61
Trinity Road	EZ	63
Whiteladies Road	CZ	66

Holiday Inn, Lower Castle St., Old Market, BS1 3AD, ☎ 294281, Telex 449720, – ■ ■ ♿ ℗. EZ s
M a la carte 3.10/5.85 ♢ 2.00 – ☕ 2.00 – **299 rm** 13.50/17.50.

Dragonara, Redcliffe Way, BS1 6NJ, ☎ 20044, Telex 449240 – ■ ■ ℗. DEZ n
M a la carte 4.15/6.30 – ☕ 2.00 – **210 rm** 16.75/22.00 **s.**

Unicorn (Rank), Prince St., BS1 4QF, ☎ 294811, Telex 44315 – ■ ■ ℗. DZ i
M a la carte 4.60/7.50 **s.** ♢ 1.50 – ☕ 1.95 – **196 rm** 12.10/18.00 **s.**

Grand (Interchange), Broad St., BS1 2EL, ☎ 291645 – ■ ■ . DZ a
180 rm.

St. Vincent's Rocks (Anchor), Sion Hill, Clifton, BS8 4BB, ☎ 39251, Group Telex 27120 – ■ wc ☎ ℗ AY c
M approx. 3.25 **t.** ♢ 1.00 – **47 rm** ☕ 9.75/18.70 **st.**

Avon Gorge (Mt. Charlotte), Sion Hill, Clifton, BS8 4LD, ☎ 38955, ← – ■ ■ wc wc ☎. AY x
M *(closed 26 December)* a la carte 3.00/5.00 – **60 rm** ☕ 12.50/16.50 **s.**

Royal (Norfolk Cap.), College Green, BS1 5TH, ☎ 23591, Group Telex 23241 – ■ wc ☎. DZ e
M a la carte 3.55/6.15 **st.** – **130 rm** ☕ 9.95/17.50 **st.**

Rodney, Clifton Down Rd, Clifton, BS8 4HY, ☎ 35422, AY r
30 rm ☕ 4.50/7.50 **t.**

Oakfield, 52-54 Oakfield Rd, Clifton, BS8 2BG, ☎ 35556 – ℗ AY n
27 rm ☕ 3.75/6.00.

Pembroke, 13 Arlington Villas, Clifton, BS8 1EG, ☎ 35550 CZ a
13 rm ☕ 4.10/8.00 **s.**

XXX **Harvey's,** 12 Denmark St., BS1 5DQ, ☎ 27665 DZ c
closed Saturday lunch, Sunday and Bank Holidays – **M** a la carte approx. 6.70 **t.**

XX **Rajdoot,** 83 Park St., BS1 5PJ, ☎ 28033, Indian rest. CZ u
closed Sunday lunch, Bank Holiday lunches and 25-26 December – **M** a la carte approx. 3.50 **t.**

XX **Du Gourmet,** 43 Whiteladies Rd, BS8 2LS, ☎ 36230 AY v
closed Sunday, Monday and Christmas – **M** (dinner only) a la carte 3.25/5.40 ♢ 1.45.

XX **Rossi's,** 35 Princess Victoria St., Clifton, BS8 4BX, ☎ 30049, Italian rest. AY a
closed Sunday – **M** a la carte 3.90/5.10 **t.** ♢ 1.30.

X **Trattoria da Renato,** 19 King St., BS1 4EF, ☎ 298291, Italian rest. DZ r
closed Saturday lunch, Sunday and Bank Holidays – **M** a la carte 2.70/5.20 **t.** ♢ 1.20.

X **Rossi's Nº 10,** 10 The Mall, Clifton, BS8 4DR, ☎ 36273, Italian rest. AY e
closed Sunday, Monday and Bank Holidays – **M** a la carte 3.05/3.75 **t.** ♢ 1.50.

at Hambrook **NE : 5 ½ m. on A 4174 by M 32 – ✉ ☎ 0272 Bristol :**

Bristol Eurocrest (Crest), Filton Rd, BS16 1QG, ☎ 564242, Telex 449376, , park – ■ ■ wc ☎ ♿ ℗. BX o
M 3.75/5.50 **s.** ♢ 1.60 – ☕ 1.80 – **156 rm** 12.60/16.10 **s.**

MICHELIN Branch, Central Trading Estate, 275-277 Bath Rd, Arnos Vale, BS4 3EF, ☎ 773681 (5 lines).

ALFA-ROMEO 54/56 Redcliffe St. ☎ 27166
AUDI-NSU, MERCEDES-BENZ 20 Whitehouse St. ☎ 669331
AUSTIN-MG-WOLSELEY 36-56 West St. ☎ 662261
AUSTIN-MG-WOLSELEY 74-80 Staple Hill Rd ☎ 654776
AUSTIN-MG-ROVER-TRIUMPH-WOLSELEY Station Rd, Kingswood ☎ 569911
AUSTIN-MG-WOLSELEY Feeder Rd ☎ 48051
AUSTIN-DAIMLER-JAGUAR-MORRIS-MG-ROVER-TRIUMPH, ROLLS ROYCE 11/15 Merchants Rd, Clifton ☎ 30361
AUSTIN-DAIMLER-JAGUAR-MORRIS-MG-ROVER-TRIUMPH-WOLSELEY 156 Cheltenham Rd ☎ 48051
BMW 33 Zetland Rd ☎ 45561
BMW, PEUGEOT Gloucester Rd North ☎ 692234
CHRYSLER 176-178 Kellaway Av. ☎ 49068
CHRYSLER-SIMCA 84 Downend Rd ☎ 567088
CITROEN 20 Whitehouse St. ☎ 669331
CITROEN, FIAT 724 Fishponds Rd ☎ 657247
DAIMLER-JAGUAR-MORRIS-MG-ROVER-TRIUMPH Avon St. ☎ 26531
DATSUN 168/176 Coronation Rd ☎ 631101
FORD 175/185 Muller Rd, Horfield ☎ 41175
FORD College Green ☎ 293881
LANCIA 47 Whiteladies Rd ☎ 37199
MORRIS-MG-WOLSELEY 280 Gloucester Rd ☎ 46283
MORRIS-MG-WOLSELEY Church Rd ☎ 556381
MORRIS-MG-WOLSELEY 135 High St. ☎ 670011
MORRIS-MG-WOLSELEY Vale Lane ☎ 665070
OPEL Westbury Rd, Westbury-on-Trym ☎ 626172
PEUGEOT 33 Zetland Rd ☎ 45561
RENAULT Marlborough St. ☎ 421816
ROVER-TRIUMPH 676 Fishponds Rd ☎ 655439
SAAB Redcliffe St. ☎ 27166
TOYOTA Gloucester Rd Patchway ☎ 693704
VAUXHALL Avon St. ☎ 70411
VAUXHALL Gloucester Rd ☎ 694331
VOLVO Berkeley Pl. ☎ 294191
VW, AUDI-NSU 55 Victoria St. ☎ 292956

BRIXHAM Devon 986 ㊴ – pop. 11,900 – ☎ 080 45.

i Brixham Theatre, Market St. ☎ 2861 (summer only).

London 230 – Exeter 30 – **Plymouth 32** – Torquay 8.

Quayside, 41-49 King St., TQ5 9TJ, ☎ 3051, ← harbour – ■ wc ℗
closed December – **M** (bar lunch) approx. 3.50 ♢ 1.30 – **31 rm** ☕ 7.00/21.00.

Smuggler's Haunt, Church Hill East, TQ5 8HH, ☎ 3050 – wc
M approx. 2.85 **t.** ♢ 0.95 – **14 rm** ☕ 6.50/13.00.

Beverley Court, Upton Manor Rd, TQ5 9RG, ☎ 3149 – ℗
May-October – **11 rm** ☕ 7.75/10.00 **t.**

XX ⚘ **Randalls,** 3 The Strand, TQ5 8EH, ☎ 3357, French rest.
closed Monday, 2 weeks June and 2 weeks October – **M** (dinner only) a la carte 4.75/5.95 **s.** 🍾 1.50
Spec. Délice de St. Emilion, Coquilles St-Jacques à la bretonne, Carré d'agneau au vinaigre.

at Churston Ferrers **W: 2 m. off A 3022 – ✉ Brixham – ☎ 0803 Churston:**

Broadsands Links ⛬, Bascombe Rd, TQ5 0JT, ☎ 842360, ≤, ⚘, 🅿 – wc ☎ **P**
M 3.80/3.95 **s.** 🍾 1.50 – **25 rm** 12.50/24.00 – P 17.00/18.80.

Churston Court, ☎ 842186, – wc **P**
M (dinner only and Sunday lunch) 4.00/4.50 **t.** 🍾 1.40 – **8 rm** 8.00/17.00.

AUSTIN-MG Churston Ferrers ☎ 080 44 (Churston) 2245
MORRIS-MG-WOLSELEY Bolton Cross ☎ 2110
RENAULT New Rd ☎ 2266
ROVER-TRIUMPH Milton St. ☎ 2474

BROAD HAVEN **Dyfed – pop. 530 – ✉ Haverfordwest – ☎ 043 783.**
i Pembrokeshire Coast National Park Countryside Unit, Car Park ☎ 412 (Easter-September).
London 257 – Haverfordwest 7.

Rosehill Country ⛬, Portfield Gate, SA62 3LX, NE: 3 ½ m. off B 341 ☎ 304, – **P**
season – **14 rm.**

BROADSTAIRS **Kent 986 ㊱ – pop. 20,048 (inc. St. Peter's) – ☎ 0843 Thanet.**
See : Bleak House (stayed in by Charles Dickens) *AC.*
Kingsgate ☎ 62140, 1 ½ m. Broadstairs Station.
i Pierremont Hall ☎ 68399 – Victoria Parade ☎ 61118 (summer only).
London 77 – Dover 22 – Maidstone 46 – Margate 3.

Castlemere ⛬, Western Esplanade, CT10 1TD, ☎ 61566, ≤, – wc **P**
M approx. 3.50 **s.** 🍾 2.30 – **40 rm** 9.00/21.10 **s.** – P 11.50/13.05 **s.**

Velindré ⛬, 10 Western Esplanade, CT10 1TG, ☎ 61485, ≤, – **P**
closed October – **M** 3.75/7.00 🍾 1.45 – **15 rm** 9.50/19.00 – P 13.50/16.50.

Royal Albion (T.H.F.), Albion St., CT10 1LU, ☎ 62116, ≤, – TV ☎
M approx. 3.00 **st.** 🍾 1.50 – **23 rm** 6.50/14.00 **st.**

Bay Tree, 12 Eastern Esplanade, CT10 1DR, ☎ 61327, ≤, – **P**
May-September – **7 rm** 5.50/9.00 **s.**

XX **Marchesi,** 18 Albion St., CT10 1LU, ☎ 62481 – **P**
closed 25 and 26 December – **M** a la carte 3.40/5.35 **t.** 🍾 1.60.

at Kingsgate **N: 2 m. on B 2052 – ✉ Broadstairs – ☎ 0843 Thanet:**

Castle Keep, Joss Bay Rd, CT10 3PQ, ☎ 65222, Telex 896570, ≤, heated, – wc ☎ **P**
M 4.00/5.00 🍾 1.00 – **29 rm** 8.50/22.50.

XX **Fayreness** with rm, Marine Drive, off Kingsgate Av., CT10 3LG, ☎ 61103, ≤, – TV wc **P**
M *(closed Monday)* a la carte 3.95/6.45 **t.** 🍾 1.50 – **8 rm** 9.00/15.00 **t.**

XX **Captain Digby,** Kingsgate Bay, CT10 3QL, ☎ 67764, ≤ – **P**
closed Sunday dinner and Monday – **M** a la carte 4.85/8.00 **t.** 🍾 1.50.

CHRYSLER-SIMCA Ramsgate Rd ☎ 63531
DATSUN ☎ 62333

BROADSTONE **Dorset – see Poole.**

BROADWATER **Herts. – see Stevenage.**

BROADWAY **Heref. and Worc. 986 ㉛ – pop. 2,503 – ☎ 038 681.**
London 93 – Birmingham 36 – Cheltenham 15 – Worcester 22.

Lygon Arms, High St., WR12 7DU, ☎ 2255, Telex 338260, « Part 15C inn », ⚘, – TV ♿ **P**.
M a la carte 5.55/8.15 **s.** 🍾 1.85 – 3.00 – **58 rm** 18.10/34.75 **st.**

Broadway, The Green, WR12 7AB, ☎ 2401, « Part 15C house », – wc ☎ **P**
23 rm.

Milestone House, 122 High St., WR12 7AL, ☎ 3432, – **P**
closed Christmas and January – **M** 3.50/4.75 **st.** 🍾 1.15 – **5 rm** 11.50/16.00 **st.** – P 12.00/15.00 **st.**

Halfway House, 89 High St., WR12 7AL, ☎ 2237 – **P**
6 rm 8.00/12.00 **st.**

XX **Hunters Lodge,** High St., WR12 7DT, ☎ 3247 – **P**
closed Sunday and Monday – **M** a la carte 4.90/7.60 **t.** 🍾 1.20.

at Willersey Hill **E: 2½ m. off A 44 – ✉ ☎ 038 681 Broadway:**

XX **Dormy House** (Interchange) ⛬ with rm, WR12 7LF, ☎ 2241, – TV wc wc ☎ **P**
M (bar lunch) a la carte 3.75/8.05 🍾 1.20 – 2.00 – **26 rm** 13.00/30.00 **st.**

MORRIS-MG-WOLSELEY Cheltenham Rd ☎ 2424

BROADWINDSOR Dorset – pop. 1,021 – ✉ Beaminster – ☎ 030 86.
London 148 – Exeter 37 – Taunton 26 – Weymouth 26.

Broadwindsor House ⛰, Beaminster Rd, DT8 3TX, ☎ 353, ≤, garden – ⇔wc Ⓟ
closed February – **M** 2.50/3.85 **s.** 🍶 1.10 – **12 rm** ☕ 4.50/10.00 **s.** – P 7.20/8.20 **s.**

BROCKENHURST Hants. – pop. 2,599 – ☎ 059 02.
18 Sway Rd ☎ 2383.
☎ 0703 (Southampton) 27948.
London 99 – Bournemouth 17 – **Southampton 14** – Winchester 27.

Balmer Lawn (Myddleton) ⛰, Lyndhurst Rd, SO4 7ZB, ☎ 3116, ≤, tennis, pool heated, garden – lift TV Ⓟ.
closed 29 December-10 January – **M** approx. 4.50 **st.** 🍶 1.15 – **60 rm** ☕ 7.50/23.00 **st.**

Carey's Manor, Lyndhurst Rd, SO4 7RH, ☎ 3551, garden – TV ⇔wc ☎ ♿ Ⓟ
M 4.45/5.45 🍶 1.45 – **49 rm** ☕ 12.25/21.75.

Forest Park, Rhinefield Rd, SO4 7ZG, ☎ 2095, ≤, tennis, pool heated, garden – TV ⇔wc ☎ ♿ Ⓟ
M a la carte 3.05/8.55 **t.** 🍶 1.45 – ☕ 1.00 – **40 rm** 9.75/21.00 **t.** – P 15.80/17.05 **t.**

Brockenhurst ⛰, Rhinefield Rd, SO4 7ZF, ☎ 2557, garden – ⇔wc ☎ Ⓟ
March-November and Christmas – **M** approx. 4.50 **t.** 🍶 1.70 – **13 rm** ☕ 9.50/22.00 **t.** – P 17.50/19.00 **t.**

Watersplash, The Rise, SO4 7ZP, ☎ 2344, pool heated, garden – ⇔wc ♿ Ⓟ
M 3.00/4.00 **st.** 🍶 1.50 – **27 rm** ☕ 8.00/18.00 **st.** – P 12.00/14.00 **st.**

AUSTIN-MORRIS-MG-WOLSELEY Sway Rd ☎ 3344
SAAB 24 Brookley Rd ☎ 3464

BROME Suffolk – see Eye.

BROMLEY CROSS Greater Manchester – see Bolton.

☞ *Michelin puts no plaque or sign*
on the hotels and restaurants mentioned in this Guide.

BROMPTON-BY-SAWDON North Yorks. – pop. 572 – ✉ Scarborough – ☎ 072 385.
London 242 – **Kingston-upon-Hull 44** – Scarborough 8 – York 31.

✕ Brompton Forge, ☎ 409 – Ⓟ.

BROMSGROVE Heref. and Worc. 986 ⑫ and ㉛ – pop. 40,683 – ☎ 0527.
ℹ 47/49 Worcester Rd ☎ 31809.
London 117 – **Birmingham 14** – **Bristol 71** – Worcester 13.

Perry Hall (Embassy), 8 Kidderminster Rd, B61 7JN, ☎ 31976 – TV ⇔wc shower wc ☎ Ⓟ.
closed Christmas – **M** approx. 3.40 🍶 1.05 – **50 rm** ☕ 10.00/14.75 **st.**

AUSTIN-MG-WOLSELEY 52 Birmingham Rd ☎ 72212
FORD 184/188 Worcester Rd ☎ 31178
MORRIS-MG-WOLSELEY 126 Worcester Rd ☎ 31313
SAAB Windsor St. ☎ 75210
VAUXHALL 137 Birmingham Rd ☎ 71244
VW, AUDI-NSU 12 Station St. ☎ 72071

BROOK Hants. – pop. 572 – ✉ Lyndhurst – ☎ 042 127 Cadnam.
London 81 – Bournemouth 33 – **Southampton 13.**

Bell, SO4 7HE, ☎ 2214, 18, garden – ⇔wc Ⓟ
M approx. 3.50 🍶 1.15 – **11 rm** ☕ 8.00/16.00.

BROXTON Cheshire – see Chester.

BRUSHFORD Somerset – pop. 457 – ✉ ☎ 0398 Dulverton.
London 195 – Exeter 24 – Minehead 18 – Taunton 24.

Carnarvon Arms, TA22 9AE, ☎ 23302, tennis, pool heated, fishing, garden, park – ⇔wc Ⓟ
closed 3 days at Christmas – **M** approx. 4.20 **t.** 🍶 1.00 – **29 rm** ☕ 6.50/15.00 **t.** – P 13.00 **t.**

Three Acres Country House ⛰, TA22 9AR, ☎ 23426, ≤, « Country house atmosphere », garden – Ⓟ
April-October – **M** approx.3.50 🍶 1.00 – **7 rm** ☕ 7.50/15.50 – P 10.00.

BUCKDEN Cambs. 986 ㉜ – pop. 2,010 – ✉ ☎ 0480 Huntingdon.
London 65 – Bedford 16 – Huntingdon 4 5.

Lion (T.H.F.), High St., PE18 9XA, ☎ 810313 – TV ☎ Ⓟ
M a la carte 4.25/5.00 **st.** 🍶 1.50 – **11 rm** ☕ 8.00/13.00 **st.**

George, High St., PE18 9XA, ☎ 810304, garden – Ⓟ
M *(closed Sunday dinner and Monday lunch)* a la carte 2.40/4.70 **t.** 🍶 1.50 – **12 rm** ☕ 6.75/15.00.

BUCKFASTLEIGH Devon – pop. 2,656 – ✆ 036 44.
London 223 – Exeter 23 – Plymouth 20.

- Furzeleigh Mill, Dart Bridge, TQ11 0JP, NE: ¾ m. on old A 38 ☎ 2245, ⛱ – 🅿
  closed 2 weeks Christmas and New Year – **16 rm.**
- **Country Fare,** 54 Fore St., TQ11 0BS, ☎ 2383
  closed Sunday dinner and Monday in winter – **M** a la carte 2.70/5.05 **t.** 🌡 1.40.

MORRIS-MG-WOLSELEY Station Rd ☎ 2303

BUCKHURST HILL Essex 986 ④ – pop. 11,683 – ✆ 01 London.
London 13 – Chelmsford 25.

- **Roebuck** (T.H.F.), IG9 1QX, ☎ 505 4636 – 📺 🛁wc ☎ 🅿.
  M a la carte 4.05/5.50 **st.** 🌡 1.50 – **27 rm** ☕ 10.50/17.50 **st.**

BUCKINGHAM Bucks. 986 ㉜ – pop. 5,075 – ✆ 028 02.
Envir. : Claydon House* (Rococo interior** : Chinese Room** staircase***, Florence Nightingale Museum) *AC*, SE : 8 m. – Stowe School 18C (south front*, Marble Saloon*, park : monuments* 18C, ≤* from the Lake Pavilions) *AC*, NW : 4 ½ m.
London 64 – Birmingham 61 – Northampton 20 – Oxford 25.

- **White Hart** (T.H.F.), Market Sq., MK18 1NL, ☎ 2131 – 📺 🛁wc ☎ 🅿.
  M a la carte 3.95/5.35 **st.** 🌡 1.50 – **21 rm** ☕ 8.50/15.00 **st.**
- **Swan and Castle,** Castle St., MK18 1BS, ☎ 3082 – 🚗 🅿
  M *(closed Sunday, Christmas and Bank Holidays)* a la carte 2.35/4.30 **t.** 🌡 1.20 – **7 rm** ☕ 6.50/11.50 **st.**

AUSTIN-MG-WOLSELEY 14/18 High St. ☎ 3153
AUSTIN-MORRIS-MG-ROVER-TRIUMPH-WOLSELEY Chandos Rd ☎ 2121
VAUXHALL School Lane ☎ 2209

BUCKLAND IN THE MOOR Devon – pop. 79 – ✆ 0364 Ashburton.
London 225 – Exeter 25 – Plymouth 28.

- **Buckland Hall** 🐎, TQ13 7HL, ☎ 52679, ≤ countryside and Holne Moor, ⛱, park – 🛁wc 🅿
  March-October – **M** 4.00/5.00 **st.** 🌡 1.00 – **6 rm** ☕ 11.00/18.00 **s.** – P 15.00/17.00 **s.**

BUCKLERS HARD Hants. – see Beaulieu.

BUCKLOW HILL Cheshire – see Knutsford.

BUDE Cornwall 986 ㉞ – pop. 4,069 – ✆ 0288.
18 ☎ 2006.
i The Castle ☎ 3111.
London 252 – Exeter 51 – Plymouth 44 – Truro 53.

- **Strand,** The Strand, EX23 8BB, ☎ 3222 – 🛗 📺 🛁wc ☎ 🅿
  M 3.00/6.00 **t.** 🌡 1.50 – ☕ 1.00 – **40 rm** 9.00/14.00.
- **Falcon,** EX23 8SD, ☎ 2005, ⛱ – 🛁wc 🚿wc 🅿
  3 May-6 October – **M** approx. 4.25 **s.** 🌡 1.30 – ☕ 2.55 – **47 rm** 9.00/21.30 **s.**
- **Burn Court,** Burn View, EX23 8DB, ☎ 2872 – 🛁wc 🚿wc
  M approx. 3.00 🌡 1.50 – **34 rm** ☕ 6.50/15.00.
- **Maer Lodge,** Maer Down, Crooklets, EX23 8NG, ☎ 3306, ⛱ – 🛁wc 🚿 🅿
  Easter-October – **M** (bar lunch) approx. 3.00 **st.** 🌡 1.50 – **24 rm** ☕ 7.00/16.00 **st.**
- **Florida,** 17-18 Summerleaze Crescent, EX23 8HJ, ☎ 2451 – 🚿wc 🅿
  April-October – **21 rm** ☕ 5.00/12.00.
- **Atlantic Beach,** 25 Downs View, EX23 8RG, ☎ 3431 – 🚿
  April-October – **8 rm** ☕ 4.00/8.00 **s.**

at Marhamchurch SE: 2 m. by A 3072 off A 39 – ✉ Bude – ✆ 028 885 Widemouth Bay:

- **Bullers Arms** with rm, EX23 0HB, ☎ 277 – 🛁wc 🚿 🅿
  closed 20 December-10 January – **M** *(closed Sunday dinner from November to March)* (buffet lunch except Sunday) a la carte 3.90/5.75 **t.** 🌡 1.30 – **12 rm** ☕ 5.20/15.90 **st.** – P 9.50/14.50 **t.**

AUSTIN-MORRIS-MG-ROVER-TRIUMPH-WOLSELEY Bencoolen Rd ☎ 2146
DAF Widemouth Bay ☎ 028 885 (Widemouth Bay) 279

BUDLEIGH SALTERTON Devon 986 ㊴ – pop. 4,157 – ✆ 039 54.
Envir. : Bicton Gardens* *AC*, N: 3 ½ m.
i 3 Fore St. ☎ 2311 (summer only).
London 215 – Exeter 16 – Plymouth 55.

- Rosemullion 🐎, Cliff Rd, EX9 6JX, ☎ 2288, ≤ – 🛗 🛁wc ☎ 🅿 – **38 rm.**
- **Southlands,** 9 Marine Par., EX9 6NS, ☎ 3497, ≤ – 🛁wc 🅿
  M 3.00/3.30 🌡 1.50 – **17 rm** ☕ 7.25/15.50 – P 9.50/10.50.

AUSTIN-MG-WOLSELEY ☎ 2277

BUDOCK VEAN Cornwall – see Falmouth.

BULKINGTON Warw. – see Nuneaton.

BULPHAN Essex – ✉ Upminster – ☎ 0375 Grays Thurrock.
London 26 – Chelmsford 17.

Ye Olde Plough House Motel, Brentwood Rd, RM14 3SR, ☎ 891592, ⚔, heated, – wc wc P
M a la carte 4.00/6.80 – 1.80 – **54 rm** 9.00/14.00 **st.**

BUNWELL Norfolk – pop. 738 – ☎ 095 389.
London 102 – Cambridge 51 – Norwich 16.

Bunwell Manor, Bunwell St., NR16 1QU, NW: 1 m. off B 1113 ☎ 317, – wc P
closed Christmas Day – **M** (dinner only) approx. 3.50 **st.** 1.45 – **14 rm** 8.00/18.00 **st.**

BURBAGE Wilts. – see Marlborough.

BURFORD Oxon. 986 ㉛ – pop. 1,255 (inc. Upton and Signet) – ☎ 099 382.
See : St. John's Church* 12C-14C. **Envir. :** Swinbrook (church: Fettiplace Monuments*) E: 3 ½ m. – Cotswold Wildlife Park* *AC*, S : 2 m.
18 ☎ 2149.
London 76 – Birmingham 55 – Gloucester 32 – Oxford 20.

Bay Tree, Sheep St., OX8 4LW, ☎ 3137, – wc P
M approx. 3.85 **t.** 1.70 – **24 rm** 7.70/17.60 **st.** – P 11.25/14.00 **st.**

Inn For All Seasons, Great Barrington, OX8 4TN, W: 3 ¼ m. on A 40 ☎ 045 14 (Windrush) 324, – wc P
closed Christmas – **M** (buttery only to non-residents) a la carte 2.40/3.90 **t.** 1.75 – **8 rm** 8.50/17.00 **st.**

Bull, High St., OX8 4RH, ☎ 2220 – wc
M *(closed Sunday dinner to non-residents and Saturday lunch)* 3.50/4.00 **st.** – 2.00 – **11 rm** 5.50/11.00 **st.**

Lamb Inn, Sheep St., OX8 4LR, ☎ 3155, – wc
M approx. 3.50 **t.** 1.25 – **14 rm** 7.00/16.00 **st.** – P 10.00/11.00 **st.**

Corner House, High St., OX8 4RJ, ☎ 3151
closed January – **M** *(closed Sunday lunch)* a la carte 3.00/4.20 **st.** 0.80 – **10 rm** 5.25/13.00 **st.**

BURGH HEATH Surrey – pop. 2,984 – ✉ Tadworth – ☎ 073 73.
London 20 – Brighton 37.

Pickard Motor (Interchange), Brighton Rd on A 217, KT20 6BW, ☎ 57222, Telex 929908 – TV wc P
M (grill rest. only) a la carte approx. 2.25 **t.** 1.30 – 1.25 – **32 rm** 11.35/15.65 **t.**

BURGH-LE-MARSH Lincs. – pop. 1,289 – ✉ Skegness – ☎ 075 483 Burgh.
London 147 – Lincoln 37.

Windmill, 46 High St., PE24 5JJ, ☎ 281 – P
M a la carte approx. 5.50 **st.**

BURHAM Kent – pop. 1,843 – ✉ Rochester – ☎ 0634 Medway.
London 35 – Maidstone 5.

Toastmaster's Inn, Church St., ME1 3SD, ☎ 61299 – P
closed Sunday, Monday, first 2 weeks September and 25-26-31 December – **M** a la carte 4.85/6.95 1.65.

BURLEY Hants. – pop. 1,552 – ✉ Ringwood – ☎ 042 53.
9 Ringwood, ☎ 2431.
London 102 – Bournemouth 17 – Southampton 17 – Winchester 30.

Burley Manor, BH24 4BS, ☎ 3314, Telex 47674, heated, – TV wc P.
M 3.75/4.55 **t.** 1.45 – 1.00 – **23 rm** 9.75/21.00 **t.** – P 16.05/19.55 **t.**

Moorhill House, BH24 4AH, ☎ 3285, – wc P
closed January and February – **M** *(closed Christmas Day)* (bar lunch) approx. 4.00 **s.** 1.25 – **22 rm** 8.00/19.00 **s.**

Highcroft, Highcroft Woods, BH24 4AG, ☎ 2525, ⚔, – – P
11 rm 9.00/13.00 **s.**

Tree House, The Cross, BH24 4BA, ☎ 3448, – P
8 rm 8.00/12.00 **st.**

BURLEY IN WHARFEDALE West Yorks. – pop. 4,768 – 094 35.
West Busk Lane 094 34 (Otley) 2081, off Bradford Rd.
London 207 – Bradford 10 – Harrogate 14 – **Leeds 13.**

Burley House, Bradford Rd, LS29 7EG, 2811 – TV wc P
M a la carte 3.30/4.85 **t.** 1.25 – 1.25 – **14 rm** 11.50/17.50 **t.**

BURN BRIDGE North Yorks. – see Harrogate.

BURNHAM Bucks. – pop. 17.751 – 062 86.
London 33 – Oxford 37 – Reading 17.

Burnham Beeches, Grove Rd, SL1 8DP, 3333, park – wc P.
M a la carte 5.25/9.40 1.50 – 2.00 – **40 rm** 10.00/18.00.

XX **Grovefield** with rm, Taplow Common Rd , SL1 8LR, 3131, – wc P
M *(closed Sunday dinner and Bank Holidays)* a la carte 4.45/5.95 **t.** – **8 rm** 12.00/ 20.00 **st.**

AUSTIN-MORRIS-MG-WOLSELEY 46/48 High St. 5255
VAUXHALL 71 Stomp Rd 4994

BURNHAM MARKET Norfolk – pop. 970 – King's Lynn – 032 873.
London 121 – King's Lynn 22 – **Norwich 35.**

X **Fishes,** Market Pl., PE31 4EG, 588, Seafood – P
closed Monday except Bank Holidays, Sunday dinner in winter and 25-26 December –
M a la carte 4.10/6.40 **t.** 1.50.

BURNHAM-ON-CROUCH Essex 986 ㊱ – pop. 4,619 – 0621 Maldon.
London 52 – Chelmsford 19 – Colchester 32 – Southend-on-Sea 25.

XX **Contented Sole,** 80 High St., CM0 8AA, 782139
closed Sunday dinner, Monday and mid December-mid January – **M** a la carte 4.25/ 6.15 **s.**

MORRIS-MG-WOLSELEY Station Rd 782130

BURNLEY Lancs. 986 ㉓ – pop. 76,513 – 0282.
Envir. : Towneley Hall* (16C-18C) SE: 1 m.
Towneley Park 38473 E: 1 ½ m. – Glen View 21045.
London 227 – Bradford 32 – **Leeds 37** – **Liverpool 55** – **Manchester 25** – **Middlesbrough 85** – Preston 21 – **Sheffield 67.**

Burnley Crest (Crest), Keirby Walk, BB11 2DH, 27611 – TV wc P.
M 2.50/3.50 **s.** 1.55 – 1.60 – **48 rm** 10.95/15.50 **s.**

Rosehill House, Rosehill Av., Manchester Rd, BB11 2PW, 27116, – P
M *(closed Sunday and 25-26 December)* 3.75/4.50 **st.** – **11 rm** 7.50/12.50 **st.**

AUSTIN-MG-WOLSELEY Church St. 21312
DAIMLER-JAGUAR-ROVER-TRIUMPH Trafalgar St. 33311
FIAT Padiham Rd 27328
FORD Caldervale Rd 28311
MORRIS Todmorden Rd 22721
SAAB Manchester Rd 26020
VAUXHALL Accrington Rd 27321
VW, AUDI-NSU Accrington Rd 31141

BURNSALL North Yorks. – pop. 109 – Skipton – 075 672.
i Burnsall Car Park 295 (summer only).
London 223 – Bradford 26 – **Leeds 29.**

Red Lion, BD23 6BU, 204, – P
M approx. 3.30 1.10 – **8 rm** 5.25.

BURTON Clywd – see Chester.

BURTON-UPON-TRENT Staffs. 986 ㉗ – pop. 49,480 – 0283.
Envir. : Keddleston Hall** (Renaissance) *AC,* NE: 16 ½ m.
Burton Rd, Branston 43207, SW: ½ m. – 43 Ashby Rd East 44551, E: 3 m.
i Town Hall 45369.
London 128 – **Birmingham 29** – **Leicester 27** – **Nottingham 27** – Stafford 27.

Edgecote, 179 Ashby Rd, DE15 0LB, 68966,
12 rm 5.40/10.80 **st.**

XXX **Riverside Inn** with rm, Riverside Drive, DE14 3EP, S: 2 ¼ m. off A 5121 63117 – TV wc P
M a la carte 4.00/7.75 **st.** – **22 rm** 10.00/14.50 **st.**

XXX **Stanhope Arms** with rm, Ashby Rd East, DE15 0PU, E: 2 ¼ m. on A 50 217954, – wc wc P.
M a la carte 3.60/5.20 **s.** – **19 rm** 7.20/14.00 **s.**

AUDI-NSU, CHRYSLER-SIMCA, TOYOTA Derby Rd 65432
AUSTIN-MORRIS-MG-WOLSELEY Derby Rd 45353
DAF Burton Rd, Branston 2726
DATSUN Scalpcliffe Rd 66677
FIAT All Saints Rd 65994
FORD Horninglow St. 61081
JAGUAR-ROVER-TRIUMPH Moor St. 45353
PEUGEOT Tutbury Rd 61565
RENAULT 118 Horninglow Rd 67811
VAUXHALL 12 Lichfield St. 61655
VOLVO New St. 62282

BURWASH East Sussex – pop. **1,140** – ☎ **0435.**
London 55 – **Brighton 27** – Hastings 19 – Maidstone 27 – Royal Tunbridge Wells 20.

Burwash Motel, High St., TN19 7HT, ☎ 882540, ←, 🌳 – TV ⌂wc ☎ P
M (grill rest. only) 4.00/5.00 **t.** 🍷 1.20 – ☕ 1.25 – **8 rm** 7.50/11.00 **st.**

BURY ST. EDMUNDS Suffolk 986 ㉜ – pop. 25,661 – ☎ 0284.
See : St. Mary's Church★ 15C (the Angel roof★★). **Envir. :** Ickworth House★ (18C) *AC*, SW : 3 m.
18 Westley Rd ☎ 5979, W : 2 m.
i Thingoe House, Northgate St. ☎ 64667 (summer only).
London 79 – Cambridge 27 – Ipswich 26 – Norwich 41.

Angel, 3 Angel Hill, IP33 1LT, ☎ 3926 – TV ⌂wc ☎ P.
M approx. 3.50 🍷 1.00 – **45 rm** ☕ 11.50/20.00.

Suffolk (T.H.F.), 36 The Butter Market, IP33 1DC, ☎ 3995 – ⌂wc ☎ P
M a la carte 5.00/8.65 **st.** 🍷 1.50 – **41 rm** ☕ 9.50/18.50 **s.**

Everards, 2 Cornhill, IP33 1BD, ☎ 5384 – P
M 2.50/2.80 **t.** 🍷 1.85 – **15 rm** ☕ 8.00/15.50 **t.**

Square House, St. Mary's Sq., IP33 2AA, ☎ 5337, 🌳 – P
12 rm.

AUSTIN-DAIMLER-JAGUAR-MG-ROVER-TRIUMPH-WOLSELEY, ROLLS ROYCE 76 Risbygate St. ☎ 3101
DAF, SAAB Barrow ☎ 810411
FIAT Mildenhall Rd ☎ 3280
FORD 5 Fornham Rd ☎ 2332
MORRIS-MG-WOLSELEY Eastgate St. ☎ 3913
RENAULT Bury Rd, Horringer ☎ 028 488 (Horringer) 362
VAUXHALL Cotton Lane ☎ 5621
VOLVO Out Risbygate ☎ 62444
VW, AUDI-NSU Northern Way, Bury St. ☎ 63441

BUSHEY Herts. 986 ④ – see Watford.

BUTTERMERE Cumbria 986 ⑲ – pop. 257 – ✉ Cockermouth – ☎ 059 685.
See : Lake★. **Envir. :** Keswick (Derwent Water★★) NE : 9 ½ m.
London 305 – Carlisle 35 – Kendal 43.

Bridge, CA13 9UZ, ☎ 252, ← – P
April-November – **M** approx. 4.25 **t.** 🍷 1.50 – **24 rm** ☕ 9.00/17.50 **t.**

Dalegarth 🐚, CA13 9XA, SE : 1 ¼ m. on B 5289 ☎ 233, ←, 🌳, park – P
April-October – **9 rm** ☕ 6.00/9.00 **st.**

BUTTINGTON Powys – pop. 1,256 – ✉ Welshpool – ☎ 093 874 Trewern.
London 180 – Birmingham 62 – Shrewsbury 17.

Garth Darwen, on A 458 ☎ 238, 🌳 – P
closed mid December-mid January – **8 rm** ☕ 6.00/9.00 **t.**

BUXTON Derbs. 986 ㉗ – pop. 20,324 – ✉ Stockport – ☎ 0298.
Envir. : Tideswell (Parish church★ 14C) NE : 9 m.
18 Townend ☎ 3453, NE : on A 6 – 18 Gadley Lane ☎ 3494, ¾ m. Buxton Station.
i St. Ann's Well, The Crescent ☎ 5106.
London 172 – Derby 38 – **Manchester 25 – Stoke-on-Trent 24.**

Lee Wood, 13 Manchester Rd, SK17 6TQ, on A 5002 ☎ 3002, 🌳 – lift ⌂wc shower wc P.
M 4.00/5.00 **s.** 🍷 1.00 – **40 rm** ☕ 8.50/16.00 **s.**

Hartington, 18 Broad Walk, SK17 6JR, ☎ 2638 – ⌂wc P
closed first 2 weeks November and 24 December-3 January – **M** (dinner only) 3.50 **t.** – **14 rm** ☕ 6.00/11.00 **t.**

AUSTIN Brierlow Bar ☎ 3801
AUSTIN-JAGUAR-MORRIS-ROVER-TRIUMPH Spring Gardens ☎ 2321
CHRYSLER 9 Scarsdale Pl. ☎ 2796
DAF London Rd ☎ 3075
FIAT 26 Lightwood Rd ☎ 2460
OPEL Leek Rd ☎ 3466
RENAULT The Old Court House ☎ 3947
SAAB Leek Rd 2494

BWLCHTOCYN Gwynedd – see Abersoch.

CADNAM Hants. 986 ㉟ – pop. 2,500 – ☎ 042 127.
London 91 – Salisbury 16 – **Southampton 8** – Winchester 19.

Le Chanteclerc, Romsey Rd, SO4 2NX, on A 31 ☎ 3271, French rest. – P
closed Sunday, Monday, 2 weeks August-September and first 2 weeks January – **M** a la carte 3.65/6.15 **t.** 🍷 1.40.

CAERLEON Gwent 986 ㉟ – pop. 6,270 – ☎ 0633 – 9.
See : Roman Amphitheatre★ *AC*.
London 144 – Cardiff 17 – Newport 3.

The Priory, High St., NP6 1XD, ☎ 421241, 🌳 – ⌂wc ☎ P.
M 3.00/3.30 **st.** – **24 rm** ☕ 10.00/14.50 **st.**

ALFA-ROMEO, AUDI-NSU, MERCEDES-BENZ Ponthir Rd ☎ 420563

CAERNARFON Gwynedd 986 ㉗ – pop. 9,260 – ☎ 0286.

See : Castle *** 13C-14C (Royal Welch Fusiliers Regimental museum*) *AC* – City walls*.

Envir. : SE: Snowdon (ascent and ✻***) 1 h 15 mn by Snowdon Mountain Railway (*AC*) from Llanberis – Llanberis (Pass**) SE : 13 m. – Dinas Dindle * SW: 5 m.

i Tourist Information Centre, Slate Quay ☎ 2232 (Easter-September).

London 249 – Birkenhead 76 – **Chester 68** – **Holyhead 30** – Shrewsbury 85.

Muriau Park, Pwllheli Rd, LL55 2YS, S: 1 ½ m. on A 487 ☎ 4647, ←, – TV ⇔wc Ⓟ
closed December and January – **6 rm** 8.50 **t.**

at Llanwnda SW: 3 ½ m. off A 487 on A 499 – ✉ Caernarfon – ☎ 0286 Llanwnda:

✕ **The Stables,** LL54 5SD, ☎ 830711 – Ⓟ
closed Sunday, Monday lunch and Christmas Day – **M** a la carte 3.55/6.10 🍾 1.75.

AUSTIN-MG-WOLSELEY Caeathraw ☎ 3096
DATSUN Bangor Rd ☎ 2475
VAUXHALL Bont Newydd ☎ 2212

CAERPHILLY Mid Glam. 986 ㉟ – pop. 40,788 – ☎ 0222.

See : Castle** 13C.

London 157 – **Cardiff 8** – Newport 11.

Hotels and restaurants see: Cardiff S: 8 m.
Newport E: **11** m.

MORRIS-MG-WOLSELEY Pontygwindy Rd ☎ 2123

CAERSWS Powys 986 ㉛ – pop. **1,205** – ☎ 068 684.

London 202 – Aberystwyth 38 – Newtown 6.

Maesmawr Hall ⑤, SY17 5SF, E: 1 m. on A 492 ☎ 255, ←, « 16C manor house in large garden », park – ⇔wc ⇔wc Ⓟ
M 4.00/6.00 🍾 1.30 – **20 rm** 9.00/18.00.

AUSTIN-MG-WOLSELEY ☎ 345

CAISTOR ST. EDMUNDS Norfolk – see Norwich.

CALNE Wilts. 986 ㉟ – pop. 9,688 – ✉ Chippenham – ☎ 0249.

Envir. : Avebury (stone circles**) E: 7 ½ m. – Bowood Mansion* (Italian) *AC*, W: 3 ½ m.

18 Bishop's Cannings ☎ 038 086 (Cannings) 627, SE: **1** m. from A 4.

London 98 – **Bristol 33** – **Southampton 56** – Swindon 19.

Lansdowne Arms, The Strand, SN11 0EH, ☎ 812488 – Ⓟ
M 2.15/3.10 **t.** 🍾 1.10 – **15 rm** 6.00/11.50 **t.**

AUSTIN-MORRIS-MG-WOLSELEY Curzon St. ☎ 812791
DATSUN London Rd ☎ 814455
ROVER-TRIUMPH Main Rd, Cherhill ☎ 812254

CALSTOCK Cornwall – pop. 4,079 (inc. Gunnislake) – ☎ 0822 Gunnislake.

London 246 – **Plymouth 22** – Tavistock 7.

Danescombe Valley ⑤, PL18 9RY, W: ½ m. by Riverside Rd ☎ 832414, ← river Tamar, « Country house atmosphere » – ⇔wc
Easter-October – **M** (dinner only by arrangement to non-residents) 4.50 🍾 1.00 – **7 rm** 6.00/15.00.

CAMBERLEY Surrey 986 ㊱ – pop. 44,967 (inc. Frimley) – ☎ 0276.

Envir. : Sandhurst (Royal Military Academy: Royal Memorial Chapel*) NW : **1 ½ m.**

London 40 – Reading 13 – **Southampton 48.**

Frimley Hall (T.H.F.), Portsmouth Rd, GU15 2BG, S: 1 ¾ m. on A 325 ☎ 28321, Telex 858446, – TV ⇔wc ☎ Ⓟ.
M 4.00/4.50 **st.** 🍾 1.50 – **77 rm** 11.50/19.00 **st.**

AUSTIN-MORRIS-MG-ROVER-TRIUMPH-WOLSELEY London Rd ☎ 63443

CAMBORNE Cornwall 986 ㊳ – pop. **16,631** – ☎ 0209.

London 306 – Falmouth 12 – Newquay 19 – Penzance 13 – **Plymouth 63** – Truro 12.

Tyack's, Church St., TR14 7DQ, on A 3047 ☎ 713252 – ⇔wc Ⓟ
M approx. 2.50 🍾 2.00 – **12 rm** 7.75/15.50 **st.**

AUSTIN-MORRIS-MG-WOLSELEY Church St. ☎ 712066
DAF, SAAB Newton Rd ☎ 713309
RENAULT Rosewarn Rd ☎ 713769

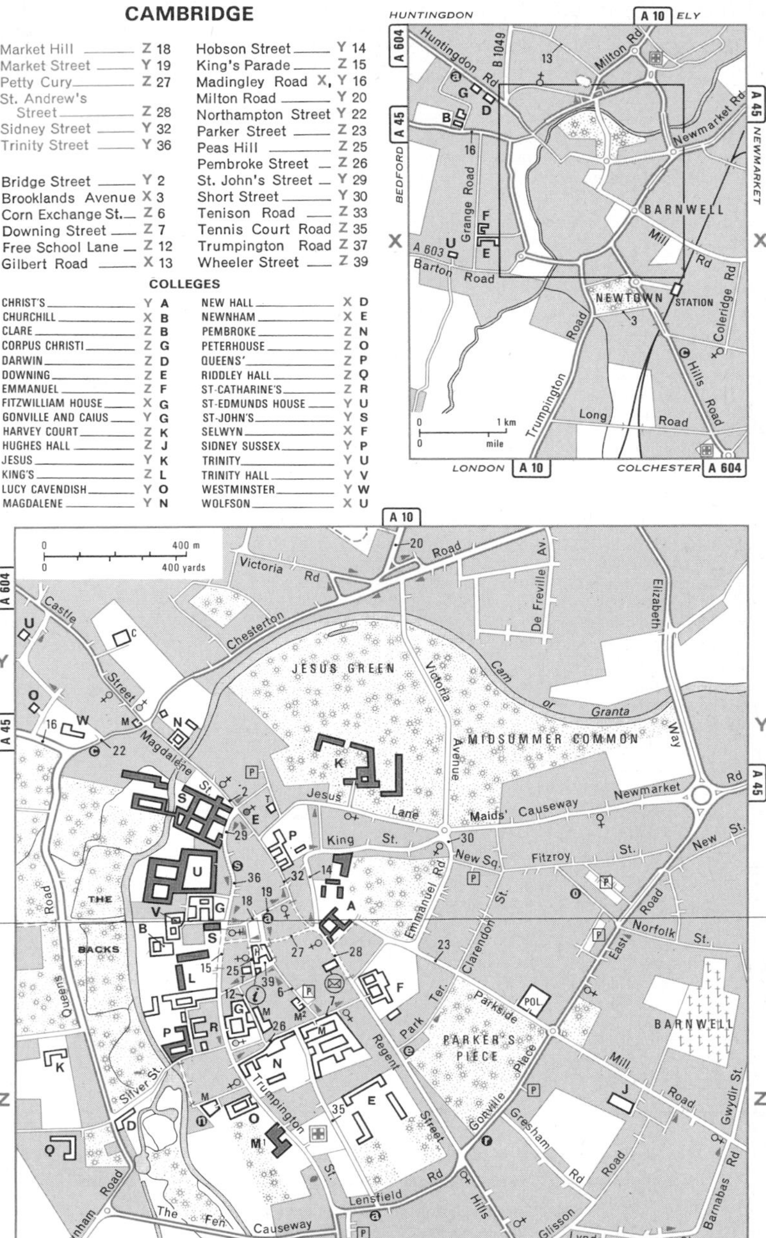
CAMBRIDGE
Market Hill Z 18
Market Street Y 19
Petty Cury Z 27
St. Andrew's Street Z 28
Sidney Street Y 32
Trinity Street Y 36
Bridge Street Y 2
Brooklands Avenue X 3
Corn Exchange St. Z 6
Downing Street Z 7
Free School Lane Z 12
Gilbert Road X 13
Hobson Street Y 14
King's Parade Z 15
Madingley Road X, Y 16
Milton Road Y 20
Northampton Street Y 22
Parker Street Z 23
Peas Hill Z 25
Pembroke Street Z 26
St. John's Street Y 29
Short Street Y 30
Tenison Road Z 33
Tennis Court Road Z 35
Trumpington Road Z 37
Wheeler Street Z 39
COLLEGES
CHRIST'S Y A
CHURCHILL X B
CLARE Z B
CORPUS CHRISTI Z G
DARWIN Z D
DOWNING Z E
EMMANUEL Z F
FITZWILLIAM HOUSE X G
GONVILLE AND CAIUS Y G
HARVEY COURT Z K
HUGHES HALL Z J
JESUS Y K
KING'S Z L
LUCY CAVENDISH Y O
MAGDALENE Y N
NEW HALL X D
NEWNHAM X E
PEMBROKE Z N
PETERHOUSE Z O
QUEENS' Z P
RIDDLEY HALL Z Q
ST-CATHARINE'S Z R
ST-EDMUNDS HOUSE Y U
ST-JOHN'S Y S
SELWYN X F
SIDNEY SUSSEX Y P
TRINITY Y U
TRINITY HALL Y V
WESTMINSTER Y W
WOLFSON X U
HUNTINGDON
A 10
ELY
A 604
Huntingdon Rd
B 1049
Milton Rd
A 45
Newmarket Rd
NEWMARKET
BEDFORD
Grange Road
BARNWELL
Mill Rd
A 603
Barton Road
NEWTOWN
STATION
Coleridge Rd
Hills Road
Trumpington Road
Long Road
1 km
mile
LONDON
COLCHESTER
400 m
400 yards
Victoria Rd
Chesterton Road
Castle Street
JESUS GREEN
Victoria Avenue
De Freville Av.
Elizabeth Way
Cam or Granta
MIDSUMMER COMMON
Magdalene St.
Jesus Lane
Maids' Causeway
Newmarket Rd
King St.
New Sq.
Fitzroy St.
New St.
Emmanuel Rd
East Road
Norfolk St.
Clarendon St.
THE BACKS
Queens Road
Parkside
Park Ter.
PARKER'S PIECE
Regent Street
POL.
BARNWELL
Mill Road
Gwydir St.
Silver St.
Trumpington St.
Gonville Place
Gresham Rd
Road
Lensfield Rd
Hills Rd
Glisson Road
Lyndewode Rd
St.
Barnabas Rd
Newnham Road
A 603
The Fen Causeway

CAMBRIDGE Cambs. 986 ㉜ – pop. 98,840 – ☎ 0223.

See : Colleges Quarter***: King's College** (King's Chapel***) Z **L** – Queens' College** (Cloister Court) Z **P** – St. John's College** (Gateway*) Y **S** – Fitzwilliam Museum** *AC* Z **M**[1] – Trinity College** (Wren Library**, Chapel*, Great Court and Gate*) Y **U** – Holy Sepulchre* (12C round church) Y **E** – Senate House* Y **S** – The Backs* YZ – Jesus College (Chapel*) Y **K** – Christ's College (Gatehouse) YZ **A**.

Envir. : Anglesey Abbey 12C (interior** and park* *AC*) NE: 6 m. by A 45 X and B 1102.

18 Bar Hill ☎ 0954 (Crafts Hill) 80555, NW : 6 ½ m. by A 604 X – 9 Dodford Lane ☎ 0954 (Crafts Hill) 76169, N: 3 m. by A 604 X.

☎ 58800 ext 106.

i Wheeler St. ☎ 58977.

London 60 – Coventry 88 – Kingston-upon-Hull 130 – Ipswich 53 – Leicester 68 – Norwich 61 – Nottingham 87 – Oxford 78.

Plan on preceding page

Garden House, Granta Pl., off Mill Lane, CB2 1RT, ☎ 63421, Telex 81463, ←, –
closed 25 to 31 December – **M** 3.85/4.50 **t.** 1.90 – 1.50 – **55 rm** 17.00/26.00 **t.** Z n

University Arms, Regent St., CB2 1AD, ☎ 51241, Telex 817311 – Z e
M a la carte 3.75/6.00 **st.** 1.20 – **120 rm** 10.00/20.00 **st.** – P 14.20/19.20 **st.**

Gonville (Interchange), Gonville Pl., CB1 1LY, ☎ 66611 – wc Z r
M 3.60/4.00 **st.** 1.15 – **62 rm** 13.25/20.00 **st.** – P 19.20 **st.**

Blue Boar (T.H.F.), 17 Trinity St., CB2 1TC, ☎ 63121 – wc Y s
M approx. 3.75 **st.** 1.50 – **48 rm** 9.00/17.50 **st.**

Helen, 167-169 Hills Rd, CB2 2RJ, ☎ 46465 – X c
closed 10 December-10 January – **M** *(closed Sunday)* (dinner only, residents only) 3.00/3.50 **t.** 1.25 – **20 rm** 5.50/11.50 **t.**

Lensfield, 53 Lensfield Rd, CB2 1EN, ☎ 55017 – wc Z a
26 rm 5.50/12.00 **t.**

Guest House, 139 Huntingdon Rd, CB3 0DQ, ☎ 52833, – X a
closed Christmas – **13 rm** 6.00/12.00 **st.**

Don Pasquale, 12 Market Hill, CB2 3NJ, ☎ 67063, Italian rest. Y a
M a la carte 4.00/7.10 **t.** 1.30.

Oyster Tavern, 21-24 Northampton St. ☎ 53110. Y c

Peking, 21 Burleigh St. ☎ 54755, Chinese rest. Y o
M a la carte 3.00/4.50.

at Fowlmere S: 8 ¾ m. off A 10 – X – by B 1368 – ✉ Royston – ☎ 076 382 Fowlmere:

Swan House, High St., SG8 7SR, ☎ 444 –
closed Sunday and 25 to 30 December – **M** a la carte 5.00/6.00 1.25.

Chequers Inn, High St., SG8 7SR, ☎ 369 –
closed Christmas Day – **M** a la carte 4.35/6.20 **s.** 1.80.

at Madingley W : 4 ½ m. off A 45 – X – ✉ ☎ 0954 Madingley:

Three Horseshoes, CB3 8AB, ☎ 210221, –
closed Christmas Day – **M** a la carte 3.90/6.05 **s.**

at Bar Hill NW: 6 ½ m. on A 604 – X – ✉ Bar Hill – ☎ 0954 Crafts Hill:

Cambridgeshire, Huntingdon Rd, CB3 8EU, ☎ 80555, Telex 817141, 18 – wc
M a la carte 3.95/5.10 **s.** 1.25 – 1.75 – **100 rm** 14.50/19.50 **s.** – P 20.00/25.00 **s.**

ALFA-ROMEO 146 Hills Rd ☎ 47296
AUSTIN-DAIMLER-JAGUAR-MORRIS-MG-ROVER-TRIUMPH-WOLSELEY 400 Newmarket Rd ☎ 65111
BENTLEY, ROLLS ROYCE 121 Chesterton Rd ☎ 69761
CITROEN, CHRYSLER-SIMCA Newmarket Rd ☎ 59151
CHRYSLER-SIMCA Babraham Rd ☎ 47072
DAF 6 Fair St. ☎ 59573
DATSUN 315 Mill Rd ☎ 42222
FORD Cherryhinton Rd ☎ 48151
MAZDA, VOLVO Harston ☎ 870123
MERCEDES-BENZ 121/129 Perne Rd ☎ 47268
MORRIS-MG-WOLSELEY 8/10 St. Barnabas Rd ☎ 58333
PEUGEOT Elizabeth Way ☎ 68686
RENAULT 217 Newmarket Rd ☎ 51616
TOYOTA Union Lane ☎ 56225
VAUXHALL 137 Histon Rd ☎ 66751
VW, AUDI-NSU 383 Milton Rd ☎ 50589

Questa guida non è un repertorio di tutti gli alberghi e ristoranti,
nè comprende tutti i buoni alberghi e ristoranti di Gran Bretagna e Irlanda.
Nell'intento di tornare utili a tutti i turisti,
siamo indotti a indicare esercizi
di tutte le classi ed a citarne soltanto un certo numero di ognuna.

CANTERBURY Kent 986 ㊱ – pop. 33,176 – ☎ 0227.

See : Christ Church Cathedral*** (Norman crypt**, Bell Harry Tower**, Great Cloister**, ≼*from Green Court) Y **A** – King's School* Y **B** – Mercery Lane* Y – Weavers* (old houses) Y **D. Envir. :** Patrixbourne (St. Mary's Church : south door*) SE : 3 m. by A 2 Z – Chilham (Village Square*, Castle* 17C, *AC*) SW : 6 m. by A 28 Z.

i The Long Market ☎ 66567 (summer only) – Sidney Cooper Centre, 22 St. Peter's St. ☎ 66567.

London 59 – Brighton 72 – Dover 16 – Maidstone 27 – Margate 17.

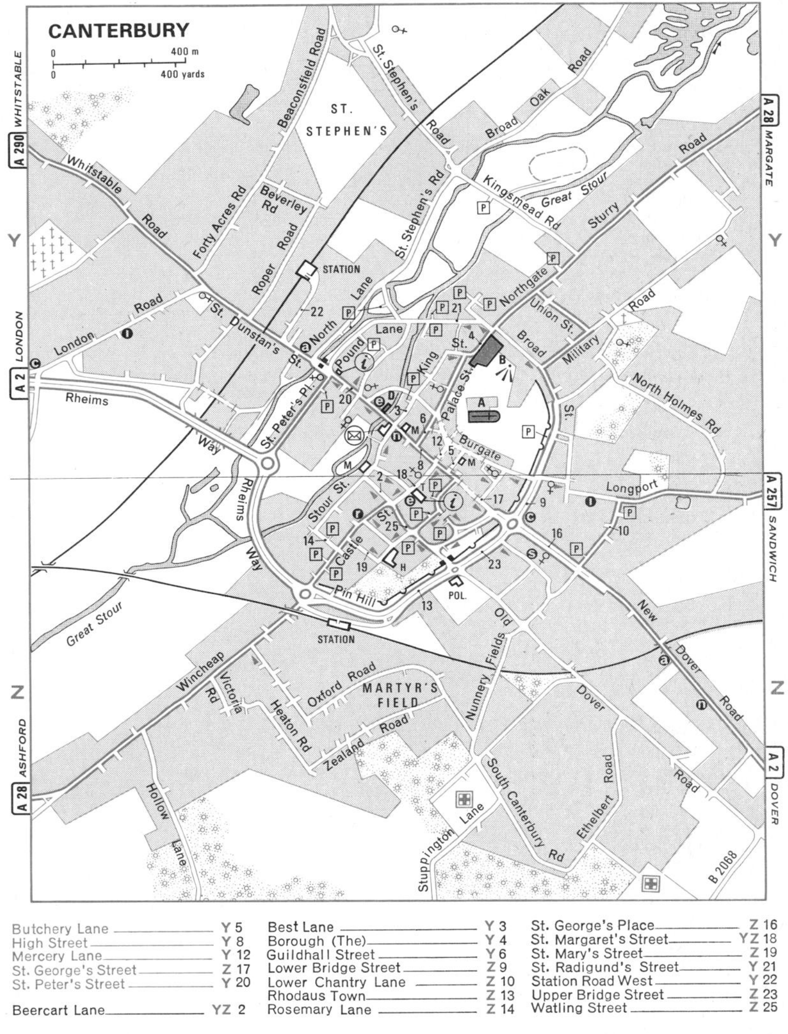

Butchery Lane .... Y 5	Best Lane .... Y 3	St. George's Place .... Z 16
High Street .... Y 8	Borough (The) .... Y 4	St. Margaret's Street .... YZ 18
Mercery Lane .... Y 12	Guildhall Street .... Y 6	St. Mary's Street .... Z 19
St. George's Street .... Z 17	Lower Bridge Street .... Z 9	St. Radigund's Street .... Y 21
St. Peter's Street .... Y 20	Lower Chantry Lane .... Z 10	Station Road West .... Y 22
	Rhodaus Town .... Z 13	Upper Bridge Street .... Z 23
Beercart Lane .... YZ 2	Rosemary Lane .... Z 14	Watling Street .... Z 25

🏨 **Chaucer** (T.H.F.), Ivy Lane, CT1 1XL, ☎ 64427 – 📺 🛁wc ☎ **P**. 🏃 — Z **c**
M 2.95/3.65 **st.** 🍷 1.50 – **51 rm** ☕ 10.00/20.00 **st.**

🏨 **County,** High St., CT1 2RX, ☎ 66266, Telex 965076 – 🛗 📺 🛁wc ☎ **P**. 🏃 — Y **n**
M a la carte 4.80/6.60 **st.** 🍷 1.50 – **74 rm** ☕ 14.00/21.00 **st.**

P.T.O. ⟶

Abbot's Barton, 36 New Dover Rd, CT1 3DT, ✆ 60341, Telex 957141, – wc P. — Z a
M 3.50/3.85 **t.** 1.35 – **35 rm** 6.75/14.50 **t.**

Slatters (County), St. Margaret's St., CT1 1AA, ✆ 63271 – TV wc P. — Z e
M a la carte 3.50/11.00 **st.** 1.20 – **30 rm** 12.90/18.90 **st.** – P 18.40/26.00 **st.**

Falstaff, 8-10 St. Dunstan's St., CT2 8AF, ✆ 62138 – TV wc P — Y a
M 3.00/3.50 **t.** 1.50 – **9 rm** 8.00/16.00 **t.**

Barcroft, 56 New Dover Rd, CT1 3DT, ✆ 69177 – P — Z n
14 rm 7.00/13.00 **st.**

Highfield, Summer Hill, Harbledown, CT2 8NH, ✆ 62772, – wc P — Y c
closed Christmas – **12 rm** 7.50/13.00 **t.**

Pilgrims, 18 The Friars, CT1 2AS, ✆ 64531 – wc — Y e
closed Christmas – **14 rm** 6.00/14.00 **st.**

Victoria Court, 59 London Rd, CT2 7HG, ✆ 65447 – P — Y i
25 rm 6.50/15.00 **st.**

Harbledown Court, 17 Summer Hill, Harbledown, ✆ 60659 – TV P — by London Rd Y
7 rm 5.00/10.00 **st.**

Red House, London Rd, CT2 8NB, ✆ 63578, – P — by London Rd Y
17 rm 5.40/14.05 **t.**

Trattoria Roma Antica, 9 Longport, CT1 1PE, ✆ 63326, Italian rest. — Z i
closed Sunday, Christmas Day and Bank Holidays – **M** a la carte 3.25/5.25 1.15.

Beehive, 52 Dover St., CT1 3MD, ✆ 61126 — Z s
closed Sunday – **M** a la carte 3.35/4.70.

Adelaide Silver Grill, Adelaide Pl., 71 Castle St., CT1 2QD, ✆ 65658 – P — Z r
closed Sunday, Christmas, Good Friday and Bank Holidays lunch – **M** (grill rest. only) a la carte 3.25/4.90 **t.** 1.80.

***at Fordwich* NE: 3 m. off A 28 – Y – ✉ 0227 Canterbury :**

George and Dragon, CT2 0BX, ✆ 710661, « 16C village inn », – wc P
closed 24 to 28 December – **M** *(closed Sunday dinner)* (buffet lunch) a la carte 5.00/7.50 **t.** – **14 rm** 7.50/16.50 **t.**

***at Wingham* E: 6 m. on A 257 – Z – ✉ Canterbury – 022 772 Wingham:**

Red Lion, High St., CT3 1BB, ✆ 217 – P
closed Sunday dinner, Monday and 25-26 December.

***at Pett Bottom* S: 4 ½ m. off A 2 via Bridge Village – Z – ✉ 0227 Canterbury :**

Duck Inn, CT4 5PB, ✆ 830354 – P
closed Monday, Tuesday, 2 weeks March and 2 weeks September – **M** a la carte approx. 7.55 1.50
Spec. Civet de fruits de mer, Caneton rôti à l'ananas flambé au Cognac, Poires au cassis.

AUDI-NSU, VAUXHALL Rose Lane ✆ 65544
AUSTIN-DAIMLER-JAGUAR-MG-ROVER-TRIUMPH-WOLSELEY 5 Rose Lane and 28/30 St. Peters St. ✆ 66161
CHRYSLER-SIMCA The Pavillion ✆ 51791
DATSUN Island Rd ✆ 710431
FIAT, CITROEN, FERRARI, ROLLS ROYCE-BENTLEY 41 St. Georges Pl. ✆ 66131
FORD 23 Lower Bridge St. ✆ 69121
LANCIA The Friars ✆ 62977
MORRIS-MG-WOLSELEY New Dover Rd ✆ 66711
OPEL-VAUXHALL Ashford Rd, Chartham ✆ 022 789 (Great Stour) 331
RENAULT Northgate ✆ 65561

CARBIS BAY Cornwall – pop. 2,615 (inc. Lelant) – ✉ 073 670 St. Ives.

London 317 – Penzance 9 – Truro 23.

St. Uny, Boskerris Rd, TR26 2NQ, ✆ 5011, ←, – wc P
May-October – **M** (bar lunch) approx. 4.00 1.25 – **32 rm** 9.50/19.00.

Carbis Bay, TR26 2NP, ✆ 5311, ←, heated, – wc P
28 April-1 October – **M** (cold lunch) 4.00/6.00 1.80 – **29 rm** 6.00/20.00 – P 9.00/16.00.

Hendras, Porthrepta Rd, TR26 2NZ, ✆ 5030, – wc P
mid May-September – **38 rm.**

Boskerris, Boskerris Rd, TR26 2NQ, ✆ 5295, ←, – wc P
Easter-mid October – **M** approx. 3.50 **st.** 1.50 – **23 rm** 7.50/17.00 **st.** – P 11.00/13.00 **st.**

CARDIFF South Glam. 986 ㉟ – pop. 279,111 – 0222.

See : National Museum BY M – Llandaff Cathedral* AY B – St. Fagan's Castle (Folk Museum)*** *AC* **by St. Fagans Rd.**

Envir. : Caerphilly (castle 13C) N: 7 m. by A 469 AY.**

18 Dinas Powis ✆ 512157, SW: 3 m. by A 4055 AZ.

Glamorgan (Rhoose) Airport ✆ 0446 (Rhoose) 710296, SW : 8 m.

i Tourist, Information Centre 3 Castle St. ✆ 27281.

London 157 – Birmingham 105 – Bristol 43 – Coventry 118.

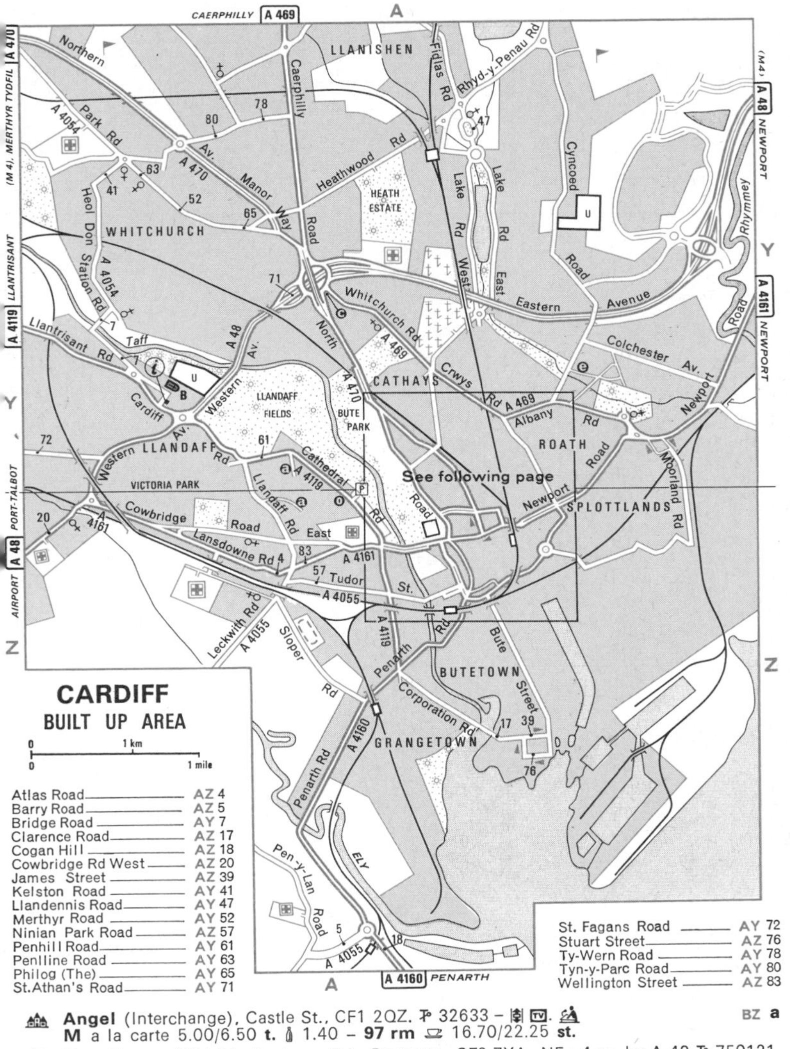

Angel (Interchange), Castle St., CF1 2QZ. ☎ 32633 – lift TV. – **M** a la carte 5.00/6.50 **t.** 1.40 – **97 rm** 16.70/22.25 **st.** — BZ **a**

Post House (T.H.F.), Pentwyn Rd., Pentwyn, CF2 7XA, NE : 4 m. by A 48 ☎ 750121, Telex 497633 – lift TV wc ☎ P. – **M** 2.95/4.00 **st.** 1.50 – 2.00 – **150 rm** 13.00/18.00 **st.** — on A 48 AY

Royal (Embassy), St. Marys St., CF1 1LL, ☎ 23321 – lift TV wc ☎. – *closed Christmas* – **68 rm** 9.50/15.00 **st.** — BZ **n**

Park (Mt. Charlotte), Park Pl., CF1 3UD, ☎ 23471 – lift TV wc ☎ P. – **M** a la carte 4.65/6.65 **st.** 1.35 – **95 rm** 11.00/20.00 **st.** — BZ **c**

Cardiff Centre (Centre), Westgate St., CF1 1JB, ☎ 388681, Telex 497258 – lift TV wc ☎. – **M** (Carvery rest.) 2.95/3.95 **s.** 1.25 – 1.50 – **160 rm** 10.75/14.50 **s.** — BZ **i**

Beverley (Crest), 75 Cathedral Rd, CF1 9OG, ☎ 43443 – wc ☎ P – **M** *(closed Sunday)* (dinner only) 2.50/3.50 **s.** 1.55 – **19 rm** 9.80/17.00 **s.** — AZ **o**

Park Lodge, 5 Kimberley Rd, Penylan ☎ 394190 – *closed 25 December-5 January* – **6 rm** 4.50/8.00 **st.** — AY **e**

CARDIFF
CENTRE

0 — 300 m
0 — 300 yards

Duke Street .... BZ 25
High Street .... BZ 35
Queen Street .... BZ
St. Mary Street .... BZ
Working Street .... BZ

Castle Street .... BZ 8
Central Square .... BZ 12
Church Street .... BZ 13
City Hall Road .... BY 15
Customhouse Street .... BZ 22
David Street .... BZ 23
Dumfries Place .... BY 26
Fitzalan Place .... BYZ 28
Glossop Road .... BY 29
Greyfriars Road .... BY 31
Guildford Street .... BZ 33
Hayes (The) .... BZ 34
King Edward VII Avenue .... BY 43

Kingsway .... BZ 44
Mary Ann Street .... BZ 49
Meteor Street .... BZ 53
Moira Terrace .... BYZ 55
Nantes (Boulevard de) .... BY 56
Penarth Road .... BZ 58
St. Andrews Crescent .... BY 69
St. Andrews Place .... BY 70
St. John Street .... BZ 73
Station Terrace .... BZ 74
West Grove .... BY 85
Wharf Street .... BZ 87
Windsor Place .... BY 89

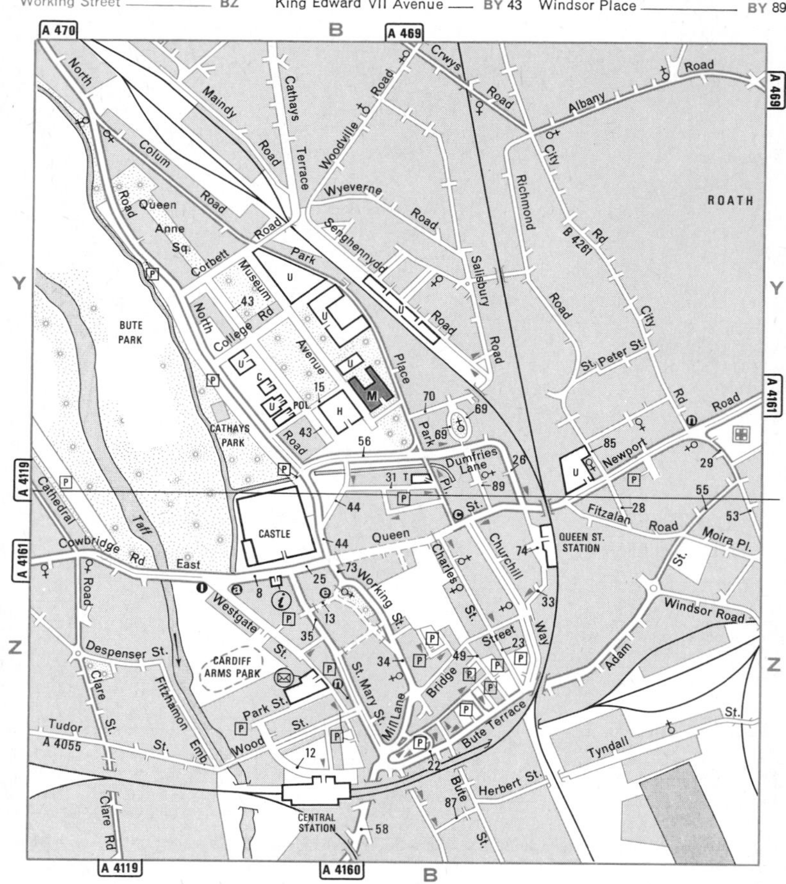

✕✕ **La Corona,** 1st floor, 47 Newport Rd, CF2 1AD, ☎ 30404 — BY **n**
closed Sunday and Bank Holidays – **M** a la carte 5.65/10.25 **t.**

✕ Positano, 9 Church St., CF1 2BG, ☎ 35810, Italian rest. — BZ **e**

✕ **Harvesters,** 5 Pontcanna St., off Cathedral Rd, CF1 9HQ, ☎ 32616 — AY **a**
closed Sunday, Monday, 3 weeks August and Christmas – **M** (dinner only) a la carte 3.95/6.40 🍷 1.40.

✕ **Gibson's,** 8 Romilly Crescent, Canton, CF1 9NR, ☎ 41264, Bistro — AZ **a**
closed Sunday, Monday and Tuesday after Bank Holidays – **M** a la carte 3.25/5.00 **t.** 🍷 1.50.

✕ Savastano's, 302 North Rd ☎ 30270, Italian rest. — AY **c**

at Castleton **(Gwent) NE: 7 m. on A 48** – AY – ✉ **Cardiff** – ☎ **0633 Castleton :**

🏨 **Mercury Motor Inn,** CF3 8OQ, ☎ 680591 – TV 🛁wc 🚿wc ☎ **P**. 🐕
M a la carte 3.80/6.80 **st.** 🍷 1.35 – ☕ 1.50 – **55 rm** 11.80/16.50 **st.**

MICHELIN Branch, Garth St., Adamsdown, CF1 2UN, ☎ 33948.

AUDI-NSU Grangetown ☎ 388932
AUSTIN-JAGUAR-MORRIS-MG-ROVER-TRIUMPH 52 Penarth Rd ☎ 43571
AUSTIN-DAIMLER-JAGUAR-MORRIS-MG-ROVER-TRIUMPH-WOLSELEY 501 Newport Rd ☎ 495591
AUSTIN-MORRIS-MG-ROVER-TRIUMPH-WOLSELEY 89/103 City Rd ☎ 492676
BMW 2a City Rd ☎ 24422
DAF 134/148 City Rd ☎ 30022
DATSUN 516 Cowbridge Rd ☎ 561212
FORD 505 Newport Rd ☎ 59511
FORD 281 Penarth Rd ☎ 21071
MERCEDES-BENZ, PEUGEOT 14 Station Rd ☎ 566260
MORRIS-MG-WOLSELEY Rhiwbina ☎ 63232
MORRIS-MG-WOLSELEY Cowbridge Rd West ☎ 591182
MORRIS-MG-WOLSELEY City Rd ☎ 22231
OPEL West Bute St. ☎ 33221
RENAULT 325 Penarth Rd ☎ 23122
SAAB Crwys Rd ☎ 35725
TOYOTA Llantrisant Rd ☎ 562345
VAUXHALL 2/12 City Rd ☎ 20531
VAUXHALL Sloper Rd ☎ 387221
VOLVO Newport Rd, St. Mellons ☎ 77183

CARDIGAN Dyfed 986 ㉚ – pop. 3,810 – ☎ 0239.

Envir.: Mwnt (site★) N: 6 m. – Gwbert-on-Sea (cliffs ≤★) NW: 3 m.

18 Gwbert-on-Sea ☎ 2035, NW: 3 m.

i Tourist Information Centre, Market Pl. ☎ 3230 (Easter - September).

London 250 – Carmarthen 30 – Fishguard 19.

at St. Dogmaels W: 1 m. on B 4546 by A 487 – ✉ ☎ 0239 Cardigan:

Glanteifi, SA43 3LL, on B 4546 ☎ 2353, ≤ Teifi estuary, – wc P
Easter-October – **11 rm** 4.25/13.00 **s.**

at Gwbert-on-Sea NW: 3 m. – ✉ ☎ 0239 Cardigan:

Cliff (Interchange), SA43 1PP, ☎ 3241, Telex 48440, ≤ bay and countryside, heated, – wc P.
M a la carte 5.55/8.35 **st.** 1.30 – **60 rm** 12.75/25.50 **st.**

AUSTIN-MORRIS-MG-ROVER-TRIUMPH-WOLSELEY Aberystwyth Rd ☎ 2365
CHRYSLER-SIMCA Aberystwyth Rd ☎ 3347
FIAT St. Dogmaels ☎ 2025
FORD ☎ 2206

***During the season,** particularly in resorts it is wise to book in advance.*
However, if you find you cannot take up a hotel booking you have made, please let the hotel know immediately.
If you are writing to a hotel abroad enclose an International Reply Coupon (available from Post Offices).

CARISBROOKE I.O.W. 986 ㊴ – see Wight (Isle of).

CARLISLE Cumbria 986 ⑲ – pop. 71,582 – ☎ 0228.

See: Castle★ (12C) *AC* AY – Cathedral★ 12C-14C AY **E.**

18 ☎ 022 872 (Scotby) 303, E: 2 m. by A 69 BY – 9 Stony Holme ☎ 34856, E: 1 m. by St. Aidan's Rd BY.

☎ 25146.

i Old Town Hall, ☎ 25517 or 25396.

London 311 – Blackpool 95 – Edinburgh 98 – Glasgow 96 – Leeds 126 – Liverpool 127 – Manchester 120 – Newcastle-upon-Tyne 58.

Plan on next page

Crown and Mitre (Interchange), English St., CA3 8HZ, ☎ 25491, Telex 64183 – TV P. BY **a**
M *(closed Saturday lunch, Sunday lunch and Sunday dinner from November to March)* a la carte 3.50/5.00 **s.** 1.60 – 1.35 – **75 rm** 9.20/16.75 **s.**

Cumbrian (Thistle), Court Sq., CA1 1QY, ☎ 31951 – TV wc P. BZ **u**
M a la carte 3.90/8.75 **s.** 1.40 – 2.00 – **69 rm** 9.50/16.00 **st.** – P 14.00/25.00 **st.**

Hilltop Motor London Rd, CA1 2PQ, SE: 1 m. on A 6 ☎ 29255, Telex 64292 – TV wc P. SE: 1 m. on A 6 BZ
M 3.00/3.80 **s.** 1.40 – 1.40 – **123 rm** 5.50/13.50 **s.**

Central, Victoria Viaduct, CA3 8AL, ☎ 20256 – wc BZ **a**
M a la carte 2.90/5.35 **t.** 1.90 – **67 rm** 5.50/11.00 **t.**

at Kingstown N: 3 m. at junction 44 of A 7 – BY – and M 6 – ✉ ☎ 0228 Carlisle:

Carlisle Crest Motel (Crest), Kingstown Rd, CA3 0HR, ☎ 31201 – TV wc P.
M 2.50/3.50 **s.** 1.55 – 1.60 – **98 rm** 10.95/15.50 **s.**

at Crosby-on-Eden NE: 4 ½ m. by A 7 – BY – on B 6264 – ✉ Carlisle – ☎ 022 873 Crosby-on-Eden:

XX **Crosby Lodge** with rm, CA6 4QZ, ☎ 618, ≤, « 18C country mansion », – wc P
closed 24 December-mid January – **M** *(closed Sunday dinner)* a la carte 3.60/8.70 **s.** 1.75 – **11 rm** 11.25/16.00 **s.**

6

CARLISLE

0 — 300 m
0 — 300 yards

Street	Ref
Botchergate	BZ
Castle Street	BY 6
English Street	BY 13
Scotch Street	BY 19
Annetwell Street	AY 2
Bridge Street	AY 3
Brunswick Street	BZ 4
Caldcotes	AY 5
Charlotte Street	AZ 7
Chiswick Street	BY 8
Church Street	AY 10
Eden Bridge	BY 12
Lonsdale Street	BY 14
Lowther Street	BY 15
Port Road	AY 16
St. Aidan's Road	BY 17
St. Nicholas Street	BZ 18
Spencer Street	BY 20
Tait Street	BZ 21
Victoria Viaduct	ABZ 24
West Tower Street	BY 26
West Walls	ABY 27

MICHELIN Branch, Willow Holme Industrial Estate, CA2 5RT, ☎ 20477.

AUSTIN-MG-WOLSELEY 53 Lowther St. ☎ 28111
BMW, VAUXHALL Viaduct Estate ☎ 29401
CHRYSLER-SIMCA 37 Warwick Rd ☎ 25177
DAIMLER-JAGUAR-ROVER-TRIUMPH Rosehill Estate ☎ 24387
DATSUN Lowther St. ☎ 31469
FIAT Lonsdale St. ☎ 25677
FIAT Church St., Caldewgate ☎ 25092
MERCEDES-BENZ, VOLVO Victoria Viaduct ☎ 28234
MORRIS-MG-WOLSELEY, ROLLS ROYCE Botchergate ☎ 26131
OPEL Wigton Rd ☎ 26269
PEUGEOT Warwick Bridge ☎ 60434
RENAULT Church St. ☎ 22423
VW, AUDI-NSU Lowther St. ☎ 26104

CARLYON BAY Cornwall – pop. **1,043** – ✉ St. Austell – **072 681** Par.

18 ☎ 4250.

London 277 – Plymouth 34 – Truro 17.

Carlyon Bay, PL25 3RD, ☎ 2304, ≤ Carlyon Bay, « Extensive gardens », heated, 18, park – park – **M** approx. 5.00 **s.** 0.85 – **74 rm** 12.00/24.00 **s.** – P 15.50/21.00 **s.**

Porth Avallen, Sea Rd, PL25 3SG, ☎ 2802, ≤ Carlyon Bay, – wc *closed mid December-mid January* – **M** *(closed Sunday dinner to non-residents)* 3.50/4.75 **s.** 1.60 – **21 rm** 8.50/18.50 **s.**

CARMARTHEN Dyfed 986 ㉚ ㉛ – pop. **13,081** – **0267**.

Envir.: Kidwelly Castle** (12C) *AC*, S: 9 m.

18 Blaenycoed Rd ☎ **87214**, **NW: 4 m.**

i South Wales Tourism Council, Darkgate ☎ 7557.

London 220 – Fishguard 45 – **Swansea 27.**

Ivy Bush Royal (T.H.F.), 11-13 Spilman St., SA31 1LG, ☎ 5111, Telex 48520 – **M** 4.00/4.75 **st.** 1.50 – **103 rm** 9.50/18.00 **st.**

AUSTIN-MG-WOLSELEY Priory St. ☎ 6622
DAIMLER-JAGUAR-MORRIS-MG-ROVER-TRIUMPH Pensarn Rd ☎ 6456
DATSUN Glasfryn ☎ 026 786 (Llanddarog) 370
FIAT Pensarn ☎ 6633
FORD The Bridge ☎ 6482
OPEL-VAUXHALL Priory St. ☎ 4171

CARTMEL Cumbria – see Grange-over-Sands.

CARTMEL FELL Cumbria – pop. 361 – ✉ Grange-over-Sands – ☎ 044 83 Newby Bridge.
London 269 – Kendal 15 – Lancaster 26.

XX **Hodge Hill,** LA11 6NQ, ☎ 480, « 16C farmhouse », – Ⓟ
closed Tuesday – **M** (dinner only and Sunday lunch) approx. 5.00 **st.**

CASTLE ACRE Norfolk – pop. 955 – ☎ 076 05.
See: Priory** (ruins 11C - 14C) *AC.*
London 101 – King's Lynn 20 – Norwich 31.

Hotels see : King's Lynn NW: 20 m.
Swaffam S: 4 m.

CASTLE ASHBY Northants. – pop. 148 – ✉ Northampton – ☎ 060 129 Yardley Hastings.
See : Castle Ashby* (16C-17C) *AC.*
London 68 – Bedford 16 – Northampton 8.

XX **Falcon Inn** with rm, NN7 1LF, ☎ 200, ←, – wc Ⓟ
M *(closed Sunday dinner)* a la carte 5.20/7.50 1.50 – **4 rm** 9.00/14.00 **st.**

CASTLE CARY Somerset – pop. 1,754 – ☎ 096 35.
London 125 – Bristol 28 – Taunton 31 – Yeovil 13.

George, Market Pl., BA7 7AH, ☎ 215 – wc Ⓟ
M approx. 4.00 **st.** 1.55 – **14 rm** 10.75/16.75 **st.**

SAAB ☎ 310

CASTLE COMBE Wilts. – pop. 414 – ✉ Chippenham – ☎ 0249.
London 110 – Bristol 23 – Chippenham 6.

Manor House, SN14 7HR, ☎ 782206, Telex 44220, « Manor house in park », –
TV Ⓟ
M a la carte 6.70/9.30 – **34 rm** 16.10/28.55 **st.**

CASTLE DONINGTON Leics. – pop. 5,113 – ✉ ☎ 0332 Derby.
East Midlands, ☎ 810621.
i East Midlands Airport ☎ 810621.
London 123 – Birmingham 38 – Leicester 23 – Nottingham 13.

Donington Manor, High St., DE7 2PP, ☎ 810253 – TV wc Ⓟ
closed 24 to 30 December – **M** approx. 2.90 **st.** 1.60 – **32 rm** 7.50/15.65 **st.**

XX **Priest House,** Kings Mills, DE7 2RR, W: 2 m. ☎ 810649, ←, Dancing (Friday and Saturday only) – Ⓟ
M (dinner only and Sunday lunch) a la carte 3.10/5.65 1.70.

CASTLETON Derbs. 986 ㉗ – pop. 729 – ✉ Sheffield (South Yorks.) – ☎ 0433 Hope Valley.
Envir. : Blue John Caverns* *AC,* W: **1** m.
i Peak National Park, Castle St. ☎ 20679.
London 173 – Manchester 27 – Sheffield 16.

Ye Olde Nag's Head, Cross St., S30 2WH, ☎ 20248 – Ⓟ
M a la carte 5.60/7.30 **st.** 2.50 – **10 rm** 10.00/19.00 **st.**

CASTLETON South Glam. – see Cardiff.

CATTERICK North Yorks. – pop. 2,391 – ✉ ☎ 0748 Richmond.
18 Leyburn Rd ☎ 074 883 (Catterick Camp) 3268, W: 5 m.
London 239 – Darlington 11 – Leeds 49 – Northallerton 14.

Bridge House (Embassy), Catterick Bridge, DL10 7PE, N: 2 ½ m. on A 6136 ☎ 818331 –
TV wc Ⓟ.
closed Christmas – **M** approx. 2.90 **st.** 1.45 – **18 rm** 7.75/13.75 **st.**

AUSTIN-MORRIS-MG-PRINCESS 18 Richmond Rd ☎ 074 883 (Catterick Camp) 3219

CATWORTH Cambs. – pop. 221 – ✉ Huntingdon – ☎ 080 14 Bythorn.
London 70 – Cambridge 29 – Northampton 29.

X Racehorse, 43 High St., PE18 0PF, ☎ 262 – Ⓟ.

CAVENDISH Suffolk – pop. 701 – ✉ Sudbury – ☎ 0787 Glemsford.
London 66 – Cambridge 29 – Ipswich 28.

XX **Alfonso's,** High St., CO10 8BB, ☎ 280372, Italian rest.
closed Sunday dinner and Monday lunch – **M** a la carte 4.10/6.50 **t.** 1.75.

CAWSAND Cornwall – pop. 600 – ✉ ☎ 0752 Plymouth.
London 253 – Plymouth 10 – Truro 53.

Criterion ⑤, Garrett St,. PL10 1PD, ☎ 822244, ≤ Plymouth Sound, « Converted fishermen's cottages » – ⋒wc
7 May-24 September – **M** (dinner only) 5.00/6.00 **t.** 1.30 – **8 rm** 7.00/16.00 **t.** – P 10.00/14.00 **t.**

CEFN BRYN West Glam.
See : ☼*** from the reservoir.
London 208 – Swansea 12.

Hotels and restaurants see : Mumbles E: **11** m.
Swansea NE: **12** m.

CHADLINGTON Oxon. – pop. 717 – ☎ 060 876.
London 74 – Cheltenham 32 – **Oxford 18** – Stratford-on-Avon 25.

Chadlington House, OX7 3LZ, ☎ 437, – Ⓟ
M 3.50/6.00 1.50 – **12 rm** 7.00/12.00 **st.** – P 12.00/16.00 **st.**

CHAGFORD Devon – pop. **1,250** – ☎ 064 73.
London 218 – Exeter 17 – **Plymouth 28.**

Gidleigh Park ⑤, TQ13 8HH, NW : 2 m., Dartmoor National Park ☎ 2225, ≤, « Country house atmosphere », ✂, ⛱, ✎, , park – ⇔wc Ⓟ
closed January and February – **M** (dinner only) approx. 6.50 – **14 rm** 12.00/22.00 – P 16.00/23.00.

Greenacres ⑤, TQ13 8AS, ☎ 3471, – Ⓟ
Easter-October – **12 rm** 6.50/12.00 **st.**

at Easton Cross NE : **1 ½** m. on **A 382** – ✉ ☎ **064 73 Chagford :**

Easton Court, TQ13 8JL, ☎ 3469, « 15C thatched house », – ⇔wc Ⓟ
March-November – **M** (dinner only) 6.00/7.00 – **8 rm** 10.00/18.00.

at Sandypark NE : **1 ½** m. on **A 382** – ✉ ☎ **064 73 Chagford :**

Mill End ⑤, TQ13 8JN, ☎ 2282, « Country house with water mill », ✎, – ⇔wc Ⓟ
closed 18 to 28 December – **M** 5.00/5.75 **s.** 1.50 – 2.25 – **18 rm** 7.25/17.00 **s.**

Great Tree ⑤, TQ13 8JS, ☎ 2491, ≤, « Country house atmosphere », , park – ⇔wc Ⓟ
closed January and February – **M** a la carte 4.50/6.60 **st.** 1.50 – **15 rm** 8.00/17.00 **st.**

CHALFONT ST. GILES Bucks. **986** ④ – pop. **7,118** – ☎ 024 07.
See : Milton's Cottage *AC*.
London 26 – Aylesbury 18.

Le Relais, London Rd, ☎ 2590, French rest. – Ⓟ
closed Sunday and Monday lunch – **M** a la carte approx. 5.15 **t.**

MORRIS-MG-WOLSELEY London Rd ☎ 3045

CHALFONT ST. PETER Bucks. – ☎ 024 07 Chalfont St. Giles.
London 22 – **Oxford 37.**

Water Hall, Amersham Rd, SL9 0PA, ☎ 2820 – Ⓟ
closed Sunday, Monday, 1 week summer and 1 week Christmas – **M** (dinner only) a la carte 4.60/5.40 1.30.

CITROEN High St. ☎ 028 13 (Gerrards Cross) 85581
OPEL Gravell Hill, Amersham Rd ☎ 028 13 (Gerrards Cross) 85372

CHANCERY Dyfed – see Aberystwyth.

CHANDLER'S FORD Hants. – pop. **7,200** – ☎ 042 15.
London 79 – **Southampton 6.5** – Winchester 7.

Hut, S05 3DJ, ✉ Eastleigh ☎ 3039, – Ⓟ
M a la carte 3.65/4.70 **t.** 1.15 – **10 rm** 6.05/8.85 **s.**

King's Court, 83 Winchester Rd, SO5 2GG, ☎ 2232 – Ⓟ
closed Sunday, Monday, Good Friday, 26 December and Bank Holidays – **M** a la carte 3.20/5.40 1.65.

FORD Bournemouth Rd ☎ 2901
RENAULT Hursley Rd ☎ 3853

CHAPEL STILE Cumbria – see Ambleside.

CHARDSTOCK Devon – pop. **1,151** – ✉ Axminster – ☎ 046 02 South Chard.
London 154 – Dorchester 33 – Exeter 32 – Taunton 23.

Tytherleigh Arms, EX13 7BE, on A 358 ☎ 214 – Ⓟ.

CHARING Kent 986 ㊱ – see Ashford.

CHARLBURY Oxon. – pop. 2,249 – ☎ 060 881.
London 72 – Birmingham 50 – Oxford 15.

Bell, Church St., OX7 3PP, ☎ 278, « Tasteful decor » – 🛁wc ☎ **P**.
M *(closed Sunday dinner to non-residents)* 3.00/3.50 **t.** – **14 rm** ☕ 8.00/18.00 **st.**

CHARLTON West Sussex – see Chichester.

CHARLTON KINGS Glos. – see Cheltenham.

CHARMOUTH Dorset – pop. 1,017 – ✉ Bridport – ☎ 029 76.
London 157 – Dorchester 22 – Exeter 31 – Taunton 27.

Fernhill, DT6 6BX, on A 3052 ☎ 492, heated – 🛁wc **P**
Easter-September – **M** (bar lunch) 3.50/3.75 **t.** 🍷 1.50 – **15 rm** ☕ 7.00/15.50 **t.**

Queen's Armes, The Street, DT6 6QF, ☎ 339, – **P**
March-October – **M** approx. 3.50 🍷 1.50 – **15 rm** ☕ 6.00/14.00 – P 10.50/12.50.

Sea Horse, Higher Sea Lane, DT6 6BB, ☎ 414, ≤, – **P**
April-October – **M** (bar lunch) approx. 3.50 **s.** 🍷 1.30 – **16 rm** ☕ 7.00/14.00 **st.**

Newlands House, Stonebarrow Lane, DT6 6RA, ☎ 212 – TV 🚿wc **P**
Easter-October – **8 rm** ☕ 4.75/9.00 **st.**

CHARNOCK RICHARD Lancs. – pop. 1,684 – ☎ 0257 Coppull.
London 215 – Liverpool 26 – Manchester 24 – Preston 10.

TraveLodge, without rest. (T.H.F.), Mill Lane, PR7 5LQ, on M 6 ☎ 791746 – TV 🛁wc ☎ ♿ **P**
108 rm ☕ 10.50/14.50 **st.**

CHASTLETON Oxon. 986 ㉛ – pop. 128.
See : Chastleton House** (Elizabethan) *AC*.
London 83 – Gloucester 35 – Oxford 26.

Hotels and restaurants see : Moreton-in-Marsh NW : 5 m.
Stow-on-the-Wold SW : 8 m.

Red Lion	Wenn der Name eines Hotels dünn gedruckt ist, dann hat uns der Hotelier Preise und Öffnungszeiten nicht angegeben.

CHATSWORTH Derbs. 986 ㉗.
See : Chatsworth *** : site**, house*** (Renaissance) garden*** *AC*.
London 164 – Derby 32 – Manchester 38 – Sheffield 16.

Hotels and restaurants see : Sheffield NE : 16 m.

CHEDDAR Somerset 986 ㉟ – pop. 3,435.
See : Cheddar Gorge*** – Gough's Caves** *AC*.
i The Library, Union St. ☎ 742769.
London 145 – Bristol 20 – Wells 7 – Weston-super-Mare 13.

Hotels see : Axbridge NW : 3 m.
Wells : SE : 7 m.

AUSTIN-MG-WOLSELEY The Cliffs ☎ 742420

CHELMSFORD Essex 986 ㉜ – pop. 58,194 – ☎ 0245.
London 33 – Cambridge 46 – Ipswich 40 – Southend-on-Sea 19.

South Lodge, 196 New London Rd, CM2 0AR, ☎ 64564, Telex 99452 – TV 🛁wc ☎ **P**
M approx. 3.75 **s.** 🍷 1.15 – ☕ 1.00 – **27 rm** 7.25/17.00 **s.**

County, 29 Rainsford Rd, CM1 2QA, ☎ 66911 – 🛁wc 🚿wc ☎ **P**.
M 3.15/3.70 **s.** 🍷 1.05 – ☕ 1.00 – **47 rm** 7.00/15.00 **s.** – P 12.75/13.65 **s.**

Tanunda, 217-219 New London Rd, CM2 0AJ, S : 1 m. on A 130 ☎ 54295 – **P**
closed Christmas – **18 rm** ☕ 5.50/10.40 **st.**

Oaklands, 240 Springfield Rd, CM2 6BP, ☎ 50357 – **P**
closed Christmas week – **8 rm** ☕ 7.00/12.00 **st.**

AUSTIN-MORRIS-MG-WOLSELEY 74 Main Rd, Broomfield ☎ 440571
DAF, VOLVO Braintree Rd, Little Waltham ☎ 024 534 (Great Leighs) 534260
CHRYSLER-SIMCA 145 Moulsham St. ☎ 61822
CITROEN Galley Wood ☎ 68366
FIAT, MERCEDES-BENZ 47 Springfield Rd ☎ 55622
FORD 39 Robjohns Rd ☎ 64111
OPEL Baddow Rd ☎ 52959
PEUGEOT Bridge St. ☎ 421233
RENAULT Southend Rd, Sandon ☎ 71113
VAUXHALL Duke St. ☎ 53674
VW, AUDI-NSU Colchester Rd, Springfield ☎ 468151

CHELTENHAM Glos. 986 ㉛ – pop. 74,356 – ☎ 0242.

See : Pittville Park* A – Municipal Art Gallery and Museum* B M. **Envir. :** Elkstone (Parish church: doorway* and arches* 12C) SE: 7 m. by A 435 A.

Staverton Airport : ☎ 0452 (Churchdown) 713351 and 712285, W: 3 ½ m. by A 40 A and near M 5 Motorway, intersection Nº 11 – **Terminal :** Royal Wells.

i Municipal Offices, The Promenade ☎ 22878 and 21333.

London 99 – Birmingham 48 – Bristol 40 – Gloucester 9 – Oxford 43.

Plan opposite

Queen's (T.H.F.), Promenade, GL50 1NN, ☎ 54724, Telex 43381, – TV P. — B n
M a la carte 4.65/7.30 **st.** 1.40 – 2.00 – **77 rm** 15.00/24.00 **st.**

Golden Valley (Thistle), Gloucester Rd, GL51 0TS, W: 2 m. on A 40 ☎ 32691, Telex 43410 – TV P. — by A 40 A
M a la carte 8.00/11.50 2.50 – 2.30 – **103 rm** 17.25/24.75.

Carlton, Parabola Rd, GL50 3AQ, ☎ 54453, – TV wc P. — B r
M 4.00/6.00 **st.** 1.20 – **49 rm** 11.00/18.00 **s.** – P 16.00 **s.**

George (T.H.F.), St. George's Rd, GL10 3DZ, ☎ 24732 – TV wc P — B u
M 3.00/3.50 **st.** 1.50 – **42 rm** 9.00/16.50 **st.**

Savoy (Interchange), Bayshill Rd, GL50 3AS, ☎ 27788, – wc P — B c
M a la carte 3.00/5.15 **st.** 1.75 – **58 rm** 10.00/18.00 **st.**

Overton, 88 St. George's Rd, GL50 4PE, ☎ 23371, – P — B e
closed 3 days at Christmas – **M** 2.75/4.00 **st.** 0.75 – **14 rm** 6.75/13.90 **st.**

Wellesley Court, Clarence Sq., GL50 4JR, ☎ 31632, – P — C a
M 2.50/2.95 **t.** 0.95 – **18 rm** 5.95/10.45 **t.**

Smiths, 4 Montpellier St., GL50 1SX, ☎ 28856 — B v
closed Sunday, Monday and Bank Holidays – **M** a la carte 4.55/6.85 **st.** 1.50.

Aubergine, Belgrave House, Imperial Sq., GL50 1QB, ☎ 31402, Bistro — B a
closed Sunday, Monday lunch and 25-26 December – **M** a la carte approx. 5.65 1.80.

at Bishop's Cleeve N: 3 ½ m. on A 435 – A – ✉ Cheltenham – ☎ 024 267 Bishop's Cleeve:

Cleeveway House, 22 Evesham Rd, GL52 4SA, ☎ 2585, – P
closed Sunday, Monday, Bank Holidays and Christmas – **M** a la carte 3.30/6.80 **t.** 1.15.

at Prestbury NE : 2 m. on A 46 – ✉ ☎ 0242 Cheltenham:

Prestbury House with rm, The Burgage, GL52 3DN, ☎ 29533, – wc wc P — A i
M a la carte 5.15/6.40 1.20 – **8 rm** 8.00/17.00.

at Southam NE: 3 m. on A 46 – A – ✉ ☎ 0242 Cheltenham:

De la Bere, GL52 3NH, ☎ 37771, « Tudor manor house », , park – TV P.
M a la carte 3.95/5.45 **st.** 1.50 – **19 rm** 11.00/20.00 **st.**

at Cleeve Hill NE: 4 m. on A 46 – A – ✉ Cheltenham – ☎ 024 267 Bishop's Cleeve:

Malvern View with rm, GL52 3PR, ☎ 2017, <, – wc wc P
closed Sunday dinner to non-residents and 3 weeks at Christmas – **M** (dinner only) 5.00/6.00 1.65 – **7 rm** 9.25/14.50.

at Charlton Kings SE: 2 ¼ m. on A 435 – ✉ ☎ 0242 Cheltenham:

Lilley Brook, Cirencester Rd, GL53 8EH, ☎ 25861, <, , park – wc wc P. — A a
M 2.00/5.00 2.00 – **32 rm** 13.00/22.00 **st.** – P 15.00/20.00 **st.**

at Shipton SE: 7 m. off A 40 – A – ✉ Cheltenham – ☎ 024 282 Andoversford:

Frogmill, GL54 4HT, W: ¾ m. junction A 436 and A 40, ☎ 547, Group Telex 261125 – wc P.
M 3.50/7.00 **t.** 1.20 – **14 rm** 6.50/16.00.

at Withington SE: 10 m. by A 435 – A – ✉ Cheltenham – ☎ 024 289 Withington:

Mill House, GL54 4BE, ☎ 204, « 15C Stone mill house », – P
closed last week October and first week November – **M** a la carte 4.25/5.80 **s.** 1.25.

at Shurdington SW: 3 ¾ m. on A 46 – A – ✉ ☎ 0242 Cheltenham :

Greenway , GL51 5UG, ☎ 862352, < , « Country house atmosphere, gardens » – wc P
M approx. 4.20 **s.** 1.60 – **14 rm** 10.00/18.00 **s.**

AUDI-NSU North St. ☎ 55301
AUSTIN-MORRIS-MG-ROVER-TRIUMPH Princess Elizabeth Way ☎ 20441
CHRYSLER-SIMCA Imperial Sq. ☎ 21121
CITROEN 16 Bath Rd ☎ 55391
DAF 41/43 Painswick Rd ☎ 22539
DAF Andoversford ☎ 045 15 (Guiting Power) 274
DAF, MAZDA 18 Andover Rd ☎ 24116
DAIMLER-JAGUAR Montpellier Spa Rd ☎ 21651
DATSUN 60/66 Fairview Rd ☎ 53880
FIAT Prestbury ☎ 7247
FIAT 172 Leckhampton Rd ☎ 23365
FORD 71 Winchcombe Rd ☎ 27061
LANCIA Swindon Rd ☎ 32167
OPEL 379 High St. ☎ 22666
PEUGEOT Kingsditch Lane ☎ 28945
ROLLS ROYCE 62/68 Swindon Rd ☎ 55374
SAAB Townsend St. ☎ 24348
VOLVO 38 Suffolk Rd ☎ 27778

CHELTENHAM

Street	Grid
High Street	BC
Pittville Street	C 27
Portland Street	C
Promenade (The)	BC 28
Winchcombe Street	C 38
Ambrose Street	B 2
Berkeley Street	C 4
Clarence Road	C 5
Clarence Street	C 6
Crescent Terrace	B 7
Deep Street	A 9
Dunalley Street	C 10
Henrietta Street	C 13
High Street (PRESTBURY)	A 14
Keynsham Road	C 15
Montpellier Avenue	B 16
Montpellier Walk	B 18
North Street	C 20
Norwood Road	B 21
Oriel Road	C 22
Parabola Road	B 23
Park (The)	B 25
Park Place	B 26
Regent Street	C 29
Royal Well Road	BC 30
St. George's Parade	B 31
St. George's Place	B 32
St. Margaret's Road	C 33
Sandford Terrace	C 34
Thatcham Lane	A 35
Western Road	B 37

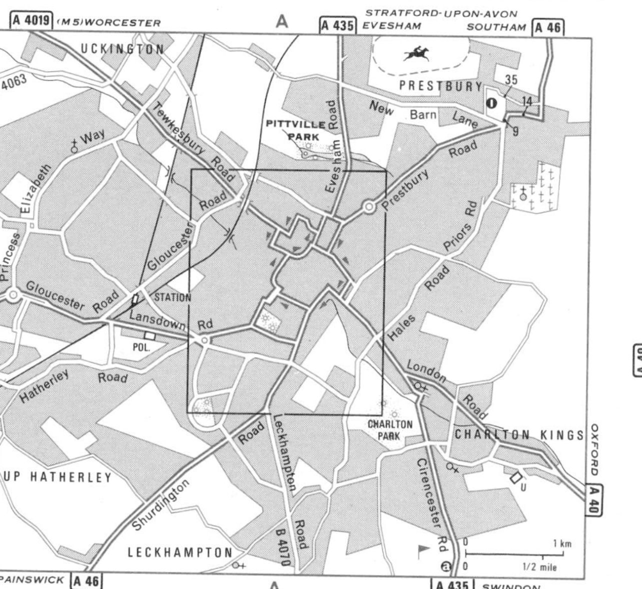

CHELWOOD GATE East Sussex – see Forest Row.

CHENIES Bucks. – pop. **1,099** – ✉ Rickmansworth – ☎ 092 78 Chorleywood.
London 30 – Aylesbury 18 – Watford 7.

Bedford Arms (Thistle), WD3 6EQ, ☎ 3301, – TV P
M a la carte 6.60/10.85 **st.** 1.40 – 2.20 – **10 rm** 16.75/25.00 **st.**

CHEPSTOW Gwent 986 ㉟ – pop. 8,082 – ☎ 029 12.
See: Castle* (stronghold) *AC.* **Envir.:** Tintern (abbey**) *AC,* N: 6 m.
i Tourist Information Centre, Old Arch Building, High St. ☎ 3772.
London 131 – **Bristol 17** – **Cardiff 28** – Gloucester 34.

Two Rivers, Newport Rd, NP6 5PR, ☎ 5151 – wc P.
M approx. 2.50 **s.** 1.20 – **27 rm** 9.50/15.50 **s.**

George (T.H.F.), Moor St., NP6 5DB, ☎ 2365 – TV wc P.
M a la carte 4.00/5.30 **st.** 1.50 – **20 rm** 8.00/15.00 **st.**

AUSTIN-MORRIS-MG-WOLSELEY Station Rd ☎ 3159
CHRYSLER-SIMCA Tutshill ☎ 3131
FORD Newport Rd ☎ 2861
OPEL Bulwork Rd ☎ 5251
VAUXHALL St. Lawrence Rd ☎ 3889

CHESTER Cheshire 986 ⑨ and ㉗ – pop. 62,911 – ☎ 0244.
See: Cathedral** 14C-16C (choir stalls and misericords**) **B** – St. John's Church* 12C **D** – The Rows* – City Walls* – Grosvenor Museum (Roman gallery*) **M**[1]. **Envir.:** Upton (Chester Zoo**) *AC,* N: 3 m. by A 5116.
18 Upton Lane ☎ 23638, by A 5116 – 18 Vicars Cross ☎ 35174, E: 2 m. by A 51 – 18 Tower's Lane ☎ 092 82 (Helsby) 2021, NE: 8 m. by A 56.
i Publicity Department, Town Hall ☎ 40144 ext 2111.
London 195 – Birkenhead 19 – **Birmingham 80** – **Liverpool 21** – **Manchester 39** – Preston 55 – **Sheffield 75** – **Stoke-on-Trent 37.**

Plan opposite

Grosvenor, Eastgate St., CH1 1LT, ☎ 24024, Telex 61240 – TV. **a**
M a la carte 6.80/10.00 1.70 – 2.40 – **100 rm** 22.70/39.50 **st.**

Queen (T.H.F.), City Rd, CH1 3AH, ☎ 28341, Telex 617101, – TV wc P. **r**
M 3.75/4.25 **st.** 1.45 – **91 rm** 11.00/18.50 **st.**

Chester Curzon (T.H.F.), Wrexham Rd, CH4 9DL, S: 2 m. on A 483 ☎ 674111, Telex 61450 – TV wc P.
M 2.95/4.00 **st.** 1.50 – 2.00 – **56 rm** 12.00/16.00 **st.**

Mollington Banastre (Interchange), Parkgate Rd, CH1 6NN, NW: 2 m. on A 540 ☎ 024 455 (Great Mollington) 471, – TV wc P.
M a la carte 4.90/6.65 **s.** 1.60 – 1.70 – **53 rm** 10.50/17.80 **s.**

The Blossoms, St. John St., CH1 1HL, ☎ 23186 – wc **e**
M 3.00/4.00 – 1.65 – **77 rm** 10.00/20.00.

Oaklands (S & N), 93 Hoole Rd, CH2 3BN, ☎ 22156, – wc P **c**
M a la carte 2.70/5.30 **st.** 1.40 – **19 rm** 8.70/14.20 **st.**

Weston, 82 Hoole Rd, CH2 3NT, ☎ 26735 – TV P **n**
closed Christmas week – **7 rm** 7.50/12.50 **s.**

Green Bough, 60 Hoole Rd, CH2 3NL, ☎ 26241 – P **i**
closed Christmas and 1 January – **11 rm** 5.00/9.00 **t.**

at Backford Cross N: 4 ½ m. by **A 5116** junction **A 41** and **A 5117** – ✉ Chester – ☎ 024 455 Great Mollington:

Wirral Mercury Motor Inn, CH1 6PE, ☎ 551, Group Telex 628064 – TV wc P.
M (grill rest.) a la carte 2.50/3.80 **st.** 1.35 – 1.50 – **102 rm** 13.00/17.50 **st.**

at Christleton E: 2 m. on A 41 – ✉ ☎ 0244 Chester:

Abbots Well Motor Inn, Whitchurch Rd, CH3 5QL, ☎ 32121, Telex 61561, – TV P.
closed Christmas Day – **M** approx. 4.65 **st.** 2.15 – 2.05 – **75 rm** 11.25/18.00 **st.**

at Broxton SE: 10 m. junction A 41 and A 534 – ✉ ☎ 082 925 Broxton:

XX Egerton Arms, ☎ 241, – P.

at Aldford S: 5 ½ m. on B 5130 – ✉ Chester – ☎ 024 465 Aldford:

XX **Grosvenor Arms,** CH3 6HJ, ☎ 247 – P
closed Sunday dinner, Good Friday dinner and Christmas Day dinner – **M** a la carte 3.75/6.15 **t.** 1.30.

at Burton (Clywd) S: 6 m. by A 483 – ✉ Wrexham – ☎ 0244 Rosset:

XX **Golden Grove Inn,** ☎ 570445, – P
closed Sunday dinner and Monday – **M** a la carte 3.05/5.50.

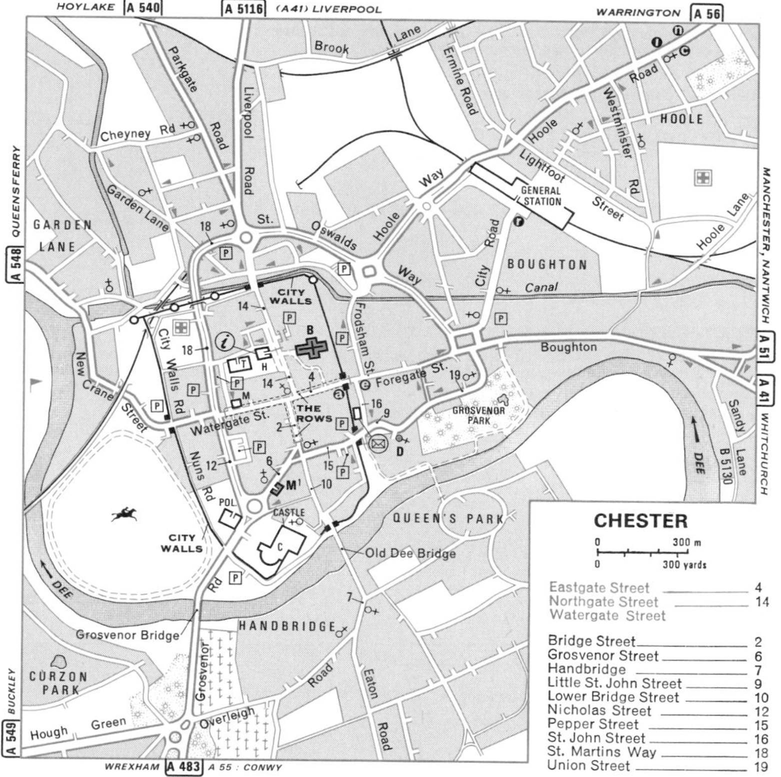

MICHELIN Branch, Winsford Way, Sealand Rd Industrial Estate, CH1 4NL, ☎ 27195.

AUSTIN-MORRIS-MG-ROVER-TRIUMPH-WOLSELEY 17 Nicholas St. ☎ 315477
AUSTIN-MORRIS-MG-ROVER-TRIUMPH Victoria Rd ☎ 45051
CHRYSLER-SIMCA Victoria Rd ☎ 22622
CITROEN, DAF Border House ☎ 672977
DAIMLER-JAGUAR, ROLLS ROYCE 8 Russell St. ☎ 25262
FORD The Newgate ☎ 20444
OPEL 21 Garden Lane ☎ 46955
PEUGEOT 36 Tarvin Rd ☎ 20336
RENAULT Hamilton Pl. ☎ 317661
SAAB Western Av. ☎ 48022
VAUXHALL Parkgate Rd ☎ 27351
VAUXHALL Hoole Lane, Broughton ☎ 24611
VOLVO 6/8 Volunteer St. ☎ 25201
VW, AUDI-NSU Saughall Rd ☎ 47363

CHESTERFIELD Derbs. 986 ㉗ – pop. 70,169 – ☎ 0246.
Envir. : Hardwick Hall** 16C (tapestries and embroideries**) *AC*, SE : 8 m – Bolsover Castle* (17C) *AC*, E : 7 m.

⛳18 Murray House, Tapton Park ☎ 73887.

i Central Library, Corporation St. ☎ 32047 or 32661.

London 152 – Derby 24 – **Nottingham 25** – **Sheffield 12.**

🏨 **Station,** Corporation St., S41 7UA, ☎ 71141 – wc ☎ Ⓟ.
M a la carte 4.00/8.25 **t.** – **56 rm** 11.00/18.00 **t.**

⌂ **Portland** (Anchor), West Bars, S40 1AY, ☎ 34502, Group Telex 27120 – wc Ⓟ
M approx. 2.50 **t.** 1.00 – **24 rm** 9.35/16.50.

at Stonedge SW : 4 ½ m. on B 5057 by A 632 – ✉ ☎ 0246 Chesterfield :

✕✕ Red Lion Inn, S45 0LW, ☎ 6142, Dancing (Wednesday and Saturday) – Ⓟ.

AUSTIN-MORRIS-MG-WOLSELEY 221 Sheffield Rd ☎ 77241
CHRYSLER-SIMCA 361 Sheffield Rd ☎ 450383
CITROEN, SAAB Pottery Lane, Whittington Moor ☎ 51611
DATSUN Ringwood Rd ☎ 77386
FIAT Soresby St. ☎ 34351
FORD Barker Lane ☎ 76341
JAGUAR-ROVER-TRIUMPH Holywell St. ☎ 77241
MORRIS-MG-WOLSELEY Park Rd ☎ 73428
OPEL-VAUXHALL Chesterfield Rd, Staveley ☎ 024 687 (Staveley) 3286
PEUGEOT Pottery Lane ☎ 74181
RENAULT North Wingfield Rd ☎ 850208
VAUXHALL 464 Chatsworth Rd ☎ 79201

CHESTER-LE-STREET Durham 986 ⑲ – pop. 20,568 – ☎ 0385.

Envir. : Lambton Lion Park** *AC*, NE: 2 m. – Lumley Castle* (14C) *AC*, E : 1 ½ m. – Beamish (North of England open Air Museum*) *AC*, NW: 3 m.

⛳18 Lumley Park ☎ 3218, E: ½ m.

London 275 – Durham 7 – Newcastle-upon-Tyne 8.

Lumley Castle, DH3 4NX, E : 1 m. on B 1284 ☎ 885326, « 14 C castle », heated, park – TV wc wc ☎ **P**.
M a la carte 5.35/8.80 🍷 0.80 – ☕ 1.50 – **48 rm** 10.50/14.00.

FIAT, VAUXHALL 187 Front St. ☎ 884221

CHESTERTON Oxon. – pop. 497 – ✉ ☎ 086 92 Bicester.

⛳18 ☎ 41204.

London 65 – Northampton 33 – Oxford 13.

XX **Kinchs,** OX6 8UE, on A 4095 ☎ 41444, « Converted barn » – **P**
closed Sunday dinner and Monday – **M** (lunch by arrangement only) 5.50/6.50 **t.** 🍷 1.30.

CHICHESTER West Sussex 986 ㊱ – pop. 20,649 – ☎ 0243.

See : Cathedral* 11C-15C BZ **A** – Market Cross* BZ **B**. **Envir. :** Fishbourne Roman Palace (mosaics*) *AC*, W : 2 m. AZ **R** – Goodwood House* (Jacobean) *AC*, NE : 4 m. by A 27 AY and A 285.

i The Council House, North St. ☎ 82226.

London 69 – Brighton 31 – Portsmouth 18 – Southampton 30.

CHICHESTER

Street	Grid
East Street	BZ
North Street	BYZ
South Street	BZ
Birdham Road	AZ 2
Bognor Road	AZ 3
Chapel Street	BY 6
Chichester Arundel Road	AY 7
Fishbourne Road	AZ 8
Florence Road	AZ 10
Hornet (The)	BZ 12
Kingsham Road	BZ 13
Lavant Road	AY 14
Little London	BY 15
Market Road	BZ 16
Northgate	BY 17
North Pallant	BZ 19
Priory Lane	BY 20
St. James's	AZ 21
St. John's Street	BZ 23
St. Martin's Square	BY 24
St. Pancras	BY 25
St. Paul's Road	BY 27
Sherborne Road	AZ 28
Southgate	BZ 29
South Pallant	BZ 31
Spitalfield Lane	BY 32
Stockbridge Road	AZ 33
Tower Street	BY 35
Westhampnett Road	AYZ 36

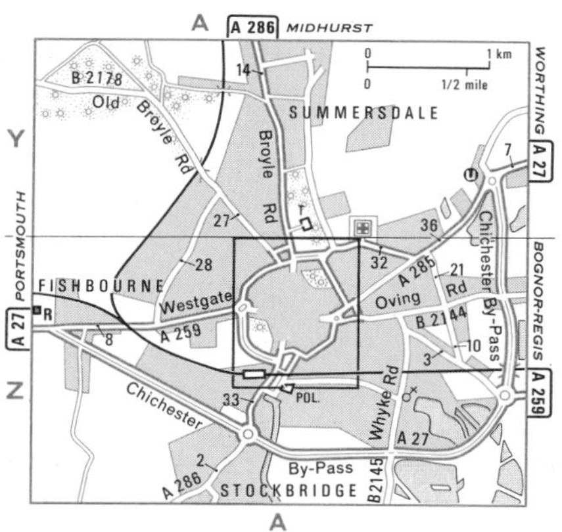

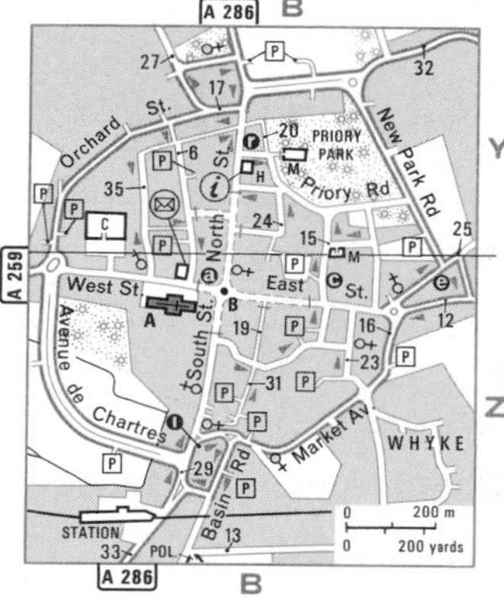

Dolphin and Anchor (T.H.F.), West St., PO19 1QE, ☎ 85121 – TV wc ☎
M 3.50/3.75 **st.** 🍷 1.50 – **54 rm** ☕ 11.00/18.00 **st.** BZ **a**

Chichester Lodge, Westhampnett Roundabout, PO19 4UL, ☎ 86351 – TV wc ☎ **P**.
34 rm. AY **u**

Ship, North St., PO19 1NH, ☎ 82028, Telex 957141 – wc ☎ **P**
M 3.50/3.85 **t.** 🍷 1.35 – **27 rm** ☕ 6.75/14.50 **t.** BY **r**

Bedford, Southgate, PO19 1DP, ☎ 85766 – **P**
M (residents only) 3.25/3.75 **t.** 🍷 1.60 – **25 rm** ☕ 5.50/11.00. BZ **i**

XX **Little London,** 38 Little London, PO19 1PL, ☎ 84899 BZ **c**
closed Sunday, Monday, October and Bank Holidays – **M** a la carte 5.95/9.60 **t.** 🍷 1.60.

XX **Christopher's,** 149 St. Pancras, PO19 1SH, ☎ 88724 BZ **e**
closed Monday in winter and Sunday – **M** approx. 6.50 **t.** 🍷 1.10.

at Chilgrove N : 6 m. on B 2141 by A 286 – AY – ✉ Chichester – ☎ 024 359 East Marden :

XX **White Horse,** PO18 9HX, ☎ 219 – Ⓟ
closed Sunday, Monday and Bank Holidays – **M** a la carte 5.30/6.70 **t.** 🌢 1.45.

at Charlton N : 6 ¼ m. off A 286 – AY – ✉ Chichester – ☎ 024 363 Singleton :

Woodstock House ⛾, PO18 0HU, ☎ 666, 🌳 – Ⓟ
closed January – **M** approx. 3.00 – **12 rm** ☕ 5.50/11.00 – P 6.85.

at Goodwood NE : 4 m. off A 285 by A 27 – AY – ✉ Chichester – ☎ 024 353 Halnaker :

Richmond Arms, PO18 0QB, ☎ 361 – TV ⛀wc ☎ Ⓟ.
M 3.45/4.50 **st.** 🌢 1.60 – **20 rm** ☕ 10.50/16.50 **st.** – P 14.00/17.00 **st.**

at Tangmere E : 3 m. on A 27 – AY – ✉ Chichester – ☎ 024 353 Halnaker :

XX **Old Timbers,** PO18 0DU, ☎ 294 – Ⓟ
closed Sunday, Tuesday, 1 week after Easter, last 2 weeks October, Christmas and Bank Holidays – **M** a la carte 4.45/6.25 🌢 1.80.

at Old Bosham W : 4 m. off A 27 – AZ – ✉ Chichester – ☎ 0243 Bosham :

Millstream (Interchange), Bosham Lane, PO18 8HL, ☎ 573234, « Tasteful decor », 🌳 – ⛀wc ☎ Ⓟ
M a la carte 4.45/6.50 **st.** 🌢 1.30 – **17 rm** ☕ 9.50/21.00 **st.**

Viking, Bosham Lane, PO18 8HG, ☎ 573109, 🌳 – Ⓟ
M approx. 3.75 **t.** 🌢 1.05 – **9 rm** ☕ 8.35/15.00 **st.**

at Funtington NW : 4 ½ m. on B 2178 – AY – ✉ Chichester – ☎ 024 358 West Ashling :

XX Hallidays of Funtington, ☎ 331 – Ⓟ.

AUSTIN-DAIMLER-JAGUAR-MORRIS-MG-ROVER-TRIUMPH-WOLSELEY South St. ☎ 82282
AUSTIN-DAIMLER-JAGUAR-MORRIS-MG-ROVER-TRIUMPH Westhampnett Rd ☎ 81331
CHRYSLER-SIMCA Market Rd ☎ 86622
FIAT Northgate ☎ 84844
FORD The Hornet ☎ 88100
LANCIA Delling Lane, Bosham ☎ 573271
MERCEDES-BENZ, VOLVO Lavant Rd ☎ 527370
RENAULT 113 The Hornet ☎ 82293
RENAULT Bath Par. ☎ 32491
VAUXHALL 55 Fishbourne Rd ☎ 82241
VW, AUDI-NSU 51/54 Bognor Rd ☎ 87684

CHIDDINGFOLD Surrey – pop. 2,449 – ☎ 042 879 Wormley.

London 45 – Brighton 40 – Guildford 12.

XXX **Crown Inn** with rm, The Green, Petworth Rd, GU8 4TX, ☎ 2255, « 13C inn » – ⛀wc ☎ Ⓟ
closed Monday and Tuesday from November to March and Christmas Day dinner – **M** a la carte 6.40/9.30 **st.** 🌢 2.00 – ☕ 1.25 – **4 rm** 16.00/20.00 **st.**

X **Crown Bistro** (at Crown Inn), The Green, Petworth Rd, GU8 4TX, ☎ 2255 – Ⓟ
closed Christmas dinner – **M** a la carte 3.20/5.00 **t.** 🌢 1.25.

CHIDDINGSTONE Kent – see Penshurst.

CHIDEOCK Dorset – pop. 555 – ✉ Bridport – ☎ 029 789.

London 153 – Dorchester 18 – Lyme Regis 7.

X **Clock House** with rm, DT6 6JW, on A 35 ☎ 423 – Ⓟ
closed Sunday lunch, Monday and Sunday in winter, January and February – **M** (bar lunch in winter) a la carte 5.35/7.80 **s.** 🌢 1.95 – ☕ 1.25 – **7 rm** 5.60/12.40 **s.**

CHIGWELL Essex 986 ④ – pop. 12,018 – ☎ 01 London.

🏌18, 🏌18 Chigwell Row ☎ 500 2097.

i Grange Farm Camping and Sports Centre, High Rd ☎ 500 0121.

London 13 – Chelmsford 22.

XXX **Ye Olde King's Head,** High Rd, IGP 6QA, ☎ 500 2021 – Ⓟ
closed Saturday lunch, Sunday and Bank Holidays – **M** a la carte 4.90/8.60 **t.**

VAUXHALL High Rd ☎ 500 4122

CHILGROVE West Sussex – see Chichester.

CHILLINGTON Devon – see Kingsbridge.

CHIPPENHAM Wilts. 986 ㉟ – pop. 18,696 – ☎ 0249.

Envir. : Corsham Court** (Elizabethan) *AC*, SW : 3 ½ m.

🏌18 Malmesbury Rd ☎ 2040, N : 1 m.

London 106 – Bristol 27 – Southampton 64 – Swindon 21.

Angel Motel (Norfolk Cap.), 8 Market Pl., SN15 3HD, ☎ 2615, Group Telex 23241 – TV ⛀wc ☎ Ⓟ
M (grill rest. only) a la carte 3.15/5.35 **st.** – **41 rm** ☕ 7.60/15.15 **st.**

CHIPPENHAM

AUSTIN-MG-WOLSELEY Allington ℡ 51134
AUSTIN-MORRIS-MG-WOLSELEY Lyneham ℡ 024 989 (Bradenstoke) 331
CHRYSLER-SIMCA 21 New Rd ℡ 2293
FIAT Pewsham ℡ 2115
FORD Cocklebury Rd ℡ 3255
MORRIS-MG-WOLSELEY London Rd ℡ 3247
RENAULT London Rd ℡ 51131
ROVER-TRIUMPH Station Hill ℡ 2215
TOYOTA Bristol Rd ℡ 3479
VAUXHALL 16/17 The Causeway ℡ 3241
VOLVO Malmesbury Rd ℡ 2016

CHIPPERFIELD Herts. – pop. **1,651** – ✉ ☎ **092 77 Kings Langley.**

London 30 – Aylesbury 21 – Watford 7.

XX **Two Brewers Inn** (T.H.F.), The Common, WD4 9BS, ℡ 65266 – P
M a la carte 5.25/9.85 **st.** 1.50.

CHIPPING CAMPDEN Glos. 986 ㉛ – pop. **1,956** – ☎ **0386 Evesham.**

See : High Street★.

London 93 – Cheltenham 21 – **Oxford 37** – Stratford-on-Avon 12.

Cotswold House, The Square, GL55 6AN, ℡ 840330, – wc P
M (bar lunch and Sunday lunch) 3.60/3.95 1.60 – 0.80 – **25 rm** 7.90/18.55.

King's Arms, The Square, GL55 6AV, ℡ 840256, – wc P
M 4.75/5.25 **t.** 1,15 – 1.20 – **14 rm** 8.50/19.60 **st.**

Seymour House, High St., GL55 6AH, ℡ 840429, – wc P
closed December and January – **M** 3.50/5.00 1.50 – **20 rm** 7.50/16.00.

Noel Arms, High St., GL55 6AT, ℡ 840317 – wc P
M approx. 3.25 **s.** 1.55 – **21 rm** 7.50/17.20 **s.**

at Mickleton N : 3 m. by B 4035 and B 4081 – ✉ Chipping Campden – ☎ 038 677 Mickleton :

Three Ways, GL55 6SB, on A 46 ℡ 231, – wc P
M 4.50/4.75 2.00 – **49 rm** 9.00/18.00.

MORRIS-MG-WOLSELEY High St. ℡ 840213
ROVER-TRIUMPH Sheep St. ℡ 840248

CHIPPING NORTON Oxon. 986 ㉛ – pop. **4,767** – ☎ **0608.**

London 77 – **Birmingham 44** – Gloucester 36 – **Oxford 21.**

White Hart (T.H.F.), High St., OX7 5AD, ℡ 2572 – wc P
M a la carte 4.00/5.15 **st.** 1.50 – **22 rm** 7.50/17.00 **st.**

Crown and Cushion, High St., OX7 5AD, ℡ 2533 – P
M 2.60/4.00 **s.** 1.50 – **12 rm** 7.00/14.00 **s.** – P 12.00/15.00 **s.**

AUSTIN-MORRIS-MG-WOLSELEY Burford Rd ℡ 2461
CHRYSLER-SIMCA ℡ 2014

CHIPPING SODBURY Avon 986 ㉟ – pop. **3,836** – ☎ **0454.**

Envir. : Dodington House★ (Renaissance) *AC*, SE : **1** m.

18, 9 ℡ 312024.

London 117 – **Bristol 11** – **Cardiff 50** – Gloucester 27.

Moda, 1 High St., BS17 6BB, ℡ 312135
closed Christmas and Easter – **9 rm** 5.50/11.00.

PEUGEOT Badmindon Rd ℡ 312552

CHIPSTEAD Surrey – pop. **4,129** (inc. Hooley) – ☎ **073 75 Downland.**

London 15 – Reigate 6.

XX **Dene Farm,** Outwood Lane ℡ 52661 – P
M a la carte 4.35/6.45 **t.** 2.50.

SAAB 2 Outwood Lane ℡ 55640

CHIRK Clwyd – pop. **3,564** – ✉ Wrexham – ☎ **069 186.**

See : Castle (gates★, interior★) *AC*. **Envir. :** W : **Vale of Ceiriog★.**

London 188 – Chester 22 – Shrewsbury 24 – Welshpool 21.

XX **Hand** with rm, Church St., LL14 5EY, on A 5 ℡ 3472, – wc P
M *(closed Sunday dinner to non-residents)* (dinner only and Sunday lunch) a la carte 3.40/6.65 **t.** 1.10 – **14 rm** 6.95/13.90 **t.**

CHITTLEHAMHOLT Devon – pop. **146** – ☎ **076 94.**

London 216 – Barnstaple 14 – Exeter 28 – Taunton 45.

Highbullen , EX37 9HD, ℡ 248, ≤, , , heated, 9, , park – wc P
M (dinner only) 5.00 **st.** 1.60 – **23 rm** (dinner included) 16.00/28.00 **st.**

CHOLLERFORD Northumb. – ✉ Hexham – ☎ **043 481 Humshaugh.**

London 303 – **Carlisle 36** – **Newcastle-upon-Tyne 21.**

George (Swallow), NE46 4EW, ℡ 205, Group Telex 53168, ≤, « Riverside gardens » – TV wc P – **22 rm.**

CHRISTCHURCH Dorset 986 ㊴ – pop. 31,463 – ☏ 020 15.
See : Priory Church★ (Norman nave★★).
Iford Bridge, ☏ 3199.
i Caravan, Saxon Sq. ☏ 4321 (summer only) – 10 Queen's Av. ☏ 5301 (winter only).
London 111 – Bournemouth 6 – Salisbury 26 – **Southampton 24** – Winchester 39.

- **King's Arms** (Crest), Castle St., BH23 1DT, ☏ 4117 – wc **P**.
  M a la carte 3.35/5.50 **s.** 1.55 – **34 rm** 9.55/16.50 **s.**
- **Park House,** 48 Barrack Rd, BH23 1PF, ☏ 2124, – **P**
  10 rm 6.00 **st.**
- **Splinters,** 12 Church St., BH23 1BW, ☏ 3454
  closed Sunday and 25-26 December – **M** (dinner only) a la carte 3.20/5.30 **t.**

AUSTIN-MG-ROVER-TRIUMPH-WOLSELEY Lyndhurst Rd ☏ 042 52 (Highcliffe) 71371
CITROEN Barrack Rd ☏ 4515
MORRIS-MG-WOLSELEY Highcliffe-on-Sea ☏ 042 52 (Highcliffe) 72333

CHRISTLETON Cheshire – see Chester.

CHURCH STRETTON Salop 986 ㉛ – pop. 3,346 – ☏ 069 42.
Links Rd ☏ 2281.
i Shropshire Hills, Church St. ☏ 2535 (summer only).
London 166 – **Birmingham 46** – Hereford 39 – Shrewsbury 14.

- **Long Mynd** , Cunnery Rd, SY6 6AG, ☏ 2244, ←, , park – wc **P**.
  M approx. 3.00 – **46 rm** 9.00/15.95.

at All Stretton NE : **1** m. on B 4370 – ✉ ☏ **069 42** Church Stretton :

- **Stretton Hall** , Shrewsbury Rd, SY6 6HG, ☏ 3224, heated, , park – wc **P**
  M 4.00/5.50 0.90 – 1.50 – **12 rm** 5.50/13.00.

at Little Stretton SW : **1** m. on B 4370 – ✉ ☏ **069 42** Church Stretton :

- **Mynd House,** Ludlow Rd, SY6 6RB, ☏ 2212, – **P**
  closed January – **12 rm** 5.60/11.20 **t.**

AUSTIN-MORRIS-MG-WOLSELEY 11 Burway Rd ☏ 2255

CHURSTON FERRERS Devon – see Brixham.

CHURT Surrey – pop. 3,443 (inc. Hindhead) – ✉ Farnham.
Envir. : Devil's Punch Bowl (←★) SE : 4 ½ m.
London 50 – Farnham 6 – **Portsmouth 34** – **Southampton 43.**

- **Frensham Pond** (Interchange) , GU10 2QD, N : 1 ½ m. off A 287 ☏ 025 125 (Frensham) 3175, ←, « Tasteful decor », – TV **P**.
  M a la carte 4.30/5.95 **s.** 2.00 – 1.20 – **19 rm** 11.00/17.00 **s.**
- **Pride of the Valley Inn** (T.H.F.) , GU10 2LE, E : 1 ½ m. off A 287 ☏ 042 873 (Hindhead) 5799, – TV wc **P**
  M a la carte 4.00/5.70 **st.** 1.50 – **11 rm** 8.00/15.00 **st.**

CITROEN ☏ 042 874 (Headley Down) 3344

CIRENCESTER Glos. 986 ㉛ – pop. 13,049 – ☏ 0285.
See : Parish Church★ (Perpendicular) – Corinium Museum★.
Cheltenham Rd ☏ 3939, N : 1 ½ m.
i Corn Hall, Market Pl. ☏ 4180. – **London 101** – **Bristol 37** – Gloucester 19 – **Oxford 37.**

- **King's Head** (Interchange), 24 Market Pl., GL7 2NR, ☏ 3322, Telex 43470 – TV **P**.
  M approx. 4.50 **st.** 2.10 – **71 rm** 13.00/21.50 **st.** – P 16.00/17.50 **st.**
- **Fleece** (T.H.F.), Market Pl., GL7 4NZ, ☏ 2680 – TV wc **P**.
  M a la carte 4.00/5.10 **st.** 1.50 – **23 rm** 7.50/15.50 **st.**
- **Corinium Court,** 12 Gloucester St., GL7 2DG, ☏ 4499, – wc **P**
  closed 24 December to 1 January – **M** *(closed Sunday)* 5.00/7.00 2.00 – **10 rm** 18.00 **t.** – P 14.00/19.00 **t.**
- **La Ronde,** 54 Ashcroft Rd, GL7 1QX, ☏ 4611
  10 rm 6.50/8.50 **t.**

at Ewen SW : **3** ¼ m. off A 429 – ✉ Cirencester – ☏ **028 577** Kemble :

- **Wild Duck Inn** with rm, GL7 6BY, ☏ 364, – TV wc **P**
  M a la carte 5.20/5.95 **s.** 2.50 – 1.75 – **7 rm** 9.75/16.50.

at Stratton NW : **1** ¼ m. on A 417 – ✉ ☏ **0285** Cirencester :

- **Stratton House,** GL7 2LE, ☏ 61761, – wc **P**
  M a la carte 4.00/4.50 **st.** 1.50 – **30 rm** 9.25/18.50 **st.**

AUSTIN-MORRIS-MG-WOLSELEY Tetbury Rd ☏ 2614
CHRYSLER-SIMCA Market Pl. ☏ 3271
CITROEN Perrotts Brook ☏ 028 583 (North Cerney) 219
RENAULT 23/25 Victoria Rd ☏ 4301
ROVER-TRIUMPH, VAUXHALL 7 Dyer St. ☏ 3314

CLACTON-ON-SEA Essex 986 ㉜ – pop. 38,070 – ☎ 0255.

See : Sea front (gardens)*.

i Town Hall, Station Rd ☎ 25501 – Central Seafront ☎ 23400 (summer only).

London 71 – Chelmsford 38 – Colchester 16.

Royal (Gd. Met.), Marine Par., CO15 1PU, ☎ 21215 – lift wc ☎ P
47 rm.

AUSTIN-MORRIS-MG-WOLSELEY 107 Old Rd ☎ 24128
DAIMLER-JAGUAR-ROVER-TRIUMPH 65-69 High St. ☎ 22422
VAUXHALL Pallister Rd ☎ 22537

CLANFIELD Oxon. – pop. 607 – ☎ 036 781.

London 76 – Oxford 20 – Swindon 17.

XXX **Plough** with rm, OX8 2RB, on A 4095 ☎ 222, garden – P
M a la carte 5.55/8.50 **st.** 2.00 – **6 rm** 11.40/24.25 **st.**

CLAPHAM Beds. – see Bedford.

CLARE Suffolk – pop. 9,796 – ✉ Sudbury – ☎ 078 727 (3 and 4 fig.) or 0787 (6 fig.).

London 63 – Cambridge 26 – Ipswich 31.

Bell, Market Hill , CO10 8NN, ☎ 7741 – TV wc ☎ P
M a la carte 5.00/8.00 1.50 – **20 rm** 8.00/15.00.

Nethergate (Interchange), Nethergate St., CO10 8NP, ☎ 279, « 16C timbered house », garden – wc P
closed December-January – **M** *(closed Saturday lunch and Sunday)* 3.50/4.50 **s.** 2.00 – **8 rm** 10.00/17.00 **s.**

CLAUGHTON Lancs. – pop. 115 – ✉ Lancaster – ☎ 0468 Hornby.

London 248 – Lancaster 6.

XX **Old Rectory** with rm, LA2 9LA, ☎ 21455, garden – P
closed 1 week Spring, 1 week Autumn, 25-26 December and Bank Holidays – **M** *(closed Sunday dinner and Monday)* a la carte 3.00/5.25 – **3 rm** 6.50/14.00 **t.**

CLAWTON Devon – pop. 303 – ✉ Holsworthy – ☎ 040 927 North Tamerton.

London 240 – Exeter 39 – Plymouth 36.

Court Barn ⑤, EX22 6PS, W: ¼ m. off A 388 ☎ 219, « ≤ large garden and countryside » – wc P
Easter-15 October – **M** 4.00/4.50 **s.** 1.20 – **8 rm** 9.00/20.00 **s.**

CLEADON Tyne and Wear – pop. 4,494 – ☎ 078 33 Boldon.

18 Dipe Lane, East Boldon ☎ 4182.

London 285 – Newcastle-upon-Tyne 10 – Sunderland 4.

X **French Blackboard,** 63 Front St., SR6 7PG, ☎ 7397, French rest. – P
closed Sunday, 25-26 December and 1 January – **M** (dinner only) a la carte 3 30/5.35 **t.** 1.25.

CLEETHORPES South Humberside 986 ㉔ – pop. 35,837 – ☎ 0472.

18 ☎ 047 281 (Humberston) 3165, S: 1 m. by A 1098 BZ.

i Alexandra Rd ☎ 66111 and 67472.

London 171 – Boston 49 – Lincoln 38 – Sheffield 77.

Plan : see Grimsby

Kingsway, Kingsway, DN35 0AE, ☎ 62836, garden – lift TV wc ☎ P. BZ a
M approx. 3.25 **s.** 1.65 – **60 rm** 9.00/16.25 **s.**

Wellow, Chichester Rd, DN35 0HL, ☎ 65589 – TV wc ☎ P
M a la carte approx. 3.10 **st.** 1.20 – **10 rm** 9.70/15.90 **st.** by Chichester Rd Y

CITROEN 80 Brereton Av. ☎ 55558
LANCIA 459a Grimsby Rd ☎ 63592
RENAULT 79 Grimsby Rd ☎ 53592
VAUXHALL 50 Taylors Av. ☎ 62961

CLEEVE HILL Glos. – see Cheltenham.

CLEVEDON Avon 986 ㉟ – pop. 14,330 – ☎ 0272.

London 138 – Bristol 15 – Taunton 34.

Walton Park, 1 Wellington Terr., BS21 7BL, ☎ 874253, ≤, garden – lift wc garage P.
M approx. 2.95 **t.** – **36 rm** 9.00/17.50 **st.** – P 14.00/16.00 **st.**

AUSTIN-MORRIS-MG Old Church Rd ☎ 872201
MORRIS-MG, CHRYSLER, FORD Bristol Rd ☎ 873701

CLIFTON-ON-DUNSMORE Warw. – see Rugby.

CLIFTONVILLE Kent – pop. 6,280 – ☎ 0843 Thanet.
London 78 – Margate 4 – Ramsgate 4,5.

Palm Springs, Palm Bay Av., CT9 3DH, ☎ 28541, ≤ – 🛗 ⇔wc Ⓟ – **48 rm.**

Ye Olde Charles Inn (Gd Met.), 382-384 Northdown Rd ☎ 21817, – Ⓟ
M *(closed Monday except Bank Holidays)* (grill rest. only) a la carte 2.60/4.50 **t.** 1.00 – **10 rm** 6.00/9.25 **t.**

RENAULT 412 Northdown Rd ☎ 20919

CLIMPING West Sussex – pop. 963 – ✉ ☎ 090 64 Littlehampton.
London 64 – Bognor Regis 5 – **Brighton 23.**

Bailiffscourt , BN17 5RW, ☎ 3952, « Reconstructed mediaeval manor », , heated, , park – TV ⇔wc ☎ Ⓟ.
M 5.00/6.00 1.20 – **23 rm** 12.50/25.00.

CLITHEROE Lancs. 986 ㉓ – pop. 13,194 – ☎ 0200.
Whalley Rd, ☎ 22618, SW: 2 m.
i Information Office, Church St. ☎ 25566.
London 236 – **Blackpool 35** – **Leeds 44** – **Liverpool 49.**

Roefield, Edisford Bridge, BB7 3LA, SW: 1 m. on B 6243 ☎ 22010, , – ⇔wc ☎ Ⓟ
M (bar lunch) 3.00/3.80 1.20 – **22 rm** 8.50/14.00.

at Sawley NE: 4 m. off A 59 – ✉ ☎ 0200 Clitheroe:

XX **Spread Eagle,** BB7 4NH, ☎ 41202, ≤ – Ⓟ
M a la carte 3.50/5.20 **st.** 1.70.

AUSTIN-MORRIS-MG-WOLSELEY Whalley Rd ☎ 23883
ROVER-TRIUMPH Moor Lane ☎ 22840
VAUXHALL Duck St., Wellgate ☎ 22222

CLOVELLY Devon 986 ㉞ – pop. 434.
See: Site**.
London 242 – Barnstaple 20 – Exeter 54.

Hotels see: Bideford E: 11 m.
Fairy Cross E: 8 m.

CLYTHA Gwent – see Abergavenny.

COBHAM Surrey 986 ⑧ – pop. 9,169 – ☎ 093 26.
Envir.: Wisley gardens** *AC,* SW: 2 ½ m. – The Clockhouse, Silvermere.
London 24 – Guildford 10.

Seven Hills Motel, Seven Hills Rd South, KT11 1EW, SW: 1 m. off A 3 ☎ 4471, Telex 929196, ≤, heated, , park – 🛗 TV ⇔wc ☎ Ⓟ.
M a la carte 4.85/5.85 **t.** 2.25 – 1.25 – **94 rm** 12.50/15.00 **t.**

XXX **Fairmile** (T.H.F.), Portsmouth Rd, KT11 1BW, NE: 1 m. on A 307 ☎ 2487, – Ⓟ
closed dinner 24 and 25 December – **M** a la carte 5.50/6.90 **t.** 1.50.

XXX **San Domenico,** Portsmouth Rd, KT11 1EL, SW: 1 m. on A 3 ☎ 3285, Italian rest. – Ⓟ
closed Sunday dinner – **M** a la carte 4.10/5.70 **t.** 2.30.

ALFA-ROMEO, PEUGEOT 42 Portsmouth Rd ☎ 4493
AUDI-NSU, BMW 22 Portsmouth Rd ☎ 7141
AUSTIN-MORRIS-MG-WOLSELEY Between St. ☎ 4444
CHRYSLER-SIMCA The Tilt ☎ 4244

COCKERMOUTH Cumbria 986 ⑲ – pop. 6,363 – ☎ 0900.
Embleton ☎ 059 681 (Bassenthwaite Lake) 223, E: 4 m.
i Riverside Car Park, Market St. ☎ 822634 (summer only).
London 305 – **Carlisle 25** – Keswick 13.

Trout, Crown St., CA13 0EJ, ☎ 823591, – TV ⇔wc Ⓟ
M 4.50/4.75 **t.** 1.55 – 1.50 – **17 rm** 7.00/14.00 **st.** – P 15.75/17.25 **t.**

AUSTIN-MG-WOLSELEY Crown St. ☎ 2282
BMW Derwent St. ☎ 82366
FORD Lorton St. ☎ 2033
MORRIS-MG-WOLSELEY Station Rd ☎ 3042
PEUGEOT Gote Rd ☎ 823017

CODICOTE Herts. – pop. 2,611 – ✉ ☎ 0438 Stevenage.
London 32 – Bedford 24 – **Cambridge 36.**

XX **George and Dragon** (T.H.F.), High St., SG4 8XE, ☎ 820452 – Ⓟ
M a la carte 5.25/13.00 **st.** 2.00.

COGGESHALL Essex – pop. 3,643 – ☎ 0376.
London 49 – Braintree 6 – Chelmsford 16 – Colchester 9.

White Hart, Market Hill, CO6 1NH, ☎ 61654, « Part 14C Guild Hall » – TV ⇔wc wc ☎ Ⓟ
M *(closed Sunday dinner and 26 December)* a la carte 4.80/7.65 0.95 – **23 rm** 10.00/16.00.

COLCHESTER Essex 986 ㉜ – pop. 76,531 – ☎ 0206.
See : Roman Walls★. **Envir. :** Layer Marney (Marney Tower★ 16C) SW : 7 m.
Layer Rd ☎ 020 634 (Layer-de-la-Haye) 276, S : 2 m.
i 4 Trinity St. ☎ 46379.
London 55 – Cambridge 48 – Ipswich 18 – Luton 67 – Southend-on-Sea 41.

George (County), 116 High St., CO1 1TD, ☎ 78494, Group Telex 25971 – TV wc ☎ P.
M 2.50/3.50 **st.** 1.20 – **36 rm** 9.00/17.00 **st.**

Rose and Crown, East St., CO1 2TZ, ☎ 76677 – wc wc P
28 rm.

Bistro Nine, 9 North Hill, CO1 1DZ, ☎ 76466, Bistro
closed Sunday, Monday and 23 December-2 January – **M** a la carte 2.85/4.55 1.35.

at Wivenhoe SE : 4 m. by A 133 and B 1027 – ✉ Colchester – ☎ 020 622 Wivenhoe :

Smugglers, 47 High St. ☎ 3582.

at Marks Tey W : 5 m. by A 12 on B 1408 – ✉ ☎ 0206 Colchester :

Marks Tey, London Rd, CO6 1DU, ☎ 210001, Telex 987176 – TV wc ☎ P.
M a la carte 3.35/7.70 **st.** 0.90 – **106 rm** 11.90/17.30 **st.**

MICHELIN Branch, Gosbecks Rd, CO2 9JT, ☎ 78451/4.

AUSTIN-MG-WOLSELEY Cowdray Av. ☎ 76291
CHRYSLER-SIMCA Wimpole Rd ☎ 7082
CHRYSLER-SIMCA Middleborough ☎ 77391
CITROEN Butt Rd ☎ 76803
DAF Ipswich Rd ☎ 77727
DAIMLER-JAGUAR-MORRIS 44 Crouch St. ☎ 77484
DAIMLER-JAGUAR-ROVER-TRIUMPH Elmstead Rd ☎ 76281
DATSUN 78 Military Rd ☎ 77295
FERRARI, TOYOTA Auto Way, Ipswich Rd ☎ 48141
FORD Maldon Rd ☎ 71171
LANCIA, PEUGEOT Gosbecks Rd ☎ 46455
OPEL-VAUXHALL Ipswich Rd ☎ 61333
RENAULT Ipswich Rd ☎ 77866
VOLVO 10 Osborne St. ☎ 77287
VW, AUDI-NSU 83/85 East Hill ☎ 77665

COLEFORD Glos. – pop. 3,627 – ✉ Gloucester – ☎ 0594 Cinderford – 18.
London 143 – Bristol 28 – Gloucester 19 – Newport 29.

Speech House (T.H.F.), Forest of Dean, GL16 7EL, NE : 3 m. on B 4226 ☎ 22607, – TV wc P
M 3.25/3.75 **st.** 1.50 – **14 rm** 7.00/18.00 **st.**

AUSTIN-MORRIS-MG-WOLSELEY ☎ 42468
DATSUN ☎ 3517

COLESHILL West Midlands 986 ⑫ and ㉛ – pop. 6,297 – ✉ Birmingham – ☎ 0675.
London 113 – Birmingham 8 – Coventry 11.

Swan (Ansells), High St., B46 3BL, ☎ 62212 – TV wc P.
M a la carte 4.40/6.40 **st.** – **35 rm** 9.70/16.00 **st.**

COLLYWESTON Lincs. – see Stamford.

COLNBROOK Berks. – see Slough.

COLWYN BAY Clwyd 986 ㉗ – pop. 25,564 – ☎ 0492.
See : Zoo★.
Old Colwyn ☎ 55581.
i North Wales Tourism Council, Glan-y-don Hall, Civic Centre ☎ 56881, Telex 61467 – Prince of Wales Theatre ☎ 30478 – Wales Tourist Board Information Centre, Penmaenhead ☎ 55719 or 56044 (Easter-September).
London 237 – Birkenhead 50 – Chester 42 – Holyhead 41.

Norfolk House, 39 Princes Drive, LL29 8PF, ☎ 31757, – wc wc ☎ P
closed 22 December-9 January – **M** 4.50/5.00 **st.** 1.40 – **35 rm** 9.50/19.50 **st.** – P 15.75/16.50 **st.**

at Penmaenhead E : 2 m. on A 55 – ✉ ☎ Colwyn Bay :

Hotel 70°, LL29 9LD, ☎ 56555, ← – TV P
M a la carte 4.40/6.05 **st.** 1.75 – **37 rm** 10.75/18.00 **st.**

at Rhos-on-Sea NW : 1 m. – ✉ ☎ 0492 Colwyn Bay :

Cabin Hill, 12 College Av. ☎ 44568
May-October – **9 rm** 3.50/12.00 **s.**

AUDI-NSU, MERCEDES-BENZ Abergele Rd ☎ 30456
AUSTIN-MG-WOLSELEY 394 Abergele Rd ☎ 55292
BENTLEY, ROLLS-ROYCE, ROVER-TRIUMPH 60 Princes Drive ☎ 30322
FIAT 268 Conwy Rd ☎ 44278
FORD Conwy Rd ☎ 2201
JAGUAR-MORRIS-MG-WOLSELEY, Conwy Rd ☎ 2281
VAUXHALL Princes Drive ☎ 30164

COLYFORD Devon – see Colyton.

COLYTON Devon – pop. 2,112 – ☎ 0297.
London 160 – Exeter 23 – Lyme Regis 7.

XX **Old Bakehouse** with rm, Dolphin St., EX13 6NA, ☎ 52518 – Ⓟ
March-December – **M** *(closed Sunday)* (dinner only) a la carte approx. 4.90 🍷 1.35 – **7 rm** ☕ 6.50/15.00.

at Colyford S: **1** m. by **B 3161** on **A 3052** – ✉ ☎ 0297 Colyton:

Old Manor ⛰, EX13 6QQ, ☎ 52862, « Converted 15C manor house », 🏸, 🌳 – ⛀wc Ⓟ
March-October – **M** (residents only) approx. 2.90 **st.** 🍷 1.05 – **10 rm** ☕ 5.30/12.20 **st.**

St. Edmund's, EX13 6QQ, ☎ 52431, 🌳 – Ⓟ
Easter and mid-May-September – **9 rm** ☕ 4.00/8.00 **s.**

COMBE MARTIN Devon 986 ㉟ – pop. 2,207 – ✉ Ilfracombe – ☎ 027 188.
⛳18 Hele Bay ☎ (0271) 62176, W: 3 ½ m.
i Exmoor National Park Information Centre, Beach Car Park ☎ 3319 (summer only).
London 218 – Exeter 56 – Taunton 58.

Higher Leigh, EX34 0NG, SE: ½ m. on A 399 ☎ 2486, ≤, 🌳, park – Ⓟ
April-October – **M** approx. 3.25 **t.** 🍷 1.50 – **11 rm** ☕ 7.00/14.00.

XX **La Gallerie** with rm, Victoria St., EX34 0JT, ☎ 2566, « Tasteful decor » – Ⓟ
March-October – **M** *(closed Sunday and Monday in winter)* (dinner only) a la carte 4.50/7.00 🍷 2.00 – **4 rm** ☕ 4.50/9.00.

MORRIS-MG-WOLSELEY Borough Rd ☎ 2391 VAUXHALL Borough Rd ☎ 3257

COMPTON Surrey – see Guildford.

CONISTON Cumbria 986 ⑲ – pop. 1,063 – ☎ 096 64.
Envir.: Tarn Hows** (lake) NE: 3 m.
i Main Car Park ☎ 533 (summer only).
London 284 – Carlisle 55 – Kendal 22 – Lancaster 42.

Sun ⛰, LA21 8HQ, ☎ 248, ≤, 🌳 – Ⓟ
March-October – **M** (dinner only) approx. 3.75 **s.** 🍷 1.20 – **10 rm** ☕ 6.20/12.40 **s.**

MORRIS-MG-WOLSELEY Coniston Lake ☎ 253

CONSTANTINE BAY Cornwall – see Padstow.

CONWY Gwynedd 986 ㉗ – pop. 12,206 – ☎ 049 263.
See: Site** – Castle** (13C) *AC* – St. Mary's Church* 14C. **Envir.:** Bodnant gardens** *AC*, SE: 7 m. – Sychnant Pass* W: 1 ½ m. – ⛳9 Penmaenmawr ☎ 3330, W: 4 m.
⛳18 ☎ 3400.
i Snowdonia National Park Office, Castle St. ☎ 2248 (Easter-September).
London 241 – Caernarfon 22 – Chester 46 – Holyhead 37.

Castle (T.H.F.), High St., LL32 8DB, ☎ 2324 – 📺 ⛀wc ☎ Ⓟ
M a la carte 3.95/5.30 **st.** 🍷 1.50 – **28 rm** ☕ 7.00/17.50 **st.**

Llys Gwilym, 3 Mountain Rd (off Cadnant Park), LL32 8PU, ☎ 2351 – Ⓟ
8 rm ☕ 4.50/9.50 **st.**

X **Alfredo's,** Lancaster Sq., LL32 8DA, ☎ 2381
M a la carte 3.65/6.40 🍷 1.40.

at Tal-y-Bont S: **5 ¼** m. on **B 5106** – ✉ Conwy – ☎ 049 267 Tyn-y-Groes:

XX **Lodge** with rm, LL32 8YX, ☎ 476, 🌳 – 📺 ⛀wc Ⓟ
M *(closed 26 December and 1 January)* a la carte 3.50/4.70 **t.** 🍷 1.75 – ☕ 1.00 – **10 rm** 10.00/15.00 **st.**

COODEN East Sussex – see Bexhill.

COOKHAM Berks. – pop. 6,249 – ✉ Maidenhead – ☎ 062 85 Bourne End.
See: Cliveden House* 19C (park**) *AC*.
⛳18 Grange Lane ☎ 27613.
London 36 – High Wycombe 7 – Reading 16.

XXX **Bel and The Dragon,** High St., SL6 9SQ, ☎ 21263
M a la carte 4.60/7.00 **t.** 🍷 2.25.

AUDI-NSU High St. ☎ 22029 CITROEN High St. ☎ 22984

COPDOCK Suffolk – see Ipswich.

COPTHORNE West Sussex – see Crawley.

CORBRIDGE Northumb. 986 ⑲ – pop. 3,177 – ✆ 043 471.
Envir.: Corstopitum Roman Fort* *AC*, NW: 1 ½ m.
i The Vicar's Pele Tower, Market Pl. ☎ 2815 (summer only).
London 300 – Hexham 3 – **Newcastle-upon-Tyne 18.**

- **Angel Inn** (S & N), Main St., NE45 5LA, ☎ 2119 – Ⓟ
  M a la carte 3.25/6.35 **t.** 1.15 – **7 rm** 6.00/10.50 **t.**
- XX **Ramblers,** 18 Front St., NE45 5AP, ☎ 2424
  closed Sunday and Monday – **M** a la carte 3.45/4.60 0.80.

ALFA-ROMEO, BMW, SAAB Stagshaw ☎ 043 472 (Great Whittington) 216
AUSTIN-MORRIS-MG-ROVER-TRIUMPH-WOLSELEY Main St. St. ☎ 2068

CORBY Northants. 986 ㉜ – pop. 47,994 – ✆ 043 471.
Envir.: Kirby Hall* (ruins 16 C) NE: 4 ½ m.
18 Stamford Rd ☎ 5222.
London 93 – **Leicester 27** – Northampton 22.

- **Strathclyde,** George St., NN17 1QQ, ☎ 3441 – wc wc Ⓟ.
  M 3.25/4.00 **s.** 0.95 – **40 rm** 10.50/14.50 **s.**

FORD Southern By-Pass ☎ 2332
MORRIS-MG-ROVER-TRIUMPH-WOLSELEY Occupation Rd ☎ 2050
VAUXHALL Rockingham Rd ☎ 2531

CORNHILL-ON-TWEED Northumb. – pop. 320 – ✆ 0890 Coldstream.
London 345 – Edinburgh 49 – **Newcastle-upon-Tyne 59.**

- **Tillmouth Park** , TD12 4UU, NE: 2 ½ m. on A 698 ☎ 2255, ←, « Country house in extensive grounds », – wc Ⓟ
  M 4.00/4.50 1.30 – **16 rm** 9.00/11.00 – P 12.00/16.00.
- Collingwood Arms (Swallow), TD12 4UH, ☎ 2424, Group Telex 53168, – wc Ⓟ – **16 rm.**

BMW, SAAB ☎ 2146

CORSE LAWN Glos. – see Gloucester.

CORSHAM Wilts. 986 ㉟ – pop. 10,117 – ✆ 0249.
See: Corsham Court** (Elizabethan) *AC*.
London 110 – **Bristol 22** – Swindon 25.

Hotels and restaurants see Bath: SW: 9 m.

CORTON Wilts. – ✉ Warminster – ✆ 098 55 Codford St. Mary.
London 104 – Salisbury 17 – Warminster 6.

- X **Dove Inn,** BA12 0SZ, ☎ 378 – Ⓟ
  closed Sunday dinner, Monday, 4 days at Christmas and Bank Holidays – **M** a la carte 4.45/5.95 **t.** 1.60.

CORWEN Clwyd 986 ㉗ – pop. 2,164 – ✆ 0490.
London 203 – Chester 33 – Holyhead 67 – Shrewsbury 39.

- Owain Glyndwr, The Square, LL21 0DL, ☎ 2115, – Ⓟ
  16 rm.
- **Crown,** LL21 0AH, ☎ 2403 – Ⓟ
  M *(closed Sunday from November to March)* a la carte 2.25/5.25 **t.** 1.50 – **6 rm** 6.00/10.00 **t.** – P 10.50/12.50 **t.**

COSSINGTON Leics. – pop. 800 – ✉ Leicester – ✆ 050 981 Sileby.
London 109 – **Leicester 6** – **Nottingham 20.**

- XX **Cossington Mill,** LE7 8UZ, W: 1 m. on B 5328 ☎ 2205, « Converted 17C mill » – Ⓟ
  closed Saturday lunch, Sunday dinner and 25 December-2 January – **M** a la carte 5.50/7.00 **t.** 0.75.

COTTENHAM Cambs. – pop. 3,540 – ✉ Cambridge – ✆ 0954.
London 66 – **Cambridge 6.**

- XX **Hunters Fen,** Twentypence Rd, CB4 4SP, N: 1 ¼ m. on B 1049 ☎ 50455 – Ⓟ
  closed Saturday lunch, Sunday, Monday, 25-26 December, last week August and first week September – **M** a la carte 3.15/4.20 0.90.

COTTINGHAM Northants. – pop. 1,730 – ✉ Market Harborough (Leics.) – ✆ 053 675 East Carlton.
London 93 – Kettering 8 – **Leicester 23.**

- XX **Hunting Lodge,** High St., LE18 8XN, ☎ 370 – Ⓟ
  closed Sunday, Monday and 1 January – **M** a la carte 3.35/5.40 1.10.

COVENTRY West Midlands 986 ⑫ and ㉛ – pop. 335,238 – 0203.

See : St. Michael's Cathedral*** (1962) : tapestry*** AV **A** – Old Cathedral* (ruins) AV **A** St. John's Church* 14C-15C AV **B** – Old houses* 16C-17C AV **DEF.**

Copeswood 451465, E: BY.

Coventry Airport: 301717, S: 3 ½ m. by Coventry Rd BZ.

The Precinct, 36 Broadgate 25555 or 20084/51517.

London 98 – Birmingham 23 – Bristol 91 – Nottingham 55.

Plans on following pages

De Vere (De Vere), Cathedral Sq., CV1 5RP, 51851, Telex 31380 – . AV **n**
M a la carte approx. 5.00 **st.** 1.45 – **213 rm** 20.00/28.50 **st.**

Leofric (Embassy), Broadgate, CV1 1LZ, 21371, Telex 311193 – . AV **c**
closed Christmas – **M** approx. 3.90 **st.** 1.55 – 1.25 – **90 rm** 12.00/18.00 **st.**

Falcon, 13-19 Manor Rd 58615 – wc wc AV **s**
M a la carte 3.85/7.75 1.50 – **35 rm** 6.00/11.50.

Hylands, 153 Warwick Rd, CV3 6AU, 501600 – wc . AZ **e**
56 rm.

Manor Park, 7 Park Rd 27472 – – **25 rm.** AV **u**

Fairlight, 14 Regent St. CV1 3EP, 24215 AV **i**
11 rm 4.00/7.00 **st.**

Ciska and Rikki, 9 Coundon Rd, CV1 4AR, 25998 AV **a**
12 rm 4.25/8.50.

Weavers, 66 St. Nicholas St., CV1 4BP, 22467 – AV **r**
14 rm 5.75/8.50 **s.**

Grandstand, Coventry F.C., King Richard St., CV2 4FW, 25392 – . BY **a**

Pagoda, Mercia House, Lower Precinct, CV1 1NQ, 25449, Chinese rest. AV **e**
M a la carte 4.25/5.40 **st.** 1.45.

at Longford N: 4 m. on A 444 – 0203 Coventry:

Novotel, Wilsons Lane, CV6 6HL, junction 3 of M 6, 88833, Telex 31545, heated – wc .
M (grill rest. only) 3.50/5.00 **st.** 1.10 – 1.90 – **100 rm** 13.50/17.00 **st.** BV **v**

at Walsgrave-on-Sowe NE: 3 m. on A 46 – 0203 Coventry:

Coventry Eurocrest (Crest), Hinckley Rd, CV2 2HP, NE: ½ m. 613261, Telex 311292 – wc . BX **e**
M 3.50/4.50 **s.** 1.60 – 1.80 – **161 rm** 12.60/16.10 **s.**

at Brandon E: 6 m. off A 428 – BZ – Coventry – 020 335 Wolston:

Brandon Hall (T.H.F.) , Main St., CV8 3FW, 2571, Telex 31472, , park – wc .
M 3.95/4.20 **st.** 1.50 – **67 rm** 12.00/21.00 **st.**

at Willenhall SE: 3 m. on A 423 – 0203 Coventry:

Coventry Crest (Crest), London Rd, CV3 4EQ, 303398 – wc BZ **u**
M 3.15/3.75 **s.** 1.55 – 1.60 – **71 rm** 10.95/15.50 **s.**

at Baginton S: 4 ½ m. off A 423 – 0203 Coventry:

Old Mill, Mill Hill, CV8 3AH, 303588, « Converted water mill » – BZ **n**
closed Sunday dinner – **M** a la carte 3.65/5.40 **t.** 1.35.

at Berkswell W: 6 ¾ m. off A 4023 – AZ – Coventry – 0676 Berkswell:

Bear Inn, Spencers Lane, CV7 7BB, 33202 –
closed Sunday – **M** a la carte 4.55/7.65 **t.** 1.65.

at Allesley NW: 3 m. on A 4114 – Coventry – 020 334 Allesley:

Post House (T.H.F.), Rye Hill, CV5 9PH, 2151, Telex 31427, – wc . AXY **s**
M 2.95/4.00 **st.** 1.50 – 2.00 – **200 rm** 13.00/18.00 **st.**

Allesley, Birmingham Old Rd, CV5 9GP, 3272 – wc . AY **r**
M 3.95/4.50 1.30 – **45 rm** 7.50/14.00.

at Keresley NW: 3 m. on B 4098 – AX – Coventry – 020 333 Keresley:

Royal Court , Tamworth Rd, CV7 8JG, 4171, , – wc .
closed 24 and 25 December – **M** approx. 3.55 **st.** 1.40 – **19 rm** 5.25/12.00.

Beechwood , Sandpits Lane, CV6 2FR, 4243, – wc
M 2.65/3.50 **st.** 1.50 – **27 rm** 6.00/12.00.

at Meriden NW: 6 m. on B 4102 by A 45 – AX – – 0676 Meriden:

Manor (De Vere) , Old Birmingham Rd, CV7 7NH, 22735, heated, – .
M a la carte approx. 5.00 **st.** 1.45 – **32 rm** 16.00/24.25 **st.**

COVENTRY

Street	Grid
Broadgate	AV 6
Corporation Street	AV
Shopping Precincts	AV
Bayley Lane	AV 3
Bishop Street	AV 5
Burges	AV 7
Canterbury Street	AV 9
Earl Street	AV 10
Fairfax Street	AV 12
Far Gosford Street	AV 13
Gosford Street	AV 15
Greyfriars Lane	AV 16
Hales Street	AV 17
Harnall Lane	AV 19
High Street	AV 22
Ironmonger Row	AV 23
Jordan Well	AV 26
Leicester Row	AV 29
Light Lane	AV 30
Little Park Street	AV 31
Oxford Road	BZ 32
Primrose Hill Street	AV 33
Queen Victoria Road	AV 35
St. Johns (Ringway)	AV 38
St. Nicholas (Ringway)	AV 39
Swanswell (Ringway)	AV 40
Trinity Street	AV 41
Upper Well Street	AV 43
Vecqueray Street	AV 45
Victoria Street	AV 46
Warwick Road	AV 48
Warwick Row	AV 49
White Street	AV 51
Windsor Street	AV 52
White Friars (Ringway)	AV 54

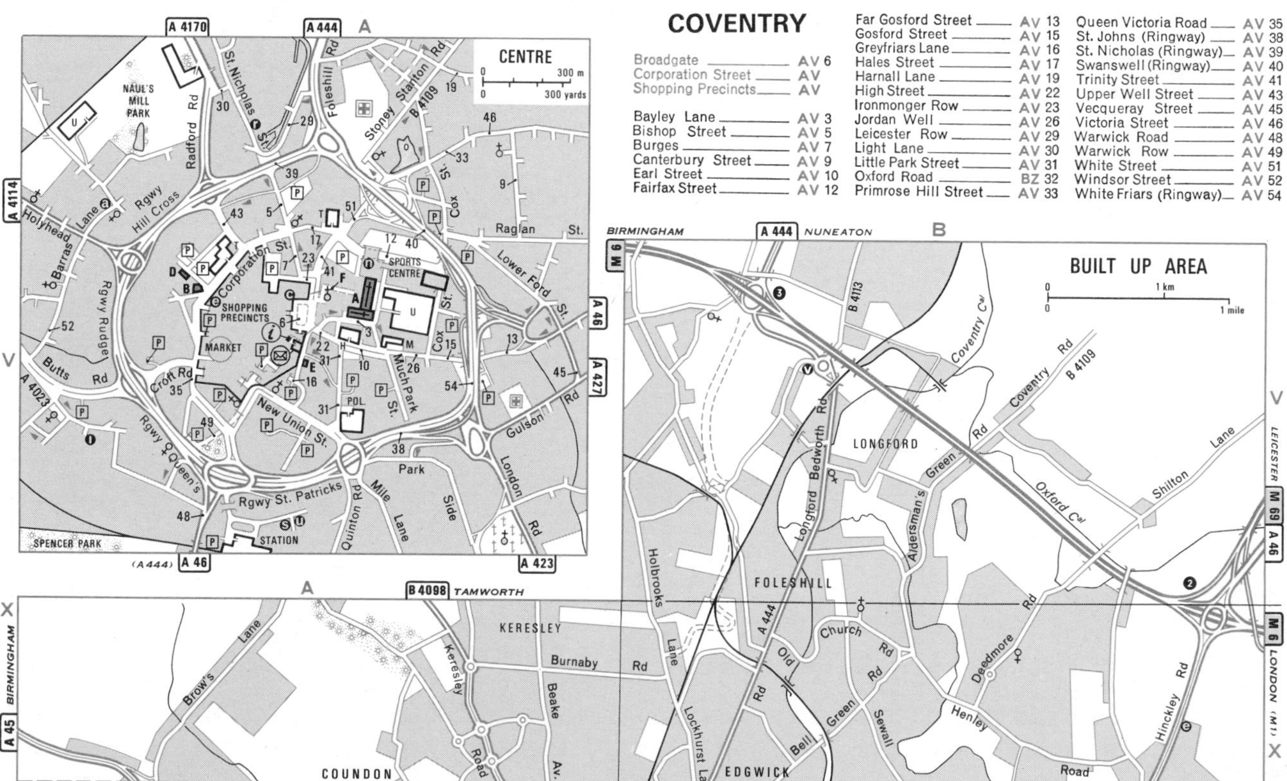

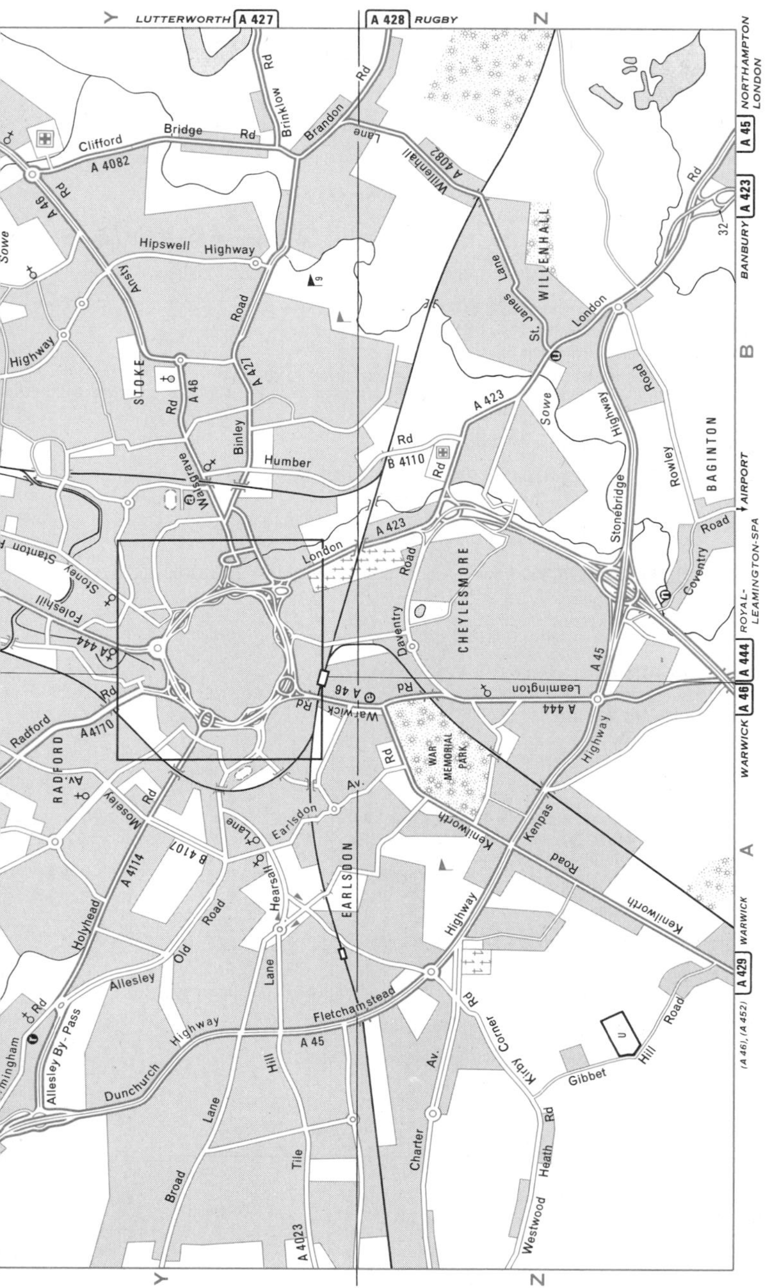
LUTTERWORTH A 427
A 428 RUGBY
Y
Z
NORTHAMPTON
LONDON
A 45
A 423
BANBURY
B
AIRPORT
ROYAL-LEAMINGTON-SPA
A 444
A 46
WARWICK
A
WARWICK
A 429
(A 46), (A 452)
Clifford
Bridge
Rd
A 4082
Brinklow
Brandon
Lane
Willenhall
A 4082
Hipswell
Highway
Ansty
Road
A 46
Sowe
STOKE
A 427
Binley
Humber
Walsgrave
WILLENHALL
James
St.
Lane
London
A 423
B 4110
Sowe
Highway
Road
Rowley
BAGINTON
Stonebridge
Coventry
Road
London
A 423
Daventry
Road
CHEYLESMORE
A 45
Leamington
A 444
Highway
Warwick
Rd
A 46
Stoney
Stanton
Foleshill
A 444
Radford
A 4170
RADFORD
Av.
Moseley
Rd
Earlsdon
Lane
B 4107
A 4114
Hearsall
EARLSDON
Av.
WAR MEMORIAL PARK
Kenilworth
Kenpas
Road
Kenilworth
Highway
Holyhead
Road
Old
Allesley
Lane
Fletchamstead
A 45
Highway
Dunchurch
Allesley By-Pass
Rd
Hill
Broad
Lane
Tile
A 4023
Charter
Av.
Rd
Corner
Kirby
Gibbet
Hill
Road
Heath
Rd
Westwood
32

COVENTRY

MICHELIN Branch, Charter Av., CV4 8AL, ☎ 462323.

ALFA-ROMEO, ASTON-MARTIN, BMW 138 Sutherland Av. ☎ 461441
AUDI-NSU, LOTUS, MERCEDES BENZ, VOLVO Spon End ☎ 56325
AUSTIN-MG-WOLSELEY 28/32 Cox St. ☎ 23242
AUSTIN-JAGUAR-MG-ROVER-TRIUMPH-WOLSELEY, FORD Holbrook Lane ☎ 87291
AUSTIN-MG-WOLSELEY Holyhead Rd ☎ 592501
CHRYSLER-SIMCA Daventry Rd ☎ 503522
CHRYSLER-SIMCA Lower Holyhead Rd ☎ 28581
FORD London Rd ☎ 58764
MORRIS-MG-WOLSELEY Warwick Rd ☎ 28661
MORRIS-MG-WOLSELEY Lockhurst Lane ☎ 88851
RENAULT 158 Walsgrave Rd ☎ 458600
ROVER-TRIUMPH Queens Rd ☎ 23366
TOYOTA Bennetts Rd, Keresley ☎ 334204
VAUXHALL 200 Fletchamstead Highway ☎ 77222
VAUXHALL Whitefriars St. ☎ 25361

COVERACK Cornwall – pop. 643 – ✉ Helston – ☎ 032 628 St. Keverne.
London 326 – Penzance 24 – Truro 29.

Coverack Headland , TR12 6SB, ☎ 243, ≤ Chynhalls Point and Blackhead, , park – wc –
Easter-October – **M** approx. 3.75 **s.** 1.20 – **34 rm** 9.00/24.00 **s.**

COWBRIDGE South Glam. 986 ㉟ – pop. **1,224** – ☎ 044 63.
Envir: Old Beaupré Castle* 14C, SE: 3 m.
London 169 – Cardiff 12 – Swansea 27.

Bear, High St., CF7 7AF, ☎ 2169 – wc wc – .
closed 22 December-1 January – **M** *(closed Sunday dinner)* a la carte 3.55/6.2
1.30 – 1.50 – **21 rm** 6.75/12.50.

COWES I. O. W. 986 ㊴ – see Wight (Isle of).

COW HONEYBOURNE Heref. and Worc. – pop. 925 – ✉ ☎ 0386 Evesham.
London 100 – Birmingham 35 – Cheltenham 21 – Worcester 21.

Thatched Tavern, 12 High St., WR11 5PQ, ☎ 830454 –
closed Sunday dinner and Christmas Day – **M** a la carte 4.20/6.40 **t.** 1.50.

CRACKINGTON HAVEN Cornwall – pop. 380 – ✉ Bude – ☎ 084 03 St. Gennys.
London 262 – Bude 11 – Truro 42.

Coombe Barton, EX23 0JG, ☎ 345 –
March-October – **M** 4.00/6.00 **t.** 1.05 – **11 rm** 7.00/14.00 **t.** – P 13.00 **t.**

CRANBROOK Kent – pop. 5,326 – ☎ 058 04.
Envir: Sissinghurst: castle* 16C (≤* 78 steps), gardens** *AC*, NE: 1 ½ m.
18 Benenden Rd ☎ 3434.
i Vestry Hall ☎ 2538 (summer only).
London 53 – Hastings 19 – Maidstone 15.

Willesley, Angley Rd, TN17 2LE, N: 1 ¾ m. on B 2189 at junction with A 229 ☎ 355
 – TV wc
closed 1 week February – **M** a la carte 3.90/6.55 **s.** – **16 rm** 12.50/20.00 **s.**

Kennel Holt , Flishinghurst, TN17 2PT, NW: 2 ¼ m. off A 229 on A 262 ☎ 2032
« Country house atmosphere », – wc
closed 1 to 15 October – **M** (residents only) (buffet lunch) approx. 4.00 **s.** 1.50
7 rm 9.00/21.00 **s.**

AUSTIN-MG-WOLSELEY Carriers Rd ☎ 2322

CRANE MOOR South Yorks. – pop. 180 – ✉ ☎ 0742 Sheffield.
London 175 – Barnsley 6 – **Sheffield 11.**

The Rock, S30 4AT, ☎ 883427, Dancing (Thursday and Saturday) – .

CRANTOCK Cornwall – see Newquay.

CRAVEN ARMS Salop 986 ㉛ – pop. **1,463** – ☎ 058 82.
Envir: Stokesay Castle* (13C) *AC*, S: 1 m.
London 165 – Birmingham 47 – Hereford 32 – Shrewsbury 21.

Craven Arms, SY7 9QJ, on A 49 ☎ 3331 – – **10 rm.**

Hotels in categories , , ,
offer every modern comfort and facility -
therefore no particulars are given.

wc wc

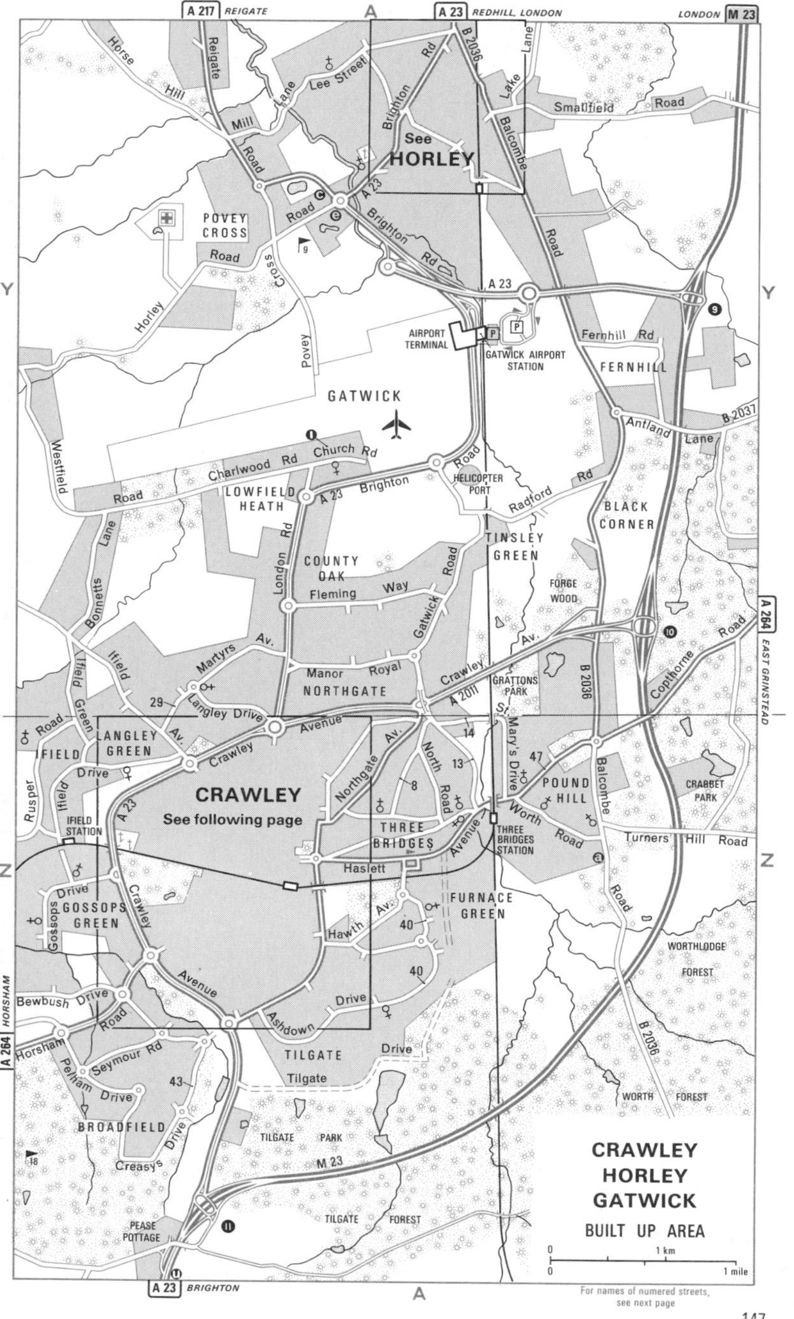
A 217 REIGATE
A 23 REDHILL, LONDON
LONDON M 23
A
Y
Z
Horse Hill
Reigate
Mill Road
Lee Street
Lane
Brighton Rd
B 2036
Lake Lane
Smallfield Road
Balcombe Road
See HORLEY
A 23
Road
Brighton Rd
POVEY CROSS
Road
Cross
Horley
Povey
AIRPORT TERMINAL
GATWICK AIRPORT STATION
Fernhill Rd
FERNHILL
GATWICK
Church Rd
Charlwood Rd
Westfield
Road
LOWFIELD HEATH
A 23
Brighton
Road
HELICOPTER PORT
Radford Rd
Antland Lane
B 2037
BLACK CORNER
TINSLEY GREEN
FORGE WOOD
Lane
Bonnetts
London Rd
COUNTY OAK
Fleming Way
Gatwick Road
A 264
EAST GRINSTEAD
Copthorne Road
Martyrs Av.
Ifield Av.
Ifield Green
Manor Royal
NORTHGATE
Crawley Av.
A 2011
GRATTONS PARK
B 2036
29
Langley Drive
Avenue
Road
LANGLEY GREEN
IFIELD
Crawley
St. Mary's Drive
14
13
47
Northgate Av.
North Road
8
POUND HILL
Balcombe
CRABBET PARK
CRAWLEY
See following page
Rusper
Ifield
Drive
A 23
IFIELD STATION
THREE BRIDGES
Worth Road
Avenue
THREE BRIDGES STATION
Turners Hill Road
Haslett
Drive
GOSSOPS GREEN
Gossops
Crawley
Av.
FURNACE GREEN
Road
Hawth
40
WORTHLODGE FOREST
40
Avenue
Bewbush Drive
Drive
Road
Ashdown
A 264 HORSHAM
Horsham
Seymour Rd
Pelham Drive
TILGATE
Drive
Tilgate
43
B 2036
WORTH FOREST
BROADFIELD
Drive
TILGATE PARK
Creasys
M 23
CRAWLEY
HORLEY
GATWICK
BUILT UP AREA
0 1 km
0 1 mile
PEASE POTTAGE
TILGATE FOREST
A 23 BRIGHTON
For names of numbered streets, see next page

CRAWLEY West Sussex 986 ㊱ – pop. 67,608 – 0293.

18 Buchan Hill 28256, S : 4 m. AZ – 9 Gatwick Manor 24470, N : 5 m. AY.

London 33 – Brighton 21 – Lewes 23 – Royal Tunbridge Wells 23.

Plan of built up area preceding page

- **George** (T.H.F.), High St., RH10 1BS, 24215, Telex 87385 – TV P. **M** 3.75/4.00 **st.** 1.50 – 2.00 – **75 rm** 12.50/19.00 **st.** — BZ **o**
- **Centre Airport** (Centre), Tushmore Roundabout, RH11 7SX, 29991, Telex 877311 – TV wc P. **M** approx. 3.95 **s.** 1.25 – 1.50 – **230 rm** 11.75/15.75 **s.** — BY **n**
- **Goffs Park,** 45 Goffs Park Rd, RH11 8AX, 35447, – TV wc wc P **M** 2.20/2.45 **s.** 0.85 – **40 rm** 6.50/10.80 **s.** — BZ **s**
- Grange without rest., 15 Brighton Rd, RH10 6AL, 35191 – TV wc P – **38 rm.** — BZ **a**

CRAWLEY HORLEY GATWICK

Street	Grid
Broad Walk	BZ 3
High Street	BYZ
Queens Square	BZ 22
The Broadway	BZ
The Martlets	BZ
Ashfield Way	BZ 2
Buckmans Road	BY 4
College Road	BZ 6
Crossways	AZ 8
Drake Road	BZ 10
Exchange Road	BY 12
Hazelwick Avenue	AZ 13
Hazelwick Mill Lane	AZ 14
Hunter Road	BZ 15
Loppetts Road	BZ 18
Orchard Street	BZ 19
Queensway	BZ 24
Southgate Road	BZ 28
Stagelands	AY 29
Station Road	BZ 30
The Boulevard	BZ 32
Titmus Drive	BZ 34
Town Mead	BY 37
Weald Drive	AZ 40
West Street	BZ 42
Woodmans Hill	AZ 43
Woolborough Road	BY 45
Wooldfield Close	BY 46
Worth Park Avenue	AZ 47

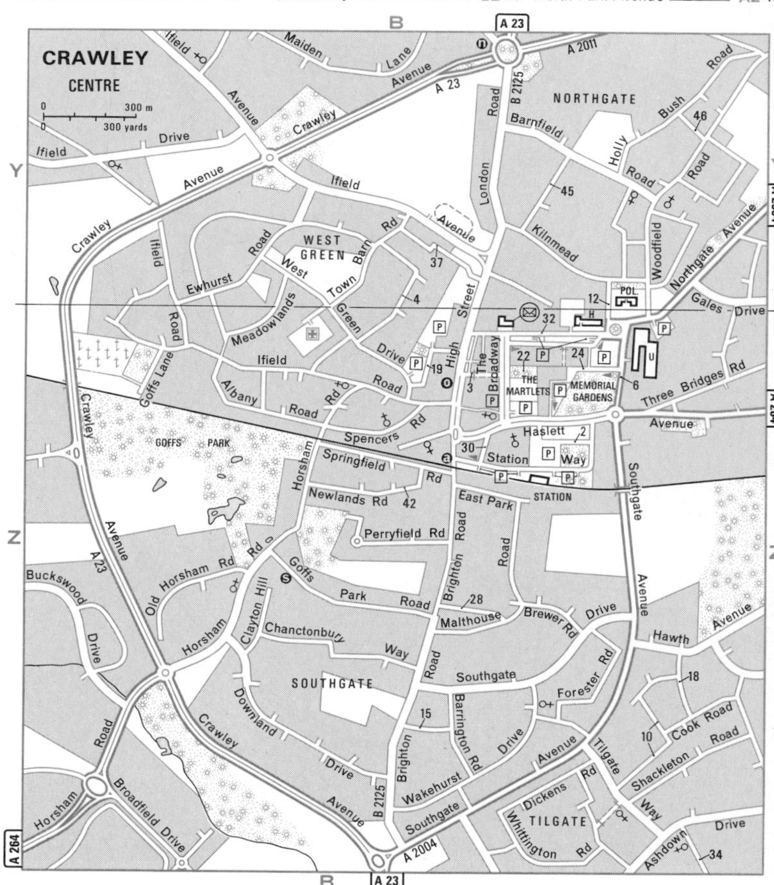

at Lowfield Heath N: 2 m. off A 23 – ✉ ☎ 0293 Crawley:

Gatwick Hickmet, RH11 0PQ, ☎ 33441, Telex 87287 – 🛗 TV ♿ **P** AY **i**
M 3.00/8.00 🍷 1.25 – **89 rm** 🛏 15.00/21.00 **st.**

at Copthorne NE: 4 ½ m. on A 264 – AY – ✉ Crawley – ☎ 0342 Copthorne:

Copthorne, Copthorne Rd, RH10 3PG, ☎ 714971, Telex 95500, 🌳, park – TV ♿ **P.**
M 3.95/5.00 **t.** 🍷 2.00 – 🛏 1.80 – **180 rm** 16.50/23.50 **t.**

at Pound Hill E: 3 m. by A 264 on B 2036 – ✉ Crawley – ☎ 029 382 Pound Hill:

Barnwood, Balcombe Rd, RH10 4RU, ☎ 882709, 🌳 – TV 🚿wc ☎ **P** AZ **a**
M (dinner only) – **21 rm.**

at Pease Pottage S: 2 m. on A 23 – ✉ ☎ 0293 Crawley:

Crawley Forest, Brighton Rd, RH11 9AD, ☎ 24101, 🌳 – 🛁wc ☎ **P.** AZ **u**
M *(closed Sunday dinner)* 3.50/5.00 🍷 1.85 – **11 rm** 🛏 8.00/14.00.

at Handcross S: 5 ½ m. off A 23 – AZ – ✉ Crawley – ☎ 044 487 Handcross:

XXX Red Lion, High St., RH17 6BP, ☎ 292 – **P.**

AUSTIN-MORRIS-MG-WOLSELEY 263/269 Haslett Av. Three Bridges ☎ 27101
CITROEN, TOYOTA 82 High St. ☎ 26325
DAF 163/165 Three Bridges Rd ☎ 36437
DAIMLER-JAGUAR-MORRIS-MG-ROVER-TRIUMPH 41 Ifield Rd ☎ 20191
DATSUN 5 Brighton Rd ☎ 35264
FIAT Ashdown Drive ☎ 21255
FORD ☎ 28381
RENAULT Orchard St. ☎ 23323
SAAB Turners Hill ☎ Crofthorne 715467
TOYOTA Overdene Drive, Ifield ☎ 37521
VAUXHALL Fleming Way ☎ 29771

CRESSAGE Salop – see Shrewsbury.

CREWE Cheshire 986 ⑨ and ㉗ – pop. 51,421 – ☎ 0270.
Envir.: Sandbach (Two Crosses* 7C, in Market Place) NE: 4 ½ m.
🚗 ☎ 4343.
i Delamere House, Delamere St. ☎ 583191.
London 174 – Chester 24 – **Liverpool 49** – **Manchester 36** – **Stoke-on-Trent 15.**

Crewe Arms (Embassy), Nantwich Rd, CW1 1DW, ☎ 3204 – TV 🛁wc ☎ **P.**
closed Christmas – **M** *(closed Sunday lunch)* approx. 3.40 **st.** 🍷 1.45 – **35 rm** 🛏 9.00/12.75 **st.**

AUSTIN-MORRIS-MG-WOLSELEY Nantwich Rd ☎ 56521
AUSTIN-MORRIS-MG-ROVER-TRIUMPH-WOLSELEY Newcastle Rd, ☎ 093 64 (Wybunbury) 320
AUSTIN-MG-WOLSELEY High St. ☎ 4064
BMW, POLSKI West St. ☎ 4317
CHRYSLER-SIMCA Oak St. ☎ 3241
CITROEN Woolstanwood ☎ 3495
DATSUN Cross Green ☎ 583437
FIAT Stewart St. ☎ 60688
FORD High Town ☎ 55241
PEUGEOT 613 Crewe Rd, Wistaston ☎ 68651
TOYOTA Earle St. ☎ 584414
VW, AUDI-NSU Macon Way ☎ 582425

CREWKERNE Somerset 986 ㉟ – pop. 4,821 – ☎ 0460.
Envir.: Cricket St. Thomas House (Wildlife Park* *AC*) W: 7 m.
London 144 – Exeter 38 – Taunton 25 – Weymouth 29.

Old Parsonage 🐎, Barn St. ☎ 73516 – **P**
8 rm 🛏 4.50/9.00 **st.**

CRICCIETH Gwynedd 986 ㉗ – pop. 1,505 – ☎ 076 671.
See: Castle ≤** *AC.*
🏌18 Ednyfed Hill ☎ 2154.
London 249 – Caernarfon 17 – Shrewsbury 85.

Bron Eifion 🐎, LL52 0SA, W: ½ m. on A 497 ☎ 2293, ≤, « 19C country house in large garden », park – 🛁wc **P**
M 4.00/5.00 – **25 rm** 🛏 (dinner included) 11.40/24.80 **st.** – P 14.70/17.85 **st.**

Lion, Y Maes, LL52 0AA, ☎ 2460, 🌳 – 🛗 🛁wc **P**
M 4.00/5.00 🍷 0.80 – **38 rm** 🛏 8.25/18.00 **t.** – P 13.70/15.00 **t.**

Parciau Mawr 🐎, LL52 0RP, W: ¼ m. on A 497 ☎ 2368, 🌳 – TV 🛁wc 🚿wc **P**
closed November – **M** *(closed Monday from December to April)* (dinner only) 4.20/5.70 🍷 1.40 – **13 rm** 🛏 13.20/20.50.

Mynydd Ednyfed 🐎, LL52 0PH, N: ¾ m. on B 4411 ☎ 2200, ≤, 🌳 – **P**
M (bar lunch) 3.75/4.00 **st.** – **10 rm** 🛏 7.00/14.00 **s.** – P 11.00/12.00 **s.**

Glyn-y-Coed, Porthmadoc Rd, LL52 0HP, ☎ 2870 – **P**
Easter-October – **10 rm** 🛏 4.00/8.00.

Bron-Aber, Pwllheli Rd, LL52 0RR, W: ¼ m. on A 497 ☎ 2539 – 🚿 **P**
Easter-October – **20 rm** 🛏 5.50/11.00.

AUDI-NSU, FORD, MERCEDES-BENZ Caernarfon Rd ☎ 2516
DAF, VOLVO Llanystumdwy ☎ 2733

CRICK Northants. – see Rugby.

CRICKHOWELL Powys 986 ㉛ – pop. 1,286 – ☎ 0873.
Llangattock ☎ 373.
i Tourist Information Centre, c/o J. A. Ward Ltd, 5b High St. ☎ 810357.
London 169 – Abergavenny 6 – Brecon 14 – Newport 25.

Gliffaes ⑤, NP8 1RH, W: 4 m. off A 40 ☎ 0874 (Bwlch) 730371, ←, « Large garden », park – wc Ⓟ
March-December – **M** (buffet lunch) approx. 4.80 **st.** – **22 rm** 10.70/21.40 **st.** – P 11.10/17.20 **st.**

Gwernvale Manor, Brecon Rd, NP8 1SE, W: 1 m. on A 40 ☎ 810212, ←, – wc Ⓟ.
M a la carte 2.80/4.40 **st.** 1.10 – **14 rm** 6.00/14.00 **st.**

CRICKLADE Wilts. 986 ㉟ – pop. 2,431 – ☎ 079 375.
London 94 – Bristol 41 – Gloucester 26 – Swindon 8.

White Hart, High St., SN6 6AA, ☎ 206 – Ⓟ
M a la carte 2.30/4.60 0.90 – **15 rm** 6.05/11.00.

Dieser Führer ist kein vollständiges Hotel- und Restaurantverzeichnis.
Um den Ansprüchen aller Touristen gerecht zu werden, haben wir uns auf eine Auswahl in jeder Kategorie beschränkt.

CROMER Norfolk 986 ㉘ – pop. 5,376 – ☎ 0263.
See: SS. Peter and Paul's Church (tower ←*). **Envir.:** Blicking Hall* (Jacobean) SW: 10 ½ m.
i North Lodge Park ☎ 2497 (summer only) – North Norfolk District Council, P.o. Box 3 ☎ 3811 (winter only).
London 134 – King's Lynn 44 – Norwich 22.

Colne House (Mt. Charlotte), Louden Rd, NR27 9EF, ☎ 2013, heated, – wc Ⓟ
M 3.25/4.25 **s.** 1.60 – **38 rm** 4.00/10.00 **s.** – P 7.55/9.70 **s.**

AUSTIN-MORRIS-MG-WOLSELEY 16 Church St. ☎ 2203
RENAULT Cabbell Rd ☎ 2557

CROOKLANDS Cumbria – ✉ Milnthorpe – ☎ 044 87.
London 257 – Kendal 6 – Lancaster 15.

Crooklands, LA7 7NW, ☎ 432 – TV wc wc Ⓟ
M approx. 3.00 **st.** 1.20 – 2.00 – **20 rm** 12.00/16.00 **t.**

CROSBY-ON-EDEN Cumbria – see Carlisle.

CROWBOROUGH East Sussex – pop. 13,236 – ☎ 089 26.
London 45 – Brighton 25 – Maidstone 26.

Crest, Beacon Rd, TN6 1AD, on A 26 ☎ 2772, – wc Ⓟ
M *(closed Christmas dinner)* 3.75/4.00 **st.** 1.50 – **29 rm** 10.25/18.25 **st.** – P 14.30/16.00 **st.**

AUSTIN-MORRIS-MG-WOLSELEY Beacon Rd ☎ 2777
CHRYSLER Church Rd ☎ 3424
DAF Mark Cross ☎ 089 285 (Rotherfield) 2447
RENAULT Crowborough Hill ☎ 2175

CROWTHORNE Berks. – pop. 6,767 – ☎ 034 46.
London 44 – Reading 12 – Southampton 52.

Waterloo, Duke's Ride, ☎ 2115, – Ⓟ
M (buffet lunch) 3.50/5.00 **t.** 1.25 – **15 rm** 7.00/14.00 **t.**

MORRIS-MG-PRINCESS Duke's Ride ☎ 2208
OPEL High St. ☎ 2067

CRUG-Y-BAR Dyfed – pop. 200 – ✉ Llanwrda – ☎ 055 83 Talley.
London 213 – Carmarthen 26 – Swansea 36.

Glanrannell Park ⑤, SA19 8SA, SW: ½ m. off B 4302 ☎ 230, ←, , park – Ⓟ
closed November and December – **M** *(open April-September)* approx. 4.00 1.50 – **11 rm** 5.50/11.00 – P 11.00/12.00.

DALTON North Yorks. – see Richmond.

DARESBURY Cheshire – pop. 330 – ✉ ☎ 0925 Warrington.
London 197 – Chester 16 – Liverpool 22 – Manchester 25.

Lord Daresbury, WA4 4BB, on A 56 ☎ 67331 – TV Ⓟ.
M 3.00/3.80 **st.** 1.75 – **108 rm** 13.50/16.00 **st.**

DARLINGTON Durham 986 ⑲ – pop. 85,938 – ☎ 0325.
Briar Close ☎ 4464, S: 1 m. on A 66.
Tees-side Airport: ☎ 032 573 (Dinsdale) 2811, E: 6 m by A 67.
i District Library, Crown St. ☎ 62034 or 69858.
London 251 – Leeds 61 – Middlesbrough 14 – Newcastle-upon-Tyne 35.

Europa Lodge (County), Blackwell Grange, DL3 8QH, SW: 2 m. on A 66 ☎ 60111, Telex 587272, – TV P.
M a la carte 5.80/7.55 **st.** 1.20 – **96 rm** 14.85/19.45 **st.**

King's Head, Priestgate, DL1 1NW, ☎ 67612 – TV wc P.
closed 3 days at Christmas – **M** a la carte 3.30/5.00 **st.** 1.20 – **72 rm** 11.50/18.00 **st.**

at Middleton One Row E: 5 m. off A 67 – ✉ Darlington – ☎ 032 573 Dinsdale :

Devonport, The Front, DL2 1AS, ☎ 2255 – wc P
M approx. 4.50 **t.** 0 80 – **15 rm** 7.50/15.00 **t.**

AUSTIN-MG-WOLSELEY Garden St. ☎ 3627
AUSTIN-MG-WOLSELEY Grange Rd ☎ 69231
DAF, SAAB 182 Woodland Rd ☎ 62440
DAIMLER-JAGUAR-ROVER-TRIUMPH Croft Rd ☎ 2728
DATSUN Haughton Rd ☎ 63384
FIAT Woodland Rd ☎ 2928
FORD St Cuthberts Way ☎ 67581
MORRIS-MG-WOLSELEY Valley St. North ☎ 67477
MORRIS-MG-WOLSELEY 24/26 Bondgate ☎ 60921
OPEL 127 Woodland Rd ☎ 66044
PEUGEOT 201/209 Northgate ☎ 67757
RENAULT 28/56 West Auckland Rd, Faverdale ☎ 53737
VAUXHALL 163 Grange Rd ☎ 66155
VW, AUDI-NSU Chesnut St. ☎ 53536

DARTINGTON Devon – see Totnes.

DARTMOUTH Devon 986 ㊴ – pop. 5,707 – ☎ 080 43.
i The Quay ☎ 2218 (summer only) – The Guildhall, Victoria Rd ☎ 2281 (winter only).
London 236 – Exeter 36 – Plymouth 35.

Dart Marina (T.H.F.), Sandquay, TQ6 9PH, ☎ 2580, ← – TV wc P
M a la carte 4.00/5.50 **st.** 1.50 – **28 rm** 9.00/16.50 **st.** – P 14.00/16.50 **st.**

Royal Castle (Anchor), 11 The Quay, TQ6 9QD, ☎ 2397, Group Telex 27120, « 1639 coaching inn » – TV wc wc
M a la carte 4.00/5.10 **t.** 1.00 – **20 rm** 9.75/18.70 **st.**

Victoria, Victoria Rd, TQ6 9EJ, ☎ 2572
M 1.90/3.00 **st.** 1.10 – **8 rm** 6.00/12.00.

XX ✿ **Carved Angel,** 2 South Embankment, TQ6 9BH, ☎ 2465
closed Sunday dinner, Monday and January – **M** (dinner only) a la carte 4.85/6.25 **st.** 1.50
Spec. Provençal fish soup, Poulet basquaise, Salmon in pastry (May-September).

XX **Taylor's,** 8 The Quay, TQ6 9PS, ☎ 2748
closed Tuesday, Christmas Day and mid January-mid February – **M** a la carte 4.15/5.50 **t.** 1.25.

at Kingswear E: over ferry – ✉ Dartmouth – ☎ 080 425 Kingswear :

Redoubt, TQ6 0DA, ☎ 295, ← Dartmouth and estuary, « Country house atmosphere », – P
season – **16 rm.**

MORRIS-MG-WOLSELEY South Embankment ☎ 2181
VAUXHALL Mayor's Av. ☎ 2134

DATCHET Berks. – pop. 3,737 – ✉ Windsor – ☎ 0753 Slough.
London 26 – Windsor 2.

Manor, The Green, SL3 9EA, ☎ 43442 – TV wc P
M a la carte 4.00/5.50 1.65 – **20 rm** 8.50/14.50 **st.**

DAIMLER-JAGUAR-MORRIS-MG-ROVER-TRIUMPH-WOLSELEY 18 Horton Rd ☎ 43254
OPEL, TOYOTA The Green ☎ 44568

DAWLISH Devon 986 ㊴ – pop. 9,519 – ☎ 0626.
18 ☎ 862255, E: 1 ½ m.
i The Lawn ☎ 863589 (summer only).
London 215 – Exeter 13 – Plymouth 40 – Torquay 11.

Lynbridge, 8 Barton Villas, The Bartons, EX7 9QJ, ☎ 862352,
Easter-October – **8 rm** 3.50/7.00 **st.**

DEAL Kent 986 ㊱ – pop. 25,432 – ☎ 030 45.
i Time Ball Tower, Sea Front ☎ 61161 ext 63.
London 77 – Dover 9 – Maidstone 45 – Margate 15.

Royal, Beach St., CT14 6JD, ☎ 5555, Telex 957141, ← – wc P
M 3.50/3.85 **t.** 1.35 – **27 rm** 6.75/14.50 **t.**

AUSTIN-MG-WOLSELEY The Marina ☎ 5143
MERCEDES-BENZ Sandwich Rd ☎ 030 46 (Sandwich) 2034
MORRIS-MG-WOLSELEY Queen St. ☎ 2214
RENAULT Sandown Rd ☎ 4239
VAUXHALL 48 Dover Rd ☎ 3366

DEDHAM Essex – pop. 1,641 – ✉ ☎ 0206 Colchester.

i Countryside Centre, Duchy Barn ☎ 323447 (summer only).

London 63 – Chelmsford 30 – Colchester 8 – Ipswich 12.

Maison Talbooth without rest., Stratford St. Mary Rd, CO7 6HN, W: ½ m. ☎ 322367, ≤, – TV P
1.50 – **9 rm** 13.50/35.00 **t.**

Dedham Vale, Stratford St. Mary Rd, CO7 6HW, W: ¾ m. ☎ 322273, ≤, wc ☎ P
M *(closed first week January)* approx. 4.00 1.55 – **12 rm** 6.50/15.00 P 13.00/15.00.

XXX **Le Talbooth,** Gun Hill, CO7 6HP, W: 1 m. ☎ 323150, ≤, «Tudor house on riverside», – P
M a la carte 6.70/11.65 **t.**

DEGANWY Clwyd – see Llandudno.

DENTON Greater Manchester 986 ⑤ – pop. 38,154 – ✉ ☎ 061 Manchester.

London 204 – Manchester 6 – Sheffield 34.

XX **Old Rectory** with rm, Meadow Lane, Haughton Green, M34 1GD, ☎ 336 7516, – TV wc ☎ P
closed Bank Holidays – **M** *(closed Saturday lunch and Sunday)* a la carte 3.80/4.90 **st.** – **24 rm** 11.50/16.00 **st.**

carte	Hotels and restaurants offering set meals generally also serve « a la carte ».

DERBY Derbs. 986 ㉗ – pop. 219,582 – ☎ 0332.

Envir.: Kedleston Hall** (Renaissance) *AC*, NW: 5 m. by Kedleston Rd X – Melbourne (St. Michael's Church: Norman nave*) S: 8 m. by A 514 X.

Allestree Park, ☎ 50616, N: 2 m. on A 6 X – by Sinfin Lane X ☎ 21226. – Mickleover ☎ 53339, W: 3 m. by A 38 X.

East Midlands, Castle Donington ☎ 810621, SE: 12 m. by A 6 X.

i Central Library, The Strand ☎ 31111 ext 2185.

London 132 – Birmingham 39 – Coventry 53 – Leicester 32 – Manchester 59 – Nottingham 16 – Sheffield 46 – Stoke-on-Trent 34.

Plan opposite

Midland (B.T.H.), Midland Rd, DE1 2SQ, ☎ 45894, – TV wc ☎ P. Z i
M a la carte 4.60/8.75 **st.** 1.25 – **63 rm** 9.75/22.00 **st.**

Pennine, Macklin St., DE1 1LF, ☎ 41741 – TV wc wc ☎ P. Z e
M (buffet lunch) approx. 3.50 **st.** 1.25 – **100 rm** 14.00/17.00 **st.**

Gables, 119 London Rd, DE1 2QR, ☎ 40633 – wc P Z o
closed Christmas – **M** a la carte 1.80/3.90 – **60 rm** 4.75/8.50.

Clarendon, Midland Rd, DE1 2SL, ☎ 44466 – P Z a
M (bar lunch) approx. 3.25 **s.** 1.20 – **45 rm** 7.65 **s.**

York (Embassy), Midland Rd, DE1 2SL, ☎ 42716 – TV wc P. Z u
closed Christmas – **M** 2.50/3.00 **st.** 1.25 – **39 rm** 6.95/12.10 **st.**

XX **La Gondola,** 220 Osmaston Rd, ☎ 32895, Italian rest. – P X c
closed Sunday and Bank Holidays – **M** a la carte 4.50/6.35 **st.** 1.40.

at Allestree N: 2 m. on A 6 – X – ✉ ☎ 0332 Derby:

XXX **Palm Court,** Duffield Rd, DE3 1ET, ☎ 58107 – P
closed Sunday dinner, Monday, Christmas and Bank Holidays – **M** a la carte 4.45/6.45 0.90.

at Shelton Lock S: 3 ½ m. on A 514 – X – ✉ ☎ 0332 Derby:

XX **Golden Pheasant,** 221 Chellaston Rd, DE2 9EE, ☎ 700112 – P
closed Sunday dinner, Christmas Day dinner and Bank Holidays – **M** a la carte 3.65/6.25 **t.** 1.50.

at Littleover SW: 2½ m. on A 5250 by A 38 – ✉ ☎ 0332 Derby:

Derby Crest Motel (Crest), Pasture Hill, DE3 7BA, ☎ 53834, – TV wc ☎ P. X a
M 2.65/4.20 **s.** 1.55 – 1.60 – **40 rm** 10.95/15.50 **s.**

AUDI-NSU, CITROEN, FIAT 35 Ashbourne Rd ☎ 31282
AUSTIN-MORRIS-MG-WOLSELEY Derwent St. ☎ 31166
AUSTIN-MORRIS-MG-WOLSELEY 158/160 Burton Rd ☎ 43224
BMW Uttoxeter New Rd ☎ 32421
CHRYSLER-SIMCA Old Chester Rd ☎ 47007
DAF 275 Nottingham Rd ☎ 44248
DAIMLER-JAGUAR-ROVER-TRIUMPH, ROLLS ROYCE London Rd ☎ 47471
DATSUN, MERCEDES-BENZ, OPEL, VAUXHALL Nottingham Rd ☎ 362661
FORD Normanton Rd ☎ 40271
PEUGEOT Nottingham Rd, Chaddesden ☎ 671221
RENAULT 1263 London Rd, Alvaston ☎ 71847
ROVER-TRIUMPH Queen St. ☎ 31166
TOYOTA Raynesway, Spondon ☎ 671225
VAUXHALL Castle Donington ☎ 810221
VOLVO Kedleston Rd ☎ 32625

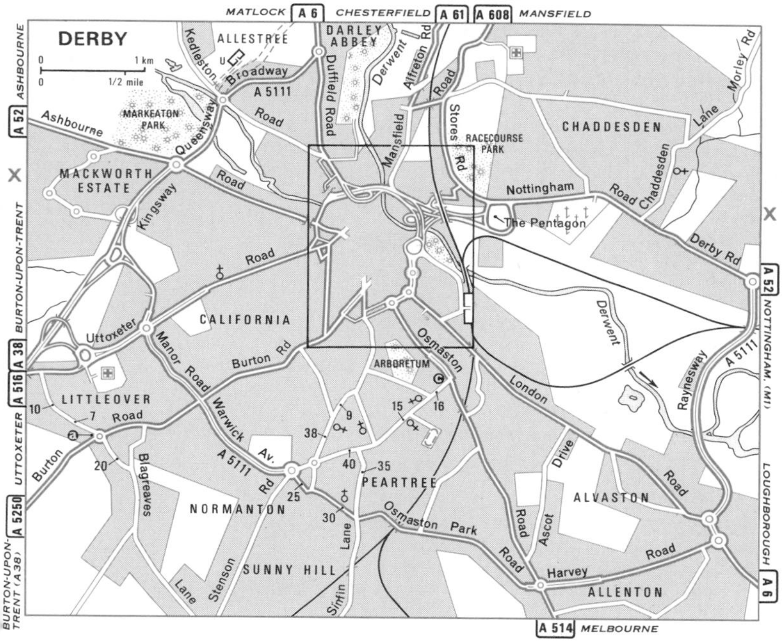

DERBY

MATLOCK A 6 CHESTERFIELD A 61 A 608 MANSFIELD

0 1 km
0 1/2 mile

ALLESTREE
DARLEY ABBEY
Kedleston
Broadway
A 5111
Road
Duffield Road
Derwent
Alfreton Rd
Road
Mansfield
Stores Rd
RACECOURSE PARK
CHADDESDEN
Lane
Morley Rd
Chaddesden
MARKEATON PARK
Ashbourne
Queensway
MACKWORTH ESTATE
Road
Kingsway
Nottingham
Road
The Pentagon
Derby Rd
Road
CALIFORNIA
Uttoxeter
Manor Road
Burton Rd
Derwent
Raynesway
A 5111
Osmaston
ARBORETUM
London
Road
LITTLEOVER
Road
Warwick Av.
A 5111
Rd
Blagreaves
Burton
PEARTREE
NORMANTON
Drive
Road
ALVASTON
Osmaston Park Road
Road
Ascot
Lane
SUNNY HILL
Stenson
Lane
Sinfin
Harvey Road
ALLENTON
X X
ASHBOURNE A 52
BURTON-UPON-TRENT A 38
UTTOXETER A 516
A 5250 BURTON-UPON-TRENT (A38)
A 52 NOTTINGHAM (M1)
LOUGHBOROUGH A 6
A 514 MELBOURNE
10 7 20 9 38 40 35 15 16 25 30

Corn Market	Z 12
Iron Gate	Y 23
Shopping Centre	Z
Victoria Street	Z 39
Albert Street	Z 2
Babington Lane	Z 3
Bold Lane	Y 4
Bradshaw Way	Z 5
Cathedral Road	Y 6
Chain Lane	X 7
Charnwood Street	Z 8
Church Street	X 9
Corden Avenue	X 10
Corporation Street	YZ 14
Dairy House Road	X 15
Douglas Street	X 16
Duffield Road	Y 17
East Street	Z 18
Full Street	Y 19
Hillsway	X 20
Hope Street	Z 21
Jury Street	Y 24
Kenilworth Avenue	X 25
King Street	Y 26
Market Place	YZ 27
Midland Road	Z 28
Mount Street	Z 29
Newdigate Street	X 30
Normanton Road	Z 31
Queen Street	Y 32
St. Mary's Gate	Z 33
St. Peter's Street	Z 34
St. Thomas Road	X 35
Sacheveral Street	Z 36
Stafford Street	Z 37
Upper Dale Road	X 38
Walbrook Road	X 40
Wardwick	Z 41

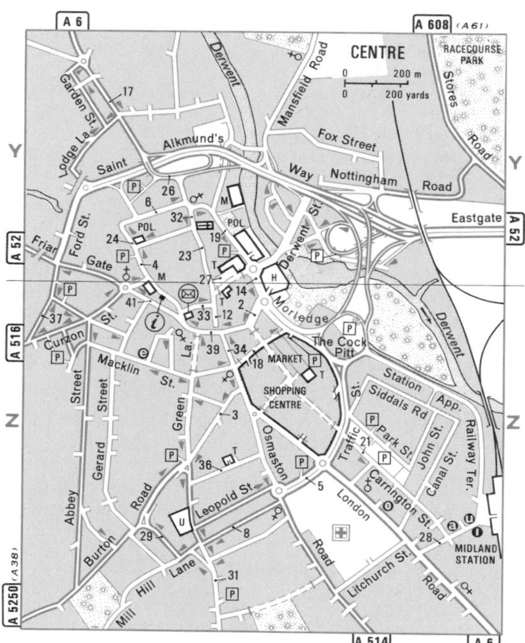

DEVIL'S BRIDGE Dyfed 986 ㉛ – pop. 150 – ✉ Aberystwyth – ☎ 097 085 Ponterwyd.
See: Nature Trail (Mynach Falls and Devil's Bridge)**.
London 230 – Aberystwyth 12 – Shrewsbury 66.

- **Hafod Arms** (Crest), SY23 3JL, ☎ 232, ≤, – P
Easter-mid October – **M** (bar lunch) 3.25/3.85 **s.** 1.55 – **22 rm** 6.50/11.00 **s.**

DEVIZES Wilts. 986 ㉟ – pop. 10,179 – ☎ 0380.
See : Museum (Bronze Age Room*) *AC* – St. John's Church (Norman choir* *AC*).
Envir. : Avebury (stone circles**) NE: 10 m. – Edington (Priory Church* 14C) SW: 10 m.
18 Bishop's Cannings ☎ 038 086 (Cannings) 627, N: 5 m.
London 98 – Bristol 38 – Salisbury 25 – Swindon 19.

- **Bear,** Market Pl., SN10 1HS, ☎ 2444 – TV wc ☎ P
M 3.00/5.00 **s.** 1.00 – **25 rm** 8.25/15.40 **s.**

AUSTIN-MG-ROVER-TRIUMPH-WOLSELEY New Park St. ☎ 5203
CHRYSLER-SIMCA The Green, Escort St. ☎ 3667
DAIMLER-MORRIS-MG-WOLSELEY New Park St. ☎ 3517
FIAT Market Lavington ☎ 2381
PEUGEOT ☎ 038 081 (Lavington) 2336
VAUXHALL Lydeway ☎ 038 084 (Chirton) 203

DISLEY Cheshire – pop. 3,986 – ✉ Stockport – ☎ 066 32.
18 Jackson's Edge ☎ 2071.
London 187 – Chesterfield 35 – Manchester 12.

- **Moorside** , Mudhurst Lane, Higher Disley, SK12 2BY, SE: 2 m. ☎ 3000, Telex 668822 – wc ☎ P.
M a la carte 5.95/8.80 **st.** 1.70 – **25 rm** 9.00/15.00 **st.**

MAZDA Fountain Sq. ☎ 2327

DITTON PRIORS Salop – pop. 693 – ✉ Bridgnorth – ☎ 074 634.
London 154 – Birmingham 34 – Ludlow 13 – Shrewsbury 21.

- **Howard Arms,** WV16 6SQ, ☎ 200 – P
closed 2 weeks September – **M** *(closed Sunday dinner, Monday and Christmas dinner)* (dinner only and Sunday lunch) 4.35/5.25 1.45.

DOLGELLAU Gwynedd 986 ㉗ – pop. 2,567 – ☎ 0341.
Envir. : Precipice walk** N: 3 m. – S: Cader Idris (road** to Cader Idris : Cregenneu lakes) – Tal-y-llyn Lake** S: 7 m. – Torrent walk* N: 2 m. – New precipice walk* N: 3 m. – Rhaiadr Ddu (Black waterfalls*) N: 4 m. – Coed-y-Brenin Forest* N: 6 m. – Bwlch Oerddrws* E: 4 m.
9 ☎ 422603.
i Snowdonia National Park and Tourist Information Centre, Beechwood House, The Bridge ☎ 422888 (Easter-September).
London 221 – Birkenhead 72 – Chester 64 – Shrewsbury 57.

- **Golden Lion Royal,** Lion St., LL40 1DN, ☎ 422579, – wc P
closed 21 December-1 January – **M** a la carte 3.70/5.30 2.00 – 1.20 – **28 rm** 8.20/11.20 – P 12.30/16.80.
- Royal Ship, Queens Sq., LL40 1AR, ☎ 422209 – wc P
23 rm.
- **Gwernan Lake** , Cader Idris Rd, LL40 1TL, SW: 2 m. ☎ 422488, ≤, , – P
Easter-October – **M** (dinner only) 3.50/4.00 – **11 rm** 5.80/11.60 **t.**

at Penmaenpool W: 2 m. on A 493 – ✉ ☎ 0341 Dolgellau:

- **George III** with rm, LL40 1YD, ☎ 422525, ≤, – wc ☎ P
M a la carte 3.50/8.65 – **6 rm** 12.00/23.00.

at Bontddu W: 5 m. on A 496 – ✉ Dolgellau – ☎ 034 149 Bontddu:

- **Bontddu Hall,** LL40 2UF, ☎ 209, ≤ estuary and garden, « Victorian mansion in large gardens » – wc wc P
May-October – **M** approx. 3.95 1.75 – **28 rm** 9.45/21.40.
- **Halfway House,** LL40 2UE, ☎ 635 – P
Easter-December – **M** (bar lunch) a la carte 3.70/5.90 1.50 – **5 rm** 6.00/16.00.

at Ganllwyd N: 6 m. on A 487 – ✉ Dolgellau – ☎ 034 140 Ganllwyd:

- **Dolmelynllyn Hall** , LL40 2HP, ☎ 273, – P
Easter-October – **M** (dinner only) 4.00 1.40 – **14 rm** (dinner included) 7.50/15.00.

AUSTIN-MORRIS-MG-ROVER-TRIUMPH-WOLSELEY Arran Rd ☎ 422631
DATSUN Bala Rd ☎ 422681
MORRIS-MG-WOLSELEY Bontddu ☎ 278

Es ist empfehlenswert, in der Hauptsaison und vor allen Dingen in Urlaubsorten, Hotelzimmer im voraus zu bestellen.

DONCASTER South Yorks. 986 ㉓ – pop. 82,668 – ☎ 0302.
18 Armthorpe Rd ☎ 030 278 (Armthorpe) 203, E : 3 m. – 18 Conisbrough ☎ 070 286 (Conisbrough) 2974, W: 3 m. on A 630.
i Central Library, Waterdale ☎ 69123.
London 173 – Kingston-upon-Hull 46 – Leeds 30 – Nottingham 46 – Sheffield 19.

Earl of Doncaster (Anchor), Bennetthorpe, DN2 6AD, ☎ 61371, Group Telex 27120 – wc. **M** approx. 1.95 **t.** 1.00 – **42 rm** 12.65/17.35 **st.**

Punch's (Embassy), Bawtry Rd, DN4 7BS, SE: 3 m. on A 638 ☎ 55235, – wc. *closed Christmas* – **M** approx. 3.25 **st.** 1.45 – **25 rm** 8.60/12.30 **st.**

Danum (Embassy), High St., DN1 1DN, ☎ 62261 – wc. *closed Christmas* – **M** approx. 2.75 **st.** 1.30 – **70 rm** 9.10/12.50 **st.**

at Sprotbrough SE: 3 m. off A 630 – ☎ 0302 Doncaster:

Edelweiss, 4 Main St., DN5 7PJ, ☎ 853923, Austrian-Swiss rest. *closed Monday* – **M** (dinner only and Sunday lunch) a la carte 4.95/6.30.

AUSTIN-MG-WOLSELEY Church Way ☎ 21541
AUSTIN-MG-WOLSELEY High Rd ☎ 853249
DAF Amershall Rd ☎ 66405
DAIMLER-JAGUAR-ROVER-TRIUMPH York Rd ☎ 66861
DATSUN Bawtry ☎ 710181
FIAT York Rd ☎ 23418
FORD York Rd ☎ 65221
FORD Barnby Dun Rd ☎ 4411
MORRIS-MG-WOLSELEY York Rd ☎ 66933
PEUGEOT Bawtry Rd ☎ 55241
RENAULT Kelham St., Balby Bridge ☎ 66912
RENAULT Thorne ☎ 0405 (Thorne) 812110
SAAB Westwoodside ☎ 752332
TOYOTA Thorne Rd, Hatfield ☎ 840348
VAUXHALL York Rd ☎ 67483
VW, AUDI-NSU York Rd Roundabout ☎ 64141

DONYATT Somerset – pop. 342 – ☎ 046 05 Ilminster.
Envir.: Cricket St. Thomas House (Wildlife Park* *AC*) SE: 8 ½ m.
London 147 – Exeter 33 – Taunton 11 – Yeovil 17.

Thatchers Pond, TA19 0RG, ☎ 3210, – *closed Monday and mid December-31 January* – **M** (cold buffet) 4.00/5.50 **t.** 1.40.

DORCHESTER Dorset 986 ㊴ – pop. 13,736 – ☎ 0305.
See : Dorset County Museum* *AC*.
Envir. : Hardy Monument ** SW: 5 m. – Maiden Castle (prehistoric fortress*) *AC*, SW: 2 m.
London 135 – Bournemouth 27 – Exeter 53 – Southampton 53.

King's Arms, 30 High East St., DT1 1EZ, ☎ 5353 – wc. **M** 2.80/3.10 **st.** 1.40 – **27 rm** 7.00/16.50 **st.**

ALFA-ROMEO, FIAT, MERCEDES-BENZ Trinity St. ☎ 4494
AUSTIN-MG 21/26 Trinity St. ☎ 3031
CITROEN, PEUGEOT Puddletown ☎ 456
DAF, VOLVO Bridport Rd ☎ 5555
DATSUN London Rd ☎ 6666
FORD Prince of Wales Rd ☎ 2211
MORRIS-MG-PRINCESS-WOLSELEY 6 High East St. ☎ 3913
VAUXHALL, BEDFORD 45 High West St. ☎ 3556

DORE South Yorks. – see Sheffield.

DORKING Surrey 986 ㊱ – pop. 22,422 – ☎ 0306.
Envir. : Box Hill ** NE: 2 ½ m. – Polesden Lacey** (19C) *AC*, NW: 4 ½ m.
London 26 – Brighton 39 – Guildford 12 – Worthing 33.

Burford Bridge (T.H.F.), Box Hill, RH5 6BX, N: 1 ½ m. on A 24 ☎ 4561, Telex 859507, heated, – . **M** 3.75/4.25 **st.** 1.60 – 2.00 – **30 rm** 15.50/20.00 **st.**

White Horse (T.H.F.), High St., RH4 4BE, ☎ 81138, heated – wc. **M** 3.75/4.00 **st.** 1.50 – **68 rm** 13.00/19.00 **st.**

Punch Bowl Motel (Anchor), Reigate Rd, RH4 1QB, ☎ 81935, Group Telex 27120 – wc. **M** (Carvery Rest.) approx. 2.15 **t.** 1.00 – **29 rm** 12.10/17.60 **st.**

at Abinger Common SW: 5 m. off A 25 – ☎ 0306 Dorking:

Jock and Jenny's, Abinger Hatch, RH5 6HZ, ☎ 730737, French rest. – .

at Peaslake SW: 8 m. off A 25 – Guildford – ☎ 0306 Dorking:

Hurtwood Inn (T.H.F.), Walking Bottom, GU5 9RR, ☎ 730851, – wc. **M** a la carte 4.10/5.70 **st.** 1.50 – **16 rm** 8.00/17.50 **st.**

at Wotton W: 3 m. on A 25 – ☎ 0306 Dorking:

Wotton Hatch, RH5 6QQ, ☎ 5665, – **M** a la carte 3.65/6.40 **t.** 1.60.

AUSTIN-DAIMLER-JAGUAR-MORRIS-MG-ROVER-TRIUMPH-WOLSELEY 105 South St. ☎ 2244
CITROEN, VAUXHALL Reigate Rd ☎ 5022

DORRINGTON Salop – see Shrewsbury.

DOVEDALE Derbs. – ✉ Ashbourne.

See : Dovedale** (valley). – **London 152** – Buxton 15 – Derby 19.

Hotels see : Thorpe SE.

DOVER Kent 986 ㊱ – pop. 34,395 – ☎ 0304.

See : Castle** 12C (≤*) *AC* Y. **Envir. :** Barfrestone (Norman Church* 11C : carvings**) NW : 6 ½ m. by A2 Z – Bleriot Memorial E : 1 m. Z **A.**

🚗 ☎ 01 (London) 603 4555.

⛴ Shipping connections with the Continent : to Boulogne (P & O Ferries : Normandy Ferries) (Sealink) (Seaspeed Hovercraft) – to Calais (Sealink) (Seaspeed Hovercraft) (Townsend Thoresen) – to Dunkerque (Sealink) – to Oostende (Sealink) – to Zeebrugge (Townsend Thoresen).

i South East England Tourist Board, Townwall St. ☎ 205108 – Town Hall ☎ 206941.

London 75 – Brighton 81.

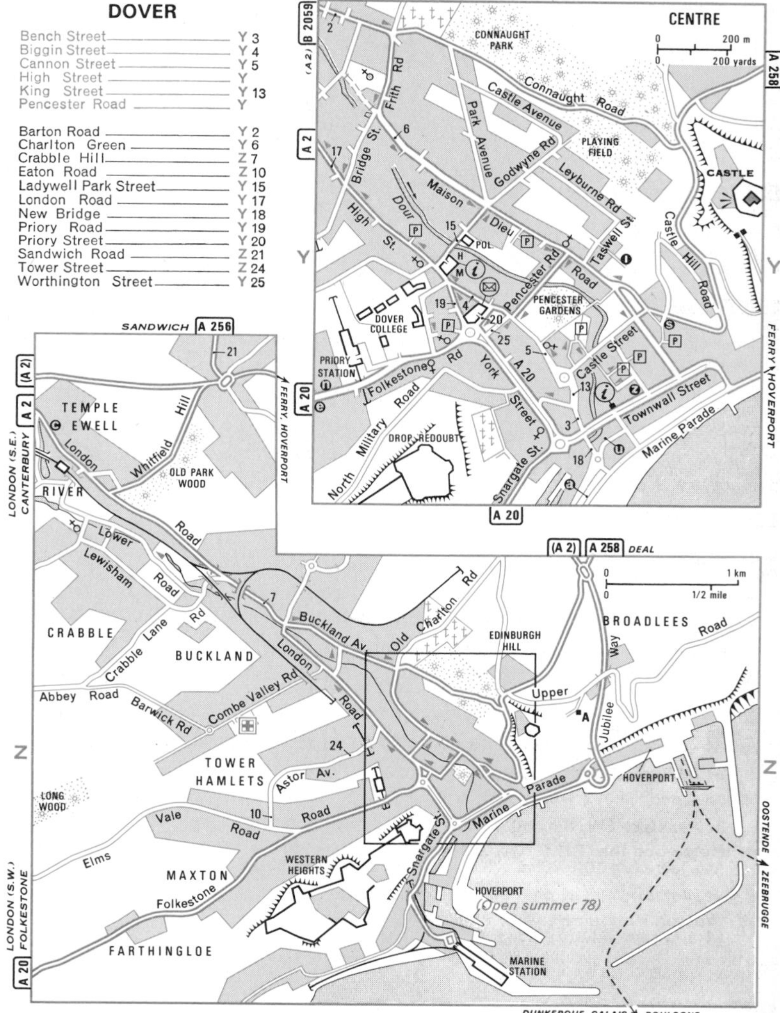

Holiday Inn, Townwall St., CT16 1JP, ☎ 203270, – 🛗 TV ♿ P — Y z
M a la carte 2.45/5.75 🍷 1.90 – ☕ 2.75 – **83 rm** 16.50/24.20 **s.**

White Cliffs, Sea Front, CT17 9BW, ☎ 203633, Telex 965422, ← – 🛗 TV 🛁wc ☎ P — Y a
64 rm.

Granham Webb, 161-165 Folkestone Rd, CT17 9SJ, ☎ 201897, – 🛁wc 🚿wc P
M 3.50/4.50 **st.** 🍷 1.30 – **26 rm** ☕ 11.50/15.00 **st.** — Y e

St. James, 2 Harold St., CT16 1LF, ☎ 204579, – 🚿wc — Y i
M 4.50/7.00 **st.** 🍷 2.00 – **19 rm** ☕ 8.00/16.00 **st.**

Mildmay, 78 Folkestone Rd, CT17 9SF, ☎ 204278 – 🛁wc 🚿wc P — Y n
closed December and January – **M** (dinner only) 3.00/4.00 **st.** 🍷 1.20 – **17 rm** ☕ 8.00/16.00 **st.** – P 14.00/16.00 **st.**

Dover Stage (County), Camden Crescent, CT16 1LF, ☎ 201001 – 🛗 ☎ P. — Y u
M a la carte 2.85/5.05 **st.** 🍷 1.20 – **42 rm** ☕ 9.20/15.50 **st.**

Hubert House, 9 Castle Hill Rd, CT16 1QW, ☎ 202253 — Y s
M *(closed Sunday and Bank Holidays)* a la carte 3.40/5.95 🍷 1.50 – **10 rm** ☕ 5.00/9.00 **t.**

at Temple Ewell NW: 2 m. on A 2 – ✉ Dover – ☎ 030 47 Kearsney:

Kearsney without rest., 121 London Rd, CT16 3BZ, ☎ 2002, – P — Z c
19 rm.

BMW Whitfield ☎ 030 47 (Kearsney) 4351
MERCEDES-BENZ, VAUXHALL Combe Valley Rd ☎ 201851
MORRIS-MG-ROVER-TRIUMPH-WOLSELEY 6/12 Folkestone Rd ☎ 201760
RENAULT London Rd, River ☎ 037 47 (Kearsney) 4155
VW, AUDI-NSU 1 Crabble Hill ☎ 206710

DREWSTEIGNTON Devon – pop. 534 – ✉ Exeter – ☎ 064 721.

London 214 – Exeter 13 – Plymouth 35.

Old Inn, The Square, EX6 6QR, ☎ 276
M 4.25/4.50 **st.** 🍷 1.45 – ☕ 1.00 – **6 rm** 4.00/8.00 **st.** – P 12.00 **st.**

DRIFFIELD North Humberside 986 ㉔ – pop. 7,895 – ✉ York – ☎ 0377.

⛳9 Sunderland Wick ☎ 43116.

London 201 – Kingston-upon-Hull 21 – Scarborough 22 – York 29.

Bell, 46 Market Pl., YO25 7AN, ☎ 43342 – P
M a la carte 3.40/3.65 **st.** 🍷 1.30 – **12 rm** ☕ 6.50/10.50 **t.**

DROITWICH Heref. and Worc. 986 ㉛ – pop. 12,748 – ☎ 090 57.

ℹ Norbury House, Friar St. ☎ 2352.

London 129 – Birmingham 20 – Bristol 66 – Worcester 6.

Château Impney, WR9 0BN, NE: 1 m. on A 38 ☎ 4411, Telex 336673, « Reproduction 16C French château », park – 🛗 TV P.
65 rm.

Raven, St. Andrews Rd., WR9 8DU, ☎ 2224, Telex 339907, – 🛗 TV P.
M a la carte 3.00/4.50 **st.** – **55 rm** ☕ 13.00/19.00 **st.**

Worcestershire (Interchange), St. Andrews Rd, WR9 8DL, on A 38 ☎ 2371, Telex 338309, – 🛗 ♿ P.
closed 1 to 4 January – **M** approx. 3.75 **s.** 🍷 1.80 – ☕ 1.25 – **100 rm** 10.00/14.00 **s.** – P 16.00/17.50 **s.**

AUSTIN-MG-WOLSELEY St. Georges Sq. ☎ 3337

DRONFIELD Derbs. 986 ㉗ – pop. 17,835 – ✉ Sheffield – ☎ 0246.

⛳18 ☎ 413149.

London 158 – Derby 30 – Nottingham 31 – Sheffield 6.

Manor with rm, 10-15 High St., S18 6PY, ☎ 413971 – P
M *(closed Sunday dinner and Monday)* a la carte 3.55/5.65 🍷 1.60 – **4 rm** ☕ 6.00/8 00.

DUDLEY West Midlands 986 ⑫ and ㉛ – pop. 185,581 – ☎ 0384.

ℹ 39 Churchill Precinct ☎ 50333.

London 133 – Birmingham 10 – Wolverhampton 7.

Station, Castle Hill, DY1 4RA, ☎ 53418 – 🛗 🛁wc ☎ P.
27 rm.

AUSTIN-MG Netherton ☎ 57841
AUSTIN-MORRIS-MG-PRINCESS-WOLSELEY 413/415 Himley Rd, Lower Gornal ☎ 54336
FIAT, LOTUS Stafford St. ☎ 213431
MAZDA, POLSKI-FIAT Queens Cross ☎ 59897
MORRIS-MG-PRINCESS 99 High St. ☎ 53791
RENAULT Trindle Rd ☎ 54591
ROVER-TRIUMPH Castle Hill ☎ 52474
VAUXHALL, BEDFORD Saltwells Rd, Netherton ☎ 0384 (Cradley Heath) 60181

DULOE Cornwall – see Looe.

DUNKIRK Avon – pop. 50 – ✉ Badminton – ☎ 045 423 Didmarton.
London 118 – Bath 15 – Bristol 19 – Cirencester 18.

✕✕ Petty France, with rm, GL9 1AF, on A 46 ☎ 361, ⛱ – TV ⛀wc ⛆wc ☎ P
closed 10 days January – **15 rm.**

DUNSOP BRIDGE Lancs. – pop. 201 – ✉ Clitheroe – ☎ 020 08.
London 245 – Burnley 22 – Preston 28.

Thorneyholme Hall ⚲, BB7 3BB, ☎ 271, ⛱ – P
M *(closed Monday in winter)* (residents only in winter) 4.00/5.00 **t.** 🍾 1.50 – **5 rm** ☕ 6.00/12.00 **t.** – P 10.50/11.50 **t.**

DUNSTABLE Beds. 986 ㉜ – pop. 31,828 – ☎ 0582.
See : Priory Church of St. Peter (West front*). **Envir. :** Woburn (Abbey*** (18C) *AC*, Wild Animal Kingdom** *AC*) NW : 9 ½ m. – Whipsnade Park* (zoo) ∢** *AC*, S : 3 m.
⛳9 Dunstable Rd ☎ (052 521) 722, N : 2 m. on A 5.
i Queensway Hall, Vernon Pl. ☎ 603326.
London 40 – Bedford 24 – Luton 4,5 – Northampton 35.

Highwayman, London Rd, LU6 3DX, SE : 1 m. on A 5 ☎ 61999 – TV ⛀wc ⛆wc ☎ P
26 rm.

Cook's Motel, 306 High St. North, LU6 1LW, ☎ 62341 – TV ⛆wc ☎ P
M a la carte 4.20/5.05 **s.** – ☕ 1.35 – **10 rm** 7.75/12.50 **st.**

Roxburgh, 42-46 Priory Rd, LU5 4HR, ☎ 64089 – ⛆wc P
M 2.00/3.50 **s.** 🍾 1.75 – **20 rm** ☕ 7.50/13.00 **s.**

Old Sugar Loaf, High St. North, LU6 1LA, ☎ 601326 – P – **10 rm.**

✕✕ Old Palace Lodge, with rm, Church St., LU5 4RT, ☎ 62201, ⛱ – ⛀wc ⛆wc ☎ P
16 rm.

AUSTIN-MORRIS-MG-WOLSELEY, VAUXHALL London Rd ☎ 62111
FORD 55 London Rd ☎ 67811
PEUGEOT Common Rd, Kensworth ☎ 872182
TOYOTA 3 Tring Rd ☎ 63231
VW, AUDI-NSU 104/112 Church St. ☎ 68796

☞ *Leggereste un giornale di ieri ?...*
Utilizzate allora la guida dell'anno !

DUNSTER Somerset 986 ㉟ – pop. 815 – ✉ Minehead – ☎ 064 382.
See : Dunster castle* 16C-19C – Yan Market*.
London 184 – Bristol 61 – Exeter 40 – Taunton 22.

Luttrell Arms (T.H.F.), 36 High St., TA24 6SG, ☎ 555, « 15C inn », ⛱ – TV ⛀wc ☎
M approx. 3.50 **st.** 🍾 1.50 – **21 rm** ☕ 8.50/17.50 **st.** – P 14.00/17.00 **st.**

Osborne House (Interchange), 31 High St., TA24 6SF, ☎ 475
March-November – **M** (dinner only) 5.90/6.50 **st.** 🍾 1.65 – **7 rm** ☕ 10.75/21.75 **st.**

DUNTON GREEN Kent – see Sevenoaks.

DURHAM Durham 986 ⑲ – pop. 24,776 – ☎ 0385.
See : Cathedral*** (Norman) (Chapel of the nine Altars**) B **A** – University (Gulbenkian Museum of Art and Archaeology** *AC*) by Elvet Hill Rd A – Castle* (Norman chapel*) *AC* B.
⛳18 Mount Oswald ☎ 2242, by South Rd B – ⛳18 Brancepath ☎ 780075, W : 4½ m. by A 690 A.
i 13 Claypath ☎ 3720.
London 267 – Leeds 77 – Middlesbrough 23 – Sunderland 12.

Plan opposite

Royal County (Swallow), Old Elvet, DH1 3JD, ☎ 66821, Group Telex 53168 – ⛓ TV P. ⛾
122 rm. B **a**

Durham Crest Motel (Crest), DH1 3SP, ✉ Croxdale ☎ 0385 (Meadowfield) 780269, S : 3 m. on A 167 B
⚲ – TV ⛀wc ☎ P
M 3.05/3.85 **s.** 🍾 1.55 – ☕ 1.60 – **33 rm** 10.95/15.50 **s.**

Three Tuns (Swallow), New Elvet, DH1 3AQ, ☎ 64326, Group Telex 53168 – ⛀wc ☎ P. ⛾ B **e**
15 rm.

✕ **Travellers Rest,** 72 Claypath, DH1 1QT, ☎ 65370 B **c**
closed Sunday, Bank Holiday Mondays – **M** (dinner only) a la carte 4.65/6.20 🍾 1.20.

✕ **De Medici,** 1st floor, 21 Elvet Bridge, DH1 3AA, ☎ 2051, Italian rest. B **u**
closed Saturday lunch, Sunday and Bank Holidays – **M** a la carte 1.75/5.45 🍾 1.20.

AUSTIN-MG-WOLSELEY 74 New Elvet ☎ 2278
CITROEN Croxdale ☎ 0388 (Spennymoor) 814671
DAIMLER-MORRIS-MG-ROVER-TRIUMPH-WOLSELEY Gilesgate Moor ☎ 67231
DATSUN 81 New Elvet ☎ 2233
OPEL-VAUXHALL Claypath ☎ 2511
VW, AUDI-NSU 20 Alma Rd, Gilesgate Moor ☎ 67215

DURHAM

0 — 200 m
0 — 200 yards

- Saddler Street — B
- Silver Street — B 22
- Alexander Crescent — A 2
- Castle Chare — A 3
- Court Lane — B 5
- Elvet Bridge — B 6
- Elvet Crescent — B 7
- Flass Street — A 8
- Framwelgate Bridge — B 9
- Framwelgate Waterside — B 10
- Gilesgate — B 12
- Market Place — B 13
- Millburngate — A 15
- Neville Street — A 16
- Pimlico Street — A 18
- Providence Row — B 20

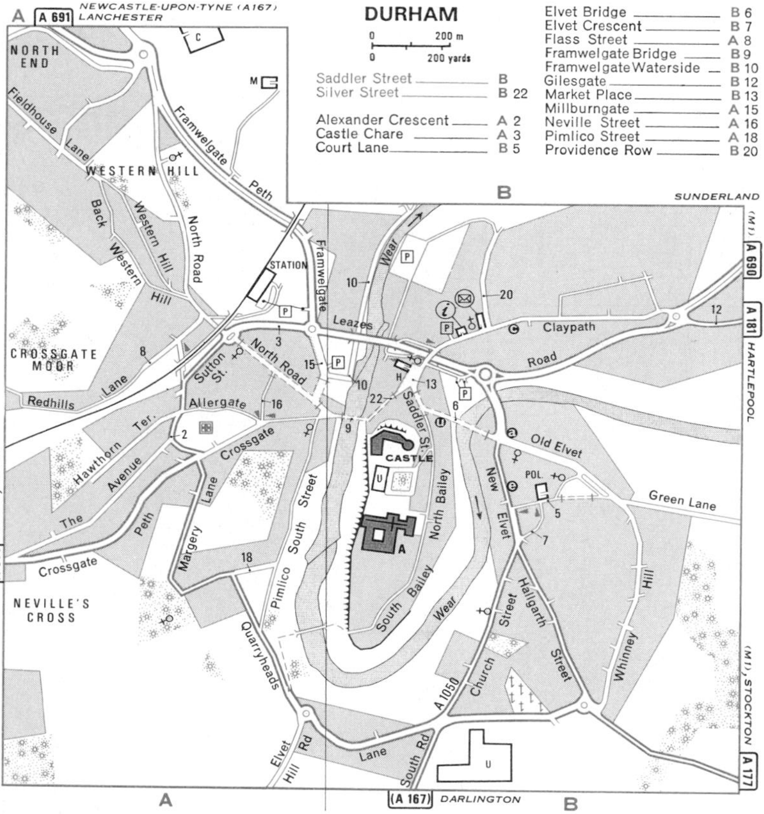

Do not mix up :

Comfort of hotels	: 🏨🏨🏨🏨 . . . 🏨, 🏠, 🏠
Comfort of restaurants	: ✕✕✕✕✕ . . . . . ✕
Quality of the cuisine	: ✿✿, ✿, M

EAGLESCLIFFE Cleveland – see Stockton-on-Tees.

EARLS COLNE Essex – pop. 2,389 – ☎ 078 75.
London 54 – Cambridge 37 – Colchester 11 – Chelmsford 21.

✕ **Draper's House,** 53 High St., CO6 2PB, ☎ 2484 – Ⓟ
closed Saturday lunch, Sunday, Monday, 30 July - 18 August, 26 to 30 December and Bank Holidays – **M** a la carte 3.70/6.05 🍷 1.50.

AUSTIN-MG-WOLSELEY Holt St. ☎ 736

EASTBOURNE East Sussex 986 ㊱ ㊵ – pop. 70,921 – ☎ 0323.
See : Grand Parade★ X. **Envir. :** Beachy Head★ (cliff), ※★ SW : 3 m. Z – Seven Sisters★ (cliffs) from Birling Gap, SW : 5 m. Z – Wilmington (the Long Man★ : prehistoric giant figure) NW : 8 m. by A 27 Y – W : scenic road★ from Eastdean by A 259 Z up to Wilmington by Westdean.
18, 9 Paradise Drive Z ☎ 30412 – 18 East Dean Rd Z ☎ 20827 – 18 Southdown Rd at Seaford ☎ 890139, W : 5 m. by A 259 Z.
ℹ 3 Cornfield Ter. ☎ 27474 – Lower Promenade ☎ 27474 (summer only) – Shopping Precinct, Terminus Rd ☎ 27474.
London 68 – Brighton 25 – Dover 61 – Maidstone 49.

EASTBOURNE

Street	Square	No.
Grove Road	V	
South Street	V	
Terminus Road	V	
Bedfordwell Road	V	2
Church Street	Z	3
Cornfield Road	V	4
Devonshire Place	X	5
Gildredge Road	V	7
Hailsham Road	Y	8
High Street	Z	9
Junction Road	V	10
Lewes Road	Y	13
Lismore Road	V	14
North Street	V	15
Pevensey Road	V	16
Polegate By-Pass	Y	18
Royal Parade	Z	20
St. Anthony's Avenue	Y	21
Station Road	Y	24
Susan's Road	V	25
The Goffs	Z	26
Trinity Trees	V	27
Upperton Road	V Z	28

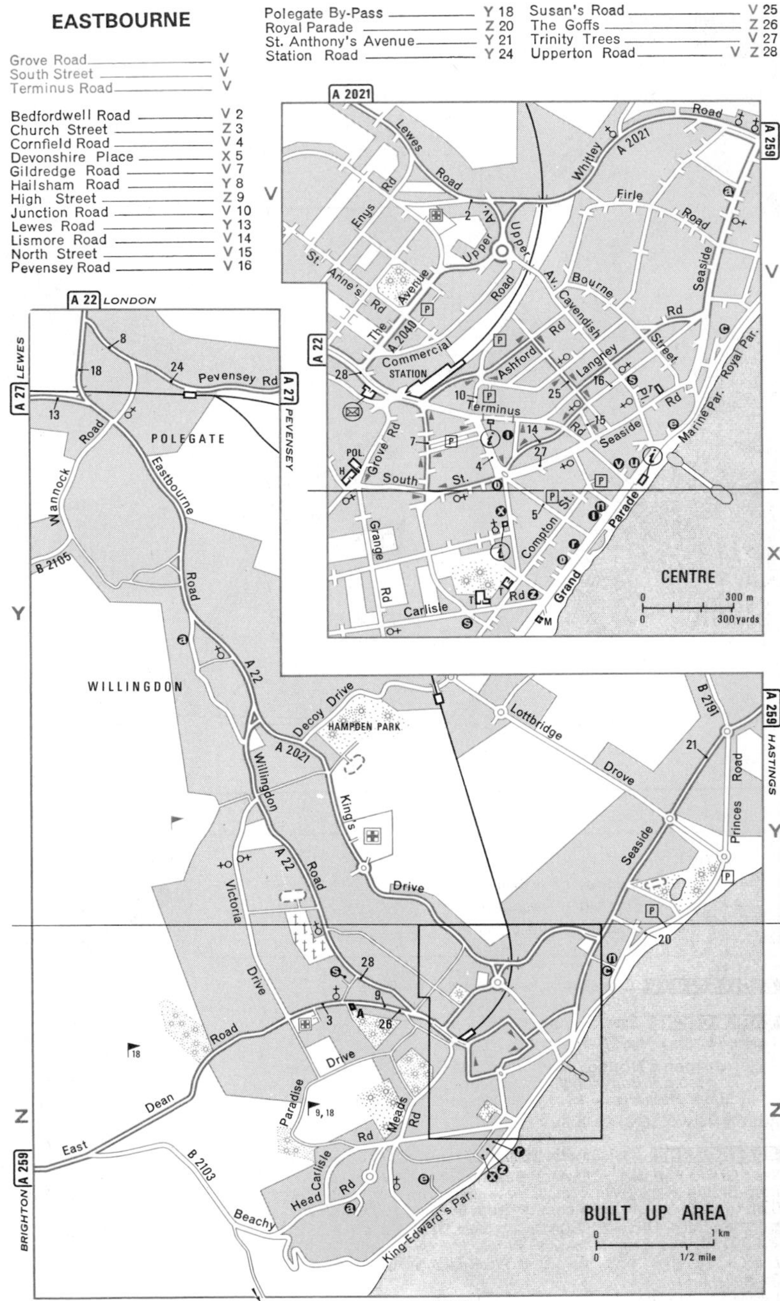

Grand (De Vere), King Edward's Par., BN21 4EQ, ☎ 22611, Telex 87332, ←, heated, – Ⓟ. Z **x**
M approx. 6.75 **st.** 1.45 – **177 rm** 18.50/37.00 **st.**

Cavendish (De Vere), 37-40 Grand Par., BN21 4DH, ☎ 27401, ← – Ⓟ. X **r**
M approx. 6.00 **st.** 1.45 – **109 rm** 17.50/34.75 **st.**

Queen's (De Vere), Marine Par., BN21 3DY, ☎ 22822, ← – Ⓟ. V **e**
M approx. 5.00 **st.** 1.45 – **106 rm** 12.75/26.75 **st.**

Burlington (Myddleton), Grand Par., BN21 3YN, ☎ 22724, Telex 87591, ← – Ⓟ. V **u**
M 4.50/5.50 **st.** 1.20 – **124 rm** 12.50/28.00 **st.** – P 14.15/21.25 **st.**

Mansion (T.H.F.), Grand Par., BN21 3YS, ☎ 27411, Group Telex 877288, ← – wc. X **i**
M 3.95/4.25 **st.** 1.50 – **103 rm** 6.00/14.00 **st.** – P 15.50/20.50 **st.**

Chatsworth, Grand Par., BN21 3YR, ☎ 30327, ← – wc wc X **n**
M approx. 3.85 **st.** – **46 rm** 10.10/21.50 **st.** – P 14.00 **st.**

Lansdowne (Interchange), King Edward's Par., BN21 4EE, ☎ 25174, ← – wc. Z **z**
M 2.80/3.75 **st.** 1.20 – **141 rm** 7.25/25.00 **st.** – P 11.75/17.00 **st.**

Wish Tower (T.H.F.), King Edward's Par., BN21 4EB, ☎ 22676, Group Telex 877288 – wc Z **r**
M 3.95/4.25 **st.** 1.50 – **74 rm** 6.00/14.00 **st.** – P 15.50/20.50 **st.**

Hydro, Mount Rd, BN20 7HZ, ☎ 20643, ←, – wc Ⓟ Z **e**
M approx. 3.60 **t.** 1.50 – **100 rm** (residents only) – P 14.00/18.00 **st.**

Eastbourne Motel, Pevensey Bay Rd, BN23 6JG, NE: 2 m. on A 259 ☎ 764188 – wc wc Ⓟ on A 259 Y
M a la carte 3.70/6.50 **s.** 1.70 – 1.75 – **82 rm** 8.75/13.75 **s.**

Sandhurst, Grand Par., BN21 4DJ, ☎ 27868, ← – wc wc X **o**
M approx.3.40 1.45 – **65 rm** 7.00/16.00 – P 10.50/13.50.

Princes, 12-20 Lascelles Ter., BN21 4BL, ☎ 22056 – wc. X **z**
M approx. 3.25 **st.** 0.90 - **50 rm** 9.25/20.30 **st.** – P 14.25/17.10 **st.**

Langham, 44-49 Royal Par., BN22 7AH, ☎ 31451, ← – wc V **c**
Easter-October – **M** approx. 3.00 **s.** 1.10 – **87 rm** 8.50/21.00 **s.** – P 11.50/14.00 **s.**

Heatherleigh, 63-66 Royal Par., BN22 7AG, ☎ 21167 – wc Z **n**
M approx. 2.50 **st.** – **45 rm** 6.25/14.50 **st.**

Farrar's, 3-5 Wilmington Gdns, BN21 4JW, ☎ 23737 – wc wc Ⓟ X **s**
M approx. 3.00 **s.** 1.50 – **42 rm** 7.00/18.00 **s.** – P 12.50/14.00 **s.**

Sussex, Cornfield Ter., BN21 4NS, ☎ 27681 – V **o**
M a la carte 3.95/5.40 **t.** 1.35 – **34 rm** 7.50/14.00 **t.**

Nirvana, 32 Redoubt Rd, BN22 7DL, ☎ 22603 Z **c**
closed Christmas week – **8 rm** 5.50/10.00 **s.**

Worcester House, 77 Pevensey Rd, BN22 8AD, ☎ 21601 V **s**
7 rm 5.30/10.60 **t.**

Crimples Flemish Room, 42-44 Meads St., BN20 7RG, ☎ 26805 Z **a**
closed Sunday dinner, Monday, 15 October-1 November and 25-26 December – **M** a la carte 2.60/4.95 **t.** 1.10.

Le Chantecler, 7 Bolton Rd ☎ 30748. V **i**

Porthole, 8 Cornfield Ter., BN21 4NN, ☎ 20767 X **x**
closed 25 and 26 December – **M** a la carte 3.75/7.10 **t.** 1.25.

La Lupa, 213 Terminus Rd, BN21 3DH, ☎ 21640, Italian rest. V **v**
M a la carte 4.75/6.80 1.10.

La Taverna, 92 Seaside, BN22 7QP, ☎ 23240, Italian rest. V **a**
closed 25 and 26 December – **M** a la carte 3.25/5.70 1.20.

Bistro Byron, 6 Crown St., BN21 1NX, ☎ 20171, Bistro Z **s**
closed Sunday and 25-26 December – **M** (dinner only) a la carte 2.55/6.30 **t.** 1.20.

at Willingdon **N: 2 ¾ m. off A 22 – ✉ 0323 Eastbourne:**

Chalk Farm, Coopers Hill, BN20 9JD, ☎ 53800, – Ⓟ Y **a**
M *(closed Sunday dinner and Monday)* a la carte 4.60/6.50 0.90 – **8 rm** 6.50/10.50.

at Pevensey **NE: 5 m. by A 259 – Y – on A 27 – ✉ 0323 Eastbourne:**

Priory Court (Interchange), BN24 5LE, ☎ 763150, – Ⓟ
M approx. 3.50 **st.** 1.60 – **17 rm** 8.00/15.00 **st.**

at Jevington **NW: 6 m. by A 259 on B 2105 – Y – ✉ Eastbourne – 032 12 Polegate:**

Hungry Monk, Jevington Rd, BN26 5QB, ☎ 2178 – Ⓟ
closed first 2 weeks October, 24-25 December and 2 weeks February – **M** 4.75/5.25.

USTIN-MG-WOLSELEY 17-25 Cornfield Rd ☎ 20255
USTIN-MG-WOLSELEY Fairlight Rd ☎ 33957
HRYSLER-SIMCA Cavendish Pl. ☎ 22771
ITROEN, LANCIA Cornfield Rd ☎ 22244
AIMLER-JAGUAR-ROVER-TRIUMPH Trinity Pl. ☎ 2577
DATSUN 46 Pevensey Rd ☎ 37339
PEUGEOT Wish Rd ☎ 36551
RENAULT 18 Lottbridge Drove ☎ 37233
ROLLS ROYCE Meads Rd ☎ 30201
VAUXHALL 336/8 Seaside ☎ 30663
VW, AUDI-NSU Lottbridge Drove ☎ 56111

EAST DEREHAM Norfolk 986 ㉘ – pop. 9,384 – ☎ 0362 Dereham.
Quebec Rd ℡ 3122.
London 109 – Cambridge 57 – King's Lynn 27 – Norwich 16.

Phœnix (T.H.F.), Church St., NR19 1DN, ℡ 2276 – TV wc ☎ P.
M 3.50/3.75 **st.** 1.50 – **27 rm** 9.50/17.50 **st.**

AUSTIN-MG Two Oaks Garage Beetley ℡ 86219
AUSTIN-MORRIS-MG-ROVER-TRIUMPH-WOLSELEY Norwich Rd ℡ 2293
FORD High St. ℡ 2281

EAST GRINSTEAD West Sussex 986 ㊱ – pop. 18,632 – ☎ 0342.
Envir : Hever Castle* (13C-20C) and gardens** *AC*, NE: 10 m.
i East Court Mansion, College Lane ℡ 23636.
London 32 – Brighton 29 – Eastbourne 33 – Lewes 21 – Maidstone 32.

Ye Olde Felbridge, London Rd, RH19 2BH, ℡ 24424, heated, – wc ☎ P.
61 rm.

at Gravetye SW: 4½ m. off B 2110 – ✉ East Grinstead – ☎ 0342 Sharpthorne:

❀ **Gravetye Manor** , RH19 4LJ, ℡ 810567, <, « 16C manor house with beautif gardens and grounds by William Robinson », , park – P
M a la carte 5.40/10.90 **t.** 1.30 – 4.50 – **15 rm** 16.00/21.00 **t.**
Spec. Gravad Lax (February-September), Champignons farcis frits, Médaillons de chevreuil Baden-Baden (Augus April).

AUSTIN-MG-WOLSELEY Sharpthorne ℡ 0342 (Sharpthorne) 234
AUSTIN-MORRIS-MG-WOLSELEY King St. ℡ 24666
CHRYSLER-SIMCA The Parade, North End ℡ 21456
FORD 220 London Rd ℡ 24344

EAST HORSLEY Surrey – pop. 3,972 – ☎ 048 65.
London 27 – Guildford 7.

Thatchers, Epsom Rd, KT24 6TB, on A 246 ℡ 4291, heated, – TV wc ☎
M 2.75/3.75 **t.** 1.25 – **22 rm** 12.50/22.00 **st.**

EAST MOLESEY Surrey – pop. 6,680 – ☎ 01 London.
London 18 – Portsmouth 59.

XX **Vecchia Roma,** 55-57 Bridge Rd, KT8 9EL, ℡ 979 5490, Italian rest.
closed Monday and 25-26 December – **M** a la carte 4.85/7.85 **t.** 1.50.

XX **Le Chien Qui Fume,** 107 Walton Rd, KT8 0DR, ℡ 979 7150
closed Sunday, Monday and Bank Holidays – **M** (lunch by reservation) a la carte 5.7 7.25 1.25.

X **Lantern,** 20 Bridge Rd, KT8 9HA, ℡ 979 1531
closed Sunday and Bank Holidays – **M** (dinner only) a la carte 4.90/7.10 **t.** 1.25.

EASTON CROSS Devon – see Chagford.

EASTON GREY Wilts. – see Malmesbury.

EAST PRAWLE Devon – pop. 150 – ✉ Kingsbridge – ☎ 054 851 Chivelstone.
London 245 – Exeter 45 – Plymouth 29.

XX **Sharper's Head** with rm, TQ7 2BZ, ℡ 263, < Sharper's Head and Lannacombe Ba « Tastefully furnished », – TV P
June-September – **M** *(open May-September)* (dinner only) a la carte 4.35/6.65 1.60 – **6 rm** 9.00/17.00 **t.**

EAST PRESTON West Sussex – pop. 4,446 – ✉ Littlehampton – ☎ 090 62 Rustington.
London 60 – Brighton 16 – Littlehampton 4 – Worthing 5.

XX **Old Forge,** The Street, BN16 1JJ, ℡ 2040 – P
closed Sunday dinner and Monday – **M** a la carte 3.35/9.15 1.35.

MORRIS-MG-WOLSELEY ℡ 4114

EDWALTON Notts. – see Nottingham.

EGHAM Surrey 986 ⑧ – pop. 30,609 – ☎ 078 43.
London 29 – Reading 21.

Runnymede, Windsor Rd, TW20 0AG, on A 308 ℡ 6171, Telex 934900, <, –
P.
M 3.80/4.40 **st.** 1.70 – **90 rm** 17.80/26.20 **st.** – P 22.80/26.80 **st.**

Great Fosters, Stroude Rd, TW20 9UR, S : 1 m. off B 388 ℡ 3822, <, « Elizabetha mansion with extensive gardens », , heated, park – P.
M 4.50/6.50 **s.** 1.50 – **38 rm** 11.50/21.00 **s.** – P 20.25/23.75 **s.**

XX **La Casina Rosa,** 5 High St. ℡ 3206, Italian rest. – P
closed Sunday, last 2 weeks August and 25-26 December – **M** a la carte 3.70/4.75 1.2

DAIMLER-JAGUAR-ROVER-TRIUMPH The Causeway ℡ 6191
DATSUN The Avenue ℡ 4743
FIAT Egham-by-pass ℡ 6222

GLWYSFACH Powys – see Machynlleth.

LSTEAD Surrey – pop. 2,548 – ✉ Farnham – ☎ 025 122.
ndon 43 – Guildford 9 – Southampton 44.

✗ **Emmerich's,** Thursley Rd, GU8 6DH, ☎ 2323 – Ⓟ
closed Sunday dinner and Monday – **M** a la carte 4.50/5.00 🍷 1.70.

LTERWATER Cumbria – see Ambleside.

LY Cambs. 986 ㉜ – pop. 9,966 – ☎ 0353.
e : Cathedral** 11C-16C (Norman nave***, lantern***).
Cambridge Rd ☎ 2751.
24 St. Mary's St. ☎ 3311.
ndon 76 – Cambridge 16 – Norwich 60.

🏨 **Lamb** (County), 2 Lynn Rd, CB7 4EJ, ☎ 3574 – Ⓟ
M 3.00/4.00 **t.** 🍷 1.25 – **26 rm** ☕ 9.00/15.00 **t.**

✗ **Old Fire Engine House,** 25 St. Mary's St., CB3 4ER, ☎ 2582
closed Sunday dinner, Good Friday and 2 weeks at Christmas – **M** a la carte 2.90/5.45 **t.** 🍷 1.00.

JSTIN-MG-WOLSELEY, CHRYSLER Lynn Rd ☎ 2981
AT 64 St. Mary's St. ☎ 2300
RD Station Rd ☎ 2345
MORRIS-MG-ROVER-TRIUMPH-WOLSELEY St. Mary's St. ☎ 2952
VOLVO Witcham ☎ 035 373 (Sutton) 403

MBOROUGH Somerset – pop. 165 – ✉ Bath (Avon) – ☎ 0761 Stratton-on-Fosse.
ndon 134 – Bath 15 – Bristol 16 – Taunton 35.

🏨 **Court,** Lynch Hill, BA3 4SA, E : ½ m. on B 3139 ☎ 232237, 🌳 – 🚿wc Ⓟ
M a la carte 2.95/3.50 **t.** 🍷 1.30 – **9 rm** ☕ 8.00/13.50 **t.**

NGLEFIELD GREEN Surrey – pop. 7,601 – ✉ ☎ 078 43 Egham.
ndon 30 – Reading 20.

✗✗✗ Bailiwick, Wick Rd, TW20 0HN, off A 30 ☎ 2223 – Ⓟ.

PPING Essex 986 ④ – pop. 11,714 – ☎ 0378.
e : Forest* – **Envir.:** Waltham Abbey (Abbey*) E : 6 m.
Forest Approach, Bury Rd ☎ 520 2758.
ndon 20 – Cambridge 40 – Chelmsford 18.

🏨 **Post House** (T.H.F.), High Rd, Bell Common, CM16 4DG, S : ¾ m. on A 11 ☎ 73137, 🌳 – TV 🛁wc ☎ Ⓟ
M 3.50/3.70 **t.** 🍷 1.50 – ☕ 2.00 – **60 rm** 13.00/18.00 **t.**

🏨 **Epping Forest Motel** (County), 234 High St., CM16 4AL, ☎ 73134 – 🛗 TV 🛁wc ☎ Ⓟ. 🐕
M approx. 3.00 **t.** 🍷 1.20 – **28 rm** ☕ 10.00/15.50.

HRYSLER-SIMCA High Rd ☎ 72266

PSOM Surrey 986 ⑧ and ㊱ – pop. 72,301 (inc. Ewell) – ☎ 037 27.
vir. : Chessington Zoo* *AC,* NW : 3 ½ m.
☎ 23363.
ndon 17 – Guildford 16.

🏨 **Drift Bridge** (Crest), Reigate Rd, KT17 3JZ, SE : 2¼ m. on A 240 by A 2022 ☎ 073 73 (Burgh Heath) 52163 – TV 🛁wc ☎ Ⓟ. 🐕
M 3.00/3.50 **s.** 🍷 1.55 – **29 rm** ☕ 10.95/16.70 **s.**

🏨 **Linden House,** 9 College Rd off Church Rd, KT17 4HF, ☎ 21447, 🌳 – 🛁wc 🚗 Ⓟ
M *(closed Sunday)* (dinner only) 2.00/4.50 🍷 1.40 – **20 rm** ☕ 7.15/14.25 **st.**

⌂ White House, Downs Hill Rd ☎ 22472, 🌳 – 🛁wc Ⓟ
10 rm.

JDI-NSU, AUSTIN-MG-WOLSELEY, CHRYSLER, EUGEOT 28/38 Upper High St. ☎ 25611
JSTIN-DAIMLER-JAGUAR-ROVER-TRIUMPH High St. ☎ 26422
RD 28 Church St. ☎ 25101
MORRIS-MG-WOLSELEY 4 Church St. ☎ 26611
RENAULT 1/3 Dorking Rd ☎ 28391
VAUXHALL 48 Upper High St. ☎ 25920
VW, AUDI-NSU Reigate Rd ☎ 073 73 (Burgh Heath) 60180

Cet ouvrage n'est pas un répertoire de tous les hôtels et restaurants, ni même de tous les bons hôtels et restaurants de Grande-Bretagne et d'Irlande.

Comme nous cherchons à rendre service à tous les touristes, nous sommes amenés à indiquer des établissements de toutes les classes et à n'en citer que quelques-uns de chaque sorte.

ERBISTOCK Clwyd – pop. 350 – ✉ Wrexham – ☎ 097 873 Overton-on-Dee.
London 184 – Chester 18 – Shrewsbury 22.

✗ **Boat Inn,** LL13 0DL, ☎ 243, ≤, – Ⓟ
closed Christmas Day dinner – **M** a la carte 5.25/6.20 **st.**

ERIDGE GREEN East Sussex – see Royal Tunbridge Wells.

ERMINGTON Devon – see Modbury.

ESHER Surrey 986 ⑧ – pop. 64,414 – ☎ 0372.
☎ 63533 – More Lane ☎ 65921.
London 20 – Portsmouth 58.

✗✗ **Borsalino,** 63 High St., KT10 9RQ, ☎ 63191
closed Saturday lunch and Sunday dinner – **M** a la carte 3.15/5.85 1.10.

AUSTIN-MORRIS-MG Kingston By-pass, Hinchley Wood ☎ 01 (London) 398 0123

ESKDALE Cumbria – pop. 450 – ✉ Holmrook – ☎ 094 03.
Envir. : Wast Water★ NE : 6 m. – Wasdale Head (site★) NE : 7 m.
London 312 – Carlisle 59 – Kendal 60.

Bower House Inn, Holmrook, CA19 1TD, W : ¾ m. ☎ 244, – wc Ⓟ
closed 24 to 27 December – **M** approx. 5.00 **t.** – **12 rm** 9.00/20.00 **st.** – P 14.0(
15.50 **st.**

ETON Berks. 986 ㊱ – see Windsor.

EVERCREECH Somerset – pop. 1,548 – ✉ Shepton Mallet – ☎ 074 983.
London 122 – Bristol 24 – Southampton 58 – Taunton 35.

Glen, Queen's Rd, BA4 6JR, ☎ 369, ≤, – wc Ⓟ
M *(closed Sunday dinner to non-residents)* approx. 3.00 – **16 rm** 5.75/13.50.

AUSTIN-MG-WOLSELEY Weymouth Rd ☎ 393

EVESHAM Heref. and Worc. 986 ㉛ – pop. 13,855 – ☎ 0386.
London 99 – Birmingham 30 – Cheltenham 16 – Coventry 32.

Evesham, Coopers Lane, WR11 6DA, ☎ 6344, « Large garden » – wc Ⓟ
M (buffet lunch) a la carte 3.55/5.40 **st.** 1.80 – **18 rm** 10.00/22.50 **st.**

Northwick Arms, Waterside, WR11 6BT, ☎ 6109 – wc Ⓟ
M 2.50/4.00 **t.** 1.00 – **22 rm** 8.00/15.50 **t.**

at Abbots Salford (Warw.) N : 5 ¼ m. by A 435 on A 439 – ✉ ☎ 0386 Evesham :

Salford Hall, WR11 5UT, ☎ 870561, « 15C and 17C hall », – Ⓟ
M 3.50/6.00 **s.** 2.00 – **10 rm** 6.50/14.00.

AUSTIN-JAGUAR-MG-ROVER-TRIUMPH-WOLSELEY Broadway Rd ☎ 6441
BMW, VW, AUDI-NSU Harvington ☎ 038 671 (Harvington) 612
CHRYSLER-SIMCA Elm Rd ☎ 2773
DAF High St. ☎ 830228
FIAT 3 Cheltenham Rd ☎ 2301
FORD Market Pl. ☎ 2525
MORRIS-MG-WOLSELEY Abbey Rd ☎ 6173
PEUGEOT High St. ☎ 2021
RENAULT 123 Pershore Rd, Hampton ☎ 2446
TOYOTA Icknield St. Honeybourne ☎ 830350
VAUXHALL Cheltenham Rd, Sedgeberrow ☎ 0386 (Ashton-under-Hill) 208
VAUXHALL 70 High St. ☎ 2614

EWEN Glos. – see Cirencester.

EXETER Devon 986 ㊴ – pop. 95,729 – ☎ 0392.
See : Cathedral★★ 12C-14C (Tierceron ribbed vault★★★, West front★, Bishop's Throne★) AZ **A**
St. Nicholas' Priory★ 11C AZ **B** – Guildhall★ 14C-15C AZ **D** – Maritime Museum★ *AC* AZ **M**[1].
Exeter Airport : ☎ 67433, Telex 42648, E : 3 m. by A 30 BY – **Terminal** : St. David's Statior
i Civic Centre, Dix's Field ☎ 77888 ext 2297.
London 201 – Bournemouth 80 – Bristol 78 – Plymouth 43 – Southampton 106.

Plan opposite

Rougemont (Mt. Charlotte), Queen St., EX4 3SP, ☎ 54982 – Ⓟ. AZ
M approx. 5.00 **s.** 1.60 – **53 rm** 12.00/18.00 **s.**

Imperial, New North Rd, EX4 4JX, ☎ 72750, « Extensive gardens » – wc
Ⓟ. AZ
M approx. 3.00 **st.** 1.25 – **30 rm** 9.00/17.50 **st.**

White Hart, 66 South St., EX1 1EE, ☎ 79897, « Part 14C inn » – wc wc
Ⓟ. AZ
closed 25 and 26 December – **M** 3.50/4.00 **t.** 1.25 – **48 rm** 10.50/17.00 **t.**

Buckerell Lodge (Crest), Topsham Rd, EX2 4SQ, SE : 1 m. on A 377 ☎ 52451, –
wc Ⓟ BY
M a la carte 3.35/5.50 **s.** 1.55 – **19 rm** 10.95/17.85 **s.**

EXETER

edford Street AZ 3
ore Street AZ
igh Street AZ

lphington Road AZ 2
ackall Road AZ 4
utts Road BY 5
ommins Road BZ 8
dmund Street AZ 9
East Wonford Hill BY 10
Frog Street AZ 12
Gladstone Road BZ 13
Ladysmith Road BZ 16
Little John's Cross Hill AY 17
Magdalen Street AZ 20
Mount Pleasant Road BY 21
New Bridge Street AZ 22
North Street AZ 23
North Street HEAVITREE BY 24
Okehampton Road AZ 26
Old Tiverton Road BZ 27
Paris Street BZ 28
Prince Charles Road BY 30
Prince of Wales Road AY 31
Richmond Road AZ 32
St. Andrew's Road AY 33
Southernhay East ABZ 34
Southernhay West AZ 35
Sweetbriar Lane BY 36
Union Road AY 37
Western Way AZ 38
Whipton Lane BY 39
Wonford Street BY 40

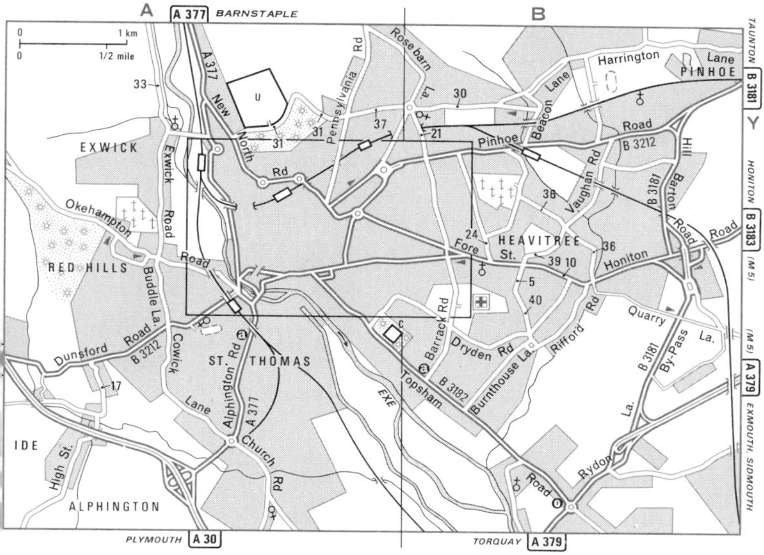

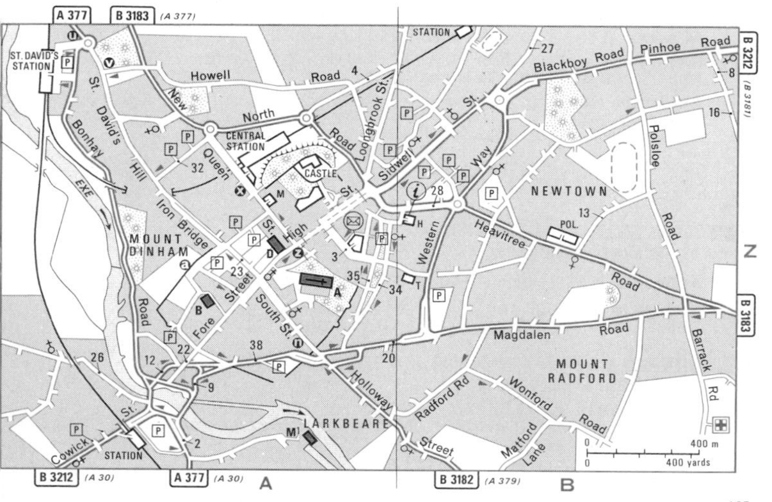

Royal Clarence (Norfolk Cap.), Cathedral Yard, EX1 1HD, ☎ 58464, Telex 23241 – lift, bath wc, shower wc, ☎ – AZ
M a la carte 3.50/5.50 **st.** – **65 rm** ☐ 10.25/21.10 **st.**

Countess Wear Lodge (County), 398 Topsham Rd, EX2 6HE, S: 2 ½ m. on A 37 – BY
☎ 039 287 (Topsham) 5441 – TV bath wc ☎ Ⓟ.
M 3.25/3.75 **t.** 1.45 – **43 rm** ☐ 11.90/18.40 **st.**

Great Western (T.H.F.), St. David's Station App., EX4 4NU, ☎ 74039 – TV bath wc ☎ – AZ
M a la carte 4.05/5.50 **st.** 1.50 – **43 rm** ☐ 7.50/19.50 **st.**

St. Andrews, 28 Alphington Rd, EX2 8HN, ☎ 76784 – Ⓟ – AY
closed 1 week at Christmas – **20 rm** ☐ 8.00/14.00 **s.**

Old Malthouse, Bartholomew St. East, EX4 3BH, ☎ 70092 – AZ
closed Sunday and Bank Holidays – **M** a la carte 3.45/5.05 2.15.

at Pinhoe **NE: 3 m. on A 38 – BY – ✉ ☎ 0392 Exeter:**

Gipsy Hill, EX1 3RN, ☎ 67806, – bath wc shower wc ☎ Ⓟ.
30 rm.

at Kennford **S : 5 m. on A 38 by A 380 – AY – ✉ ☎ 0392 Kennford :**

Exeter Mercury Motor Inn, Exeter By-Pass, EX6 7UX, ☎ 832121 – TV bath wc Ⓟ
60 rm.

Haldon Thatch, Telegraph Hill, EX6 7XX, off A 38 ☎ 832273 – Ⓟ
closed Tuesday lunch, Monday and January – **M** a la carte 5.00/6.35 1.40.

ASTON-MARTIN, DAIMLER-JAGUAR, FERRARI, Frog St., Inner By-pass ☎ 75237
AUSTIN-MG-WOLSELEY 88 Polsloe Rd ☎ 73261
AUSTIN-MORRIS-MG-WOLSELEY Alphington St. ☎ 58241
AUSTIN-MG-WOLSELEY 85/88 Sidwell St. ☎ 54923
AUSTIN-MORRIS-MG-WOLSELEY Marsh Barton Rd ☎ 74161
CHRYSLER-SIMCA Honiton Rd ☎ 68187
CITROEN, FIAT Trusham Rd, Marsh Barton ☎ 7731
DAF Exhibition Way ☎ 74529
FORD 9 Marsh Barton Rd ☎ 76561
MORRIS-MG-WOLSELEY 55 Sidwell St. ☎ 78342
PEUGEOT 11 Verney St. ☎ 55372
RENAULT Summerland St. ☎ 77225
ROLLS ROYCE, ROVER-TRIUMPH Paris St. ☎ 77244
SAAB Ladysmith Rd ☎ 73990
VOLVO 42 Magdalen Rd ☎ 57097

EXFORD Somerset – pop. 452 – ✉ Minehead – ☎ 064 383.

London 194 – Exeter 35 – Minehead 13 – Taunton 32.

Crown, TA24 7PP, ☎ 243 – bath wc Ⓟ
March-November – **M** 3.50/4.25 **st.** 1.40 – **18 rm** ☐ 7.00/15.25 – P 9.00/12.00.

EXMOUTH Devon 986 ㊴ – pop. 25,827 – ☎ 039 52.

i Alexandra Ter. ☎ 3744 (summer only) – Town Hall ☎ 4356 (winter only).

London 210 – Exeter 11.

Imperial (T.H.F.), The Esplanade, EX8 2SW, ☎ 74761, ≤, heated, – lift TV Ⓟ
M a la carte 4.10/5.60 **st.** 1.50 – **41 rm** ☐ 13.00/19.00 **st.** – P 16.25/21.00 **st.**

Devoncourt, 16 Douglas Av., EX8 2EX, ☎ 72277, ≤, heated, – lift Ⓟ
M approx. 3.30 1.50 – **62 rm** ☐ 8.25/16.50 – P 12.25/13.75.

Royal Beacon, The Beacon, EX8 2AF, ☎ 4886 – lift bath wc Ⓟ
M 3.50/7.00 **st.** 1.75 – **32 rm** ☐ 7.50/17.00 **st.** – P 12.00 **st.**

Balcombe House, 7 Stevenstone Rd, EX8 2EP, NE: 1 m. off A 376 ☎ 6349,
shower wc Ⓟ
Easter-October – **10 rm** ☐ 7.00/13.00.

AUSTIN-MG-WOLSELEY 12 High St. ☎ 2048
CHRYSLER-SIMCA St. Andrews Rd ☎ 3045
RENAULT 4 Church Rd ☎ 72921
ROVER-TRIUMPH The Parade ☎ 72266
VAUXHALL Salterton Rd ☎ 4366
VW, AUDI-NSU Belvedere Rd ☎ 4303

EYE Suffolk 986 ㉜ – pop. 1,660 – ☎ 037 987.

London 93 – Ipswich 20 – Norwich 23.

at Brome **NW: 2 m. on A 140 by B 1077 – ✉ ☎ 037 987 Eye:**

Grange Motel, IP23 8AP, ☎ 456 – TV bath wc ☎ Ⓟ
M a la carte 4.00/7.00 1.25 – ☐ 1.00 – **22 rm** 9.00/13.00 **st.**

FAIRBOURNE Gwynedd – pop. 400 – ☎ 034 16.

London 229 – Dolgellau 8 – Shrewsbury 65.

Brackenhurst, LL38 2HX, ☎ 226, ≤, – Ⓟ
closed 21 October-21 November – **M** *(closed Sunday)* approx. 2.50 **t.** 1.60 – **13 r**
☐ 4.25/9.00 **st.**

Liety Heulog, 2-4 Alyn Rd ☎ 228 – Ⓟ
12 rm.

FAIRFORD Glos. 986 ㉛ – pop. 1,840 – ☏ 0285.
See : St. Mary's Church (stained glass windows** 15C-16C).
London 99 – Bristol 46 – Gloucester 28 – Oxford 27.

- Bull, Market Pl., GL7 4AA, ☏ 712535, – wc P.
  16 rm.
- Pink's, London Rd, GL7 4AR, ☏ 712355 – P.

MORRIS-MG-WOLSELEY ☏ 222

FAIRY CROSS Devon – pop. 274 (inc. Alwington) – ✉ Bideford – ☏ 023 75 Horns Cross.
London 235 – Barnstaple 13 – Exeter 47.

- **Portledge**, EX39 5BX, ☏ 262, ←, « Part 13C and 17C manor house », heated, park – wc P
  May-early October – **M** 5.25/6.25 **t.** – **35 rm** 12.75/25.50 **t.**

FAKENHAM Norfolk 986 ㉘ – pop. 4,462 – ☏ 0328.
Envir. : Castle Acre (priory** ruins 11C-14C) *AC*, SW : 12 m.
☏ 2867.
London 112 – Cambridge 61 – King's Lynn 22 – Norwich 26.

- Crown (Gd. Met.), Market Pl., NR21 9BG, ☏ 2010 – P
  12 rm.

AUSTIN-MORRIS-MG-ROVER-TRIUMPH-WOLSELEY Holt Rd ☏ 2277
CHRYSLER-SIMCA Norwich Rd ☏ 2251
DATSUN Norwich Rd ☏ 2266
FORD Oak St. ☏ 2317
OPEL Greenway Lane ☏ 2200
VAUXHALL Hempton Rd ☏ 3331

Se scrivete ad un albergo all'estero
allegate alla vostra lettera un tagliando-riposta internazionale
(disponibile presso gli uffici postali).

FALFIELD Avon – pop. 658 – ✉ Gloucester (Glos.) – ☏ 045 48.
London 129 – Bristol 16 – Gloucester 18 – Newport 30.

- Park, S : 1 m. on A 38 ☏ 550, – P
  10 rm.

FALLOWFIELD Greater Manchester – see Manchester.

FALMOUTH Cornwall 986 ㊳ – pop. 18,041 – ☏ 0326.
See : Pendennis Castle 16C (←*) *AC*.
Swanpool Rd ☏ 311262 – at Budock Vean ☏ 032 68 (Mawnan Smith) 288, SW : 7 m.
Town Hall, The Moot ☏ 312300.
London 308 – Penzance 26 – Plymouth 65 – Truro 11.

- **Falmouth,** Cliff Rd, TR11 4NZ, ☏ 312671, ←, heated, – P
  M 4.00/4.50 **st.** 1.50 – **73 rm** 11.60/28.00 **st.** – P 16.00/19.00 **st.**
- **Bay,** Cliff Rd, TR11 4NU, ☏ 312094, ←, – TV P
  closed 25 and 26 December – **M** approx. 4.50 **st.** 1.70 – **39 rm** 8.45/20.00 **st.** – P 14.65/17.75 **st.**
- **Green Bank,** Green Bank, TR11 2SR, ☏ 312440, ← harbour – wc P
  M approx. 3.60 2.00 – **45 rm** 7.50/15.00.
- **Green Lawns,** Western Ter., TR11 4QJ, ☏ 312734, – TV wc P
  closed Christmas – **M** approx. 3.50 **s.** 1.25 – **31 rm** 7.75/26.15 **st.**
- **Penmere Manor**, Mongleath Rd, TR11 5BY, ☏ 311356, heated, – wc P
  Easter-October – **M** (bar lunch) approx. 3.50 **st.** – **30 rm** 8.00/20.00 **st.**
- **St. Michaels,** Stracey Rd, TR11 4NB, ☏ 312707, ←, « Large garden » – wc wc P
  M 3.75/4.20 – **50 rm** 7.00/16.00.
- **Palm Beach,** 2 Queen Mary Rd, TR11 4DP, ☏ 313812, – wc P
  Easter-November and Christmas – **M** *(open all year)* 3.50/4.00 1.10 – **28 rm** 6.00/14.00 – P 13.00/14.00.
- **Tresillian House,** Stracey Rd, TR11 4DW, ☏ 312425 – wc wc
  M approx. 3.00 **s.** 1.25 – **13 rm** 5.00/10.00 **s.**
- **Gyllyngvase House,** Gyllyngvase Rd, TR11 4DJ, ☏ 312956, – wc P
  March-October – **17 rm** 5.95/11.90 **t.**
- **Cotswold House,** 49 Melvill Rd, TR11 4DF, ☏ 312077 – P
  closed Christmas – **11 rm** 7.50/16.00 **t.**
- **Cheriton,** Stracey Rd, TR11 4DW, ☏ 312289
  12 rm 5.50/11.00 **st.**

✗ **Peter's,** 26-28 Arwenack St., TR11 3JW, ☏ 312377, Bistro
M a la carte 3.00/4.00 **t.** 🍷 1.25.

✗ **Twenty One,** 21 Church St., TR11 3EG, ☏ 311486
closed Sunday to Wednesday in winter – **M** (dinner only) 3.00/3.90 **t.** 🍷 1.50.

✗ **Continental,** 29 High St., ☏ 313003
closed Sunday, 25-26 December and 4 weeks in winter - **M** (dinner only) à la cart 3.40/5.60 **t.** 🍷 1.40.

at Mawnan Smith **SW: 5 m. off B 3291 – ✉ Falmouth – ☎ 0326 Mawnan Smith:**

Meudon 🐎, TR11 5HT, E: ½ m. ☏ 250541, « ≤ Attractive gardens », park – TV Ⓟ
closed January and February – **M** approx. 4.75 **st.** 🍷 1.75 – **38 rm** ⊇ 14.00/41.00 **st.** P 20.00/25.00 **st.**

at Budock Vean SW : 7 m. via Mawnan Smith – ✉ Falmouth – ☎ 0326 Mawna Smith :

Budock Vean 🐎, TR11 5LG, ☏ 250288, ≤, %, ⬚, 9, ⛱, park – lift Ⓟ
closed mid January - end February – **M** approx. 5.00 – **54 rm** (full board only) – P 21.5

AUSTIN-MG-WOLSELEY Dracaena Av. ☏ 312338
DAIMLER-JAGUAR-ROVER-TRIUMPH-MERCEDES-BENZ The Moor ☏ 312316
DATSUN Dracaena Av. ☏ 311616
FORD Ponsharden ☏ 032 67 (Penryn) 2331
RENAULT Falmouth Rd, Penryn ☏ 032 67 (Penryn) 26
TOYOTA North Par. ☏ 313029
VW, AUDI-NSU Dracaena Av. ☏ 312283

FAREHAM Hants. 986 ㉟ ㊱ – pop. 80,403 – ☎ 032 92.

Envir. : Porchester castle* (ruins 3C-12C), Keep ≤* *AC*, SE : 2 ½ m.

London 77 – Portsmouth 9 – Southampton 13 – Winchester 19.

Red Lion, East St., PO16 0BP, ☏ 234113 – Ⓟ
M (closed Sunday dinner) a la carte 2.80/3.85 **t.** 🍷 1.70 – **20 rm** ⊇ 10.00/15.00 **t.**

AUSTIN-MG-WOLSELEY 216 West St. ☏ 2488
FIAT, LANCIA Newgate Lane ☏ 82811
MORRIS-MG-WOLSELEY 36 West St. ☏ 2771
MORRIS-MG-ROVER-TRIUMPH East St. ☏ 2277

FARINGDON Oxon. 986 ㉛ ㉟ – pop. 3,898 – ☎ 0367.

London 79 – Bristol 55 – Oxford 17 – Reading 34.

Bell, Market Pl., SN7 7HP, ☏ 20534 – Ⓟ
closed 25 and 26 December – **M** *(closed Sunday dinner)* a la carte 3.30/5.20 ⊇ 1.30 – **9 rm** 5.00/11.00.

BMW Church St. ☏ 20614
PEUGEOT Marlborough St. ☏ 20141

FARNBOROUGH Hants. 986 ㊱ – pop. 41,474 – ☎ 0252.

See : St. Michael's Abbey church* 19 C (Imperial crypt *AC*).

⛳9 Ively Rd, W : 1 m.

London 41 – Reading 17 – **Southampton 44** – Winchester 33.

Queens (Anchor), Lynchford Rd, GU14 6AZ, S : 1 ½ m. on Farnborough Rd (A 32 ☏ 45051, Group Telex 27120 – TV ⌂wc ☎ Ⓟ.
M approx. 3.25 **t.** 🍷 1.00 – **79 rm** ⊇ 13.20/18.70.

at Frimley Bridges **N : 1 m. on A 325 – ✉ ☎ 0276 Camberley:**

✗✗ **Auctioneer,** GU14 8DF, ☏ 23559 – Ⓟ
closed Saturday lunch, Sunday and Bank Holidays – **M** a la carte 4.50/6.40 🍷 1.20.

ALFA-ROMEO 13 Cross St. ☏ 46291
AUSTIN-MORRIS-MG-WOLSELEY 116 Farnborough Rd ☏ 41345
FORD Elles Rd ☏ 44344

FARNE ISLANDS Northumb.

See : Islands** (Sea Bird Sanctuary and grey seals, by boat from Seahouses *AC*).

Hotel see : Bamburgh.

FARNHAM Surrey 986 ㊱ – pop. 31,248 – ☎ 025 13.

See : Castle keep 12C (square tower*) *AC*. **Envir. :** Birdworld* (zoological bird gardens) *A* SW : 3 ½ m.

⛳9 Farnham Park ☏ 3319.

London 45 – Reading 22 – **Southampton 39** – Winchester 28.

Bush (Anchor), The Borough, GU9 7NN, ☏ 5237, Group Telex 27120, ⛱ – TV ⌂w ☎ Ⓟ
M a la carte 4.00/5.10 **t.** 🍷 1.00 – **49 rm** ⊇ 9.75/18.70 **st.**

✗✗ **Bishop's Table** with rm, 27 West St., GU9 7DX, ☏ 5545, ⛱ – TV ⌂wc ⌂wc ☎
closed Bank Holidays – **M** *(closed Sunday dinner)* a la carte 3.55/11.35 **s.** 🍷 1.25 **11 rm** ⊇ 7.90/14.00 **s.**

✗ **Merriman,** 30 Downing St., GU9 7PD, ☏ 6463, French rest.
closed Sunday – **M** a la carte 4.15/7.45 **s.** 🍷 1.50.

at Seale E: 4 m. on A 31 – ✉ Farnham – ☎ 025 18 Runfold:

Hog's Back (Embassy), GU10 1EX, ☎ 2345, – 📺 wc ☎ P
closed Christmas – **M** approx. 3.40 1.55 – **13 rm** 8.50/13.00 **st.**

AUSTIN-MORRIS-MG-WOLSELEY East St. ☎ 6201
DAIMLER-JAGUAR-ROVER-TRIUMPH East St. ☎ 22911
FIAT 81-84 East St. ☎ 2967
MERCEDES-BENZ 48/50 Shortheath Rd ☎ 6266
MORRIS-MG-WOLSELEY Lower Bourne ☎ 5610
SAAB Frensham ☎ 025 125 (Frensham) 2002
VAUXHALL Union Rd ☎ 21185
VW, AUDI-NSU, PORSCHE West St. and Crondall Lane ☎ 5616

FARNLEY TYAS West Yorks. – see Huddersfield.

FARNSFIELD Notts. – pop. 2,500 – ✉ Newark – ☎ 0623 Mansfield.
Envir.: Newstead Abbey** 16C (gardens**) *AC*, SW: 9 m.
London 145 – Nottingham 13 – Sheffield 31.

White Post Inn, Mansfield Rd, W 1 ¼ m. on A 614 ☎ 882215 – P.

FARRINGTON GURNEY Avon – pop. 647 – ✉ Bristol – ☎ 0761 Temple Cloud.
London 132 – Bath 13 – **Bristol 12** – Wells 8.

Old Parsonage with rm, BS13 5UB, ☎ 52211, – wc P
M *(closed Sunday dinner and Monday to non-residents)* a la carte 4.50/6.40 1.35 – **3 rm** 7.00/16.00.

FAWLEY Bucks. – pop. 398 – ✉ Henley-on-Thames (Oxon.) – ☎ 049 163 Turville Heath.
London 45 – Oxford 25 – Reading 12.

Walnut Tree, Fawley Green, RG9 6JE, ☎ 360 – P
closed Sunday and Christmas Day – **M** (dinner only) 8.50/10.00 **st.**

FEERING Essex – pop. 1,569 – ✉ Colchester – ☎ 0376 Kelvedon.
London 47 – Colchester 9 – Chelmsford 14.

Old Anchor, on old A 12 ☎ 70469 – P
10 rm.

RENAULT London Rd ☎ 0376 (Kelvedon) 70388

FELINDRE-FARCHOG Dyfed – see Newport (Dyfed).

FELIXSTOWE Suffolk 986 ㉜ – pop. 18,925 – ☎ 039 42.
Shipping connections with the Continent: to Dunkerque (Sealink) – to Gothenburg (Tor Line) – to Rotterdam: Europoort (Transport Ferry Service) – to Zeebrugge (Townsend Thoresen).
i 91 Undercliffe Rd West ☎ 2126 or 3303 – Tourist Information Caravan, No. 2 Gate, The Docks ☎ 78359 (summer only).
London 84 – Ipswich 11.

Orwell Moat House, Hamilton Rd, IP11 7DX, ☎ 5511, – 📺 P.
M a la carte 3.50/4.50 **st.** 1.50 – 1.70 – **65 rm** 11.25/17.00 **st.** – P 19.65/21.65 **st.**

De Novo, Orwell Rd, IP11 4ZX, ☎ 78441 – wc ☎ P.
M 3.50/4.00 1.70 – **28 rm** 7.50/13.50 – P 14.00/16.00.

AUSTIN-MORRIS-MG-ROVER-TRIUMPH-WOLSELEY Crescent Rd ☎ 3221
CHRYSLER-SIMCA Garrison Lane ☎ 5591

FENSTANTON Cambs. – see St. Ives.

FERNDOWN Dorset – pop. 11,752 – ☎ 0202.
London 108 – Bournemouth 6 – Dorchester 27 – Salisbury 23.

Dormy (De Vere), New Rd, BH22 8ES, on A 347 ☎ 872121, ←, heated, – 📺 P.
M approx. 5.25 **st.** 1.45 – **81 rm** 15.25/30.50 **st.**

Coach House Motel, Tricketts Cross, BH22 9NW, on A 31 ☎ 871222 – 📺 wc P
M approx. 3.00 **s.** 1.50 – 1.25 – **32 rm** 9.75/13.50 **st.**

ROVER-TRIUMPH New Rd ☎ 6255
ROVER-TRIUMPH 553 Ringwood Rd ☎ 2212
TOYOTA Ringwood Rd ☎ 2201
VAUXHALL Wimborne Rd ☎ 872055
WOLSELEY Victoria Rd ☎ 71649

FILEY North Yorks. 986 ㉔ – pop. 5,336 – ☎ 072 381.
i John St. ☎ 0723 (Scarborough) 512204 (summer only).
London 251 – Kingston-upon-Hull 40 – Scarborough 7.5 – York 41.

White Lodge, The Crescent, YO14 9JX, ☎ 0723 (Scarborough) 512268, ←, – wc
Easter-October – **M** 2.75/4.50 1.60 – **22 rm** 9.00/20.00 – P 12.00/14.50.

FINDON West Sussex – see Worthing.

FINGEST Bucks. – pop. 3,080 (inc. Lane End) – ✉ Henley-on-Thames (Oxon.) – ☎ 049 163 Turville Heath.

London 42 – High Wycombe 8 – **Oxford 24** – Reading 16.

✗ **Chequers Inn,** RG9 6QD ℡ 335, ⛱ – Ⓟ
M a la carte 4.70/8.05 **t.** 🍷 1.50.

FISHBOURNE I.O.W. 986 ㊴ – Shipping Services: see Wight (Isle of).

FISHGUARD Dyfed 986 ㉚ – pop. 3,039 – ☎ 0348.

See: ≤** on Goodwick. **Envir.:** Porthgain (cliffs ☀***) – Strumble Head (≤** from the lighthouse) NW: 5 m. – Trevine (≤**) SW: 8 m. – Bryn Henllan (site*) NE: 5 m. – Abereiddy (site*) SW: 13 m.

🚗 ℡ 01 (London) 723 7000 ext 3148.

⛴ to Rosslare (Sealink) 1-2 daily (Sundays: Summer only) (3 h. 30 mn).

ℹ Town Hall, ℡ 873484 (Easter-September).

London 267 – **Cardiff 110** – Gloucester 157 – Holyhead 166 – Shrewsbury 134 – **Swansea 72.**

🏠 **Cartref,** High St., SA65 9AW, ℡ 872430
M 2.70/3.25 **st.** 🍷 1.40 – **16 rm** 🛏 6.00/12.00 **st.** – P 10.75/11.25 **st.**

✗ **The Bistro** with rm, Main St., SA65 9HG, ℡ 873365 – Ⓟ
Easter-mid October – **M** *(closed Sunday in summer, Sunday and Monday in winter, November and 25-26 December)* a la carte 4.10/6.30 🍷 1.20 – **5 rm** 🛏 5.00/10.00 **t.**

at Goodwick NW: **1 ½** m. – ✉ ☎ 0348 Fishguard:

🏨 **Fishguard Bay** 🐚, Quay Rd, SA64 0BT, ℡ 873571, Telex 48503, 🏊 heated, ⛱, park – 🛗 🛁wc 🚿 Ⓟ. 🏕
M 3.15/4.00 **s.** 🍷 1.75 – **61 rm** 🛏 8.00/18.00 **s.**

AUSTIN Clive Rd ℡ 872254

MORRIS-MG-ROVER-TRIUMPH West St. ℡ 872253

En haute saison, et surtout dans les stations, il est prudent de retenir à l'avance.

FITTLEWORTH West Sussex – pop. 895 – ✉ Pulborough – ☎ 079 882.

London 52 – **Brighton 28** – Chichester 15 – Worthing 17.

🏠 **Swan,** Lower St., RH20 1EN, ℡ 429 – Ⓟ
M a la carte 2.45/5.55 **t.** 🍷 1.50 – **7 rm** 🛏 7.25/16.00 **st.**

FLEET Hants. 986 ㊱ – pop. 69,900 – ☎ 025 14.

London 46 – Guildford 14 – Reading 16 – **Southampton 42.**

✗✗ **Fleet Chantelle,** 33 Reading Rd South, GU13 9QP, ✉ Aldershot ℡ 3775 – Ⓟ
closed Saturday lunch, Sunday, 24 December-10 January and Bank Holidays – **M** a la carte 3.60/5.25 **t.** 🍷 1.35.

AUSTIN-MORRIS 66 Albert St. ℡ 3303

LANCIA 42 Reading Rd South ℡ 3425

FLEETWOOD Lancs. 986 ㉓ – pop. 28,599 – ☎ 039 17.

⛳18 Princes Way ℡ 3114, W: from Promenade.

⛴ to the Isle of Man: Douglas (Isle of Man Steam Packet Co.) 2-5 weekly Summer only (4 h).

ℹ Marine Hall, Esplanade ℡ 71141.

London 245 – **Blackpool 10** – Lancaster 28 – **Manchester 53.**

🏠 North Euston, Esplanade, FY7 6BN, ℡ 3375 – 🛗 🛁wc 🚿wc ☎ Ⓟ
64 rm.

AUSTIN-ROVER-TRIUMPH Poulton Rd ℡ 2575

FLITTON Beds. – pop. 717 – ✉ Ampthill – ☎ 0525 Silsoe.

London 48 – Bedford 11 – Luton 10.

✗✗ **White Hart Inn,** MK45 5DY, ℡ 60403 – Ⓟ
closed Sunday and Bank Holidays – **M** (dinner only) a la carte 3.70/5.75 **t.** 🍷 1.30.

FOLKESTONE Kent 986 ㊱ – pop. 43,801 – ☎ 0303.

See: Site*. **Envir.:** The Warren* (cliffs) E: 2 m. by A 20 X – Acrise Place* *AC*, NW: 6 m. by A 260 X.

⛳18 Sene, ℡ 66726, N: 2 m. of Hythe on B 2065, W: by A 259 X.

⛴ Shipping connections with the Continent: to Boulogne, Calais and Oostende (Sealink).

ℹ South East England Tourist Board, Harbour St. ℡ 58594 – The Precinct ℡ 53840.

London 72 – **Brighton 74** – **Dover 7** – Maidstone 35.

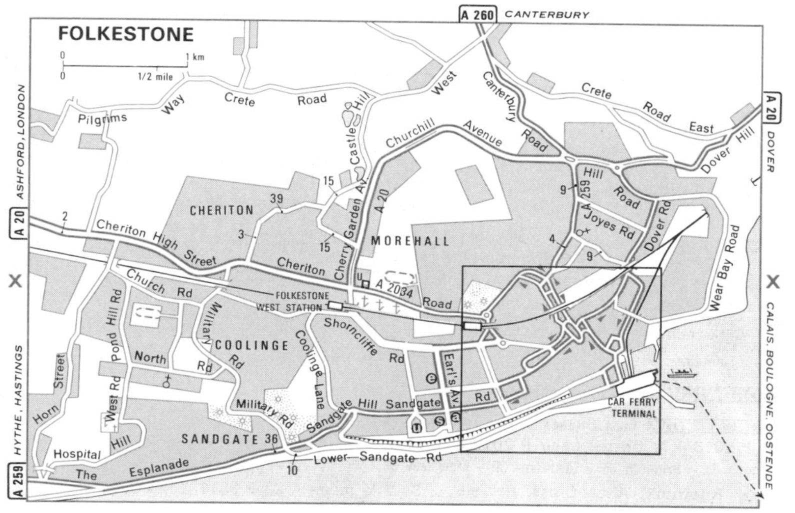

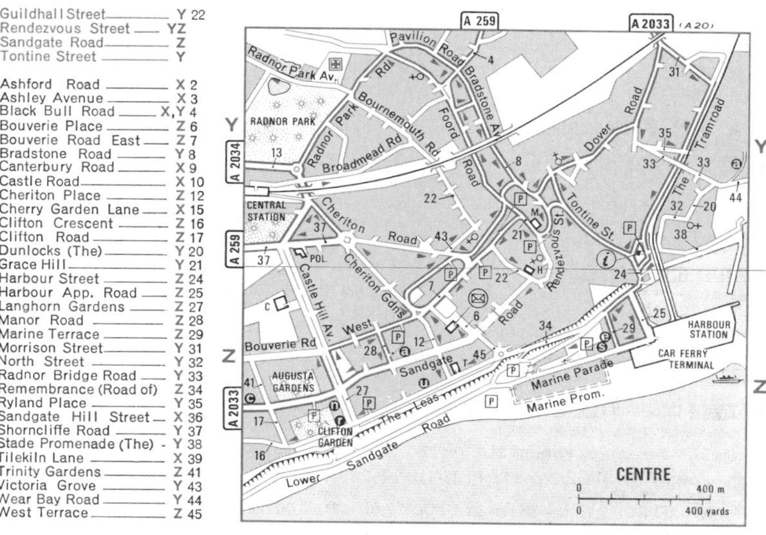

Burlington (Interchange), Earl's Av., CT20 2HR, ☎ 55301, Telex 27950, ≤, – Ⓟ X s
58 rm.

Clifton (T.H.F.), The Leas, CT20 2EA, ☎ 53191, ≤ – wc. Z r
M 3.50/3.75 **st.** 1.50 – **55 rm** 8.50/17.50 **st.** – P 13.50/18.00 **st.**

Garden House, 142 Sandgate Rd, CT20 2EY, ☎ 52278, – wc Ⓟ Z c
M 3.25/4.00 1.40 – **41 rm** 8.50/15.40.

Chilworth Court, 39-41 Earl's Av., CT20 2BW, ☎ 55673, – wc wc Ⓟ X e
24 rm.

Southcliff, 25-26 The Leas, CT20 2DY, ☎ 56075, ≤, – wc Ⓟ. Z u
M *(dinner only and Sunday lunch)* – **20 rm** 5.75/12.00 – P 8.00/10.00.

P.T.O. ⟶

Beaumont, 5 Marine Terr., CT20 1PZ, ☎ 52740 — Z e
8 rm 4.50/9.00 **st.**

Wearbay, 25 Wear Bay Crescent, CT19 6AX, ☎ 52586, – — Y a
closed January – **7 rm** 5.00/11.15 **st.**

Gran Canaria, 4-5 Marine Par., CT20, ☎ 51247, ≤ – — Z s
18 rm 6.50/12.00 **st.**

Emilio's Portofino, 124a Sandgate Rd, CT20 2BW, ☎ 55762, Italian rest. — Z a
closed Monday, Christmas Day and Bank Holidays – **M** a la carte 3.05/4.30 1.10.

La Tavernetta, Leaside Court, Clifton Gdns, CT20 2ED, ☎ 54955, Italian rest. — Z n
closed Sunday, first 2 weeks February and Bank Holidays – **M** a la carte 3.05/5.65 **t.** 1.20.

Nicola's l'Escargot, 3 Trinity Crescent, CT20 2ES, ☎ 53864 — X a
closed Sunday – **M** a la carte 3.90/4.90 1.20.

New Metropole Vintage Room, The Leas, CT20 2LS, ☎ 55114 – P. — X u

AUSTIN-DAIMLER-JAGUAR Bouverie St. ☎ 55501
CHRYSLER-SIMCA 1/3 Park Rd ☎ 75114
CITROEN, FIAT, ROLLS ROYCE, VAUXHALL Caesars Way, Cheriton ☎ 76431
DAF Hamstreet ☎ 2207
FORD 104 Ford Rd ☎ 51222
LANCIA Etchinghill ☎ 0303 (Lyminge) 862113
MORRIS-MG-ROVER-TRIUMPH-WOLSELEY 141/143 Sandgate Rd ☎ 55331
RENAULT 360 Cheriton Rd, Cheriton ☎ 75412

FORDWICH Kent – see Canterbury.

FOREST ROW East Sussex – pop. 4,484 – 034 282.

18 ☎ 2018 – 18 Chapel Lane ☎ 2010 and 2751.

London 35 – Brighton 26 – Eastbourne 30 – Maidstone 32.

Roebuck, Wych Cross, RH18 5JL, S: 2 ¼ m. on A 22 ☎ 3811, Telex 957088 – TV P.
M 4.50/5.00 **st.** 2.20 – 1.95 – **35 rm** 10.00/15.50 **st.** – P 20.65 **st.**

at Chelwood Gate S: 3 ½ m. on A 275 by A 22 – ✉ Hayward's Heath – 082 574 Chelwood Gate:

Red Lion, Lewes Rd, RH17 5DE, ☎ 265 – P
closed Sunday in summer, Sunday dinner in winter and Bank Holidays – **M** (bar lunch) a la carte 3.95/5.00 1.50.

CITROEN 92-93 Hartfield Rd ☎ 2724
LANCIA Wych Cross and Hartfield Rd ☎ 3864

FOSSEBRIDGE Glos. – ✉ Northleach – 028 572.

London 88 – Cirencester 7 – Gloucester 25 – Oxford 33.

Fossebridge Inn, GL54 3JJ, ☎ 310, – wc P
closed 24 December - 14 March – **M** (buttery rest. only) a la carte 2.60/3.90 **t.** 1.60 – **12 rm** 8.00/18.00 **t.**

FOUNTAINS (Abbey) North Yorks. 986 ㉓.

See: Abbey*** (ruins 12C-13C, floodlit in summer) Studley Royal Gardens** and Fountains Hall* (17C) *AC*.

London 226 – Leeds 30 – Middlesbrough 39 – York 27.

Hotels and restaurants see : Harrogate SE: 9 m.
Ripon NE: 3 m.

FOWEY Cornwall 986 ㊳ – pop. 2,369 – 072 683.

i Toyne Carter, 1 Albert Quay ☎ 3274.

London 277 – Newquay 24 – Plymouth 34 – Truro 22.

Fowey, The Esplanade, PL23 1HX, ☎ 2551, ≤ Fowey estuary and Polruan, – wc P
M 4.00/5.00 1.25 – **35 rm** 10.00/22.00 – P 17.00/20.00.

Riverside, 32 Passage St., PL23 1DE, ☎ 2275, ≤ – wc
M *(open Easter-10 October)* (dinner only) 4.50/7.50 1.30 – **14 rm** 6.50/17.00.

Square Rig, 14 North St., PL23 1DD, ☎ 2328, ≤ Fowey harbour – TV wc wc
9 rm.

Old Quay House, 28 Fore St., PL23 1AQ, ☎ 3302 – wc
closed Christmas and 1 January – **M** (snack lunch) approx. 3.25 **st.** – **15 rm** 6.75/15.50 **st.** – P 9.00/11.00 **st.**

Cordon Bleu, 3 Esplanade, PL23 1HY, ☎ 2359
closed Sunday and mid December-mid March – **M** (dinner only) approx. 4.50 **t.**

at Golant NW: 3 m. off B 3269 – ✉ 072 683 Fowey:

Cormorant, PL23 1LL, ☎ 3426, ≤ river Fowey, – wc P
M (bar lunch) a la carte 3.50/4.85 1.50 – **10 rm** 8.50/17.00.

ALFA-ROMEO Polvillion Rd ☎ 3393

FOWLMERE Cambs. – see Cambridge.

FRAMFIELD East Sussex – see Uckfield.

FRAMLINGHAM Suffolk – pop. 2,258 – ✉ Woodbridge – ☎ 0728.
See: Castle ramparts★ (Norman ruins) *AC*.
London 92 – Ipswich 19 – Norwich 42.

- **Crown** (T.H.F.), Market Hill, IP13 9AP, ☎ 723521, « 16C inn » – TV ⊟wc Ⓟ
  M approx. 3.50 **st.** 1.50 – **15 rm** 8.50/16.00 **st.**

FORD Market Hill ☎ 723215

FRAMPTON ON SEVERN Glos. – pop. 1,231 – ☎ 045 274 Saul.
London 121 – Bristol 29 – Gloucester 11.

- Old Vicarage, ☎ 562, – Ⓟ – **21 rm.**

FRESHWATER BAY I.O.W. – see Wight (Isle of).

FRESSINGFIELD Suffolk – pop. 730 – ✉ Diss – ☎ 037 986.
London 103 – Ipswich 30 – Norwich 23.

- ✕ ✿ **Fox and Goose,** IP21 5PB, ☎ 247 – Ⓟ
  closed Tuesday and 25-26 December – **M** (reservations only) a la carte 4.70/8.00
  Spec. Truite aux amandes, Entrecôte bordelaise, Rum chocolate truffle.

FRILFORD Oxon. – see Abingdon.

FRIMLEY BRIDGES Hants. – see Farnborough.

FRINTON-ON-SEA Essex 986 ㉜ – pop. 4,113 – ☎ 025 56.
London 72 – Chelmsford 39 – Colchester 17.

- **Maplin,** Esplanade, CO13 9EL, ☎ 3832, heated – TV ⊟wc ☎
  closed January – **M** *(closed Monday to non-residents)* 3.90/5.00 **st.** 2.10 – **11 rm**
  9.00/19.00 **st.**

  at Kirby Cross W: 1 ½ m. on B 1033 – ✉ ☎ 025 56 Frinton-on-Sea:

- **Linnets,** 2 Thorpe Rd, CO13 0LD, ☎ 4910, – ⊟wc Ⓟ
  April-October – **M** *(closed Sunday dinner and Monday)* 3.50/4.00 **st.** 1.60 – **16 rm**
  6.50/15.00 **s.** – P 10.00/12.00 **s.**

AUSTIN-MORRIS-MG-WOLSELEY Connaught Av. ☎ 4311
CHRYSLER-SIMCA ☎ 4383
FIAT, VOLVO 132 Connaught Av. ☎ 4341
TOYOTA Frinton Rd, Kirby Cross ☎ 4141

FROGGATT-EDGE Derbs. – pop. 185 – ✉ Sheffield (South Yorks.) – ☎ 0433 Grindleford.
See: ☼★.
London 164 – Chesterfield 12 – Sheffield 11.

- ✕ Chequers Inn, S30 1ZB, on B 6054 ☎ 30231 – Ⓟ.

FROME Somerset 986 ㉟ – pop. 13,401 – ☎ 0373.
Envir.: Longleat House★★ (Elizabethan) *AC* and Lion Reserve★★ *AC*, SE: 7 m. – Stourhead House★ (18C) *AC* and park ★★ *AC*, S: 10 m. – Nunney Castle★ (ruins 14C) SW: 3 ½ m. – Westbury Hill (White Horse★, ≤★) NE: 8 m.
London 115 – Bristol 28 – Southampton 51 – Taunton 43.

- **Mendip Lodge,** Bath Rd, BA11 2HP, ☎ 3223, ≤, – TV ⊟wc ☎ Ⓟ
  M 4.50/6.00 **t.** – 1.20 – **40 rm** 13.00/19.00 **st.** – P 17.00/19.00 **st.**
- **Portway,** Portway, Christchurch St. East, BA11 1QH, ☎ 3508, – ⊟wc ☎ Ⓟ
  M 4.00/4.25 **st.** 0.90 – **22 rm** 8.50/15.50 **st.**
- ✕✕ **La Cambusa,** 8 The Bridge, BA11 1AR, ☎ 3567, Italian rest.
  closed Sunday and Bank Holidays – **M** a la carte 3.35/5.35 1.10.

AUSTIN-MG-WOLSELEY Rodden Rd ☎ 3489
MORRIS-MG-WOLSELEY Christchurch St. East ☎ 3351
RENAULT Manor Rd ☎ 5881
ROVER-TRIUMPH 33 Christchurch St. East ☎ 2685
VAUXHALL The Portway ☎ 3366

FUNTINGTON West Sussex – see Chichester.

GAINSBOROUGH Lincs. 986 ㉘ – pop. 17,415 – ☎ 0427.
See: Old Hall★★ (15C) *AC*.
London 150 – Lincoln 19 – Nottingham 42 – Sheffield 34.

Hotels and restaurant see : Bawtry NW: 12 m.
Scunthorpe NE: 17 m.

AUSTIN-MG-WOLSELEY North St. ☎ 2178
CHRYSLER-SIMCA North St. ☎ 2505
FORD Trinity St. ☎ 3146
MORRIS-ROVER-TRIUMPH, VAUXHALL North St. ☎ 2251

GANLLWYD Gwynedd – see Dolgellau.

GARFORTH West Yorks. – see Leeds.

GARGRAVE North Yorks. – pop. 1,426 – ✉ Skipton – ☎ 075 678.
London 222 – Leeds 30 – Preston 37.

Anchor Inn, BD23 3NA, ☎ 666, – TV wc P
M (dinner only and Sunday lunch) 2.70/5.50 1.50 – **10 rm** 5.75/12.50.

GATESHEAD Tyne and Wear 986 ⑲ – pop. 94,469 – ☎ 0632.
Envir. : Lambton Lion Park** AC, SE: 8 ½ m.
18 Mossheaps ☎ 876014.
i Central Library, Prince Consort Rd ☎ 773478.
London 282 – Durham 16 – Middlesbrough 38 – Newcastle-upon-Tyne 1 – Sunderland 11.

Plan: see Newcastle-upon-Tyne

Five Bridges (Rank), High West St., NE8 1PE, ☎ 771105, Telex 53534 – TV P.
M *(closed Saturday lunch, Sunday and Bank Holidays)* a la carte 4.10/5.70 **s.** 1.50 – 1.90 – **103 rm** 12.75/25.50 **s.** CZ r

Springfield (Embassy), Durham Rd, NE9 5BT, ☎ 774121 – TV wc P. BX s
closed Christmas – **M** approx. 3.15 **st.** 1.45 – **32 rm** 10.80/14.00 **st.**

Italia, 580a Durham Rd, NE9 6HX, ☎ 879362, Italian rest. by A 1 BX
closed Sunday – **M** a la carte 2.40/4.15 **t.** 1.20.

AUSTIN-MORRIS-MG-WOLSELEY Bensham Rd ☎ 771291
AUSTIN-MG-WOLSELEY St. James Sq. ☎ 771135
FORD 685/691 Durham Rd ☎ 878191
VAUXHALL 106/108 Lobley Hill Rd ☎ 0632 (Dunston) 604691

Prévenez immédiatement l'hôtelier si vous ne pouvez pas occuper la chambre que vous avez retenue.

GATWICK AIRPORT West Sussex – see hotels at Crawley and Horley.

GERRARDS CROSS Bucks. – pop. 6,524 – ☎ 028 13.
London 22 – Aylesbury 22 – Oxford 36.

Bull (De Vere), Oxford Rd, SL9 7PA, on A 40 ☎ 85995, – TV P.
M a la carte approx. 5.00 **st.** 1.45 – **38 rm** 15.50/23.75 **st.**

BMW, VAUXHALL 44 Oak End Way ☎ 88321
CHRYSLER-SIMCA Oxford Rd Tatling End ☎ 82545
MORRIS-MG-WOLSELEY, VOLVO Packhorse Rd ☎ 85555
PEUGEOT Market Pl. ☎ 86635

GISBURN Lancs. 986 ㉓ – pop. 433 – ✉ Clitheroe – ☎ 020 05.
London 243 – Manchester 37 – Preston 25.

Stirk House, BB7 4LJ, SW: 1 m. on A 59 ☎ 581, – TV wc P.
M 3.25/3.60 1.75 – **32 rm** 9.00/16.00.

GITTISHAM Devon – pop. 220 – ✉ ☎ 0404 Honiton.
London 164 – Exeter 14 – Sidmouth 9 – Taunton 21.

Combe House with rm, EX14 0AD, ☎ 2756, ←, « Country house atmosphere », park – wc P
closed January and February – **M** (bar lunch and Sunday lunch) a la carte 4.85/6.90 1.80 – 1.00 – **13 rm** 8.50/21.00.

GLASBURY-ON-WYE Powys – ☎ 049 74.
London 185 – Brecon 12 – Hereford 24 – Swansea 56.

Maesllwch Moat House with rm, HR3 5LH, ☎ 226, – wc P
M (bar lunch) 4.00/5.00 **t.** – **10 rm** 6.00/11.00 **t.**

GLASTONBURY Somerset 986 ㉟ – pop. 6,558 – ☎ 0458.
See : Abbey* (ruins 12C) – Tribunal* 15C. **Exc.** : Cheddar (Cheddar Gorge*** – Gough's Caves** AC) NW: 13 ½ m. via Wells.
i 7 Northload St. ☎ 32954 (summer only).
London 136 – Bristol 26 – Taunton 22.

George and Pilgrims, 1 High St., BA6 9DP, ☎ 31146, « Part 15C Inn » – wc
M (Sunday dinner cold buffet only) 4.00/5.00 **t.** 0.85 – **13 rm** 7.00/16.00 **st.**

Nº 3, 3 Magdalene St., BA6 9EW, ☎ 32129, – P
closed Sunday dinner, Monday, 1 month in Spring and in Autumn – **M** (dinner only and Sunday lunch) 7.50/9.50 1.50.

AUSTIN-MG-WOLSELEY Street Rd ☎ 2137
FORD Magdalene St. ☎ 3355
RENAULT Mill Lane ☎ 2741

GLEN PARVA Leics. – see Leicester.

GLENRIDDING Cumbria – see Ullswater.

GLOUCESTER

Eastgate Shopping Centre Y
Eastgate Street Y 10
Northgate Street Y 16
Southgate Street Y

Barnwood By-Pass Z 3
Bruton Way Y 5
Commercial Road Y 6
Cotteswold Road Z 8
Derby Road Z 9
Great Western Road Y 12
Heathville Road Y 13
King Edward's Avenue Z 14
Lower Westgate Street Y 15
Parkend Road Z 17
Parliament Street Y 18
Pitt Street Y 19
Quay Street Y 20
Royal Oak Road Y 21
St. Aldate Street Y 22
St. Johns Lane Y 23
Southern Avenue Z 24
Spa Road Y 26
Stroud Road Z 28
Tredworth Road Z 30
Worcester Street Y 31

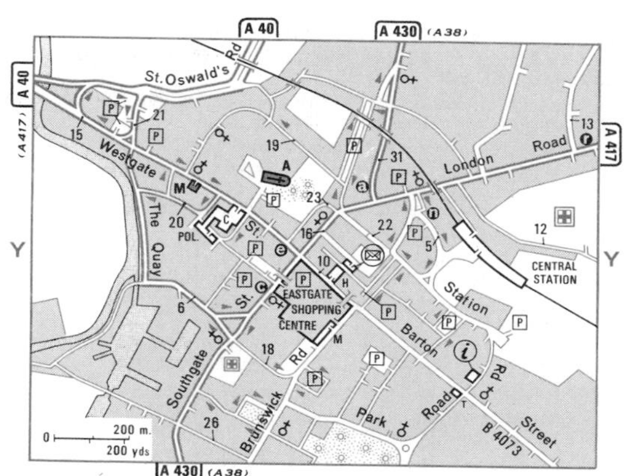

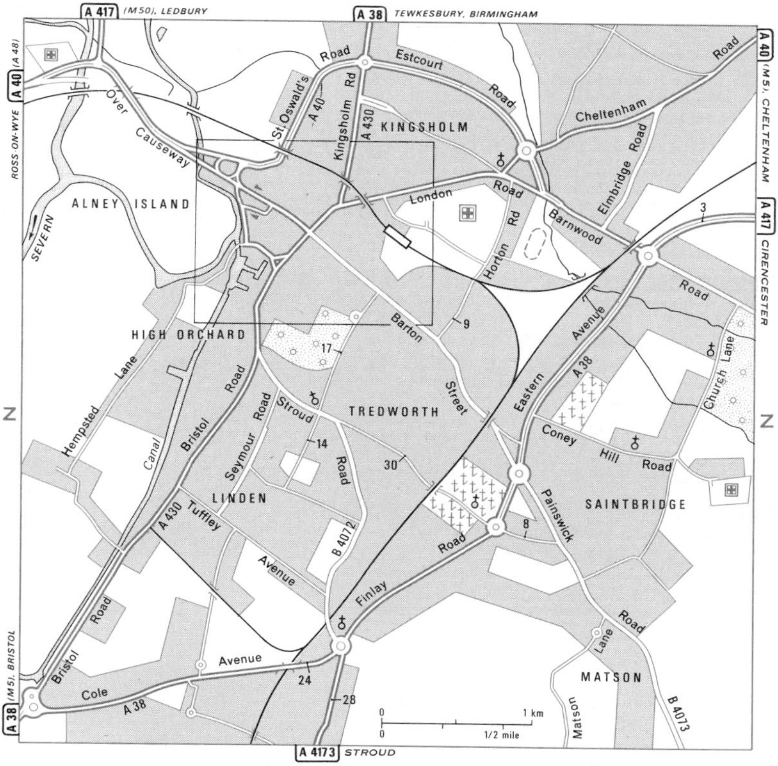

GLOUCESTER Glos. 986 ㉛ – pop. 90,232 – ✆ 0452.

See : Cathedral** 12C-14C (Great Cloister*** 14C) Y **A** – Bishop Hooper's Lodging (Folk Museum)* 15C Y **M**.

Staverton Airport : ☎ 713351 and 712285, NE : 5 m. by A 40 Z and near M 5 Motorway, intersection Nº 11 – **Terminal :** Market Parade.

i Gloucester Leisure Centre, Station Rd ☎ 36498 and 36788.

London 103 – Birmingham 51 – Bristol 33 – Cardiff 60 – Coventry 57 – Northampton 87 – Oxford 48 – Southampton 101 – Swansea 87 – Swindon 34.

Plan on preceding page

Tara, Upton Hill, GL4 8DE, by Upton-St. Leonards S : 3 m. on B 4073 ☎ 67412, ≤ Severn Valley, heated, – TV wc wc ☎ P. by B 4073 Z
M a la carte 3.20/6.80 1.25 – **20 rm** 9.00/18.00.

New County (Norfolk Cap.), Southgate St., GL1 2DU, ☎ 24977 – wc ☎. Y **c**
36 rm.

Fleece, 19 Westgate St., GL1 2NR, ☎ 22762 – P Y **e**
M 2.00/3.15 **t.** 1.65 – **43 rm** 5.00/12.00 **t.**

New Wellington (Embassy), Bruton Way, ☎ 20022 – TV wc – **23 rm.** Y **n**

Stanley House, 87 London Rd, GL1 3HH, ☎ 20140 – P Y **r**
14 rm 4.50/9.50.

Hucclecote Garden, 164 Hucclecote Rd, GL3 3SH, E : 2 ½ m. off A 417, ☎ 67374, – P by A 417 Z
12 rm 5.50/11.00.

Don Pasquale, 19 Worcester St., GL1 3AJ, ☎ 25636, Italian rest. Y **a**
closed Sunday, 2 weeks in July-August and Bank Holidays – **M** a la carte 3.00/5.55.

at Corse Lawn N : **11** m. on B 4211 by A 417 – Z – ✉ Gloucester – ✆ 045 278 Tirley :

Corse Lawn House, GL19 4LZ, ☎ 479 – P
M a la carte 4.00/5.50 1.40.

AUSTIN-DAIMLER-JAGUAR-ROVER-TRIUMPH 209/211 Westgate St. ☎ 34581
AUSTIN-MORRIS-MG-WOLSELEY Mercia Rd ☎ 29531
BMW London Rd ☎ 23456
CHRYSLER-SIMCA London Rd ☎ 24081
CITROEN, FIAT 143 Westgate St. ☎ 23252
DAF-POLSKI South Gate St. ☎ 22353
DATSUN 176 Barton St. ☎ 22922
FORD Eastern Av. ☎ 21731
MERCEDES-BENZ, TOYOTA Southgate St. ☎ 26741
PEUGEOT 72/76 Barton St. ☎ 32731
RENAULT St. Oswalds Rd ☎ 35051
VAUXHALL ☎ 66621
VAUXHALL Shepherd Rd, Cole Av. ☎ 26711
VOLVO 56a Barton St., Eastgate St. ☎ 25251
VW, AUDI-NSU 98/106 Barton St. ☎ 25251

GLYNGARTH Gwynedd – see Menai Bridge.

GOATHLAND North Yorks. – pop. 458 – ✉ Whitby – ✆ 094 786.

Envir. : Whitby (Abbey ruins* 13C, *AC*, Old St. Mary's Church* 12C, East Terrace ≤*) NE : 7 ½ m.

London 248 – Middlesbrough 36 – York 38.

Mallyan Spout , YO22 5AN, ☎ 206, , – TV wc wc P
closed 6 to 30 January – **M** (dinner only and Sunday lunch) 4.00/4.25 **t.** 1.65 – **23 rm** 7.00/18.50 **t.**

Goathland Hydro , YO22 5LZ, ☎ 296, – wc P
Easter-mid October – **M** 2.15/2.65 **st.** 1.95 – **33 rm** 8.35/18.90 **st.**

Goathland with rm, YO22 5LY, ☎ 203 – wc P
M approx. 3.50 **st.** 1.50 – **9 rm** 6.00/14.00 **st.** – P 11.00 **st.**

GODALMING Surrey 986 ㊱ – pop. 18,669 – ✆ 048 68.

London 38 – Guildford 5 – Southampton 51.

King's Arms Royal (Embassy), High St., GU7 1EB, ☎ 21545 – P
M 2.00/2.25 **st.** 1.60 – **17 rm** 5.80/11.60 **st.**

Pike's, 78 High St., GU7 1DU, ☎ 29191
closed Sunday, Monday and 2 weeks after Easter – **M** a la carte 3.25/5.10 1.15.

AUSTIN-MORRIS-MG-WOLSELEY, DATSUN The Wharf ☎ 5201
CHRYSLER-SIMCA Farncombe ☎ 7743
CITROEN Guildford Rd ☎ 23555
VAUXHALL Ockford Rd ☎ 5666

GODSTONE Surrey 986 ㊱ – pop. 5,568 – ✆ 088 384.

London 22 – Brighton 36 – Maidstone 28.

White Hart, 71 High St., Godstone Green, RH9 8DT, ☎ 2521 – P
closed Christmas Day dinner – **M** a la carte 4.80/6.25 **t.** 1.60.

at South Godstone S : 2 ¼ m. off A 22 – ✉ Godstone – ✆ 034 285 South Godstone :

La Bonne Auberge with rm, Tilburstow Hill, RH9 8JY, ☎ 3184, , , park – P
closed mid January-mid February – **M** *(closed Sunday dinner and Monday except Bank Holidays)* a la carte 4.80/7.70 **t.** 1.90 – **5 rm** 5.50/15.00 **t.**

BEDFORD, VAUXHALL Eastbourne Rd ☎ 2000

GOLANT Cornwall – see Fowey.

GOMSHALL Surrey – pop. 3,705 – ✉ Guildford – ☎ 048 641 Shere.
London 31 – Brighton 44 – Guildford 7 – Maidstone 47.

- **Black Horse,** GU5 9NP, ☎ 2242, – P
  M 4.50/6.00 **t.** 1.50 – **6 rm** 6.50/12.00 **t.**

GOODWICK Dyfed – see Fishguard.

GOODWOOD West Sussex – see Chichester.

GORLESTON-ON-SEA Norfolk 986 ㉘ – see Great Yarmouth.

GOSFORTH Cumbria 986 ⑲ – pop. 1,076 – ☎ 094 05.
London 314 – Kendal 62 – Workington 20.

- **Gosforth Hall** , CA20 1AZ, E: ½ m. on Wasdale Rd ☎ 322, « 17C manor », , – P
  closed Christmas and 1 January – **M** (dinner only) 4.50/5.00 1.60 – **6 rm** 6.50/13.00.

GOSFORTH Tyne and Wear – see Newcastle-upon-Tyne.

GOUDHURST Kent – pop. 2,950 – ✉ Cranbrook – ☎ 058 03.
London 45 – Hastings 22 – Maidstone 13.

- **Goudhurst,** TN17 1HA, W: 1 m. on A 262 ☎ 200, – P
  M a la carte 3.25/5.00 **t.** 1.70 – **6 rm** 6.50/13.00 **t.**
- XX **Star and Eagle** with rm, High St., TN17 1AL, ☎ 512 – P
  closed 3 days at Christmas – **M** *(closed Sunday dinner and Monday lunch)* a la carte 3.50/6.50 **t.** – **6 rm** 8.00/12.00 **t.**

GOVETON Devon – see Kingsbridge.

GRANGE-IN-BORROWDALE Cumbria – see Keswick.

GRANGE-OVER-SANDS Cumbria 986 ㉓ – pop. 3,474 – ☎ 044 84.
Envir.: Cartmel (Priory Church* 12C: chancel**) NW: 1 ½ m.
18 Meathop Rd ☎ 3180, ½ m. Grange Station – 9 ☎ 2536.
i Victoria Hall, Main St. ☎ 4331 (summer only).
London 267 – Kendal 13 – Lancaster 24.

- **Graythwaite Manor** , Fernhill Rd, LA11 7JE, ☎ 2001, ≤ gardens and sea, « Extensive flowered gardens », , park – wc P
  M approx. 4.75 **t.** 1.45 – **27 rm** (dinner included) 12.00/27.00 **st.**
- **Netherwood** , Lindale Rd, LA11 6ET, ☎ 2552, ≤, – wc P
  M approx. 3.50 **st.** 1.15 – **23 rm** 6.00/13.00 **st.** – P 10.75 **st.**
- **Grange** (Interchange), Lindale Rd, LA11 6EJ, ☎ 3666 – wc P
  M approx. 4.85 **st.** 1.00 – **32 rm** 7.80/18.80 **st.** – P 14.80/18.05 **st.**
- Somerset House, Kents Bank Rd, LA11 7EY, ☎ 2631
  season – **8 rm.**
- **Elton Private,** Windermere Rd, LA11 6EQ, ☎ 2838
  closed Christmas – **9 rm** 4.75/9.00 **st.**
- XX **Hardcragg Hall** with rm, Grange Fell Rd, LA11 6BJ, ☎ 3353, ≤, « Renovated 16C manor », – P
  closed Christmas – **M** *(closed Sunday and Monday except Bank Holidays to non-residents)* (dinner only) 5.50/6.00 – **7 rm** 6.00/10.00.

at Kents Bank SW: 1 ¾ m. off B 5277 – ✉ ☎ 044 84 Grange-over-Sands:

- Kents Bank, Kentsford Rd ☎ 2054, ≤ – P
  season – **11 rm.**

at Cartmel NW: 3 m. – ✉ Grange-over-Sands – ☎ 044 854 Cartmel:

- **Aynsome Manor** , LA11 6HH, ☎ 276, – wc P
  M *(closed Sunday dinner and Christmas)* (bar lunch for residents only except Sunday) 5.00/5.75 **t.** 1.50 – **16 rm** 7.25/16.00 **t.** – P 9.95/11.50 **t.**

AUSTIN-MORRIS-MG-WOLSELEY Station Sq. ☎ 2612 BMW Lindale Corner ☎ 2284

GRANTHAM Lincs. 986 ㉘ – pop. 27,943 – ☎ 0476.
See: St. Wulfram's Church* 13C. **Envir.:** Belton House* (Renaissance) *AC*, NE: 2 m. – Belvoir Castle 19C (interior*) W: 8 m.
18 Belton Lane, Londonthorpe Rd ☎ 3355, N: 2 m. – 18 Great North Rd ☎ 045 683 (Great Ponton) 275, S: 6 m. on A 1.
London 113 – Leicester 31 – Lincoln 29 – Nottingham 24.

Angel and Royal (T.H.F.), 4 High St., NG31 6PN, ✆ 5816, « 13C stone walled restaurant and bar » – TV ⇔wc ☎ P.
M a la carte 4.10/5.35 **st.** 1.50 – **32 rm** 9.50/18.00 **st.**

George, High St., NG31 6NN, ✆ 3286 – TV ⇔wc ☎ P.
closed Christmas – **M** 3.50/4.00 1.70 – **37 rm** 10.00/20.00 **t.**

King's, North Par., NG31 8AU, ✆ 5881 – ⇔wc ☎ P
M approx. 2.70 **t.** 1.25 – **15 rm** 6.55/13.10 **st.** – P 11.00 **st.**

Hop Sing, Tudor House, 21 Westgate, NG31 6LU, ✆ 2302, Chinese rest.
M 1.20/3.60 **t.** 1.25.

AUSTIN-MG-WOLSELEY North St. ✆ 61066
CHRYSLER-SIMCA 66 London Rd ✆ 2595
DATSUN Barrowby High Rd ✆ 4443
FORD 30/40 London Rd ✆ 5195
RENAULT London Rd ✆ 61338
ROVER-TRIUMPH 50/58 London Rd ✆ 2651
VAUXHALL Watergate ✆ 3267
VOLVO Barrowby Rd ✆ 4114

GRAPPENHALL Cheshire – see Warrington.

GRASMERE Cumbria 986 ⑲ – pop. 990 – ✆ 096 65.

i Broadgate News Agency ✆ 245.

London 280 – Carlisle 43 – Kendal 18.

Grasmere Red Lion, Lion, LA22 9SS, ✆ 456, – ⇔wc ☎ P
March-November – **M** (bar lunch) 5.50/7.50 **st.** 1.75 – **39 rm** 9.90/19.55 **st.**

Gold Rill, Langdale Rd, LA22 9PU, ✆ 486 <, heated, – ⇔wc P
late March-early November – **M** 4.50/8.00 **st.** 1.50 – **23 rm** (dinner included) 15.75/39.50 **st.**

Michael's Nook, LA22 9RP, E: ¼ m. off A 591 ✆ 496, < mountains and countryside, « Tastefully furnished and with fine gardens » – TV ⇔wc wc ☎ P
M 7.00/8.00 1.75 – **10 rm** 12.50/33.00.

Swan (T.H.F.), LA22 9RF, on A 591 ✆ 551, <, – ⇔wc ☎ P
M a la carte 4.00/5.50 **st.** 1.50 – **31 rm** 10.00/19.00 **st.**

Rothay Bank, Broadgate, LA22 9RH, ✆ 334, – wc ☎ P
season – **15 rm.**

Oak Bank, Broadgate, LA22 9TA, ✆ 217, – ⇔wc P
Easter-October – **M** (dinner only) (residents only) 4.50/6.00 **st.** 1.30 – **12 rm** 6.50/14.00 **st.**

Moss Grove, LA22 9SW, ✆ 251 – P
Easter-November – **M** (dinner only) 4.00/5.00 **st.** 1.15 – **16 rm** 6.60/13.20 **st.**

Meadow Brow, LA22 9RR, N: ¾ m. by A 591 ✆ 275, < mountains and valley, – P
closed Christmas and 1 January – **8 rm** 6.00/12.00 **t.**

Bridge House,, Stock Lane, LA22 9SN, ✆ 425, – ⇔wc P
Easter-October – **12 rm** 7.00.

Ben Place,, LA22 9RD, E: ¼ m. off A 591 ✆ 372, – P
March-October – **13 rm** (dinner included) 8.65/17.30 **t.**

GRAVESEND Kent 986 ㊱ – pop. 54,106 – ✆ 0474.

London 25 – Dover 54 – Maidstone 16 – Margate 53.

Europa Lodge Tollgate (County), Watling St., DA12 5UD, S: 2 m. at junction A 2 and A 227 ✆ 52768 – TV ⇔wc P
M *(closed Christmas Day)* (grill rest. only) 3.00/5.00 **t.** 1.40 – **114 rm** 10.00/15.00.

AUSTIN-MG-WOLSELEY St. James St. ✆ 4598
CITROEN Rochester Rd ✆ 65211
DAF, DATSUN 50 Singlewell Rd ✆ 66148
FORD 1/3 Pelham Rd ✆ 64411
MORRIS-MG-ROVER-TRIUMPH-WOLSELEY The Grove ✆ 65236
RENAULT West St. ✆ 67801
TOYOTA 10/12 High St. ✆ 4550
VAUXHALL Overcliffe ✆ 63566

GRAVETYE East Sussex – see East Grinstead.

GRAYSWOOD Surrey – see Haslemere.

GREASBY Merseyside – pop. 6,860 – ✆ 051 Liverpool.

London 223 – Chester 19 – Liverpool 7.

Manor Farm, 91 Greasby Rd, Wirral, L49 3NF, ✆ 677 7034 – P

GREAT BARDFIELD Essex – pop. 944 – ✉ Braintree – ✆ 0371 Great Dunmow.

London 49 – Cambridge 30 – Chelmsford 20 – Colchester 26.

Corn Dolly, High St., CM7 4SP, ✆ 810554
closed Sunday dinner, Monday, Tuesday and 24 to 26 December – **M** 4.80/6.00 1.50.

GREAT BARR West Midlands – see Birmingham.

GREAT BROUGHTON Cleveland – pop. 1,000 – ✉ Middlesbrough – ☎ 064 97 Wainstones.
London 250 – Middlesbrough 11 – Northallerton 17 – York 46.

✗ **Wainstones** with rm, Helmesley Rd ☎ 268, – Ⓟ
M a la carte 4.70/5.80 **t.** 1.45 – **9 rm** 6.00/11.00 **t.** – P 11.50/12.50 **t.**

GREAT CHESTERFORD Essex – see Saffron Walden.

GREAT CORNARD Suffolk – see Sudbury.

GREAT DUNMOW Essex 986 ㉜ – pop. 3,827 – ☎ 0371.
London 42 – Cambridge 27 – Chelmsford 13 – Colchester 24.

Saracen's Head (T.H.F.), High St., CM6 1AG, ☎ 3901 – TV wc Ⓟ.
M a la carte 4.10/5.20 **st.** 1.50 – **15 rm** 8.50/16.00 **st.**

BMW The Downs ☎ 2884

GREAT WALTHAM Essex – pop. 2,104 – ✉ ☎ 0245 Chelmsford.
London 38 – Cambridge 35 – Chelmsford 5.

✗✗ **Windmill,** Little Waltham, CM3 1AB, on A 130 ☎ 360292 – Ⓟ
M a la carte 3.40/5.70 1.10.

GREAT WITLEY Heref. and Worc. – pop. 460 – ✉ Worcester – ☎ 029 921.
London 136 – Birmingham 26 – Worcester 12.

✗✗ **Hundred House,** WR6 6HS, on A 443 ☎ 215 – Ⓟ
closed Sunday dinner, Monday dinner and Christmas Day – **M** (buffet lunch) 2.50/6.50.

VW, AUDI-NSU, SAAB Worcester Rd ☎ 202

GREAT YARMOUTH Norfolk 986 ㉘ – pop. 50,236 – ☎ 0493.
18 Warren Rd, Gorleston ☎ 61082 – 18 Beach House ☎ 70214, N: 3 m.
Shipping connections with the Continent: to Scheveningen (Norfolk Line).
i Town Hall, 14 Regent St. ☎ 4313/4 – Marine Parade ☎ 2195 (summer only).
London 126 – Cambridge 81 – Ipswich 53 – Norwich 20.

Carlton, Kimberley Ter., Marine Par., NR30 3JE, ☎ 55234, Telex 97249 – .
M a la carte 3.85/7.05 1.50 – **96 rm** 8.25/20.00 – P 14.00/21.00.

Star (County), Hall Quay, NR30 1HG, ☎ 2294 – wc Ⓟ.
M a la carte 4.00/6.10 **st.** 1.20 – **42 rm** 8.50/17.50 **s.**

at Gorleston-on-sea S: 3 m. on A 12 – ✉ ☎ 0493 Great Yarmouth:

Cliff, Cliff Hill, NR31 6DH, ☎ 62179 – Ⓟ
M 3.50/4.50 **t.** 1.50 – **31 rm** 8.00/20.00 – P 12.00/14.00.

AUSTIN-DAIMLER-MORRIS-MG-ROVER-TRIUMPH-WOLSELEY 55 St. Nicholas Rd ☎ 55431
AUSTIN-MG-WOLSELEY 91/102 Regent Rd ☎ 56836
CHRYSLER-SIMCA Drudge Rd ☎ 64158
CHRYSLER-SIMCA North Quay ☎ 4266
CITROEN Repps ☎ 069 27 (Potter Heigham) 271
DAF, VOLVO Beccles Rd, Bradwell ☎ 65316
FORD South Gates Rd ☎ 4922
RENAULT Suffolk Rd ☎ 55142
VAUXHALL Station Rd ☎ 3677
VW, AUDI-NSU South Denes Rd ☎ 57711

GREAT YELDHAM Essex – pop. 1,290 – ✉ Halstead – ☎ 078 723 (3 and 4 fig.) or 0787 (6 fig.).
Envir.: Castle Hedingham (Norman keep*) *AC*, SE: 2 ½ m.
London 56 – Cambridge 27 – Chelmsford 23 – Colchester 21.

✗✗ **White Hart,** Poole St., CO9 4HJ, ☎ 250, – Ⓟ
closed Christmas Day dinner – **M** a la carte 4.60/6.50 1.65.

CHRYSLER-SIMCA ☎ 218

GRETA BRIDGE Durham – pop. 85 – ✉ Barnard Castle – ☎ 083 37 Whorlton.
Envir.: Barnard Castle (Bowes Museum** *AC*, castle* ruins 12C-14C) NW: 3 m.
London 253 – Carlisle 63 – Leeds 63 – Middlesbrough 32.

Morritt Arms, DL12 9SE, ☎ 232, – wc Ⓟ
M approx. 4.25 **st.** 1.60 – **26 rm** 8.50/17.00 **st.** – P 14.00/15.00 **st.**

GRIMLEY Heref. and Worc. – pop. 574 – ✉ Hallow – ☎ 0905 Worcester.
London 129 – Kidderminster 13 – Worcester 5.

✗ **Wagon Wheel Inn,** WR2 6LU, ☎ 640340 – Ⓟ
M (buffet only Sunday and Monday) a la carte 3.50/5.95 **t.**

GRIMSBY South Humberside 986 ㉔ – pop. 95,540 – ☎ 0472.
London 172 – Boston 50 – Lincoln 36 – Sheffield 75.

Plan on next page

Humber Royal (Crest), Littlecoates Rd, DN34 4LX, ☎ 50295 – TV wc Ⓟ. Y c
M 3.50/4.50 **s.** 1.60 – 1.80 – **54 rm** 11.50/15.80 **s.**

Grimsby Crest Motel (Crest), St. James Sq., DN31 1EP, ☎ 59771 – TV wc Ⓟ. AZ n
M 2.90/4.15 **s.** 1.50 – 1.60 – **132 rm** 10.95/15.50 **s.**

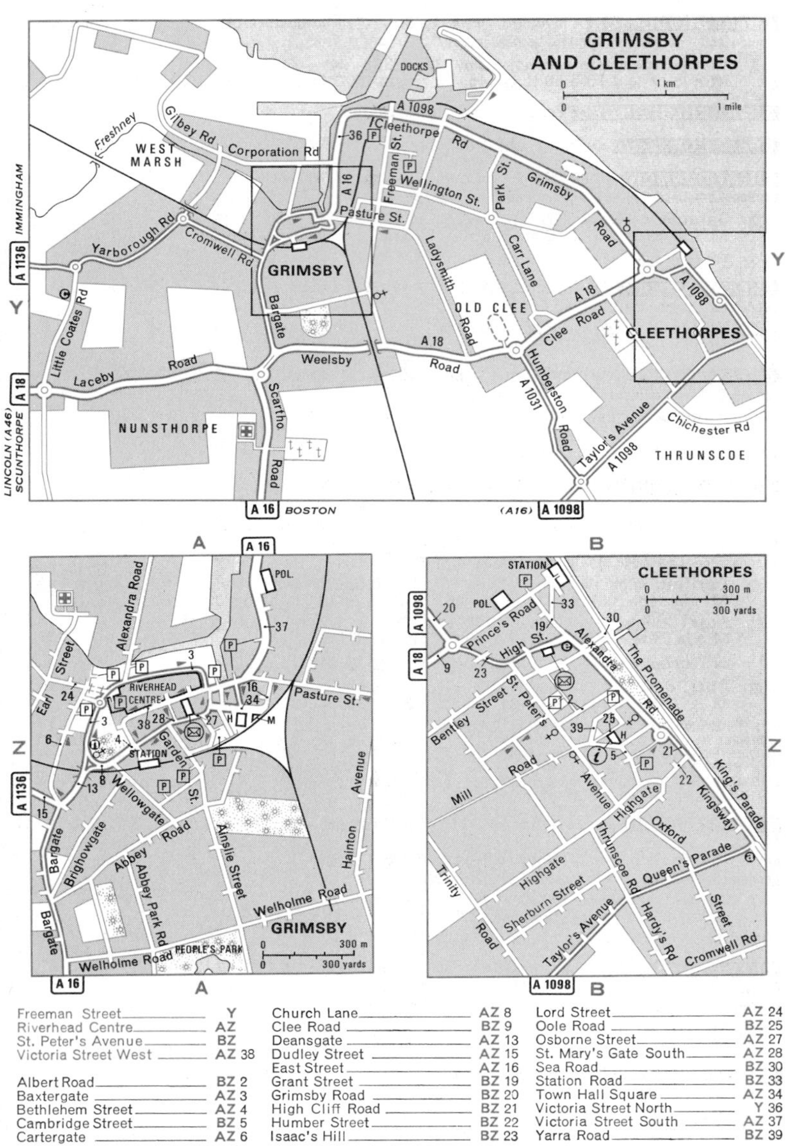

ALFA-ROMEO, SIMCA Alexandra Rd ☎ 58625
AUSTIN-MG-WOLSELEY 166/168 Hainton Av. ☎ 52461
AUSTIN-MG-ROVER-TRIUMPH-WOLSELEY 415 Victoria St. ☎ 56161
CHRYSLER-SIMCA Victoria St. ☎ 57151
DAF Rendel St. ☎ 57362
DAIMLER-JAGUAR-MORRIS-MG-WOLSELEY Brighowgate ☎ 58851

DATSUN 210/212 Victoria St. ☎ 53572
FIAT Wellowgate ☎ 55951
FORD Corporation Rd ☎ 58941
MERCEDES-BENZ, SAAB Bradley Cross Rd ☎ 79274
OPEL 123 Cromwell Rd ☎ 59371
PEUGEOT 33 Louth Rd ☎ 79207
RENAULT Chelmsford Av. ☎ 70111
VAUXHALL Brighowgate ☎ 58486

☛ *Benutzen Sie den Hotelführer des laufenden Jahres.*

GRIMSTHORPE Lincs. – pop. 313 – ✉ Bourne – ☎ 077 832 Edenham.
London 105 – Lincoln 43 – Nottingham 38.

XX **Black Horse Inn** with rm, PE10 0LY, ☎ 247, ⛱, English rest. – Ⓟ
closed Sunday and Christmas Day – **M** a la carte 4.35/6.50 🍾 1.25 – **4 rm** ⊡ 7.50/10.00.

GUILDFORD Surrey 986 ㊱ – pop. 57,213 – ☎ 0483.
See: Cathedral* (1961). **Envir.**: Clandon Park** (Renaissance House) *AC*, NE: 2 m. – Polesden Lacey** (19C) *AC*, NE: 11 m.
i Civic Hall, London Rd ☎ 67314.
London 33 – Brighton 43 – Reading 27 – Southampton 49.

🏨 **Angel** (T.H.F.), High St., GU1 3DR, ☎ 64555 – TV ⛀wc ☎
M a la carte 4.10/6.30 **st.** 🍾 1.50 – **24 rm** ⊡ 11.50/19.00 **st.**

🏨 **White Horse** (Embassy), Upper High St., GU1 3JG, ☎ 64511 – TV ⛀wc ☎
closed Christmas – **M** 2.50/3.00 **st.** 🍾 1.65 – **38 rm** ⊡ 8.75/15.75 **st.**

XX **Mad Hatter,** 1st floor, 5-6 Sydenham Rd, GU1 3RT, ☎ 63011
closed Sunday and Bank Holidays – **M** a la carte 4.00/5.75 🍾 1.25.

XX **Swiss,** 14 Park St., GU1 4XB, ☎ 61458
closed Sunday, Monday and 24 to 31 December – **M** a la carte 3.65/5.00 **t.** 🍾 1.30.

at West Clandon NE: 5 m. on A 247 by A 246 – ✉ ☎ 0483 Guildford:

XXX **Onslow Arms Inn,** The Street, GU4 7TE, ☎ 222447 – Ⓟ
closed Sunday dinner and Monday – **M** a la carte 4.25/6.85 🍾 1.70.

at Compton SW: 4 m. on B 3000 by A 3100 – ✉ Guildford – ☎ 048 68 Godalming:

XX **Withies Inn,** Withies Lane, GU3 1JA, ☎ 21158, « Garden with shaded pergola » – Ⓟ
closed Sunday dinner and Christmas Day – **M** a la carte 3.50/7.00 🍾 1.50.

AUDI-NSU Old Portsmouth Rd, Peasmarsh ☎ 62570
AUSTIN-MG-WOLSELEY Working Rd ☎ 60251
AUSTIN-MG-WOLSELEY Walnut Tree Close ☎ 77371
CHRYSLER-SIMCA By-Pass Rd ☎ 76931
DAIMLER-JAGUAR-ROVER-TRIUMPH 113 Portsmouth Rd ☎ 62907
DATSUN 224 London Rd ☎ 75326
FIAT, LANCIA, MERCEDES-BENZ Aldershot Rd ☎ 60751
FORD Woodbridge Meadow ☎ 60601
MORRIS-MG-WOLSELEY, ROLLS ROYCE Woodbridge Rd ☎ 69231
PEUGEOT 26 High St. ☎ 048 647 (Bramley) 8159
RENAULT 8 North St. ☎ 65242
TOYOTA Pitch Pl. Worplesdon ☎ 048 631 (Worplesdon) 3166
VAUXHALL Working Rd ☎ 37731

GULWORTHY Devon 986 ㊴ – see Tavistock.

GUNNISLAKE Cornwall – pop. 4,079 (inc. Calstock) – ☎ 0822.
Envir.: Cotehele House* (Tudor) *AC*, SW: 2 ½ m.
London 244 – Bude 37 – Exeter 43 – Plymouth 20 – Tavistock 5.

🏠 **Tavistock Arms,** Fore St., PL18 9BN, ☎ 832217 – Ⓟ
M *(closed Sunday, Christmas dinner and 26 December)* (bar lunch) a la carte 4.75/6.25 **t.** 🍾 1.00 – **7 rm** ⊡ 5.50/11.00 **t.**

GWBERT-ON-SEA Dyfed – see Cardigan.

HACKNESS North Yorks – see Scarborough.

HADLEIGH Suffolk 986 ㉜ – pop. 5,620 – ☎ 047 338.
London 72 – Cambridge 49 – Colchester 17 – Ipswich 10.

X **Taviton's,** 103 High St., IP7 5EJ, ☎ 2820, Wine bar
closed Sunday, Monday, Banks Holidays, 2 weeks in spring and 3 weeks in summer – **M** a la carte 2.25/4.70 🍾 1.00.

CHRYSLER-SIMCA 132 High St. ☎ 3525
MORRIS-MG-WOLSELEY 115 High St. ☎ 3286
RENAULT 272 London Rd ☎ 554563

HAGLEY Heref. and Worc. – pop. 4,551 – ☎ 056 286.
London 132 – Birmingham 11 – Kidderminster 6.

XX **Lyttleton Arms** (Ansells), Bromsgrove Rd, DY9 9LJ, ☎ 2213, ⛱ – Ⓟ
M a la carte 3.80/7.00 **st.** 🍾 1.80.

HALE Greater Manchester – see Altrincham.

HALEBARNS Greater Manchester – see Altrincham.

HALESWORTH Suffolk 986 ㉜ – pop. 3,236 – ☎ 098 67.
London 103 – Ipswich 30 – Norwich 25.

X **Bassett's,** London Rd, IP19 8LS, on A 144 ☎ 3154
closed Sunday, March and 25-26 December – **M** (dinner only) 4.65/5.30 **t.** 🍾 1.15.

AUSTIN-MG-PRINCESS-VANDEN PLAS ☎ 3213
BMW, HONDA Norwich Rd ☎ 3666
MAZDA Hotton Rd ☎ 3129
VAUXHALL London Rd ☎ 2138

HALIFAX West Yorks. 986 ㉓ – pop. 91,272 – ☎ 0422.
18 Holywell Green ☎ 042 27 (Elland) 4108 – 18 Highroad Well ☎ 53608, N : 3 m. – 9 Norland ☎ 31355, S : 3 m.
i The Piece Hall ☎ 68725.
London 205 – Bradford 8 – Burnley 21 – Leeds 15 – Manchester 28.

White Swan (T.H.F.), Princess St., HX1 1TS, ☎ **54227** – wc.
M a la carte 3.95/5.35 **st.** 1.50 – **50 rm** 10.00/18.00 **st.**

AUSTIN-DAIMLER-JAGUAR-ROVER-TRIUMPH Huddersfield Rd ☎ 65944
AUSTIN-MG-WOLSELEY 68 Horton St. ☎ 60304
CHRYSLER-SIMCA Skircoat Rd ☎ 53701
DAF Boothtown ☎ 67516
FIAT, CITROEN Queens Rd ☎ 67711
FORD Skircoat Rd ☎ 62957
MORRIS-MG-WOLSELEY 14 Portland Pl. ☎ 60392
OPEL 7 Horton St. ☎ 65846
PEUGEOT Wakefield Rd, Copley ☎ 67302
POLSKI Rochdale Rd ☎ 65036
RENAULT Hope St. ☎ 52087
ROLLS ROYCE, BENTLEY Haley Hill ☎ 65944
SAAB Saville Park Rd ☎ 59425
VAUXHALL Northgate ☎ 62851
VOLVO 354 Pellon Lane ☎ 61961
VW, AUDI-NSU Denholme Gate Rd, Hipperholme ☎ 201681

HALLAND East Sussex – pop. 762 – ✉ Lewes – ☎ 082 584.
London 48 – Brighton 16 – Eastbourne 16 – Royal Tunbridge Wells 19.

XX **Halland Motel and Old Forge Rest.** with rm, BN8 6PW, on A 22 ☎ 456, – wc Ⓟ
closed 25 and 26 December – **M** a la carte 3.65/9.90 **t.** 1.85 – 1.50 – **12 rm** 8.50/14.50 **t.**

HALSE TOWN Cornwall – see St. Ives.

HALSTEAD Essex 986 ㉜ – pop. 7,632 – ☎ 078 74.
London 51 – Cambridge 34 – Chelmsford 18 – Colchester 14.

XX **Fernando's**, 26 High St., CO9 2AP, ☎ 2001
closed Sunday – **M** a la carte 4.20/15.00 1.50.

AUDI-NSU Gosfield ☎ 2131
BMW 13 High St. ☎ 2012
CITROEN Sible Hedingham ☎ 0787 (Hedingham) 60538
SAAB Colchester Rd ☎ 2183

HALSTEAD Kent – pop. 1,734 – ✉ Sevenoaks – ☎ 095 97 Badgers Mount.
London 20 – Maidstone 21.

XX **Monte Carlo**, London Rd, Polhill, TN13 1BH, on A 21 ☎ 236, Italian rest. – Ⓟ
closed Saturday lunch, Sunday dinner, Monday and Bank Holidays – **M** a la carte 4.95/7.75.

HAMBROOK Avon – see Bristol.

HAMSTEAD MARSHALL Berks. – pop. 199 – ✉ Newbury – ☎ 048 85 Kintbury.
London 72 – Newbury 5 – Southampton 39.

X **White Hart**, RG15 0HW, ☎ 201, – Ⓟ
closed Sunday dinner, Monday and Bank Holidays – **M** a la carte 3.55/5.45 **t.** 0.90.

HANDCROSS West Sussex – see Crawley.

HANDFORTH Greater Manchester – see Wilmslow.

HANLEY Staffs. 986 ⑨ and ㉗ – see Stoke-on-Trent.

HARBERTONFORD Devon – pop. 974 – ✉ Totnes – ☎ 080 423.
London 228 – Exeter 28 – Plymouth 24 – Torquay 13.

XX **Hungry Horse**, Old Rd, TQ9 7TA, ☎ 441 – Ⓟ
closed Sunday, Monday, 1 to 15 October, 16 January-14 February and Bank Holidays – **M** (dinner only) a la carte 4.10/5.30 1.85.

HAREWOOD West Yorks. 986 ㉓ – pop. 3,459 – ✉ Leeds – ☎ 097 336.
See : Harewood House** 18C : the Bird Garden* *AC*.
London 201 – Harrogate 7 – Leeds 8.

Harewood Arms, LS17 9LH, ☎ 235 – wc Ⓟ
11 rm.

HARLECH Gwynedd 986 ㉗ – pop. 1,405 – ☎ 076 673.
See : Castle** (13C) *AC*, site and ⩽ from the castle*. **Envir.** : Llanbedr (Cwm Bychan*) S : 3 ½ m. – Vale of Ffestinoig* NE : 9 m. – Blaenau Ffestinoig (site : slate quarries*) NE : 15 m.
18 ☎ 203.
i Snowdonia National Park and Tourist Information Centre, Gwyddfor House, High St. ☎ 658 (Easter-September).
London 241 – Chester 72 – Dolgellau 21.

🏨 **Maes-y-Neuadd** ♨, LL47 6YA, NE: 2 ½ m. off B 4573 ☎ 200, ≤, « Part 14C country house », garden, park – ⌂wc Ⓟ
Easter-October – **M** (dinner only) 4.00/5.60 🍾 1.70 – **13 rm** ☐ 9.80/19.60.

🏨 **St. Davids,** ☎ 366, ≤ sea and golf courses, ⛱ heated, garden – lift ⌂wc ☎ ♿ Ⓟ. 🏞
M approx. 4.00 **t.** – **80 rm** ☐ 8.00/18.00 **t.** – P 12.00 **t.**

Noddfa, LL46 2UB, ☎ 319, ≤ – ⌂wc Ⓟ
M a la carte 3.30/5.90 🍾 1.60 – **8 rm** ☐ 8.00/17.00 – P 14.00/18.00.

at Llanbedr S: 3 m. on A 496 – ✉ ☎ 034 123 Llanbedr:

Cae Nêst Hall ♨, LL45 2NL, ☎ 349, « Country house atmosphere », garden – Ⓟ
April-December – **M** (dinner only and Sunday lunch - bar lunch in summer) 3.55/4.20 🍾 1.75 – **9 rm** ☐ 6.90/15.00 – P 10.50/11.70.

TOYOTA Main St. ☎ 432

HARLOW Essex 986 ㉜ – pop. 78,087 – ☎ 0279.

London 26 – Cambridge 34 – Chelmsford 20.

🏨 **Saxon Inn Motor,** Southern Way, CM18 7BA, on A 11 ☎ 22441, Telex 81658 – TV ⌂wc ☎ Ⓟ. 🏞
M approx. 2.85 **s.** 🍾 1.80 – ☐ 1.75 – **100 rm** 11.00/14.00 **s.**

at Old Harlow :

XX **Gables,** 1 Fore St., CM17 0AA, ☎ 27108
closed Sunday, Monday lunch, 2 weeks mid summer and Bank Holidays – **M** a la carte 4.35/7.35 🍾 1.75.

AUSTIN-JAGUAR-ROVER-TRIUMPH First Av., The Stow ☎ 27541
CHRYSLER-SIMCA Harrolds Rd ☎ 32111
DATSUN, PEUGEOT Tillwicks Rd ☎ 22381
FORD Edinburgh Way ☎ 21166
RENAULT Station Rd ☎ 39631
VAUXHALL Potter St. ☎ 22391
VW, AUDI-NSU Wych Elm ☎ 21461

HARNHAM Wilts. – see Salisbury.

HARPENDEN Herts. 986 ㉜ – pop. 24,188 – ☎ 058 27.

Envir. : Luton Hoo* (interior: Wernher Collection**) and park* *AC*, NW: 4 m.

London 32 – Luton 6.

🏨 **Harpenden Moat House,** 18 Southdown Rd, AL5 1PE, ☎ 64111, garden – TV Ⓟ
M a la carte 5.20/7.20 – ☐ 1.50 – **35 rm** 11.00/15.50 **s.**

🏨 **Glen Eagle,** 1 Luton Rd, AL5 2PX, ☎ 60271, garden – lift TV ⌂wc ☎ Ⓟ. 🏞
M (*closed Christmas Day dinner*) a la carte 5.10/7.20 🍾 1.50 – ☐ 1.80 – **41 rm** 12.50/20.00 **t.**

Milton, 25 Milton Rd, AL5 5LA, ☎ 2331, garden – Ⓟ
9 rm ☐ 5.00/10.00.

AUSTIN-MG-WOLSELEY 74 High St. ☎ 4545
CHRYSLER 86/90 High St. ☎ 60141
RENAULT Southdown Rd ☎ 5217
VAUXHALL 17 Luton Rd ☎ 5252
VOLVO Station Rd ☎ 64311

HARROGATE North Yorks. 986 ㉓ – pop. 62,427 – ☎ 0423.

See : Harlow Car gardens** by B 6162 Z. **Envir.** : Fountains Abbey*** (ruins 12C-13C, floodlit in summer), Studley Royal Gardens** and Fountains Hall* (17C) *AC*, NW: 9 m. by A 61 Y.

⛳18 Starbeck, nr. Harrogate ☎ 042 376 (Knaresborough) 3158, E : 2 m. by A 59 YZ – ⛳18 Oakdale, off Kent Rd Y ☎ 2806 – ⛳18 Pannal, ☎ 871641, S: 2 ½ m. by A 61 Z.

i Royal Baths Assembly Rooms, Crescent Rd ☎ 65912.

London 211 – Bradford 18 – Leeds 15 – Newcastle-upon-Tyne 76 – York 22.

Plan on next page

🏨 **Majestic** (T.H.F.), Ripon Rd, HG1 2HU, ☎ 68972, Telex 57918, 🎾, ⛱ heated, garden – lift TV Ⓟ. 🏞 Y c
M a la carte 4.70/8.90 **st.** 🍾 1.45 – ☐ 2.00 – **159 rm** 11.50/21.00 **st.**

🏨 **Old Swan,** Swan Rd, HG1 2SR, ☎ 504051, Telex 57922, 🎾, garden, park – lift ♿ Ⓟ. 🏞 Y e
M a la carte 2.65/5.80 **st.** 🍾 1.85 – **145 rm** ☐ 17.00/35.00 **st.**

🏨 **Crown** (T.H.F.), Crown Pl., HG1 2RZ, ☎ 67755, Telex 57652 – lift TV Ⓟ. 🏞 Z i
M a la carte 4.20/8.70 **st.** 🍾 1.45 – ☐ 2.00 – **112 rm** ☐ 11.00/20.50 **st.**

🏨 **Cairn** (Interchange), Ripon Rd, HG1 2JD, ☎ 504005, 🎾, garden – lift Ⓟ. 🏞 Y n
M a la carte 4.05/6.50 **st.** – **141 rm** ☐ 14.00/24.00 **st.**

🏨 **St. George** (Interchange), 1 Ripon Rd, HG1 2SY, ☎ 61431, Telex 57995 – lift ⌂wc ☎ Ⓟ. 🏞 Y o
M 3.65/4.00 **s.** 🍾 1.60 – **73 rm** ☐ 10.00/23.00 **s.** – P 15.50/18.50 **s.**

Gilmore, 98 Kings Rd, HG1 5HH, ☎ 503699 – Ⓟ Y s
18 rm ☐ 4.00/8.00.

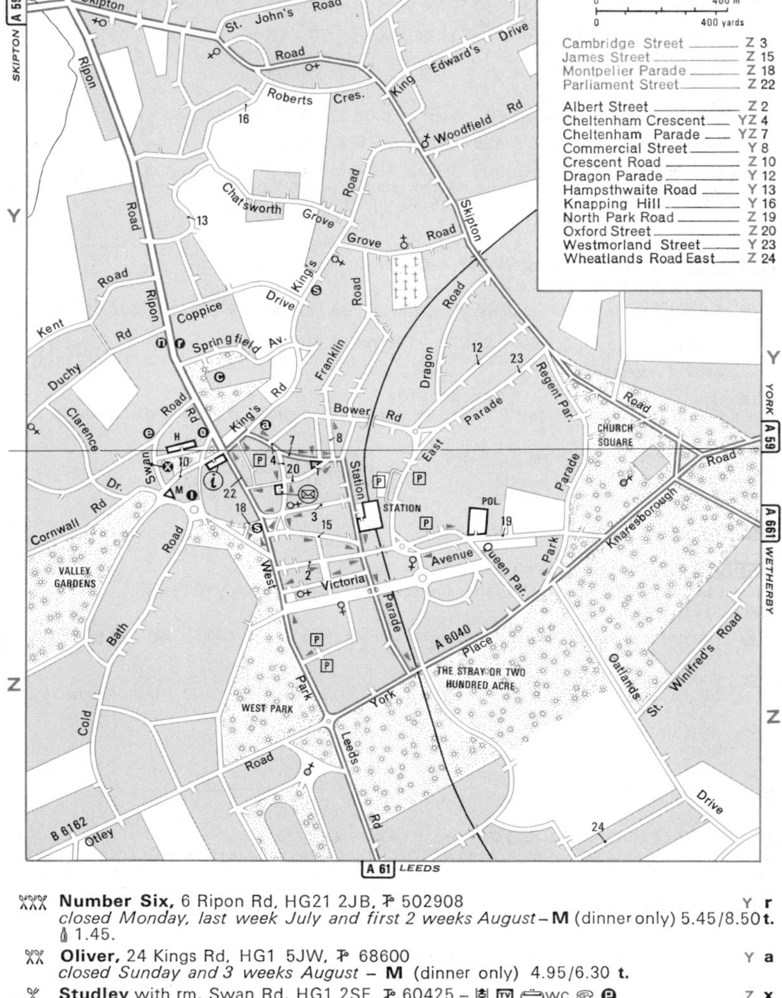

XXX **Number Six,** 6 Ripon Rd, HG21 2JB, ☎ 502908 Y **r**
closed Monday, last week July and first 2 weeks August – **M** (dinner only) 5.45/8.50 **t.** 🍷 1.45.

XX **Oliver,** 24 Kings Rd, HG1 5JW, ☎ 68600 Y **a**
closed Sunday and 3 weeks August – **M** (dinner only) 4.95/6.30 **t.**

X **Studley** with rm, Swan Rd, HG1 2SE, ☎ 60425 – ⇕ TV ⌂wc ☎ Ⓟ Z **x**
M a la carte 4.20/5.25 **t.** 🍷 1.50 – **17 rm** ☕ 9.50/19.50 **t.**

X Drum and Monkey, 5 Montpelier Gardens ☎ 2650, Seafood. Z **s**

at Burn Bridge S : 4 m. off A 61 – Z – ✉ ☎ 0423 Harrogate :

XX **Roman Court,** 55 Burn Bridge Rd, HG3 1PB, ☎ 879933, Italian rest. – Ⓟ
closed Saturday lunch, Sunday and Monday – **M** 5.25/8.75 **t.** 🍷 2.00.

AUSTIN-DAIMLER-JAGUAR-MG-ROVER-TRIUMPH-WOLSELEY, ROLLS ROYCE 91 Leeds Rd ☎ 87263
CHRYSLER-SIMCA West Park ☎ 4601
DAF Starbeck ☎ 886351
DATSUN Cheltenham Mount ☎ 66001
FIAT Leeds Rd, Pannal ☎ 879236
FORD Station Par. ☎ 61061
MORRIS-MG-WOLSELEY West Park ☎ 61751
PEUGEOT Pannal ☎ 879231
RENAULT 23 Station Par. ☎ 504153
SAAB Roseville Av. ☎ 883070
VAUXHALL 19 York Pl. ☎ 64511
VOLVO East Parade ☎ 2390
VW, AUDI-NSU Otley Rd, Killinghall ☎ 55141

Im Juli und August sind die Hotels oft überfüllt.
Außerhalb dieser Zeit werden Sie besser bedient.

HARTFORD Cheshire – pop. 3,587 – ✆ 0606 Northwich.
London 188 – Chester 15 – Liverpool 31 – Manchester 25.

Hartford Hall, School Lane, CW8 1PW, SW: 2 ½ m. off A 556 by A 533, ☎ 75711, – wc P
M a la carte 2.55/4.50 **t.** 1.40 – 1.00 – **20 rm** 10.00/17.50 **t.**

CHRYSLER 322 Chester Rd ☎ 0606 (Sandiway) 888188
FORD Chesterway, Northwich ☎ 0606 (Northwich) 6141
MAZDA 199 Witton St. ☎ 2485
POLSKI 141 Runcorn Rd, Barnton, Northwich ☎ 0606 (Northwich) 74293
VAUXHALL London Rd ☎ 3434

HARTLEPOOL Cleveland 986 ⑲ – pop. 97,094 – ✆ 0429.
18 Hart Warren ☎ 4398.
i Victor Square, Victoria Rd ☎ 68366 (summer only) – Civic Centre ☎ 66522 (winter only).
London 263 – Durham 19 – Middlesbrough 9 – Sunderland 21.

Grand (B.T.H.), Swainson St., TS24 8AA, ☎ 66345 – TV P.
M a la carte 5.30/10.75 **st.** 1.30 – **47 rm** 10.95/22.25 **st.**

AUDI-NSU 52/54 Park Rd ☎ 2345
CHRYSLER-SIMCA Victoria Rd ☎ 5365
MORRIS-MG-ROVER-TRIUMPH-WOLSELEY 128/130 York Rd ☎ 66393
VAUXHALL Blackhall ☎ 078 323 (Peterlee) 3655
VAUXHALL Oxford Rd ☎ 67719

HARTWELL Bucks. – see Aylesbury.

HARWICH and DOVERCOURT Essex 986 ㉜ – pop. 14,960 – ✆ 025 55.
9 Parkeston Rd ☎ 3616.
Shipping connections with the Continent : to Bremerhaven, Hamburg (Prins Ferries) – to Dunkerque (Sealink) – to Esbjerg (DFDS Seaways) – to Kristiansand and Oslo (Fred. Olsen-Bergen Line) – to Hoek van Holland (Sealink).
i Parkeston Quay, Parkeston ☎ 6139 (summer only).
London 74 – Chelmsford 41 – Colchester 19 – Ipswich 23.

Cliff, Marine Par., CO12 3RD, ☎ 3345 – wc wc P
M a la carte 4.35/6.50 1.05 – **32 rm** 6.00/13.50.

HASLEMERE Surrey 986 ㊱ – pop. 13,277– ✆ 0428.
Envir.: Petworth House*** 17C (paintings*** and carved room***) *AC*, SE: **11** m.
London 47 – Brighton 46 – Southampton 44.

Lythe Hill, Petworth Rd, GU27 3BQ, E: 1 ½ m. on B 2131 ☎ 51251, Telex 858402, ≤, , , . park – TV P.
M 4.25/5.75 **st.** 1.35 – 1.50 – **34 rm** 7.50/21.00 **st.** – P 17.00/25.00 **st.**

Georgian, High St., GU27 2JY, ☎ 51555, – wc P
M 2.25/3.35 **st.** 1.30 – **23 rm** 8.50/17.50 **st.**

XXX **Auberge de France,** Petworth Rd, GU27 3BQ, E: 1 ½ m. on B 2131 ☎ 4131, Telex 858402, ≤ , French rest. – P
closed Monday, Tuesday lunch and 26 December-1 March – **M** a la carte 5.50/7.20 **st.** 2.20.

at Grayswood NE: **1** ¼ m. on A 286 – ✉ ✆ 0428 Haslemere:

XX **Wheatsheaf Inn,** GU27 2DP, ☎ 4440 – P
closed Sunday dinner, Monday and Christmas Holidays – **M** a la carte 4.25/6.10 **t.** 1.20.

AUSTIN-MG-WOLSELEY Hindhead Rd ☎ 3216
CHRYSLER-SIMCA West St. ☎ 3333
FORD Farnham Lane ☎ 3222
JAGUAR-ROVER-TRIUMPH Grayswood Rd ☎ 2303
MORRIS-MG-WOLSELEY Kings Rd ☎ 4222
PEUGEOT High St. ☎ 52552
VAUXHALL 101/107 Camelsdale Rd ☎ 3678

HASTINGS and ST. LEONARDS East Sussex 986 ㊱ – pop. 72,410 – ✆ 0424.
See : Norman Castle (ruins) ** *AC* BZ – Alexandra Park* AY – White Rocks gardens ≤* ABZ – Public Museum and Art Gallery (pottery*, Durbar Hall*) BZ **M.**
18 Beauport Park, St. Leonards, ☎ 52977, NW: **3** m. by B **2159** AY.
i 4 Robertson Ter. ☎ 424242.
London 65 – Brighton 37 – Folkestone 37 – Maidstone 34.

Plan on next page

Beauport Park , Battle Rd, TN38 8EA, NW: 3 ½ m. on A 2100, ☎ 51222, ≤, « Country house atmosphere, formal gardens », heated, park – TV P on B 2159 AY
M a la carte 4.00/5.50 **st.** 1.30 – **20 rm** 8.50/18.50 **st.** – P 12.25/14.50 **st.**

XX Saraceno, 64 Eversfield Pl. ☎ 432358, Italian rest. AZ **e**

X **Mitre,** 56 High St., TN34 3EN, ☎ 427000, French rest. BY **a**
closed Sunday dinner, Monday and February – **M** (dinner only and Sunday lunch) a la carte 3.45/5.60 **t.** 1.50.

HASTINGS AND ST. LEONARDS

Street	Grid	No.
King's Road	AZ	22
London Road	AZ	
Norman Road	AZ	
Queen's Road	BZ	
Robertson Street	BZ	27
Wellington Place	BZ	35
Bourne (The)	BY	4
Castle Street	BZ	7
Castle Hill Road	BZ	8
Cornwallis Gardens	BZ	9
Cornwallis Terrace	BZ	10
Dane Road	AY	12
Denmark Place	BZ	13
Dorset Place	BZ	15
Gensing Road	AZ	16
George Street	BY	18
Grosvenor Crescent	AY	19
Harold Place	BZ	20
High Street	BY	21
Priory Street	BZ	24
Rock-a-Nore Road	BY	30
St. Helen's Park Road	BY	32
Silchester Road	AZ	33
Warrior Square	AZ	34
Wellington Square	BZ	36
White Rock Road	BZ	38

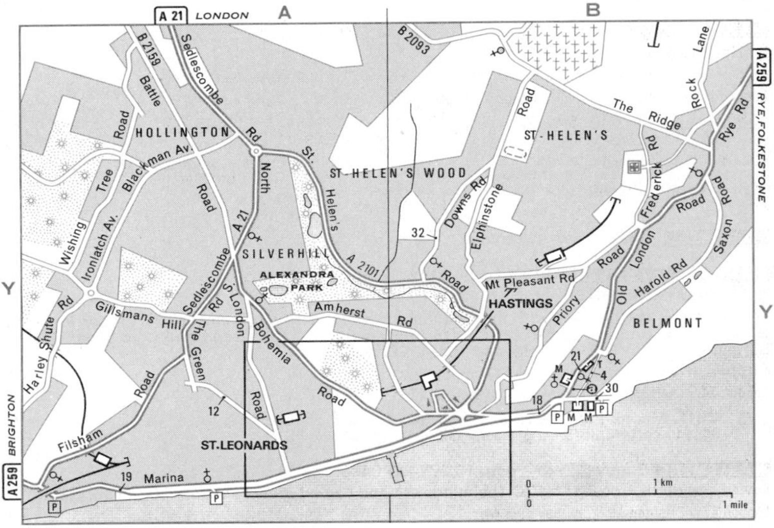

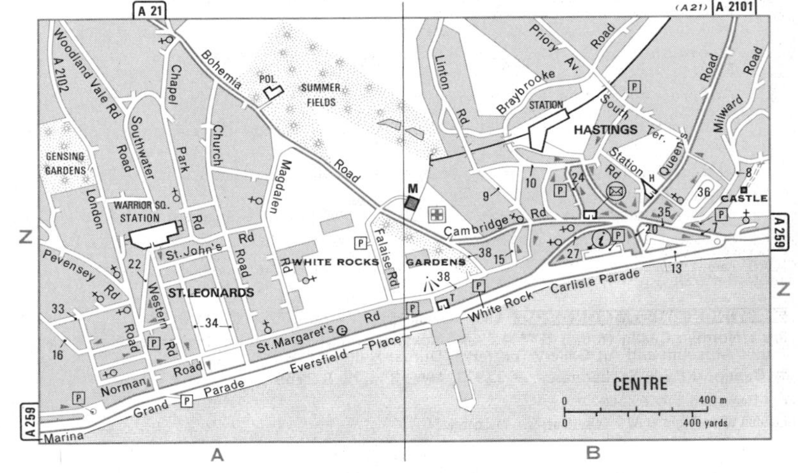

AUSTIN-MG-WOLSELEY 18 Cambridge Rd ☎ 426607
DAF Winchelsea Rd ☎ 424445
DAIMLER-JAGUAR-ROVER-TRIUMPH 107 Sedlescombe Rd North ☎ 420641
FIAT Bexhill Rd ☎ 433533
FORD Braybrooke Rd ☎ 2727
RENAULT 109/111 Sedlescombe Rd North ☎ 432982
VAUXHALL 36/39 Western Rd, St. Leonards ☎ 424545
VW, AUDI-NSU 111/113 Bexhill Rd ☎ 424146

HATCH BEAUCHAMP Somerset – see Taunton.

HATFIELD Herts. 986 ㉜ – pop. 25,990 – ☎ 070 72.
See : Hatfield House*** *AC* (gardens* and Old Palace*).
London 27 – Bedford 38 – Cambridge 39.

Comet (Embassy), 301 St. Albans Rd West, AL10 9RH, junction A 1 and A 414, ☎ 65411, – TV wc P.
closed Christmas – **M** approx. 3.15 **st.** 1.55 – **44 rm** 11.25/15.50 **st.**

Salisbury, The Broadway, Old Hatfield, AL9 5JB, ☎ 62220 – P
closed Sunday dinner, Good Friday, 25-26 December and Bank Holidays – **M** a la carte 4.80/7.35.

ALFA-ROMEO, CHRYSLER-SIMCA By-Pass ☎ 64521
AUSTIN-MORRIS-MG-ROVER-TRIUMPH-WOLSELEY 1 Great North Rd ☎ 64366
FIAT North Parade ☎ 62908
PEUGEOT 42 Beaconsfield Rd ☎ 71226

HATHERLEIGH Devon 986 ㉟ – pop. 915 – ✉ Okehampton – ☎ 083 781.
London 230 – Exeter 29 – Plymouth 38.

George, Market St., EX20 3JN, ☎ 454, « 15C inn », – wc P
M *(closed November)* 3.50/4.00 0.75 – **13 rm** 6.00/13.00.

at Sheepwash NW: 4 ½ m. off A 3072 – ✉ Beaworthy – ☎ 040 923 Black Torrington:

Half Moon Inn, EX21 5NE, ☎ 232, « 17C Inn », – wc P
M (dinner only) 4.75 **t.** 1.25 – **10 rm** 6.95/16.25 – P 10.30/11.50.

AUSTIN-MG-WOLSELEY Market Pl. ☎ 210
MORRIS-MG-WOLSELEY ☎ 244

HATHERSAGE Derbs. – pop. 1,458 – ✉ Sheffield (South Yorks.) – ☎ 0433 Hope Valley.
London 165 – Manchester 33 – Sheffield 10.

George, Main Rd, S30 1BB, ☎ 50436, – wc P
M a la carte 3.25/6.45 **t.** 1.30 – **10 rm** 10.10/17.45 **t.**

AUSTIN-ROVER-TRIUMPH Main Rd ☎ 50341

HAVERFORDWEST Dyfed 986 ㉚ – pop. 9,104 – ☎ 0437.
Envir.: Porthgain (cliffs ***) NW: 16 m. – St. Ann's Head** SW: 14 m. – Martin's Haven (**) SW: 14 m. – Newgale (<**) NW: 9 m. – Dale (site*) SW: 12 m.
i Pembrokeshire Coast National Park and Wales Tourist Board Centre 40 High St. ☎ 3110 (Easter September).
London 250 – Fishguard 15 – Swansea 57.

Mariners (Embassy), Mariners Sq., SA61 2DU, ☎ 3353 – TV wc P
closed Christmas – **M** approx. 3.80 **st.** 1.45 – **29 rm** 7.55/12.50.

Pembroke House-Chez Gilbert with rm, Spring Gdns, SA61 2EN, ☎ 3652 – wc wc P
M *(closed Sunday lunch)* a la carte 3.85/4.75 **s.** 1.00 – **23 rm** 6.50/12.00 **s.**

AUSTIN-DAIMLER-JAGUAR-MG-ROVER-TRIUMPH WOLSELEY Jubilee Gdns ☎ 4511
CHRYSLER-SIMCA ☎ 2468
DATSUN, JAGUAR-MORRIS-MG-WOLSELEY Slebech ☎ 251
FIAT Portfield ☎ 3414
FORD Dew St. and Salutation Sq. ☎ 2215
RENAULT St. Thomas Green ☎ 5151
SAAB Johnston ☎ 0437 (Johnston) 377
VAUXHALL Bridgend Sq. ☎ 2717

HAWKCHURCH Devon – pop. 431 – ✉ Axminster – ☎ 029 77.
London 155 – Dorchester 27 – Exeter 31 – Taunton 24.

Fairwater Head, EX13 5TX, ☎ 349, <, – wc P
March-November – **M** approx. 4.00 **st.** 1.70 – **14 rm** 11.65/20.75 **st.**

HAWKHURST Kent 986 ㊱ – pop. 4,107 – ☎ 058 05.
Envir. : Bedgebury Pinetum* *AC*, NW : 2 m. – Bodiam Castle* 14C (ruins) *AC*, SE: 5 m.
High St. ☎ 2396.
London 50 – Folkestone 34 – Hastings 15 – Maidstone 19.

Royal Oak, Highgate, TN18 4EP, ☎ 2184, – P
M a la carte 3.25/4.30 **t.** 1.30 – **11 rm** 5.00/9.50 **st.**

Tudor Arms with rm, Rye Rd, TN18 5DA, E: ½ m. on A 268, ☎ 2312, « < over rose garden », – wc P
M a la carte 4.00/6.25 **t.** 1.35 – 0.60 – **10 rm** 6.00/15.00 **st.**

MORRIS-MG Rye Lane ☎ 3251
ROVER-TRIUMPH Horns Rd ☎ 2020

HAWKSHEAD Cumbria 986 ⑲ – pop. 684 – ✉ Ambleside – ☎ 096 66.
i Main Car Park ☎ 525 (summer only).
London 281 – Carlisle 52 – Kendal 19.

Tarn Hows, LA22 0PR, NW: 1 ½ m., ☎ 330, <, heated, , park – wc P
closed January-February – **M** approx. 6.00 **t.** 1.30 – **25 rm** 10.00/22.00 – P 20.00 **t.**

Red Lion Inn, LA22 0NS, ☎ 213 – P
M (bar lunch) 4.00/6.50 **st.** 1.50 – **8 rm** 6.00/12.00 **st.**

Highfield House ⑤, Hawkshead Hill, LA22 0PN, W: ½ m. on B 5285 ☎ 344, ≤, ⛱ – Ⓟ
closed 16 November-31 January – **11 rm** ☕ 5.50/11.00 **t.**

at Near Sawrey SE: **1 ½ m. on B 5285** – ✉ **Ambleside** – ☎ **096 66 Hawkshead:**

Sawrey House ⑤, LA22 0LF, on B 5285 ☎ 387, ≤, ⛱ – Ⓟ
March-4 November – **10 rm** ☕ 5.00/10.00 **s.**

HAYLING ISLAND Hants. – ✉ ☎ 070 12 Havant.

London 77 – Brighton 45 – Southampton 28.

Post House (T. H. F.), Northney Rd, PO11 0NQ, ☎ 5011, Telex 86620, 🏊 heated – TV ♿ Ⓟ.
M 2.95/4.00 **st.** 🍾 1.50 – ☕ 2.00 – **96 rm** 14.00/20.00 **st.**

Three Musketeers, Station Rd, West Town ☎ 3226, French rest. – Ⓟ.

HAYWARDS HEATH West Sussex **986** ㊱ – pop. **17,654** – ☎ **0444.**

⛳18 High Beech ☎ 044 47 (Lindfield) 2310, N: 2 m.

London 44 – Brighton 15 – Eastbourne 29 – Lewes 12.

Hayworthe Arms, Market Pl., RH16 1DB, ☎ 412808 – 🛁wc Ⓟ
M 2.75/3.05 **t.** 🍾 1.30 – **20 rm** ☕ 6.90/13.60 **t.**

Hilton Park ⑤, Cuckfield, RH17 5EG, W: 1 m. on A 272 ☎ 54555, ⛱ – 🛁wc Ⓟ
M (buffet lunch) 4.00/5.00 **st.** 🍾 1.90 – **15 rm** ☕ 10.00/19.00 **st.** – P 11.00/14.00 **st.**

AUSTIN-DAIMLER-JAGUAR-ROVER-TRIUMPH Mill Green Rd ☎ 50404
BMW 275a Chelwood Gate ☎ 082 574 (Chelwood Gate) 456
FORD 22/24 Wivelsfield Rd ☎ 50222
MORRIS-MG-WOLSELEY The Broadway ☎ 51511
ROLLS-ROYCE-BENTLEY Market Pl. ☎ 51511
VAUXHALL 104 Franklynn Rd ☎ 50115

HEALD GREEN Greater Manchester – pop. **14,755** – ☎ **061 Manchester.**

London 192 – Manchester 10.

Moss Nook, Ringway Rd, M22 5NA, ☎ 437 4778 – Ⓟ
closed Sunday and 3 weeks from 25 December – **M** (dinner only) a la carte approx. 7.75 **t.**

La Bonne Auberge, 224 Finney Lane, SK7 3AN, ☎ 437 5701, French rest. – Ⓟ
closed Sunday, Monday dinner and Bank Holidays – **M** a la carte 3.10/5.20 🍾 1.50.

HECKFIELD Hants. – pop. **340** – ✉ **Basingstoke** – ☎ **073 583.**

London 52 – Basingstoke 10 – Reading 9.

Andwells, RG27 0LN, on A 33 ☎ 202 – Ⓟ
M a la carte 5.95/10.35 **t.**

HEDDONS MOUTH Devon – ✉ **Barnstaple** – ☎ **059 83 Parracombe.**

London 209 – Exeter 57 – Minehead 23 – Taunton 48.

Hunters Inn ⑤, Parracombe, EX31 4PY, ☎ 230, ≤, ⛱ – 🛁wc Ⓟ
March-October – **M** (dinner only) 4.50/5.00 **t.** 🍾 1.00 – **12 rm** ☕ 9.50/22.00 **t.**

HELFORD Cornwall – pop. **289** (inc. Manaccan) – ✉ **Helston** – ☎ **032 623 Manaccan.**

London 324 – Falmouth 15 – Penzance 22 – Truro 27.

Riverside with rm, TR12 6JU, ☎ 443, « Converted cottage »
M *(closed Sunday dinner, Monday and 24 December-February)* (dinner only and Sunday lunch) 6.50/8.00 **st.** 🍾 2.00 – **3 rm** ☕ 13.00/14.00 **st.**

HELMSLEY North Yorks. **986** ㉔ – pop. **1,278** – ☎ **043 92.**

See: Castle* (ruins 12C) *AC*. **Envir.:** Rievaulx Abbey** (ruins 12C-13C) *AC*, NW: 2 ½ m. – Byland Abbey* (ruins 12C) *AC*, SW: 6 m. by Ampleforth.

London 234 – Middlesbrough 29 – York 24.

Black Swan (T.H.F.), Market Pl., YO6 5BJ, ☎ 466, ⛱ – TV 🛁wc ☎ Ⓟ
M a la carte 4.10/6.10 **st.** 🍾 1.50 – **38 rm** ☕ 12.00/18.00 **st.** – P 16.00/20.00 **st.**

Feversham Arms (Interchange), 1 High St., YO6 5AG, ☎ 346 – 🛁wc Ⓟ
M *(closed 24 to 30 December)* approx. 4.00 🍾 1.10 – **10 rm** ☕ 7.00/14.00 – P 13.00/14.00.

HEMEL HEMPSTEAD Herts. **986** ㉜ – pop. **15,207** – ☎ **0442** – ⛳18.

i Pavilion, The Marlowes ☎ 64451.

London 30 – Aylesbury 16 – Luton 10 – Northampton 46.

Post House (T.H.F.), Breakspear Way, HP2 4UA, NE: 2 ½ m. on A 4147, ☎ 51122, ⛱ – 🛗 TV 🛁wc ☎ Ⓟ.
M 3.50/3.95 **st.** 🍾 1.50 – **91 rm** 13.00/18.00 **st.**

South Lea, 8 Charles St., HP1 1JH, ☎ 3061 – Ⓟ
11 rm.

Southville, 9 Charles St., HP1 1JH, ☎ 51387 – Ⓟ
12 rm ☕ 5.00/10.00 **st.**

✗ **White Hart,** 30-32 High St., HP3 0HG, ☎ 42458 – Ⓟ
closed Saturday, Sunday, last 2 weeks August and Bank Holidays – **M** (lunch only) 3.00/6.00.

✗ **Spinning Wheel,** 80 High St., HP1 3AQ, ☎ 64309
closed 25 and 26 December – **M** (dinner only) 3.50/5.00 **st.** 🍾 1.95.

AUSTIN-MG-WOLSELEY Leverstock Green ☎ 53522
AUSTIN-MG-WOLSELEY London Rd ☎ 51611
AUSTIN-MORRIS-MG-ROVER-TRIUMPH Redbourn Rd ☎ 63013
CHRYSLER-SIMCA High St. ☎ 50401
FIAT, VAUXHALL Two Waters Rd ☎ 51212
FORD 499 London Rd ☎ 2841
MORRIS-MG-WOLSELEY Fletcherway, Highfield ☎ 2061
RENAULT Warners End Rd ☎ 2751

HENLEY-IN-ARDEN Warw. 986 ㉛ – pop. 1,577 – ⊙ 056 42.
London 104 – Birmingham 15 – Stratford-on-Avon 8 – Warwick 8,5.

✗✗ **Beaudesert,** Birmingham Rd, B95 5QR, N: 1 ¼ m. on A 34 ☎ 2675 – Ⓟ
closed Sunday dinner, Monday and 3 weeks August-September – **M** (dinner only and Sunday lunch) 5.90/8.00 **st.**

AUSTIN-MG 57 High St. ☎ 2543

Prices For notes on the prices quoted in this Guide, see p. 16.

HENLEY-ON-THAMES Oxon. 986 ㊱ – pop. 11,431 – ⊙ 049 12.
Envir.: Greys Court★ *AC*, NW: 2 ½ m.
i West Hill House, 4 West St. ☎ 2626.
London 42 – Oxford 23 – Reading 9.

✗ **Cherub,** 49-51 Market Pl., RG9 2AA, ☎ 3060
closed Monday – **M** a la carte 3.60/5.85 **t.** 🍾 1.70.

AUSTIN-MORRIS-MG-ROVER-TRIUMPH-WOLSELEY 49 Station Rd ☎ 4136
FIAT 66 Bell St. ☎ 3077
FORD 12 Station Rd ☎ 2955
RENAULT 47 Station Rd ☎ 3555
ROVER-TRIUMPH 58 Reading Rd ☎ 77933

HEREFORD Heref. and Worc. 986 ㉛ – pop. 46,503 – ⊙ 0432.
See : Cathedral★★ 12C-13C (the Mappa Mundi★ 13C) A **A** – The Old House★ 17C A **B**. **Envir. :** Abbey Dore★ (12C-17C) SW : 12 m. by A 465 B.
⛳18 Raven's Causeway, Wormsley ☎ 043 271 (Canon Pyon) 219, NW: 6 m. by A 438 B.
i Blue School St. ☎ 68430.
London 133 – Birmingham 51 – Cardiff 56.

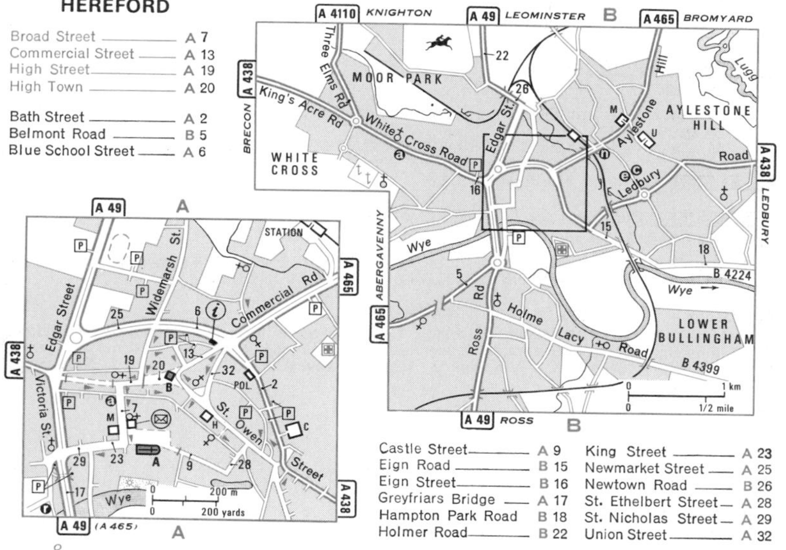

Green Dragon (T.H.F.), Broad St., HR4 9BG, ☎ 2506, Telex 35491 – TV Ⓟ. A a
M 3.90/5.25 **st.** 1.45 – **93 rm** 10.00/18.00 **st.** – P 14.00/18.50 **st.**

Oaklands, 43 Bodenham Rd, HR1 2TP, ☎ 2775, – wc wc Ⓟ B c
M *(closed Sunday dinner)* 2.75/3.25 **t.** 1.50 – **19 rm** 6.95/15.50 **t.**

Litchfield Lodge, Bodenham Rd, HR1 2TS, ☎ 3258 – Ⓟ B e
10 rm 4.50/8.50.

Somerville, 12 Bodenham Rd, HR1 2TS, ☎ 3991, – Ⓟ B n
9 rm 5.85/14.00 **st.**

Alexander House, 61 Whitecross Rd, HR4 0DQ, ☎ 4882 – Ⓟ B a
closed 24 to 26 December – **8 rm** 5.75/11.50 **st.**

XX **Greyfriars,** 23 Greyfriars Av., HR4 0BE, ☎ 67274, ≼, – Ⓟ A r
closed Sunday and Monday dinner – **M** a la carte 2.45/7.85 1.10.

AUSTIN-MG-WOLSELEY Commercial Rd ☎ 6456
CHRYSLER-SIMCA Blue School St. ☎ 2354
CITROEN Bridge St. ☎ 2341
DAF, MAZDA Kings Acre Rd ☎ 66974
DAIMLER-JAGUAR-MORRIS-MG-ROVER-TRIUMPH 91/97 Widemarsh St. ☎ 67611
DATSUN, VW, AUDI-NSU Muchgowarne ☎ 053 186 (Bosbury) 605
FIAT Bath St. ☎ 4134
FORD Commercial Rd ☎ 6494
LANCIA Whitestone ☎ 043 275 (Bartestree Cross) 464
MORRIS-MG WOLSELEY Callow ☎ 3074
PEUGEOT 101/105 St. Owen St. ☎ 6268
RENAULT White Cross Rd ☎ 2589
VAUXHALL Blackfriars St. ☎ 67441
VOLVO 14 Commercial Rd ☎ 6275

HERNE BAY Kent 986 ㊱ – pop. 25,198 – ✆ 022 73.

Envir. : Reculver (Church twin towers* *AC*) E : 3 m.

i Council Offices, 1 Richmond St. ☎ 66031.

London 63 – Dover 24 – Maidstone 31 – Margate 12.

St. George, Western Esplanade, CT6 8JA, ☎ 3776, – Ⓟ
M 3.00/3.50 **t.** 1.30 – **15 rm** 7.00/12.00 **t.** – P 9.60/11.00 **t.**

MORRIS-MG-WOLSELEY Kings Rd ☎ 3871

HERSTMONCEUX East Sussex – pop. 2,036 – ✆ 032 181.

See : Castle 15C (home of the Royal Greenwich Observatory), site and grounds** *AC*.

Envir. : Michelham Priory (site*) *AC*, SW : 6 m.

London 63 – Eastbourne 12 – Hastings 14 – Lewes 16.

XX **Sundial,** Gardner St., BN27 4LA, ☎ 2217, French rest. – Ⓟ
closed Sunday dinner, Monday, 3 weeks August and 3 weeks January – **M** a la carte 5.35/7.20 1.40.

at Boreham Street SE : 2 m. on A 271 – ✉ ✆ 032 181 Herstmonceux :

White Friars (Interchange), BN27 4SE, ☎ 2355, « Attractive garden » – wc Ⓟ
closed January – **M** *(closed Sunday dinner and Monday to non-residents)* 4.00/4.75 **st.** 1.40 – **15 rm** 8.00/20.00 **st.** – P 11.50/13.80 **st.**

VAUXHALL Buckwell Hill ☎ 2211

HERTINGFORDBURY Herts. – pop. 703 – ✉ ✆ 0992 Hertford.

London 26 – Luton 18.

White Horse Inn (T.H.F.), Hertingfordbury Rd, SG14 2LB, ☎ 56791, – TV wc Ⓟ
M a la carte 4.30/5.25 **st.** 1.50 – **30 rm** 13.00/18.00 **st.**

HESLEDEN Durham – see Peterlee.

HEVERSHAM Cumbria – pop. 703 – ✉ ✆ 044 82 Milnthorpe.

London 258 – Kendal 6 – Lancaster 15.

XX **Blue Bell** with rm, The Prince's Way, LA7 7EE, on A 6 ☎ 3159 – wc Ⓟ
M approx. 5.25 **st.** – **20 rm** 8.00/14.00 **st.** – P 14.00/15.00 **st.**

HEXHAM Northumb. 986 ⑲ – pop. 9,806 – ✆ 0434.

See : Abbey Church* 13C. **Envir. :** Hadrian's Wall** with its forts and milecastles (Chesters Fort*, museum *AC*) NW : 5 ½ m. – Housesteads Fort**, museum *AC*, NW : 14 m. – Derwent Reservoir (site*) SE : 7 m. – Vindolanda* (fort and town) *AC*, NW : 14 ½ m. – Steel Rigg ≼* of wall, W : 19 m.

18 Spital Park ☎ 2057.

i The Manor Office, Hallgates ☎ 5225.

London 303 – Carlisle 37 – Newcastle-upon-Tyne 21.

Royal, Priestpopple, NE46 1PQ, ☎ 2270 – TV wc Ⓟ
15 rm.

Beaumont, Beaumont St., NE46 3LZ, ☎ 2331
M *(closed Monday lunch)* a la carte 2.15/3.45 **t.** 1.00 – **19 rm** 8.50/14.00 **t.**

CHRYSLER West Rd ℡ 3861
CITROEN ℡ 3615
DATSUN Haugh Lane ℡ 4527
FIAT Tyne Mills ℡ 3013
VAUXHALL Parkwell ℡ 2411
VOLVO ℡ 2184
VW, AUDI-NSU Station Garage ℡ 2179

HIGHAM Derbs. – pop. 4,909 (inc. Shirland) – ✉ Derby – ☎ 077 383 Alfreton.
London 147 – Derby 16 – **Nottingham 20** – **Sheffield 20.**

XX **Higham Farm** with rm, Main Rd, Old Higham, DE5 6EH, ℡ 3812, park – TV wc wc ☎ P
M a la carte 4.40/6.80 **s.** 1.20 – **12 rm** 10.50/21.00 **s.**

HIGH WYCOMBE Bucks. 986 ㊱ – pop. 59,340 – ☎ 0494.
Envir. : Hughenden Manor★ (site★, Disraeli Museum) *AC*, N : 1 m. – West Wycombe (Manor House★ 18C, *AC*, St. Lawrence's Church : from the tower 74 steps, *AC*, ☼★) NW : 2 ½ m.
i District Council, Queen Victoria Rd ℡ 26100.
London 34 – Aylesbury 17 – **Oxford 26** – Reading 18.

Falcon, High St., HP11 2AX, ℡ 22173 – P
M 2.90/3.85 **st.** – **11 rm** 6.50/11.00 **st.**

Clifton Lodge, 210 West Wycombe Rd ℡ 29062, – P – **15 rm.**

MICHELIN Branch, Copyground Lane, HP12 3HA, ℡ 25391.

AUSTIN-DAIMLER-JAGUAR-MG-ROVER-TRIUMPH-WOLSELEY 111/121 London Rd ℡ 26180
CITROEN Naphill ℡ 024 024 (Naphill) 3270
DAF Lane End ℡ 881354
DATSUN, VAUXHALL London Rd ℡ 30021
FORD Oxford Rd ℡ 23111
OPEL West Wycombe Rd ℡ 32545
RENAULT Desborough Av. ℡ 36331
ROVER-TRIUMPH 125 Amersham Rd ℡ 23832
TOYOTA Littleworth Rd, Downley ℡ 23628

HILLINGTON Norfolk – pop. 230 – ✉ King's Lynn – ☎ 048 56.
London 112 – King's Lynn 7,5 – **Norwich 39.**

XX **Ffolkes Arms,** PE31 6BJ, on A 148 ℡ 210 – P
closed Christmas Day – **M** a la carte 4.05/5.60 **s.** 1.80.

HILLMORTON Warw. – see Rugby.

HIMLEY West Midlands – pop. 739 – ✉ Dudley – ☎ 090 77 Wombourne.
London 136 – **Birmingham 15.**

Himley House, DY3 4LD, on A 449 ℡ 2468, – TV wc wc ☎ P
M *(closed Sunday dinner)* a la carte 2.50/9.30 **t.** 1.20 – **24 rm** 8.00/12.00 **t.**

HINDHEAD Surrey 986 ㊱ – pop. 3,443 (inc. Churt) – ☎ 042 873.
London 47 – Guildford 14 – **Portsmouth 31** – Winchester 32.

X **Woodcock Inn,** Churt Rd, Beacon Hill, GU26 6PD, ℡ 4079 – P
closed 1 to 19 August and Christmas Day – **M** (dinner only and Sunday lunch) a la carte 3.80/5.00 **t.** 1.35.

HINDON Wilts. – pop. 534 – ✉ Salisbury – ☎ 074 789.
London 107 – Bath 28 – Bournemouth 40 – Salisbury 15.

Lamb, SP3 6DP, ℡ 225, – P
M 3.75/4.50 **st.** 1.10 – **12 rm** 6.00/12.00 **st.** – P 11.50/12.50 **st.**

HINTLESHAM Suffolk – pop. 486 – ☎ 047 387.
London 73 – Colchester 18 – **Ipswich 5.**

XXX ✿ **Hintlesham Hall,** IP8 3QP, ℡ 268, park – P
M 7.00/8.00
Spec. Pâté aux herbes, Rack of Lamb with walnuts, Elizabeth Moxon's lemon posset.

HITCHIN Herts. 986 ㉜ – pop. 25,295 – ☎ 0462.
London 40 – Bedford 14 – **Cambridge 26** – Luton 9.

Sun (Crest), Sun St., SG5 1AF, ℡ 2092 – P.
M a la carte 3.35/5.55 **s.** 1.55 – **27 rm** 9.70/15.40 **s.**

at Little Wymondley SE : 2 ½ m. on A 602 – ✉ Hitchin – ☎ 0438 Stevenage :

Blakemore, SG4, 7JJ, ℡ 55821, Telex 825479, heated, – TV P.
M 3.00/4.50 1.50 – **42 rm** 14.00/20.00.

Redcoats Farmhouse, SG4 7JL, ℡ 3500, – wc P
closed Christmas – **M** *(closed Sunday, Monday, Tuesday and Bank Holidays)* (dinner only) a la carte 5.10/7.20 1.90 – **8 rm** 8.00/14.50.

AUSTIN-DAIMLER-MG-ROVER-TRIUMPH Queen St. ℡ 50311
CITROEN High St., Graveley ℡ 0438 (Stevenage) 66177
MORRIS-MG-PRINCESS Walsworth Rd ℡ 4436
SAAB The Heath, Breachwood Green ℡ 043 887 (Whitwell) 300

HOCKLEY HEATH West Midlands – pop. 3,507 – ✉ Solihull – ☎ 056 43 Lapworth.
London 108 – Birmingham 11 – Coventry 14 – Warwick 10.

Barn Motel, Stratford Rd, B94 6NX, ☎ 2144 – TV wc ☎ P
36 rm.

HOGSTHORPE Lincs. – pop. 542 – ✉ ☎ 0754 Skegness.
London 146 – Boston 30 – Grimsby 38 – Lincoln 48.

Belmont, Thames St., PE25 1QZ, ☎ 72288, – P
closed Sunday – **M** (dinner only) 3.10/9.50 1.75.

HOLFORD Somerset – pop. 283 – ✉ Bridgwater – ☎ 027 874.
London 171 – Bristol 48 – Minehead 15 – Taunton 22.

Alfoxton Park, TA5 1SG, W : 1 ½ m., ☎ 211, ≤, « Country house atmosphere », heated, , park – wc wc P
M (dinner only and Sunday lunch) 4.00 1.60 – **18 rm** 10.00/19.50.

Combe House, TA5 1RZ, SW : 1 m. ☎ 382, « Country house atmosphere », , –
wc P
April-October – **M** (dinner only) 4.00/5.50 **t.** 1.20 – **15 rm** 7.00/15.75 **t.** – P 11.00/13.00 **t.**

HOLKHAM Norfolk 986 ㉘ – pop. 272 – ✉ ☎ 032 871 Wells-next-the-Sea.
See : Holkham Hall** (18C) *AC.*
London 124 – King's Lynn 32 – **Norwich 38.**

Pour un bon usage des plans de villes, voir les signes conventionnels p. 27.

HOLLINGBOURNE Kent – see Maidstone.

HOLMBRIDGE West Yorks. – pop. 1,083 – ✉ Huddersfield – ☎ 048 489 Holmfirth.
London 189 – Huddersfield 9 – **Leeds 24** – **Sheffield 24.**

Fernleigh House, Bank Lane, HD7 1NG, ☎ 2603 – P
closed Saturday lunch, Sunday dinner, Monday, 15 July-7 August and 26 to 28 December –
M 4.00/6.50 **t.** 1.00.

HOLME UPON SPALDING MOOR North Humberside – pop. 1,712 – ✉ York – ☎ 069 63.
London 205 – Doncaster 32 – **Kingston-upon-Hull 22** – **Leeds 36** – York 23.

Ye Olde Red Lion, 25 Old Rd, YO4 4AD, ☎ 220 – P
closed Sunday and Christmas Day – **M** (dinner only) a la carte 2.70/5.15 **t.** 1.50.

HOLMROCK Cumbria – pop. 254 – ☎ 094 04.
London 311 – Kendal 59 – Workington 23.

Lutwidge Arms, CA19 1UH, on A 595 ☎ 230, – P
season – **10 rm.**

HOLNEST PARK Dorset – see Sherborne.

HOLT Norfolk 986 ㉘ – pop. 2,532 – ☎ 026 371.
London 124 – King's Lynn 34 – **Norwich 22.**

Feathers, 6 Market Pl., NR25 6BW, ☎ 2318, – wc P
23 rm.

HOLYHEAD Gwynedd 986 ㉖ – pop. 10,620 – ☎ 0407.
Envir. : South Stack (cliffs*) W : 3 ½ m.
to Dun Laoghaire (Sealink) 1-4 daily (3 h 30 mn).
i Tourist Information Centre, Marine Sq., Salt Island Approach ☎ 2622 (Easter-September).
London 269 – Birkenhead 94 – **Cardiff 224** – Chester 83 – Shrewsbury 106 – **Swansea 186.**

Hotels and restaurant see : Rhosneigr SE : 13 m.
Treardurr Bay S : 2 ½ m.

FORD ☎ 492

HOLY ISLAND Northumb. – pop. 200 – ☎ 0289.
See : Castle (16C) ≤** *AC* – Priory* (ruins 12C) *AC.*
London 341 – Berwick-upon-Tweed 13 – **Newcastle-upon-Tyne 59.**

Hotels see : Berwick-upon-Tweed NW : 13 m.

HOLYWELL BAY Cornwall – see Newquay.

HOPE Derbs. – pop. 850 – ✉ Sheffield (South Yorks.) – ☎ 0433 Hope Valley.
Envir. : Blue John Caverns* *AC*, W : 2 m.
London 172 – Manchester 28 – Sheffield 15.

XX **House of Anton,** 95 Castleton Rd, S30 2RD, on A 625 ☎ 20380 – Ⓟ
M 6.25/9.00 **t.** 🍷 1.80.

HOPE COVE Devon – see Salcombe.

HORLEY Surrey 986 ㊱ – pop. 18,593 – ☎ 029 34.
London 27 – Brighton 26 – Royal Tunbridge Wells 22.

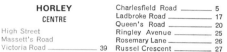

Plan of built up area see : Crawley

Europa Lodge (County), Longbridge Roundabout, RH6 0AB, ☎ 5599, Telex 877138 – 🛗 TV ⌂wc ☎ ♿ Ⓟ. 🏌
See plan of Crawley AY **e**
M (buffet lunch Saturday and Sunday) 3.50/5.00 **st.** 🍷 1.20 – **110 rm** ☕ 13.50/19.45 **st.**

Gatwick Post House (T.H.F.), Povey Cross Rd, RH6 0VA, ☎ 71621, Telex 877351, 🏊 heated – 🛗 TV ⌂wc ☎ ♿ Ⓟ. 🏌
See plan of Crawley AY **c**
M a la carte 4.65/6.20 **st.** 🍷 1.50 – ☕ 2.00 – **149 rm** 14.00/24.50 **st.**

Chequers (Thistle), Brighton Rd, RH6 8PH, ☎ 6992, 🏊 heated – TV ⌂wc ☎ ♿ Ⓟ. 🏌
78 rm. **a**

Skylane, Brighton Rd, RH6 8QG, ☎ 6971 – TV ⌂wc Ⓟ
See plan of Crawley by A 23 AY
M approx. 2.85 **st.** 🍷 1.15 – ☕ 1.50 – **59 rm** 12.50/17.50 **st.**

White House without rest., Brighton Rd, RH6 7HD, ☎ 4322, 🚗 – TV Ⓟ **c**
16 rm.

MORRIS-MG-WOLSELEY Massetts Rd ☎ 5176
PEUGEOT Keppers Corner, Burstow ☎ 0342 (Copthorne) 712017

HORLEY
CENTRE

High Street
Massett's Road
Victoria Road 39
Charlesfield Road 5
Ladbroke Road 17
Queen's Road 20
Ringley Avenue 25
Rosemary Lane 26
Russel Crescent 27

RENAULT 61 Brighton Rd ☎ 72566

HORNBY Lancs. – pop. 695 – ✉ Lancaster – ☎ 0468.
London 251 – Kendal 20 – Lancaster 8.

XX Castle, with rm, Main St. ☎ 21204 – Ⓟ
11 rm.

HORNCASTLE Lincs. 986 ㉘ – pop. 4,102 – ☎ 065 82.
i Town Hall, Boston Rd ☎ 3513.
London 140 – Lincoln 21.

Rodney, North St., LN9 5DX, ☎ 3583 – TV Ⓟ
M approx. 2.25 **st.** 🍷 1.25 – **13 rm** ☕ 5.00/9.50 **t.**

MORRIS Fulletby ☎ 065 84 (Tetford) 217
VAUXHALL Boston Rd ☎ 3566

HORNING Norfolk – pop. 975 – ✉ Norwich – ☎ 069 23.
London 123 – Great Yarmouth 17 – Norwich 11.

Petersfield House (Mt. Charlotte) 🌳, Lower St., NR12 8PF, ☎ 741, 🚗 – ⌂wc Ⓟ
M approx. 4.00 **s.** 🍷 1.60 – **12 rm** ☕ 13.75/21.00 **s.**

Red Lion

If the name of the hotel
is not in bold type,
on arrival ask the hotelier his prices.

HORNS CROSS Devon – pop. 170 – ✉ Bideford – ☎ 023 75.
Envir. : Clovelly (site**) W : 6 m.
London 237 – Barnstaple 15 – Exeter 48.

- **Hoops Inn,** EX39 5DL, ☎ 222, – P
April-September – **M** a la carte 4.35/5.00 **st.** 1.90 – **16 rm** 8.50/15.60 **st.**

HORNSEA North Humberside 986 ㉔ – pop. 7,031 – ☎ 040 12.
18 Rolston Rd ☎ 2020.
i Information Bureau, Floral Hall, Promenade ☎ 2919 (summer only).
London 194 – **Kingston-upon-Hull 14** – Scarborough 33.

- **Luigi's,** Broadway, HU18 1QA, ☎ 3101
closed Monday – **M** a la carte 2.60/5.50 1.20.

HORSFORTH West Yorks. 986 ⑧ – see Leeds.

HORSHAM West Sussex 986 ㊱ – pop. 26,446 – ☎ 0403.
18 Mannings Heath ☎ 65224, SE : 3 m. A 281.
London 39 – **Brighton 23** – Guildford 20 – Lewes 25 – Worthing 20.

- **Ye Olde King's Head,** 35 Carfax, RH12 1EG, ☎ 3126 – wc ☎ P
M a la carte 2.85/5.10 **t.** 1.20 – **16 rm** 10.00/18.50 **st.** – P 15.70/17.30 **t.**

AUSTIN-MG Plummers Plain ☎ 76244
AUSTIN Guildford Rd ☎ 61393
AUSTIN-MORRIS Springfield Rd ☎ 4311
OPEL, VAUXHALL Broadbridge Heath ☎ 61101
PEUGEOT Lyons Corner, Slinfold ☎ 0403 (Slinfold) 790766
RENAULT 108 Crawley Rd ☎ 2274
ROVER-TRIUMPH North St. ☎ 3291
VOLVO 51 North Par. ☎ 60281

HORTON Dorset – pop. 411 – ✉ Wimborne – ☎ 025 884 Witchampton.
London 110 – Bournemouth 14 – Dorchester 30 – Salisbury 22.

- Horton Inn, BH21 5AD, NW : 1 m. on B 3078 ☎ 252, – wc ☎ P – **6 rm.**

HORTON Northants. – pop. 424 – ✉ ☎ 0604 Northampton.
London 66 – Bedford 18 – Northampton 6.

- **French Partridge,** Newport Pagnell Rd, NN7 2AP, ☎ 870033 – P
closed Sunday, Monday, last 2 weeks July, first week August and Bank Holidays – **M** (dinner only) 5.50 **st.**

HORTON-CUM-STUDLEY Oxon. – pop. 432 – ✉ Oxford – ☎ 086 735 Stanton St. John.
London 57 – Aylesbury 23 – **Oxford 7.**

- **Studley Priory** , OX9 1AZ, ☎ 203, « Converted priory in park », – wc wc ☎ P.
M 3.75/4.75 1.40 – **20 rm** 9.65/26.45 **st.**

HOTON Leics. – pop. 255 – ✉ Loughborough – ☎ 0509 Wymeswold.
London 120 – **Leicester 13** – Loughborough 2,5 – **Nottingham 12.**

- **Packe Arms,** Rempstone Rd, LE12 5SJ, ☎ 880662 – P
M (buffet lunch) 3.50/5.00 **st.** 1.60.

HOUGHTON CONQUEST Beds. – see Bedford.

HOVE East Sussex 986 ㊱ – see Brighton and Hove.

HOVINGHAM North Yorks. – pop. 305 – ✉ York – ☎ 065 382.
Envir. : Castle Howard** (18C) *AC*, SE : 5 m.
London 235 – **Middlesbrough 36** – York 25.

- **Worsley Arms,** YO6 4LA, ☎ 234, – wc P
closed Christmas Day – **M** 4.50/6.50 **st.** 1.75 – **14 rm** 9.50/16.00 **st.**

HOW CAPLE Heref. and Worc. – see Ross-on-Wye.

HOWDEN North Humberside 986 ㉔ – pop. 12,651 – ☎ 0430.
See : St. Peter's Church* 12C-14C.
London 196 – **Kingston-upon-Hull 23** – **Leeds 37** – York 22.

- Bowmans, Bridgegate, ON14 7JG, ☎ 30805 – TV wc P – **13 rm.**

HOYLAKE Merseyside 986 ⑤ and ㉗ – pop. 32,277 – ☎ 051 Liverpool.
18 Carr Lane ☎ 632 2530.
London 226 – Chester 22 – **Liverpool 10.**

- Stanley, King's Gap, Wirral, L47 2AH, ☎ 632 3311 – wc P – **16 rm.**
- **Sandtoft,** 70 Alderley Rd, Wirral, L47 2BA, ☎ 632 2204
closed Christmas – **9 rm** 7.75/11.90 **st.**

HUDDERSFIELD West Yorks. 986 ⑫ and ㉓ – pop. 131,190 – ☎ 0484.

Meltham ☎ 850227, W: 5 m. – Crosland Heath ☎ 53216, W: 3 m. – Maple St., off Somerset Rd ☎ 22304.

London 191 – Bradford 11 – Leeds 15 – Manchester 25 – Sheffield 26.

Pennine President, Ainley Top, HD3 3RH, NW: 2 ½ m. at junction A 629 and M 62, exit 24 ☎ 0422 (Elland) 75431, Telex 517346 – wc. **P**.
M 2.75/3.00 **s.** 0.80 – 1.20 – **118 rm** 12.50/16.00 **s.** – P 15.00/16.50 **s.**

George (T.H.F.), St. George's Sq., HD1 1JA, ☎ 25444 – wc.
M a la carte 4.10/5.55 **st.** 1.50 – **60 rm** 10.50/20.00 **st.**

Quo Vadis, 4 St. Peter's St., HD1 1LJ, ☎ 35440, Italian rest.
closed Sunday and Bank Holidays – **M** a la carte approx. 4.00/5.60 **t.** 1.50.

at Farnley Tyas S: 5 ½ m. off A 616 – ✉ ☎ **0484 Huddersfield:**

Golden Cock, HD4 6UN, ☎ 661979 – **P**
M a la carte 3.70/6.35 **st.** 1.25.

ALFA-ROMEO, DAF, PEUGEOT Northgate ☎ 20822
AUSTIN-MG-ROVER-TRIUMPH 100 Wakefield Rd ☎ 35341
BMW Somer Rd ☎ 25435
CHRYSLER-SIMCA Viaduct St. ☎ 33401
CITROEN Scar Lane ☎ 56164
DAIMLER-JAGUAR-MORRIS-MG-WOLSELEY, ROLLS ROYCE-BENTLEY Southgate ☎ 29461
DATSUN Northgate ☎ 35251
FORD Southgate ☎ 29675
LANCIA Lockwood Rd ☎ 29344
OPEL Wakefield Rd ☎ 20566
POLSKI Savile St. ☎ 53911
RENAULT 4 Queensgate ☎ 39351
ROVER-TRIUMPH 100 Wakefield Rd ☎ 3534
SAAB Kirkheaton ☎ 29754
TOYOTA Fartown ☎ 23201
VAUXHALL 386 Leeds Rd ☎ 23191
VOLVO Northgate ☎ 31362
VW, AUDI-NSU Bradford Rd ☎ 42001

If you find you cannot take up a hotel booking you have made, please let the hotel know immediately.

HULL North Humberside 986 ㉔ – see Kingston-upon-Hull.

HUNDLETON Dyfed – pop. 541 – ✉ Pembroke – ☎ 064 681 Castle Martin.

London 254 – Carmarthen 34 – Pembroke 2.

Corston, Axton Hill, SW: 2 ¼ m. off B 4320 ☎ 242, – **P**
12 rm 3.50/7.00 **s.**

HUNGERFORD Berks. 986 ㉟ – pop. 4,083 – ☎ 048 86.

Envir.: Littlecote House* (Tudor) *AC*, NW: 3 ½ m.

Chaddleworth ☎ 574, N: 2 ½ m.

London 74 – Bristol 57 – Oxford 28 – Reading 26 – Southampton 46.

Bear, Charnham St., RG17 0EL, on A 4 ☎ 2512, – wc **P**.
M approx. 3.00 1.60 – **25 rm** 7.00/13.00.

AUSTIN-MORRIS-MG 17/19 Bridge St. ☎ 2279
BMW Bath Rd ☎ 2772
FIAT Bath Rd ☎ 2033

HUNSTANTON Norfolk 986 ㉘ – pop. 3,911 – ☎ 048 53.

Envir.: Sandringham House* (not open) and park** *AC*, S: 9 ½ m.

i Le Strange Terrace ☎ 2610.

London 120 – Cambridge 60 – Norwich 45.

Le Strange Arms, Golf Course Rd, PE36 6JJ, N: 1 m. off A 149 ☎ 2810, – wc **P**
M 3.50/4.10 **st.** 1.40 – **26 rm** 7.25/16.00 **st.** – P 12.00/12.75 **st.**

AUSTIN-MORRIS-MG-ROVER-TRIUMPH-WOLSELEY 12 Kings Lynn Rd ☎ 2828
CITROEN Southend Rd ☎ 2683
VAUXHALL ☎ 2842

HUNTINGDON Cambs. 986 ㉜ – pop. 16,557 (inc. Godmanchester) – ☎ 0480.

See: Cromwell Museum – All Saints' Church (interior*). **Envir.:** Hinchingbrooke House* (Tudor mansion-school) W: 1 m. – Ramsey (Abbey Gatehouse* 15C) NE: 11 ½ m.

High Leys, ☎ 64459, E: 5 m.

London 69 – Bedford 21 – Cambridge 16.

Old Bridge, 1 High St., PE18 6TQ, ☎ 52681 – wc **P**
closed Christmas Day – **M** a la carte 4.30/5.85 **s.** 1.80 – **26 rm** 7.50/18.00 **st.**

George (T.H.F.), George St., PE18 6AB, ☎ 53096 – wc **P**.
M a la carte 4.00/5.25 **st.** 1.50 – **21 rm** 9.00/16.50 **st.**

AUSTIN-MORRIS-MG-WOLSELEY 13 Hartford Rd ☎ 56441
BMW, PEUGEOT, VAUXHALL Brookside ☎ 52694
ROVER-TRIUMPH St. Peters Rd ☎ 53614

HURLEY-ON-THAMES Berks. – pop. 2,203 – ✉ Maidenhead – ☎ 062 882 Littlewick Green.

London 38 – Oxford 26 – Reading 12.

Ye Olde Bell with rm, High St., SL6 5LX, ☎ 4244, – wc **P**
M a la carte approx. 8.85 **t.** – 2.65 – **9 rm** 10.50/22.00 **t.**

HURST GREEN Lancs. – pop. **1,100** – ✉ Whalley – ☎ 025 486 Stonyhurst.
London 235 – Blackburn 12 – Burnley 13 – Preston 12.

Shireburn Arms, BB6 9QJ, ☎ 208, « Tastefully furnished part 18C house », – TV wc P
M *(closed Monday lunch)* a la carte 3.70/4.95 **t.** 1.50 – **8 rm** 7.00/16.00 **t.**

HUSBANDS BOSWORTH Leics. 986 ㉜ – pop. 820 – ✉ Lutterworth – ☎ 0858 Market Harborough.
London 88 – Birmingham 40 – Leicester 14 – Northampton 17.

XX **Fernie Lodge,** Berridges Lane, LE16 6LE, ☎ 880551 – P
closed Sunday, Monday, Saturday lunch and Bank Holidays – **M** 4.75/5.00 **t.**

HYTHE Kent 986 ㊱ – pop. 11,959 – ☎ 0303.
See : St. Leonard's Church (≤* from the churchyard) – Canal.
9 Princes Parade ☎ 67441.
Lydd Airport: ☎ 0679 (Lydd) 20409, SW: **13** m.
London 67 – Folkestone 4 – Hastings 33 – Maidstone 30.

Imperial, Princes Par., CT21 6AE, ☎ 67441, ≤, heated, 9, park – P.
M a la carte 4.25/6.40 **t.** 2.60 – **82 rm** 13.00/26.00 **t.** – P 18.50 **t.**

Stade Court, West Par., CT21 6DT, ☎ 68263, ≤ – wc P
M 3.60/4.50 **t.** 1.50 – **30 rm** 9.30/20.00 **t.** – P 12.00/13.55 **t.**

XX **Gambrinos,** 74 High St., CT21 5AL, ☎ 60571 – P
closed Sunday and 2 weeks January – **M** a la carte 3.40/4.75 1.10.

AUSTIN-MORRIS-MG-WOLSELEY 70/72 High St. ☎ 66131
PEUGEOT The Green ☎ 60511
SAAB 215 Seabrook Rd ☎ 38467

IBSLEY Hants. – pop. 565 (inc. Harbridge) – ✉ ☎ 042 54 Ringwood.
London 105 – Bournemouth 14 – Salisbury 14 – Winchester 33.

X **Old Beams,** BH24 3PP, on A 338 ☎ 3387, « 14C thatched cottage » – P
closed Sunday dinner – **M** approx. 3.50 **t.**

IDEN East Sussex – see Rye.

ILFRACOMBE Devon 986 ㉟ – pop. 9,859 – ☎ 0271.
See : Tors Walks*, Capstone Hill ≤*.
18 Hele Bay ☎ 62176, E: **1** m.
i The Promenade ☎ 63001.
London 223 – Exeter 54 – Taunton 61.

Harleigh House, Wilder Rd, EX34 9AE, ☎ 63850 – wc
Easter and mid May-mid October – **M** (bar lunch) 2.75/3.25 1.20 – **32 rm** 5.20/11.90.

St. Helier, Hillsborough Rd, EX34 9QQ, ☎ 63862, – P
Easter and May-October – **M** 2.50/2.80 1.40 – **35 rm** 5.00/10.00 – P 8.50/9.50.

at Berrynarbor E: 3 m. on A 399 – ✉ Ilfracombe – ☎ 027 188 Combe Martin :

XX **Old Sawmill,** ☎ 2259 – P
closed Sunday, 17 April-3 May, 9 to 24 October and 8 to 15 January – **M** (dinner only) a la carte 2.90/4.55.

at Lee W: 3 ¼ m. – ✉ ☎ 0271 Ilfracombe :

Lee Bay, ☎ 63503, ≤, heated, , park – wc P – *May-October*
53 rm.

AUSTIN Highfield Rd ☎ 62229
CHRYSLER West Down ☎ 3140

ILKLEY West Yorks. 986 ㉓ – pop. 21,849 – ☎ 094 33 (4 and 5 fig.) or 0943 (6 fig.).
18 Myddleton ☎ 3505 and 4783 – 9 High Wood ☎ 3727.
London 209 – Bradford 13 – Harrogate 17 – **Leeds 16** – Preston 46.

Craiglands (T.H.F.), Cowpasture Rd, LS29 8RQ, ☎ 607676, Telex 51137, – TV P.
M 4.00/4.75 **st.** 1.45 – **73 rm** 11.00/19.50 **st.**

Crescent (Crest), Brook St., LS29 8DG, ☎ 3534 – wc P
M (dinner only and Sunday lunch) 3.00/3.50 **s.** 1.55 – **21 rm** 9.70/14.90 **s.**

XXX ✿✿ **Box Tree Cottage,** Church St., LS29 9EH, ☎ 608484, « Tasteful decor »
closed 1 week in February, 2 weeks in June, Sunday and Monday except Christmas and 1 January – **M** (dinner only) 7.50/10.50 2.50
Spec. Terrine de trois poissons de mer (February-September), Cuisses de volaille au cidre, Noisette d'agneau Edward VII.

AUSTIN-DAIMLER-JAGUAR-ROVER-TRIUMPH, ROLLS ROYCE-BENTLEY Ben Rydding ☎ 3431
CHRYSLER-SIMCA Skipton Rd ☎ 2863
MORRIS Skipton Rd ☎ 2717
VAUXHALL Bradford Rd, Menston ☎ 0943 (Menston) 75147

ILLOGAN Cornwall – see Redruth.

ILMINSTER Somerset 986 ㉟ – pop. 3,374 – ☎ 046 05.
London 144 – Exeter 34 – Taunton 12.

- **Horton Cross Motel,** TA19 9PT, W: 1 ½ m. on A 303 ☎ 2144, – TV wc ☎ ♿ P
  M 3.50/6.00 t. 1.20 – 1.75 – **23 rm** 12.00/17.00 **st.**

AUSTIN-FIAT Station Rd ☎ 2443

IMMINGHAM South Humberside 986 ㉔ – pop. 10,259 – ☎ 0469.
Envir. : Thornton Abbey (ruins 14C) : the Gatehouse* *AC*, NW : 8 m. – Thornton Curtis (St. Lawrence's Church* : Norman and Gothic) NW : 10 m.
Shipping connections with the Continent : to Gothenburg (Tor Line).
London 181 – Grimsby 9 – Lincoln 38 – Scunthorpe 22.

- **Pelham,** Washdyke Lane, DN40 2HL, ☎ 74191 – TV wc ☎ P
  M a la carte 2.00/3.45 **st.** 1.15 – **10 rm** 9.70/15.90 **st.**

VAUXHALL Pelham Rd ☎ 2212

INGATESTONE Essex – pop. 4,823 (inc. Fryerning) – ☎ 027 75.
London 27 – Chelmsford 6.

- XXX **Heybridge Moat House,** Roman Rd, CM4 9AB, ☎ 3000, Dancing (Friday and Saturday) – P
  closed Sunday dinner – M a la carte 4.30/8.80 **t.** 1.50.

at Margaretting NE : 1 m. off A 12 – ✉ ☎ 027 76 Ingatestone :

- XXXX **Furze Hill,** CM4 0EW, ☎ 4755, « Tastefully converted Victorian house », Dancing (Friday and Saturday), heated, – P
  closed Sunday dinner and Bank Holidays – M a la carte 4.95/7.00 **t.**

INSTOW Devon – pop. 722 – ✉ Bideford – ☎ 027 186 (3 fig.) or 0271 (6 fig.).
London 228 – Barnstaple 6 – Exeter 46.

- **Commodore,** Marine Parade, EX39 4JN, ☎ 347, ≤, – TV P.
  M *(closed Christmas Day)* 3.95/4.55 1.75 – **20 rm** 12.00/19.50.

IPSWICH Suffolk 986 ㉜ – pop. 123,312 – ☎ 0473.
See : St. Margaret's Church (the roof*) – Christchurch Mansion (museum)* – Ancient House* 16C, 30 Butter Market – Pykenham House* 16C, 7 Northgate St.
18, 9 Purdis Heath ☎ 78941, E : 3 m. 18 Rushmere Heath ☎ 77109.
i Town Hall, Princes St. ☎ 55851.
London 73 – Norwich 42.

- **Post House** (T.H.F.), London Rd, IP2 0UA, SW : 2 ¼ m. on A 12 ☎ 212313, heated – TV wc ☎ P.
  M 3.40/3.80 **st.** 1.50 – 2.00 – **118 rm** 13.00/18.00 **st.**
- **Marlborough,** 73 Henley Rd, IP1 3SP, ☎ 57677, – TV wc ☎ P
  M 3.20/3.50 1.65 – **26 rm** 9.50/18.00.
- **Great White Horse** (T.H.F.), Tavern St., IP1 3AH, ☎ 56558 – wc ☎.
  M 3.75 **st.** 1.50 – **56 rm** 9.00/17.00 **s.**
- **Gables,** 17 Park Rd, IP1 3SX, ☎ 54252, – P
  12 rm 4.25/8.50 **s.**
- X **Rosie's Place,** 200 St. Helens St., IP4 2LH, ☎ 55236, Bistro
  closed Monday, Tuesday, Christmas Day, 1 week in Spring, 2 weeks in summer and 1 week in Autumn – M (dinner only) a la carte 4.00/5.05 **st.** 1.10.

at Belstead SW : 2 ½ m. – ✉ ☎ 0473 Ipswich :

- **Belstead Brook** , Belstead Rd, IP2 9HB, ☎ 216456, , park – TV wc ☎ P.
  M a la carte 5.40/9.05 – **24 rm** 13.00/18.00.

at Copdock SW : 4 m. on A 12 – ✉ Ipswich – ☎ 047 386 Copdock :

- **Copdock International** (Interchange), London Rd, IP8 3JD, ☎ 444, – TV wc ☎ P.
  closed 24 to 30 December – M 3.50/4.75 **s.** 1.35 – **47 rm** 12.50/19.50 **s.**

AUDI-NSU St. Helen St. ☎ 50545
AUSTIN-MG 935 Woodbridge Rd ☎ 76929
AUSTIN-MG-WOLSELEY Barrack Lane ☎ 54202
AUSTIN-DAIMLER-JAGUAR, ROLLS ROYCE-BENTLEY Majors Corner ☎ 52271
DAF 488 Woodbridge Rd ☎ 78465
DATSUN 176/182 Norwich Rd ☎ 53173
FIAT Burrell Rd ☎ 57845
FORD Princes St. ☎ 55401
MAZDA, POLSKI Fuchsia Lane ☎ 74535
MORRIS-MG-WOLSELEY Felixstowe Rd ☎ 75431
OPEL Burrell Rd ☎ 57845
PEUGEOT 162/166 London Rd ☎ 54461
RENAULT 301/305 Norwich Rd ☎ 43021
ROVER-TRIUMPH 88 Princes St. ☎ 214231
SAAB Dales Rd ☎ 42547
VAUXHALL St. Helens St. ☎ 56363
TOYOTA 301/5 Woodbridge Rd ☎ 76927
VW, AUDI-NSU Knightsdale Rd ☎ 43044

IRONBRIDGE Salop 986 ㉗ – see Telford.

IVER Bucks. – pop 11,207 – ✆ 0753.
London 28 – Reading 24 – Watford 17.

XX **Les Escargots,** High St., SL0 9ND, ℗ 653778, French rest.
closed Saturday lunch, Sunday and Bank Holiday Mondays – **M** a la carte 4.95/9.40 **s.** 1.80.

AUSTIN-MORRIS-MG-ROVER-TRIUMPH High St. ℗ 653463

IVER HEATH Bucks. – pop. 5,200 – ✆ 028 16 Fulmer.
London 21 – Reading 25.

Bridgettine Convent, Fulmer Common Rd, SL0 0NR, ℗ 2645, – Ⓟ
13 rm 4.00/8.00 **st.**

IVINGHOE Bucks. – pop. 945 – ✉ Leighton Buzzard – ✆ 0296 Cheddington.
9 ℗ 668881.
London 42 – Aylesbury 9 – Luton 11.

XXX King's Head (T.H.F.), Station Rd, LU7 9EB, ℗ 668388 – Ⓟ.

JAMESTON Dyfed – see Manorbier.

JEVINGTON East Sussex – see Eastbourne.

KELLING Norfolk – pop. 571 – ✉ ✆ 026 371 Holt.
London 127 – Cromer 8.5 – Norwich 25.

XX **Kelling Park** with rm, Weybourne Rd, NR25 7ER, S: 1 ½ m. ℗ 2235, « Gardens and aviary » – wc Ⓟ
Easter-mid October and weekends only in winter – **M** a la carte 3.60/5.80 1.30 – **6 rm** 7.55/15.10.

KENDAL Cumbria 986 ⑲㉓ – pop. 21,596 – ✆ 0539.
See : Abbot Hall Art Gallery (Museum of Lakeland Life and Industry★) *AC*.
Envir. : Levens Hall★ (Elizabethan) *AC* and Topiary Garden★ *AC*, SW: 5 ½ m.
18 The Heights ℗ 24079.
i Town Hall, ℗ 23649 ext 253.
London 262 – Bradford 64 – Burnley 60 – Carlisle 53 – Lancaster 21 – Leeds 71 – Middlesbrough 79 – Newcastle-upon-Tyne 94 – Preston 42 – Sunderland 89.

Woolpack (Swallow), Stricklandgate, LA9 4ND, ℗ 23852, Group Telex 53168 – TV wc wc Ⓟ
M a la carte 2.70/6.00 **st.** 1.00 – 0.75 – **53 rm.**

County (Thistle), Station Rd, LA9 6BC, ℗ 22461 – TV wc Ⓟ
31 rm.

Shenstone Country , LA8 8AA, S: 2 m. on A 6 ℗ 21023, – Ⓟ
closed 25 and 26 December – **M** (dinner only and Sunday lunch) approx. 3.00 **st.** 1.00 – **13 rm** 6.75/13.50 **st.**

at Meal Bank NE: 2 m. off A 685 – ✉ ✆ 0539 Kendal:

High Laverock House , LA8 9DJ, ℗ 23082, – wc Ⓟ
M (bar lunch) a la carte 3.50/5.15 **t.** 1.20 – **8 rm** 9.00/16.00 **t.**

ALFA-ROMEO, MERCEDES-BENZ, VAUXHALL Ings ℗ 0539 (Staveley) 442
AUSTIN-MG-WOLSELEY Sandes Av. ℗ 21695
DAIMLER-JAGUAR-MORRIS-MG-ROVER-TRIUMPH, ROLLS ROYCE 84/92 Highgate ℗ 23610
DATSUN, VAUXHALL Sandes Av. ℗ 24420
FIAT 113 Stricklandgate ℗ 20967
FORD Kendal ℗ 23534
PEUGEOT Mint Close, Industrial Estate ℗ 24396
VW, AUDI-NSU Longpool ℗ 24331
VW, AUDI-NSU, PORSCHE Longpool ℗ 24331

KENILWORTH Warw. 986 ⑫ and ㉛ – pop. 20,098 – ✆ 0926.
See : Castle★ (12C) *AC*.
18 Crew Lane ℗ 54296.
i 11 Smalley Pl. ℗ 52595.
London 102 – Birmingham 19 – Coventry 5 – Warwick 5.

De Montfort (De Vere), The Square, CV8 1ED, ℗ 55944 – TV Ⓟ.
M approx. 4.50 **st.** 1.45 – **99 rm** 16.00/26.00 **st.**

Queen and Castle, Castle Hill, CV8 1ND, ℗ 54153 – Ⓟ
8 rm.

Clarendon House, 6-8 High St., CV8 1LZ, ℗ 54694 – Ⓟ
closed 26 December and 1 January – **M** a la carte 3.50/4.20 **s.** – **12 rm** 6.50/8.50 **s.**

XX ✿ **Bosquet,** 97a Warwick Rd, CV8 1HP, ℗ 52463
closed Sunday, Monday, 1 week Christmas, 1 week Easter, first 3 weeks August and Bank Holidays – **M** (dinner only) a la carte 5.40/7.40 **t.** 1.35
Spec. Soufflé de merlan Bosquet, Filet de bœuf lardé Philomène, Crêpe aux fraises.

JAGUAR-ROVER-TRIUMPH Whitemoor Rd ℗ 58443
LANCIA Station Rd ℗ 53073

KENNFORD Devon – see Exeter.

KENNINGTON Kent – see Ashford.

KENTS BANK Cumbria – see Grange-over-Sands.

KERESLEY West Midlands – see Coventry.

KESWICK Cumbria 986 ⑲ – pop. 5,183 – ☎ 0596.

See : Derwent Water**. **Envir. :** Castlerigg (stone circle) ☼* E: 2 m. **Exc. :** Langdale Valley** S: 19 m.

i The Moot Hall, Market Sq. ☎ 72645 (summer only) – Council Offices, 50 Main St. ☎ 72645 (winter only).

London 292 – Carlisle 31 – Kendal 30.

- **Keswick** (T.H.F.) ⛺, Station St., CA12 4NQ, ☎ 72020, Telex 64200, ⛺ – 🛗 ⛺ Ⓟ
  M a la carte 4.20/6.30 **st.** 🛈 1.60 – **72 rm** ⛺ 9.00/22.00 **st.** – P 16.50/20.00 **st.**
- **Royal Oak** (T.H.F.), Station St., CA12 5HH, ☎ 72965 – 🛗 TV ⛺wc ☎ Ⓟ. ⛺
  M a la carte 4.05/5.50 **st.** 🛈 1.50 – **66 rm** ⛺ 8.00/17.50 **st.** – P 13.00/17.50 **st.**
- **Skiddaw,** 29-31 Main St., CA12 5BN, ☎ 72071 – 🛗 TV ⛺wc Ⓟ
  M 4.00/4.50 **s.** – **49 rm** ⛺ 7.30/20.60 **s.** – P 10.00/12.00 **s.**
- **Millfield,** Penrith Rd, CA12 4HB, ☎ 72099, ⛺ – 🛗 ⛺wc ⛺
  closed February – **M** (bar lunch) approx. 3.50 🛈 1.00 – **24 rm** ⛺ 8.30/15.80.
- **Lairbeck** ⛺, Vicarage Hill, CA12 5QB, ☎ 73373, ⛺ – ⛺wc Ⓟ
  M (bar lunch) 3.25/4.00 **t.** 🛈 2.35 – **14 rm** ⛺ 6.75/13.50 **t.** – P 10.90/14.50 **t.**
- **Lyzzick Hall** ⛺, Under Skiddaw, CA12 4PY, NW: 2 ½ m. on A 591 ☎ 72277, ⛺ heated, ⛺ – ⛺ Ⓟ
  March-November – **18 rm** ⛺ 6.25/14.50 **s.**
- **Gale** ⛺, Under Skiddaw, CA12 4PL, NW: 1 ¾ m. off A 591 on Ormathwaite Rd ☎ 72413, ≤ Derwent Valley and countryside, ⛺ – Ⓟ
  March-November – **13 rm** ⛺ 6.50/9.00 **st.**
- **Cumbria,** 1 Derwentwater Pl., CA12 4DR, ☎ 73171 – Ⓟ
  April-October – **9 rm** ⛺ 5.00/10.00 **st.**
- **Walpole,** 35 Station Rd, CA12 4NA, ☎ 72072 – ⛺wc
  18 rm ⛺ 4.90/11.35 **st.**
- Highfield, The Heads, CA12 5ER, ☎ 72508, ≤
  season – **11 rm.**

at Borrowdale S : 3 ¼ m. on B 5289 – ✉ Keswick – ☎ 059 684 Borrowdale:

- **Lodore Swiss** ⛺, CA12 5UX, ☎ 285, Telex 64305, ≤ mountains and lake, ⛺, ⛺, ⛺ heated, ⛺, park – 🛗 TV ⛺ Ⓟ
  16 March-6 November – **M** a la carte 5.40/7.70 **st.** 🛈 1.90 – **72 rm** ⛺ 15.50/31.00 **st.** – P 20.00 **st.**
- Borrowdale, CA12 5UV, ☎ 224, ⛺ – ⛺wc ⛺wc Ⓟ
  M (bar lunch) – **37 rm.**
- **Leathes Head House** ⛺, CA12 5UY, ☎ 247, ≤, ⛺ – ⛺wc Ⓟ
  Easter-early November – **M** (bar lunch) approx. 5.50 **st.** 🛈 1.90 – **12 rm** ⛺ 10.00/21.40 **st.**
- **Mary Mount** ⛺, CA12 5UU, ☎ 223, ≤ lake and hills, « Country house atmosphere », ⛺, park – ⛺wc ☎ Ⓟ
  M (bar lunch) approx. 4.40 **t.** 🛈 1.90 – **9 rm** ⛺ 9.80/19.60 **t.**

at Grange-in-Borrowdale S : 4 ¾ m. off B 5289 – ✉ Keswick – ☎ 059 684 Borrowdale:

- **Borrowdale Gates** ⛺, CA12 5UQ, ☎ 204, ≤, ⛺ – ⛺wc Ⓟ
  April-October – **M** (buffet lunch) approx. 3.90 **st.** 🛈 1.70 – **12 rm** ⛺ 8.00/17.70 **s.** – P 11.00 **s.**

at Rosthwaite S : 6 m. by B 5289 – ✉ Keswick – ☎ 059 684 Borrowdale:

- Scafell ⛺, CA12 5XB, ☎ 208, ≤, ⛺ – ⛺wc Ⓟ
  season – **23 rm.**
- **Royal Oak,** CA12 5XB, ☎ 214 – ⛺wc ♿ Ⓟ
  closed 1 to 27 December – **12 rm** ⛺ 7.00/13.00 **t.**

at Braithwaite W : 2 m. on B 5292 off A 594 – ✉ Keswick – ☎ 059 682 Braithwaite:

- **Ivy House** ⛺, CA12 5SY, ☎ 338, « Country house atmosphere », ⛺ – ⛺wc Ⓟ
  Easter-November – **M** (dinner only) 8.00 🛈 1.50 – **12 rm** ⛺ (dinner included) 14.00/32.00.
- **Middle Ruddings,** CA12 5RY, on A 66 ☎ 436, ⛺ – ⛺wc Ⓟ
  closed mid January-mid February – **M** approx. 3.25 🛈 1.00 – **13 rm** ⛺ 6.30/14.40.

CHRYSLER Keswick ☎ 72606
FIAT, VOLVO Lake Rd ☎ 72064
ROVER-TRIUMPH High Hill ☎ 72768

KETTERING Northants. 986 ㉜ – pop. 42,668 – ☎ 0536.
i Public Library, Sheep St. ☎ 82143 and 85211.
London 84 – Bedford 25 – Leicester 26 – Northampton 14 – Stamford 22.

- **George,** Sheep St., NN16 0AN, ☎ 2705 – wc Ⓟ.
  M approx. 3.00 **s.** – **50 rm** 7.40/12.95 **s.**

DAF, VOLVO Stamford St. ☎ 053 687 (Wadcroft) 3351
FIAT Britannia Rd ☎ 3098
JENSEN, TVR 28-30 Queensberry Rd ☎ 3351
LANCIA Northampton Rd ☎ 790224
PEUGEOT 6 Station Rd ☎ 873491
RELIANT Ebenezer Pl. ☎ 2196
RENAULT Windmill Av. ☎ 2392
TOYOTA Britannia Rd ☎ 3571
VAUXHALL London Rd ☎ 85371

KETTLEWELL North Yorks. – pop. 333 (inc. Starbotton) – ✉ Skipton – ☎ 075 676.
London 231 – Bradford 33 – Leeds 40.

- **Race-Horses,** Town Foot, BD23 5QZ, ☎ 233, – wc Ⓟ
  closed 2 weeks early November – **M** 6.00/7.50 **st.** 1.25 – **16 rm** 11.50/25.00 **st.** – P 20.75 **st.**

KEYNSHAM Avon 986 ㉟ – pop. 19,018 – ✉ Bristol – ☎ 027 56.
18 Manor Rd, Saltford ☎ 022 17 (Saltford) 3220, SE : 2 m.
London 127 – Bath 8 – Bristol 4.

- **Grange,** 42 Bath Rd, BS18 1SD, on B 3116 ☎ 2130 – wc Ⓟ
  M (dinner only) 2.70/3.00 **st.** 1.50 – **35 rm** 8.00/14.00 **st.** – P 12.50/14.00 **st.**
- **Uplands Farmhouse,** Wellsway, BS18 2SY, S : 1 ¼ m. on B 3116 ☎ 5764, – Ⓟ
  8 rm 5.50/9.00.

CHRYSLER-SIMCA 20 Bath Rd ☎ 2908

KEYSTON Cambs. – pop. 259 (inc. Bythorn) – ✉ Huntingdon – ☎ 080 14 Bythorn.
London 75 – Cambridge 29 – Northampton 24.

- **Pheasant Inn,** Village Loop Rd, PE18 0RE, ☎ 241 – Ⓟ
  closed 25 and 26 December – **M** a la carte 3.90/5.45 **s.**

KIDDERMINSTER Heref. and Worc. 986 ㉛ – pop. 47,326 – ☎ 0562.
London 139 – Birmingham 17 – Shrewsbury 34 – Worcester 15.

- **Gainsborough House,** Bewdley Hill, DY11 6BS, ☎ 64041, – TV wc Ⓟ.
  M (buffet lunch) 4.10/4.50 **st.** 2.00 – **40 rm** 12.50/18.70 **st.** – P 20.50/25.00 **st.**

at Stone SE : 2 ½ m. on A 448 – ✉ Kidderminster – ☎ 056 283 Chaddesley Corbett :

- **Stone Manor** with rm, DY10 4PJ, ☎ 555, ≤, heated, park – TV wc Ⓟ
  M a la carte 3.50/5.50 1.65 – **6 rm** 12.00/17.00 **st.**

ALFA-ROMEO, TOYOTA Mill St. ☎ 3708
AUSTIN-MG-WOLSELEY George St. ☎ 2255
BMW Mustow Green ☎ 056 283 (Chaddesley Corbett) 435
DATSUN Stourport Rd ☎ 63024
FIAT, LANCIA Stourport Rd ☎ 68211
FORD Worcester Rd ☎ 62661
JAGUAR-ROVER-TRIUMPH Worcester Rd ☎ 5056
MORRIS-MG-WOLSELEY Worcester Rd ☎ 3626
VAUXHALL Worcester Rd ☎ 2202
VOLVO Worcester Rd ☎ 65411

KIDWELLY Dyfed 986 ㉛ – pop. 3,084.
See : Castle** (12C) *AC.*
London 215 – Carmarthen 10 – Swansea 20.

Hotels see : Carmarthen N : 10 m.
Llanelli SE : 9 m.

KINGHAM Oxon. – pop. 831 – ☎ 060 871.
London 81 – Gloucester 32 – Oxford 25.

- **Mill** , OX7 6UH, ☎ 255, – Ⓟ
  M approx. 3.50 **t.** 1.30 – **11 rm** 7.50/14.50 **t.**
- **Langston Arms,** OX7 6UP, on B 4450 ☎ 319, – TV wc Ⓟ
  M 3.00/5.50 **t.** 1.25 – **8 rm** 6.50/13.00 **t.**

KINGSBRIDGE Devon 986 ㊴ – pop. 3,545 – ☎ 0548.
Bigbury ☎ 054 881 (Bigbury-on-Sea) 207, W: 7 ½ m.
The Quay ☎ 3195 (summer only).
London 236 – Exeter 36 – Plymouth 20 – Torquay 21.

Crabshell Motor Inn. Embankment Rd, TQ7 1JZ, ☎ 3301, ≤ – TV wc P
M a la carte approx. 4.00 **st.** 1.30 – 1.50 – **30 rm** 11.50/13.50 **s.**

Kingsbridge Motel without rest, The Quay, TQ7 1HN, ☎ 2540 – TV wc P
closed 20 December-8 January – 1.25 – **19 rm** 7.50/11.00 **s.**

Harbour Lights, 13 Ebrington St., TQ7 1DE, ☎ 2418
Easter-October – **M** (dinner only) 4.25 1.20 – **6 rm** 10.50/13.00.

Old Brewhouse, Union Rd, TQ7 1EF, ☎ 3232 – P.

at Goveton NE: 2 m. off A 381 – ✉ ☎ 0548 Kingsbridge:

Buckland-Tout-Saints (Interchange), TQ7 2DS, ☎ 2586, ≤, « Queen Anne mansion in well kept gardens », park – wc wc P
April-October – **M** 5.00/6.50 1.35 – **17 rm** (dinner included) 16.15/29.70.

at Chillington SE: 5 m. by A 379 – ✉ ☎ 0548 Kingsbridge:

Oddicombe House, TQ7 2JD, ☎ 234, ≤, – P
Easter-October – **M** 3.90/4.50 1.50 – **8 rm** 9.00/20.00.

at Thurlestone W: 4 m. off A 381 – ✉ Kingsbridge – ☎ 054 857 Thurlestone:

Thurlestone (Interchange), TQ7 3NN, ☎ 382, ≤, « Attractive park », heated, – wc P.
M 4.00/5.00 **t.** 2.00 – **77 rm** 10.50/22.50 – P 18.00/22.00.

MORRIS-MG-ROVER-TRIUMPH-WOLSELEY The Quay ☎ 2323
RENAULT Aveton Gifford ☎ 054 855 (Loddiswell) 248
VAUXHALL Embankment Rd ☎ 2140

KINGSGATE Kent – see Broadstairs.

KING'S HEATH West Midlands – see Birmingham.

KING'S LYNN Norfolk 986 ㉘ – pop. 30,107 – ☎ 0553.
See: St. Margaret's Church* (17C, chancel 13C) – St. Nicholas' Chapel* (Gothic). **Envir.:** Sandringham House* (not open) and park** *AC,* NE: 6 m. – Long Sutton (St. Mary's Church*: Gothic) W: 12 m.
King's Lynn Museum, Old Market St., ☎ 5001.
London 105 – Cambridge 45 – Leicester 75 – Norwich 44.

Duke's Head (T.H.F.), Tuesday Market Pl., PE30 1JS, ☎ 4996, Telex 817349 – TV P.
M a la carte 4.80/6.70 **st.** 1.50 – 2.00 – **72 rm** 13.00/20.00 **st.**

AUSTIN Gayton ☎ 055 386 (Gayton) 204
AUSTIN-DAIMLER-JAGUAR-MORRIS-MG-ROVER-TRIUMPH, ROLLS ROYCE-BENTLEY Church St. and 24 St. James St. ☎ 63133
CHRYSLER-SIMCA Lynn Rd, Heacham ☎ 0485 (Heacham) 70243
CHRYSLER-SIMCA, CITROEN Kings Lynn ☎ 4281
FIAT, LANCIA St. Germans ☎ 055 385 (St. Germans) 296
FORD South Gates ☎ 3444
OPEL Valingers Rd ☎ 23500
RENAULT Hardwick Rd ☎ 2644
TOYOTA, LOTUS Tottenhill ☎ 055 381 (Watlington) 306
VAUXHALL North St. ☎ 3861
VW, AUDI-NSU 123/5 Wootton Rd ☎ 672875

KINGSTEIGNTON Devon – pop. 5,757 – ✉ ☎ 0626 Newton Abbot.
London 214 – Exeter 14 – Plymouth 33 – Torquay 9.

Old Rydon Inn, Rydon Rd, TQ12 3QG, ☎ 4626, – P
closed Monday and 3 weeks January – **M** a la carte 7.50/11.50 **t.** 1.90.

KINGSTON-UPON-HULL North Humberside 986 ㉔ – pop. 285,970 – ☎ 0482 Hull.
Envir.: Beverley (Minster** 13C-15C, St. Mary's Church* 14C-15C) NW: 8 ½ m. by A 1079 Z – Burton Constable Hall* (16C) *AC,* NE: 8 m. by A 165 Z.
Kirk Ella ☎ 658919, W: 5 m. by A 164 Z – Willerby Rd ☎ 656309, W: by Spring Bank West Z – Salthouse Rd ☎ 74242, E: 3 m. Z.
Shipping connections with the Continent: to Rotterdam: Europoort, Zeebrugge (North Sea Ferries).
Central Library, Albion St. ☎ 223344 – King George Dock ☎ 702118.
London 180 – Leeds 60 – Nottingham 87 – Sheffield 68.

Plan on next page

Royal Station (B.T.H.), 170 Ferensway, HU1 3UF, ☎ 25087, Telex 52450 – TV P. Y a
M a la carte 6.30/13.75 **st.** 1.30 – **100 rm** 11.55/28.10 **st.**

Hull Centre (Centre), Paragon St., HU1 3PJ, ☎ 26462, Telex 52431 – TV wc Y e
M approx. 2.95 **s.** 1.25 – 1.50 – **125 rm** 10.75/14.50 **s.**

KINGSTON-UPON-HULL

Street	Grid	No.
Carr Lane	Y	
George Street	X	
Jameson Street	XY	
King Edward Street	Y	19
Paragon Street	Y	29
Prospect Street	X	
Whitefriargate	Y	49
Albion Street	X	2
Bond Street	X	3
Cannon Street	X	4
Caroline Street	X	6
Chapman Street	X	7
Commercial Road	Y	8
Dock Office Row	X	10
Dock Street	X	12
Great Union Street	X	13
Grimston Street	X	15
Humber Dock Street	Y	16
Jarrat Street	X	17
Lockwood Street	X	21
Lowgate	Y	23
Market Place	Y	24
Maybury Road	Z	25
Mytongate	Y	27
Prince's Avenue	Z	31
Prince's Dock Street	Y	32
Queen's Road	Z	33
Queen's Street	Y	35
Queen's Dock Avenue	X	36
Reform Street	X	37
St. Luke's Street	Y	39
St. Mark's Street	X	40
Scott Street	X	42
Southcoates Avenue	Z	43
Southcoates Lane	Z	44
Waterhouse Lane	Y	48
Wilberforce Drive	X	50
Worship Street	X	52

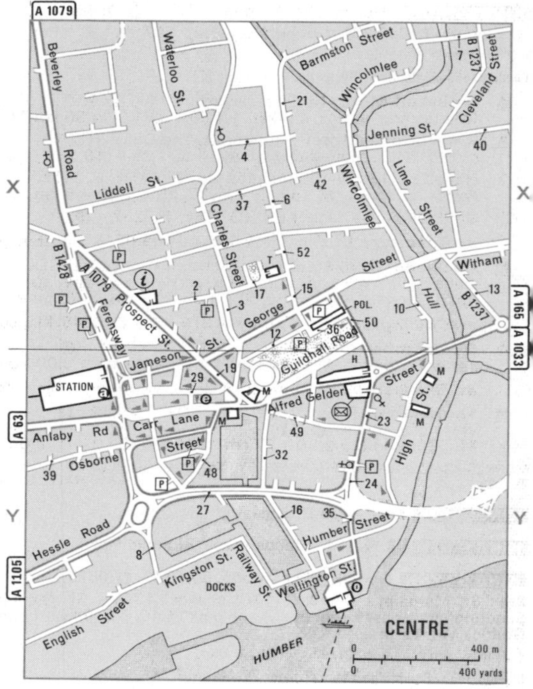

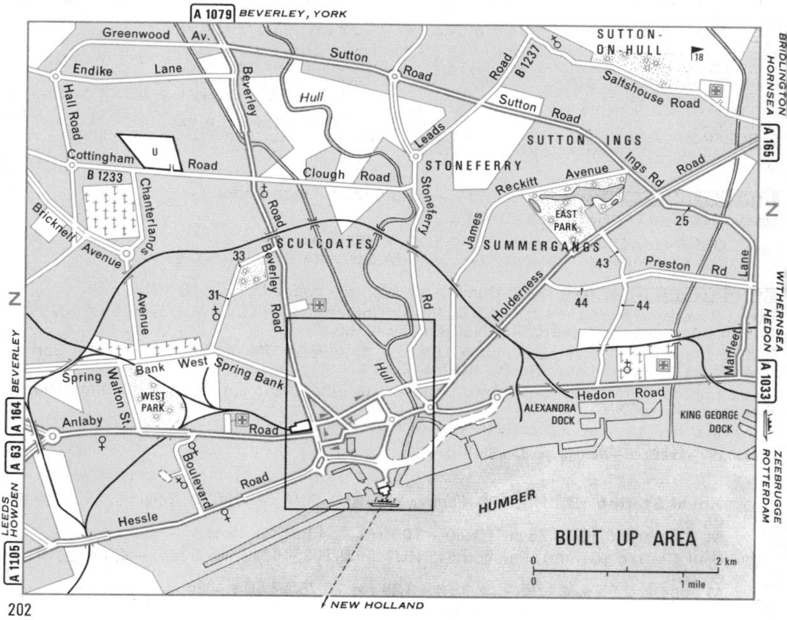

A 1079 BEVERLEY, YORK

BRIDLINGTON HORNSEA

WITHERNSEA HEDON

ZEEBRUGGE ROTTERDAM

LEEDS HOWDEN BEVERLEY

NEW HOLLAND

BUILT UP AREA

0 2 km

0 1 mile

XXX **Cerutti's,** 10 Nelson St., HU1 1XE, ☎ 28501, Seafood Y o
closed Saturday lunch, Sunday and Bank Holidays – **M** a la carte 4.55/8.25 **t.** 🍷 1.90.

at Willerby NW: **5 m.** off **A 164** by **A 63** – Z – ✉ Willerby – ☎ **0482 Hull:**

Willerby Manor, Well Lane, HU10 6ER, ☎ 652616, park – TV wc ☎ **P.**
M a la carte 4.85/6.60 **st.** 🍷 1.15 – **37 rm** 8.85/15.60 **st.**

at North Ferriby W: **7 m.** on **A 63** – Z – ✉ Kingston-upon-Hull – ☎ **0482 Hull:**

Hull Crest Motel (Crest), Ferriby High Rd, HU14 3LG, ☎ 645212, Telex 52558 – TV wc ☎ **P**
M a la carte 3.35/5.50 **s.** 🍷 1.55 – 1.60 – **54 rm** 10.95/15.50 **s.**

MICHELIN Branch, Springfield Way, Anlaby, Hull, HU10 6RJ, ☎ 561191.

AUDI-NSU, MERCEDES-BENZ 169 George St. ☎ 20370
AUSTIN-MORRIS-MG-WOLSELEY 561 Holderness Rd ☎ 76233
AUSTIN-MG-WOLSELEY 132 Anlaby Rd ☎ 24373
BMW, PEUGEOT 54 Anlaby Rd ☎ 25071
CHRYSLER-SIMCA Anlaby Rd ☎ 23631
DAF 61 Boothferry Rd ☎ 52078
DATSUN Witham ☎ 24131
FIAT 96 Boothferry Rd ☎ 506976
FORD 182/198 Kingston Rd ☎ 657136
FORD 172 Anlaby Rd ☎ 25732
MORRIS-MG-WOLSELEY 386 Beverley Rd ☎ 42337
MORRIS-MG-WOLSELEY Clough Rd ☎ 42154
MORRIS-MG-WOLSELEY 13/17 Boothferry Rd ☎ 506911
RENAULT Holderness High Rd ☎ 74436
TOYOTA Clarence St. ☎ 20039
VAUXHALL 230/6 Anlaby Rd ☎ 23681
VOLVO Hessle Rd ☎ 52010
VW, AUDI-NSU 1/13 Boothferry Rd ☎ 649124

*Die **Michelin-Karte** 1 : 1.000.000 hilft Ihnen, große Strecken schnell zurückzulegen.*

KINGSTOWN Cumbria – see Carlisle.

KINGSWEAR Devon – see Dartmouth.

KINGSWINFORD West Midlands 986 ⑫ – pop. **14,065** (inc. Wallheath) – ☎ 038 44 (4 and 5 fig.) or 0384 (6 fig.).
London 134 – **Birmingham 14** – Stafford 22 – Worcester 32.

Summerhill House (Ansells), Swindon Rd, DY6 9XA, ☎ 5254, – wc **P.**
M *(closed Saturday lunch and Sunday dinner)* 3.85/4.60 **st.** 🍷 1.80 – **10 rm** 10.60/14.15 **st.**

AUSTIN-MORRIS 45 Dudley Rd ☎ 4231

KINGTON Heref. and Worc. 986 ㉛ – pop. **2,000** – ☎ **054 43.**
18 ☎ 340, N: **1** m.
i 2 Mill St. ☎ 202.
London 152 – Brecon 29 – Hereford 19 – Leominster 14.

Oxford Arms, Duke St., HR5 3DR, ☎ 322 – wc **P**
M (grill rest.) a la carte 2.30/4.00 – **10 rm** 5.50/11.75.

X **Penrhos Court,** Lyonshall, HR5 3LN, E: 1 ½ m. on A 44 ☎ 720 – **P**
April-December – **M** *(closed Monday)* (dinner only) approx. 5.00 **t.** 🍷 1.35.

KINTBURY Berks. – pop. **2,060** – ✉ Newbury – ☎ **048 85.**
London 73 – Newbury 6 – Reading 23.

XX **Dundas Arms** with rm, RG15 0UT, ☎ 263, ←, – wc **P**
closed Sunday, Monday, Christmas and Bank Holidays – **M** (dinner only) 6.20/7.50 **t.** 🍷 2.00 – **6 rm** 10.50/15.00 **t.**

KINVER West Midlands – see Stourbridge.

KIRBY CROSS Essex – see Frinton-on-Sea.

KIRKBY Merseyside – pop. **59,918** – ☎ **051 Liverpool.**
Envir. : Knowsley Safari Park** *AC*, SE : 4 m.
18 Ingoe Lane.
i Municipal Buildings ☎ 548 6555.
London 213 – **Liverpool 6.**

Golden Eagle (Embassy), Cherryfield Drive, L32 8SB, ☎ 546 4355 – TV wc ☎ **P**
closed Christmas – **M** approx. 2.70 **st.** 🍷 1.50 – **79 rm** 10.50/15.00 **st.**

KIRKBY LONSDALE Cumbria 986 ㉓ – pop. **1,506** – ✉ Carnforth – ☎ **0468.**
9 Casterton Rd ☎ **71796, 1** m. on Sedbergh Rd.
i The Art Store ☎ 71603.
London 259 – **Carlisle 62** – Kendal 13 – Lancaster 17 – **Leeds 58.**

Royal, 2 Main St., LA6 2AE, ☎ 71217, – wc **P**
M approx. 3.10 🍷 1.40 – **22 rm** 7.50/17.00 – P 11.95.

KIRKBY STEPHEN Cumbria 986 ⑲ – pop. **1,539** – ☎ 0930.

Envir.: Brough (Castle ruins 12C-14C : keep ※* *AC*) N : 4 m.

London 284 – Carlisle 52 – Kendal 24.

- **King's Arms,** Market St., CA17 4QN, ☎ 71378, – Ⓟ
  M 4.50/5.00 **t.** – **11 rm** 8.50/17.00 **t.**

KISLINGBURY Northants. – pop. **1,046** – ✉ ☎ 0604 Northampton.

London 75 – Coventry 33 – Northampton 4.

- **Cromwell Cottage,** NN7 4AG, ☎ 830288 – Ⓟ
  closed Sunday – **M** a la carte approx. 4.00 **t.** 1.20.

KNARESBOROUGH North Yorks. 986 ㉓ – pop. **11,878** – ☎ 0423.

18 Boroughbridge Rd ☎ 3219, N : 1 ¼ m.

i Market Place (summer only).

London 217 – Bradford 21 – Harrogate 3 – **Leeds 18** – York 18.

- **Dower House,** Bond End, HG5 9AL, ☎ 863302 , – wc wc Ⓟ
  M approx. 4.25 **t.** 2.00 – **18 rm** 7.50/18.50 **s.**

FORD York Place ☎ 2291 OPEL-VAUXHALL Bond End ☎ 21919

KNIGHTON Powys 986 ㉛ – pop. **208** – ☎ 054 72 (3 fig.) or 0547 (4 fig.).

9 The Frydd, S : ½ m.

i Offa's Dyke Association, The Old Primary School ☎ 753 (Easter-September).

London 165 – Aberystwyth 57 – **Birmingham 56** – Shrewsbury 33.

- **Norton Arms,** Broad St., LD7 1BT, ☎ 321, – wc Ⓟ.
  M approx. 3.25 **s.** – 1.50 – **11 rm** 5.50/13.00 **s.**

AUSTIN-JAGUAR-MORRIS-MG-ROVER-TRIUMPH, FORD ☎ 645

KNIGHTWICK Heref. and Worc. – pop. **114** – ✉ Worcester – ☎ 088 62.

London 132 – Hereford 20 – Leominster 18 – Worcester 8.

- **Talbot,** ☎ 235, – Ⓟ
  M (bar lunch) a la carte 2.75/4.35 1.20 – **7 rm** 5.50/12.00 **s.**

KNOWLE West Midlands – pop. **7,676** – ✉ Solihull – ☎ 056 45.

London 108 – **Birmingham 9** – **Coventry 10** – Warwick 11.

- **Greswolde Arms** (Ansells), 1657 High St., B93 0LP, ☎ 2711 – wc Ⓟ
  M (grill rest.) 2.50/5.00 **st.** 1.70 – **19 rm** 9.65/14.70 **st.**
- **Florentine,** 15 Kenilworth Rd, B93 0JB, ☎ 6449, Italian rest.
  closed Sunday, Monday lunch and Bank Holidays – **M** a la carte 3.80/5.80 **s.** 0.80.

AUSTIN-MG-ROVER-TRIUMPH Grange Rd, Dorridge ☎ 6131 MORRIS-MG-WOLSELEY Station Rd ☎ 4221

KNOWL HILL Berks. – pop. **495** – ✉ Twyford – ☎ 062 882 Littlewick Green.

London 38 – Maidenhead 5 – Reading 8.

- **Bird in Hand,** Bath Rd, RG10 9UP, ☎ 2781, – Ⓟ
  closed Christmas Day dinner – **M** a la carte 5.50/6.60 **t.** 1.65.

KNOWSLEY Merseyside – see Liverpool.

KNUTSFORD Cheshire 986 ⑤ and ㉗ – pop. **13,776** – ☎ 0565.

Envir. : Tatton Hall* (Georgian) and gardens** *AC*, N : 2 m. – Jodrell Bank (Concourse building-radiotelescope *AC*) SE : 8 ½ m.

i Council Offices, Toft Rd ☎ 2611.

London 187 – Chester 25 – **Liverpool 33** – **Manchester 18** – **Stoke-on-Trent 30.**

- **Royal George,** King St., WA16 6EE, ☎ 4151 – TV wc Ⓟ.
  M a la carte 4.90/6.10 2.00 – 1.00 – **24 rm** 10.75/18.00 **st.**
- **Longview,** 55 Manchester Rd, WA16 0LX, ☎ 2119 – Ⓟ
  10 rm 5.15/9.95 **st.**
- **La Belle Epoque** with rm, 60 King St., WA16 6DT, ☎ 3060, « Art nouveau »,
  M *(closed Sunday and Bank Holidays)* (dinner only) a la carte 4.75/6.45 1.40 – **5 rm** 7.75/11.75 **t.**
- **David's Place,** 10 Princess St., WA16 6DD, ☎ 3356
  closed Sunday dinner and Monday – **M** a la carte 5.45/7.90 1.50.

at Lower Peover S : 3 m. by A 50 on B 5081 – ✉ Knutsford – ☎ 056 581 Lower Peover :

- **Bells of Peover,** ☎ 2269, « Attractive gardens » – Ⓟ
  closed Monday – **M** a la carte 5.65/6.85 **t.** 1.80.

at Bucklow Hill NW: 3 ½ m. junction **A 556 and A 5034** – ⊠ Knutsford – 0565 Bucklow Hill :

Swan, Chester Rd, WA16 6RD, 830295, Telex 666911 – wc wc **M** a la carte 2.75/5.00 **st.** 1.95 – **48 rm** 13.50/16.00 **st.**

ALFA-ROMEO London Rd, Allostock 056 581 (Lower Peover) 2899
FORD Garden Rd 4141
MORRIS-MG-WOLSELEY Bucklow Hill 830041
RENAULT Toft Rd 4294

LACOCK Wilts. – pop. **1,318** – ⊠ Chippenham – **024 973.**

See : Lacock Abbey* (16C) *AC.*

London 109 – Bath 16 – **Bristol 30** – Chippenham 3.

Sign of the Angel, 6 Church St., SN15 2LB, 230, *closed 23 to 31 December* – **M** *(closed Saturday lunch and Sunday dinner)* 5.00/6.00 **s.** 1.30 – **7 rm** 12.00/16.00 – P 15.00/17.00.

LAKE SIDE Cumbria – see Newby Bridge.

LAKE VYRNWY Powys 986 ㉗ – pop. **324** – ⊠ Oswestry (Salop) – **069 173** Llanwddyn.

London 204 – Chester 52 – Llanfyllin 10 – Shrewsbury 40.

Lake Vyrnwy , SY10 0LY, 244, lake Vyrnwy, , , , park – wc *closed 15 January-28 February* – **M** 3.00/3.50 **st.** 1.00 – **30 rm** 7.00/16 00 **st.**

Valid for late 1977 the prices shown may be revised if the cost of living changes to any great extent. In any event they should be considered as basic.

LAMBERHURST Kent – pop. **1,297** – ⊠ Royal Tunbridge Wells – **089 278.**

Envir. : Scotney Castle gardens (trees*, Bastion view*) *AC,* SE: **1** m.

London 43 – Hastings 21 – Maidstone 17.

George and Dragon with rm, TN3 8QD, 605, – **M** *(closed dinner 24 December)* a la carte 3.20/6.65 **t.** 1.40 – **3 rm** 7.00/9.50 **t.**

LAMBTON Tyne and Wear – pop. **480.**

See : Lambton Lion Park** *AC.*

London 274 – **Newcastle-upon-Tyne 10** – Sunderland 8.

Hotels and restaurant see : Chester-le-Street SW: 2 m.
Gateshead NW: 7 ½ m.

LAMORNA COVE Cornwall – ⊠ Penzance.

Envir. : Land's End** W: **7** ½ m.

London 323 – Penzance 5 – Truro 31.

Lamorna Cove , TR19 6XH, 073 673 (Mousehole) 411, , heated, – wc wc **M** (bar lunch) a la carte 4.50/5.60 **t.** 2.00 – **21 rm** 11.00/22.50 **t.** – P 17.50/20.55 **t.**

Menwinnion , TR19 6BJ, W : 1 m. off B 3315, 073 672 (St. Buryan) 233, « Country house atmosphere », – wc *mid February-October and Christmas* – **M** (by arrangement only) 3.75/4.00 0.95 – **8 rm** 6.50/14.50.

LAMPETER Dyfed 986 ㉛ – pop. **2,189** – **0570.**

18 422793.

London 223 – Brecon 41 – Carmarthen 22 – **Swansea 50.**

Black Lion Royal, High St., SA48 7JP, 422172 – wc **M** a la carte 2.95/4.95 1.70 – **15 rm** 7.50/16.00 **t.**

AUSTIN-MORRIS-MG Cwmann 366

LANCASTER Lancs. 986 ㉓ – pop. **49,584** – **0524.**

18 Ashton Hall 0524 (Galgate) 751247, S: 3 m. on A 588.

i 7 Dalton Sq. 2878.

London 243 – **Blackpool 26** – Bradford 62 – Burnley 41 – **Leeds 69** – **Middlesbrough 96** – Preston 22.

Portofino, 23 Castle Hill, LA1 1YN, 2388 *closed Sunday and Bank Holidays* – **M** a la carte 3.60/5.00 **t.** 1.25.

AUSTIN-DAIMLER-JAGUAR-MG-WOLSELEY 110 Penny St. 2233
CHRYSLER-SIMCA Bulk Rd 63373
FORD Parliament St. 3553
MORRIS-MG Brookhouse 0524 (Caton) 770501
MORRIS-MG Penny St. 2424
RENAULT Aldrens Lane 67221
VAUXHALL, CITROEN Penny St. 2442

LANCHESTER Durham 986 ⑲ – pop. 4.962 – ☎ 0207.
London 275 – Durham 8 – Newcastle-upon-Tyne 13.

✕ **Kings Head** (S & N) with rm, Village Green, DH7 0EX, ☎ 520054 – Ⓟ
M a la carte 2.20/4.05 **t.** 🍷 0.70 – **5 rm** ☕ 5.50/9.75 **t.**

MORRIS-MG ☎ 520336

LANERCOST Cumbria – pop. 655 – ✉ ☎ 069 77 Brampton.
See : Priory* (ruins 14C) *AC.* **Envir. :** Bewcastle (churchyard Runic Cross 8C) N : 8 ½ m.
London 320 – Carlisle 12 – Newcastle-upon-Tyne 48.

🏠 **New Bridge,** ⛰, CA8 2HG, ☎ 2224, 🎣 – 🛁wc Ⓟ
March-October – **M** (buffet lunch) a la carte 3.10/4.75 **t.** 🍷 1.60 – **13 rm** ☕ 8.00/17.00 **t.**

LANGHAM Leics. – pop. 875 – ✉ ☎ 0572 Oakham.
London 105 – Leicester 23 – Nottingham 26.

✕✕ Noel Arms, Bridge St., LE15 7HU, ☎ 2931 – Ⓟ.

LANGSTONE Gwent – see Newport.

LANREATH Cornwall – pop. 352 – ✉ Looe – ☎ 050 32.
London 269 – Plymouth 26 – Truro 34.

🏠 **Punch Bowl Inn,** PL13 2NX, ☎ 218, 🌳 – 🛁wc 🚿 Ⓟ
April-October – **M** a la carte 3.90/4.10 **s.** 🍷 1.15 – **19 rm** ☕ 7.25/16.50 **s.**

LASTINGHAM North Yorks. – pop. 88 – ✉ York – ☎ 075 15.
London 244 – Scarborough 26 – York 32.

🏠 **Lastingham Grange** ⛰, YO6 6TH, ☎ 345, « Country house atmosphere », 🌳 – 🛁wc Ⓟ
Easter-mid November **M** 5.00/5.50 **t.** – **15 rm** ☕ 8.50/19.00 **t.** – P 13.50/14.50 **t.**

LAVENHAM Suffolk 986 ㉜ – pop. 1,480 – ✉ Sudbury – ☎ 078 724 (3 and 4 fig.) or 0787 (6 fig.).
See : SS. Peter and Paul's Church : the Spring Parclose* (Flemish).
London 66 – Cambridge 39 – Colchester 22 – Ipswich 19.

🏠 **Swan** (T.H.F.), High St., CO10 9QA, ☎ 477, « Part 14C timbered inn », 🌳 – Ⓟ. 🏔
M a la carte 4.60/6.00 **st.** 🍷 1.50 – ☕ 2.00 – **42 rm** 13.50/22.00 **st.**

PEUGEOT ☎ 228

LAWRENNY Dyfed – pop. 106 – ✉ Kilgetty – ☎ 064 67 Carew.
London 250 – Carmarthen 30 – Haverfordwest 16.

🏠 **Lawrenny Arms** ⛰, Lawrenny Quay, SA68 0PR, ☎ 367, ≤ river Cleddau – 📺 🛁wc Ⓟ
M (buffet lunch) approx. 2.95 **t.** 🍷 1.75 – **12 rm** ☕ 8.30/13.60 **t.** – P 9.50 **t.**

LEAMINGTON SPA Warw. 986 ㉛ – see Royal Leamington Spa.

LECHLADE Glos. 986 ㉛ ㉟ – pop. 1,689 – ☎ 0367.
London 97 – Gloucester 32 – Oxford 23 – Swindon 11.

✕ **Trout Inn,** St. John's Bridge, Faringdon Rd, GL7 3HA, SE : ¾ m. on A 417 ☎ 52313, 🌳 – Ⓟ
closed Monday except Bank Holidays and 25-26 December – **M** a la carte 4.40/6.55 **t.** 🍷 1.20.

LEDBURY Heref. and Worc. 986 ㉛ – pop. 3,911 – ☎ 0531.
See : Church Lane*. **Envir. :** Birtsmorton Court* (15C) *AC,* SE : 7 m.
i St. Katherine's, High St. ☎ 2461 and 3429.
London 119 – Hereford 14 – Newport 46 – Worcester 16.

🏠 **Feathers,** High St., HR8 1DS, ☎ 2600, « Heavily timbered 16C inn » – Ⓟ
M (buffet lunch) 4.00/4.75 – **13 rm** ☕ 7.00/14.50.

AUSTIN-MORRIS-MG-ROVER-TRIUMPH New St. ☎ 2233
CHRYSLER-SIMCA The Homenn ☎ 2053

LEE Devon – see Ilfracombe.

LEEDS West Yorks. 986 ㉓ – pop. 496,009 – ☎ 0532.

See: St. John's Church* 17C DZ **A. Envir.:** Harewood House** 18C: the Bird Garden* *AC*, N: 8 m. by A 61 CV – Temple Newsam House* 17C (interior**) *AC*, E: 4 m. CX – Kirkstall Abbey* (ruins 12C) *AC*, NW: 3 m. BV.

18 Temple Newsam Rd, Halton ☎ 645214, E: 3 m. CX – 18 Armley Ridge Rd, Armley ☎ 638232, W: 2 m. BV – 18 Layton Rise ☎ (0532) 586819, NW: 6 m. BV – 9 Town St., Middleton ☎ 700449, S: 3 m. CX.

Leeds & Bradford Airport: ☎ (0532) 503431, NW: 8 m. by A 65 and A 658 BV – **Terminal:** Vicar Lane, Bus Station, Leeds.

i Central Library, Calverley St. ☎ 462453/4.

London 193 – Liverpool 70 – Manchester 42 – Newcastle-upon-Tyne 93 – Nottingham 67.

Plans on following pages

Queen's (B.T.H.), City Sq., LS1 1PL, ☎ 31323, Telex 55161 – DZ e
M a la carte 7.05/10.50 **st.** 1.40 – **193 rm** 14.50/28.00 **st.**

Dragonara, Neville St., LS1 4BX, ☎ 442000, Telex 557143 – DZ r
M 3.05/4.25 – 2.00 – **237 rm** 16.00/21.00 **s.**

Merrion, Merrion Centre, Wade Lane, LS2 8NH, ☎ 39191, Telex 55459 – DZ a
M 3.50/4.00 **s.** 1.30 – 1.75 – **120 rm** 13.00/17.50 **s.**

Metropole (T.H.F.), King St., LS1 2HQ, ☎ 450841 – CZ o
M 3.75/4.25 **st.** 1.50 – **113 rm** 10.00/18.50 **st.**

Parkway (Embassy), Otley Rd, LS16 8AG, NW: 6 m. on A 660 ☎ 672551, – wc by A 660 BV
closed Christmas – **M** approx. 3.80 **st.** 1.55 – **45 rm** 9.50/14.50 **st.**

Wellesley, Wellington St., LS1 4HJ, ☎ 30431 – wc CZ a
closed 25 and 26 December – **M** (grill rest. only) 1.85/3.85 **st.** 1.20 – **50 rm** 8.45/15.20 **st.**

Golden Lion (T.H.F.), Lower Briggate, LS1 4AE, ☎ 36454 – DZ s
M approx. 3.00 **st.** 1.50 – **82 rm** 8.50/15.50 **st.**

Terrazza, Minerva House, 16 Greek St., LS1 5RU, ☎ 32880, Italian rest. CDZ n
closed Sunday – **M** a la carte 4.95/8.50 **t.**

Embassy, 333 Roundhay Rd, LS8 4HT, NE: 2 ½ m. off A 58 ☎ 622135 – BY v
M (dinner only) 3.75/4.85 1.10.

Quebec, Quebec St., LS1 2HA, ☎ 456723 CZ c
M a la carte 3.50/4.40 **s.** 1.35.

Rules, 188 Selby Rd, LS15 0LF, ☎ 604564 CV u
closed Sunday, Monday, 1 week February, 1 week August and Bank Holidays – **M** (dinner only) a la carte 4.20/5.00 1.40.

Get Stuffed Dining Chambers, 19 York Pl., LS1 2EX, ☎ 455965, Bistro CZ i
closed Sunday and Bank Holiday Mondays – **M** (dinner only) a la carte 3.50/5.50 **t.** 1.30.

at Seacroft NE: 5 ½ m. at junction of A 64 and A 6120 – ✉ ☎ 0532 Leeds:

Windmill (Stakis), Mill Green View, LS14 5QP, ☎ 732323 – wc CV a
M a la carte 2.70/5.50 1.75 – **40 rm** 12.50/18.00.

at Garforth E: 6 m. at junction A 63 and A 642 – ✉ Leeds – ☎ 097 38 (4 and 5 fig.) or 0532 (6 fig.) Garforth:

Mercury Motor Inn, Wakefield Rd, LS26 1LH, ☎ 866556 – wc CV e
M a la carte approx. 3.80 **st.** 1.35 – 1.50 – **120 rm** 13.50/17.50 **st.**

at Oulton SE: 6 ¼ m. by A 61 – ✉ ☎ 0532 Leeds:

Leeds Crest Motel (Crest), The Grove, LS26 8EJ, at junction of A 639 and A 642 ☎ 826201 – wc CX z
M 2.60/4.95 **s.** 1.55 – 1.60 – **40 rm** 10.95/15.50 **s.**

at Pudsey W: 4 ½ m. by A 647 – ✉ Leeds – ☎ 0274 Bradford:

Tiberio, 68 Galloway Lane, LS28 8LE, W: 1 ½ m. on B 6154 ☎ 665895, Italian rest.
closed Sunday and July – **M** a la carte 2.20/6.20 **s.** 1.30. BV o

at Horsforth NW: 5 m. off A 6120 by A 65 – ✉ ☎ 0532 Leeds:

Low Hall, Calverley Lane, LS18 4ES, ☎ 588221, « Elizabethan house » – BV a
closed Sunday, Monday and Bank Holidays – **M** a la carte 2.95/6.25 **st.** 1.55.

Roman Garden, Hall Park, LS18 5JY, ☎ 587962, ≤, Italian rest. – BV i
closed Saturday lunch, Sunday and Monday – **M** 5.25/8.75 **t.** 2.00.

MICHELIN Branch, Gelderd Rd, LS12 6EU, ☎ 630461.

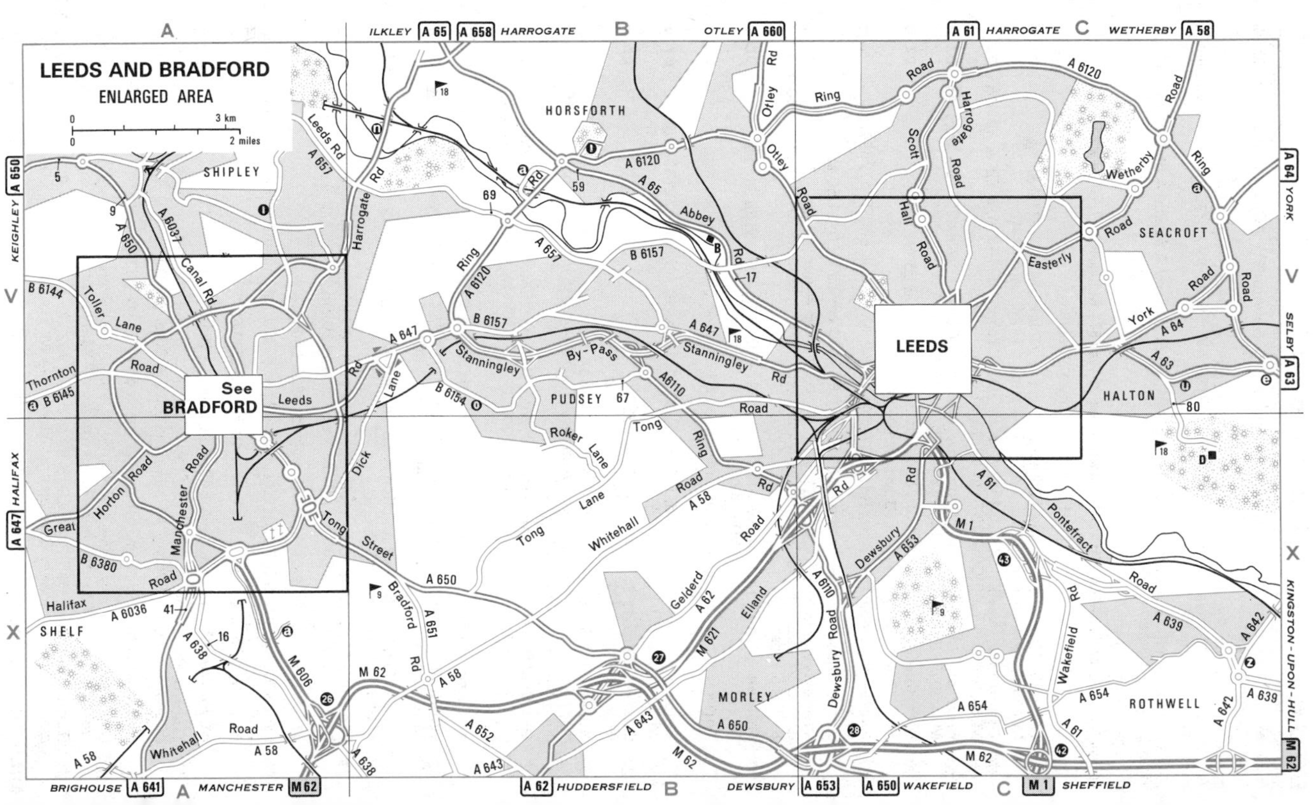

LEEDS AND BRADFORD
ENLARGED AREA
0 3 km
0 2 miles
ILKLEY A 65
A 658 HARROGATE
OTLEY A 660
A 61 HARROGATE
WETHERBY A 58
A 64 YORK
SELBY A 63
KINGSTON-UPON-HULL M 62
KEIGHLEY A 650
HALIFAX A 647
BRIGHOUSE A 641
MANCHESTER M 62
A 62 HUDDERSFIELD
DEWSBURY A 653
A 650 WAKEFIELD
M 1 SHEFFIELD
A
B
C
V
X
LEEDS
See BRADFORD
SHIPLEY
HORSFORTH
SEACROFT
HALTON
PUDSEY
MORLEY
ROTHWELL
SHELF
Ring Road
Harrogate Road
Scott Hall Road
Wetherby Road
Easterly Road
York Road
Otley Rd
Otley Road
Abbey Rd
Stanningley Rd
Stanningley By-Pass
Leeds Rd
Leeds Road
Harrogate Rd
Canal Rd
Toller Lane
Thornton Road
Horton Road
Manchester Road
Great Horton Road
Halifax
Tong Street
Dick Lane
Bradford Rd
Tong Lane
Roker Lane
Tong Road
Whitehall Road
Gelderd Road
Elland Road
Dewsbury Road
Dewsbury Rd
Wakefield Rd
Pontefract Road
Whitehall Road
A 6120
A 65
A 657
A 647
A 6110
B 6157
B 6154
A 6037
A 650
B 6144
B 6145
B 6380
A 6036
A 638
M 606
M 62
A 58
A 651
A 652
A 643
A 62
M 621
A 653
A 61
A 639
A 642
A 654
A 64
A 63
M 1

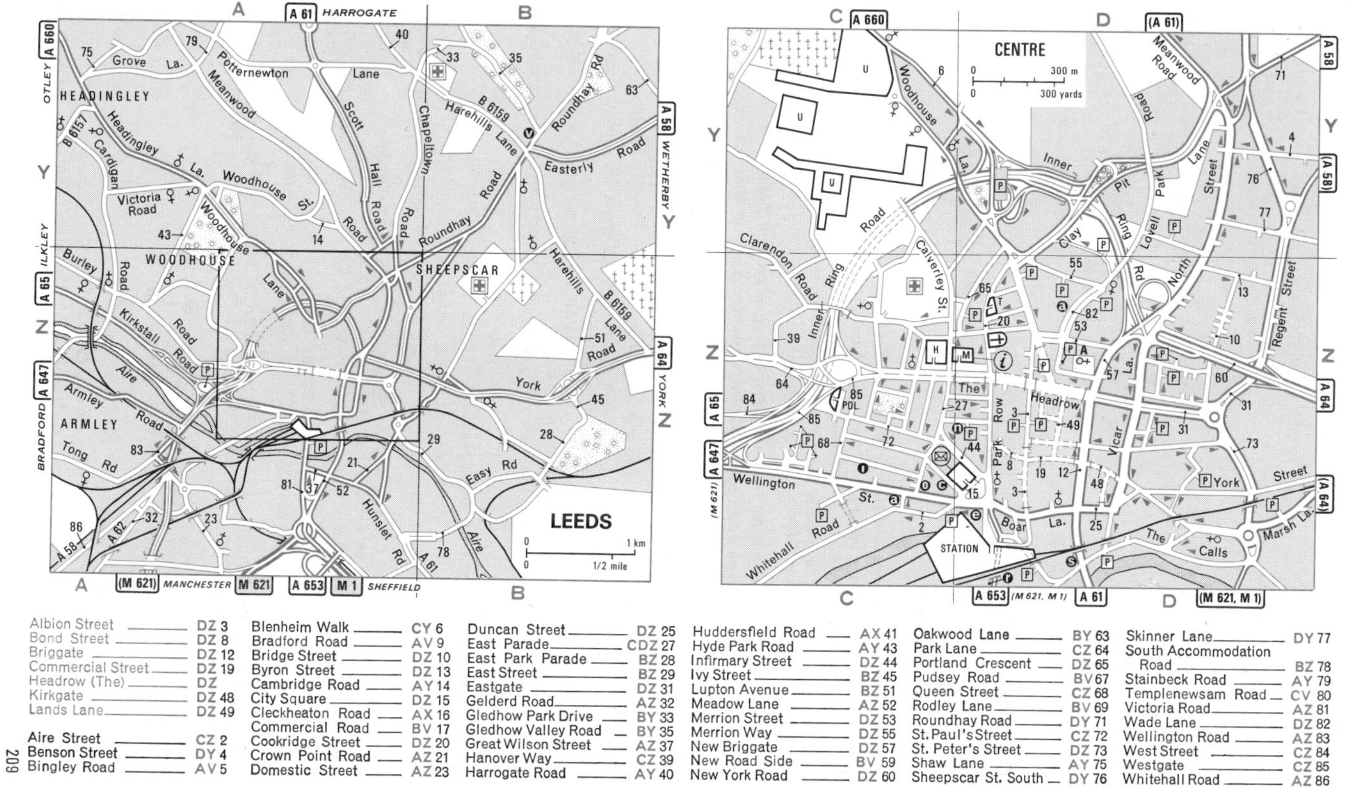

Street	Ref
Albion Street	DZ 3
Bond Street	DZ 8
Briggate	DZ 12
Commercial Street	DZ 19
Headrow (The)	DZ
Kirkgate	DZ 48
Lands Lane	DZ 49
Aire Street	CZ 2
Benson Street	DY 4
Bingley Road	AV 5
Blenheim Walk	CY 6
Bradford Road	AV 9
Bridge Street	DZ 10
Byron Street	DZ 13
Cambridge Road	AY 14
City Square	DZ 15
Cleckheaton Road	AX 16
Commercial Road	BV 17
Cookridge Street	DZ 20
Crown Point Road	AZ 21
Domestic Street	AZ 23
Duncan Street	DZ 25
East Parade	CDZ 27
East Park Parade	BZ 28
East Street	BZ 29
Eastgate	DZ 31
Gelderd Road	AZ 32
Gledhow Park Drive	BY 33
Gledhow Valley Road	BY 35
Great Wilson Street	AZ 37
Hanover Way	CZ 39
Harrogate Road	AY 40
Huddersfield Road	AX 41
Hyde Park Road	AY 43
Infirmary Street	DZ 44
Ivy Street	BZ 45
Lupton Avenue	BZ 51
Meadow Lane	AZ 52
Merrion Street	DZ 53
Merrion Way	DZ 55
New Briggate	DZ 57
New Road Side	BV 59
New York Road	DZ 60
Oakwood Lane	BY 63
Park Lane	CZ 64
Portland Crescent	DZ 65
Pudsey Road	BV 67
Queen Street	CZ 68
Rodley Lane	BV 69
Roundhay Road	DY 71
St. Paul's Street	CZ 72
St. Peter's Street	DZ 73
Shaw Lane	AY 75
Sheepscar St. South	DY 76
Skinner Lane	DY 77
South Accommodation Road	BZ 78
Stainbeck Road	AY 79
Templenewsam Road	CV 80
Victoria Road	AZ 81
Wade Lane	DZ 82
Wellington Road	AZ 83
West Street	CZ 84
Westgate	CZ 85
Whitehall Road	AZ 86

AUSTIN-MG-WOLSELEY 27 Burley Rd ℡ 39291
AUSTIN-MG-ROVER-TRIUMPH 495 Harrogate Rd ℡ 684391
BMW Bramhope ℡ 097 335 (Arthington) 2238
BMW York Rd ℡ 643772
CHRYSLER-SIMCA Regent St. ℡ 31914
CHRYSLER Crossgates ℡ 641573
CHRYSLER-SIMCA Armley Rd ℡ 34554
CHRYSLER-SIMCA Wike Ridge Lane ℡ 661129
DAF ℡ 702341
DAIMLER-JAGUAR, ROLLS ROYCE-BENTLEY Roseville Rd ℡ 32721
DATSUN Meadow Rd ℡ 444531
DATSUN Street Lane ℡ 661048
DATSUN, SAAB Apperley Lane, Yeadon ℡ 0532 (Rawdon) 502231
FIAT, CITROEN Water Lane ℡ 38091
FORD 98 Roundhay Rd ℡ 629301
FORD Abeford Rd ℡ 097 38 (Garforth) 3261
FORD Whitehall Rd ℡ 639174
LANCIA 251 Whitehall Rd ℡ 634418
MERCEDES-BENZ 39/41 Lovell Park Rd ℡ 31153
MORRIS-MG-WOLSELEY North St. ℡ 32731
MORRIS-MG-WOLSELEY North Lane ℡ 51948
MORRIS-MG-WOLSELEY Church Lane, Crossgates ℡ 645151
MORRIS-MG-WOLSELEY Stanningley Rd ℡ 097 35 (Pudsey) 3181
PEUGEOT 633 Roundhay Rd ℡ 656565
PEUGEOT South Milford ℡ 0977 (South Milford) 2539
RENAULT Regent St. ℡ 30837
ROVER-TRIUMPH, ASTON MARTIN Regent St. ℡ 38201
SAAB Wellington Rd ℡ 633331
TOYOTA Regent St. ℡ 444223
VAUXHALL 123 Hunslet Rd ℡ 39911
VAUXHALL Roseville Rd ℡ 41551
VOLVO Wellington Rd ℡ 36412
VW, AUDI-NSU Gelderd Rd ℡ 633431

LEE-ON-THE-SOLENT Hants. – pop. 6,266 – ✆ 0705.

London 81 – Portsmouth 13 – Southampton 15 – Winchester 23.

- **Belle Vue,** 39 Marine Par. East, PO13 9BW, ℡ 550258 – ⌸wc ⌸wc Ⓟ
  M 2.50/3.50 **t.** 1.80 – **34 rm** 9.50/15.50 **st.**

DATSUN High St. ℡ 551785
SAAB 178 Portsmouth Rd ℡ 550448

During the season, *particularly in resorts, it is wise to book in advance.*
However, if you find you cannot take up a hotel booking you have made, please let the hotel know immediately.
If you are writing to a hotel abroad enclose an International Reply Coupon (available from Post Offices.)

En saison, *surtout dans les stations fréquentées, il est prudent de retenir à l'avance.*
Cependant, si vous ne pouvez pas occuper la chambre que vous avez retenue, prévenez immédiatement l'hôtelier.
Si vous écrivez à un hôtel étranger, joignez à votre lettre un coupon-réponse international (disponible dans les bureaux de poste).

LEICESTER Leics. 986 ㉗ ㉘ – pop. 284,208 – ✆ 0533.

See : Museum of local archaeology, Jewry Wall and baths★ *AC* BY **M¹** – Museum and Art Gallery★ CY **M²** – St. Mary de Castro's Church★ 12C BY **A.**

18 Rothley ℡ 053 724 (Rothley) 2019, N : 6 m. by A 46 AX – 18 Evington Lane ℡ 736035, E : 2 m. AY – 18 Braunstone ℡ 872339, W : 4 m. AY.

✈ East Midlands Airport : Castle Donington ℡ 0332 (Derby) 810621, NW : 22 m. by A 50 AX and M1.

i 12 Bishop St. ℡ 20644.

London 103 – Birmingham 41 – Coventry 26 – Nottingham 24.

Plans on following pages

- Holiday Inn, St. Nicholas Circle, LE1 5LX, ℡ 51161, Telex 341281, ⌸ – ⌸ TV ♿ Ⓟ. ⌸ **190 rm.** — BY c
- **Grand** (Embassy), 73 Granby St., LE1 6ES, ℡ 56222 – ⌸ TV ⌸ Ⓟ. ⌸ — CY o
  closed Christmas – **M** approx. 3.65 **st.** 1.40 – **93 rm** 10.45/16.85.
- **Leicester Centre** (Centre), Humberstone Gate, LE5 3AT, ℡ 20471, Telex 341460 – ⌸ TV ⌸wc ☎ Ⓟ. ⌸ — CX n
  M approx. 2.95 **s.** 1.25 – 1.50 – **222 rm** 10.45/14.50 **s.**
- Abbey Motor (Thistle), Abbey St., LE1 3TE, ℡ 50666, ≤ – ⌸ TV ⌸wc ⌸wc ☎. ⌸ **68 rm.** — CX a
- **Belmont** (Interchange), De Montfort St., LE1 7GR, ℡ 24177 – ⌸ ⌸wc ⌸wc ☎ Ⓟ. ⌸
  closed Christmas week – **M** *(closed Sunday)* 3.50/4.50 **st.** 1.75 – **55 rm** 9.25/19.00 **st.** — CY c
- **Daval,** 292 London Rd, LE2 3ND, ℡ 708234 – Ⓟ — AY a
  closed Christmas week – **14 rm** 5.50/9.95.
- **Gables,** 368 London Rd, LE2 2PN, ℡ 706969 – Ⓟ — AY c
  9 rm 5.00/8.00.
- Golden Fish, 127 Granby St., ℡ 22151, Chinese rest. — CY a

at Scraptoft **E : 3¼ m. off A 47** – AX – ✉ ✆ **0533 Leicester :**

- White House, 359 Scraptoft Lane, LE5 2HW, ℡ 415951, Dancing (Friday and Saturday) – Ⓟ.

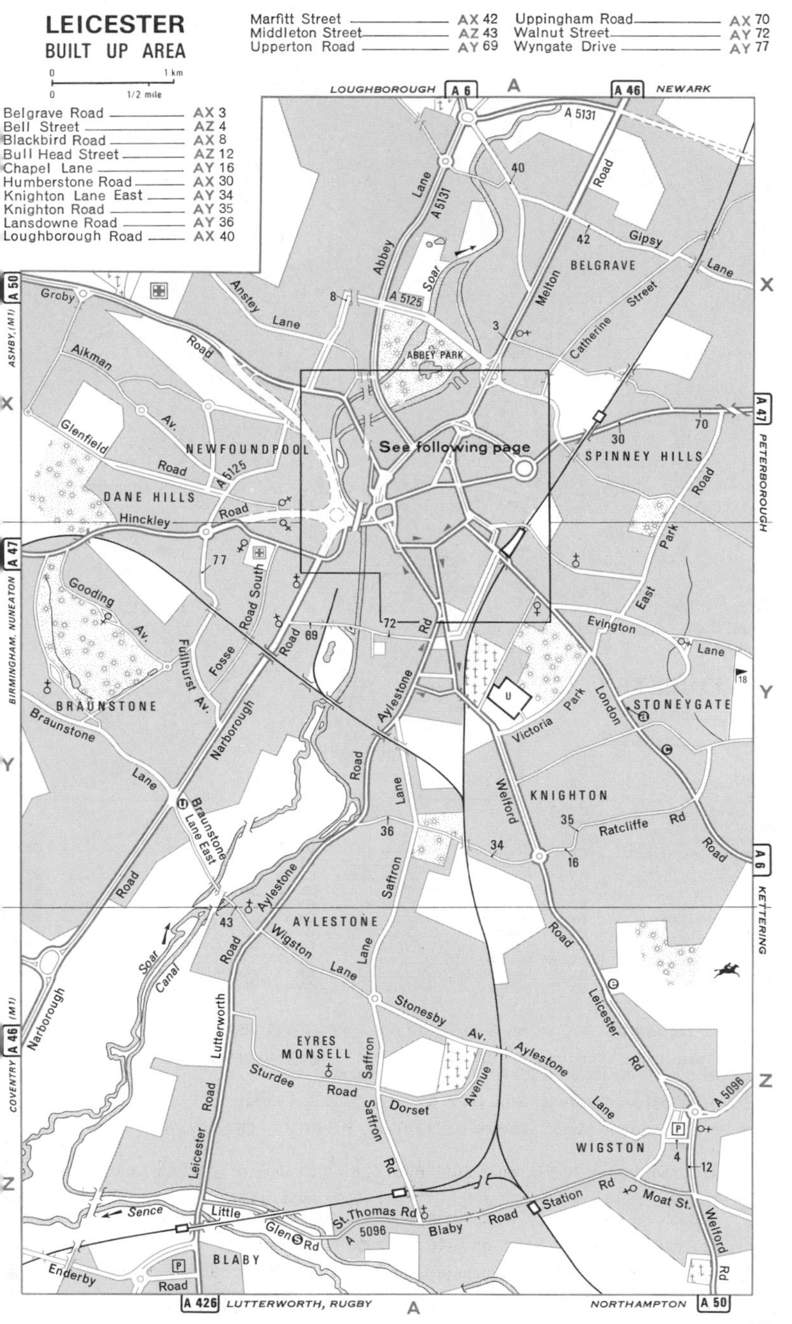

LEICESTER
BUILT UP AREA
0 1 km
0 1/2 mile
Belgrave Road AX 3
Bell Street AZ 4
Blackbird Road AX 8
Bull Head Street AZ 12
Chapel Lane AY 16
Humberstone Road AX 30
Knighton Lane East AY 34
Knighton Road AY 35
Lansdowne Road AY 36
Loughborough Road AX 40
Marfitt Street AX 42
Middleton Street AZ 43
Upperton Road AY 69
Uppingham Road AX 70
Walnut Street AY 72
Wyngate Drive AY 77
LOUGHBOROUGH A 6
A 46 NEWARK
A 47 PETERBOROUGH
A 6 KETTERING
A 50 ASHBY, (M1)
A 47 BIRMINGHAM, NUNEATON
A 46 (M1) COVENTRY
A 426 LUTTERWORTH, RUGBY
NORTHAMPTON A 50
See following page
BELGRAVE
NEWFOUNDPOOL
SPINNEY HILLS
DANE HILLS
BRAUNSTONE
STONEYGATE
KNIGHTON
AYLESTONE
EYRES MONSELL
WIGSTON
BLABY
ABBEY PARK

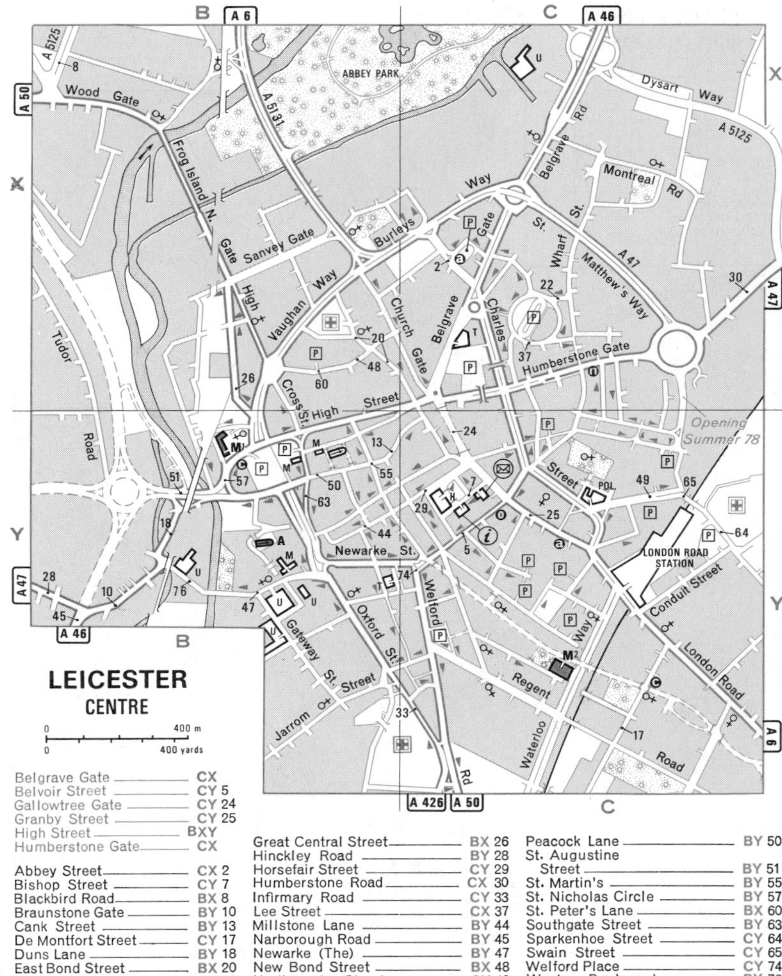

Belgrave Gate	CX
Belvoir Street	CY 5
Gallowtree Gate	CY 24
Granby Street	CY 25
High Street	BXY
Humberstone Gate	CX
Abbey Street	CX 2
Bishop Street	CY 7
Blackbird Road	BX 8
Braunstone Gate	BY 10
Cank Street	BY 13
De Montfort Street	CY 17
Duns Lane	BY 18
East Bond Street	BX 20
Fleet Street	CX 22
Great Central Street	BX 26
Hinckley Road	BY 28
Horsefair Street	CY 29
Humberstone Road	CX 30
Infirmary Road	CY 33
Lee Street	CX 37
Millstone Lane	BY 44
Narborough Road	BY 45
Newarke (The)	BY 47
New Bond Street	BX 48
Northampton Street	CY 49
Peacock Lane	BY 50
St. Augustine Street	BY 51
St. Martin's	BY 55
St. Nicholas Circle	BY 57
St. Peter's Lane	BX 60
Southgate Street	BY 63
Sparkenhoe Street	CY 64
Swain Street	CY 65
Welford Place	CY 74
Western Boulevard	BY 76

at Oadby SE: 3 ¼ m. on A 5096 by A 6 – AY – ✉ ☎ 0533 Leicester :

🏨 **Hermitage,** Wigston Rd, LE2 5QE, ☎ 719441 – 🛗 ⛀wc ☎ **P**. 🏨
M 3.50/6.00 🍷 1.50 – **29 rm** ☕ 11.00/16.00 **s.**

at Wigston Fields S: 3 m. on A 50 – ✉ ☎ 0533 Leicester:

🏨 Wigston Stage Motel, Welford Rd, LE8 1JF, ☎ 886161 – TV ⛀wc ⛆wc ☎ **P**. 🏨 AZ **e**
80 rm.

at Glen Parva S: 5 m. on A 5096 by A 426 – ✉ Leicester – ☎ 053 76 Wigston:

XXX **Manor,** The Ford, Little Glen Rd, LE2 9TL, ☎ 774604, « 15C manor house » – **P** AZ **s**
closed Saturday lunch, Sunday and Bank Holidays – **M** a la carte 4.60/6.60.

at Braunstone SW: 2 m. on A 46 – ✉ ☎ 0533 Leicester:

🏨 **Post House** (T.H.F.), Braunstone Lane East, LE3 2FW, ☎ 896688, Telex 341009 – 🛗
TV ⛀wc ☎ ♿ **P**. 🏨 AY **u**
M a la carte 3.35/5.00 **st.** 🍷 1.50 – ☕ 2.00 – **171 rm** 13.00/18.00 **st.**

at Narborough SW: 6 m. off A 46 – AZ – ✉ ☎ 0568 Leicester:

Charnwood, 48 Leicester Rd, LE9 5DF, ☎ 862218, – **P**
21 rm ☕ 8.00/12.50 **st.**

at Leicester Forest East W: 3 m. on A 47 – AY – ✉ ☎ 0533 Leicester:

Europa Lodge (County), Hinckley Rd, LE3 3GH, ☎ 394661, Group Telex 25971 – TV wc ☎ **P**.
M 3.25/3.75 **st.** 🌢 1.20 – **31 rm** ☕ 13.10/17.00 **st.** – P 15.00/18.00 **st.**

MICHELIN Branch, 33 Blackbird Av., Blackbird Rd, LE4 0AD, ☎ 25596.

AUDI-NSU, MERCEDES-BENZ Churchgate ☎ 25841
AUSTIN-MG-WOLSELEY High St., Evington ☎ 73657
AUSTIN, CHRYSLER Leicester Rd ☎ 881601
AUSTIN-MG-WOLSELEY Narborough Rd South ☎ 824316
AUSTIN-MG-WOLSELEY 230 Belgrave Gate ☎ 56631
AUSTIN-MG-WOLSELEY Stoughton Drive North ☎ 736362
BMW Harborough Rd ☎ 2303
CHRYSLER-SIMCA 91 Abbey Lane ☎ 61501
CITROEN 289/297 Melton Rd ☎ 63371
CITROEN Queens Rd ☎ 708947
DAF 7 Pitte St. ☎ 21007
DAIMLER-JAGUAR-ROVER-TRIUMPH Dover St. ☎ 27252
DATSUN Thurcaston Rd ☎ 666861
DATSUN Conduit St. ☎ 544301
FIAT 459 Aylestone Rd ☎ 831052
FIAT 47 Blackbird Rd ☎ 53137
FORD Belgrave Gate ☎ 50501
FORD Welford Rd ☎ 706215
HONDA 220 Loughborough Rd ☎ 61117
MORRIS-MG-WOLSELEY 40/44 Braunstone Gate ☎ 24728
MORRIS-MG-WOLSELEY Green Lane Rd ☎ 767551
MORRIS-MG-WOLSELEY, ROLLS ROYCE Welford Rd ☎ 548757
OPEL-VAUXHALL Aylestone Rd ☎ 547515
PEUGEOT Mayfield Corner ☎ 543675
RENAULT 60/62 Northgate St. ☎ 28612
SAAB Nelson St. ☎ 50928
TOYOTA Catherine St. ☎ 62628
VAUXHALL Evington ☎ 730421
VOLVO 31 London Rd ☎ 24751
VW, AUDI-NSU 670/686 Melton Rd, Thurcaston ☎ 693731
VW, AUDI-NSU Church Gate ☎ 25841

☞ *Keine Aufnahme in den **Michelin-Führer** durch*
— falsche Information oder
— Bezahlung!

LEIGH Greater Manchester 986 ⑤ and ㉓ – pop. 46,181 – ☎ 0942.

Kenyon Hall, Culcheth ☎ 092 576 (Culcheth) 3130, S: by A 574.

London 205 – Liverpool 25 – Manchester 12 – Preston 25.

Greyhound Motor (Embassy), Warrington Rd, WN7 3XQ, S: 1 m. at junction A 580 and A 574 ☎ 671256 – TV wc ☎ **P**
closed Christmas – **M** (grill rest. only) approx. 4.50 **st.** 🌢 1.60 – ☕ 1.60 – **64 rm** 10.75/13.75 **st.**

AUSTIN-MG-ROVER-TRIUMPH Chapel St. ☎ 71126
CHRYSLER-SIMCA Brown St. North ☎ 354264
DAF-OPEL Wigan Rd ☎ 71951
DATSUN 39 Plank Lane ☎ 673334
RENAULT Wigan Rd ☎ 76236
VAUXHALL 196 Chapel St. ☎ 71326

LEOMINSTER Heref. and Worc. 986 ㉛ – pop. 7,079 – ☎ 0568.

See: Priory Church* 14C (the north aisle* 12C). **Envir.:** Berrington Hall* (Georgian) *AC*, N: 3 m. – Croft Castle* (15C) *AC*, NW: 6 m.

i The Library, South St. ☎ 2384.

London 141 – Birmingham 47 – Hereford 13 – Worcester 26.

Talbot, West St., HR6 8OP, ☎ 2121 – TV wc wc **P**
M *(closed Christmas)* (grill rest. only) 2.50/4.00 🌢 1.75 – **31 rm** ☕ 8.00/18.20 **st.** – P 17.00/19.50.

Royal Oak, South St., HR6 8JA, ☎ 2610 – wc **P**
M a la carte 2.65/4.75 **t.** 🌢 1.20 – **18 rm** ☕ 6.00/12.50 **t.** – P 10.00 **t.**

AUSTIN-MG-ROVER-TRIUMPH-WOLSELEY Broad St. ☎ 2787
CHRYSLER-SIMCA, OPEL The Bargates ☎ 2337
DAIMLER-JAGUAR-MORRIS-MG-WOLSELEY South St. ☎ 2545

LETCHWORTH Herts. 986 ㉜ – pop. 30,945 – ☎ 046 26.

London 40 – Bedford 22 – **Cambridge 22** – Luton 14.

Broadway (Crest), The Broadway, SG6 3NS, ☎ 5651 – TV wc ☎ **P**.
M a la carte 3.35/5.55 **s.** 🌢 1.55 – **32 rm** ☕ 11.50/18.00 **s.**

Letchworth Hall, Letchworth Lane, SG6 3NP, S: 1 m. off A 505 ☎ 3747, ←, ,
 – TV wc ☎ **P**
M 2.30/3.50 **t.** 🌢 1.50 – **19 rm** ☕ 9.70/14.50 **st.**

AUSTIN-MG-WOLSELEY Jubilee Rd ☎ 73161
FORD 18/24 Station Rd ☎ 3722
OPEL Norton Way North ☎ 4850
RENAULT Norton Way North ☎ 6341

LEWDOWN Devon – ✉ Okehampton – ☎ 056 683.

London 234 – Exeter 33.

- **Coach House Motel** without rest., EX20 4DS, on A 30 ☏ 322, ≤ – TV ⇔wc ⋒wc P
closed 25 and 26 December – **50 rm** ☐ 8.50/15.00 **t.**

LEWES East Sussex 986 ㊱ – pop. 14,159 – ☎ 079 16.

See : Norman Castle (ruins) site and ≤*, 45 steps, *AC* – Anne of Cleves' House* (1559) *AC.*
Envir.: Glynde Place (pictures*) *AC,* E: 3 ½ m. – Firle Place* (mansion 15C-16C) *AC,* SE: 4 ½ m. – Ditchling Beacon ≤* W: 7 ½ m. – Glyndebourne Opera Festival (May-August) *AC,* E: 3 m.

18 Chapel Hill ☏ 3245, Opp. Junction Cliffe High/South St.

i 187 High St. ☏ 6151 ext 57.

London 53 – Brighton 8 – Hastings 29 – Maidstone 43.

- **The Shelleys,** High St., BN7 1XS, ☏ 2361, ⚘ – ⇔wc ☎ P
M a la carte 2.95/5.50 **s.** 1.20 – ☐ 1.50 – **21 rm** 7.50/16.50 **s.**
- **White Hart** (Interchange), 55 High St., BN7 1XE, ☏ 4676 – ⇔wc ☎ P
M a la carte 3.10/5.30 2.00 – **28 rm** ☐ 9.00/19.00 **s.**
- XX **Trumps,** 19-20 Station St., BN7 2DB, ☏ 3906
closed Sunday, Monday and 3 weeks January – **M** (dinner only) a la carte 5.15/5.90 **t.** 1.45.
- X **Pelham Arms (Sussex Kitchen),** High St., BN7 1XL, ☏ 6149 – P
closed Sunday, Monday, Bank Holidays, last week August and first week September – **M** a la carte 3.00/4.40 **t.** 1.25.
- X **Nitchevo,** 199 High St., BN7 2NS, ☏ 2343, Mid European rest.
closed Sunday, Wednesday and Bank Holidays – **M** (dinner only) a la carte 4.75/7.10 **st.** 1.50.
- X **La Cucina,** 13 Station St., BN7 2DA, ☏ 6707, Italian rest.
closed Sunday and 24 December-21 January – **M** a la carte 3.30/5.40 1.20.

at Selmeston SE: 6 ½ m. off A 27 – ✉ Polegate – ☎ 032 183 Ripe:

- XX **Corin's,** Church Farm, BN26 6TZ, ☏ 343, « 17C farmhouse », ⚘ – P
closed Monday and February – **M** (dinner only) approx. 5.00 **t.** 1.20.

AUSTIN-MG Western Rd ☏ 3221
MORRIS-MG Cliffe Bridge ☏ 2245
RENAULT 96/106 Malling St. ☏ 4136
ROVER-TRIUMPH Station St. ☏ 4461

LICHFIELD Staffs. 986 ⑧ and ㉗ – pop. 22,660 – ☎ 054 32.

See : Cathedral** 12C-14C.

18 Tamworth Rd ☏ 0543 (Whittington) 212, 2 ½ m. Lichfield Station.

i 21 Dam St. ☏ 52109.

London 128 – Birmingham 16 – Derby 23 – Stoke-on-Trent 30.

- **Little Barrow,** Beacon St., WS13 7AA, ☏ 53311 – TV ⇔wc ☎ P.
closed Christmas – **M** approx. 4.25 **st.** 1.40 – ☐ 2.00 – **24 rm** 9.00/12.00.
- **George,** Bird St., WS13 6PR, ☏ 23061 – TV ⇔wc ⋒wc ☎ P.
M approx. 3.60 **st.** 1.80 – **38 rm** ☐ 7.20/17.70 **st.**
- **Angel Croft,** Beacon St., WS13 7AA, ☏ 23147, ⚘ – ⋒wc P
M *(closed Sunday dinner)* 3.50/4.50 1.35 – **13 rm** ☐ 6.00/12.00.

AUSTIN-MORRIS-MG-ROVER-TRIUMPH St. John St. ☏ 51451
CHRYSLER-SIMCA Beacon St. ☏ 2329
FORD Birmingham Rd ☏ 3196
RENAULT Birmingham Rd ☏ 53571

LIFTON Devon – pop. 820 – ☎ 056 684.

Envir.: Launceston (castle*: Norman ruins *AC,* St. Mary Magdalene's Church : carving outside walls* 16C) E: 3 ½ m.

London 238 – Bude 24 – Exeter 37 – Launceston 4 – Plymouth 32.

- **Arundell Arms** (Interchange), Fore St., PL16 0AA, ☏ 244, ⚲, ⚘ – ⇔wc P
closed 3 days at Christmas – **M** (buffet lunch) approx. 5.00 **st.** 1.55 – **27 rm** ☐ 11.50/21.00 **st.**

This Guide is not a comprehensive list of all hotels and restaurants, nor even of all good hotels and restaurants in Great Britain and Ireland.

Since our aim is to be of service to all motorists, we must show establishments in all categories and so we have made a selection of some in each.

LIMPSFIELD Surrey – pop. 3,352 – ✉ ☎ 088 33 Oxted.
London 24 – Brighton 39 – Maidstone 25.

XX **Lodge,** High St., RH8 0DR, ☎ 2996 – Ⓟ
closed Sunday and Bank Holidays except 25 December – **M** a la carte 3.90/8.90 **t.** 🍷 1.65.

LINCOLN Lincs. 986 ㉘ – pop. 74,269 – ☎ 0522.
See : Cathedral*** 11C-15C (Angel Choir**, Library: Magna Carta *AC*) Y **A** – Jew's House** 12C Y **B** – Castle* (11C) *AC* Y – Newport Arch* (Roman) Y **E** – Stonebow and Guildhall* 15C-16C Z **S. Envir. :** Doddington Hall* (Elizabethan) *AC*, SW: 7 m. by A 15 Z and A 46.
⛳18 Carholme ☎ 23725 by A 57 Z – ⛳18 Lincoln ☎ 042 771 (Torksey) 210, W: 12 m. by A 57 Z.
i 90 Bailgate ☎ 29828 – City Hall, Beaumont Fee ☎ 32151.
London 143 – Bradford 79 – **Cambridge 93** – Kingston-upon-Hull 37 – **Leeds 70** – **Leicester 49** – **Norwich 104** – **Nottingham 36** – **Sheffield 46** – York 80.

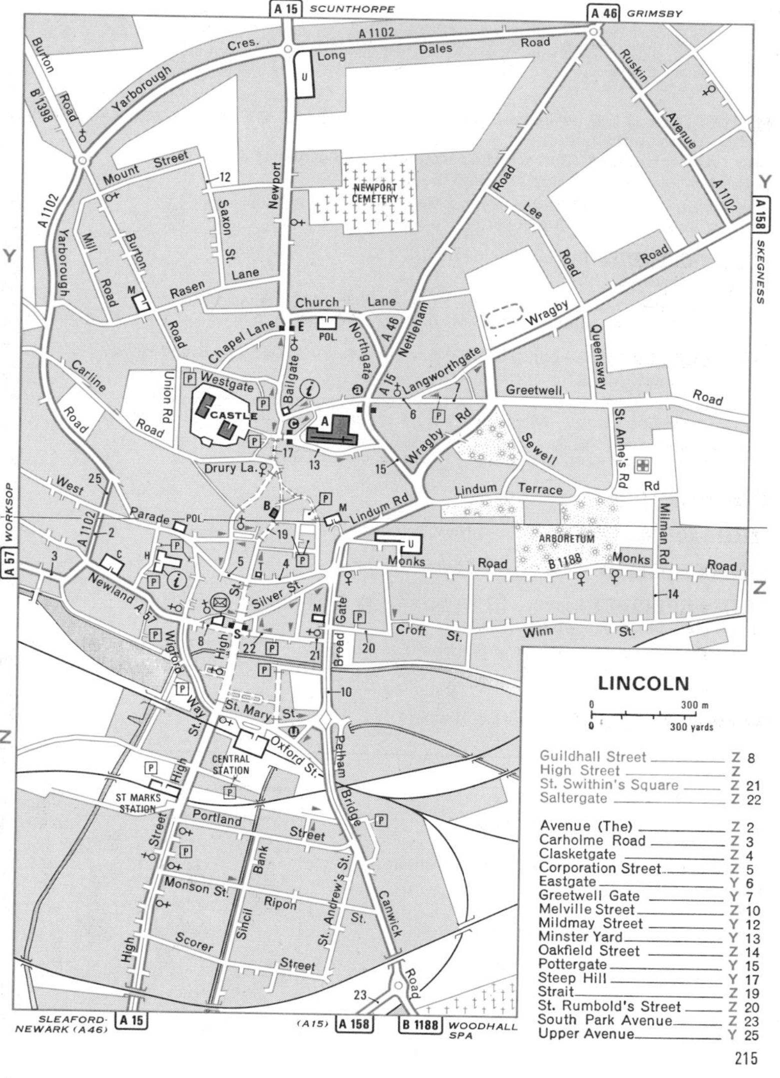

🏨 **White Hart,** Bailgate, LN1 3AR, ☎ 26222, Telex 56304, « Antique furniture » – 🛗 📺 🚗 🅟. 🏌 – Y c
M 3.75/4.50 **s.** 🍷 1.50 – **62 rm** ☕ 15.00/27.50 **s.** – P 21.50/23.50 **s.**

🏨 **Eastgate** (T.H.F.), Eastgate, LN2 1PN, ☎ 20341, Telex 56316 – 🛗 📺 ♿ 🅟. 🏌 – Y a
M 4.25/4.75 **st.** 🍷 1.45 – ☕ 2.00 – **72 rm** 13.00/19.50 **st.**

🏨 **Grand,** St. Mary's St., LN5 7EP, ☎ 24211 – 🛁wc ☎ 🅟 – Z u
M 3.00/3.70 **st.** 🍷 1.70 – **51 rm** ☕ 9.00/19.00 **st.** – P 12.60/18.50 **st.**

at Branston SE: 4 ½ m. on B 1188 – Z – ✉ ☎ 0522 Lincoln:

🏨 **Moor Lodge,** 23 Sleaford Rd, LN4 1HU, ☎ 791366 – 🛁wc 🅟
M 3.50/4.50 **st.** 🍷 1.40 – **28 rm** ☕ 9.00/20.00 **st.** – P 14.50/16.50 **st.**

MICHELIN Branch, Moorland Close, off Tritton Rd, LN6 7JL, ☎ 64023.

ALFA-ROMEO, FIAT, PEUGEOT 233 Newark Rd ☎ 22329
AUSTIN-MG-WOLSELEY 53/55 St. Catherines ☎ 20201
BMW, TOYOTA South Park Av. ☎ 21345
DAIMLER-JAGUAR-ROVER-TRIUMPH, BENTLEY-ROLLS ROYCE St. Rumbold St. ☎ 27117
DAF Outer Circle Rd ☎ 27916
DAF Portland St. ☎ 22097
DATSUN 148/150 Newark Rd ☎ 26122
LANCIA Boultham Park Rd ☎ 31735
MORRIS-MG St. Marys St. ☎ 33351
OPEL Skellingthorpe ☎ 62670
RENAULT 116 High St. ☎ 21262

LINSLADE Beds. 986 ㉜ – pop. 23,599 (inc. Leighton) – ✉ ☎ 052 53 (4 and 5 fig.) or 0525 (6 fig.) Leighton Buzzard.

Envir.: Ascott House** (Rothschild Collection**) and gardens* *AC*, SW: 2 m.

London 49 – Aylesbury 10 – Bedford 19 – Luton 13 – Northampton 30.

XX **Globe Inn,** Bletchley Rd, NW: 1 ½ m. on B 488 ☎ 3338 – 🅟
closed Monday – **M** a la carte 3.10/6.10 **s.**

LITTLE CHALFONT Bucks. – ☎ 024 04.

London 29 – Oxford 35 – Reading 28.

X **Marcello,** 1-2 Chalfont House, Station Rd ☎ 2498, Italian Bistro
closed Sunday, August and Bank Holidays – **M** approx. a la carte 5.05 **t.** 🍷 1.60.

LITTLE HAVEN Dyfed – pop. 150 – ✉ Haverfordwest – ☎ 043 783 Broad Haven.

London 258 – Haverfordwest 8.

🏨 Haven Fort 🐎, SA62 3UH, ☎ 401, ≤ sea and countryside – 🛁wc 🚿wc 🅟
March-September – **M** (dinner only) a la carte 4.20/7.50 **s.** 🍷 1.25 – **15 rm.**

🏨 **Little Haven** 🐎, Strawberry Hill, SA62 3UT, ☎ 285, ≤ – 🛁wc 🅟
M (bar lunch) approx. 4.00 **t.** – **15 rm** ☕ 6.50/15.00 **t.**

LITTLEOVER Derbs. – see Derby.

LITTLESTONE-ON-SEA Kent – see New Romney.

LITTLE STRETTON Salop – see Church Stretton.

LITTLE THORNTON Lancs. – ✉ Blackpool – ☎ 0253 Poulton-le-Fylde.

London 240 – Blackpool 5 – Lancaster 20.

XX **River House** 🐎 with rm, Skippool Creek, FY5 5LF, ☎ 883307, ≤, 🌳 – 📺 ☎ 🅟
M *(closed Monday)* (by arrangement only) a la carte 5.45/10.40 **t.** 🍷 1.55 – **4 rm** ☕ 9.00/18.00 **t.** – P 14.00/15.00 **t.**

LITTLE WYMONDLEY Herts. – see Hitchin.

LIVERPOOL Merseyside 986 ⑤ and ㉓ ㉗ – pop. 610,113 – ☎ 051.

See : Walker Art Gallery** CY **M**[1] – City of Liverpool Museums* CY **M**[2] – Anglican Cathedral* (1904) CZ **A** – Roman Catholic Cathedral* (1967) DZ **B. Envir. :** Knowsley Safari Park** *AC*, NE : 8 m. by A 57 BX – Speke Hall* (16C) *AC*, SE : 7 m. by A 561 BX.

Allerton Park ☎ 428 1046, S : 5 m. by B 5180 BX – Naylor's Rd, Gateacre ☎ 428 2189, E : 7 m. by B 5178 BX – Lee Park, Gateacre ☎ 428 1085, SE : 7 m. by B 5178 BX.

☎ 427 4101, SE : 6 m. by A 561 BX – **Terminal :** Pier Head and Lime St.

to Belfast (P & O Ferries) 6-8 weekly (10 h) – to Dublin (B & I Line) 6-8 weekly (7 to 8 h 45 mn) – to the Isle of Man : Douglas (Isle of Man Steam Packet Co.) Summer 1-7 daily; Winter Monday/Saturday 1 daily (4 h 15 mn).

i Municipal Buildings, Dale St. ☎ 227 3911 – 187 St. John's Centre, Elliot St. ☎ 709 3631 or 8681.

London 214 – Birmingham 99 – Leeds 70 – Manchester 36.

Town plans : Liverpool pp. 2-5

Atlantic Tower (Thistle), 30 Chapel St., L3 9RE, ☎ 227 4444, Telex 627070, ← – TV. **226 rm.** CY **r**

Adelphi (B.T.H.), Ranelagh Pl., L3 5UL, ☎ 709 7200, Telex 62644, – TV. **M** 4.25/5.75 **st.** 1.30 – **165 rm** 11.80/26.05 **st.** CZ **o**

Holiday Inn, Paradise St., L1 8JD, ☎ 709 0181, Telex 627270, – TV P. **M** 4.50/5.00 1.90 – 2.25 – **275 rm** 13.50/19.00. CZ **n**

St. George's (T.H.F.), St. John's Precinct, Lime St., L1 1NQ, ☎ 709 7090, Telex 627630 – TV P. **M** 4.20/4.90 **st.** 1.45 – 2.00– **155 rm** 15.00/20.00 **st.** CY **v**

Liverpool Centre (Centre), Lord Nelson St., L3 5QB, ☎ 709 7050, Telex 627954 – TV wc P. **M** (Carvery rest.) 2.95/3.95 **s.** 1.25 – 1.50 – **175 rm** 10.75/14.50 **s.** CY **i**

Alexandra Court, Alexandra Drive, L17 8TE, SE : 3 m. by A 561 ☎ 727 2551, – wc P **M** *(closed Saturday, Sunday and Bank Holidays)* (dinner only) approx. 3.25 1.50 – **24 rm** 9.95/13.90. BX **n**

Lord Nelson, Lord Nelson St., L3 5PD, ☎ 709 4362 – wc **M** a la carte 3.35/6.50 1.75 – **63 rm** 9.00/12.50 **st.** CY **e**

Shaftesbury, Mount Pleasant, L3 5SA, ☎ 709 4421 – wc. **M** approx. 3.00 1.00 – **70 rm** 9.50/12.50 **st.** CZ **c**

Green Park, 4-6 Greenbank Drive, L17 1AN, SE : 2 ½ m. by A 562 ☎ 733 3382, – TV P **M** 2.00/3.50 **s.** 1.20 – **22 rm** 5.50/10.50 **s.** BX **u**

XXX **Oriel,** 16 Water St., L2 8TH, ☎ 236 4664 CY **s**
closed Saturday lunch, Sunday, last 2 weeks August, first week September and Bank Holidays – **M** a la carte 6.60/8.75 **st.** 2.15.

XXX **Tower,** St. John's Precinct, L1 1LL, ☎ 709 8895, « Revolving restaurant with city and docks » CYZ **a**
closed 26 December – **M** a la carte 5.05/6.95 **s.** 1.95.

XX **Jenny's Seafood,** Old Ropery, Fenwick St., L2 7NT, ☎ 236 0332, Seafood CZ **e**
closed Saturday lunch, Sunday and Bank Holidays – **M** a la carte 3.30/6.35 **t.** 1.40.

at Waterloo N : 5 ¾ m. off A 565 – ✉ ☎ 051 Liverpool :

Royal, Bath St., L22 5PS, ☎ 928 2332 – TV wc wc P **20 rm.** AV **a**

at Netherton N : 6 m. off A 59 – AV – ✉ ☎ 051 Liverpool :

Park, Park Lane West, L30 3SU, ☎ 525 7555 – TV wc wc P. **M** 3.50/4.50 **st.** 2.00 – **54 rm** 11.50/14.00 **st.**

at Blundellsands N : 6 ½ m. off A 565 – AV – ✉ ☎ 051 Liverpool :

Blundellsands, Agnes Rd, L23 6TN, ☎ 924 6515 – TV wc P. **M** 3.85/4.40 **t.** – **44 rm** 9.75/22.00 **t.** – P 16.95/18.20 **t.**

at Knowsley NE : 7 m. on A 580 – BV – ✉ ☎ 051 Liverpool :

Liverpool Crest Motel (Crest), East Lancashire Rd, L34 9HA, ☎ 546 7531 – TV wc P. **M** (buffet lunch) 2.30/3.60 **s.** 1.50 – 1.60 – **50 rm** 10.95/15.50 **s.**

at Aigburth SE : 4 m. by A 561 – BX – ✉ ☎ 051 Liverpool :

Grange, 14 Holmefield Rd, L19 3PG, ☎ 427 2950, – wc P
closed Christmas week – **M** (dinner only) 3.25/4.55 0.70 – **28 rm** 8.50/13.00.

P.T.O. →

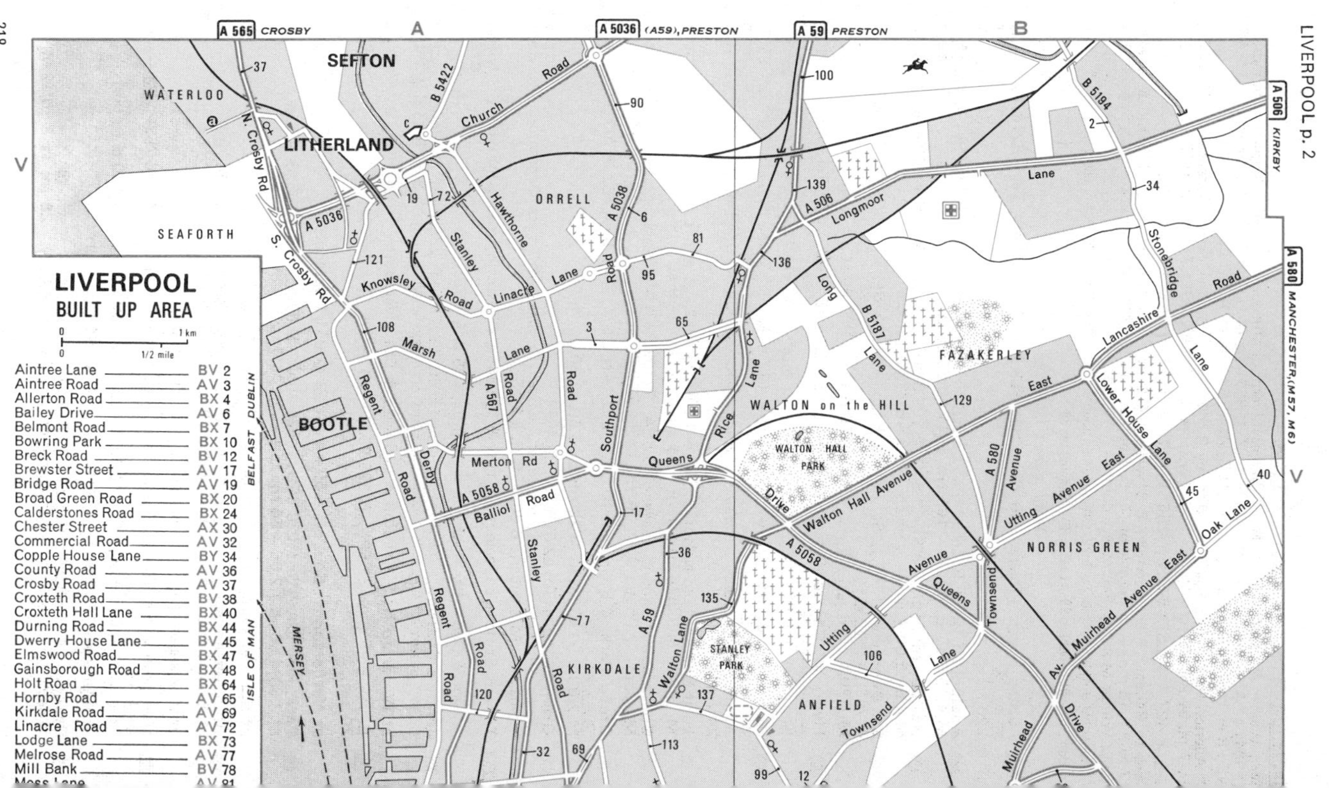

A 565 CROSBY
A 5036 (A59), PRESTON
A 59 PRESTON
A 506 KIRKBY
A 580 MANCHESTER,(M57, M6)
A
B
V
SEFTON
WATERLOO
LITHERLAND
SEAFORTH
ORRELL
BOOTLE
KIRKDALE
ANFIELD
WALTON on the HILL
FAZAKERLEY
NORRIS GREEN
WALTON HALL PARK
STANLEY PARK
MERSEY
BELFAST DUBLIN
ISLE OF MAN
N. Crosby Rd
S. Crosby Rd
Church Road
B 5422
A 5038
Hawthorne
Stanley
Linacre Lane
Knowsley Road
Marsh Lane
Regent Road
Derby Road
A 567
Merton Rd
A 5058
Balliol Road
Southport Road
Stanley Road
Queens Drive
Rice Lane
Long Lane
B 5187
Longmoor Lane
A 506
B 5194
Stonebridge Lane
Lancashire Road
Lower House Lane
East Lancashire Road
A 580
Utting Avenue East
Oak Lane
Muirhead Avenue East
Walton Hall Avenue
Queens Avenue
Townsend Lane
Utting Avenue
Townsend Avenue
Walton Lane
A 59
Muirhead Av.
Drive
LIVERPOOL
BUILT UP AREA
0 1 km
0 1/2 mile
Aintree Lane BV 2
Aintree Road AV 3
Allerton Road BX 4
Bailey Drive AV 6
Belmont Road BX 7
Bowring Park BX 10
Breck Road BV 12
Brewster Street AV 17
Bridge Road AV 19
Broad Green Road BX 20
Calderstones Road BX 24
Chester Street AX 30
Commercial Road AV 32
Copple House Lane BY 34
County Road AV 36
Crosby Road AV 37
Croxteth Road BV 38
Croxteth Hall Lane BX 40
Durning Road BX 44
Dwerry House Lane BV 45
Elmswood Road BX 47
Gainsborough Road BX 48
Holt Road BX 64
Hornby Road AV 65
Kirkdale Road AV 69
Linacre Road AV 72
Lodge Lane BX 73
Melrose Road AV 77
Mill Bank BV 78

Street	Grid	No.
Netherton Way	AV	90
New Chester Road	AX	91
Northfield Road	AV	95
Oakfield Road	BV	99
Ormskirk Road	BV	100
Pinehurst Avenue	BV	106
Rimrose Road	AV	108
Rocky Lane	BX	112
St. Domingo Road	AV	113
St. Oswald's Street	BX	119
Sandhills Lane	AV	120
Seaforth Road	AV	121
Sefton Park Road	BX	123
Stopgate Lane	BV	129
Tunnel Road	BX	133
Walton Road	ABV	135
Walton Vale	BV	136
Walton Breck Road	AV	137
Warbreck Moor	BV	139
Wellington Road	BX	141
West Derby Road	BX	144

For Street Index
See Liverpool p. 5 and 6

LIVERPOOL
CENTRE

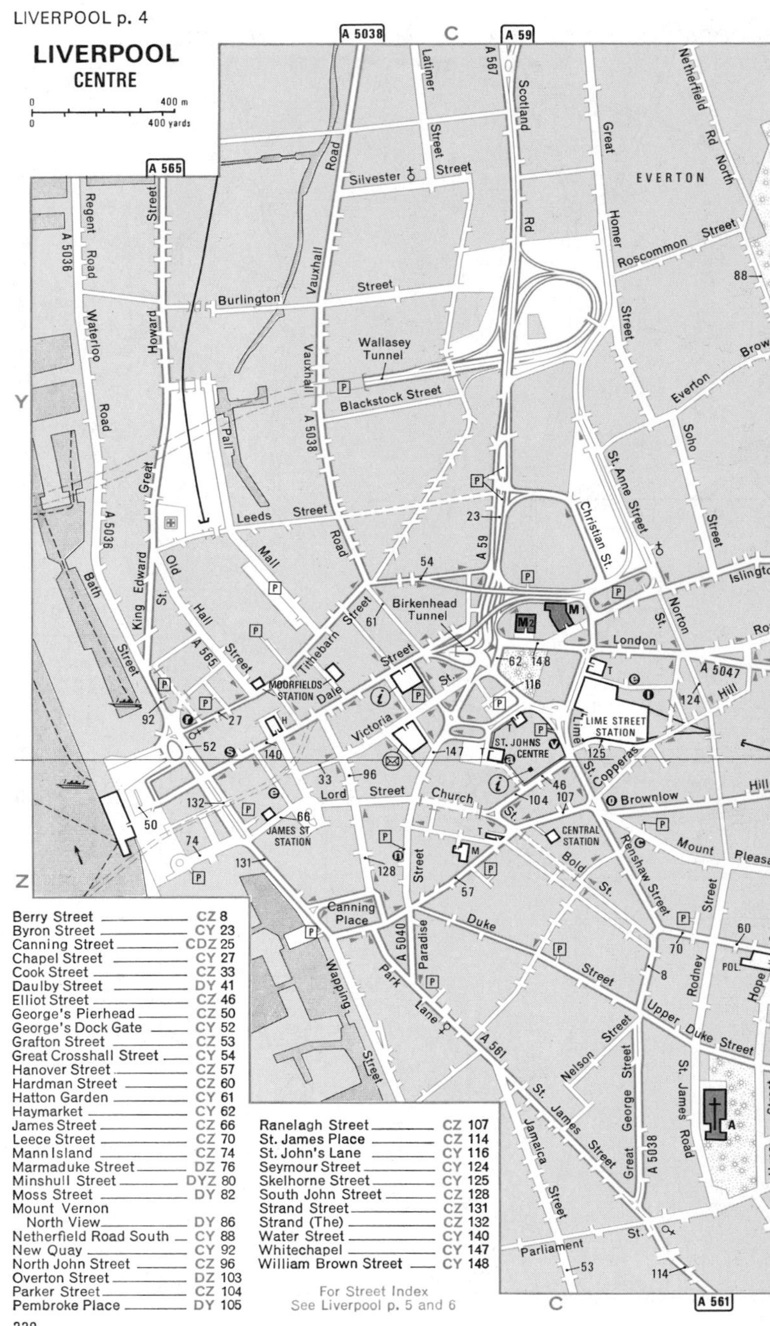

For Street Index
See Liverpool p. 5 and 6

STREET INDEX

Concluded on next page

STREET INDEX TO LIVERPOOL TOWN PLANS (concluded)

Hardman St. p. 4 CZ 60
Hatton Garden p. 4 CY 61
Haymarket p. 4 CY 62
Hawthorne Rd p. 2 AV
Heyworth St. p. 5 DY
High St. p. 3 BX
Holt Rd p. 3 BX 64
Hope St. p. 4 CZ
Hornby Rd p. 2 AV 65
Islington p. 4 CY
Jamaica St. p. 4 CZ
James St. p. 4 CZ 66
Jubilee Drive p. 5 DY
Kelvin Rd p. 3 AX
Kensington p. 5 DY
King St. p. 3 AX
King Edward St. p. 4 CY
Kingsley Rd p. 5 DZ
Kingsway p. 3 AX
Kirkdale Rd p. 2 AV 69
Knowsley Rd p. 2 AV
Laird St. p. 3 AX
Latimer St. p. 4 CY
Leece St. p. 4 CZ 70
Leeds St. p. 4 CY
Lime St. p. 4 CY
Linacre Rd p. 2 AV 72
Linacre Lane p. 2 AV
Liscard Rd p. 3 AX
Lodge Lane p. 3 BX 73
London Rd p. 4 CY
Long Lane p. 2 BV
Longmoor Lane p. 2 BV
Lord St. p. 4 CZ
Lower House Lane p. 2 BV
Low Hill p. 5 DY
Manor Rd p. 3 AX
Mann Island p. 4 CZ 74
Marmaduke St. p. 5 DZ 76
Marsh Lane p. 2 AV
Mather Av. p. 3 BX
Melrose Rd p. 2 AV 77
Menlove Av. p. 3 BX
Merton Rd p. 2 AV
Mill Bank p. 2 BV 78
Minshull St. p. 5 DY 80
Moss Lane p. 2 AV 81
Moss St. p. 5 DY 82
Mount Pleasant p. 4 CZ
Mount Vernon N. View p. 5 DY 86
Muirhead Av. p. 2 BV
Muirhead Av. E. p. 2 BV
Myrtle St. p. 5 DZ
Nelson St. p. 4 CZ
Netherfield Rd N. p. 4 CY
Netherfield Rd S. p. 4 CY 88
Netherton Way p. 2 AV 90
New Chester Rd p. 3 AX 91
New Quay p. 4 CY 92
North Crosby Rd p. 2 AV
Northfield Rd p. 2 AV 95
North John St. p. 4 CZ 96
Norton St. p. 4 CY
Oakfield Rd p. 2 BV 99
Oak Lane p. 2 BV
Old Hall St. p. 4 CY
Ormskirk Rd p. 2 BV 100
Overbury St. p. 5 DZ
Overton St. p. 5 DZ 103
Oxford St. p. 5 DZ
Paddington p. 5 DZ
Pall Mall p. 4 CY
Paradise St. p. 4 CZ
Parker St. p. 4 CZ 104
Park Lane p. 4 CZ
Park Rd p. 3 AX
Parliament St. p. 4 CZ
Pembroke Pl. p. 5 DY 105
Picton Rd p. 3 BX
Pinehurst Av. p. 2 BV 106
Poulton Rd p. 3 AX
Prescot Rd p. 3 BX
Prescot St. p. 5 DY
Prince's Rd p. 5 DZ
Queens Drive p. 3 BX
Queensway p. 3 AX
Ranelagh St. p. 4 CZ 107
Rathbone Rd p. 3 BX
Regent Rd p. 2 AV
Renshaw St. p. 4 CZ
Rice Lane p. 2 AV
Rimrose Rd p. 2 AV 108
Rocky Lane p. 3 BX 112
Rodney St. p. 4 CZ
Roscommon St. p. 4 CY
Rose Lane p. 3 BX
St. Anne St. p. 4 CY
St. Domingo Rd p. 2 AV 113
St. James Pl. p. 4 CZ 114
St. James Rd p. 4 CZ
St. James St. p. 4 CZ
St. John's Lane p. 4 CY 116
St. Johns Centre p. 4 CY
St. Oswald's St. p. 3 BX 119
Sandhills Lane p. 2 AV 120
Scotland Rd p. 4 CY
Seaforth Rd p. 2 AV 121
Sefton Park Rd p. 3 BX 123
Seymour St. p. 4 CY 124
Shaw St. p. 5 DY
Sheil Rd p. 3 BX
Silvester St. p. 4 CY
Skelhorne St. p. 4 CY 125
Smithdown Lane p. 5 DZ
Smithdown Rd p. 3 BX
Soho St. p. 4 CY
South Crosby Rd p. 2 AV
South John St. p. 4 CZ 128
Southport Rd p. 2 AV
Stanley Rd p. 2 AV
Stonebridge Lane p. 2 BV
Stopgate Lane p. 2 BV 129
Strand St. p. 4 CZ 131
Strand (The) p. 4 CZ 132
Tithebarn St. p. 4 CY
Townsend Av. p. 2 BV
Townsend Lane p. 2 BV
Tunnel Rd p. 3 BX 133
Ullet Rd p. 3 BX
Upper Duke St. p. 4 CZ
Upper Hill St. p. 5 DZ
Upper Parliament St. p. 5 DZ
Utting Av. p. 2 BV
Utting Av. E. p. 2 BV
Vauxhall Rd p. 4 CY
Victoria St. p. 4 CY
Walton Lane p. 2 AV
Walton Rd p. 2 AV 135
Walton Vale p. 2 BV 136
Walton Breck Rd p. 2 AV 137
Walton Hall Av. p. 2 BV
Wapping St. p. 4 CZ
Warbreck Moor p. 2 BV 139
Water St. p. 4 CY 140
Waterloo Rd p. 4 CY
Wellington Rd p. 3 BX 141
West Derby Rd p. 3 BX 144
West Derby St. p. 5 DY
Whitechapel p. 4 CY 147
William Brown St. p. 4 CY 148

at Woolton **SE: 5 ½ m. on A 562 – ✉ ⊛ 051 Liverpool:**

XX **Elephant,** 1 Woolton St., L25 5NH, ☎ 428 2711 – Ⓟ by A 562 BX
M a la carte 2.35/5.85 **t.** 🌢 1.05.

MICHELIN Branch, Knowsley Park Industrial Estate, Prescot, L34 9HT, ☎ 548 6242.

AUSTIN-ROVER-TRIUMPH 232 Aigburth Rd ☎ 727 5002
AUSTIN-MORRIS 72/74 Coronation Rd ☎ 924 6411
AUSTIN-MG-WOLSELEY 782 Queens Drive, Stoneycroft ☎ 228 6464
AUSTIN-DAIMLER-JAGUAR-MG-WOLSELEY Hanover St. ☎ 709 9636
BMW Rice Lane ☎ 525 6241
CHRYSLER 44/46 Sandy Rd ☎ 928 3898
CHRYSLER Edge Lane ☎ 924 4210
CHRYSLER-SIMCA Speke Hall Rd ☎ 486 8511
CITROEN Speke Hall Rd ☎ 427 6464
CITROEN 607 West Derby Rd ☎ 228 3670
DAIMLER-JAGUAR-ROVER-TRIUMPH, ROLLS ROYCE-BENTLEY 66/72 Mill Lane ☎ 228 0919
DATSUN 164 Allerton Rd ☎ 724 4699
FIAT East Prescott Rd ☎ 228 9151
FORD Woodend Av. ☎ 486 3211
FORD Linacre Lane ☎ 922 8201
FORD 35 Hardman St. ☎ 709 6622
MORRIS-MG-WOLSELEY 308/310 Kensington ☎ 263 0661
MORRIS-MG-WOLSELEY 175 Lower House Lane ☎ 546 5671
MORRIS-MG-WOLSELEY 84/88 Rose Lane ☎ 724 2377
MORRIS-MG-WOLSELEY 179/181 Duke St. ☎ 709 3437
MORRIS-MG-WOLSELEY 1 Aigburth Rd ☎ 727 2204
MORRIS-MG-WOLSELEY Crosby Rd North ☎ 928 6434
OPEL 215 Knowsley Rd ☎ 922 7585
PEUGEOT Ullet Rd ☎ 727 1413
RENAULT 47/49 Brook Rd West ☎ 924 2387
RENAULT Speke Hall Rd ☎ 486 8846
SAAB 574 Aigburth Rd ☎ 427 3500
SAAB 203 Queens Drive ☎ 228 3964
TOYOTA Gale Rd ☎ 546 8228
VAUXHALL 224 Smithdown Rd, Sefton Park ☎ 733 3262
VAUXHALL 143 Prescot Rd ☎ 263 3488
VAUXHALL 42/44 Irvine St. ☎ 709 7693
VOLVO Fox St. ☎ 207 4364
VW, AUDI-NSU Moor Lane, Thornton ☎ 924 9186
VW, AUDI-NSU Wilson Rd, Huyton ☎ 489 9771

Questa guida non è un repertorio di tutti gli alberghi e ristoranti,
nè comprende tutti i buoni alberghi e ristoranti di Gran Bretagna ed Irlanda.
Nell'intento di tornare utili a tutti i turisti,
siamo indotti ad indicare esercizi
di tutte le classi ed a citarne soltanto un certo numero di ognuna.

LIZARD Cornwall 986 ㊳ – pop. 1,000 – ☎ 032 629.
See : Lizard Point*. **Envir. :** Kynance Cove* *AC*, NW : 1 ½ m.
London 326 – Penzance 24 – Truro 29.

Housel Bay ⚘, Housel Bay, TR12 7PG, ☎ 417, ≤ Housel bay, – wc Ⓟ
Easter-October – **M** (cold lunch) approx. 3.55 **s.** 1.10 – **27 rm** 6.80/20.25 **s.** – P 9.85/12.20 **s.**

LLANARMON DYFFRYN CEIRIOG Clwyd – pop. 161 – ✉ Llangollen – ☎ 069 176.
London 196 – Chester 33 – Shrewsbury 32.

Hand ⚘, LL20 7LD, ☎ 666, – wc Ⓟ
closed February – **M** approx. 4.00 **st.** – **14 rm** 9.00/16.00 **st.** – P 15.00/16.00 **st.**

West Arms ⚘, LL20 7LD, ☎ 665, – wc Ⓟ
M (buffet lunch except Sunday) approx. 3.90 **st.** 1.60 – **15 rm** 9.00/18.00 **t.** – P 12.00/14.00 **t.**

LLANBEDR Gwynedd – see Harlech.

LLANDEILO Dyfed 986 ㉛ – pop. 1,799 – ☎ 055 82.
Envir.: Talley (abbey and lakes*) N : 7 m.
Llandybie nr. Ammanford ☎ 026 975 (Llandybie) 472.
London 218 – Brecon 34 – Carmarthen 15 – **Swansea 25.**

Cawdor Arms, Rhosmaen St., SA19 6EN, ☎ 3500 – wc Ⓟ
M (dinner only October-Easter) approx. 4.00 **s.** 1.50 – **15 rm** 9.00/15.50 **s.**

at Rhosmaen N : 1 m. on A 40 – ✉ ☎ 055 82 Llandeilo :

Plough Inn, SA19 6NP, ☎ 3431 – Ⓟ
closed Sunday, 1 week November and Christmas Day – **M** a la carte 4.20/5.90.

AUSTIN-MORRIS-MG-TRIUMPH 28 Rhosmaen St. ☎ 2297

LLANDOGO Gwent – pop. 290 – ✉ Monmouth – ☎ 059 453 St. Briavels.
London 140 – Bristol 26 – Gloucester 43 – Newport 25.

Old Farmhouse, NP5 4TL, on A 466 ☎ 303 – wc Ⓟ
closed 2 weeks November – **M** 3.25/4.00 **t.** 1.25 – **27 rm** 7.50/17.00 **st.** – P 12.00/20.00 **st.**

LLANDOVERY Dyfed 986 ㉛ – pop. 2,002 – ☎ 0550.
i Brecon Beacons National Park, Central Car Park, 8 Broad St. ☎ 20693 (Easter-September).
London 204 – Brecon 21 – Carmarthen 28 – **Swansea 38.**

Picton Court ⚘, S : on Myddfai Rd, SA20 0JT, ☎ 20320 – wc Ⓟ
8 rm.

Broadway, 13 Market Sq. ☎ 20297
9 rm 5.00/10.00 **st.**

LLANDRINDOD WELLS Powys 986 ㉛ – pop. 3,381 – ☎ 0597.
☎ 2010, E : 1 m.
i Tourist Information Centre, Town Hall ☎ 2600.
London 202 – Brecon 28 – Carmarthen 59 – Shrewsbury 59.

Metropole (Interchange), Temple St., LD1 5DY, ☎ 2881, Telex 35237, – wc Ⓟ.
M approx. 4.30 **st.** 1.90 – **138 rm** 8.90/18.00 **st.** – P 16.10/17.60 **st.**

AUSTIN-DAIMLER-JAGUAR-MORRIS-MG-ROVER-TRIUMPH-WOLSELEY Temple St. ☎ 2214
CHRYSLER Temple St. ☎ 2121
VAUXHALL Tremont Rd ☎ 2461

LLANDUDNO Gwynedd 986 ㉗ – pop. 19,077 – ☎ 0492.
See : Great Orme's Head (≤** from the summit) by Ty-Gwyn Rd A – Tour of the Great Orme's Head**. **Envir. :** Bodnant gardens** *AC*, SE : 10 ½ m. by A 496 A.
72 Bryniau Rd ☎ 75325 A.
to the Isle of Man : Douglas (Isle of Man Steam Packet Co.) Summer 2-4 weekly (3 h).
i Information Centre, 1-2 Chapel St. ☎ 76413 – Information Office, Arcadia Theatre ☎ 76413 (July-August only).
London 242 – Birkenhead 55 – Chester 47 – Holyhead 43.

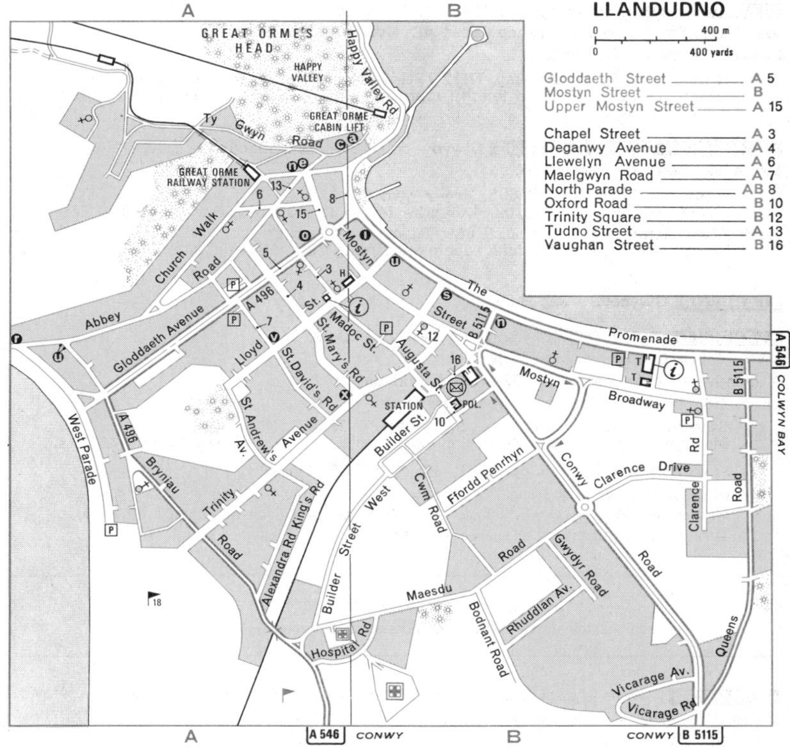

St. George's, St. George's Pl., LL30 2LG, ☎ 77544 – [lift] [TV] (P). – **M** approx. 4.00 **s.** 1.25 – **79 rm** 7.50/19.00 **s.** – P 12.50/17.50 **s.** B **u**

Empire, 73 Church Walks, LL30 2HE, ☎ 77260, Telex 617161 – [lift] [TV] (P) – *closed Christmas and 1 January* – **M** approx. 4.75 **s.** 2.30 – **51 rm** 8.00/16.00 **s.** – P 11.50/18.00 **s.** A **e**

Marine (T.H.F.), Promenade, LL30 1AN, ☎ 77521 – [lift] [TV] (P). [garage] – **M** 3.50/3.75 **st.** 1.90 – **79 rm** 7.50/15.00 **st.** – P 14.50/16.50 **st.** B **n**

Gogarth Abbey, West Shore, LL30 2QY, ☎ 76212, [view] – [hotel]wc (P) – *closed January and February* – **M** approx. 4.00 **t.** 1.50 – **41 rm** 7.50/11.25 **t.** – P 12.00/16.00 **t.** A **r**

Clarence, Gloddaeth Av., LL30 2DS, ☎ 76485 – [lift] – *Easter-October* – **M** approx. 2.90 **s.** 1.60 – **74 rm** 8.25/16.50. A **o**

Southcliffe, Hill Terrace, LL30 2LS, ☎ 76277, [view] – [hotel]wc – *April-October* – **M** approx. 2.50 **t.** 1.20 – **32 rm** 5.00/12.30 – P 7.75/8.15. AB **c**

Esplanade, 1-5 Glan-y-Mor Parade, Promenade, LL30 1LL, ☎ 76687 – [lift] [hotel]wc (P). [garage] – **M** 3.00/3.50 2.00 – **55 rm** 6.50/16.50 – P 10.00/12.50. B **i**

Headlands, Hill Terrace, LL30 2LS, ☎ 77485, [view] – *Easter-September* – **M** approx. 2.50 **t.** 1.30 – **19 rm** 5.50/11.00 – P 7.90/8.20. AB **a**

Lockyers, Promenade, LL30 2XS, ☎ 76053 – [lift] – *Easter-mid October* – **M** 2.00/2.75 1.65 – **52 rm** 7.00/17.00 – P 8.50/10.50. B **s**

Clontarf, West Shore, LL30 2AS, ☎ 77621 – [hotel]wc (P) – *Easter-October* – **M** 2.50/3.50 **s.** 1.40 – **10 rm** 5.00/13.50 **s.** – P 8.75/9.75 **s.** A **u**

Cranleigh, Great Orme's Rd, West Shore, LL30 2AR, ☎ 77688 – (P) – *Easter-October* – **13 rm** 5.75/11.50. A **u**

Leamore, 40 Lloyd St., LL30 2YG, ☎ 75552 – *Easter-October* – **12 rm** 5.00/10.00 **st.** A **v**

- Bella Vista Private, 72 Church Walk, LL30 2HG, ☎ 76855 — A n
  closed December-1 January – **12 rm** 4.35/8.65 **st.**
- Buile Hill, 46 St. Mary's Rd, LL30 2UE, ☎ 76972 — AB x
  closed December and January – **13 rm** 6.50/13.00 **t.**

at Deganwy **S : 2 ½ m. by A 546** – A – ✉ **Conwy** – **0492 Deganwy :**

- **Deganwy Castle,** LL31 9DA, ☎ 83358, ≤, – TV wc ☎ P
  M (bar lunch except Sunday) approx. 4.25 **s.** 2.25 – **30 rm** 8.50/20.00 **s.**

AUSTIN Nant-y-Gamor Rd ☎ 78156
CHRYSLER-SIMCA Conwy Rd ☎ 77461
CITROEN Herkomer Rd ☎ 77607
FORD 141 Mostyn St. ☎ 77511

LLANELLI Dyfed 986 ㉛ – pop. 26,383 – 055 42.

London 206 – Carmarthen 20 – Swansea 11.

- **Stradey Park** (T.H.F.), Furnace, SA15 4HA, ☎ 58171, Telex 48521 – TV wc ☎ P.
  M 4.00/4.50 **st.** 1.50 – **86 rm** 11.00/17.00 **st.** – P 14.00/17.00 **st.**
- **Stepney** (Crest), Park St., SA15 3YE, ☎ 2155 – ☎ P
  M *(closed Sunday dinner)* 3.25/4.25 **s.** 1.55 – **34 rm** 10.50/15.20 **s.**

AUSTIN-ROVER-TRIUMPH Vauxhall St. ☎ 3371
FORD Sandy Rd ☎ 3120
MORRIS-MG-WOLSELEY Pwll ☎ 3666
SIMCA Marsh St. ☎ 4609
VAUXHALL Sandy Rd ☎ 59284

Would you read yesterday's paper ?
Then use this year's guide.

LLANFYLLIN Powys 986 ㉗ – pop. 1,118 – 069 184.

London 188 – Chester 42 – Shrewsbury 24 – Welshpool 11.

- **Bodfach Hall**, SY22 5HS, NW : 1 m. on B 4391 ☎ 272, ≤, « Country house in extensive gardens », park – wc P
  March-October – **M** (dinner only) 3.00/5.50 **st.** – **10 rm** 9.00/16.50 **st.**
- **Cain Valley,** High St., SY22 5AQ, ☎ 366 – wc P
  M 2.95/3.95 **t.** 1.00 – **12 rm** 6.30/11.50 **t.**

LLANGADOG Dyfed 986 ㉛ – pop. 1,186 – 055 03.

London 218 – Carmarthen 15 – Swansea 29.

- **Plas Glansevin**, SA19 9HY, E : 1 ½ m. on Myddfai Rd ☎ 238, ≤, – P
  M *(closed Monday, Tuesday and 24-25 December)* approx. 4.75 **st.** – **8 rm** 6.95/16.00 **st.**

LLANGAMMARCH WELLS Powys – 059 12.

London 200 – Brecon 17 – Builth Wells 8.

- **Lake**, LD4 4BS, E : ¾ m. ☎ 202, ≤, , park – wc P
  mid March-early November – **M** 4.00/5.00 1.00 – **27 rm** 6.00/13.00 – P 10.00/12.00.

LLANGOLLEN Clwyd 986 ⑨ and ㉗ – pop. 3,117 – 0978.

See : Plas Newydd** (the house of the Ladies of Llangollen) *AC*. **Envir. :** Horseshoe Pass* NW : 4 ½ m.

18 ☎ 860040, E : 1 ½ m.

i Tourist Information Centre, Town Hall ☎ 860828.

London 194 – Chester 23 – Holyhead 76 – Shrewsbury 30.

- **Bryn Howel**, LL20 7UW, E : 2 ¾ m. on A 539 ☎ 860331, ≤, – TV wc ☎ P.
  M 3.50/3.75 **st.** 1.30 – **38 rm** 7.25/17.75 **st.**
- **Hand** (Mt. Charlotte), Bridge St., LL20 8PL, ☎ 860303, ≤, – wc wc P
  M a la carte 3.50/5.75 **s.** 1.45 – **61 rm** 9.00/18.90 **st.**
- **Royal** (T.H.F.), Bridge St., LL20 8PG, ☎ 860202, ≤, – TV wc ☎ P.
  M 3.25/3.85 **st.** 1.45 – **39 rm** 7.00/14.00 **st.** – P 12.75/15.00 **st.**
- **Chain Bridge,** LL20 8BS, W : 2 m. by A 5 ☎ 860215, ≤ river Dee – wc wc ☎ P
  M (grill lunch) 3.30/3.50 – **34 rm** 5.00/12.00.

AUSTIN-MORRIS-MG-WOLSELEY Berwyn St. ☎ 2270
CHRYSLER Regent St. ☎ 2776

LLANGYNIDR Powys – pop. 520 – ✉ Crickhowell – 0874 Bwlch.

Envir.: Bwlch (≤* of the Usk Valley) N : 2 ½ m. – Tretower Court and castle* NE : 3 ½ m.

London 174 – Brecon 11 – Newport 30.

- **Coach and Horses,** Cwm Crawnon Rd, NP8 1LS, on B 4558 ☎ 730245, – P
  M a la carte 3.70/5.35 **st.** 1.50.

LLANGYNOG Powys – pop. 265 – ✉ Oswestry (Salop) – ☎ 069 174 Pennant.
London 193 – Chester 46 – Shrewsbury 30.

- **New Inn,** ☎ 229 – Ⓟ
  M 2.50/4.00 **s.** – **8 rm** 3.50/7.00 **s.** – P 6.50/7.50 **s.**

LLANRHAEADR Clwyd – pop. 891 – ✉ Denbigh – ☎ 074 578 Llanynys.
London 214 – Chester 28 – Shrewsbury 50.

- **Bryn Morfydd**, LL16 4NP, ☎ 280, ≤ Vale of Clwyd, heated, park – TV wc wc Ⓟ.
  M approx. 3.00 **t.** – **21 rm** 12.50/21.00 **t.**

AUSTIN-MG-WOLSELEY ☎ 227

LLANRWST Gwynedd 986 ㉗ – pop. 2,743 – ☎ 0492.
See : Gwydir Castle*. **Envir.:** Capel Garmon (Burial Chamber*) SE: 6 m.
i Snowdonia National Park Countryside Centre, Glan-y-Borth ☎ 640604.
London 230 – Holyhead 50 – Shrewsbury 66.

- **Gwesty Plas Maenan**, LL26 0YR, N: 4 m. on A 470 ☎ 049 269 (Dolgarrog) 232, ≤, park – TV Ⓟ.
  M a la carte 2.65/4.50 **t.** 1.30 – 1.00 – **15 rm** 10.00/17.00 **t.**
- **Meadowsweet** with rm, Station Rd, LL26 0DS, ☎ 640732
  March-October – (open all year except Sunday to Wednesday in winter) (dinner only) a la carte 3.75/6.05 1.25 – **4 rm** 5.50/10.50.

MORRIS-MG-ROVER-TRIUMPH ☎ 640381

LLANTWIT MAJOR South Glam. – pop. 6,503 – ☎ 044 65.
London 175 – Cardiff 18 – Swansea 33.

- **Quaintways,** Colhugh St., CF6 9RE, ☎ 2321 – Ⓟ
  closed Sunday and 26 December – **M** (dinner only) a la carte 3.65/6.30 **t.** 1.20.

TOYOTA 2 Colhugh St. ☎ 3466

LLANWNDA Gwynedd – see Caernarfon.

LLANWRTYD WELLS Powys 986 ㉛ – pop.488 – ☎ 059 13.
See : Cambrian Mountains : road** from Llanwrtyd to Tregaron. **Envir.:** Rhandir-mwyn (≤* of Afon Tywi Valley) SW: 12 m.
London 214 – Brecon 32 – Carmarthen 39.

- **Abernant Lake** (Mt. Charlotte), LD5 4RR, ☎ 250, heated, park – wc Ⓟ
  M 3.00/4.00 **s.** 1.50 – **56 rm** 4.00/10.00 **s.** – P 7.55/9.70 **s.**

  at Abergwesyn NW: 4 ½ m. – ✉ Builth Wells – ☎ 059 13 Llanwrtyd Wells:

- **Llwynderw**, LD5 4TW, ☎ 238, ≤ countryside and hills, – wc Ⓟ
  Easter-October – **M** *(mid March-October)* (dinner only) (by arrangement only to non residents) approx. 7.00 2.00 – **12 rm** (dinner included) 18.00/36.00 **st.**

LLWYNMAWR Clwyd – pop. 740 – ✉ Llangollen – ☎ 069 172 Glynceiriog.
London 192 – Shrewsbury 28 – Wrexham 15.

- **Golden Pheasant**, LL20 7BB, ☎ 281, ≤ Ceiriog Valley, – wc Ⓟ
  M a la carte 3.50/4.75 **st.** 1.40 – **14 rm** 11.50/28.00 **st.** – P 15.00/17.50 **st.**

LOFTUS Cleveland 986 ⑳ – pop. 7,760 – ✉ Saltburn by the Sea – ☎ 0287.
London 264 – Leeds 73 – Middlesbrough 17 – Scarborough 36.

- **Grinkle Park**, Easington, TS13 4UB, ☎ 40515, ≤, park – TV wc Ⓟ
  M a la carte 4.25/5.35 **st.** – **17 rm** 8.30/15.65 **st.** – P 14.10/19.00 **st.**

London

LONDON (Greater) 986 ④ ⑧ and ㊱ – pop. 7,452,346 – ✆ 01.

Heathrow, ✆ 759 4321.

Gatwick, ✆ 0293 (Crawley) 28822, p. 12 : by A 23 DZ.

BA Air Terminal : Buckingham Palace Rd, Victoria, SW1, ✆ 834 2323, p. 26 AX.

British Caledonian Airways, Victoria Air Terminal : Victoria Station, SW1, ✆ 833 9411, p. 26 BX.

BA, West London Air Terminal : Cromwell Rd, SW7, ✆ 370 5411, p. 24.

Euston ✆ 387 9400 ext 4461 – Kensington Olympia ✆ 603 4555 – King's Cross ✆ 837 4200 ext 4700 – Paddington ✆ 723 7000 ext 3148.

i London Tourist Board, Head Office : 4 Grosvenor Gardens, SW1W 0DU, ✆ 730 0791, Telex 919041.
Victoria Station (adjacent to Platform 15), Buckingham Palace Rd, SW1, ✆ 739 0202.
British Tourist Authority, 64 James's St., SW1, ✆ 629 9191.

N'oubliez pas qu'il existe des limitations de vitesse au Royaume Uni en dehors de celles mentionnées sur les panneaux.

60 mph (= 96 km/h) sur route.
70 mph (= 112 km/h) sur route à chaussées séparées et autoroute.

SIGHTS
CURIOSITÉS
LE CURIOSITÀ
SEHENSWÜRDIGKEITEN

HISTORIC BUILDINGS AND MONUMENTS

Palace of Westminster*** (Houses of Parliament) p. 19 NX – Tower of London*** p. 16 QU – Banqueting House** p. 19 NV – Buckingham Palace** (Changing of the Guard**) p. 26 BV – Kensington Palace** p. 18 JV – Lincoln's Inn** p. 27 FV – Royal Hospital Chelsea** p. 25 FU – St. James's Palace** p. 23 EP – South Bank Arts Centre** (Royal Festival Hall*) p. 19 NV – The Temple** p. 15 NU – Tower Bridge** p. 20 QV – Albert Memorial* p. 24 CQ – Apsley House* (Wellington Museum) p. 22 BP – Burlington House* (Museum of Mankind) p. 23 EM – Charterhouse* p. 16 PT – Commonwealth Institute* p. 17 HX – County Hall* p. 19 NX – Design Centre* p. 23 FM – HMS Discovery* p. 27 FX – George Inn*, Southwark p. 20 QV – Gray's Inn* p. 15 NT – Guildhall* p. 16 PT – Dr Johnson's House* p. 16 PT **A** – Lancaster House* p. 23 EP – London Bridge* p. 20 QV – Mansion House* p. 16 QU **P** – The Monument* (☼*) p. 16 QU **G** – Royal Exchange* p. 16 QU **V** – Somerset House* p. 27 EV – Staple Inn* p. 15 NT **Y** – Stock Exchange* p. 16 QU – Westminster Bridge* p. 19 NX.

CHURCHES

St. Paul's Cathedral*** (Dome ☼***) p. 16 PU – Westminster Abbey*** p. 19 MX – St. Bartholomew the Great** p. 16 PT **K** – St. Mary-at-Hill** p. 16 QU **B** – Southwark Cathedral** p. 20 QV – Temple Church** p. 15 NU **D** – Christ Church* p. 16 PT **E** – Queen's Chapel* p. 23 EP – St. Bride's* p. 16 PU **J** – St. Clement Danes* p. 27 FV – St. Dunstan-in-the-East* p. 16 QU **F** – St. Giles Cripplegate* p. 16 PT **N** – St. Helen Bishopsgate* p. 16 QU **R** – St. Margaret Lothbury* p. 16 QT **S** – St. Martin-in-the-Fields* p. 27 DX – St. Mary Abchurch* p. 16 QU **X** – St. Olave* p. 16 QU **Y** – St. Stephen Walbrook* p. 16 QU **Z**.

PARKS

Regent's Park*** (London Zoo***) p. 14 KS – Hyde Park** p. 18 JU – St. James's Park** p. 19 MV – Kensington Gardens* p. 18 JV.

STREETS AND SQUARES

Bedford Square** p. 15 MT – Belgrave Square** p. 26 AV – The Mall** p. 23 GN – Nash Terraces**, Regent's Park p. 14 KS – Piccadilly** p. 23 EM – The Thames** pp. 18-20 – Trafalgar Square** p. 27 DX – Whitehall** p. 19 MV – Barbican* p. 16 PT – Bond Street* pp. 22-23 CK-DM – Burlington Arcade* p. 23 DM – Carlton House Terrace* p. 23 GN – Cheyne Walk* p. 18 JZ – Fitzroy Square* p. 15 LT – Jermyn Street* p. 23 EN – Merrick Square* p. 20 PX – Montpelier Square* p. 25 EQ – Portman Square* p. 22 AJ – Queen Anne's Gate* p. 19 MX – Regent Street* p. 23 EM – St. James's Square* p. 23 FN – St. James's Street* p. 23 EN – Shepherd Market* p. 22 CN – Soho Square* p. 23 FJ – Strand* p. 27 DX – Trinity Church Square* p. 20 PX – Victoria Embankment* p. 27 EX – Waterloo Place* p. 23 FN.

MUSEUMS

British Museum*** p. 15 MT – National Gallery*** p. 23 GM – Science Museum*** p. 24 CR – Tate Gallery*** p. 19 MY – Victoria and Albert Museum*** p. 25 DR – Courtauld Institute Galleries** p. 15 MT **M** – Museum of London** p. 16 PT **M** – National Portrait Gallery** p. 23 GM – Natural History Museum** p. 24 CS – Queen's Gallery** p. 26 BV – Wallace Collection** p. 22 AH – Geological Museum* p. 24 CR – Imperial War Museum* p. 20 PX – Madame Tussaud's* p. 14 KT **M** – Museum of Mankind* p. 23 DM – National Army Museum* p. 25 FU – Percival David Foundation of Chinese Art* p. 15 MS **M** – Sir John Soane's Museum* p. 15 NT **M** – Wellington Museum* p. 22 BP.

OUTER LONDON

Hampton Court*** (Hampton Court) p. 8 BZ – Kew Gardens*** (Kew) p. 8 BY – Windsor Castle*** by A4, M4 AX – Chiswick House** (Chiswick) p. 8 BCY **R** – Chiswick Mall** (Chiswick) p. 8 CY – Cutty Sark** (Greenwich) p. 9 EXY **A** – Fenton House** (Hampstead) p. 13 GR – Ham House** (near Richmond) p. 8 BY **N** – Kenwood House** (Hampstead Heath) p. 8 DV **E** – Kew Palace** (Kew Gardens) p. 8 BY **S** – National Maritime Museum** (Greenwich) p. 9 EXY **A** – Osterley Park** (Hounslow) p. 8 BY – Richmond Bridge** p. 8 BY **A** – Richmond Green** p. 8 BY **A** – Richmond Park** p. 8 BY – Royal Air Force Museum** (Hendon) p. 8 CV **M** – Royal Naval College** (Greenwich) p. 9 EXY **A** – Syon Park** (Brentford) p. 8 BY – Canonbury Square* (Islington) p. 16 PR – Dulwich Gallery* p. 9 EY **L** – Geffrye Museum* (Shoreditch) p. 9 EX **M** – Hogarth's House* (Chiswick) p. 8 CX **A** – Old Royal Observatory* (Greenwich Park) p. 9 EXY **A** – St. Katharine Dock* (Tower Hamlets) p. 9 EX **B**.

THE BOROUGHS AND THEIR AREAS

Those with recommended hotels and restaurants are printed in red

Greater London is divided, for administrative purposes, into 32 boroughs plus the City; these sub-divide naturally into minor areas, usually grouped around former villages or quarters, which often maintain a distinctive character.

LES ,, BOROUGHS '' ET LEURS ,, AREAS ''

Nous signalons en rouge ceux ayant des hôtels et restaurants cités

Le Grand Londres (GREATER LONDON) est composé de la City et de 32 arrondissements administratifs (Borough) eux-mêmes divisés en quartiers ou villages ayant conservé leur caractère propre (Area).

I DISTRETTI AMMINISTRATIVI (BOROUGHS) ED I LORO QUARTIERI (AREAS)

Segnaliamo in rosso quelli che hanno alberghi e ristoranti citati

La Grande Londra (GREATER LONDON) e' composta dalla City e da 32 distretti amministrativi (Borough) divisi a loro volta in quartieri o villaggi che hanno conservato il loro proprio carattere (Area).

DIE ,, BOROUGHS '' UND IHRE ,, AREAS ''

Die mit empfohlenen Hotels und Restaurants sind rot gedruckt

Groß-London (GREATER LONDON) besteht aus der City und 32 Verwaltungsbezirken (Borough); diese sind wiederum in kleinere Bezirke (Area) unterteilt, deren Mittelpunkt ehemalige Dörfer oder Stadtviertel sind, die oft ihren eigenen Charakter bewahrt haben.

BOROUGH	PAGE Plan	PAGE Est.	AREA
Barking pp. 8 and 9			Barking (eastern)
			Dagenham (southern)
Barnet pp. 8 and 9			Barnet
			Church End
			Cricklewood
			East Barnet
			East Finchley
		43	Finchley
			Friern Barnet
		43	Golders Green
		43	Hendon
			The Hyde (also Brent)
			Mill Hill
			North Finchley
			Whetstone
Bexley pp. 8 and 9		43	Bexley
			Chislehurst (northern)
			Crayford
			Erith
		43	Sidcup (also Bromley)
		43	Welling
Brent pp. 8 and 9			The Hyde (also Barnet)
			Kilburn
		43	Wembley
			Willesden
Bromley pp. 8 and 9			Anerley
		43	Beckenham
		44	Bickley
		44	Bromley
		44	Chislehurst (southern)
		44	Farnborough
		44	Orpington
			Penge
			Sidcup (also Bexley)
			Sydenham

AREA	PAGE Plan	PAGE Est.	BOROUGH
Abbey Wood			Greenwich
Acton			Ealing
Airport Area (Heathrow)			Hounslow
Aldersgate		46	City of London
Aldgate		46	City of London
Anerley			Bromley
Balham			Wandsworth
Barking (eastern)			Barking
Barking (western)			Newham
Barnes		56	Richmond-upon-Thames
Barnet			Barnet
Battersea		57	Wandsworth
Bayswater and Maida Vale	13	58	Westminster (City of)
Beckenham		43	Bromley
Beddington and Wallington			Sutton
Belgravia	18	59	Westminster (City of)
Bermondsey			Southwark
Bethnal Green			Tower Hamlets
Bexley		43	Bexley
Bickley		44	Bromley
Bishopsgate		46	City of London
Blackheath		55	Lewisham (also Greenwich)
Bloomsbury	15	44	Camden
Bow			Tower Hamlets
Brentford		50	Hounslow
Brixton			Lambeth
Brixton Hill			Lambeth
Brockley			Lewisham
Bromley		44	Bromley
Bromley		55	Lewisham
Brompton			Kensington and Chelsea (Royal Borough of)
Bushey Heath		49	Harrow
Camberwell			Southwark
Carshalton Beeches			Sutton

BOROUGH	PAGE Plan	PAGE Est.	AREA
Camden	15	44	Bloomsbury
pp. 13 to 16	15	45	Euston
	13	45	Finchley Road
	13	45	Hampstead
			High Holborn
	15	46	Holborn (also City)
			Kentish Town
	15	46	King's Cross (also Islington)
	15	46	Regent's Park
			St. Pancras
	14	46	Swiss Cottage
City of London		46	Aldersgate
pp. 13 to 16		46	Aldgate
		46	Bishopsgate
		46	Cheapside
		46	Holborn (also Camden)
		46	Queenhithe
Croydon			Coulsdon and Purley
pp. 8 and 9		47	Croydon
		47	Norbury
			Norwood
			Purley and Coulsdon
		47	Sanderstead
		47	Shirley
		47	South Croydon
			South Norwood
Ealing			Acton
pp. 8 and 9		47	Ealing
			Hanwell
			Southall
			West Ealing
Enfield			Cockfosters
pp. 8 and 9		48	Edmonton
		48	Enfield
		48	Hadley Wood
			Lower Edmonton
			New Southgate
		48	Palmers Green
			Southgate
			Upper Edmonton
Greenwich			Abbey Wood
pp. 8 and 9			Blackheath
			Charlton
		48	Eltham
		48	Greenwich
			Woolwich (south Thames)
Hackney			Clapton
pp. 8 and			Finsbury Park
			Hackney
			Homerton
			Shoreditch
			Stoke Newington

AREA	PAGE Plan	PAGE Est.	BOROUGH
Catford		55	Lewisham
Central Harrow		49	Harrow
Charlton			Greenwich
Cheam and Sutton			Sutton
Cheapside		46	City of London
Chelsea	25	51	Kensington and Chelsea (Royal Borough of)
Chigwell (southern)			Redbridge
Chingford			Waltham Forest
Chislehurst (northern)			Bexley
Chislehurst (southern)		44	Bromley
Chiswick			Hounslow
Church End			Barnet
Clapham		57	Wandsworth (also Lambeth)
Clapton			Hackney
Cockfosters			Enfield
Coombe			Kingston-upon-Thames
Coulsdon and Purley			Croydon
Cranford		50	Hounslow
Crayford			Bexley
Cricklewood			Barnet
Croydon		47	Croydon
Dagenham (southern)			Barking
Dagenham (northern)			Redbridge
Deptford			Lewisham
Dulwich Village		57	Southwark
Ealing		47	Ealing
Earl's Court	24	52	Kensington and Chelsea (Royal Borough of)
East Barnet			Barnet
Eastcote		49	Hillingdon
East Dulwich			Southwark
East Finchley			Barnet
East Ham			Newham
Edmonton		48	Enfield
Eltham		48	Greenwich
Enfield		48	Enfield
Erith			Bexley
Euston	15	45	Camden
Farnborough		44	Bromley
Feltham			Hounslow
Finchley		43	Barnet
Finchley Road	13	45	Camden
Finsbury	15	50	Islington
Finsbury Park			Hackney
Finsbury Park			Haringey
Forest Gate			Newham
Forest Hill			Lewisham
Friern Barnet			Barnet
Fulham	17	48	Hammersmith
Golders Green		43	Barnet
Greenwich		48	Greenwich
Hackney			Hackney
Hadley Wood		48	Enfield
Hammersmith	17	48	Hammersmith
Hampstead	13	45	Camden

BOROUGH	PAGE Plan	PAGE Est.	AREA
ammersmith	17	48	Fulham
. 17 to 20	17	48	Hammersmith
			Shepherd's Bush
	17	49	West Kensington
aringey			Finsbury Park
. 8 and 9		49	Highgate
			Hornsey
		49	Muswell Hill
			South Tottenham
			Tottenham
			Wood Green
arrow		49	Bushey Heath
. 8 and 9		49	Central Harrow
			Harrow on the Hill
			Harrow Weald
			Kenton
		49	Pinner
		49	Stanmore
avering		49	Hornchurch
. 8 and 9			Romford
llingdon		49	Eastcote
. 8 and 9			Harlington
			Hayes
		49	Heathrow (Airport)
		50	Hillingdon
		50	Northwood
		50	Ruislip
			Uxbridge
			West Drayton
			Yiewsley
ounslow			Airport Area (Heathrow)
. 8 and 9		50	Brentford
			Chiswick
		50	Cranford
			Feltham
			Heston
		50	Hounslow
		50	Isleworth
ington	15	50	Finsbury
. 13 to 16			Highbury
			Holloway
	15	50	Islington
			King's Cross
			Upper Holloway
nsington and			Brompton
elsea (Royal	25	51	Chelsea
rough of)	24	52	Earl's Court
. 17 to 20	17	53	Kensington
	13	54	North Kensington
			Notting Hill
	24	54	South Kensington
			West Brompton

AREA	PAGE Plan	PAGE Est.	BOROUGH
Hampton Court		56	Richmond-upon-Thames
Hanwell			Ealing
Harlington			Hillingdon
Harrow on the Hill			Harrow
Harrow Weald			Harrow
Hayes			Hillingdon
Heathrow (Airport)		49	Hillingdon
Hendon		43	Barnet
Herne Hill			Lambeth (also Southwark)
Heston			Hounslow
Highbury			Islington
Highgate		49	Haringey
High Holborn			Camden
Hillingdon		50	Hillingdon
Holborn	15	46	Camden (also City)
Holloway			Islington
Homerton			Hackney
Hornchurch		49	Havering
Hornsey			Haringey
Hounslow		50	Hounslow
Hyde (The)			Barnet (also Brent)
Hyde Park and Knightsbridge	18	59	Westminster (City of)
Ilford		56	Redbridge
Isleworth		50	Hounslow
Islington	15	50	Islington
Kennington			Lambeth (also Southwark)
Kensington	17	53	Kensington and Chelsea (Royal Borough of)
Kentish Town			Camden
Kenton			Harrow
Kew		56	Richmond-upon-Thames
Kilburn			Brent
King's Cross	15	46	Camden (also Islington)
Kingston		55	Kingston-upon-Thames
Lambeth			Lambeth
Lee			Lewisham
Lewisham			Lewisham
Leyton			Waltham Forest
Leytonstone		57	Waltham Forest
Lower Edmonton			Enfield
Malden			Kingston-upon-Thames
Manor Park			Newham
Mayfair	15	59	Westminster (City of)
Merton			Merton
Mill Hill			Barnet
Mitcham			Merton
Morden			Merton
Mortlake			Richmond-upon-Thames
Muswell Hill		49	Haringey

BOROUGH	PAGE Plan	PAGE Est.	AREA
Kingston-upon-Thames pp. 8 and 9			Coombe
		55	Kingston-upon-Thames
			Malden
			Surbiton
Lambeth pp. 17 to 20			Brixton
			Brixton Hill
			Clapham (also Wandsworth)
			Herne Hill (also Southwark)
			Kennington
			Lambeth
			South Lambeth (also Wandsworth)
			Stockwell
			Streatham
		55	Waterloo
			West Norwood
Lewisham pp. 8 and 9		55	Blackheath (also Greenwich)
			Brockley
		55	Bromley
		55	Catford
			Deptford
			Forest Hill
			Lee
			Lewisham
			New Cross
Merton pp. 8 and 9			Merton
			Mitcham
			Morden
			West Wimbledon
		56	Wimbledon
Newham pp. 8 and 9			Barking (western)
			East Ham
			Forest Gate
			Manor Park
			North Woolwich
			Plaistow
			Stratford
			Victoria Docks
			West Ham
			Woolwich (north Thames)
Redbridge pp. 8 and 9			Chigwell (southern)
			Dagenham (northern)
		56	Ilford
		56	South Woodford
			Wanstead
			Woodford
Richmond-upon-Thames pp. 8 and 9		56	Barnes
		56	Hampton Court
		56	Kew
			Mortlake
		56	Richmond
			Twickenham

AREA	PAGE Plan	PAGE Est.	BOROUGH
New Cross			Lewisham
New Southgate			Enfield
Norbury		47	Croydon
North Finchley			Barnet
North Kensington	13	54	Kensington an Chelsea (Royal Borough of)
North Woolwich			Newham
Northwood		50	Hillingdon
Norwood			Croydon
Notting Hill			Kensington an Chelsea (Royal Borough of)
Orpington		44	Bromley
Paddington			Westminster (City of)
Palmers Green		48	Enfield
Peckam			Southwark
Penge			Bromley
Pinner		49	Harrow
Plaistow			Newham
Poplar			Tower Hamlets
Purley and Coulsdon			Croydon
Putney		57	Wandsworth
Queenhithe		46	City of London
Regent's Park	15	46	Camden
Regent's Park and Marylebone	14	60	Westminster (City of)
Richmond		56	Richmond-upon-Thames
Romford			Havering
Rotherhithe			Southwark
Ruislip		50	Hillingdon
St. James's	19	62	Westminster (City of)
St. John's Wood			Westminster (City of)
St. Pancras			Camden
Sanderstead		47	Croydon
Shepherd's Bush			Hammersmith
Shirley		47	Croydon
Shoreditch			Hackney
Sidcup		43	Bexley (also Bromley)
Soho	15	63	Westminster (City of)
South Croydon		47	Croydon
Southgate			Enfield
Southall			Ealing
South Kensington	24	54	Kensington an Chelsea (Royal Borough of)
South Lambeth			Lambeth (also Wandsworth)
South Norwood			Croydon
South Tottenham			Haringey
Southwark			Southwark
South Woodford		56	Redbridge
Spitalfields			Tower Hamlets

BOROUGH	PAGE Plan	PAGE Est.	AREA
Southwark pp. 17 to 20			Bermondsey
			Camberwell
		57	Dulwich Village
			East Dulwich
			Herne Hill (also Lambeth)
			Kennington
			Peckham
			Rotherhithe
			Southwark
			Walworth
Sutton pp. 8 and 9			Beddington and Wallington
			Carshalton
			Beeches
			Cheam and Sutton
		57	Sutton
			Wallington
Tower Hamlets pp. 8 and 9			Bethnal Green
			Bow
			Poplar
			Spitalfields
			Stepney
		57	Tower Hamlets
			Wapping
			Whitechapel
Waltham Forest pp. 8 and 9			Chingford
			Leyton
		57	Leytonstone
			Walthamstow
		57	Woodford Green
Wandsworth pp. 8 and 9			Balham
		57	Battersea
		57	Clapham (also Lambeth)
		57	Putney
			South Lambeth (also Lambeth)
			Tooting
			Wandsworth (western)
Westminster (City of) pp. 13 to 16	13	58	Bayswater and Maida Vale
	18	59	Belgravia
	18	59	Hyde Park and Knightsbridge
	15	59	Mayfair
			Paddington
	14	60	Regent's Park and Marylebone
	19	62	St. James's
			St. John's Wood
	15	63	Soho
	15	64	Strand
	19	64	Victoria
			West End
			Westminster

AREA	PAGE Plan	PAGE Est.	BOROUGH
Stanmore		49	Harrow
Stepney			Tower Hamlets
Stockwell			Lambeth
Stoke Newington			Hackney
Strand	15	64	Westminster (City of)
Stratford			Newham
Streatham			Lambeth
Surbiton			Kingston-upon-Thames
Sutton		57	Sutton
Swiss Cottage	14	46	Camden
Sydenham			Bromley
Tooting			Wandsworth
Tottenham			Haringey
Tower Hamlets		57	Tower Hamlets
Twickenham			Richmond-upon-Thames
Upper Edmonton			Enfield
Upper Holloway			Islington
Uxbridge			Hillingdon
Victoria	19	64	Westminster (City of)
Victoria Docks			Newham
Wallington			Sutton
Walthamstow			Waltham Forest
Walworth			Southwark
Wanstead			Redbridge
Wandsworth (western)			Wandsworth
Wapping			Tower Hamlets
Waterloo		55	Lambeth
Welling		43	Bexley
Wembley		43	Brent
West Brompton			Kensington and Chelsea (Royal Borough of)
West Drayton			Hillingdon
West Ealing			Ealing
West End			Westminster (City of)
West Ham			Newham
West Kensington	17	49	Hammersmith
Westminster			Westminster (City of)
West Norwood			Lambeth
West Wimbledon			Merton
Whetstone			Barnet
Whitechapel			Tower Hamlets
Willesden			Brent
Wimbledon		56	Merton
Woodford			Redbridge
Woodford Green		57	Waltham Forest
Wood Green			Haringey
Woolwich (south Thames)			Greenwich
Woolwich (north Thames)			Newham
Yiewsley			Hillingdon

Town plans : *roads most used by traffic and those on which guide listed hotels and restaurants stand are fully drawn; the beginning only of lesser roads is indicated.*

Plans de villes : *Les rues sont sélectionnées en fonction de leur importance pour la circulation et le repérage des établissements cités. Les rues secondaires ne sont qu'amorcées.*

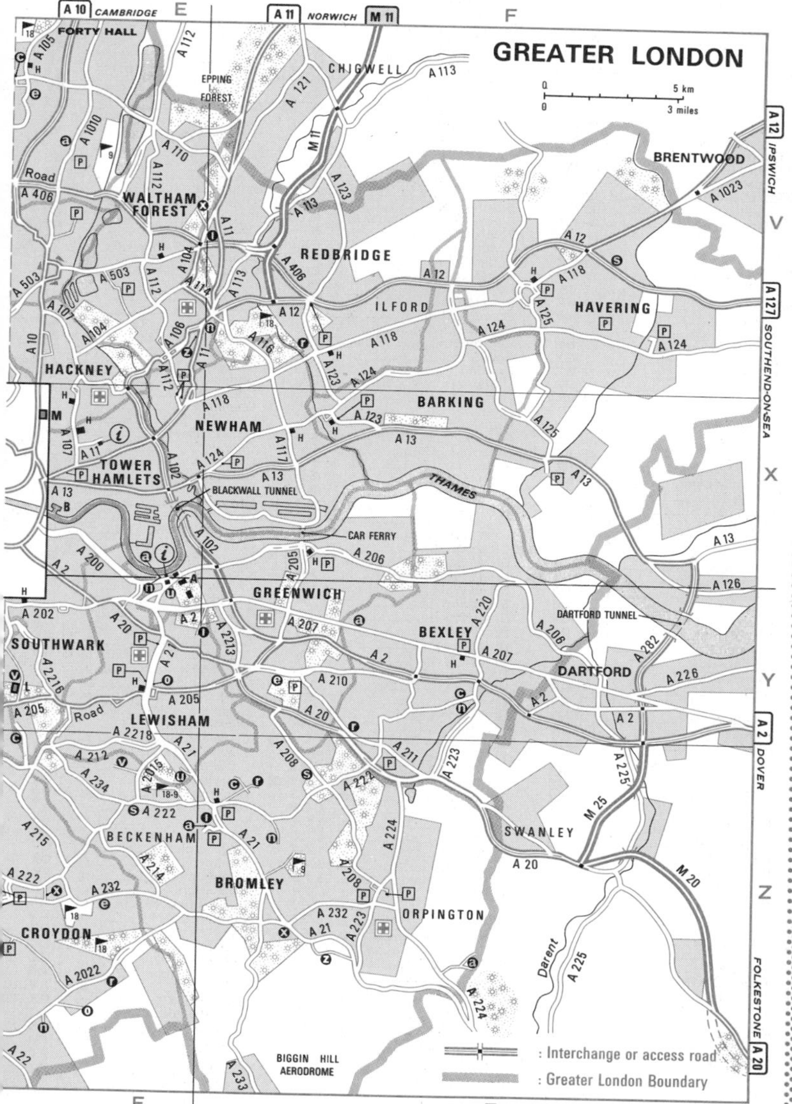

Piante di città : *le vie sono selezionate in funzione della loro importanza per la circolazione e l'ubicazione degli edifici citati. Non indichiamo che l'inizio delle vie secondarie.*

Stadtpläne: *Die Auswahl der Straßen wurde unter Berücksichtigung des Verkehrs und der Zufahrt zu den erwähnten Häusern getroffen. Die weniger wichtigen Straßen werden nur angedeutet.*

Continued on next page

STREET INDEX TO LONDON TOWN PLANS (continued)

Concluded p 21

See also plan pp 14-15
WALLACE COLLECTION
REGENT'S PARK AND MARYLEBONE
Portman Square
Cavendish Sq.
Grosvenor Square
Berkeley Square
CITY OF WESTMINSTER
MAYFAIR
MARBLE ARCH
HYDE PARK
HYDE PARK AND KNIGHTSBRIDGE
Serpentine Road
Park Lane
Oxford Street
Piccadilly
GREEN PARK
Shepherd Market
APSLEY HOUSE WELLINGTON MUSEUM
BOND ST
0 200 m
0 200 yards

Street index: See pp 10-12 and 21

CAMDEN · BLOOMSBURY · SOHO · STRAND · ST. JAMES'S · VICTORIA

Oxford Street is closed to private traffic, Mondays to Saturdays : from 7 am to 7 pm between Portman Street and St. Giles Circus

...an pp 18-19

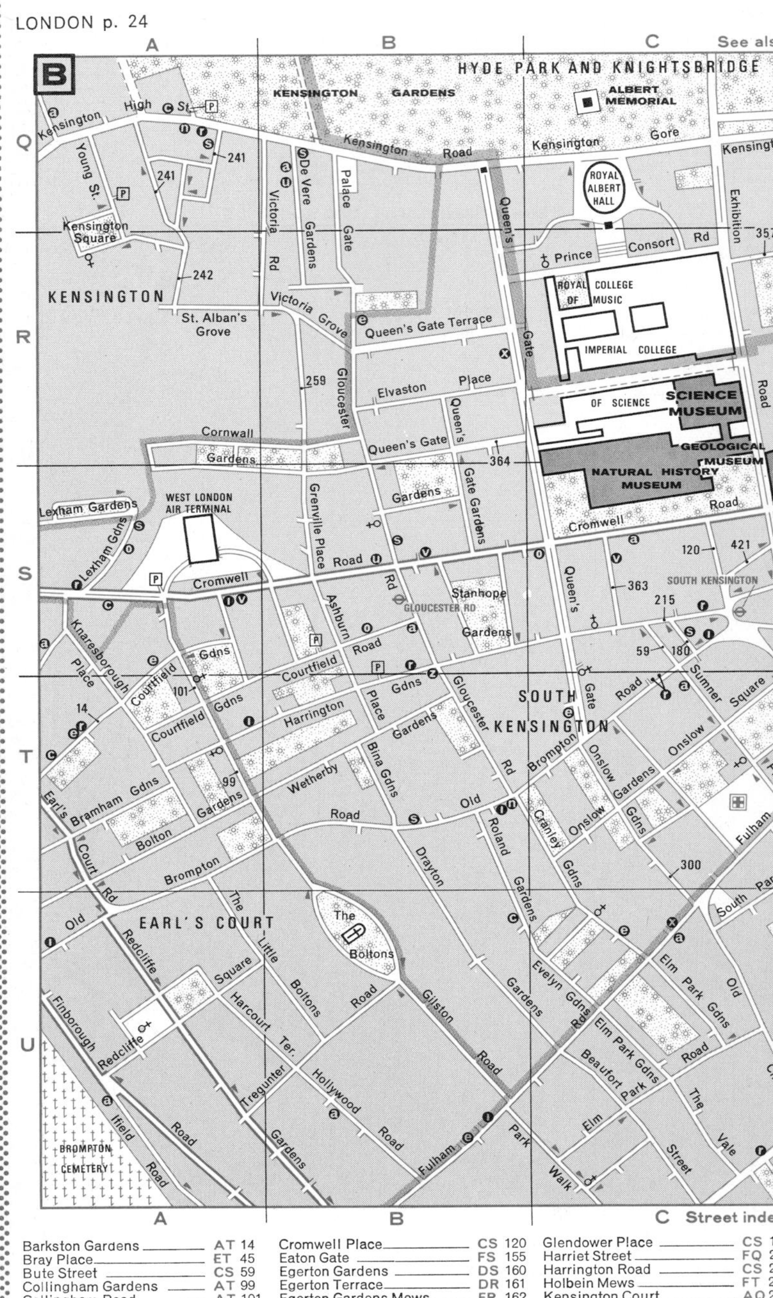
A
B
C
See als
B
HYDE PARK AND KNIGHTSBRIDGE
KENSINGTON GARDENS
ALBERT MEMORIAL
Kensington High St.
Kensington Road
Kensington Gore
ROYAL ALBERT HALL
Young St.
Kensington Square
KENSINGTON
De Vere Gardens
Victoria Rd
Palace Gate
Queen's Gate
Exhibition Rd
Prince Consort Rd
ROYAL COLLEGE OF MUSIC
IMPERIAL COLLEGE OF SCIENCE
SCIENCE MUSEUM
GEOLOGICAL MUSEUM
NATURAL HISTORY MUSEUM
St. Alban's Grove
Victoria Grove
Queen's Gate Terrace
Gloucester Rd
Elvaston Place
Cornwall Gardens
Queen's Gate Gardens
Queen's Gate Gardens
Lexham Gardens
Lexham Gdns
WEST LONDON AIR TERMINAL
Grenville Place
Cromwell Road
Cromwell Road
SOUTH KENSINGTON
GLOUCESTER RD
Stanhope Gardens
Ashburn Road
Knaresborough Place
Courtfield Gdns
Courtfield Road
Harrington Gdns
Harrington Road
Sumner Place
Onslow Square
SOUTH KENSINGTON
Gloucester Rd
Queen's Gate
Bina Gdns
Wetherby Gardens
Collingham Gardens
Bramham Gdns
Bolton Gardens
Earl's Court Rd
Old Brompton Road
Brompton Rd
Onslow Gardens
Onslow Gdns
Cranley Gdns
Roland Gardens
Drayton Gardens
Fulham Road
South Parade
EARL'S COURT
The Boltons
The Little Boltons
Redcliffe Square
Redcliffe Gardens
Finborough Road
Harcourt Ter.
Tregunter Road
Hollywood Road
Gilston Road
Evelyn Gdns
Elm Park Gdns
Elm Park Road
Beaufort Street
Park Walk
Elm Park Gdns
The Vale
Old Church St
BROMPTON CEMETERY
Ifield Road
Fulham Road
Q
R
S
T
U
241
242
259
364
357
421
120
363
215
180
59
101
14
99
300
C
Street inde

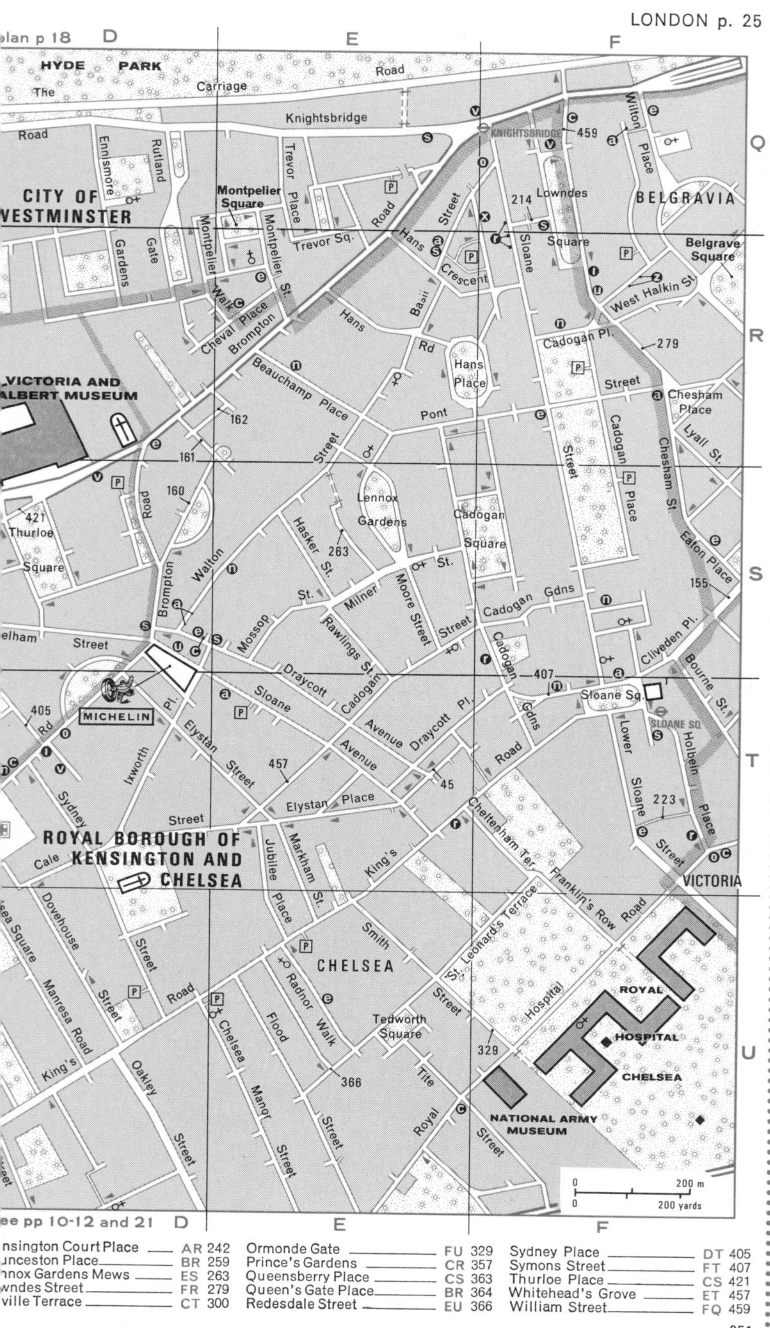

...nsington Court Place	AR	242
...unceston Place	BR	259
...nnox Gardens Mews	ES	263
...wndes Street	FR	279
...ville Terrace	CT	300
Ormonde Gate	FU	329
Prince's Gardens	CR	357
Queensberry Place	CS	363
Queen's Gate Place	BR	364
Redesdale Street	EU	366
Sydney Place	DT	405
Symons Street	FT	407
Thurloe Place	CS	421
Whitehead's Grove	ET	457
William Street	FQ	459

See also plan pp 18-19

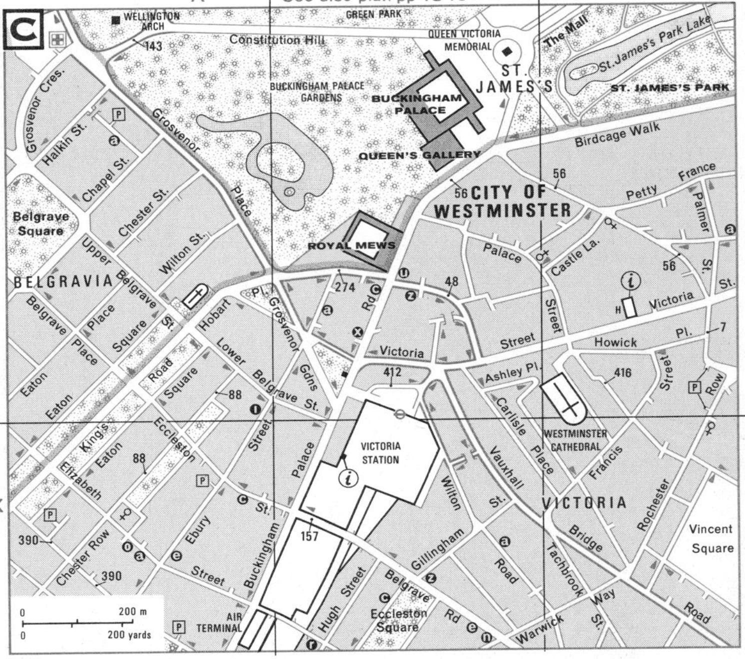

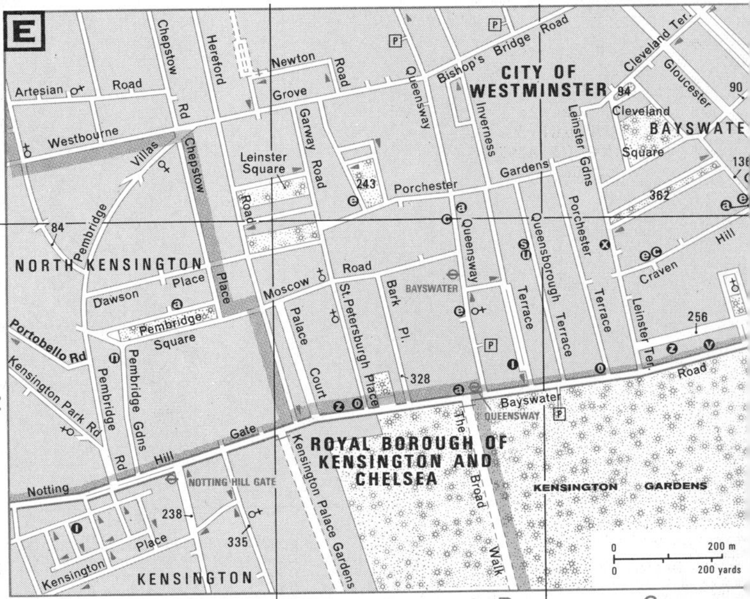

A B C

C

WELLINGTON ARCH
GREEN PARK
Constitution Hill
143
QUEEN VICTORIA MEMORIAL
The Mall
St. James's Park Lake
ST. JAMES'S
ST. JAMES'S PARK
BUCKINGHAM PALACE GARDENS
BUCKINGHAM PALACE
QUEEN'S GALLERY
Birdcage Walk
Grosvenor Cres.
Halkin St.
Chapel St.
Grosvenor Place
Chester St.
Belgrave Square
Wilton St.
Upper Belgrave St.
ROYAL MEWS
56 CITY OF WESTMINSTER
56
Petty France
Palmer St.
Palace St.
Castle La.
56
BELGRAVIA
Belgrave Place
Place
Square
Hobart Pl.
Grosvenor Rd
274
48
Victoria St.
H Victoria
Howick Pl.
7
Eaton
Eaton
Road
Square
Lower Belgrave St.
Grosvenor Gdns
Victoria
412
Ashley Pl.
416
Street
Row
88
King's
Eccleston
Street
Palace
Street
VICTORIA STATION
Carlisle Place
WESTMINSTER CATHEDRAL
Francis
Elizabeth
Eaton
88
Vauxhall
Wilton
X
St.
VICTORIA
Rochester
Vincent Square
390
Chester Row
Ebury
157
Buckingham
Bridge
390
Street
Gillingham
Road
Tachbrook
Hugh Street
Belgrave Rd
Eccleston Square
Way
St.
Road
Warwick
AIR TERMINAL
0 200 m
0 200 yards

E

Artesian Road
Chepstow Rd
Hereford
Newton Road
Grove
Queensway
Bishop's Bridge Road
CITY OF WESTMINSTER
Cleveland Ter.
Gloucester
94
90
Westbourne
Villas
Chepstow
Leinster Square
Garway Road
Inverness
Leinster Gdns
Cleveland Square
BAYSWATER
136
243
Porchester
Gardens
362
Road
84
Pembridge
Queensway
Queensborough Terrace
Porchester Terrace
Hill
NORTH KENSINGTON
Place
Place
Road
Moscow
Craven
Dawson
Bark Pl.
BAYSWATER
Terrace
Pembridge Square
Palace Court
St. Petersburgh Place
Leinster Ter.
256
Portobello Rd
Pembridge Rd
Pembridge Gdns
Kensington Park Rd
328
Bayswater Road
Z
The Broad Walk
QUEENSWAY
Gate
Hill
Notting
Kensington Palace Gardens
ROYAL BOROUGH OF KENSINGTON AND CHELSEA
NOTTING HILL GATE
KENSINGTON GARDENS
238
335
Place
Kensington
KENSINGTON
0 200 m
0 200 yards

A B C

See also plan pp 17-18

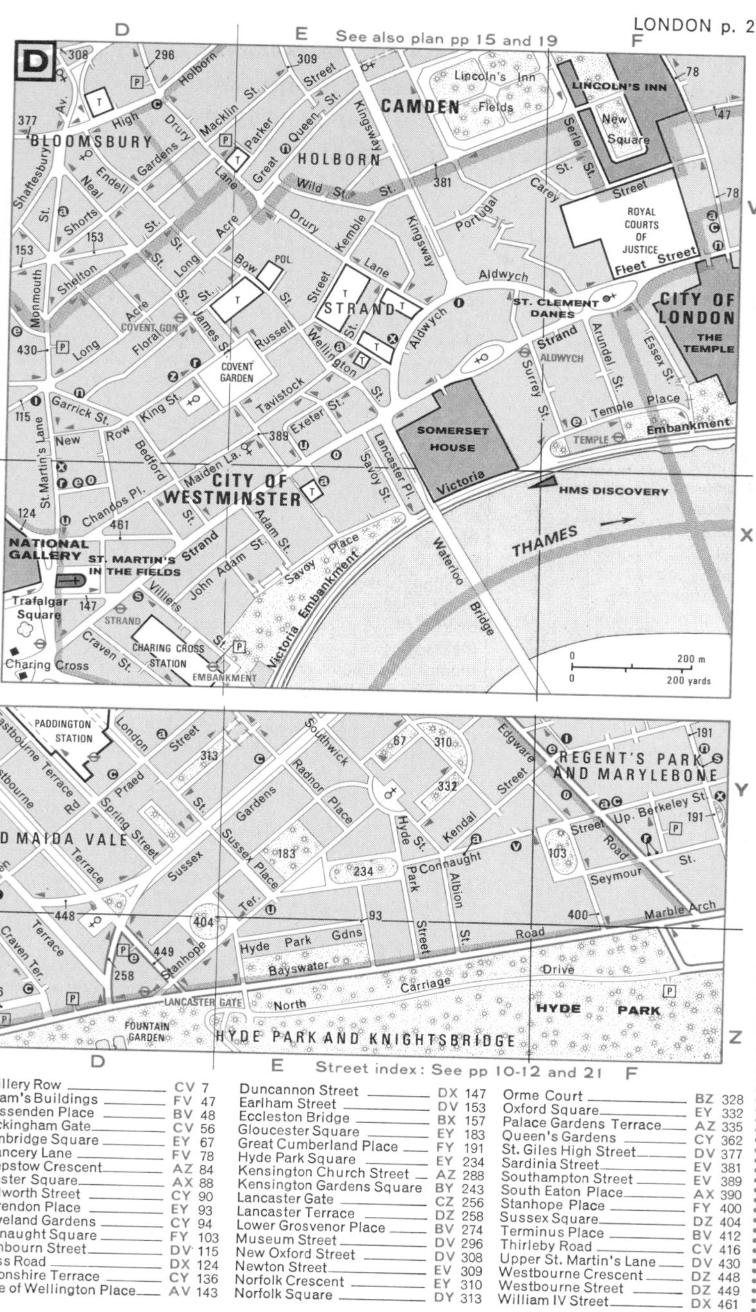
D
E
F
See also plan pp 15 and 19
CAMDEN
HOLBORN
BLOOMSBURY
Lincoln's Inn Fields
LINCOLN'S INN
New Square
ROYAL COURTS OF JUSTICE
Fleet Street
CITY OF LONDON
THE TEMPLE
STRAND
ST. CLEMENT DANES
ALDWYCH
COVENT GARDEN
COVENT GDN
SOMERSET HOUSE
CITY OF WESTMINSTER
HMS DISCOVERY
THAMES
NATIONAL GALLERY
ST. MARTIN'S IN THE FIELDS
Trafalgar Square
Charing Cross
CHARING CROSS STATION
EMBANKMENT
STRAND
TEMPLE
Victoria Embankment
Waterloo Bridge
High Holborn
Shaftesbury Av.
Kingsway
Aldwych
Drury Lane
Long Acre
St. Martin's Lane
Savoy Place
Temple Place
Embankment
V
X
0
200 m
200 yards
PADDINGTON STATION
REGENT'S PARK AND MARYLEBONE
ND MAIDA VALE
Eastbourne Terrace
Westbourne Terrace Rd
London Street
Praed Street
Spring Street
Sussex Gardens
Southwick Street
Radnor Place
Edgware Road
Up. Berkeley St.
Kendal Street
Connaught Street
Seymour Street
Hyde Park Street
Albion St.
Marble Arch
Hyde Park Gdns
Bayswater Road
North Carriage Drive
LANCASTER GATE
FOUNTAIN GARDEN
HYDE PARK
HYDE PARK AND KNIGHTSBRIDGE
Craven Ter.
Stanhope
Y
Z
Street index: See pp 10-12 and 21

ALPHABETICAL LIST OF HOTELS AND RESTAURANTS
LISTE ALPHABÉTIQUE DES HOTELS ET RESTAURANTS
ELENCO ALFABETICO DEGLI ALBERGHI E RISTORANTI
ALPHABETISCHES HOTEL- UND RESTAURANTVERZEICHNIS

L

M

N

O

P

Q - R

S

T

U - V

W

In addition to establishments indicated by XXXXX ... X, many hotels possess good class restaurants.

RESTAURANTS CLASSIFIED ACCORDING TO TYPE
RESTAURANTS CLASSÉS SUIVANT LEUR GENRE
RISTORANTI CLASSIFICATI SECONDO IL LORO GENERE
RESTAURANTS NACH ART UND EINRICHTUNG GEORDNET

Borough	Area	Restaurant	Page
		BISTRO	
Barnet	Finchley	X **Aubergade (L')**	43
Camden	Hampstead	X **Chateaubriand**	46
City of London	City of London	X **Bistingo (Le)**	47
Croydon	Norbury	X **Mr. Bunbury's**	47
Greenwich	Greenwich	X **Meantime**	48
—	—	X **Papillon (Le)**	48
—	—	X **Spread Eagle**	48
Hammersmith	Fulham	X **Red Onion Bistro**	48
—	—	X **Trencherman Bistro**	48
Islington	Islington	X **M'sieur Frog**	50
Kensington & Chelsea (Royal Borough of)	Chelsea	X **Bistingo (Le)**	52
	Kensington	X **Bistingo (Le)**	54
—	South Kensington	X **Bistingo (Le)**	55
Kingston-upon-Thames	Kingston	X **Cloud's**	55
Lewisham	Blackheath	X **Goulue (La)**	55
Richmond-upon-Thames	Barnes	X **River Bistro**	56
—	Richmond	X **Bistro Village**	56
Wandsworth	Battersea	X **Jacks Place**	57
—	Clapham	X **Wine and Dine**	57
—	Putney	X **Cassis**	57
Westminster (City of)	Bayswater & Maida Vale	X **Bistingo (Le)**	59
—	—	X **Chef (Le)**	59
—	Belgravia	X **Other Bistro (The)**	59
—	Mayfair	X **Bistingo (Le)**	60
—	Regent's Park & Marylebone	X **Bistro 57**	62
—	—	X **Bois St. Jean (Au)**	62
—	Soho	X **Bistingo (Le)**	63
—	Victoria	X **Bumbles**	65
—	—	X **Pimlico**	65
—	—	X **Poule au Pot (La)**	65
		DANCING	
Hammersmith	Fulham	XX **Barbarella**	48
Hillingdon	Northwood	XX **Belair Swiss**	50
Kensington & Chelsea (Royal Borough of)	South Kensington	XX **Stable**	55
Redbridge	Ilford	XX **Mario's (Friday and Saturday only)**	56
Westminster (City of)	Bayswater & Maida Vale	X **Concordia Notte**	59
—	Mayfair	XXX **Tiberio**	60
—	St. James's	XX **Dolce Notte (La)**	62
—	Strand	XXX **Bussola (La)**	64

Borough	Area	Restaurant	Page
		SEAFOOD	
Camden	Bloomsbury	XX **Wheeler's Antoine**	45
—	—	X **Trattoria dei Pescatori**	45
City of London	City of London	XXX **Bill Bentley's**	46
—	—	XXX **Wheeler's Fenchurch**	46
—	—	XX **Wheeler's City**	47
Croydon	Croydon	XX **Hook, Line and Sinker**	47
Kensington & Chelsea (Royal Borough of)	Chelsea	XX **Poissonnerie de l'Avenue**	51
	—	XX **Suquet (Le)**	51
—	Earl's Court	XX **Croisette (La)**	53
—	Kensington	XX **Wheeler's Alcove**	53
Westminster (City of)	Belgravia	XXX **Wheeler's Carafe**	59
—	Mayfair	XXXX **Scott's**	60
—	—	XX **Golden Carp**	60
—	Regent's Park & Marylebone	XX **Fisherman's Wharf**	61
—	St. James's	X **Wheeler's**	62
		ARMENIAN	
Kensington & Chelsea (Royal Borough of)	Kensington	X **Armenian**	53
		AUSTRIAN	
Westminster (City of)	Regent's Park & Marylebone	XX **Kerzenstüberl**	61
		CHINESE	
City of London	City of London	X **City Friends**	47
Kensington & Chelsea (Royal Borough of)	Earl's Court	X **Golden Duck**	53
	Kensington	XX **Sailing Junk**	53
—	—	X **Lee Yuan**	53
Richmond-upon-Thames	Richmond	XX **Kew Rendezvous**	56
—	—	X **Richmond Rendezvous**	56
—	—	X **Richmond Rendezvous (Annexe)**	56
Westminster (City of)	Bayswater & Maida Vale	XX **Lotus House**	58
—	—	X **Kam Tong**	59
—	Hyde Park & Knightsbridge	XX **Mr. Chow**	59
—	Regent's Park & Marylebone	XX **Lords Rendezvous**	61
—	—	XX **Manchurian**	61
—	Soho	XX **China Garden**	63
—	—	XX **Gallery Rendezvous**	63
—	—	XX **Soho Rendezvous**	63
—	—	X **Dumpling Inn**	63
—	—	X **Village (The)**	63
—	Strand	X **Poons of Covent Garden**	64
		ENGLISH	
Camden	Hampstead	X **Turpin's**	46
City of London	City of London	XXX **Baron of Beef**	46
Kensington & Chelsea (Royal Borough of)	Chelsea	X **Busby's**	52
	—	X **Hungry Horse**	52
Westminster (City of)	Belgravia	X **Upper Crust in Belgravia**	59
—	St. James's	XXX **Stone's Chop House**	62
—	—	XXX ✿ **Wilton's**	62
—	Strand	XXX **Simpson's in the Strand**	64
—	Victoria	XXX **Lockets**	65
—	—	XX **Tate Gallery Rest.**	65

FRENCH

Borough	Area	Restaurant	Page
Bromley	Orpington	XXX **Chelsfield Park**	44
Camden	Bloomsbury	XXX **Etoile (L')**	45
—	—	XXX **Savarin (Au)**	45
—	—	X **Brasserie du Coin**	45
—	—	X **Mon Plaisir**	45
—	Hampstead	XXX **Keats**	46
—	—	X **Cellier du Midi (Le)**	46
City of London	City of London	XXX ✿ **Poulbot (Le)** (basement)	46
—	—	XX **Gaulois (Le)**	47
—	—	X **Bubb's**	47
—	—	X **Gamin (Le)**	47
—	—	X **Germainerie (La)**	47
Harrow	Central Harrow	XX **Old Etonian**	49
Kensington & Chelsea (Royal Borough of)	Chelsea	XXXX ✿ ✿ **Gavroche (Le)**	51
	—	XX **Bagatelle**	52
—	—	XX **Coq au Vin**	51
—	—	XX **Fin Bec (Au)**	51
—	—	XX **Français (Le)**	51
—	—	XX ✿ **Ma Cuisine**	51
—	—	XX **Marcel**	51
—	—	X **Brasserie (La)**	52
—	Kensington	XXX **Belvedere**	53
—	—	XXX ✿ **Bressan (Le)**	53
—	—	XX **Pomme d'Amour (La)**	53
—	—	XX **Toque Blanche (La)**	53
—	—	X **Ark (The)**	54
—	North Kensington	XX **Chez Moi**	54
Richmond-upon-Thames	Barnes	XX **Petit Bedon (Le)**	56
—	Hampton Court	XX **Bastians**	56
—	Kew	X **Jasper's Bun in the Oven**	56
Wandsworth	Battersea	X **Lavender Hill**	57
Westminster (City of)	Mayfair	XXX **Napoule (La)**	60
—	—	XXX **Snooty Fox**	60
—	Regent's Park & Marylebone	XX **P'tit Montmartre (Le)**	61
—	St. James's	XXXX **Ecu de France (A l')**	62
—	Soho	XXXXX **Café Royal Grill**	63
—	—	XXXXX **Relais du Café Royal (Le)**	63
—	—	XXX **Jardin des Gourmets (Au)**	63
—	Strand	XX **Chez Solange**	64
—	—	X **Cellier de Medici**	64

GREEK

Borough	Area	Restaurant	Page
Camden	Bloomsbury	XXX **White Tower**	45
Westminster (City of)	Bayswater & Maida Vale	X **Kalamaras Taverna**	59
—	Regent's Park & Marylebone	X **Hellenic**	62

HUNGARIAN

Borough	Area	Restaurant	Page
Westminster (City of)	Soho	XX **Gay Hussar**	63

INDIAN & PAKISTANI

Borough	Area	Restaurant	Page
Hammersmith	Hammersmith	XX **Anarkali**	48
Kensington & Chelsea (Royal Borough of)	Chelsea	XX **Tandoori**	52
—	Earl's Court	XX **Naraine**	53
—	South Kensington	X **Jamshid's**	55
—	—	X **Star of India**	55
Merton	Wimbledon	XX **Rawalpindi**	56
Redbridge	South Woodford	X **Meghna Grill**	56
Waltham Forest	Leytonstone	XX **Tandoori Golden Curry**	57
Westminster (City of)	Bayswater & Maide Vale	X **Ganges**	59
—	Belgravia	XXX **Salloos**	59
—	Hyde Park & Knightsbridge	XX **Shezan**	59
—	Mayfair	XXX **Tandoori**	60
—	—	XX **Gaylord**	60
—	Regent's Park & Marylebone	XX **Gaylord**	61
—	—	X **Indira**	62
—	Soho	X **Ganges**	63
—	Victoria	XXX **Kundan**	65

ITALIAN

Borough	Area	Restaurant	Page
Barnet	Finchley	XX **Luigi's " Belmont "**	43
—	—	X **Otello**	43
Bexley	Sidcup	X **Botte (La)**	43
Bromley	Beckenham	X **Gran Sasso**	43
—	Bromley	XX **Chariot Wheel**	44
Camden	Bloomsbury	X **Belmonte**	45
—	—	X **Conca d'Oro**	45
—	Finchley Road	XX **Trattoria del Buonamico**	45
—	Hampstead	XX **Baita (La)**	46
—	—	X **Villa Bianca**	46
City of London	City of London	XX **Terrazza-Est**	46
Croydon	Sanderstead	X **Elio**	47
—	Shirley	XX **Baita di Piero (La)**	47
—	South Croydon	X **Trattoria Bella Venezia**	47
Hammersmith	Fulham	XX **Barbarella**	48
Haringey	Highgate	XX **San Carlo**	49
Harrow	Bushey Heath	X **Alpine**	49
—	Stanmore	X **Signor Tonino**	49
Hillingdon	Eastcote	X **Trombino**	49
Kensington & Chelsea (Royal Borough of)	Chelsea	XX **Ben Accolto (Al)**	52
—	—	XX **Don Luigi**	52
—	—	XX **Famiglia (La)**	52
—	—	XX **Girasole (Il)**	52
—	—	XX **Meridiana**	51
—	—	XX **Sale e Pepe**	52
—	—	XX **Sambuca**	52
—	—	XX **San Frediano**	52
—	—	XX **Santa Croce**	52
—	—	X **Como Lario**	52
—	—	X **Leonardo Ristorante**	52
—	—	X **San Quintino**	52

ITALIAN (continued)

Borough	Area	Restaurant	Page
Kensington & Chelsea (Royal Borough of)	Earl's Court	XX **Pontevecchio**	53
	—	X **Palio di Siena (Il)**	53
—	—	X **Scala (La)**	53
—	Kensington	XX **Franco Ovest**	53
—	—	XX **Gatamelata**	53
—	—	XX **Gondoliere**	53
—	—	XX **Trattoo**	53
—	—	X **Paesana (La)**	54
—	South Kensington	XX **Giorno e la Notte (Il)**	55
—	—	XX **Pulcinella**	55
—	—	X **Alpino**	55
Merton	Wimbledon	XX **San Lorenzo Fuoriporta**	56
Richmond-upon-Thames	Richmond	XX **Franco's**	56
—	—	XX **Veranda (La)**	56
Southwark	Dulwich Village	XX **Gemma-San Martino**	57
Sutton	Sutton	XX **Trattoria Toscana**	57
Waltham Forest	Leytonstone	X **Trattoria Parmigiana**	57
Wandsworth	Putney	XX **Forchetta (La)**	57
Westminster (City of)	Bayswater & Maida Vale	XX **Canaletto**	59
—	—	XX **Lupa (La)**	59
—	—	XX **San Marino**	58
—	—	XX **Trat-West**	58
—	—	X **Concordia**	59
—	Hyde Park & Knightsbridge	XX **Montpeliano**	59
—	Mayfair	XXX **Tiberio**	60
—	—	XX **Genova (La)**	60
—	—	X **Trattoria Fiori**	60
—	Regent's Park & Marylebone	XX **Loggia (La)**	61
—		XX **Rossetti**	62
—	—	XX **Sandro**	61
—	—	XX **Tonino's**	61
—	—	X **Barbino (Il)**	62
—	—	X **Biagi's**	62
—	—	X **Vecchio Parioli**	62
—	St. James's	XX **Dolce Notte (La)**	62
—	—	XX **Frank's**	62
—	Soho	XXX **Gennaro's**	63
—	—	XXX **Leonis Quo Vadis**	63
—	—	XX **Capannina (La)**	63
—	—	XX **Paparazzi (I)**	63
—	—	XX **Romeo e Giulietta**	63
—	—	XX **Rugantino**	63
—	—	XX **Terrazza (La)**	63
—	—	XX **Venezia**	63
—	—	X **Hostaria Romana**	63
—	—	X **Peter Mario**	63
—	—	X **Trattoria Imperia**	63
—	Strand	XXX **Bussola (La)**	64
—	—	XX **San Martino**	64
—	—	X **Colosseo**	64
—	—	X **Laguna 50**	64
—	—	X **Luigi's**	64

Borough	Area	Restaurant	Page
ITALIAN *(continued)*			
Westminster (City of)	Victoria	XX **Gran Paradiso**	65
—	—	XX **Massimo**	65
—	—	X **Mimmo d'Ischia**	65
JAPANESE			
City of London	City of London	XX **Aykoku Kaku**	46
—	—	X **Ginnan**	47
Westminster (City of)	Mayfair	X **Tokyo**	60
—	Regent's Park & Marylebone	XX **Masako**	61
—	—	XX **Mikado**	62
—	Soho	XX **Fuji**	63
—	—	X **Hokkai**	63
LEBANESE			
Kensington & Chelsea (Royal Borough of)	Chelsea	X **Lebanese Food Centre-Beirut Restaurant**	52
MALAYSIAN			
Westminster (City of)	Regent's Park & Marylebone	X **Singapore**	62
POLYNESIAN			
Westminster (City of)	Mayfair	XXX **Trader Vics (at Hilton)**	60
SWISS			
Westminster (City of)	Soho	XX **Chesa (Swiss Centre)**	63
—	—	X **Rendezvous (Swiss Centre)**	63
TURKISH			
Westminster (City of)	Regent's Park & Marylebone	X **Nibub Lokanta**	62
VEGETARIAN			
Westminster (City of)	Soho	X **Crank's**	63

RESTAURANTS OPEN ON SUNDAY (L : lunch - D : dinner) AND RESTAURANTS TAKING LAST ORDERS AFTER 11.30 p.m.

RESTAURANTS OUVERTS LE DIMANCHE (L : déjeuner - D : dîner) ET RESTAURANTS PRENANT LES DERNIÈRES COMMANDES APRÈS 23 h 30

RISTORANTI APERTI LA DOMENICA (L : colazione - D : pranzo) E RISTORANTI CHE ACCETTANO ORDINAZIONI DOPO LE 23. 30

RESTAURANTS, DIE SONNTAGS GEÖFFNET SIND (L : Mittagessen - D : Abendessen), BZW. BESTELLUNGEN AUCH NACH 23.30 UHR ANNEHMEN

Borough	Area	Restaurant	Sunday	11.30 p. m.	Page
Barnet	Finchley	XX **Luigi's « Belmont »**	L D		43
—	—	X **Aubergade (L')**	D		43
—	—	X **Otello**	L D		43
Bexley	Bexley	XX **King's Head**	L		43
Bromley	Chislehurst	XX **London Steak House**	L D		44
—	—	XX **George at Farnborough (The)**	L D		44
—	Orpington	XXX **Chelsfield Park**	L D		44
Camden	Bloomsbury	XX **Top of the Tower**	L D		45
—	—	XX **Wheeler's Antoine**	L D		45
—	—	X **Trattoria dei Pescatori**		x	45
—	Finchley Road	XX **Trattoria del Buonamico (11.45)**	L D	x	45
—	Hampstead	XXX **Keats**	L D	x	46
—	—	XX **Baita (La)**	L D	x	46
—	—	X **Chateaubriand**		x	46
—	—	X **Turpin's**	L		46
—	—	X **Villa Bianca**	L D	x	46
—	Holborn	XXX **Opera (L') (12.00)**		x	46
—	Regent's Park	XX **Barque and Bite**		x	46
—	Swiss Cottage	XX **Peter's**	L D	x	46
City of London	City of London	X **Bistingo (Le) (12.00)**		x	47
—	—	X **City Friends (12.00)**		x	47
Croydon	South Croydon	X **Trattoria Bella Venezia**		x	47
Greenwich	Eltham	XX **Reine (La)**	L		48
—	Greenwich	X **Spread Eagle**	L		48
Hammersmith	Fulham	XX **Barbarella (12.00)**		x	48
—	—	X **Carlo's Place**	D		48
—	—	X **Trencherman Bistro**	L		48
—	Hammersmith	XX **Anarkali (11.45)**	L D	x	48
Haringey	Highgate	XX **San Carlo**		x	49
Harrow	Pinner	X **Giralda (La)**	L D		49
Hillingdon	Northwood	XX **Belair Swiss (11.45)**		x	50
Hounslow	Brentford	XXX **Camellia**	L D		50
Islington	Islington	XX ✿ **Carrier's**		x	50
—	—	XX **Frederick's**		x	50
—	—	X **M'sieur Frog**		x	50
Kensington & Chelsea (Royal Borough of)	Chelsea	XXXX ✿✿ **Gavroche (Le) (11.45)**		x	51
—	—	XXX **Brompton Grill**	D		51
—	—	XXX **Minotaur**	L D		51
—	—	XXX **Waltons of Walton Street**	L	x	51

Borough	Area	Restaurant	Sunday	11.30 p. m.	Page
Kensington & Chelsea (Royal Borough of)	Chelsea	XX **Coq au Vin**	L D	x	51
	—	XX **Daphne's**		x	51
—	—	XX **Don Luigi**	L D	x	52
—	—	XX **Drakes**	L D		51
—	—	XX **Famiglia (La)**	L D		52
—	—	XX **Girasole (Il) (11.45)**		x	52
—	—	XX **Meridiana (12.00)**		x	51
—	—	XX **Poissonnerie de l'Avenue**		x	51
—	—	XX **Salamis (11.45)**		x	52
—	—	XX **San Frediano (11.45)**		x	52
—	—	XX **Santa Croce**		x	52
—	—	XX **Suquet (Le)**	L D		51
—	—	XX **Tandoori**	L D	x	52
—	—	X **Bistingo (Le) (11.45)**	L D	x	52
—	—	X **Brasserie (La)**	L D	x	52
—	—	X **Como Lario**		x	52
—	—	X **Hungry Horse**	L D	x	52
—	—	X **San Quintino**		x	52
—	Earl's Court	XX **Croisette (La)**	L D		53
—	—	XX **Naraine (12.00)**	L D	x	53
—	—	XX **Pontevecchio**	L D	x	53
—	—	X **Golden Duck**	L D	x	53
—	—	X **Palio di Siena (Il) (11.45)**	L D	x	53
—	Kensington	XXX **Belvedere**	L D	x	53
—	—	XX **Franco Ovest**		x	53
—	—	XX **Sailing Junk**	D	x	53
—	—	XX **Trattoo**	L D	x	53
—	—	X **Ark (The)**	D		54
—	—	X **Armenian**	D		53
—	—	X **Bistingo (Le) (11.45)**		x	54
—	—	X **Lee Yuan (11.45)**	L D	x	53
—	—	X **Paesana (La) (11.50)**		x	54
—	North Kensington	XXX **Leith's**	D	x	54
—	—	XX **Julie's**	L D	x	54
—	South Kensington	XX **Giorno e la Notte (11.45)**		x	55
—	—	XX **Pulcinella**		x	55
—	—	XX **Stable (1.30)**		x	55
—	—	X **Alpino**	L D		55
—	—	X **Bistingo (Le) (11.45)**	L D	x	55
—	—	X **Chanterelle (12.00)**	D	x	55
—	—	X **Jamshid's**		x	55
—	—	X **Star of India (11.45)**		x	55
Kingston-upon-Thames	Kingston	XX **London Steak House**	L D		55
—	—	X **Cloud's**	L		55
Lambeth	Waterloo	XX **National Theatre Rest.**	D		55
Lewisham	Catford	XX **Casa Cominetti**	L		55
Merton	Wimbledon	XX **San Lorenzo Fuoriporta**		x	56
Redbridge	South Woodford	X **Meghna Grill**	L D		56
Richmond-upon-Thames	Barnes	XX **Petit Bedon (Le)**		x	56
	—	X **River Bistro**		x	56
—	Richmond	XX **Franco's (12.00)**	L D	x	56
—	—	XX **Kew Rendezvous**	L D	x	56
—	—	XX **Veranda (La)**		x	56
—	—	X **Bistro Village**	L D	x	56
—	—	X **Richmond Rendezvous (Annexe)**	L D	x	56
—	—	X **Richmond Rendezvous**	L D	x	56

Borough	Area	Restaurant	Sunday	11.30 p. m.	Page
Southwark	Dulwich Village	X **London Steak House**	L D		57
Waltham Forest	Leytonstone	XX **Tandoori Golden Curry**		x	57
Wandsworth	Battersea	XX **Alonso's**		x	57
Westminster (City of)	Bayswater & Maida Vale	XX **Lotus House**	L D	x	58
		XX **San Marino**		x	58
—	—	XX **Trat-West**		x	58
—	—	X **Bistingo (Le)**	L D	x	59
—	—	X **Concordia**		x	59
—	—	X **Concordia Notte (12.30)**		x	59
—	—	X **Kalamaras Taverna**		x	59
—	Belgravia	XXX **Wheeler's Carafe**	L D		59
—	—	X **Other Bistro (The) (11.45)**	L D	x	59
—	—	X **Upper Crust in Belgravia**	L D		59
—	Hyde Park & Knightsbridge	XX **Mr. Chow**	L D	x	59
		XX **Montpeliano**		x	59
—	—	XX **Shezan**		x	59
—	Mayfair	XXXX **Scott's**	L D		60
—	—	XXX **Snooty Fox (11.45)**		x	60
—	—	XXX **Tandoori (12.30)**		x	60
—	—	XXX **Tiberio (1.30)**		x	60
—	—	XXX **Trader Vics (at Hilton)**		x	60
—	—	XX **Gaylord**		x	60
—	—	X **Bistingo (Le) (11.45)**	L D	x	60
—	—	X **Dukes**		x	60
—	Regent's Park & Marylebone	XXX **Oslo Court**	L		61
		XX **Fisherman's Wharf**	L D		61
—	—	XX **Gaylord**	L D	x	61
—	—	XX **Lords Rendezvous**	L D	x	61
—	—	XX **Manchurian**	L D	x	61
—	—	XX **P'tit Montmartre (Le)**		x	61
—	—	XX **Rossetti (11.45)**	L D	x	62
—	—	XX **Sandro**		x	61
—	—	X **Biagi's**		x	62
—	—	X **Hellenic**	L D		62
—	—	X **Indira**	L D	x	62
—	—	X **Nibub Lokanta**	L D	x	62
—	—	X **Vecchio Parioli (Saturday only)**	L D	x	62
—	St. James's	XXXX **Ecu de France (A l')**	D	x	62
—	—	XXX **Hunting Lodge**		x	62
—	—	XXX **Lafayette**		x	62
—	—	XXX **Stone's Chop House**		x	62
—	—	XX **Dolce Notte (La) (12.00)**		x	62
—	—	XX **Frank's**	L D	x	62
—	Soho	XXXXX **Café Royal Grill**	L D		63
—	—	XXXXX **Relais du Café Royal (Le)**	L D		63
—	—	XXX **Gennaro's**		x	63
—	—	XXX **Leonis Quo Vadis (11.45)**	D	x	63
—	—	XX **Capannina (La)**	L D	x	63
—	—	XX **Chesa (Swiss Centre)**	L D	x	63
—	—	XX **China Garden (12.45)**		x	63
—	—	XX **Gallery Rendezvous (11.45)**	L D	x	63
—	—	XX **Fuji**	L D	x	63
—	—	XX **Paparazzi (I)**	L D	x	63
—	—	XX **Romeo e Giuletta**	L D		63
—	—	XX **Rugantino**		x	63

Borough	Area	Restaurant	Sunday	11.30 p. m.	Page
Westminster (City of)	Soho	XX **Soho Rendezvous (11.45)**	L D	x	63
—	—	XX **Terrazza (La)**	L D	x	63
—	—	XX **Venezia**		x	63
—	—	X **Bistingo (Le)**	L D	x	63
—	—	X **Dumpling Inn (11.45)**	L D	x	63
—	—	X **Ganges**		x	63
—	—	X **Hokkai**	D		63
—	—	X **Hostaria Romana**	L D	x	63
—	—	X **Peter Mario**		x	63
—	—	X **Rendezvous (Swiss Centre) (12.00)**	L D	x	63
—	—	X **Trattoria Imperia**		x	63
—	—	X **Village (The) (12.00)**	L D	x	63
—	Strand	XXX **Bussola (La) (12.00)**		x	64
—	—	XXX **Inigo Jones (11.45)**		x	64
—	—	XX **Chez Solange**		x	64
—	—	XX **Grange (11.45)**		x	64
—	—	XX **San Martino (11.45)**		x	64
—	—	X **Colosseo**		x	64
—	—	X **Laguna 50**		x	64
—	—	X **Luigi's**		x	64
—	—	X **Poons of Covent Garden (11.45)**	L D	x	64
—	Victoria	XX **Eatons**		x	65
—	—	XX **Gran Paradiso**		x	65
—	—	XX **Massimo**		x	65
—	—	X **Mimmo d'Ischia**		x	65
—	—	X **Pimlico**	L D		65
—	—	X **Poule au Pot (La)**	L D		65
—	—	X **Tent (The)**	L D		65

LONDON p. 42

LICENSING HOURS: WHEN DRINKING ALCOHOLIC BEVERAGES IS PERMITTED IN PUBS AND BARS AND OTHER LICENSED PREMISES (The general rule).

HEURES PERMISES POUR LA CONSOMMATION DES BOISSONS ALCOOLISÉES (Règle générale).

ORARI CONSENTITI PER LA CONSUMAZIONE DI BEVANDE ALCOLICHE (Regola Generale).

AUSSCHANKZEITEN FÜR ALKOHOLISCHE GETRÄNKE (Allgemeine Regelung).

	from de	to à	from de	to à	
Weekdays (other than Good Friday and Christmas Day) **Jours de Semaine** (autres que Vendredi-Saint et Jour de Noël)	**11.00**	**15.00**	**18.00**	**22.30**	**Giorni della Settimana** (esclusi Venerdì Santo e Natale) **Wochentags** (außer Karfreitag und Weihnachten)
Sundays, Good Friday, Christmas Day **Dimanches, Vendredi-Saint, Jour de Noël**	**12.00**	**14.00**	**19.00**	**22.30**	**Domeniche, Venerdì Santo, Natale** **Sonntags, Karfreitag und Weihnachten**
	dalle von	alle bis	dalle von	alle bis	

Children under 14 are not allowed in the bars of licensed premises (Public Houses, Hotels and Restaurants) where alcoholic drinks may be bought and consumed. The sale of alcoholic drink to minors under the age of 18 is illegal.

Unlicensed hotels and restaurants are not permitted to sell alcoholic beverages, including beer, at any time.

L'accès dans les bars des lieux autorisés à la vente des boissons alcoolisées (Public Houses, Hôtels, Restaurants) est interdit aux enfants de moins de 14 ans. La vente de boissons alcoolisées est interdite aux personnes de moins de 18 ans.

Les établissements sans licence (unlicensed) ne peuvent vendre, à aucun moment, aucune boisson alcoolisée.

E'vietato ai ragazzi minori di 14 anni l'ingresso ai bars dei locali autorizzati alla vendita di bevande alcoliche (Public Houses, Alberghi, Ristoranti).

E' vietata la vendita di bevande alcoliche ai minori di 18 anni. Gli esercizi senza licenza (unlicensed) non possono vendere bevande alcoliche in nessun momento.

Kindern unter 14 Jahren ist der Besuch von Lokalen (Bars) mit Alkoholausschank (Public houses, Hotels, Restaurants) untersagt. Der Verkauf von alkoholischen Getränken an Jugendliche unter 18 Jahren ist verboten.

Betriebe ohne Konzession (unlicensed) dürfen grundsätzlich keinen Alkohol verkaufen.

BOROUGHS and AREAS

☎ of Greater London : 01 except special cases.

BARNET pp. 8 and 9.

Finchley – ✉ N3/N12/NW11.

XX **Luigi's "Belmont",** 2-4 Belmont Parade, Finchley Rd, NW11 6XP, ☎ 455 0210, Italian rest.
closed Monday and Bank Holidays – **M** a la carte 3.45/5.45 **t.** 🍷 1.25. CV **x**

X **Otello,** 241 Regents Park Rd, N3 3LA, ☎ 346 5232, Italian rest. – Ⓟ CV **c**
closed Christmas Day and Easter Day – **M** a la carte 3.15/8.60 🍷 1.25.

X **L'Aubergade,** 816 Finchley Rd, NW11 6XL, at Temple Fortune ☎ 455 8853, French Bistro
closed 24 December-1 January and Bank Holidays – **M** (dinner only) a la carte 4.40/6.20 **t.** 🍷 2.00. CV **v**

Golders Green – ✉ NW11.

Croft Court, 44-46 Ravenscroft Av., NW11 8AY, ☎ 455 9175, – wc CV **n**
17 rm 7.50/16.00 **t.**

XXX ✿ **Le Connaisseur,** 10a Golders Green Rd, NW11 8LL, ☎ 455 4882 CV **z**
closed Saturday lunch, Sunday, Easter Saturday, 24 December and Bank Holidays – **M** a la carte 4.70/7.65 **t.** 🍷 2.50
Spec. Brioche à la moëlle, Paupiettes de sole Daumont, Médaillons de veau au saumon fumé.

Hendon – ✉ NW4/NW7.

18 off Sanders Lane ☎ **346 7810.**

Hendon Hall, Ashley Lane, NW4 1HF, ☎ 203 3341, heated, – TV Ⓟ. CV **e**
M 2.50/3.50 **st.** – **57 rm** 12.25/18.00 **st.**

TraveLodge (T.H.F.) without rest., at Scratchwood Service Area on M1, NW7 3HB, ☎ 906 0611 – TV wc Ⓟ. BV **n**
100 rm 10.50/14.00 **st.**

BEXLEY pp. 8 and 9.

i Town Hall at Erith ✉ Kent, CA8 1TL, ☎ 303 7777.

Bexley – ✉ Kent – ☎ Crayford.

XX **King's Head,** 65 High St., DA5 1AA, ☎ 526112 – Ⓟ FY **c**
closed Sunday dinner and Christmas Day – **M** a la carte 3.80/5.25 **t.** 🍷 1.65.

XX **Le Boulot,** 80 High St., DA5 1LB, ☎ 29905 FY **n**
M a la carte 3.70/5.70 🍷 1.50.

Sidcup – ✉ Kent.

X **La Botte,** 9 Marechal Neil Par., Main Rd, DA15 7PB, ☎ 300 5233, Italian rest. FY **r**
closed Sunday and 25-26 December – **M** (dinner only) a la carte 4.25/5.70 **t.**

Welling – ✉ Kent.

X Station (Centurion Rest.), 124 Bellegrove Rd, DA16 3QR, ☎ 303 4141 – Ⓟ. FY **a**

BRENT pp. 8 and 9.

Wembley – ✉ Middx.

18 Bridgewater Rd ☎ **902 0218** – 9 Whitton AS. Greenford ☎ **902 4555.**

London Eurocrest (Crest), Empire Way, HA9 8DL, ☎ 902 8839, Telex 923842 – TV Ⓟ. BV **o**
M a la carte 4.50/6.75 **s.** 🍷 1.50 – 1.80 – **335 rm** 15.60/19.00 **s.**

BROMLEY pp. 8 and 9.

i Town Hall, Widmore Rd ☎ 464 3333.

Beckenham – ✉ Kent.

18, 9 ☎ **650 2292.**

Four Chimneys , 18 Brackley Rd, BR3 1RQ, ☎ 650 5225, – wc Ⓟ EZ **v**
14 rm 4.00/9.00.

X **Gran Sasso,** 189a-191 High St. ☎ 658 3614, Italian rest. EZ **s**
closed Sunday and Bank Holidays – **M** a la carte 4.10/6.60 **t.** 🍷 1.30.

Bickley – ✉ Kent.

Glendevon House, 80 Southborough Rd, BR1 2EN, ☎ 467 2183, — FZ n
8 rm ☕ 5.20/11.00 **st.**

Bromley – ✉ Kent.

Magpie Hall Lane ☎ **462 7014.**

Bromley Continental, 56 Plaistow Lane ☎ 460 3606, – Ⓟ — FZ c
13 rm ☕ 6.50/13.00 **st.**

Grianan, 23 Orchard Rd, BR1 2PR, ☎ 460 1795, – Ⓟ — FZ r
10 rm.

XX **Chariot Wheel,** 21-22 Westmoreland Pl., Bromley South Shopping Centre, BR2 0TE, ☎ 460 8477, Italian rest. — FZ i
closed Sunday, Monday and Bank Holidays – **M** a la carte 3.80/8.55 **t.** 1.50.

X **Capisano,** 9 Simpsons Rd, BR2 9AP, ☎ 464 8036 — EZ a
closed Sunday, Monday lunch and Bank Holidays – **M** a la carte 3.95/5.25 **t.** 1.50.

Chislehurst – ✉ Kent.

X **London Steak House,** 7a High St. ☎ 467 0278 — FZ s
M a la carte 4.65/6.40 **t.** 1.20.

Farnborough – ✉ Kent – Farnborough.

XXX New Fantail, Locksbottom, BR6 8NF, ☎ 54848 – Ⓟ. — FZ x

XX **The George at Farnborough,** High St. ☎ 52005 – Ⓟ — FZ z
M a la carte 3.40/5.50 **t.** 0.95.

Orpington – ✉ Kent – Orpington.

XXX Chelsfield Park with rm, Bucks Cross Rd, Chelsfield Village ☎ 39325, French rest., ←, – TV wc Ⓟ. — FZ a
13 rm.

CAMDEN Except where otherwise stated see pp. 13-16.

i Town Hall, Euston Rd, NW1 2RU, ☎ 278 4444.

Bloomsbury – ✉ NW1/W1/WC1.

Drury Lane (Gd. Met.), 10 Drury Lane, High Holborn, WC2B 5RE, ☎ 836 6666, Telex 8811395 – TV . — p. 27 DV c
M 7.50/8.50 **st.** – ☕ 2.25 – **128 rm** 26.00/32.00 **s.**

Russell (T.H.F.), Russell Sq., WC1B 5BE, ☎ 837 6470, Telex 24615 – TV. — NT o
M (Carvery Rest.) approx. 4.95 **st.** 1.65 – ☕ 2.50 – **312 rm** 22.00/29.50 **st.** – P 25.95/33.20 **st.**

Cora, Upper Woburn Pl., WC1H 0HT, ☎ 387 5111 – wc . — MS z
150 rm.

Bonnington, 92 Southampton Row, WC1B 4BH, ☎ 242 2828, Telex 261591 – wc . — NT s
M a la carte 4.20/6.20 **st.** – **268 rm** ☕ 10.00/20.00 **st.**

Bloomsbury Centre (Centre), Coram St., WC1N 1HT, ☎ 837 1200, Group Telex 22113 – TV wc Ⓟ. — MNS c
M approx. 2.95 **s.** 1.25 – ☕ 1.50 – **250 rm** 11.75/15.75 **s.**

Royal National, 3a Bedford Way, WC1H 0DG, ☎ 637 2488, Group Telex 263951 – TV wc — MT v
M approx. 4.00 – **754 rm.**

Bedford, 83 Southampton Row, WC1B 4AD, ☎ 636 7822, Group Telex 263951 – TV wc . Ⓟ — NT x
M approx. 4.00 – **181 rm.**

Imperial, Southampton Row, WC1B 5BB, ☎ 837 3655, Group Telex 263951 – TV wc Ⓟ. — NT i
M approx. 4.00 – **450 rm.**

President, 9 Russell Sq., WC1N 1DB, ☎ 837 8844, Group Telex 263951 – TV wc Ⓟ — NT e
M approx. 4.00 – **447 rm.**

Tavistock, Tavistock Sq., WC1H 9EU, ☎ 636 8383, Group Telex 263951 – TV wc Ⓟ — MS x
M approx. 4.00 – **301 rm.**

Kingsley (T.H.F.), Bloomsbury Way, WC1A 2SD, ☎ 242 5881, Telex 21157 – wc . — NT r
178 rm.

Montague (Norfolk Cap.), Montague St., WC1B 5BJ, ☎ 637 1001, Group Telex 23241 – wc — MT n
M (coffee shop only) approx. 3.75 – **120 rm** ☕ 10.25/20.15 **st.**

Crescent, 49-50 Cartwright Gdns, WC1H 9EL, ☎ 387 1515 MS **a**
29 rm ☐ 5.50/15.00 **st.**

Harlingford, 61-63 Cartwright Gdns, WC1H 9EL, ☎ 387 1551 MS **n**
40 rm ☐ 7.00/11.00 **st.**

Wansbeck, 5-6 Bedford Pl., WC1B 5JD, ☎ 636 6232 NT **a**
23 rm.

Staunton, 13-15 Gower St., WC1E 6HE, ☎ 580 2740 MT **c**
closed 4 days at Christmas – **23 rm** ☐ 5.00/10.00 **s.**

Arran House, 77 Gower St., WC1E 6HJ, ☎ 636 2186 – MT **e**
25 rm ☐ 6.00/13.00 **st.**

XXX **L'Etoile,** 30 Charlotte St., W1P 1HJ, ☎ 636 7189, French rest. LT **e**
closed Saturday, Sunday, Easter, first 3 weeks August and Christmas – **M** a la carte 6.55/8.60 **t.** 1.45.

XXX **White Tower,** 1 Percy St., W1P 0ET, ☎ 636 8141, Greek rest. MT **u**
closed Saturday, Sunday, 3 weeks August and Bank Holidays – **M** a la carte 5.30/10.45 2.00.

XXX **Au Savarin,** 8 Charlotte St., W1P 1HE, ☎ 636 7134, French rest. LT **e**
closed Sunday, last 3 weeks August and Bank Holidays – **M** a la carte 10.30/21.55 1.35.

XX **Lacy's,** 26-28 Whitfield St., W1P 5RD, ☎ 636 2323 MT **a**
closed Saturday lunch and Sunday – **M** a la carte 5.50/8.90 **t.**

XX **Top of the Tower,** Maple St., W1P 6BR, ☎ 636 3000, London, « Revolving restaurant » LT **z**
closed Christmas Day – **M** a la carte 6.30/8.80 2.60.

XX **Wheeler's Antoine,** 40 Charlotte St., W1P 1HP, ☎ 636 2817, Seafood LT **e**
closed Saturday and Christmas – **M** a la carte 4.80/8.50 **t.** 1.75.

X **Trattoria dei Pescatori,** 57 Charlotte St., W1P 1LA, ☎ 580 3289, Italian Seafood
closed Sunday and Bank Holidays – **M** a la carte 4.00/6.95 **t.** 1.45. LT **v**

X **Conca d'Oro,** 54 Red Lion St., WC1 4PD, ☎ 242 6964, Italian rest. NT **c**
closed Saturday lunch, Sunday, 2 weeks August and Bank Holidays – **M** a la carte 2.95/4.45 **t.** 1.30.

X **Mon Plaisir,** 21 Monmouth St., WC2H 9DD, ☎ 836 7243, French rest. p. 27 DV **a**
closed Saturday, Sunday and Bank Holidays – **M** a la carte 2.90/3.95 1.15.

X **Brasserie du Coin,** 54 Lambs Conduit St., WC1N 3LN, ☎ 405 1717, French rest.
closed Saturday, Sunday and Bank Holidays – **M** a la carte 3.30/5.00 1.05. NT **z**

X Belmonte, 31 Rathbone Pl., W1, ☎ 636 8965, Italian rest. MT **s**

Euston – ✉ NW1.

Kennedy (Gd. Met.), 43 Cardington St., NW1 2LP, ☎ 387 4400, Telex 28250 – wc . LS **r**
M (dinner only) a la carte approx. 5.80 **st.** 1.50 – ☐ 1.15 – **319 rm** 17.00/23.00 **s.**

Finchley Road – ✉ NW1/NW3.

Nether Court, Frith Lane ☎ 346 2436.

Charles Bernard, 5 Frognal, NW3 6AL, ☎ 794 0101, Telex 23560 – wc GR **s**
M 2.75 **s.** 1.20 – **57 rm** ☐ 14.00/20.00 **s.**

Dawson House, 72 Canfield Gdns, NW6 3ED, ☎ 624 0079, HR **a**
15 rm ☐ 5.50/11.00 **st.**

Clearview House, 161 Fordwych Rd, NW2, ☎ 452 9773 CV **r**
6 rm.

XX **Trattoria del Buonamico,** 122a Finchley Rd, NW3 5HT, ☎ 794 5784, Italian rest. JR **o**
closed 25 and 26 December – **M** a la carte 3.65/5.90 **t.** 1.10.

Hampstead – ✉ NW3.

Swiss Cottage, 4 Adamson Rd, NW3 3HR, ☎ 722 2281, « Antique furniture collection » – wc wc JR **n**
67 rm.

Clive, Primrose Hill Rd, NW3 3NA, ☎ 586 2233, Telex 22759 – wc wc . KR **a**
84 rm.

Post House (T.H.F.), 215 Haverstock Hill, NW3 4RB, ☎ 794 8121, Telex 262494 – wc GR **r**
M a la carte 4.10/5.35 **st.** 1.50 – ☐ 2.00 – **140 rm** 14.00/20.00 **st.**

Sandringham, 3 Holford Rd, NW3 1AD, ☎ 435 1569, GR **u**
13 rm ☐ 5.00/10.00.

Frognal Lodge, 14 Frognal Gdns, NW3 6UX, ☎ 435 8238 – wc GR **v**
15 rm.

The Buckland, 6 Buckland Crescent, NW3, ☎ 722 5574 – wc JR **e**
☐ 0.50 – **14 rm** 7.50/15.00 **st.**

XXX **Keats,** 3-4 Downshire Hill, NW3 1NR, ☎ 435 1499, French rest. GR **i**
closed 2 weeks August and Bank Holidays – **M** (dinner only and Sunday lunch) a la carte 6.25/10.45 **t.** 🍷 2.50.

XX **La Baita,** 200 Haverstock Hill, NW3 2AG, ☎ 794 4126, Italian rest. GR **e**
closed 25 and 26 December – **M** a la carte 3.00/6.75 **t.** 🍷 1.25.

X **Villa Bianca,** 1 Perrin's Court, NW3 1QR, ☎ 435 3131, Italian rest. GR **c**
closed Bank Holidays – **M** a la carte 4.65/6.10 **t.** 🍷 1.20.

X **Turpin's,** 118 Heath St., NW3 1DR, ☎ 435 3791, English rest. GR **a**
closed Sunday dinner, Monday and Bank Holidays – **M** (dinner only and Sunday lunch) a la carte 4.70/6.00 **t.** 🍷 1.35.

X **Le Cellier du Midi,** 28 Church Row, NW3 6UP, ☎ 435 9998, French rest. GR **x**
closed Sunday and Bank Holidays – **M** (dinner only) a la carte 4.85/6.85 **t.** 🍷 1.50.

X **Chateaubriand,** 48 Belsize Lane, NW3 5AR, ☎ 435 4882, Bistro GR **n**
closed Sunday and 25-26 December – **M** (dinner only) a la carte 4.85/5.85 **t.** 🍷 1.70.

Holborn – ✉ WC2.

XXX **L'Opera,** 32 Great Queen St., WC2B 5AA, ☎ 405 9020 p. 27 EV **n**
closed Saturday lunch, Sunday and Christmas Day – **M** a la carte 5.40/8.10 **t.** 🍷 1.50.

King's Cross – ✉ N1.

🏨 **Great Northern** (B.T.H.), N1 9AN, ☎ 837 5454 – 🛗 📺 🛁wc ☎. 🚗 MNS **s**
M 3.50/6.50 **st.** 🍷 1.60 – **69 rm** ☕ 15.00/29.00 **st.**

Regent's Park – ✉ NW1.

🏨 **White House** (Rank), Albany St., NW1 3UP, ☎ 387 1200, Telex 24111 – 🛗 📺 ♿. 🚗
M *(closed Saturday lunch, Sunday and Bank Holidays except Christmas lunch)* a la carte 5.80/7.85 🍷 1.65 – ☕ 2.50 – **600 rm** 14.75/25.00 **s.** LS **o**

XX **Barque and Bite,** Opposite 15, Prince Albert Rd, NW1 7SR, ☎ 485 8137, « Old canal barge » KR **n**
closed Saturday lunch, Sunday, Christmas and Bank Holidays – **M** a la carte 4.60/5.70 🍷 1.40.

Swiss Cottage – ✉ NW3.

🏨 **Holiday Inn,** 128 King Henry's Rd, NW3 3ST, ☎ 722 7711, Telex 267396, 🏊 – 🛗 📺 ♿ 🅟. 🚗 JR **a**
M a la carte 4.60/7.50 – ☕ 2.50 – **297 rm** 22.00/28.00.

XX **Peter's,** 65 Fairfax Rd, NW6 4EE, ☎ 624 5804 JR **i**
closed Christmas Day – **M** (dinner only and Sunday lunch) a la carte 4.90/5.90 **t.**

CITY OF LONDON Except where otherwise stated see pp. 13-16.

i St. Paul's Churchyard, EC4, ☎ 606 3030 ext 2456/7.

🏨 **Great Eastern** (B.T.H.), Liverpool St., EC2M 7QN, ☎ 283 4363, Telex 886812 – 🛗 📺 ♿. 🚗 QT **r**
M approx. 4.00 **st.** 🍷 1.60 – **157 rm** ☕ 14.00/31.00 **st.**

XXX ✿ **Le Poulbot** (basement), 45 Cheapside, EC2V 6AR, ☎ 236 4379, French rest. PU **i**
closed Saturday, Sunday and Bank Holidays – **M** (lunch only) a la carte 9.00/11.50 **st.** 🍷 2.60
Spec. Filets de sole Leonora, Marmite du pêcheur, Piccatta de veau à ma façon.

XXX **Baron of Beef,** Gutter Lane, Gresham St., EC2V 6BR, ☎ 606 6961, English rest. PT **r**
closed Saturday, Sunday and Bank Holidays – **M** a la carte 5.95/10.00.

XXX **Wheelton Room,** 62 Crutched Friars, EC3N 2DD, ☎ 709 9622 QU **r**
closed Saturday, Sunday and Bank Holidays – **M** (lunch only) a la carte 6.00/10.00 🍷 2.50.

XXX City Yacht (T.H.F.), 1 Addle St., EC2V 7EU, ☎ 606 8536. PT **c**

XXX **Bill Bentley's,** Swedeland Court, 202 Bishopsgate, EC2M 4NR, ☎ 283 1763, Seafood
closed Saturday and Sunday – **M** (lunch only) a la carte 4.45/8.60 🍷 1.50. QY **e**

XXX **Wheeler's Fenchurch,** 9-13 Fenchurch Buildings, EC3P 3HY, ☎ 488 4848, Seafood
closed Saturday, Sunday and Bank Holidays – **M** (lunch only) a la carte approx. 8.50 **t.** 🍷 1.75. QU **n**

XXX **Cotillion Room,** Bucklersbury House, 18 Walbrook, EC4N 8EL, ☎ 248 4735 PU **s**
closed Saturday, Sunday and Bank Holidays – **M** (lunch only) a la carte 5.10/7.15 **t.** 🍷 1.60.

XXX Essex Rib Roast, Dunster House, Mark Lane, EC3R 7DP, ☎ 626 5513. QU **o**

XX **Terrazza-Est,** 125 Chancery Lane, WC2A 1PP, ☎ 242 2601, Italian rest. p. 27 FV **n**
closed Saturday lunch, Sunday and Bank Holidays – **M** a la carte 5.55/8.45 🍷 1.20.

XX Aykoku-Kaku, 9 Walbrook, EC4, ☎ 236 9020, Japanese rest. PQU **u**

XX **Wheeler's City,** 19-21 Great Tower St., EC3R 5AQ, ☎ 626 3685, Seafood QU **e**
closed Saturday, Sunday, Easter, Christmas Day, 1 January and Bank Holidays – **M** (lunch only) a la carte approx. 8.50 **t.** 🍷 1.75.

XX **Le Gaulois,** 119 Chancery Lane, WC2A 1PP, ☎ 405 7769, French rest. p. 27 FV **c**
closed Saturday, Sunday and Bank Holidays – **M** a la carte 3.75/4.80 🍷 2.50.

XX **Court,** 116 Newgate St., EC1A 7AE, ☎ 600 1134 PT **n**
closed Saturday, Sunday and Bank Holidays – **M** (lunch only) a la carte approx. 4.90 🍷 1.40.

X **Le Gamin,** 32 Old Bailey, EC4M 7HS, ☎ 236 7931, French rest. PU **a**
closed Saturday, Sunday and Bank Holidays – **M** (lunch only) a la carte 3.05/4.20 **st.** 🍷 1.60.

X **Bubb's,** 329 Central Markets, Farringdon St., EC1A 9NB, ☎ 236 2435, French rest. PT **a**
closed Saturday, Sunday, August and Bank Holidays – **M** a la carte approx. 4.20 🍷 1.10.

X **Ginnan,** 5 Cathedral Pl., St. Paul's, EC4, ☎ 236 4120, Japanese rest. PT **e**
closed Saturday, Sunday and Bank Holidays – **M** a la carte 3.55/5.65 🍷 0.80.

X Mincing Lane Grill Room, Plantation House, Mincing Lane, EC3M 3OX, ☎ 626 4479. QU **c**

X **La Germainerie,** 120 Chancery Lane, WC2A 1PP, ☎ 405 0290, French rest. p. 27 FV **a**
closed Saturday, Sunday and Bank Holidays – **M** (lunch only) a la carte 3.35/4.15 🍷 2.50.

X George and Vulture (T.H.F.), George Yard, Lombard St., EC3 9DL, ☎ 626 9710. QU **a**

X City Friends, 34 Old Bailey, EC4, ☎ 248 5189, Chinese rest. PU **c**

X **Le Bistingo,** 65 Fleet St., EC4, ☎ 353 4436, Bistro PU **e**
closed Sunday – **M** a la carte 2.95/4.25 **t.** 🍷 1.30.

CROYDON pp. 8 and 9.

i Taberner House, Park Lane, Croydon, CR9 3JS, ☎ 686 4433.

Croydon – ✉ Surrey.

18 9 Featherbed Lane ☎ 657 0281, E: 3 m.

🏨 **Aerodrome** (Anchor), Purley Way, CR9 4LT, ☎ 688 5185, Group Telex 27120, – TV wc ☎ P. DZ **c**
M a la carte 4.00/5.10 **t.** 🍷 1.00 – **65 rm** 9.75/17.05 **st.**

XX **Hook, Line and Sinker,** 3 George St., CR10 1LA, ☎ 688 8604, Seafood DZ **s**
closed Sunday, Monday dinner and Bank Holidays – **M** a la carte 4.10/8.30 **st.** 🍷 1.40.

Norbury

X **Mr. Bunbury's,** 1154 London Rd, SW16 4DS, ☎ 764 3939, Bistro DZ **n**
closed Sunday and Bank Holidays – **M** (dinner only) a la carte 3.35/5.25 **t.** 🍷 1.25.

Sanderstead – ✉ Surrey.

🏨 **Selsdon Park,** Addington Rd, CR2 8YA, ☎ 657 8811, Telex 945003, ←, heated, 18, park – TV P. EZ **o**
M a la carte 6.75/9.00 **s.** 🍷 2.50 – **160 rm** 21.00/32.00 **s.**

X **Elio,** 17 Limpsfield Rd, CR2 9LA, ☎ 657 2953, Italian rest. EZ **n**
closed Sunday and Bank Holidays – **M** a la carte 3.35/4.80 🍷 1.35.

Shirley – ✉ Surrey.

XX La Baita di Piero, 138 Wickam Rd ☎ 654 5622, Italian rest. EZ **e**

South Croydon – ✉ Surrey.

Briarley, 8-10 Outram Rd, CR0 6XE, ☎ 654 1000, – wc P EZ **x**
21 rm 7.00/14.00 **st.**

XX **Pastori's Farmhouse,** 88 Selsdon Park Rd, Addington, CR2 8JT, ☎ 657 2576 – P EZ **r**
closed Sunday and Monday – **M** a la carte 4.00/6.25 🍷 1.35.

X **Trattoria Bella Venezia,** 248 Brighton Rd, CR2 6AH, ☎ 686 2680, Italian rest. DZ **a**
closed Sunday, Monday lunch, 25-26 December and 1 January – **M** a la carte 4.30/7.80 🍷 1.50.

EALING pp. 8 and 9.

Ealing – ✉ W5.

18 Church Rd, Hanwell ☎ 567 4230.

i Town Hall, New Broadway, W5, ☎ 579 2424.

🏨 **Carnarvon,** Ealing Common, W5 3HN, ☎ 992 5399, Telex 935114 – TV wc ☎ P. BX **s**
M a la carte 3.35/5.05 **st.** 🍷 1.70 – **150 rm** 16.30/23.30 **st.**

🏨 **Kenton House,** 5 Hillcrest Rd, Hanger Hill, W5 2JL, ☎ 997 8436 – TV wc wc ☎ P
M (dinner only) a la carte 3.10/4.90 🍷 1.45 – **50 rm** 17.50/26.00 **st.** BJ **e**

Sussex House, 37 Hamilton Rd, W5 2EE, ☎ 567 3176, BX **a**
10 rm 6.50/13.00 **st.**

ENFIELD pp. 8 and 9.

Edmonton – ✉ N9/N18.
Picketts Lock Lane ☎ 803 3611.
✕ Viking, 52-54 Church St., N9, ☎ 807 2555. EV a

Enfield – ✉ Middx.
See : Forty Hall (park★).
Enfield Municipal GC., Whitewebbs Park ☎ 363 4458, N : 1 m.
Royal Chace, 162 The Ridgeway, EN2 3AR, ☎ 366 6500, ≤, heated, – TV ♿ Ⓟ. DV a
M a la carte 5.90/10.05 **s.** 1.65 – 1.50 – **50 rm** 10.25/14.75 **st.**
Holtwhites, 92 Chase Side, EN2 0QN, ☎ 363 0124, Telex 299670 – wc wc Ⓟ
M (dinner only) a la carte 3.90/8.00 **t.** 1.75 – **30 rm** 10.00/17.00 **t.** EV c
✕✕✕ Norfolk, 80 London Rd, EN2, ☎ 363 0979. EV e

Hadley Wood – ✉ Herts.
West Lodge Park, off Cockfosters Rd, near Barnet, EN4 0PY, ☎ 440 8311, ≤, park – TV ♿ Ⓟ. DV s
M a la carte 4.95/5.95 **s.** 1.50 – **54 rm** 15.00/23.00 **s.**

Palmers Green – ✉ N13.
✕✕ **Pilgrims Rest,** 16-18 Hazelwood Lane, N13 5EX, ☎ 886 2454 DV o
closed Sunday and Bank Holidays – **M** a la carte 3.45/6.20 **t.** 1.30.

MICHELIN Branch, Eley's Estate Angel Rd, N18, ☎ 803 7341.

Red Lion — Si le nom d'un hôtel figure en petits caractères, demandez à l'arrivée les conditions à l'hôtelier.

GREENWICH pp. 8 and 9.

Eltham – ✉ SE9.
✕✕ **La Reine** (King's Arms), 60 Eltham High St., SE9 1BT, ☎ 859 0606 FY e
closed Sunday dinner – **M** a la carte 3.85/6.50 **t.** 1.90.

Greenwich – ✉ SE10.
i King William Walk, Cutty Sark Gardens, SE10, ☎ 854 888 (summer only).
✕ **Meantime,** 47-49 Greenwich Church St., SE10 9BL, ☎ 858 8705, Bistro EX a
closed Sunday, Monday and Bank Holidays – **M** a la carte 4.45/5.50 **t.** 1.25.
✕ **Le Papillon,** 57 Greenwich Church St., SE10 9BL, ☎ 858 2668, Bistro EY n
closed Sunday and Christmas Day – **M** a la carte 3.60/5.50 1.15.
✕ **Spread Eagle,** 2 Stockwell St., SE10 9JN, ☎ 858 5861, Bistro EY u
closed Sunday dinner and Bank Holidays – **M** (dinner only and Sunday lunch) a la carte 3.50/5.60 **t.** 1.10.

HAMMERSMITH Except where otherwise stated see pp. 17-20.

Fulham – ✉ SW6.
Lindsay, without rest., 422-428 Fulham Rd, SW6 1DU, ☎ 385 8561 – wc Ⓟ
59 rm. HZ s
✕✕ **Newton's,** 576 King's Rd, SW6 2DY, ☎ 736 1804 JZ a
closed Sunday and 25-26 December – **M** (dinner only) 3.25/6.50 1.00.
✕✕ **Barbarella,** 428 Fulham Rd, SW6 1DU, ☎ 385 9434, Italian rest., Dancing HZ x
closed Sunday and Bank Holidays – **M** (dinner only) a la carte 4.70/6.00 2.50.
✕ **Carlo's Place,** 855 Fulham Rd, SW6 5HJ, ☎ 736 4507 pp. 8 and 9 CY r
closed Monday, Easter week, August and Christmas week – **M** (dinner only) a la carte 5.00/6.25 **t.** 1.40.
✕ Red Onion Bistro, 636 Fulham Rd, SW6, ☎ 736 0920, Bistro. pp. 8 and 9 CY e
✕ **Trencherman Bistro,** 271 New King's Rd, SW6 4RD, ☎ 736 4988, Bistro
closed Saturday lunch, Sunday dinner, Good Friday and 25-26 December – **M** a la carte 3.55/5.25 **t.** 1.10. pp. 8 and 9 CY s

Hammersmith – ✉ W6/W12/W14.
i Town Hall, King St., W6, ☎ 748 3020.
Cunard International, 1 Shortlands, W6 8DR, ☎ 741 1555, Telex 934539 – TV ♿ Ⓟ. GY a
M a la carte 4.10/7.25 **s.** 1.40 – 2.25 – **640 rm** 20.00/26.00 **s.**
✕✕ **Anarkali,** 303-305 King St., W6 9NH, ☎ 748 1760, Indian rest. pp. 8 and 9 CX c
M a la carte 3.20/5.90 1.75.

West Kensington – ✉ SW6/W14.

West Centre (Centre), Lillie Rd, SW6 1UQ, ☎ 385 1255, Telex 917728 – wc ☎ Ⓟ. HZ **e**
M approx. 2.95 **s.** 1.25 – 1.50 – **502 rm** 11.75/15.75 **s.**

Lily, 23-33 Lillie Rd, SW6 1UG, ☎ 381 1881, Telex 918922 – wc ☎ Ⓟ HZ **o**
M 2.50/4.50 **s.** 1.95 – **98 rm** 12.00/18.00 **s.**

HARINGEY pp. 8 and 9.

Highgate – ✉ N6.

San Carlo, 2 High St., Highgate, N6, ☎ 340 5823, Italian rest. DV **e**

Muswell Hill – ✉ N10.

Silverdale, 27 Queens Av., N10 3PE, ☎ 444 9783, DV **c**
36 rm 6.00/9.00 **st.**

HARROW pp. 8 and 9.

Bushey Heath – ✉ Herts.

Alpine, 135 High Rd, W2 1JA, ☎ 950 2024, Italian rest. – Ⓟ. BV **a**

Central Harrow – ✉ Middx.

Cumberland, 1 St. John's Rd, HA1 2EF, ☎ 863 4111, – wc wc ☎ Ⓟ BV **u**
63 rm.

Old Etonian, 38 High St., Harrow Hill, HA1 3LL, ☎ 422 8482, French rest. BV **c**
closed Saturday lunch, Sunday and Bank Holidays – **M** a la carte 5.30/6.65 2.30.

London Steak House, 51 High St., Harrow Hill, HA1 3MX, ☎ 422 8473. BV **r**

Pinner – ✉ Middx.

The Ember, 141 Marsh Rd ☎ 866 9764 AV **r**
closed Saturday lunch, Sunday and Bank Holidays – **M** a la carte 4.60/7.85 1.70.

La Giralda, 66 Pinner Green, HA5 2AB, ☎ 868 3429 AV **o**
M 3.50/4.00 0.95.

Stanmore – ✉ Middx.

Signor Tonino, 85 Stanmore Hill, HA7 3DZ, ☎ 954 0147, Italian rest. BV **i**
closed Sunday – **M** (dinner only) a la carte 3.90/5.20 0.95.

HAVERING pp. 8 and 9.

Hornchurch – ✉ Essex – Ingrebourne.

Fairlane Motor Inn, Southend Arterial Rd (A 127), RM11 3UJ, ☎ 46789, Telex 897315 – wc ☎ Ⓟ. FV **s**
M approx. 4.25 **st.** 1.85 – **145 rm** 11.75/17.00 **st.**

HILLINGDON pp. 8 and 9.

Eastcote – ✉ Middx.

Trombino, 4 Black Horse Parade, Eastcote High Rd ☎ 868 5599, Italian rest. AV **v**

Sambuca, 113 Field End Rd, HA5 1QG, ☎ 866 7500. AV **a**

Heathrow Airport – ✉ Middx.

Sheraton Skyline, Bath Rd, Harlington, Hayes, UB3 5BP, ☎ 759 2535, Telex 934254, « Exotic indoor garden with » – Ⓟ. AXY **x**
M 5.50/12.50 **st.** – 2.90 – **350 rm** 26.00/31.00 **st.**

Holiday Inn, Stockley Rd, West Drayton, UB7 9NA, ☎ West Drayton 45555, Telex 934518, , , 9 – Ⓟ. AX **c**
M a la carte 4.40/6.80 **s.** 1.75 – 2.45 – **281 rm** 17.00/22.00.

Excelsior (T.H.F.), Bath Rd, West Drayton, UB7 0DU, ☎ 759 6611, Telex 24525, heated – Ⓟ. AY **s**
M a la carte 3.10/7.30 **st.** 1.40 – 2.20 – **666 rm** 19.50/26.00 **st.**

The Heathrow, Bath Rd, Hounslow, TW6 2AQ, ☎ 897 6363, Telex 934660, ←, – Ⓟ. AY **n**
680 rm.

Sheraton Heathrow, Colnbrook by-pass, West Drayton, UB7 0HJ, ☎ 759 2424, Telex 934331, – Ⓟ. AY **i**
M (grill rest.) 3.60/6.00 **st.** – 2.50 – **440 rm** 22.00/26.50.

Post House (T.H.F.), Sipson Rd, West Drayton, UP7 0JU, ☎ 759 2323, Telex 934280 – AXY e
M a la carte 4.80/6.40 **st.** 1.60 – 2.00 – **594 rm** 16.00/22.50 **st.**

Skyway (T.H.F), 140 Bath Rd, Hayes, UB3 5AW, ☎ 759 6311, Telex 23935, heated – AXY v
M a la carte 4.85/6.90 **st.** 1.55 – 2.00 – **440 rm** 13.50/19.00 **st.**

Ariel (T.H.F.), Harlington Corner, Bath Rd, Hayes, UB3 5AJ, ☎ 759 2552, Telex 21777 – wc AXY z
M a la carte 3.60/6.35 **st.** 1.50 – 2.00 – **177 rm** 15.00/22.00 **st.**

Arlington (Norfolk Cap.), Shepiston Lane, Hayes, UB3 1LP, ☎ 573 6162, Group Telex 23241 – wc wc AX r
M approx. 4.15 **st.** 1.25 – 1.65 – **80 rm** 13.00/17.55 **st.**

Hillingdon – Middx – Uxbridge.

i Civic Centre, High St., Uxbridge ☎ 50111 ext 3670.

Master Brewer Motel, Western Av., Hillingdon Circus, UB10 9NR, ☎ 51199 – wc AVX c
M (grill rest.) 3.00/4.50 **t.** 1.25 – 1.50 – **64 rm** 13.50/16.00 **st.**

Northwood – Middx – Northwood.

18 The Drive ☎ 26485.

Belair Swiss, Rickmansworth Rd, HA6 2QW, ☎ 22206, Dancing AV e
closed Saturday lunch and Sunday – **M** a la carte 4.40/7.60 1.25.

Ruislip – Middx – Ruislip.

18 Ickenham Rd ☎ 32004.

Barn without rest., West End Rd, HA4 6JD, ☎ 36057, – wc AV n
54 rm 8.00/15.00.

HOUNSLOW pp. 8 and 9.

Brentford – Middx.

Camellia, Syon Park, TW8 8JF, ☎ 568 0778, – BY u
closed Christmas dinner and 26 December – **M** a la carte 5.45/7.65 **t.** 1.35.

Cranford – Middx.

Berkeley Arms (Embassy), Bath Rd, TW5 9QE, ☎ 897 2121, Telex 935728, – AY o
closed Christmas – **M** a la carte 5.50/7.65 **st.** 1.50 – 1.65 – **42 rm** 15.75/21.00 **st.**

Hounslow – Middx.

Master Robert Motel, 366 Great West Rd, TW5 0BD, ☎ 570 6261, – wc wc AY a
M a la carte 3.25/5.35 **t.** 1.25 – 1.50 – **63 rm** 13.50/15.00 **st.**

Isleworth – Middx.

18 Syon Lane ☎ **560 8777, ½ m. from Gillettes Corner (A 4).**

Osterley Motel, 764 Great West Rd, TW7 5NA, ☎ 568 9981 – wc BY r
32 rm.

ISLINGTON pp. 13-16.

Finsbury – WC1/EC1.

Royal Scot (Thistle), 100 King's Cross Rd, WC1X 9BR, ☎ 278 2434, Telex 27657 – wc NS n
349 rm.

London Ryan, Gwynne Pl., King's Cross Rd, WC1X 9QN, ☎ 278 2480, Telex 27728 – wc NS a
M (bar lunch) 4.00/4.75 **t.** 1.40 – 1.25 – **213 rm** 17.50/24.00 **st.**

Islington – N1.

i Town Hall, Upper St. ☎ 226 1234.

Carrier's, 2 Camden Pass., N1 8ED, ☎ 226 5353 PR e
closed Sunday, Easter Saturday and Bank Holidays – **M** 10.00/12.50 2.25
Spec. Brandade of smoked trout, Bœuf à la ficelle, Petit pot au chocolat à l'orange.

Frederick's, Camden Pass., N1 8EG, ☎ 359 2888 PR a
closed Sunday, 1 January and Bank Holidays – **M** a la carte 4.20/7.10 1.30.

M'sieur Frog, 31a Essex Rd, N10 3PT, ☎ 226 3495, Bistro PR n
closed Sunday, Monday and August – **M** (dinner only) a la carte 5.00/6.00 **t.** 1.15.

KENSINGTON and CHELSEA (Royal Borough of).

Chelsea – ✉ SW1/SW3/SW10 – Except where otherwise stated see pp. 24 and 25.

Carlton Tower, 2 Cadogan Pl., SW1X 9PY, ☎ 235 5411, Telex 21944 – **M** Chelsea Room a la carte 8.75/14.75 **s.** 1.50 – Rib Room a la carte 8.50/14.50 **s.** 2.50 – 3.50 – **244 rm** 52.00/60.00 **s.** FR **n**

Sheraton Park Tower, 101 Knightsbridge, SW1X 7RN, ☎ 235 8050, Telex 917222 – FQ **v**
M a la carte 8.05/11.85 **st.** 1.85 – 3.50 – **289 rm** 47.00/55.00 **s.**

✿ **Capital,** 22-24 Basil St., SW3 1AT, ☎ 589 5171, Telex 919042 – ER **a**
M a la carte approx. 7.35 1.95 – 3.25 – **60 rm** 31.05/43.50 **st.**
Spec. Cœur d'artichaut farci à la Nissarda, Quenelles de brochet à l'armoricaine, Carré d'agneau persillé aux herbes de Provence.

Holiday Inn, 17-25 Sloane St., SW1X 9NU, ☎ 235 4377, Telex 919111, –
M (grill rest.) approx. 7.00 **s.** 1.90 – 2.25 – **217 rm** 31.00/37.00. FR **r**

Cadogan, 75 Sloane St., SW1X 9SG, ☎ 235 7141, Telex 267893 – FR **e**
M 5.00/8.00 **st.** 2.50 – 2.60 – **74 rm** 23.00/34.00.

Ladbroke Belgravia, 20 Chesham Pl., SW1X 8HQ, ☎ 235 6040, Telex 919020 –
M a la carte 5.65/7.35 – 2.20 – **110 rm** 28.00/35.00 **s.** FR **a**

Basil Street, 8 Basil St., SW3 1AH, ☎ 730 3411, Group Telex 21879 – FQ **o**
M 5.00/6.00 **st.** 1.50 – 1.75 – **109 rm** 22.50/32.50 **st.**

Wilbraham, Wilbraham Pl., Sloane St., SW1X 9AE, ☎ 730 8296 – wc FS **n**
M *(closed Sunday and Bank Holidays)* a la carte 3.95/5.25 **s.** 2.20 – 1.40 – **54 rm** 10.00/19.50 **s.**

Royal Court (Norfolk Cap.), Sloane Sq., SW1W 8EG, ☎ 730 9191, Group Telex 23241 – wc FST **a**
M a la carte 3.55/4.40 **st.** 1.60 – **102 rm** 12.30/23.95 **st.**

Fenja without rest., 69 Cadogan Gdns, SW3 2RB – wc FS **r**
18 rm 17.00/31.60 **st.**

Campden Court without rest., 28 Basil St., SW3 1AT, ☎ 589 6286 – wc ER **s**
17 rm 12.50/20.00 **s.**

Willett without rest., 32 Sloane Gardens, Sloane Sq., SW1W 8DJ, ☎ 730 0634 – wc FT **s**
17 rm 7.50/12.50 **st.**

XXXX ✿✿ **Le Gavroche,** 61-63 Lower Sloane St., SW1W 8DH, ☎ 730 2820, French rest. FT **e**
closed Sunday and Bank Holidays – **M** (dinner only) a la carte 12.25/17.50 **t.** 2.00
Spec. Papillote de saumon fumé Claudine, Caneton Gavroche, Sablé aux fraises.

XXX **Waltons of Walton Street,** 121 Walton St., SW3 2HP, ☎ 584 0204 DS **a**
closed Sunday dinner and Bank Holidays – **M** 9.00/13.50.

XXX **Minotaur,** Chelsea Cloisters, Sloane Av., SW3 3DN, ☎ 584 8608 ET **a**
closed Saturday lunch – **M** a la carte 5.00/6.70 **t.** 1.50.

XXX **Brompton Grill,** 243 Brompton Rd, SW3 2EP, ☎ 589 8005 DR **e**
closed Sunday lunch and Bank Holidays – **M** a la carte 5.40/7.40 2.00.

XX **Le Français,** 259 Fulham Rd, SW3 6HY, ☎ 352 4748, French rest. CU **a**
closed Sunday, July and Bank Holidays – **M** a la carte 6.10/9.00 **t.** 2.20.

XX **Daphne's,** 112 Draycott Av., SW3 3AE, ☎ 589 4257 DS **e**
closed Sunday and Bank Holidays – **M** (dinner only) a la carte 4.60/7.05 1.35.

XX **Parke's,** 4-5 Beauchamp Pl., SW3 1NG, ☎ 589 1390 ER **n**
closed Sunday, Easter and Christmas – **M** approx. 11.00.

XX **Drakes,** 2a Pond Pl., Fulham Rd, SW3 6SP, ☎ 584 4555 DT **v**
closed Christmas Day and Bank Holidays – **M** a la carte 3.65/4.55 **t.** 1.25.

XX ✿ **Ma Cuisine,** 113 Walton St., SW3 2JY, ☎ 584 7585, French rest. DS **a**
closed Saturday, Sunday, July and Bank Holidays – **M** a la carte 5.75/7.20 **t.** 1.95
Spec. Filet de bar bordelaise (June-October), Ballotine de volaille Lucien Tendret, Tartelettes aux fruits de saison.

XX **Poissonnerie de l'Avenue,** 82 Sloane Av., SW3 3DZ, ☎ 589 2457, Seafood DS **u**
closed Sunday and Bank Holidays – **M** a la carte 4.75/8.00 **t.** 1.50.

XX **Marcel,** 14 Sloane St., SW1X 9NB, ☎ 235 4912, French rest. FQR **r**
closed Sunday and Bank Holidays – **M** a la carte approx. 7.60 1.10.

XX **Au Fin Bec,** 100 Draycott Av., SW3 3AD, ☎ 584 3600, French rest. ES **s**
closed Sunday, August and Bank Holidays – **M** a la carte 4.10/6.30 1.30.

XX **Le Suquet,** 104 Draycott Av., SW3, ☎ 581 1785, French rest., Seafood DS **c**
closed Monday and Bank Holidays – **M** a la carte 6.10/9.60 **t.**

XX **Meridiana,** 169 Fulham Rd, SW3 6SP, ☎ 589 8815, Italian rest. DT **i**
closed Sunday and Bank Holidays – **M** a la carte 4.60/6.80 1.50.

XX **Coq au Vin,** 8 Harriet St., Lowndes Sq., SW1X 9JW, ☎ 235 3969, French rest. FQ **s**
closed Saturday lunch, 25-26 December and Bank Holidays – **M** a la carte 5.10/7.65 1.80.

XX **Don Luigi,** 33c King's Rd, SW3 4LX, ☏ 730 3023, Italian rest. — ET **r**
M a la carte 4.65/7.20.

XX Il Girasole, 126 Fulham Rd, SW3, ☏ 370 6656, Italian rest. — CU **x**

XX Sale e Pepe, 13-15 Pavillion Rd, SW1, ☏ 235 0098, Italian rest. — FQ **x**

XX **Bewick's,** 87-89 Walton St., SW3 2HP, ☏ 584 6711 — ES **n**
closed Sunday – **M** a la carte 4.50/6.90 🍷 1.45.

XX **Santa Croce,** 112 Cheyne Walk, Chelsea Embankment, SW10 0DJ, ☏ 352 7534, Italian rest. — pp. 17-20 JZ **n**
closed Sunday and Bank Holidays – **M** a la carte 3.80/5.20 **t.** 🍷 1.15.

XX **San Frediano,** 62-64 Fulham Rd, SW3 6HH, ☏ 584 8375, Italian rest. — DT **n**
closed Sunday and Bank Holidays – **M** a la carte 3.40/5.40 **t.** 🍷 1.15.

XX Sambuca, 6 Symons St., SW3, ☏ 730 6571, Italian rest. — FT **n**

XX **Bagatelle,** 5 Langton St., SW10, ☏ 351 4185, French rest. — pp. 17-20 JZ **u**
closed Sunday, Christmas and Bank Holidays – **M** a la carte 4.35/6.00 **t.** 🍷 1.45.

XX **Tandoori,** 153 Fulham Rd, SW3 6SN, ☏ 589 7749, Indian and Pakistani rest. — DT **o**
closed 24 to 26 December – **M** (dinner only and Sunday lunch) a la carte 4.80/5.55 🍷 1.50.

XX **September,** 457 Fulham Rd, SW10 9UZ, ☏ 352 0206 — pp. 17-20 JZ **c**
closed Sunday – **M** (dinner only) a la carte 4.35/5.60 **t.** 🍷 1.40.

XX **Al Ben Accolto,** 58 Fulham Rd, SW3 6HH, ☏ 589 0876, Italian rest. — DT **c**
closed Sunday and Bank Holidays – **M** a la carte 3.35/4.70 🍷 1.05.

XX **La Famiglia,** 7 Langton St., SW10 0JL, ☏ 351 0761, Italian rest. — pp. 17-20 JZ **r**
closed Bank Holidays – **M** a la carte 3.50/5.10 🍷 1.55.

XX **Salamis,** 204 Fulham Rd, SW10 9PJ, ☏ 352 9827 — BU **e**
closed Sunday – **M** a la carte 4.25/7.55 🍷 1.25.

X Lebanese Food Centre-Beirut Restaurant, 11 Sloane St., SW1X 9LE, ☏ 235 1896, Lebanese rest. — FR **r**

X Como Lario, 22 Holbein Pl., Pimlico Rd, SW1N 8NL, ☏ 730 2954, Italian rest. — FT **r**

X **La Brasserie,** 272 Brompton Rd, SW3 2AW, ☏ 584 1668, French rest. — DS **s**
closed 25 and 26 December – **M** a la carte 4.25/5.30 **t.** 🍷 1.10.

X **Hungry Horse,** 196 Fulham Rd, SW10 9PN, ☏ 352 7757, English rest. — BU **i**
closed 2 weeks August/September, Good Friday and Christmas Day – **M** a la carte 3.60/5.35 🍷 1.25.

X **Busby's,** 79 Royal Hospital Rd, SW3 4HN, ☏ 352 7179, English rest. — EU **c**
closed Sunday and Bank Holidays – **M** (dinner only) 2.95 🍷 0.85.

X San Quintino, 45-47 Radnor Walk, SW3 4BP, ☏ 352 2698, Italian rest. — EU **e**

X Leonardo Ristorante, 397 Kings Rd, SW10, ☏ 352 4146, Italian rest. — pp. 17-20 JZ **v**

X **Le Bistingo,** 332-334 King's Rd, SW3 5UR, ☏ 352 4071, Bistro — CU **r**
closed Christmas Day – **M** a la carte 3.30/4.25 **t.** 🍷 1.25.

MICHELIN Branch, 81 Fulham Rd, SW3 6RD, ☏ 581 2381. — DST

Earl's Court – ✉ SW5/SW10 – Except where otherwise stated see pp. 24 and 25.

🏨 **Barkston** (T.H.F.), Barkston Gdns, SW5 0EN, ☏ 373 7851 – |‡| TV. 🅰 — AT **c**
M a la carte approx. 3.65 **st.** 🍷 1.30 – ☕ 1.60 – **69 rm** 16.50/20.50 **st.**

🏨 Hogarth, 27-35 Hogarth Rd, SW5 0QQ, ☏ 370 6831 – |‡| TV 🛁wc ☎ Ⓟ. 🅰 — AS **a**
M (coffee shop only) a la carte 3.25 **st.** 🍷 0.95 – ☕ 1.50 – **66 rm.**

🏨 **Kensington Court,** 33-35 Nevern Pl., SW5 9NP, ☏ 370 5151 – |‡| TV 🛁wc ☎ — pp. 17-20 HY **n**
M (dinner only) 3.45/4.00 **st.** – ☕ 1.75 – **35 rm** 14.90/22.35 **st.**

🏨 Burns, 18-26 Barkston Gdns, SW5 0EN, ☏ 373 3151 – |‡| TV 🛁wc ☎ — AT **e**
M (grill rest.) (dinner only and Sunday lunch) – **100 rm.**

🏨 **George,** 5-11 Templeton Pl., SW5 9NB, ☏ 370 1092, Telex 916122, 🛎 – |‡| TV 🛁wc 🚿wc ☎ Ⓟ — pp. 17-20 HY **r**
M 3.50/5.50 **t.** 🍷 1.50 – ☕ 1.30 – **130 rm** 14.05/23.80 **t.** – P 19.00/24.00 **t.**

🏨 Manor Court, without rest., 33-35 Courtfield Gdns, SW5, ☏ 373 8585, Telex 885230 – |‡| 🛁wc ☎ – **78 rm.** — AS **e**

🏨 Oliver, 198 Cromwell Rd, SW5 0SN, ☏ 370 6881 – |‡| TV 🛁wc 🚿wc ☎ — pp. 17-20 HY **a**
48 rm.

🏨 **Terstan** without rest., 29-31 Nevern Sq., SW5 9PE, ☏ 373 5368 – |‡| 🛁wc — pp. 17-20 HY **v**
57 rm ☕ 7.50/13.50 **st.**

⌂ **Mowbray Court,** 28-32 Penywern Rd, SW5 5UQ, ☏ 370 2316 – 🛁wc — pp. 17-20 HZ **c**
25 rm ☕ 7.00/13.00 **st.**

⌂ **Beaver,** 57-59 Philbeach Gdns, SW5 9ED, ☏ 373 4553 – ☎ — pp. 17-20 HZ **a**
closed 24 to 31 December – ☕ 0.90 – **50 rm** 7.00/13.00 **st.**

⌂ **Andora,** 44-48 West Cromwell Rd, SW5 9QL, ☏ 373 4546 – 🚿wc ☎ — CS **a**
☕ 1.00 – **47 rm** 11.00/16.00 **s.**

⌂ Henly House, 30 Barkston Gdns, SW5 0EN, ☏ 373 3770 – 🚿 – **21 rm.** — AT **r**

XX **La Croisette,** 168 Ifield Rd, SW10 9AF, ☎ 373 3694, Seafood AU **a**
closed Monday, August and Bank Holidays – **M** 8.50 **t.**

XX **Pontevecchio,** 256 Old Brompton Rd, SW5 9HR, ☎ 373 9082, Italian rest. AU **i**
closed Bank Holidays – **M** a la carte 4.05/5.30 🍾 1.40.

XX **Naraine,** 10 Kenway Rd, SW5 0RR, ☎ 370 3853, Indian rest. pp. 17-20 HY **i**
closed Monday and Bank Holidays – **M** a la carte 3.35/3.95 🍾 1.30.

X La Scala, 12 Kenway Rd, SW5, ☎ 370 3898, Italian rest. pp. 17-20 HY **z**

X **Il Palio di Siena,** 133 Earl's Court Rd, SW5 9HR, ☎ 373 8060, Italian rest.
M a la carte 4.60/5.65 **t.** pp. 17-20 HY **c**

X **Golden Duck,** 6 Hollywood Rd, SW10 9HY, ☎ 352 3500, Chinese rest. BU **a**
closed Bank Holidays – **M** (dinner only, Saturday lunch and Sunday lunch) 3.50/4.50 🍾 1.25.

Kensington – ✉ SW7/W8/W11/W14 – **Except where otherwise stated see pp. 17-20.**
i Town Hall, Kensington High St., W8, ☎ 937 5464.

Royal Garden (Rank), Kensington High St., W8 4PT, ☎ 937 8000, Telex 263151, ≤ – ⧉ 📺 ♿ 🅟. 🚗 pp. 24 and 25 AQ **c**
M a la carte 3.80/7.05 **s.** 🍾 1.70 – ☕ 2.60 – **433 rm** 28.00/34.00 **s.**

Kensington Close (T.H.F.), Wrights Lane, W8 5SP, ☎ 937 8170, Telex 23914, 🏊 – ⧉ 📺 🅟. 🚗 HY **c**
M (Carvery Rest.) a la carte 3.60/4.60 **st.** 🍾 1.65 – ☕ 2.00 – **528 rm** 18.00/24.00 **st.**

Kensington Palace (Thistle), De Vere Gdns, W8 5AF, ☎ 937 8121, Telex 262422 – ⧉ 📺. 🚗 pp. 24 and 25 BQ **a**
M approx. 4.50 **s.** 🍾 1.50 – ☕ 2.00 – **312 rm** 18.00/28.00 **st.**

Kensington Hilton, 179-199 Holland Park Av., W11 4UL, ☎ 603 3355, Telex 919763 – ⧉ 📺 ♿ 🅟. 🚗 GV **s**
M a la carte 3.70/8.80 **st.** 🍾 1.30 – ☕ 2.95 – **611 rm** 23.00/28.00 **st.**

De Vere (De Vere), 60 Hyde Park Gate, W8 5AS, ☎ 584 0051, Group Telex 22121 – ⧉ 📺 ♿. 🚗 pp. 24 and 25 BQ **s**
M a la carte 2.50/5.00 **st.** 🍾 1.45 – ☕ 1.50 – **81 rm** 15.00/32.00 **st.**

Tara, Wrights Lane, W8 5SR, ☎ 937 7211, Telex 918835 – ⧉ 📺 ♿ 🅟. 🚗 HX **u**
M 3.70/6.50 **s.** 🍾 1.95 – ☕ 1.70 – **840 rm** 17.00/21.00.

Royal Kensington, 380 Kensington High St., W14 8NL, ☎ 603 3333, Telex 22229 – ⧉ 📺. 🚗 GX **o**
M (grill rest.) a la carte 6.05/7.70 🍾 1.60 – ☕ 3.00 – **409 rm** 21.00/24.00 **s.**

Prince of Wales, 16-26 De Vere Gdns, W8 5AG, ☎ 937 8080 – ⧉ 📺 🛁wc ☎. 🚗 pp. 24 and 25 BQ **u**
M a la carte 3.50/6.25 **s.** 🍾 1.75 – ☕ 2.00 – **315 rm** 13.00/23.00 **s.** – P 16.50/18.50 **s.**

XXX **Belvedere,** Holland House off Abbotsbury Rd, Holland Park, W8 6LU, ☎ 602 1865, ≤, 🪑 GX **a**
M a la carte 5.20/12.10 **t.**

XXX ✿ **Le Bressan,** 14 Wrights Lane, W8 6TF, ☎ 937 8525, French rest. HX **a**
closed Saturday lunch, Sunday, August and Bank Holidays – **M** a la carte 7.30/11.30 🍾 2.60
Spec. Quenelles de saumon ou de brochet sauce Nantua, Steak au poivre en chemise, Soufflé glacé au Grand Marnier.

XX Wheeler's Alcove, 17 Kensington High St., W8 5NP, ☎ 937 1443, Seafood. pp. 24 and 25 AQ **n**

XX **La Toque Blanche,** 21 Abingdon Rd, W8 6AH, ☎ 937 5832, French rest. HX **n**
closed Saturday lunch, Sunday, Easter, August, Christmas and Bank Holidays – **M** a la carte 5.50/7.00 **t.** 🍾 1.40.

XX **Trattoo,** 2 Abingdon Rd, W8 6AF, ☎ 937 4448, Italian rest. HX **e**
M a la carte 4.35/8.50.

XX **La Pomme d'Amour,** 128 Holland Park Av., W11 4UE, ☎ 229 8532, French rest. GV **e**
closed Saturday lunch, Sunday and Bank Holidays – **M** a la carte 4.60/5.95 🍾 1.15.

XX **Gondoliere,** 3 Gloucester Rd, SW7 4PP, ☎ 584 8062, Italian rest. pp. 24 and 25 BR **e**
closed Saturday lunch, Sunday and Bank Holidays – **M** a la carte 4.15/6.05 **t.** 🍾 1.45.

XX **Gatamelata,** 343 Kensington High St., W8 6NW, ☎ 603 3613, Italian rest. GHX **s**
closed Sunday and Bank Holidays – **M** a la carte 4.65/6.05 🍾 1.45.

XX **Franco Ovest,** 3 Russell Gardens, W14 8EZ, ☎ 602 1242, Italian rest. GX **u**
closed Sunday and Bank Holidays – **M** a la carte 3.95/5.40 🍾 1.35.

XX **Sailing Junk,** 59 Marloes Rd, W8 6LE, ☎ 937 9691, Chinese rest. HX **x**
M (dinner only) 5.55 **st.** 🍾 1.60.

X **Lee Yuan,** 40 Earl's Court Rd, W8 6EJ, ☎ 937 7047, Chinese rest. HX **r**
closed 25 and 26 December – **M** a la carte 4.00/5.25 🍾 1.00.

X **Armenian,** 20 Kensington Church St., W8 4EP, ☎ 937 5828, Armenian rest. pp. 24 and 25 AQ **a**
closed Sunday lunch, Good Friday and Christmas Day – **M** a la carte 3.30/4.35 🍾 1.25.

P.T.O. ⟶

✕ **The Ark,** 35 Kensington High St., W8 5BA, ☎ 937 4294, French rest.
closed Sunday lunch, 4 days at Easter and 4 days at Christmas – **M** a la carte 3.95/4.8 🍾 1.35. pp. 24 and 25 AQ

✕ **La Paesana,** 30 Uxbridge St., W8 7TA, ☎ 229 4332, Italian rest. pp. 26 and 27 AZ
closed Sunday and Bank Holidays – **M** a la carte 3.05/5.80 **t.** 🍾 1.05.

✕ Le Bistingo, 7 Kensington High St., W8 5NP, ☎ 937 0932, Bistro. pp. 24 and 25 AQ

North Kensington – ✉ W2/W10/W11 – **Except where otherwise stated see pp. 13-16**

Hyde Park West, 25 Pembridge Sq., W2 4DR, ☎ 229 3400, Telex 27380 – 🛗 ⛀wc ⛆wc ☎ pp. 26 and 27 AZ
M (snack rest. only) 2.10/3.45 – ☕ 1.00 – **76 rm** 15.00/20.40 **st.**

Portobello, 22 Stanley Gdns, W11 2NG, ☎ 727 2777, Group Telex 21879 – 🛗 📺 ⛆wc ☎ GU
closed 5 days at Christmas – **M** (residents only) a la carte 3.60/5.80 **s.** 🍾 1.60 ☕ 2.50 – **26 rm** 14.30/40.00.

Pembridge Court, 34 Pembridge Gdns, W2 4DX, ☎ 229 9977, Telex 298 363 ⛀wc ⛆wc ☎ pp. 26 and 27 AZ
M *(closed Sunday)* (dinner only and Saturday lunch) a la carte 3.40/5.35 **t.** – **37 rm** ☕ 12.50/16.50 **s.**

✕✕✕ **Leith's,** 92 Kensington Park Rd, W11 2PN, ☎ 229 4481 GU
closed 4 days at Christmas and Bank Holidays – **M** (dinner only) approx. 9.00.

✕✕ **Chez Moi,** 3 Addison Av., Holland Park, W11 4QS, ☎ 603 8267, French rest.
closed Sunday, last 3 weeks August and Bank Holidays – **M** (dinner only) a la carte 5.25/6.75 🍾 1.75. pp. 17 - 20 GV

✕✕ **Julie's,** 135 Portland Rd, W11 4LW, ☎ 229 8331 pp. 17 - 20 GV
closed Bank Holidays – **M** (dinner only and Sunday lunch) a la carte 5.00/6.55 **t.** 🍾 1.50

South Kensington – ✉ SW5/SW7/W8 – **pp. 24 and 25.**

Gloucester (Rank), 4-18 Harrington Gdns, SW7 4LH, ☎ 373 6030, Telex 917505 🛗 📺 ♿ Ⓟ. 🏋 BS
M a la carte 4.20/8.40 **st.** 🍾 1.65 – ☕ 2.60 – **559 rm** 31.05/36.80 **s.**

Elizabetta (Gd. Met.), 162 Cromwell Rd, SW5 0TT, ☎ 370 4282, Telex 918978 – 🛗 AS
M a la carte 3.20/4.50 **st.** 🍾 1.60 – ☕ 1.25 – **84 rm** 17.50/24.00 **s.**

Penta (Gd. Met.), 97 Cromwell Rd, SW7 4ON, ☎ 370 5757, Telex 919663 – 🛗 📺 ♿ Ⓟ 🏋 BS
M 4.00/5.00 **st.** 🍾 1.75 – ☕ 1.15 – **914 rm** 19.00/27.00 **s.**

Rembrandt (Gd. Met.), Thurloe Pl., SW7 2RS, ☎ 589 8100, Telex 917575 – 🛗 ⛀wc ⛆wc ☎. 🏋 DS
M approx. 4.25 **st.** 🍾 1.35 – ☕ 1.15 – **173 rm** 8.50/22.00 **s.**

Eden Plaza, 68-69 Queen's Gate, SW7 5JT, ☎ 370 6111, Telex 916228 – 🛗 📺 ⛀wc ⛆wc ☎ CS
M 3.00/6.00 **st.** 🍾 1.25 – **61 rm** ☕ 18.95/26.95 **st.**

Blakes, 33-35 Roland Gdns, SW7 3PF, ☎ 370 6701 – 🛗 📺 ⛀wc ☎ BU
33 rm.

Bailey's, Gloucester Rd, SW7, ☎ 373 8131 – ⛀wc ☎ BS
150 rm.

Adelphi without rest., 127-129 Cromwell Rd, SW7 4DT, ☎ 373 7177 – 🛗 ⛀wc ☎ AS
59 rm ☕ 16.90/24.90 **st.**

Norfolk (Norfolk Cap.), 2-10 Harrington Rd, SW7 3ER, ☎ 589 8191, Group Tele 23241 – 🛗 ⛀wc ☎. 🏋 CS
M (Angus Steak House) a la carte 3.00/7.80 – **70 rm** 12.30/23.95.

Regency, 100-105 Queen's Gate, SW7 5AG, ☎ 370 4595, Telex 267594 – 🛗 📺 ⛀wc ⛆wc ☎. 🏋 CT
M 4.00/6.00 **st.** 🍾 1.00 – ☕ 0.75 – **192 rm** 19.90/25.90 **st.**

Cranley Gardens, 6-12 Cranley Gdns, SW7, ☎ 373 3232, Telex 24159 – 🛗 📺 ⛀wc ⛆wc ☎ BT
84 rm.

Vanderbilt, 76 Cromwell Rd, SW7 5BT, ☎ 584 0491, Telex 919867 – 🛗 ⛀wc ☎ BS
M a la carte 3.00/4.35 **s.** 🍾 1.50 – **88 rm** ☕ 10.00/20.00 **s.**

Embassy House, 31 Queen's Gate, SW7 5JA, ☎ 584 7222, Telex 27727 – 🛗 📺 ⛀wc ⛆wc ☎ BR
M approx. 3.25 **st.** 🍾 1.40 – **86 rm** ☕ 9.00/20.00 **st.**

Richwood, 25 Cranley Gdns, SW7, ☎ 589 5281, Telex 24159, 🌳 – 🛗 📺 ⛀wc ⛆wc ☎ CU
58 rm.

Edwardian. 40-44 Harrington Gdns, SW7 4LT, ☎ 370 4444 – 🛗 📺 ⛀wc ⛆wc ☎ AT
M (grill rest.) (dinner only) 3.50/5.00 **st.** 🍾 2.00 – ☕ 1.20 – **83 rm** 15.00/21.00 **st.**

Alexander without rest., 9 Sumner Pl., SW7 3EE, ☎ 581 1591 – ⛀wc ☎ CT
☕ 1.50 – **39 rm** 11.00/22.00 **st.**

Apollo, 18-22 Lexham Gdns, W8 5JE, ☎ 373 3236, Telex 264189 – 🛗 ⛀wc ☎ AS
M (dinner only) approx. 2.50 – ☕ 2.00 – **57 rm** 6.00/11.00 **st.**

Queensberry Court without rest., 7-11 Queensberry Pl., SW7 2EA, ☎ 589 3693 – wc wc ☎ CS **v**
42 rm 7.70/14.50 **s.**

Buckingham, 94-102 Cromwell Rd, SW7 4ER, ☎ 373 7131, Telex 8951330 – wc ☎ BS **u**
M approx. 3.00 **s.** 1.00 – **98 rm** 10.00/17.00 **s.**

Atlas without rest., 24-30 Lexham Gdns, W8 5JE, ☎ 373 7873, Telex 264189 – wc ☎ AS **s**
1.00 – **69 rm** 6.00/11.00 **st.**

Montana, 67-69 Gloucester Rd, SW7 4PG, ☎ 584 7654, Telex 24159 – TV wc wc ☎ BS **s**
58 rm.

Concord, 155 Cromwell Rd, SW5 0TQ, ☎ 370 4151 AS **c**
18 rm 7.50/12.50 **s.**

Il Giorno e la Notte, 60 Old Brompton Rd, SW7 3DY, ☎ 584 4028, Italian rest. CT **r**
closed Sunday and Bank Holidays – **M** a la carte 4.35/6.30 1.35.

Stable, 123 Cromwell Rd, SW7 4ET, ☎ 370 1203, Dancing AS **v**
closed Sunday and Bank Holidays – **M** (dinner only) a la carte 6.25/7.65 **t.** 1.50.

Pulcinella, 30 Old Brompton Rd, SW7 3DL, ☎ 589 0529, Italian rest. CS **i**
closed Sunday and Bank Holidays – **M** a la carte 3.95/4.65 1.15.

Chanterelle, 119 Old Brompton Rd, SW7 3RN, ☎ 373 7390 BT **i**
closed Sunday lunch and 25 to 27 December – **M** a la carte 3.85/5.40 **t.** 1.25.

Jamshid's, 6 Glendower Pl., SW7 3DP, ☎ 584 2309, Indian and Pakistani rest.
closed Sunday and 25-26 December – **M** a la carte 2.30/4.30 1.20. CS **s**

Star of India, 154 Old Brompton Rd, SW5 0BE, ☎ 373 2901, Indian rest. BT **s**

Le Bistingo, 56 Old Brompton Rd, SW7, ☎ 589 1929, Bistro CT **r**
closed Christmas Day.

Alpino, 154 Gloucester Rd, SW7 4TD, ☎ 370 5625, Italian rest. BST **z**
M a la carte 2.40/3.45 **t.** 1.35.

KINGSTON-UPON-THAMES – Surrey – pp. 8 and 9.

18 Hampton Wick ☎ **977 6645, W: 2 ½ m.** – 18 **Traps Lane, New Malden,** ☎ **942 0654.**

Kingston – Surrey.

London Steak House, 17 High St., KT1 1LA, ☎ 546 3788 BZ **a**
closed Christmas Day – **M** a la carte 2.55/5.65 **t.** 1.30.

Cloud's, 14 Kingston Hill, KT2 5HR, ☎ 549 5984, Bistro BZ **c**
closed Saturday lunch, Sunday dinner and Bank Holidays – **M** a la carte 3.10/4.65 **t.** 1.20.

LAMBETH pp. 17-20.

Waterloo – SE1.

National Theatre Rest., National Theatre, South Bank, SE1 9PX, ☎ 928 2033 – Ⓟ NV **c**
M (dinner only) a la carte 5.90/6.90 **st.** 1.40.

LEWISHAM pp. 8 and 9.

Blackheath – SE3.

La Goulue, 17 Montpelier Vale, SE3 0TJ, ☎ 852 9226, Bistro. EFY **i**

Bromley – SE3.

Bromley Court , Bromley Hill, BR1 4JD, ☎ 464 5011, Telex 896310, ←, – TV Ⓟ. EZ **u**
M 4.25/5.45 1.55 – 2.00 – **130 rm** 13.25/17.85.

Catford – SE6.

Casa Cominetti, 129 Rushey Green, SE6 4AA, ☎ 697 2314 EY **o**
closed Sunday dinner and 25-26 December – **M** a la carte 3.75/6.60 **t.** 1.30.

MICHELIN Branch, Thomas Lane, SE6 4RZ, ☎ 690 0064/3511.

Ne confondez pas :

Confort des hôtels : ... , ,
Confort des restaurants : XXXXX X
Qualité de la table : ✿✿, ✿, M

MERTON pp. 8 and 9.

Wimbledon – ✉ SW19.
i Town Hall, Broadway, SW 19, ☎ 946 8070.

- **Wimbledon,** 78 Worple Rd, SW19 4HZ, ☎ 946 9265 – Ⓟ — CZ a
  9 rm 6.75/10.25 **st.**
- **Dog and Fox,** 24 High St., SW19 5EA, ☎ 946 6565 — CZ i
  closed Sunday and Bank Holidays – **M** a la carte 4.20/7.25.
- San Lorenzo Fuoriporta, Worple Rd Mews, SW19, ☎ 946 8463, Italian rest. — CZ e
- **Le Café Royal,** 72 High St., SW19 5DX, ☎ 946 0238 — CZ u
  closed Sunday, Good Friday, 25-26 December and Bank Holidays – **M** a la carte 4.20/7.40 **t.** 🍾 1.50.
- Rawalpindi, 26 High St., SW19, ☎ 946 2798, Indian rest. — CZ

REDBRIDGE pp. 8 and 9.

Ilford – ✉ Essex.
⛳18 Wanstead Park Rd ☎ **554 5174.**
i Town Hall, High Rd, IG1 1DD, ☎ 478 3020.

- Mario's, 251 Cranbrook Rd, IG1 4TG, ☎ 554 2921, Dancing (Friday and Saturday only) — FV

South Woodford – Essex.

- **Meghna Grill,** 219 High Rd, E18 2PB, ☎ 504 0923, Indian rest. — EFV
  M approx. 4.00.

☞ *Michelin hängt keine Schilder an die empfohlenen Hotels und Restaurants.*

RICHMOND-UPON-THAMES pp. 8 and 9.

Barnes – ✉ SW13.

- **Le Petit Bedon,** 8-9 Rocks Lane, SW13 0DB, ☎ 876 2554, French rest. — CY
  closed Sunday and Bank Holidays – **M** (dinner only) a la carte approx. 5.75 🍾 2.40.
- River Bistro, 15 Barnes High St., SW13, ☎ 876 1471, French Bistro. — CY

Hampton Court – ✉ Middx.

- **Greyhound** (T.H.F.), Hampton Court Rd, East Molesey, KT8 9BZ, ☎ 977 8121 – wc Ⓟ. — BZ
  M (grill rest. only) 1.75/2.95 **st.** 🍾 1.50 – **29 rm** 10.00/18.00 **st.**
- **Bastians,** Hampton Court Rd, East Molesey, KT8 9BY, ☎ 977 6074, French rest. — BZ
  closed Saturday lunch, Sunday and Bank Holidays – **M** a la carte 4.90/6.25 🍾 2.30.

Kew – ✉ Surrey.

- **Jasper's Bun in the Oven,** 9-11 Kew Green ☎ 940 3987, French rest. — BY
  closed Sunday and Bank Holidays – **M** a la carte 4.30/5.85 **t.** 🍾 1.20.

Richmond – ✉ Surrey.
⛳18, ⛳18 Richmond Park ☎ **876 3205.**
i Old Richmond Town Hall, Hill St., TW1 3LT, ☎ 892 0032.

- **Richmond Gate,** Richmond Hill, TW10 6RP, ☎ 940 0061, Telex 928556, – wc Ⓟ. — BY
  M 4.00/5.00 – **50 rm** 15.00/21.50 **s.**
- **Valchera's,** 30 The Quadrant, TW9 1DN, ☎ 940 0648 — BY
  closed Sunday, last week July, first 2 weeks August and Bank Holidays – **M** a la cart 3.10/6.30 🍾 1.45.
- **Kew Rendezvous,** 110 Kew Rd, TW9 1ND, ☎ 948 4343, Chinese rest. — BY
  closed 25 and 26 December – **M** a la carte 4.00/5.50 🍾 1.50.
- **Franco's,** 5 Petersham Rd, TW9 1EN, ☎ 940 9051, Italian rest. — BY
  M a la carte 4.25/5.70 **t.** 🍾 1.10.
- **La Veranda,** 102 Kew Rd, TW9 1RZ, ☎ 940 8938, Italian rest. — BY
  closed Sunday and Bank Holidays – **M** a la carte 4.60/6.50 **t.** 🍾 1.25.
- **Richmond Rendezvous** (Annexe), 1 Wakefield Rd, TW9 1RX, ☎ 940 6869, Chinese res — BY
  closed 25 and 26 December – **M** a la carte 3.70/5.10 🍾 2.20.
- **Richmond Rendezvous,** 1 Paradise Rd, TW9 1RX, ☎ 940 5114, Chinese rest. — BY
  closed 25 and 26 December – **M** a la carte 3.70/5.10 🍾 2.20.
- **Bistro Village,** 27f The Quadrant, TW9 1DG, ☎ 948 2786, Bistro — BY
  closed 25 and 26 December – **M** a la carte 2.75/4.05 **t.** 🍾 1.15.

SOUTHWARK pp. 8 and 9.

Dulwich Village – ✉ SE21.

XX **Gemma-San Martino,** 129 Gipsy Hill, SE19 1QS, ☎ 670 1396, Italian rest. — EZ **c**
closed Sunday, Easter Day and Christmas Day – **M** a la carte 3.15/5.15 🍾 1.35.

X **London Steak House,** 96-98 Dulwich Village, SE21 7AQ, ☎ 693 6880 — EY **v**
M a la carte 4.55/5.35 **t.** 🍾 1.30.

SUTTON pp. 8 and 9.

Sutton – ✉ Surrey.

🏠 **The Dene,** 39 Cheam Rd, SM1 2AT, ☎ 642 3170, 🌳 – TV 🛁wc — CZ **n**
17 rm ☕ 6.00/13.00 **s.**

🏠 **Thatched House,** 135 Cheam Rd, SM1 2BN, 🌳 – 🚿wc Ⓟ — CZ **c**
18 rm ☕ 6.50/13.00 **st.**

XX **Trattoria Toscana,** 6-7 Station Par., Brighton Rd ☎ 642 3341, Italian rest. — DZ **e**
closed Sunday and Bank Holidays – **M** a la carte 3.20/4.15 **t.** 🍾 1.25.

TOWER HAMLETS Except where otherwise stated see pp. 8 and 9.

Tower Hamlets – ✉ E1.

i Information Centre, 88 Roman Rd, E2 0PG, ☎ 980 3749.

🏨 **Tower** (Royal London), St. Katharine's Way, E1 9LD, ☎ 481 2575, Telex 885934, ≤ Tower Bridge and river Thames – 🛗 TV Ⓟ. 🛎 — pp. 17-20 QV **r**
M a la carte 8.50/12.00 **st.** 🍾 2.20 – ☕ 1.50 – **826 rm** 29.25/40.00 **st.**

WALTHAM FOREST pp. 8 and 9.

Leytonstone – ✉ E11.

XX Tandoori Golden Curry, 734 High Rd, E11, ☎ 539 5429, Indian rest. — EFV **n**

X **Trattoria Parmigiana,** 715 High Rd, E11 4RD, ☎ 539 1700, Italian rest. — EV **z**
closed Sunday – **M** a la carte approx. 5.50 **t.** 🍾 0.90.

Woodford Green – ✉ Essex.

🏨 **Waltham Forest,** 30 Oak Hill, IG8 9NY, ☎ 505 4511 – 🛗 TV 🛁wc 🚿wc ☎ Ⓟ. 🛎 — EV **x**
M 4.00/5.75 **t.** 🍾 1.75 – ☕ 2.00 – **50 rm** 14.50/16.00 **st.**

WANDSWORTH pp. 8 and 9.

i Municipal Buildings, SW18, ☎ 874 6464.

Battersea – ✉ SW8/SW11.

XX **Alonso's,** 32 Queenstown Rd, SW8 3RX, ☎ 720 5986 — DY **e**
closed Saturday lunch, Sunday and Bank Holidays – **M** 5.85/6.10.

X **Lavender Hill,** 245 Lavender Hill, SW11 1JW, ☎ 223 4129, French rest. — DY **u**
closed Sunday, Monday, Tuesday and 2 weeks January – **M** (dinner only) 5.80/6.40 **t.** 🍾 1.20.

X **Jacks Place,** 12 York Rd, SW11 3PX, ☎ 228 8519, Bistro — DY **v**
closed Sunday, Monday and Bank Holidays – **M** (dinner only) a la carte 3.80/6.10 🍾 1.20.

Clapham – ✉ SW11.

XX **Hathaways,** 13 Battersea Rise, SW11 1HG, ☎ 228 3384 — DY **i**
closed Sunday, 2 weeks July and Bank Holidays – **M** (dinner only) a la carte 4.50/5.60 **t.** 🍾 1.25.

X **Wine and Dine,** 50 Battersea Rise, SW11 1EG, ☎ 228 1206, French Bistro — DY **n**
closed Saturday lunch, Sunday and Bank Holidays – **M** a la carte 3.45/4.35 🍾 1.15.

Putney – ✉ SW15.

XX **La Forchetta,** 3 Putney Hill, SW15 6BA, ☎ 785 6749, Italian rest. — CY **o**
closed Sunday and Bank Holidays – **M** a la carte 3.00/3.85 🍾 1.05.

X **Cassis,** 30 Putney High St., SW15 1SQ, ☎ 788 8668, French Bistro — CY **c**
closed Saturday lunch, Sunday and Bank Holidays – **M** a la carte 3.65/5.85 **t.** 🍾 1.30.

En dehors des établissements désignés par XXXXX... X,
il existe dans de nombreux hôtels,
un restaurant de bonne classe.

WESTMINSTER (City of)

i Westminster City Hall, Victoria St., SW1E 6QW, ☎ 828 8070.

Bayswater and Maida Vale – ✉ W2/W9 – Except where otherwise stated see pp. 26 and 27.

Royal Lancaster (Rank), Lancaster Ter., W2 2TY, ☎ 262 6737, Telex 24822, ≤ – 🛗 📺 ♿ Ⓟ. 🏠 DZ e
M a la carte 8.25/11.60 **s.** 🌢 1.85 – ☕ 2.70 – **433 rm** 27.00/45.00 **s.**

Great Western Royal (B.T.H.), Praed St., W2 1HE, ☎ 723 8064, Telex 263972 – 🛗 📺 ♿. 🏠 DY c
M 4.55/6.90 **st.** 🌢 1.40 – **170 rm** ☕ 20.50/28.50 **st.**

Metropole, Edgware Rd, W2 2XH, ☎ 402 4141, Telex 23711, ≤ – 🛗 📺. 🏠 pp. 13-16 JT c
M a la carte 6.90/10.60 **s.** 🌢 1.20 – ☕ 2.55 – **555 rm** 20.00/25.00.

Post House (T.H.F.), 104 Bayswater Rd, W2 3HL, ☎ 262 4461, Telex 22667, ≤ – 🛗 📺 🛁wc ☎ Ⓟ. 🏠 CZ o
M a la carte 3.25/4.80 **st.** 🌢 1.50 – ☕ 2.00 – **175 rm** 16.00/22.50 **st.**

London Embassy, 150 Bayswater Rd, W2 4RT, ☎ 229 1212, Telex 27727 – 🛗 📺 🛁wc ☎ Ⓟ. 🏠 PZ o
M a la carte 4.55/6.50 **st.** 🌢 1.40 – ☕ 1.25 – **193 rm** 23.50/33.00 **st.**

Leinster Towers (Anchor), 25-31 Leinster Gdns, W2 3AU, ☎ 262 4591, Group Telex 27120 – 🛗 📺 🛁wc 🚿wc CZ x
M a la carte 4.35/6.70 **t.** 🌢 1.00 – **166 rm** ☕ 14.85/23.10 **st.**

White's (T.H.F.), Bayswater Rd, 90-92 Lancaster Gate, W2 3NR, ☎ 262 2711, Group Telex 23922 – 🛗 📺 🛁wc ☎ Ⓟ CZ v
M a la carte 5.00/6.65 **t.** 🌢 1.80 – ☕ 1.50 – **59 rm** 19.00/28.00 **t.**

Park Court (T.H.F.), 75 Lancaster Gate, W2 3NN, ☎ 402 4272, Group Telex 23922, 🌳 – 🛗 📺 🛁wc ☎. 🏠 CZ z
M (coffee shop only) a la carte 3.45/6.65 **t.** 🌢 1.45 – ☕ 1.00 – **442 rm** 15.50/23.00 **st.**

Clarendon Court (Interchange), Edgware Rd, W9 1AG, ☎ 286 8080, Telex 27374 – 🛗 📺 🛁wc 🚿wc ☎. 🏠 pp. 13-16 JS a
M *(closed Saturday lunch and Sunday)* 5.50/6.00 **st.** 🌢 1.50 – ☕ 1.50 – **155 rm** 11.00/ 27.00 **s.** – P 22.50/25.00 **s.**

Coburg (Myddleton), 129 Bayswater Rd, W2 4RJ, ☎ 229 3654, Telex 268235 – 🛗 📺 🛁wc ☎. 🏠 BZ a
M a la carte 3.60/5.00 **st.** 🌢 1.75 – **120 rm** ☕ 12.50/26.00 **st.** – P 20.00 **st.**

Grosvenor Court (Gd. Met.), 144 Praed St., W2 1HU, ☎ 262 3464, Group Telex 25971 – 🛗 📺 🛁wc ☎ DY a
M (coffee shop only) approx. 2.25 **st.** 🌢 1.40 – ☕ 1.00 – **93 rm** 11.00/17.00 **s.**

Inverness Court, 1-9 Inverness Ter., W2 3JL, ☎ 229 1444 – 🛗 📺 🛁wc 🚿wc ☎ BZ i
M 3.25/6.00 **s.** 🌢 1.70 – ☕ 1.50 – **184 rm** 12.00/18.00 **s.** – P 15.50/22.00 **s.**

Carlyle, 27 Devonshire Ter., W2 3DP, ☎ 262 2204, Telex 22487 – 🛗 📺 🛁wc ☎ CY e
156 rm.

Westland, 154 Bayswater Rd, W2 4HP, ☎ 229 9191 – 🛗 📺 🛁wc ☎ BZ z
M a la carte 3.85/6.15 🌢 2.00 – **30 rm** ☕ 13.95/18.90.

Averard, without rest., 10-11 Lancaster Gate, W2 3EL, ☎ 723 8877, Telex 24939 – 🛗 🛁wc 🚿wc ☎ DZ c
62 rm.

Century, without rest., 18 Craven Hill Gns, W2, ☎ 262 6644, Telex 24939 – 🛗 📺 🛁wc ☎ CZ c
59 rm.

Allandale House, 3 Devonshire Ter., Lancaster Gate, W2 3DN, ☎ 723 8311 – 🛁wc CY a
17 rm ☕ 9.50/16.00.

Caring, 24 Craven Hill Gdns, Leinster Ter., W2 3EA, ☎ 262 8708 – 📺 🛁wc CZ e
24 rm ☕ 7.00/14.50 **st.**

Garden Court, 30-31 Kensington Gardens Sq., W2 4BG, ☎ 229 2553 – 🛁wc BY e
40 rm ☕ 7.50/12.00.

McCormacks, 2 Devonshire Ter., W2, ☎ 723 9433 – 🛁wc 🚿wc ☎ – **20 rm.** CY c

Trevose, 68-70 Queensborough Ter., W2 3SH, ☎ 229 5974 – 🛁 BZ u
32 rm ☕ 7.50/14.00 **st.**

Berkeley Court, 94 Sussex Gdns, W2 1UH, ☎ 723 4801 – 🚿 EY c
16 rm ☕ 6.00/10.00 **st.**

Park Lodge, 73 Queensborough Ter., W2 3SU, ☎ 229 6424 – 🛁wc – **26 rm.** BZ s

Trat-West, 143 Edgware Rd, W2 2HR, ☎ 723 8203, Italian rest. pp. 13-16 KT i
closed Sunday – **M** a la carte 4.60/7.50.

San Marino, 26 Sussex Pl., W2 2TH, ☎ 723 8395, Italian rest. EY u
closed Sunday and Bank Holidays – **M** a la carte 4.05/6.45 🌢 1.20.

Lotus House, 61-69 Edgware Rd, W2 2HZ, ☎ 262 4341, Chinese rest. FY o
closed 25 and 26 December – **M** a la carte 3.80/5.00 **t.**

XX **La Lupa,** 23 Connaught St., W2 2AY, ☎ 723 0540, Italian rest. EY v
closed Sunday and 25-26 December – **M** a la carte 3.40/6.50 **t.** 🍷 2.50.

XX **Canaletto,** 451 Edgware Rd, W2 1TH, ☎ 262 7027, Italian rest. pp. 13-16 JT v
closed Saturday lunch, Sunday and Bank Holidays – **M** a la carte 3.80/6.30 🍷 1.50.

X **Concordia Notte,** 29-31 Craven Rd, W2 3BX, ☎ 402 4985, Italian rest., Dancing DY r
closed Sunday – **M** (dinner only) a la carte 4.70/7.00 **t.** 🍷 0.90.

X **Concordia,** 29-31 Craven Rd, W2 3BX, ☎ 402 4985, Italian rest. DY r
closed Sunday – **M** a la carte 4.70/7.00 **st.** 🍷 0.90.

X **Le Chef,** 41 Connaught St., W2 2AY, ☎ 262 5945, French Bistro EY a
closed Saturday lunch, Sunday, Monday, August and Bank Holidays – **M** a la carte 3.85/5.35 🍷 0.90.

X Kam Tong, 59 Queensway, W2, ☎ 229 6065, Chinese rest. BZ e

X **Kalamaras Taverna,** 76-78 Inverness Mews, W2, ☎ 727 9122, Greek rest. BY a
closed Sunday and Bank Holidays – **M** (dinner only) a la carte 2.95/5.40 🍷 1.30.

X **Le Bistingo,** 117 Queensway, W2, ☎ 727 0743, French Bistro BYZ c
closed Christmas Day – **M** a la carte 2.85/4.30 **st.** 🍷 1.30.

X Ganges, 101 Praed St., W2, ☎ 723 4096, Indian and Pakistani rest. pp. 13-16 JT x

Belgravia – ✉ SW1 – **Except where otherwise stated see pp. 24 and 25.**

🏨 Berkeley, Wilton Pl., SW1X 7RL, ☎ 235 6000, Telex 919252, 🏊 – 🛗 📺 ♿ 🚗 . 🏋 FQ e
M Restaurant *(closed Saturday)* – **Le Perroquet** *(closed Sunday)* – **152 rm.**

🏨 Lowndes, 21 Lowndes St., SW1 9ES, ☎ 235 6020, Telex 919065 – 🛗 📺 – **80 rm.** FR i

🏨 Eaton Court, without rest., 85 Eaton Pl., SW1, ☎ 235 1152 – 📺 🛁wc – **17 rm.** FS e

🏠 **Headfort Place,** 17 Headfort Pl., SW1X 8BY, ☎ 235 2607 pp. 26 and 27 AV a
closed Christmas – **24 rm** ☕ 7.75/16.00 **t.**

XXX **Salloos,** 62-64 Kinnerton St., SW1, ☎ 235 4444, Pakistani rest. FQ a
closed Sunday and Bank Holidays – **M** a la carte 4.60/6.35.

XXX **Wheeler's Carafe,** 15-16 Lowndes St., SW1X 9EY, ☎ 235 2525, Seafood FR u
closed Monday, Easter, Christmas, 1 January and Bank Holidays – **M** a la carte approx. 8.50 **t.** 🍷 1.75.

X **Upper Crust in Belgravia,** 9 William St., SW1X 9HL, ☎ 235 8444, English rest. FQ c
closed 25 and 26 December – **M** a la carte 3.75/4.50 **t.** 🍷 1.30.

X **Motcombs,** 26 Motcomb St., SW1X 8JU, ☎ 235 6382 FR z
closed Sunday, Easter, Christmas and Bank Holidays – **M** a la carte 3.20/5.10 **t.** 🍷 1.70.

X **The Other Bistro,** 27 Motcomb St., SW1X 8JU, ☎ 235 1668, Bistro FR z
closed Bank Holidays – **M** a la carte 3.50/6.30 **t.** 🍷 1.30.

Hyde Park and Knightsbridge – ✉ SW1/SW7 – **pp. 24 and 25.**

🏨 **Hyde Park** (T.H.F.), 66 Knightsbridge, SW1 7LA, ☎ 235 2000, Telex 262057, ← – 🛗 📺. 🏋 EQ v
M a la carte 4.50/9.50 **st.** 🍷 2.00 – ☕ 3.50 – **182 rm** 35.00/50.00 **st.**

XX **Shezan,** 16-22 Cheval Pl., Montpelier St., SW7 1ES, ☎ 589 7918, Indian and Pakistani rest. ER c
closed Sunday and Bank Holidays – **M** a la carte 6.20/7.50.

XX **Mr Chow,** 151 Knightsbridge, SW1X 7PA, ☎ 589 7347, Chinese rest. EQ s
closed 25 and 26 December – **M** a la carte 4.30/6.20 🍷 1.60.

XX **Montpeliano,** 13 Montpelier St., SW7 1HQ, ☎ 589 0032, Italian rest. ER e
closed Sunday and Bank Holidays – **M** a la carte 3.50/5.40 🍷 1.15.

Mayfair – ✉ W1 – **pp. 22 and 23.**

🏨 **Dorchester,** Park Lane, W1A 2HJ, ☎ 629 8888, Telex 887704 – 🛗 📺 ♿ 🅿. 🏋 BN z
M The Terrace *(closed Sunday)* a la carte 7.15/11.10 **st.** 🍷 1.50 – **Grill** a la carte 6.55/11.65 **st.** 🍷 1.50 – ☕ a la carte only – **290 rm** 35.00/50.00 **st.**

🏨 Claridge's, Brook St., W1A 2JQ, ☎ 629 8860, Telex 21872 – 🛗 📺 ♿. 🏋 BL c
M Restaurant a la carte 6.60/10.35 **t.** 🍷 1.45 – **Causerie** a la carte 6.60/13.10 **t.** 🍷 1.45 – ☕ 1.90 – **205 rm.**

🏨 Inn on the Park, Hamilton Pl., Park Lane, W1A 1AZ, ☎ 499 0888, Telex 22771, ← – 🛗 📺 ♿ 🅿. 🏋 BP a
M Four Seasons a la carte 8.50/13.50 🍷 1.75 – **Vintage Room** approx. 13.50 **st.** – ☕ 3.50 – **228 rm.**

🏨 **Grosvenor House** (T.H.F.), Park Lane, W1A 3AA, ☎ 499 6363, Telex 24871, 🏊 – 🛗 📺 ♿ 🅿. 🏋 AM a
M a la carte 5.50/10.75 **st.** 🍷 2.25 – ☕ 3.00 – **478 rm** 32.00/44.00 **st.**

🏨 ✿✿ Connaught, 16 Carlos Pl., W1Y 6AL, ☎ 499 7070 – 🛗 📺 BM e
M a la carte 8.95/16.50 **t.** – **105 rm**
Spec. : Pâté de turbot, Filets de sole Princesse, Rosette de veau à l'orange riz Madras.

🏨 **Inter-Continental,** 1 Hamilton Pl., Hyde Park Corner, W1V 0QY, ☎ 409 3131, Telex 25853 – 🛗 📺 ♿ 🅿. 🏋 BP o
M a la carte 6.35/10.50 **st.** 🍷 2.00 – ☕ 4.00 – **497 rm** 48.00/55.00 **s.**

Hilton, 22 Park Lane, W1A 2HH, ☎ 493 8000, Telex 24873, < London – TV ♿. BP **e**
M a la carte 7.30/13.00 **t.** 2.50 – 4.00 – **509 rm** 38.90/47.55 **s.**

Athenaeum (Rank), 116 Piccadilly, W1V 0BJ, ☎ 499 3464, Telex 261589 – TV CP **s**
M a la carte 8.25/13.50 **t.** 2.40 – 3.35 – **111 rm** 34.50/45.50 **s.**

May Fair (Gd. Met.), Berkeley St., W1A 2AW, ☎ 629 7777, Telex 262526 – TV. DN **z**
3.00 – **390 rm** 25.00/38.00 **s.**

Brown's (T.H.F.), 21-24 Dover St., W1A 4SW, ☎ 493 6020, Telex 28686 – TV. DM **e**
M a la carte 7.70/14.25 **st.** 1.75 – 2.85 – **127 rm** 29.00/42.00 **st.**

Westbury (T.H.F.), New Bond St., W1Y 0PD, ☎ 629 7755, Telex 24378 – TV ♿ Ⓟ. DM **a**
279 rm.

Bristol, 1 Berkeley St., W1X 6NE, ☎ 493 8282, Telex 24561 – TV ♿ Ⓟ. DN **r**
M a la carte 7.50/10.30 **s.** 2.35 – 3.25 – **189 rm** 43.00/45.00 **s.**

Britannia (Gd. Met.), 42 Grosvenor Sq., W1X 0DX, ☎ 629 9400, Telex 23941 – TV ♿ Ⓟ. BM **i**
M a la carte 5.10/8.90 **st.** 1.70 – 3.00 – **434 rm** 32.00/42.00 **s.**

Londonderry, 19 Park Lane, W1Y 8AP, ☎ 493 7292, Telex 263292, < – TV Ⓟ BP **r**
143 rm.

Chesterfield (Gd. Met.), 34-36 Charles St., W1X 8LX, ☎ 491 2622, Telex 269394 – TV CN **c**
M a la carte 6.50/12.60 **st.** 1.80 – 2.95 – **87 rm** 24.00/34.00 **s.**

Europa (Gd. Met.), Grosvenor Sq., W1A 4AW, ☎ 493 1232, Telex 268101 – TV ♿ Ⓟ. BL **n**
M approx. 5.25 **st.** 2.50 – 2.25 – **275 rm** 28.00/39.00 **s.**

Washington (Gd. Met.), Curzon St., W1Y 8DT, ☎ 499 7030, Telex 24540 – TV wc ☎. CN **n**
M 3.50/4.50 **st.** 1.50 – 1.20 – **160 rm** 20.00/27.00 **s.**

XXXXX **Mirabelle** (De Vere), 56 Curzon St., W1Y 8DL, ☎ 499 4636, CN **a**
closed Sunday and Bank Holidays – **M** a la carte 12.00/17.75 1.45.

XXXX **Scott's,** 20 Mount St., W1Y 5RB, ☎ 629 5248, Seafood BN **r**
M a la carte 8.55/11.75 1.95.

XXX **Tiberio,** 22 Queen St., W1X 7PJ, ☎ 629 3561, Italian rest., Dancing CN **z**
closed Sunday – **M** a la carte 5.65/14.05.

XXX **Snooty Fox,** 52 Hertford St., W1Y 7HJ, ☎ 629 1786, French rest. BN **c**
closed Saturday lunch, Sunday and Bank Holiday Mondays – **M** approx. 5.50 1.60.

XXX Trader Vics (at Hilton), 22 Park Lane, W1A 2HH, ☎ 493 7586, Polynesian rest. BP **e**

XXX **La Napoule,** 8-10 North Audley St., W1Y 1WK, ☎ 629 4178, French rest. AL **e**
closed Saturday lunch, Sunday and Bank Holidays – **M** a la carte 5.15/9.75 **t.** 2.00.

XXX **Tandoori,** 37a Curzon St., W1Y 7AF, ☎ 629 0600, Indian and Pakistani rest. BN **i**
closed Sunday and 25-26 December – **M** a la carte 5.25/6.60 1.40.

XX **Marquis,** 121a Mount St., W1Y 5HB, ☎ 499 1256 BM **u**
closed Sunday and Bank Holidays – **M** a la carte 5.00/6.65 **t.** 1.75.

XX **La Genova,** 32 North Audley St., W1Y 1WG, ☎ 629 5916, Italian rest. AL **u**
closed Sunday and Bank Holidays – **M** a la carte 3.05/7.20 1.00.

XX **Golden Carp,** 8a Mount St., W1Y 5AD, ☎ 499 3385, Seafood BM **x**
closed Saturday lunch, Sunday and Bank Holidays – **M** a la carte 4.00/15.60 **t.** 1.80.

XX **Gaylord,** 16 Albemarle St., W1 3HA, ☎ 629 8542, Indian rest. DM **u**
M 3.50/4.50 1.20.

X **Trattoria Fiori,** 87-88 Mount St., W1Y 5HG, ☎ 499 1447, Italian rest. BM **o**
closed Sunday and Bank Holidays – **M** a la carte 3.20/6.20 **t.** 1.20.

X **Tokyo,** 7 Swallow St., W1R 7HD, ☎ 734 2269, Japanese rest. EM **i**
closed Sunday – **M** a la carte 6.40/9.50 **s.** 1.50.

X Le Bistingo, 5 Trebeck St., W1, ☎ 499 3292, Bistro. CN **r**

X **Dukes,** 55-59 Duke St., W1M 5HD, ☎ 499 5000 BK **s**
closed Sunday and Bank Holidays – **M** a la carte 2.70/4.60 **t.** 1.30.

Regent's Park and Marylebone – ✉ NW1/NW6/NW8/W1 – Except where otherwise stated see pp. 22 and 23.

Churchill, 30 Portman Sq., W1H 0AJ, ☎ 486 5800, Telex 264831 – TV ♿ Ⓟ. AJ **x**
M a la carte 5.10/11.20 1.50 – 3.00 – **489 rm** 33.00/41.00.

Selfridge, 400 Orchard St., W1H 0JS, ☎ 408 2080, Telex 22361 – TV ♿ Ⓟ. AK **e**
M a la carte 5.00/9.70 **s.** 1.30 – 2.50 – **298 rm** 31.70/41.00 **st.**

Portman, 22 Portman Sq., W1H 9FL, ☎ 486 5844, Telex 261526 – TV ♿ Ⓟ. AJ **o**
M a la carte 7.50/10.50 **st.** 2.50 – 3.90 – **287 rm** 35.00/46.00.

Montcalm, Great Cumberland Pl., W1H 7DJ, ☎ 402 4288, Telex 28710 – TV. pp. 26 and 27 FY **x**
M a la carte 8.00/12.00 **st.** 1.75 – 3.50 – **112 rm** 30.00/40.00 **st.**

Holiday Inn, 134 George St., W1M 6DN, ☎ 723 1277, Telex 27983, – TV ♿ Ⓟ. pp. 26 and 27 FY **i**
M 4.50/8.80 **s.** 1.90 – 2.50 – **243 rm** 28.00/36.00.

St. George's (T.H.F.), Langham Pl., W1N 8QS, ₱ 580 0111, Telex 27274, ≤ – |♦| TV ♿ pp. 13-16 LT **a**
M a la carte 8.65/11.25 **st.** ₫ 2.00 – ☕ 2.75 – **85 rm** 25.00/35.00 **st.**

Cumberland (T.H.F.), Marble Arch, W1A 4RF, ₱ 262 1234, Telex 22215 – |♦| TV ♿ P. 🏃 AK **n**
M 4.50/4.75 **t.** ₫ 1.75 – ☕ 3.00 – **894 rm** 24.00/33.00 **t.**

Westmoreland at Lords (Gd. Met.), 18 Lodge Rd, NW8 7JT, ₱ 722 7722, Telex 23101 – |♦| TV P. 🏃 pp. 13-16 JS **v**
M a la carte 3.55/10.25 **st.** ₫ 1.50 – ☕ 1.10 – **335 rm** 20.00/27.00 **st.**

Durrants, 26-32 George St., W1H 6BJ, ₱ 935 8131 – |♦| TV ⛀wc ☎. 🏃 AH **e**
M a la carte 4.95/9.00 **t.** ₫ 1.50 – **86 rm** ☕ 14.00/23.00 **s.**

Londoner (Gd. Met.), 57 Welbeck St., W1M 8HS, ₱ 935 4442, Group Telex 22569 – |♦| TV ⛀wc ☎. 🏃 BJ **v**
M approx. 4.25 **st.** – ☕ 1.15 – **121 rm** 21.60/29.15 **st.** – P approx. 32.25 **st.**

Clifton Ford (Gd. Met.), 47 Welbeck St., W1M 8DN, ₱ 486 6600, Group Telex 22569 – |♦| TV ⛀wc ☎ ♿ 🚗. 🏃 BH **a**
M approx. 4.25 **st.** – ☕ 1.15 – **219 rm** 21.60/29.15 **st.** – P approx. 32.25 **st.**

Harewood, Harewood Row, NW1 6SE, ₱ 262 2707, Telex 24159 – |♦| TV ⛀wc ☎ pp. 13-16 KT **x**
M a la carte 1.65/4.50 **t.** ₫ 1.15 – ☕ 1.50 – **82 rm.**

Berners (Gd. Met.), 10 Berners St., W1A 3BE, ₱ 636 1629, Telex 25759 – |♦| ⛀wc 🚿wc ☎. 🏃 EJ **a**
M approx. 4.10 **st.** ₫ 1.40 – ☕ 1.10 – **238 rm** 8.50/22.00 **s.**

Stratford Court (Gd. Met.), 350 Oxford St., W1N 0BY, ₱ 629 7474, Group Telex 25971 – |♦| TV ⛀wc ☎ BJK **n**
M (coffee shop only) a la carte 2.20/3.10 **st.** ₫ 1.35 – ☕ 1.15 – **137 rm** 17.00/25.00 **s.**

Regent Centre (Centre), Carburton St., W1P 8EE, ₱ 388 2300, Telex 22453 – |♦| TV ⛀wc ☎ P pp. 13-16 LT **i**
M (coffee shop only) approx. 3.50 **s.** ₫ 1.25 – ☕ 1.75 – **350 rm** 13.85/17.50 **s.**

Concorde without rest., 50 Great Cumberland Pl., W1H 7HD, ₱ 402 6169 – |♦| ⛀wc 🚿wc ☎ pp. 26 and 27 FY **n**
☕ 1.00 – **28 rm** 12.50/18.00 **s.**

Hallam, without rest., 12 Hallam St., W1N 5LJ, ₱ 580 1166 – |♦| ⛀wc 🚿wc ☎ pp. 13-16 LT **r**
27 rm.

Somerset House, 6 Dorset Sq., Baker St., NW1 6QA, ₱ 723 0741 – ⛀wc ☎ pp. 13-16 KT **u**
27 rm ☕ 12.50/21.00 **t.**

Portman Court, 30 Seymour St., W1H 5WD, ₱ 402 5401 – ⛀wc 🚿 ☎ AK **a**
☕ 0.50 – **30 rm** 7.00/13.50 **s.**

Rose Court, 35 Great Cumberland Pl., W1H 8DJ, ₱ 262 7241 – |♦| ⛀wc 🚿wc ☎ pp. 26 and 27 FY **s**
45 rm.

XXX **Geneviève,** 13-14 Thayer St., W1M 5LD, ₱ 486 2244 BH **s**
closed Saturday lunch, Sunday and Christmas Day – **M** a la carte 5.80/6.90 **t.** ₫ 1.50.

XXX **Oslo Court,** Prince Albert Rd, Regent's Park, NW8, ₱ 722 8795 pp. 13-16 JKS **s**
closed Sunday dinner, Monday, 2 weeks Easter, last 2 weeks August and first week September – **M** a la carte 5.15/8.75 **t.** ₫ 1.50.

XXX **Odins,** 27 Devonshire St., W1N 1RJ, ₱ 935 7296 pp. 13-16 KT **n**
closed Saturday lunch, Sunday, Easter, Christmas and Bank Holidays – **M** 7.50/8.50 **t.**

XX **Le P'tit Montmartre,** 15-17 Marylebone Lane, W1M 5FE, ₱ 935 9226, French rest.
closed Saturday lunch, Sunday and Bank Holidays – **M** a la carte 4.55/7.10 ₫ 1.50. BJ **z**

XX **Fisherman's Wharf,** 73 Baker St., W1M 1AH, ₱ 935 0471, Seafood pp. 13-16 KT **e**
closed Christmas Day – **M** a la carte 4.10/8.20 **t.** ₫ 1.30.

XX La Loggia, 68 Edgware Rd, W2 2EG, ₱ 723 0554, Italian rest. pp. 26 and 27 FY **a**

XX **Bill Bentley's,** 239 Baker St., NW1 6RE, ₱ 935 3130 pp. 13-16 KST **a**
closed Sunday and Bank Holidays – **M** a la carte 4.10/7.55 **t.** ₫ 1.05.

XX **Gaylord,** 79-81 Mortimer St., W1N 7TB, ₱ 580 3615, Indian and Pakistani rest. pp. 13-16 LT **c**
M 2.25/3.25 ₫ 1.20.

XX **Manchurian,** 42 Baker St., W1M 1DH, ₱ 935 0331, Chinese rest. AH **i**
closed 25-26 December and Bank Holidays – **M** a la carte 4.35/9.25 **st.** ₫ 2.25.

XX **Tonino's,** Berkeley Court, 12 Glentworth St., NW1 5PG, ₱ 935 4220, Italian rest.
closed Sunday and Bank Holidays – **M** a la carte 4.50/6.10 ₫ 2.70. pp. 13-16 KT **c**

XX **Lords Rendezvous,** 24 Finchley Rd, NW8, ₱ 586 4280, Chinese rest. pp. 13-16 JR **r**
M approx. 5.00.

XX **Sandro,** 114 Crawford St., W1H 1AG, ₱ 935 5736, Italian rest. pp. 13-16 KT **r**
closed Saturday lunch, Sunday and Bank Holidays – **M** a la carte 4.15/5.90 ₫ 1.70.

XX **Kerzenstüberl,** 9 St. Christopher's Pl., W1M 6DU, ₱ 486 3196, Austrian rest. BJ **a**
closed Saturday lunch, Sunday, Bank Holidays, and mid August-mid September – **M** a la carte 4.65/7.65 ₫ 1.95.

XX **Masako,** 6-8 St. Christopher's Pl., W1M 5HB, ₱ 935 1579, Japanese rest. BJ **e**
closed Sunday, Easter Monday, summer Bank Holiday, 25-26 December and 1 January – **M** a la carte 4.50/8.60 ₫ 0.75.

XX **Rossetti,** 23 Queens Grove, St. John's Wood, NW8 6PR, ℗ 722 7141, Italian rest. *closed Bank Holidays* – **M** a la carte 4.30/6.50 **t.** ₰ 1.30. pp. 13-16 JR **c**

XX **Mikado,** 110 George St., W1H 6DJ, ℗ 935 8320, Japanese rest. AH **s** *closed Saturday lunch, Sunday, 1 week August and Bank Holidays* – **M** a la carte 7.00/11.30 ₰ 3.00.

X Biagi's, 39 Upper Berkeley St., W1H 7PG, ℗ 723 0394, Italian rest. pp. 26 and 27 FY **c**

X **Au Bois St. Jean,** 122 St. John's Wood High St., NW8 7SG, ℗ 722 0400, French Bistro *closed Sunday and Bank Holidays* – **M** a la carte 5.05/7.35 **t.** ₰ 1.50. pp. 13-16 JS **r**

X **Vecchio Parioli,** 129 Crawford St., W1H 1AA, ℗ 935 3791, Italian rest. pp. 13-16 KT **s** **M** a la carte 3.80/4.50 **t.** ₰ 1.20.

X **Indira,** 62 Seymour St., W1, ℗ 402 6733, Indian rest. pp. 26 and 27 FY **r** **M** a la carte 2.45/4.30.

X **Nibub Lokanta,** 112-114 Edgware Rd, W2 2DZ, ℗ 262 6636, Turkish rest. pp. 26 and 27 FY **e** *closed 25-26 December and lunch 1 January* – **M** a la carte 4.65/6.35 **t.** ₰ 2.50.

X **Il Barbino,** 64 Seymour St., W1, ℗ 402 6866, Italian rest. pp. 26 and 27 FY **r** *closed Sunday and Bank Holidays* – **M** a la carte 3.80/5.50 **t.** ₰ 1.15.

X **Hellenic,** 30 Thayer St., W1M 5LJ, ℗ 935 1257, Greek rest. BH **c** **M** a la carte 3.45/4.65 ₰ 1.50.

X Bistro 57, 57 St. John's Wood High St., NW8 5AR, ℗ 722 0450, Bistro pp. 13-16 JS **n** **M** (dinner only and Sunday lunch).

X **Singapore,** 62 Marylebone Lane, Wigmore St., W1, ℗ 486 2004, Malaysian rest. *closed Sunday and Bank Holidays* – **M** a la carte approx. 3.85 **st.** ₰ 1.20. BJ **c**

St. James's W1/SW1/WC2 – pp. 22 and 23.

Ritz, Piccadilly, W1A 2JS, ℗ 493 8181, Telex 267200 – lift TV ♿ DN **a** **M** a la carte 9.00/17.00 **st.** ₰ 1.50 – ☕ 2.50 – **140 rm** 35.00/70.00 **st.**

Dukes (quiet), 35 St. James's Pl., SW1A 1NY, ℗ 491 4840, Telex 28283 – lift TV EP **x** **M** a la carte 5.85/8.95 ₰ 1.50 – **52 rm** 27.30/43.50 **st.**

Stafford (quiet), 16 St. James's Pl., SW1A 1NJ, ℗ 493 0111, Telex 28602 – lift TV DN **u** **61 rm.**

Quaglino's (T.H.F), 16 Bury St., SW1Y 6AJ, ℗ 930 6767 – lift TV. EN **n** **M** 6.00/9.50 **st.** ₰ 1.75 – ☕ 2.75 – **41 rm** 26.00/36.00 **st.**

Cavendish (T.H.F.), Jermyn St., SW1Y 6JF, ℗ 930 2111, Telex 263187 – lift TV ♿ P. EN **i** **M** a la carte 6.00/9.00 **st.** ₰ 2.25 – ☕ 3.50 – **255 rm** 32.00/42.00 **st.**

Royal Trafalgar (Royal London), Whitcomb St., WC2H 7HL, ℗ 930 4477, Group Telex 24616 – lift TV bath wc phone GM **r** **M (Angus Steak House)** a la carte 4.40/7.15 ₰ 1.75 – ☕ 2.75 – **108 rm** 20.00/28.00 **s.**

Royal Angus (Royal London), 39 Coventry St., W1V 7FH, ℗ 930 4033, Group Telex 24616 – lift TV bath wc shower wc phone FGM **a** **M** (coffee shop only) a la carte 2.40/5.15 **st.** ₰ 1.70 – ☕ 2.75 – **95 rm** 19.00/25.00 **s.**

Pastoria (Gd. Met.), St. Martin's St., WC2H 7HL, ℗ 930 8641, Group Telex 25971 – lift bath wc phone GM **v** **M** *(closed Saturday lunch, Sunday and Bank Holidays)* a la carte 2.75/4.80 **t.** ₰ 1.35 – ☕ 1.10 – **52 rm** 8.50/22.00 **s.**

XXXX **A L'Ecu de France,** 111 Jermyn St., SW1Y 6HB, ℗ 930 2837, French rest. FM **s** *closed Saturday lunch, Sunday lunch, Easter Day and Christmas Day* – **M** a la carte 7.15/13.70 ₰ 1.75.

XXX **Stone's Chop House,** Panton St., SW1Y 4DX, ℗ 930 0037, English rest. GM **c** *closed Sunday, Good Friday and Christmas Day* – **M** a la carte 2.80/6.70 **t.** ₰ 1.20.

XXX Hunting Lodge (T.H.F.), 16-18 Lower Regent St., SW1Y 4PH, ℗ 930 4222. FM **o**

XXX **Lafayette,** 32 King St., SW1 6RJ, ℗ 930 1131 EN **v** *closed Saturday, Sunday and Bank Holidays* – **M** a la carte 5.50/9.00 **t.** ₰ 1.50.

XXX ✿ **Wilton's,** 27 Bury St., SW1Y 6AL, ℗ 930 8391, English rest. EN **u** *closed Friday dinner, Saturday, Sunday, last week July and first week August* – **M** a la carte 8.30/14.80 **t.** ₰ 2.50
Spec. Oysters (September-April), Lobster, Game (season).

XX **Frank's,** 63 Jermyn St., SW1Y 6LX, ℗ 493 3645, Italian rest. EN **z** **M** a la carte 3.80/5.45 ₰ 0.95.

XX La Dolce Notte, 55 Jermyn St., SW1, ℗ 499 1168, Italian rest., Dancing. EN **e**

X **Wheelers,** 12a Duke of York St., SW1 6LB, ℗ 930 2460, Seafood EN **a** *closed Sunday, Easter, 25-26 December, 1 January and Bank Holidays* – **M** a la carte approx. 8.50 **t.** ₰ 1.75.

X **Richoux at the Caprice,** Arlington House, Arlington St., SW1A 1RJ, ℗ 493 9025 DN **e** *closed Sunday, 25-26 December and Bank Holidays* – **M** a la carte 4.10/6.80 ₰ 1.60.

Soho - ✉ W1/WC2 - pp. 22 and 23.

XXXXX **Café Royal Grill** (T.H.F.), 68 Regent St., W1R 6EL, ☎ 437 9090, French rest. EM **a**
M a la carte 6.15/11.45 **st.**

XXXXX **Le Relais du Café Royal** (T.H.F.), 68 Regent St., W1R 6EL, ☎ 437 9090, French rest.
M a la carte 8.20/11.45 **t.** 🍷 2.55. EM **a**

XXX **Leonis Quo Vadis,** 26-29 Dean St., W1V 6LL, ☎ 437 9585, Italian rest. FK **u**
closed Sunday lunch, Good Friday, Easter Sunday and Christmas Day – **M** a la carte 5.00/8.75 🍷 1.30.

XXX Gennaro's (T.H.F.), 44-45 Dean St., W1V 5AP, ☎ 437 3950, Italian rest. FK **s**

XXX **Au Jardin des Gourmets,** 5 Greek St., Soho Sq., W1V 5LA, ☎ 437 1816, French rest.
closed Saturday lunch, Sunday and Christmas Day – **M** a la carte 5.70/7.50 **t.** 🍷 1.50. GJ **a**

XX **Gay Hussar,** 2 Greek St., W1V 6NB, ☎ 437 0973, Hungarian rest. GJ **c**
closed Sunday, Christmas Day and Bank Holidays – **M** a la carte 5.50/7.50.

XX **La Terrazza,** 19 Romilly St., W1T 5GT, ☎ 734 2504, Italian rest. FL **i**
M a la carte 4.80/7.80.

XX **Fuji,** 36-40 Brewer St., W1R 3HP, ☎ 734 0957, Japanese rest. FL **c**
closed Monday, Easter and 23 December-6 January – **M** a la carte 6.00/14.40.

XX China Garden, 66 Brewer St., W1R 3PJ, ☎ 437 6500, Chinese rest. EM **o**

XX **Chesa** (Swiss Centre), 2 New Coventry St., W1V 3HG, ☎ 734 1291, Swiss rest. GM **n**
closed Christmas Day – **M** a la carte 5.00/5.95.

XX **Soho Rendezvous,** 21 Romilly St., W1V 5TG, ☎ 437 1486, Chinese rest. GL **o**
closed 25 and 26 December – **M** a la carte 3.30/7.70.

XX **Romeo e Giulietta,** 11 Sutton Row, W1V 5FE, ☎ 734 4914, Italian rest. GJ **e**
M a la carte approx. 5.60.

XX **I Paparazzi,** 52-54 Dean St., W1V 5HJ, ☎ 437 1703, Italian rest. GL **a**
closed Bank Holidays – **M** a la carte 3.65/4.75 🍷 1.55.

XX **Gallery Rendezvous,** 53-55 Beak St., W1R 3LF, ☎ 437 4446, Chinese rest. EL **c**
closed 25 and 26 December – **M** a la carte 4.00/6.00 🍷 2.50.

XX **Venezia,** 21 Great Chapel St., W1V 5HA, ☎ 437 6506, Italian rest. FJ **a**
closed Saturday lunch, Sunday and Bank Holidays – **M** a la carte 4.95/6.40 🍷 1.30.

XX **Rugantino,** 26 Romilly St., W1V 5TQ, ☎ 437 5302, Italian rest. GK **u**
closed Sunday and Bank Holidays – **M** a la carte 4.95/5.75 🍷 1.45.

XX **La Capannina,** 24 Romilly St., W1V 5TG, ☎ 437 2473, Italian rest. GL **x**
closed Bank Holidays – **M** a la carte 4.60/6.50 **t.**

X **Peter Mario,** 47 Gerrard St., W1V 7LP, ☎ 437 4170, Italian rest. GL **n**
closed Sunday and Bank Holidays – **M** a la carte 3.55/5.25 **t.** 🍷 1.15.

X **Hostaria Romana,** 70 Dean St., W1V 5HB, ☎ 734 2869, Italian rest. FK **s**
M a la carte 3.80/4.60 **t.** 🍷 0.95.

X **Trattoria Imperia,** 19 Charing Cross Rd, WC2H 0ES, ☎ 930 8364, Italian rest. GM **z**
closed Sunday and Bank Holidays – **M** 6.00/9.00 **t.** 🍷 1.30.

X **Rendezvous** (Swiss Centre), 2 New Coventry St., W1V 3HG, ☎ 734 1291, Swiss rest.
closed Christmas Day – **M** a la carte 2.90/5.75. GM **n**

X **Crank's,** 8 Marshall St., W1V 1FE, ☎ 437 9431, Vegetarian rest. EK **a**
closed Sunday, Easter, Christmas and Bank Holidays – **M** (buffet only) a la carte approx. 2.65 **st.** 🍷 0.75.

X **Dumpling Inn,** 15a Gerrard St., W1V 7NL, ☎ 437 2567, Chinese rest. GL **e**
closed 25 and 26 December – **M** a la carte 4.00/5.60 🍷 2.40.

X **Hokkai,** 59-61 Brewer St., W1V 3FB, ☎ 734 5826, Japanese rest. ELM **e**
closed Sunday lunch and Bank Holidays – **M** a la carte 3.35/6.55.

X **The Village,** 61-63 Shaftesbury Av., W1V 7AA, ☎ 437 5021, Chinese rest. FL **a**
M a la carte 3.00/6.10 🍷 1.20.

X **Le Bistingo,** 57-59 Old Compton St., W1V 5PN, ☎ 437 0784, French Bistro FL **n**
closed Christmas Day – **M** a la carte 2.85/3.80 **st.** 🍷 1.30.

X **Ganges,** 40 Gerrard St., W1V 7LP, ☎ 437 0284, Indian and Pakistani rest. GL **r**
closed Sunday and Christmas Day – **M** a la carte 2.60/3.90 **t.** 🍷 1.10.

Strand – ✉ WC2 – p. 27.

Savoy, Strand, WC2R 0BP, ☎ 836 4343, Telex 24234 – EX a
M Restaurant *(closed Sunday)* a la carte 7.75/13.25 **t.** 1.45 – **Savoy Grill** *(closed Saturday)* a la carte 7.20/13.10 **t.** 1.45 – 2.75 – **301 rm** 32.00/63.00 **st.**

Waldorf (T.H.F.), Aldwych, WC2B 4DD, ☎ 836 2400, Telex 24574 – EV x
M a la carte 4.70/9.00 **st.** – 2.60 – **310 rm.**

Charing Cross (B.T.H.), Strand, WC2N 5HX, ☎ 839 7282, Telex 261101 –
M a la carte 7.35/10.45 **st.** 1.45 – **207 rm** 26.00/36.00 **st.** DX s

Howard, 12 Temple Pl., WC2R 2PR, ☎ 836 3555, Telex 268047 – FV e
141 rm.

Strand Palace (T.H.F.), Strand, WC2R 0JJ, ☎ 836 8080, Telex 24208 – EV u
M (Carvery rest.) approx. 4.25 **t.** – 1.50 – **786 rm** 16.50/24.50 **t.**

Ivy, 1-5 West St., WC2H 9NE, ☎ 836 4751 DV e
closed Saturday lunch and Sunday – **M** a la carte 6.40/10.40 1.50.

Simpson's in the Strand, 100 Strand, WC2R 0EW, ☎ 836 9112, English rest. EV o
closed Sunday, Good Friday and Christmas Day – **M** a la carte 4.30/8.95 **t.** 1.20.

Inigo Jones, 14 Garrick St., WC2E 9BJ, ☎ 836 6456, « Converted Mission house » DV n
closed Saturday lunch, Sunday and Bank Holidays – **M** a la carte 6.20/8.50 1.55.

La Bussola, 42-49 St. Martin's Lane, WC2, ☎ 240 1148, Italian rest., Dancing. DX r

Grange, 39 King St., WC2E 8JS, ☎ 240 2939 DV z
closed Saturday lunch, Sunday and Bank Holidays – **M** 6.20/8.50 **t.** 1.65.

Chez Solange, 35 Cranbourn St., WC2H 7AD, ☎ 836 5886, French rest. DV i
closed Sunday and Bank Holidays – **M** a la carte 3.95/6.70 **t.** 1.95.

San Martino, 46 St. Martin's Lane, WC2N 4EJ, ☎ 240 2336, Italian rest. DX x
closed Saturday lunch, Sunday, Christmas Day and Bank Holidays – **M** a la carte 3.70/5.60 1.30.

Forum, Bush House, Aldwych, WC2B 4PA, ☎ 836 9828 EV i
closed Saturday, Sunday and Bank Holidays – **M** (lunch only) a la carte 4.40/6.05 **t.** 1.40.

Poons of Covent Garden, 41 King St., WC2, ☎ 240 1743, Chinese rest. DV r
closed 25 and 26 December – **M** approx. 5.00 2.00.

Laguna 50, 50 St. Martin's Lane, WC2N 4EA, ☎ 836 0960, Italian rest. DX u
closed Saturday lunch, Sunday and Bank Holidays – **M** a la carte 3.75/5.50 **t.** 1.00.

Colosseo, 12 May's Court, St. Martin's Lane, WC2N 4BS, ☎ 836 6140, Italian rest. DX e
closed Saturday lunch, Sunday and Bank Holidays – **M** a la carte 3.85/5.80 **t.** 1.00.

Cellier de Medici, 8 May's Court, St. Martin's Lane, WC2N 4BS, ☎ 836 9180, French rest. DX o
closed Saturday lunch, Sunday and Bank Holidays – **M** a la carte approx. 4.05 **t.** 1.35.

Luigi's, 15 Tavistock St., WC2E 7PA, ☎ 240 1795, Italian rest. EV a
closed Sunday and Bank Holidays – **M** a la carte 3.85/6.85 **t.** 1.25.

Victoria – ✉ SW1 – Except otherwise stated see p. 26.

Goring, Beeston Pl., Grosvenor Gdns, SW1W 0JW, ☎ 834 8211, Telex 919166 –
M 6.00/9.00 **st.** 1.50 – 3.00 – **100 rm** 24.00/30.00 **st.** – P 36.00/40.00 **st.** BV a

Royal Horseguards (Royal London), 2 Whitehall Court, SW1A 2EJ, ☎ 839 3400, Telex 917096 – pp. 17-20 NV a
M 5.25/5.75 **s.** 2.00 – 2.75 – **285 rm** 22.00/28.00 **s.**

Royal Westminster (Royal London), Buckingham Palace Rd, SW1W 0QT, ☎ 834 1302, Telex 916821 – BV z
M a la carte 4.60/6.60 **t.** 1.30 – 2.75 – **136 rm** 27.00/35.00 **s.**

St. Ermin's (Gd. Met.), Caxton St., SW1H 0QW, ☎ 222 7888, Telex 917731 – CV a
M a la carte 4.50/6.55 **st.** 1.75 – 1.15 – **241 rm** 18.00/26.00 **s.**

Rubens (Gd. Met.), 39 Buckingham Palace Rd, SW1W 0PS, ☎ 834 6600, Telex 916577 – wc BV u
M a la carte 3.90/5.00 **st.** 1.50 – 1.00 – **145 rm.**

Eccleston (Norfolk Cap.), Eccleston Sq., SW1V 1PS, ☎ 834 8042, Group Telex 23241 – wc BX z
M *(closed Saturday and Sunday lunch)* a la carte 2.30/8.10 **st.** 1.60 – **120 rm** 12.30/23.95 **st.**

Ebury Court, 26 Ebury St., SW1W 0LU, ☎ 730 8147 – wc AV i
M a la carte 3.45/6.30 1.35 – **38 rm** 12.00/24.00 **st.**

Lime Tree, 135-137 Ebury St., SW1W 9RA, ☎ 730 8191 – wc wc AX e
closed 1 week at Christmas – **49 rm** 8.00/15.00.

Elizabeth, 37 Eccleston Sq., SW1V 1PB, ☎ 828 6812 – BX c
23 rm 9.00/20.00 **st.**

Hamilton House, 60-64 Warwick Way, SW1V 1SA, ✆ 821 7113 pp. 17-20 LY **a**
21 rm ☕ 10.00/20.00 **st.**

Belgrave House, 30-32 Belgrave Rd, SW1V 1RG, ✆ 834 8620 BX **e**
37 rm ☕ 8.65/16.20 **st.**

Hansel and Gretel, 64-76 Belgrave Rd, SW1V 2BS, ✆ 828 1806 BX **n**
72 rm ☕ 8.00/10.00.

XXX **Lockets,** Marsham Court, Marsham St., SW1P 3DR, ✆ 834 9552, English rest. pp. 17-20 MY **z**
closed Saturday, Sunday and Bank Holidays – **M** a la carte 6.70/8.10 **t.** 1.50.

XXX **Kundan,** 3 Horseferry Rd, SW1P 2AN, ✆ 834 3434, Indian and Pakistani rest.
closed Sunday and Bank Holidays – **M** a la carte 5.15/5.75 1.80. pp. 17-20 NXY **a**

XX **Pomegranates,** 94 Grosvenor Rd, SW1V 3LG, ✆ 828 6560 pp. 17-20 LMZ **a**
closed Sunday and Bank Holidays – **M** a la carte 5.80/8.60 1.50.

XX **Eatons,** 49 Elizabeth St., SW1W 9PP, ✆ 730 0074 AX **a**
closed Saturday lunch, Sunday and Bank Holidays – **M** a la carte 4.60/5.80 **s.** 1.60.

XX **Tate Gallery Rest.,** Tate Gallery, Millbank, SW1P 4RG, ✆ 834 6754, English rest.
closed Sunday, Good Friday, 24 to 26 December and 1 January – **M** (lunch only) a la carte 5.10/6.35 1.15. pp. 17-20 NY **c**

XX **Massimo,** 42 Buckingham Palace Rd, SW1W 0RE, ✆ 834 8283, Italian rest. BV **x**
closed Saturday lunch, Sunday and Bank Holidays – **M** a la carte 5.80/9.85 **t.** 1.85.

XX **Gran Paradiso,** 52 Wilton Rd, SW1V 1DE, ✆ 828 5818, Italian rest. BX **a**
closed Saturday lunch, Sunday and Bank Holidays – **M** a la carte 4.50/5.55 **t.** 1.05.

XX **La Fontana,** 101 Pimlico Rd, SW1W 8PH, ✆ 730 6630 pp. 24 and 25 FT **o**
closed Saturday lunch, Sunday and Bank Holidays – **M** a la carte 4.80/6.30 **t.** 1.25.

X **The Tent,** 15 Eccleston St., SW1W 9LX, ✆ 730 6922 AX **c**
closed Saturday, Easter Christmas and Bank Holidays – **M** 3.45 **t.** 1.40.

X Mimmo d'Ischia, 61 Elizabeth St., SW1W 9PP, ✆ 730 5406, Italian rest. AX **o**

X **Pimlico,** 89 Pimlico Rd, SW1W 9PH, ✆ 730 5323, Italian Bistro pp. 24 and 25 FT **c**
closed Tuesday lunch, Monday and Bank Holidays – **M** a la carte 4.05/4.95 **t.** 1.25.

X **La Poule au Pot,** 231 Ebury St., SW1W 8UT, ✆ 730 7763, French Bistro
M a la carte 6.00/7.00. pp. 17-20 KY **n**

X **Bumbles,** 16 Buckingham Palace Rd, SW1W 0QP, ✆ 828 2903, Bistro BV **c**
closed Saturday lunch, Sunday and Bank Holidays – **M** a la carte 4.00/5.00 **t.** 1.45.

CAR DEALERS AND REPAIRERS

GARAGISTES RÉPARATEURS

OFFICINE MECCANICHE

REPARATURWERKSTÄTTEN

BOROUGH

BARNET	ALFA ROMEO, VOLVO 205 Regents Park Rd ☎ 346 6616 DAF, PEUGEOT Hendon Way ☎ 202 6105	DAIMLER, JAGUAR, ROVER Lyttleton Rd ☎ 458 7111 RENAULT Finchley Lane ☎ 203 1145
BRENT	AUSTIN-MG 28/30 Watford Rd ☎ 904 4567 CHRYSLER-SIMCA Watford Rd ☎ 904 0971	BRITISH LEYLAND, FORD Neasden Lane ☎ 450 8000 CITROEN Abbey Rd, Park Royal ☎ 965 7757
BROMLEY	CITROEN, LANCIA, MERCEDES-BENZ Bromley Hill ☎ 460 1194 FORD Masons Hill ☎ 460 9101	AUSTIN 10 Masons Hill ☎ 460 4693
CAMDEN	DAF, HONDA 96A Clifton Hill ☎ 328 4422 PEUGEOT 93/103 Drummond St. ☎ 387 3621 DATSUN 617 Finchley Rd ☎ 435 2254 FORD 591 Commercial Rd ☎ 790 1851	CITROEN 133B Upper St., Islington ☎ 226 3437 CITROEN 265 Finchley Rd ☎ 435 8532 FIAT, POLSKI Randolph St. ☎ 485 8716
CROYDON	MERCEDES-BENZ, VW, AUDI 375/379 Brighton Rd ☎ 681 3881 PEUGEOT 468/472 Purley Way ☎ 681 2600	RENAULT 117 Whitehorse Rd ☎ 684 5591 FORD 15/19 Brighton Rd ☎ 686 8888
EALING	RENAULT Western Av. ☎ 992 3481 BMC, DAF Woodstock Av. ☎ 567 8685 RENAULT Western Av. ☎ 998 1515	CITROEN, PEUGEOT Western Av. ☎ 992 5181 CHRYSLER, HILLMAN, HUMBER, SUNBEAM Hastings Rd ☎ 567 1475
ENFIELD	DAF, LADA, RELIANT Cornwall Rd ☎ 428 1985	PEUGEOT 70/76 London Rd ☎ 363 3950
GREENWICH	CHRYSLER-SIMCA 43/53 Trafalgar Rd ☎ 858 4881 PEUGEOT Footscray Rd ☎ 850 2889	RENAULT 2/12 Dorset Rd ☎ 857 2231
HAMMERSMITH	CITROEN 258/264 Goldhawk Rd ☎ 743 9558	COLT MITSUBISHI, FIAT 181-183 Warwick Rd ☎ 370 3152
HARINGEY	RENAULT 177 Archway Rd ☎ 340 8467	BEDFORD, VAUXHALL Tottenham Lane ☎ 340 8051
HARROW	BRITISH LEYLAND Marsh Rd ☎ 866 2111	FORD 364/372 High Rd ☎ 247 4377

BOROUGH		
HAVERING	FORD Jutsums Lane ℡ Romford 45091 CITROEN 132 Hornchurch Rd ℡ Hornchurch 54212	VAUXHALL 134 London Rd, Romford ℡ Romford 22311
HILLINGDON	FORD 215/218 High St. ℡ Uxbridge 33444	RENAULT 36 George St., Staines ℡ 58176
HOUNSLOW	DAF, OPEL, RELIANT 644 Hanworth Rd ℡ 894 1951	
KENSINGTON & CHELSEA	AUSTIN-MG-ROVER-TRIUMPH 107/109 Old Brompton Rd ℡ 589 3621 FORD 7/17 Ansdell St. ℡ 937 7207	FORD 133 Old Brompton Rd ℡ 373 3333
KINGSTON-UPON-THAMES	VAUXHALL High St. ℡ 546 7193	
LAMBETH	VAUXHALL 80 Clapham Rd ℡ 735 4211	CITROEN, FIAT 64 Wandsworth Rd ℡ 622 0042
LEWISHAM	BEDFORD, VAUXHALL 2/22 Burnt Ash Rd, Lee Green ℡ 852 1202	
MERTON	CITROEN 256 Wimbledon Park Rd ℡ 788 4577 FIAT 213/217 The Broadway ℡ 540 9991 VOLVO, VW 151 Hartfield Rd ℡ 540 1615	RENAULT 14 Morden Rd ℡ 542 2454 AUSTIN, VANDEN PLAS 9 Revelstoke Rd ℡ 946 5686 PEUGEOT 165/177 The Broadway ℡ 540 8728
NEWHAM	VAUXHALL 125/131 High St. ℡ 534 6699	
REDBRIDGE	MORRIS 543 High Rd ℡ 478 2225	
RICHMOND-UPON-THAMES	CHRYSLER-SIMCA 1/6 North Rd ℡ 878 0271	AUSTIN-DAIMLER-JAGUAR-MG-ROVER-TRIUMPH 174/176 Sheen Rd ℡ 940 6441
SOUTHWARK	BEDFORD, VAUXHALL 100 Enid St. ℡ 237 4661	VW, AUDI 434/450 Old Kent Rd ℡ 231 0031
SUTTON	DAF, VOLVO 56/58 Cheam Rd ℡ 642 2206	FORD 268 High St. ℡ 643 3388
TOWER HAMLETS	VAUXHALL 343 Mile End Rd ℡ 980 3633	
WALTHAM FOREST	VAUXHALL 400 Hoe St. ℡ 520 8241	CHRYSLER-SIMCA Nightingale Lane ℡ 989 5155
WANDSWORTH	AUSTIN-MORRIS-MG-PRINCESS-ROVER-TRIUMPH, VANDEN PLAS, VAUXHALL 15/25 East Hill ℡ 228 6480	DAIMLER-JAGUAR-MORRIS-MG-ROVER-TRIUMPH, ROLLS ROYCE BENTLEY 100 York Rd ℡ 228 6444
WESTMINSTER	VAUXHALL 466/490 Edgware Rd ℡ 723 0024	

MICHELIN Branch 81 Fulham Rd, SW3 6RD, ℡ 581 2381.

LONG EATON Notts. – see Nottingham.

LONGFORD West Midlands – see Coventry.

LONG MELFORD Suffolk 986 ㉜ – pop. 2,870 – ☎ 078 725.
See : Holy Trinity Church* 15C.
London 62 – Cambridge 34 – Colchester 18 – Ipswich 24.

- **Bull** (T.H.F.), Hall St., CO10 9JG, ☎ 494, « Part 15C coaching inn » – TV P
  M a la carte 4.50/5.80 **st.** 1.50 – **25 rm** 12.00/18.50 **st.**
- **Crown** with rm, Hall St., CO10 9JL, ☎ 366, – P
  M a la carte 4.70/6.00 **t.** 1.75 – **8 rm** 7.50/12.00 **t.**

LONGNOR Staffs. – pop. 352 – ✉ Buxton – ☎ 029 883.
London 161 – Derby 29 – Manchester 31 – Stoke-on-Trent 22.

- **Ye Olde Cheshire Cheese,** High St., SK17 0NS, ☎ 218 – P
  M a la carte 4.80/7.60 **s.** 1.35.

LONG SUTTON Somerset – pop. 704 – ✉ Langport – ☎ 045 824.
London 136 – Ilchester 6 – Taunton 16.

- **Devonshire Arms** (Interchange) with rm, TA10 9LP, ☎ 271, « Country house atmosphere », – P
  M *(closed Sunday dinner to non-residents)* a la carte 3.15/4.25 **t.** 1.40 – **6 rm** 9.25/18.50 **st.** – P 13.60/15.10 **st.**

LOOE Cornwall 986 ㊳ – pop. 4,090 – ☎ 050 36.
18 ☎ 050 34 (Widegates) 247, E: 3 m.
i The Guildhall, Fore St. ☎ 2702 (summer only).
London 264 – Plymouth 21 – Truro 39.

- **Hannafore Point,** Marine Drive, PL13 2DG, ☎ 3273, ≤ Looe Bay – wc P.
  M approx. 4.00 **t.** 1.20 – **40 rm** 11.00/22.00 **t.** – P 15.50/20.00 **t.**
- **Rock Towers,** Hannafore Rd, PL13 2DQ, ☎ 2140, ≤ sea and bay – wc P
  M 3.50/5.50 1.00 – **22 rm** 6.75/18.50.
- **Klymiarven** , Barbican Hill, PL13 1BH, ☎ 2333, ≤ Looe, – wc P
  March-December – **M** (cold lunch) a la carte 2.85/4.45 1.25 – **15 rm** 8.00/17.50

at Duloe N: 3 ½ m. on B 3254 by A 387 – ✉ ☎ 050 36 Looe:

- **Duloe Manor** , PL14 4PW, ☎ 2795, , heated, , park – wc P
  Easter-October – **M** (dinner only) 4.50 1.50 – **11 rm** 9.50/21.50 **st.**

LOSTWITHIEL Cornwall 986 ㊳ – pop. 1,905 – ☎ 0208.
Envir.: Restormel Castle* (ruins 12C-13C) *AC*, N: **1** m.
London 273 – Plymouth 30 – Truro 23.

- **Carotel Motel,** 6 Edgcombe Rd, PL22 0DD, ☎ 872223 – TV wc wc P
  M (dinner only from October to April) a la carte 2.15/3.10 **s.** 0.80 – 1.20 – **32 rm** 6.00/11.00 **s.**
- Royal Talbot, PL22 0AG, on A 390 ☎ 498 – P
  9 rm.

LOUGHBOROUGH Leics. 986 ㉗ ㉘ – pop. 45,875 – ☎ 0509.
9 Joe Moores Lane ☎ 0509 (Woodhouse Eaves) 890035, S: 6 m.
i John Storer House, Wards End ☎ 30131.
London 117 – Birmingham 41 – Leicester 11 – Nottingham 15.

- **King's Head** (Embassy), High St., LE11 2GL, ☎ 214893 – TV P.
  closed Christmas – **M** approx. 2.95 **st.** 1.50 – **80 rm** 8.75/15.25 **st.**
- **Sunnyside,** The Coneries, LE11 1D7, ☎ 216217 – P
  11 rm 3.75/7.50 **s.**
- **Harlequin,** 11 Swan St., LE11 0BJ, ☎ 215235, Italian rest.
  closed Sunday and 25-26 December – **M** a la carte 3.20/4.85 **t.** 1.20.
- **Roman Inn,** 18 Baxter Gate, LE11 1TH, ☎ 66704 – P
  M a la carte 3.15/4.30 **t.** 1.10.

AUSTIN-JAGUAR-MORRIS-MG-ROVER-TRIUMPH-WOLSELEY Woodgate ☎ 66771
FORD Derby Rd ☎ 67721
MORRIS-MG-WOLSELEY The Coneries ☎ 214854
PEUGEOT Nottingham Rd ☎ 67657
VW, AUDI-NSU 28 Market St. ☎ 63244

LOUTH Lincs. 986 ㉘ – pop. 11,757 – ☎ 0507.
See: St. James' Church* 15C.
Crowtree Lane ☎ 2554.
Town Hall, Eastgate ☎ 2391.
London 155 – Boston 33 – Grimsby 17 – Lincoln 26.

- **King's Head,** Mercer Row, LN11 9JG, ☎ 2965 – P
  closed Christmas – **M** a la carte 2.80/5.60 **st.** 1.10 – **16 rm** 7.00/12.00 **st.**

LOWER LIMPLEY STOKE Avon – see Bath.

LOWER PEOVER Cheshire – see Knutsford.

LOWER SWELL Glos. – see Stow-on-the-Wold.

LOWESTOFT Suffolk 986 ㉜ – pop. 52,267– ☎ 0502.
Amenities Department, The Esplanade ☎ 65989 and 62111.
London 116 – Ipswich 43 – Norwich 30.

- **Victoria,** Kirkley Cliff, NR33 0BZ, ☎ 4433, ≤, heated – TV wc P.
  M a la carte 5.00/7.50 **st.** 0.90 – **52 rm** 11.75/17.50 **st.** – P 13.75/15.00 **st.**
- **Royal George,** The Esplanade, NR33 0QP, ☎ 65337, ≤, heated – TV wc P
  M a la carte 2 45/6.75 1.45 – **36 rm** 9.00/15.40.
- **Windsor,** Kirkley Cliff, ☎ 65138
  M approx. 2.80 **s.** 1.20 – 1.00 – **10 rm** 5.00/10.00 **s.**

AUSTIN-DAIMLER-JAGUAR-MORRIS-MG-ROVER-TRIUMPH 97/99 London Rd South ☎ 61711
DATSUN High St. ☎ 65301
FIAT Beccles Rd, Oulton Broad ☎ 63622
FORD Whapload Rd ☎ 3553
MAZDA 2/8 Bridge Rd, Oulton Broad ☎ 3797
RENAULT 9 London Rd ☎ 2783
VAUXHALL London Rd South ☎ 3512
VW, AUDI-NSU Cooke Rd, South Lowestoft Industrial Estate ☎ 2583

LOWESWATER Cumbria – pop. 202 – ✉ Cockermouth – ☎ 090 085 Lorton.
London 304 – Carlisle 33 – Keswick 12.

- **Scale Hill** , CA13 9UX, ☎ 232, ≤, – wc P
  March-November – **M** 4.50/5.00 **st.** 1.75 – **19 rm** 9.00/18.00 **st.** – P 13.00/14.00 **st.**

LOWFIELD HEATH West Sussex – see Crawley.

LOWICK GREEN Cumbria – see Ulverston.

LOW LAITHE North Yorks. – ✉ ☎ 0423 Harrogate.
London 222 – Leeds 26 – York 30.

- XXX **Knox Manor,** Summerbridge, HG3 4DQ, ☎ 780473, – P
  closed Tuesday, last 2 weeks February and last 2 weeks November – **M** (dinner only and Sunday lunch) 3.75/6.75 **t.** 1.60.

LUDLOW Salop 986 ㉛ – pop. 7,466 – ☎ 0584.
See: Castle* (ruins 11C-16C) *AC* – Parish Church* 13C – Feathers Hotel* early 17C – Broad Street* 17C.
Bromfield ☎ 058 477 (Bromfield) 285, N: 2 m on A 49.
County Museum, 13 Castle St. ☎ 3857 (summer only).
London 162 – Birmingham 39 – Hereford 24 – Shrewsbury 29.

- **Feathers,** Bull Ring, SY8 1AA, ☎ 2919, « Part Elizabethan house » – TV wc P
  M 4.00 **st.** 1.40 – **29 rm** 12.00/22.00 **st.** – P 17.00/20.00 **st.**
- Angel, Broad St., SY8 1NG, ☎ 2531 – wc P.
  17 rm.
- **Overton Grange,** SY8 4AD, S: 1 ½ m. on A 49 ☎ 3500, – P
  closed 25 and 26 December – **M** a la carte 2.30/3.60 1.30 – **17 rm** 6.50/16.00 **st.**
- **The Cliff,** Dinham, SY8 2JE, ☎ 2063, ≤, – P
  15 rm 4.50/9.00 **s.**
- **The Croft,** Dinham, SY8 1EJ, ☎ 2076
  8 rm 4.00/8.00 **t.**
- **Cecil,** Sheet Rd ☎ 2442, – P
  10 rm 3.50/7.00 **s.**

AUSTIN-MORRIS-MG-ROVER-TRIUMPH-WOLSELEY Corve St. ☎ 2301

LUSTLEIGH Devon – pop. 555 – ☎ 064 77.
London 217 – Exeter 17 – Plymouth 35.

- X **Moorwood Cottage,** TQ13 9SN, NW: 1 ½ m. on A 382 ☎ 341 – P
  closed Sunday and Christmas Day – **M** (dinner only) a la carte 3.85/5.80 **s.** 1.45.

LUTON Beds. 986 ㉜ – pop. 161,405 – ✆ 0582.

See: Luton Hoo* (Wernher Collection**) and park* *AC*. **Envir.:** Whipsnade Park* (zoo) ≤** *AC*, SW: 7 ½ m.

18 London Rd ☎ 31421, S: 1 m. on A 6.

Fire Station Airport ☎ 36061 ext 66, E: 1 ½ m.

i Central Library, Bridge St. ☎ 32629 – Consumer Advice Centre, 25 George St. ☎ 413237.

London 36 – Cambridge 35 – Ipswich 86 – Oxford 43 – Southend-on-Sea 60.

- Strathmore (Thistle), Arndale Centre, LU1 2TR, ☎ 34199, Telex 825763 – TV P. **151 rm.**
- **Luton Eurocrest** (Crest), Dunstable Rd, Waller Av., LU4 9RU, NW: 2 m. on A 505 ☎ 55911, Telex 825048 – TV wc P. **M** 3.00/3.50 **s.** 1.55 – 1.80 – **99 rm** 11.50/15.80 **s.**
- **Luton Crest Motel** (Crest), 641 Dunstable Rd, LU4 8RQ, NW: 2 ¾ m. on A 505 ☎ 55955 – TV wc P. **M** 4.10/4.25 **s.** 1.55 – 1.60 – **139 rm** 10.95/15.50 **s.**

AUSTIN-MG-WOLSELEY 691 Dunstable Rd ☎ 51408
AUSTIN-MG-WOLSELEY 51/61 Park St. ☎ 28521
BMW 82/88 Marsh Rd ☎ 56622
DAIMLER-JAGUAR-ROVER-TRIUMPH Park St. West ☎ 411311
DATSUN 619 Hitchin Rd ☎ 35332
FORD Chaul End Lane ☎ 31133
MORRIS-MG-WOLSELEY Leagrave Rd ☎ 51221
RENAULT Castle St. ☎ 28461
VAUXHALL 15 Hitchin Rd ☎ 22268
VAUXHALL Memorial Rd ☎ 52577
VAUXHALL 540/550 Dunstable Rd ☎ 55944

LUTTERWORTH Leics. – pop. 5,965 – ✉ Leicester – ✆ 045 55.

London 92 – Birmingham 34 – Leicester 15 – Northampton 24.

- Denbigh Arms, 24 High St., LE17 4AD, ☎ 3537 – TV wc P **25 rm.**

CHRYSLER-SIMCA Bitteswell Rd ☎ 2177

*To go a long way quickly, use **Michelin maps** at a scale of 1/1 000 000*

LYDFORD Devon – pop. 2,241 – ✉ Okehampton – ✆ 082 282.

Envir.: Gorge* *AC*, SW: 1 ½ m.

London 231 – Exeter 30 – Plymouth 23.

- **Castle Inn,** EX20 4BH, ☎ 242 **M** *(closed Christmas Day)* (buffet lunch) a la carte 3.50/4.95 **t.** 1.00 – **5 rm** 6.00/10.00 **t.**

LYDNEY Glos. 986 ㉛ – pop. 6,455 – ✉ Gloucester – ✆ 059 44.

9 ☎ 2614.

London 140 – Bristol 26 – Gloucester 19 – Newport 25.

- **Feathers,** High St., GL15 5DN, ☎ 2826 – wc P **M** *(closed Sunday)* a la carte 3.55/5.15 1.60 – **16 rm** 6.50/12.00.

AUSTIN-MG-ROVER-TRIUMPH Newerne St. ☎ 2446
AUSTIN-MORRIS-MG High St. ☎ 2481
DAF Bream ☎ 0594 (Whitecroft) 247
RENAULT Gloucester Rd ☎ 2364
TOYOTA Swan Rd ☎ 2131

LYME REGIS Dorset 986 ㊴ – pop. 3,403 – ✆ 029 74.

18 Timber Hill ☎ 2043.

i The Guildhall, Bridge St. ☎ 2138.

London 160 – Dorchester 25 – Exeter 31 – Taunton 27.

- **Alexandra,** Pound St., DT7 3HZ, ☎ 2010, ≤, – wc wc P *20 March-5 November* – **M** 3.50/4.40 **st.** 1.45 – **23 rm** 10.20/19.50 **st.**
- **Mariners,** Silver St., DT7 3HS, ☎ 2753, – wc P *February-October* – **M** 4.00/6.65 **s.** 1.70 – **16 rm** (dinner included) 11.95/23.90 **s.** – P 13.85/16.65 **s.**
- **Kersbrook,** Pound Rd, DT7 3HX, ☎ 2596, – P *Easter-September* – **8 rm** 4.50/10.50 **t.**
- **Toni's,** 14-15 Monmouth St., DT7 3PR, ☎ 2079, Italian rest. *Easter-September* – **M** *(closed Sunday)* (dinner only) a la carte 3.65/5.60 **t.** 1.50.

at Rousdon (Devon) W: 3 m. on A 3052 – ✉ ✆ 029 74 Lyme Regis:

- **Orchard Country,** DT7 3XW, ☎ 2972, – wc P *closed November* – **M** *(closed Monday lunch and Tuesday lunch from October to February)* approx. 3.45 **t.** 1.00 – **11 rm** 5.50/12.50 **t.** – P 11.05 **t.**

at Uplyme (Devon) NW: 1 ¼ m. on A 3070 – ✉ ✆ 029 74 Lyme Regis:

- **Devon,** DT7 3TQ, ☎ 3231, heated, , park – wc P *Easter-mid October* – **M** approx. 4.00 **st.** 1.50 – **21 rm** 9.50/19.00 **st.** – P 18.00 **st.**

LYMINGTON Hants. 986 ㉟ – pop. 35,733 – ☎ 0590.

to the Isle of Wight : Yarmouth (Sealink) Monday/Thursday 15 daily; Friday/Saturday/Sunday 7-28 daily (30 mn).

London 104 – Bournemouth 18 – **Southampton 19** – Winchester 32.

- **Stanwell House,** 15 High St., SO4 9AA, ☎ 77123 – wc
  M 4.10/5.10 **st.** 1.30 – **17 rm** 6.90/16.80 **st.**
- **Farino,** 53 New St., SO4 9BP, ☎ 77140, – P
  10 rm 6.00/9.00 **s.**
- **The Slipway,** The Quay, SO4 9AY, ☎ 74545, ≤
  closed Tuesday and Wednesday lunch – **M** a la carte 4.50/6.60 1.50.
- **Limpets,** 9 Gosport St., SO4 9BG, ☎ 75595, French rest.
  closed Monday, Sunday dinner from November to Easter and 4 weeks from Christmas – **M** (dinner only and Sunday lunch from November to Easter) a la carte 4.25/6.30 **t.** 1.60.
- **Flounders,** 5 Quay St., SO4 8LS, ☎ 77364, Bistro
  closed Sunday in winter, Monday and November – **M** (dinner only) a la carte 3.30/4.55 **t.** 1.40.

at Mount Pleasant NW : 2 m. off A 337 – ✉ Lymington – ☎ 059 068 Sway :

- **Passford House** , SO4 8LS, ☎ 2398, , heated, , park – TV wc P
  M approx. 4.50 1.50 – **40 rm** 10.50/19.00 – P 15.00/16.50.

at Sway NW : 4 m. off A 337 on B 3055 – ✉ Lymington – ☎ 059 068 Sway :

- **White Rose,** Station Rd, SO4 0BA, ☎ 2754, heated, – wc P
  M approx. 3.50 **t.** 1.25 – **11 rm** 7.50/20.00 **t.**
- **Pine Trees** , Mead End Rd, SO4 0EE, ☎ 2288, « Victoriana decor », – wc P
  closed 25 and 26 December – **M** (lunch by arrangement) 5.00/6.00 **st.** 1.20 – 0.75 – **7 rm** 9.00/15.00 **st.**

AUSTIN-MORRIS-MG-WOLSELEY 76 High St. ☎ 2378 VAUXHALL Bath Rd ☎ 3981
FIAT Sway ☎ 2212

LYMM Cheshire 986 ⑤ – pop. 10,497 – ☎ 092 575.

18 Whitbarrow Rd ☎ 2177.

London 193 – Chester 24 – **Liverpool 23** – **Manchester 15.**

- **Dingle,** 26 Rectory Lane, WA13 0AH, ☎ 2297, – TV wc wc P
  M *(closed Sunday dinner and Bank Holidays)* a la carte 4.50/7.10 2.00 – **32 rm** 11.50/16.50 – P 18.10.

LYNDHURST Hants. 986 ㉟ – pop. 2,948 – ☎ 042 128.

See : New Forest*.

18 ☎ 2450.

i Main Car Park ☎ 2269 (summer only).

London 95 – Bournemouth 20 – **Southampton 10** – Winchester 23.

- **Crown,** 9 High St., SO4 7NF, ☎ 2722, – TV P.
  M 4.90/6.40 **st.** – **48 rm** 12.00/22.00 **st.**
- **David Bell's Forest Lodge,** Pike's Hill, Romsey Rd, SO4 7AS, ☎ 2365, heated, – TV wc wc P
  closed February – **M** (residents only from October to January) 5.00/6.00 **st.** 1.75 – **12 rm** 10.50/22.00 **st.** – P 18.75/21.50 **st.**
- **Ormonde House,** Southampton Rd, SO4 7BN, ☎ 2806, – P
  closed January – **16 rm** 5.00/13.00 **st.**

AUSTIN-MORRIS-MG-WOLSELEY High St. ☎ 2861 OPEL Romsey Rd ☎ 2609

LYNMOUTH Devon 986 ㉟ – pop. 1,984 (inc. Lynton) – ☎ 059 85 Lynton.

See : Site*.

i Lee Rd, at Lynton ☎ 2225.

London 205 – Exeter 59 – Taunton 43.

- Tors , EX35 6NA, ☎ 3236, ≤ sea and bay, heated – wc P – *season* – **39 rm.**
- **Bath,** EX35 6EH, ☎ 2238 – wc P
  mid March-October – **M** 3.50/5.00 **st.** 1.30 – **26 rm** 5.25/16.00 **st.**

LYNTON Devon 986 ㉟ – ☎ 059 85.

i Lee Rd ☎ 2225.

London 206 – Exeter 59 – Taunton 44.

- **Lynton Cottage** , North Walk, EX35 6ED, ☎ 2342, ≤, – wc P
  mid March-October – **M** (bar lunch) approx. 4.00 1.00 – **22 rm** 10.25/18.50 **st.** – P 14.00/15.00 **st.**
- **Crown,** Sinai Hill, EX35 6AR, ☎ 2253 – wc P
  M a la carte 2.85/6.75 **st.** 2.00 – **18 rm** 7.75/17.00 **st.**

LYTHAM ST. ANNE'S Lancs. 986 ㉓ – pop. 40,299 – ☎ 0253 St. Anne's.
Lytham Hall Park, ☎ 736741, E : 2 m. – Ballam Rd ☎ 734782.
i The Square ☎ 725610 (summer only) – Town Hall ☎ 721222 (winter only).
London 237 – Blackpool 7 – Liverpool 44 – Preston 13.

Grand (Crest), 77 South Promenade, FY8 1NB, ☎ 722155 – wc
M approx. 3.20 **s.** 1.55 – **37 rm** 9.90/15.65 **s.**

at Lytham SE : 3 m. – ✉ ☎ 0253 Lytham :

Clifton Arms, West Beach, FY8 5QJ, ☎ 739898 –
M a la carte 3.55/7.30 **t.** 1.70 – **43 rm** 13.70/26.30 **t.** – P 18.85/20.20 **t.**

AUSTIN-DAIMLER-MG-WOLSELEY Kings Rd ☎ 728051
JAGUAR-MORRIS-MG Henry St. ☎ 736670

MACHYNLLETH Powys 986 ㉗ – pop. 1,768 – ☎ 0654.
Envir. : SE : Llyfnant Valley* via Glaspwll.
Maes-y-Gollen ☎ 2000.
i Tourist Information Centre, Owain Glyndwr Institute, Maengwyn St. ☎ 2401.
London 220 – Shrewsbury 56 – Welshpool 37.

Wynnstay (T.H.F.), Maengwyn St., SY80 8AE, ☎ 2003 – wc
M a la carte 3.95/5.35 **st.** 1.50 – **27 rm** 6.50/14.00 **st.**

at Eglwysfach SW : 6 m. off A 487 – ✉ Machynlleth – ☎ 065 474 Glandyfi :

Ynyshir Hall, SY20 8TA, ☎ 209, ≤, « Country house in large gardens », park –
wc
Easter-October – **M** *(closed Sunday dinner to non-residents)* (bar lunch) approx. 3.50
1.60 – **10 rm** 8.00/18.00.

at Pennal (Gwynedd) W : 4 ½ m. on A 493 – ✉ Machynlleth (Powys) – ☎ 065 475
Pennal :

Llugwy, SY20 9JX, ☎ 228, ≤, – TV wc
M (bar lunch) a la carte approx. 4.75 1.00 – **10 rm** 10.50/19.00.

Riverside, ☎ 285, –
M (bar lunch) – **7 rm.**

AUSTIN-MORRIS-MG-WOLSELEY ☎ 2108

MADINGLEY Cambs. – see Cambridge.

MAIDENCOMBE Devon – see Torquay.

MAIDENHEAD Berks. 986 ㊱ – pop. 45,288 – ☎ 0628.
i Central Library, St. Ives Rd ☎ 25657.
London 35 – Oxford 32 – Reading 13.

Maidenhead Eurocrest (Crest), Shoppenhangers Rd, SL6 2RA, ☎ 23444, Telex 847502
– TV wc .
M *(closed Saturday lunch)* 3.50/4.00 **s.** 1.70 – 1.75 – **194 rm** 14.60/19.00 **s.**

Bear (Anchor), 8-10 High St., SL6 1QJ, ☎ 25183, Group Telex 27120 –
M a la carte 4.00/5.10 **t.** 1.00 – **12 rm** 9.90/15.95 **st.**

XXX **Shoppenhangers Manor** (Crest) (at Maidenhead Eurocrest), Manor Lane, SL6 2RA
☎ 23444, –
closed Sunday and Bank Holidays – **M** a la carte 6.65/8.60 1.75.

XX **La Riva,** Ray Mead Rd, SL6 8NJ, ☎ 33522 –
closed Sunday – **M** a la carte 4.10/5.70 **t.**

XX **Michel et Valérie,** 7 Glynwood House, Bridge Av., SL6 1RS, ☎ 22450, French rest
closed Sunday and Bank Holidays – **M** a la carte 3.75/5.30 1.90.

AUSTIN-MORRIS-MG-WOLSELEY Braywick Rd ☎ 25321
BMW Altwood Rd ☎ 37611
DAIMLER-JAGUAR-MORRIS-MG-ROVER-TRIUMPH-WOLSELEY 128 Bridge Rd ☎ 32311
DAIMLER-JAGUAR Marshgate Trading Eastate, Taplow ☎ 2637
DATSUN, TOYOTA Littlewick Green ☎ 062 882 (Littlewick Green) 2572
FIAT Woodlands Park ☎ 062 882 (Littlewick Green) 321
FORD Bell St. ☎ 25111
FORD Bath Rd, Taplow ☎ 29711
PEUGEOT Furze Platt ☎ 27524
RENAULT 7 Bath Rd ☎ 21331
ROLLS ROYCE, VOLVO 34 Market St. ☎ 25371
VAUXHALL 128 Bridge Rd ☎ 32311

Les hôtels ou restaurants agréables
sont indiqués dans le guide par un signe rouge.
Aidez-nous en nous signalant les maisons où,
par expérience, vous savez qu'il fait bon vivre.
Votre guide Michelin 1979 sera encore meilleur.

XXXXX ... X

MAIDSTONE Kent 986 ㊱ – pop. 70,987 – ☎ 0622.

See: All Saints' Church* – Carriage Museum* *AC* – Chillington Manor (Museum and Art Gallery*). **Envir.:** Leeds Castle* *AC*, SE: 4 ½ m. – Aylesford (The Friars carmelite priory: great courtyard*) NW: 3 ½ m.

i The Gatehouse, Old Palace Gardens ☎ 671361.

London 38 – Brighton 51 – Cambridge 90 – Colchester 73 – Croydon 32 – **Dover 43** – Southend-on-Sea 47.

- **Royal Star** (Embassy), 15 High St., ME14 1JA, ☎ 55721 – TV wc wc ☎ P. – *closed Christmas* – **M** approx. 3.25 **st.** 1.75 – **37 rm** 8.80/13.75 **st.**
- XX **Dino's,** 14 London Rd, ME16 8QL, ☎ 52460, Italian rest. – P – *closed Sunday* – **M** a la carte 3.45/5.85 **t.** 1.25.

at Sandling **N: 1 ½ m. on A 229 – ✉ ☎ 0622 Maidstone:**

- **Veglios** without rest., Chatham Rd, ME14 3AP, ☎ 55459 – TV wc wc P – **28 rm** 7.50/12.00 **st.**

at Hollingbourne **SE: 5 m. off A 20 on B 2163 – ✉ Maidstone – ☎ 062 780 Hollingbourne:**

- **Great Danes** (Rank), Ashford Rd, ME17 1RE, S: 1 ¾ m. on A 20 ☎ 381, Telex 96198, park – TV P. – **M** a la carte 5.20/7.15 **s.** 1.35 – 2.00 – **78 rm** 13.30/18.80 **s.**

MICHELIN Branch, St. Michaels Close, Forstal Trading Estate, Aylesford, ME20 7HR, ☎ 76228.

AUSTIN-DAIMLER-JAGUAR-MORRIS-MG-ROVER-TRIUMPH Bircholt Rd ☎ 65461
AUSTIN-MORRIS-MG-WOLSELEY Ashford Rd ☎ 54744
CHRYSLER-SIMCA Mill St. ☎ 53333
FIAT 29 Union St. ☎ 52071
FORD Ashford Rd ☎ 56781
MERCEDES-BENZ, PEUGEOT, ROLLS ROYCE 215/233 Sutton Rd ☎ 55531
PEUGEOT Sutton Rd ☎ 61161
OPEL-VAUXHALL Park Wood, Sutton Rd ☎ 55531
RENAULT Sutton Rd ☎ 50881
VAUXHALL London Rd, Ditton ☎ 0732 (West Malling) 843227

MALDON Essex 986 ㉜ – pop. 13,891 – ☎ 0621.

London 42 – Chelmsford 9 – Colchester 17.

- **Blue Boar** (T.H.F.), Silver St., CM9 7QE, ☎ 52681 – TV wc ☎ P – **M** a la carte 4.30/5.35 **st.** 1.50 – **25 rm** 11.50/17.00 **st.**

AUSTIN-MORRIS-MG-WOLSELEY Heybridge ☎ 52468
BMW, FIAT Spital Rd ☎ 52131
CHRYSLER ☎ 2172
FORD 1 Spital Rd ☎ 2345
VAUXHALL 127/131 High St. ☎ 52424

MALLWYD Gwynedd 986 ㉗ – pop. 459 – ✉ Machynlleth (Powys) – ☎ 065 04 Dinas Mawddwy.

Envir.: N: Road* from Dinas Mawddwy to Pandy – Aberangell Clipiau (site*) SE: 3 m. – NW: Road* from Cross Foxes Hotel to Dinas Mawddwy.

London 209 – Aberystwyth 29 – Dolgellau 12 – Shrewsbury 45.

- **Brigands Inn,** SY20 9HJ, ☎ 208, – wc P – *April-October and Christmas* – **M** approx. 4.50 **s.** 0.90 – **13 rm** 5.75/13.50 **t.** – P 11.25/13.25 **s.**

MALMESBURY Wilts. 986 ㉟ – pop. 2,527 – ☎ 066 62.

See: Abbey Church* 12C-14C (porch**). **Envir.:** Badminton House* (17C) *AC*, SW: 10 m. – Dodington House (Renaissance) *AC*, SW: 15 m.

London 108 – Bristol 28 – Gloucester 24 – Swindon 19.

- **Old Bell,** Abbey Row, SN16 0BW, ☎ 2344, – TV wc P. – **M** (buffet lunch) a la carte 4.00/5.70 **t.** 1.65 – **19 rm** 9.00/19.00 **t.**
- X **Suffolk Arms,** Tetbury Hill, SN16 9JW, on B 4014 ☎ 2271 – P – *closed Sunday dinner and 25-26 December* – **M** a la carte 3.10/6.20 **t.** 1.60.

at Easton Grey W: 2 m. on B 4040 – ✉ ☎ 066 62 Malmesbury:

- **Whatley Manor** , SN16 0PL, ☎ 2888, ≤, « Tasteful decor and furnishings », heated, , park – TV wc ☎ P – **M** a la carte 5.75/9.50 **t.** 1.30 – **8 rm** 25.00/33.00 **t.**

AUSTIN-MG-WOLSELEY Bristol Rd ☎ 2211
PEUGEOT Gloucester Rd ☎ 3434

MALTON North Yorks. 986 ㉔ – pop. 3,986 – ☎ 0653.

Envir.: Castle Howard** (18C) *AC*, SW: 6 m. – Flamingo Park Zoo* *AC*, N: 4 ½ m.

18 Welham Park ☎ 2959.

London 229 – Kingston-upon-Hull 36 – Scarborough 24 – York 17.

- **Talbot** (T.H.F.), Yorkersgate, YO17 0AS, ☎ 4031 – TV wc ☎ P – **M** a la carte 4.00/6.00 **st.** 1.50 – **24 rm** 7.00/14.50 **st.** – P 11.50/15.00 **st.**

AUSTIN-MORRIS-MG-WOLSELEY Wintringham ☎ 094 42 (Rillington) 242
AUSTIN-MG-WOLSELEY 4 Welham Rd ☎ 2165
BMW, VAUXHALL York Rd ☎ 2252
VOLVO Horse Market Rd ☎ 3019

MALVERN Heref. and Worc. 986 ㉛ – pop. 29,051 – ☎ 068 45.

See : Great Malvern (Priory Church* **11C**).

Wood Farm, Malvern Wells ☎ 3905, NE : 5 m.

i Grange Rd ☎ 4700 ext 276 or 279.

London 127 – Birmingham 34 – Cardiff 66 – Gloucester 24.

Foley Arms (Interchange), 14 Worcester Rd, WR14 4QW, ☎ 3397, ≤, – wc ☎ **P**.
M a la carte 4.80/6.15 **st.** 1.50 – **27 rm** 10.00/22.00 **st.** – P 14.00/18.00 **st.**

Gold Hill, Avenue Rd, WR14 3AL, ☎ 4000, – wc wc **P**
M approx. 3.50 **t.** 0.75 – **21 rm** 5.50/13.75 **t.** – P 10.50/14.00 **t.**

Walmer Lodge, 49 Abbey Rd, WR14 3HH, ☎ 4139,
M *(closed Sunday and Monday to non-residents)* (dinner only) a la carte 3.80/4.5
1.05 – **10 rm** 4.50/13.00.

Thornbury, Avenue Rd, WR14 3AR, ☎ 2278, – **P**
M (cold lunch) 2.70/5.00 1.10 – **20 rm** 5.40/12.80 – P 8.40.

Bredon House, 34 Worcester Rd, WR14 4AA, ☎ 5323, ≤, – **P**
8 rm 4.50/9.00 **st.**

Cotford, Graham Rd, WR14 2JW, ☎ 2427, – **P**
11 rm 5.50/6.00 **st.**

at Welland SE : 4 ½ m. on B 4208 – ✉ Malvern – ☎ 068 43 Hanley Swan :

Holdfast Cottage, , WR13 6NA, W : ¾ m. ☎ 288, – **P**
mid April-October – **8 rm** 6.50/13.00.

at Malvern Wells S : 2 m. by A 449 – ✉ ☎ 068 45 Malvern :

Cottage in the Wood , Holywell Rd, WR14 4LG, ☎ 3487, ≤ Severn and Evesham Vales, – wc ☎ **P**
closed 24 December-1 January – **M** 5.00/5.75 **s.** 1.50 – 1.75 – **20 rm** 10.00 20.00 **s.**

at Wynds Point S : 4 m. on A 449 – ✉ Malvern – ☎ 0684 Colwall :

Malvern Hills, WR13 6DW, ☎ 40237 – **P**
M (buffet lunch except Sunday) 4.75/9.00 **st.** 1.50 – **14 rm** 9.50/16.50 **st.** –
P 15.25/20.25 **st.**

at West Malvern W : 2 m. on B 4232 – ✉ ☎ 068 45 Malvern :

Broomhill, West Malvern Rd, WR14 4AY, ☎ 64367, ≤ hills and countryside, – **P**
March-October – **M** (dinner only) 3.00 1.30 – **12 rm** 5.00/11.00.

CITROEN 62 Court Rd ☎ 3393
DAIMLER-JAGUAR-ROVER-TRIUMPH Worcester Rd ☎ 3301
SIMCA Leigh Sinton ☎ 0886 (Leigh Sinton) 32351
VAUXHALL Link Top ☎ 3336
VOLVO Pickersleigh Rd ☎ 61498

MANCHESTER Greater Manchester 986 ⑤ and ㉓ – pop. 543,650 – ☎ 061.

See : Town Hall* **19C** DZ **H** – City Art Gallery* DZ **M** – Whitworth Art Gallery* BY **M** – Cathedral **15C** (chancel*) DZ **B** – John Ryland's Library (manuscripts*) CZ **A. Envir. :** Heaton Hall* (**18C**) *AC*, N : 5 m. AX **M.**

Heaton Park, ☎ 061 773 (Prestwich) 1085, N : by A 576 ABX – Ford Lane, Northenden ☎ 998 2743, S : by A 34 BY – Booth Rd, Audenshaw ☎ 370 1641, E : by A 635 BY – Woodhouses, Failsworth ☎ 681 4534, N : 5 m. BX.

☎ 437 5233, S : 15 m. by A 5103 AY and M 56 – **Terminal :** Victoria Station.

i County Hall Extension, Piccadilly Gardens ☎ 247 3694 – Town Hall ☎ 236 3377.

London 201 – Birmingham 86 – Glasgow 216 – Leeds 42 – Liverpool 36 – Nottingham 69.

Plans on following pages

Piccadilly (Embassy), Piccadilly Plaza, M60 1QR, ☎ 236 8414, Telex 668765, ≤ – **P**. DZ **s**
closed Christmas – **M** a la carte 5.50/8.75 **st.** 1.70 – 2.35 – **245 rm** 18.00/23.00 **st.**

Midland (B.T.H.), Peter St., M60 2DS, ☎ 236 3333, Telex 667797 – . CDZ **n**
closed 2 days at Christmas – **M** 4.45/5.10 **st.** 1.40 (see also **French Restaurant**) – **308 rm** 21.50/32.25 **st.**

Portland (Thistle), Piccadilly Gardens, M1 6DP, ☎ 228 3567, Telex 669157 – . DZ **v**
221 rm.

Grand (T.H.F.), Aytoun St., M1 3DR, ☎ 236 9559, Telex 667580 – . DZ **u**
M 4.20/4.70 **st.** 1.45 – 2.00 – **146 rm** 14.00/20.50 **st.**

XXX **French Restaurant** (at Midland H.) (B.T.H.), Peter St., M60 2DS, ☎ 236 3333, Telex 667797 CDZ **n**
closed Sunday, August, 3 days at Christmas and Bank Holidays – **M** a la carte 7.20/10.25 **st.** 🍾 1.40.

XXX **L'Elysée,** 44 Princess St., M1 6DE, ☎ 236 1652, French rest. DZ **x**
M a la carte 3.85/7.15 🍾 1.40.

XXX **Via Veneto,** 35 George St., M1 4HQ, ☎ 236 4887, Italian rest. DZ **z**
closed Saturday lunch and Sunday – **M** a la carte 4.30/5.70.

XXX **Terrazza,** 14 Nicholas St., M1 4FE, ☎ 236 4033, Italian rest. DZ **r**
closed Sunday – **M** a la carte 4.80/8.30 **t.** 🍾 2.65.

XX **Isola Bella,** 6a Booth St., M2 4AW, ☎ 236 6417, Italian rest. DZ **e**
closed Sunday and Bank Holidays – **M** a la carte 4.10/8.20 🍾 1.30.

XX **Royal Exchange,** 1st floor, St. Ann's Sq., M2 7DH, ☎ 833 9682 DZ **c**
closed Sunday and Christmas Day – **M** a la carte 3.45/5.80 **t.** 🍾 1.70.

XX **Casa España,** 100 Wilmslow Rd, M14 5AJ, S : 2 m. on A 34 ☎ 224 6826, Spanish rest.
closed Sunday and Bank Holidays – **M** a la carte 3.20/5.55. BY **v**

XX **Manzil,** 328-344 Stockport Rd, M13 0LE, SE : 2 m. on A 6 ☎ 273 3688, Indian rest. – Ⓟ BY **a**
closed Christmas Day – **M** 3.25/4.00 **st.**

X Don Luigi, 48 Princess St. ☎ 236 2860, Italian rest. DZ **x**

X **Woo Sang,** 1st floor, 19-21 George St., M1 4AG, ☎ 236 3697, Chinese rest. DZ **a**
M a la carte 3.50/5.60 **t.**

X **Danish Food Centre** (Copenhagen Room), Cross St., M2 7BY, ☎ 832 9924, Smorrebrod DZ **n**
closed Sunday and Bank Holidays – **M** a la carte 3.50/6.60 **st.** 🍾 1.65.

at Whalley Range S : 2 ½ m. – ⊠ ⊙ **061 Manchester :**

🏠 **Simpson's,** 122 Withington Rd, M16 8FB, ☎ 226 2235, 🚗 – 🛁wc ☎ Ⓟ AY **a**
closed 24 December to 1 January – **M** a la carte 3.30/4.85 🍾 1.35 – **38 rm** ☕ 8.50/13.00.

at Fallowfield S : 3 m. on B 5093 – ⊠ ⊙ **061 Manchester :**

🏨 **Willow Bank,** 340-342 Wilmslow Rd, M14 6AF, ☎ 224 0461 – TV 🛁wc ☎ Ⓟ BY **x**
M approx. 3.00 **s.** 🍾 1.25 – ☕ 2.00 – **122 rm** 6.50/13.50 **s.**

🏨 Brookhouse, 393 Wilmslow Rd, M20 9WA, ☎ 224 2015 – TV 🛁wc ☎ Ⓟ BY **z**
M a la carte 4.65/7.70 **s.** 🍾 1.75 – ☕ 1.35 – **38 rm.**

🏠 **Lansdowne,** 346 Wilmslow Rd, M14 6AB, ☎ 224 6244, Telex 667822 – 🛁wc 🚿wc ☎ Ⓟ BY **r**
M (buffet lunch) 3.50/5.50 🍾 0.80 – **51 rm** ☕ 9.50/12 50 **t.**

X **Armenian Rest. and Granada Hotel** with rm, 404 Wilmslow Rd, M20 9BN, ☎ Rest. 434 3480, Hotel ☎ 445 5908 – Ⓟ BY **c**
M *(closed Saturday lunch, Sunday lunch, Good Friday, Easter Sunday and 25-26 December)* a la carte 3.60/6.10 🍾 1.15 – **11 rm** ☕ 5.50/9.50 **st.**

at Withington S : 4 m. by B 5093 – BY – ⊠ ⊙ **061 Manchester :**

🏠 **Elm Grange,** 561 Wilmslow Rd, M20 9GJ, ☎ 445 3336 – 🛁wc ☎ Ⓟ
M 2.25/3.50 🍾 1.25 – **26 rm** ☕ 5.50/13.00.

at Northenden S : 6 ½ m. by A 5103 – AY – ⊠ ⊙ **061 Manchester :**

🏨 **Post House** (T.H.F.), Palatine Rd, M22 4FH, ☎ 998 7090, Telex 669248 – 🛗 TV 🛁wc ☎ ♿ Ⓟ. 🏛
M 2.95/4.00 **st.** 🍾 1.50 – ☕ 2.00 – **201 rm** 14.00/20.00 **st.**

at Manchester Airport S : 9 m. by A 5103 – AY – and M 56 – ⊠ ⊙ **061 Manchester :**

🏨 **Excelsior** (T.H.F.), M22 5NS, ☎ 437 5811, Telex 668721, 🏊 heated – 🛗 TV ♿ Ⓟ. 🏛
M a la carte 5.40/9.05 **st.** 🍾 1.50 – ☕ 2.00 – **255 rm** 16.00/22.00 **st.**

ICHELIN Branch, Ferris St., off Louisa St., Openshaw, M11 1BS, ☎ 223 2010 and 3274.

LFA-ROMEO 250 Plymouth Grove ☎ 224 3325
USTIN-DAIMLER-JAGUAR-MG-WOLSELEY 776/8 hester Rd ☎ 865 4433
USTIN-MG-WOLSELEY 156 Barlow Moor Rd ☎ 4 1133
USTIN-MG-WOLSELEY Moseley Rd ☎ 224 6265
USTIN-MORRIS-MG-ROVER-TRIUMPH-WOLSELEY 1 Wilmslow Rd ☎ 224 2894
USTIN-MG-WOLSELEY 186 Bury New Rd ☎ 792 2261
USTIN-MG-WOLSELEY Gill St. ☎ 205 2792
MW, OPEL Gt Bridgewater St. ☎ 832 8781
HRYSLER-SIMCA Chester Rd ☎ 834 6677
HRYSLER-SIMCA 81/85 Barlow Moor Rd ☎ 445 7818
HRYSLER-SIMCA 199 Wilmslow Rd ☎ 224 7282
TROEN 66 Port St. ☎ 236 1341
AF 1 Midland St. ☎ 273 4425
ATSUN 770 Chester Rd ☎ 865 1151
ATSUN Victoria Rd ☎ 330 3840
ATSUN 845 Manchester Rd ☎ 766 3089
ORD 391 Palatine Rd ☎ 998 3427
ORD Oxford Rd ☎ 224 7301
ORD 660 Chester Rd ☎ 872 7711
FORD 3/5 New Wakefield St. ☎ 236 4168
MERCEDES-BENZ, VW, AUDI-NSU 345 Chapel St., Salford ☎ 832 7871
MORRIS-MG-WOLSELEY 267 Palatine Rd ☎ 998 3201
MORRIS-MG-WOLSELEY 654 Chester Rd ☎ 832 8781
MORRIS-MG-WOLSELEY Kenyon Lane ☎ 681 3084
OPEL Middleton Rd ☎ 740 2812
PEUGEOT 22 Rochdale Rd ☎ 833 0752
RENAULT Blackfriars Rd ☎ 832 6121
RENAULT 412 Ashton Old Rd ☎ 273 2101
ROLLS ROYCE-BENTLEY Carnavon St. ☎ 833 0548
ROVER-TRIUMPH 208 Bury New Rd ☎ 792 4343
TOYOTA New Cross Oldham Rd ☎ 832 7466
VAUXHALL 141 Waterloo Rd ☎ 792 4321
VAUXHALL Blackfriars Rd ☎ 834 8200
VAUXHALL 80/90 Port St., Gt Ancoats St. ☎ 236 4311
VAUXHALL 94 Whithington Rd ☎ 226 1122
VAUXHALL Egerton Rd ☎ 224 1114
VAUXHALL 799 Chester Rd ☎ 872 2141
VAUXHALL 674 Wilmslow Rd ☎ 445 6414
VAUXHALL Manchester Rd, Denton ☎ 336 3911
VOLVO Rowsley St. ☎ 223 7272

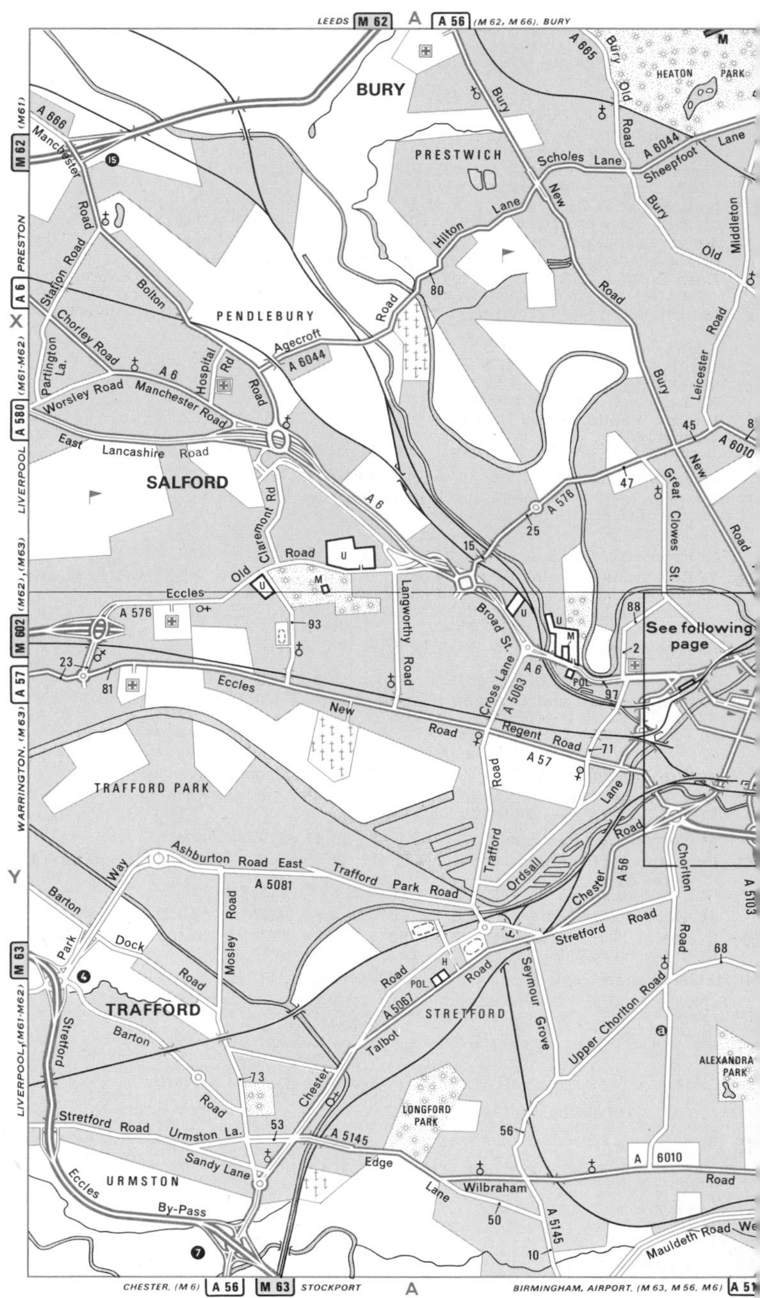
LEEDS M 62
A
A 56 (M 62, M 66), BURY
BURY
PRESTWICH
HEATON PARK
PENDLEBURY
SALFORD
TRAFFORD PARK
TRAFFORD
STRETFORD
URMSTON
LONGFORD PARK
ALEXANDRA PARK
See following page
M 62
A 6 PRESTON
X
A 580 LIVERPOOL
M 602
A 57 WARRINGTON, (M 63)
Y
M 63 LIVERPOOL, (M61-M62)
CHESTER, (M 6) A 56
M 63 STOCKPORT
BIRMINGHAM, AIRPORT, (M 63, M 56, M6)

MANCHESTER
BUILT UP AREA

0 — 1 km
0 — 1 mile

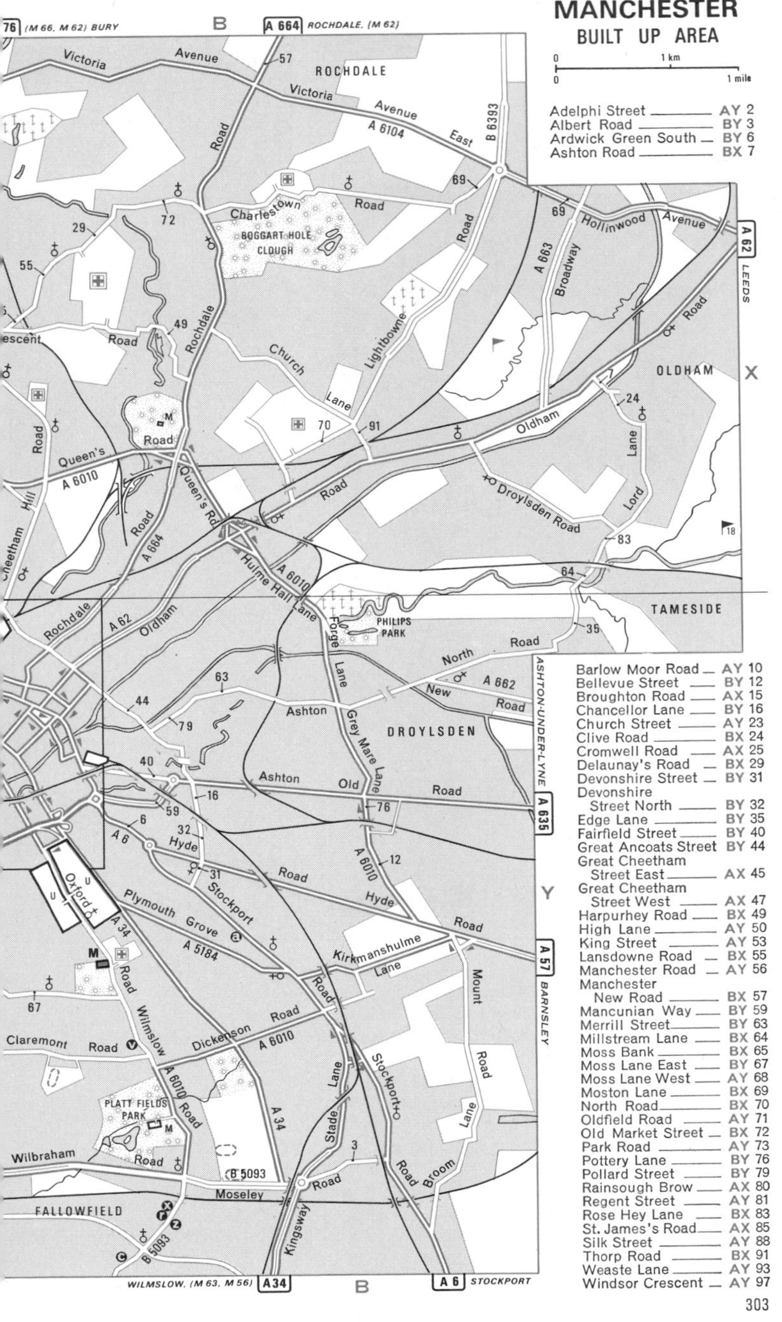

MANCHESTER
CENTRE

0 — 400 m
0 — 400 yards

Street	Grid
Deansgate	CZ
Lower Mosley Street	DZ
Market Place, Market Street	DZ
Mosley Street	DZ
Princess Street	DZ

Street	Grid
Albert Square	CDZ 4
Aytoun Street	DZ 8
Blackfriars Street	CZ 13
Charlotte Street	DZ 17
Cheetham Hill Road	DZ 19
Chorlton Street	DZ 20
Church Street	DZ 21
Dale Street	DZ 27
Dawson Street	CZ 28
Ducie Street	DZ 33
Egerton Street	CZ 36
Fairfield Street	DZ 39

Street	Grid
Great Ducie Street	CZ
John Dalton Street	CZ
King Street	DZ
Medlock Street	CZ
Parker Street	DZ
Peter Street	CZ
St. Ann's Street	CZ
St. Peter's Square	DZ
Spring Gardens	DZ
Viaduct Street	CZ
Whitworth Street West	CZ
Windmill Street	CZ

Carte — In den Hotels und Restaurants, für die ein Menu zu festem Preis angegeben ist, kann man jedoch im allgemeinen auch nach der Karte essen.

MANORBIER Dyfed – pop. **1,168** – ☎ 083 482.
See : Castle* (13C) *AC.* **Envir. :** Freshwater West (site*) W: 5 m.
London 253 – Carmarthen 33 – Haverfordwest 18.

- **Castle Mead** ⌂, SA70 7TA, ☎ 358, ≤ Manorbier Bay, ⌂ – wc Ⓟ
  Easter-October – **M** (bar lunch) approx. 3.00 **st.** ⌂ 1.30 – **11 rm** ⌂ 6.00/14.50 **st**

at Jameston W: 2 m. on A 4139 – ✉ ☎ 083 482 Manorbier:

- **Tudor Lodge** ⌂, SA70 7SS, ☎ 320, ⌂ – Ⓟ
  Easter-October – **M** (dinner only) 3.50/5.00 **t.** ⌂ 1.50 – **10 rm** ⌂ (dinner included) 9.00/18.00.

MARGARETTING Essex – see Ingatestone.

MARHAMCHURCH Cornwall – see Bude.

MARKET DEEPING Lincs. 986 ㉘ – pop. 2,816 – ✆ 0778.
London 94 – Cambridge 44 – Leicester 41 – Lincoln 42.

Deeping Stage, Market Pl., PE6 8EA, ☎ 343234 – P
8 rm.

MARKET DRAYTON Salop 986 ⑨ and ㉗ – pop. 7,088 – ✆ 0630.
London 161 – Birmingham 44 – Chester 33 – Shrewsbury 19 – Stoke-on-Trent 16.

Corbet Arms, High St., TF9 1PY, ☎ 2037 – TV wc P
M 2.40/2.70 **s.** 1.00 – **8 rm** 9.00/15.00 **st.**

AUSTIN-MG-WOLSELEY Shrewsbury Rd ☎ 4257
CHRYSLER-SIMCA, MAZDA Shrewsbury Rd ☎ 2027
DAIMLER-MORRIS-MG-ROVER-TRIUMPH-WOLSELEY Cheshire St. ☎ 2444
VOLVO Queen St. ☎ 2462
VW, AUDI-NSU, DAF, MERCEDES-BENZ Shrewsbury Rd ☎ 3861

MARKET HARBOROUGH Leics. 986 ㉜ – pop. 14,539 – ✆ 0858.
i Public Library, 53 The Square ☎ 2649.
London 87 – Birmingham 47 – Leicester 15 – Northampton 17.

XX **Three Swans** with rm, 21 High St., LE16 7NJ, ☎ 3247 – wc P
M a la carte 4.15/5.55 – **13 rm** 8.00/12.00.

XX **Peacock Inn,** St. Mary's Rd, LE16 7QT, ☎ 2269 – P
closed Sunday dinner – **M** a la carte 3.90/5.50 **t.** 1.50.

at Marston Trussell W : 3 ¼ m. by A 427 – ✉ ✆ 0858 Market Harborough :

Sun Inn, LE16 9TY, ☎ 5531 – wc P
M a la carte 3.90/7.00 **st.** – **10 rm** 10.50/13.50 **st.**

AUSTIN-MORRIS-MG-WOLSELEY, FORD Leicester Rd ☎ 4281
DAIMLER-JAGUAR-ROVER-TRIUMPH Northampton Rd ☎ 5511
FORD Leicester Rd ☎ 4821

MARKS TEY Essex – see Colchester.

MARLBOROUGH Wilts. 986 ㉟ – pop. 6,108 – ✆ 067 25.
See : Marlborough College* 17C. **Envir. :** Avebury (stone circles**) W : 6 m.
18 The Common ☎ 2147, N : 1 m.
London 84 – Bristol 47 – Southampton 40 – Swindon 12.

Ailesbury Arms, High St., SN8 1AB, ☎ 3451, – TV wc wc P
M 3.00/4.00 **t.** – 1.00 – **30 rm** 7.60/16.00 **t.** – P 11.50/13.50 **t.**

Castle and Ball (T.H.F.), High St., SN8 1DZ, ☎ 2002 – TV wc P
M a la carte 4.05/5.40 **st.** 1.50 – **30 rm** 8.00/15.50 **st.**

at Burbage SE : 5 ½ m. off A 346 – ✉ Marlborough – ✆ 0672 Burbage :

Savernake Forest (Interchange), SN8 3AY, ☎ 810206, – wc P
M (buffet lunch) a la carte 1.55/4.55 0.95 – **14 rm** 7.00/16.00 **t.**

AUSTIN-JAGUAR-MG-ROVER-TRIUMPH London Rd ☎ 2381
MERCEDES-BENZ George Lane ☎ 3535
MORRIS-MG-WOLSELEY 80/83 High St. ☎ 2076
RENAULT London Rd ☎ 2564

MARLOW Bucks. 986 ㊱ – pop. 11,749 – ✆ 062 84.
i Court Garden, Pound Lane ☎ 72033/4.
London 35 – Aylesbury 22 – Oxford 29 – Reading 14.

Compleat Angler, Marlow Bridge, SL7 1RG, ☎ 4444, Telex 848644, < river Thames, « Riverside setting and gardens », – TV P.
M a la carte 5.70/8.90 **s.** 1.50 – 2.50 – **42 rm** 19.50/28.00 **s.**

XX **Cavaliers,** 24-26 West St., SL7 2NB, ☎ 2544
closed Monday lunch – **M** a la carte 5.65/7.45 **t.** 1.40.

X Dino's Trattoria La Veneziana, 5 High St. ☎ 4919, Italian rest.

at Bisham S : 1 m. on B 482 – ✉ ✆ 062 84 Marlow :

XX **Bull,** Marlow Rd, SL7 1RR, ☎ 4734 – P
M a la carte 3.90/5.90 1.75.

AUSTIN-MORRIS-MG-WOLSELEY West St. ☎ 2215

MARPLE Greater Manchester 986 ⑤ – pop. 23,665 – ✉ Stockport – ✆ 061 Manchester.
London 202 – Manchester 11 – Sheffield 37.

West Towers, Church Lane, SK6 7LB, ☎ 427 2968 – wc wc P
38 rm.

MARSTON TRUSSELL Leics. – see Market Harborough.

MARTOCK Somerset – pop. 2,703 – ✆ 093 582.

London 139 – Taunton 22 – Yeovil 9.

- **White Hart,** Market Sq., TA12 6JQ, ☎ 2246 – Ⓟ
  M (bar lunch) a la carte 2.10/3.10 – **9 rm** 4.50/9.00.

AUSTIN-MG-WOLSELEY ☎ 2547

MARTON Cleveland – see Middlesbrough.

MATLOCK BATH Derbs. 986 ㉗ – pop. 1,107 – ✆ 0629 Matlock.

See: Site★. **Envir.:** Haddon Hall★★ (14C-16C) *AC*, NW: 6 m. – Riber Castle (ruins) ≤★ (Faun Reserve and Wildlife Park *AC*) SE: 2½ m.

i The Pavilion ☎ 55082.

London 152 – Derby 18 – Manchester 45 – Nottingham 25 – Sheffield 23.

- **New Bath** (T.H.F.), New Bath Rd, DE4 3PX, ☎ 3275, heated, – wc Ⓟ.
  M 4.00/4.50 **st.** 1.50 – **56 rm** 14.00/20.00 **st.**

AUSTIN-MORRIS-MG-ROVER-TRIUMPH-WOLSELEY Bakewell Rd ☎ 3291
FORD 41 Causeway Lane ☎ 2231
VAUXHALL Bakewell Rd ☎ 2131

MAWNAN SMITH Cornwall – see Falmouth.

MAYFIELD East Sussex – pop. 3,847 – ✆ 043 55.

London 46 – Brighton 25 – Eastbourne 22 – Lewes 17 – Royal Tunbridge Wells 9.

- **Middle House,** High St., TN20 6AB, ☎ 2146, – Ⓟ
  M 4.50/6.00 **s.** 1.20 – **7 rm** 7.00/15.00 **s.**

MORRIS-MG-WOLSELEY High St. ☎ 3386

MEAL BANK Cumbria – see Kendal.

MEASHAM Leics. – pop. 3,620 – ✆ 0530.

London 119 – Birmingham 26 – Derby 18 – Leicester 18 – Nottingham 25.

- **Measham Inn,** Tamworth Rd, DE12 7DY, ☎ 70095 – wc Ⓟ.
  M a la carte 2.45/4.85 **t.** 1.10 – **32 rm** 8.00/13.00 **t.**

AUSTIN-MORRIS-MG-WOLSELEY High St. ☎ 70545

MELBOURN Cambs. – pop. 2,851 – ✉ ✆ 0763 Royston (Herts.).

London 44 – Cambridge 10.

- **Pink Geranium,** 25 Station Rd, SG8 6JP, ☎ 60215 – Ⓟ
  closed Sunday, Monday and last 2 weeks August – **M** (dinner only) a la carte 3.35/4.35

MELTON MOWBRAY Leics. 986 ㉘ – pop. 19,336 – ✆ 0664.

Thorpe Arnold ☎ 2118, NE: 2 m.

i Carnegie Museum, Thorpe End ☎ 69946.

London 113 – Leicester 15 – Northampton 45 – Nottingham 18.

- **King's Head,** Nottingham St., LE13 1NW, ☎ 2110 – wc wc Ⓟ.
  M approx. 3.30 1.20 – **13 rm** 6.50/13.00.
- **Bell,** 2 Nottingham St., LE13 1NW, ☎ 2026 – wc Ⓟ
  M approx. 2.90 **st.** – **14 rm** 6.35/12.70 **st.**
- **Harboro** (Anchor), Burton St., LE13 1AF, ☎ 2529, Group Telex 27120 – wc Ⓟ
  M approx. 2.90 **t.** 1.00 – **18 rm** 8.80/14.85 **st.**
- **Westbourne,** 11a Nottingham Rd, LE13 0NP, ☎ 3556 – Ⓟ
  11 rm 3.75/7.50 **st.**

CHRYSLER Scalford ☎ 066 476 (Scalford) 278
FIAT Mill St. ☎ 2559
MORRIS-MG-ROVER-TRIUMPH-WOLSELEY 16 Burton St. ☎ 3394
SIMCA Albert St. ☎ 2235
VOLVO 56 Scalford Rd ☎ 3241

MENAI BRIDGE Gwynedd 986 ㉗ – pop. 2,612 – ✆ 0248.

See: Menai Strait★ (channel), Menai Suspension Bridge ≤★. **Envir.:** Bryn Celli Du (buria chamber★) SW: 3½ m.

i Wales Tourist Information Centre, Coed Cyrnol ☎ 712626 (Easter-September).

London 249 – Birkenhead 70 – Holyhead 21 – Shrewsbury 85.

- Anglesey Arms, LL59 5EA, on A 5 ☎ 712305, – wc Ⓟ – **17 rm.**

  at Glyngarth NE: 2 m. on A 545 – ✉ ✆ 0248 Menai Bridge:

- Gazelle, LL59 5PD, ☎ 713364, ≤ Menai Straits and hills – Ⓟ
  M (Sunday, residents only) approx. 3.45 **t.** – **14 rm.**

MENTMORE Bucks. – pop. 208 – ✉ Leighton Buzzard – ☎ 0296 Cheddington.
London 46 – Aylesbury 10 – Luton 15.

XX **Stag Inn,** The Green, LU7 0QG, ☎ 668423 – Ⓟ
closed Monday – **M** a la carte 3.70/6.15 🍷 1.50.

MERE Wilts. – pop. 2,085 – ☎ 074 786.
i The Square ☎ 341.
London 113 – Exeter 65 – Salisbury 26 – Taunton 40.

Old Ship, Castle St., BA12 6JE, on A 303 ☎ 258 – TV wc ☎ Ⓟ
M approx. 3.25 **st.** 🍷 1.00 – **24 rm** 7.50/14.50 **st.**

AUSTIN-MG-ROVER-TRIUMPH ☎ 244
CITROEN Castle St. ☎ 404

MERIDEN West Midlands – see Coventry.

MERTHYR TYDFIL Mid Glam. 986 ㉛ – pop. 55,317 – ☎ 0685.
9 Cilsanws Mountain, Cefn Coed ☎ 3308.
i Sports and Leisure Centre ☎ 71491.
London 181 – Brecon 17 – **Cardiff 24 – Swansea 30.**

Baverstock's, Heads of the Valleys Rd, CF47 8DE, W: 3 m. on A 465 by A 4102 – TV wc ☎ Ⓟ.
M 3.00/3.40 – **26 rm** 9.00/15.00.

AUSTIN-MORRIS-MG-ROVER-TRIUMPH ☎ 2611
FORD Pentrebach Rd ☎ 3442

MEVAGISSEY Cornwall 986 ㊳ – pop. 2,151 – ☎ 072 684.
London 286 – Plymouth 43 – Truro 19.

Tremarne , Polkirt Hill, PL26 6UY, ☎ 2213, heated – wc Ⓟ
Easter-mid October – **M** (*mid May-mid October*) (dinner only) approx. 3.75 🍷 1.20 – **15 rm** 7.50/16.50.

Treloen, Polkirt Hill, PL26 6UX, ☎ 2406, <, – Ⓟ
closed January – **M** a la carte 2.20/4.50 **s.** 🍷 1.95 – **12 rm** 6.95/17.90 **s.**

MICKLETON Glos. – see Chipping Campden.

MIDDLESBROUGH Cleveland 986 ⑲ – pop. 157,740 – ☎ 0642.
18 Brass Castle Lane ☎ 36430, S: 3 m. by A 172 BZ.
✈ Tees-side Airport : ☎ 032 573 (Dinsdale) 2811, SW: 13 m. by A 66 AZ and A 19 on A 67.
i 125 Albert Rd ☎ 245750 ext 3580.
London 250 – **Kingston-upon-Hull 85 – Leeds 61 – Newcastle-upon-Tyne 39.**

Plan on next page

Ladbroke Dragonara, Fry St., TS1 1JH, ☎ 248133, Telex 58266 – TV Ⓟ. BY c
M a la carte 3.45/5.65 **s.** 🍷 1.95 – 2.30 – **207 rm** 13.50/20.00 **s.**

Middlesbrough Crest Motel (Crest), Marton Way, TS4 3BS, S: 2 m. on A 172 ☎ 87651 – TV wc ☎ Ⓟ. BZ a
M 2.50/3.50 **s.** 🍷 1.55 – 1.60 – **53 rm** 10.95/15.50 **s.**

at Marton SE: 4 m. on A 172 – BZ – ✉ ☎ 0642 Middlesbrough:

Marton Hotel and Country Club, Stokesley Rd, TS7 8DU, ☎ 37141 – TV wc ☎ Ⓟ.
M 2.70/6.50 **t.** 🍷 1.25 – **54 rm** 9.00/12.50 **t.** – P 14.15/21.80 **t.**

at Acklam SW: 2 m. on A 174 by Acklam Rd – AZ – ✉ ☎ 0642 Middlesbrough:

Blue Bell Motor Inn (Swallow), TS5 7HL, ☎ 593939, Group Telex 53168 – TV wc ☎ Ⓟ
60 rm.

AUSTIN-MG-ROVER-WOLSELEY Eastbourne Rd ☎ 86658
AUSTIN-MG-ROVER-TRIUMPH-WOLSELEY 336 Stokesley Rd, Marton ☎ 37171
AUSTIN-MG-WOLSELEY 339 Linthorpe Rd ☎ 87606
BMW 1 Manor Close ☎ 710566
CHRYSLER-SIMCA 134 Marton Rd ☎ 42873
FIAT Newport Rd ☎ 49346
FORD North Ormesby Rd ☎ 2452
MORRIS-MG-WOLSELEY St. Barnabas Rd ☎ 86706
MORRIS-MG-WOLSELEY Ormesby ☎ 37227
MORRIS-MG-WOLSELEY 132 Park Lane ☎ 46031
OPEL 370 Linthorpe Rd ☎ 822884
RENAULT Longlands Rd ☎ 44651
ROVER-TRIUMPH Marton Rd ☎ 46065
VAUXHALL Marton Rd ☎ 43415
VAUXHALL Bluebell Corner, Acklam Rd ☎ 37131
VW, AUDI-NSU Ormesby Rd, Park End ☎ 37971

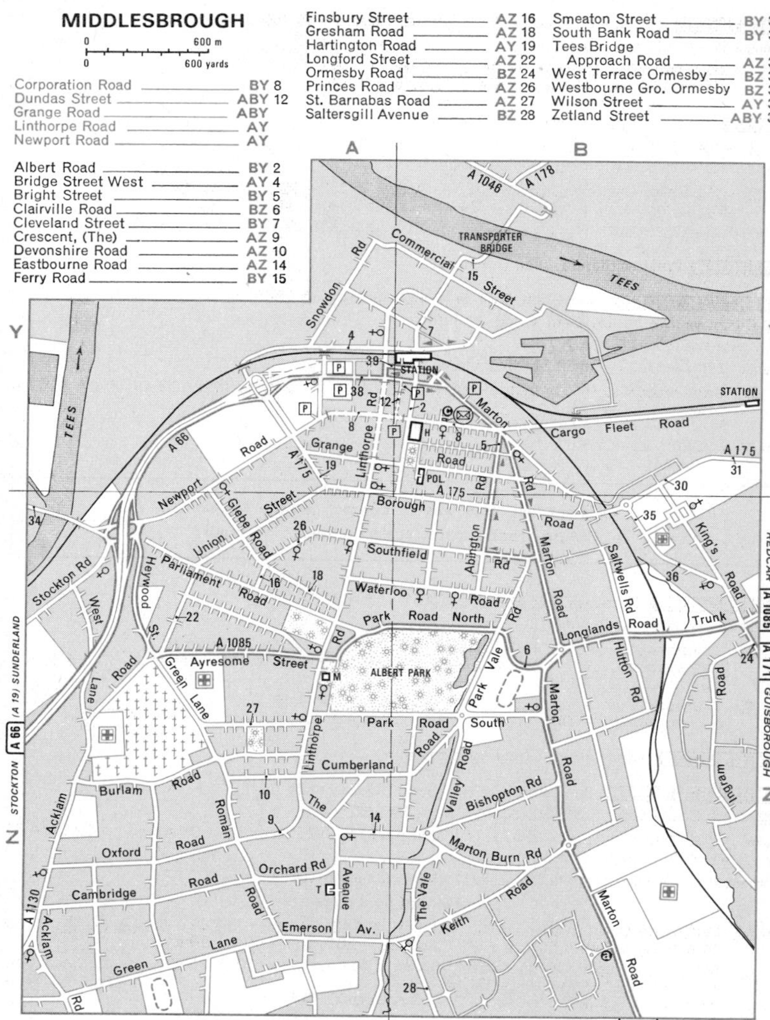

MIDDLETON ONE ROW Durham – see Darlington.

MIDDLETON-ON-SEA West Sussex – pop. **2,708** – ✉ Bognor Regis – ☎ 024 369.
London 65 – Bognor Regis 4 – Brighton 26.

🏠 **Villa Plage,** Elmer Rd, PO22 6HZ, ☎ 2251, ⇐ – Ⓟ
Easter-December – **M** *(closed Monday)* approx. 2.75 **t.** 🍷 1.35 – **7 rm** ☕ 7.50/15.00 **t.**

RENAULT Harefield Rd, Elmer Rd ☎ 3557

MIDDLETON STONEY Oxon. – pop. 196 – ✉ Bicester – ☎ 086 989.
London 66 – Northampton 30 – Oxford 12.

✕✕ **Jersey Arms** with rm, Ardley Rd, OX6 8SE, ☎ 234 – wc Ⓟ
closed Christmas – **M** (dinner only) a la carte 3.40/4.95 **st.** 🍷 1.25 – **11 rm** ☕ 7.50/19.00 **st.**

MIDDLE WALLOP Hants. – pop. 2,800 – ✉ Stockbridge – ☎ 026 478 Wallop.
London 80 – Salisbury 11 – Southampton 21.

XX **Fifehead Manor** with rm, SO20 8EG, on A 343 ☎ 566, « 16C converted manor house », – TV wc P
M *(closed Sunday dinner)* a la carte 4.25/5.25 **t.** 1.30 – **6 rm** 11.00/18.00 **st.** – P 15.00/18.00 **st.**

MIDHURST West Sussex 986 ㊱ – pop. 2,169 – ☎ 073 081.
See : Cowdray House (Tudor ruins)* *AC.*
18 Cowdray Park ☎ 2088, NE : **1** m. on A 272.
London 57 – Brighton 38 – Chichester 12 – Southampton 41.

Spread Eagle, South St., GU29 9NN, ☎ 2211, Telex 86853, « 15C hostelry » – TV wc ☎ P
28 rm.

Angel, North St., GU29 9DN, ☎ 2421, – TV wc P
M 3.50/5.00 **t.** 1.40 – **18 rm** 8.00/15.50 **t.**

XX **Mida,** Wool Lane, GU29 9BY, ☎ 3284
closed Sunday dinner, Monday, 2 weeks Easter and last 2 weeks October – **M** a la carte approx. 6.05.

XX **Knockers,** Knockhundred Row, GU29 9DQ, ☎ 3712
closed Sunday and 25 to 29 December – **M** a la carte 4.65/8.05 1.50.

AUSTIN-MG-ROVER-TRIUMPH-WOLSELEY Petersfield Rd ☎ 2443 MORRIS Rumbolds Hill ☎ 2162

MILDENHALL Suffolk 986 ㉜ – pop. 9,269 – ☎ 0638.
9 Worlington ☎ 712216.
London 73 – Cambridge 22 – Ipswich 38 – Norwich 41.

Bell, High St., IP28 7EA, ☎ 712134 – wc P
M a la carte 3.50/5.45 2.00 – **19 rm** 6.50/11.00 – P 10.50.

MILFORD HAVEN Dyfed 986 ㉚ – pop. 13,751 – ☎ 064 62.
Envir. : Martin's Haven ** W : **11** m. – St. Ann's Head ** by Dale (site*) W : **12** m.
9 Hubberston ☎ 2368.
London 257 – Carmarthen 37 – Fishguard 22.

Lord Nelson, Hamilton Ter., SA73 3AW, ☎ 3265, – wc P
M approx. 3.95 **st.** 1.10 – **27 rm** 7.00/16.50 **st.**

MILFORD-ON-SEA Hants. – pop. 3,625 – ✉ Lymington – ☎ 059 069.
London 109 – Bournemouth 15 – Southampton 24 – Winchester 37.

South Lawn, Lymington Rd, SO4 0RF, ☎ 3261, – wc P
closed January – **M** (dinner only and Sunday lunch) 3.75/4.50 1.55 – **12 rm** 8.50/17.00.

Kingsland, Westover Rd ☎ 2670, – P
closed Christmas – **15 rm** 6.00/9.00 **s.**

X **Mill House,** 1 High St., SO4 0QF, ☎ 2611
closed Sunday dinner and Monday – **M** a la carte 3.05/4.35 **t.** 1.10.

AUSTIN-MORRIS-MG-ROVER-TRIUMPH-WOLSELEY High St. ☎ 2161 AUSTIN-MORRIS-MG-WOLSELEY High St. ☎ 2378

MILTON ABBAS Dorset – pop. 788 – ✉ Blandford – ☎ 0258.
See : Village* 18C.
London 127 – Bournemouth 23 – Weymouth 19.

Milton Manor , ☎ 880254, « Country house atmosphere », – P
March-October – **M** (residents only) approx. 3.40 **st.** 1.45 – **11 rm** 6.20/12.40 **st.** – P 12.00 **st.**

MILTON COMMON Oxon. – pop. 300 – ☎ 084 46 Great Milton.
London 50 – Oxford 9.

Belfry, Brimpton Grange, OX9 2JW, M 40 exit 7NW off A 329 ☎ 381, – TV wc ☎ P.
M 3.25/3.95 1.25 – 1.00 – **32 rm** 8.50/14.50 – P 13.50/15.50.

MILTON DAMEREL Devon – pop. 409 – ✉ Holsworthy – ☎ 040 926.
London 249 – Barnstaple 21 – Plymouth 48.

Woodford Bridge, EX22 7LL, ☎ 252, « 15C thatched inn », , – wc P
M approx. 4.00 0.80 – **16 rm** 7.00/16.00.

MILTON ERNEST Beds. – see Bedford.

MILTON ON STOUR Dorset – pop. 4,050 (inc. Gillingham) – ✉ ☎ 074 76 Gillingham.
London 115 – Shaftesbury 6 – Taunton 42.

- **Milton Lodge,** SP8 4PR, ☎ 2262, heated, – wc
  M 4.50/5.50 0.90 – **10 rm** 7.00/9.50 – P 13.00/16.00.

MINEHEAD Somerset 986 ㉟ – pop. 8,055 – ☎ 0643.
18 Warren Rd ☎ 2057.
i Market House, ☎ 2624.
London 187 – Bristol 64 – Exeter 43 – Taunton 25.

- **Beach** (T.H.F.), The Avenue, TA24 5AP, ☎ 2193, heated – TV wc
  M a la carte 4.00/5.30 **st.** 1.50 – **41 rm** 7.50/14.50 **st.** – P 16.00/19.50 **st.**
- **Northfield**, Northfield Rd, TA24 5PU, ☎ 2864, « ≤ gardens », – wc
  M 2.60/4.30 **t.** 1.00 – **22 rm** 8.65/19.45 **t.** – P 9.20/11.35 **t.**
- Wellington, Wellington Sq., TA24 5LJ, ☎ 4371 –
  29 rm.
- **Benares**, Northfield Rd, TA24 5PT, ☎ 2340, ≤, – wc
  Easter and mid May-mid October – **M** (dinner only) 3.50/4.00 **t.** 1.20 – **23 rm** 7.50/18.00.
- **York,** The Avenue, TA24 5AN, ☎ 2037 – wc
  closed November – **M** (dinner only from October to May) 3.50/4.25 **st.** 1.50 – **24 rm** 7.00/16.00 **st.**

AUSTIN-MORRIS-MG-WOLSELEY North Rd ☎ 2336
FIAT, VAUXHALL Townsend Rd ☎ 3379
RENAULT Blue Anchor ☎ 064 382 (Dunster) 82571
VW, AUDI-NSU Mart Rd ☎ 2108

MINSTER LOVELL Oxon. – pop. 1,085 – ✉ Witney – ☎ 099 387 Asthall Leigh.
London 72 – Gloucester 36 – Oxford 16.

- XX **Old Swan** (Embassy) with rm, OX8 5RB, ☎ 614, –
  M a la carte 5.05/8.00 **t.** 1.75 – **6 rm** 9.50/15.00 **t.**

MITCHELL Cornwall – see Newquay.

MITHIAN Cornwall – pop. 420 – ✉ ☎ 087 255 St. Agnes.
Envir. : St. Agnes Beacon (the Beacon ✻**) W : 3 m.
London 298 – Newquay 10 – Penzance 25 – Truro 7.

- **Rose-in-Vale**, TR5 0QD, ☎ 2202, ≤, « Country house atmosphere », heated, – wc wc
  Easter-early October – **M** (dinner only) 2.75 1.30 – **17 rm** 6.25/14.00.

MODBURY Devon 986 ㊴ – pop. 1,131 – ✉ Ivybridge – ☎ 054 883.
London 237 – Exeter 37 – Plymouth 12.

- XX **Exeter Inn,** Church St., PL21 0QR, ☎ 239, « 15C inn »
  M (bar lunch) a la carte 2.15/4.05 **t.** 1.85.

at Ermington NW : 2 ½ m. by A 379 on B 3210 – ✉ Ivy Bridge – ☎ 054 883 Modbury :

- **Ermewood House,** PL21 9NS, ☎ 321, – wc wc
  M (dinner only) 2.45/3.50 **t.** – 0.85 – **12 rm** 7.00/15.00 **t.** – P 11.50/14.50 **t.**

MONK FRYSTON North Yorks. – pop. 539 – ✉ Lumby – ☎ 0977 South Milford.
London 190 – Kingston-upon-Hull 42 – Leeds 13 – York 20.

- **Selby Fork** (Anchor), LS25 5LF, W : 2 ¼ m. on A 1 by A 63 ☎ 682711, Group Telex 27120, – TV .
  M a la carte 4.00/5.10 **t.** 1.00 – **115 rm** 12.65/17.60 **st.**
- **Monk Fryston Hall**, LS25 5DU, ☎ 682369, , park – wc .
  M approx. 4.00 **t.** 1.80 – **18 rm** 9.00/16.50 **t.**

MONKSPATH STREET West Midlands – see Solihull.

MONMOUTH Gwent 986 ㉛ – pop. 6,570 – ☎ 0600.
Envir. : Tintern Abbey** *AC*, SE : 11 m. – SE : Wye Valley* – Raglan (castle* 15C) SW : 7 m. – Skenfrith (castle and church*) NW : 6 m.
9 Leasebrook Lane ☎ 2212.
i Tourist Information Centre, c/o Nelson Museum ☎ 3899 (Easter-September).
London 147 – Gloucester 26 – Newport 24 – Swansea 64.

- **King's Head,** Agincourt Sq., NP5 3DY, ☎ 2177 – TV wc .
  M 4.00/4.75 1.40 – **33 rm** 10.00/20.00.
- **Beaufort Arms** (T.H.F.), Agincourt Sq., NP5 3BT, ☎ 2411 – wc
  M a la carte 3.95/5.35 **st.** 1.50 – **26 rm** 7.50/15.00 **st.**

at Whitebrook S: 8 ¼ m. off A 466 – ✉ Monmouth – ☎ 060 082 Trelleck:

XX ✿ **Crown Inn** with rm, NP5 4TX, ☎ 254, ←, French rest. – wc wc P
closed 1 January-14 February and 2 weeks November – **M** *(closed Sunday dinner, Monday lunch and from November to Easter: Monday dinner and Tuesday lunch)* a la carte 4.50/7.65 1.35 – **8 rm** 7.25/14.50 **st.**
Spec. Pâté de poisson aux algues marines et au beurre blanc, Médaillon de chevreuil à l'eau de vie de genièvre et au sureau (November-March), Selle d'agneau farcie de brioche aux fines herbes à la sauce paloise (April-October).

AUSTIN-MG-WOLSELEY St. James Sq. ☎ 2773
FORD 77/79 Monnow St. ☎ 2366
MORRIS-MG-WOLSELEY 110/114 Monnow St. ☎ 2501
VAUXHALL Wonastow Rd ☎ 2896

MONTACUTE Somerset – see Yeovil.

MORECAMBE Lancs. 986 ㉓ – pop. 41,908 (inc. Heysham) – ☎ 0524.

See: Marineland★ *AC*.
18 Clubhouse ☎ 418050 – 18 Trumacar Park, Heysham ☎ 0524 (Heysham) 51011, SW: 2 m.
i Marine Rd Central ☎ 414110 and 417120 ext. 249.
London 248 – Blackpool 29 – Carlisle 70 – Lancaster 4.

Midland, Marine Rd, LA4 4BZ, ☎ 417180, ← – TV wc wc P
M 3.50/4.00 1.60 – **44 rm** 9.20/18.50 – P 12.50/15.00.

The Elms, Bare, LA4 6DD, ☎ 411501, – wc P
M 3.25/3.90 **s.** 1.20 – **41 rm** 7.75/15.50 **s.** – P 12.50 **s.**

Strathmore, Marine Rd East, LA4 5AP, ☎ 411314 – wc P
M 2.85/6.00 **st.** 1.40 – **67 rm** 8.75/19.50 **st.**

Prospect, 363 Marine Rd East, LA4 5AQ, ☎ 412133
Easter-November – **15 rm** 3.75/7.50 **s.**

AUSTIN-MG-WOLSELEY Marine Rd West ☎ 414134
FORD Clarke St. ☎ 5061
MORRIS-MG-WOLSELEY Thornton Rd ☎ 414141
PEUGEOT Torrisholme ☎ 412478
SAAB, VOLVO Marlborough Rd ☎ 417437
TOYOTA West Gate ☎ 415636
VAUXHALL Bare Lane ☎ 410205
VW, AUDI-NSU Heysham Rd ☎ 415833

MORETONHAMPSTEAD Devon 986 ㊴ – pop. 1,440 – ☎ 064 74.

18 ☎ 355.
London 213 – Exeter 12 – **Plymouth 38.**

Manor House (B.T.H.), TQ13 8RE, SW: 2 m. on B 3212 ☎ 355, Telex 42794, ←, 18, park – TV P
M a la carte 8.55/16.10 **st.** 1.20 – **68 rm** 23.00/40.00 **st.**

at North Bovey SW: 2 m. – ✉ Newton Abbot – ☎ 064 74 Moretonhampstead:

Glebe House, TQ13 8RA, ☎ 544, ←, – wc wc P – **11 rm.**

MORETON-IN-MARSH Glos. 986 ㉛ – pop. 2,477 – ☎ 0608.

Envir.: Chastleton House★★ (Elizabethan) *AC*, SE: 3 ½ m.
i Council Offices, High St. ☎ 50881.
London 86 – Birmingham 40 – Gloucester 31 – **Oxford 29.**

Manor House (Interchange), High St., GL56 0LJ, ☎ 50501, Telex 837151, « Tasteful decor, gardens » – TV wc P.
closed Christmas – **M** a la carte 5.40/8.20 **st.** 2.00 – **34 rm** 10.00/25.30 **st.**

White Hart Royal (T.H.F.), High St., GL56 0BA, ☎ 50731, – TV wc P.
M a la carte 4.10/5.50 **st.** 1.50 – **24 rm** 8.00/15.00 **st.**

XX **Redesdale Arms** (Crest) with rm, High St., GL56 0BN, ☎ 50308 – wc P
M (buffet lunch) a la carte 3.35/5.50 **s.** 1.50 – **15 rm** 8.50/16.00 **s.**

ALFA-ROMEO Oddington Service Station ☎ 0451 (Stow-on-the-Wold) 30132
BMW ☎ 50323
MORRIS-MG-ROVER-TRIUMPH-WOLSELEY London Rd ☎ 50585
RENAULT Little Compton ☎ 74202

MORPETH Northumb. 986 ⑲ – pop. 14,054 – ☎ 0670.

Envir.: Brinkburn Priory (site★, church★: Gothic) *AC*, NW: 10 m.
18 ☎ 2065, S: 1 m. on A 197.
London 301 – Edinburgh 93 – Newcastle-upon-Tyne 15.

Queen's Head (S & N), Bridge St., NE61 1NB, ☎ 2083 – P
M 3.00/4.00 **st.** – **13 rm** 7.85/13.65 **st.**

X **Gourmet,** 59 Bridge St., NE61 1PQ, ☎ 56200
closed Sunday, Monday, 3 weeks February and Bank Holidays – **M** a la carte 4.10/9.20 1.50.

AUSTIN-MORRIS-MG-ROVER-TRIUMPH Oldgate ☎ 3286
FORD 53/55 Bridge St. ☎ 2323
MORRIS-MG Queen St., Amble ☎ 066 571 (Amble) 247
RENAULT Cliton ☎ 2538

MORTEHOE Devon – pop. **1,261** – ✉ ☎ **027 187** Woolacombe.
London 237 – Barnstaple 15 – Exeter 55.

- **Rockham Bay,** EX34 7EG, ☎ 347 – ⇔wc ☎ Ⓟ
  Easter-mid October – **M** 4.00/6.00 **t.** 🌢 1.50 – **34 rm** ⊐ 5.50/25.00 **t.** – P 13.00/18.00 **t.**
- **Castle Rock,** EX34 7EB, ☎ 465, ≤, ⚐ – ⇔wc ⟹ Ⓟ
  May-September – **M** 2.75/3.25 🌢 1.25 – **29 rm** ⊐ 7.00/18.00.

MOULTON Northants. – see Northampton.

MOULTON North Yorks. – pop. **198** – ✉ Richmond – ☎ **032 577** Barton.
London 243 – Leeds 53 – Middlesbrough 25 – Newcastle-upon-Tyne 43.

- ✗✗ **Black Bull Inn,** DL10 6QJ, ☎ 289, « Victoriana decor and Brighton Belle Pullman coach » – Ⓟ
  closed Sunday and 24 to 31 December – **M** a la carte 4.20/8.35 **t.**

MOUNT PLEASANT Hants. – see Lymington.

MOUSEHOLE Cornwall – pop. **1,079** – ☎ **073 673.**
London 321 – Penzance 3 – Truro 29.

- **Lobster Pot,** TR19 6PT, ☎ 251, ≤ – ⇔wc ⫿wc
  Mid February-mid November – **M** approx. 3.75 🌢 1.50 – **23 rm** ⊐ 4.75/17.50.

MUDEFORD Dorset – pop. **4,654** – ✉ ☎ **020 15** (4 and 5 fig.) or **0202** (6 fig.) Christchurch.
London 113 – Bournemouth 7 – Christchurch 2 – Winchester 24.

- **Avonmouth** (T.H.F.), BH23 3NT, ☎ 3434, ≤ Christchurch harbour, ⛱ heated, ⚐ – TV ⇔wc ☎ ♿ Ⓟ. 🏕
  M a la carte 4.10/6.00 **st.** 🌢 1.50 – **48 rm** ⊐ 10.00/20.00 **st.** – P 15.00/20.50 **st.**

☞ *Pour aller loin rapidement, utilisez les **cartes Michelin** à 1/1 000 000.*

MULLION Cornwall – pop. **1,346** – ✉ Helston – ☎ **0326.**
See : Mullion Cove (site★).
⛳18 Cury ☎ 240 2967, N : 3 m.
London 323 – Falmouth 21 – Penzance 21 – Truro 26.

- **Polurrian** 🐦, TR12 7EN, SW : ½ m. ☎ 240421, ≤ Mounts Bay, 🎾, ⛱ heated, ⚐ – ⇔wc Ⓟ
  mid May-September – **M** approx. 4.60 **st.** 🌢 1.30 – **54 rm** ⊐ 8.70/27.00 **st.** – P 16.20/19.25 **st.**
- **Mullion Cove** 🐦, TR12 7EP, SW : 1 ¼ m. ☎ 240328, ≤ Mullion Cove and Mounts Bay, 🎾, ⛱ – ⇔wc Ⓟ
  M 3.00/3.50 🌢 1.00 – **45 rm** ⊐ 6.50/19.00 – P 10.50/12.00.

MUMBLES West Glam. **986** ㉟ – pop. **13,712** – ✉ ☎ **0792** Swansea.
See: Mumbles Head★. **Envir.:** Cefn Bryn (✲★★★ from the reservoir) W : **12** m.
London 202 – Swansea 6.

- **Osborne** (Embassy), Rotherslade Rd, Langland Bay, SA3 4QL, W : ¾ m. ☎ 66274, ≤, ⚐ – 🛗 TV ⇔wc ☎ Ⓟ. 🏕
  closed Christmas – **M** approx. 3.50 **st.** 🌢 1.50 – **42 rm** ⊐ 8.25/15.50 **st.**
- Langland Court 🐦, Langland Court Rd, Langland Bay, SA3 4TD, W : 1 m. ☎ 68505, ≤, ⚐ – TV ⇔wc ⫿ ⟹ Ⓟ
  30 rm.
- Ashleigh, 690 Mumbles Rd, Southend, SA3 4EE, ☎ 68926
  15 rm.
- **Carlton,** 654-656 Mumbles Rd, Southend, SA3 4EA, ☎ 60450 – ⫿
  closed last 2 weeks December – **20 rm** ⊐ 6.00/11.50 **t.**
- ✗✗✗ **Norton House** with rm, 17 Norton Rd, SA3 5TQ, ☎ 66174 – Ⓟ
  closed 3 weeks at Easter – **M** *(closed Sunday)* (dinner only) a la carte 4.60/6.20 **t.** – ⊐ 0.80 – **4 rm** 10.00/15.00 **t.**
- ✗ **Quo Vadis,** 614-616 Mumbles Rd, Southend, SA3 4EF, ☎ 60706, Italian rest.
  M a la carte 5.10/6.80 **t.** 🌢 1.50.

MUNDESLEY-ON-SEA Norfolk **986** ㉘ – pop. **1,536** – ☎ **0263** Mundesley.
⛳9 ☎ 720279.
London 132 – Great Yarmouth 30 – Norwich 20.

- **Continental** (Mt. Charlotte), Cromer Rd, NR11 8DB, ☎ 720271, 🎾, ⛱ heated, ⚐ – 🛗 ⇔wc Ⓟ
  May-mid September – **M** 3.25/3.75 **s.** 🌢 1.60 – **55 rm** ⊐ 5.25/20.50 **s.** – P 7.55/9.70 **s.**

NANNERCH Clywd – pop. 262 – ✉ Mold – ☎ 035 283 Hendre.
London 213 – Birkenhead 26 – Chester 18 – Shrewsbury 46.

✗ **Rising Sun Inn,** CH7 5HG, on A 541 ☎ 205 – Ⓟ
closed Sunday dinner – **M** a la carte 2.55/5.40.

NANTWICH Cheshire 986 ⑨ and ㉗ – pop. 11,683 – ☎ 0270.
ℹ The Library, Beam St. ☎ 63914.
London 176 – Chester 20 – Liverpool 45 – Stoke-on-Trent 17.

Alvaston Hall, Middlewich Rd, CW5 6PD, NE: 2 m. on A 530 by A 51 ☎ 64341, – TV wc Ⓟ.
32 rm.

✗✗ **Churche's Mansion,** 156 Hospital St., CW5 5RY, ☎ 65933, « 16C half-timbered house », – Ⓟ
closed Sunday dinner and 25 to 28 December – **M** 5.00/6.00 **st.** 1.60.

VAUXHALL Station Rd ☎ 64027

NARBERTH Dyfed 986 ㉚ – pop. 937 – ☎ 0834.
London 240 – Fishguard 25 – Swansea 47.

✗✗ **Robeston House** with rm, Robeston Wathen, SA67 8AU, NW: 1 ¾ m. by B 4314 on A 40 ☎ 860392, – wc Ⓟ
M *(closed Sunday)* (lunch by arrangement) 4.95/7.00 1.30 – **5 rm** 7.50/15.00.

NARBOROUGH Leics. – see Leicester.

NATIONAL EXHIBITION CENTRE West Midlands – see Birmingham.

NEAR SAWREY Cumbria – see Hawkshead.

NEATH West Glam. 986 ㉛㉟ – pop. 28,619 – ☎ 0639.
18 Cadoxton ☎ 3615.
London 194 – Cardiff 35 – Swansea 9.

Cimla Court, 77 Cimla Rd, SA11 3TT, ☎ 3771 – wc Ⓟ
closed Christmas Day – **M** (grill rest. only) approx. 2.50 1.50 – **30 rm** 6.50/13.15.

Castle, The Parade, SA11 1RE, ☎ 3581 – wc
M (grill rest. only) – **36 rm.**

AUSTIN-MG-ROVER-TRIUMPH-WOLSELEY Gnoll Park Rd ☎ 3911
FORD 17/22 Alfred St. ☎ 2601
RENAULT 57 Windsor Rd ☎ 2708
VAUXHALL Angel St. ☎ 4441

NEEDINGWORTH Cambs. – see St. Ives.

NEFYN Gwynedd 986 ㉖ – pop. 2,086 – ☎ 075 882.
See: Site*. **Envir.:** Braich y Pwll (<** from the 2nd car park) SW: 18 m.
London 265 – Caernarfon 20.

Nanhoron Arms, St. Davids Rd, LL53 6EA, ☎ 203 – wc Ⓟ
M (cold buffet lunch in summer) 3.25/3.60 1.40 – **20 rm** 5.75/15.50.

Caeau Capel, Rhodfa'r Mor, LL53 6EB, ☎ 240, – wc Ⓟ
Easter-September – **M** 3.50/5.00 0.80 – **20 rm** 4.00/10.00.

AUSTIN-MORRIS-MG Church St. ☎ 206
VAUXHALL ☎ 344

NETHERTON Merseyside – see Liverpool.

NEWARK-ON-TRENT Notts. 986 ㉘ – pop. 24,646 – ☎ 0636 Newark.
18 Kelwick, Coddington ☎ 063 684 (Fenton Claypole) 241, E: 4 m.
ℹ The Ossington, Beast Market Hill ☎ 71156.
London 127 – Lincoln 16 – Nottingham 20 – Sheffield 42.

Robin Hood (Anchor), Lombard St., NG24 1XB, ☎ 3858 – TV wc Ⓟ.
M 2.15/3.50 **t.** 1.05 – **19 rm** 11.00/15.75 **t.**

Ram, Castle Gate, NG24 1AZ, ☎ 2255 –
21 rm.

Midland, Muskam Rd ☎ 73788 – Ⓟ
9 rm.

AUSTIN-MG-WOLSELEY 18 Balderton Gate ☎ 73888
CHRYSLER-SIMCA 23/25 London Rd ☎ 5335
FIAT Sleaford Rd ☎ 3405
FORD Farndon Rd ☎ 4131
JAGUAR-MORRIS-MG-ROVER-TRIUMPH-WOLSELEY Castle Gate ☎ 4456
OPEL Farndon Rd ☎ 5431
RENAULT 36/40 Albert St. ☎ 4619
SAAB North Muskham ☎ 3232
VAUXHALL 69 Northgate ☎ 3413
VW-AUDI-NSU Northern Rd ☎ 4484

NEWBURY Berks. 986 ㉟ – pop. 23,634 – ☎ 0635.

i The Granary, Wharf Rd ☎ 42400.

London 67 – Bristol 66 – Oxford 28 – Reading 17 – Southampton 38.

Chequers (T.H.F.), 6-8 Oxford St., RG13 1JB, ☎ 43666, – TV wc ☎ P. **M** 2.95/3.95 **st.** 1.50 – **69 rm** 9.50/18.00 **st.**

Bacon Arms, 10 Oxford St., RG13 1JB, ☎ 40408 – P **M** a la carte 3.55/5.45 **t.** 1.75 – **11 rm** 6.05/11.55 **st.**

Guest House, 133 Andover Rd, RG14 6JJ, ☎ 41359, – P **11 rm.**

La Riviera, 26 The Broadway, RG13 1AU, ☎ 47499 *closed Wednesday, Easter, 2-3 weeks April, Christmas and Bank Holidays* – **M** a la carte 2.90/5.45 1.25.

AUSTIN-MG-WOLSELEY The Broadway ☎ 40678
CHRYSLER-SIMCA Kings Rd ☎ 49444
CITROEN Newtown Rd ☎ 41911
DAF West Kings Close ☎ 47232
DAIMLER-JAGUAR-MORRIS-MG-ROVER-TRIUMPH 123 London Rd ☎ 43181
FORD London Rd ☎ 1103
PEUGEOT Hermitage ☎ 257
RENAULT, VAUXHALL London Rd ☎ 41020
VAUXHALL 24 Greenham Rd ☎ 41501
VOLVO 45 Bartholomew St. ☎ 40168

NEWBY BRIDGE Cumbria – pop. 200 – ✉ Ulverston – ☎ 044 83.

London 269 – Kendal 16 – Lancaster 27.

Swan, LA12 8NB, ☎ 681, ←, – wc ☎ P **M** a la carte 4.70/8.00 **st.** 2.20 – **36 rm** 11.00/18.00 **st.**

at Lake Side N: **1** m. – ✉ Ulverston – ☎ 044 83 Newby Bridge:

Richard's, LA12 8NA, ☎ 381 – P *closed Monday except Bank Holidays and 10 January to Easter* – **M** a la carte 4.65/5.65 **t.** 1.50.

NEWCASTLE EMLYN Dyfed 986 ㉚ – pop. 651 – ☎ 0239.

Envir.: Cenarth Falls★ W: 3 m. – Cilgerran (castle★ 13C) *AC*, W: 9 m. – New Quay (site★) NE: 12 ½ m. **Exc.:** E: Teifi Valley★.

London 240 – Carmarthen 20 – Fishguard 29.

Emlyn Arms, Bridge St., SA38 9DU, ☎ 710317 – TV wc ☎ P **M** 3.50/5.00 **s.** 1.80 – **38 rm** 6.50/18.00 **s.**

AUSTIN-MG-WOLSELEY New Rd ☎ 245

NEWCASTLE-UNDER-LYME

Staffs. 986 ⑨ and ㉗ – pop. 77,126 – ☎ 0782 Stoke-on-Trent.

Envir.: Little Moreton Hall★★ (16C) *AC*, N: 8 m. by A 34.

18 ☎ 078 271 (Keele Park) 582 by A 525 v – 18 Trentham Park ☎ 657315, S: 4 m. v.

London 161 – Birmingham 46 – Liverpool 56 – Manchester 43.

Plan of Built up Area: see Stoke-on-Trent

Clayton Lodge (Embassy), Clayton Rd, Clayton, ST5 4AF, S: 1 ¼ m. on A 519 ☎ 613093 – TV wc ☎ P. v e *closed Christmas* – **M** approx. 3.70 **st.** 1.30 – **51 rm** 8.75/15.50 **st.**

Post House (T.H.F.), Clayton Rd, Clayton, ST5 4DL, S: 2 m. on A 519 ☎ 625151, Telex 36531 – TV wc ☎ P. v n **M** 2.95/4.00 **st.** 1.50 – 2.00 – **106 rm** 13.00/18.00 **st.**

NEWCASTLE-UNDER-LYME CENTRE

High Street

Albert Street	2
Blackfriars Road	4
Church Street	6
Iron Market	8
Merrial Street	10
Vessey Terrace	12

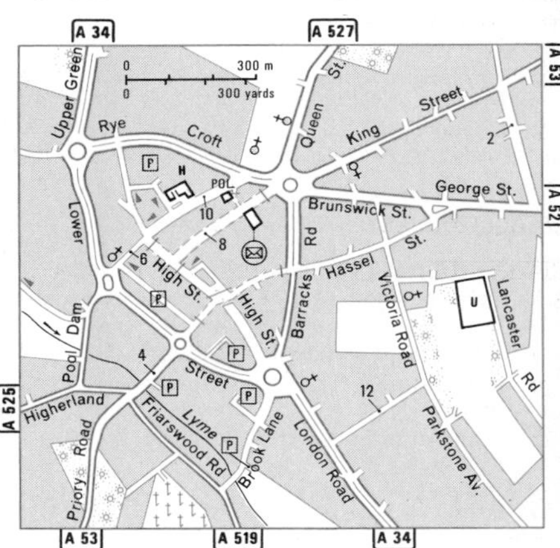

AUSTIN-DAIMLER-MORRIS-MG Brook Lane ☎ 618461
FIAT Keele Rd ☎ 622141
FORD Silverdale Rd ☎ 614631
JAGUAR-ROVER-TRIUMPH Brunswick St. ☎ 617321
RENAULT Keele Rd ☎ 610749
VOLVO Knutton Rd ☎ 564524
VW, AUDI-NSU Talke Rd ☎ 563711

NEWCASTLE-UPON-TYNE Tyne and Wear 986 ⑲ – pop. 222,209 – ☎ 0632.

See: Cathedral* 14C CZ **A**.

Three Mile Bridge, Gosforth ℡ 851775, N: 3 m. by A 1 AV – Broadway East, Gosforth, ℡ 856710, N: 3 m. by Kenton Rd AV – Chimney Mills, Spital Tongues ℡ 28236 AV – Whorlton Grange, Westerhope, ℡ 869125, W: 5 m. by B 6324 AV.

Newcastle Airport, ℡ 860966, NW: 5 m. by A 696 AV – **Terminal**: Bus Assembly: Central Station Forecourt.

to London/Bristol/Newton Abbot ℡ 611234 ext 2295 – to Inverness ℡ 0904 (York) 53022 ext 2067.

Shipping connections with the Continent: to Bergen, Stavanger, Kristiansand and Oslo, (Fred Olsen-Bergen Line) – to Esbjerg (DFDS Seaways) NE: by A 1058 BV.

i Central Library, Princess Sq. ℡ 610691 – Prudential Building, 140-150 Pilgrim St. ℡ 28795.

London 282 – Edinburgh 108 – Leeds 93.

Plans on following pages

Royal Station (B.T.H.), Neville St., NE99 1DW, ℡ 20781, Telex 53681 – **M** a la carte 5.60/9.35 **st.** 1.25 – **113 rm** 12.75/26.00 **st.** CZ **i**

Swallow (Swallow), Newgate St., NE1 5SX, ℡ 25025, Group Telex 53168, ← – **92 rm.** CZ **o**

Newcastle Centre (Centre), Newbridge St., NE1 8BS, ℡ 26191, Telex 53467 – wc **M** approx. 2.95 **s.** 1.25 – 1.50 – **180 rm** 10.75/14.50 **s.** CY **n**

County (Thistle), Neville St., NE99 1AH, ℡ 22471 – wc **105 rm.** CZ **a**

Royal Turks Head (Thistle), Grey St., NE1 6EL, ℡ 26111 – wc **103 rm.** CY **r**

Moors, 56 Pilgrim St. ℡ 610774. CY **s**

Moulin Rouge, 27 Sandhill, NE1 3VF, ℡ 20377 CZ **x**
closed Sunday and Bank Holidays – **M** a la carte 6.00/10.00 **s.** 1.30.

Dante's, 1-3 Market St., NE1 6JE, ℡ 22816. CY **c**

Mario, 59 Westgate Rd ℡ 20708, Italian rest. CZ **u**

Fisherman's Wharf, 15 The Side, NE1 3JE, ℡ 21057 CZ **v**
closed Saturday lunch, Sunday and Bank Holidays – **M** a la carte 5.20/7.75 **s.** 1.60.

Roma, 22 Collingwood St., NE1 1JF, ℡ 20612, Italian rest. CZ **e**
closed Sunday and August – **M** a la carte 4.45/6.85 **t.** 2.45.

Jim and Carole's Kitchen, 89-91 Blenheim St. ℡ 24660. CZ **z**

at Gosforth N: 4 ¾ m. on A 1 – AV – ✉ Newcastle-upon-Tyne – ☎ 089 426 Wideopen:

Gosforth Park (Thistle), High Gosforth Park, NE3 5HN, on B 1318 ℡ 4111, Telex 53655, ←, park – **102 rm.**

at Seaton Burn N: 8 m. on A 1 – AV – ✉ Newcastle-upon-Tyne – ☎ 089 426 Wideopen:

Holiday Inn, NE13 6BP, N: ¾ m. ℡ 5432, Telex 53271, – **M** a la carte 5.45/9.25 1.70 – 2.00 – **151 rm.**

at Wallsend E: 4 m. on A 1058 – BV – ✉ ☎ 0632 Newcastle-upon-Tyne:

Europa Lodge (County), Coast Rd, NE28 9HP, E: 1 ¼ m. junction A 1058 and A 108, ℡ 628989, Telex 53583 – **M** 4.00/4.75 **st.** 1.40 – **182 rm** 13.50/18.00 **st.**

at Newcastle Airport NW: 6 m. on A 696 – AV – ✉ Woolsington – ☎ 0661 Ponteland:

Airport (Stakis), NE13 8DJ, ℡ 24911, ← – wc **M** a la carte 4.75/7.15 **st.** 1.50 – **100 rm** 12.00/17.50 **st.**

MICHELIN Branch, Benton Sq., Industrial Trading Estate, NE12 9TP, ℡ 666266.

ALFA-ROMEO Diana St. ℡ 22314
AUSTIN-MG-WOLSELEY Westgate Rd ℡ 37901
AUSTIN-MG-WOLSELEY 21/33 George St. ℡ 34591
AUSTIN-MG-WOLSELEY 87 Osborne Rd ℡ 811677
AUSTIN-MG-ROVER-TRIUMPH-WOLSELEY Warwick St. ℡ 24367
CHRYSLER-SIMCA, MAZDA-POLSKI Benton Rd ℡ 666361
CITROEN Elswick Rd ℡ 37281
DAF Westgate Rd ℡ 31082
DAF Four Lane Ends ℡ 666331
DAIMLER-JAGUAR-MORRIS-MG-ROVER-TRIUMPH, ROLLS ROYCE Forth St. ℡ 28981
DATSUN 62 Westmorland Rd ℡ 28281
DATSUN Benfield Rd ℡ 659171
FIAT, LANCIA Railway St. ℡ 32131
FORD Main St. ℡ 0661 (Ponteland) 4261
FORD Market St. ℡ 611471
FORD Scotswood Rd ℡ 39161
JAGUAR-MORRIS-MG-ROVER-TRIUMPH-WOLSELEY Etherstone Av. ℡ 663311
MORRIS-MG-WOLSELEY Denton Burn ℡ 675967

P.T.O. →

NEWCASTLE-UPON-TYNE

Street	Grid	No.
Adelaide Terrace	AX	2
Askew Road	AX	3
Atkinson Road	AX	4
Bath Street	BX	6
Bensham Road	AX	7
Benton Bank	BV	8
Buddle Street	BV	14
Church Avenue	AV	17
Church Road	AV	18
Clayton Road	BV	21
Coldwell Lane	BX	26
Coldwell Street	BX	27
Condercum Road	AX	30
Derwentwater Road	AX	32
Fossway	BV	35
Haddrick's Mill Road	BV	41
Heathery Lane	BV	42
High Street West	BV	44
Jesmond Dene Road	BV	45
Killingworth Road	BV	46
Lobley Hill Road	AX	48
Matthew Bank	BV	53
Neptune Road	BV	60
Red Hall Drive	BV	71
Saltwell Road	BX	80
Shipdon Road	AX	82
Springfield Road	AV	85
Station Road	BX	87
Stephenson Road	BV	90
Sunderland Road	BX	93
Sutton Street	BV	95
Swalwell Bank	AX	96
Waverdale Avenue	BV	99
West Farm Avenue	BV	100
Whickham Bank	AX	103

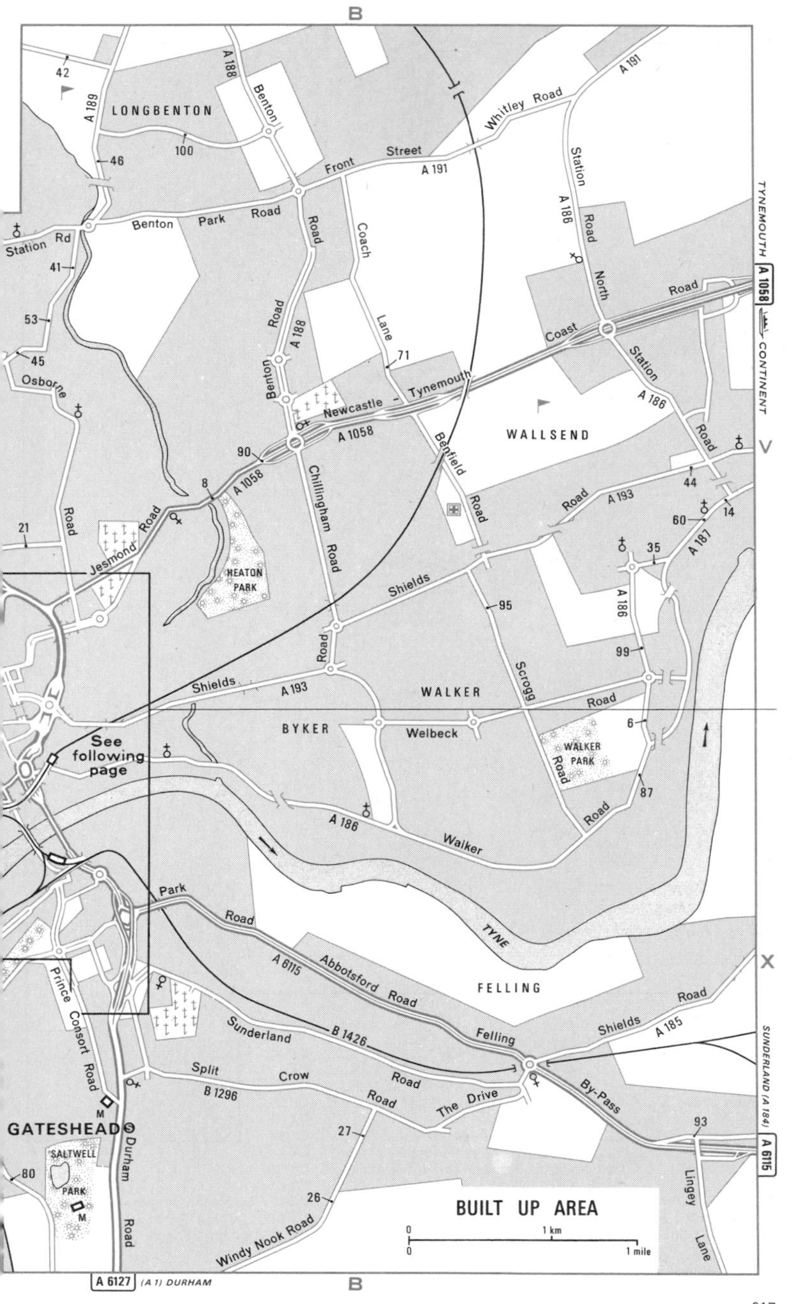
B
LONGBENTON
WALLSEND
WALKER
BYKER
FELLING
GATESHEAD
HEATON PARK
WALKER PARK
SALTWELL PARK
TYNE
See following page
BUILT UP AREA
0 1 km
0 1 mile
TYNEMOUTH A 1058
CONTINENT
SUNDERLAND (A 184) A 6115
A 6127 (A 1) DURHAM
V
X
Benton Park Road
Front Street
Whitley Road
Station Road
North Road
Coast Road
Newcastle - Tynemouth
Coach Lane
Benton Road
Chillingham Road
Benfield Road
Shields Road
Scrogg Road
Welbeck Road
Walker Road
Jesmond Road
Osborne Road
Station Rd
Park Road
Abbotsford Road
Felling Shields Road
By-Pass
Sunderland Road
Split Crow Road
The Drive
Prince Consort Road
Durham Road
Windy Nook Road
Lingey Lane
A 188
A 189
A 191
A 186
A 1058
A 193
A 187
A 6115
B 1426
B 1296
A 185
42
100
46
41
53
45
90
8
21
71
44
14
60
35
99
95
6
87
93
27
26
80

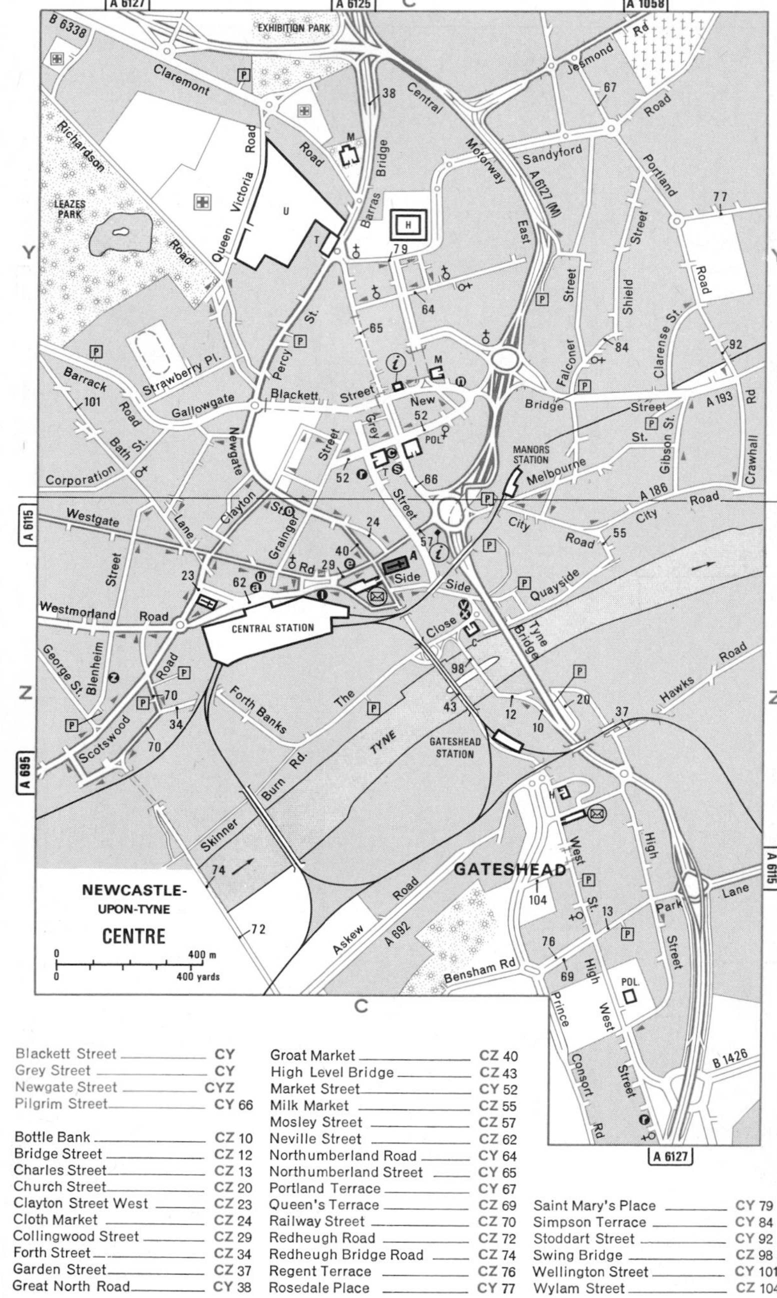
NEWCASTLE-
UPON-TYNE
CENTRE
0
400 m
0
400 yards
A 6127
A 6125
A 1058
A 6115
A 695
A 6127
C
Y
Z
B 6338
EXHIBITION PARK
Claremont
Road
Richardson
Road
LEAZES
PARK
Queen
Victoria
Road
Barras
Bridge
Central
Motorway
East
A 6127 (M)
Jesmond
Rd
Road
Sandyford
Portland
Road
Shield
Street
Falconer
Street
Clarense St.
Percy
St.
Barrack
Road
Strawberry Pl.
Gallowgate
Blackett
Street
New
Grey
Street
POL.
Newgate
Street
Bath
St.
Corporation
Westgate
Road
Clayton
St.
Grainger
Rd
Side
Lane
Street
Westmorland
Road
CENTRAL STATION
George St.
Blenheim
Road
Scotswood
Forth Banks
The
TYNE
Skinner
Burn
Rd.
MANORS
STATION
Melbourne
Bridge
Street
St.
Gibson St.
Crawhall
Rd
A 193
A 186
Road
City
City
Road
Quayside
Close
Tyne
Bridge
Hawks
Road
GATESHEAD
STATION
GATESHEAD
West
St.
High
Street
Park
Lane
Askew
Road
A 692
Bensham Rd
Prince
Consort
Rd
High
West
Street
B 1426
POL.
38
67
77
79
64
65
84
92
101
52
52
66
24
40
29
57
55
23
62
70
34
70
98
43
12
10
20
37
74
72
104
13
76
69

MORRIS-MG-WOLSELEY Great North Rd ☎ 858194
MORRIS-MG-WOLSELEY Brinkburn St. ☎ 659277
PEUGEOT 388 West Rd ☎ 35683
RENAULT Shiremoor ☎ 532318
RENAULT Scotswood Rd ☎ 30101
SAAB, LOTUS 111 New Bridge St. ☎ 25964
SAAB Front St. ☎ 887298
SAAB Whitley Rd, Longbenton ☎ 668223
VAUXHALL Two Ball Lonnen ☎ 39211
VAUXHALL Great North Rd ☎ 089 426 (Wideopen) 3176
VAUXHALL West Moor ☎ 661050
VW, AUDI-NSU Fossway ☎ 657121

NEW DENHAM Bucks. – **pop. 7,543** – ✉ ⊙ **0895 Uxbridge.**
London 20 – Aylesbury 25 – **Oxford 40.**

XXX Giovanni's, at Denham Lodge, Oxford Rd, UB9 4AA, on A 4020 ☎ 31568, Italian rest. – 🅿.

NEWDIGATE Surrey – **pop. 1,404** – ⊙ **030 677.**
London 32 – **Brighton 32** – Guildford 18.

XX **The Forge,** Parkgate Rd, RH5 5DZ, N: 1 m. ☎ 582 – 🅿
closed Sunday, Monday, 2 weeks winter, 26 December and 2 weeks summer – **M** a la carte 4.80/7.30 **t.**

NEWHAVEN East Sussex 986 ㊱㊵ – **pop. 10,009** – ✉ **Newhaven** – ⊙ **0323 Seaford.**
⛳9 **Brighton Rd ☎ 4049.**
⛴ **Shipping connections with the Continent : to Dieppe (Sealink) 2-6 daily (3 h 45 mn).**
i Car Ferry Terminal Car Park ☎ 4970 (summer only).
London 63 – **Brighton 9** – Eastbourne 14 – Lewes 7.

🏨 **Newhaven Mercury Motor Inn,** Bishopstone Rd, BN25 2RA, SE: 1 ½ m. on A 259 ☎ 891055, Telex 628064 – TV 🛁wc ☎ 🅿. 🏠
M (grill rest.) a la carte approx. 3.80 **st.** 🍾 1.35 – ☕ 1.50 – **70 rm** 10.80/15.50.

FORD Drove Rd ☎ 5303

NEWLYN Cornwall – see Penzance.

Carte

Dans les hôtels et restaurants
cités avec des menus à prix fixes,
il est généralement possible de se faire servir également à la carte.

NEWMARKET Suffolk 986 ㉜ – **pop. 12,951** – ⊙ **0638.**
⛳18 **Cambridge Rd ☎ 2131, SW: 1 m.**
London 64 – **Cambridge 13** – **Ipswich 40** – **Norwich 48.**

🏨 **White Hart** (T.H.F.), High St., CB8 8JP, ☎ 3051 – TV 🛁wc ☎ 🚗 🅿. 🏠
M a la carte 4.10/4.50 **st.** 🍾 1.50 – **23 rm** ☕ 8.00/16.00 **st.**

🏨 **Rutland Arms,** 33 High St., CB8 8NB, ☎ 4251 – 🛁wc ☎ 🅿
M 2.50/3.80 **s.** 🍾 1.20 – **48 rm** ☕ 8.40/14.50 **s.**

XX **Bedford Lodge** with rm, Bury Rd, CB8 7BX, on A 1304 ☎ 3175, 🌳 – TV 🛁wc 🚿wc ☎ 🅿
M a la carte 4.50/5.80 **st.** 🍾 1.35 – **12 rm** ☕ 7.50/14.50 **t.**

MORRIS-MG-WOLSELEY Park Lane ☎ 2474
TOYOTA Bury Rd ☎ 2130
VAUXHALL All Saints Rd ☎ 4982
VOLVO Dullingham ☎ 063 876 (Stetchworth) 244

NEW MILTON Hants. – **pop. 4,373** – ✉ **Bournemouth (Dorset)** – ⊙ **042 52 Highcliffe.**
London 106 – Bournemouth 12 – **Southampton 21** – Winchester 34.

🏨 **Chewton Glen** 🐦, Christchurch Rd, BH25 6QS, ☎ 5341, Telex 41456, ≤ gardens, « Country house atmosphere », 🎾, 🏊 heated, 🌳, park – TV 🅿. 🏠
M a la carte 6.50/10.50 **st.** 🍾 1.60 – ☕ 2.50 – **42 rm** 20.00/40.00 **st.**

AUSTIN-MG-WOLSELEY Christchurch Rd ☎ 611198
DATSUN 25 Station Rd ☎ 610034
FORD Fernhill Lane ☎ 612121
MORRIS-MG-WOLSELEY Old Milton Rd ☎ 614665
RENAULT 56 Old Milton Rd ☎ 612296
VAUXHALL Ashley Cross Rd, Ashley ☎ 615989

NEWNHAM Glos. 986 ㉛ – **pop. 1,201** – ⊙ **059 47.**
London 115 – **Bristol 33** – Gloucester 12 – Newport 32.

🏠 **Victoria,** High St., GL14 1AD, ☎ 221, 🌳 – 🛁wc 🅿
M (bar lunch in winter) 3.10/3.50 **t.** 🍾 1.20 – **11 rm** ☕ 6.50/15.00.

NEWPORT Glos. – see Berkeley.

NEWPORT I.O.W. 986 ㊴ – see Wight (Isle of).

NEWPORT Gwent 986 ㉟ – **pop. 112,286** – ⊙ **0633.**
Envir. : Caerphilly (castle** 13C) W: 9 m.
⛳18 **Great Oak, Rogerstone ☎ 063 343 (Rhiwderin) 2683 and 4496, W: 3 m. on A 467** – ⛳18 **☎ 063 341 (Llanwern) 3038, E: 3 m.**
London 145 – **Bristol 31** – **Cardiff 12** – Gloucester 48.

Gateway Motor Motel, The Coldra, Chepstow Rd, NP6 2YG, E: 3 m. on A 48 ☎ 063 341 (Llanwern) 2777 – TV wc ☎ ♿ P.
M 4.00/4.30 **s.** 1.20 – **90 rm** 11.90/16.90 **s.** – P 16.20/18.20 **s.**

Queen's (Anchor), 19 Bridge St., NPT 4RN, ☎ 62992, Group Telex 27120 – TV wc ☎.
M approx. 2.15 **t.** 1.00 – **42 rm** 9.50/17.60 **st.**

Westgate (T.H.F.), Commercial St., NPT 1TT, ☎ 66244 – TV wc ☎.
M 3.25/3.50 **st.** 1.50 – **68 rm** 9.50/17.50 **st.**

Conti's Grill, 1st floor, 40-41 Llanarth St., NPT 1HR, ☎ 63684
closed Sunday – **M** a la carte 3.05/7.45 1.50.

at Langstone **E: 4 ½ m. on A 48 – ✉ Newport – ☎ 063 341 Llanwern:**

New Inn Motel (Ansells), Chepstow Rd, NP6 2JN, ☎ 2426 – wc ☎ P
M 3.30/4.00 **st.** 1.80 – **30 rm** 11.55/14.85 **st.**

AUSTIN-MORRIS-MG-WOLSELEY Commercial St. ☎ 58451
AUSTIN-DAIMLER-JAGUAR-MORRIS-MG-WOLSELEY Corporation Rd ☎ 72381
AUSTIN-MORRIS-MG-WOLSELEY Cardiff Rd ☎ 63847
CHRYSLER-SIMCA Town Wharf ☎ 53666
CITROEN Chepstow Rd ☎ 71955
DATSUN Spytty Rd ☎ 74891
FIAT, VAUXHALL Turner St. ☎ 59771
FORD Agincourt St. ☎ 52233
MORRIS-MG-WOLSELEY Bassaleg Rd ☎ 63717
RENAULT Queens Hill ☎ 51317
ROVER-TRIUMPH 41/59 Clarence Pl. ☎ 62901
ROVER-TRIUMPH Bassaleg Rd ☎ 53771
VW, AUDI-NSU Maeglas Industrial Estate ☎ 211326

NEWPORT Dyfed – pop. 1,062 – ☎ 0239.

See: Site*. Envir.: Pentre Ifan (burial chamber*) SE: 4 ½ m.
9 Newport Sands ☎ 244.
London 258 – Fishguard 7.

Pantry, Market St., SA42 0PH, ☎ 820420 – P.

at Felindre-Farchog **E: 3 m. on A 487 – ✉ Crymych – ☎ 0239 Newport:**

Ye Olde Salutation Inn, SA41 3UY, ☎ 820348, – wc P
14 rm.

NEWPORT Salop 986 ㉗ – pop. 6,931 – ☎ 0952.

London 150 – Birmingham 33 – Shrewsbury 18 – **Stoke-on-Trent 21.**

Royal Victoria, St. Mary's St., TF10 7AB, ☎ 810831 – wc ☎ P
21 rm.

CHRYSLER-SIMCA 23 High St. ☎ 811076

NEWPORT PAGNELL Bucks. 986 ㉜ – pop. 6,334 – ☎ 0908.

London 57 – Bedford 13 – Luton 21 – Northampton 15.

TraveLodge (T.H.F.) without rest., M 1 Service Area 3, MK16 8DS, W: 1 ½ m. off A 422 on M 1 ☎ 610878 – TV wc ☎ P
100 rm 10.00/13.50 **st.**

Swan Revived, High St., MK16 8AR, ☎ 610565 – TV wc wc ☎ P – **31 rm.**

Glovers, 18-20 St. John St., MK16 9HT, ☎ 090 862 (Goldcrest) 6398
closed Saturday lunch, Sunday, Monday dinner, 1 to 14 August, 24 December-2 January and Bank Holidays – **M** a la carte 5.50/8.20 **st.** 1.65.

AUDI-NSU, VW Tickford St. ☎ 611642
PEUGEOT High St. ☎ 611715

NEWQUAY Cornwall 986 ㊳ – pop. 15,017 – ☎ 063 73.

Envir.: St. Agnes Beacon (the Beacon ☀) SW: 13 ½ m. by A 3075** Y.
i Morfa Hall, Cliff Rd ☎ 2119/2716/2822.
London 286 – Exeter 83 – Penzance 34 – **Plymouth 48** – Truro 14.

Plan opposite

Bristol, Narrowcliff, TR7 2PQ, ☎ 5181, ←, – TV P Z **r**
closed 3 weeks October – **M** 4.50/5.00 **s.** 1.30 – **110 rm** 8.50/22.00 **s.** – P 13.00/18.00 **s.**

Riviera (Interchange), Lusty Glaze Rd, TR7 3AA, ☎ 4251, ←, heated, – TV P. Z **o**
closed 25 and 26 December – **M** approx. 4.00 **st.** 1.20 – **54 rm** 10.00/26.60 **st.**

Windsor, Mount Wise, TR7 2AY, ☎ 5188, heated, – wc P Z **n**
Easter-October – **M** 3.25/3.75 **t.** 1.20 – **51 rm** 8.00/20.00.

Trebarwith , Trebarwith Crescent, TR7 1BZ, ☎ 2288, ← bay, , – wc P Z **a**
May-October – **M** approx. 4.25 **st.** 1.25 – **51 rm** 8.00/18.00 **st.**

Kilbirnie, Narrowcliff, TR7 2RS, ☎ 5155, , – wc P Z **e**
closed 3 weeks November and 4 days at Christmas – **M** approx. 4.25 **t.** – **65 rm** 10.25/23.50.

Edgcumbe, Narrowcliff, TR7 2RR, ☎ 2061, , heated – TV wc wc P Z **u**
March-November – **M** a la carte 3.55/6.15 **t.** 1.50 – **88 rm** 11.00/23.50 **t.**

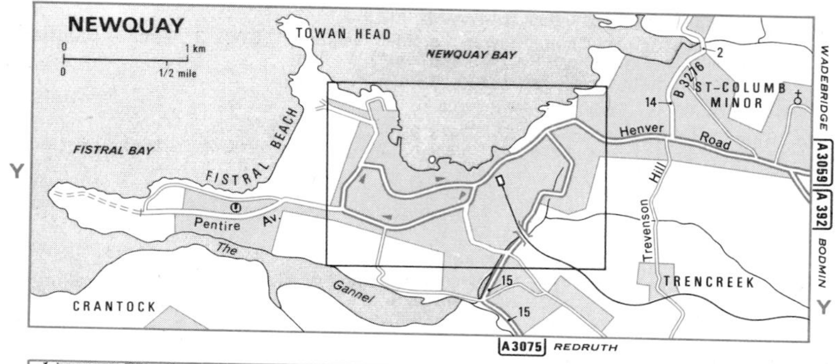

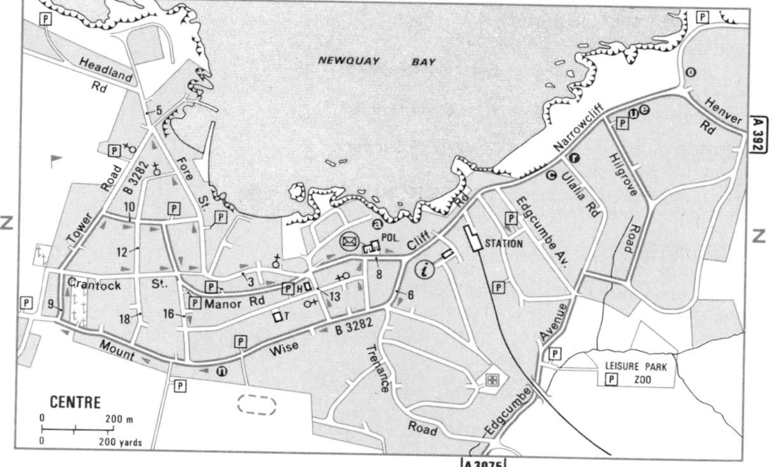

Bank Street	Z 3	Beacon Road	Z 5	Marcus Hill	Z 13
East Street	Z 8	Berry Road	Z 6	Porth Way	Y 14
Fore Street	Z	Higher Tower Road	Z 9	Trevemper Road	Y 15
Alexander Road	Y 2	Hope Terrace	Z 10	St. Georges Road	Z 16
		Jubilee Street	Z 12	St. John's Road	Z 18

Water's Edge, Esplanade Rd, TR7 1QA, ☎ 2048, ≤ Fistral Bay, – wc wc ℗ *May-October* – **M** approx. 4.00 🌡 1.00 – **23 rm** ☕ 9.00/19.50. Y u

Cliffdene, Narrowcliff, TR7 2RA, ☎ 3094 – ℗ *season* – **68 rm.** Z c

at Mitchell SE: 6 m. by A 392 on A 30 – Y – ✉ Newquay – ☎ 087 251 Mitchell:

Pillars with rm, TR8 5AT, ☎ 243 – wc ℗
M *(closed Sunday and Monday)* (dinner only) a la carte 3.10/6.55 **s.** – **5 rm** ☕ 8.00/12.50.

at Crantock SW: 4 m. off A 3075 – Y – ✉ Newquay – ☎ 063 77 Crantock:

Crantock Bay, West Pentire, TR8 5SE, W: ¾ m. ☎ 229, ≤ Crantock Bay, – wc ℗
Easter-early October – **M** approx. 3.50 **t.** 🌡 1.70 – **35 rm** ☕ 7.50/22.80 **t.**

Manor House, West Pentire, TR8 5SE, W: ¾ m. ☎ 229, – wc ℗
Easter-October – **M** approx. 3.50 **t.** 🌡 1.70 – **9 rm** ☕ 7.00/17.00 **t.**

at Holywell Bay SW: 7 m. off A 3075 – Y – ✉ Newquay – ☎ 063 77 Crantock:

Holywell Bay, TR8 5PT, ☎ 242, – wc ℗
May-September – **M** (dinner only) 3.50 **s.** – **43 rm** ☕ (dinner included) 10.00/21.00.

DAF Newlyn East ☎ 087 251 (Mitchell) 347
MORRIS-MG-WOLSELEY Quintrell Downs ☎ 2410
VOLVO Sommercourt ☎ 087 251 (Mitchell) 386

NEW ROMNEY Kent 986 ㊱ – pop. 3,447 – ☎ 067 93.

Envir. : Lydd (All Saints' Church tower : groined vaulting*) SW : 3 ½ m. – Brookland (St. Augustine's Church : belfry* 15C, Norman font*) W : 6 m.

Lydd Airport ☎ 0679 (Lydd) 20409, S : 5 m.

London 71 – Folkestone 14 – Hastings 23 – Maidstone 33.

Blue Dolphins, Dymchurch Rd, TN28 8BE, ☎ 3224 – Ⓟ
closed 2 weeks late Autumn – **M** *(closed Sunday to non-residents)* 2.85/3.50 ₰ 1.05 – **6 rm** 5.00/9.50 – P 10.25/11.50.

Rome House, 10 High St., TN28 8BZ, ☎ 2002 – Ⓟ
closed Sunday dinner, Monday, 15 to 30 October and 1 week January – **M** a la carte 4.60/6.15 **s.** ₰ 1.75.

at Littlestone-on-Sea E : 1 ½ m. on B 2070 – ✉ ☎ 067 93 New Romney :

Dormy House, Marine Par., TN28 8QF, ☎ 3233, – wc Ⓟ
M 3.20/4.60 **s.** ₰ 1.65 – **32 rm** 10.10/20.20 **s.**

FIAT The Avenue, Littlestone ☎ 2184

NEWSTEAD Notts. – pop. 2,976.

See : Abbey** 16C (gardens**) *AC.*

London 139 – Nottingham 9 – Sheffield 30.

Hotels and restaurants see : Nottingham S : 9 m.

Keine bezahlte Reklame im Michelin-Führer.

NEWTON Suffolk – pop. 376 – ✉ ☎ 0787 Sudbury.

London 67 – Colchester 12 – Ipswich 18.

Saracen's Head. Sudbury Rd, CO10 0QJ, ☎ 72536 – Ⓟ
closed Sunday dinner and Monday – **M** a la carte 3.40/5.00 **t.**

NEWTON ABBOT Devon 986 ㊴ – pop. 19,399 – ☎ 0626.

18 ☎ 2460, N : 3 m.

to London/Stirling/Crewe/Sheffield/Newcastle-upon-Tyne ☎ 66490.

London 216 – Exeter 16 – Plymouth 31 – Torquay 7.

Globe, Courtenay St., TQ12 2QH, ☎ 4106 – wc Ⓟ
24 rm.

Queen's, Queen's St., TQ12 2EZ, ☎ 5216 – wc
M 2.75/3.50 **st.** ₰ 1.30 – **35 rm** 8.30/17.75 **st.**

ALFA-ROMEO, VOLVO Wolborough St. ☎ 2545
AUSTIN-MORRIS-MG-ROVER-TRIUMPH-WOLSELEY 64/72 Wolborough St. ☎ 4141
CHRYSLER-SIMCA 177/187 Queen St. ☎ 3838
FIAT The Avenue ☎ 2526
FORD Wolborough St. ☎ 5081
MORRIS, ROLLS ROYCE 48 Wolborough St. ☎ 3652
RENAULT 173 Exeter Rd, Kingsteignton ☎ 3545
SAAB, VAUXHALL 83/85 Queen St. ☎ 2653
TOYOTA Highweek ☎ 4702
VW, AUDI-NSU The Avenue ☎ 2641

NEWTON FERRERS Devon – pop 1,815 – ☎ 0752 Plymouth.

London 242 – Exeter 42 – Plymouth 11.

Court House , Court Rd, PL8 1AQ, ☎ 872324, « Country house atmosphere », heated, – Ⓟ
closed January – **M** 4.00/4.50 **s.** ₰ 1.60 – **11 rm** 7.50/18.00 **t.**

River Yealm , Yealm Rd, PL8 1BL, ☎ 872419, ≤ estuary – wc Ⓟ
M (buffet lunch) approx. 4.00 ₰ 1.70 – **19 rm** 7.00/16.00.

NEWTON POPPLEFORD Devon – pop. 1,352 (inc. Harpford) – ☎ 0395 Colaton Raleigh.

London 208 – Exeter 10 – Sidmouth 4.

Bridge End House with rm, Harpford, EX10 0NG, on A 3052 ☎ 68411 – Ⓟ
closed Monday, 25-26 December and last 3 weeks January – **M** a la carte 3.50/6.20 **t.** ₰ 1.55 – **3 rm** 3.85/7.70 **st.**

NEWTON SOLNEY Derbs. – pop. 528 – ✉ Burton-upon-Trent (Staffs.) – ☎ 028 389 Repton.

London 131 – Burton-upon-Trent 3 – Derby 11.

Newton Park (Embassy) , DE15 0SS, ☎ 703568, ≤, , park – TV wc Ⓟ.
closed Christmas – **M** approx. 3.40 **st.** ₰ 1.40 – **25 rm** 9.75/15.75 **st.**

NEWTOWN Powys 986 ㉛ – pop. 6,115 (inc. Llanllwchaiarn) – ☎ 0686.

i Tourist Information Centre, Shortbridge St. Car Park ☎ 25580 (Easter-September).

London 196 – Aberystwyth 44 – Chester 56 – Shrewsbury 32.

The Bear, Broad St., SY16 2LU, ☎ 26964 – wc wc Ⓟ
M 3.00/4.00 **st.** ₰ 1.80 – **42 rm** 8.00/17.50 **st.** – P 10.00/12.00 **st.**

at Abermule **NE: 4 ½ m. on A 483 – ✉ ☎ 068 686 Abermule:**

Dolforwyn Hall ⛰, SY15 6JG, N: ½ m. on A 483 ☎ 221 – Ⓟ
closed 24 December-2 January – **M** 3.25/3.75 **st.** 🍷 1.35 – **8 rm** 🛏 6.00/14.00 **st.** – P 11.50/12.50 **st.**

AUSTIN-MORRIS-MG-ROVER-TRIUMPH-WOLSELEY Pool Rd ☎ 6357
DAF Powys ☎ 055 16 (Trefeglwys) 202
FORD Pool Rd ☎ 6014

NEWTOWN LINFORD **Leics. – pop. 1,046 – ☎ 053 05 Markfield.**
London 112 – Birmingham 51 – Derby 27 – **Leicester 6 – Nottingham 27.**

XX Grey Lady, N: ¾ m. ☎ 3558 – Ⓟ.

NINFIELD **East Sussex – pop. 1,096 – ✉ Battle – ☎ 0424.**
London 62 – Brighton 28 – Hastings 9 – Lewes 20.

Moor Hall ⛰, High St., TN33 9JT, ☎ 892330, 🎾, 🏊 heated, 🌳, park – 🛁wc 🚿wc Ⓟ
M approx. 3.50 🍷 1.40 – **22 rm** 🛏 8.00/19.00 **s.**

NITON **I.O.W. – see Wight (Isle of).**

NORTHALLERTON **North Yorks. 986 ⑲ – pop. 6,726 – ☎ 0609.**
Envir. : Bedale (Parish church* 13C-14C) SW: 7 ½ m.
London 238 – Leeds 48 – Middlesbrough 24 – York 33.

Golden Lion (T.H.F.), High St., DL7 8PP, ☎ 2404 – TV 🛁wc ☎ Ⓟ. 🏨
M a la carte 4.00/5.30 **st.** 🍷 1.50 – **28 rm** 🛏 8.50/17.50 **st.**

XX **McCoys at the Tontine,** Staddlebridge, DL6 3JD, NE: 8 ½ m. by A 684 on A 19 ☎ 060 982 (East Harlsey) 207, « 1930's decor » – Ⓟ
closed Sunday and Bank Holidays – **M** a la carte 5.35/7.35 🍷 1.35.

XX **Romanby Court,** High St., DL7 8EG, ☎ 4918
closed Sunday, Monday, 3 weeks August and Bank Holidays – **M** 4.30/5.75 **t.**

AUSTIN-MG-WOLSELEY Brompton Rd ☎ 891
MORRIS-ROVER-TRIUMPH 84 High St. ☎ 2372
RENAULT Leeming Bar ☎ 2388
SAAB East Rd ☎ 3921

NORTHAMPTON **Northants. 986 ㉒ – pop. 126,642 – ☎ 0604.**
See : Church of the Holy Sepulchre* 12C – Central Museum and Art Gallery (collection of footwear*).
i 21 St. Giles St. ☎ 34881 ext 404/537.
London 70 – Cambridge 51 – Coventry 31 – Leicester 36 – Luton 35 – **Oxford 45.**

Saxon Inn, Silver St., NN1 2TA, ☎ 22441, Telex 311142 – 🛗 TV Ⓟ. 🏨
M approx. 2.85 **s.** 🍷 1.80 – 🛏 1.75 – **134 rm** 11.50/14.00 **s.**

Angel (County) Bridge St., NN1 1NA, ☎ 21661 – Ⓟ
M *(closed Sunday dinner)* 2.95/3.95 **st.** 🍷 1.20 – **45 rm** 🛏 9.55/15.90 **st.**

X **Ca d'Oro,** 334 Wellingborough Rd, NN1 4ES, ☎ 32660, Italian rest.
M (dinner only) a la carte 5.30/6.90 🍷 2.00.

X **Napoleon's Bistro,** 9-11 Welford Rd, Kingsthorpe, NN2 8AE, N: 1 ¾ m. by A 508 on A 50 ☎ 713899, French Bistro
closed Saturday lunch, Sunday, Monday and Bank Holidays – **M** a la carte 3.70/6.00 **t.** 🍷 1.50.

at Weston Favell **NE: 3 ½ m. off A 45 – ✉ ☎ 0604 Northampton:**

Westone (County) ⛰, Ashley Way, NN3 3EA, ☎ 406262, 🌳 – 🛗 TV Ⓟ. 🏨
M 3.50/4.25 **st.** 🍷 2.70 – **65 rm** 🛏 13.00/20.00.

at Moulton **NE: 4 ¼ m. off A 43 – ✉ ☎ 0604 Northampton:**

Poplars, 33 Cross St., NN3 1RZ, ☎ 43983 – 🚿wc Ⓟ
21 rm 🛏 5.00/12.00 **t.**

ALFA ROMEO 78 St. Michaels Rd ☎ 38411
AUSTIN-MG-WOLSELEY, ROLLS ROYCE Bedford Rd ☎ 39645
CHRYSLER-SIMCA Bridge St. ☎ 36271
CITROEN 194/200 Kingsthorpe Rd ☎ 713 202
DAF Harlestone Rd ☎ 51315
DAIMLER-JAGUAR-ROVER-TRIUMPH 22 Wellingborough Rd ☎ 401141
DATSUN 159/185 Abington Av. ☎ 714303
FIAT 91/93 Harborough Rd, Kingsthorpe ☎ 711 333
MORRIS-MG-ROVER-TRIUMPH Weedon Rd ☎ 54041
OPEL Acre Lane ☎ 3413
PEUGEOT 112/116 Abington Av. ☎ 31249
RENAULT 74 Kingsthorpe Rd ☎ 714555
ROVER-TRIUMPH 46/50 Sheep St. ☎ 35471
TOYOTA 348 Wellingborough Rd ☎ 31086
VOLVO Bedford Rd ☎ 21363
VW, AUDI-NSU, MERCEDES-BENZ 42/50 Harborough Rd ☎ 716716

NORTH BOVEY **Devon – see Moreton Hampstead.**

NORTHENDEN **Greater Manchester – see Manchester.**

NORTH FERRIBY **North Humberside – see Kingston-upon-Hull.**

NORTHLEACH Glos. 986 ㉛ – pop. 1,150 (inc. Eastington) – ☎ 045 16.
See: SS. Peter and Paul's Church: South Porch and the brasses* (Perpendicular).
Envir.: Chedworth (Roman Villa*) *AC*, SW: 4 m.
London 86 – Birmingham 53 – Gloucester 22 – Oxford 30.

XX **Old Woolhouse,** The Square, GL54 3EE, ☎ 366, French rest.
closed Sunday, 25-26 December and mid May-mid June – **M** (dinner only) 7.00 **st.**

NORTHOPHALL Clwyd – pop. 1,200 – ✉ Mold – ☎ 0244 Deeside.
London 206 – Birkenhead 18 – Chester 10.

Chequers Inn, Delyn, CH4 6HJ, on A 55 ☎ 816181, – TV wc ☎ P.
M 3.65/4.00 **st.** 1.60 – **18 rm** 9.75/14.50 **st.** – P 12.50/15.00 **st.**

NORTH STIFFORD Essex – ✉ Grays – ☎ 0375 Grays Thurrock.
London 22 – Chelmsford 24 – Southend-on-Sea 20.

Europa Lodge (County), Stifford Clays Rd, RM16 1UE, ☎ 71451, – TV P
M 3.25/3.50 **st.** 1.20 – **60 rm** 12.50/18.00 **st.**

NORTH WARNBOROUGH Hants. – see Odiham.

P 9.00/9.50 **Full Board prices**
given are intended as a rough guide.
If you are planning a stay, make enquiries at the hotel.

NORWICH Norfolk 986 ㉘ – pop. 122,083 – ☎ 0603.
See: Cathedral** 11C-12C (bosses** of nave vaulting) Y **A** – Castle (museum**) *AC* Z **M** – St. Peter Mancroft's Church* (Perpendicular) Z **B**.
Envir.: Wymondham (Abbey Church*: Perpendicular) SW: 9 m. by A 11 X – Norfolk Wildlife Park* *AC*, NW: 12 m. by A 1067 V.
✈ ☎ 411923, N: 3 ½ m by A 140 V.
i Augustine Steward House, 14 Tombland ☎ 20679 or 23445.
London 112 – Kingston-upon-Hull 141 – Leicester 117 – Nottingham 123.

Plan opposite

Norwich (Interchange), 121-131 Boundary Rd, NR3 2BA, on A 1047 ☎ 410431, Group Telex 975247 – TV P. V **r**
M a la carte 4.10/7.10 **st.** 1.50 – 1.35 – **84 rm** 12.00/15.25 **st.** – P 17.65 **st.**

Post House (T.H.F.), Ipswich Rd, NR4 6EP, S: 2 ¼ m. on A 140 ☎ 56431, heated – TV wc ☎ P. on A 140 X
M 3.50/4.00 **st.** 1.50 – 2.00 – **120 rm** 13.00/18.00 **st.**

Maid's Head, Tombland, NR3 1LB, ☎ 28821 – TV wc wc ☎ P Y **u**
M 3.10/3.60 **t.** 1.75 – 2.15 – **82 rm** 11.75/17.00 **t.** – P 16.60/19.85 **t.**

Nelson, Prince of Wales Rd, NR1 1DX, ☎ 28612, Group Telex 975247, – TV wc ☎ P. Z **a**
M (buttery lunch) a la carte 3.85/6.40 **st.** 1.70 – 1.40 – **43 rm** 12.20/16.25 **t.**

Castle (De Vere), Castle Meadow, NR1 3PZ, ☎ 611511 – TV wc ☎. Z **n**
M approx. 3.75 **st.** 1.45 – **78 rm** 13.75/21.25 **st.**

XX **Savoy,** 50 Prince of Wales Rd, NR1 1NN, ☎ 20732, Greek rest. – P YZ **s**
M a la carte 3.10/6.90 **t.** 1.50.

XX Belmonte, 60 Prince of Wales Rd, NR1 1LT, ☎ 22533, Portuguese and Italian rest. Z **c**

XX **Marco's,** 17 Pottergate, NR2 1DS, ☎ 24044, Italian rest. YZ **e**
closed Sunday, Monday and Bank Holidays – **M** a la carte 4.00/9.00.

X Hobbs, 19 Fye Bridge St., NR3 1LJ, ☎ 21825. Y **o**

at Thorpe St. Andrew E: 2 ¼ m. on A 47 – X – ✉ ☎ 0603 Norwich:

Oaklands, 89 Yarmouth Rd, NR7 0HH, ☎ 34471, – wc P
closed 24 and 25 December – **M** 2.60/3.25 **st.** – **37 rm** 6.25/11.75 **st.**

at Blofield E: 8 m. off A 47 – X – ✉ ☎ 0603 Norwich:

XX **La Locanda,** Fox Lane, NR13 4LW, ☎ 713787, Italian rest. – P
closed Sunday and Bank Holidays – **M** a la carte 3.85/7.00 **t.** 1.65.

at Caistor St. Edmund S: 4 m. off A 140 – X – ✉ Norwich – ☎ 050 86 Framingham Earl:

Caistor Hall , NR14 8QN, ☎ 2245, , park – wc P
M approx. 2.50 1.50 – **18 rm** 5.50/10.50.

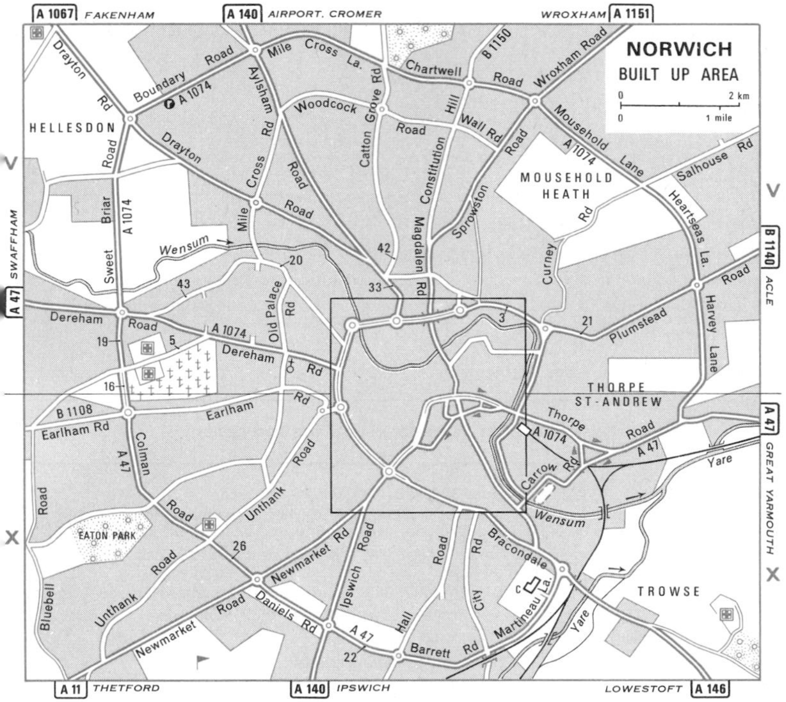

NORWICH
BUILT UP AREA

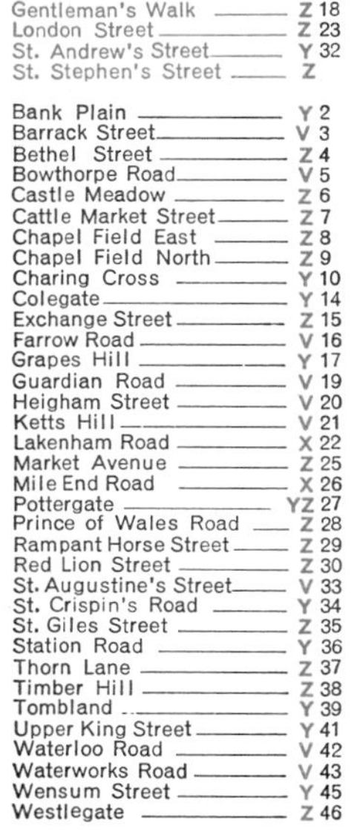
Elm Hill — Y
Gentleman's Walk — Z 18
London Street — Z 23
St. Andrew's Street — Y 32
St. Stephen's Street — Z

Bank Plain — Y 2
Barrack Street — V 3
Bethel Street — Z 4
Bowthorpe Road — V 5
Castle Meadow — Z 6
Cattle Market Street — Z 7
Chapel Field East — Z 8
Chapel Field North — Z 9
Charing Cross — Y 10
Colegate — Y 14
Exchange Street — Z 15
Farrow Road — V 16
Grapes Hill — Y 17
Guardian Road — V 19
Heigham Street — V 20
Ketts Hill — V 21
Lakenham Road — X 22
Market Avenue — Z 25
Mile End Road — X 26
Pottergate — YZ 27
Prince of Wales Road — Z 28
Rampant Horse Street — Z 29
Red Lion Street — Z 30
St. Augustine's Street — V 33
St. Crispin's Road — Y 34
St. Giles Street — Z 35
Station Road — Y 36
Thorn Lane — Z 37
Timber Hill — Z 38
Tombland — Y 39
Upper King Street — Y 41
Waterloo Road — V 42
Waterworks Road — V 43
Wensum Street — Y 45
Westlegate — Z 46

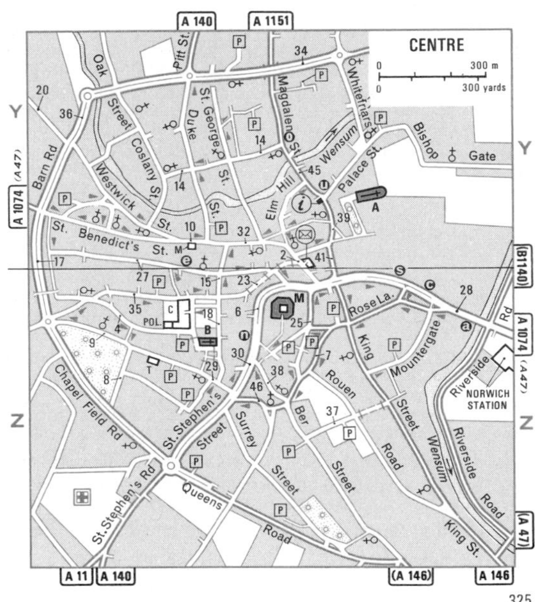

at Stoke Holy Cross S: 5 m. off A 140 – ✕ – ✉ Norwich – ☎ 050 86 Framingham Earl:

XX Old Mill, Mill Rd, NR14 8PA, ☎ 3337 – Ⓟ.

MICHELIN Branch, 81 Barn Rd, NR2 4UB, ☎ 614427/8/9.

ALFA ROMEO, MERCEDES-BENZ, VW, AUDI-NSU Heigham Causeway, Heigham St. ☎ 61211
AUSTIN-MG-WOLSELEY Ipswich Rd, Long Stratton ☎ 30491
BMW, MAZDA Castle Hill ☎ 21471
CHRYSLER-SIMCA, JENSEN, VW, AUDI-NSU 116 Prince of Wales Rd ☎ 28811
CITROEN, RELIANT Whiffler Rd ☎ 43643
DAF, TOYOTA Rouen Rd ☎ 21629
DAIMLER-JAGUAR-ROVER-TRIUMPH 31 King St. ☎ 29607
DATSUN Constitution Hill ☎ 43944
DATSUN 79 Mile Cross Lane ☎ 410661
FIAT, LANCIA Aylsham Rd ☎ 45345
FORD 39 Palace St. ☎ 27787
FORD 37 Surrey St. ☎ 29011
MORRIS-MG-WOLSELEY Melrose Rd ☎ 52534
MORRIS-MG-WOLSELEY Norwich Rd, Stoke Holy Cross ☎ 050 86 (Framingham Earl) 218
MORRIS-MG-WOLSELEY 106/110 Prince of Wales Rd ☎ 28271
MORRIS-MG-WOLSELEY 162 Cromer Rd ☎ 46946
OPEL 36 Duke St. ☎ 29825
PEUGEOT Vulcan Rd South ☎ 49237
PEUGEOT, VAUXHALL Mountergate ☎ 23111
RENAULT 22 Heigham St. ☎ 28911
ROLLS ROYCE-BENTLEY King St. ☎ 28383
ROVER-TRIUMPH Earlham Rd ☎ 21393
SAAB 32/36 Harvey Lane ☎ 33536
VAUXHALL Mile Cross, Aylsham Rd ☎ 410861
VOLVO Westwick St. ☎ 26192

NOTTAGE Mid Glam. – see Porthcawl.

NOTTINGHAM Notts. 986 ㉗㉘ – pop. 300,630 – ☎ 0602.

See: Castle* (Renaissance) and museum* *AC* CZ **M**. **Envir.:** Newstead Abbey** 16C and gardens** *AC*, N: 9 m. by B 683 AY – Wollaton Hall* (16C) *AC*, W: 3 ½ m. AZ **M**.

18 Bulwell Hall Park Links ☎ 278021, N: 5 m. AY – 18 Beeston, ☎ 257062, S: 4 m. by A 52 AZ – 9 Plains Rd, Mapperley ☎ 265611 BY.

✈ East Midlands Airport: Castle Donington ☎ 0332 (Derby) 810621, SW: 15 m. by A 648 AZ.

ℹ 18 Milton St. ☎ 40661 – at Long Eaton: Central Library, Tamworth Rd ☎ 060 76 (Long Eaton) 5426.

London 132 – Birmingham 50 – Leeds 67 – Manchester 69.

Plans on following pages

Albany (T.H.F.), St. James's St., NG1 6BN, ☎ 40131, Telex 37211 – lift TV ♿ Ⓟ. – **M** a la carte 5.30/10.80 **t.** 1.45 – 2.00 – **160 rm** 19.50/27.00 **st.** CYZ **a**

Savoy, Mansfield Rd, NG5 2BT, N: 1 m. on A 60 ☎ 602621 – lift TV Ⓟ – **M** 3.50/5.60 **t.** 0.95 – **125 rm** 12.50/18.00 **t.** BY **u**

Victoria, Milton St., NG1 3PZ, ☎ 49561, Telex 37401 – lift TV Ⓟ. – **M** a la carte 3.50/7.40 **st.** 1.50 – 1.50 – **167 rm** 14.00/17.00 **st.** DY **a**

Strathdon (Thistle), 44 Derby Rd, NG1 5FT, ☎ 48501 – lift TV wc wc ☎ Ⓟ. – **M** *(closed 25-26 December and 1 January)* (bar lunch) approx. 4.00 **s.** 1.20 – 2.00 – **64 rm** 14.00/20.00 **st.** CY **c**

George, George St., NG1 3BP, ☎ 45641 – lift wc ☎. – **66 rm.** DY **e**

Pelham, Pelham Rd ☎ 604829 – Ⓟ – **10 rm.** ABY **a**

XX **Rhinegold,** Fletcher Gate, NG5 1NB, ☎ 51294 DY **v**
closed Sunday and 25 July-6 August – **M** a la carte 4.10/5.30 **s.** 0.90.

XX La Contessa, 14-16 St. James St., NG1 6FG, ☎ 43448, Italian rest. CY **o**

XX **Trattoria Conti,** 14-16 Wheeler Gate, NG1 2NB, ☎ 44056, Italian rest. CY **n**
closed Sunday, first 3 weeks August and Bank Holidays – **M** a la carte 4.55/7.20 1.90.

X **Old English,** 189 Mansfield Rd, NG1 3FS, N: ½ m. on A 60 ☎ 42025 CY **s**
closed Sunday, 26 to 30 December and Bank Holidays – **M** (dinner only) 3.55/4.55 **st.** 1.20.

X **Le Bistro,** 20 St. James's St., NG1 6FG, ☎ 42993, Bistro CY **i**
closed Sunday and last 2 weeks August – **M** a la carte 2.95/3.45 1.45.

at Trent Bridge S: 2 m. on A 52 – ✉ ☎ 0602 Nottingham:

Bridgford, Pavilion Rd, NG2 5FD, ☎ 868661, ← – lift TV Ⓟ. – **M** approx. 8.00 **st.** 1.55 – **90 rm** 16.00/19.00 **st.** – P 22.50 **st.** BZ **i**

at Edwalton S: 3 m. on A 606 – ✉ ☎ 0602 Nottingham:

Edwalton Hall, NG12 4AE, ☎ 231116, – ☎ Ⓟ – **M** 3.00/3.80 **s.** 1.20 – **13 rm** 7.70/14.50 **s.** BZ **r**

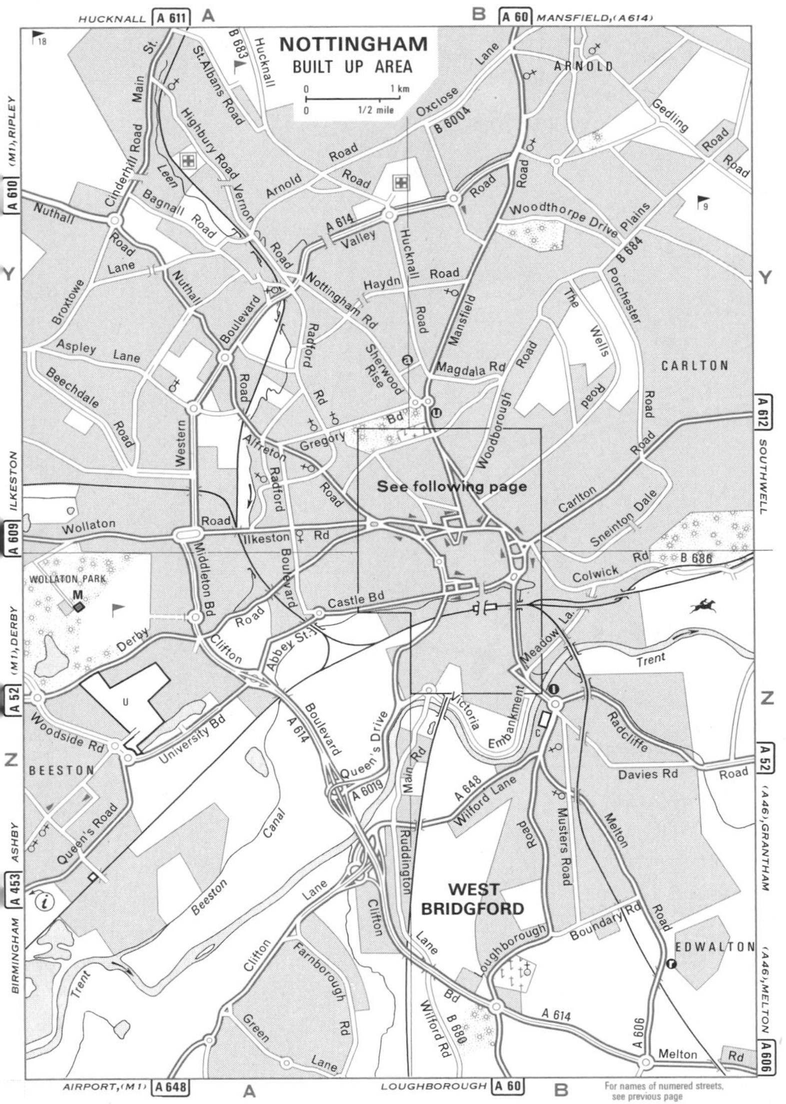

at Toton SW: 6 ½ m. on A 453 – Z – ✉ Nottingham – ☎ 060 76 Long Eaton:

Manor, Nottingham Rd, NG9 6EF, ☎ 3487 – Ⓟ
17 rm ☕ 5.50/11.00 **s.**

Grange Farm, Nottingham Rd, NG9 6EJ, ☎ 69426 – Ⓟ
closed Sunday, spring Bank Holiday week and Bank Holidays – **M** 3.95/4.80 **t.** 🍷 1.90.

at Long Eaton SW: 8 m. on B 6002 by A 52 – AZ – ✉ Nottingham – ☎ 060 76 Long Eaton:

Novotel, Bostock Lane, NG10 4EP, ☎ 60106, Telex 377585, heated, – TV wc ☎ ♿ Ⓟ.
M (grill rest. only) 3.75 **st.** – ☕ 1.70 – **112 rm** 13.70/17.00 **st.**

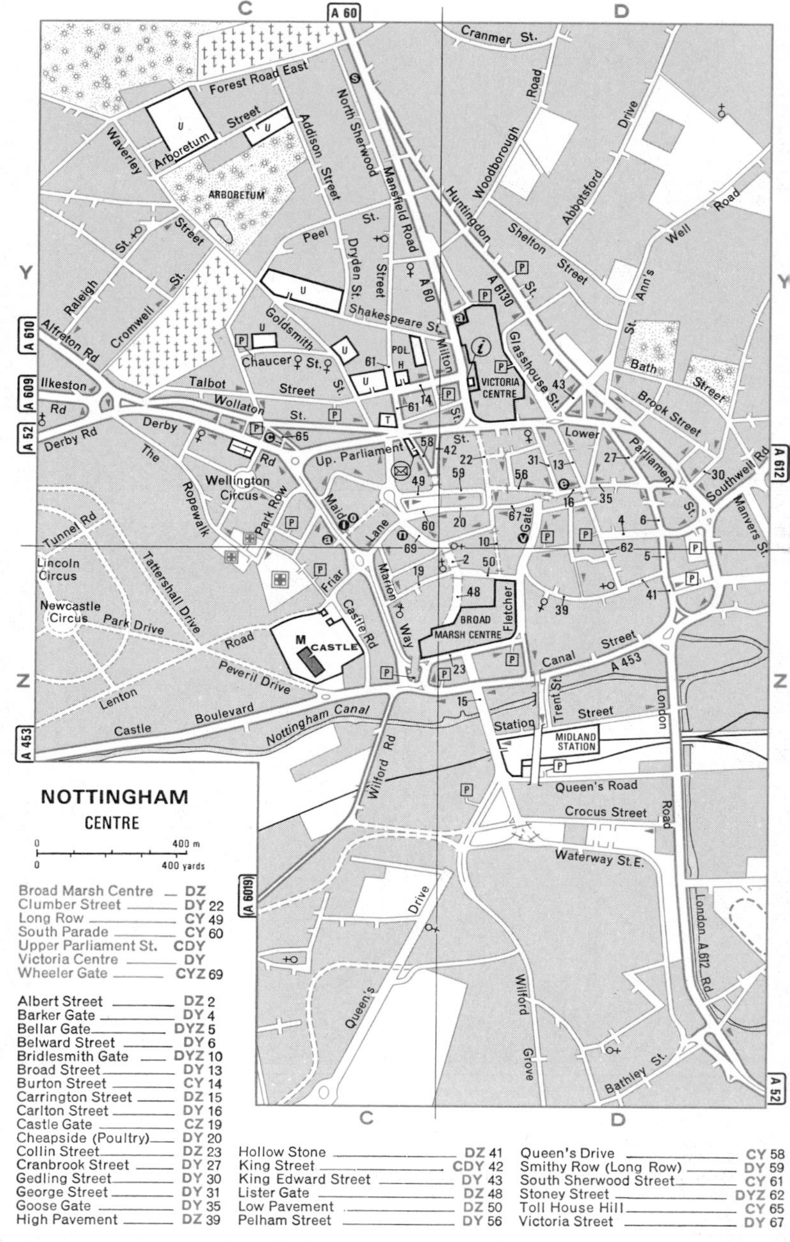

Broad Marsh Centre — DZ
Clumber Street — DY 22
Long Row — CY 49
South Parade — CY 60
Upper Parliament St. CDY
Victoria Centre — DY
Wheeler Gate — CYZ 69

Albert Street — DZ 2
Barker Gate — DY 4
Bellar Gate — DYZ 5
Belward Street — DY 6
Bridlesmith Gate — DYZ 10
Broad Street — DY 13
Burton Street — CY 14
Carrington Street — DZ 15
Carlton Street — DY 16
Castle Gate — CZ 19
Cheapside (Poultry) — DY 20
Collin Street — DZ 23
Cranbrook Street — DY 27
Gedling Street — DY 30
George Street — DY 31
Goose Gate — DY 35
High Pavement — DZ 39

Hollow Stone — DZ 41
King Street — CDY 42
King Edward Street — DY 43
Lister Gate — DZ 48
Low Pavement — DZ 50
Pelham Street — DY 56

Queen's Drive — CY 58
Smithy Row (Long Row) — DY 59
South Sherwood Street — CY 61
Stoney Street — DYZ 62
Toll House Hill — CY 65
Victoria Street — DY 67

I prezzi

Per ogni chiarimento sui prezzi qui riportati, consultate le spiegazioni a p. 32.

at Sandiacre W: 8 m. on A 52 – AZ – ✉ ☎ 0602 Nottingham:

Post House (T.H.F.), Bostocks Lane, NG10 5NJ, ☎ 397800, Telex 377378 – TV wc ☎ ♿ P.
M 2.95/4.00 **st.** 1.50 – 2.00 – **106 rm** 13.00/18.00 **st.**

MICHELIN Branch, Glaisdale Drive East, NG8 4JN, ☎ 293251.

ALFA-ROMEO, CITROEN 325/333 Mansfield Rd ☎ 606666
AUSTIN-MORRIS-MG-ROVER-TRIUMPH-WOLSELEY Talbot St. ☎ 56051
AUSTIN-MG-WOLSELEY 136 Burton Rd, Carlton ☎ 248808
AUSTIN-MG-WOLSELEY Church St. ☎ 77781
AUSTIN-MORRIS-MG Melton Rd, West Bridgford ☎ 811386
AUSTIN-MORRIS-MG Nuthall Rd ☎ 71697
AUSTIN-MG-ROVER-TRIUMPH-WOLSELEY Hucknall Rd, Bulwell ☎ 272915
CHRYSLER-SIMCA Sherwood St. ☎ 46381
CHRYSLER-SIMCA Lenton Lane ☎ 863301
CHRYSLER-SIMCA 136/138 Loughborough Rd ☎ 814320
DAF 61a Mansfield Rd ☎ 45635
DAIMLER-JAGUAR-MG-ROVER-TRIUMPH, ROLLS ROYCE-BENTLEY Derby Rd ☎ 77701
DATSUN Woodborough Rd ☎ 623324
DATSUN Main St., Bulwell ☎ 272226
DATSUN Castle Rd ☎ 46674
FIAT 375/381 Mansfield Rd ☎ 623251
FORD London Rd ☎ 56282
FORD Derby Rd ☎ 46111
JENSEN Watnall ☎ 060 743 (Kimberley) 2781
MORRIS-MG-WOLSELEY Clifton Bridge Roundabout, Lenton Lane ☎ 56131
MORRIS-MG-WOLSELEY 199 Mansfield Rd ☎ 268655
OPEL Beechdale Rd ☎ 293023
PEUGEOT Loughborough Rd ☎ 862121
RENAULT Ilkestone Rd ☎ 781938
RENAULT Sawley, Long Eaton ☎ 060 76 (Long Eaton) 3121
SAAB 499/509 Woodborough Rd ☎ 606674
VAUXHALL Clifton Lane, Clifton ☎ 211228
VAUXHALL 5 Haywood Rd, Mapperley ☎ 603231
VAUXHALL Lenton Lane, Dunkirk ☎ 71162
VAUXHALL Main St., Bulwell ☎ 279216
VOLVO Holly Lane ☎ 221141
VOLVO 50 Plains Rd ☎ 266336
VW, AUDI-NSU 180 Loughborough Rd ☎ 813813

NUNEATON Warw. 986 ⑫ and ㉛ – pop. 67,027 – ☎ 0682.

Envir.: Arbury Hall* (Gothic house 18C) *AC*, SW: 4 m.

18 Green Lane, Garden Suburb, ☎ 624 1190 – 18 Uppermill ☎ 045 77 (Saddleworth) 2059, E: 5 m.

i Nuneaton Library, Church St. ☎ 384027/8.

London 107 – Birmingham 25 – Coventry 10 – Leicester 18.

Chase (Ansells), Higham Lane, CV11 6AG, NE: 1 m. off A 47 ☎ 383406, – TV wc P.
M 3.45/3.65 **st.** 1.75 – **28 rm** 12.00/15.30 **st.**

Nuneaton Crest Motel (Crest), Watling St., CV11 5JH, NE: 2 ½ m. at junction A 47 and A 5 ☎ 329711 – TV wc ☎ P.
M (bar lunch) 2.65/3.30 **s.** 1.50 – 1.60 – **47 rm** 10.95/15.50 **s.**

Abbey Grange, Manor Court Rd, CV12, ☎ 385535 – TV P
9 rm 7.00/12.00.

at Bulkington SE: 4 m. by B 4114 on B 4112 – ✉ Nuneaton – ☎ 0203 Bedworth:

Weston Hall, Weston Lane, CV12 9RU, ☎ 315475, , park – wc P.
closed 1 week at Christmas – **M** a la carte 3.45/5.75 **t.** 1.15 – **32 rm** 7.30/12.40 **t.**

AUSTIN-MG-WOLSELEY Leicester Rd ☎ 4145
CHRYSLER-SIMCA 208/214 Edward St. ☎ 383339
DAF Whittleford Rd ☎ 323603
FIAT Haunchwood Rd ☎ 382807
FORD Hinckley Rd ☎ 4101
JAGUAR-MORRIS-MG Weddington Rd ☎ 383471
RENAULT Nuneaton Rd, Bulkington ☎ 383344
ROVER-TRIUMPH Avenue Rd ☎ 67867
SAAB Lutterworth Rd ☎ 382093
VAUXHALL Arbury Rd, Stockingford ☎ 384833
VW, AUDI-NSU Edward St. ☎ 385665

NUNNINGTON North Yorks. – pop. 189 – ✉ Helmsley – ☎ 043 95.

London 229 – Malton 11 – **Middlesbrough 35** – York 19.

Ryedale Lodge with rm, YO6 5XB, W: 1 ½ m. ☎ 246, – wc P
M *(closed Monday dinner, Christmas Day, 1 January and Easter Day)* (dinner only) approx. 5.00 1.50 – **3 rm** 7.00/14.00.

OADBY Leics. 986 ㉗㉘ – see Leicester.

OAKHAM Leics. 986 ㉘ – pop. 6,414 – ☎ 0572.

i Public Library, Catmos St. ☎ 2918.

London 103 – Leicester 26 – Northampton 35 – **Nottingham 28.**

Crown (Interchange), 16 High St., LE15 6AP, ☎ 3631 – TV wc ☎ P.
M 2.60/3.35 **t.** 1.40 – **26 rm** 9.75/14.10 **t.**

George, Market Pl., LE15 6DT, ☎ 2284 – P
M approx. 3.00 **t.** 1.00 – **10 rm.**

AUSTIN-MORRIS-MG-ROVER-TRIUMPH-WOLSELEY Burley Rd ☎ 2657

OAKLEY Hants. – see Basingstoke.

OBORNE Dorset – see Sherborne.

OCKHAM Surrey – pop. 447 – ✉ Esher – ☎ 048 643 Ripley.
London 29 – Guildford 8.

XXX **Hautboy Inn** with rm, Alms Heath, GU23 6NP, ☎ 3553, ⛱ – ⛀wc Ⓟ
M a la carte 5.10/6.90 **t.** 🍷 1.50 – **5 rm** ☕ 12.50 **t.** – P 14.00 **t.**

ODIHAM Hants. 986 ㊱ – pop. 4,310 – ☎ 025 671.
London 51 – Reading 16 – Winchester 25.

🏠 **George,** High St., RG25 1LP, ☎ 2081 – Ⓟ
M a la carte 4.05/5.95 🍷 2.00 – **6 rm** ☕ 6.00/12.00 **st.**

at North Warnborough SE: 1 m. on A 287 – ✉ Basingstoke – ☎ 025 671 Odiham

XX **Mill House,** RG25 1ET, ☎ 2953, ⛱ – Ⓟ
closed Sunday, Monday and first 2 weeks January – **M** a la carte 5.30/7.15 🍷 1.50.

at Well SE: 3 ½ m. – ✉ Basingstoke – ☎ 045 824 Long Sutton:

X **Chequers Inn,** Long Sutton ☎ 605, French rest. – Ⓟ
closed Sunday, Monday and February – **M** a la carte 2.95/5.35 🍷 1.50.

ALFA-ROMEO, MERCEDES-BENZ The Square ☎ 2294

ODSTOCK Wilts. – see Salisbury.

OLD BOSHAM West Sussex – see Chichester.

OLDHAM Greater Manchester 986 ⑤ and ㉓ – pop. 105,913 – ☎ 061 Manchester.
⛳18 Lees New Rd ☎ 624 4986 – ⛳18 High Barn ☎ 624 2154.
i Local Interest Centre, Greaves St. ☎ 620 8930.
London 212 – Leeds 36 – Manchester 7 – Sheffield 38.

🏨 **The Bower,** Hollinwood Av., OL9 8DE, SW: 2 ½ m. by A 62 on A 6104 ☎ 682 7254 – TV ⛀wc ☎ Ⓟ. 🏊
M a la carte 4.00/4.85 **st.** – **28 rm** ☕ 10.50/12.50 **st.**

🏨 Belgrade, Manchester St., OL8 1UZ, ☎ 624 0555, Telex 667782 – ⇅ TV ⛀wc ☎ Ⓟ. 🏊
130 rm.

RENAULT Manchester Rd, Hollinwood ☎ 624 1979

OLD HARLOW Essex – see Harlow.

OLLERTON Notts. 986 ㉘ – pop. 7,855 – ✉ Newark – ☎ 0623 Mansfield.
London 151 – Leeds 53 – Lincoln 25 – Nottingham 19 – Sheffield 27.

🏠 **Hop Pole,** Church St., NG22 9AD, ☎ 822573 – Ⓟ
M a la carte 2.85/5.05 🍷 1.60 – **10 rm** ☕ 6.00/10.50 – P 9.50/10.00.

OLNEY Bucks. – pop. 2,750 – ☎ 0234 Bedford.
London 62 – Bedford 11 – Oxford 45.

XX **Four Pillars,** 60 High St., MK46 4BE, ☎ 711563, ⛱
closed 25 and 26 December – **M** a la carte 3.25/5.25 **s.** 🍷 1.75.

OMBERSLEY Heref. and Worc. – pop. 2,209 – ✉ Droitwich – ☎ 0905 Worcester.
London 130 – Birmingham 24 – Kidderminster 4 – Worcester 5.

XX **Venture In,** WR9 0EW, ☎ 620552 – Ⓟ
closed Sunday, Monday and 3 weeks August – **M** a la carte 5.25/8.10 **t.** 🍷 1.95.

ORFORD Suffolk – pop. 673 – ✉ Woodbridge – ☎ 039 45.
London 93 – Ipswich 20 – Norwich 48.

🏠 **Crown and Castle** (T.H.F.), IP12 2LJ, ☎ 205, ⛱ – TV ⛀wc ☎ Ⓟ
M a la carte 4.00/4.80 **st.** 🍷 1.50 – **20 rm** ☕ 8.50/15.00 **st.**

X **King's Head Inn** with rm, Front St., IP12 2LW, ☎ 271 – Ⓟ
M *(closed Sunday dinner and Monday)* a la carte 3.40/5.10 🍷 2.00 – **4 rm** ☕ 8.50/13.00

X **Butley-Orford Oysterage,** Market Hill, IP12 2LH, ☎ 277, Seafood
closed 25 and 26 December – **M** (lunch only in January and February) a la carte 2.90/4.25 **t.** 🍷 1.40.

ORMESBY ST. MARGARET Norfolk – pop. 2,588 – ✉ ☎ 0493 Great Yarmouth.
London 132 – Great Yarmouth 5 – Norwich 20.

XX **Ormesby Lodge** 🐌 with rm, Decoy Rd, NR29 3LG, at junction of Hemsby Rd ☎ 730910, ⛱ – TV ⛀wc Ⓟ
closed October – **M** *(closed Sunday and Christmas)* (dinner only) a la carte 2.65/8.65 – **5 rm** ☕ 8.00/16.00.

OSWESTRY Salop 986 ㉗ – pop. 12,018 – ☎ 0691.
ℹ Babbinswood, Whittington ☎ 069 187 (Whittington Castle) 488 (summer only).
London 182 – Chester 28 – Shrewsbury 18.

Wynnstay (T.H.F.), 43 Church St., SY11 2SZ, ☎ 5261 – TV wc ☎ P
M a la carte 3.95/5.35 **st.** 1.50 – **31 rm** 8.00/15.50 **st.**

AUSTIN-MG-WOLSELEY Lower Brook St. ☎ 2285
BMW Victoria Rd ☎ 2413
CHRYSLER-SIMCA Willow St. ☎ 2301
FORD Salop Rd ☎ 4141
MORRIS-MG-ROVER-TRIUMPH-WOLSELEY Salop Rd ☎ 3237
RENAULT ☎ 2233
ROVER-TRIUMPH Victoria Rd ☎ 3581
VAUXHALL ☎ 2235
VW, AUDI-NSU Station Rd ☎ 3491

OTTERBURN Northumb. 986 ⑮ – pop. 564 – ☎ 083 02 (3 fig.)or 0830 (5 fig.).
London 313 – Carlisle 54 – Edinburgh 74 – Newcastle-upon-Tyne 31.

Percy Arms (Swallow), NE19 1NR, ☎ 261, – wc ☎ P.
32 rm.

Otterburn Tower (S & N), NE19 1NP, ☎ 673, – wc P
15 rm.

OTTERY ST. MARY Devon 986 ㊴ – pop. 5,834 – ☎ 040 481.
See: St. Mary's Church★ 13C-16C.
London 167 – Exeter 12 – Taunton 24.

XX **The Lodge,** Silver St., EX11 1DB, ☎ 2356
closed Sunday dinner, Monday, Good Friday, 25 and 26 December, 1 week November and 3 weeks February – **M** a la carte 3.20/5.70 **t.** 1.50.

OULTON West Yorks. 986 ⑫ – see Leeds.

OULTON BROAD Suffolk – pop. 8,718 – ✉ ☎ 0502 Lowestoft.
London 117 – Great Yarmouth 10 – Ipswich 44 – Norwich 30.

Golden Galleon Motel, Bridge Rd, NR32 3LR, ☎ 2157 – TV wc P
M a la carte 2.05/4.75 **t.** – **27 rm** 9.20/16.40 **st.**

OUNDLE Northants. 986 ㉜ – pop. 3,739 – ✉ Peterborough – ☎ 083 22.
London 89 – Leicester 37 – Northampton 30.

Talbot (Anchor), New St., PE8 4EA, ☎ 3621, Group Telex 27120 – TV wc ☎ P
M approx. 2.80 **t.** 1.00 – **21 rm** 9.35/14.85.

XX Barnwell Mill, PE8 5PB, S: ¾ m. on A 605 ☎ 2621, « Converted mill » – P.

AUSTIN-MG-WOLSELEY 1 Station Rd ☎ 3542
MORRIS-MG-WOLSELEY 1 Benefield Rd ☎ 3519

OVERCOTE FERRY Cambs. – see St. Ives.

OVINGTON Northumb. – pop. 373 – ✉ ☎ 0661 Prudhoe-on-Tyne.
London 295 – Hexham 9 – Newcastle-upon-Tyne 13.

Highlander Inn, NE42 6DH, ☎ 32016, – wc wc ☎ P
M *(closed Sunday to non-residents and Christmas Day)* a la carte 3.60/5.55 – **15 rm** 5.50/10.00.

OWER Hants. – see Romsey.

OWLSWICK Bucks. – ✉ Aylesbury – ☎ 084 44 Princes Risborough.
London 47 – Oxford 20.

Shoulder of Mutton, HP17 9RH, ☎ 4304, – TV wc ☎ P
M (dinner only) approx. 4.50 – **10 rm** 8.50/13.00.

OXFORD Oxon. 986 ㉛ – pop. 108,805 – ☎ 0865.
See: Colleges Quarter★★★: Merton College★ (Old Library★★★, hall★, quadrangle★, chapel windows and glass★) BZ **L** – Christ Church College★ (hall★★, cathedral★, quadrangle★, tower★) BZ **D** – Bodleian Old Library★★ (painted ceiling★★) BZ **M**² – Divinity School (carved vaulting★★) BZ **M**² – Magdalen College★★ (cloister★★, chapel★) BZ **K** – New College (cloister★, chapel★) BZ **Y** – All Souls College (chapel★) BZ **A** – University College (gateway★) BZ **V** – Corpus Christi College (quadrangle and sundial★) BZ **E** – Radcliffe Camera★ BZ **O** – Sheldonian Theatre★ BZ **M**³ – High Street★ BZ **9** – Ashmolean Museum★★ BY **M**¹. **Envir.:** Blenheim Palace★★★ 18C (park★★) *AC*, NW: 7 m. on A 34 AY.
18 Banbury Rd ☎ 54415, N: by A 423 AY.
ℹ St. Aldates ☎ 48707 or 49811.
London 58 – Birmingham 63 – Brighton 99 – Bristol 69 – Cardiff 101 – Coventry 50 – Southampton 67.

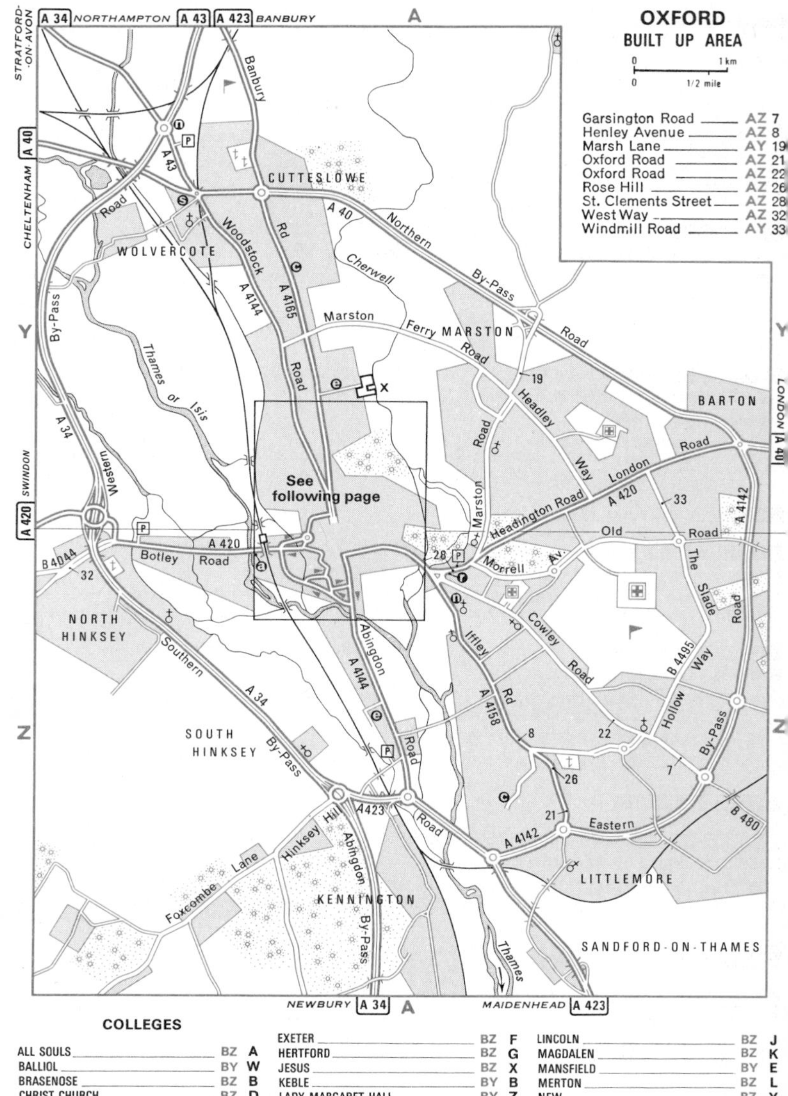

COLLEGES

ALL SOULS	BZ	A
BALLIOL	BY	W
BRASENOSE	BZ	B
CHRIST CHURCH	BZ	D
CORPUS CHRISTI	BZ	E
EXETER	BZ	F
HERTFORD	BZ	G
JESUS	BZ	X
KEBLE	BY	B
LADY MARGARET HALL	BY	Z
LINACRE	BZ	I
LINCOLN	BZ	J
MAGDALEN	BZ	K
MANSFIELD	BY	E
MERTON	BZ	L
NEW	BZ	Y
NUFFIELD	BZ	N

Randolph (T.H.F.), Beaumont St., OX1 2LN, ☎ 47481, Telex 83446 – lift TV Ⓟ. BZ **n**
M 3.95/4.25 **st.** 🍷 1.60 – ☕ 2.00 – **114 rm** 14.00/20.50 **st.**

Linton Lodge (Interchange), 11-13 Linton Rd off Banbury Rd, OX2 6UJ, ☎ 53461, – lift TV wc ☎ ♿ Ⓟ. AY **e**
M 3.25/5.00 **t.** 🍷 1.60 – ☕ 1.75 – **72 rm** 13.10/23.75 **s.**

TraveLodge (T.H.F.) without rest., Pear Tree Hill Roundabout, Woodstock Rd, OX2 8JZ, ☎ 54301, Telex 83202, heated – TV wc ☎ ♿ Ⓟ. AY **n**
101 rm ☕ 10.50/14.00 **st.**

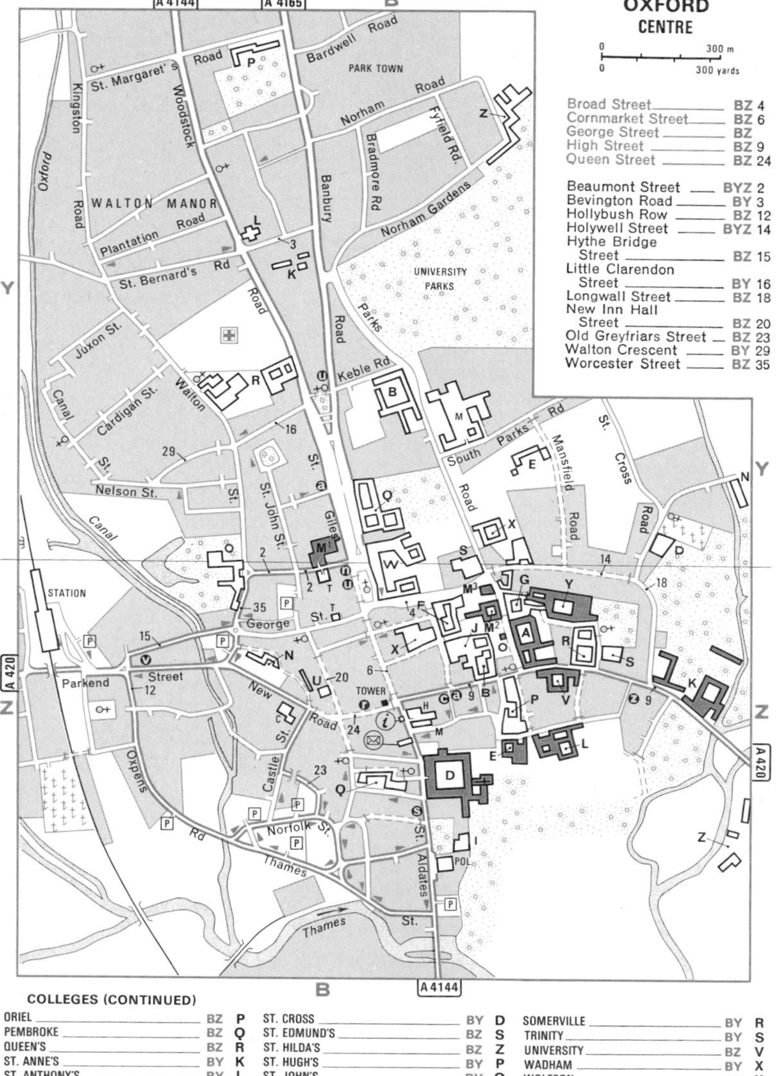

COLLEGES (CONTINUED)

ORIEL	BZ	P	ST. CROSS	BY	D	SOMERVILLE	BY	R
PEMBROKE	BZ	Q	ST. EDMUND'S	BZ	S	TRINITY	BY	S
QUEEN'S	BZ	R	ST. HILDA'S	BZ	Z	UNIVERSITY	BZ	V
ST. ANNE'S	BY	K	ST. HUGH'S	BY	P	WADHAM	BY	X
ST. ANTHONY'S	BY	L	ST. JOHN'S	BY	Q	WOLFSON	AY	X
ST. CATHERINE'S	BY	N	ST. PETER'S	BZ	U	WORCESTER	BY	O

Oxford Lodge Motel (County), Wolvercote Roundabout, OX2 8AL, ☎ 59933 – wc P. — AY **s**
M a la carte 3.75/4.75 **st.** 1.35 – **89 rm** 13.35/20.20 **st.**

Royal Oxford (Embassy), Park End St., OX1 1HR, ☎ 48432 – wc P. — BZ **v**
closed Christmas – **M** 2.50/3.00 **st.** 1.45 – **23 rm** 8.75/15.50 **st.**

Eastgate (Anchor), The High, OX1 4BE, ☎ 48244, Group Telex 27120 – wc P. — BZ **z**
M approx. 3.25 **t.** 1.00 – **46 rm** 9.75/16.50 **st.**

P.T.O. →

Old Parsonage, 1-3 Banbury Rd, OX2 6NN, ☎ 54843, – Ⓟ BY u
closed Christmas week – **M** (dinner only and Sunday lunch) a la carte 3.10/4.25 **t.** 1.25 – **34 rm** 5.50/11.00 **t.**

Isis, 45-53 Iffley Rd, OX4 1ED, ☎ 48894 – wc Ⓟ AZ n
M a la carte 3.75/5.50 1.50 – **36 rm** 8.50/17.50 **t.**

St. Giles, 56 St. Giles, OX1 3LU, ☎ 54620 BY a
10 rm 7.00/12.00 **st.**

Willow Reaches, 1 Wytham St., OX1 4SU, ☎ 43767, AZ e
closed January – **7 rm** 10.00/15.00 **st.**

Old Black Horse, 102 St. Clements, OX4 1AR, ☎ 44691 – Ⓟ AZ r
closed Christmas – **20 rm** 6.00/11.00 **t.**

River, 17 Botley Rd, OX2 0AA, ☎ 43475, – Ⓟ AZ a
closed Christmas to 1 January – **18 rm** 7.00/15.00 **t.**

XXX ✿ **Elizabeth,** 84 St. Aldates, OX1 1RA, ☎ 42230 BZ s
closed Monday, last 3 weeks August, Good Friday and 24 to 26 December – **M** (dinner only and Sunday lunch) a la carte 5.35/9.15 **s.** 2.50
Spec. Quenelles de saumon sauce Nantua, Suprême de volaille au vin blanc, Sorbet au champagne.

XX **Saraceno,** 15 Magdalen St., OX1 3AE, ☎ 49171, Italian rest. BZ u
closed Sunday – **M** a la carte 4.55/6.65 **t.** 1.25.

XX ✿ **La Sorbonne,** 1st floor, 130a High St., OX1 4DH, ☎ 41320, French rest. BZ c
closed Sunday, last 2 weeks August and Bank Holidays – **M** a la carte 5.15/6.75 **t.** 0.95
Spec. Suprême de volaille à l'estragon, Râble de lièvre sauce poivrade, Crêpes fourrées flambées au Calvados.

XX **Les Quat'Saisons,** 272 Banbury Rd ☎ 53540, French rest. AY c
closed Sunday and 24 December-2 January – **M** a la carte 3.70/5.60 **t.** 0.80.

XX **Tudor Cottage,** 56 Church Way, Iffley, OX4 4EF, ☎ 777690, – Ⓟ AZ c
closed Sunday, Monday and Bank Holidays – **M** (dinner only) a la carte 5.90/7.25 **t.** 1.50.

X **Bleu Blanc Rouge,** 129 High St., OX1 3HY, ☎ 42883, French rest. BZ a
closed Tuesday, 2 weeks July and 1 week August – **M** 4.50 **st.** 0.95.

X **La Cantina di Capri,** 34 Queen St., OX1 1ER, ☎ 47760, Italian rest. BZ r
closed Monday – **M** a la carte 3.75/5.95 **t.** 1.20.

AUSTIN-MG-WOLSELEY Park End St. ☎ 21421
AUSTIN-MORRIS-MG-WOLSELEY Oxford Rd, Kidlington ☎ 086 75 (Kidlington) 4363
AUSTIN-MG-WOLSELEY Abingdon Rd ☎ 42241
BMW, VAUXHALL 280 Banbury Rd ☎ 511461
CHRYSLER-SIMCA 311/321 Banbury Rd ☎ 53232
CITROEN 281 Banbury Rd ☎ 54521
DAF, SAAB 75 Woodstock Rd ☎ 57028
DAIMLER-JAGUAR-ROVER-TRIUMPH Woodstock Rd ☎ 59955
DATSUN, VAUXHALL 72 Rose Hill ☎ 774696
FIAT, LANCIA, PEUGEOT, ROLLS ROYCE Banbury Rd ☎ 59944
FORD West Way ☎ 4996
MERCEDES-BENZ, PEUGEOT, VW, AUDI-NSU 2 Oxford Rd ☎ 086 75 (Kidlington) 3732
MORRIS-WOLSELEY Magdalen Rd ☎ 47307
OPEL, VAUXHALL Botley Rd ☎ 722455
PEUGEOT Benson ☎ 0491 (Wallingford) 35656
RENAULT 265 Iffley Rd ☎ 40101

OXTED Surrey – pop. 9,970 – ☎ 088 33.

London 23 – Brighton 38 – Maidstone 26.

Hoskins, Station Rd West, RH8 9EF, ☎ 2338 – wc Ⓟ
M 2.95/3.60 **s.** 1.00 – **10 rm** 10.00/16.00.

XX **Barons,** 28-30 Station Rd East, RH8 0PG, ☎ 3988
closed Sunday, Monday and Bank Holidays – **M** 2.00/3.75 **t.** 1.50.

AUSTIN-JAGUAR-MORRIS-MG-ROVER-TRIUMPH Station Rd East ☎ 3325

PADSTOW Cornwall 986 ㊳ – pop. 2,802 – ☎ 084 13 (3 fig.) or 0841 (6 fig.).

London 288 – Exeter 78 – **Plymouth 45** – Truro 23.

Metropole (T.H.F.), Station Rd, PL28 8DB, ☎ 486, ≤ Camel estuary, heated, – Ⓟ
M a la carte 4.10/5.70 1.50 – **42 rm** 14.00/26.00 **st.**

XX **Blue Lobster,** North Quay, PL28 8AF, ☎ 451, Seafood
closed 2 weeks November – **M** (dinner only) a la carte 4.20/7.30 **t.**

at Constantine Bay **W : 3 m. off B 3276 – ✉ ☎ 0481 St. Merryn :**

Treglos , PL28 8JH, ☎ 520727, ≤, – wc Ⓟ
mid March-November – **M** 3.95/4.50 1.25 – **40 rm** 9.00/20.00 **s.**

PAIGNTON Devon 986 ㊴ – pop. 35,100 – ☎ 0803.

See : Oldway Mansion* (Renaissance) *AC* Y **E** – Zoo* *AC* by A 385 Z. **Envir. :** Compton Castle* (13C-16C) *AC*, NW : 4 m. by Marldon Rd Y.

i Festival Hall, Esplanade Rd ☎ 558383.

London 226 – Exeter 26 **– Plymouth 29.**

Plan of Built up Area : See Torquay

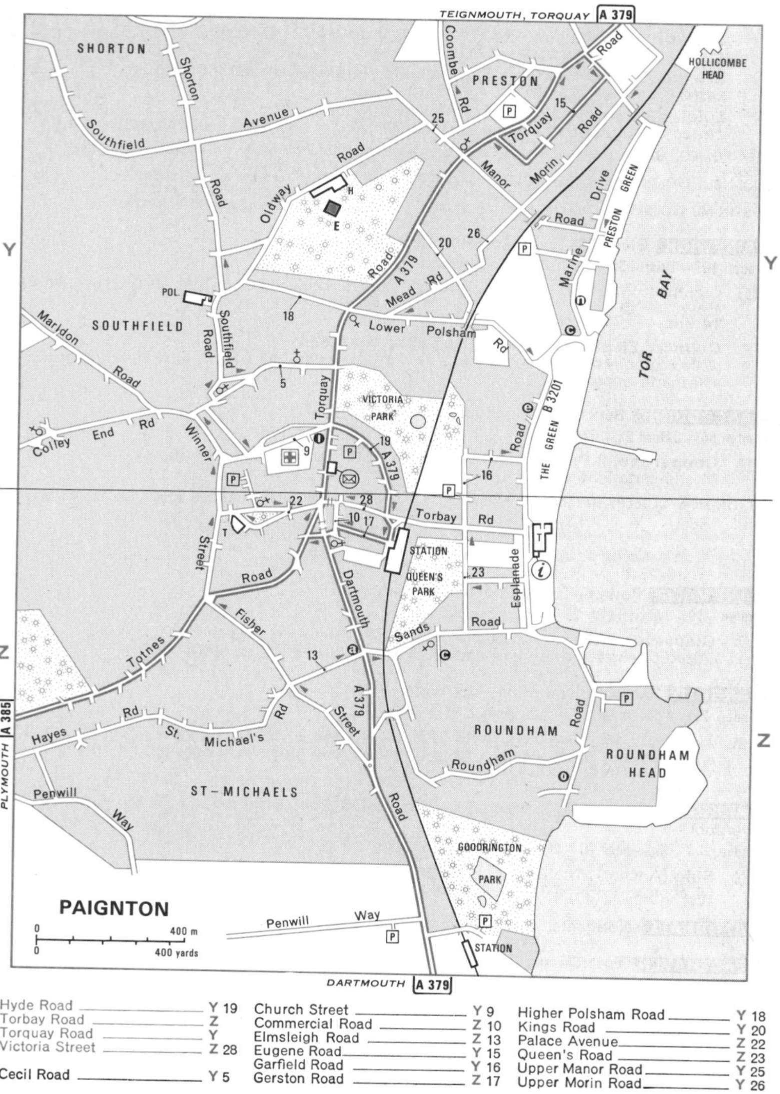

Hyde Road ______ Y 19	Church Street ______ Y 9	Higher Polsham Road ______ Y 18
Torbay Road ______ Z	Commercial Road ______ Z 10	Kings Road ______ Y 20
Torquay Road ______ Y	Elmsleigh Road ______ Z 13	Palace Avenue ______ Z 22
Victoria Street ______ Z 28	Eugene Road ______ Y 15	Queen's Road ______ Z 23
Cecil Road ______ Y 5	Garfield Road ______ Y 16	Upper Manor Road ______ Y 25
	Gerston Road ______ Z 17	Upper Morin Road ______ Y 26

Redcliffe, 4 Marine Drive, TQ3 2NL, ☎ 556224, ≤, heated, – **P**.
M 3.50/4.50 **st.** 0.80 – **70 rm** 10.00/23.00 **st.** – P 12.00/17.50 **st.** Y **n**

Palace (T.H.F.), Esplanade Rd, TQ4 6BJ, ☎ 555121, heated, – TV **P**.
M a la carte 4.10/5.70 **st.** 1.50 – **57 rm** 11.00/24.50 **st.** – P 15.75/20.50 **st.** Y **e**

Middlepark, 3 Marine Drive, TQ3 2NJ, ☎ 559025, – **P**
season – **24 rm.** Y **c**

St. Ann's, 6 Alta Vista Rd, TQ4 6BZ, ☎ 557360, ≤, – wc **P**
April-November – **M** (dinner only) 2.50/5.00 1.50 – **25 rm** 6.00/14.00 **s.** Z **o**

P.T.O. →

- **Stantor,** 7 St. Andrews Rd, TQ4 6HA, ℡ 557156 – wc Ⓟ — Z c
  May-October – **15 rm** 4.50/11.00 **s.**
- **Erleigh Court Private,** 1 Elmsleigh Rd, TQ4 5AX, ℡ 551565 – Ⓟ — Z a
  Easter-October – **15 rm** 4.00/8.00 **s.**
- **Luigi,** 59 Torquay Rd, TQ3 3DT, ℡ 556185, Italian rest. — Y i
  closed Sunday and 25-26 December – **M** (dinner only) a la carte 4.05/6.35 1.50.

ALFA-ROMEO, BMW, SAAB Collaton St. Mary ℡ 558567
AUDI-NSU, LANCIA, MERCEDES-BENZ Bishop's Pl. ℡ 556234
AUSTIN-MG-WOLSELEY 69 Torquay Rd ℡ 551818
CHRYSLER-SIMCA 375 Torquay Rd ℡ 523555
FIAT Totnes Rd ℡ 554484
FORD 338 Torquay Rd ℡ 543433
TOYOTA Dartmouth Rd ℡ 554721
VAUXHALL Steartfield Rd ℡ 559122

PAINSWICK Glos. 986 ㉛ – pop. 2,895 – ✉ Stroud – ✆ 0452.
London 107 – Bristol 35 – Cheltenham 10 – Gloucester 7.

- Cranham Wood with rm, Kemps Lane, Tibbiwell, GL6 6YB, ℡ 812160, – TV wc Ⓟ
  14 rm.
- **Country Elephant,** New St., GL6 6XA, ℡ 813564
  closed Sunday dinner, Monday and 25-26 December – **M** (dinner only and Sunday lunch) a la carte approx. 4.70.

PANGBOURNE Berks. 986 ㊱ – pop. 2,503 – ✆ 073 57.
London 56 – Oxford 22 – Reading 6.

- **Copper Inn,** 2 Church Rd, RG8 7AR, ℡ 2244, – TV wc Ⓟ.
  M a la carte 5.35/6.05 1.20 – **14 rm** 14.80/18.50 **st.**

AUSTIN-MG-WOLSELEY Reading Rd ℡ 2376
JENSEN, LANCIA, MERCEDES-BENZ Station Rd ℡ 3322

A Londres, en toutes saisons,
il est prudent de réserver sa chambre à l'avance.

PANT MAWR Powys – ✉ ✆ 055 15 Llangurig.
London 219 – Aberystwyth 21 – Shrewsbury 55.

- **Glansevern Arms,** SY18 6SY, on A 44 ℡ 240, – Ⓟ
  closed Christmas week – **M** approx. 3.30 1.50 – **6 rm** 5.50/11.00.

PARBOLD Lancs. – pop. 1,994 – ✉ Wigan – ✆ 025 76.
London 212 – Liverpool 18 – Manchester 33 – Preston 18.

- **Lindley,** Lancaster Lane, WN8 7AB, on B 5246 ℡ 2804 – TV wc wc Ⓟ
  closed 25 and 26 December – **M** *(closed Saturday lunch)* a la carte 2.90/4.40 **t.** 1.20 – **10 rm** 10.00/14.00 **t.**

PARKGATE Cheshire 986 ⑤ and ㉗ – pop. 2,939 (inc. Leighton) – ✉ Neston – ✆ 051 Liverpool.
London 206 – Birkenhead 10 – Chester 11 – Liverpool 12.

- **Ship** (Anchor), The Parade, L64 6SA, ℡ 336 3931, Group Telex 27120 – TV wc Ⓟ
  M approx. 2.85 **t.** 1.00 – **19 rm** 9.10/14.85 **st.**

PATTISHALL Northants. – see Towcester.

PEACEHAVEN East Sussex – pop. 8,472 – ✆ 079 14.
Brighton Rd, Newhaven ℡ 079 12 (Newhaven) 4049.
London 60 – Brighton 6.5 – Eastbourne 16 – Lewes 10.

- **Brighton Motel,** 1 South Coast Rd, BN9 8SY, ℡ 3736 – TV wc Ⓟ
  M (grill rest. only) a la carte 2.70/4.45 **t.** 1.00 – 1.50 – **19 rm** 8.00/12.00 **st.**
- **La Mer,** 20 Steyning Av., BN9 8JL, ℡ 2291 – Ⓟ
  closed Sunday dinner, Monday and February – **M** a la carte 4.25/6.00.

PEASE POTTAGE West Sussex – see Crawley.

PEASLAKE Surrey – see Dorking.

PEASMARSH East Sussex – see Rye.

PELYNT Cornwall – pop. 712 – ✉ Looe – ✆ 050 32 Lanreath.
London 269 – Plymouth 26 – Truro 36.

- Jubilee Inn, PL13 2JZ, on B 3359 ℡ 312, « Part 16 C inn », – wc Ⓟ
  10 rm 7.80/17.60.

PEMBREY Dyfed – pop. 6,317 – ✉ ☎ 055 46 Burry Port.
Envir.: Kidwelly Castle** (12C) *AC*, N: 4 m.
London 211 – Carmarthen 14 – **Swansea 16.**

- **Ashburnham,** Ashburnham Rd, SA16 0TH, ☎ 2328 – Ⓟ
 M 2.85/5.25 **t.** 0.90 – **13 rm** 6.25/12.50 **st.**

PEMBRIDGE Heref and Worc. – pop. 827 – ✉ Leominster – ☎ 054 47.
London 148 – Hereford 15 – Leominster 7.5.

- New Inn, The Square, HR6 9DZ, ☎ 427, – Ⓟ
 7 rm.

PEMBROKE Dyfed 986 ㉚ – pop. 14,197 – ☎ 064 63.
See: Site* – Castle**. **Envir.:** Lamphey (Bishop's palace*) *AC*, E: 2 m. – Carew (castle* 13C) *AC*, NE: 4 ½ m.
Defensible Barracks, Pembroke Dock ☎ 3817.
i Pembroke Coast National Park, Drill Hall, Main St. ☎ 2148 (Easter-September).
London 252 – Carmarthen 32 – Fishguard 26.

- **Old Kings Arms,** 13 Main St., SA71 4JS, ☎ 3611 – TV wc Ⓟ
 M a la carte 3.30/5.00 1.25 – **21 rm** 10.50/18.00 **st.**

CHRYSLER-SIMCA Albion Sq. ☎ 2688
ROVER-TRIUMPH Main St. ☎ 3169

PEMBROKESHIRE (Coast) ** Dyfed 986 ㉚.
See: From Cemaes Head to Strumble Head**: Newport (site*) – Pentre Ifan (burial chamber*) – Bryn Henllan (site*) – Fishguard ≤** – Strumble Head (≤** from the lighthouse). From Strumble Head to Solva**: Trevine ≤** – Porthgain (cliffs ☼***) – Abereiddy (site*) – St. David's Head** – Whitesand Bay** – Solva (site*).
From Solva to Dale**: Newgale ≤** – Martin's Haven ☼** – St. Ann's Head ≤** – Dale ≤*.
From Dale to Freshwater West*: Freshwater West (site*).
From Freshwater West to Pendine Sands** (Stack Rocks**) – St. Govan's Chapel (site*) – Freshwater East (site*) – Manorbier (castle*) – Tenby (site**) – Amroth (site*) – Pendine Sands*.

PENALLY Dyfed – pop. 1,080 – ✉ ☎ 0834 Tenby.
London 249 – Carmarthen 29 – Tenby 2.

- **Abbey** , SA70 7PY, ☎ 2143 – Ⓟ
 closed October – **8 rm** 7.00/13.00.

PENARTH South Glam. 986 ㉟ – pop. 24,000 – ☎ 0222.
Lavernock Rd ☎ 707048.
i Tourist Information Centre, West House ☎ 707201 (Easter-September).
London 161 – Cardiff 4.

- XXX **Caprice,** 1st floor, 1 Beach Cliff, The Esplanade, CF6 2AS, ☎ 702424, ≤
 closed Sunday and Bank Holidays – **M** a la carte 5.25/7.75 **t.** 1.75.

at Swanbridge **S: 2 ½ m. off B 4267 – ✉ Penarth – ☎ 0222 Sully:**

- XXX **Sully House** with rm, Lavernock Beach Rd, CF6 2XR, ☎ 530448, – TV wc Ⓟ
 M *(closed Saturday lunch, Sunday and Bank Holiday Mondays)* a la carte 5.25/6.50 **t.** 1.60 – **5 rm** 13.00/18.50 **t.**

CHRYSLER-SIMCA Windsor Rd ☎ 707214

PENDOGGETT Cornwall – pop. 60 – ✉ Bodmin – ☎ 020 888 Port Isaac.
London 264 – Newquay 22 – Truro 30.

- XX **Cornish Arms** with rm, St. Kew, PL30 3HH, ☎ 263, – Ⓟ
 M a la carte 3.70/4.85 1.35 – **6 rm** 7.50/15.10.

PENGETHLEY Heref. and Worc. – see Ross-on-Wye.

PENMACHNO Gwynedd – see Betws-y-Coed.

PENMAENHEAD Clwyd – see Colwyn Bay.

PENMAENPOOL Gwynedd – see Dolgellau.

PENNAL Gwynedd – see Machynlleth (Powys).

PENN STREET Bucks. – pop. 250 – ✉ Amersham – ☎ 049 47 Holmer Green.
London 32 – Oxford 30.

XX **Hit or Miss Inn,** HP7 0PX, ℡ 3109 – Ⓟ
closed Sunday dinner and Monday – **M** a la carte 4.85/6.30 **t.** 🍷 1.50.

PENRITH Cumbria 986 ⑲ – pop. **11,306** – ☎ 0768.
Envir. : Lowther (Wildlife Park* *AC*) S : 5 m.
⛳18 ℡ 2217 and 5429, E: ½ m. on Salkeld Rd.
i Robinson's School, Middlegate ℡ 4671 (summer only).
London 290 – Carlisle 24 – Kendal 31 – Lancaster 48.

🏠 **George,** Devonshire St., CA11 7SU, ℡ 2696 – 🛁wc Ⓟ. 🏊
M 3.25/4.50 🍷 1.25 – **32 rm** ☕ 7.00/17.00.

AUDI-NSU, CITROEN Ullswater Rd ℡ 4545
AUSTIN-MG-WOLSELEY 18/19 King St. ℡ 3312
AUSTIN-MORRIS-MG-ROVER-TRIUMPH Victoria Rd ℡ 2666
CHRYSLER-SIMCA Roper St. ℡ 3641
FIAT King St. ℡ 4691
FORD Old London Rd ℡ 2307
RENAULT 11 King St. ℡ 2371
TOYOTA 15 Victoria Rd ℡ 4555
VAUXHALL Scotland Rd ℡ 3756

Benachrichtigen Sie sofort das Hotel,
wenn Sie ein bestelltes Zimmer nicht belegen können.

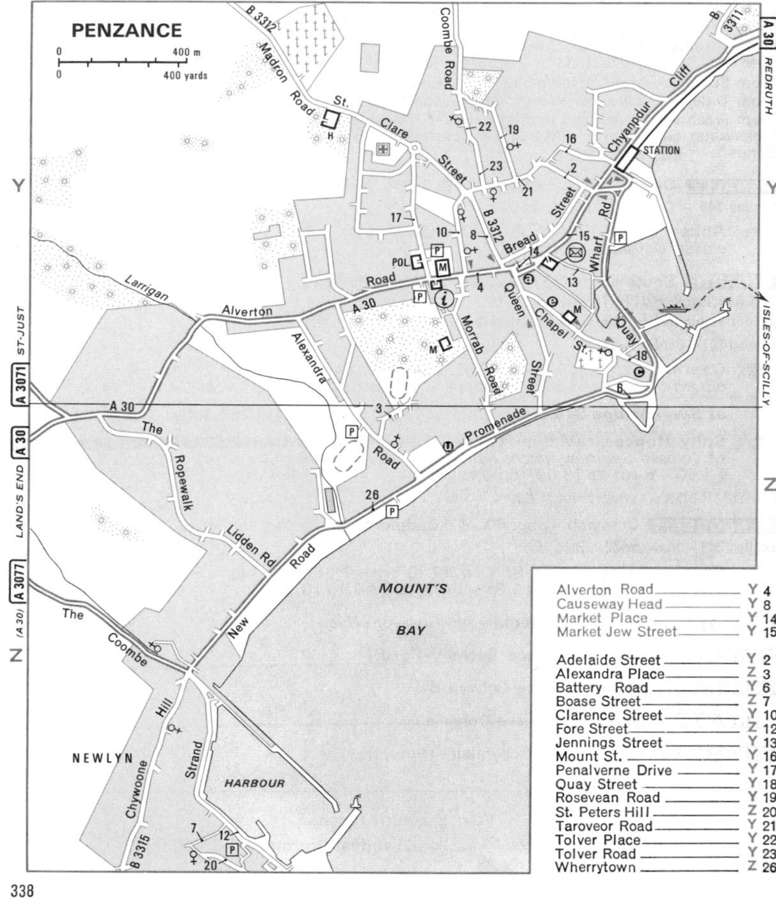

PENSHURST Kent 986 ㉟ – pop. 1,620 – ☎ 089 284.

See : Penshurst Place* (castle 14C) *AC*. **Envir. :** Chiddingstone (castle : Egyptian and Japanese collections* *AC*) NW : 5 m.

London 38 – Maidstone 19 – Royal Tunbridge Wells 6.

Leicester Arms, High St. TN11 8BT, ☎ 551, ≤, – TV wc P
M a la carte 4.25/6.45 **t.** – **7 rm** 9.50/16.00 **t.**

at Chiddingstone NW : 5 m. – ✉ Edenbridge – ☎ 089 284 Penshurst :

Castle Inn, TN8 7AH, ☎ 247,
closed Wednesday lunch, Tuesday, Christmas Day and January – **M** a la carte 6.70/8.60 **st.** 1.50.

PENZANCE Cornwall 986 ㊳ – pop. 19,415 – ☎ 0736.

Envir. : St. Michael's Mount** *AC*, E : 3 m. by A 30 Y – Land's End** SW : 10 m. by A 30 Z. Access to the Isles of Scilly by helicopter.

to London ☎ 5831.

to the Isles of Scilly : St. Mary's (Isles of Scilly Steamship Co.) Summer Monday to Saturday 1 daily ; Winter 3 weekly (2 h 45 mn).

i Alverton St. ☎ 2341.

London 318 – Exeter 110 – **Plymouth 75** – Taunton 149.

Plan opposite

Queens, Promenade, TR18 4HG, ☎ 2371, ≤ – wc P — Z **u**
M approx. 3.60 1.30 – **44 rm** 7.00/18.00.

Trevaylor, on Newmill Rd, TR20 8UR, NE : 1 ¾ m. off B 3311 ✉ Gulval ☎ 2882, ≤, « Country house atmosphere », – wc P — by B 3311 Y
23 March-2 April and 8 May-8 October – **M** (residents only) a la carte approx. 3.85 **t.** 1.00 – **8 rm** 5.80/12.00 **t.**

Union, Chapel St., TR18 4AE, ☎ 2319 – — Y **e**
M (dinner only) 3.50/4.00 – **28 rm** 8.00/15.00.

Le Tarot, 19 Quay St., TR18 4BD, ☎ 3118, French rest. — Y **c**
April-December – **M** *(closed Sunday, Monday in April, May and October to December)* – **M** (dinner only) a la carte 5.30/6.35 1.75.

Bistro One, 46 New St., TR18 2LZ, ☎ 4408 — Y **a**
closed Sunday, Monday in winter and Bank Holidays – **M** (dinner only) a la carte 4.30/5.85 1.55.

at Newlyn W : 2 m. on **B 3315** – Z – ✉ ☎ 0736 Penzance :

Higher Faugan, TR18 5NS, ☎ 2076, heated, , park – wc wc P
M (buffet lunch) approx. 5.40 **st.** 1.50 – **17 rm** 10.80/23.75 **st.**

AUSTIN-MORRIS-MG-ROVER-TRIUMPH-WOLSELEY Coinage Hall St. ☎ 2307
CHRYSLER-SIMCA Newlyn ☎ 2038
PEUGEOT Hayle Terr. ☎ 753143

PERSHORE Heref. and Worc. 986 ㉛ – pop. 6,150 – ☎ 038 65.

i Council Offices, 37 High St. ☎ 2442.

London 106 – **Birmingham 32** – Cheltenham 22 – Stratford-on-Avon 21 – Worcester 9.

Angel Inn, 9 High St., WR10 1AF, ☎ 2046, , – wc P
M 3.30/3.75 **t.** 1.05 – **17 rm** 7.75/14.50 **t.** – P 12.00/18.00 **t.**

Zhivago's, 22 Bridge St., WR10 1AT, ☎ 3828
closed Sunday and Bank Holidays – **M** a la carte 3.50/8.45 **t.** 1.45.

AUSTIN-MORRIS-MG-ROVER-TRIUMPH High St. ☎ 2255

PETERBOROUGH Cambs. 986 ㉘㉜ – pop. 70,100 – ☎ 0733.

See : Cathedral** 12C-13C (nave : painted roof***). **Envir. :** Crowland : Abbey Church* (8C ruins), Triangular Bridge* 13C, NE : 8 m.

18 Nene Parkway ☎ 267701, W : 3 m. on A 47.

i Central Library, Broadway ☎ 69105/6 – Town Hall, Bridge St. ☎ 63141 and 51219.

London 85 – Cambridge 35 – Leicester 41 – Lincoln 51.

Great Northern (B.T.H.), Station Rd, PE1 1QL, ☎ 52331, – TV wc P.
closed Christmas – **M** a la carte 6.00/8.25 **st.** 1.50 – **49 rm** 11.90/23.50 **st.**

Bull, Westgate, PE1 1RB, ☎ 61364 – wc P.
M a la carte 4.45/6.40 **t.** 1.30 – **125 rm** 10.50/16.00 **t.**

at Whittlesey SE : 7 m. on A 605 – ✉ ☎ 0733 Peterborough :

Falcon, London St., PE7 1BH, ☎ 203247 – P
M a la carte 4.70/5.95 **s.** 1.75.

P.T.O. →

at Wansford W : 8 m. off A 47 – ✉ Peterborough – ☎ 0780 Stamford :

Haycock Inn, Great North Rd, Bridge End, PE8 6JA ☎ 782223, – TV ⇔wc ☎ Ⓟ
closed Christmas Day – **M** a la carte 3.90/5.45 **s.** 1.80 – **20 rm** 9.00/18.00 **st.**

ALFA-ROMEO, DAF, MAZDA 659 Lincoln Rd ☎ 52141
AUSTIN-MG-WOLSELEY, ROLLS ROYCE-BENTLEY 7 Oundle Rd ☎ 66011
BMW Cowgate ☎ 66173
CHRYSLER-SIMCA, POLSKI Lincoln Rd ☎ 71739
CHRYSLER-SIMCA, VOLVO 343 Eastfield Rd ☎ 64566
CITROEN, FIAT Oxney Rd ☎ 67201
DAIMLER-JAGUAR-ROVER-TRIUMPH Broadway ☎ 61201
DATSUN, MAZDA 50/64 Burghley Rd ☎ 65787
FORD 27/39 New Rd ☎ 65271
LANCIA Midland Rd ☎ 53146
MERCEDES-BENZ, PEUGEOT High St., Eye ☎ 222363
MORRIS-MG-WOLSELEY Broadway ☎ 54661
RENAULT Thorney Rd, Newborough ☎ 073 123 (Newborough) 625
SAAB The Broadway ☎ 240218
VAUXHALL Eastfield Rd ☎ 53231
VW, AUDI-NSU 21/27 Burton St. ☎ 65857

PETERLEE Durham 986 ⑲ – pop. **21,821** – ☎ **078 323 (4 fig.) or 0783 (6 fig.).**
Castle Eden ☎ 042 981 (Castle Eden) 220, S : 2 m.
i Arts and Information Centre, The Upper Chare ☎ 864450.
London 270 – Durham 13 – **Middlesbrough 19** – Sunderland 11.

Norseman (Thistle), Bede Way, SR8 1BU, ☎ 2161 – TV ⇔wc ☎ Ⓟ
26 rm.

at Hesleden S : 3 ½ m. by **A 1088** and **B 1281** – ✉ Hartlepool (Cleveland) – ☎ 042 981 Castle Eden :

Golden Calf with rm, Front St., SR8 3UJ, ☎ 493 – Ⓟ
M 4.95/5.60 **st.** 1.30 – **4 rm** 5.75/10.50 **st.**

PETT BOTTOM Kent – see Canterbury.

PETWORTH West Sussex 986 ㊱ – pop. **2,506** – ☎ **0798.**
See : Petworth House★★★ (17C paintings★★★ and carved room★★★) *AC.*
London 54 – Brighton 31 – Portsmouth 33.

Hotels and restaurants see : Haslemere NW : **11** m.
Midhurst W : 6 ½ m.

PEVENSEY East Sussex – see Eastbourne.

PICKERING North Yorks. 986 ㉔ – pop. **4,545** – ☎ **0751.**
See : SS. Peter and Paul's Church (wall paintings★ 15C) – Norman castle★ (ruins) : ≤★ *AC.*
i North York Moors Railway, The Station ☎ 72508.
London 237 – Middlesbrough 43 – Scarborough 19 – York 25.

Forest and Vale, 2 Hungate, YO18 7DL, ☎ 72722, ≤, – ⇔wc Ⓟ
M 4.00/5.50 **s.** – **15 rm** 7.00/16.00 **s.**

CHRYSLER Middleton ☎ 72557
MERCEDES-BENZ, SAAB Eastgate ☎ 72251

PIDDLETRENTHIDE Dorset – pop. **501** – ☎ **030 04.**
Envir. : Athelhampton Hall★ (15C) *AC,* SE : 6 m.
London 135 – Bournemouth 27 – Dorchester 7 – Sherborne 13.

Old Bakehouse with rm, DT2 7QX, S : 1 m. on B 3143 ☎ 305, heated – TV ⇔wc Ⓟ
M (dinner only) a la carte 3.95/6.75 **s.** 1.00 – **8 rm** 9.50/16.00 **s.**

PILLATON Cornwall – pop. **334** – ✉ Saltash – ☎ **0579 St. Dominick.**
London 254 – Plymouth 11.

Weary Friar, PL12 6QS, ☎ 50238, « Part 12C inn » – TV ⇔wc Ⓟ
M 3.50/4.00 **s.** 0.70 – **13 rm** 8.40/16.80.

PINHOE Devon – see Exeter.

PLAXTOL Kent – pop. **911** – ✉ Sevenoaks – ☎ **073 276.**
London 32 – Brighton 41 – Hastings 35 – Maidstone 15.

Forge, The Street, TN15 0QE, ☎ 446, « 16C forge », – Ⓟ
closed Monday and 1 January – **M** a la carte 4.95/7.60 2.00.

PLAYDEN East Sussex – see Rye.

*Ne prenez pas toujours vos vacances en **juillet-août** ;*
certaines régions sont plus belles en d'autres mois.

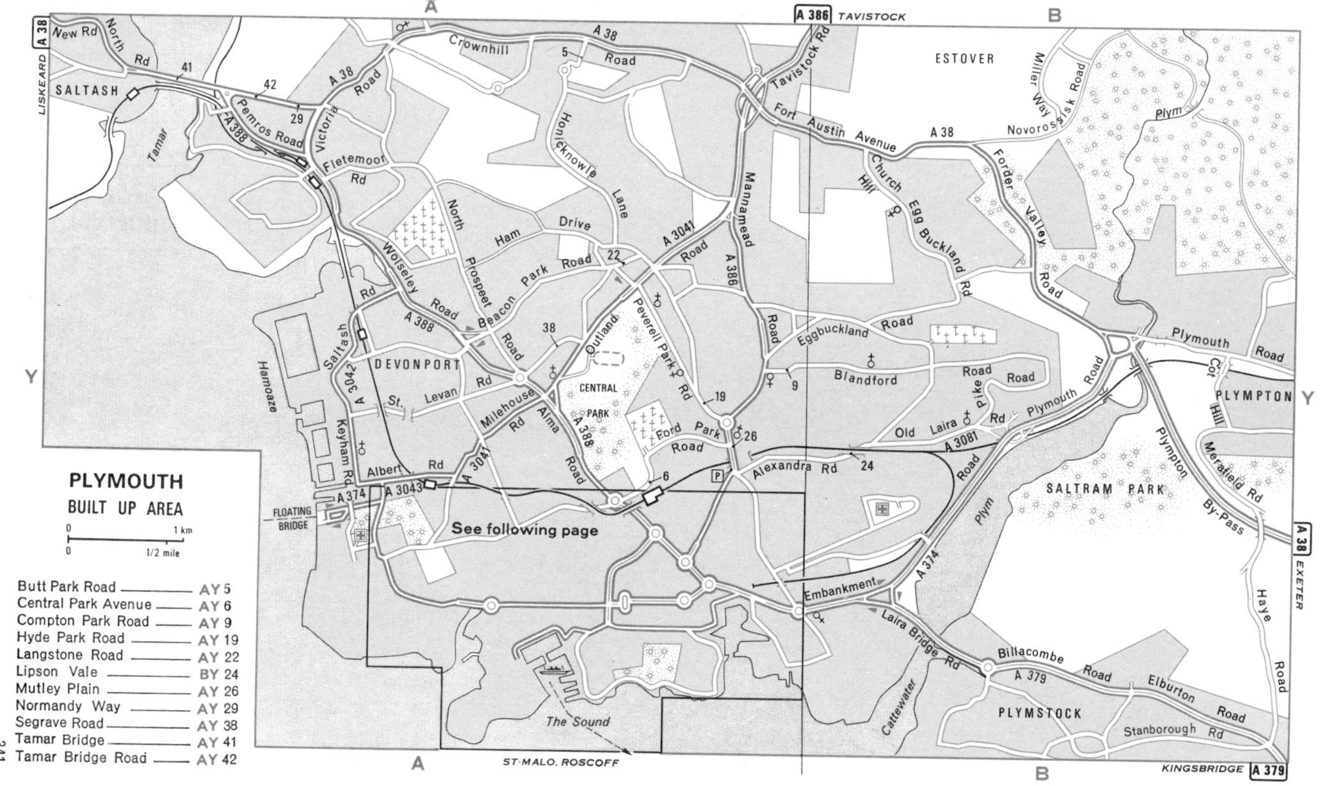

PLYMOUTH

BUILT UP AREA

0 — 1 km
0 — 1/2 mile

Street	Square
Butt Park Road	AY 5
Central Park Avenue	AY 6
Compton Park Road	AY 9
Hyde Park Road	AY 19
Langstone Road	AY 22
Lipson Vale	BY 24
Mutley Plain	AY 26
Normandy Way	AY 29
Segrave Road	AY 38
Tamar Bridge	AY 41
Tamar Bridge Road	AY 42

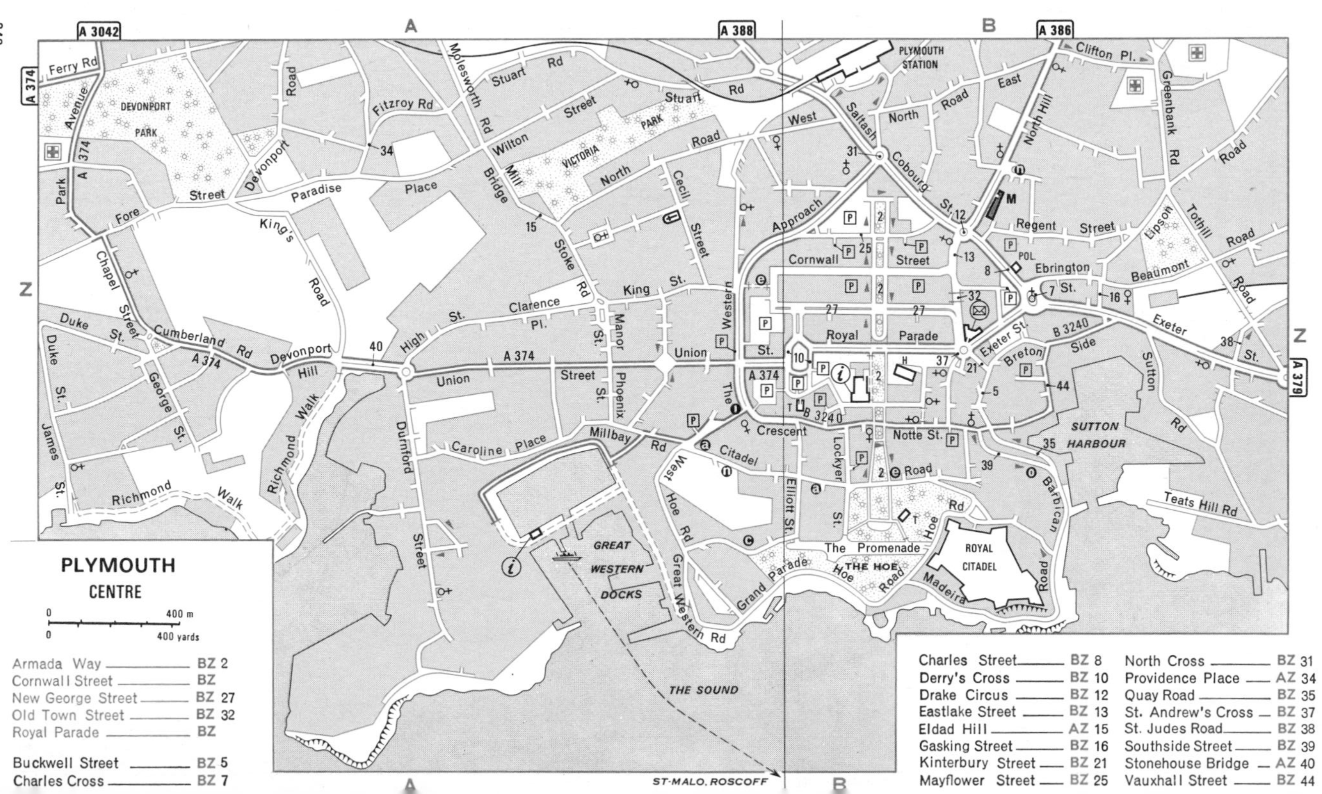
PLYMOUTH
CENTRE
0 400 m
0 400 yards
Armada Way BZ 2
Cornwall Street BZ
New George Street BZ 27
Old Town Street BZ 32
Royal Parade BZ
Buckwell Street BZ 5
Charles Cross BZ 7
Charles Street BZ 8
Derry's Cross BZ 10
Drake Circus BZ 12
Eastlake Street BZ 13
Eldad Hill AZ 15
Gasking Street BZ 16
Kinterbury Street BZ 21
Mayflower Street BZ 25
North Cross BZ 31
Providence Place AZ 34
Quay Road BZ 35
St. Andrew's Cross BZ 37
St. Judes Road BZ 38
Southside Street BZ 39
Stonehouse Bridge AZ 40
Vauxhall Street BZ 44
ST-MALO, ROSCOFF
THE SOUND
GREAT WESTERN DOCKS
SUTTON HARBOUR
ROYAL CITADEL
THE HOE
PLYMOUTH STATION
DEVONPORT PARK
VICTORIA PARK

PLYMOUTH Devon 986 ㊴ – pop. 239,452 – ☎ 0752.

See : The Hoe** BZ – Municipal Museum and Art Gallery* BZ **M. Envir. :** Buckland Abbey* (13C) *AC*, N : 7 m. by A 386 ABY – Antony House* (Renaissance) *AC*, W : 5 m. by A 374 AY.

Staddon Heights, Plymstock ☎ 42475, SW : by Stamborough Rd BY – at Yelverton ☎ 082 285 (Yelverton) 3618, N : 8 m. by A 386 ABY.

to London ☎ 63272.

Shipping connections with the Continent : to Roscoff (Brittany Ferries) – to St-Malo (Brittany Ferries).

i Civic Centre, ☎ 68000 – Ferry Terminal, Millbay Docks ☎ 27789 (summer only).

London 243 – Bristol 120 – Southampton 148.

Plans on preceding pages

Holiday Inn, Armada Way, PL1 2HJ, ☎ 62866, Telex 45637, ≤ city and sea, – TV **P**. BZ **e**
M *(closed Sunday lunch)* 3.75/10.00 1.80 – 2.25 – **222 rm** 13.00/15.00.

Mayflower Post House (T.H.F.), Cliff Rd, The Hoe, PL1 3DL, ☎ 62828, ≤ Plymouth Sound, heated – TV wc **P**. AZ **c**
M 3.80/4.50 1.50 – 2.00 – **104 rm** 13.50/19.00 **st.**

Duke of Cornwall (Interchange), Millbay Rd, PL1 3LG, ☎ 266256, Telex 45424 – TV wc **P**. AZ **a**
closed 22 to 28 December – **M** a la carte 3.55/5.70 **t.** 1.30 – **70 rm** 9.00/17.00 **t.**

Continental, Millbay Rd, PL1 3LD, ☎ 20782 – wc **P** AZ **i**
M a la carte 4.00/7.55 **t.** 1.55 – **64 rm** 8.50/14.50 **t.**

Chichester, 280 Citadel Rd, The Hoe, PL1 2PZ, ☎ 62746 BZ **a**
10 rm 4.50/8.00 **s.**

Carnegie, 172 Citadel Rd, The Hoe, PL1 3BD, ☎ 60937 AZ **n**
10 rm 4.75/9.50 **t.**

Bella Napoli, 41-42 Southside St., Barbican, PL1 2LW, ☎ 67772, Italian rest. BZ **o**
closed Sunday and 25-26 December – **M** a la carte 3.60/9.70 **t.** 1.30.

Chez Nous, 13 Frankfort Gate, ☎ 266793, French rest. AZ **e**
closed Sunday and February – **M** (dinner only in winter) a la carte 4.80/10.40 **t.** 2.00.

Marquee, 1 Sherwell Arcade, PL4 8LH, ☎ 266832 BZ **n**
closed Sunday and Bank Holidays – **M** a la carte 3.05/6.05 **t.** 1.40.

at Yelverton N : 9 ½ m. on A 386 – ABY – ✉ ☎ 082 285 Yelverton :

Moorland Links , PL20 6DA, S : 1 m. ☎ 2245, ≤, , , , park – TV **P**
M 4.50/5.25 **s.** 1.50 – 2.10 – **26 rm** 12.25/16.10 **s.**

MICHELIN Branch, South Milton St., Cattedown, PL4 0QB, ☎ 65458.

AUSTIN-MG Peverell ☎ 771392
AUSTIN-MG-WOLSELEY Derry's Cross ☎ 23451
AUSTIN-MG-WOLSELEY Roborough ☎ 772767
CHRYSLER-SIMCA, BMW Union St. ☎ 69202
CITROEN Colebrook Rd ☎ 336606
DAIMLER-JAGUAR-ROVER-TRIUMPH Valley Rd, Plympton ☎ 38373
DATSUN Newnham Rd ☎ 36462
DATSUN The Crescent ☎ 68332
FIAT Valley Rd, Plympton ☎ 338306
FORD Millbay ☎ 68040
HONDA Albert Rd ☎ 51810
MERCEDES-BENZ, PEUGEOT 58/64 Embankment Rd ☎ 63003
MORRIS-MG Pridham Lane ☎ 771493
LANCIA Budshead Rd ☎ 771123
RENAULT 23 Wolsley Rd, Milehouse ☎ 53484
VAUXHALL Bretonside ☎ 67111
VAUXHALL Cattledown Rd ☎ 68886
VOLVO 87 Crownhill Rd ☎ 772345
VW, AUDI-NSU Durnford St., Stonehouse ☎ 68351

POCKLINGTON North Humberside – pop. 4,176 – ✉ York – ☎ 075 92.

London 213 – Kingston-upon-Hull 25 – York 13.

Feathers (S & N), 56 Market Pl., YO4 2QF, ☎ 3155 – wc **P**
14 rm.

AUSTIN-MORRIS-MG-WOLSELEY, CHRYSLER-SIMCA, VAUXHALL 2 Railway St. ☎ 2021

POLKERRIS Cornwall – pop. 75 – ✉ ☎ 072 681 Par.

London 277 – Newquay 22 – Plymouth 34 – Truro 20.

Rashleigh Inn, PL24 2TL, ☎ 3991, ≤ – **P**
Easter-November – **M** *(closed Sunday and Christmas Day)* (buffet lunch) approx. 4.50 1.50.

POLPERRO Cornwall 986 ㊳ – pop. 1,600 – ✉ Looe – ☎ 050 38.

See : Village*.

London 271 – Plymouth 28.

House on Props, The Harbour, PL13 2RB, ☎ 310
closed Monday, Tuesday in winter and January-mid February – **M** a la carte 6.15/9.25 1.60.

Captain's Cabin, Lansallos St., PL13 2QU, ☎ 292
March-December – **M** *(closed Sunday)* a la carte 4.55/6.75 **t.** 1.20.

14

PONTERWYD Dyfed – pop. 280 – ✉ Aberystwyth – ☎ 097 085.

i Tourist Information Centre, c/o Llywernog Silver Lead Mine ☎ 620 (Easter-September).

London 228 – Aberystwyth 12 – Chester 88 – Shrewsbury 64.

- Dyffryn Castell, Dyffryn Castell, SY23 3LB, E: 2 m. on A 44 ☎ 237, ← – Ⓟ
  6 rm.

PONTLYFNI Gwynedd – pop. 375 – ✉ Caernarfon – ☎ 028 686 Clynnog Fawr.

London 257 – Caernarfon 8.

- **Bron Dirion**, LL54 5EU, SE : ¾ m. off A 499 ☎ 346, ←, – Ⓟ
  March-October – **M** (dinner only) 2.50/3.00 🍷 1.50 – **9 rm** (dinner included) 6.00
  12.00 **s.**

POOLE Dorset 986 ㊴ – pop. 107,161 – ☎ 020 13.

See : Compton Acres Gardens* *AC* AY. **Envir.** : Wareham : St. Martin's Church* (Norman) St. Mary's Church (font* 12C) W : 8 ½ m by A 35 AY.

i Civic Centre ☎ 5151 ext 26 or 42 - Arndale Centre ☎ 3322.

London 116 – Bournemouth 4 – Dorchester 23 – Weymouth 28.

Plan : see Bournemouth

- **Dolphin,** 180 High St., BH15 1DU, ☎ 3612 – wc Ⓟ. by A 35 AY
  M (grill rest. only) a la carte 2.75/4.80 **s.** 🍷 1.40 – **61 rm** 9.75/19.50 **s.** – P 12.75
  16.75 **s.**
- Avalon, 14 Pinewood Rd, Branksome Park, BH13 6JS, ☎ 0202 (Bournemouth) 760917 -
  Ⓟ BY e
  closed 1 January – **M** (dinner only) – **14 rm** (dinner included) 7.00/17.00 **s.**
- **Dene,** 16 Pinewood Rd, Branksome Park, BH13 6JS, ☎ 0202 (Bournemouth) 761143 -
  Ⓟ BY c
  12 rm 5.50/12.00 **s.**
- **Blue Shutters,** 109 North Rd, Parkstone, BH14 0LU, ☎ 0202 (Parkstone) 748129 -
  Ⓟ by A 35 AY
  closed December – **11 rm** 4.00/8.00 **s.**
- **Isabel's,** 32 Station Rd, Lower Parkstone, BH14 8UD, ☎ 0202 (Bournemouth) 747885
  closed Sunday, 4 days at Christmas and November – **M** (dinner only) a la carte 4.20/
  5.60 **t.** 🍷 1.50. AY a
- **John B's,** 20 High St. ☎ 2440 by A35 AY
  closed Saturday lunch and Sunday – **M** (hot buffet lunch) a la carte 3.65/5.80 **t.**
  🍷 1.35.
- **Edelweiss,** 232 Ashley Rd, Upper Parkstone, BH14 9BZ, ☎ 0202 (Parkstone) 747703
  Austrian rest. AY e
  closed Tuesday and January – **M** (dinner only) a la carte 4.10/6.70 **t.** 🍷 1.60.

at Broadstone : N : 4 m. off A 35 – AY – ✉ ☎ 020 124 (4 fig.) or 0202 (6 fig.) :

- **Fairlight,** 1 Golf Links Rd, BH18 8BE, ☎ 694316, – Ⓟ
  8 rm 5.00/10.00 **st.**

AUSTIN-MG-WOLSELEY The Quay ☎ 4187
CITROEN 490 Blandford Rd ☎ 020 122 (Lychett Minster) 3636
CITROEN Broadstone ☎ 020 124 (Broadstone) 3501
MORRIS-ROVER-TRIUMPH West Quay Rd ☎ 77511
PEUGEOT Station Rd ☎ 745000
RENAULT Haven Rd ☎ 707387
VAUXHALL Poole Rd, Branksome ☎ 0202 (Bournemouth) 763361
VW, AUDI-NSU 3 Commercial Rd ☎ 0202 (Parkstone) 740850

POOL-IN-WHARFEDALE West Yorks. – pop. 1,672 – ✉ Otley – ☎ 0532 Arthington.

London 203 – Bradford 10 – Harrogate 8 – **Leeds 10.**

- **Pool Court,** Pool Bank, LS21 1EH, ☎ 842288 – Ⓟ
  closed Sunday, Monday, last week July, first week August and first 2 weeks January – **M** (dinner only) 5.95/7.25.

AUSTIN-MG-WOLSELEY Main St. ☎ 842318

PORLOCK WEIR Somerset 986 ㉟ – pop. 95 – ✉ Minehead – ☎ 0643 Porlock.

London 193 – **Bristol 70** – Exeter 49 – Taunton 31.

- Anchor, TA24 8PB, ☎ 862636, ←, – wc Ⓟ
  21 rm.
- **West Porlock House**, West Porlock, TA24 8NX, SE : 1 m. ☎ 862492, ←, – Ⓟ
  February-October – **M** 3.75/4.75 **st.** 🍷 1.40 – **8 rm** 6.50/13.00 **st.**
- **Ship Inn** with rm, TA24 8PB, ☎ 862753 –
  M 3.25/4.50 🍷 1.40 – **6 rm** 5.00/12.00.

PORT GAVERNE Cornwall – ✉ ☎ 020 888 Port Isaac.

London 266 – Newquay 24 – Truro 32.

- **Port Gaverne**, PL29 3FQ, ☎ 244 – wc Ⓟ
  closed February – **M** (dinner only) 4.50/5.50 **st.** 🍷 1.60 – **20 rm** 8.50/19.00 **st.**

PORTHCAWL Mid Glam. 986 ㉟ – pop. 14,103 – ☎ 065 671.
i Wales Tourist Office, The Old Police Station, St. John's St ☎ 6639 (Easter-September).
London 183 – Cardiff 28 – Swansea 18.

- **Seabank** (Interchange), Promenade, CF36 3LU, ☎ 2261, ≤, heated – TV **P**.
  M a la carte 5.00/6.50 **t.** 1.80 – **80 rm** 12.35/22.35 **t.** – P 20.00/25.00 **t.**
- **Atlantic,** West Drive, Sea Front, CF36 3LT, ☎ 5011, ≤, – TV wc **P**
  M (bar lunch) 3.00/3.50 **t.** 0.90 – **15 rm** 9.75/17.50 **t.**
- **Fairways,** West Drive, Sea Front, CF36 3LS, ☎ 2085, ≤ – wc **P**
  M (bar lunch except Sunday) 3.00/3.50 1.40 – **25 rm** 8.00/18.00.
- **Seaways,** 28 Mary St., CF36 3YA, ☎ 3510
  10 rm 5.00/9.00 **s.**

at Nottage N: ¾ m. – ✉ ☎ **065 671** Porthcawl:

- Rose and Crown, ☎ 4849 – wc **P**
  8 rm.

AUSTIN-MORRIS-MG-WOLSELEY Lias Rd ☎ 6221

PORTHGAIN Dyfed – pop. 122.
See: Cliffs ☼★★★.
London 266 – Fishguard 14 – Haverfordwest 16 – St. David's 8.

Hotels and restaurant see : Fishguard NE: 14 m.
St. Davids SW: 8 m.

PORT ISAAC Cornwall – pop. 966 – ☎ 020 888.
London 266 – Newquay 24 – Tintagel 14 – Truro 32.

- Slipway, PL29 3RH, ☎ 264 – wc
  season – **11 rm.**

PORTLAND Dorset 986 ㊴ – pop. 12,329 – ☎ 0305.
London 149 – Dorchester 14 – Weymouth 6.

- **Pennsylvania Castle** , Wakeham, DT5 1HZ, ☎ 820561, ≤, – wc wc **P**
  M a la carte 3.40/5.20 **t.** 1.30 – **12 rm** 7.50/16.00 **t.**

DAF Victoria Sq. ☎ 820478

PORTLOE Cornwall – pop. 200 – ✉ Truro – ☎ 087 250 Veryan.
London 296 – St. Austell 15 – Truro 15.

- **Lugger,** TR2 5RD, ☎ 322, ≤ – wc **P**
  mid February-mid November – **M** (dinner only and Sunday lunch) approx. 5.00 **t.** 1.00 –
  20 rm (dinner included) 12.50/20.00 **t.**

PORTMADOC Gwynedd 986 ㉗ – pop. 3,683 – ☎ 0766.
18 Morfa Bychan ☎ 2037, W: 2 m.
i Wales Tourist Office, c/o Festiniog Railway, Wharf Station ☎ 2981.
London 245 – Caernarfon 20 – Chester 70 – Shrewsbury 81.

- **Royal Sportsman** (T.H.F.), High St., LL49 9HB, ☎ 2015 – wc **P**
  M a la carte 3.95/5.35 1.50 – **21 rm** 7.00/14.00 **st.** – P 12.50/13.50 **st.**

PORTMEIRION Gwynedd – pop. 200 – ✉ ☎ 076 674 Penrhyndeudraeth.
London 244 – Chester 69 – Dolgellau 23 – Holyhead 52.

- **Portmeirion** , LL48 6ER, ☎ 228, ≤ village and estuary, « Picturesque private village », , heated, , park – TV **P**.
  Easter-October – **M** a la carte 6.75/9.00 1.50 – **50 rm** 22.00/38.00 **s.**

PORTSCATHO Cornwall – pop. 800 – ✉ Truro – ☎ 087 258.
London 298 – Plymouth 55 – Truro 16.

- **Gerrans Bay,** Gerrans, TR2 5ED, ☎ 338 – wc **P**
  Easter-October – **M** *(closed Sunday dinner)* 4.75 **st.** 1.50 – **16 rm** 8.50/19.50 **st.**
- **Roseland House** , Rosevine, TR2 5EW, N: 2 m. off A 3078 ☎ 320, ≤ Gerrans Bay, , park – wc **P**
  Easter-mid October – **M** approx. 3.80 **s.** 1.20 – **18 rm** 10.00/24.00 **s.**
- **Rosevine** , TR2 5EW, N: 2 m. off A 3078 ☎ 206, ≤, – wc wc **P**
  closed October – **M** approx. 6.00 1.50 – **18 rm** (dinner included) 14.25/30.00.

Carte

Negli alberghi e ristoranti per i quali
indichiamo dei pasti a prezzo fisso,
è generalmente possibile ordinare anche alla carta.

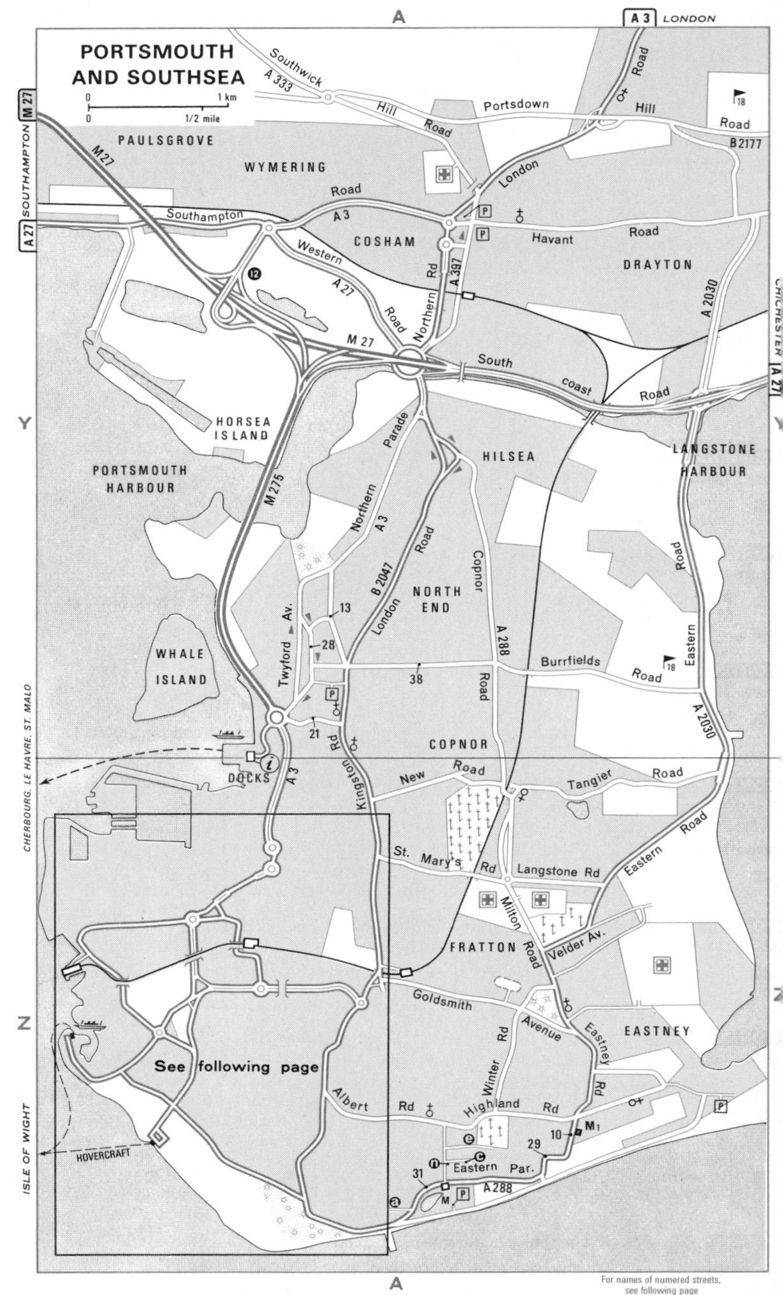

For names of numbered streets, see following page

PORTSMOUTH AND SOUTHSEA

rundel Street .... BY
harlotte Street .... BY 9
ommercial Road .... BY
almerston Road .... BZ
ricorn Centre .... BY

lec Rose Lane .... BY 2
lfred Road .... BY 5

Anglesea Road .... BY 6
Bellevue Terrace .... BZ 7
Bradford Road .... BY 8
Cromwell Road .... AZ 10
Edinburgh Road .... BY 12
Gladys Avenue .... AY 13
Grove Road South .... BZ 15
Guildhall Walk .... BY 16
Hampshire Terrace .... BY 17
Hard (The) .... BY 18
Isambard Brunel Road .... BY 19
King's Terrace .... BZ 20

Kingston Crescent .... AY 21
Landport Terrace .... BZ 22
Lennox Road South .... BZ 24
Museum Road .... BZ 25
Ordnance Row .... BY 26
Outram Road .... BZ 27
Stamshaw Road .... AY 28
St. George's Road .... AZ 29
St. Helen's Parade .... AZ 31
St. Michael's Road .... BY 33
Southsea Terrace .... BZ 36
Stubbington Avenue .... AY 38

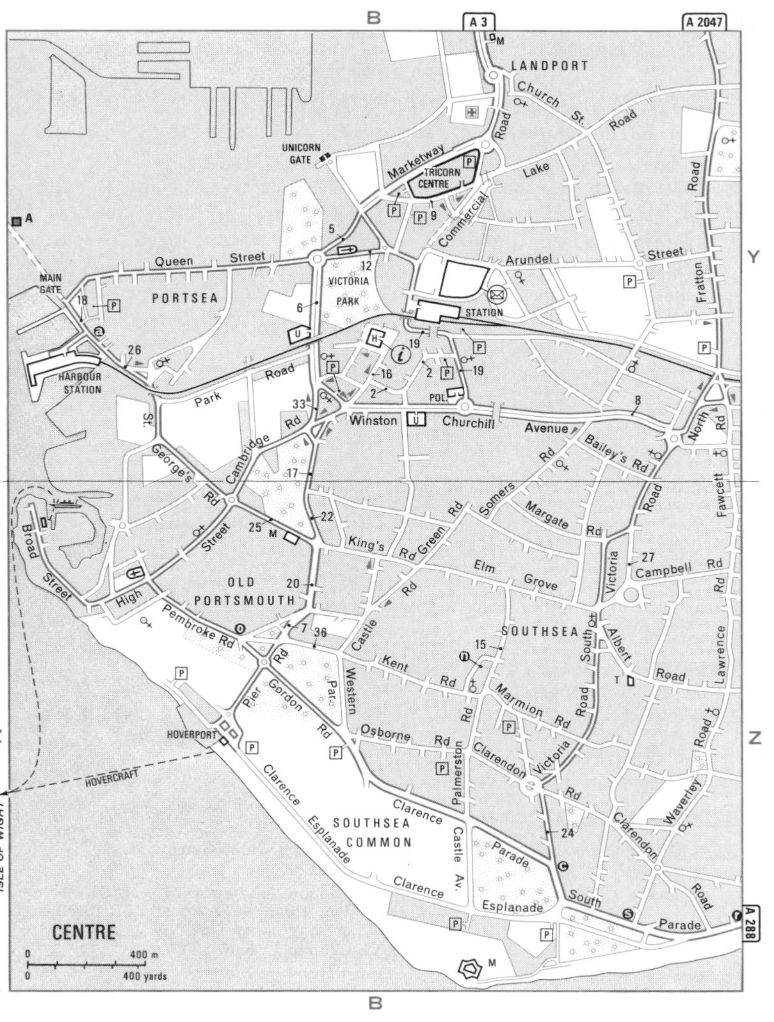

Town plans: roads most used by traffic and those on which guide listed hotels and restaurants stand are fully drawn; the beginning only of lesser roads is indicated.

PORTSMOUTH and SOUTHSEA Hants. 986 ㊱㊵ – pop. 197,431 – ☎ 0705.

See : H.M.S. Victory*** and Victory Museum* *AC* BY **A** by Main Gate – Royal Marines' Museum*, at Eastney AZ **M**¹.

Great Salterns ☎ 64549 AY – Crookhorn Lane, Widley ☎ 070 18 (Cosham) 72210 N : 1 m. off B 2177 AY.

Shipping connections with the Continent : to Cherbourg, Le Havre (Townsend Thoresen) – to St-Malo (Brittany Ferries) – to the Isle of Wight : Fishbourne (Sealink) Monday/Thursday 20-29 daily ; Friday/Saturday/Sunday 11-35 daily (45 mn).

to the Isle of Wight : Ryde (Sealink) 9-22 daily (25 to 40 mn) – from Southsea to the Isle of Wight : Ryde (Hovertravel) 11-24 daily summer only (7 mn).

i Guildhall Sq. ☎ 834092 – Ferry Terminal, Albert Johnson Docks ☎ 819688 (summer only).

London 77 – Southampton 20.

Plans on preceding pages

Pendragon (T.H.F.), Clarence Par., Southsea, PO5 2HY, ☎ 23201 – wc **P**
M 2.95/4.00 **st.** 1.50 – **55 rm** 9.50/17.00 **st.** BZ **c**

Portsmouth Centre (Centre), Pembroke Rd, PO1 2NS, ☎ 27651, Telex 86397 – wc **P**. BZ **o**
M approx. 2.95 **s.** 1.25 – 1.50 – **119 rm** 10.75/14.50 **s.**

Royal Beach (Mt. Charlotte), South Parade, Southsea, PO4 0RN, ☎ 31281 – wc **P**. BZ **r**
M a la carte 3.75/5.75 **s.** 1.60 – **125 rm** 10.80/19.25 **s.**

Keppels Head (Anchor), 24-26 The Hard, PO1 3DT, ☎ 21954, Group Telex 27120 – wc **P** BY **a**
M (Captain's Table and grill room only) approx. 2.15 **t.** 1.00 – **20 rm** 9.90/14.85 **st.**

Tudor Court, Queen's grove, Southsea, PO5 3HH, ☎ 20174, BZ **n**
closed Christmas – **10 rm** 6.00/9.00 **st.**

Salisbury, 57-59 Festing Rd, Southsea ☎ 23606 – **P** AZ **n**
25 rm 5.40/10.80 **st.**

Chequers, Salisbury Rd, Southsea, PO4 9RH, ☎ 27399 – **P** AZ **c**
24 rm 5.90/10.80 **t.**

Averano, 65 Granada Rd, Southsea, PO4 0RQ, ☎ 20079 – **P** AZ **a**
12 rm 4.90/9.75 **st.**

Homeleigh, 42 Festing Grove, Southsea, PO4 9QD, ☎ 23706 AZ **e**
10 rm 4.25/8.50 **s.**

Murray's, 27a South Par., Southsea, PO5 2JF, ☎ 32322 BZ **s**
closed Sunday in winter and 25-26 December – **M** a la carte 3.80/6.00 1.55.

AUSTIN-DAIMLER-JAGUAR-MORRIS-MG-ROVER-TRIUMPH Granada Rd, Southsea ☎ 35311
AUSTIN-MG-WOLSELEY 1 Stubbington Av. ☎ 62216
AUSTIN-MORRIS-MG-ROVER-TRIUMPH, PEUGEOT Hambledon Rd ☎ 070 14 (Waterlooville) 54641
CHRYSLER-SIMCA Grove Rd South, Southsea ☎ 23261
DAIMLER-ROVER-TRIUMPH, ROLLS ROYCE 41 Castle Rd, Southsea ☎ 27261
DATSUN 135/153 Fratton Rd ☎ 27551
FIAT 117 Copnor Rd ☎ 691621
FORD Southampton Rd ☎ 070 18 (Cosham) 70944
MERCEDES-BENZ 76 Castle Rd, Southsea ☎ 812951
MORRIS-MG-WOLSELEY Havant Rd, Drayton ☎ 74041
RENAULT 28 Milton Rd ☎ 815151
TOYOTA Gamble Rd ☎ 60734
VAUXHALL London Rd, Hilsea ☎ 61321
VOLVO 23 Bedhampton Rd ☎ 070 12 (Havant) 72953
VW, AUDI-NSU 41/53 Highland Rd ☎ 815111

PORT TALBOT West Glam. 986 ㉟ – pop. 50,729 – ☎ 063 96.

London 187 – Cardiff 32 – Swansea 9.

Executive, Princess Margaret Way, Aberavon Beach, SA12 6QP, ☎ 4949 – **P**
M 3.00/5.80 **st.** 1.70 – **69 rm** 14.00/21.00 **st.**

AUSTIN-MORRIS-MG Baglan ☎ 813247
FORD Acacia Av. ☎ 2112

POUND HILL West Sussex – see Crawley.

POUNDISFORD PARK Somerset – see Taunton.

PRAA SANDS Cornwall – pop. 300 – ✉ Penzance – ☎ 073 676 Germoe.

London 321 – Penzance 8 – Truro 24.

Lesceave Cliff , TR20 9TX, ☎ 2325, ← Mounts Bay, – wc **P**
Easter-October – **M** (dinner only) 4.75/6.00 **st.** 0.80 – **17 rm** 7.50/18.00 **st.**

Prah Sands, Chy-an-Dour Rd, TR20 9SY, ☎ 2438, ←, , – wc **P**
Easter-September – **M** 3.00/4.00 **t.** 1.50 – **26 rm** 6.00/13.60.

Cet ouvrage n'est pas un répertoire de tous les hôtels et restaurants, ni même de tous les bons hôtels et restaurants de Grande Bretagne et d'Irlande.

Comme nous cherchons à rendre service à tous les touristes, nous sommes amenés à indiquer des établissements de toutes les classes et à n'en citer que quelques-uns de chaque sorte.

PRESTBURY Cheshire – pop. 2,891 – ☎ 0625.
Envir. : Adlington Hall* (15C) *AC*, N : 3 ½ m.
London 184 – Liverpool 43 – Manchester 17 – Stoke-on-Trent 25.

Mottram Hall ⅀, Mottram St. Andrew, SK10 4QT, NW : 2 ½ m. on A 538 ☎ 48135, Telex 668181, ≤, « Tastefully renovated 18C mansion in park », ✂, ⚘, 🛋 – TV P. 🅰
M a la carte 3.45/6.55 **t.** – **44 rm** ☕ 17.50/24.50 **t.**

XXX **Bridge,** New Rd, SK10 4DQ, ☎ 49326, « Brookside terrace and gardens » – P
closed Sunday – **M** a la carte 4.50/6.90 🍷 2.20.

XX **Oskar's,** New Rd, SK10 4AW, ☎ 49640
closed Sunday dinner and Christmas Day dinner – **M** a la carte 5.45/7.60.

XX **Legh Arms,** Main St., SK10 4DG, ☎ 49130 – P
closed Christmas Day dinner – **M** a la carte 4.90/7.10 🍷 1.50.

PRESTBURY Glos. – see Cheltenham.

PRESTEIGNE Powys 986 ㉛ – pop. 1,213 – ☎ 054 44.
See : Church (Flemish Tapestry*). **Envir.** : Old Radnor (church*) SW : 7 ½ m.
London 159 – Llandrindod Wells 20 – Shrewsbury 39.

Radnorshire Arms (T.H.F.), High St., LD8 2BE, ☎ 406, 🛋 – 🛁wc P
M a la carte 3.95/5.35 **st.** 🍷 1.50 – **17 rm** ☕ 7.00/14.00 **st.**

PRESTON Lancs. 986 ㉓ – pop. 98,088 – ☎ 0772.
Envir. : Samlesbury Old Hall* (14C) *AC*, E : 3 ½ m.
⛳18 Lea ☎ 726480, W : 3 m. – ⛳18 Blundell Lane ☎ 43207, W : 1 ½ m. – ⛳9 Glenluce Drive, Farringdon Park ☎ 51390.
i Town Hall, Lancaster Rd ☎ 53731.
London 223 – Blackpool 17 – Burnley 21 – Liverpool 31 – Manchester 32 – Stoke-on-Trent 67.

Preston Eurocrest (Crest), The Ringway, PR1 3AU, ☎ 59411, Telex 677147 – lift TV 🛁wc ☎ ♿ P. 🅰
M 3.00/4.00 **s.** 🍷 1.60 – ☕ 1.80 – **133 rm** 11.00/14.80 **s.**

Whitburn, 111 Garstang Rd, PR2 3EB, ☎ 717973 – P
13 rm ☕ 4.50/9.00 **st.**

at Samlesbury E : 2 ½ m. at junction M 6 and A 59 – ✉ Preston – ☎ 077 477 Samlesbury :

Tickled Trout, Preston New Rd, PR5 0UJ, ☎ 671, ≤, ⚘, 🛋 – TV 🛁wc ☎ ♿ P. 🅰
M a la carte 4.00/5.45 🍷 1.00 – **66 rm** ☕ 14.00/19.00.

MICHELIN Branch, 39-41 Rough Hey Rd, Grimsargh, PR2 5AR, ☎ 57057.

AUSTIN-MG-WOLSELEY 366/368 Blackpool Rd ☎ 717726
BMW Garstang Rd ☎ 0772 (Broughton) 863922
CHRYSLER-SIMCA Manchester Rd ☎ 58384
CITROEN Garstang Rd ☎ 718852
DAF, SAAB Emmanuel St. ☎ 21581
DAIMLER-JAGUAR-MORRIS-MG-ROVER-TRIUMPH, ROLLS ROYCE-BENTLEY Corporation St. ☎ 54242
DATSUN Chorley Rd ☎ 53911
FIAT 306/310 Ribbleton Lane ☎ 21326
FORD Penwortham ☎ 44471
FORD Marsh Lane ☎ 54083
MORRIS-MG 213/227 Lancaster Rd ☎ 54239
PEUGEOT 314/318 Ribbleton Lane ☎ 709060
RENAULT Manchester Rd ☎ 58389
TOYOTA 350 Blackpool Rd ☎ 719841
VOLVO Strand Rd ☎ 50501
VW, AUDI-NSU Blackpool Rd, Ashton ☎ 724391

PRIDDY Somerset – pop. 270 – ✉ Wells – ☎ 074 987.
London 140 – Bristol 21 – Taunton 36 – Wells 8.

X **Miners' Arms,** BA5 3DB, NE : 2 m. junction of B 3134 and B 3135 ☎ 217 – P
closed Sunday dinner, Monday and Christmas – **M** a la carte 2.50/5.05 **t.** 🍷 1.50.

PRINCETHORPE Warw. – pop. 489 – ✉ Rugby – ☎ 0926 Marton.
London 92 – Coventry 6.5 – Rugby 6 – Warwick 9.

XX **Woodhouse** with rm, Leamington Rd, CV23 9PZ, W : 1 m. on B 4453 ☎ 632303, ≤, ✂, 🏊 heated, 🛋 – TV P
closed Sunday dinner, Monday and 24 to 26 December – **M** a la carte 5.00/6.75 **s.** 🍷 1.60 – **7 rm** ☕ 8.00/17.50 **st.**

PUDDINGTON Cheshire – pop. 348 – ✉ Wirral – ☎ 051 Liverpool.
London 203 – Birkenhead 12 – Chester 8.

Craxton Wood ⅀, Parkgate Rd, L66 9PB, (A 540) ☎ 339 4717, « ≤ picturesque grounds and gardens », ✂, 🛋, park – 🛁wc ☎ P
M (*closed Sunday and Bank Holidays*) a la carte 5.15/6.95 🍷 2.50 – **12 rm** ☕ 10.00/16.00.

PUDSEY West Yorks. 986 ⑫ – see Leeds.

PULBOROUGH West Sussex 986 ㊱ – pop. 3,316 – ☎ 079 82.
Envir. : Hardham (church : wall paintings* 12C) S : 1 m.
London 49 – Brighton 25 – Guildford 25 – **Portsmouth 35.**

✕ **Stane Street Hollow,** Codmore Hill, RH20 2BG, ☎ 2819 – Ⓟ
closed Saturday lunch, Sunday, Monday, 2 weeks April, 3 weeks October and Ban Holidays – **M** a la carte 4.10/5.10 **t.** 🍷 1.80.

✕ Waters Edge, Station Rd, RH20 1AH, (A 283) ☎ 2451, ≤ – Ⓟ.

AUSTIN-MORRIS-MG-ROVER-TRIUMPH London Rd ☎ 2407
SAAB London Rd ☎ 079 881 (Bury) 691

PURFLEET Essex – pop. 430 – ☎ 040 26.
London 17 – Chelmsford 25.

🏨 **Royal** (T.H.F.), High St., RM16 1QA, ☎ 5432 – TV ⛀wc ☎ Ⓟ
M a la carte 2.10/3.55 **t.** 🍷 1.50 – **28 rm** ☕ 11.00/16.00 **st.**

PUTSBOROUGH Devon – pop. 1,342 – ✉ Braunton – ☎ 027 189 (3 fig.) or 0271 (6 fig. Croyde.
London 233 – Barnstaple 11 – **Exeter 51** – Ilfracombe 9.

🏨 **Putsborough Sands** 🐚, EX33 1LB, ☎ 555, ≤, 🏊 heated – ⛀wc Ⓟ
Easter-September – **M** *(closed 1 week after Easter to 7 May)* 4.00/5.00 **st.** – **62 rm** ☕ 8.00/18.00 **t.** – P 12.00/15.50 **t.**

RADLETT Herts. 986 ④ – pop. 9,110 – ☎ 092 76.
London 21 – Luton 15.

🏨 **Red Lion** (T.H.F.), Watling St., WD7 7NP, ☎ 5341 – TV ⛀wc ☎ Ⓟ
M a la carte 4.10/5.50 **st.** 🍷 1.50 – **17 rm** ☕ 9.00/16.50 **st.**

AUSTIN-MORRIS-MG-WOLSELEY 411 Watling St. ☎ 5681
BMW 74/6 Watling St. ☎ 4851
TOYOTA Station Rd ☎ 6711

RAINFORD Merseyside – pop. 8,404 – ✉ St. Helens – ☎ 074 488.
London 208 – Liverpool 12 – Manchester 24.

✕ **Royal Oak,** East Lancashire Rd, WA10 5QN, S : 3 m. on A 580 by B 5203 ☎ 2465 – Ⓟ
closed Sunday, Monday dinner and Bank Holidays – **M** (buffet lunch) a la carte 3.30/4.90 **t.** 🍷 1.25.

RAKE West Sussex – pop. 523 – ✉ Petersfield (Hants.) – ☎ 073 082 Liss.
London 54 – Guildford 21 – Petersfield 5.

✕✕ **Les Gourmets,** GU33 7PH, on A 3 ☎ 2377, 🌳, French rest. – Ⓟ
closed Sunday, Monday, 1 week in autumn and 10 days in February – **M** a la carte 3.45/5.95 🍷 1.60.

RAMSBURY Wilts. – pop. 1,390 – ✉ Marlborough – ☎ 067 22.
London 79 – Southampton 51 – Swindon 13.

✕✕ **Bell Inn,** The Square, SN8 2PE, ☎ 230 – Ⓟ
closed Sunday dinner, Monday, Christmas Day, Good Friday and Bank Holidays – **M** a la carte 5.50/7.25 **s.** 🍷 1.50.

✕✕ **Bleeding Horse,** High St., SN8 2QW, ☎ 200 – Ⓟ
closed Monday, Tuesday lunch, first 2 weeks August, 1 week Christmas and 1 week Easter **M** 4.00/5.00.

RAMSGATE Kent 986 ㊱ – pop 39,561 – ☎ 0843 Thanet.
See : St. Augustine's Abbey Church (interior*). **Envir.** : Minster-in-Thanet (abbey : remains 7C-12C) W : 4 ½ m.
⛴ Shipping connections with the Continent : to Calais (Hoverlloyd by Hovercraft).
ℹ South East England Tourist Board, International Hoverport ☎ 57115 – Queen Street District Offices, Queen St ☎ 581261.
London 77 – Dover 20 – Maidstone 44 – Margate 4.

🏨 **Savoy,** 43 Grange Rd, CT11 9NA, ☎ 52637 – TV ⛀wc 🚿wc ☎ Ⓟ
closed February – **M** *(closed Sunday in winter)* a la carte 2.80/4.00 **st.** 🍷 1.50 – **23 rm** ☕ 7.00/16.00 **st.**

🏨 **Court Stairs Hotel and Country Club** 🐚, Pegwell Rd, CT11 0JE, ☎ 51850, ≤ 🌳 – ⛀wc Ⓟ
M 5.05/7.05 🍷 1.50 – ☕ 1.25 – **12 rm** 8.10/18.90 **t.**

🏨 **San Clu,** Victoria Par., East Cliff, CT11 8DT, ☎ 52345, ≤ – 🛗 ⛀wc Ⓟ
M approx. 3.25 **st.** 🍷 1.50 – **54 rm** ☕ 7.80/22.20 **st.** – P 9.90/14.40 **st.**

AUSTIN-MORRIS-MG-ROVER-TRIUMPH Grange Rd ☎ 51456
DAF Turner St. ☎ 53687
FORD Boundary Rd ☎ 53784
VAUXHALL West Cliff Rd ☎ 53877
VW, AUDI-NSU St. Lawrence ☎ 52333

RAMSGILL North Yorks. – ✉ ☎ 0423 Harrogate.
London 229 – Leeds 33 – York 37.

Yorke Arms, HG3 5RL, ☎ 75243 – ⊟wc Ⓟ
M 4.50/5.50 ♁ 1.30 – **16 rm** ⊡ 10.00/22.00 – P 15.00/20.00.

RANTON Staffs. – see Stafford.

RAVENSCAR North Yorks. – see Scarborough.

READING Berks. 986 ㊱ – pop. 132,939 – ☎ 0734.
Envir.: Stratfield Saye* *AC*, S: 7 m. by A 33 x – Mapledurham House* *AC*, NW: 3 ½ m. by A 329 x.
to St. Austell ☎ 01 (London) 603 4555.
i Civic Offices, Civic Centre ☎ 55911.
London 48 – Brighton 71 – Bristol 77 – Croydon 46 – Luton 52 – Oxford 28 – Portsmouth 55 – Southampton 48.

Plans on next page

Post House (T.H.F.), Basingstoke Rd, RG2 0SL, S: 2 ½ m. on A 33 ☎ 85485, Telex 849160, heated – TV ⊟wc ☎ Ⓟ. X **a**
M 3.50/4.00 **st.** ♁ 1.50 – ⊡ 2.00 – **121 rm** 14.00/20.00 **st.**

Ship (Anchor), 2-6 Duke St., RG1 4RU, ☎ 583455, Group Telex 27120 – TV ⊟wc ☎ Ⓟ Z **e**
M (Carvery rest.) approx. 2.15 **t.** ♁ 1.00 – **35 rm** ⊡ 9.35/18.15 **st.**

ALFA-ROMEO, PEUGEOT 108 Bath Rd ☎ 586425
AUSTIN Bath Rd ☎ 27636
AUSTIN-DAIMLER-JAGUAR-MG-ROVER-TRIUMPH 38 Portman Rd ☎ 585011
BMW, DAF 291 Oxford Rd ☎ 54204
CHRYSLER Christchurch Rd ☎ 85242
CITROEN Chatham St. ☎ 57008
DAF Earley ☎ 61402
DATSUN 67 Caversham Rd ☎ 50432
DATSUN 209/211 Shinfield Rd ☎ 81620
FIAT Wolsey Rd, Caversham ☎ 582521
FORD 160 Basingstoke Rd ☎ 85333
MORRIS-MG-WOLSELEY 660 Wokingham Rd ☎ 61602
OPEL 705 London Rd ☎ 63333
RENAULT Chatham St. ☎ 583322
TOYOTA 814 Oxford Rd ☎ 57368
TOYOTA 569/575 Basingstoke Rd ☎ 81278
VOLVO 406/412 London Rd ☎ 67321
VW, AUDI-NSU Erleigh Rd ☎ 666111
VW, AUDI-NSU Oxford Rd ☎ 413434

REDBOURN Herts. – pop. 4,853 – ✉ St. Albans – ☎ 058 285.
18 9 Luton Lane ☎ 3493.
London 31 – Luton 6 – Northampton 42.

Aubrey Park (Interchange), Hemel Hempstead Rd, AL3 7AF, SW: 1 ¼ m. on B 487 ☎ 2105, heated, park – TV ⊟wc ☎ Ⓟ.
M 4.00/5.00 **s.** ♁ 1.50 – ⊡ 1.45 – **57 rm** 12.50/18.00 **s.**

PEUGEOT 271 Oxford Rd ☎ 50534

REDBOURNE South Humberside – pop. 348 – ✉ Gainsborough – ☎ 065 24 Kirton Lindsey.
London 162 – Lincoln 19 – Scunthorpe 10.

Red Lion, Gainsborough Rd DN21 4QR, ☎ 302 – Ⓟ
M approx. 5.50 ♁ 1.60 – **9 rm** ⊡ 6.00/11.00 **st.**

REDCAR Cleveland 986 ⑲ ⑳ – pop. 12,270 – ☎ 064 93.
18 ☎ 3693 – 18 Wilton, ☎ 064 95 (Eston Grange) 4626, W: 3 m. on A 174.
i Beach Centre, The Esplanade ☎ 3332 and 4657.
London 263 – Leeds 70 – Middlesbrough 9 – York 57.

Royal York, 27 Coatham Rd, TS10 1RP, ☎ 6221 – TV ⊟wc ☎ Ⓟ.
M a la carte 3.90/5.85 **t.** ♁ 1.25 – **51 rm** ⊡ 9.50/13.50 **t.**

Swan (Crest), High St., TS10 3DE, ☎ 3678 – TV ⊟wc ☎
M (grill rest. only) a la carte 3.35/5.50 **s.** ♁ 1.55 – **37 rm** ⊡ 9.00/14.95 **s.**

DAF, VOLVO Queen St. ☎ 3589
MORRIS-MG-WOLSELEY Longbeck Estate, Marske ☎ 2943
PEUGEOT, TOYOTA Redcar Lane ☎ 73231

REDDITCH Heref. and Worc. 986 ㉛ – pop. 40,839 – ☎ 0527.
18 Plymouth Rd ☎ 60140.
i Kingfisher House, Kingfisher Walk ☎ 60806.
London 111 – Birmingham 15 – Cheltenham 33 – Stratford-on-Avon 15.

Southcrest, Mount Pleasant, B97 4JG, ☎ 67521, Telex 338455, park – ⊟wc ⊟wc ☎ Ⓟ.
28 rm.

at Astwood Bank S: 4 m. on A 441 – ✉ Redditch – ☎ 052 789 Astwood Bank:

Nevill Arms, S: 1 m. on A 441 ☎ 2603 – Ⓟ
closed Sunday dinner and Monday – **M** a la carte 3.20/4.80 **t.** ♁ 0.95.

AUSTIN-MG-WOLSELEY Hewell Rd Garage ☎ 65341
CITROEN Birmingham Rd ☎ 63636
JAGUAR-ROVER-TRIUMPH 530 Evesham Rd ☎ 052 789 (Astwood Bank) 2305
TOYOTA Mount Pleasant ☎ 63711
VW, AUDI-NSU George St. ☎ 62417

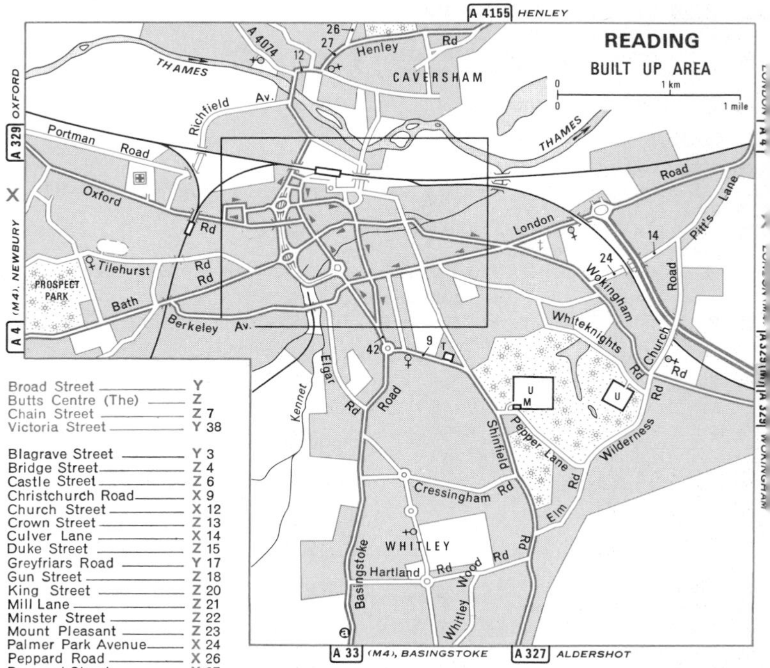

READING

BUILT UP AREA

Broad Street — Y
Butts Centre (The) — Z
Chain Street — Z 7
Victoria Street — Y 38

Blagrave Street — Y 3
Bridge Street — Z 4
Castle Street — Z 6
Christchurch Road — X 9
Church Street — X 12
Crown Street — Z 13
Culver Lane — X 14
Duke Street — Z 15
Greyfriars Road — Y 17
Gun Street — Z 18
King Street — Z 20
Mill Lane — Z 21
Minster Street — Z 22
Mount Pleasant — Z 23
Palmer Park Avenue — X 24
Peppard Road — X 26
Prospect Street — X 27
St. Mary's Butts — Z 29
Station Hill — Y 30
Station Road — Y 31
Tilehurst Road — Z 33
Tudor Road — Y 34
Valpy Street — Y 37
Watlington Street — Z 4
West Street — Y 4
Whitley Street — X 4

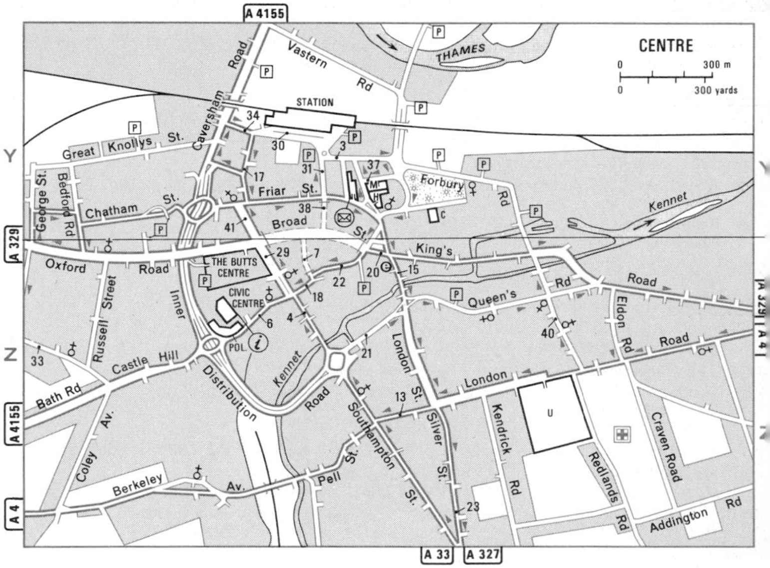

CENTRE

REDHILL Surrey 986 ㊱ – pop. 56,223 (inc. Reigate) – ☎ 0737.
Envir.: Box Hill ≤** W: 9 m.
London 22 – **Brighton 31** – Guildford 20 – Maidstone 34.

- **Ashleigh House,** 39 Redstone Hill, RH1 4BG, ☎ 64763, – Ⓟ
  9 rm 7.50/15.00 **st.**

AUSTIN-JAGUAR-ROVER-TRIUMPH 22/36 Bell St., Reigate ☎ 43333
AUSTIN-MG-WOLSELEY Sidlow Bridge, Reigate ☎ 45749
DAIMLER-MORRIS-MG-WOLSELEY, ROLLS ROYCE London Rd, Reigate ☎ 46881
FIAT West St., Reigate ☎ 47334
MORRIS-MG-WOLSELEY Allingham Rd, Reigate ☎ 43805
RENAULT 50/64 Church St., Reigate ☎ 45482
VOLVO Lesbourne Rd, Reigate ☎ 44781

REDLYNCH Wilts. – see Salisbury.

REDRUTH Cornwall 986 ㊳ – pop. 10,549 – ☎ 0209.
London 303 – Newquay 17 – Penzance 17 – **Plymouth 60** – Truro 9.

- XX **Basset Count House,** Carnkie, TR16 6RZ, SW: 1 ¼ m. off B 3297 ☎ 215181 – Ⓟ
  closed Sunday and Monday lunch – **M** a la carte 3.50/6.55.

  at Illogan NW: 3 ¼ m. by B 3300 – ✉ Redruth – ☎ 0209 Portreath:

- XX Avery Court, TR16 4QZ, ☎ 842256, – Ⓟ.

ROVER-TRIUMPH Illogan ☎ 842230
VAUXHALL Highway Illogan ☎ 5502

RHOSMAEN Dyfed – see Llandeilo.

RHOSNEIGR Gwynedd – pop. 1.200 – ☎ 0407.
See: Site*.
18 ☎ 219.
London 267 – Holyhead 13.

- **Glan Neigr,** LL64 5JA, ☎ 810516, – Ⓟ
  M (bar lunch) approx. 3.00 **st.** 1.50 – **8 rm** 6.50/13.00 **st.**
- X **Dolphin,** Maelog Rd, LL64 5JD, ☎ 810302
  closed Sunday all year; Monday and Tuesday from October to Easter – **M** (dinner only) a la carte 3.80/4.60 1.00.

RHOS-ON-SEA Clwyd – see Colwyn Bay.

RHOSSILY Dyfed – pop. 333.
See: Site and ≤ ***.
London 214 – Swansea 18.

Hotels and restaurants see: Swansea NE: 18 m.

RHYL Clwyd 986 ㉗ – pop. 21,821 – ☎ 0745.
Envir.: Rhuddlan (castle* 13C) *AC*, S: 3 m.
9 Coast Rd ☎ 53171 – 18 Rhuddlan ☎ 590217, S: 3 m.
i Tourist Information Centre, Central Promenade, ☎ 55068 (Easter-September) – Town Hall Information Bureau ☎ 31515.
London 229 – Birkenhead 42 – Chester 34 – Holyhead 53.

- **Westminster,** 10-12 East Parade, LL18 3HA, ☎ 2241 – wc Ⓟ
  M 3.05/5.30 **st.** 1.30 – **53 rm** 9.50/13.50 **st.** – P 11.00/16.00 **st.**

AUSTIN-MORRIS-MG-ROVER-TRIUMPH-WOLSELEY Elwy St. ☎ 2301
FORD Vale Rd ☎ 4436
PEUGEOT Foel Rd ☎ 570307
TOYOTA Vale Rd ☎ 53336
VW Ffforddlas Rd ☎ 4011

RICHMOND North Yorks. 986 ⑲ – pop. 7,245 – ☎ 0748.
See: Castle* (Norman ruins) *AC*. **Envir:** Bolton Castle* (15C) *AC*, ≤ *, SW: 13 m.
18 Bend Hagg ☎ 2457.
i District Council Offices, Swale House, Frenchgate ☎ 4221 (winter only) – Friary Gardens, Queen's Rd ☎ 3525 (summer only).
London 243 – **Leeds 53** – **Middlesbrough 26** – **Newcastle-upon-Tyne 44.**

- King's Head (Swallow), Market Pl., DL10 4NS, ☎ 2311 – TV wc.
  23 rm.
- **Frenchgate,** 59-61 Frenchgate, DL10 7AE, ☎ 2087, – TV wc wc Ⓟ
  closed 19 March-1 April and 22 October-4 November – **M** *(closed Sunday and Christmas to non-residents)* a la carte 3.70/5.20 **t.** 1.50 – **12 rm** 8.00/16.75 **t.**
- A 66 Motel, Smallways, DL11 7QW, NW: 8 m. on A 66 by B 6274 ☎ 083 37 (Whorlton) 334 – TV Ⓟ
  6 rm.

P.T.O. →

at Dalton NW: 7 m. – ✉ Richmond – ☎ 083 321 Barningham:

✕ **Traveller's Rest,** DL11 7HU, ☎ 225 – Ⓟ
closed Sunday, Christmas Day and 1 January – **M** (dinner only) a la carte 3.35/5.25 **t.**
🍾 1.35.

AUSTIN-MG-WOLSELEY Victoria Rd ☎ 2539
CHRYSLER Catterick Village ☎ 074 881 (Old Catterick) 334
DATSUN, VAUXHALL Dundas St. ☎ 3956
MERCEDES-BENZ Brompton on Swale ☎ 074 881 (Old Catterick) 306

RICKMANSWORTH Herts. 986 ④ – pop. 29,574 – ☎ 092 37 (5 fig.) or 0923 (6 fig.).
⛳18 Moor Lane ☎ 73163.
ℹ 17-23 High St. ☎ 76611.
London 27 – Watford 5.

🏨 Victoria, Victoria Close, WD3 4EQ, junction A 404 and A 412 ☎ 75211 – TV Ⓟ
M *(closed Sunday dinner)* – **9 rm.**

AUSTIN-MORRIS-MG-WOLSELEY 10 High St. ☎ 73101
RENAULT Moneyhill Par. ☎ 73621

RIEVAULX North Yorks. 986 ㉓ – pop. 126.
See: Abbey** (ruins 12C-13C) *AC.*
London 236 – Middlesbrough 27 – York 26.

Hotels see: Helmsley SE: 2 ½ m.
Thirsk SW: 11 m.

RINGWOOD Hants. 986 ㉟ – pop. 10,237 – ☎ 042 54.
Envir.: Fordingbridge (St. Mary's Church*) 13C, N: 6 ½ m.
⛳9 Ringwood ☎ 042 53 (Burley) 2431, NE: 4 m.
London 102 – Bournemouth 11 – Salisbury 17 – Southampton 20.

🏨 **Little Moortown House,** 244 Christchurch Rd, BH24 3AS, S: ½ m. ☎ 3325, 🌳 – 🚿wc Ⓟ
M (lunch by arrangement) 3.50/4.30 🍾 1.40 – **6 rm** 🛏 6.25/13.50 – P 12.25/13.55.

at St. Leonards SW: 2 ½ m. on A 31 – ✉ Ringwood – ☎ 0202 Ferndown:

🏠 **Avon Forest,** Ringwood Rd, BH24 2QL, ☎ 872699 – Ⓟ
closed January – **10 rm** 🛏 5.50/11.00 **st.**

RIPLEY Surrey – pop. 2,210 – ☎ 048 643.
Envir.: Wisley gardens** *AC,* NE: 1 m.
London 28 – Guildford 6.

✕✕✕ **Clock House,** Portsmouth Rd, GU23 6AF, ☎ 2777, 🌳
M a la carte 4.80/6.15 **t.** 🍾 1.40.

✕✕ **Talbot,** Portsmouth Rd, GU23 6BD, ☎ 3188, 🌳 – Ⓟ
closed Sunday dinner – **M** a la carte 5.45/10.25 **st.**

RIPON North Yorks. 986 ㉓ – pop. 10,989 – ☎ 0765.
See: Cathedral* 12C-15C. **Envir.:** Fountains Abbey*** (ruins 12C-13C, floodlit in summer), Studley Royal Gardens** and Fountains Hall* (17C) *AC,* SW: 3 m. – Newby Hall* (18C) *AC* (the tapestry room** and gardens* *AC*) SE: 3 ½ m. – Brimham Rocks* SW: 8 ½ m.
⛳9 Palace Rd ☎ 3640, N: 1 m. on A 6108.
ℹ Information Kiosk, Market Sq. ☎ 4625 (summer only).
London 222 – Leeds 26 – Middlesbrough 35 – York 23.

🏨 **Ripon Spa** (Interchange), Park St., HG4 2BU, ☎ 2172, ≤, 🌳 – 🛗 TV 🛁wc ☎ Ⓟ
M 3.75/5.50 **st.** 🍾 1.70 – **40 rm** 🛏 8.75/22.00 **st.**

✕ **Old Deanery,** Minster Rd, HG4 1QS, ☎ 3518 – Ⓟ
closed Sunday, Monday and 25-26 December – **M** (buffet lunch) a la carte 3.45/7.40
🍾 1.50.

AUSTIN-DAIMLER-JAGUAR-MORRIS-MG-ROVER-TRIUMPH-WOLSELEY Borrage Bridge ☎ 2371
DAF, VOLVO Palace Rd ☎ 2461
FIAT, MERCEDES-BENZ, VAUXHALL Kirkby Rd ☎ 4491
FORD North St. ☎ 2324

RIVENHALL END Essex – see Witham.

ROCHDALE Greater Manchester 986 ⑤ and ㉓ – pop. 91,454 – ☎ 0706.
⛳18 Marland ☎ 49801, West boundary – ⛳18 Endefield Rd ☎ 46024, 3 m. M 62 exit 20.
London 221 – Burnley 15 – Leeds 31 – Manchester 11.

🏨 Flying Horse, Town Hall Sq., OL16 1AA, ☎ 46412 – **21 rm.**

at Bamford W: 2 ½ m. on B 6222 – ✉ Rochdale – ☎ 0706 Heywood:

🏨 Crimble 🐎, Crimble Lane, OL11 4AH, ☎ 68591, 🌳 – 🛁wc Ⓟ – **13 rm.**

AUSTIN-MORRIS-MG-WOLSELEY John St. ☎ 38491
AUSTIN-DAIMLER-JAGUAR-MG-ROVER-TRIUMPH-WOLSELEY Manchester Rd, Castleton ☎ 32717
CHRYSLER-SIMCA Oldham Rd ☎ 47984
DAF Water St. ☎ 45964
FORD Station Approach ☎ 44614
RENAULT Milnrow Rd ☎ 31288
VOLVO 249 Oldham Rd ☎ 59967

ROCHESTER Kent 986 ㉟ – pop. 55,519 – ☎ 0634 Medway.

See : Castle*, ☼** (142 steps) *AC* – Cathedral* (interior**) – Eastgate House* 1590 – Fort Pitt Hill ≤* – to Brompton : Royal Engineers' Museum*. **Envir. :** Cobham Hall (Gilt Hall*) *AC*, W : 4 m.

i 85 High St. ☎ 0634 (Medway) 43666.

London 30 – **Dover 47** – Maidstone 8 – Margate 46.

Hotels and restaurants see : Gravesend NW : 6 ½ m.
Maidstone S : 8 m.

AUSTIN-DAIMLER-JAGUAR-MG-WOLSELEY Commercial Rd, Strood ☎ 79741
CHRYSLER-SIMCA High St. ☎ 42231
TOYOTA Maidstone Rd ☎ 41906
VAUXHALL Station Rd, Strood ☎ 79661

ROCK Cornwall – pop. 350 – ✉ Wadebridge – ☎ 020 886 Trebetherick.

18, 9 ☎ 3216.

London 288 – Newquay 22 – **Plymouth 45** – Truro 30.

St. Enodoc, PL27 6LA, ☎ 2311, ≤, – P
March-September – **M** (bar snacks) 4.00/4.50 **st.** 1.30 – **12 rm** 9.00/12.00.

RODBOROUGH Glos. – see Stroud.

ROKE Oxon. – see Benson.

ROMSEY Hants. 986 ㉟ – pop. 10,043 – ☎ 0794.

See : Abbey Church* 12C-13C (interior**).

18 Shootash Hill ☎ 0794 (Lockerley) 40459, SE : 3 m. on A 27 – 18 Ampfield Par Three ☎ 68480, NE: on A 31.

London 82 – Bournemouth 28 – Salisbury 16 – **Southampton 8** – Winchester 10.

White Horse (T.H.F.), Market Pl., SO5 8ZJ, ☎ 512431 – TV wc P
M a la carte 4.20/6.30 **st.** 1.50 – **33 rm** 11.00/17.50 **st.**

at Ower SW : 3 m. by A 31 on A 36 – ✉ Romsey – ☎ 042 136 Ower :

New Forest Lodge (County), SO5 0ZJ, ☎ 333, – TV wc P.
M a la carte 3.50/6.10 **t.** – **43 rm** 17.30/19.45 **t.**

AUSTIN-MORRIS-MG-ROVER-TRIUMPH-WOLSELEY Winchester Rd ☎ 512850
PEUGEOT 45/55 Winchester Hill ☎ 513185
VAUXHALL 24 Middlebridge St. ☎ 513806

ROSS-ON-WYE Heref. and Worc. 986 ㉛ – pop. 6,405 – ☎ 0989.

Envir. : Symond's Yat Rock (≤**) SW : 6 m. – Goodrich (Castle* : ruins 12C-14C) *AC*, SW : 3 ½ m.

18 ☎ 098 982 (Gorsley) 267, E : 5 m.

i 20 Broad St. ☎ 2768.

London 118 – Gloucester 15 – Hereford 15 – Newport 35.

Chase, Gloucester Rd, HR9 5LH, on A 40 ☎ 3161, – wc P.
M a la carte 4.90/6.35 **st.** – **38 rm** 9.90/19.80 **s.**

Royal (T.H.F.), Palace Pound, HR9 5HZ, ☎ 2769, – TV wc P
M approx. 3.05 **st.** 1.50 – **32 rm** 7.00/18.50 **st.**

Swan, Edde Cross St., HR9 7BZ, ☎ 2169 – P
M approx. 3.00 **t.** – **19 rm** 7.55/14.05 **t.** – P 12.95 **t.**

Chasedale, Walford Rd, HR9 5PQ, ☎ 2423, – wc P
March-October – **M** 3.00/3.50 1.25 – **17 rm** 6.50/15.00 – P 13.00/13.50.

Orles Barn, Wilton ☎ 2155, heated, – P
9 rm.

Ashburton, Gloucester Rd, ☎ 2987 – P
12 rm.

at Weston-under-Penyard E : 2 m. on A 40 – ✉ ☎ 0989 Ross-on-Wye :

Wye, HR9 7NT, ☎ 3541, , park – TV wc P.
M 3.50/3.75 **s.** 1.50 – **53 rm** 9.00/15.00 **s.** – P 12.00/15.00 **s.**

at Pengethley W : 4 m. on A 49 – ✉ Ross-on-Wye – ☎ 098 987 Harewood End :

Pengethley, HR9 6LL, ☎ 211, ≤, heated, , park – wc P
M 3.95/4.35 **s.** 1.50 – **13 rm** 12.00/21.00 **s.**

AUSTIN-MG-WOLSELEY Cantilupe Rd ☎ 2400
CHRYSLER Brook End St. ☎ 2440
MORRIS-MG-WOLSELEY Wilton Rd ☎ 2447
RENAULT Overross St. ☎ 3666

ROSTHWAITE Cumbria 986 ⑲ – see Keswick.

ROTHAY BRIDGE Cumbria – see Ambleside.

ROTHLEY Leics. – pop. 3,679 – ☎ 0533 Leicester.

Rothley Park ☎ 2019.

London 108 – Leicester 5 – Loughborough 6.

- **Rothley Court**, Westfield Lane, LE7 7LG, W: ½ m. on B 5328 ☎ 302618, ←, wc ☎ Ⓟ
  M *(closed Sunday dinner)* 4.50/5.50 **t.** 1.75 – **14 rm** 10.50/18.50 **st.**
- **Rothley,** 35 Mount Sorrel Lane, LE7 7PS, ☎ 302531 – Ⓟ
  8 rm 5.25/10.00 **s.**

BMW, FERRARI 929/931 Loughborough Rd ☎ 2484

ROTTINGDEAN East Sussex – pop. 8,637 – ⊠ ☎ 0273 Brighton.

London 58 – Brighton 4 – Lewes 9 – Newhaven 5.

- White Horse, Marine Drive, BN2 7HR, ☎ 31955 – wc ☎ Ⓟ
  22 rm.

ROUSDON Devon – see Lyme Regis.

ROWLEY REGIS West Midlands 986 ⑫ – pop. 12,753 – ⊠ ☎ 021 Birmingham.

London 132 – Birmingham 9 – Wolverhampton 10.

- **Highfield House,** Waterfall Lane, B65 0BH, ☎ 559 1066 – Ⓟ
  12 rm 4.00/8.00 **s.**

ROWSLEY Derbs. – pop. 221 – ⊠ Matlock – ☎ 062 983 Darley Dale.

Envir.: Chatsworth*** (site***, house***: Renaissance, Garden***) *AC*, N: 3½ m. – Haddon Hall** (14C-16C) *AC*, W: 1½ m.

London 157 – Derby 23 – Manchester 40 – Nottingham 30.

- **Peacock** (Embassy), DE4 2EB, ☎ 3518, « 17C stone house, with antiques », wc ☎ Ⓟ
  closed Christmas – **M** approx. 5.35 1.60 – **20 rm** 8.25/17.75 **st.**

ROYAL LEAMINGTON SPA Warw. 986 ⑫ and ㉛ – pop. 45,064 – ☎ 0926.

Whitnash ☎ 20298, S: 1½ m. by A 452 – Newbold Terrace East ☎ 21157, off Willes Rd.

i South Lodge, Jephson Gardens, The Parade ☎ 311470.

Plan of Built up Area see: Warwick

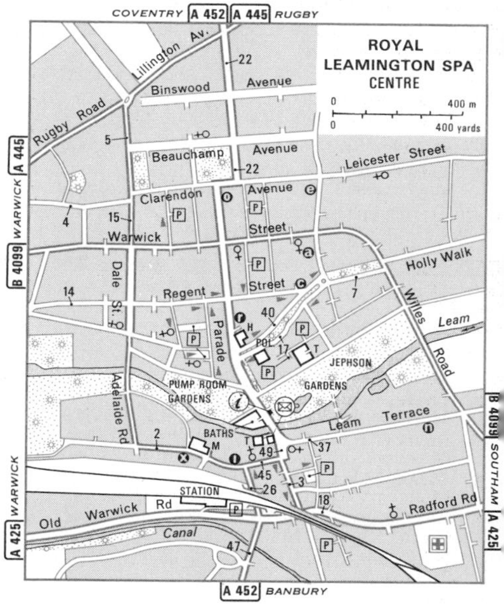

Parade
Regent Street
Warwick Street

Avenue Road	2	Clarendon Place	15
Bath Street	3	Hamilton Terrace	17
Beauchamp Hill	4	High Street	18
Binswood Street	5	Kenilworth Road	22
Brandon Parade	7	Lower Avenue	26
Church Hill	14	Priory Terrace	37
		Regent Grove	40
		Spencer Street	45
		Tachbrook Road	47
		Victoria Terrace	49

- **Manor House** (De Vere), Avenue Rd CV31 3NJ, ☎ 23251 – TV Ⓟ. i
  M approx. 4.25 **st.** 1.45 – **55 rm** 13.65/24.00 **st.**
- **Clarendon** (T. H. F.), The Parade, CV32 4DJ, ☎ 22201 – TV wc ☎ Ⓟ. o
  M 3.00/3.30 **st.** 1.50 – **54 rm** 9.00/19.00 **st.**
- **Regent** (Interchange), 77 The Parade, CV32 4AX, ☎ 27231 – wc ☎ Ⓟ. r
  M approx. 4.30 **st.** – **87 rm** 10.50/19.50 **st.**
- **Falstaff,** 18-20 Warwick New Rd, CV32 5JG, ☎ 21219 – TV wc wc Ⓟ.
  M 3.50/5.00 1.85 – **35 rm** 8.00/17.00 **s.** see plan of Warwick Z u

Amersham, 34 Kenilworth Rd, CV32 6JE, ☎ 21637 – Ⓟ see plan of Warwick Z **c**
closed 23 to 27 December – **M** (dinner only) (residents only) approx. 3.00 🍾 1.50 – **13 rm** ☕ 6.00/12.00.

Angel, 143 Regent St., CV32 4NZ, ☎ 23683 – 🛁wc 🚿 Ⓟ **c**
M *(closed Sunday and Bank Holidays)* approx. 2.80 🍾 1.05 – ☕ 1.50 – **13 rm** 6.00/12.00.

Park, 17 Avenue Rd, CV31 3PG, ☎ 28376 – 🛁wc 🚿wc Ⓟ **x**
M (lunch by arrangement) 3.00/3.50 🍾 1.20 – **16 rm** ☕ 5.50/12.50.

Veleta, 42 Warwick New Rd ☎ 21380 – Ⓟ see plan of Warwick by A 452 Z
12 rm ☕ 4.75/9.50 **t.**

Westella, 26 Leam Terr., CV31 1BB, ☎ 22710 – Ⓟ **n**
10 rm ☕ 4.50/8.50 **st.**

Chesford House, 12 Clarendon St., CV32 5ST, ☎ 20924 – Ⓟ **e**
closed Christmas – **8 rm** ☕ 4.70/8.55 **st.**

XXX **Mallory Court** with rm, Harbury Lane, Bishops Tachbrook, CV33 9QB, S : 2 m. by A 452 ☎ 30214, « Tasteful decor », ≤, ⛱, park – TV 🛁wc Ⓟ
M *(closed Sunday dinner, Monday lunch and Saturday lunch to non-residents)* 7.95/11.00 **st.** 🍾 1.50 – **6 rm** ☕ 11.00/18.25 **st.** see plan of Warwick Z **a**

XX **Il Portico,** 50 Clarendon St., CV32 4PE, ☎ 24471, Italian rest. **a**
closed Saturday lunch, Sunday and Bank Holidays – **M** a la carte 3.70/5.25 🍾 1.00.

XX **The Vaults** (at Regent Hotel), The Parade, CV32 4AX, ☎ 27231 – Ⓟ **r**
closed Sunday and Bank Holidays – **M** a la carte 3.65/6.25 🍾 1.50.

AUSTIN-MG Fenny Compton Wharf ☎ 77244
AUSTIN-MORRIS-MG Old Milverton Rd ☎ 35533
CHRYSLER-SIMCA Spencer St. ☎ 30115
DAIMLER-JAGUAR-ROVER-TRIUMPH Beauchamp Rd ☎ 38111
FORD Sydenham Drive ☎ 29411
MORRIS-MG-WOLSELEY The Parade ☎ 27156
PEUGEOT Hall Rd ☎ 22311
ROVER-TRIUMPH 14/24 Russell St. ☎ 21171
ROVER-TRIUMPH Dormer Pl. ☎ 36511
TOYOTA Wood St. ☎ 24681
VAUXHALL Old Warwick Rd ☎ 20861
VOLVO High St. ☎ 21381

ROYAL TUNBRIDGE WELLS Kent 986 ㊱ – pop. 44,612 – ☎ 0892.

See : The Pantiles* (promenade 18C) – Town Hall Museum (wood-mosaic articles*) B **M.**

i Town Hall ☎ 26121.

London 37 – Brighton 33 – Folkestone 48 – Hastings 29 – Maidstone 18.

ROYAL TUNBRIDGE WELLS

High Street B 14
Mount Pleasant Road B 25
Pantiles (The) B 26

Benhall Mill Road A 3
Bishop's Down A 4
Calverley Park Gardens B 7
Clarence Road B 8
Crescent Road B 9
Fir Tree Road A 10
Grosvenor Road B 12
Hall's Hole Road A 13
High Rocks Lane A 16
Hungershall Park Road A 17
Lansdowne Road B 18
Lower Green Road A 20
Major York's Road A 22
Mount Ephraim A 23
Mount Ephraim Road B 24
Prospect Road A 27
Rusthall Road A 28
St. John's Road B 29
Tea Garden Lane A 30
Upper Grosvenor Road B 31
Vale Road B 33
Victoria Road B 34
Warwick Park B 35

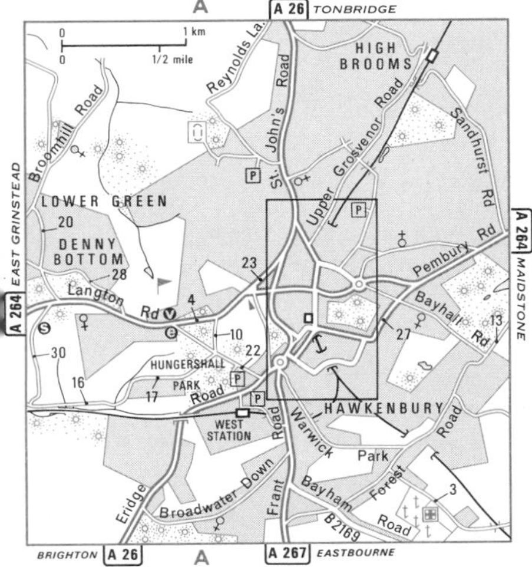

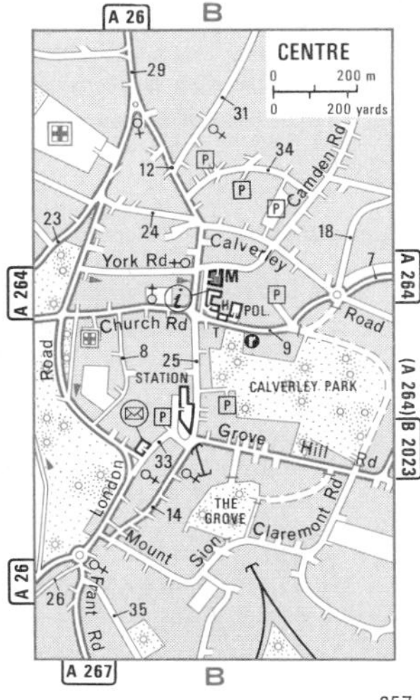

Spa (Interchange), Mount Ephraim, TN4 8XJ, ☎ 20331, Telex 957188, ≤, garden, park – lift TV Ⓟ.
M a la carte 5.20/6.45 **t.** 1.70 – 1.50 – **80 rm** 14.00/22.00 **st.** A v

Calverley, Crescent Rd, TN1 2LY, ☎ 26455, ≤, garden – lift bath wc ☎ Ⓟ B r
M 3.25/3.50 **t.** 1.25 – **39 rm** 8.50/18.00.

Beacon without rest., Tea Garden Lane, TN3 9JH, ☎ 24252, garden – bath wc shower wc Ⓟ A s
9 rm 7.00/16.00 **st.**

High Rocks Inn, TN3 9JJ, W: 2 m. ☎ 26074, « Attractive garden » – Ⓟ
closed Monday – **M** a la carte 3.35/5.75 **t.** 1.50. by High Rocks Lane A

Alpine Rose, 9-11 Langton Rd, TN4 8XA, ☎ 21575, Swiss rest. A e
closed Monday – **M** a la carte 3.30/4.95 **t.** 1.15.

at Southborough **N : 2 m. on A 26 – A – ✉ ☎ 0892 Royal Tunbridge Wells :**

Weavers, London Rd, TN4 0PU, ☎ 29896 – Ⓟ
closed Sunday dinner, Monday, 1 week February, 26 to 30 December and Bank Holidays – **M** a la carte 4.10/5.80 **t.** 1.45.

at Eridge Green **SW : 3 m. on A 26 – A – ✉ Royal Tunbridge Wells – ☎ 089 276 Groombridge :**

Nevill Crest and Gun, ☎ 209, garden – Ⓟ.

at Speldhurst **NW : 3 ½ m. off A 26 – A – ✉ Royal Tunbridge Wells – ☎ 089 286 Langton :**

George and Dragon Inn, TN3 0NN, ☎ 3125, « Part 13C inn » – Ⓟ
closed Saturday lunch, Sunday dinner and Monday – **M** a la carte 5.05/6.70 **t.** 1.30.

AUSTIN-MG-WOLSELEY Calverley Rd ☎ 27174
CHRYSLER-SIMCA 49 Mount Pleasant ☎ 27202
CITROEN, FIAT, LANCIA 321 St. Johns Rd ☎ 35111
DAIMLER-JAGUAR 34 Hastings Rd, Pembury ☎ 089 282 (Pembury) 2294
DAIMLER-JAGUAR-ROVER-TRIUMPH 12/16 London Rd ☎ 26461
DATSUN 13/17 London Rd ☎ 29292
FORD 3 Mount Ephraim ☎ 20323
MORRIS-MG-WOLSELEY 41/43 St. Johns Rd ☎ 24131
PEUGEOT London Rd ☎ 28122
RENAULT Currie Rd St John's ☎ 20628
SAAB, TOYOTA St. James Rd ☎ 31345
VAUXHALL 39 St. Johns Rd ☎ 20211

RUABON Clwyd 986 ⑨ and ㉗ – pop. 5,663 – ✉ Wrexham – ☎ 097 881.

London 190 – Chester 17 – Shrewsbury 26 – Stoke-on-Trent 30.

Wynnstay Arms, High St., LL14 6BL, ☎ 3836 – TV Ⓟ.
M *(closed Sunday dinner)* a la carte 3.60/6.00 **st.** 1.40 – **9 rm** 7.25/14.50 **st.**

RUAN-HIGH-LANES Cornwall – pop. 236 – ✉ Truro – ☎ 087 250 Veryan.

London 293 – St. Austell 12 – Truro 12.

Polsue Manor, TR2 5LU, W: 1 m. off A 3078 ☎ 270, ≤, garden – bath wc Ⓟ
Easter-first week October – **M** *(closed Sunday dinner to non-residents)* (buffet lunch) 4.00/5.50 1.40 – **13 rm** 7.50/15.75 **s.**

RUGBY Warw. 986 ㉛ – pop. 59,396 – ☎ 0788.

Envir. : Stanford-on-Avon (castle 17C: park* *AC*) NE: 5 m.

i Borough Library, St. Matthews St. ☎ 2687.

London 88 – Birmingham 33 – Leicester 21 – Northampton 20 – Warwick 17.

Three Horse Shoes, Sheep St., CV21 3BX, ☎ 4585 – TV bath wc shower wc ☎
M 4.25/5.00 1.35 – 1.75 – **31 rm** 12.00/16.50.

Grosvenor House, 81 Clifton Rd ☎ 3437
9 rm.

Andalucia, 10 Henry St., CV21 2QA, ☎ 76404, Spanish rest.
closed Christmas Day dinner – **M** a la carte 4.10/7.60 1.30.

at Clifton-on-Dunsmore **NE : 2 ¾ m. off B 5414 – ✉ ☎ 0788 Rugby :**

Clifton Court, Lilbourne Rd, CV23 0BB, ☎ 65033, garden – TV bath wc shower wc ☎ Ⓟ
M *(closed Saturday lunch and Sunday)* a la carte 3.00/5.95 **s.** 1.00 – **14 rm** 12.00/17.00 **s.**

at Hillmorton **SE : 2 m. on A 428 – ✉ ☎ 0788 Rugby :**

Hillmorton Manor, 78-86 High St. CV21 4EE, ☎ 76512 – shower wc Ⓟ
M 3.00/4.00 **s.** 1.65 – **18 rm** 8.00/16.50 **s.**

at Crick **SE : 5 m. on A 428 – ✉ Northampton – ☎ 0788 Rugby :**

Post House (T.H.F.), NN6 7XR, W: ½ m. on A 428 ☎ 822101, Telex 311107 – TV Ⓟ.
M 3.00/4.00 **st.** 1.50 – 2.00 – **96 rm** 14.00/20.00 **st.**

DAF Leicester Rd ☎ 2685
DATSUN Temple St. ☎ 3094
JAGUAR-MORRIS-MG-ROVER-TRIUMPH-WOLSELEY Railway Terrace ☎ 3477
MORRIS-MG-WOLSELEY 339/341 Hillmorton Rd ☎ 2784
RENAULT 100 Railway Terrace ☎ 2660
ROVER-TRIUMPH, VAUXHALL Bilton Rd ☎ 2063

RUGELEY Staffs. 986 ㉗ – pop. 22,230 – ☎ 088 94.
Envir. : Blithfield Hall* (Elizabethan) *AC*, N : 5 m.
London 135 – Birmingham 23 – Stafford 9 – **Stoke-on-Trent 23.**

Eaton Lodge, 118 Wolseley Rd, WF15 2ET, ☎ 3454 – Ⓟ – **7 rm.**

at Armitage SE : 3 m. on A 513 – ✉ Rugeley – ☎ 0543 Armitage :

✕ **Old Farmhouse,** WS15 4AT, ☎ 490353, – Ⓟ
closed Saturday, Sunday, Monday lunch, 29 May-4 June, last week July, first week August, 2 to 8 October and Bank Holidays – **M** 4.00/6.00 **t.** 1.35.

at Brereton S : ¾ m. on A 51 – ✉ ☎ 088 94 Rugeley :

Cedar Tree, 118 Main Rd, WS15 1DY, ☎ 4241, – wc Ⓟ
closed 25 and 26 December – **M** *(closed Sunday dinner)* 3.50/6.00 **t.** 1.60 – **12 rm** 6.50/12.50 **st.**

AUSTIN-MORRIS-MG 6 Market St. ☎ 3385
PEUGEOT Brereton Rd ☎ 2248
SAAB Market St. ☎ 2347

RUNCORN Cheshire 986 ⑤ and ㉗ – pop. 35,999 – ☎ 092 85 (5 fig.) or 0928 (6 fig.).
Clifton Rd ☎ 72093.
i 57 Church St. ☎ 76776 or 69656.
London 202 – Liverpool 14 – Manchester 29.

Runcorn Eurocrest (Crest), Wood Lane, Beechwood, WA7 3HA, SE : ¼ m. off junction 12 ☎ 714000, Telex 627426 – TV wc Ⓟ.
M a la carte 4.50/6.70 **s.** 1.60 – 1.80 – **141 rm** 11.50/15.80 **s.**

AUSTIN-MORRIS-MG Balfour St. ☎ 72271
DAF, MAZDA 51 Halton Rd ☎ 63099
VAUXHALL Victoria Rd ☎ 74333

RUSHLAKE GREEN East Sussex – pop. **1,195** (inc. Warbleton) – ✉ Heathfield – ☎ 043 56.
London 57 – Eastbourne 14 – Hastings 15 – Royal Tunbridge Wells 21.

Priory , TN21 9RG, N : 1 m. ☎ 553, ≤, « Country house atmosphere-Former Priory », , , park – TV wc Ⓟ
closed 25 December-7 January – **M** *(closed Monday to non-residents)* 5.75/6.75 **t.** 1.40 – **10 rm** 12.00/18.25 **t.**

RUSHYFORD Durham – pop. 339 – ✉ Ferryhill – ☎ 038 886.
London 260 – Durham 10 – **Leeds 70 – Middlesbrough 18.**

Eden Arms (Swallow), DL17 0LL, ☎ 541, Group Telex 53168 – TV wc Ⓟ.
41 rm.

RUSTINGTON West Sussex – pop. 8,904 – ✉ Littlehampton – ☎ 090 62.
Ham Manor ☎ 3288 – Littlehampton ☎ 7170, W : bank river Arun.
London 63 – Brighton 16 – Southampton 47.

Broadmark, Broadmark Lane, BN16 2JN, ☎ 4281, ≤ – TV wc Ⓟ
17 rm.

AUSTIN-DAIMLER-JAGUAR-ROVER-TRIUMPH Ash Lane ☎ 73333
FIAT, SIMCA Sea Lane ☎ 2052

RUTHIN Clwyd 986 ㉗ – pop. 4,338 – ☎ 082 42.
See : Church*.
Pwllglas ☎ 2296, S : 2 ½ m.
London 210 – Birkenhead 31 – Chester 23 – Shrewsbury 46.

Ruthin Castle , Corwen Rd, LL15 2NU, ☎ 2664, Telex 61169, ≤, , , park – wc Ⓟ.
M a la carte 1.75/5.80 **t.** 1.25 – **64 rm** 11.50/23.00 **t.** – P 17.50 **t.**

Castle, St. Peter's Sq., LL15 1AA, ☎ 2479 – TV wc Ⓟ.
M (dinner only) 3.50/5.00 **st.** 1.00 – 0.75 – **25 rm** 7.75/16.50 **st.**

AUSTIN-MG-WOLSELEY Llanfair D.C. ☎ 2969
OPEL Well St. ☎ 2645

RYDAL Cumbria – see Ambleside.

RYDE I.O.W. 986 ㊴㊵ – see Wight (Isle of).

Außer den mit XXXXX . . . X gekennzeichneten Häusern haben auch sehr viele Hotels ein gutes Restaurant.

RYE East Sussex 986 ㊱ – pop. 4,449 – ☎ 079 73.

See : Old Town★ (chiefly : Mermaid Street) – Ypres Tower ≤★. **Envir.** : Winchelsea (Church of St. Thomas the Martyr★ 1283 : tombs★★ 12C) SW : 3 m.

i Council Offices, Ferry Rd ☎ 2293.

London 65 – Brighton 48 – Folkestone 26 – Maidstone 32.

- **Mermaid,** Mermaid St., TN31 7EY, ☎ 3065, Telex 957141, « 15C inn » – bath wc shower wc Ⓟ
  M a la carte 3.75/6.15 **t.** 1.35 – **29 rm** 7.25/15.00 **t.**
- **George** (T.H.F.), High St., TN31 7JT, ☎ 2114 – TV bath wc shower wc Ⓟ
  M a la carte 4.05/5.70 **st.** 1.50 – **22 rm** 10.50/16.00 **st.**
- **Hope Anchor,** Watchbell St., TN31 7HA, ☎ 2216, ≤ – bath wc
  M approx. 4.00 1.30 – **13 rm** 7.00/14.80.
- **Mariners** without rest., High St., TN31 7JF, ☎ 3480, garden – bath wc
  16 rm 5.75/13.00 **st.**
- **Saltings,** Hilders Cliff, High St., TN31 7JF, ☎ 3838 – bath wc Ⓟ
  M a la carte 4.15/5.95 **t.** 1.75 – **19 rm** 7.00/15.00 **t.**
- **Durrant House,** 2 Market St., TN31 7LA, ☎ 3182, garden – bath wc
  Easter-Christmas – **8 rm** 7.00/14.00 **st.**
- XX **Flushing Inn,** Market St., TN31 7LA, ☎ 3292
  closed Monday dinner, Tuesday, fourth week September to third week October and 26 December-9 January – **M** a la carte 4.75/9.00 **t.** 1.80.
- XX **Monastery** with rm, 6 High St., TN31 7JE, ☎ 3272, garden – shower
  April-October – **M** *(closed Tuesday all year, Wednesday and Thursday from October to March)* (dinner only from April to September) a la carte 3.85/6.00 **t.** 2.20 – **7 rm** 13.50/15.00 **st.**
- X **Old Forge,** 24 Wish St., TN31 7DA, ☎ 3227
  closed Sunday, Monday in winter, Tuesday lunch, 2 weeks Autumn and 2 weeks February – **M** a la carte 3.25/6.55 **t.** 1.35.

at Playden N : 1 m. on A 268 – ✉ ☎ 079 73 Rye :

- **Playden Oasts,** TN31 7UL, ☎ 3502, garden – bath wc Ⓟ
  M (dinner only and Sunday lunch) approx. 4.25 – **6 rm** 12.00.

at Iden N : 2 m. on B 2082 by A 268 – ✉ Rye – ☎ 079 78 Iden :

- X **Bell Inn,** TN31 7PU, ☎ 242 – Ⓟ
  M a la carte 3.90/4.75 **t.** 1.00.

at Rye Foreign N : 2 ½ m. on A 268 – ✉ Rye – ☎ 079 721 Peasmarsh :

- **Rumpel's Motel,** London Rd, TN31 7SY, ☎ 494, garden – TV bath wc Ⓟ
  M 3.50/4.50 **t.** 1.20 – **12 rm** 7.50/12.00 **s.** – P 15.00/17.00 **t.**

at Peasmarsh NW : 4 m. on A 268 – ✉ Rye – ☎ 079 721 Peasmarsh :

- XX **Flackley Ash** with rm, London Rd ☎ 381, garden – bath wc Ⓟ
  closed 24 December-12 January – **M** *(closed Tuesday, Wednesday and Thursday)* (dinner only) a la carte 3.65/4.50 **t.** 1.60 – **7 rm** 8.50/15.00 **t.**

AUSTIN-MORRIS-MG-ROVER-TRIUMPH Bedford Pl. ☎ 3334
MERCEDES-BENZ Lydd Rd ☎ 079 75 (Camber) 293

SAFFRON WALDEN Essex 986 ㉜ – pop. 9,971 – ☎ 0799.

See : Parish church★ (Perpendicular) – Audley End House★ (Jacobean : interior★★) *AC.*

London 46 – Cambridge 15 – Chelmsford 25.

- **Saffron,** 8-10 High St., CB10 1AZ, ☎ 22676 – bath wc shower ☎ Ⓟ
  M *(closed Sunday and Christmas to 1 January)* 3.25/5.00 **s.** 1.15 – 1.25 – **16 rm** 8.00/14.00 **s.** – P 15.75/19.75 **s.**

at Great Chesterford N : 4 m. on A 11 – ✉ Saffron Walden – ☎ 079 983 Great Chesterford :

- XX Crown House, ☎ 515 – Ⓟ.

AUSTIN-MORRIS-MG High St. ☎ 27909
DAF High St. ☎ 40281
FORD Station Rd ☎ 3203
ROVER-TRIUMPH 66 High St. ☎ 3597
RENAULT 13/15 Station St. ☎ 23238

ST. AGNES Cornwall – pop. 4,747 – ☎ 087 255.

See : The Beacon ※★★.

London 302 – Newquay 12 – Penzance 26 – Truro 9.

- **Rosemundy House** ⑤, Rosemundy Hill, TR5 0UF, ☎ 2101, heated swimming pool, garden – bath wc shower wc Ⓟ
  April-mid October – **M** 2.50/3.00 **st.** 1.50 – **41 rm** 10.00/20.00.
- **Trevaunance Point** ⑤, Quay Rd, Trevaunance Cove ☎ 3235, ≤ bay and cliffs, garden – Ⓟ
  M (bar lunch) 3.50/4.50 1.20 – **13 rm** 7.50/9.50.

ST. ALBANS Herts. 986 ㉜ – pop. 52,174 – ☎ 0727.

See: Site** – Cathedral and Abbey Church* (Norman Tower*). **Envir.:** Hatfield House*** *AC* (gardens* and Old Palace*) E: 6 m. – Verulamium (Roman remains* and museum) *AC,* W: 2 m.

18 Batchwood Hall ☎ 52100.

i Town Hall, 37 Chequer St. ☎ 64511/2.

London 27 – Cambridge 41 – Luton 10.

- Noke (Thistle), Watford Rd, AL2 3DS, SW: 2 ½ m. at junction A 405 and A 412 ☎ 54252 – TV wc ☎ P. **55 rm.**
- **Sopwell House** (Interchange), Cotton Mill Lane, AL1 2HQ, SE: 1 ½ m. off A 6 by Milehouse Lane ☎ 64477, park – TV wc ☎ P. **M** a la carte 4.45/7.35 2.20 – 2.00 – **18 rm** 12.00/18.00 **s.**
- **St. Michael's Manor**, Fishpool St., AL3 4RY, ☎ 64444, « Manor house, lake, ≤ garden », park – TV wc P. **M** 3.95/4.50 **s.** – **22 rm** 9.00/16.00 **s.**
- White Hart, 25 Holywell Hill, AL1 1EZ, ☎ 53624 – P – **10 rm.**
- **Black Lion,** 196 Fishpool St., AL3 4SB, ☎ 51786 – P **M** 2.50/7.00 2.50 – 0.75 – **10 rm** 6.90/9.80.
- **Melford House,** 24 Woodstock Rd North, AL1 4QQ, ☎ 53642 – P **12 rm** 6.00/12.00.

AUSTIN-DAIMLER-JAGUAR-MG-ROVER-TRIUMPH-ROLLS ROYCE-BENTLEY Acrewood Way, Hatfield Rd ☎ 66522
AUSTIN-JAGUAR-MG-WOLSELEY-ROLLS ROYCE Catherine St. ☎ 54342
CHRYSLER-SIMCA 220 London Rd ☎ 63377
CITROEN 22 Guildford Rd ☎ 50401
DAF 2/4 Grange St. ☎ 57208
FORD London Rd ☎ 60191
OPEL 101 Holywell Hill ☎ 65756
RENAULT 99/111 London Rd ☎ 52345
ROVER-TRIUMPH Park St., Frogmore ☎ 72626
TOYOTA 318 Watford Rd ☎ 0923 (Watford) 54630
VAUXHALL 185 Marshallwick Lane ☎ 65730
VAUXHALL 100 London Rd ☎ 50601
VW, AUDI-NSU 260/264 Hatfield Rd ☎ 60536

ST. ASAPH Clwyd 986 ㉗ – pop. 3,095 – ☎ 0745.

London 224 – Chester 29 – Shrewsbury 59.

- **Oriel House,** Upper Denbigh Rd, LL17 0LW, S: ¾ m. on A 525 ☎ 582716, – TV wc wc P. **M** a la carte 4.90/7.20 **st.** – **17 rm** 10.00/20.00 **st.**

AUSTIN-MORRIS-MG-ROVER-TRIUMPH-WOLSELEY, RENAULT Bod Ewr, Cornes ☎ 582345

ST. AUSTELL Cornwall 986 ㊳ – pop. 25,158 – ☎ 0726.

18 Carlyon Bay ☎ 072 681 (Par) 4250, E: 2 m.

to London/Reading, Worcester, Crewe ☎ 5671/2.

London 281 – Newquay 16 – Plymouth 38 – Truro 14.

- **White Hart,** Church St., PL25 4AT, ☎ 2100 – wc **M** 2.90/3.20 1.30 – **18 rm** 6.50/14.00.

at Tregrehan W: 2 ½ m. off A 390 – ✉ St. Austell – ☎ 072 681 Par:

- XX **Boscundle Manor** with rm, PL25 3RL, ☎ 3557, – P **M** *(closed Sunday in winter to non-residents)* a la carte 4.55/6.40 **st.** – **5 rm** 9.00/16.00 **st.**

AUSTIN-DAIMLER-JAGUAR-MG Gover Rd ☎ 5571
CITROEN 77 Fore St. ☎ 072 685 (Stenalees) 241
DATSUN East Hill ☎ 5624
FIAT Bucklers Lane ☎ 5667
FORD Slades Rd ☎ 2333
MORRIS-MG-ROVER-TRIUMPH-WOLSELEY Carlyon Bay ☎ 2451
PEUGEOT Gwendra, St.Stephen ☎ 822566
RENAULT Woodland Rd ☎ 5551

ST. DAVID'S Dyfed 986 ㉚ – pop. 1,638 – ☎ 043 788.

See: Cathedral** 12C (site*) – Bishop's palace* *AC.* **Envir.:** Whitesand Bay** and St. David's Head** NW: 2 m. – Newgale (≤**) SE: 7 m. – Solva (site*) E: 3 m.

i Wales Tourist Information Centre, opposite Guildhall ☎ 747 (Easter-September).

London 266 – Carmarthen 46 – Fishguard 16.

- **Warpool Court**, SA62 6BN, ☎ 300, ≤ sea and countryside, – wc wc P *closed 27 December-27 January* – **M** a la carte 4.85/7.45 **t.** – **25 rm** 11.30/19.10 **st.** – P 14.20 **st.**
- **Old Cross,** Cross Sq., SA62 6SP, ☎ 387, – wc P *March-11 November* – **M** (dinner only) a la carte 4.10/6.80 **t.** 1.30 – **17 rm** 6.45/10.90.
- **St. Nons,** Catherine St., SA62 6RJ, ☎ 239, – wc P **M** (buffet lunch) (residents only) a la carte 3.80/6.30 0.95 – **20 rm** 11.00/14.50.

at Whitesand Bay NW: 2 m. – ✉ ☎ 043 788 St. David's:

- **Whitesands Bay**, SA62 6PT, ☎ 403, ≤ Whitesand Bay, park – TV wc P *Easter-mid October* – **M** 4.50/6.00 **t.** 1.60 – **30 rm** 11.00/26.00 – P 15.50/17.50.

ST. DOGMAELS Dyfed – see Cardigan.

ST. HELENS Merseyside 986 ⑤ and ㉓ ㉗ – pop. 104,341 – ☎ 0744.
Envir.: Knowsley Safari Park** *AC*, W: 6 m.
Sherdley Park ☎ 813149, E: 2 m. on A 570.
London 204 – Liverpool 14 – Manchester 21 – Preston 25.

- **Fleece,** 15 Church St., WA10 1BA, ☎ 26546 – wc. *closed 23 to 28 December* – **M** 4.00/5.00 **st.** 2.50 – **70 rm** 11.50/15.00 **st.**

AUSTIN-MG-WOLSELEY Knowsley Rd ☎ 34441
CHRYSLER-SIMCA Knowsley Rd ☎ 32411
DAIMLER-JAGUAR-MORRIS-MG-ROVER-TRIUMPH-WOLSELEY 18 Dentons Green Lane ☎ 20934
FORD City Rd ☎ 26381
MORRIS-MG-WOLSELEY 449 Prescot Rd ☎ 26686
PEUGEOT East Lancashire Rd ☎ 27373
RENAULT Jackson St. ☎ 26681
ROVER-TRIUMPH Elephants Lane ☎ 811565
VAUXHALL Knowsley Rd ☎ 35221

ST. IVES Cornwall 986 ㊳ – pop. 9,839 – ☎ 073 670.
See: Parish church* 15C. **Envir.:** Marazion (St. Michael's Mount** *AC*) S: 8 ½ m.
i The Guildhall, Street-an-Pol ☎ 6297.
London 319 – Penzance 10 – Truro 25.

- **Tregenna Castle** (B.T.H.), TR26 2DE, ☎ 5254, Telex 45128, heated, park – M a la carte 6.95/10.80 1.75 – **76 rm** 14.55/28.55 **st.**
- **Porthminster,** The Terrace, TR26 2BN, ☎ 5221, heated, – wc **M** a la carte 3.40/4.50 1.15 – **50 rm** 10.00/20.00 – P 14.00/18.00.
- **St. Ives Bay,** The Terrace, TR26 2BP, ☎ 5106, – wc *14 April-September* – **M** a la carte 3.75/9.00 **st.** 1.00 – **52 rm** 6.80/15.40 **st.** – P 9.50/10.90 **st.**
- **Garrack**, Burthallan Lane, Higher Lane, TR26 3AA, ☎ 6199, – wc *Easter-October* – **M** (bar lunch) approx. 3.75 1.45 – **21 rm** 9.00/21.00.
- **Chy-an-Dour,** Treloyhan Av., TR26 2AD, ☎ 6436, – **M** 2.75/3.25 – **29 rm** 7.70/16.40 – P 11.00/12.50.
- Chy-an-Drea, The Terrace, TR26 2BP, ☎ 5076, – wc *season* – **36 rm.**
- **Outrigger,** Street-an-Pol, TR26 2DR, ☎ 5936 *closed Monday and December* – **M** (dinner only) a la carte 3.50/6.05 **t.** 1.75.

at Halsetown S: 2 m. on B 3311 – ✉ ☎ 073 670 St. Ives:

- **Chef's Kitchen,** TR26 3NA, ☎ 6218 *closed Sunday and Christmas Day* – **M** (dinner only) a la carte 3.25/7.20 **s.** 1.50.

CITROEN ☎ 5442

ST. IVES Cambs. 986 ㉜ – pop. 7,148 – ☎ 0480.
See: Bridge* 15C.
High Leys ☎ 64459.
London 75 – Cambridge 14 – Huntingdon 6.

- **Golden Lion,** Market Hill, PE17 4AL, ☎ 63159 – wc **M** a la carte 4.00/7.00 **st.** 1.50 – **20 rm** 7.50/14.50 **st.**
- **St. Ives Motel,** London Rd, PE17 4EX, S: ½ m. on A 1096 ☎ 63857, – wc **M** a la carte 3.40/5.60 **t.** 1.75 – 1.35 – **15 rm** 9.15/12.80 **t.**
- **Slepe Hall** with rm, Ramsey Rd, PE17 4RB, ☎ 63122 – wc **M** a la carte 4.45/11.30 1.75 – **15 rm** 10.80/19.25 **st.**

at Needingworth E: 2 ½ m. on A 1123 – ✉ ☎ 0480 St. Ives:

- **Chestnuts,** 85 High St., PE17 3SB, ☎ 63456 – *closed Sunday dinner and 24 to 26 December* – **M** a la carte 3.65/6.10 1.00.

at Overcote Ferry E: 3 ½ m. off A 1123 – ✉ ☎ 0480 St. Ives:

- **Pike and Eel**, Overcote Lane, PE17 4SG, ☎ 63336, – *closed 24 to 26 December* – **M** *(open all year)* a la carte 3.40/5.25 **s.** – **10 rm** 7.50/9.25 **s.**

at Fenstanton S: 2 m. by A 1096 on A 604 – ✉ ☎ 0480 St. Ives:

- Tudor Inn, High St., PE18 9LN, ☎ 62532, – wc **10 rm.**

AUSTIN-MG-WOLSELEY 2 Quadrant ☎ 62871
FIAT, LANCIA Station Rd ☎ 62641
FORD Ramsey Rd ☎ 63184
MORRIS-MG-WOLSELEY Station Rd ☎ 63322

ST. LEONARDS Hants. – see Ringwood.

ST. MARGARET'S BAY Kent – pop. 2,185 – ✉ ☎ 0304 Dover.
London 79 – Dover 4 – Ramsgate 19.

- **Granville**, Granville Rd, CT15 6DT, ☎ 852212, sea and coastline, – wc **M** *(closed Tuesday)* approx. 4.00 1.70 – 1.60 – **20 rm** 6.00/14.00.

ST. MARY'S Cornwall – see Scilly (Isles of).

ST. MARY'S HOO Kent – pop. 155 – ✉ Rochester – ☎ 0634 Medway.
London 35 – Rochester 8,5.

XX **Coombe House,** ME3 8RN, ☎ 270583 – Ⓟ
closed Sunday and Monday – **M** a la carte 4.95/6.60 **s.**

ST. MAWES Cornwall 986 ㊳ – pop. 870 – ✉ Truro – ☎ 032 66.
See : Castle 16C (≤*) *AC.*
London 299 – Plymouth 56 – Truro 18.

Tresanton, TR2 5DR, ☎ 544, ≤ estuary, – wc
February-October and 1 week at Christmas – **M** approx. 5.00 1.80 – **29 rm** (full board only) – P 15.50/23.00.

Rising Sun, The Square, TR2 5DJ, ☎ 233, ≤ – wc
closed 1 week at Christmas – **M** a la carte 5.05/7.00 – **20 rm** 10.00/21.50.

Pen Eglos , Riviera Lane, TR2 5BG, ☎ 302, ≤ bay – wc Ⓟ
March-October – **M** (dinner only) 4.50 **st.** 1.50 – **13 rm** 7.50/21.00.

Green Lantern, Marine Parade, TR2 5DW, ☎ 502
closed mid December - mid February – **M** (dinner only and Sunday lunch) approx. 4.50 1.00 – **10 rm** 6.00/12.00.

Manor House, TR2 5AG, ☎ 392, ≤ – wc
season – **20 rm.**

AUSTIN-MORRIS-MG-WOLSELEY ☎ 200

ST. MICHAEL'S MOUNT Cornwall 986 ㊳.
See : St. Michael's Mount** *AC.*

Hotels and restaurants see : Penzance W : 3 m.
St. Ives N : 8 ½ m.

ST. MICHAEL'S-ON-WYRE Lancs. – pop. 529 – ✉ Preston – ☎ 099 58.
London 234 – Blackpool 11 – Lancaster 14 – Preston 11.

XX **Rivermede** with rm, PR3 0UB, ☎ 267, , – Ⓟ
closed 25 December-31 January – **M** *(closed Tuesday)* (dinner only) 6.25/7.95 **t.** 1.90 – **3 rm** 8.75/16.75 **s.**

ST. NEOTS Cambs. 986 ㉜ – pop. 15,204 – ☎ 0480 Huntingdon.
See : St. Mary's Church* 15C.
18 Cross Hall Rd ☎ 75617, W : 1 m.
London 60 – Bedford 11 – Cambridge 17 – Huntingdon 9.

XX **Chequers Inn,** St. Mary's St., PE19 2TA, Eynesbury S : ½ m. on B 1046 ☎ 72116 – Ⓟ
closed Christmas Day – **M** a la carte 4.40/6.45 **s.** 1.80.

AUSTIN-MORRIS-MG 11 New St. ☎ 73237
FORD Cambridge St. ☎ 73321
ROVER-TRIUMPH 42 Huntingdon St. ☎ 73578

SALCOMBE Devon 986 ㊴ – pop. 2,496 – ☎ 054 884.
i Shadycombe Rd ☎ 2736.
London 243 – Exeter 43 – Plymouth 27 – Torquay 28.

Marine, Cliff Rd, TQ8 8JH, ☎ 2251, Telex 45185, ≤ estuary, heated – TV Ⓟ
March-November – **M** a la carte 7.60/10.30 **st.** 1.75 – **51 rm** 16.50/35.00 **st.** – P 24.50/32.00 **st.**

Tides Reach, South Sands, TQ8 8LJ, ☎ 2888, ≤ estuary, – TV wc Ⓟ
March-October – **M** approx. 6.00 1.50 – **40 rm** 11.00/29.00 **s.** – P 18.00/20.00 **s.**

St. Elmo , Sandhills Rd, TQ8 8JR, ☎ 2233, – wc Ⓟ
May-October – **M** 4.00/4.60 **s.** 1.10 – **32 rm** 5.00/16.00 **s.** – P 10.50/14.00 **s.**

Bolt Head , South Sands, TQ8 8LL, ☎ 2780, ≤ estuary, heated – wc Ⓟ
Easter-mid October – **M** (snack lunch) approx. 4.20 1.55 – **20 rm** 8.90/17.80 – P 12.35/14.75.

Castle Point , Sandhills Rd, TQ8 8JP, ☎ 2167, ≤ estuary, – wc Ⓟ
Easter- October – **M** (snack lunch) 4.25 **t.** 1.30 – **21 rm** 8.00/22.00.

Sunny Cliff, Cliff Rd, TQ8 8JU, ☎ 2207, ≤ estuary, heated, – wc Ⓟ
mid March-October – **M** (snack lunch) 3.00 **st.** 1.60 – **17 rm** 6.30/14.20 **st.** – P 11.35 **st.**

Grafton Towers , Moult Rd, TQ8 8LG, ☎ 2882, ≤, – wc Ⓟ
Easter-October – **M** (cold lunch) 3.50/4.00 **t.** 1.25 – **15 rm** 8.00/18.00 – P 10.00/13.00.

P.T.O. ⟶

Hazeldene, Sandhills Rd, TQ8 8JP, ☎ 2802, ≤, ✂, ⚘ – ⌂wc Ⓟ
April-October – **M** (dinner only) 2.50 🌡 0.95 – **10 rm** ☕ 6.50/18.00.

Penn Torr, Herbert Rd, TQ8 8HN, ☎ 2234 – ⌂wc Ⓟ
Easter-September – **M** (dinner only) 2.25/4.50 **s.** 🌡 1.20 – **10 rm** ☕ (dinner included) 7.00/14.00 **s.**

Bay View, Bennett Rd, TQ8 8JJ, ☎ 2238, ≤ estuary – Ⓟ
Easter-September – **11 rm** ☕ 7.50/16.00 **t.**

Woodgrange, Devon Rd, TQ8 8HJ, ☎ 2439, ⚘ – ⌂wc Ⓟ
Easter-September – **11 rm** ☕ (dinner included) 8.00/16.00 **t.**

XX **Galley,** 5 Fore St., TQ8 8BY, ☎ 2828, ≤
closed Sunday to Thursday from mid November to March and Christmas Day – **M** (dinner only Friday and Saturday) a la carte 4.10/6.00 **t.** 🌡 1.40.

at Hope Cove W: 4 m. – ✉ Kingsbridge – ☎ 054 854 Galmpton:

Cottage ⛰, TQ7 3HJ, ☎ 555, ≤ Bolt Tail and Bigbury Bay, ⚘ – ⌂wc ♿ Ⓟ
closed January – **M** approx. 5.30 **s.** 🌡 1.50 – **36 rm** ☕ 7.60/28.30 **s.**

Lantern Lodge ⛰, TQ7 3HE, ☎ 280, ≤, ⚘ – ⌂wc ⌂wc Ⓟ
Easter-October – **M** (dinner only) (residents only) 4.50 🌡 1.20 – **15 rm** ☕ 7.00/14.00.

SALE Greater Manchester 986 ⑤ and ㉓ ㉗ – pop. 55,769 – ☎ 061 Manchester.

⛳18 Sale Lodge, Golf Rd ☎ 973 3404.

London 193 – Liverpool 35 – Manchester 5.

Normanhurst, 195 Brooklands Rd, M33 3PJ, ☎ 973 1982, ⚘ – ⌂wc Ⓟ
M (dinner only) (residents only) 2.25 **s.** 🌡 1.30 – **50 rm** ☕ 5.25/9.90 **s.**

AUSTIN-MORRIS-MG-WOLSELEY 77/79 Cross St. ☎ 969 1421

CHRYSLER-SIMCA 253 Washway Rd ☎ 973 8224

Red Lion	Si le nom d'un hôtel figure en petits caractères, demandez à l'arrivée les conditions à l'hôtelier.

SALFORDS Surrey – ✉ ☎ 0737 Redhill.

London 24 – Brighton 29.

Mill House, Brighton Rd, RH1 5BT, ☎ 67277, ⚘ – ⌂wc ⌂wc Ⓟ
M *(closed 26 December)* approx. 2.85 🌡 0.95 – ☕ 1.20 – **31 rm** 6.00/12.50.

SALISBURY Wilts. 986 ㉟ – pop. 35,302 – ☎ 0722.

See: Cathedral*** 13C (cloister***, chapter house***, Library : Magna Carta* *AC*) Z **A**.
Envir.: Stonehenge (Megalithic monument)*** *AC*, NW: 10 m. by A 345 Y – Old Sarum (excavations 12C-13C)* *AC*, N : 2 m. by A 345 Y – Longford Castle* (16C) *AC*, SE : 2 ½ m. by A 338 Z – Breamore House* (Elizabethan) *AC*, S : 8 ½ m. by A 338 Z – Wilton House* 17C-19C (interior**) *AC*, W : 2 ½ m. by A 30 Y.

⛳18, ⛳9 Netherhampton ☎ 072 274 (Wilton) 2131, by A 3094 Z – ⛳18 Great Dunford ☎ 072 273 (Middle Woodford) 231 N: 4 m. by A 345 Y.

i 10 Endless St. ☎ 4956 – Fisherton St. ☎ 27675/4432/6272.

London 91 – Bournemouth 28 – Bristol 53 – Southampton 23.

Plan opposite

White Hart (T.H.F.), 1 St. John's St., SP1 2SD, ☎ 27476 – TV ⌂wc ☎ Ⓟ. 🏋 — Z **s**
M 3.75/4.25 **st.** 🌡 1.50 – ☕ 2.00 – **72 rm** 8.00/17.00 **st.**

Cathedral, 7 Milford St., SP1 2AJ, ☎ 20144 – lift ⌂wc — Y **a**
M a la carte 4.45/6.30 **st.** 🌡 1.35 – **32 rm** ☕ 9.85/17.35 **st.**

Kings Arms, St. John's St., SP1 2SB, ☎ 27629, « Part 13C and part 15C inn » – ⌂wc — Z **r**
M 3.00/4.00 **t.** 🌡 1.10 – **16 rm** ☕ 9.00/17.00 **t.**

Byways House, 31 Fowlers Rd, off Milford Hill, SP1 2QP, ☎ 28364, ⚘ — Z **e**
10 rm ☕ 5.75/11.50 **t.**

Glen Lyn, Milford Hill, SP1 2QZ, ☎ 27880, ⚘ — Y **n**
9 rm.

XX ✿ **Cranes,** 90-92 Crane St., SP1 2QD, ☎ 3471, French rest. — Z **a**
closed Sunday, Monday, 3 weeks June, 3 weeks after Christmas, Easter Saturday, Tuesday after Bank Holidays and Bank Holidays – **M** a la carte 6.30/7.75 **st.** 🌡 1.50
Spec. Tartelettes aux crabes, Civet of Venison (October-January), Home-made ice-creams.

XX **The Haunch of Venison,** Minster St., SP1 1TB, ☎ 22024, « 14C timbered inn » — Y **e**
closed Sunday, Monday, 2 weeks November and Bank Holidays – **M** a la carte 4.85/7.70 **t.** 🌡 1.90.

XX **Provençal,** 14 Ox Row, Market Pl., SP1 1EU, ☎ 28923, French rest. — Y **c**
closed Sunday from November to March and Christmas – **M** (dinner only) a la carte 5.40/6.30 **t.** 🌡 1.30.

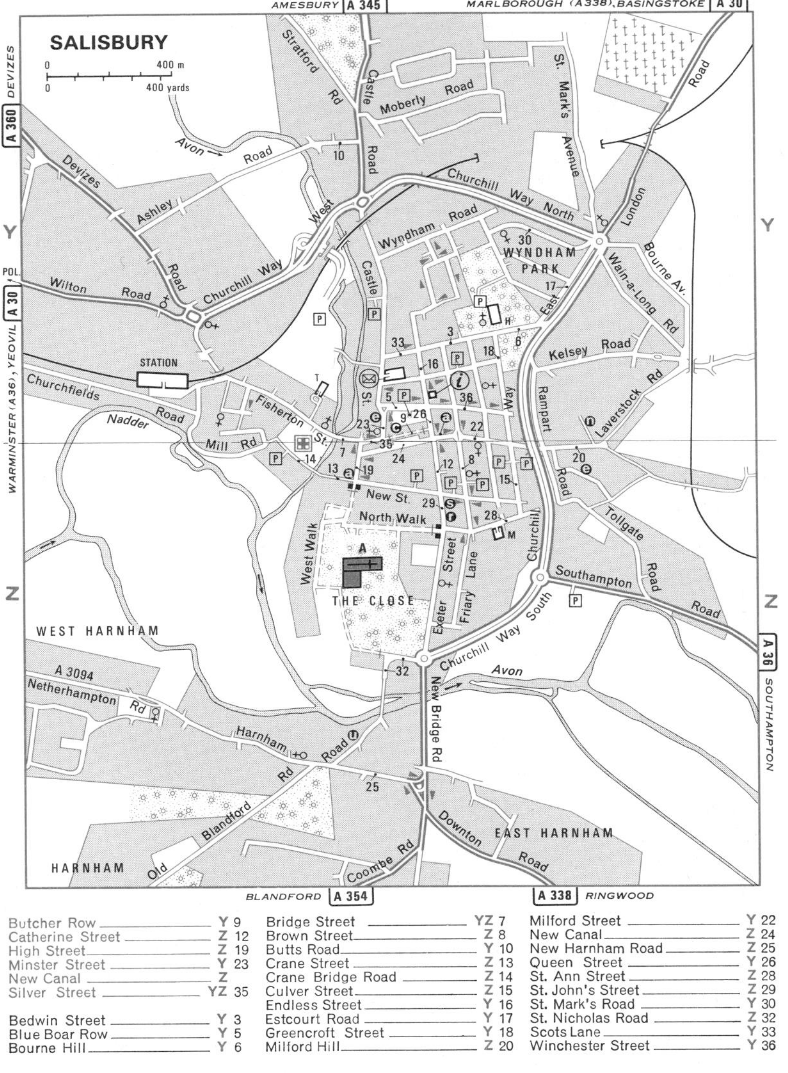

Butcher Row Y 9
Catherine Street Z 12
High Street Z 19
Minster Street Y 23
New Canal Z
Silver Street YZ 35

Bedwin Street Y 3
Blue Boar Row Y 5
Bourne Hill Y 6

Bridge Street YZ 7
Brown Street Z 8
Butts Road Y 10
Crane Street Z 13
Crane Bridge Road Z 14
Culver Street Z 15
Endless Street Y 16
Estcourt Road Y 17
Greencroft Street Y 18
Milford Hill Z 20

Milford Street Y 22
New Canal Z 24
New Harnham Road Z 25
Queen Street Y 26
St. Ann Street Z 28
St. John's Street Z 29
St. Mark's Road Y 30
St. Nicholas Road Z 32
Scots Lane Y 33
Winchester Street Y 36

at Winterslow NE: 6 m. on A 30 – Y – ✉ Salisbury – ☎ 0980 Winterslow:

Pheasant, SP5 1BN, ☎ 862374 – wc Ⓟ
M a la carte 2.75/3.95 **st.** 1.00 – 1.00 – **9 rm** 6.50/13.00 **st.**

at Redlynch SE: 8 ½ m. by A 338 – Z – off B 3080 – Salisbury – ☎ 079 439 Earldoms:

Langley Wood, Timberley Lane SE: 1 m. ☎ 348, – Ⓟ
closed Sunday, 25-26 December and 1 January – **M** (dinner only) a la carte 4.10/5.95 **t.** 1.20.

at Odstock S: 2 ½ m. off A 338 – Z – ✉ ☎ 0722 Salisbury:

Yew Tree Inn, SP5 4JE, ☎ 29786, French rest. – Ⓟ
closed Sunday, Monday and Bank Holidays – **M** a la carte 4.35/6.20 0.85.

at Harnham **SW: 1 ½ m. off A 3094 – ✉ ☎ 0722 Salisbury:**

Rose and Crown (County), Harnham Rd, SP2 8JQ, ☎ 27908, ≤, « Garden on riverside » – TV ⇔wc ☎ ♿ P
M a la carte 3.65/5.50 **t.** 🍷 1.40 – **28 rm** ☕ 14.05/19.45 **st.** Z u

at Wilton **NW: 2 ½ m. on A 30 – Z – ✉ Salisbury – ☎ 072 274 Wilton:**

Pembroke Arms, Minster St., SP2 0BH, ☎ 3127 – P – **8 rm.**

AUSTIN-MG-WOLSELEY 41/45 Winchester St. ☎ 6681
CHRYSLER-SIMCA Scamels Rd ☎ 28321
CITROEN Stephenson Rd ☎ 24136
DAF Downton Rd ☎ 4886
DAIMLER-JAGUAR-ROVER-TRIUMPH Brunell Rd ☎ 23131
FIAT Castle St. ☎ 5668
FORD Castle St. ☎ 28443
MORRIS-MG, ROLLS ROYCE Southampton Rd ☎ 5251
PEUGEOT Southampton Rd ☎ 5268
RENAULT 114/120 Wilton Rd ☎ 28328
SAAB Dowton Rd, Redlynch ☎ 20340
VAUXHALL Brunell Rd ☎ 23522
VOLVO Telford Rd ☎ 3650
VW, AUDI-NSU 16 Lower Rd, Churchfields ☎ 27162

SALTBURN BY THE SEA Cleveland 986 ⑳ – pop. 19,595 – ☎ 028 72.

18 Hob Hill ☎ 2812. – **London 264** – **Leeds 74** – **Middlesbrough 13** – York 61.

Zetland, Marine Par., TS12 1AR, ☎ 2961, ≤ – lift ⇔wc P.
M a la carte 4.25/8.55 **t.** 🍷 0.80 – **45 rm** ☕ 8.50/20.00 **t.**

Queen, Station St., TS12 1AE, ☎ 3371 – TV ⇔wc ⇒wc ☎.
M (bar lunch) approx. 3.05 – **18 rm.**

AUSTIN-MG-WOLSELEY Holmbeck Garage, Skelton ☎ 50247
VAUXHALL High St., Brotton ☎ 028 77 (Brotton) 265

SAMLESBURY Lancs. – see Preston.

SANDIACRE Notts. – see Nottingham.

SANDLING Kent – see Maidstone.

SANDOWN I.O.W. 986 ㊴ ㊵ – see Wight (Isle of).

SANDWICH Kent 986 ㊱ – pop. 4,490 – ☎ 030 46.

18, 18, 9 Sandwich Bay ☎ 2247.
London 71 – Canterbury 12 – **Dover 13** – Maidstone 39 – Margate 9.

Bell, 2 Upper Strand St., CT13 9EF, ☎ 2836 – TV ⇔wc ☎ P
M a la carte 5.05/6.95 🍷 1.50 – ☕ 1.50 – **27 rm** 8.85/15.10.

The Cave, 15 Harnet St., CT13 9ES, ☎ 2274
closed Sunday lunch, Monday except Bank Holidays and 25 December-24 January – **M** a la carte 3.90/6.20 🍷 1.55.

Kingpost, 31 Harnet St., CT13 9ES, ☎ 3021, French rest.
closed Tuesday and 25-26 December – **M** a la carte 3.85/4.95 **t.** 🍷 1.85.

AUSTIN-MG-WOLSELEY Market Hall ☎ 3066

SANDYPARK Devon – see Chagford.

SAUNDERSFOOT Dyfed – pop. 3,150 – ☎ 0834.

London 245 – Carmarthen 25 – Fishguard 34 – Tenby 3.

St. Brides, St. Brides Hill, SA69 9NH, ☎ 812304, Telex 48350, ≤ Saundersfoot Bay, heated – TV ⇔wc ☎ P
M a la carte 4.65/6.45 **st.** 🍷 1.65 – **52 rm** ☕ 11.00/23.00 **st.** – P 15.00/17.50 **st.**

Glen Beach ⑤, Swallow Tree Woods, SA69 9DE, ☎ 813430, garden – ⇒wc P
M (buffet lunch) 3.00/3.25 🍷 1.10 – **14 rm** ☕ 8.00/16.00 – P 12.00/14.00.

Malin House, St. Brides Hill, SA69 9NP, ☎ 812344, garden – ⇔wc ⇒wc P
Easter-October – **13 rm** ☕ 6.50/15.00.

Jalna, Stammers Rd, SA69 9HH, ☎ 812282 – ⇔wc P
Easter-October – **14 rm** ☕ 5.00/10 00 **s.**

Merlewood, St. Brides Hill, SA69 9NP, ☎ 812421, heated, garden – P
closed 1 December-6 January – **21 rm** ☕ (dinner included) 8.45/16.85.

SAUNDERTON Bucks. – pop. 256 – ✉ Aylesbury – ☎ 084 44 Princes Risborough.

London 42 – Aylesbury 9 – **Oxford 20.**

Rose and Crown, Wycombe Rd, HP17 9NP, S : on A 4010 ☎ 5299 – P
closed Christmas week – **M** *(closed Sunday and Bank Holidays lunch)* a la carte 3.75/5.25 🍷 1.50 – **9 rm** ☕ 7.00/12.00 **s.**

SAUNTON Devon – pop. 200 – ✉ Braunton – ☎ 027 189 (3 fig.) or 0271 (6 fig.) Croyde.

London 230 – Barnstaple 8 – Exeter 48.

Saunton Sands, EX33 1LQ, ☎ 212, ≤, tennis, pool, garden – lift P
Easter-October – **M** a la carte 5.75/7.15 **s.** 🍷 1.10 – ☕ 1.10 – **95 rm** 8.15/29.80 **s.** – P 16.50/21.75 **s.**

SAWBRIDGEWORTH Herts. – pop. 7,089 – ✆ 0279 Bishops Stortford.
London 29 – Cambridge 31.

XX **Straw Hat,** London Rd, CM21 0AJ, S: 1 m. on A 11 ☎ 722434 – Ⓟ
closed Sunday, Monday and Tuesday after Bank Holidays – **M** a la carte 3.75/6.10 **t.**
🍾 1.40.

AUSTIN-MG-WOLSELEY London Rd ☎ 723401

SAWLEY Lancs. – see Clitheroe.

SCALBY North Yorks. 986 ㉔ – see Scarborough.

Ensure that you have up to date **Michelin maps** in your car.

SCARBOROUGH North Yorks. 986 ㉔ – pop. 44,440 – ✆ 0723.
See : Castle 12C (≤*) *AC* Y.
⛳18 **North Cliff Av. ☎ 60786 and 4529, NW: 2 m. by A 165** Y – ⛳18 **Deepdale Av., off Filey Rd ☎ 60522, S: 1 m. by A 165** Z.
i St. Nicholas Cliff ☎ 72261.
London 253 – Kingston-upon-Hull 47 – Leeds 67 – Middlesbrough 52.

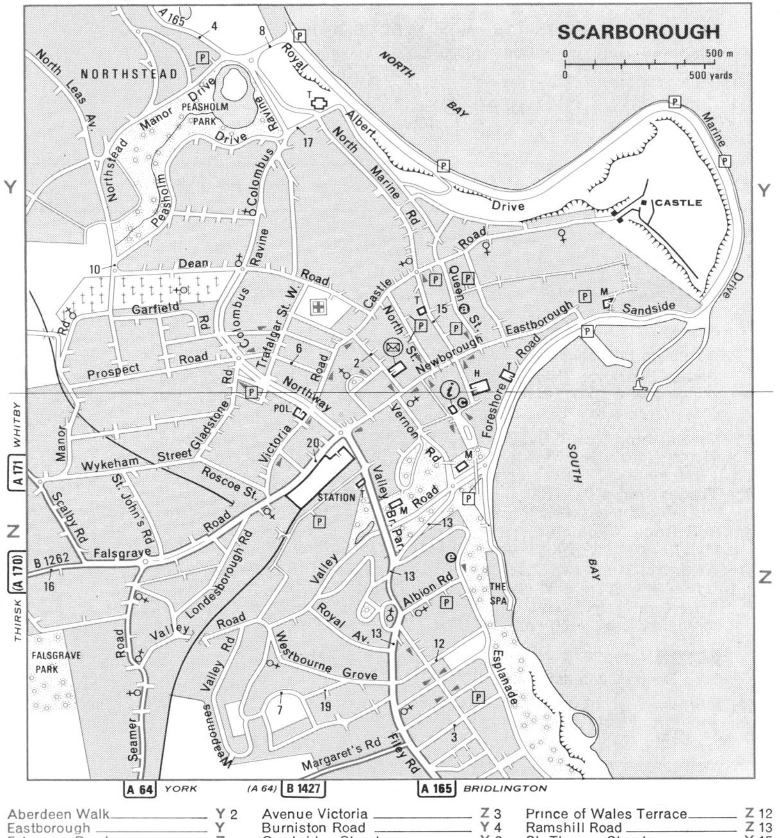

Crown, Esplanade, YO11, ℡ 73491 – lift TV P — z e
83 rm.

Royal, St. Nicholas St., YO11 2HE, ℡ 64333 – lift. — z c
M 3.75/6.00 **st.** 1.60 – **135 rm** 7.00/18.00 **st.** – P 12.50/17.00 **st.**

Holbeck Hall, Holbeck Hill, YO11 2XX, ℡ 74374, ←, « Country house atmosphere », – wc P — by A 165 z
closed January – **M** a la carte 2.30/5.05 **t.** 1.40 – **29 rm** 10.00/21.00 **t.**

Lanterna, 33 Queen St., YO11 1HJ, ℡ 63616, Italian rest. — Y a
closed Sunday, Monday and March – **M** a la carte 4.00/5.30 1.20.

at Ravenscar **N : 10 ½ m. off A 171 – z – ✉ ☎ 0723 Scarborough :**

Raven Hall, YO13 0ET, ℡ 870353, ← Robin Hoods Bay, « Country house atmosphere », heated, 9, park – wc P
May-October – **M** 4.00/6.00 **t.** 0.90 – **60 rm** 10.50/25.00 **t.**

at Scalby **NW : 3 m. on A 171 – z – ✉ ☎ 0723 Scarborough :**

The Gatehouse, 17-19 High St., YO13 0PT, ℡ 62840 – P
closed Monday, Tuesday, 2 weeks Easter and 2 weeks September – **M** (dinner only and Sunday lunch) a la carte 3.35/6.30 **t.** 1.90.

at Hackness **NW : 7 m. by A 171 – z – ✉ ☎ 0723 Scarborough :**

Hackness Grange, YO13 0JW, ℡ 82281, ←, « Country house atmosphere », park – wc wc P
M 5.50/6.50 **t.** 1.25 – **16 rm** 14.00/28.00 **st.** – P 19.50/23.00 **st.**

AUSTIN-MORRIS-MG-WOLSELEY Valley Bridge Rd ℡ 60221
CHRYSLER-SIMCA Northway ℡ 63533
CITROEN Main St. ℡ 072 383 (West Ayton) 3421
DAF, LANCIA, MAZDA Falconers Rd ℡ 60322
DAIMLER-JAGUAR-ROVER-TRIUMPH 60 Ramshill Rd ℡ 62495
DATSUN Northway ℡ 69131
FORD Vine St. ℡ 5581
OPEL Main St., ℡ 072 383 (West Ayton) 2242
PEUGEOT 13/17 North Marine Rd ℡ 66541
RENAULT Clifton St. ℡ 60791
VAUXHALL Seamer Rd ℡ 60335
VW, AUDI-NSU Cayton Bay ℡ 0723 (Cayton Bay) 883111

SCILLY (Isles of) Cornwall 986 ㊳ – pop. 2,020.

See : Archipelago.**

St. Mary's – pop. 1,958 – ✉ St. Mary's – ☎ 072 04 Scillonia.

See : Hugh Town (the Garrison ←*).

9 ℡ 692.

Access to Penzance by helicopter.

to Penzance (Isles of Scilly Steamship Co.) Summer : Monday to Saturday 1 daily ; Winter : 3 weekly (2 h 45 mn).

i Town Hall, ℡ 536.

Godolphin, Church St., TR21 0JR, ℡ 22316 – wc
March-October – **M** 4.60/5.20 **st.** 1.30 – **29 rm** 7.00/16.00 **st.** – P 13.00/15.55 **st.**

Tregarthen's, TR21 0PP, ℡ 22540, ←, – wc
mid March-mid October – **M** 4.00/5.00 – **32 rm** 8.00/20.00 **s.** – P 13.00/17.00 **s.**

Bell Rock, Church St., TR21 0JS, ℡ 22575, heated – wc
March-October – **M** 4.50/5.00 – **16 rm** 13.05/25.50.

Atlantic, Hugh St. TR21 0LL ℡ 22417, ← St. Mary's harbour – wc
February-October – **M** approx. 3.50 – **28 rm** 8.50/19.00.

Star Castle, TR21 0LS, ℡ 22317, « Elizabethan fortress »,
M approx. 3.50 – **20 rm** 6.00/12.00 – P 11.00.

Tresco – pop. 246 – ✉ Tresco – ☎ 072 04 Scillonia.

See : Tresco Gardens *AC*.**

Island, TR24 0PU, ℡ 22883, ← Islands, « Gardens », heated, park – wc
March-mid October – **M** approx. 6.00 **st.** 1.75 – **28 rm** 10.75/21.50 **st.** – P 21.50/24.50 **st.**

SCOTCH CORNER North Yorks. 986 ⑲ – ✉ ☎ 0748 Richmond.

London 243 – Leeds 53 – Middlesbrough 22 – Newcastle-upon-Tyne 40.

Vintage, Middleton Tyas, DL10 6NP, ℡ 2961 – P
closed Christmas Day and 1 January – **M** a la carte 3.30/4.95 **t.** 1.35 – **4 rm** 5.50/11.00 **t.** – P 12.50/13.50 **t.**

SCRAPTOFT Leics. – see Leicester.

SCUNTHORPE South Humberside 986 ㉔ – pop. 70,907 – ☎ 0724.
Envir. : Normanby Hall* (Regency) : Wildlife park* *AC*, N : 4 m.
18 Holme Lane, Bottesford ☎ 66476, SE : 2 m.
i Central Library, Carlton St. ☎ 60161.
London 167 – **Leeds 54** – Lincoln 30 – **Sheffield 45.**

Royal (Anchor), Doncaster Rd, DN15 7DE, ☎ 68181, Group Telex 27120 – TV wc ☎ P.
M 1.80/2.25 **t.** 1.00 – **28 rm** 9.75/17.05 **st.**

AUSTIN-MORRIS-MG-WOLSELEY Normandy Rd ☎ 4534
BMW 12 Scotter Rd ☎ 64251
CHRYSLER-SIMCA Smith St. ☎ 69322
DATSUN Old Crosby ☎ 4542
FIAT 187 Ashby Rd ☎ 61191
FORD Station Rd ☎ 61144
OPEL Winterton Rd ☎ 61083
RENAULT Robert St. ☎ 2616
ROVER-TRIUMPH 76 Doncaster Rd ☎ 67101
TOYOTA Brigg Rd ☎ 2011
VAUXHALL 136/144 Ashby High St. ☎ 67474
VAUXHALL Ferry Rd ☎ 3284
VW, AUDI-NSU 14/16 Collum Lane ☎ 3716

SEACROFT West Yorks. – see Leeds.

SEAFORD East Sussex 986 ㊱ ㊵ – pop. 16,226 – ☎ 0323.
Envir. : Charleston Manor* *AC*, NE : 4 m.
18 Southdown Rd ☎ 890139.
i Council Offices, Sutton Rd ☎ 892224.
London 67 – **Brighton 13** – Eastbourne 10 – Lewes 11.

Viking, Dane Rd, BN25 1DZ, ☎ 890840 – wc ☎ P
35 rm.

AUSTIN-MORRIS-MG-WOLSELEY Sutton Park Rd ☎ 890864

SEAL Kent – see Sevenoaks.

SEALE Surrey – see Farnham.

SEASCALE Cumbria – pop. 2.200 – ☎ 094 02 (3 and 4 fig.) or 0940 (5 fig.).
18 The Banks ☎ 202.
London 314 – Kendal 62 – Workington 23.

Scawfell, Seafront, CA20 1QU, ☎ 400, ← – wc P
M 3.00/5.00 **t.** 0.75 – **34 rm** 7.00/14.00 **t.**

SEATON Devon 986 ㊴ – pop. 4,139.
18 Axe Cliff ☎ 20499.
i Sea Front ☎ 21660 (summer only) – 18 Seaton Down Rd ☎ 21345 (winter only).
London 162 – Dorchester 32 – Exeter 23 – Taunton 28.

Hawkeshyde Motel, Harepath Hill, EX12 2TF, N : 1 m. on A 3052 ☎ 20932, ←, heated – TV wc P
closed 25-26 December and 1 January – **M** *(closed 15 December-10 January)* (dinner only and cold buffet lunch in season) 3.00 – 1.45 – **26 rm** 9.00/12.00.

Copperfields, Fore St., EX12 2LE, ☎ 22294
closed Sunday – **M** (lunch by arrangement) a la carte 3.00/4.60 1.30.

SEATON BURN Tyne and Wear – see Newcastle-upon-Tyne.

SEATON CAREW Cleveland – pop. 7,332 – ✉ ☎ 0429 Hartlepool.
18 Tees Rd ☎ 66249.
London 263 – Durham 21 – **Middlesbrough 7** – Sunderland 23.

Staincliffe (Swallow), The Cliff, TS25 1AB, ☎ 64301, Group Telex 53168, ←, – TV wc ☎ P.
22 rm.

SEAVINGTON ST. MARY Somerset – pop. 212 – ✉ Ilminster – ☎ 0460 South Petherton.
London 142 – Taunton 14 – Yeovil 11.

Pheasant with rm, TA19 0QH, ☎ 40502, – wc ☎ P
closed Sunday dinner, 2 weeks end September, 25-26 December and 2 weeks end February – **M** (buffet lunch) a la carte 3.15/5.40 **t.** 1.65 – **11 rm** 6.60/15.60 **t.**

SEDGEFIELD Durham 986 ⑲ – pop. 5,337 – ✉ Stockton-on-Tees (Cleveland) – ☎ 0740.
London 261 – Hartlepool 14 – **Middlesbrough 13** – **Newcastle-upon-Tyne 28.**

Hardwick Hall , TS21 2EH, NW : 1½ m. on A 177 ☎ 20253, ←, , park – TV wc ☎ P
M approx. 5.00 – **17 rm** 13.00/17.50.

SEDLESCOMBE East Sussex – pop. 1,318 – ✉ Battle – ☎ 042 487.

London 56 – Hastings 7 – Lewes 26 – Maidstone 27.

- **Brickwall,** The Green, TN33 0QA, ☎ 253, heated, – wc *closed January* – **M** 3.25/3.75 **t.** 1.75 – **16 rm** 8.00/18.00 **t.** – P 12.50/13.50 **t.**
- **Holmes House,** The Green, TN33 0QA, ☎ 450 *closed Sunday dinner and Monday* – **M** a la carte 3.30/5.55 **st.** 1.50.

SELBY North Yorks. 986 ㉓㉔ – pop. 11,616 – ☎ 0757.

See : Abbey Church** 12C-16C.

18 Mill Lane, Brayton ☎ 075 782 (Gateforth) 234, SW : 3 m.

London 197 – Kingston-upon-Hull 34 – Leeds 21 – York 14.

- **Londesborough Arms,** Market Pl., YO8 0NS, ☎ 2885 – wc . **M** 2.60/3.50 **st.** 1.50 – **31 rm** 7.50/12.50 **st.**

AUSTIN-MG-ROVER-TRIUMPH-WOLSELEY Gowthorpe ☎ 3023
DAF Chapel Haddlesey ☎ 075 787 (Burn) 638
VAUXHALL Brook St. ☎ 3258

SELMESTON East Sussex – see Lewes.

SELSEY West Sussex – pop. 6,491 – ☎ 024 361.

9 ☎ 2203. – London 78 – Brighton 40 – Chichester 9.

- **Thatched House** , 23 Warner Rd, PO20 9DD, ☎ 2207, – **M** a la carte 3.15/4.90 0.95 – 1.50 – **8 rm** 6.00/13.00.
- **Conifers** , Seal Sq., Seal Rd, PO20 0HP, ☎ 2436, – wc **M** 3.50/4.50 – **12 rm** 6.50/19.00 **st.**

SENNEN COVE Cornwall – pop. 704 – ☎ 073 687.

Envir. : Land's End** S : 2 m. – Porthcurno (Minack Theatre) site* *AC,* SE : 5 m.

London 328 – Penzance 10 – Truro 36.

- **Old Success Inn,** TR19 7DG, ☎ 232, ← – wc *Easter-mid-October* – **M** (bar lunch) approx. 3.50 2.40 – **18 rm** 4.50/11.00.

SETTLE North Yorks. 986 ㉓ – pop. 2,171 – ☎ 072 92.

9 Giggleswick ☎ 3580, off A 65.

i National Park Information Centre, Town Hall ☎ 3617 (summer only).

London 232 – Bradford 34 – Kendal 30 – Leeds 41.

- **Royal Oak,** Market Pl., BD24 9ED, ☎ 2561 – *closed Christmas Day* – **M** *(closed Wednesday lunch)* 3.75/4.00 **st.** – **6 rm** 8.00/12.50 **st.** – P 13.25 **st.**

AUSTIN-MORRIS-MG-ROVER-TRIUMPH-WOLSELEY Station Rd ☎ 2323

SEVENOAKS Kent 986 ㊱ – pop. 18,247 – ☎ 0732.

See: Knole** (15C-17C) *AC.* **Envir.:** Lullingstone (Roman Villa: mosaic panels*) *AC,* N : 6 m.

18 Darenth Valley ☎ 095 92 (Otford) 2922, N : 3 m.

London 26 – Guildford 40 – Maidstone 17.

- **Crossway,** Seal Hollow Rd, TN13 3RX, ☎ 54245, – TV **M** *(closed Sunday lunch)* (dinner only) a la carte 2.55/4.70 **s.** 1.00 – **11 rm** 7.50/14.50 **s.**
- **Moorings** without rest., 73 Hitchen Hatch Lane, TN13 3BE, ☎ 52589, – TV **9 rm** 9.50/13.50 **st.**
- **Al Mottarone,** 7 Tubs Hill Par., TN13 3AF, ☎ 54385, Italian rest. – *closed Sunday* – **M** a la carte 4.30/5.50 1.10.
- **Le Chantecler,** 43 High St., TN13 1JF, ☎ 54662 *closed Sunday, last 2 weeks August and first week September* – **M** a la carte 3.35/5.70 1.40.

at Dunton Green N : 3 m. by A 2028 – ✉ Sevenoaks – ☎ 073 273 Dunton Green :

- **Emma** without rest., London Rd, TN13 2TD, ☎ 681 – TV wc . **M** (see **Donnington Manor**) – 1.95 – **40 rm** 9.70/15.60 **s.**
- **Donnington Manor,** London Rd, TN13 2TD, ☎ 326, Italian rest. – **M** a la carte 4.10/6.75 **s.** 1.75.

at Seal NE : 2 m. on A 25 – ✉ ☎ 0732 Sevenoaks :

- **Copper Kettle,** 67 High St., TN15 0EG, ☎ 61481 – **M** *(closed Sunday dinner, Monday, 25 to 30 December and Bank Holidays)* a la carte 3.90/7.80 **st.** 1.50.

CITROEN Tonbridge Rd ☎ 53328
DAF High St. ☎ 62435
FIAT London Rd ☎ 58177
FORD The Vine ☎ 52341
MORRIS-MG, ROLLS ROYCE-BENTLEY 166 High St. ☎ 52371
PEUGEOT London Rd, Dunton Green ☎ 073 273 (Dunton Green) 292
RENAULT 128 Seal Rd ☎ 51337
ROVER-TRIUMPH 71 St. Johns Hill ☎ 55174
SAAB Station Approach ☎ 0732 (Borough Green) 883044
TOYOTA Badgers Mount ☎ 095 97 (Badgers Mount) 218
VAUXHALL 92/96 London Rd ☎ 56105

SHAFTESBURY Dorset 986 ㉟ – pop. 3,976 – ☎ 0747.
Envir.: Longleat House** (Elizabethan) *AC* and Lion Reserve** *AC*, NW: 18 m. by Warminster – Old Wardour castle* (ruins 14C) *AC*, site*, NE: 5 m.
London 115 – Bournemouth 31 – **Bristol 47** – Dorchester 29 – Salisbury 20.

- **Grosvenor** (T.H.F), The Commons, SP7 8JA, ☎ 2282 – TV wc ☎.
  M a la carte 4.05/5.60 **st.** 1.50 – **48 rm** 7.00/20.50 **st.** – P 14.00/18.00 **st.**
- **Royal Chase** (Interchange), Royal Chase Roundabout, SP7 8DB, (A 30/A 350) ☎ 3355, – wc ☎ P
  M a la carte 3.50/7.00 **st.** 1.55 – **18 rm** 8.85/23.00 **st.** – P 12.50/16.50 **st.**

FIAT High St. ☎ 2117
MORRIS-MG-WOLSELEY Salisbury Rd ☎ 2295
PEUGEOT ☎ 2939

SHALDON Devon – pop. 1,535 – ✉ Teignmouth – ☎ 062 687.
London 217 – Exeter 17 – **Plymouth 37** – Torquay 7.

- **Chequered Lantern,** Shaldon Village, 21 Fore St., TQ14 0DE, ☎ 2384, Bistro
  Easter-November – **M** *(closed Sunday and Monday)* (dinner only) a la carte 3.75/4.55 **t.** 1.05.

SHANKLIN I.O.W. – see Wight (Isle of).

SHARDLOW Derbs. – pop. 906 (inc. Great Wilne) ✉ ☎ 0332 Derby.
London 124 – Derby 6 – **Leicester 23** – **Nottingham 13.**

- **Lady in Grey,** 5 Wilne Lane, DE7 2HA, ☎ 792331, – P
  closed Sunday dinner, Monday and Bank Holidays – **M** a la carte 3.70/6.50.

SHAW Wilts. – pop. 800 – ✉ ☎ 0225 Melksham.
London 112 – **Bristol 23** – Salisbury 35.

- **Shaw Farm,** SN12 8EF, on A 365 ☎ 702836, heated, – P
  10 rm 5.50/11.00 **t.**

SHEEPWASH Devon – see Hatherleigh.

SHEERNESS Kent 986 ㊱ – pop. 13,691 – ☎ 079 56.
See: ≤* from the pier. **Envir.:** Minster (abbey: brasses*, effigied tombs*) SE: 2 ½ m.
Shipping connections with the Continent: to Vlissingen and Dunkerque (Olau-Line).
i Garrison Rd, Sheerness Docks, Sheppey ☎ 5324.
London 52 – Canterbury 24 – Maidstone 20.

Hotels and restaurants see: Maidstone SW: 20 m.

AUSTIN-MORRIS-MG Queenborough Corner ☎ 3133

SHEFFIELD South Yorks. 986 ⑫ and ㉗ – pop. 520,327 – ☎ 0742.
See: Abbeydale Industrial Hamlet* (steel and scythe works) *AC*, SW: by A 621 AZ.
18 Hemsworth Rd ☎ 54402, S: 3 ½ m. AZ – 18 Beauchief ☎ 360648, SW: by B 6068 AZ – 18 Darnall ☎ 42237, E: by A 57 BZ. – 18 Birley Lane ☎ 390099, S: 4 m. on A 616 BZ.
☎ 20002 ext 2254.
i Central Library, Surrey St. ☎ 734760/1/4.
London 168 – **Leeds 34** – **Liverpool 79** – **Manchester 40** – **Nottingham 42.**

Plans on following pages

- **Hallam Tower** (T.H.F.), Manchester Rd (A 57), S10 5DX, ☎ 686031, Telex 547293, ≤, – TV P. AZ **o**
  M 4.20/4.90 **st.** 1.45 – 2.00 – **135 rm** 16.50/24.00 **st.**
- **Grosvenor House** (T.H.F.), Charter Sq., S1 3EH, ☎ 20041, Telex 54312 – TV P. CZ **a**
  M 4.20/4.90 **st.** 1.45 – 2.00 – **121 rm** 17.00/24.50 **st.**
- **Royal Victoria** (B.T.H.), Victoria Station Rd, S4 7YE, ☎ 78822 – TV P. DY **c**
  closed Bank Holiday weekends – **M** *(closed Friday dinner, Saturday, Sunday and Bank Holidays)* 4.10/6.00 **st.** 1.30 – **63 rm** 15.10/28.10 **st.**
- **Rutland,** 452 Glossop Rd, S10 2PY, ☎ 665215 – wc ☎ P. AZ **e**
  M approx. 3.75 **st.** 1.50 – **100 rm** 11.25/22.50 **st.**
- Omega, Brincliffe Hill, off Psalter Lane, S11 9DF, ☎ 55171, Dancing (Tuesday to Saturday) – P. AZ **n**
- **La Casina Bianca,** 74 Abbeydale Rd, S7 1FD, ☎ 57292, Italian rest. AZ **r**
  M (dinner only) a la carte 2.20/7.00 1.30.

at Dore SW: 5 m. off A 621 – AZ – ✉ ☎ 0742 Sheffield:

- **Dore Grill,** 38 Church Lane, S17 3GS, ☎ 365948 – P
  M a la carte 4.30/6.65 **st.** 1.95.

MICHELIN Branch, 80 Catley Rd, S9 5LX, ☎ 441195/6/7.

SHEFFIELD
BUILT UP AREA

0 — 1 km
0 — 1 mile

Abbey Lane	AZ 2	Hemsworth Road	AZ 27
Barrow Road	BY 4	Holywell Road	BY 29
Bawtry Road	BY 5	Main Road	BZ 32
Bradfield Road	AY 7	Middlewood Road	AY 33
Brocco Bank	AZ 8	Newhall Road	BY 36
Broughton Lane	BY 10	Westbourne Road	AZ 47
Burngreave Road	AY 12	Western Bank	AZ 48
Ecclesfield Road	BY 17	Woodhouse Road	BZ 50
Handsworth Road	BZ 24		

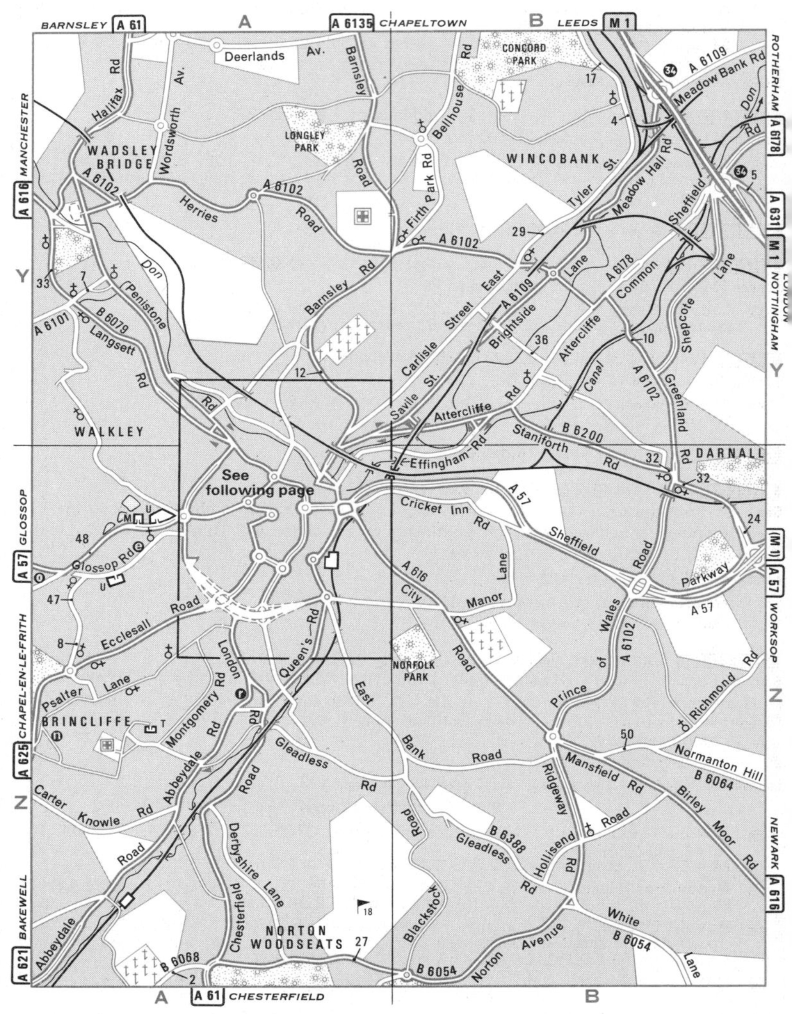

ALFA-ROMEO Scotland St. ☎ 70567
AUDI-NSU Middleswood Rd ☎ 348807
AUSTIN-MG-WOLSELEY 968 Abbeydale Rd ☎ 362292
AUSTIN-MG-WOLSELEY 850882 Ecclesall Rd ☎ 662797
AUSTIN-MORRIS-MG-WOLSELEY Ecclesall ☎ 71141
CHRYSLER-SIMCA, VAUXHALL Ecclesall Rd ☎ 664471
CHRYSLER-SIMCA Bradfield Rd ☎ 344256
CITROEN Northfield Rd ☎ 662441
DAF Lepping Lane ☎ 345247
DATSUN 252 Crookes ☎ 665913
DATSUN 1/7 Meersbrook Rd ☎ 57315
FIAT 918/920 Chesterfield Rd ☎ 54248
FORD 53/67 London Rd ☎ 29091
FORD 196 Gibraltar St. ☎ 29631
FORD Brown St. ☎ 78271
LOTUS Broad Lane ☎ 25048
MERCEDES-BENZ 115 Ecclesall Rd South ☎ 368161
MORRIS-MG 113/115 Abbeydale Rd ☎ 50685
MORRIS-MG 168 Penistone Rd ☎ 348801
MORRIS-MG-WOLSELEY 286 Sandygate Rd ☎ 302021

SHEFFIELD
CENTRE

0 — 400 m
0 — 400 yards

- Angel Street ______ DY 3
- Commercial Street ______ DZ 15
- Fargate ______ CZ
- High Street ______ DZ
- Leopold Street ______ CZ 31
- West Street ______ CZ
- Blonk Street ______ DY 6
- Castlegate ______ DY 13
- Charter Row ______ CZ 14
- Cumberland Street ______ CZ 16
- Fitzwilliam Gate ______ CZ 19
- Flat Street ______ DZ 20
- Furnival Street ______ CZ 21
- Gibraltar Street ______ CY 23
- Haymarket ______ DY 25
- Moorfields ______ CY 35
- Pinstone Street ______ CZ 37
- Queen Street ______ CY 38
- Shalesmoor ______ CY 39
- Snig Hill ______ DY 40
- Waingate ______ DY 44
- Westbar Green ______ CY 45

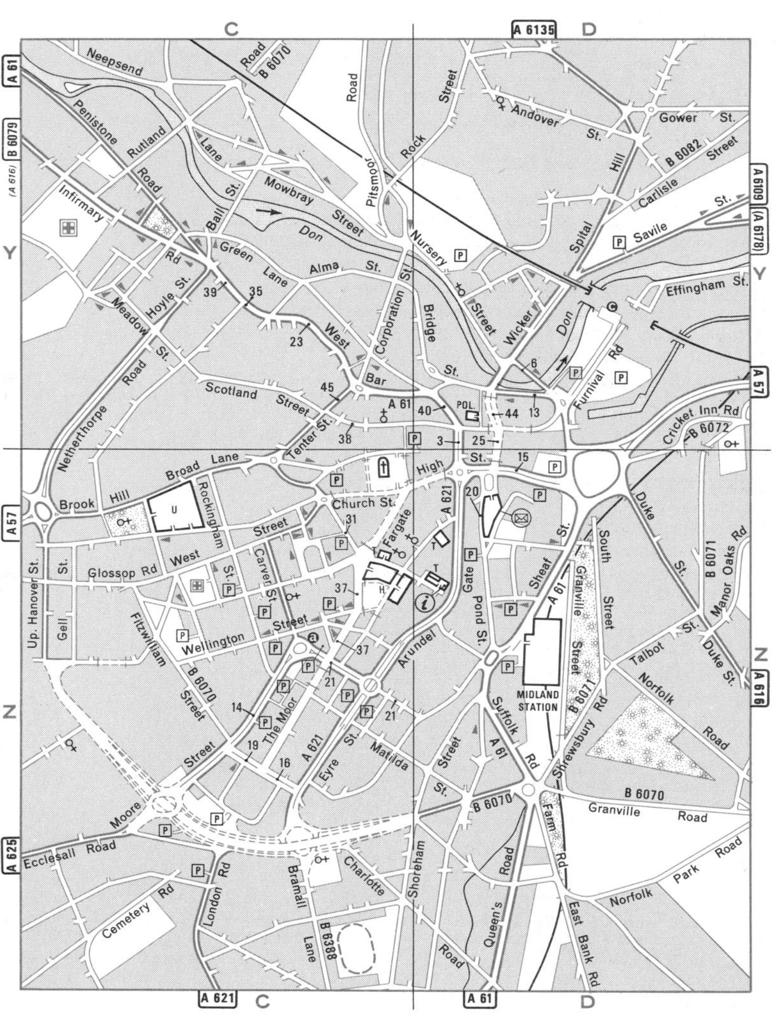

MORRIS-MG-WOLSELEY Broadfield Rd ☎ 52404
OPEL 53 Upper Hanover St. ☎ 29487
PEUGEOT London Rd ☎ 581041
RENAULT 885 Chesterfield Rd ☎ 585423
RENAULT 30/46 Suffolk Rd ☎ 21378
RENAULT 176 Penistone Rd North ☎ 344879
ROLLS ROYCE-BENTLEY Peel St., Bromhill ☎ 71141
ROVER-TRIUMPH 75 Herries Rd ☎ 387155
TOYOTA Ellin St. ☎ 78717
TOYOTA City Rd ☎ 396993
VAUXHALL 44/46 Savile St. ☎ 29281
VOLVO 43/67 Ecclesall Rd ☎ 78705
VOLVO Netherthorpe Rd ☎ 78739
VW, AUDI-NSU 1 Ecclesall Rd South ☎ 668441

SHEFFIELD PARK East Sussex – ✉ Uckfield – ☎ 082 573 Danehill.
See : Sheffield Park Gardens* (the five lakes**) *AC*.
London 45 – Brighton 18.

SHELDON Warw. – see Birmingham.

SHELTON LOCK Derbs. – see Derby.

SHEPPERTON Middx. – pop. 10,765 – ☎ 093 22 Walton-on-Thames.
London 25.

Elizabethan ⛨, Felix Lane, TW17 8NP, E: 1 ¼ m. on B 375 ☎ 41404, Telex 928170, ⛱, 🌳 – |♦| TV ⛀wc ☎ **P**. 🏕
M approx. 3.75 **t.** – ☕ 1.50 – **183 rm** 12.50/17.00 **t.**

Warren Lodge, Church Sq., TW17 9JZ, ☎ 42972, ←, 🌳 – TV ⛀wc ⛆wc ☎ **P**
43 rm.

at Upper Halliford NE: **1** m. off **A 244** – ✉ Weybridge – ☎ 093 27 Sunbury-on-Thames:

Goat, 47 Upper Halliford Rd, TW17 8RX, ☎ 82415 – **P**
closed Sunday dinner and Monday – **M** a la carte 4.00/5.75 **t.** 🍷 1.20.

AUSTIN-MG-WOLSELEY Station Approach ☎ 24811
DAF High St. ☎ 40121
DATSUN Walton Bridge Rd ☎ 26784

SHEPTON MALLET Somerset 986 ㉟ – pop. 5,920 – ☎ 0749.
See : SS. Peter and Paul's Church (carved barrel roof* 15C).
⛳18 Gurney Slade ☎ 074 984 (Oakhill) 205, N: 3 m. (A 37).
London 127 – Bristol 20 – Southampton 63 – Taunton 31.

Charlton House with rm, BA4 4PR, E: 1 m. on A 361 ☎ 2008, ←, 🌳 – ⛀wc ⛆ **P**
closed Christmas – **M** *(closed Sunday dinner)* a la carte 2.75/6.15 **t.** – ☕ 0.75 – **10 rm** 9.60/16.80 **t.**

DAF Townsend Rd ☎ 2864
MORRIS-MG High St. ☎ 2976
VAUXHALL Paul St. ☎ 2030

SHERBORNE Dorset 986 ㉟ – pop. 7,272 – ☎ 093 581.
See : Abbey Church* 15C (choir: fan vaulting**).
⛳18 Clatcombe ☎ 2475, N: 1 m.
London 128 – Bournemouth 39 – Dorchester 19 – Salisbury 36 – Taunton 31.

Post House (T.H.F.), Horsecastles Lane, DT9 6BB, W: 1 m. on A 30 ☎ 3191 – TV ⛀wc ☎ ♿ **P**. 🏕
M a la carte 3.50/3.85 **st.** 🍷 1.50 – ☕ 2.00 – **60 rm** 13.00/18.00 **st.**

Eastbury, Long St., DT9 3BY, ☎ 3387, 🌳
M 2.50/2.75 **t.** 🍷 1.15 – **16 rm** ☕ 6.50/13.00 **t.**

at Oborne NE: 2 m. off A 30 – ✉ ☎ 093 581 Sherborne:

The Grange, ☎ 3463, ←, 🌳 – **P**
closed Sunday dinner and Monday – **M** a la carte 3.70/6.20 **t.** 🍷 1.30.

at Holnest Park SE: 5 ½ m. by A 352 – ✉ Sherborne – ☎ 096 321 Holnest:

Manor Farm Country House ⛨, DT9 6HA, ☎ 474, ←, 🌳 – **P**
March-November – **M** (dinner only) 2.50/2.75 – **8 rm** ☕ 5.00/10.00.

MERCEDES-BENZ Yeovil Rd ☎ 3350
MORRIS-MG-ROVER-TRIUMPH Long St. ☎ 3262
VOLVO Digby Rd ☎ 2436

SHIFNAL Salop 986 ㉗ – pop. 5,070 – ✉ ☎ 0952 Telford.
See: St. Andrew's Church* 12C-16C.
London 150 – Birmingham 28 – Shrewsbury 16.

Park House, Park St., TF11 9BA, ☎ 460128, ⛱ heated, 🌳 – TV ⛀wc ⛆wc ☎ **P**. 🏕
M *(closed 24 to 28 December)* a la carte 5.30/8.00 **s.** 🍷 1.80 – **10 rm** ☕ 10.00/18.00 **t.**

AUSTIN-MG Chepside ☎ 460412
MORRIS Western Heath ☎ 095 270 (Great Chatwell) 252

SHIPLEY West Midlands – see Wolverhampton.

Pour les 🏨🏨🏨, 🏨🏨, 🏨, nous ne donnons pas
le détail de l'installation,
ces hôtels possédant, en général, tout le confort.

⛀wc ⛆wc
☎

Take a great tread forward

Drive the Michelin XZX

The long distance runner

Michelin radial tyres

SR CATEGORY

XZX

The XZX follows the classic Michelin steel-braced radial configuration combined with a newly designed tread and is suitable for fitment to cars capable of speeds up to 180 km/h (113 mph)

- Exceptional adhesion particularly in the wet due to the modified tread design that highlights the need for efficient water dispersal
- Tread life is well up to the high standards set by Michelin
- Excellent comfort and low noise levels
- Reduces fuel consumption

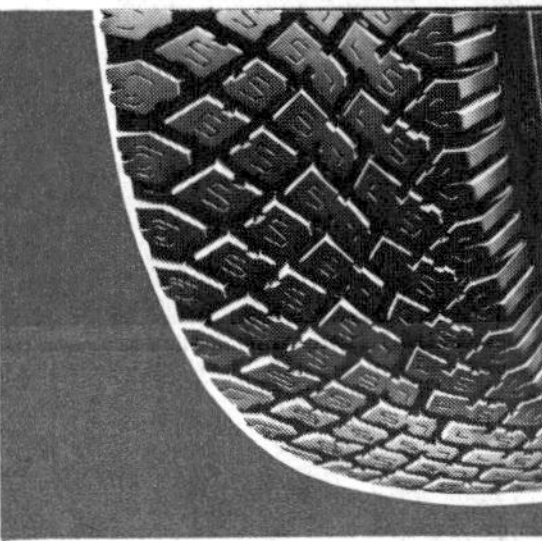

XRN

A new Michelin tyre designed for all the year round motoring. Suitable for fitment to cars capable of speeds up to 180 km/h (113 mph)

- Asymmetric tread pattern ensures stability and road holding on dry roads and excellent performance in difficult conditions of rain, snow and mud
- Supple radial casing giving excellent ride comfort
- Reduces fuel consumption

HR CATEGORY

TRX

An entirely new generation of radials with a unique super low profile allied to a new wheel and rim combination

- Outstanding road holding and vehicle control
- Super adhesion, wet or dry
- Exceptional passenger and vehicle protection
- Maintains the high mileage characteristic of Michelin radials

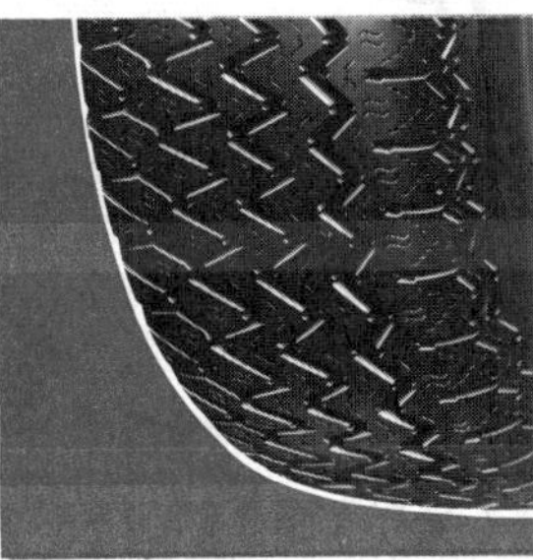

XVS

The XVS is an asymmetric tyre complementary to the XAS and suitable for fitment to cars with a maximum speed capability of up to 210 km/h (130 mph) and able to sustain speeds at or near that figure

- Designed for sustained high speed performance
- Exceptional adhesion on wet and dry surfaces
- Reduces fuel consumption
- Remarkable comfort

VR CATEGORY

XDX

The XDX is designed to meet the requirements of cars capable of speeds in excess of 210 km/h (130 mph) but having a maximum of 227 km/h (142 mph)

- Excellent road holding and stability
- Unusual ride comfort for a VR tyre
- Quiet running not normally associated with tyres in the VR category
- Low power absorption (leading to fuel economy)

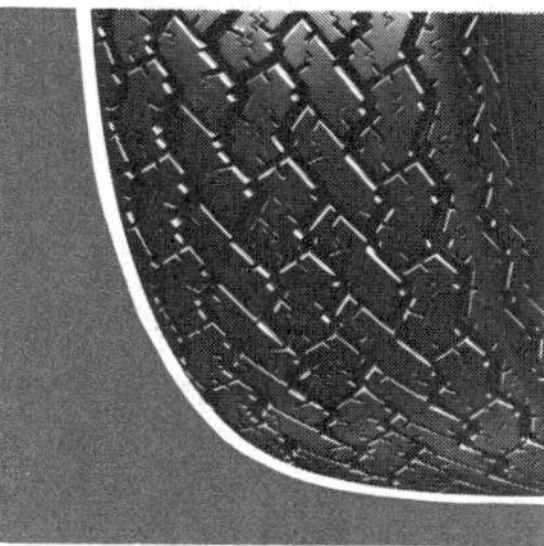

XWX

The XWX is designed for high performance cars with a speed capability well in excess of 210 km/h (130 mph)

- Provides excellent stability at very high speeds
- Exceptional grip and road holding

R CATEGORY

XM + S tyres

Designed to give exceptional adhesion and traction in adverse conditions. Suitable for speeds up to 160 km/h (100 mph) or 150 km/h (90 mph) if studded

- Radial winter tyre
- Suitable for normal road use
- Extra adhesion in snow, mud or adverse conditions
- Moulded holes for studs
- Reduces fuel consumption

XM + S8/88

The XM + S8/88 are improved winter radials suitable for speeds up to 160 km/h (100 mph) or 150 km/h (90 mph) if studded

- Excellent grip on snow, ice and muddy conditions
- Extremely good stability
- Moulded holes for studs
- Reduces fuel consumption

Michelin tyre fitment and pressure guide

***Alignment:** with Michelin radial tyres all round the best alignment is parallel to 1.5mm ($\frac{1}{16}$ in) toe-in, except for models marked with an asterisk, where it should be parallel to 1.5mm ($\frac{1}{16}$ in) toe-out.

Pressures: the pressures shown in the fitment chart are in pounds per square inch (lb/in²). Where additional pressure is required for full load conditions or sustained high speed or both this is indicated by (L), for full load and (S) for speed or (LS) for a combination of full load and sustained high speed.

Towing: An increase in pressure of 4 lb/in² to the rear tyres of the car is recommended in all cases of towing unless an increase in rear tyre pressures has already been shown for (L), (S) or (LS), in which case use the latter.

XRN, XM + S, XM + S8, XM + S88. These tyres may replace XZX/ZX tyres on cars shown in the fitment tables.

XRN. Use XZX/ZX pressures.

XM + S, XM + S8, XM + S88. It is recommended that these tyres are fitted in complete sets. If fitted, increase XZX/ZX pressures by 3 lb/in² except for Minis and derivatives where standard XZX/ZX pressures should be used.

Fitting of Michelin radial tubeless tyres
Most sizes of Michelin radial tyres are available in tubeless versions, but they may only be fitted as such providing certain conditions are fulfilled. Please consult your tyre specialists for full information.

XAS, XVS, XDX, XWX. It is preferred that these tyres are fitted in complete sets only. If it is necessary to mix these tyres, consult Michelin.

TRX. These tyres must be fitted in complete sets only.

Car Make and Model	Michelin Radial Fitment	Pressure Front	Rear
ALFA ROMEO			
Alfasud 5M, ti	145 SR 13XZX/ZX	28	22
Alfetta 1·8	165 SR 14XZX/ZX	26	29
AUDI			
Audi 80, 80L, 80S, 80LS 80GL	155 SR 13XZX/ZX	25,28(L)	25,30(L)
80GL Estate	155 SR 13XZX/ZX	25,26(L)	25,32(L)
Audi 80GT	175/70 SR 13XZX/ZX	23,26(L)	23,29(L)
80GTE	175/70 HR 13XVS	23,26(L)	23,29(L)
Audi 100, 100S, 100GL, 100LS	165 SR 14XZX/ZX	26,29(L)	26,32(L)
Audi 100GL 5E	185/70 HR 14XVS	28,30(L)	28,30(L)
Audi 100 Coupé S Auto	185/70 SR 14ZX	26,29(L)	26,32(L)
Audi 100 Coupé S Manual	185/70 HR 14XVS	26,29(L)	26,32(L)
AUSTIN – see Leyland.			
BMW			
1502, 1600, 1600Ti, 1600-2, 1602, 2002	165 SR 13XZX/ZX	26,26(L)	26,29(L)
2002 Ti	165 HR 13XAS	26,26(L)	26,29(L)
2002 Tii	165 HR 13XAS	28,28(L)	28,30(L)
316, 318	165 SR 13XZX/ZX	26,28(L)	26,29(L)
320	165 SR 13XZX/ZX	28,29(L)	28,30(L)
320i	185/70 HR 13XVS	28,29(L)	28,30(L)
518	175 SR 14XZX/ZX	28,29(L)	28,30(L)
520, 520A, 520i	195/70 HR 14XVS	28,30(L)	28,34(L)
525, 525 Auto	175 HR 14XAS	30,32(L)	30,36(L)
528	195/70 HR 14XVS	30,32(L)	30,35(L)
2500	175 HR 14XAS	30,32(L)	28,34(L)
2800 (Sept 73 onwards)	195/70 HR 14XVS	30,32(L)	28,34(L)
2800CS	195/70 HR 14XVS	32	32
3.0L	195/70 HR 14XVS	32,32(L)	32,36(L)
3.0Si, 3.3Li	195/70 VR 14XDX	32,32(L)	32,36(L)
3.0CS, CSi, CSA	195/70 VR 14XDX	29,32(L)	29,32(L)
3.0CSL	195/70 VR 14XDX	30,34(L)	30,35(L)
3.3L	195/70 VR 14XDX	29,33(L)	30,35(L)
630CS 633CSi	195/70 VR 14XWX	34,35(L)	30,35(L)
CHRYSLER – see also Hillman			
Avenger 1300, 1600, DL, S & Estates, 1600GT, 1600GLS	155 SR 13XZX/ZX	24,24(L)	24,30(L)
Avenger Heavy-Duty Estate	155 SR 13XZX/ZX	24,24(L)	24,36(L)
180, 2 litre	175 SR 14XZX/ZX	22,23(LS)	26,28(LS)
Alpine GL,S, GLS	155 SR 13XZX/ZX	26,28(L) or (S)	26,29(L) or (S)
CITROEN			
2CV, Dyane 4 and 6, 2CV6	125–15X	20	26
Ami 8	125–15X	26	26
Ami Super and Super Estate	135 SR 15ZX	26	28
GS 1015 and 1220 All Models	145 SR 15ZX	26	28
DS21 (1969 onwards)	180 HR 15XAS	29	26
DS21 (Fuel Injection)	185 HR 15XAS	29	26
D Super, D Super 5, DS23	180 HR 15XAS	29	26
DS23 Injection	185 HR 15XAS	30	26
DS23 Break, DS23 Family Estate	180 HR 15XAS	29	32

*(L) (S) (LS) See notes at head of table

Car Make and Model	Michelin Radial Fitment	Pressure Front	Rear
CITROEN			
CX 2000	185 SR 14XZX/ZX (Front) 175 SR 14XZX/ZX (Rear)	28	30
CX 2000	185HR14XVS (Front) 175HR14XVS (Rear)	28	30
CX2200 Diesel Saloon	1·85SR14XZX/ZX(Front)	30	
	175SR14XZX/ZX(Rear)		30
CX2200 Diesel Safari	185 SR 14XZX/ZX	34	32
CX2400 Super CX2400 Pallas	185 HR 14XVS(Front)	28	
	175 HR 14XVS(Rear)		30
CX2400 G.T.I.	185 HR 14XVS	30	32
CX2400 Prestige	185 HR 14XVS	32	32
COLT			
Lancer 1400, 1600 Saloons	155 SR 13XZX/ZX	22	22
Celeste 1600ST, 1600GS, 2000	165 SR 13XZX/ZX	26	28
Galant 1600 Estate	165 SR 13XZX/ZX	24,26(L)	24,26(L)
Galant GT0 2000	185/70 HR 13XVS	26	26
DAF – see Volvo			
DAIMLER			
Sovereign 2.8 3.4 4.2 Sovereign Series II Vanden Plas 4.2 Saloon	205/70 VR 15XDX	25,31(LS)	26,36(LS)
Double Six Double Six Vanden Plas	205/70 VR 15XDX	26,34(LS)	26,36(LS)
DATSUN			
100A Cherry, B110/1200 Saloon and Coupé	155 SR 12XZX/ZX	21	21
100A Cherry Estate	155 SR 12XZX/ZX	24,24(L)	24,28(L)
B110/1200 Estate	155 SR 12XZX/ZX	24,24(L)	24,32(L)
120 A Coupé	155 SR 12XZX/ZX	21	21
120Y MkII Saloon & Coupé	155 SR 13XZX/ZX	24	24
120Y MkII Estate	155 SR 13XZX/ZX	24,24(L)	24,28(L)
140J, 160J, 160J SSS	165 SR 13XZX/ZX	24,28(L)	24,28(L)
160B, 180B 160B, 180B Estate	165 SR 13XZX/ZX	26,26(L)	26,30(L)
Bluebird 180B SSS Coupé	165 SR 14XZX/ZX	24,28(L)	24,28(L)
2000 Estate	175 SR 14XZX/ZX	21,26(LS)	21,36(LS)
200L & GL Laurel Saloon & Coupé	165 SR 14XZX/ZX	24	24
240C Saloon	175 SR 14XZX/ZX	26,30(LS)	26,30(LS)
260C Saloon & Coupé	175 HR 14XAS	26,30(LS)	26,30(LS)
260C Estate	175 SR 14XZX/ZX	26,30(LS)	26,34(LS)
260Z Sports 260Z 2+2	195/70 VR 14XDX	28,33(LS)	28,33(LS)
FIAT			
124, 124S, 124Special T	155 SR 13XZX/ZX	24	26
124 Sports Coupé 1400	165 SR 13XZX/ZX	26	29
124 Sports Coupé 1600, 1800	165 SR 13XZX/ZX	29	29
124 Estate	165 SR 13XZX/ZX	23,23(L)	29,32(L)
126	135 SR 12XZX/ZX	20	29
127L (2 door)	135 SR 13XZX/ZX	24	27
127CL, 1050CL (3 door)	135 SR 13XZX/ZX	24,24(L)	27,31(L)
128, 128S, Coupé Rally, 3P	145 SR 13XZX/ZX	26	24
128 3P	145 SR 13XZX/ZX	26,28(L)	26,28(L)

*(L) (S) (LS) See notes at head of table

Car Make and Model	Michelin Radial Fitment	Pressure Front	Rear
FIAT			
128 Estate	145 SR 13XZX/ZX	27	28
X 1-9	165/70 SR 13ZX	26	28
130B (3·2 litre)	205/70 HR 14XVS	29	32
130 BC Coupé (3·2 litre)	205/70 HR 14XVS	32	32
131 1300 & 1600	155 SR 13XZX/ZX	26	28
131 1300, 1600 Estates	165 SR 13XZX/ZX	26	32
132 Special, GLS1600,1800	185/70 SR 13ZX	26	28
132 (1600, 2000) (77 onwards)	175/70 SR 14ZX		
	180/65 HR 390TRX	26	28
FORD			
Fiesta L, S, Ghia	145 SR 12XZX/ZX	23,26(L)	26,29(L)
Escort MkI 1100, 1300	155 SR 12XZX/ZX	22	28
Escort MkI Estates 1100 & 1300	155 SR 12XZX/ZX	22,22(L)	28,32(L)
Escort MkI 1300GT	155 SR 12XZX/ZX	24	28
Escort MkI Sport & Executive	165 SR 13XZX/ZX	20,23(L)	23,30(L)
Escort MkII 1100	155 SR 12XZX/ZX	22,25(L)	28,36(L)
	155 SR 13XZX/ZX	22,25(L)	25,36(L)
Escort MkII 1100 Estate	155 SR 12XZX/ZX	22,25(L)	28,36(L)
Heavy-Duty	155 SR 12XZX/ZX Reinforced	22,25(L)	28,36(L)
Escort MkII Popular 'Base' 1100 & 1300	155 SR 12XZX/ZX	22,25(L)	28,36(L)
1100 Popular 'Plus'	155 SR 12XZX/ZX	22,25(L)	28,36(L)
1300 Popular 'Plus'	155 SR 13XZX/ZX	22,25(L)	25,36(L)
Escort MkII 1300, L, GL, Ghia 1300, 1300 Estate	155 SR 13XZX/ZX	22,25(L)	25,36(L)
1300 Estate Heavy-Duty	155 SR 13XZX/ZX Reinforced	22,25(L)	25,36(L)
Escort MkII 1300, 1600 Sport	175/70 SR 13ZX	22,23(L)	25,30(L)
Escort MkII 1600	155 SR 13XZX/ZX	22,92(L)	25,36(L)
Escort MkII RS 1800, RS 2000	175/70 HR 13XVS	24	22
Cortina MkIII Saloons until September 73	165 SR 13XZX/ZX	23,26(L)	23,28(L)
	175 SR 13XZX/ZX	20,23(L)	20,26(L)
September 73 until 76	165 SR 13XZX/ZX	26,26(L)	26,30(L)
Cortina MkIII Family Estates (until 76)	165 SR 13XZX/ZX	23,26(L)	23,36(L)
	175 SR 13XZX/ZX	20,23(L)	20,31(L)
CortinaMkIII Saloons (76 onwards)	165 SR 13XZX/ZX	26,28(L)	26,36(L)
Cortina MkIII Estates (76 onwards)	165 SR 13XZX/ZX	26,28(L)	26,40(L)
Cortina MkIV Saloons	165 SR 13XZX/ZX	25,28(L)	25,36(L)
Cortina MkIV Estates	165 SR 13XZX/ZX	25,28(L)	25,40(L)
Cortina MkIV Estates Heavy-Duty	175 SR 13 ZX Reinforced	21,25(L)	24,40(L)
Capri 1300 and GT 1600 and GT, 2000GT	165 SR 13XZX/ZX	24	27
Capri 3000, E GT, GXL	185/70 HR 13XVS	26	26
Capri II 1300, 1600, 2000	165 SR 13XZX/ZX	21,27(LS)	27,31(LS)
Capri II 3000	185/70 HR 13XVS	22,28(LS)	22,28(LS)
Granada 2 litre	175 SR 14XZX/ZX	21,24(L)	23,27(L)
	185 SR 14XZX/ZX	20,23(L)	21,26(L)
Granada 2·5 litre	175 SR 14XZX/ZX	24,26(L)	24,30(L)
	185 SR 14XZX/ZX	23,24(L)	23,27(L)
Granada 3 litre Automatic Ghia and Coupé	175 SR 14XZX/ZX	24,26(L)	24,30(L)
	185 SR 14XZX/ZX	23,24(L)	23,27(L)
Granada 3 litre Manual Ghia and Coupé	175 HR 14XAS	24,26(L)	24,30(L)
	185 HR 14XVS	23,24(L)	23,27(L)
Granada 3,000 S	195/70 HR 14XVS	24,27(L)	24,33(L)
Consul and Granada Estate 2 litre	185 SR 14XZX/ZX	21,23(L)	21,28(L)
Granada Estate 3 litre Auto	185 SR 14XZX/ZX	24,27(L)	24,33(L)
Granada Estate 3 litre Man	185 HR 14XVS	24,27(L)	24,33(L)

*(L) (S) (LS) See notes at head of table

Car Make and Model	Michelin Radial Fitment	Pressure Front	Rear
FORD			
Granada 2000L; 2300L, GL; 2800 Auto, GL & Ghia	175 SR 14XZX/ZX 185 SR 14XZX/ZX	24,27(L)	24,33(L)
Granada 2800i, GL & Ghia	175 HR 14XAS/XVS 185 HR 14XVS	26,27(L)	26,36(L)
Granada 2800i S	190/65 HR 390 TRX	24,27(L)	24,36(L)
HILLMAN – see also Chrysler			
Imp (all Models)	155 SR 12XZX/ZX	18	30
Hunter, DL,S	155 SR 13XZX/ZX	24	24
Hunter Estate	165 SR 13XZX/ZX	24	26
HONDA			
Civic 1500	155 SR 12XZX/ZX	24	24
Accord	155 SR 13XZX/ZX	24	24
JAGUAR			
XJ6, XJ6L, XJ6C, 2·8, 3·4, 4·2	205/70 VR 15XDX	25,31(LS)	26,36(LS)
XJ12, XJ12L, XJ12C	205/70 VR 15XDX	26,34(LS)	16,36(LS)
E Type V12	205/70 VR 15XWX	24,38(S)	28,40(S)
XJS	205/70 VR 15XWX	26 <120 mph	26
		32 >120 mph	32
LANCIA			
Beta 1300, 1400	155 SR 14ZX	24,27(LS)	24,27(LS)
Beta 1600, 1800, 2000 Beta 1800 ES, 2000 ES Beta 1600 Coupé	175/70 SR 14ZX	24,27(LS)	24,27(LS)
Beta 1800, 2000 Coupé	175/70 HR 14XVS	24,27(LS)	24,27(LS)
Beta HPE 1600/2000 Spider 1600/2000	175/70 SR 14ZX	24,27(LS)	24,27(LS)
Beta Monte Carlo	185/70 HR 13XVS	25	28
LEYLAND			
*Mini, Mini Cooper Mini Countryman Mini Clubman & Estate	145 SR 10XZX/ZX	28	26
*Mini Cooper 'S' 1275 GT (until 74)	145 SR 10XAS	26	26
*1100, 1300, 1100 Princess 1300GT	155 SR 12XZX/ZX	23	26
*1100, 1300 Countryman	155 SR 12XZX/ZX	23,23(L)	26,29(L)
Allegro 1100, 1300 MkI	145 SR 13XZX/ZX	26	30
Allegro 1500, 1750 MkI & Vanden Plas MkI	155 SR 13XZX/ZX	26	30
Allegro Estate 1300 MkI 1500 MkI	145 SR 13XZX/ZX 155 SR 13XZX/ZX	26	30
Allegro 1100, 1300, 1500 MkII Vanden Plas MkII, 1750 MkII	145 SR 13XZX/ZX 155 SR 13XZX/ZX	26	24
Allegro Estate 1300 MkII 1500 MkII	145 SR 13XZX/ZX 155 SR 13XZX/ZX	26,26(L)	24,28(L)
Marina 1·3, 1·8	145 SR 13XZX/ZX	26	28
Marina 1·8TC; 2-1·8, 1·8S, HL, GT	155 SR 13XZX/ZX	26	28
Marina, Marina 2-Estate	155 SR 13XZX/ZX	24	32
Maxi 1500, 1750 1750HL	155 SR 13XZX/ZX 165 SR 13XZX/ZX	26	24
1800 MkII, 1800, 2200 MkIII	165 SR 14XZX/ZX	30	24

*(L) (S), (LS) See notes at head of table

Car Make and Model	Michelin Radial Fitment	Pressure Front	Rear
MAZDA			
1000, DL	155 SR 13XZX/ZX	26	26
1300, Estate	155 SR 13XZX/ZX	26, 26(L)	26, 30(L)
818 Saloon & Coupé	155 SR 13XZX/ZX	26	26
818 Estate	155 SR 13XZX/ZX	26, 26(L)	26, 30(L)
616	165 SR 13XZX/ZX	26	26
929 Saloon & Coupé	175 SR 13XZX/ZX	24	24
929 Estate	175 SR 13XZX/ZX	24, 24(L)	24, 28(L)
MERCEDES BENZ			
200/8, 220/8, 200D/8 220D/8, 230/8 (until 76)	175 SR 12ZX-P	29	34
200, 200D, 220D, 240D, 230.4, 230.6, 250 (76 onwards)	175 SR 14ZX-P	29 <100 mph 34 >100 mph	32 36
230SL	185 HR 14XVS-P	26	32
250S, 250SE	185 HR 14XVS-P	29	34
250CE	175 HR 14XAS-P	29,32(S)	34,36(S)
280, 280C, 280E, 280CE (until 76)	185 HR 14XVS-P	29	34
280, 280C, 280E, 280CE (76 onwards)	195/70 HR 14XVS-P	29 <100 mph 34 >100 mph	32 36
280S, 280SE (Post 1972)	185 HR 14XVS-P	30,34(L)	34,36(L)
280SL, SLC	185 HR 14XVS-P	32	36
280SE 3·5 and 300SEL 3·5	205/70 VR 14XDX 205/70 VR 14XWX	32	36
350SE 3·5 litre	205/70 HR 14XVS	30,34(L)	34,36(L)
350SL, 350SLC, 450SL, 450 SLC	205/70 VR 14XDX 205/70 VR 14XWX	32	36
350SE 4·5 Litre, 450SE 450 SEL 4·5	205/70 VR 14XDX 205/70 VR 14XWX	30,34(L)	34,36(L)
450 SEL 6·9 Litre	215/70 VR 14XWX	32,35(L)	32,35(L)
MG			
*1100 & 1300	155 SR 12XZX/ZX	23	26
Midget Mk I, II, III & 1500	145 SR 13XZX/ZX	22,22(L)	24,26(L)
MGB Tourer , GT	165 SR 14XZX/ZX	21,21(L)	24,26(L)
MGB GT V8	175 HR 14XAS	21,26(L)	25,32(L)
MORRIS – see Leyland			
OPEL			
Kadett Economy	155 SR 12XZX/ZX	19,22(L)	24,30(L)
Kadett DL, Special, Coupé, City DL, City Special	155 SR 13XZX/ZX	20,22(L)	25,29(L)
Kadett Estate	155 SR 13XZX/ZX	22,23(L)	29,35(L)
Kadett 1·2 Coupé Rallye	175/70 SR 13ZX	19,20(L)	22,26(L)
Kadett GTE Coupé	175/70 HR 13XVS	25 28(L)	25,32(L)
Ascona 1·6 & 1·9 (75 onwards)	165 SR 13XZX/ZX	25,29(L)	25,29(L)
Ascona Estate 1·6, 1·6S & 1·9S	165 SR 13XZX/ZX	26,26(L)	29,38(L)
Manta 1·6 & 1·9 (75 on)	165 SR 13XZX/ZX	25,29(L)	25,29(L)
Manta Berlinetta 1·6 & 1·9 (75 onwards)	185/70 SR 13ZX	23,26(L)	23,26(L)
Rekord 11 (1972) 1·7, 1·7S	6.40 SR 13ZX	29	35

*(L) (S) (LS) See notes at head of table

Car Make and Model	Michelin Radial Fitment	Pressure Front	Rear
OPEL			
1·9SH & Coupés	175 SR 14XZX/ZX	26,26(L)	26,29(L)
Rekord II 2,000 S Saloon	175 SR 14XZX/ZX	26,26(L)	26,29(L)
Rekord II 2, 100S Diesel Saloon	175 SR 14XZX/ZX	29,29(L)	29,35(L)
Rekord II Estate 1·7, 1·7S 1·9SH, 2000S	175 SR 14ZX	26	32
	6.40 SR 13ZX	26,26(L)	32,44(L)
Commodore GS, 2·5H	165 HR 14XAS	26,29(S)	26,30(S)
Commodore GS, 2·5E, 2·8H & Coupés	165 HR 14XAS	29,32(S)	30,35(S)
PEUGEOT			
104 GL	135 SR 13XZX/ZX	28	32
104 SL	135 SR 13XZX/ZX	26	29
104 Coupé	135 HR 13XAS	26	32
204	135 SR 14ZX	25	29
204 Estate	145 SR 14ZX	25,25(L)	30,38(L)
304 GL	145 SR 14XZX/ZX	26	30
304 GL Estate, SL Estate	145 SR 14XZX/ZX	26	39
304 SLS	145 SR 14XZX/ZX	26	30
504 L	165 SR 14XZX/ZX	26	30
504 L Estate, GL Estate, Family Estate	185 SR 14XZX/ZX Reinforced	23	46
504 L Diesel	165 SR 14XZX/ZX	25	29
504 L, Family Diesel Estates	185 SR 14XZX/ZX Reinforced	25	46
504 GL, GL Diesel	175 SR 14XZX/ZX	26	30
504 Ti	175 HR 14XAS	23	28
504 V6 (L.H.D.)	190/65 HR 390 TRX	20	26
604 SL & Auto	175 HR 14XAS- P	26	30
604 SL V6	175 HR 14XAS	26,30(L) or (S)	30,35(L) or (S)
604	190/65 HR 390 TRX	22	30
PRINCESS			
1800, 1800 HL, 2200 HL, 2200 HLS	185/70 SR 14ZX	26	24
RENAULT			
R4, R4L, R4TL	135 SR 13XZX/ZX	20	23
R5, R5L, R5TL, R5GTL	145 SR 13XZX/ZX	23,26(LS)	26,29(LS)
R5TS	145 SR 13XZX/ZX	23,25(LS)	28,29(LS)
R6, R6L	135 SR 13XZX/ZX	22,25(LS)	25,28(LS)
R6TL (4 seat)	135 SR 13XZX/ZX	22,23(LS)	26,29(LS)
(5 seat)	145 SR 13XZX/ZX	20,22(LS)	25,26(LS)
R12L, R12TL	145 SR 13XZX/ZX	23,26(LS)	26,29(LS)
R12TS	145 SR 13XZX/ZX	23,26(LS)	26,29(LS)
R12 Estate	155 SR 13XZX/ZX	23,25(LS)	26,29(LS)
R14TL	145 SR 13XZX/ZX	25	28
R15TL, R15TS	155 SR 13XZX/ZX	26,29(LS)	28,30(LS)
R15GTL	145 SR 13XZX/ZX	26,29(LS)	28,30(LS)
R16, R16TL	145 SR 14ZX	23,25(LS)	29,32(LS)
R16TS, R16TX	155 SR 14ZX	26,25(LS)	26,32(LS)
R17TL	155 SR 13XZX/ZX	26,29(LS)	28,30(LS)
R17TS, R17 Gordini	165 HR 13XAS	28,30(LS)	30,32(LS)
R20TL (Manual)	165 SR 13XZX/ZX	28,30(L)	28,30(L)
R20TL (Auto)	165 SR 13XZX/ZX	29,32(L)	28,30(L)
30 TS (Manual)	175 HR 14XAS	26,29(S)	28,31(S)
30 TS (Automatic)	175 HR 14XAS	28,31(S)	30,33(S)
ROVER			
2000 & TC.2200 & TC	165 SR 14XZX/ZX	30	28
3500, 3500S	185 HR 14XVS	28,30(L)	30,34(L)
2300, 2600 SD1	175 HR 14XVS	28,30(L)	30,32(L)
3,500 SD1	185 HR 14XVS	26,26(L)	26,30(L)

*(L) (S) (LS) See notes at head of table

Car Make and Model	Michelin Radial Fitment	Pressure Front	Rear
ROVER			
3·5 litre	6.70-15X	26,30(S)	26,30(S)
Range Rover	205 R16 XM+S	25,25(L)	25,35(L)
SAAB			
96 V4	155 SR 15ZX	24	22
99 (1.85, 2.0 litre)	155 SR 15ZX	28,30(L)	28,30(L)
99 GL, GLE	165 SR 15ZX	28,30(L)	28,30(L)
99 EMS (Aug 75 on)	165 HR 15XAS	28,30(L)	28,30(L)
SIMCA			
1000 S, SR, GLS, 1000 LS Rally and Rally 1	145 SR 13XZX/ZX	16,19(LS)	26,29(LS)
1100, LE, LX	145 SR 13XZX/ZX	25,26(LS)	26,29(LS)
1100S, 1204S	145 HR 13XAS	26,28(LS)	26,29(LS)
1100 Estate GLS	155 SR 13XZX/ZX	23,23(L)	26,32(L)
1300, 1301, 1301 Special 1500, 1501, 1501 Special	165 SR 13ZX	23,26(LS)	25,28(LS)
1301, 1501 Estates 1501, 1301 Special Estates	175 SR 13ZX	23,23(L)	26,32(L)
SINGER – for Chamois and Chamois Sports models – See Hillman Imp			
TOYOTA			
Publica 1000 Saloon & Coupé	155 SR 12XZX/ZX	24,26(L)	24,28(L)
Corolla 1200 Saloon & Coupé	155 SR 12XZX/ZX	22	24
Corolla 1200 Estate	155 SR 12XZX/ZX Reinforced	24,24(L)	26,30(L)
Corolla 30 Saloon & Coupé	155 SR 13XZX/ZX	24	24
Corolla 30 Estate	155 SR 13XZX/ZX	24,24(L)	24,28(L)
Carina & Celica 1600 (until 76)	165 SR 13XZX/ZX	24	26
Celica Liftback ST	165 SR 14XZX/ZX	23,23(L)	23,26(L)
Celica Liftback GT	185/70 HR 14XVS	23,23(L)	23,26(L)
Carina (76 onwards)	165 SR 13XZX/ZX 185/70 SR 13ZX	24,26(L)	26,30(L)
Crown 2600	175 SR 14XZX/ZX	26,26(L)	26,28(L)
Crown Estate	185 SR 14XZX/ZX Reinforced	24,26(L)	26,30(L)
TRIUMPH			
Toledo	155 SR 13XZX/ZX	24	28
Dolomite 1300, 1500, 1850	155 SR 13XZX/ZX	26	30
Dolomite Sprint	155 HR 13XAS	26	30
2000 Mk I, II	175 SR 13ZX	26,26(L)	26,34(L)
2000 Estate Mk I, II	175 SR 13ZX	26,26(L)	26,34(L)
2000TC	175 SR 13ZX	26	26
2·5 PI Mk I, II	175 SR 13ZX	26	30
2·5 PI Estate Mk I, II	175 HR 13XAS	26,26(L)	26,34(L)
2500 TC, and Estate	175 SR 13ZX	26	30
2500 S	175 HR 14XAS	26	30
2500 S Estate	175 HR 14XAS	26	34
Spitfire Mk I, II, III & IV	145 SR 13XZX/ZX	22	28
	155 SR 13XZX/ZX	21	26
Spitfire 1500	155 SR 13XZX/ZX	21	26
Triumph GT6	155 SR 13XZX/ZX	20	24
TR5, TR6	165 HR 15XAS	22	26
TR7	175/70 SR 13ZX	24	28
Stag	185 HR 14XVS	26	30
VAUXHALL			
Viva HC (All models)	155 SR 13XZX/ZX 165 SR 13XZX/ZX 175/70 SR 13ZX	24,26(L)	24,30(L)
Magnum Saloons & Coupés	155 SR 13XZX/ZX 175/70 SR 13ZX	24,26(L)	24,30(L)

*(L) (S) (LS) See notes at head of table

Car Make and Model	Michelin Radial Fitment	Pressure Front	Rear
VAUXHALL			
Magnum/Viva HC Estates	155 SR 13XZX/ZX 155 SR 13XZX/ZX 165 SR 13XZX/ZX	24,30(L)	24,30(L)
Firenza DL, SL and Sport	165 SR 13ZX	24,24(L)	24,26(L)
Chevette all Saloons	155 SR 13XZX/ZX until Sept. 76	21,25(L)	24,28(L)
	175/70 SR 13ZX Sept. 76 onwards	21,22(L)	25,29(L)
Chevette Estate	155 SR 13XZX/ZX 175/70 SR 13ZX	21,24(L)	25,34(L)
Victor 1800 & Est, 2300 & Est	175 SR 13ZX	24,28(LS)	24,28(LS)
VX4/90 FE Ventora FE Victor 3300 Estate FE	185/70 SR 14ZX	24,28(LS)	24,28(LS)
Cavalier 1600, 1900	165 SR 13XZX/ZX	24,29(L)	24,29(L)
Cavalier 1900 Coupé	185/70 SR 13ZX	23,26(L)	23,26(L)
VX 1800, 2300 Saloons & Estates	175 SR 13ZX	24,28(LS)	24,28(LS)
VX 2300 GLS, VX 4/90 E Saloons & Estates	185/70 SR 14ZX	24,28(LS)	24.28(LS)
VOLKSWAGEN			
1200, 1300, 1500 Beetle	155 SR 15ZX	19	28
1600 Super (1302)	155 SR 15ZX	19	28
1303, 1303S, 1303 LS	155 SR 15ZX	19	28
412 Est (all models)	165 SR 15ZX	19,19(L)	30,36(L)
412 (all models)	155 SR 15ZX	20,23(L)	26,32(L)
K70 & S & LS	165 SR 14ZX	22,25(L)	22,28(L)
Passat LS. LS	155 SR 13XZX/ZX	26	26
Passat LS, TS	165/70 SR 13ZX	26	26
Passat GLS	175/70 SR 13ZX	26	26
Scirocco 1100L, 1500S	155 SR 13XZX/ZX	26	26
Scirocco 1500 TS, LS	175/70 SR 13ZX	26	26
Scirocco GTI	175/70 HR 13XVS	25,26(L)	25,32(L)
Golf & L	155 SR 13XZX/ZX	26	26
Golf S & LS	175/70 SR 13ZX	26	26
Golf GLS	155 SR 13XZX/ZX	25,26(L)	25,32(L)
Polo, L & N	135 SR 13XZX/ZX	23,26(L)	23,29(L)
Polo, LS	145 SR 13XZX/ZX	22,25(L)	22,28(L)
VOLVO			
44, 55, 55 Coupé & Estate	135 SR 14XZX/ZX	23	29
55 Marathon	155 SR 13XZX/ZX	20	25
66, 66 Coupé & Estate	135 SR 14XZX/ZX 155 SR 13XZX/ZX	23 20	26 23
66 Marathon, Coupé & Estate	155 SR 13XZX/ZX	20	23
142, 142S, 144, 144S	165 SR 15ZX	26,28(L)	28,32(L)
145 Estate	165 SR 15ZX Reinforced	26,27(L)	28,40(L)
164	165 SR 15ZX	28,29(L)	28,35(L)
164 (Aug 72 onwards)	175 SR 15ZX	25,26(L)	26,30(L)
164E	175 HR 15XAS	25,26(L)	26,30(L)
343 DL	155 SR 13XZX/ZX	24,24(L)	29,32(L)
221 Estate, 223 Estate	165 SR 15ZX Reinforced	23,25(L)	28,41(L)
244L	165 SR 14XZX/ZX	26,28(L)	28,34(L)
244 DL	175 SR 14XZX/ZX	26,26(L)	28,32(L)
244 GL	185/70 SR 14ZX	28,28(L)	28,33(L)
245 L & DL & E Estate	185 SR 14XZX/ZX	28,29(L)	28,35(L)
264 DL (Carburetter)	175 SR 14XZX/ZX	27,27(L)	27,32(L)
264 L, DL (Fuel Injection)	185 SR 14XZX/ZX	28,28(L)	28,34(L)
264 GL & GLE	185/70 HR 14XVS	28,29(L)	28,35(L)
265 DL & GL Estate	185 SR 14XZX/ZX	27,28(L)	27,34(L)

WOLSELEY – for Hornet, 1100, 1300, 18-22 Series, 18/85 and Six – See equivalent Austin models.

*†(L) (S) (11) See notes at head of table

SHIPSTON-ON-STOUR Warw. 986 ㉛ – pop. 2,773 – ☎ 0608.
Envir. : Compton Wynyates★ (Tudor mansion 15C-16C) : site★, gardens★ *AC*, NE 4 ½ m.
London 85 – Birmingham 34 – Oxford 29.

- George, Market Sq., CV36 4AJ, ☎ 61453 – ⛀wc Ⓟ
  17 rm.
- XX Old Mill, with rm, Mill Rd, CV36 4AW, on B 4035 ☎ 61880, ⛰, ⛱ – Ⓟ
  5 rm.

AUSTIN-MORRIS-MG Church St. ☎ 61430

SHIPTON Glos. – see Cheltenham.

SHIPTON-UNDER-WYCHWOOD Oxon. – pop. 860 – ☎ 0993.
London 81 – Birmingham 50 – Gloucester 37 – **Oxford 25.**

- **Shaven Crown,** High St., OX7 6BA, ☎ 830330, « 13C monks' hostel » – Ⓟ
  M 4.00/6.00 **t.** 🍾 1.80 – **12 rm** ☕ 7.00/18.00 **t.**
- XX **Lamb Inn** with rm, OX7 6DQ, ☎ 830465, ⛱ – ⛀wc Ⓟ
  M *(closed Sunday and Monday dinner)* (bar lunch) 5.50/6.50 **s.** 🍾 1.80 – ☕ 1.10 – **3 rm** 7.00/14.00 **s.**

SHORNE Kent – pop. 2,622 – ✉ Gravesend – ☎ 047 482.
London 27 – Gravesend 4 – Maidstone 12 – Rochester 4.

- **Inn on the Lake,** DA12 3HB, on A 2 ☎ 3333, ≤, ⛰, ⛱, park – TV ⛀wc ☎ ♿ Ⓟ. 🏛
  M a la carte 4.25/6.25 **st.** 🍾 1.75 – **78 rm** ☕ 12.50/16.50 **st.**

SHOTTISHAM Suffolk – pop. 164 – ✉ Woodbridge – ☎ 039 441.
London 87 – Ipswich 14 – Woodbridge 6.

- Wood Hall ⛰, IP12 3EG, on B 1083 ☎ 283, ⛱ – ⛀wc Ⓟ
  16 rm.

SHREWSBURY Salop 986 ㉗ – pop. 56,188 – ☎ 0743.
See : Abbey church★ 11C-14C **D** – St. Mary's Church★ (Jesse Tree window★) **A** – Grope Lane★ 15C. **Envir. :** Wroxeter★ (Roman city and baths) *AC*, SE : 6 m. by A 458 and A 5 – Condover Hall★ (15C) *AC*, S : 5 m. by A 49.
⛳9 ☎ 64050, junction A 5/A 49, Meole Brace S : by A 49.
i The Square ☎ 52019.
London 163 – Birmingham 45 – Cardiff 109 – Chester 42 – Derby 65 – Gloucester 77 – **Manchester 72 – Stoke-on-Trent 35 –** Swansea 118.

Plan on next page

- **Lion** (T.H.F.), Wyle Cop, SY1 1UY, ☎ 53107 – 🛗 TV ⛀wc ☎ Ⓟ. 🏛 **c**
  M 3.00/3.50 **st.** – ☕ 1.50 – **64 rm** 8.50/20.00 **st.**
- **Prince Rupert,** Butcher Row, SY1 1UQ, ☎ 52461 – 🛗 TV ⛀wc ☎ **n**
  M 4.50/5.00 **st.** 🍾 1.50 – **61 rm** ☕ 11.00/19.00 **st.**
- Lord Hill, 131 Abbey Foregate, SY2 6AX, ☎ 52601 – ⛀wc 🚿wc ☎ Ⓟ. 🏛 **e**
  M approx. 2.95 **st.** 🍾 1.80 – **26 rm.**
- **Ainsworth's Radbrook Hall,** Radbrook Rd, SY3 9BQ, W : 1 m. on A 488 ☎ 4861, ⛱ – TV ⛀wc 🚿wc ☎ Ⓟ
  M 2.40/3.40 **st.** 🍾 0.90 – **29 rm** ☕ 7.00/12.50 **st.**
- **Beauchamp** (S & N), 100 The Mount, SY3 8PG, ☎ 3230, ⛱ – ⛀wc 🚿wc Ⓟ **a**
  M approx. 3.50 **st.** 🍾 1.50 – **25 rm** ☕ 7.00/13.85 **st.** – P 13.50 **st.**
- XX **Penny Farthing,** 23 Abbey Foregate, SY2 5EG, ☎ 56119 **s**
  closed Sunday, Monday and 3 weeks June – **M** a la carte 4.65/5.80 🍾 1.65.

at Albrighton N : 3 m. on A 528 – ✉ Shrewsbury – ☎ 093 96 Bomere Heath :

- XX **Albright Hussey,** SY4 3AF, ☎ 523, « 15C timbered manor house with garden » – Ⓟ
  closed Sunday dinner, Monday and last 2 weeks August – **M** a la carte 4.30/5.85.

at Cressage SE : 8 ½ m. by A 458 – ✉ Shrewsbury – ☎ 095 289 Cressage :

- XX **Old Hall** with rm, ☎ 298, ≤, ⛰, ⛱ – Ⓟ
  closed Sunday dinner and Monday – **M** 4.50/7.00 **t.** 🍾 1.30 – **5 rm** ☕ 9.00/16.00 **t.**

at Dorrington S : 7 m. on A 49 – ✉ Shrewsbury – ☎ 074 373 Dorrington :

- XX **Olde Hall,** Hereford Rd, SY5 7JD, ☎ 465 – Ⓟ
  closed Sunday dinner, Monday, last week August and first 2 weeks September – **M** a la carte 3.40/6.80 🍾 2.20.

15

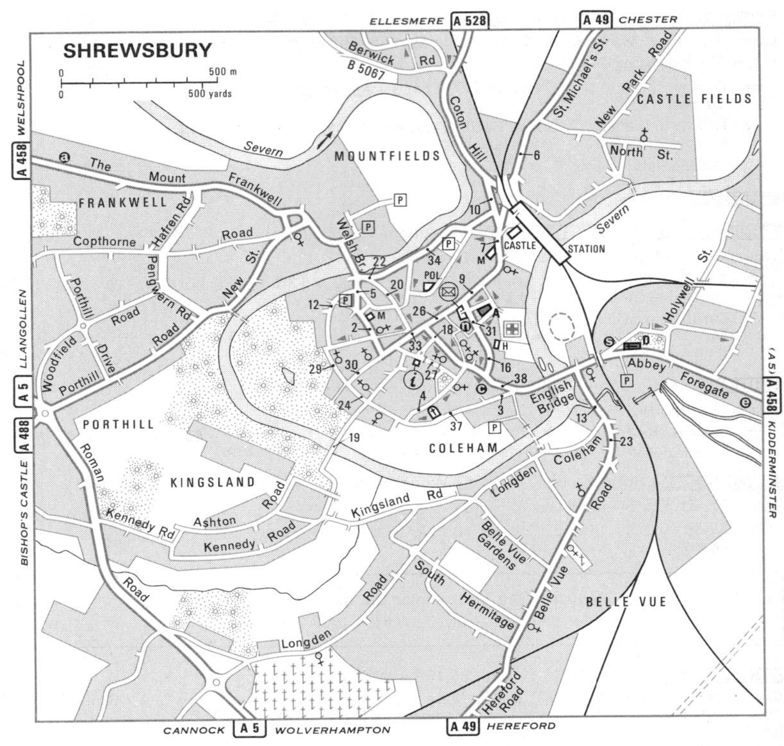

High Street	18
Pride Hill	26
Shoplatch	33
Barker Street	2
Beeches Lane	3
Belmont	4
Bridge Street	5
Castle Foregate	6
Castle Gates	7
Castle Street	9
Chester Street	10
Claremont Bank	12
Coleham Head	13
Dogpole	16
Kingsland Bridge	19
Mardol	20
Mardol Quay	22
Moreton Crescent	23
Murivance	24
Princess Street	27
St. Chad's Terrace	29
St. John's Hill	30
St. Mary's Street	31
Smithfield Road	34
Town Walls	37
Wyle Cop	38

AUSTIN-MG-WOLSELEY Chester St. ☎ 57231
BMW Castle Foregate ☎ 3250
CHRYSLER-SIMCA 170 Abbey Foregate ☎ 56326
CITROEN New St. ☎ 4039
DAIMLER-JAGUAR-MORRIS-MG Wyle Cop ☎ 52471
FORD Coton Hill ☎ 3631
OPEL-VAUXHALL St. Julian's Friars ☎ 52321
RENAULT 159 Abbey Foregate ☎ 57711
SAAB Ellesmere Rd ☎ 093 96 (Bomere Heath) 351
VOLVO Featherbed Lane ☎ 51251

SHURDINGTON Glos. – see Cheltenham.

SIDFORD Devon – see Sidmouth.

SIDMOUTH Devon 986 ㊴ – pop. 12,076 – ✆ 039 55.

18 Cotmaton Rd ☎ 3023.

i Esplanade, ☎ 6441 (summer only).

London 170 – Exeter 14 – Taunton 27 – Weymouth 45.

- **Victoria,** Esplanade, EX10 8RY, ☎ 2651, <, heated, – P
  M 5.50/7.00 2.00 – 2.00 – **65 rm** 12.00/24.00 – P 16.00/18.50.
- **Westcliff,** Manor Rd, EX10 8RU, ☎ 3252, heated, – wc P
  M 3.50/4.50 **s.** 1.30 – **38 rm** 9.80/22.00 – P 10.75/13.00.
- **Fortfield,** Station Rd, EX10 8NU, ☎ 2403, – wc P
  M a la carte 4.00/5.65 **st.** 1.10 – **60 rm** 8.00/25.50 **st.** – P 12.00/16.50 **st.**
- **Salcombe Hill House**, Beatlands Rd, EX10 8JQ, ☎ 4697, – wc P
  M 2.45/3.20 **st.** 1.55 – **31 rm** 8.65/17.30 – P 9.50/11.50.

Royal Glen, Glen Rd, EX10 8RW, ☎ 3221, « 17C house furnished with many antiques », – wc Ⓟ
M a la carte 2.25/4.05 **t.** 2.00 – **30 rm** 8.65/24.00 **t.** – P 12.30/14.40 **t.**

Bedford, Station Rd, EX10 8NR, ☎ 3047, ← – wc
March-November – **M** 3.75/4.50 **st.** 1.40 – **42 rm** 9.00/20.00 **st.** – P 12.50/15.50 **st.**

Faulkner and Royal York, Esplanade, EX10 8AZ, ☎ 3043, ← – wc
M 2.60/3.20 1.20 – **72 rm** 8.85/17.70 – P 11.50.

Woodlands, Cotmaton Cross, EX10 8HG, ☎ 3120, – wc Ⓟ
M approx. 2.50 1.30 – **30 rm** 9.00/17.50.

at Sidford **N : 2 m. – ✉ ☎ 039 55 Sidmouth :**

XX **Applegarth** with rm, Church St., EX10 9QP, ☎ 3174, « Garden » – Ⓟ
closed October and part November – **M** *(closed Sunday dinner and Monday lunch to non-residents)* a la carte 3.85/5.80 **t.** 1.10 – **8 rm** 8.00/16.00 **st.**

AUSTIN-MG-WOLSELEY ☎ 2931
CHRYSLER-SIMCA Vicarage Rd ☎ 2433
DAF Mill St. ☎ 3433
DATSUN Sidford ☎ 3334
FIAT Crossways, Sidford ☎ 3595
FORD High St. ☎ 5725
MORRIS-MG Salcombe Rd ☎ 2522

SILCHESTER Hants. – **pop. 766 – ✉ Reading (Berks.) – ☎ 0734.**

London 62 – Basingstoke 8 – Reading 14 – Winchester 26.

Romans, Little London Rd, RG7 2PN, ☎ 700421, heated, – wc Ⓟ
closed 22 July-7 August – **M** *(closed Saturday lunch and Sunday dinner)* 4.50/6.00 1.20 – **18 rm** 9.50/14.00.

SILLOTH Cumbria 986 ⑲ – **pop. 2,662 – ✉ Carlisle – ☎ 0965.**

18 ☎ **31304.**

i Central Garage, Waver St. ☎ 31276.

London 333 – Carlisle 22.

Golf, 2 Criffel St., CA5 4AB, ☎ 31438 – TV wc Ⓟ
M 3.20/3.50 1.35 – **23 rm** 6.50/11.50 **st.**

at Skinburness **NE : 2 m. off B 5302 – ✉ Carlisle – ☎ 0965 Silloth :**

Skinburness, CA5 4QY, ☎ 31468, – wc Ⓟ.
M (bar lunch) 3.25/4.50 1.45 – **23 rm** 8.20/14.00 **t.**

AUSTIN-MG Solway St. ☎ 351
FORD West End ☎ 449

SIMONSTONE Lancs. – **pop. 854 – ✉ Burnley – ☎ 0282 Padiham.**

London 235 – Burnley 5 – Lancaster 36 – Preston 17.

Higher Trapp, Trapp Lane, BB12 7QW, N : 1 m. off A 671 ☎ 72781, ←, , park – wc wc Ⓟ
M a la carte 3.95/5.65 **st.** 1.80 – **12 rm.**

SITTINGBOURNE Kent 986 ㊱ – **pop. 30,913 (inc. Milton) – ☎ 0795.**

London 44 – Canterbury 15 – Maidstone 12.

Coniston, 70 London Rd, ME10 1NT, ☎ 72907 – TV wc Ⓟ.
M approx. 4.00 – **38 rm** 8.00/15.00.

X **Nina's** with rm, 43 High St., ME10 4AW, ☎ 24670 – TV
closed Christmas Day and Bank Holidays – **M** *(closed Sunday and Monday dinner)* a la carte 3.80/8.95 1.50 – **6 rm** 9.25/15.75.

AUSTIN-MORRIS-MG Bapchild ☎ 23085
FORD Crown Quay Lane ☎ 70711
RENAULT Bapchild ☎ 76222
TOYOTA, VAUXHALL 52 West St. ☎ 23333

SKEGNESS Lincs. 986 ㉘ – **pop. 13,580 – ☎ 0754.**

18 **Seacroft ☎ 3020, S : 1 ½ m. –** 18 **North Shore ☎ 3298.**

i Council Offices, North Parade ☎ 5441 – Tower Esplanade ☎ 4821 (summer) and ☎ 4761 (winter).

London 145 – Lincoln 41.

County, North Par., PE25 2UB, ☎ 2461, ← – wc Ⓟ.
M 3.00/3.45 – **45 rm** 8.55/17.25 – P 11.75/17.75.

Crown, Drummond Rd, Seacroft, PE25 3AB, ☎ 3084 – wc Ⓟ
27 rm.

AUSTIN-MORRIS-MG Roman Bank ☎ 3671
CHRYSLER Beacon Way ☎ 2556
FIAT Beresford Av. ☎ 2079
FORD 17/25 Burgh Rd ☎ 2421

SKELMERSDALE Lancs. 986 ⑤ – **pop. 30,582 (inc. Holland) – ☎ 0695.**

London 210 – Liverpool 19 – Manchester 27 – Preston 22.

Balcony Farm Inn, Prescot Rd, East Pimbo SE : 2 m. by A 506 ☎ 20401 – wc Ⓟ
12 rm.

FORD Wigan Rd ☎ 23434
MORRIS-MG Railway Rd ☎ 21042

SKELWITH BRIDGE Cumbria – see Ambleside.

SKINBURNESS Cumbria – see Silloth.

SKIPTON North Yorks. 986 ㉓ – pop. 12,437 – ☎ 0756.
See : Castle* (14C) *AC.*
Short Lee Lane, off Grassington Rd ☎ 3257, NW : **1** m.
London 217 – Kendal 45 – **Leeds 26** – Preston 36 – York 43.

Highfield, 58 Keighley Rd, BD23 2NB, ☎ 3182
10 rm 5.00/9.50 **st.**

Oats, Chapel Hill, BD23 1NL, ☎ 3604 – Ⓟ
closed Sunday, Monday and Bank Holidays – **M** 7.50/9.00 **t.**

SLEAFORD Lincs. 986 ㉘ – pop. 7,975 – ☎ 0529.
See : St. Denis' Church* 12C-15C.
South Rauceby ☎ 052 98 (South Rauceby) 273.
London 119 – Leicester 45 – Lincoln 17 – **Nottingham 39.**

Lion, 7 Northgate, NG34 7BH, ☎ 302127 – Ⓟ
M *(closed Christmas Day)* approx. 2.35 **t.** – **10 rm** 4.50/8.25 **t.**

White Hart, 32 Southgate, NG34 7RY, ☎ 303120 – wc Ⓟ
M 2.80/4.00 0.80 – **17 rm** 5.00/11.00.

CHRYSLER-SIMCA Boston Rd ☎ 302518
MORRIS-MG Carre St. ☎ 303034
ROVER-TRIUMPH 86 Southgate ☎ 302921
VAUXHALL 50 Westgate ☎ 2919

SLOUGH Berks. 986 ④ and ㊱ – pop. 87,075 – ☎ 0753.
Envir. : Eton (college**) S : 2 m.
London 29 – Oxford 39 – Reading 19.

Holiday Inn, Ditton Rd, Langley, SL3 8PR, ☎ 44244, Telex 848646, – TV Ⓟ.
M (buffet lunch) a la carte 3.25/5.65 **s.** 1.90 – 2.10 – **234 rm** 15.00/18.00.

at Colnbrook SE : 3 m. on A 4 – ✉ Slough – ☎ 028 12 Colnbrook :

Heathrow Ambassádor, Brands Rd, London Rd, SL3 8QB, ☎ 4001, Telex 847903 –
wc Ⓟ.
110 rm.

AUSTIN-MORRIS-MG-WOLSELEY Petersfield Av. ☎ 23031
AUSTIN-MORRIS-MG-ROVER-TRIUMPH 57 Farnham Rd ☎ 24001
DAF Beaconsfield Rd ☎ 028 14 (Farnham Common) 2301
FORD Petersfield Av. ☎ 36111
VAUXHALL 134 Bath Rd ☎ 24581
VW, AUDI-NSU Colnbrook-By-Pass ☎ 028 12 (Colnbrook) 2708

SMALL DOLE West Sussex – pop. 3,903 – ✉ Henfield – ☎ 0903 Steyning.
London 49 – Brighton 13 – Horsham 13 – Worthing 11.

Golding Barn, Henfield Rd, BN5 9XH, S : 1 m. on A 2037, ☎ 813344, – Ⓟ
closed Sunday dinner and Monday – **M** a la carte 3.90/6.85 **t.** 1.40.

SMETHWICK West Midlands 986 ⑫ – see Birmingham.

SNOWDON Gwynedd 986 ㉗.
See: Ascent and *** (1 h 15 mn from Llanberis by Snowdon Mountain Railway *AC*).

Hotel and restaurant see : Caernarfon NW : 9 m.

SOLIHULL West Midlands 986 ⑫ and ㉛ – pop. 107,095 – ☎ 021 Birmingham.
Stratford Rd ☎ 744 6001.
i Library Theatre Box Office, Homer Rd ☎ 705 0060.
London 109 – Birmingham 7 – Coventry 13 – Warwick 13.

George (Embassy), The Square, B91 3RF, ☎ 704 1241 – TV Ⓟ.
closed Christmas – **M** approx. 3.40 **st.** 1.50 – **46 rm** 11.25/16.50 **st.**

St. Johns, 651 Warwick Rd, B91 1AT, ☎ 705 6777, Telex 339352 – TV wc Ⓟ.
M a la carte 4.00/7.00 **st.** 1.80 – **219 rm** 14.50/18.50 **st.**

Hillfield Hall, Hillfield Rd, B91 3JF, S : 1 m. off Church Hill Rd ☎ 704 9292 – Ⓟ
closed Sunday dinner, Monday and 1 January – **M** a la carte 5.25/7.50 **t.** 1.50.

at Monkspath Street SW : 2 m. on A 34 – ✉ Solihull – ☎ 021 Birmingham :

Da Corrado, 1097 Stratford Rd, Shirley, B90 4EB, ☎ 744 1977, Italian rest. – Ⓟ
closed Sunday and Bank Holidays – **M** a la carte 2.65/4.40 **t.** 1.60.

La Villa Bianca, 1036 Stratford Rd, B90 4EE, ☎ 744 7232, Italian rest. – Ⓟ.

AUSTIN-DAIMLER-JAGUAR-MORRIS-MG-ROVER-TRIUMPH Stratford Rd, Shirley ☎ 744 4405
AUSTIN-MORRIS-MG-WOLSELEY 707 Warwick Rd ☎ 705 3028
BMW Shirley ☎ 744 4488
CHRYSLER-SIMCA 386 Warwick Rd ☎ 704 1427
DAF Station Lane ☎ 056 43 (Lapworth) 2933
FORD 361/369 Stratford Rd ☎ 744 4456
RENAULT Stratford Rd, Hockley Heath ☎ 056 43 (Lapworth) 2244

SOMERTON Somerset – pop. 3,267 – ✆ 0458.
London 137 – Exeter 52 – Southampton 74 – Taunton 17.

Red Lion, Broad St., TA11 7NJ, ☎ 72339, Telex 46240 – TV wc ☎ P.
M (bar lunch) 6.00/8.00 **t.** 1.25 – 1.50 – **16 rm** 10.00/16.50.

SOMPTING West Sussex – see Worthing.

SONNING-ON-THAMES Berks. – pop. 1,469 – ✆ 0734 Reading.
London 48 – Reading 4.

XXX **French Horn** with rm, RG4 0TN, ☎ 692204, ≤ river Thames and gardens, – TV wc P
M a la carte 5.40/10.70 **t.** 2.00 – **3 rm** 12.00/25.00 **t.**

XX **White Hart** with rm, Thames St., RG4 0UT, ☎ 692277, ≤, « Rose gardens on river bank » – wc ☎ P.
M a la carte 6.00/8.90 1.80 – **17 rm** 14.00/19.65.

SOUTHAM Glos. – see Cheltenham.

SOUTHAM Warw. 986 ㉛ – pop. 4,506 – ✉ Royal Leamington Spa – ✆ 092 681.
London 91 – Coventry 11 – Northampton 23 – Warwick 9.

Craven Arms, Market Hill, CV33 0HE, ☎ 2452 – P
M a la carte 2.70/4.15 **s.** 0.75 – **7 rm** 5.00/9.50 **s.** – P 8.00/12.00 **s.**

DATSUN Oxford St. ☎ 2181 VAUXHALL Bull St. ☎ 2240

*Im **Juli** und **August** sind die Hotels oft überfüllt.*
Außerhalb dieser Zeit werden Sie besser bedient.

SOUTHAMPTON Hants. 986 ㉟ – pop. 215,118 – ✆ 0703.
See : Docks★ – Tudor House Museum★ (16C) *AC* AZ **M**[1] – God's House Tower★ 12C (Museum of Archaeologia) AZ **M**[2]. **Envir.** : Netley (abbey★ ruins 13C) *AC*, SE : 3 m. BZ **A**.
18 Basset ☎ 768151, N : 2m. BY – 18, 9 West Side Basset Av. ☎ 68407 AY.
Southampton Airport : ☎ 0703 (Eastleigh) 612341, N : 4 m. BY.
Shipping connections with the Continent : to Cherbourg (Townsend Thoresen) – to Le Havre (Townsend Thoresen and P & O Ferries : Normandy Ferries) – to Bilbao (Swedish Lloyd) – to the Isle of Wight : Cowes (Red Funnel Services) Monday/Saturday 7-14 daily ; Sunday 4-11 daily (1 h 10 mn).
to the Isle of Wight : Cowes (Red Funnel Services : hydrofoil) Monday/Saturday 10-12 daily ; Sunday 3-11 daily (20 mn) and (Solent Seaspeed) frequent services (20 mn).
i Canute Rd (opposite Dock Gate 3) ☎ 20438 – The Precinct, Above Bar St. ☎ 23855 ext 615.
London 84 – Bristol 76 – Plymouth 148.

Plans on following pages

Polygon (T.H.F.), Cumberland Pl., SO9 4GD, ☎ 26401, Telex 47175 – TV P. AZ **n**
M 3.75/4.25 **st.** 1.50 – 2.00 – **119 rm** 13.00/23.00 **st.**

Post House (T.H.F.), Herbert Walker Av., SO1 0GY, ☎ 28081, Telex 477368, heated – TV wc ☎ P. AZ **o**
M 3.70/4.20 **st.** 1.50 – 2.00 – **132 rm** 13.00/18.00 **st.**

Dolphin (T.H.F.), 35 High St., SO9 2DS, ☎ 26178 – TV wc ☎ P. AZ **i**
M 3.25/3.75 **st.** 1.50 – 2.00 – **72 rm** 12.00/18.00 **st.**

Royal, Cumberland Pl., SO9 4NY, ☎ 23467 – wc. AZ **c**
M 3.00/3.50 **st.** 1.50 – **105 rm** 9.50/17.50 **st.**

Cotswold (Interchange), 119 Highfield Lane, Portswood Junction, SO9 1YQ, ☎ 559555, Telex 477476 – wc ☎ P BY **e**
closed 25 and 26 December – **M** *(closed 26 December)* 3.85/4.40 **st.** 1.30 – **50 rm** 10.70/18.00 **st.**

Berkeley (Interchange), 8-10 Cranbury Ter., SO9 1LZ, ☎ 23511, Telex 477678, – TV wc wc ☎ P AZ **a**
M 4.00/4.75 **t.** 1.50 – **40 rm** 9.50/18.00 **st.**

Wessex, 66-68 Northlands Rd, SO1 2LH, ☎ 31744, – wc ☎ P AY **r**
closed 2 days at Christmas – **M** (dinner only) 2.00/2.50 **s.** 1.50 – **38 rm** 6.80/13.00 **s.**

Elizabeth House, 43-44 The Avenue, SO1 2SX, ☎ 24327 – P AY **e**
closed 25 November-27 December – **M** *(closed Saturday and Sunday)* (dinner only) 2.00/3.00 **st.** 1.00 – **17 rm** 6.00/14.00 **st.**

Rosida, 25-27 Hill Lane, SO1 5AB, ☎ 28501 – P AZ **s**
36 rm 6.50/13.00 **t.**

The Lodge, 1 Winn Rd, The Avenue, SO2 1EH, ☎ 557537 – P AZ **a**
closed 23 to 31 December – **10 rm** 4.50/9.00 **t.**

P.T.O. →

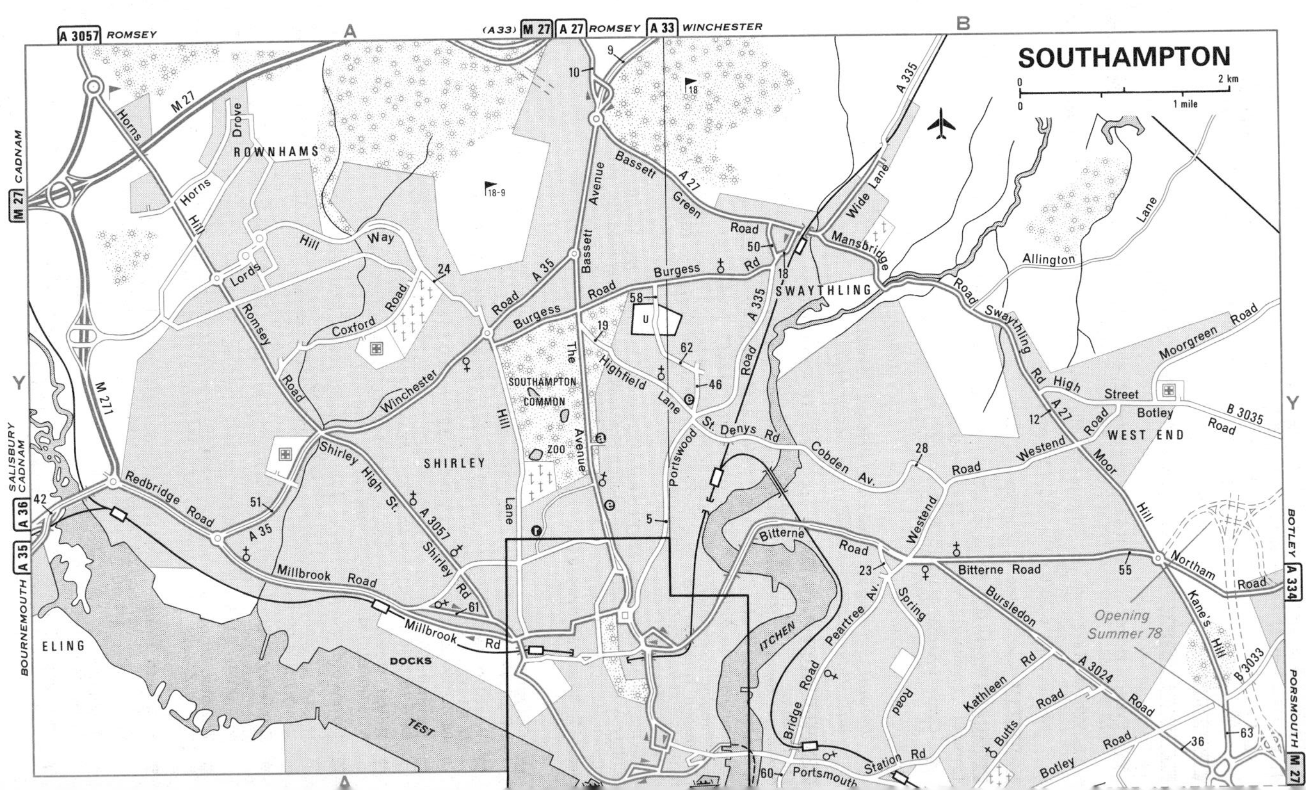
SOUTHAMPTON
0 2 km
0 1 mile
A 3057 ROMSEY
(A33) M 27 A 27 ROMSEY A 33 WINCHESTER
M 27 CADNAM
A 36 SALISBURY CADNAM
A 35 BOURNEMOUTH
BOTLEY A 334
PORSMOUTH M 27
A
B
Y
ROWNHAMS
SWAYTHLING
WEST END
SHIRLEY
ELING
DOCKS
TEST
ITCHEN
SOUTHAMPTON COMMON
ZOO
Opening Summer 78
Horns Hill
Drove
M 27
Lords Hill Way
Coxford Road
Romsey Road
Winchester Road
M 271
Redbridge Road
A 35
Millbrook Road
Millbrook Rd
Shirley High St.
A 3057
Shirley Rd
Hill Lane
Burgess Road
Bassett Avenue
The Avenue
Highfield Lane
Burgess Rd
Bassett Green Road
A 27
A 335
Wide Lane
Mansbridge Road
Allington Lane
Swaythling Rd
High Street
Moorgreen Road
Botley Road
B 3035
Westend Road
Moor Hill
Cobden Av.
St. Denys Rd
Portswood Road
Bitterne Road
Northam Road
Kane's Hill
B 3033
Bursledon Road
A 3024
Peartree Av.
Spring Road
Bridge Road
Kathleen Rd
Butts Road
Botley Road
Station Rd
Portsmouth
U
18-9
18
9
10
24
19
58
62
46
50
18
5
51
42
61
28
12
23
55
36
63
60

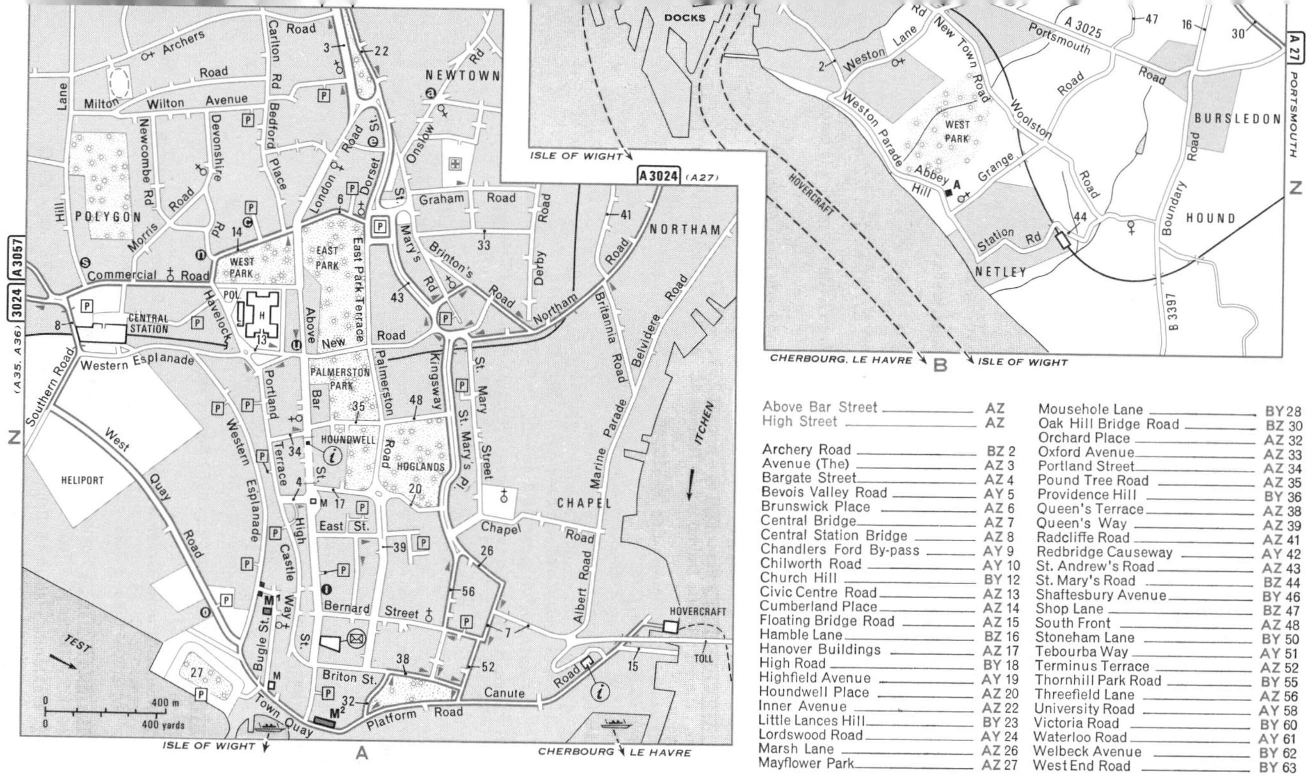

Above Bar Street	AZ
High Street	AZ
Archery Road	BZ 2
Avenue (The)	AZ 3
Bargate Street	AZ 4
Bevois Valley Road	AY 5
Brunswick Place	AZ 6
Central Bridge	AZ 7
Central Station Bridge	AZ 8
Chandlers Ford By-pass	AY 9
Chilworth Road	AY 10
Church Hill	BY 12
Civic Centre Road	AZ 13
Cumberland Place	AZ 14
Floating Bridge Road	AZ 15
Hamble Lane	BZ 16
Hanover Buildings	AZ 17
High Road	BY 18
Highfield Avenue	AY 19
Houndwell Place	AZ 20
Inner Avenue	AZ 22
Little Lances Hill	BY 23
Lordswood Road	AY 24
Marsh Lane	AZ 26
Mayflower Park	AZ 27
Mousehole Lane	BY 28
Oak Hill Bridge Road	BZ 30
Orchard Place	AZ 32
Oxford Avenue	AZ 33
Portland Street	AZ 34
Pound Tree Road	AZ 35
Providence Hill	BY 36
Queen's Terrace	AZ 38
Queen's Way	AZ 39
Radcliffe Road	AZ 41
Redbridge Causeway	AY 42
St. Andrew's Road	AZ 43
St. Mary's Road	BZ 44
Shaftesbury Avenue	BY 46
Shop Lane	BZ 47
South Front	AZ 48
Stoneham Lane	BY 50
Tebourba Way	AY 51
Terminus Terrace	AZ 52
Thornhill Park Road	BY 55
Threefield Lane	AZ 56
University Road	AY 58
Victoria Road	BY 60
Waterloo Road	AY 61
Welbeck Avenue	BY 62
West End Road	BY 63

XX **Olliver's,** 18 Ordnance Rd, off London Rd, ℡ 24789 – Ⓟ AZ e
closed Sunday and 25-26 December – **M** 4.95/5.50 **t.** 🍾 1.60.

XX **London Steak House,** Civic Centre Rd, SO1 0FL, ℡ 24394 AZ u
closed 25 and 26 December – **M** a la carte 3.35/5.50 **t.** 🍾 1.30.

MICHELIN Branch, Solent Industrial Estate, Shamblehurst Lane, Hedge End, SO3 2FQ, ℡ 048 92 (Botley) 2381.

AUSTIN-MG The Causeway ℡ 042 16 (Totton) 5021
AUSTIN-MG-WOLSELEY 170 Portsmouth Rd ℡ 47761
AUSTIN-MORRIS-MG-WOLSELEY The Avenue ℡ 28801
AUSTIN-MG-WOLSELEY 102 High Rd ℡ 554346
AUSTIN-DAIMLER-JAGUAR-MORRIS-MG-WOLSELEY, ROLLS ROYCE The Avenue ℡ 28811
BMW Dorset St. ℡ 29003
CHRYSLER Southampton Rd ℡ 042 127 (Cadnam) 2250
CHRYSLER-SIMCA Portswood Rd ℡ 554081
CITROEN Northam Bridge ℡ 26907
DAF 30/38 Bellemoor Rd ℡ 773088
DAIMLER-JAGUAR-ROVER-TRIUMPH Marsh Lane ℡ 30911
DATSUN, JENSEN 234 Winchester Rd ℡ 778316
DATSUN 21/23 St. Denys Rd ℡ 559533
FIAT 115/125 Lodge Rd ℡ 25518
FORD 362/364 Shirley Rd ℡ 775331
FORD Palmerston Rd ℡ 28331
MERCEDES-BENZ 110/112 Lodge Rd ℡ 22828
MORRIS-MG-WOLSELEY High St., West End ℡ 042 18 (West End) 3773
OPEL 14 Park St. ℡ 771929
PEUGEOT Winchester Rd, Shirley ℡ 771899
RENAULT 8/18 Cobden Av., Bitterne Park ℡ 555771
TOYOTA 159 Bitterne Rd ℡ 32056
VAUXHALL Portsmouth Rd, Sholing ℡ 449232
VOLVO Millbrook Roundabout ℡ 777616

SOUTHBOROUGH Kent 986 ㉛ – see Royal Tunbridge Wells.

SOUTH BRENT Devon – pop. 1,876 – ✆ 036 47.
London 228 – Exeter 28 – **Plymouth 16** – Torquay 17.

🏠 **Glazebrook House,** Glazebrook, TQ10 9JE, SW: 1 m. ℡ 3322, ≤, heated, park – wc Ⓟ
M *(closed Sunday, Tuesday and 25-26 December)* (dinner only) a la carte 2.80/6.45 **t.** 🍾 1.50 – **11 rm** 7.50/15.00.

If you find you cannot take up a hotel booking you have made, please let the hotel know immediately.

SOUTHEND-ON-SEA Essex 986 ㊱ – pop. 162,770 – ✆ 0702.
Envir.: Hadleigh Castle (ruins) ≤* of Thames *AC*, W: 3 m. – Southend Airport (Historic Aircraft museum) N: 2 m.
18 Eastwood Rd, Leigh-on-Sea ℡ 525345.
✈ ℡ 40201/6, N: 2 m.
i Pier Hill ℡ 44091 and 49451 ext 556 – Civic Centre, Victoria Av. ℡ 49451.
London 41 – **Cambridge 58** – Croydon 46 – **Dover 85.**

XX **Schulers,** 161 Eastern Esplanade, SS1 2YB, ℡ 610172
closed Monday – **M** a la carte 4.20/5.40 **t.** 🍾 1.60.

at Southend Airport N: 2 m. – ✉ ✆ 0702 Southend-on-Sea:

🏨 **Airport Moat House,** Aviation Way, SS2 6UL, ℡ 546344 – TV wc ☎ ♿ Ⓟ.
M 3.75/4.75 **t.** 🍾 1.75 – 1.85 – **65 rm** 11.50/15.00 **t.**

AUSTIN-MORRIS-MG Priory Crescent ℡ 67766
AUSTIN-MG, ROLLS ROYCE-BENTLEY Station Rd ℡ Thorpe Bay 582233
CHRYSLER-SIMCA 139/155 West Rd ℡ 47861
CITROEN 759/765 Southchurch Rd ℡ 64749
DATSUN 661 London Rd at Westcliff-on-Sea ℡ 35147
FIAT 22 Belle Vue Pl. ℡ 610482
FORD Arterial Rd ℡ 524501
LANCIA, PEUGEOT, SAAB Station Rd, Thorpe Bay ℡ 588200
RENAULT 499/505 London Rd, Westcliff-on-Sea ℡ 4494
TOYOTA 57 West Rd ℡ 46288
VW, AUDI-NSU, MERCEDES-BENZ 2 Comet Way ℡ 526411

SOUTH GODSTONE Surrey – see Godstone.

SOUTH LEIGH Oxon. – pop. 353 – ✉ ✆ 0993 Witney.
London 69 – Cheltenham 32 – **Oxford 13.**

XX **Mason Arms,** OX8 6XQ, ℡ 2485 – Ⓟ
closed Sunday dinner and Monday – **M** approx. 6.00 **st.** 🍾 1.60.

SOUTH MIMMS Herts. – ✉ ✆ 0707 Potters Bar.
London 21 – Luton 17.

🏨 **South Mimms Crest Motel** (Crest), Bignalls Corner, EN6 3NH, ℡ 43311, – TV wc ☎ Ⓟ.
M 2.60/4.00 **s.** 🍾 1.55 – 1.60 – **132 rm** 10.95/15.50 **s.**

SOUTH PETHERTON Somerset – pop. 2,549 – ✆ 0460.
London 138 – Taunton 21 – Yeovil 8.

XX **Oaklands** with rm, 8 Palmer St., TA13 5DB, ℡ 40272, – TV Ⓟ
M *(closed Sunday dinner and Monday)* (dinner only and Sunday lunch) 3.45/5.25 **t.** 🍾 1.50 – **3 rm** 7.00/10.00 **t.**

SOUTHPORT Merseyside 986 ㉓ – pop. 84,574 – ✆ 0704.
Envir. : Rufford Old Hall* 15C (the Great Hall**) *AC*, E : 9 m.
18 Park Rd ☎ 56221 – 18 Cockle Dick's Lane off Cambridge Rd ☎ 30226 – 18 Liverpool Rd ☎ 78092, S : 3 m.
i Cambridge Arcade ☎ 33133.
London 221 – Liverpool 20 – Manchester 38 – Preston 19.

- **Prince of Wales,** Lord St., PR8 1JS, ☎ 36688, – P.
  M a la carte 5.55/6.25 1.15 – **94 rm** 13.50/22.50.
- **Royal Clifton,** Promenade, PR8 1RB, ☎ 33771 – wc P.
  M 3.00/3.75 – **120 rm** 9.50/17.00 – P 11.50/14.50.
- **Bold,** Lord St., PR9 0BE, ☎ 32578 – wc P.
  M a la carte 2.80/4.45 – **26 rm** 8.00/16.00.
- **Red Rum,** 86-88 Lord St., PR8 1JT, ☎ 35111 – TV wc wc P
  M approx. 3.00 1.50 – **25 rm** 6.50/15.00.
- **Knowsley,** 2 Knowsley Rd, Promenade, PR9 0HG, ☎ 30190 – P
  closed November – **16 rm** 4.00/8.00 **s.**
- **Bistroquet,** 3 Stanley St., PR9 0BY, ☎ 37451, Bistro
  closed Sunday – **M** (dinner only) a la carte 3.45/4.90 1.25.

ALFA-ROMEO, SAAB 609 Liverpool Rd ☎ 79080
AUSTIN-MG-ROVER-TRIUMPH-WOLSELEY 6/16 Roe Lane ☎ 33555
DAF, PEUGEOT 642 Liverpool Rd ☎ 26861
FORD 4 Virginia St. ☎ 57921
MORRIS-MG-ROVER-TRIUMPH Regent St. Lord St. ☎ 40616
OPEL 89/91 Bath St. North ☎ 35535
RENAULT 33 Liverpool Rd ☎ 66161
TOYOTA 205 Liverpool Rd ☎ 68515
VAUXHALL King St. ☎ 32286
VOLVO 51 Weld Rd ☎ 66613
VW, AUDI-NSU Zetland St. ☎ 31091

SOUTHSEA Hants. 986 ㊵ – see Portsmouth and Southsea.

SOUTH SHIELDS Tyne and Wear 986 ⑲ – pop. 100,659 – ✆ 089 43 (4 and 5 fig.) or 0632 (6 fig.)
18 Cleadon Hill ☎ 60475, Hillcrest, off the Lonnen.
i South Foreshore, Sea Rd ☎ 557411 (summer only) – Central Library, Catherine St. ☎ 568841 (winter only).
London 284 – Newcastle-upon-Tyne 9 – Sunderland 6.

- Sea (Swallow), Sea Rd, NE33 2LD, ☎ 66227, Group Telex 53168 – TV wc wc P. – **25 rm.**

AUSTIN-MG-ROVER-TRIUMPH Burrow St. ☎ 62451

SOUTH STAINLEY North Yorks. – pop. 155 – ✉ ✆ 0423 Harrogate.
London 217 – Harrogate 6 – Ripon 5 – York 25.

- **Red Lion,** HG3 3ND, ☎ 770132, – P
  closed Christmas Day – **M** 4.50/4.85 **t.**

SOUTHWELL Notts. 986 ㉘ – pop. 5,129 – ✆ 0636.
See : Minster* 12C-13C.
London 135 – Lincoln 24 – Nottingham 14 – Sheffield 34.

- **Saracen's Head** (Anchor), Market Pl., NG25 0HE, ☎ 812701, Group Telex 27120 – TV wc P.
  M approx. 3.00 **t.** 1.00 – **23 rm** 12.95/17.90 **st.**

MORRIS-MG King St. ☎ 812146

SOUTHWOLD Suffolk 986 ㉜ – pop. 1,998 – ✆ 050 272 (4 fig.) or 0502 (6 fig.).
i Town Hall, Market Pl. ☎ 722366.
London 108 – Great Yarmouth 24 – Ipswich 35 – Norwich 34.

- Swan, Market Pl., IP18 6EG, ☎ 722186, – wc P
  52 rm.
- **Crown,** High St., IP18 6DP, ☎ 2275 – wc P
  M approx. 3.30 **t.** 1.15 – **24 rm** 5.85/13.00 **t.** – P 11.00/12.35 **t.**
- **Pier Avenue,** Station Rd, IP18 6LB, ☎ 2632 – P
  M 3.50/4.50 – **12 rm** (dinner included) 11.00/25.00 **st.** – P 14.00/16.00 **st.**

PEUGEOT Station Rd ☎ 2125

Non confondete :

Confort degli alberghi : ... , ,
Confort dei ristoranti : XXXXX X
Qualità della tavola : ✿✿, ✿, M

SOUTH ZEAL Devon – ✉ Okehampton – ☎ 083 784 Sticklepath.
London 218 – Exeter 17 – **Plymouth 36** – Torquay 27.

Oxenham Arms, EX20 2JT, ☎ 244, « 12C inn », – wc P
closed 11 January-February – **M** 4.00/5.25 **t.** 1.50 – **9 rm** 8.50/15.00 **t.**

SPALDING Lincs. 986 ㉘ – pop. 16,951 – ☎ 0775.
See : Parish church* 13C – Ayscoughfee Hall* 15C.
Surfleet ☎ 077 585 (Surfleet) 386, N : 4 m.
i Ayscoughfee Hall, Churchgate ☎ 5468.
London 106 – **Leicester 51** – Lincoln 44 – **Nottingham 54.**

White Hart (T.H.F.), Market Pl., PE11 1SU, ☎ 5668 – TV wc P.
M a la carte 4.10/5.25 **st.** 1.50 – **28 rm** 8.50/17.00 **st.**

Cley Hall, 22 High St., PE11 1TX, ☎ 5157, – P
closed Sunday, 2 weeks mid June and Bank Holiday Mondays – **M** (lunch by arrangement) a la carte 3.80/5.55 1.50.

Isobel's Pantry, 4 Church Gate, PE11 2PB, ☎ 2193 – P
closed Sunday and Monday – **M** a la carte 4.25/6.65 1.00.

AUSTIN Albion St. ☎ 4445
AUSTIN-MORRIS-MG Whaplode Drive ☎ 265
AUSTIN-MORRIS-MG-ROVER-TRIUMPH-WOLSELEY Pinchbeck Rd ☎ 3651
CHRYSLER-SIMCA Swan St. ☎ 2893
DAF, VOLVO High Rd ☎ 040 66 (Moulton) 307
FORD St. Johns Rd ☎ 3671
RENAULT 24/40 Commercial Rd ☎ 3991
VAUXHALL Pinchbeck Rd ☎ 3391

SPELDHURST Kent – see Royal Tunbridge Wells.

SPROTBROUGH South Yorks. – see Doncaster.

STAFFORD Staffs. 986 ㉗ – pop. 55,001 – ☎ 0785.
See : High House* 16C – St. Mary's Church (Norman font*). **Envir. :** Eccleshall (Parish church* 12C) NW : 7 m.
i Borough Hall, Eastgate St. ☎ 3181.
London 142 – **Birmingham 26** – Derby 32 – Shrewsbury 31 – **Stoke-on-Trent 17.**

Tillington Hall, Eccleshall Rd, ST16 1JJ, NW : 1 ½ m. on A 5013 ☎ 53531, – TV wc P.
M approx. 3.15 **st.** 1.30 – **63 rm** 12.50/14.75 **st.**

Vine, Salter St., ST16 2JU, ☎ 51071 – P – **23 rm.**

Swan, 46 Greengate St., ST16 2JA, ☎ 58142 – P
M (grill rest. only) approx. 3.20 **st.** 1.35 – **30 rm** 7.05/14.40 **st.**

Romaline, 73 Wolverhampton Rd, ST17 4AW, ☎ 54100 – P
15 rm 7.00/15.00 **s.**

at Ranton W : 7 ¼ m. by A 518 – ✉ Ranton – ☎ 078 575 Seighford :

Yew Tree, Long Compton, ST18 9JT, S : 1 m. ☎ 278, – P
closed Sunday dinner, Monday and 26 December – **M** a la carte 3.45/6.85 1.30.

ALFA-ROMEO, BMW, FIAT Walton-on-the-Hill ☎ 61293
AUSTIN-DAIMLER-JAGUAR-MG-ROVER-TRIUMPH Lichfield Rd ☎ 51366
CHRYSLER-SIMCA Milford ☎ 61226
DATSUN Wolverhampton Rd ☎ 2407
FORD Eccleshall Rd ☎ 51331
MORRIS-MG-WOLSELEY Friars Terrace ☎ 3131
MORRIS-MG-ROVER-TRIUMPH-WOLSELEY Silkmore Lane ☎ 51415
OPEL Sandon Rd ☎ 51641
PEUGEOT Newport Rd ☎ 51084
RENAULT Wolverhampton Rd ☎ 52118
SAAB Yarlet Bank Sce Sta. ☎ 088 97 (Sandon) 248

STAINES Surrey 986 ⑧ and ㊱ – pop. 56,712 – ☎ 0784.
Laleham Reach, Chertsey ☎ 093 28 (Chertsey) 62188, S : 2 m.
London 26 – Reading 25.

Pack Horse (Anchor), Thames St., TW18 4SF, ☎ 54221, Group Telex 27120, – TV P.
M approx. 3.25 **t.** 1.00 – **13 rm** 9.90/15.40 **st.**

Swan with rm, The Hythe, TW18 3JB, ☎ 52494, – P
M a la carte 3.00/4.10 **st.** 1.25 – **7 rm** 7.75/9.50 **st.**

AUSTIN-DAIMLER-MORRIS-MG-ROVER-TRIUMPH-WOLSELEY, CHRYSLER 48-54 London Rd ☎ 55301
FORD 268 London Rd ☎ 51143
MORRIS-MG-ROVER-TRIUMPH 30-38 Church St. ☎ 55281

STAINTON Cumbria – pop. 500 – ✉ ☎ 0768 Penrith.
London 291 – **Carlisle 25** – Keswick 16.

Limes Country, Redhills, CA11 0DT, S : 1 m. off A 592 ☎ 3343, – P
closed 2 weeks November and Christmas Day – **8 rm** 4.75/7.50.

STALISFIELD GREEN Kent – see Ashford.

STAMFORD Lincs. 986 ㉘ – pop. 14,662 – ☎ 0780.
See : Burghley House** 16C (paintings : Heaven Room***) *AC.*
ℹ Council Offices, St. Mary's Hill ☎ 4444.
London 92 – **Leicester 31** – Lincoln 50 – **Nottingham 45.**

- **George,** 71 St. Martins, PE9 2LB, ☎ 2101, « 17C coaching inn with walled monastic garden » – TV P.
  closed Christmas Day – **M** a la carte 5.05/7.30 **s.** 1.80 – **47 rm** 10.00/19.00 **st.**
- **Crown,** All Saints Pl., PE9 2AG, ☎ 3136 – TV P
  M 2.75/4.00 **st.** 1.60 – **18 rm** 8.50/12.00 **s.**

at Collyweston SW : 3 ¾ m. on A 43 – ✉ Stamford – ☎ 078 083 Duddington :

- Cavalier, PE9 3PQ, ☎ 288 – TV P
  8 rm.

AUSTIN-MORRIS-MG 36/40 St. Pauls St. ☎ 3174
CHRYSLER 69 Scotgate ☎ 3323
FORD Station Rd ☎ 2941
PEUGEOT 53/56 Scotgate ☎ 4003
ROVER-TRIUMPH Wharf Rd ☎ 2561
TOYOTA Collyweston ☎ 078 083 (Duddington) 271
VAUXHALL Rock House, Scotgate ☎ 51826

STANDISH Lancs. 986 ⑤ – pop. 11,174 – ✉ Wigan – ☎ 0257.
London 210 – **Liverpool 22** – **Manchester 21** – Preston 15.

- **Cassinelli's Almond Brook Motor Inn,** WN6 0SR, W : 1 m. on B 5239 ☎ 421504 – TV wc P.
  M approx. 4.00 **st.** 1.80 – **21 rm** 12.00/15.00 **st.** – P 18.20 **st.**

STANTON WICK Avon – pop. 700 – ✉ Pensford – ☎ 076 18 Compton Dando.
London 129 – Bath 10 – **Bristol 8** – Taunton 41.

- XX **Carpenters Arms,** BS18 4BX, off A 368 ☎ 202 – P
  closed Sunday dinner and Monday – **M** a la carte 3.85/6.60.

STAVERTON Devon – pop. 551 – ✉ Totnes – ☎ 080 426.
London 226 – Exeter 26 – **Plymouth 24** – Torquay 13.

- **Sea Trout Inn,** TQ9 6PA, ☎ 274 – P
  M (grill rest. only) 4.00/6.00 1.75 – **6 rm** 7.50/15.00.

STEETON North Yorks. – pop. 58 – ✉ Keighley – ☎ 0535.
London 211 – Bradford 13 – Skipton 6.5.

- XX **Curregate** with rm, Skipton Rd, BD20 6PE, ☎ 53204, Italian rest., – wc P
  M a la carte 4.45/6.70 **t.** 1.50 – **8 rm** 9.50/16.00 **s.**

STEPPINGLEY Beds. – pop. 214 – ✉ ☎ 052 57 Flitwick.
London 48 – Bedford 12 – Luton 13.

- XX **French Horn,** MK45 5BA, ☎ 2051 – P
  closed Sunday dinner and Monday – **M** a la carte 2.40/5.90 1.20.

STEVENAGE Herts. 986 ㉜ – pop. 67,016 – ☎ 0438.
Envir. : Knebworth House (furniture*) S : 3 m.
London 36 – Bedford 25 – **Cambridge 27.**

- **Grampian,** The Forum, SG1 1EJ, ☎ 50661, Telex 825697 – TV wc.
  M 3.00/4.00 **s.** 1.75 – **100 rm** 10.50/15.00 **s.** – P 14.95/15.95 **s.**
- Cromwell, High St., Old Town, SG1 3AZ, ☎ 59111, – TV wc wc P.
  57 rm.

at Broadwater S : 1 ½ m. on B 197 – ✉ ☎ 0438 Stevenage :

- **Roebuck Inn** (T.H.F.), SG2 8DS, ☎ 4171 – TV wc P
  M a la carte 4.50/5.75 **st.** 1.50 – **40 rm** 12.50/18.00 **st.**

ALFA-ROMEO, BMW Hertford Rd, Broadwater ☎ 51565
AUSTIN-JAGUAR-MORRIS-MG-ROVER-TRIUMPH-WOLSELEY 146 High St. ☎ 2400
AUSTIN-MG-WOLSELEY Shephall Way ☎ 3245
CHRYSLER-SIMCA, VW, AUDI-NSU 1 London Rd ☎ 54691
DATSUN Broadwater Crescent ☎ 53642
FORD Gunnels Wood Rd ☎ 3636
VAUXHALL 124/6 High St. ☎ 51113

STEYNING West Sussex – pop. 3,284 – ☎ 0903.
See : St. Andrew's Church (the nave* 12C).
London 52 – **Brighton 12** – Worthing 10.

- XXX **Springwells** with rm, High St., BN4 3GG, ☎ 812446, – TV wc P
  M *(closed Sunday dinner)* a la carte 4.85/6.25 1.20 – **5 rm** 8.50/11.50.

at Bramber SE : ¾ m. on A 283 – ✉ ☎ 0903 Steyning :

- XXX **Old Tollgate,** The Street, BN4 3WE, ☎ 813362, « Tasteful decor », – P
  closed Sunday dinner, Monday and January – **M** a la carte 6.30/8.45 **t.** 1.35.

AUSTIN-MORRIS-MG-ROVER-TRIUMPH-WOLSELEY 66 High St. ☎ 812202

STOCK Essex – pop. 1,798 – Ingatestone – 0277.

London 30 – Chelmsford 6 – Southend-on-Sea 20.

Stockpot, 61-63 Mill Rd, CM4 9NL, 840278 –
closed Monday – **M** (dinner only and Sunday lunch) a la carte 4.50/7.70 **s.** 1.20.

STOCKBRIDGE Hants. 986 ㉟ – pop. 431 – 026 481.

London 75 – Salisbury 14 – Winchester 9.

Carbery, Salisbury Hill, on A 30 771, –
closed Christmas – **11 rm** 4.50/9.00.

MORRIS-MG High St. 711
SAAB Middle Wallop 026 478 (Middle Wallop) 460

STOCKPORT Greater Manchester 986 ⑤ and ㉗ – pop. 139,644 – 061 Manchester.

Envir.: Bramall Hall* (14C-16C) *AC*, S: 1 ½ m. – Lyme Park* (16C-18C) *AC*, SE: 4 ½ m.

Heaton Mersey 432 2134 – Club House, Hazel Grove 483 4217, S: 3 m.

9 Princes St. 480 0315.

London 201 – Liverpool 42 – Manchester 6 – Sheffield 37 – Stoke-on-Trent 34.

Alma Lodge (Embassy), 149 Buxton Rd, SK2 6EL, 483 4431 – wc .
closed Christmas – **M** 2.90/3.30 **st.** 1.50 – **72 rm** 11.50/14.80 **st.**

AUSTIN-MG-WOLSELEY Buxton Rd 480 4244
AUSTIN-MG-WOLSELEY 91 Heaton Moor Rd 432 9416
BMW, DAF, SAAB 31/33 Buxton Rd 483 6271
CHRYSLER-SIMCA 110 Buxton Rd 480 0831
CITROEN 309 Manchester Rd 432 6403
DAIMLER-JAGUAR-ROVER-TRIUMPH Town Hall Sq. 480 7966
DATSUN Lancashire Hill 480 4423
FIAT Heaton Lane 480 6661
FORD Adswood Rd 480 0211
MORRIS-MG Wellington Rd North 432 6201
RENAULT 79 Lancashire Hill 480 9528
RENAULT 57 London Rd 483 0621
VAUXHALL Wellington Rd South 480 6146
VAUXHALL 398 Wellington Rd North 432 3232

STOCKTON-ON-TEES Cleveland 986 ⑲ – pop. 81,274 – 0642.

Yarm Rd, Eaglescliffe 780098, S: 3 m.

London 251 – Leeds 61 – Middlesbrough 4.

Swallow (Swallow), 10 John Walker Sq., TS18 1AQ, 69721, Group Telex 53168 –
.
123 rm.

at Eaglescliffe S: 3 ½ m. on A 19 – 0642 Stockton-on-Tees:

Parkmore, 636 Yarm Rd, TS16 0DH, 780324, – wc wc
26 rm.

MICHELIN Branch, Clarence Row, TS18 2HD, 64650 and 63207.

AUDI-NSU, MERCEDES-BENZ 45 Norton Rd 65361
AUSTIN-MG-WOLSELEY Yarm Lane 63194
AUSTIN-MG-WOLSELEY Bishop St. 65351
CHRYSLER-SIMCA Church Rd 612621
DAF Billingham Rd 551541
DAF 100 Yarm Lane 611544
DATSUN Church Rd 65691
FORD 87 Oxbridge Lane 65471
JAGUAR-ROVER-RANGE-ROVER-TRIUMPH 47/55 Yarm Lane 62643
MORRIS-MG 502/6 Yarm Rd, Eaglescliffe 63513
MORRIS-MG-WOLSELEY 102 Yarm Lane 63161
OPEL 318 Bishopton Rd West 65007
PEUGEOT 5 Parkfield Rd 68467
RENAULT Skinner St. 66681
SAAB Chapel St. 69781
TOYOTA 336 Norton Rd 553003
VAUXHALL Portrack Lane 64386
VAUXHALL Boathouse Lane 67804
VOLVO Prince Regent St. 63251

STOKE GABRIEL Devon – see Totnes.

STOKE GOLDINGTON Bucks. – pop. 431 – Newport Pagnell – 090 855.

London 63 – Bedford 17 – Northampton 10.

Hollow Tree Farm, High St., MK16 8NP, 256, –
closed Sunday, Monday and last 2 weeks July – **M** a la carte 3.25/5.20.

STOKE HOLY CROSS Norfolk – see Norwich.

STOKE MANDEVILLE Bucks. – see Aylesbury.

STOKE-ON-TRENT Staffs. 986 ⑨ and ㉗ – pop. 265,258 – ☎ 0782.

See : Gladstone Pottery Museum* *AC.* V **M. Envir. :** Little Moreton Hall ** (16C) *AC,* NW: 8 m. on A 34 U.

18 Trentham Park, ☎ 657315, S: 3 m. V.

i Hanley Library, Bethesda St., Hanley ☎ 263568/21242/25108.

London 160 – Birmingham 45 – Leicester 57 – Liverpool 58 – Manchester 38 – Nottingham 50 – Sheffield 60.

STOKE-ON-TRENT NEWCASTLE-UNDER-LYME BUILT UP AREA

0 – 2 km / 0 – 1 mile

Street	Ref
Alexandra Road	U 3
Bedford Road	U 5
Christchurch Street	V 10
Church Lane	U 12
Cobridge Road	U 15
Davenport Street	U 16
Deansgate	V 18
Elder Road	U 20
Etruria Vale Road	U 22
Hanley Road	U 24
Heron Street	V 27
High Street	U 28
King William Street	U 32
Manor Street	V 36
Mayne Street	V 37
Moorland Road	U 38
Park Hall Road	V 40
Porthill Road	U 45
Scotia Road	U 46
Snow Hill	U 48
Stoke Road	U 51
Strand (The)	V 52
Victoria Park Road	U 56
Watlands View	U 57

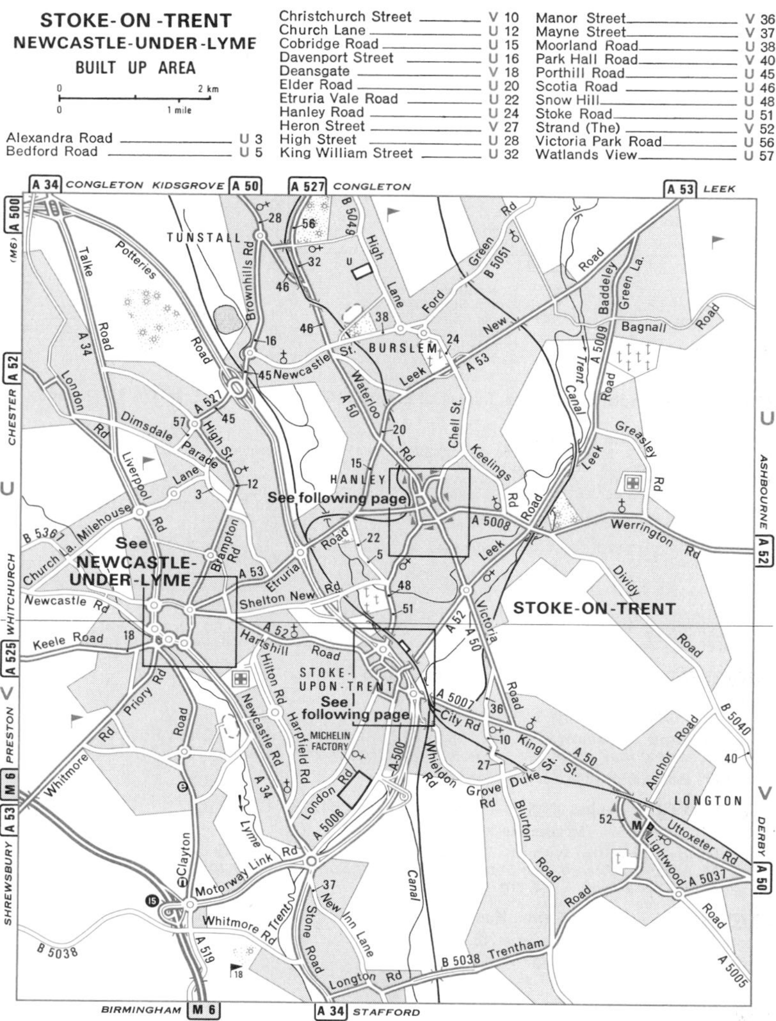

🏨 **North Stafford** (T.H.F.), Station Rd, ST4 2AE, ☎ 48501, Telex 36287 – **M** 2.95/4.25 **st.** 0.75 – 2.00 – **70 rm** 12.50/19.50 **st.** X **a**

at Hanley NW: 2 m. on A 5006 – ✉ ☎ 0782 Stoke-on-Trent :

🏨 **Grand** (T.H.F.), 66 Trinity St., ST1 5NB, ☎ 22361 – wc **M** 3.30 **st.** 1.50 – **96 rm** 9.50/19.00 **st.** Y **c**

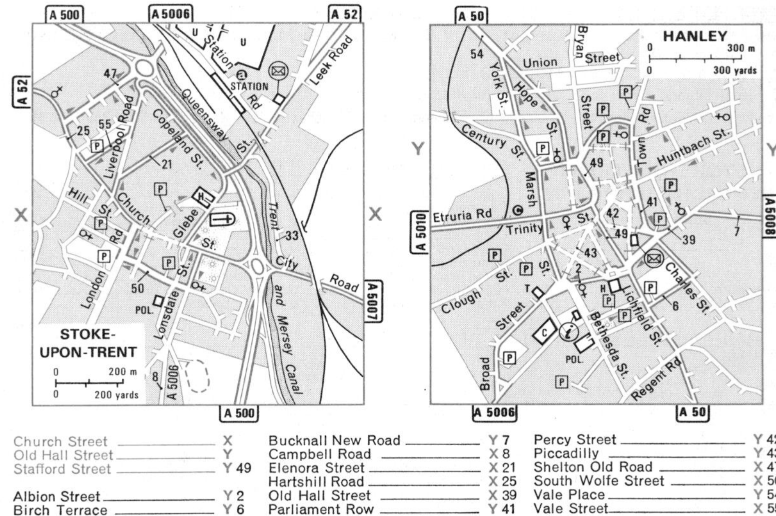

Church Street ______ X
Old Hall Street ______ Y
Stafford Street ______ Y 49
Albion Street ______ Y 2
Birch Terrace ______ Y 6
Bucknall New Road ______ Y 7
Campbell Road ______ X 8
Elenora Street ______ X 21
Hartshill Road ______ X 25
Old Hall Street ______ X 39
Parliament Row ______ Y 41
Percy Street ______ Y 42
Piccadilly ______ Y 43
Shelton Old Road ______ X 47
South Wolfe Street ______ X 50
Vale Place ______ Y 54
Vale Street ______ X 55

MICHELIN Branch, Jamage Rd, Industrial Estate, Talke Pits, ST7 1QF, ☎ 078 16 (Kidsgrove) 71211/2/3/4.

ASTON MARTIN Wharf St. ☎ 45691
AUSTIN-MORRIS-MG Endon ☎ 078 250 (Endon) 3160
AUSTIN-MORRIS-MG-DAIMLER-JAGUAR-ROVER-TRIUMPH, ROOLS ROYCE Victoria Rd, Fenton ☎ 4811
AUSTIN-MORRIS-MG-ROVER-TRIUMPH Clough St. ☎ 23841
AUSTIN-MORRIS-MG-ROVER-TRIUMPH Broad St. ☎ 25523
AUSTIN-MORRIS-MG-WOLSELEY 35 Lawton Rd ☎ 093 63 (Alsager) 2146
AUSTIN-MG-WOLSELEY Lee New Rd, Hanley ☎ 29985
AUSTIN-MG-WOLSELEY 292 Waterloo Rd, Cobridge ☎ 22210
BMW, PEUGEOT, VAUXHALL Duke St., Fenton ☎ 315119
CHRYSLER-SIMCA Leek Rd ☎ 24371
CHRYSLER-SIMCA Newcastle Rd ☎ 614621
CHRYSLER-SIMCA Lightwood Rd ☎ 317124
CITROEN Uttoxeter Rd ☎ 312235
DAF King St. ☎ 311111
DATSUN Providence Sq. ☎ 23451
FIAT Victoria Rd, Hanley ☎ 22875
FIAT Lightwood Rd, Longton ☎ 319212
FORD King St. ☎ 33051
FORD Clough St. ☎ 29591
MORRIS-MG Trentham ☎ 657348
MORRIS-MG-WOLSELEY Victoria Rd ☎ 45551
OPEL Clayton Lane ☎ 613061
RENAULT Werrington Rd, Bucknall ☎ 25406
SAAB High Lane ☎ 84527
TOYOTA Leek Rd ☎ 264888
VAUXHALL Victoria Rd, Fenton ☎ 46431
VW, AUDI-NSU Botteslow St., Hanley ☎ 29966

STOKE POGES Bucks. – pop. 4,898 – ☎ 028 16 Fulmer.

⛳9 ☎ 3332.

London 32 – Oxford 38 – Slough 3.

XX **Fox and Pheasant,** SL2 4EZ, on B 416, Slough to Gerrards Cross Rd, ☎ 2047 – Ⓟ
closed Sunday dinner, Monday and Bank Holidays – **M** a la carte 4.25/6.80 **t.**

RENAULT Bells Hill ☎ 028 14 (Farnham Common) 2365

STOKESLEY Cleveland 986 ⑲ – pop. 3,007 – ☎ 0642.

London 247 – Leeds 57 – Middlesbrough 9 – York 44.

X **Golden Lion Inn** with rm, 27 High St. ☎ 710265 – wc Ⓟ
M *(open 27 March-mid September) (closed Sunday dinner to non-residents)* a la carte 4.40/5.85 🍾 1.30 – **13 rm** ☕ 5.50/11.00.

STONE Glos. – pop. 555 (inc. Ham) – ✉ Berkeley – ☎ 045 48 Falfield.

London 130 – Bristol 17 – Gloucester 18.

Elms, ☎ 279, – Ⓟ
10 rm ☕ 5.25/10.50 **s.**

STONE Heref. and Worc. – see Kidderminster.

STONEDGE Derbs. – see Chesterfield.

STONEHENGE Wilts. 986 ㉟.

See : Megalithic Monument*** *AC.*

Hotels and restaurants see : Amesbury **E: 2 m.**
Salisbury **S: 10 m.**

STONEY CROSS Hants. – pop. 146 – ✉ Lyndhurst – ☎ 042 127 Cadnam.
London 94 – Bournemouth 19 – Southampton 12.

- **Compton Arms,** Ringwood Rd, SO4 7GN, ☎ 2134, – wc ☎ P
M a la carte 5.60/7.90 **st.** – 2.00 – **12 rm** 7.75/14.00 **st.** – P 16.30 **st.**

STONY STRATFORD Bucks. 986 ㉜ – pop. 4.335 (inc. Calverton) – ✉ ☎ 0908 Milton Keynes.
London 63 – Bedford 19 – Northampton 17 – Oxford 33.

- **Cock,** 72 High St., MK11 1AH, ☎ 562109 – P
M 3.25/4.35 – **10 rm** 8.00/14.00.
- Old George, High St., MK11 1AH, ☎ 562181.

STORRINGTON West Sussex – pop. 3,277 – ☎ 090 66.
Envir.: Parham House* (Elizabethan) *AC*, W: **1** ½ m.
London 54 – Brighton 20 – Portsmouth 36 – Worthing 9.

- **Manley's,** Manleys Hill, RH20 4BT, ☎ 2331 – P
closed Sunday dinner, Monday, 7 January-17 February and Bank Holidays except Christmas Day – **M** a la carte 4.95/6.75 **t.** 1.10.

MORRIS-MG-WOLSELEY The Square ☎ 3282

STOURBRIDGE West Midlands 986 ⑫ and ㉛ – pop. 55,660 – ☎ 038 43.
London 147 – Birmingham 14 – Wolverhampton 10 – Worcester 21.

- Talbot, High St., DY8 1DW, ☎ 4350 – wc P.
20 rm.
- **Bell,** Market St., DY8 1DW, ☎ 5641 – P
M *(closed Sunday dinner)* 2.00/3.50 **t.** 1.00 – **20 rm** 8.50/14.50 **t.**
- **The Limes,** 260 Hagley Rd, Pedmore, DY9 0RW, ☎ 056 286 (Hagley) 2689, – P
closed 23 December-1 January – **10 rm** 6.50/11.00 **st.**

at Kinver W: **5** ½ **m. by A 458 and A 449** – ✉ **Stourbridge** – ☎ **038 483 Kinver:**

- **Whittington Inn,** DY7 6NY, E: 1 ½ m. on A 449 ☎ 2110, « Part 14C manor house », – P
closed Sunday – **M** (bar lunch) approx. 5.50 1.50.

ALFA-ROMEO, BEDFORD, OPEL, VAUXHALL 131/135 Hagley Rd, Oldswinford ☎ 3031
DAIMLER-MORRIS-MG Stourbridge Rd, Lye ☎ 038 482 (Lye) 2788
FORD Hagley Rd ☎ 3131
CITROEN Enville St. ☎ 77272
OPEL The Hayes, Lye ☎ 038 482 (Lye) 3001
PEUGEOT High St., Amblecote ☎ 3158
RENAULT Norton Rd ☎ 36655

STOURPORT-ON-SEVERN Heref. and Worc. 986 ㉛ – pop. 20,100 – ☎ 029 93.
London 137 – Birmingham 21 – Worcester 12.

- **Swan** (Ansells), High St., DY13 8BX, ☎ 2050 – wc P
M *(closed Sunday dinner)* approx. 2.35 **st.** 1.80 – **33 rm** 9.25/14.15 **st.**

FORD Vale Rd ☎ 2304

STOW-ON-THE-WOLD Glos. 986 ㉛ – pop. 1,737 – ☎ 0451.
Envir.: Chastleton House** (Elizabethan) *AC*, NE: **8** m.
London 86 – Birmingham 44 – Gloucester 27 – Oxford 30.

- **Stow Lodge,** The Square, GL54 1AB, ☎ 30485, – TV wc P
March-December – **M** (bar lunch) approx. 4.25 **s.** – **17 rm** 15.00/30.00 **s.**
- **Unicorn** (Crest), Sheep St., GL54 1HQ, ☎ 30257 – wc P
M (buffet lunch) a la carte 3.35/5.55 **s.** 1.55 – **19 rm** 9.50/16.00 **s.**
- **Talbot** (Crest), The Square, GL54 1BQ, ☎ 30631 – wc P
M 2.90/6.30 **s.** 1.55 – **36 rm** 9.50/16.00 **s.**
- **Royalist,** Digbeth St., GL54 1BN, ☎ 30670 – wc wc P
M (bar lunch) a la carte 3.75/5.90 **s.** 1.35 – **13 rm** 6.60/15.40 **s.**
- **King's Arms,** The Square, GL54 1AF, ☎ 30602 – P
March-October – **M** (dinner only) a la carte 3.00/4.50 1.10 – **9 rm** 6.30/12.60 **st.**
- **Fosse Manor** with rm, Fosse Way, GL54 1JX, S: 1 ¼ m. on A 429 ☎ 30354, – wc wc P
M a la carte 4.00/5.75 1.60 – **19 rm** 9.50/15.50.
- **Rafters,** Park St., GL54 1AG, ☎ 30200
closed Sunday dinner, Monday, Sunday lunch from October to March, 24 December, Bank Holidays and January – **M** a la carte 4.95/6.00 **t.** 1.45.

at Upper Slaughter SW: **3** ¼ **m. off A 436** – ✉ ☎ **0451 Bourton-on-the-Water:**

- **Lords of the Manor** , GL54 2JD, ☎ 20243, « Country house, tasteful decor », , park – wc ☎ P
M a la carte 4.60/5.55 1.45 – **12 rm** 20.50.

P.T.O. ⟶

at Lower Swell W : 1 ¼ m. on A 436 – ✉ ☎ 0451 Stow-on-the-Wold :

✕ **Old Farmhouse** with rm, GL54 1LF, ☎ 30232, 🚗 – Ⓟ
closed 25 December-mid January – **M** *(closed Sunday dinner and Monday lunch to non-residents)* (buffet lunch) approx. 5.50 **st.** 🍾 1.20 – **5 rm** ☕ 9.40/15.70 **st.**

SAAB Well Lane ☎ 30226

STRATFORD-ON-AVON Warw. 986 ㉛ – pop. 19,452 – ☎ 0789.

See : Shakespeare's birthplace* (16C) *AC* A **A** – Hall's Croft* (16C) *AC* A **B** – Anne Hathaway's cottage* *AC*, W : by Shottery Road A – Holy Trinity Church* 14C-15C A **D. Envir. :** Upton House (pictures***, porcelain**) SE : 15 m. by A 422 B – Charlecote Park (castle 16C : interior*) *AC*, NE : 5 m. by B 4086 B.

⛳18 E : by Tiddington Rd B ☎ 2669.

i Judith Shakespeare House, 1 High St. ☎ 3127/66185/66175.

London 96 – Birmingham 23 – Coventry 18 – Oxford 40.

STRATFORD-ON-AVON

0 300 m
0 300 yards

Bridge Street B 8
Henley Street A 29
High Street A 31
Sheep Street AB 35
Wood Street A 47

Benson Road B 3
Bridge Foot B 6
Chapel Lane A 13
Church Street A 16
College Lane A 19
Ely Street A 22
Evesham Place A 24
Greenhill Street A 27
Guild Street A 28
Scholars Lane A 33
Tiddington Road B 38
Trinity Street A 40
Waterside B 43
Windsor Street A 45

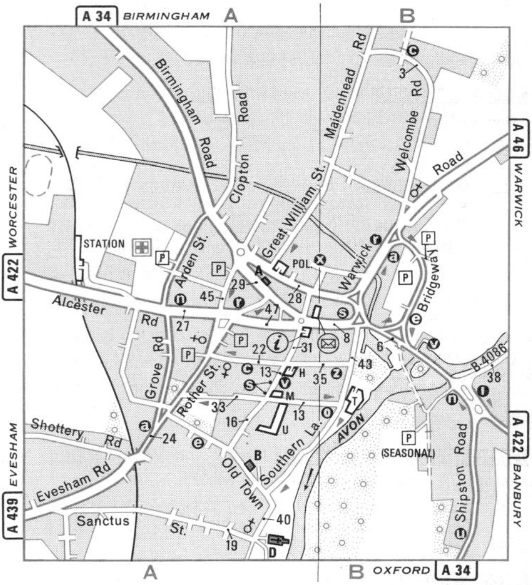

For maximum information from town plans : Consult the conventional signs key, p. 19.

Stratford-on-Avon Hilton, Bridgefoot, CV37 6YR, ☎ 67511, Telex 311127, 🚗 – 🛗 📺 ♿ Ⓟ. 🏃 B **e**
M a la carte 6.75/9.10 **t.** 🍾 2.10 – ☕ 2.50 – **253 rm** 16.10/20.40 **t.**

Welcombe (B.T.H.) 🐎, Warwick Rd, CV37 0NR, NE : 1 ½ m. on A 46 ☎ 3611, Telex 31347, ≤, « 19 C mansion in own grounds », ⛳9, 🚗, park – 📺 ♿ Ⓟ. 🏃 on A 46 B
M approx. 5.50 **st.** 🍾 1.25 – **90 rm** ☕ 25.00/38.00 **st.**

Shakespeare (T.H.F.), Chapel St., CV37 6ER, ☎ 3631, Telex 311181, « Part 16C house » – 🛗 📺 Ⓟ. 🏃 A **v**
M 3.50/3.75 – ☕ 2.00 – **66 rm** 13.00/19.50 **st.**

Alveston Manor (T.H.F.), Clopton Bridge, CV37 7HP, ☎ 4581, Telex 31324, 🚗 – 📺 Ⓟ. 🏃 B **i**
M 3.30/3.50 **st.** 🍾 1.50 – ☕ 2.00 – **112 rm** 13.80/18.50 **st.**

Falcon (County), Chapel St., CV37 6HA, ☎ 5777, 🚗 – 🛗 📺 Ⓟ. 🏃 A **s**
M approx. 4.25 **st.** 🍾 1.20 – **68 rm** ☕ 14.40/20.70 **s.**

Swan's Nest (T.H.F.), Bridgefoot, CV37 7LT, ☎ 66761, Telex 31419, 🚗 – 📺 Ⓟ. 🏃 B **n**
M 4.35/4.50 **st.** 🍾 1.50 – **71 rm** ☕ 11.00/20.00 **st.**

White Swan (T.H.F.), Rother St., CV37 6NH, ☎ 3606 – 📺 🛁wc ☎ A **r**
M 3.00/3.50 **st.** 🍾 1.50 – **55 rm** ☕ 9.50/17.50 **st.**

Arden, 44 Waterside, CV37 6BA, ☎ 3874, 🚗 – 🛁wc Ⓟ B **o**
M 3.50/4.25 **st.** 🍾 1.30 – **60 rm** ☕ 9.00/20.50 **st.**

Haytor 🐎, Avenue Rd, CV37 6UX, ☎ 3420, 🚗 – 🛁wc 🚿wc Ⓟ B **c**
closed 23 to 29 December – **M** *(25 March-22 December)* approx. 3.50 **s.** 🍾 1.10 – **20 rm** ☕ 7.70/16.50 **s.**

Grosvenor House (Interchange), 12 Warwick Rd, CV37 6YT, ☎ 69213, Telex 311699, – TV ⇌wc ⋔wc ☎ Ⓟ. B r
M 3.20/3.60 **s.** 1.10 – **48 rm** 9.00/19.00 **s.** – P 14.50/16.50 **st.**

Red Horse (Norfolk Cap.), Bridge St., CV37 6AE, ☎ 3211, Group Telex 23241 – ⇌wc ☎ Ⓟ. B s
M (grill rest. only) a la carte 3.25/5.40 **st.** – **60 rm** 9.10/19.90 **st.**

Stratheden, 5 Chapel St., CV37 6EP, ☎ 2837 A s
closed 2 weeks Christmas-1 January – **10 rm** 5.00/12.00.

Grosvenor Villa, 9 Evesham Place, CV37 6HT, ☎ 66192 A a
7 rm 4.00/8.00 **st.**

The Fold, Payton St., CV37 6UA, ☎ 2493, – Ⓟ AB x
closed 2 January-mid March – **24 rm.**

Marlyn, 3 Chestnut Walk, CV37 6HG, ☎ 3752 A e
closed Christmas – **8 rm** 5.50/11.00 **st.**

Bradbourne, 44 Shipston Rd S: ½ m. on A 34 ☎ 4178, by A 34 B
8 rm 4·25/8.50 **st.**

XX **Le Provençal** with rm, 121 Shipston Rd, CV37 7LW, S: ¾ m. on A 34 ☎ 3906, French rest. – Ⓟ
March-November – **M** *(closed Sunday and Monday)* a la carte 4.70/5.35 **s.** 1.50 – **11 rm** 4.50/9.00. B u

XX Giovanni, 8 Ely St., CV37 6LW, ☎ 3528, Italian rest. A c

XX **Piper at the Gates of Dawn,** Stratford Marine, Clopton Bridge ☎ 69821, ≤ river Avon, « Floating restaurant », English rest. – Ⓟ B v
Sailings : lunch 1.00 daily, dinner 7.30, 8.30 and 9.30 p.m. – **M** a la carte 5.35/6.25 1.60.

X **Christophi's,** 21-23 Sheep St., CV37 6EF, ☎ 3546, Greek rest. B z
closed Sunday – **M** a la carte 3.50/4.25 1.30.

X **Buccaneer** (Wayside Hotel), 11 Warwick Rd, CV37 6YW, ☎ 2550 – Ⓟ B a
closed Monday and Bank Holidays – **M** (dinner only) a la carte 3.80/5.85 **s.** 1.55.

X **Marianne,** 3 Greenhill St., CV37 6LF, ☎ 3563, French rest. A n
closed Sunday, 12 October and Bank Holidays – **M** a la carte 3.85/6.85 1.30.

AUSTIN-DAIMLER-JAGUAR-MORRIS-MG-ROVER-TRIUMPH Birmingham Rd ☎ 68121
FIAT Western Rd ☎ 3532
MORRIS-MG-WOLSELEY Waterside ☎ 3801
PEUGEOT Eversley Garage, Alderminster ☎ 078 987 (Alderminster) 331
RENAULT Western Rd ☎ 67911
VOLVO Western Rd ☎ 2468
VAUXHALL Rother St. ☎ 66254

STRATTON Glos. – see Cirencester.

STRATTON ST. MARGARET Wilts. – see Swindon.

STREET Somerset 986 ㉟ – pop. 8,143 – 0458.
London 138 – Bristol 28 – Taunton 20.

Wessex, High St., BA16 0EF, ☎ 43383 – TV ⇌wc ☎ Ⓟ.
M (bar lunch) approx. 3.50 **s.** 1.25 – **46 rm** 8.00/13.50 **s.**

BEDFORD, VAUXHALL 189 High St. ☎ 42288
MORRIS-MG-ROVER-TRIUMPH Creeches Lane, Walton ☎ 2735

STREETLY West Midlands – see Birmingham.

STRETTON Cheshire – see Warrington.

STROUD Glos. 986 ㉛ – pop. 19,152 – 045 36.
Envir. : Severn Wildfowl Trust* *AC,* W: **11** m.
i Council Offices, High St. ☎ 4252.
London 113 – Bristol 30 – Gloucester 9.

Downfield, 134 Cainscross Rd, GL5 4HN, ☎ 4496 – Ⓟ
11 rm 5.00/10.00 **st.**

X **Mr. Baillie's,** 203 Slad Rd, GL5 1RL, NE: 1 m. on B 4070 ☎ 5331, – Ⓟ
closed Sunday dinner, Monday, Tuesday after Bank Holidays and 1 to 23 January – **M** approx. 5.60 **st.** 1.70.

at Brimscombe **SE: 2 ¼ m. on A 419 – ⊠ Stroud – 045 388 Brimscombe:**

Burleigh Court , GL5 2PF, SW: ½ m. off Burleigh Rd ☎ 3804, ≤, – ⋔wc Ⓟ
M 3.50/6.50 **st.** 0.90 – **11 rm** 10.00/15.50 **st.** – P 16.00/19.00 **st.**

at Rodborough **S: ¾ m. by A 46 – ⊠ Stroud – 045 387 Amberley:**

Bear, Rodborough Common, GL5 5DE, E: 1 ½ m. ☎ 3522, – TV ⇌wc ☎ Ⓟ
M a la carte 4.55/7.55 **st.** 1.40 – **30 rm** 12.50/19.50 **st.**

AUSTIN-MORRIS-MG-ROVER-TRIUMPH Caincross Rd ☎ 3671
CHRYSLER-SIMCA Windmill Rd, Minchinhampton ☎ 045 388 (Brimscombe) 3408
CHRYSLER-SIMCA Stonehouse ☎ 045 382 (Stonehouse) 2139
DATSUN Westword Rd, Ebley ☎ 4919
FORD London Rd ☎ 4311
OPEL, SAAB London Rd ☎ 2861
RENAULT London Rd ☎ 4203

STUDLAND Dorset – pop. 620 – ✉ Swanage – ☎ 092 944.

18, 9 ☎ 210.

London 130 – Bournemouth 22 – Dorchester 26.

Knoll House, BH19 3AH, ☎ 251, ≪, heated, 9, park – P
Easter-October – **M** approx. 4.60 **st.** 1.40 – **111 rm** 11.15/26.30 **st.**

Manor House , Studland Bay, BH19 3AU, ☎ 288, « Country house atmosphere », park – wc wc P
Easter-mid October – **M** 3.50/4.00 **t.** 1.25 – **15 rm** 6.60/14.00 **t.**

STURMINSTER NEWTON Dorset 986 ㉟ – pop. 2,111 – ☎ 0258.

London 123 – Bournemouth 30 – Bristol 49 – Salisbury 28 – Taunton 41.

XX **Plumber Manor** with rm, Hazelbury Bryan Rd, DT10 2AF, SW: 1 ¾ m. ☎ 72507, « Tastefully furnished country house », park – wc P
closed 1 to 15 November and February – **M** *(closed Sunday from November to March and Monday* (dinner only) 6.00/6.50 **t.** 1.40 – **6 rm** 12.00/18.00 **st.**

XX **Townhouse,** Church St., DT10 1DB, ☎ 72874
closed Sunday and Tuesday dinner – **M** (by arrangement) a la carte 4.40/5.10 **t.** 1.75.

AUSTIN-MG-WOLSELEY Station Rd ☎ 72303

SUDBURY Derbs. – pop. 868 – ✉ Derby – ☎ 028 372 Marchington.

See: Sudbury Hall** (17C) *AC.*

London 138 – Birmingham 33 – Derby 13 – Stoke-on-Trent 23.

Boar's Head Motel, Station Rd, DE6 5GX, S: 1 m. on A 515 ☎ 344 – wc P
M a la carte 3.65/4.95 **st.** 1.45 – 1.25 – **11 rm** 6.50/9.50 **s.**

Red Lion	Se il nome di albergo è stampato in carattere magro, chiedete arrivando le condizioni che vi saranno praticate.

SUDBURY Suffolk 986 ㉜ – pop. 8,166 – ☎ 078 73.

i Sudbury Library, Market Hill ☎ 72092/76029.

London 59 – Cambridge 37 – Colchester 15 – Ipswich 21.

Mill, Walnut Tree Lane, CO10 0BD, ☎ 75544, Telex 919161, ≤ – TV wc P.
M 3.00/3.50 **t.** 1.00 – **31 rm** 11.75/18.00 **t.** – P 12.00 **t.**

Four Swans, 10 North St., CO10 6RB, ☎ 72793 – wc P
M 2.25/2.75 **st.** 1.20 – 1.45 – **17 rm** 8.75/14.00 **st.**

at Great Cornard **S: 1 m. on A 133 – ✉ ☎ 078 73 Sudbury:**

Oriel Lodge, Kings Hill, CO10 0EH, ☎ 72456 – P
11 rm 5.90/11.80 **st.**

CHRYSLER Acton Sq. ☎ 72745
DAF, DATSUN Edgeworth Rd ☎ 73172
MORRIS-MG-WOLSELEY Station Rd ☎ 72321
PEUGEOT Cornard Rd ☎ 75621
SAAB Lavenham ☎ 228
VAUXHALL Cornard Rd ☎ 72301

SUNBURY-ON-THAMES Surrey 986 ⑧ – pop. 40,186 – ☎ 093 27.

London 23 – Reading 29.

XX **Castle,** 21 Thames St., TWX 5QF, ☎ 83647 – P
M 6.00/9.50 **t.**

SUNDERLAND Tyne and Wear 986 ⑲ – pop. 217,079 – ☎ 0783.

18 Coxgreen ☎ 078 324 (Hylton) 2518, W: 2 m. by A 183 A.

London 277 – Leeds 88 – Middlesbrough 29 – Newcastle-upon-Tyne 12.

Plans opposite

Seaburn (Swallow), Queen's Par., SR6 8DB, N: 2 ½ m. on A 183 ☎ 078 329 (Whitburn) 2041, Group Telex 53168, ≤ – TV wc P. A c
61 rm.

Mowbray Park (Thistle), Borough Rd, SR1 1PR, ☎ 78221 – TV wc . B a
60 rm.

Roker, Roker Terrace, CA13 9SS, ☎ 71786 – wc P A e
M (steak bar only) approx. 3.50 **t.** 1.50 – **48 rm** 7.05/14.40 **t.**

AUSTIN-MG-WOLSELEY 23 Roker Av. ☎ 70881
BMW, DATSUN, MERCEDES-BENZ Ryhope Rd ☎ 58225
CHRYSLER-SIMCA Newcastle Rd ☎ 78811
DAF Newcastle Rd ☎ 73204
DAIMLER-JAGUAR-MORRIS-MG-ROVER-TRIUMPH-WOLSELEY 190 Roker Av. ☎ 56221
FORD Trimdon St. ☎ 70491
OPEL Roker Baths Rd ☎ 74996
PEUGEOT Allison Rd, West Boldon ☎ 078 33 (Boldon) 2726
RENAULT Newcastle Rd ☎ 58225
SAAB Grangetown ☎ 73915
SAAB Toward Rd ☎ 77538
VAUXHALL Paley St. ☎ 42841
VOLVO North Hylton Rd ☎ 70314
VW, AUDI-NSU Blue Bell Corner Station Rd ☎ 40215

SUNDERLAND

Central Area .... B
Fawcett Street .... B
High Street West .... B 15
Holmeside .... B
John Street .... B 17

Albion Place .... B 2
Barnes Park Road .... A 3
Bedford Street .... B 4
Borough Road .... B 5
Bridge Street .... B 6
Charlton Road .... A 8
Chester Road .... B 10
Fulwell Road .... A 12
Green Terrace .... B 13
Harbour View .... A 14
Kayll Road .... A 18
New Durham Road .... B 19
Northern Way .... A 20
Ormonde Street .... A 21
Pallion Road .... A 22
Riverside Road .... A 23
Roker Terrace .... A 24
St. Luke's Terrace .... A 26
St. Mary's Way .... B 27
Shields Road .... A 29
Southwick Road .... B 30
Station Road .... A 32
Sunderland Road .... A 33
Trimdon Street .... A 35
Vine Place .... B 36

Plans de villes :
Les noms des principales voies commerçantes sont inscrits en rouge au début des légendes rues.

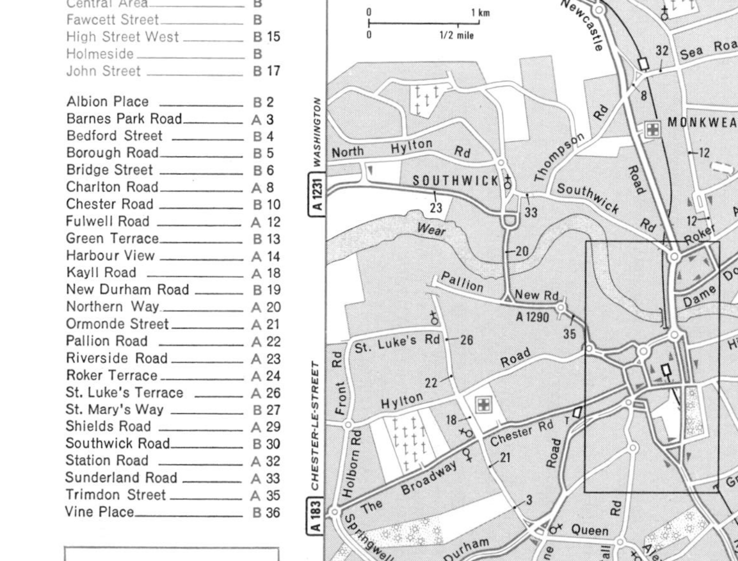

SUTTON BENGER Wilts. – pop. 542 – ✉ Chippenham – ☎ 0249 Seagry.
London 101 – Bath 18 – Bristol 26 – Swindon 16.

XXX **Bell House** with rm, SN15 4RE, ☎ 720401, – TV wc ☎ P
M a la carte 5.20/9.90 – 2.00 – **13 rm** 12.00/18.00.

SUTTON COLDFIELD West Midlands 986 ⑫ and ㉗ ㉛ – see Birmingham.

SWAFFHAM Norfolk 986 ㉘ – pop. 4,280 – ☎ 0760.
Envir.: Castle Acre (priory** ruins 11C-14C) *AC*, N: 4 m. – Oxburgh Hall* (15C) *AC*, SW: 7 ½ m.
London 97 – Cambridge 46 – King's Lynn 16 – Norwich 27.

George (Gd Met.), Station St., PE37 7LJ, ☎ 21238 – P
M approx. 3.50 **t.** 1.20 – **18 rm** 7.30/13.00 **t.**

VAUXHALL Lynn St. ☎ 21239

SWALLOWFIELD Berks. – pop. 1,864 – ✉ ☎ 0734 Reading.
London 49 – Reading 6.

XX **Mill House,** Basingstoke Rd, RG7 1PY, on A 33 ☎ 883124, – P
closed Sunday dinner and Christmas Day dinner – **M** a la carte 3.60/6.65 1.15.

SWANAGE Dorset 986 ㊴ – pop. 8,556 – ☎ 092 92.
Envir.: Corfe Castle* (Norman ruins) ≤* *AC*, NW: 6 m.
ℹ The White House, Shore Rd ☎ 2885.
London 130 – Bournemouth 22 – Dorchester 26 – Southampton 52.

The Pines, Burlington Rd, BH19 1LT, ☎ 2166, ≤ – lift wc P
M 3.50/4.00 1.10 – **50 rm** 7.00/16.00.

Ship, 23 High St., BH19 2LR, ☎ 2078
M approx. 2.75 **t.** 1.65 – **18 rm** 6.50/13.00 **t.**

Sefton, Gilbert Rd, BH19 1DU, ☎ 3469, – P
March-November – **14 rm** 7.15/15.45 **st.**

Suncliffe, 1 Burlington Rd, BH19 1LB, ☎ 3299, – P
season – **17 rm.**

Havenhurst, 3 Cranborne Rd, BH19 1EA, ☎ 4224 – P
closed 1 to 24 December – **16 rm** 5.50/10.50 **st.**

Boyne, 1 Cliffe Av., BH19 1LX, ☎ 2939 – P
March-October – **15 rm** 6.50/16.00.

X **Rif-Raf's Cauldron,** 5 High St., BH19 2LN, ☎ 2671
closed Sunday from October to March – **M** (dinner only from October to March) a la carte 2.65/4.10 1.15.

CHRYSLER 281 High St. ☎ 2877
ROVER-TRIUMPH 3 Courthill ☎ 2888
VAUXHALL Valley Rd ☎ 092 93 (Corfe Castle) 215

SWANBRIDGE South Glam. – see Penarth.

SWANLEY Kent – pop. 16,435 – ☎ 0322.
London 17 – Maidstone 19.

XX **Bull,** London Rd, Birchwood, BR8 7QB, ☎ 62086 – P
closed Sunday and Bank Holidays – **M** a la carte 4.10/6.15 1.40.

SWANSEA West Glam. 986 ㉟ – pop. 173,413 – ☎ 0792.
Envir.: Cefn Bryn (✻*** from the reservoir) W: 12 m. by A 4118 A – Oxwich Bay* SW: 10 m. by A 4118 A – **Exc.**: Rhossili (site and ≤***) W: 18 m. by A 4118 A.
18 Langland Bay, Mumbles ☎ 66023, W: 6 m. by A 4067 A – 18 Jersey Marine, Neath ☎ 0792 (Skewen) 812198, E: 3 ½ m. by A 483 A.
to Cork (B & I Line) 4-6 weekly (10 h).
ℹ Tourist Information Centre, Crumlin Burrows, Jersey Marine ☎ 462403/462498 – Oystermouth Square, The Mumbles ☎ 61302 (Easter-September) – Fairwood Common ☎ 27671/27660 (Easter-September).
London 196 – Bristol 82 – Birmingham 130 – Cardiff 41 – Liverpool 225 – Stoke-on-Trent 171.

Plans opposite

Dragon (T.H.F.), 39 The Kingsway, SA1 5LS, ☎ 51074, Telex 48309 – lift TV P. B a
M 3.50/4.00 **st.** 1.70 – 2.00 – **118 rm** 14.00/21.00 **st.**

Dolphin (Interchange), Whitewalls St., SA1 3AB, ☎ 50011 – lift TV wc ☎. B e
closed Christmas Day – **M** 3.45/3.70 **st.** 1.50 – **65 rm** 12.50/16.50 **st.**

XX **Grosvenor House,** 134 St. Helens Rd, SA1 4BL, ☎ 462884, Italian rest. A c
closed Sunday, Bank Holiday lunches and 3 days after Christmas – **M** a la carte 3.20/6.20 **t.** 1.50.

XX **Oyster Perches,** 45 Uplands Crescent, Uplands, SA2 0NP, ☎ 59173 A a
closed Sunday dinner and Christmas – **M** a la carte 3.60/7.60 **st.** 1.85.

XX **Drangway,** 66 Wind St., SA9 1AH, ☎ 461397 B c
closed Sunday, Monday, first 2 weeks August and Bank Holidays – **M** a la carte 5.95/10.95 **st.** 1.70.

SWANSEA

Street	Grid	No.
College Street	B	13
Kingsway (The)	B	
Oxford Street	B	
Princess Way	B	
Alexandra Road	B	2
Bathurst Street	B	3
Belle Vue Way	B	4
Carmarthen Road	B	7
Castle Street	B	8
Christina Street	B	9
Clarence Terrace	B	10
Clase Road	A	12
De La Beche Street	B	14
Fabian Way	B	15
Gower Road	A	16
Grove Place	B	17
Martin Street	A	20
Nelson Street	B	22
Ravenhill Road	A	23
Rutland Street	B	24
Station Road	A	25
St. Helen's Road	A	27
St. Mary's Square	B	28
Thomas Street	B	31
Union Street	B	32
Uplands Crescent	A	34
Vivian Road	A	35
Walter Road	A	36
Wellington Street	B	38
William Street	B	39
Woodfield Street	A	40
York Street	B	42

Zum besseren Verständnis der Stadtpläne lesen Sie bitte die Zeichenerklärung auf Seite 43.

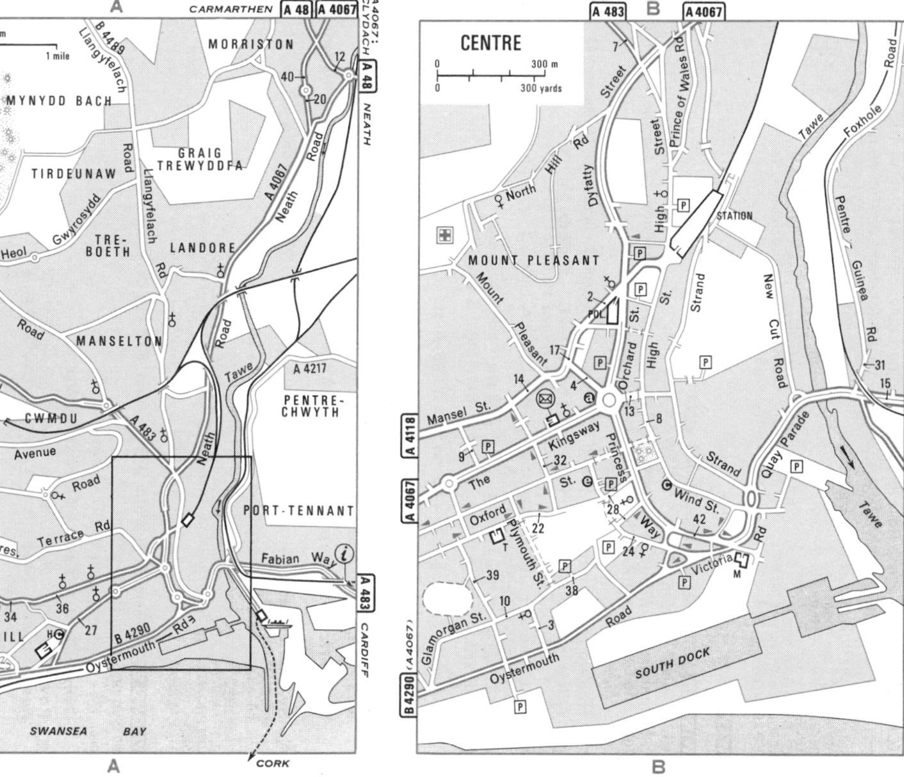

MICHELIN Branch, Bruce Rd, Fforestfach Trading Estate, Fforestfach, SA5 4HS, ✆ 33990.

AUSTIN, MORRIS-MG-ROVER-TRIUMPH 375 Carmarthen Rd ✆ 52941
AUSTIN-DAIMLER-JAGUAR-MORRIS-MG-ROVER-TRIUMPH 511 Carmarthen Rd ✆ 53281
CHRYSLER-SIMCA Neath Rd ✆ 73391
CITROEN Gors Rd ✆ 582048
DAF Blackpill ✆ 66209
DATSUN Sway Rd ✆ 75271
FORD Garngoch ✆ 2233
MORRIS-MG-WOLSELEY 10 Wyndham St. ✆ 53232
MORRIS-MG-WOLSELEY Cwmbwria ✆ 53885
PEUGEOT 1/24 Pentrechwyth Rd ✆ 54147
RENAULT Eaton Rd, Manselton ✆ 53125
SAAB Llangyfelach ✆ 71960
VAUXHALL William St. ✆ 41311
VAUXHALL Neath Rd, Morriston ✆ 75101
VW, AUDI-NSU Gorseinon Rd ✆ 0792 (Gorseinon) 894951

SWAY Hants. – see Lymington.

SWINDON Wilts. 986 ㉟ – pop. 91,033 – ✆ 0793.

Envir. : Lydiard Tregoze (church* 15C) W : 4 m.

18 Shrivenham ✆ 0793 (Shrivenham) 782946, E : 4 m. – 18 Ogbourne St. George, ✆ 067 284 (Ogbourne St. George) 217, S : 7 m. on A 345.

i 32 The Arcade, Brunel Centre ✆ 30328.

London 87 – Bournemouth 69 – **Bristol 40** – **Cardiff 72** – **Coventry 70** – **Oxford 29** – Reading 39 – **Southampton 67.**

Wiltshire (Rank), Fleming Way, SN1 1TN, ✆ 28282 – lift TV P.
M a la carte 3.65/5.50 **s.** 1.30 – 1.75 – **85 rm** 12.00/17.00 **s.**

Post House (T.H.F.), Marlborough Rd, SN3 6AQ, SE : 2 ¾ m. on A 345 ✆ 24601, heated – TV wc ✆ P.
M 4.20/4.50 **st.** 1.50 – 2.00 – **103 rm** 13.00/18.00 **st.**

Goddard Arms (Anchor), High St., Old Town, SN1 3EW, ✆ 692313 – TV wc ✆ P.
M approx. 3.25 **t.** 1.00 – **40 rm** 9.20/18.70 **st.**

at Blunsdon **N : 4 m. on A 419 – ✉ Swindon – ✆ 079 372 Blunsdon :**

Blunsdon House (Interchange), The Ridge, SN2 4AD, ✆ 72701, – lift TV wc ✆ P.
M 3.75 **st.** 1.50 – **37 rm** 8.75/17.50 **st.** – P 12.25/19.50 **st.**

at Stratton St. Margaret NE : 2 m. on A 420 – ✉ Swindon – ✆ 079 382 Stratton St. Margaret :

Swindon Crest Motel (Crest), Oxford Rd, SN3 4TL, NE : 1 ½ m. on A 420 ✆ 2921 – TV wc ✆ P
M a la carte 2.90/6.20 **s.** 1.55 – 1.60 – **50 rm** 11.00/15.50 **s.**

ALFA-ROMEO Shrivenham ✆ 0793 (Shrivenham) 782721
AUSTIN-MG-WOLSELEY Drove Rd ✆ 34035
DAIMLER-JAGUAR-ROVER-TRIUMPH Dorcan Way ✆ 5283
FIAT, VAUXHALL, VOLVO 32/36 High St. ✆ 20971
FORD 30 Marlborough Rd ✆ 20002
MORRIS-MG-WOLSELEY Victoria Rd ✆ 22205
RENAULT Elgin Drive ✆ 693841
VAUXHALL 13/21 The Street, Moredon ✆ 23457
VW, AUDI-NSU Eldene Drive ✆ 31333

SYMOND'S YAT Heref. and Worc. 986 ㉛ – **pop. 807** – ✆ **060 081.**

See : Symond's Yat Rock ≤**.

London 126 – Gloucester 23 – Hereford 17 – Newport 31.

Symond's Yat (East) – ✉ Ross-on-Wye :

Royal , HR9 6JL, ✆ 238, ≤, – wc wc P
closed January – **M** (bar lunch) a la carte 5.50/8.50 **st.** 1.30 – **23 rm** 8.25/17.90 **st.** – P 14.80/15.50 **st.**

Symond's Yat (West) – ✉ Ross-on-Wye :

Wye Rapids , HR9 6BL, ✆ 366, ≤, – wc P
M (bar lunch) 3.50/4.00 0.80 – **20 rm** 7.50/16.50.

TALKIN Cumbria – pop. 150 – ✉ ✆ 069 77 Brampton.

18 ✆ 2255.

London 320 – **Carlisle 12** – **Newcastle-upon-Tyne 52.**

XX **Tarn End** with rm, Talkin Tarn, CA8 1LS, 2 m. S. of Brampton off B 6413 ✆ 2340, ≤, – P
closed October and Christmas Day – **M** a la carte 4.55/6.80 0.95 – **6 rm** (dinner included) 11.00/22.00.

TALLAND-BY-LOOE Cornwall – ✉ Looe – ✆ 050 38 Polperro.

London 269 – **Plymouth 26** – Truro 40.

Talland Bay , PL13 2JA, ✆ 228, ≤, « Country house atmosphere », heated, – TV wc P
closed December and January – **M** a la carte 5.75/8.50 1.25 – **19 rm** 10.50/26.00.

TAL-Y-BONT Gwynedd – see Conwy.

TAL-Y-CAFN Gwynedd – ✉ Colwyn Bay – ☎ 049 267 Tynygroes.
Envir.: Bodnant Gardens** *AC,* NE: **1** m.
London 238 – Colwyn Bay 7.

Ferry, LL28 5RT, ☎ 202, ≤, 🐟, 🌳 – 🛁wc **P**
M a la carte 3.90/5.25 **t.** – **14 rm** 🛏 5.50/14.50.

TAL-Y-LLYN Gwynedd – pop. 620 – ✉ Towyn – ☎ 065 477 Abergynolwyn.
See : Lake**.
London 224 – Dolgellau 9 – Shrewsbury 60.

Tynycornel, LL36 9AJ, on B 4405 ☎ 282, ≤, 🐟, 🌳, park – 🛁wc ☎ **P**
March-November – **M** *(open all year except Monday to Thursday from December to February)* (dinner only and Sunday lunch) approx. 4.95 **t.** – **19 rm** 🛏 8.65/16.80 **t.**

TANGMERE West Sussex – see Chichester.

TANKERTON Kent – see Whitstable.

Michelin n'accroche pas de panonceau aux hôtels et restaurants qu'il signale.

TAUNTON Somerset 986 ㉟ – pop. 37,444 – ☎ 0823.
See : St. Mary Magdalene's Church* 15C. **Envir.:** Trull (Parish church : carved woodwork* 16C) SW : 2 m.
18 Corfe ☎ 082 342 (Blagdon Hill) 240, S: 5 m. on B 3170.
i The Library, Corporation St. ☎ 84077/53424.
London 171 – Bournemouth 68 – **Bristol 48** – Exeter 32 – **Plymouth 74** – **Southampton 89** – Weymouth 49.

Castle, Castle Green, TA1 1NF, ☎ 2671, « Part 11C castle with Norman garden » – lift TV ♿ 🚗 **P**.
M a la carte 5.75/7.15 **s.** 1.60 – 🛏 2.30 – **50 rm** 10.90/26.30 **s.** – P 17.45/23.40 **s.**

County (T.H.F.), East St., TA1 3LT, ☎ 87651 – lift TV 🛁wc ☎ **P**.
M a la carte 4.10/5.50 **st.** 1.50 – **76 rm** 🛏 8.50/17.50 **st.**

Corner House, Park St., TA1 4DG, ☎ 2665 – **P**
closed 22 December-2 January – **M** 2.75/3.00 **st.** 1.50 – **23 rm** 🛏 7.70/15.50 **st.** – P 11.20/12.30 **st.**

XX Well House, Poundisford Park S: 3 ¾ m. off B 3170 ☎ 082 342 (Blagdon Hill) 566 – **P**
closed Sunday dinner and Monday.

at Hatch Beauchamp SE: 6 m. on A 358 – ✉ Taunton – ☎ 082 348 Hatch Beauchamp:

XXX **Farthings,** TA3 6SG, ☎ 664 – **P**
closed Sunday dinner, Monday, Tuesday lunch and 3 weeks February – **M** (buffet lunch except by arrangement) a la carte 4.70/6.55 **t.** 1.70.

at Bishop's Hull W: 1 ¾ m. off A 38 – ✉ ☎ 0823 Taunton:

Meryan House, Bishop's Hull Rd, TA1 5EG, ☎ 87445, 🌳 – **P**
8 rm 🛏 6.00/10.00.

at Bishop's Lydeard NW: 5 m. by A 358 – ✉ Taunton – ☎ 0823 Bishop's Lydeard:

X **Rose Cottage Inn,** TA4 3LR, SE: 1 m. on A 358 ☎ 432394 – **P**
closed Sunday and 23 December-15 January – **M** (bar lunch) a la carte 3.50/6.40.

MICHELIN Branch, Cornishway West, Galmington Trading Estate, TA1 5NA, ☎ 85796.

AUDI-NSU, MERCEDES-BENZ Silver St. ☎ 88371
AUSTIN-DAIMLER-JAGUAR-ROVER-TRIUMPH South St. ☎ 88991
CHRYSLER-SIMCA 30/33a East Reach ☎ 87871
CITROEN, FIAT 43/45 East St. ☎ 2607
FORD 151/6 East Reach ☎ 85481
LANCIA Blagdon Hill ☎ 342254
MORRIS-MG-WOLSELEY 30 Wellington Rd ☎ 81081
OPEL Priory Av. ☎ 87611
RENAULT 138 Bridgwater Rd, Bathpool ☎ 412559
SAAB 60 East Reach ☎ 88351
TOYOTA 16 Kingston Rd ☎ 88288

TAVISTOCK Devon 986 ㊴ – pop. 7,620 – ☎ 0822.
Envir. : Launceston (castle* : Norman ruins *AC,* St. Mary Magdalene's Church: carving outside walls* 16C) NW: 13 m.
18 Down Rd ☎ 2049, SW: 1 m.
London 239 – Exeter 38 – **Plymouth 15.**

Bedford (T.H.F.), 1 Plymouth Rd, PL19 8BB, ☎ 3221 – TV 🛁wc ☎
M a la carte 4.05/5.50 **st.** 1.50 – **33 rm** 🛏 7.00/16.50 **st.** – P 14.50/18.00 **st.**

at Gulworthy W: 3 m. on A 390 – ✉ Tavistock – ☎ 0822 Gunnislake:

XX ✿ **Horn of Plenty,** PL19 8JD, ☎ 832528, ≤ Tamar Valley and Bodmin Moor, 🌳 – **P**
closed Thursday, Friday lunch and Christmas Day – **M** a la carte 5.00/7.85 1.85
Spec. Sweetbreads in home made brioche, Quenelles of fresh salmon (season), Lamb in pastry with mint béarnaise sauce.

TOYOTA Vigo Bridge ☎ 3735

TEBAY Cumbria – pop. 636 – ✉ ☎ 058 74 Orton.

London 272 – Carlisle 41 – Kendal 12.

- **Tebay Mountain Lodge Motel** without rest., M 6 Motorway Service Area, CA10 3SB, Ᵽ 351 – TV wc ☎ P
  0.65 – **32 rm** 9.00/12.50.

TEDBURN ST. MARY Devon – pop. 586 – ✉ Exeter – ☎ 064 76.

London 209 – Exeter 8.5 – **Plymouth 51.**

- **King's Arms Inn,** on A 30 Ᵽ 224 – P
  closed Christmas Day – **M** a la carte 3.00/4.70 **t.** – **9 rm** 5.50/10.00 **t.**

TEIGNMOUTH Devon 986 ㊴ – pop. **12,575** – ☎ **062 67.**

18 Ᵽ **3614, N: 2 m.**

i The Den Ᵽ 6271 (summer only).

London 216 – Exeter 16 – Torquay 8.

- **London,** 24 Bank St., TQ14 8AW, Ᵽ 2776, heated – wc
  M 3.00/4.00 **t.** 1.40 – **26 rm** 7.00/13.00 **t.** – P 13.00/15.00 **t.**
- **Belvedere,** Barnpark Rd, TQ14 8PJ, Ᵽ 4561 – wc P
  13 rm 5.50/11.00 **st.**
- **Inglewood,** Third Drive, Landscore Rd, TQ14 9JT, Ᵽ 4572, heated, – P
  15 rm 6.00/12.00 **st.**
- **Overstowey,** Dawlish Rd, TQ14 8TQ, on A 379 Ᵽ 4251, – P
  10 rm 4.95/9.90.
- **Churchill's,** 6-8 Den Rd, TQ14 8AP, Ᵽ 4311, French rest.
  closed Sunday dinner from October to May and Monday – **M** a la carte 3.90/6.20 1.20.
- **Minadab,** 60 Teignmouth Rd, TQ14 8UT, NW: 1 m. on A 379 Ᵽ 2044 – P
  closed Tuesday – **M** a la carte 4.15/10.70 1.20.

AUSTIN-MORRIS-MG-ROVER-TRIUMPH 106 Bitton Park Rd Ᵽ 2501

RENAULT Bridge Rd, Shaldon Ᵽ 062 687 (Shaldon) 2369

TELFORD Salop 986 ㉗ – pop. 17,163 – ☎ 0952.

Envir. : Ironbridge Gorge Museum* (Iron Bridge**) *AC*, S: 5 m. – Buildwas Abbey* (ruins 12C) S: 7 m.

18 Wrekin Ᵽ 44032 – 18 Sutton Hill Ᵽ 586052.

i Ironbridge Gorge Museum Trust Ᵽ 3522/3 (February to November).

London 152 – Birmingham 33 – Shrewsbury 12 – **Stoke-on-Trent 29.**

- **Buckatree Hall**, Ercall Lane, The Wrekin, TF6 5AL, off Holyhead Rd S: 1 ½ m. Ᵽ 51821, , park – TV wc ☎ P
  M a la carte 5.35/7.45 – **18 rm** 13.85/20.10.
- **Charlton Arms,** Church St., Wellington, TF1 1DG, Ᵽ 51351 – wc ☎ P.
  M 3.20/3.60 **t.** 1.30 – **26 rm** 8.25/13.20 **t.**

at Ironbridge S: 5 m. by A 442 on A 4169 – ✉ ☎ 095 245 Ironbridge:

- The Valley, Buildwas Rd, Coalbrookdale, TF8 7DW, Ᵽ 3280, <, , – P
  12 rm.

AUSTIN-MORRIS-MG-WOLSELEY Market St. Wellington Ᵽ 44896

DATSUN Church St. Ᵽ 42671
FORD, RENAULT Watling, St. Wellington Ᵽ 44162

TEMPLE EWELL Kent – see Dover.

TEMPLE SOWERBY Cumbria – pop. 279 – ✉ Penrith – ☎ 093 06 Kirkby Thore.

London 297 – Carlisle 31 – Kendal 38.

- King's Arms, Ᵽ 211, – P
  12 rm.

TENBURY WELLS Heref. and Worc. 986 ㉛ – pop. 2,151 – ☎ 0584.

i Teme St. Ᵽ 810465.

London 146 – Birmingham 35 – Hereford 22 – Shrewsbury 37.

- **Royal Oak,** Market St., WR15 8BQ, Ᵽ 810417, – P
  closed Christmas – **M** *(closed Sunday dinner to non-residents)* 2.00/4.00 1.75 – **6 rm** 6.50/10.50.

TENBY Dyfed 986 ㉚ – pop. 4,994 – ☎ 0834.

See : Site**.

18 **The Burrows** Ᵽ **2787.**

i South Pembrokeshire District Council and Pembrokeshire Coast National Park, Guildhall, The Norton Ᵽ 2402 (South Pembs.) and Ᵽ 3510 (Nat. Park).

London 247 – Carmarthen 27 – Fishguard 36.

Imperial, The Paragon, SA70 7HR, ☎ 3737, ≤ sea and bay, – TV wc P
M a la carte 5.55/8.10 **st.** 1.70 – **48 rm** 12.45/27.35 **st.** – P 17.85/22.55 **st.**

Tenby House, Tudor Sq. SA70 7AJ, ☎ 2000 – wc P
closed October – **M** 2.75/3.50 1.10 – **12 rm** 5.75/12.00.

Royal Lion, 1 High St., SA70 7EX, ☎ 2127 – wc P
March-November – **M** *(open all year)* 3.00/4.50 **t.** 1.10 – **33 rm** 6.50/15.00 **t.**

Cobourg, High St., SA70 7EU, ☎ 2009 – wc
May-September – **M** 2.70/3.70 **st.** 1.25 – **30 rm** 5.00/18.00 **s.** – P 11.00/12.50 **st.**

Heywood Lodge, Heywood Lane, ☎ 2684, – P
Easter-October – **14 rm** 4.50/10.00 **s.**

AUSTIN-MORRIS-MG-TRIUMPH-WOLSELEY Warren St. ☎ 2202
VAUXHALL Greenhill Rd ☎ 2459

TENTERDEN Kent 986 ㊱ – pop. 5,930 – ☎ 058 06.

Envir.: Small Hythe (Ellen Terry's House* *AC*) S: 2 m.

i Town Hall, High St. ☎ 3572 (summer only).

London 56 – Canterbury 26 – Folkestone 26 – Hastings 20 – Maidstone 18.

White Lion, TN30 6DB, ☎ 2921 – wc P
M approx. 3.50 **t.** 1.40 – **12 rm** 10.50/15.50 **t.**

TETBURY Glos. 986 ㉟ – pop. 3,461 – ☎ 0666.

London 113 – Bristol 27 – Gloucester 19 – Swindon 24.

White Hart, Market Pl., GL8 8ES, ☎ 52436 – TV.
M 4.25/6.00 **st.** 0.90 – **10 rm** 10.45/20.00 **st.**

XXX **The Close** with rm, 8 Long St., GL8 8AQ, ☎ 52272, – TV wc wc P
M 4.95/7.00 **st.** 2.60 – 2.00 – **11 rm** 11.50/24.00 **st.**

***at Westonbirt* SW: 2 ½ m. on A 433 – ✉ Tetbury – ☎ 066 66 Westonbirt:**

Hare and Hounds (Interchange), GL8 8QL, ☎ 233, , , park – wc P
M 4.00/4.50 **st.** 1.55 – **26 rm** 8.50/20.00 **st.** – P 13.50/15.00 **st.**

FIAT Hampton St. ☎ 52340
VW, AUDI-NSU London Rd ☎ 52473

TEWKESBURY Glos. 986 ㉛ – pop. 8,749.

See: Abbey Church* 12C-14C.

18 Lincoln Green ☎ 295405, S: ½ m.

i The Crescent, Church St. ☎ 295027 (summer only) – Town Hall, High St. ☎ 294639 (winter only).

London 108 – Birmingham 39 – Gloucester 11.

Royal Hop Pole (Crest), Church St., GL20 5RT, ☎ 293236, , – wc P
M a la carte 3.35/5.50 **s.** 1.55 – **24 rm** 9.50/16.00 **s.**

X **Luigi's,** 69-70 Church St., GL20 5RX, ☎ 294353, Italian rest.
closed Monday and 25 and 26 December – **M** a la carte 4.60/6.45 1.40.

AUSTIN-MORRIS-MG-WOLSELEY Gloucester Rd ☎ 293122
CHRYSLER-SIMCA Bredon Rd ☎ 293071
VAUXHALL Ashchurch Rd ☎ 292398

THAKEHAM West Sussex – pop. 1,103 – ✉ Storrington – ☎ 079 83 West Chiltington.

London 53 – Brighton 22 – Worthing 12.

Abingworth Hall , RH20 3EF, on B 2139 ☎ 2257, , heated, , , park – wc P
M 2.50/3.00 1.20 – **28 rm** 9.50/21.00 **s.**

THAME Oxon. 986 ㉜ – pop. 5,948 – ☎ 084 421.

See: St. Mary's Church* 13C. Envir.: Rycote Chapel* (15C) *AC*, W: 3 ½ m.

London 48 – Aylesbury 9 – Oxford 13.

Spread Eagle (Interchange), 16 Cornmarket, OX9 2BR, ☎ 3661 – wc P.
closed 28 to 30 December – **M** *(closed Monday lunch)* a la carte 5.35/8.40 **t.** 1.50 – 1.65 – **29 rm** 10.55/20.00 **t.**

Jolly Sailor, Wellington St. ☎ 2682 – P
12 rm.

AUSTIN-MG-ROVER-TRIUMPH-WOLSELEY Queens Rd ☎ 2726
CHRYSLER-SIMCA North St. ☎ 2921
MORRIS-MG 44 Upper High St. ☎ 2011
VAUXHALL Park St. ☎ 2505

THETFORD Norfolk 986 ㉜ – pop. 13.727 – ☎ 0842.

18 Brandon Rd ☎ 2258.

i Ancient House Museum, White Hart St. ☎ 2599.

London 83 – Cambridge 32 – Ipswich 33 – King's Lynn 30 – Norwich 29.

🏨 **Bell** (T.H.F.), King St., IP24 2AZ, ☎ 4455 – 📺 🛁wc ☎ Ⓟ. 🏨
M 3.50/3.75 **st.** 🍾 1.50 – **42 rm** 🛏 12.50/19.50 **st.**

🏨 **Anchor,** Bridge St., IP24 3AE, ☎ 3329 – Ⓟ. 🏨
M 2.85/5.50 **t.** 🍾 1.25 – **12 rm** 🛏 5.75/11.00 **t.**

AUSTIN-MORRIS-MG-ROVER-TRIUMPH-WOLSELEY Guildhall St. ☎ 4427

THIRLSPOT Cumbria – pop. 100 – ✉ ☎ 0596 Keswick.

London 286 – Kendal 24 – Keswick 6.

🏨 King's Head, CA12 4TN, ☎ 72393, ≤ – 🛁wc Ⓟ
15 rm.

THIRSK North Yorks. 986 ㉓ – pop. 2,884 – ☎ 0845.

See: St. Mary's Church* (Gothic). **Envir.:** Sutton Bank (≤**) E : 6 m. on A 170 – Rievaulx Abbey** (ruins 12C-13C) *AC*, NE : 11 m.

i Sutton Bank Information Centre, Sutton ☎ 084 56 (Sutton) 436.

London 227 – **Leeds 37** – **Middlesbrough 24** – York 24.

🏨 **Golden Fleece** (T.H.F.), Market Pl., YO7 1LL, ☎ 23108 – 📺 🛁wc ☎ Ⓟ
M a la carte 4.00/5.30 **st.** 🍾 1.50 – **20 rm** 🛏 8.00/15.50 **st.** – P 12.25/16.50 **st.**

AUSTIN-MORRIS Stockton Rd ☎ 22057
OPEL Long St. ☎ 23152
PEUGEOT Station Rd ☎ 22370

THORNABY-ON-TEES Cleveland 986 ⑲ – pop. 4,025 – ✉ Middlesbrough.

London 250 – **Leeds 62** – **Middlesbrough 3** – York 49.

🏨 **Post House** (T.H.F.), Low Lane, TS17 9LW, SE : 3 m. by A 1045 on A 1044 ☎ 0642 (Middlesbrough) 591213, Telex 58426 – 📺 🛁wc ☎ ♿ Ⓟ. 🏨
M 2.95/4.00 **st.** 🍾 1.50 – 🛏 2.00 – **140 rm** 12.00/16.00 **st.**

🏨 Golden Eagle (Thistle), Trenchard Av., TS17 0DA, ☎ 0642 (Stockton-on-Tees) 62511 – 🛗 📺 🛁wc ☎ ♿ Ⓟ. 🏨
57 rm.

FORD Master Rd ☎ 69696
SIMCA Acklam Rd ☎ 0642 (Stockton) 65181

THORNBURY Avon 986 ㉟ – pop. 9,900 – ✉ Bristol – ☎ 0454.

Envir. : Berkeley Castle** (12C) *AC*, NE : 8½ m. – Severn Bridge* W : 4 m.

London 128 – **Bristol 12** – Gloucester 23 – Swindon 43.

XXX ✿ **Thornbury Castle,** Castle St., BS12 1HH, ☎ 412647, « 15C castle » – Ⓟ
closed Sunday dinner, Monday and 5 days at Christmas – **M** (dinner only and Sunday lunch) approx. 9.00 🍾 2.25
Spec. Mousseline de saumon en croûte, Quenelles de veau à l'estragon, Suprême de volaille au Pernod.

THORNTON West. Yorks. – see Bradford.

THORNTON HOUGH Merseyside – ✉ Neston – ☎ 051 Liverpool.

London 207 – Chester 12 – **Liverpool 13.**

🏨 **Thornton Hall** 🐦, Neston Rd, Wirral, L63 1JF, ☎ 336 3938, ≤, 🌳 – 📺 🛁wc ☎ Ⓟ
M 2.80/3.25 🍾 2.00 – **26 rm** 🛏 11.00/16.00.

THORPE Derbs. – pop. 161 – ✉ Ashbourne – ☎ 033 529 Thorpe Cloud.

Envir.: N : Dovedale (valley)** – Ashbourne (St. Oswald's Church* 13C) SE : 3 m.

London 151 – Derby 16 – **Sheffield 33** – **Stoke-on-Trent 26.**

🏨 **Izaak Walton** 🐦, Dovedale, DE6 2AY, W : 1 m. ☎ 261, ≤ Dovedale, 🎣, 🌳 – 🛁wc ☎ Ⓟ. 🏨
M a la carte 4.55/8.40 **t.** 🍾 1.80 – **26 rm** 🛏 8.25/16.50 **t.** – P 15.35 **t.**

🏨 **Peveril of the Peak** (T.H.F.) 🐦, DE6 2AW, ☎ 333, ≤, 🌳 – 🛁wc ☎ Ⓟ. 🏨
M a la carte 4.25/5.20 **st.** 🍾 1.50 – **29 rm** 🛏 9.00/17.00 **st.** – P 13.00/18.00 **st.**

THORPE ST. ANDREW Norfolk – see Norwich.

THREE COCKS Powys – pop. 221 – ✉ Brecon – ☎ 049 74 Glasbury (Heref. and Worc.).

London 184 – Brecon 11 – Hereford 25 – **Swansea 55.**

XX **Three Cocks** with rm, LD3 0SL, on A 438 ☎ 215, 🌳 – Ⓟ
M a la carte 3.60/6.40 **t.** 🍾 1.40 – **7 rm** 🛏 5.00/10.00 **t.**

THRESHFIELD North Yorks. – pop. 465 – ✉ ☎ 0756 Grassington.

London 225 – Bradford 27 – Burnley 26 – **Leeds 34.**

🏨 **Wilson Arms,** Station Rd, BD23 5EL, on B 6265 ☎ 752666, 🌳 – 🛁wc ☎ 🚗 Ⓟ
M approx. 5.00 **st.** 🍾 1.30 – **23 rm** 🛏 13.50/23.00 **st.**

THURLESTONE Devon – see Kingsbridge.

THURSTASTON Merseyside – pop. 237 – ✉ West Kirby – ☎ 051 Liverpool.
London 210 – Birkenhead 7.5 – Chester 15.

✕✕ **Cottage Loaf,** Telegraph Rd, L48 0RB, on A 540 ☎ 648 1635 – Ⓟ
closed Monday and Christmas Day – **M** a la carte 4.35/5.65 **t.**

TILBURY Essex 986 ㊱ – ☎ 037 52.
Shipping connections with the Continent: to Helsinki and Leningrad (Baltic Shipping Co.)
London 24 – Southend-on-Sea 20.

Hotels and restaurants see : London W: 24 m.

TINTAGEL Cornwall 986 ㊳ – pop. 1,372 – ☎ 084 04.
See : Castle (ruins 12C) : site*, <** *AC* – Old Post Office* (14C) *AC*.
London 264 – Exeter 63 – **Plymouth 49** – Truro 41.

Bossiney House, Bossiney, PL34 0AX, ☎ 240, <, – wc wc Ⓟ
Easter-October – **M** (dinner only) 3.75 **st.** 1.80 – **19 rm** 8.00/16.50 **st.**

TINTERN Gwent – pop. 647 – ✉ Chepstow – ☎ 029 18.
See : Abbey** (ruins) *AC*.
i Tourist Information Centre, Tintern Abbey Car Park ☎ 431.
London 137 – **Bristol 23** – Gloucester 40 – Newport 22.

Beaufort (Embassy), NP6 6SF, on A 466 ☎ 202, – TV wc wc Ⓟ
closed Christmas – **M** approx. 2.90 **st.** 1.50 – **27 rm** 8.25/14.50 **st.**

Royal George (T.H.F.), NP6 6SF, ☎ 205, – TV wc Ⓟ
M a la carte 3.95/5.35 **st.** 1.50 – **18 rm** 6.00/13.50 **st.** – P 12.50/15.00 **st.**

Wye Valley, NP6 6SF, ☎ 441 – Ⓟ
M (bar lunch, grill rest. only) 2.25/3.50 **st.** 1.25 – **10 rm** 5.50/9.75 **t.** – P 9.50 **st.**

✕ **Fountain Inn,** NP6 6QW, W: 2 m. on Raglan Rd ☎ 303 – Ⓟ
closed Sunday dinner and Christmas Day – **M** (dinner only and Sunday lunch) a la carte 3.35/5.75 1.25.

TITCHWELL Norfolk – pop. 131 – ✉ Kings Lynn – ☎ 048 521 Brancaster.
London 126 – **Cambridge 66** – **Norwich 41.**

Manor, PE31 8BB, on A 149 ☎ 221, – wc Ⓟ
M (bar lunch) a la carte 3.00/5.00 **t.** 1.75 – **9 rm** 8.00/15.00 **t.**

TIVERTON Devon 986 ㉟ – pop. 15,566 – ☎ 088 42.
Envir. : Cullompton (St. Andrew's Church* 15C) SE: 9 m.
London 192 – Exeter 14 – Taunton 23.

Tiverton Motel, Blundells Rd, EX16 4DB, on A 373 ☎ 3427 – TV wc Ⓟ.
M (grill rest. only) a la carte approx. 4.10 – 1.25 – **30 rm** 8.75/13.50.

at Bolham N: 1 ¼ m. on A 396 – ✉ ☎ 088 42 Tiverton :

Hartnoll Country House, Bolham Rd, EX16 7RA, ☎ 2777, <, « Country house atmosphere », – wc Ⓟ
M a la carte 3.00/4.15 0.70 – **13 rm** 7.00/ 13.50.

AUSTIN-MORRIS-MG-ROVER-TRIUMPH-WOLSELEY Blundells Rd ☎ 56666
CHRYSLER 31 Lea St. ☎ 2170
MAZDA, SAAB Normansland ☎ 088 481 (Witheridge) 538

TONBRIDGE Kent 986 ㊱ – pop. 31,016 – ☎ 0732.
See : Tonbridge School* (1553). **Envir. :** Sevenoaks (Knole House** 15C-17C) *AC*, NW: 7 m. – Ightam Mote* (Manor House 14C-15C) *AC*, site* N : 7 m.
18 Poult Wood ☎ 64039.
London 33 – **Brighton 37** – Hastings 31 – Maidstone 14.

Rose and Crown (T.H.F.), High St., TN9 1DD, ☎ 357966, – TV wc Ⓟ.
M 3.50/3.75 **st.** – **46 rm** 14.00/20.00 **st.**

✕ **A la Bonne Franquette,** 20 Barden Rd, TN9 1TX, ☎ 358457, French rest.
closed Sunday, Wednesday lunch, Saturday lunch and Bank Holidays – **M** a la carte 3.25/5.10 **t.**

AUSTIN-MG-WOLSELEY Quarry Hill ☎ 354555
BMW 88 Priory St. ☎ 63520
DAIMLER-JAGUAR-ROVER-TRIUMPH Cannon Lane ☎ 64444
VAUXHALL Avebury Av. ☎ 3316
VW, AUDI-NSU, MERCEDES-BENZ Vale Rd ☎ 355822

TORCROSS Devon – pop. 150 – ✉ Kingsbridge – ☎ 054 858.
London 242 – Dartmouth 9 – Exeter 42 – **Plymouth 26.**

Torcross, TQ7 2TQ, ☎ 206, < – wc Ⓟ
March-November – **M** (dinner only) 3.00/3.50 **t.** 1.00 – **20 rm** 8.25/16.50 **t.**

SAAB ☎ 205

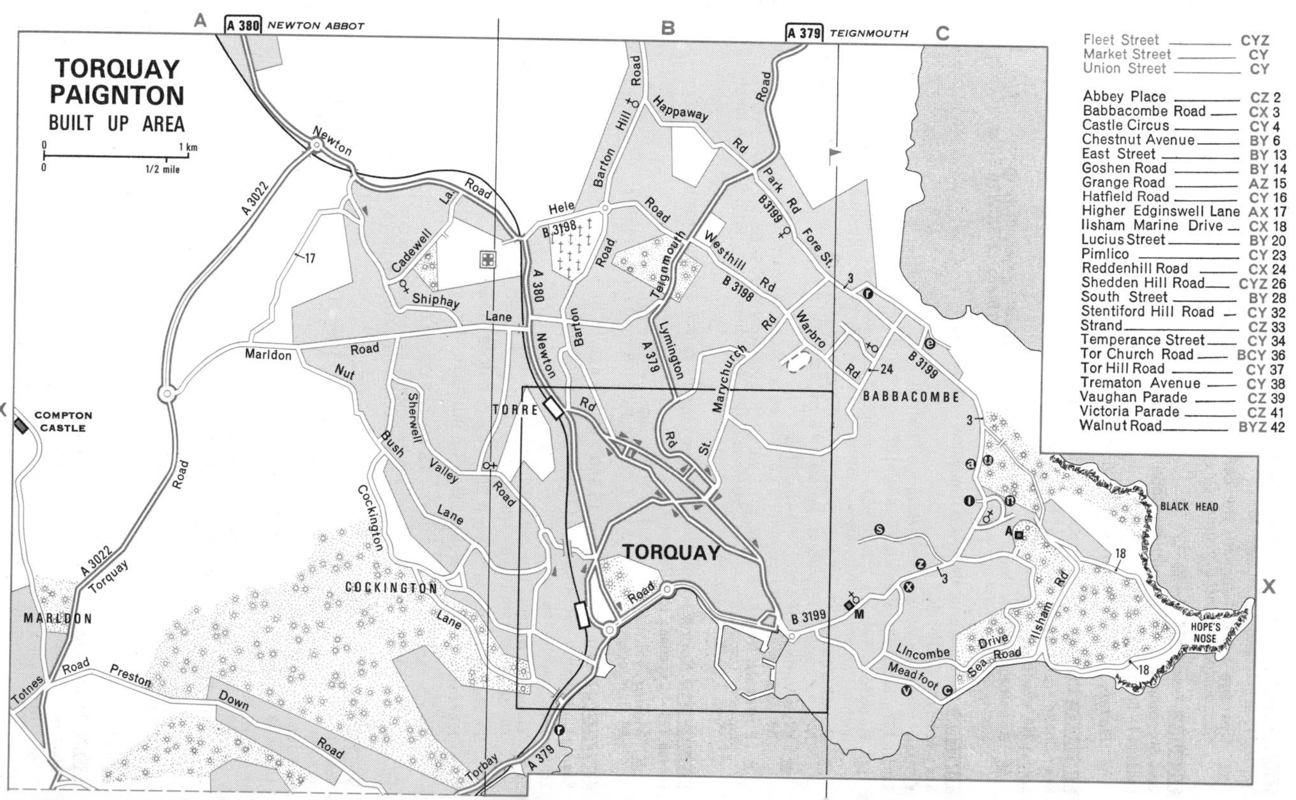
TORQUAY
PAIGNTON
BUILT UP AREA
0 1 km
0 1/2 mile
A 380 NEWTON ABBOT
A 379 TEIGNMOUTH
A
B
C
X
Fleet Street CYZ
Market Street CY
Union Street CY
Abbey Place CZ 2
Babbacombe Road CX 3
Castle Circus CY 4
Chestnut Avenue BY 6
East Street BY 13
Goshen Road BY 14
Grange Road AZ 15
Hatfield Road CY 16
Higher Edginswell Lane AX 17
Ilsham Marine Drive CX 18
Lucius Street BY 20
Pimlico CY 23
Reddenhill Road CX 24
Shedden Hill Road CYZ 26
South Street BY 28
Stentiford Hill Road CY 32
Strand CZ 33
Temperance Street CY 34
Tor Church Road BCY 36
Tor Hill Road CY 37
Trematon Avenue CY 38
Vaughan Parade CZ 39
Victoria Parade CZ 41
Walnut Road BYZ 42
TORQUAY
BABBACOMBE
TORRE
COCKINGTON
MARLDON
COMPTON CASTLE
BLACK HEAD
HOPE'S NOSE
A 3022
A 380
A 379
B 3198
B 3199

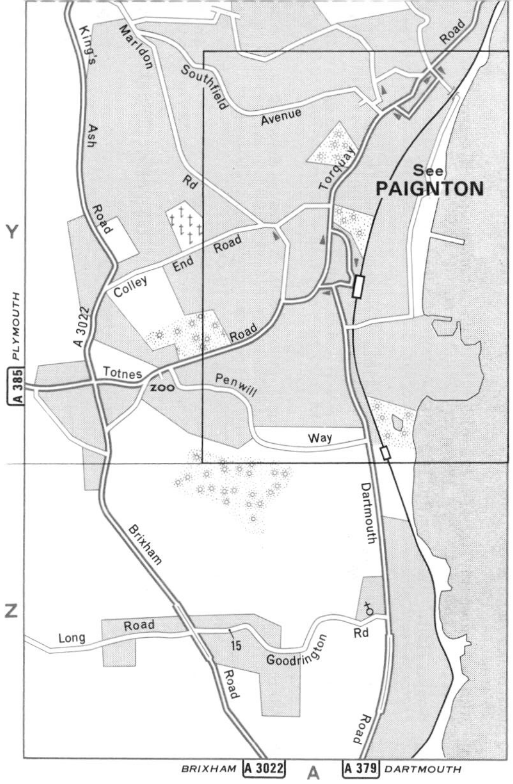

TORQUAY
CENTRE

0 — 400 m
0 — 400 yards

See
PAIGNTON

A 380 · A 379 · A 385 PLYMOUTH · BRIXHAM A 3022 · A 379 DARTMOUTH · B 3202 · B 3199

Y · Z · A · B · C

UPTON · TORRE · CHELSTON · UPTON PARK · ABBEY GARDENS · PRINCESS GARDENS · TORRE STATION · TORQUAY STATION · POL. · ZOO

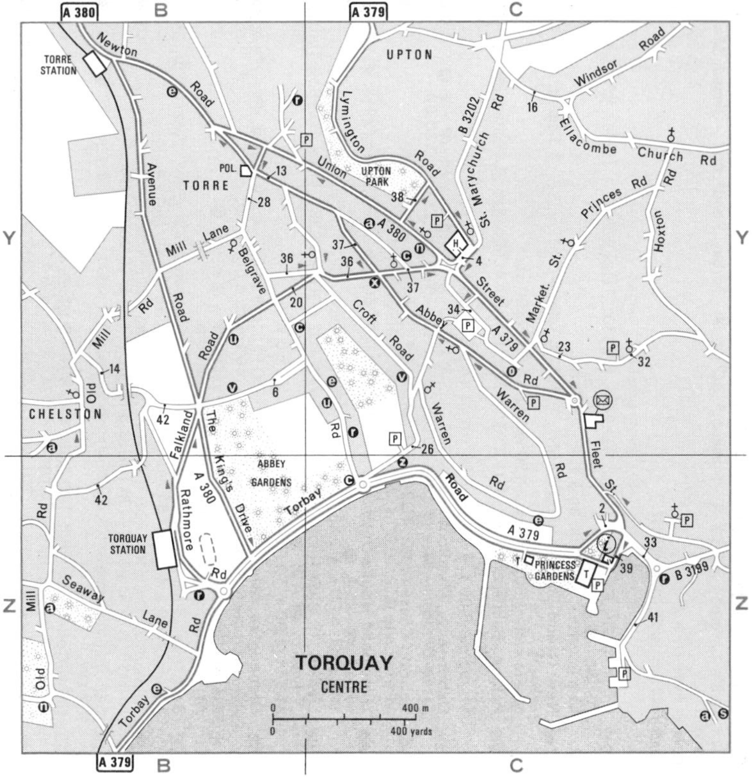

Newton Road · Avenue Road · Mill Lane · Belgrave Road · Union Street · Lymington Road · St. Marychurch Rd · Windsor Road · Ellacombe Church Rd · Princes Rd · Hoxton Rd · Market St. · Abbey Road · Croft Road · Warren Rd · Fleet St. · Torbay Road · The King's Drive · Falkland Road · Rathmore Rd · Old Mill Rd · Seaway Lane · Mill Lane · Old Rd

King's Ash Road · Marldon Rd · Southfield Avenue · Torquay Road · Colley End Road · Totnes Road · Penwill Way · Dartmouth Road · Brixham Road · Long Road · Goodrington Rd

TORQUAY Devon 986 ㊴ – pop. 109,257 (inc. Brixham and Paignton) – ☎ 0803.

See : Kent's Cavern** *AC* CX **A** – Museum* *AC* CX **M** – Torbay Road* BCZ – Ilsham Marine Drive*.

i Vaughan Parade ☎ 27428.

London 223 – Exeter 23 – Plymouth 32.

Plans on preceding pages

Imperial (T.H.F.), Park Hill Rd, TQ1 2DG, ☎ 24301, Telex 42849, ≤ Torbay, ✗, ⛱ heated, ⛱, ⛱ – ⧉ ♿ Ⓟ. ⛱ — CZ a
M a la carte 7.25/12.00 **st.** 🌢 1.65 – **170 rm.**

New Grand, Promenade, TQ2 6NT, ☎ 25234, Telex 42891, ≤, ✗, ⛱ heated, ⛱ – ⧉ ♿ 🚗. ⛱ — BZ r
M a la carte 5.50/8.75 **st.** – **120 rm** ⊏ 14.00/30.00 **st.**

Palace, Babbacombe Rd, TQ1 3TG, ☎ 22271, Telex 42606, ✗, ⛱ heated, ⛱, ⛳9, ⛱, park – ⧉ ♿ 🚗 Ⓟ. ⛱ — CX u
M approx. 5.00 **t.** 🌢 1.00 – **138 rm** ⊏ 14.00/27.00 **t.** – P 18.00/32.40 **t.**

Osborne ⛱, Meadfoot Beach, TQ1 2LL, ☎ 22232, ≤, ✗, ⛱ heated, ⛱ – ⧉ Ⓟ — CX c
Easter-October – **M** a la carte 7.10/8.50 🌢 2.50 – **100 rm** ⊏ 12.20/30.00.

Toorak, Chestnut Av., TQ2 5JS, ☎ 27135, ✗, ⛱ heated, ⛱ – Ⓟ. ⛱ — BY v
M a la carte 6.50/10.00 **s.** 🌢 1.45 – **89 rm** ⊏ 10.00/22.00 **s.**

Livermead House (Interchange), Sea Front, TQ2 6QJ, ☎ 24361, Telex 42918, ≤, ✗, ⛱ heated, ⛱ – ⧉ ♿ Ⓟ — BZ e
M approx. 4.00 **s.** 🌢 1.35 – **77 rm** ⊏ 6.85/19.50 **s.**

Livermead Cliff (Interchange), Sea Front, TQ2 6RQ, ☎ 22881, Telex 42918, ≤ Torbay, ⛱ heated, ⛱ – ⧉ Ⓟ. ⛱ — BX r
M 3.50/4.00 **s.** 🌢 1.35 – **62 rm** ⊏ 6.85/20.50 **s.**

Gleneagles, Asheldon Rd, Wellswood, TQ1 2QS, ☎ 23637, ≤, ⛱ heated, ⛱ – 🛁wc Ⓟ — CX n
April-October – **M** approx. 3.75 🌢 1.45 – **40 rm** ⊏ 8.00/16.00.

Kistor, Belgrave Rd, TQ2 5HF, ☎ 23219, ⛱, ⛱ – ⧉ 🛁wc Ⓟ — CY r
M 3.00/3.50 **s.** 🌢 1.25 – **45 rm** ⊏ 8.50/22.00 **s.**

Belgrave, Belgrave Rd, TQ2 5HE, ☎ 28566, ⛱ heated – ⧉ 🛁wc 🚿wc ☎ Ⓟ. ⛱ — CZ c
M 3.50/5.00 **s.** 🌢 1.30 – **64 rm** ⊏ 9.50/21.50 **s.** – P 15.25/16.50 **s.**

Nepaul, 27 Croft Rd, TQ2 5UD, ☎ 22745, ≤, ⛱ – ⧉ 🛁wc ☎ 🚗 Ⓟ — CY v
M 3.50/3.75 **s.** 🌢 1.25 – **38 rm** ⊏ 8.50/15.00 **s.** – P 10.00/13.00 **s.**

San Remo, Belgrave Rd, TQ2 5HH, ☎ 25548, ⛱ heated, ⛱ – TV 🛁wc ☎ Ⓟ — CY e
46 rm.

Palm Court, Sea Front, TQ2 5HD, ☎ 24881 – ⧉ TV 🛁wc ☎ Ⓟ — CZ z
M 3.40/4.00 **s.** 🌢 1.20 – **75 rm** ⊏ 7.95/21.80 **s.** – P 13.00/15.90 **s.**

Devonshire, Park Hill Rd, TQ1 2DY, ☎ 24850, Telex 42712, ✗, ⛱ heated, ⛱ – 🛁wc Ⓟ — CZ s
M 3.30/3.70 **s.** 🌢 1.20 – **55 rm** ⊏ 9.50/22.50 **s.** – P 8.40/14.50 **s.**

Queens, Victoria Par., TQ1 2AY, ☎ 24324, Telex 42906 – ⧉ 🛁wc ☎ — CZ r
M approx. 3.30 🌢 1.60 – **73 rm** ⊏ 8.90/20.50 – P 11.95/12.45.

Manor House, Seaway Lane, TQ2 6PS, ☎ 65164, ≤, ⛱ – 🛁wc Ⓟ — BZ a
26 rm.

Alpine, Warren Rd, TQ2 4TP, ☎ 27612, ≤ Torbay and harbour, ⛱ – ⧉ 🛁wc 🚿wc ☎ — CZ e
M approx. 3.50 **st.** 🌢 1.20 – **18 rm** ⊏ 7.25/30.50 **st.** – P 12.00/17.25 **st.**

Roslin Hall, 1 Belgrave Rd, TQ2 5HG, ☎ 24373, ⛱ heated, ⛱ – 🛁wc Ⓟ — CY u
Easter-November and Christmas – **M** approx. 3.20 **s.** 🌢 1.70 – **54 rm** ⊏ 5.50/13.00 **s.** – P 7.00/11.50 **s.**

Cavendish, Belgrave Rd, TQ2 5HN, ☎ 23682, ⛱ heated – 🛁wc 🚿wc Ⓟ — BY c
Easter-October – **M** approx. 3.70 **t.** 🌢 1.50 – **58 rm** ⊏ 9.90/22.80 **t.** – P 11.40/14.50 **t.**

Lansdowne, Babbacombe Rd, TQ1 1PW, ☎ 22822, ⛱ heated, ⛱ – 🛁wc Ⓟ — CX z
Easter and mid May-mid October – **M** 3.00/4.25 **s.** 🌢 1.45 – **33 rm** ⊏ 7.50/20.00 **s.** – P 10.00/14.00 **s.**

Windsor, Abbey Rd, TQ2 5NR, ☎ 23757, Telex 42906, ⛱ heated – 🛁wc Ⓟ — CY x
M approx. 2.50 🌢 1.50 – **43 rm** ⊏ 7.00/22.00 **t.** – P 8.50/14.00 **t.**

Coppice, Barrington Rd, Wellswood, TQ1 2QJ, ☎ 27786, ⛱ – 🛁wc Ⓟ — CX i
Easter-October – **M** (bar lunch) 3.00/3.50 🌢 1.05 – **18 rm** ⊏ 5.00/13.50 – P 8.50/9.50.

Nethway, Falkland Rd, TQ2 5JR, ☎ 22151, ⛱ – 🛁wc 🚿wc Ⓟ — BY u
March-November – **M** (dinner only) a la carte approx. 3.50 🌢 1.25 – **22 rm** ⊏ 5.00/12.00 **s.** – P 8.00/9.00 **s.**

Hyperion, Underhill Rd, TQ2 6QU, off Cockington Lane ☎ 67196 – 🛁wc 🚿wc Ⓟ — BZ n
season – **35 rm.**

Clevedon, Meadfoot Sea Rd, TQ1 2LQ, ☎ 24260 – Ⓟ — CX v
April-October – **15 rm** ⊏ 6.50/13.00.

Manor Mead, St. Matthew's Rd, TQ12 6JA, ☎ 65016 – Ⓟ — BY a
21 rm.

Howard, 373 Babbacombe Rd, TQ1 3TB, ☎ 25944 – 🚿 — CX a
12 rm ⊏ 8.00/16.00 **st.**

The Skerries, 25 Morgan Av., TQ2 5RR, ☎ 23618 — CY a
13 rm 3.50/7.00 **st.**

Dalmeny House, 15 Morgan Av., Castle Circus, TQ2 5RP, ☎ 22936 – **13 rm.** — CY c

Audrey Court, Lower Warbery Rd, TQ1 1QS, ☎ 24563, – Ⓟ — CX s
20 rm 5.00/10.00 **s.**

Marina, Tor Vale, TQ1 4EB, ☎ 37626 – Ⓟ – *season* – **15 rm.** — BY r

Concorde, 26 Newton Rd, TQ2 5BZ, ☎ 22330, – Ⓟ — BY e
January-October – **17 rm** 5.00/10.00 **t.**

Fanny's Dining Room, 53 Abbey Rd, TQ2 5HQ, ☎ 28605, « Victorian decor » — CY o
closed Sunday and Christmas – **M** (dinner only) a la carte 4.35/6.60 1.75.

John Dory, 7 Lisburne Sq., TQ2 2PT, ☎ 25217, Seafood — CX x
closed Sunday, Monday, 2 weeks November, 25-26 December and 2 weeks February – **M** (dinner only) a la carte 3.80/5.80 **s.** 1.25.

Mattie's Eating House, 172 Union St., Castle Circus, TQ2 5QP, ☎ 27471 — CY n
M (bar lunch Monday to Friday) a la carte 3.45/5.40 **s.** 1.65.

at Maidencombe **N : 3 ½ m. on A 379 – BX – ✉ 0803 Torquay:**

Maidencombe House, Teignmouth Rd, TQ1 4SF, ☎ 36611, ←, heated, – wc ☎ Ⓟ
M (dinner only) 3.50 1.75 – **32 rm** 6.50/13.00.

at Babbacombe **NE : 1 ½ m. – ✉ 0803 Torquay:**

Babbacombe Cliff, Beach Rd, TQ1 3LY, ☎ 37128, ←, heated, – wc Ⓟ — CX e
26 rm.

Norcliffe, Babbacombe Downs Rd, TQ1 3LF, ☎ 38456, ←, – wc Ⓟ — CX r
Easter-October – **M** 2.50/3.00 **st.** 1.00 – **22 rm** 8.00/16.00 **s.**

CHRYSLER-SIMCA St. Marychurch Rd ☎ 38221
CITROEN Walnut Rd ☎ 65858
DAF ☎ 27403
DAIMLER-JAGUAR-ROVER-TRIUMPH Market St. ☎ 26333
DATSUN 50 Torwood St. ☎ 28555
JENSEN, LOTUS Torwood St. ☎ 27591
OPEL Torwood St. ☎ 24347
PEUGEOT 141 Newton Rd ☎ 63626
RENAULT Woodland Close ☎ 63291
RENAULT Barnton Hill Rd ☎ 39444

TORRINGTON Devon 986 ㉞ ㉟ – pop. 3,050 – 080 52.

See : Castle Hill ←*.

☎ 023 72 (Bideford) 2792.

London 225 – Bideford 7 – Exeter 36 – **Plymouth 51** – Taunton 54.

Castle Hill, South St., EX38 8AA, ☎ 2339 – Ⓟ
M 3.50/5.00 **t.** – **9 rm** 7.50/15.00.

ALFA-ROMEO The Square ☎ 2555
AUSTIN-MORRIS-MG-WOLSELEY Well St. ☎ 2229

TOTLAND BAY I.O.W. 986 ㊴ – see Wight (Isle of).

TOTNES Devon 986 ㊴ – pop. 5,772 – 0803.

See : Guildhall* 16C – St. Mary's Church (rood screen* 15C). **Envir. :** Berry Pomeroy Castle* (ruins 13C-17C) *AC,* NE : 2 ½ m.

i The Plains ☎ 863168 (summer only).

London 224 – Exeter 24 – **Plymouth 23** – Torquay 9.

Seymour, Bridgetown, TQ9 5AA, ☎ 862114 – wc Ⓟ.
M 4.00/5.00 1.50 – **30 rm** 9.50/16.00 – P 14.00/16.00.

Royal Seven Stars, The Plains, TQ9 5DD, ☎ 862125 – wc Ⓟ
M *(closed Christmas Day dinner)* 3.50/3.85 **t.** – **18 rm** 10.00/19.00.

Chateau Bellevue, Newton Rd, TQ9 5BB, N : 1 m. on A 381 ☎ 862608, heated, – wc wc Ⓟ
M (bar lunch) (residents only) approx. 3.50 1.00 – **18 rm** 8.00/18.00.

Mount Plym, Higher Plymouth Rd, TQ9 5PH, ☎ 863757, – Ⓟ
10 rm 4.00/8.00 **t.**

Ffoulkes, 30 High St., TQ9 5RY, ☎ 863853
closed Sunday, Monday lunch, 2 weeks October-November and 2 weeks March – **M** a la carte 3.90/6.05 1.50.

Elbow Room, 6 North St., TQ9 5NZ, ☎ 863480
closed Sunday, Monday and 26 December – **M** (dinner only) a la carte 4.95/7.40 **t.**

at Stoke Gabriel **SE : 4 m. by A 385 – ✉ Totnes – 080 428 Stoke Gabriel:**

Gabriel Court , TQ9 6SF, ☎ 206, , heated, – wc Ⓟ
M 4.50/5.25 1.25 – **25 rm** 9.00/19.50 – P 14.50/19.00.

at Dartington **NW : 2 m. off A 385 – ✉ 0803 Totnes:**

Cott Inn with rm, TQ9 6HE, ☎ 863777 – Ⓟ
M a la carte 5.00/8.00 – 2.00 – **6 rm** 7.50/15.00.

AUSTIN-MG-WOLSELEY, VAUXHALL The Plains ☎ 862247
MAZDA Station Rd ☎ 862404

TOTON Notts. – see Nottingham.

TOWCESTER Northants. 986 ㉜ – pop. 3,768 – ☎ 0327.
Farthingstone ☎ 291, W: 6 m. M 1 Junction 16.
London 70 – Birmingham 50 – Northampton 9 – Oxford 36.

- **Saracen's Head,** Watling St. West, NN12 7BX, ☎ 50414 – Ⓟ
M a la carte 3.00/4.70 **st.** 1.50 – **12 rm** 7.00/10.00 **st.**
- Brave Old Oak, Watling St. East, NN12 8LB, ☎ 50533 – ☎ Ⓟ – **11 rm.**

at Pattishall NW: 5 m. off A 5 – ✉ Towcester – ☎ 032 735 Pattishall:

- **Cornhill Manor** , NN12 8LQ, NW: ¾ m. off A 5 ☎ 203, , park – wc ☎ Ⓟ.
M a la carte 3.50/5.00 **t.** 1.95 – **15 rm** 9.00/16.00 **st.**

MORRIS-MG-WOLSELEY Quinbury End ☎ 032 732 (Blakesley) 208

TREARDDUR BAY Gwynedd – pop. 1,000 – ✉ Holyhead – ☎ 0407.
See: Site*.
London 270 – Holyhead 2.

- **Trearddur Bay** (Interchange), LL65 2UN, ☎ 860301, Telex 61609, , , – TV wc ☎ Ⓟ
M 3.50/6.00 1.75 – **28 rm** 6.50/18.00 – P 13.50/17.00.

TREBETHERICK Cornwall – pop. 1,148 – ✉ Wadebridge – ☎ 020 886.
Rock ☎ 3216, S: 2 m.
London 287 – Newquay 22 – Truro 30.

- **Bodare** , Daymer Bay, PL27 6SA, ☎ 3210, – wc wc Ⓟ
March-October – **M** (bar lunch) 3.00/4.50 0.70 – **18 rm** 6.00/13.00 – P 8.00/10.00.

TREGREHAN Cornwall – see St. Austell.

TRENTBRIDGE Notts. – see Nottingham.

TRESCO Cornwall – see Scilly (Isles of).

TREYARNON BAY Cornwall – pop. 100 – ✉ Padstow – ☎ 0841 St. Merryn.
Constantine Bay ☎ 0841 (St. Merryn) 208, N: 1 m.
London 292 – Newquay 9 – Truro 23.

- **Waterbeach** , PL28 8JW, ☎ 520292, ≤, , – wc Ⓟ
end April-mid October – **M** approx. 4.50 **s.** 1.80 – **23 rm** 8.00/23.00 **s.** – P 11.00/15.00 **s.**

TRING Herts. 986 ㉜ – pop. 9,178 – ☎ 044 282.
See: Church of St. Peter and St. Paul (interior: stone corbels*).
London 38 – Aylesbury 7 – Luton 14.

- **Rose and Crown** (T.H.F.), High St., HP23 5AH, ☎ 4071 – TV wc ☎ Ⓟ.
M a la carte 4.00/5.50 **st.** 1.50 – **16 rm** 8.50/15.50 **st.**
- **Trattoria Pinocchio,** 56-57 High St., HP23 5AG, ☎ 4210
closed 25 and 26 December – **M** a la carte 3.00/4.85 1.00.

AUSTIN-MORRIS-MG-WOLSELEY 110 Western Rd ☎ 4144
RENAULT 22 Western Rd ☎ 3027
ROVER-TRIUMPH Brook St. ☎ 2455

TROUTBECK Cumbria – see Windermere.

TRURO Cornwall 986 ㊳ – pop. 14,849 – ☎ 0872.
See: Country Museum*. **Envir.:** Trelissick gardens* *AC*, S: 4½ m.
Treliske ☎ 2640, W: 2 m. on A 390.
i Municipal Buildings, Boscawen St. ☎ 4555.
London 297 – Exeter 87 – Penzance 26 – Plymouth 52.

- **Brookdale,** Tregolls Rd, TR1 1JZ, ☎ 3513 – TV wc wc Ⓟ
M 3.00/4.00 **s.** – **56 rm** 7.50/18.80 **s.**
- **Royal,** Lemon St., TR1 2QB, ☎ 2099 – wc Ⓟ
M 3.00/4.00 – **36 rm** 5.75/13.50.
- **Carlton,** 49 Falmouth Rd, TR1 2HL, ☎ 2450 – wc wc Ⓟ
closed 1 to 23 October and 23 December-3 January – **M** (dinner only) a la carte approx. 3.65 1.30 – **24 rm** 6.10/11.75.
- **Pencowl,** 12-14 Ferris Town, ☎ 4946
15 rm 4.85/8.00.
- **Roundhouse,** 37 St. Austell St., TR1 1SE, ☎ 2218 – Ⓟ
closed Sunday – **M** a la carte 4.10/5.20 **t.** 1.20.

AUSTIN-DAIMLER-JAGUAR-MORRIS-MG-WOLSELEY, ROLLS ROYCE Newquay Rd ☎ 2581
CHRYSLER Bissoe ☎ 0872 (Devoran) 863073
DAF, TOYOTA Calenick St. ☎ 2995
FORD Lemon Quay ☎ 3933
ROVER-TRIUMPH 10 City Rd ☎ 4321
VAUXHALL Faimantle St. ☎ 6231
VW, AUDI-NSU Three Milestone ☎ 3954

TUDDENHAM Suffolk – pop. 327 – ✉ Bury St. Edmunds – ☎ 0638 Mildenhall.
London 73 – Cambridge 22 – Ipswich 37.

XX Tuddenham Mill, IP28 6SQ, ☎ 713552, « Converted water mill » – Ⓟ.

TUNBRIDGE WELLS Kent 986 ㊱ – see Royal Tunbridge Wells.

TURVEY Beds. – see Bedford.

TUTBURY Staffs. – pop. 3,025 – ✉ ☎ 0283 Burton-upon-Trent.
London 132 – Birmingham 33 – Derby 11 – Stoke-on-Trent 27.

XX **Ye Olde Dog and Partridge Inn** with rm, High St., DE13 9LS, ☎ 813030, « 15C timbered inn » – TV Ⓟ
closed Sunday dinner and 25-26 December – **M** a la carte 4.60/6.30 – **5 rm** ☕ 7.00/14.00.

TUXFORD Notts. 986 ㉘ – pop. 2,145 – ✉ Newark – ☎ 0777.
London 141 – Leeds 53 – Lincoln 18 – Nottingham 26 – Sheffield 29.

🏠 **Newcastle Arms,** NG22 0LA, ☎ 870208 – TV ⛀wc ⫫ ☎ 🚗 Ⓟ. 🏠
M 4.50/6.50 🍷 1.50 – **13 rm** ☕ 9.00/15.00.

TWO BRIDGES Devon – pop. 30 – ✉ Yelverton – ☎ 0822 Postbridge.
London 226 – Exeter 25 – Plymouth 17.

⌂ **Cherrybrook** 🐦, PL20 6SP, NE: 1 m. on B 3212 ☎ 88260, ≤ – Ⓟ
closed Christmas and 1 January – **8 rm** ☕ 5.15/10.25 **st.**

TYNEMOUTH Tyne and Wear 986 ⑲ – pop. 69,338 – ☎ 089 45 North Shields.
See: Priory and castle: ruins* (11C) *AC*.
⛳18 Spital Dene ☎ 74578.
i Grand Parade ☎ 70251.
London 290 – Newcastle-upon-Tyne 8 – Sunderland 7.

🏨 Grand (Crest), Grand Parade, NE30 3ER, ☎ 72106, ≤ – 🛗 TV ⛀wc ☎ Ⓟ. 🏠
38 rm.

🏨 Park (Thistle), Grand Parade, NE30 4JQ, ☎ 71406, ≤ – TV ⛀wc ☎ Ⓟ. 🏠
26 rm.

FIAT 5/7 Tynemouth Rd ☎ 71830
RENAULT Preston North Rd, Preston Grange ☎ 70352

UCKFIELD East Sussex 986 ㊱ – pop. 5,973 – ☎ 0825.
⛳18 Piltdown ☎ 082 572 (Newick) 2033, W: 2 ½ m.
London 45 – Brighton 17 – Eastbourne 20 – Maidstone 34.

X Sussex Barn, Ringles Cross, TN22 1HB, N: 1 m. on A 22 ☎ 3827 – Ⓟ.

at Framfield SE: 1¾ m. on B 2102 – ✉ Uckfield – ☎ 082 582 Framfield:

X **Coach House,** The Street, TN22 5NL, ☎ 636 – Ⓟ
closed Sunday dinner, Monday, 25-26 December, 1 week May and 2 weeks October –
M a la carte 5.20/7.15 **t.** 🍷 1.60.

AUSTIN-MORRIS-MG-ROVER-TRIUMPH 84/86 High St. ☎ 4255
OPEL London Rd, Maresfield ☎ 2477
PEUGEOT London Rd ☎ 4151
VAUXHALL 143/145 High St. ☎ 2786

ULLSWATER Cumbria 986 ⑲ – ✉ Penrith – ☎ 085 36 Pooley Bridge.
See : Lake*.
i Car Park, Glenridding ☎ 085 32 (Glenridding) 414 (summer only).
London 295 – **Carlisle 29** – Kendal 31 – Penrith 6.

Sharrow Bay Country House ⛰, CA10 2LZ, S: 2 m. on Howtown Rd ☎ 301, ≤ lake and hills, « Lake-side setting, tasteful decor », 🌳 – ⛀wc ☎ ♿ 🚗 Ⓟ
closed December and January – M approx. 7.50 **s.** – **26 rm** ☕ 12.50/33.00 **s.**

at Watermillock on A 592 – ✉ Penrith – ☎ 085 36 Pooley Bridge :

Leeming on Ullswater ⛰, CA11 0JJ, on A 592 ☎ 444, ≤ lake, hills and gardens, « Elegant installation and finely laid out gardens », park – Ⓟ
M a la carte 3.95/4.85 🍾 0.90 – ☕ 1.20 – **17 rm** 10.00/20.00.

at Glenridding – ✉ Penrith – ☎ 085 32 Glenridding:

Glenridding, CA11 0PB, on A 592 ☎ 228, ≤, 🌳 – ⛀wc Ⓟ
M approx. 3.75 **st.** 🍾 1.30 – **33 rm** ☕ 8.00/16.00 **st.** – P 14.50 **st.**

ULVERSTON Cumbria 986 ㉓ – pop. 11,907 – ☎ 0229.
Envir.: Furness Abbey* (ruins 13C - 15C) *AC*, SW: 6 ½ m.
i 17 Fountain St. ☎ 52299.
London 278 – Kendal 25 – Lancaster 36.

Lonsdale House, Daltongate, LA12 7BD, ☎ 52598, 🌳 – TV ⛀wc ☎
M a la carte 3.65/5.20 🍾 1.70 – **13 rm** ☕ 7.00/15.00.

Sefton House, 34 Queen St., LA12 7AF, ☎ 52190 – 🚿
8 rm ☕ 4.50/9.40 **st.**

at Lowick Green NE: 5 m. on A 5092 by A 590 – ✉ Ulverston – ☎ 022 986 Greenodd :

Farmers Arms, LA12 8DJ, ☎ 376 – Ⓟ
9 rm.

at Baycliff S: 4 m. on A 5087 – ✉ Ulverston – ☎ 022 988 Bardsea :

Fisherman's Arms, Coast Rd, LA12 9RJ, ☎ 387 – ⛀wc Ⓟ
closed 25 and 26 December – **M** approx. 3.75 **st.** 🍾 0.75 – **12 rm** ☕ 6.00/16.00.

UNDERBARROW Cumbria – pop. 362 (inc. Bradleyfield) – ✉ Kendal – ☎ 044 88 Crosthwaite.
London 266 – **Blackpool 49** – **Carlisle 56** – Kendal 3.5.

Greenriggs Country House ⛰, LA8 8HF, E: ½ m. ☎ 387, ≤, 🌳 – ⛀wc Ⓟ
March-November and week-ends in winter – **M** (dinner only) 5.00/6.00 **st.** 🍾 1.20 – **12 rm** ☕ (dinner included) 12.00/26.00 **st.**

UPLYME Dorset – see Lyme Regis.

UPPER HALLIFORD Middx. – see Shepperton.

UPPER SLAUGHTER Glos. – see Stow-on-the-Wold.

UPPINGHAM Leics. 986 ㉘ – pop. 3,250 – ☎ 057 282.
London 101 – **Leicester 19** – Northampton 28 – **Nottingham 35.**

Falcon, High St. East, LE15 9PY, ☎ 3535, 🌳 – ⛀wc 🚿wc ☎ Ⓟ. 🏔
22 rm.

UPTON Cheshire – pop. 10,441.
See : Chester zoo** *AC*.
London 196 – Birkenhead 14 – Chester 2 – **Manchester 39.**

Hotels and restaurants see : Chester S: 2 m.

UPTON NOBLE Somerset – pop. 89 – ✉ Shepton Mallet – ☎ 074 985.
London 122 – Bath 22 – Exeter 63 – Frome 7.

✕ **Lamb Inn,** Church St., BA4 6AS, ☎ 308 – Ⓟ
closed Sunday, Monday and Bank Holidays – **M** (dinner only) 4.75/5.75 **st.** 🍾 1.50.

UPTON UPON SEVERN Heref. and Worc. 986 ㉛ – pop. 2,048 – ☎ 068 46.
i Church Lodge, 69 Old St. ☎ 2318.
London 116 – Hereford 25 – Stratford-on-Avon 29 – Worcester 11.

White Lion, High St., WR8 0HJ, ☎ 2551 – ⛀wc ☎ Ⓟ
M 2.00/3.00 🍾 1.00 – **14 rm** ☕ 7.25/14.50.

Pool House, Hanley Rd, WR8 0PA, NW: ½ m. on B 4211 ☎ 2151, ≤, ⛰, 🌳 – Ⓟ
Easter-October – **12 rm** ☕ 5.00/10.00 **t.**

USK Gwent 986 ㉛㉟ – pop. 2,033 – ☎ 029 13.
See : Valley*.
i Tourist Information Centre, Old Smithy Gallery, Maryport St. ☎ 2207.
London 144 – **Bristol 30** – Gloucester 39 – Newport 10.

Three Salmons, Bridge St., NP5 1BQ, ☎ 2133, – wc P
M a la carte 4.65/8.75 **st.** 1.75 – **30 rm** 8.50/15.00 **st.**

Glen-yr-Afon House, Pontypool Rd, NP5 1SY, ☎ 2302, – wc P
closed 25 December to 31 December – **M** approx. 2.70 **t.** 1.20 – **14 rm** 7.30/10.80 **st.**

AUSTIN-MG-WOLSELEY ☎ 2136
MORRIS-MG-WOLSELEY ☎ 2014

UTTOXETER Staffs. 986 ㉗ – pop. 9,039 – ☎ 088 93.
London 145 – **Birmingham 33** – Derby 19 – Stafford 13 – **Stoke-on-Trent 16.**

White Hart (Ansells), Carter St., ST14 8EU, ☎ 2437 – wc wc P
M a la carte 3.50/5.50 **st.** – **16 rm** 11.00/16.00 **st.**

AUSTIN-JAGUAR-MG-ROVER-TRIUMPH 20/24 Carter St. ☎ 2255
CHRYSLER-SIMCA Market St. ☎ 2858
MORRIS-MG, VAUXHALL Derby Rd ☎ 2301

VENTNOR I.O.W. 986 ㊴㊵ – see Wight (Isle of).

VERYAN Cornwall – pop. 876 – ✉ Truro – ☎ 087 250.
London 291 – St. Austell 13 – Truro 13.

Nare, Carne Beach, TR2 5PF, ☎ 279, ← Gerrans Bay, heated, – wc P
40 rm.

WADDESDON Bucks. 986 ㉜ – pop. 1,939 – ☎ 029 665.
See : Waddesdon Manor (Rothschild Collection***) *AC.*
London 52 – Aylesbury 6 – **Birmingham 66** – **Oxford 25.**

WADDINGTON Lancs. – pop. 885 – ✉ ☎ 0200 Clitheroe.
London 237 – **Blackpool 36** – **Leeds 45** – **Liverpool 50.**

Ye Moorcock Inne, BB7 3AA, N : 2 m. on B 6478 ☎ 22333, ←, – wc P
M a la carte 3.65/6.20 **st.** 1.10 – **5 rm** 9.75/15.50 **st.**

WADEBRIDGE Cornwall 986 ㊳ – pop. 3,553 – ☎ 020 881.
London 280 – Exeter 70 – **Plymouth 37** – Truro 23.

Molesworth Arms, Molesworth St., PL27 7DP, ☎ 2055 – wc P
M 2.00/4.50 **t.** 1.00 – **13 rm** 5.00/12.00 **t.** – P 8.00/14.00 **t.**

AUSTIN-MORRIS-MG Molesworth St. ☎ 2121
ROVER-TRIUMPH Brooklyn Garage ☎ 2758

WAKEFIELD West Yorks. 986 ⑫ and ㉓ – pop. 59,590 – ☎ 0924.
Envir. : Temple Newsam House* 17C (interior**) *AC*, N : 8 ½ m. – Pontefract (castle* : ruins 12C-13C) *AC*, E : 9 m.
18 Flushdyke, Ossett ☎ 092 43 (Ossett) 3275, N : 2 m. – 18 Woodthorpe ☎ 55104, S : 3 m. – 18 Lupset Park, Horbury Rd ☎ 74316 – 9 Painthorpe Lane ☎ 55083, near junction 39 on M 1.
London 188 – **Leeds 9** – **Manchester 38** – **Sheffield 23.**

Post House (T.H.F.), Queen's Drive, Ossett, WF5 9BE, W : 2 ½ m. on A 638 ☎ 276388, Telex 55407, – P.
M 2.95/4.00 **st.** 1.50 – 2.00 – **96 rm** 14.00/20.00 **st.**

Swallow (Swallow), Queen St., WF1 1JR, ☎ 72111 – wc P.
64 rm.

AUSTIN-MG 160 Westgate ☎ 74222
BMW, DATSUN Barnsley Rd ☎ 55904
CHRYSLER-SIMCA, FIAT Ings Rd ☎ 76771
FORD Barnsley Rd ☎ 74801
JAGUAR-ROVER-TRIUMPH Doncaster Rd ☎ 77261
MORRIS-MG-WOLSELEY Ings Rd ☎ 70100
MORRIS-MG-WOLSELEY Robin Hood ☎ 0532 (Leeds) 822254
OPEL Chapelthorpe ☎ 50336
RENAULT 129 New Rd, Middlestown ☎ 0924 (Horbury) 2087
TOYOTA Stanley Rd ☎ 73493
VAUXHALL 106/118 Horbury Rd ☎ 75588
VAUXHALL 68 Ings Rd ☎ 72812
VOLVO Barnsley Rd ☎ 55126

WALBERTON West Sussex – see Arundel.

WALBERSWICK Suffolk – pop. 423 – ✉ ☎ 050 272 (4 fig.) or 0502 (6 fig.) Southwold.
London 106 – Great Yarmouth 28 – **Ipswich 33** – **Norwich 32.**

Anchor, Main St., IP18 6UA, ☎ 2112, – wc P
14 rm.

P 9.00/9.50

Les **prix de pension** sont donnés, dans le guide,
à titre indicatif.
Pour un séjour consultez toujours l'hôtelier.

WALL Northumb. – pop. 423 – ✉ Hexham – ☎ 043 481 Humshaugh.
Envir.: Chesters Roman fort* (museum) *AC*, N: **1** m.
London 305 – Carlisle 37 – Newcastle-upon-Tyne 22.

XX **Hadrian** with rm, NE46 4EE, ☎ 232, ⛱ – Ⓟ
M a la carte 3.60/6.10 🍶 2.80 – **8 rm** ☕ 8.50/15.75.

WALLASEY Merseyside 986 ⑤ and ㉓ ㉗ – pop. **97,215** – ☎ **051** Liverpool.
Bayswater Rd ☎ **051 639 (New Brighton) 3630.**
i Pier Entrance, New Brighton ☎ 051 639 (New Brighton) 3929 (summer only).
London 219 – Birkenhead 3,5 – **Liverpool 5.**

St. Hilary, Grove Rd, L45 3HF, ☎ 639 3947, ⛱ – Ⓟ
M (dinner only and Sunday lunch) (residents only) a la carte 3.20/4.90 **st.** – **14 rm** ☕ 8.00/14.75 **st.**

AUSTIN-MORRIS-MG-PRINCESS-ROVER-TRIUMPH, VANDEN PLAS Harrison Drive ☎ 639 6181

WALLINGFORD Oxon. 986 ㉟ ㊱ – pop. **6,182** – ☎ **0491.**
London 54 – Oxford 12 – Reading 16.

George, High St., OX10 0BS, ☎ 36665 – TV ⛀wc ☎ Ⓟ.
M (dinner for residents only) 3.00/3.40 **t.** 🍶 1.65 – **18 rm** ☕ 10.50/17.50 **t.**

Shillingford Bridge, OX10 8LZ, N: 2 m. on A 329 ☎ 086 732 (Warborough) 8567, ≤, heated, ⛱ – ⛀wc ⛀wc Ⓟ.
M a la carte 4.10/6.60 **t.** 🍶 1.70 – **20 rm** ☕ 7.00/16.00 **t.**

WALLSEND Tyne and Wear – see Newcastle-upon-Tyne.

WALMLEY West Midlands – see Birmingham.

WALSALL West Midlands 986 ⑫ and ㉗ – pop. **184,734** – ☎ **0922.**
London 126 – Birmingham 9 – Coventry 29 – Shrewsbury 36.

Plan of Enlarged Area: See Birmingham p. 2-3

Walsall Crest Motel (Crest), Birmingham Rd, WS5 3AB, SE: 1 m. on A 34 ☎ 33555 – 🛗 TV ⛀wc ☎ Ⓟ CT **e**
M 2.75/3.80 **s.** 🍶 1.55 – ☕ 1.60 – **106 rm** 10.95/15.50 **s.**

County, 45 Birmingham Rd, WS1 2NG, ☎ 32323 – ⛀wc ☎ Ⓟ CT **u**
46 rm.

at Walsall Wood NE: 3 ½ m. on A 461 – CT – ✉ Walsall – ☎ 054 33 Brownhills:

Barons Court, Walsall Rd, WS9 9AH, ☎ 6543 – 🛗 TV Ⓟ.
M *(closed Saturday lunch and Sunday dinner)* – **M** 4.00/5.00 **t.** 🍶 2.75 – **42 rm** ☕ 9.60/16.20 **t.**

AUSTIN-MORRIS-MG Hatherton Rd ☎ 32911
CHRYSLER-SIMCA Charlotte St. ☎ 21723
DAIMLER-JAGUAR-ROVER-TRIUMPH Wolverhampton St. ☎ 26567
FORD Wolverhampton St. ☎ 21212
PEUGEOT 57/8 Lower Forster St. ☎ 27321
RENAULT Day St. ☎ 613232
SAAB West Bromwich Rd ☎ 22695
VAUXHALL 126 Lichfield St. ☎ 25111
VW, AUDI-NSU Pleck Rd ☎ 25562

WALSGRAVE-ON-SOWE West Midlands – see Coventry.

WALSHFORD North Yorks. – see Wetherby.

WALTON-ON-THAMES Surrey 986 ⑧ – pop. **51,134** (inc. Weybridge) – ☎ **093 22.**
i Town Hall, New-Zealand Av. ☎ 25141.
London 22 – Portsmouth 60.

X **Angelo's,** 70 Terrace Rd, KT12 2SF, NE: 1¼ m. on A 3050 ☎ 41964, Italian rest.
closed Sunday – **M** a la carte 6.20/8.20 🍶 1.50.

AUSTIN-DAIMLER-JAGUAR-MORRIS-MG New Zealand Av. ☎ 20404
RENAULT Station Av. ☎ 23736

WANSFORD Cambs. 986 ㉘ – see Peterborough.

WANTAGE Oxon. 986 ㉟ – pop. **8,034** – ☎ **023 57.**
Envir.: White Horse ≤*.
London 75 – Bristol 58 – Oxford 15 – Reading 25.

Bear, Market Pl., OX12 8AB, ☎ 3781 – Ⓟ
15 rm.

AUSTIN-MG Wallingford St. ☎ 3355
MORRIS Main St. Grove ☎ 3534
SAAB East Hanney ☎ 023 587 (West Hanney) 257
VW, AUDI-NSU, CHRYSLER-SIMCA Grove Rd ☎ 65511

WARE Herts. 986 ㉜ – pop. **14,727** – ☎ **0920.**
London 24 – Cambridge 30 – Luton 22.

Cannons, Baldock St., SG12 9DR, N: ½ m. on A 10 ☎ 5011 – 🛗 TV ⛀wc ☎ Ⓟ.
M *(closed Christmas)* a la carte 4.60/5.85 **st.** 🍶 2.40 – ☕ 1.65 – **50 rm** 13.50/16.50 **st.**

WAREHAM Dorset 986 ㊴ – pop. 4,368 – ☎ 092 95.
See : St. Martin's Church* (Norman), St. Mary's Church (font* 12C).
London 123 – Bournemouth 13 – Weymouth 19.

✗ **Olivers,** 46 West St., BH20 4JZ, ☎ 6164
closed Monday, 2 weeks in Autumn and 2 weeks in Spring – **M** (dinner only) a la carte 4.25/5.10 **st.** 1.30.

WARK Northumb. – pop. 689 – ✉ Hexham – ☎ 0660.
London 309 – Carlisle 42 – Newcastle-upon-Tyne 27.

Battlesteads, NE48 3LS, ☎ 30209, – **P**
closed Christmas Day – **M** a la carte approx. 3.85 **t.** – **6 rm** 6.00/10.00 **t.**

WARRINGTON Cheshire 986 ⑤ and ㉗ – pop. 68,317 – ☎ 0925.
See : St. Elphin's Church (chancel* 14C).
18 Hill Warren ☎ 61620, S: 3 m. – 18 Warrington Rd ☎ 66775, S: 2 m.
i 80 Sankey St. ☎ 36501.
London 195 – Chester 20 – **Liverpool 18** – **Manchester 21** – Preston 28.

Patten Arms, Parker St. (Bank Quay Station), WA1 1LS, ☎ 36602 – TV wc wc ☎ **P**
46 rm.

Hill Cliffe Hydro, London Rd, WA4 5BS, S: 2 ¼ m. on A 49 ☎ 63638, – wc **P**
closed Bank Holidays – **M** *(closed Sunday dinner)* approx. 4.50 **t.** 1.50 – **11 rm** 7.25/11.00.

Birchdale, Birchdale Rd, Stockton Heath, WA4 5AW, S: 1 ¾ m. off A 49 ☎ 63662, – **P**
M *(closed Saturday and Sunday)* (dinner only) approx. 2.80 **st.** 1.30 – **22 rm** 5.00/9.00 **st.**

at Grappenhall SE: 2 m. off A 50 – ✉ ☎ 0925 Warrington:

Fir Grove Inn, Knutsford Old Rd, WA4 2LD, ☎ 67471 – TV wc wc ☎ **P**.
M *(closed Saturday lunch, Sunday and Bank Holidays)* a la carte 4.50/7.10 2.00 – **38 rm** 11.50/16.50.

at Stretton S: 3 ½ m. by A 49 on B 5356 – ✉ Warrington – ☎ 092 573 Norcott Brook:

Old Vicarage, Stretton Rd, WA4 4NS, ☎ 238, – wc **P**
M 3.60/5.10 **s.** 1.00 – **37 rm** 6.50/13.70 **s.**

AUSTIN-MG-WOLSELEY Wilderspool Causeway ☎ 33515
AUSTIN-MORRIS-MG-ROVER-TRIUMPH-WOLSELEY Castle St. ☎ 0606 (Northwich) 75333
CHRYSLER Manchester Rd ☎ 3027
DAIMLER-JAGUAR-ROVER-TRIUMPH Warrington Rd, Penketh ☎ 725611
FORD Winwick Rd ☎ 34484
HONDA 60 Winwick St. ☎ 34713
MORRIS-MG-WOLSELEY Padgate Lane ☎ 50011
RENAULT Farrell St. ☎ 30448
VW, AUDI-NSU, DAF 101 Knutsford Rd ☎ 62723

Oltre ai ristoranti indicati con
XXXXX ... X,
si può trovare un buon ristorante
anche in molti alberghi.

WARWICK Warw. 986 ㉛ – pop. 18,296 – ☎ 0926.
See : Castle** (14C) *AC* Y – St. Mary's Church* 12C-18C Y **A** – Lord Leycester's Hospital* Y **B**.
9 Warwick Golf Centre ☎ 44316 Y.
i Court House, Jury St. ☎ 42212.
London 96 – Birmingham 20 – Coventry 11 – Oxford 43.

Plan on next page

Woolpack (Crest), Market Pl., CV34 4SD, ☎ 41684 – wc. — Y **a**
M 2.85/3.45 **s.** – 1.55 – **26 rm** 10.95/16.10 **s.**

Lord Leycester (Norfolk Cap.), Jury St., CV34 4EJ, ☎ 41481, Group Telex 23241 – wc ☎ **P**. — Y **c**
M a la carte 3.15/5.25 **st.** – **43 rm** 7.90/17.55 **st.**

Warwick Arms, 17 High St., CV34 4AT, ☎ 42759 – **P** — Y **n**
M 3.25/3.50 1.35 – **34 rm** 7.15/15.10.

XXX **Westgate Arms,** Old Bowling Green St., CV34 4DD, ☎ 42362, – **P** — Y **u**
closed Sunday and Bank Holiday Mondays – **M** a la carte 3.45/7.50 1.25.

XX **Aylesford,** 1 High St., CV34 4AP, ☎ 42799, Italian rest. — Y **e**
closed Sunday – **M** a la carte 4.80/6.65.

FIAT Wharf St. ☎ 46231
RENAULT Emscote Rd ☎ 41235

WARWICK ROYAL LEAMINGTON SPA

High Street	Y 19
Jury Street	Y
Market Place	Y 27
Smith Street	Y
Swan Street	Y 46
Birmingham Road	Z 6
Bowling Green Street	Y 7
Brook Street	Y 9
Butts (The)	Y 12
Castle Hill	Y 13
Church Street	Y 15
Lakin Road	Y 23
Linen Street	Y 25
North Rock	Y 33
Old Square	Y 34
Old Warwick Road	Z 36
Radford Road	Z 38
St. John's Road	Y 42
St. Nicholas Church Street	Y 44
Theatre Street	Y 48
West Street	Y 50

Les plans de villes sont orientés le Nord en haut.

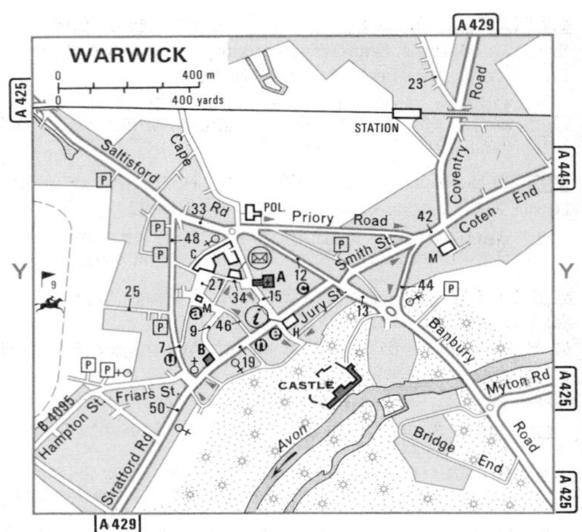

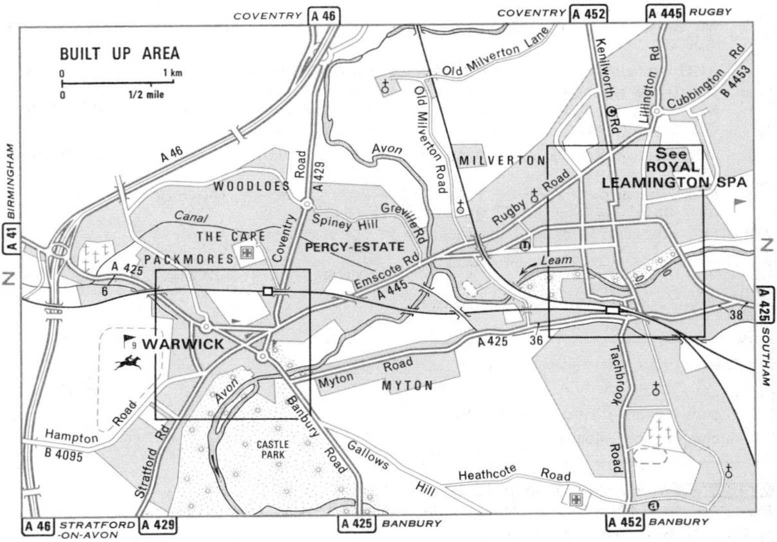

BUILT UP AREA

0 1 km
0 1/2 mile

COVENTRY A 46 — COVENTRY A 452 — A 445 RUGBY — A 41 BIRMINGHAM — A 425 SOUTHAM — A 46 STRATFORD-ON-AVON — A 429 — A 425 BANBURY — A 452 BANBURY

WOODLOES — THE CAPE — PACKMORES — PERCY-ESTATE — MILVERTON — WARWICK — MYTON — CASTLE PARK — See ROYAL LEAMINGTON SPA

WASHINGTON Tyne and Wear 986 ⑲ – pop. 24,057 – ✉ Tyneside – ☎ 0632.

London 278 – Durham 13 – Middlesbrough 32 – Newcastle-upon-Tyne 7.

Post House (T.H.F.), 5 Emerson District, NE37 1LB, via interchange A 1231 on A 1 (M) off A 1231, ☎ 462264, Telex 537574 – 🛗 TV ⌂wc ☎ 🅟. **M** 2.95/4.00 **st.** 🌡 1.50 – ☕ 2.00 – **145 rm** 13.00/18.00 **st.**

AUSTIN-MG-WOLSELEY Village Lane ☎ 460607

WASHINGTON West Sussex 986 ㊱ – see Ashington.

WATCHET Somerset 986 ㉟ – pop. 2,900 – ☎ 098 459.

Envir.: Cleeve Abbey* (ruins 13C) SW: 2 m.

London 180 – Bristol 57 – Taunton 18.

Downfield, 16 St. Decumans Rd, TA23 0HR, ☎ 31267, 🌳 – 🅟
M (dinner only) 2.50/4.00 **t.** 🌡 1.30 – **8 rm** ☕ 5.50/10.00.

WATERHEAD Cumbria – see Ambleside.

WATERLOO Merseyside – see Liverpool.

WATERLOOVILLE Hants. – pop. **10,109** – ✉ Portsmouth – ☎ **070 14.**
London 68 – Brighton 44 – Portsmouth 9 – Southampton 21.

Far End, 31 Queen's Rd, PO7 7SB, ☎ 3242, – Ⓟ
closed 23 December-1 January – **8 rm** 7.00/14.00 **s.**

WATERMILLOCK Cumbria – see Ullswater.

WATFORD Herts. 986 ④ and ㉜㊱ – pop. **78,465** – ☎ **0923.**
London 21 – Aylesbury 23.

Beehive, Elton Way, WDE 8HA, Watford By-Pass N : 3 ½ m. on A 41 at junction A 4008 ☎ 35881, Telex 923422 – wc & Ⓟ. – **116 rm.**

Caledonian, St. Albans Rd, WD1 1RN, ☎ 29212 – wc . **M** 2.75/3.25 **t.** 1.75 – **90 rm** 11.50/14.00 **t.**

AUSTIN-DAIMLER-JAGUAR-MORRIS-MG-ROVER-TRIUMPH-WOLSELEY 425/445 St. Albans Rd ☎ 22311
AUSTIN-MG-WOLSELEY 16 St. Albans Rd ☎ 25283
CHRYSLER-SIMCA 59/61 St. Albans Rd ☎ 35517
DAF, MERCEDES-BENZ, SAAB High Rd at Bushey Heath ☎ 950 3311
FORD 6/10 High Rd at Bushey Heath ☎ 950 7512
MORRIS-MG Pinner Rd ☎ 28680
PEUGEOT Aldenham ☎ 092 76 (Radlett) 2177
SAAB Sutton Rd ☎ 26596
VAUXHALL, VOLVO 329 St. Albans Rd ☎ 31716

WATLINGTON Oxon. – pop. **2,055** – ☎ **049 161.**
London 45 – Oxford 14 – Reading 14.

Martha's Kitchen, 27 Couching St., OX9 5QG, ☎ 2673, Bistro
closed Sunday dinner, Monday, 24 December, 1 to 10 January and Bank Holidays – **M** a la carte 2.95/4.00 **t.** 1.05.

WATTON Norfolk 986 ㉘ – pop. **3,343** – ☎ **0953.**
London 133 – Cambridge 47 – King's Lynn 25 – Norwich 21.

Willow House, Norwich Rd, IP25 6AE, ☎ 881181 – Ⓟ
closed Sunday dinner and Monday – **M** a la carte 3.90/5.50.

WEDMORE Somerset – pop. **2,400** – ☎ **0934.**
London 140 – Bristol 24 – Taunton 25.

George, Church St., BS28 4AB, ☎ 712124 – Ⓟ
M (bar lunch) a la carte 2.90/4.55 **t.** 1.25 – **10 rm** 7.50/14.00 **t.**

VW, AUDI-NSU Latcham ☎ 712170

WELL Hants. – see Odiham.

WELLAND Heref. and Worc. – see Malvern.

WELLESBOURNE HASTINGS Warw. – pop. **3,215** – ☎ **0789** Stratford-on-Avon.
London 96 – Birmingham 26 – Stratford-on-Avon 6 – Warwick 7.

King's Head, CV35 9LT, ☎ 840206 – Ⓟ
M *(closed last week July to third week August and Christmas Day)* (snack lunch) 3.00/5.30 **t.** 1.10 – **9 rm** 7.00/14.50.

JAGUAR Warwick Rd ☎ 840208

WELLINGBOROUGH Northants. 986 ㉜ – pop. **37,656** – ☎ **0933.**
Envir. : Higham Ferrers (St. Mary's Church* 13C-14C) E : 5 ½ m.
London 73 – Cambridge 43 – Leicester 34 – Northampton 10.

Hind (County), Sheep St., NN8 1BL, ☎ 222827 – Ⓟ
M 2.70/3.50 **st.** 1.10 – **28 rm** 7.00/13.00 **st.**

High View, 156 Midland Rd, NN8 1NG, ☎ 226060
19 rm 4.90/8.65 **t.**

CHRYSLER-SIMCA Finedon Rd ☎ 76651
FIAT Broad Green ☎ 223924
FORD Park Rd ☎ 3484
MORRIS-MG-WOLSELEY 57/61 Broad Green ☎ 2988
MORRIS-MG-WOLSELEY Oxford St. ☎ 2403
ROVER-TRIUMPH St. John's St. ☎ 224918
TOYOTA Alma St. ☎ 76173
VAUXHALL Oxford St. ☎ 223252

WELLINGTON Somerset 986 ㉟ – pop. **9,359** – ☎ **0823** Greenham.
i Bowermans Travel, 6 South St. ☎ 2716.
London 178 – Exeter 27 – Taunton 7.

Beam Bridge with rm, TA21 0HB, SW : 2 ½ m. on A 38 ☎ 672223 – Ⓟ
M *(closed Sunday dinner)* a la carte 3.05/5.10 **s.** 1.00 – **7 rm** 5.95/11.00 **st.**

AUSTIN-MORRIS-MG 44 High St. ☎ 2648

WELLS Somerset 986 ㉟ – pop. 8,604 – ✆ 0749.
See : Cathedral*** 13C-15C (West front***, Chapter House***, Retro-choir**) – Vicar's Close* 14C – Deanery* 15C – Bishop's Palace* 13C – St. Cuthbert's Church*. **Envir. :** Cheddar (Cheddar Gorge*** – Gough's Caves** *AC*) NW: 8 m. – Croscombe (Church: Jacobean panelling*) E: 3 m. – Wookey Hole Caves* *AC*, NW: 2 m.
9 ☎ 72868, E: Horrington Rd.
London 132 – Bristol 20 – Southampton 68 – Taunton 28.

- **Swan** (Interchange), Sadler St., BA5 2RX, ☎ 78877, Group Telex 449658 – TV wc wc ☎ P.
  M 4.25/4.50 **st.** – **26 rm** 10.50/23.00 **st.**
- **Star,** High St., BA5 2SQ, ☎ 73055 – wc
  M 4.00/5.00 **s.** 1.30 – **18 rm** 9.95/19.65 **st.**
- **Crown,** Market Pl., BA5 2RP, ☎ 73457 – wc ☎ P.
  M a la carte 2.95/6.50 **t.** 1.30 – **10 rm** 11.50/20.50 **t.**
- **Red Lion** without rest., Market Pl., BA5 2RP, ☎ 72616, Group Telex 449658 – wc wc ☎ P.
  29 rm 10.50/23.00 **st.**
- **White Hart,** Sadler St., BA5 2RR, ☎ 72056 – wc P
  M a la carte 2.85/4.70 1.25 – **15 rm** 9.50/16.50.

AUSTIN-DAIMLER-JAGUAR-MORRIS-MG-ROVER-TRIUMPH-WOLSELEY Glastonbury Rd ☎ 72626
CHRYSLER-SIMCA Priory Rd ☎ 73834
MORRIS-MG-WOLSELEY Chamberlain St. ☎ 72040
VAUXHALL New St. ☎ 72099

WELWYN Herts. – pop. 8,134 – ✆ 043 871.
London 30 – Bedford 31 – Cambridge 32.

- **Heath Lodge Motel** , Danesbury Park Rd, AL6 9SL, NE: 1 m. off B 197 ☎ 5101, – TV wc wc ☎ P
  closed 25 December-2 January and Bank Holidays – **M** *(closed Sunday dinner)* 3.00/7.00 – **20 rm** 7.00/14.00.
- **Clock Motel,** Clock Roundabout, AL6 9XA, junction A 1M and A 1000, ☎ 6911 – TV wc wc ☎ P.
  M 3.25/3.65 1.25 – **21 rm** 10.00/14.00 **s.** – P 15.60/16.40 **s.**

FORD By Pass Rd ☎ 5185
VW, AUDI-NSU 54 Great North Rd ☎ 5911

WELWYN GARDEN CITY Herts. 986 ㉜ – pop. 40,448 – ✆ 070 73 Welwyn Garden.
18 Panshanger ☎ 33350.
i Council Offices, The Campus ☎ 24411.
London 28 – Bedford 34 – Cambridge 34.

- **Homestead Court,** Homestead Lane, AL7 4LX, P.O. Box 115 ☎ 24336, – TV wc wc ☎ P.
  closed Christmas and Bank Holidays – **M** approx. 4.50 **st.** – **58 rm** 12.50/19.00 **st.** – P 16.80 **st.**

AUSTIN-DAIMLER-JAGUAR-MORRIS-MG-ROVER-TRIUMPH-WOLSELEY Stanborough Rd ☎ 26367
RENAULT Great North Rd ☎ Hatfield 64567
VAUXHALL Lemsford Lane ☎ 22665

WENTBRIDGE West Yorks. – pop. 130 – ✉ Pontefract – ✆ 097 764.
London 183 – Leeds 19 – Nottingham 55 – Sheffield 28.

- **Wentbridge House,** WF8 3JJ, ☎ 444, – TV wc ☎ P.
  closed 24 and 25 December – **M** *(closed dinner 26 December)* a la carte 6.25/9.50 **s.** 1.80 – 1.80 – **16 rm** 9.00/25.50 **s.**
- XX **Swiss Cottage,** Great North Rd, WF8 3JL, ☎ 300, Dancing (Monday to Saturday) – P
  closed Christmas Day – **M** a la carte 2.20/6.60 1.75.

at Barnsdale Bar S: 1 ½ m. on A 1 – ✉ Pontefract – ✆ 097 764 Wentbridge:

- **TraveLodge** (T.H.F.) without rest., Trunk Rd, WF8 3JB, on A 1 ☎ 711 – TV wc ☎ P
  71 rm 10.00/13.50 **st.**

WEOBLEY Heref. and Worc. – pop. 881 – ✆ 054 45.
London 145 – Brecon 30 – Hereford 12 – Leominster 9.

- **Unicorn,** High St., HR4 8SL, ☎ 230 – P
  M (bar lunch) a la carte 2.20/3.25 1.00 – **11 rm** 5.50/10.50.
- XX **Red Lion** with rm, Broad St., HR4 8SE, ☎ 220, « Renovated part 14C inn » – TV wc ☎ P
  M a la carte 4.45/5.70 **st.** 1.00 – **7 rm** 12.00/16.00 **st.**

WEST BROMWICH West Midlands 986 ⑫ – see Birmingham.

WEST CHILTINGTON West Sussex – pop. 1,765 – ✉ Pulborough – ✆ 079 83.
London 50 – Brighton 22 – Worthing 12.

- **Roundabout** (Interchange), Monkmead Lane, RH20 2PF, S: 1 ¼ m. ☎ 3123, – wc wc P
  closed January – **M** *(closed Sunday dinner and Monday to non-residents)* 5.00/7.00 **st.** 1.75 – **15 rm** 11.85/18.25 **st.**

WEST CLANDON Surrey – see Guildford.

WESTERHAM Kent 986 ㊱ – pop. 4,641 – ☎ 0959.
Envir. : Chartwell* (Sir Winston Churchill's country home, Museum) *AC*, S : **2** m.
London 24 – **Brighton 45** – Maidstone 22.

- King's Arms (Embassy), Market Sq., TN16 1AN, ☎ 63246 – TV ⌂wc P
  16 rm.
- XXX **Le Marquis de Montcalm,** Quebec Sq., TN16 1TD, ☎ 62139, ⛱ – P
  closed Sunday dinner, Monday and Bank Holidays except Christmas and 1 January – **M** a la carte 4.00/6.90 🍾 1.50.
- XX **Crown at Westerham,** London Rd, TN16 1DF, ☎ 63030 – P
  closed Monday – **M** a la carte 4.20/5.30 **t.** 🍾 0.95.

AUSTIN-MORRIS-MG High St. ☎ 62212 VW, AUDI-NSU London Rd ☎ 64333

WESTGATE-ON-SEA Kent 986 ㊱ – pop. 6,512 – ☎ 0843 Thanet.
London 72 – Maidstone 40 – Margate 2.

- **Westgate Lodge,** 36 Westgate Bay Av., CT8 8TA, ☎ 31278, ⛱
  April-October – **12 rm** ☕ 5.50/11.00.
- XX **Angelo's Blue Room,** 18 Cuthbert Rd, CT8 8NR, ☎ 31646, Italian rest.
  closed Sunday dinner and Monday – **M** a la carte 5.40/7.65 **t.** 🍾 1.60.

MORRIS-MG 1 Cuthbert Rd ☎ 32060

WEST LULWORTH Dorset – pop. **1,003** – ✉ Wareham – ☎ 092 941.
See : Lulworth Cove*. **Envir.** : Durdle Door** W : **1** m.
London 129 – Bournemouth 21 – Dorchester 17 – Weymouth 19.

- **Lulworth Cove,** BH20 5RQ, ☎ 333, ≤ – TV ⌂wc ⛆wc P
  closed February – **M** a la carte 3.60/5.05 🍾 1.50 – **14 rm** ☕ 5.00/14.00 – P 11.10/13.10.
- **Bishop's Cottage,** ☎ 261, ⛱
  March-October – **13 rm** ☕ 4.75/9.50.
- **Gatton House,** BH20 5RU, ☎ 252, ⛱ – P
  closed November and December – **10 rm** ☕ 6.00/12.00.
- X **Castle Inn** with rm, BH20 5RN, ☎ 311 – TV ⌂wc P
  closed January – **M** a la carte 3.25/5.90 🍾 1.75 – **12 rm** ☕ 7.00/15.00.

WEST MALVERN Heref. and Worc. – see Malvern.

WEST MEON Hants. – pop. 704 – ✉ Petersfield – ☎ 073 086.
London 64 – **Portsmouth 23** – **Southampton 19** – Winchester 13.

- X **West Meon Hut,** GU32 1JX, N : 1 ½ m. junction A 272 and A 32 ☎ 291 – P
  M a la carte 3.40/5.50 **t.** 🍾 1.15.

WESTON Devon – ✉ ☎ 0404 Honiton.
London 164 – Exeter 15 – Sidmouth 10.

- **Deer Park** ⛭, EX14 0PG, ☎ 2064, ≤, 🎾, heated, 🎣, ⛱, park – TV ⌂wc ☎ P
  M 3.50/5.00 🍾 1.25 – **30 rm** ☕ 8.50/22.00.

WESTON BIRT Glos. – see Tetbury.

WESTON FAVELL Northants. – see Northampton.

WESTON-ON-THE-GREEN Oxon. – pop. 519 – ✉ Bicester – ☎ 086 95 Bletchington.
London 66 – Northampton 33 – **Oxford 9.**

- Weston Manor (Interchange) ⛭, OX6 8QW, ☎ 621, « 16C manor, Tudor gardens », heated, park – TV ⌂wc ☎ P. 🏊
  20 rm.

WESTON-SUPER-MARE Avon 986 ㉟ – pop. 50,894 – ☎ 0934.
See : Sea front ≤*.
18 Worlebury ☎ 23214, 2 m. from station BY.
i Beach Lawns ☎ 26838.
London 147 – **Bristol 24** – Taunton 32.

Plan on next page

- **Grand Atlantic** (T.H.F.), Beach Rd, BS23 1BA, ☎ 26543, ≤, 🎾, 🏊, ⛱ – 🛗 TV P. 🏊 BZ **e**
  M a la carte 4.40/6.50 **st.** 🍾 1.50 – **79 rm** ☕ 15.00/27.00 **st.** – P 18.50/21.00 **st.**
- **Royal** (Norfolk Cap.), South Par., BS23 1JP, ☎ 23601, Group Telex 23241, ⛱ – 🛗 ⌂wc ⛆wc ☎ P. 🏊 BZ **a**
  M approx. 3.50 – **36 rm** ☕ 8.80/18.95.
- **Royal Pier,** Birnbreck Rd, BS23 2EF, ☎ 26644, ≤ – 🛗 ⌂wc ☎ P AY **a**
  Easter-October – **M** approx. 2.85 **s.** 🍾 1.40 – **46 rm** ☕ 10.20/22.00 **s.** – P 11.85/14.30 **s.**
- X Cosa Nostra, Kewstoke Rd ☎ 32549, ≤, Italian rest. AY **c**

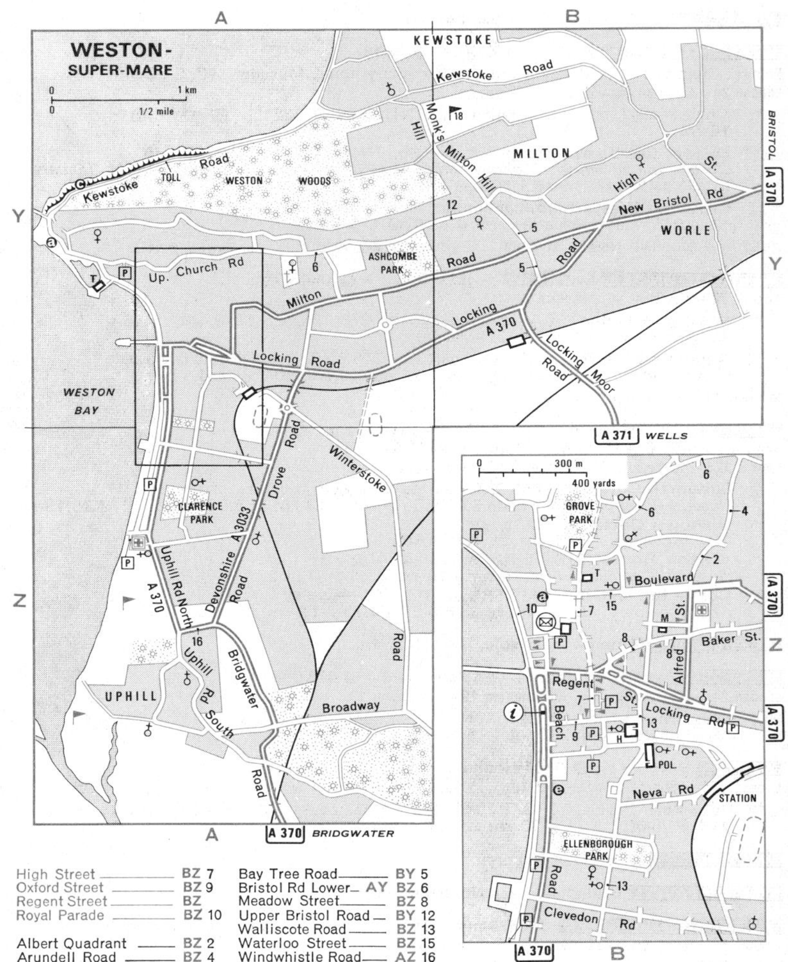

High Street	BZ 7	Bay Tree Road	BY 5
Oxford Street	BZ 9	Bristol Rd Lower	AY BZ 6
Regent Street	BZ	Meadow Street	BZ 8
Royal Parade	BZ 10	Upper Bristol Road	BY 12
		Walliscote Road	BZ 13
Albert Quadrant	BZ 2	Waterloo Street	BZ 15
Arundell Road	BZ 4	Windwhistle Road	AZ 16

AUSTIN-MG-WOLSELEY Drove Rd ☎ 25382
AUSTIN-MG-WOLSELEY 55 Upper Church Rd ☎ 21161
CITROEN Baker St. ☎ 23995
DAF, MAZDA 264 Milton Rd ☎ 25707
DAIMLER-JAGUAR-MORRIS-MG-ROVER-TRIUMPH-WOLSELEY Alfred St. ☎ 21451

FIAT 108/110 Milton Rd ☎ 26428
FORD Locking Rd ☎ 28291
PEUGEOT Broadway ☎ Bleadon 812479
RENAULT Locking Rd ☎ 25242
SAAB Main Rd ☎ 0934 (Bleadon) 812546
VAUXHALL 13 Langford Rd ☎ 23904

WESTON-UNDER-PENYARD Heref. and Worc. – see Ross-on-Wye.

WEST RUNTON Norfolk – pop. 1,467 – ✉ Cromer – ☎ 026 375.

London 136 – King's Lynn 42 – **Norwich 24.**

- **Links Country Park,** NR27 9QH, ☎ 691, 9, – wc wc **P.**
  M a la carte 4.95/9.40 **st.** 2.00 – **21 rm** 15.50/27.00 **st.**
- **Mirabelle,** Station Rd, NR27 9QD, ☎ 396 – **P**
  closed Sunday dinner from November to May and Monday – **M** a la carte 3.70/6.30 1.40.

In alta stagione, e soprattutto nelle stazioni turistiche,
è prudente prenotare con un certo anticipo.

WEST WITTERING West Sussex – pop. 2,520 – ✉ Chichester – ☎ 024 366.
London 77 – Brighton 38 – Chichester 7,5.

- **Roman Way Hotel and Country Club,** PO20 8QA, on A 286 ☎ 2229, , , – wc Ⓟ
  M a la carte 2.85/5.00 **t.** 🌢 1.40 – ☕ 1.50 – **10 rm** 9.20/12.95 **t.**

WETHERAL Cumbria – pop. 4,081 – ✉ Carlisle – ☎ 0228.
London 311 – Carlisle 6 – Newcastle-upon-Tyne 56.

- Crown , CA4 8ES, ☎ 60208, – Ⓟ – **20 rm.**
- **Fantails,** The Green, CA4 8EG, ☎ 60239 – Ⓟ
  closed 26 December, 1 January and 26 February-16 March – **M** a la carte 2.35/6.15 **t.** 🌢 1.30.

WETHERBY West Yorks. 986 ㉓ – pop. 7,332 – ☎ 0937.
18 Linton Lane ☎ 2527, 1 m. centre.
i Council Offices, 24 Westgate ☎ 62706.
London 208 – Harrogate 8 – Leeds 13 – York 14.

- **Wetherby Turnpike Motor Inn,** Leeds Rd, Wetherby Roundabout, LS22 5HE, junction A 661 and A 1 ☎ 63881 – TV wc Ⓟ.
  M 2.50/2.75 **st.** 🌢 1.50 – ☕ 1.50 – **70 rm** 13.50/18.00 **st.**
- XXX **Linton Spring,** Sicklingall Rd, LS22 9XX, W : 1 ¾ m. ☎ 65353, – Ⓟ
  closed Saturday lunch, Sunday dinner and Monday – **M** 7.00/12.00 **t.** 🌢 2.00.
- XX **Cardinal,** 16 Bank St., LS22 4NQ, ☎ 63613 – Ⓟ
  closed Monday – **M** (dinner only) 5.60/6.25 **t.**

at Walshford N : 4 m. on A 1 – ✉ ☎ 0937 Wetherby :

- XXX **Bridge Inn,** LS22 5HS, ☎ 62345 – Ⓟ
  closed Sunday dinner and Monday – **M** 6.45/10.95 **st.**

AUSTIN-MORRIS-MG-TRIUMPH-WOLSELEY North St. ☎ 2623
FORD 62/66 North St. ☎ 2029

WEYBOURNE Norfolk – pop. 430 – ✉ Holt – ☎ 026 370.
London 128 – Cromer 7.5 – Norwich 26.

- **Maltings,** NR25 7SY, on A 149 ☎ 275 – wc Ⓟ
  M 3.95/4.50 **st.** 🌢 1.20 – **17 rm** ☕ 12.80/16.00 **st.**
- XX **Gasché's Swiss,** High St., NR25 7SY, on A 149 ☎ 220 – Ⓟ
  closed Sunday dinner, Monday and Christmas Day – **M** a la carte 5.40/7.10 **t.** 🌢 0.95.

WEYBRIDGE Surrey 986 ⑧ – pop. 51,134 (inc. Walton-on-Thames) – ☎ 0932.
i Town Hall, Walton-on-Thames ☎ 28844.
London 23.

- Ship (Thistle), Monument Green, KT13 8BQ, ☎ 48364 – TV wc Ⓟ. – **39 rm.**
- XX **Casa Romana,** 2 Temple Hall, Monument Hill, KT13 8RH, ☎ 43470, Italian rest. – Ⓟ
  closed Monday, Easter Sunday dinner and 25-26 December – **M** a la carte 5.45/7.35 **t.** 🌢 1.35.
- XX **London Steak House,** 7 Temple Market, KT13 9DL, ☎ 42826
  M a la carte 3.25/5.60 **t.** 🌢 1.35.
- X **Chez Antoine,** 108 Oatlands Drive, KT13 9HL, ☎ 43131, French rest.
  closed Sunday lunch and Monday – **M** a la carte 5.30/8.00 🌢 1.40.

AUSTIN-MORRIS-MG Woodham Lane, New Haw ☎ 093 23 (Byfleet) 42870
AUSTIN-MG-WOLSELEY 30 Queens Rd ☎ 42233
DAIMLER-JAGUAR-ROVER-TRIUMPH 105 Queens Rd ☎ 429221
FIAT, LANCIA Brooklands Rd ☎ 093 23 (Byfleet) 49521
FORD Monument Hill ☎ 46231
RENAULT 51/59 Baker St. ☎ 48247
VAUXHALL 170 Oatlands Drive ☎ 42318

WEYMOUTH Dorset 986 ㊴ – pop. 42,349 (inc. Melcombe Regis) – ☎ 030 57 (4 and 5 fig.) or 0305 (6 fig.).
Envir. : Hardy Monument ※** NW : 10 m. – Abbotsbury (the Swannery* *AC*, the gardens* *AC*) NW : 8 ½ m.
18 ☎ 4994.
Shipping connections with the Continent : to Cherbourg (Sealink) – to Guernsey (Sealink) 3-7 weekly (4 h 45 m to 6 h 30 mn) – to Jersey (Sealink) Summer 2 daily ; Winter 3-6 weekly (6 h 30 mn to 9 h).
i Publicity Office, 12 The Esplanade ☎ 72444.
London 143 – Bournemouth 35 – Bristol 69 – Exeter 57 – Swindon 88.

- **Ingleton,** 7 Greenhill, DT4 7SW, ☎ 5804 – wc wc Ⓟ
  M 3.00/4.00 **t.** 🌢 1.30 – ☕ 2.50 – **13 rm** 7.00/16.00.

AUSTIN-MG-ROVER-TRIUMPH-WOLSELEY Victoria St. ☎ 5454
CHRYSLER-SIMCA 172 Dorchester Rd ☎ 6311
FORD Dorchester Rd ☎ 2284
RENAULT 148/162 Dorchester Rd ☎ 2222
VAUXHALL Chickerell Rd ☎ 3384

WHALLEY RANGE Greater Manchester – see Manchester.

WHIPPINGHAM I.O.W. – see Wight (Isle of).

WHITCHURCH Bucks. – pop. 729 – ✉ Aylesbury – ☎ 029 664.
London 51 – Bedford 28 – **Oxford 30.**

- **Priory,** High St., HP22 4JS, ☎ 239, – **P**
  M (dinner and residents only) 3.50/4.00 **s.** 1.50 – **11 rm** 8.00/12.00 **s.**

WHITCHURCH Salop – 986 ⑨ and ㉗ – pop. 7,143 – ☎ 0948.
18, 9 Terrick Rd ☎ 3584, N: 1 m.
London 171 – **Birmingham 54** – Chester 22 – **Manchester 43** – Shrewsbury 20.

- **Redbrook Hunting Lodge,** Wrexham Rd, Redbrook, SY13 3ET, W: 2 ½ m. on A 525 ☎ 094 873 (Redbrook Maelor) 204, – wc **P**
  M a la carte 3.50/8.40 **st.** 1.20 – **12 rm** 7.00/14.00 **st.** – P 11.00/12.50 **st.**

AUSTIN-MG, VANDEN PLAS Brownlow St. ☎ 2826
MORRIS-MG-ROVER-TRIUMPH-LAND ROVER Newport Rd ☎ 3333

WHITEBROOK Gwent – see Monmouth.

WHITESAND BAY Dyfed – see St. David's.

WHITFIELD Northants. – see Brackley.

WHITLEY BAY Tyne and Wear 986 ⑲ – pop. 37,817 – ☎ 0632.
Envir. : Seaton Delaval Hall* (18C) *AC*, NW: 6 m.
i Promenade ☎ 524494 (summer only) – Municipal Offices ☎ 523211 (winter only).
London 292 – **Newcastle-upon-Tyne 10** – Sunderland 10.

- **Ambassador,** 38-42 South Par., NE26 2RQ, ☎ 531218 – TV wc **P**
  M *(closed Christmas Day)* a la carte 5.80/9.00 **t.** – **28 rm** 9.00/16.50 **t.**

AUSTIN-DAIMLER-MORRIS-MG-ROVER-TRIUMPH-WOLSELEY Cauldwell Lane ☎ 22231
DATSUN Claremont Rd ☎ 523347
FORD Whitley Rd ☎ 22225
MAZDA Fox Hunters Rd ☎ 528282
VAUXHALL Earsdon Rd West Monkseaton ☎ 23355
VW, AUDI-NSU Hillheads Rd ☎ 528225

WHITLEY BRIDGE West Yorks. – pop. 361 – ✉ Goole – ☎ 0977.
London 190 – **Kingston-upon-Hull 40** – **Leeds 20** – York 22.

- **Maine Motor Inn,** Weeland Rd, Eggborough, DN14 0RY, ☎ 661395 – TV **P**
  M 3.50/6.50 **t.** 0.85 – **15 rm** 9.00/14.00 **t.**

WHITSTABLE Kent 986 ㊱ – pop. 25,449 – ☎ 0227.
i Division Office, 1 Tankerton Rd ☎ 272233.
London 58 – **Dover 22** – Maidstone 26 – Margate 19.

- **Windmill Motel,** 35 Borstal Hill, CT5 4ND, ☎ 272866 – TV wc wc **P**
  M a la carte 5.05/7.05 **t.** 2.00 – **12 rm** 8.50/12.00 **t.**
- XX **Giovanni's,** 49-51 Canterbury Rd, CT5 4HH, ☎ 273034, Italian rest. – **P**
  closed Monday and Bank Holidays except Christmas Day – **M** a la carte 5.20/7.85 **t.** 2.10.

at Tankerton E: ¾ m. – ✉ ☎ 0227 Whitstable:

- **Marine,** 33 Marine Par., CT5 2BE, ☎ 272672, ←, – wc **P**
  M 2.50/2.75 1.35 – **32 rm** 9.50/20.00 – P 10.50/15.00.
- X Le Pousse Bedaine, 101 Tankerton Rd ☎ 272056, French bistro.

AUSTIN-MORRIS-MG, PEUGEOT Tankerton Rd ☎ 272244
RENAULT Tower Parade ☎ 61477

WHITTLESEY Cambs. 986 ㉘㉜ – see Peterborough.

WICKEN Northants. – pop. 376 – ✉ Milton Keynes (Bucks.) – ☎ 090 857.
London 65 – Bedford 21 – Northampton 15 – **Oxford 31.**

- **Wicken Country** , Cross Tree Rd, MK19 6BX, ☎ 239, – TV wc wc **P**
  M *(closed 24 to 27 December)* 3.50/8.00 **st.** 1.50 – 1.00 – **12 rm** 7.00/16.00 – P 15.00/18.00.

WICKHAM Hants. – pop. 3,896 – ☎ 0329.
London 74 – **Portsmouth 12** – **Southampton 11** – Winchester 16.

- **Old House,** The Square, PO17 5JG, ☎ 833049, « Tastefully renovated Georgian house », – wc **P**
  closed 17 days July-August, 10 days Christmas and Bank Holidays – **M** *(closed Monday lunch and Sunday)* a la carte 4.85/5.60 **s.** 1.70 – **10 rm** 12.00/18.00 **s.**

WICKHAM MARKET Suffolk – pop. 1,436 – 0728.
London 85 – Great Yarmouth 41 – Ipswich 12 – Norwich 43.

White Hart (Interchange) with rm, High St., IP13 0RB, ☎ 746203 – Ⓟ
M a la carte 3.30/4.95 **s.** 1.10 – **10 rm** 10.00/18.00 **s.**

MORRIS-MG-WOLSELEY 18 High St. ☎ 6161

WIDECOMBE IN THE MOOR Devon – pop. 523 – ✉ Newton Abbot – 036 42.
Envir. : Dartmeet Bridge (site*) SW : 5 m.
London 223 – Exeter 23 – Plymouth 31.

Wooder Manor (Interchange) , TQ13 7TR, N : ¾ m. ☎ 240, Telex 267867, – wc Ⓟ
March-November – **M** approx. 5.25 **s.** 1.45 – **10 rm** 11.20/20.30 **s.**

WIDEMOUTH BAY Cornwall – 028 885.
London 255 – Bude 4 – Truro 53.

Trelawny, Marine Drive, EX23 0AH, ☎ 328 – Ⓟ
Easter-October – **M** *(May-September)* (dinner only) 3.00/4.00 1.25 – **10 rm** 5.50/11.00.

DAF ☎ 279

WIGAN Greater Manchester 986 ⑤ and ㉓ – pop. 81,147 – 0942.
Haigh ☎ 42050, NW : 3 m. – Arley Hall, Haigh ☎ 0257 (Standish) 421360, N : 4 m.
London 206 – Liverpool 19 – Manchester 18 – Preston 18.

Brocket Arms (Embassy), Mesnes Rd, WN1 2DD, ☎ 46283 – TV wc Ⓟ.
closed Christmas – **M** approx. 2.70 **st.** 1.50 – **24 rm** 10.00/12.95 **st.**

AUSTIN-MG-WOLSELEY 240 Warrington Rd ☎ 36231
CHRYSLER-SIMCA Nicol Rd 0942 (Ashton in Makerfield) ☎ 76588
CITROEN Crompton St. ☎ 42281
DAIMLER-JAGUAR-MORRIS-MG-ROVER-TRIUMPH-WOLSELEY Wallgate ☎ 44977
DATSUN Woodhouse ☎ 34141
FORD Clayton St. ☎ 41393
VAUXHALL Chapel St., Pemberton ☎ 214028
VAUXHALL Mesnes St. ☎ 43271
VOLVO Platt St. ☎ 66594
VW, AUDI-NSU 32 Whelly ☎ 41493

WIGHT (Isle of) 986 ㊴㊵ – pop. 95,752.
from Cowes to Southampton (Red Funnel Services) Monday/Saturday 7-14 daily; Sunday 4-11 daily (1 h 10 mn) – from Yarmouth to Lymington (Sealink) Monday/Thursday 15 daily; Friday/Saturday/Sunday 7-28 daily (30 mn) – from Fishbourne to Portsmouth (Sealink) Monday/Thursday 20-29 daily; Friday/Saturday/Sunday 11-35 daily (45 mn).

from Cowes to Southampton (Solent Seaspeed Hovercraft) 12-13 daily (20 mn) and (Red Funnel Services: hydrofoil) Monday/Saturday 10-12 daily; Sunday 3-11 daily (20 mn) – from Ryde to Southsea (Hovertravel) 11-24 daily Summer only (7 mn) – from Ryde to Portsmouth (Sealink) 9-22 daily (25 to 40 mn).

Bembridge – pop. 3,272 – ✉ 098 387 Bembridge.
Newport 14.

Elms Country , Swaines Rd, PO35 5XS, ☎ 2248, – TV wc wc Ⓟ
March-22 October – **M** *(open Thursday to Saturday in winter)* 3.50/5.50 1.35 – **14 rm** 5.00/11.00 – P 11.50/12.50.

Highbury, Lane End Rd, PO35 5SU, ☎ 2838, heated – wc
closed 23 to 28 December – **M** 3.25/4.75 – **9 rm** 6.50/13.50 – P 12.15/14.00.

PEUGEOT High St. ☎ 2121

Bonchurch – pop. 521 – ✉ 0983 Ventnor.

Winterbourne , PO38 1RQ, ☎ 852535, ←, « Country house atmosphere », – TV wc wc Ⓟ
mid January-mid November – **M** approx. 6.50 **st.** – **20 rm** 11.85/28.75 **st.** – P 19.00/23.75 **st.**

Peacock Vane , PO38 1RG, ☎ 852019, ←, « Unique decor, country house atmosphere », heated, , park – TV wc Ⓟ
closed mid January-mid February – **M** approx. 6.00 **s.** 1.30 – **11 rm** 8.00/20.00 **s.** – P 15.00/20.00 **s.**

Bonchurch Manor , Bonchurch Shute, PO38 1NU, ☎ 852868, ←, « Country house atmosphere », – wc Ⓟ
closed November – **M** *(closed Sunday)* 3.50/4.50 **s.** 1.25 – **11 rm** 8.00/18.00 **s.** – P 13.50/15.50 **s.**

Lake, Shore Rd, PO38 1RF, ☎ 852613, – Ⓟ
Easter-October – **M** 2.75/3.95 1.25 – **24 rm** 5.00/10.00 **st.** – P 9.00 **st.**

Carisbrooke – pop. 3,217 – ✉ 098 381 Newport.
Newport 1.5.

Clatterford House , Clatterford Shute, PO30 1PD, ☎ 3969, – Ⓟ
May-October – 0.75 – **7 rm** 7.00/14.00 **st.**

Cowes – pop. 18,910 – ✉ ☎ 098 382 Cowes.
Envir. : Osborne House* (19C) *AC*, E: 1 m.
⛳9 Baring Rd ☎ 3529.
Newport 4.

- **Holmwood,** 65 Queens Rd, PO31 8BW, ☎ 2508, ≤ Solent – ⇔wc ⋒wc ☎ Ⓟ
M a la carte 5.50/9.00 – **20 rm** ⊐ 8.75/15.00.

Freshwater Bay – pop. 4,171 – ✉ ☎ 098 383 Freshwater.
⛳18 ☎ 2400.
Newport 13.

- **Farringford** ⟡, Bedbury Lane, PO40 9PE, ☎ 2500, ≤, ⁂, ⛱ heated, ⛱, park – ⇔wc ☎ Ⓟ
Easter-November – **M** approx. 4.75 **t.** 🍷 2.00 – **40 rm** 15.00/30.00 **t.** – P 18.00 **t.**
- **Albion,** PO40 9RA, ☎ 3631, ≤ – ⇔wc ☎ Ⓟ
Easter-September – **M** approx. 4.50 **s.** – **42 rm** ⊐ 6.05/15.60 **st.**
- **Saunders,** PO40 9QX, ☎ 2322, ⛱ – Ⓟ
Easter-mid October – **13 rm** ⊐ 5.40/8.70 **t.**

DAF Avenue Rd ☎ 2179

Newport – pop. 22,309 – ✉ ☎ 098 381 (4 fig.) or 0983 (6 fig.) Newport.
Envir. : Carisbrooke Castle** 12C-16C (keep ≤*) *AC* – Shorwell (St. Peter's Church* 15C) SW: 5 m.
⛳9 St. George's Down, Shide, SE: 1 m.
i 21 High St. ☎ 4343/4.

- ✗ Bugle, with rm, 117 High St., PO30 1TP, ☎ 2800 – Ⓟ – **24 rm.**

AUDI-NSU, MERCEDES-BENZ Medina Avenue ☎ 3232
AUSTIN-DAIMLER-JAGUAR-MORRIS-MG-ROVER-TRIUMPH-WOLSELEY River Way ☎ 3555
BMW ☎ 3684

Niton – pop. 1,742 – ✉ ☎ 0983 Niton.
Newport 12.

- **Windcliffe House** ⟡, Sandrock Rd, PO38 2NG, ☎ 730215, ⛱ heated – Ⓟ
Easter-October – **12 rm** ⊐ 7.65/15.30 **s.**

Ryde – pop. 19,845 – ✉ ☎ 0983 Ryde.
⛳9 Ryde House Park ☎ 2088.
i Amenities Section, Esplanade Pavilion ☎ 62905 (summer only).
Newport 7.5

- **Yelf's** (T.H.F.), Union St., PO33 2LG, ☎ 64062 – TV ⇔wc ☎. ⛱
M approx. 3.50 **st.** 🍷 1.50 – **32 rm** ⊐ 8.00/16.00 **st.**

ALFA-ROMEO Brading Rd ☎ 4166
AUSTIN-MG-WOLSELEY Elmfield ☎ 2717
CHRYSLER-SIMCA 186 High St. ☎ 2281
OPEL Havenstreet ☎ 0983 (Wootton Bridge) ☎ 882455
ROVER-TRIUMPH Victoria St. ☎ 3661
VW, AUDI-NSU Fishbourne Lane ☎ 0983 (Wootton Bridge) 882465

Sandown – pop. 4,593 – ✉ ☎ 098 384 Sandown.
⛳18 ☎ 3170.
Newport 9.

- **St. Catherine's,** 1 Winchester Park Rd, PO36 8HJ, ☎ 2392 – ⇔wc ⋒wc
closed November and December – **M** (dinner only) 2.75/4.50 🍷 1.15 – **18 rm** ⊐ 7.75/16.65 **st.**

Shanklin – pop. 7,240 – ✉ ☎ 098 386 Shanklin.
See : Old Village (thatched cottages)* – The Chine* *AC*. **Envir. :** Brading (Roman Villa: mosaics* *AC*) N: 3 ½ m.
i 67a High St. ☎ 2942 – Esplanade ☎ 4214 (summer only).
Newport 9.

- **Cliff Tops,** 1-5 Park Rd, PO37 6BB, ☎ 3262, ≤, ⛱ heated, ⛱ – 🛗 Ⓟ
M 4.45/6.20 **st.** 🍷 1.40 – **98 rm** ⊐ 11.70/24.00 **st.** – P 14.70/20.00 **st.**
- **Shanklin,** Clarendon Rd, PO37 6DL, ☎ 2286, ≤ – 🛗 ⇔wc ♿ Ⓟ
M a la carte 2.75/6.40 🍷 1.20 – **87 rm** ⊐ 10.10/20.20 **st.**
- **Luccombe Hall,** Luccombe Rd, PO37 6RL, ☎ 2719, ≤, ⁂, ⛱ heated, ⛱ – ⇔wc ⋒wc ♿ Ⓟ
closed 18 December-13 January – **M** (dinner only from November to March) 3.50/4.50 **t.** 🍷 1.15 – **33 rm** ⊐ 11.00/18.75 **t.**
- **Auckland,** 10 Queens Rd, PO37 6AN, ☎ 2960 – TV ⇔wc Ⓟ
closed last 2 weeks November and first 2 weeks January – **M** approx. 3.80 **st.** – **29 rm** ⊐ 7.60/21.60 **st.**
- **Delphi Cliff,** 7 St. Boniface Cliff Rd, PO37 6ET, ☎ 2179, ≤, ⛱ – ⇔wc Ⓟ
Easter-mid October – **12 rm** ⊐ 7.00/18.50 **st.**

Totland Bay – pop. 1,724 – ✉ ☎ 098 383 Freshwater.
Envir.: Alum Bay (coloured sands*) and the Needles* SW: **1** m.
Newport 13.

Sentry Mead, Madeira Rd, PO39 0BJ, ☎ 3212, ⛱ – ⌂wc Ⓟ
late March-early November and Christmas – **M** 3.30/4.00 🍷 1.20 – **14 rm** ☕ 6.00/14.00 – P 11.00/13.00.

Randolph, Granville Rd, PO39 0AX, ☎ 2411, ⛱
closed November and December – **8 rm** ☕ 4.50/9.00 **s.**

Brandlehow, Ward Rd, PO39 0BD, ☎ 2238
Easter-October – **9 rm** ☕ 4.00/8.00 **s.**

Ventnor – pop. 6,435 – ✉ ☎ 0983 Ventnor.
Envir. : St. Catherine's Point (≤* from the car-park) W: 5 m.
⛳9 Steephill Down Rd ☎ 853326.
i 34 High St. ☎ 853625 (summer only).
Newport 10.

Royal (T.H.F.), Belgrave Rd, PO38 1JJ, ☎ 852186, ⛱ heated, ⛱ – lift TV ⌂wc ☎ Ⓟ
M a la carte 4.10/5.50 **st.** 🍷 1.50 – **66 rm** ☕ 7.00/14.50 **st.**

Ventnor Towers, 54 Madeira Rd, PO38 1QT, ☎ 852277, ≤, 🎾, ⛱ heated, ⛱ – ⌂wc Ⓟ
Easter-mid October – **M** 4.00/4.50 **st.** 🍷 1.30 – **32 rm** ☕ 8.15/17.80 **st.** – P 12.30/14.70 **st.**

Madeira Hall 🌿, Trinity Rd, PO38 1NS, ☎ 852624, ⛱ heated, ⛱ – Ⓟ
mid March-mid October – **12 rm** ☕ 5.15/10.30 **st.**

AUSTIN-MORRIS-MG-WOLSELEY Victoria St. ☎ 852650

Whippingham – ✉ ☎ 098 382 Cowes.
Newport 3,5.

Padmore House 🌿, Beatrice Av., PO32 6LP, ☎ 3210, « Country house atmosphere », ⛱ heated, ⛱ – TV ⌂wc 🚿 ☎ Ⓟ
M 4.50/5.75 🍷 2.75 – **11 rm** ☕ 10.00/18.00.

Yarmouth – pop. 984 – ✉ ☎ 0983 Yarmouth.
i The Quay ☎ 760015/6 (summer only).
Newport 10.

George, Quay St., PO41 0PE, ☎ 760331, ⛱ – ⌂wc
Easter-October – **M** 4.25/5.50 🍷 1.75 – **25 rm** ☕ 9.00/21.00.

Jireh House, St. James Sq., PO41 0MP, ☎ 760513
9 rm ☕ 4.50/9.00 **s.**

SAAB Mill Rd ☎ 760436

WIGSTON FIELDS Leics. – see Leicester.

WIGTON Cumbria 986 ⑲ – pop. 4,880 – ☎ 096 54.
London 322 – Carlisle 11.

Greenhill Mansion 🌿, Red Dial, CA7 8LS, S: 2 m. on A 595, ☎ 2414, ≤, park – Ⓟ
M 5.00/6.00 **st.** 🍷 1.80 – **10 rm** ☕ 8.50/12.50 **st.**

CHRYSLER-SIMCA Bolton Low House ☎ 3361 MORRIS-MG-WOLSELEY ☎ 2670

WILLENHALL West Midlands – see Coventry.

WILLERBY North Humberside – see Kingston-upon-Hull.

WILLERSEY Heref. and Worc. – see Broadway.

WILLINGDON East Sussex – see Eastbourne.

WILLITON Somerset 986 ㉟ – pop. 2,948 – ☎ 0984.
London 177 – Minehead 8 – Taunton 16.

White House, 11 Long St., TA4 4QW, ☎ 32306 – ⌂wc Ⓟ
May-October – **M** (dinner only) 4.30/5.00 **t.** 🍷 1.70 – **14 rm** ☕ 8.60/15.20.

PEUGEOT 2 High St. ☎ 32761 ROVER-TRIUMPH Fore St. ☎ 8817

WILMCOTE Warw. – pop. 1,005 – ✉ ☎ 0789 Stratford-on-Avon.
See : Mary Arden's House* (16C) *AC.*
London 101 – Birmingham 20 – Stratford-on-Avon 5 – Warwick 10.

Swan House, The Green, CV37 9XJ, ☎ 67030, ⛱ – Ⓟ
9 rm.

WILMINGTON Devon – pop. 202 – ✉ Honiton – ☎ 040 483.
London 162 – Dorchester 33 – Exeter 20 – Taunton 28.

- **Home Farm,** EX14 9JR, on A 35 ☎ 278, « Converted 17C thatched farm house », – wc P
closed January-15 February – **M** *(closed Sunday dinner)* 5.00/7.00 **st.** – **9 rm** 10.00/22.00 **st.**

WILMINGTON East Sussex – pop. 225 – ✉ ☎ 032 12 Polegate.
London 62 – Brighton 17 – Eastbourne 7 – Hastings 20.

- **Crossways,** BN26 5SG, on A 27 ☎ 2455, – P
8 rm 6.00/11.00 **st.**

WILMSLOW Cheshire 986 ⑤ and ㉗ – pop. 29,040 – ☎ 099 64 (5 fig.) or 0625 (6 fig.).
Great Warford ☎ 056 587 (Mobberley) 2579, SW: 1 ½ m.
London 189 – Liverpool 38 – Manchester 12 – Stoke-on-Trent 27.

- Valley Lodge, Altrincham Rd, SK9 4LR, NW: 2 ¾ m. on A 538 ☎ 29201 – TV wc P. – **66 rm.**
- Stanneylands, Stanneylands Rd, SK9 4EY, N: 1 m. off A34 ☎ 525225, – TV wc wc P.
28 rm.

at Handforth N: 3 m. on A 34 – ✉ Wilmslow:

- **Belfry,** Stanley Rd, SK9 3LD, ☎ 061 (Manchester) 437 0511 – TV P.
M a la carte 4.30/7.60 **st.** 1.75 – 1.50 – **91 rm** 12.35/16.45 **st.**
- **Pinewood,** 180 Wilmslow Rd, SK9 3LG, ☎ 099 64 (Wilmslow) 29211, – TV P.
M 3.85/5.00 **s.** 1.00 – 1.50 – **64 rm** 11.25/15.50 **s.** – P 14.85/20.00 **s.**

CHRYSLER-SIMCA 51 Water Lane ☎ 23210
JENSEN, LANCIA Station Rd ☎ 27356
MORRIS-MG-WOLSELEY Dean Rd, Handforth ☎ 29271
RENAULT ☎ 23669
VAUXHALL Water Lane ☎ 27331

WILSHAMSTEAD Beds. – see Bedford.

WILTON Wilts. – see Salisbury.

P 9.00/9.50	Die im Führer angegebenen **Pensionspreise** sind nur Richtpreise. Einigen Sie sich vor einem Aufenthalt mit dem Hotelier über den endgültigen Pensionspreis.

WIMBORNE MINSTER Dorset 986 ㉟ ㊴ – pop. 4,997 – ☎ 0202 Wimborne.
See: Minster* 12C-15C. **Envir.:** Bere Regis (Parish church: nave roof* 15C) SW: 12 m.
London 112 – Bournemouth 10 – Dorchester 23 – Salisbury 27 – Southampton 30.

- **King's Head** (T.H.F.), The Square, BH21 1JA, ☎ 883135 – TV wc P
M a la carte 4.20/5.70 **st.** 1.50 – **29 rm** 7.50/15.50 **st.** – P 13.75/18.00 **st.**

AUSTIN-MG-WOLSELEY 41 Leigh Rd ☎ 3537
FORD Poole Rd ☎ 0202 (Bournemouth) 3333
JAGUAR-ROVER-TRIUMPH Wimborne Rd ☎ 4211
MORRIS-MG-WOLSELEY West St. ☎ 2261
MORRIS-MG-WOLSELEY 133 Wareham Rd ☎ 020 124 (Broadstone) 3681
VAUXHALL 11 Wimborne Rd, Colehill ☎ 2154

WINCANTON Somerset 986 ㉟ – pop. 2,576 – ☎ 0963.
Envir.: Stourhead House* (18C) *AC* and park** *AC*, NE: 9 m.
i County Library, 7 Carrington Way ☎ 32173.
London 119 – Bristol 37 – Taunton 34 – Yeovil 16.

- **Holbrook House** (Interchange), Castle Cary Rd, BA9 8BS, W: 1 ½ m. on A 371 ☎ 32377, « Country mansion », heated, , park – wc wc P
M 3.25/3.50 **st.** 1.25 – **20 rm** 9.50/21.00 **st.** – P 14.75/15.25 **st.**

AUSTIN-MORRIS-MG-ROVER-TRIUMPH-WOLSELEY Station Rd ☎ 2021

WINCHCOMBE Glos. 986 ㉛ – pop. 4,070 – ☎ 0242.
Envir.: Sudeley Castle* (12C-15C) *AC*, SE: 1 m.
London 107 – Cheltenham 8 – Gloucester 17 – Stratford-on-Avon 23.

- **George,** High St., GL54 5LJ, ☎ 602331, – wc P
M a la carte 2.90/6.90 1.70 – **16 rm** 8.00/17.00.

WINCHESTER Hants. 986 ㉟ – pop. 31,107 – ☎ 0962.
See: Cathedral*** 11C-13C B **A** – Winchester College** 14C B **B** – Pilgrim's Hall* 14C B **E** – St. Cross Hospital* 12C-15C A **D**. **Envir.:** Marwell Zoological Park** *AC*, SE: 5 m. on A 333 A.
i City Offices, Colebrook St. ☎ 68166.
London 72 – Bristol 76 – Oxford 52 – Southampton 12.

WINCHESTER

High Street ____ B

Alresford Road ____ A 2
Andover Road ____ B 3
Bereweeke Road ____ A 5
Bridge Street ____ B 6
Broadway ____ B 8
Chilbolton Avenue ____ A 9
City Road ____ B 10
Clifton Terrace ____ B 12
East Hill ____ B 15
Eastgate Street ____ B 16
Easton Lane ____ A 18
Friarsgate ____ B 19
Garnier Road ____ A 20
Kingsgate Road ____ A 22
Magdalen Hill ____ B 23
Middle Brook Street ____ B 25
Park Road ____ A 26
Petersfield Road ____ A 28
Quarry Road ____ A 29
St. George's Street ____ B 32
St. Paul's Hill ____ B 33
St. Peter Street ____ B 34
Southgate Street ____ B 35
Stoney Lane ____ A 36
Stockbridge Road ____ B 37
Sussex Street ____ B 38
Union Street ____ B 39
Upper High Street ____ B 40

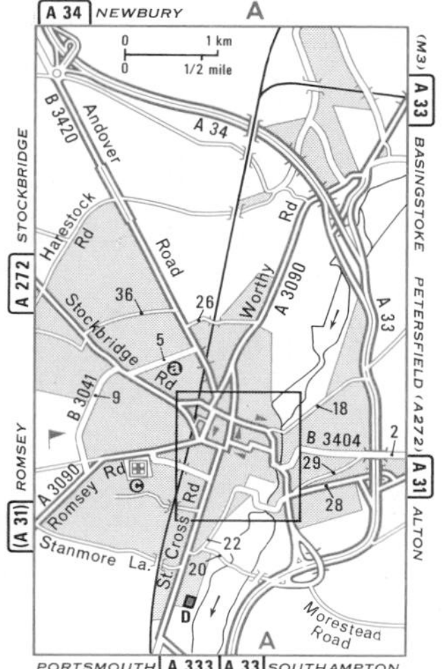

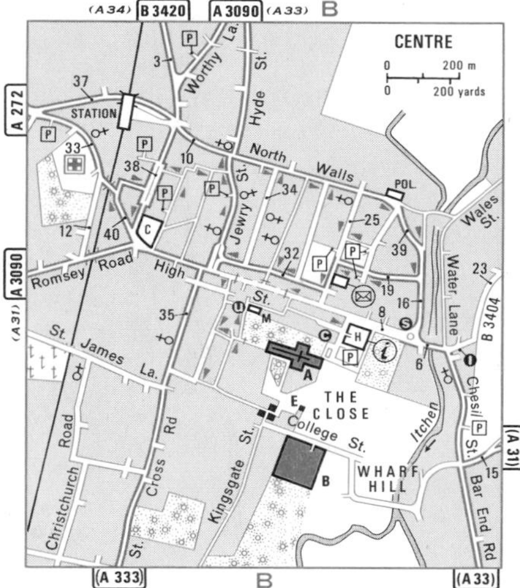

Wessex (T.H.F.), Paternoster Row, SO23 9LG, ℡ 61611, Telex 47419, < – **P.** B c
M 3.75/4.25 **st.** 1.60 – 2.00 – **93 rm** 16.00/21.00 **st.**

Chantry Mead, 22 Bereweeke Rd, SO22 6AJ, ℡ 2767, – wc **P** A a
closed 23-December-1 January – **M** (dinner only and Sunday lunch) a la carte 2.60/3.90 1.50 – **20 rm** 5.95/17.30 **t.**

Westacre, Sleepers Hill, SO22 4NE, ℡ 68403, – wc **P** A c
M 2.50/3.25 1.40 – **14 rm** 6.00/12.00.

Old Chesil Rectory, 1 Chesil St., SO23 8HU, ℡ 3177, Italian rest. B i
closed Monday and Christmas Day – **M** a la carte 3.85/5.80 **t.** 1.20.

Splinters, 9 Great Minster St., SO23 9HA, ℡ 64004, Bistro B u
closed Sunday and February – **M** a la carte 3.65/6.50 **t.** 1.25.

Sesto's, 3 Eastgate St., SO23 8EB, ℡ 69739, Italian rest. B s
closed Sunday and Bank Holidays – **M** a la carte 2.90/5.55 1.05.

ASTON-MARTIN Hursley ℡ 0962 (Hursley) 218
AUSTIN-MG-WOLSELEY St. Swithun St. ℡ 68461
BMW Kingsworthy ℡ 881414
CHRYSLER-SIMCA 2/4 St. Cross Rd ℡ 61855
DATSUN Stockbridge Rd ℡ 2255
FIAT, TOYOTA Station Hill ℡ 62175
FORD Bar-End Rd ℡ 62211
MORRIS-MG-WOLSELEY Easton Lane, The By-pass ℡ 69182
MORRIS-MG-WOLSELEY St. Cross Rd ℡ 61555
VAUXHALL Gordon Rd ℡ 69544
VW, AUDI-NSU St. Cross Rd ℡ 66331

WINDERMERE Cumbria 986 ⑲ – pop. 8,065 – 096 62.

See : Lake★. Envir. : Kirkstone Pass (on Windermere <★) N : 7 m by A 592 Y.

Cleabarrow ℡ 3123, by A 5074 Z **and B 5284.**

Victoria St. ℡ 4561 – Glebe Rd, Bowness ℡ 2244 (summer only).

London 272 – Blackpool 55 – Carlisle 50 – Kendal 10.

Plan on next page

Langdale Chase , LA23 1LW, N : 3 m. on A 591 ℡ 096 63 (Ambleside) 2201, < lake and mountains. « Extensive grounds with lake frontage », park – **P**
closed December and January – **M** approx. 6.00 **st.** 1.85 – **33 rm** 11.50/29.00 **st.** – P 20.00/23.50 **st.** on A 591 Y

Priory, Rayrigg Rd, LA23 1EX, ℡ 4377, < lake and mountains, – wc **P** by A 592 Y
M (bar lunch except Sunday) approx. 4.50 1.50 – **15 rm** 14.00/26.00.

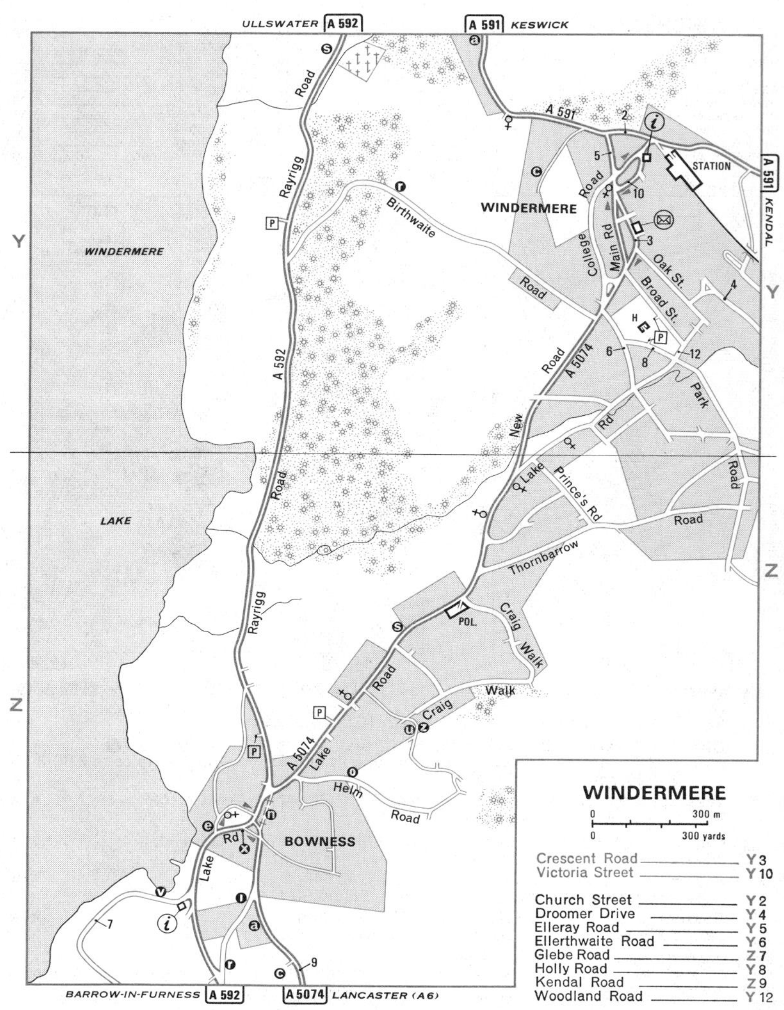

Wild Boar, Crook Rd, LA23 3NF, SE: 4 m. by A 5074 on B 5284 ☎ 3178, – wc by A 5074 Z
M approx. 6.55 **st.** 1.40 – **40 rm** 12.20/21.40 **st.** – P 17.00/21.30 **st.**

Miller Howe, Rayrigg Rd, LA23 1EY, ☎ 2536, lake and mountains, « Tasteful decor », – wc wc Y **s**
March-2 January – **M** (dinner only) 8.00 **s.** 2.10 – **13 rm** (dinner included) 18.00/52.00.

Holbeck Ghyll Country House, Holbeck Lane, LA23 1LU, NW: 3 ½ m. off A 591 ☎ 096 63 (Ambleside) 2375, « Country house atmosphere », – wc by A591 Y
March-October – **M** approx. 4.50 **st.** 1.60 – **11 rm** 12.00/25.00 **st.**

Birthwaite Edge Country House, Birthwaite Rd, LA23 1BS, ☎ 2861, – wc wc Y **r**
Easter-October – **M** (dinner only) 3.50/4.00 **t.** – **14 rm** 12.75/17.50 **t.**

Hide-a-Way, Phoenix Way, LA23 1DB, ☎ 3070, – wc Ⓟ Y c
M approx. 3.75 **st.** 1.00 – **13 rm** 5.50/11.00 **st.** – P 11.50 **st.**

Willowsmere, Ambleside Rd, LA23 1ES, ☎ 3575, – wc Ⓟ Y a
March-November – **15 rm** 6.00/14.00 **t.**

at Bowness-on-Windermere S : **1** m. – ✉ 096 62 Windermere:

Old England (T.H.F.), LA23 3DP, ☎ 2444, Telex 65194, ≤ lake and mountains, heated, – TV Ⓟ. Z e
M a la carte 4.20/6.30 **st.** 1.60 – 2.00 – **90 rm** 14.00/26.50 **st.** – P 19.00/25.00 **st.**

Belsfield (T.H.F.), Kendal Rd, LA23 3EL, ☎ 2448, Telex 65238, ≤ lake and mountains, – TV Ⓟ. Z i
M a la carte 4.20/6.30 **st.** 1.60 – **73 rm** 13.00/23.00 **st.** – P 17.25/22.00 **st.**

Windermere Hydro, Helm Rd, LA23 3BA, ☎ 4455, Telex 65196, ≤ – TV wc Ⓟ. Z o
closed January and February – **M** 3.00/5.00 **st.** 1.50 – **97 rm** 12.00/24.00 **st.**

Linthwaite, Crook Rd, LA23 3JA, by A 5074 on B 5284 ☎ 3688, ≤ Belle Isle, lake and mountains, « Extensive grounds and private lake », , park – wc Ⓟ
Easter-November – **M** (dinner only) 4.00/5.00 1.05 – **13 rm** (dinner included) 11.00/28.00. by A 5074 Z

Burnside (T.H.F.), Kendal Rd, LA23 3EP, ☎ 2211, ≤, – wc wc Ⓟ.
M a la carte 4.20/5.50 **st.** 1.60 – **31 rm** 11.50/21.00 **st.** – P 17.00/19.00 **st.** Z c

Cranleigh, Kendal Rd, LA23 3EW, ☎ 3293 – wc Z a
March-November and Christmas – **M** 3.50/4.00 **st.** 1.35 – **11 rm** 7.00/16.00 **st.**

St. Martin's, Lake Rd, LA23 3DE, ☎ 3731 – Ⓟ Z x
March-October – **M** (dinner only) approx. 4.00 **st.** 1.50 – **15 rm** 6.50/15.50 **st.** – P 11.50/12.75 **st.**

Burn How Motel, Back Belsfield Rd, LA23 3EW, ☎ 4486, – TV wc Ⓟ Z r
March-October – **M** (dinner only) 3.00/5.00 **st.** 1.35 – 1.50 – **18 rm** 12.00/18.50 **st.**

Craig Foot, Lake Rd, LA23 2JF, ☎ 3902, – Ⓟ Z s
April-October – **11 rm** 6.50/13.00 **s.**

Westbourne, Biskey Howe Rd, LA23 2JR, ☎ 3625 – Ⓟ Z z
9 rm 6.25/12.50 **st.**

Eastbourne, Biskey Howe Rd, LA23 2JR, ☎ 3525 Z u
9 rm 3.50/7.00 **s.**

Shepherds Aquarius, Bowness Bay, LA23 3HE, ☎ 4040, ≤ lake, Dancing (Friday and Saturday) – Ⓟ Z v
M a la carte 6.70/10.00 **st.** 2.00.

Porthole Eating House, 3 Ash St., LA23 3EB, ☎ 2793 Z n
closed Tuesday, December and January – **M** (dinner only and Sunday lunch) a la carte 4.60/5.65 1.50.

at Troutbeck N : 4 m. off A 592 – Y – ✉ Windermere – 096 63 Ambleside:

Mortal Man , LA23 1PL, ☎ 3193, ≤, – Ⓟ
closed mid November-mid February – **11 rm.**

AUSTIN-MG-ROVER-TRIUMPH-WOLSELEY, JENSEN College Rd ☎ 2451
CHRYSLER-SIMCA Main Rd ☎ 2441

WINDSOR Berks. 986 ⑧ and ㊱ – pop. 30,114 – 075 35.

See : Castle*** (St. George's Chapel***) Z. **Envir.** : Eton (College**) N : **1** m. Z. **Exc.** : Runnymede (signing of the Magna Carta, 1215, museum) *AC*, SE : 4 m. by A 308 Y.

i Windsor Central Station ☎ 52010 (summer only).

London 28 – Reading 19 – Southampton 59.

Plan on next page

Castle (T.H.F.), High St., SL4 1LJ, ☎ 51011 – TV Ⓟ. Z c
M 3.75/4.00 **st.** 1.60 – **63 rm** 14.00/21.00 **st.**

Old House, Thames St., SL4 1PX, ☎ 61354, ≤, « Former residence of Sir Christopher Wren » – wc Ⓟ – **39 rm.** Z v

Ye Harte and Garter, 21 High St., SL4 1PH, ☎ 63426 – TV wc Z e
45 rm.

Royal Adelaide (Crest), 42-46 Kings Rd, SL4 2AG, ☎ 63916 – wc Ⓟ Z a
M (dinner only) 2.70/4.75 **s.** 1.50 – **34 rm** 10.20/16.00.

Don Peppino, 28-30 Thames St., SL4 1PU, ☎ 60081, Italian rest. Z x
closed Sunday dinner, Good Friday and 25-26 December – **M** a la carte 3.75/5.45 1.35.

Ye Old Kings Head, 7 Church St., SL4 1PE, ☎ 68952 Z i
closed Sunday – **M** a la carte 4.30/5.50 **t.** 1.60.

La Taverna, 2 River St., SL4 1OU, ☎ 63020, Italian rest. Z n
closed Sunday, Good Friday and 25-26 December – **M** a la carte 3.15/5.00 1.35.

P.T.O. →

WINDSOR

North is at the top on all town plans.

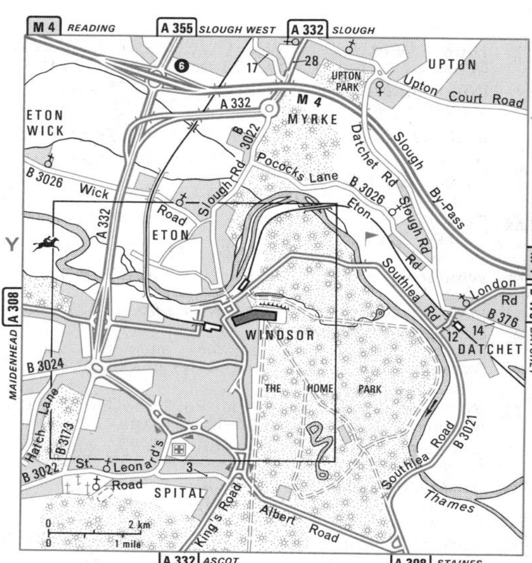

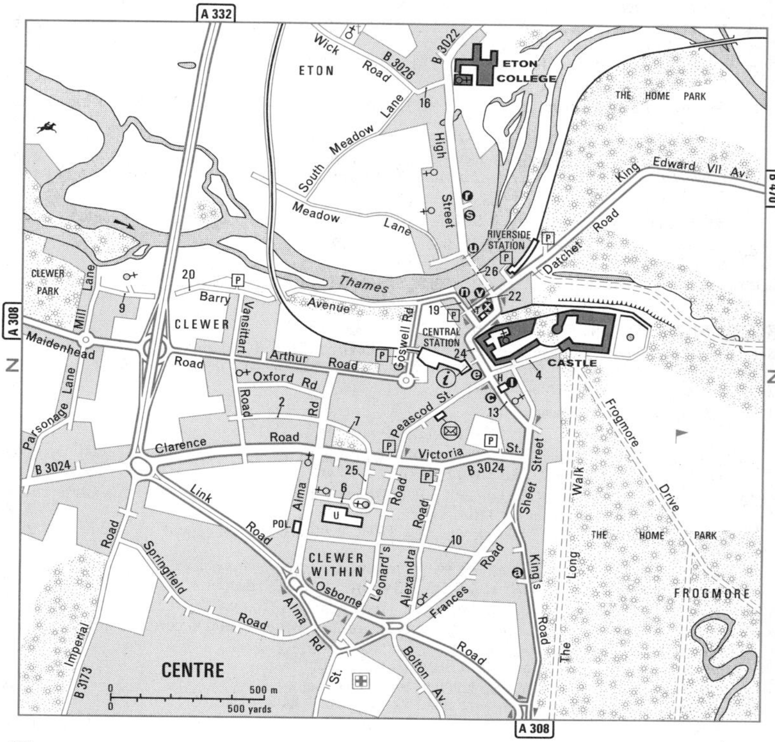

A 332
ETON
Wick Road
B 3026
B 3022
ETON COLLEGE
THE HOME PARK
South Meadow Lane
High Street
Meadow Lane
King Edward VII Av.
B 470
Datchet Road
RIVERSIDE STATION
Thames
CLEWER PARK
Mill Lane
Barry Avenue
Vansittart Road
CLEWER
Goswell Rd
CENTRAL STATION
CASTLE
A 308
Maidenhead Road
Arthur Road
Oxford Rd
Parsonage Lane
Peascod St.
Frogmore Drive
Clarence Road
Victoria St.
Sheet Street
B 3024
Link Road
Alma Road
The Long Walk
POL.
CLEWER WITHIN
St. Leonard's Road
Alexandra Road
Frances Road
King's Road
Springfield Road
Osborne Road
Imperial Road
Alma Rd
THE HOME PARK
FROGMORE
Bolton Av.
B 3173
CENTRE
0 500 m
0 500 yards
A 308
Z

at Eton – ✉ ☎ 075 35 Windsor:

XX **Antico,** 42 Eton High St., SL4 6AX, ☎ 63977, Italian rest. Z **s**
closed Sunday and 25 to 27 December – **M** a la carte 5.20/7.30 **t.** 1.70.

XX Cock Pit, 47-49 Eton High St. ☎ 60944, Italian rest. Z **r**

XX **House on the Bridge,** 71 High St., Windsor Bridge, SL4 6AA, ☎ 60914, ← – P
closed 26 December and lunch 27 December – **M** 4.75/7.50 **s.** 1.25. Z **u**

AUSTIN-MG-ROVER-TRIUMPH-WOLSELEY 37/39 Sheet St. ☎ 68131
CHRYSLER-SIMCA 72/74 Arthur Rd ☎ 64068
DATSUN Dedworth Rd ☎ 69191
LANCIA 195 Clarence Rd ☎ 60707
VAUXHALL 2/6 Frances Rd ☎ 60131

WINGHAM Kent – see Canterbury.

WINKFIELD Berks. – pop. 8,689 – ✉ Bracknell – ☎ 034 47 Winkfield Row.
London 36 – Maidenhead 9 – Reading 16.

XX Jolly Gardener, Maidens Green, SW: ¾ m. on B 3022 ☎ 2284 – P.

FORD Hatchet Lane ☎ 2591

WINSFORD Somerset – pop. 294 – ✉ Minehead – ☎ 064 385.
London 194 – Exeter 31 – Minehead 10 – Taunton 32.

Royal Oak Inn, TA24 7JE, ☎ 232 – P
closed December and January – **M** (bar lunch) a la carte 3.95/6.10 **st.** – **12 rm** 8.95/19.50 **st.**

WINTERSLOW Wilts. – see Salisbury.

WISBECH Cambs. 986 ㉘ – pop. 17,016 – ☎ 0945.
Envir.: March (St. Wendreda's Church 15C: the Angel roof*) SW: 10 m.
London 106 – Cambridge 47 – Leicester 62 – Norwich 57.

White Lion, 5 South Brink, PE13 1JD, ☎ 3221 – wc P.
M a la carte 3.50/5.55 1.20 – **23 rm** 8.60/16.60 **st.**

AUDI-NSU, MERCEDES-BENZ, VAUXHALL Elm High Rd ☎ 2471
AUSTIN-MORRIS-MG 46 Norwich Rd ☎ 4342
FIAT, VOLVO Sutton Rd ☎ 3082
FORD Elm Rd ☎ 2681
MORRIS-MG-ROVER-TRIUMPH Harecroft Rd ☎ 2771
RENAULT Old Lynn Rd ☎ 2662

WITHAM Essex 986 ㉜ – pop. 17,381 – ☎ 0376.
London 42 – Cambridge 46 – Chelmsford 9 – Colchester 13.

White Hart, 39 Newland St., CM8 2AF, ☎ 512245 – wc P.
M a la carte 3.55/5.00 **t.** 1.50 – **14 rm** 9.50/12.50 **t.**

at Rivenhall End NE: 1 ½ m. by B 1389 on A 12 – ✉ ☎ 0376 Witham:

Rivenhall Motor Inn, CM8 3HF, on A 12 ☎ 516969 – TV wc P
M approx. 3.00 **t.** 1.75 – 1.50 – **26 rm** 8.50/12.50 – P 14.00/18.00.

AUSTIN-MORRIS-MG Newland St. ☎ 513272
DATSUN London Rd ☎ 515575
FORD Colchester Rd ☎ 513496
VAUXHALL Maldon Rd ☎ 513326

WITHINGTON Glos. – see Cheltenham.

WITHINGTON Greater Manchester – see Manchester.

WIVENHOE Essex 986 ㉜ – see Colchester.

WOBURN Beds. 986 ㉜ – pop. 796 – ✉ Milton Keynes – ☎ 052 525.
See: Woburn Abbey*** (18C) *AC*, Wild Animal Kingdom** *AC*.
London 49 – Bedford 13 – Luton 13 – Northampton 24.

Bedford Arms, 1 George St., MK17 9PX, ☎ 441 – TV wc P.
M 3.50/3.75 **st.** 1.40 – **41 rm** 12.00/18.00 **st.** – P 15.50/17.50 **st.**

WOBURN SANDS Bucks. – pop. 2,046 – ✉ Milton Keynes – ☎ 0908.
London 53 – Bedford 13 – Northampton 19.

Swan, High St., MK17 8RH, ☎ 583204, – P
M *(closed Sunday dinner)* (dinner only and Sunday lunch) 3.00/4.50 **t.** 1.50 – **11 rm** 5.70/10.50 **st.**

WOKING Surrey 986 ⑧ and ㊱ – pop. 75,952 – ☎ 048 62.
Envir.: Clandon Park** (Renaissance House) *AC*, SE: 6 m.
i Centre Halls, New Town Centre ☎ 64848.
London 31 – Southampton 55.

XX **Mayford Manor** with rm, Guildford Rd, Mayford, GU22 0SQ, S: 2 ½ m. on A 320 ☎ 66166, – TV wc P
M a la carte 4.15/6.65 1.20 – **6 rm** 8.50/10.60.

DAF Albert Drive ☎ 61517
AUSTIN-DAIMLER-MORRIS-MG-WOLSELEY 82 Goldsworth Rd ☎ 61444
DATSUN Guildford Rd ☎ 048 67 (Brookwood) 4988
DATSUN 67 High St. ☎ 61725
FORD 123/4 Maybury Rd ☎ 3323
JAGUAR-ROVER-TRIUMPH 2 White Rose Lane ☎ 4515
PEUGEOT Hermitage Rd ☎ 048 67 (Brookwood) 4324
POLSKI, RENAULT Vicarage Rd ☎ 099 05 (Chobham) 8031
RENAULT 24/26 Guildford Rd ☎ 66572
TOYOTA St. John's Rd ☎ 64641
VW, AUDI-NSU Portsmouth Rd ☎ 048 643 (Ripley) 2361

WOLVERHAMPTON West Midlands 986 ⑫ and ㉗ – pop. 269,112 – ☎ 0902.

See : St. Peter's Church* 15C B **A.**

Bushbury ☎ 20506, N : 1 ½ m. A.

London 132 – Birmingham 15 – Liverpool 89 – Shrewsbury 30.

Plan of Enlarged Area : See Birmingham p. 2-3

WOLVERHAMPTON

Street	Square
Darlington Street	B
Mander Centre	B
Victoria Street	B 24
Wulfrun Centre	B
Alfred Squire Road	A 2
Birmingham New Road	A 3
Bridgnorth Road	A 6
Cleveland Street	B 7
Garrick Street	B 8
Lichfield Road	A 10
Lichfield Street	B 12
Market Street	B 14
Princess Street	B 15
Queen Square	B 17
Railway Drive	B 20
Salop Street	B 22
Thompson Avenue	A 23
Wolverhampton Road	A 26

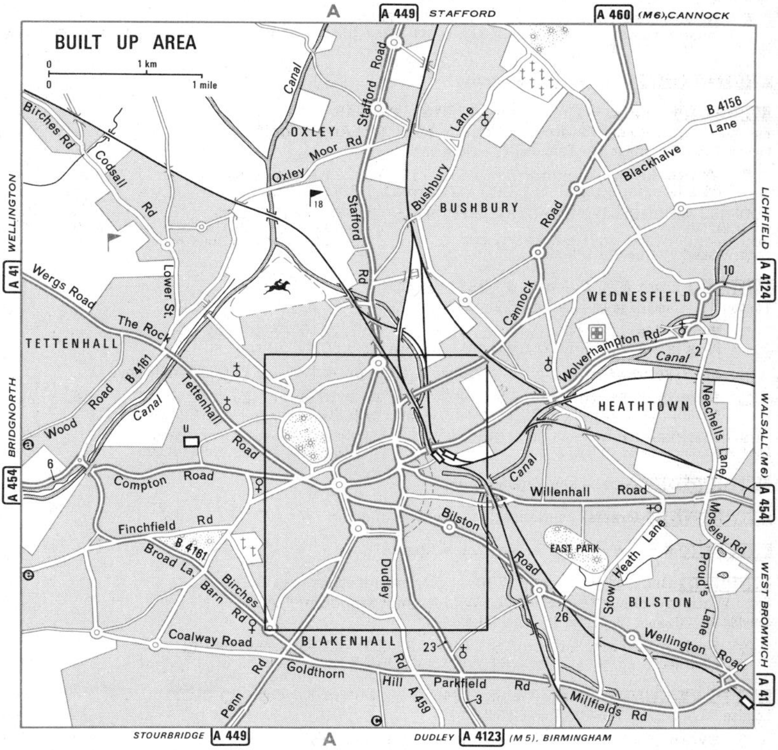

Mount (Embassy) 🔖, Mount Rd, Tettenhall Wood, WV6 8HL, W : 2 ½ m. off A 454 ☎ 752055, ≤, park – TV P. A a
closed Christmas – **M** approx. 3.75 **st.** 1.60 – **62 rm** 10.50/15.75 **st.**

Park Hall (Embassy) 🔖, Park Drive, off Ednam Rd, Goldthorn Park, WV4 5AJ, S : 2 m. by A 449 ☎ 31121, – TV wc P. A c
closed Christmas – **M** approx. 3.75 **st.** 1.95 – **56 rm** 13.00/15.80 **st.**

Connaught, 44-50 Tettenhall Rd, WV1 4SW, ☎ 24433, Telex 338490 – TV wc wc P. B s
61 rm.

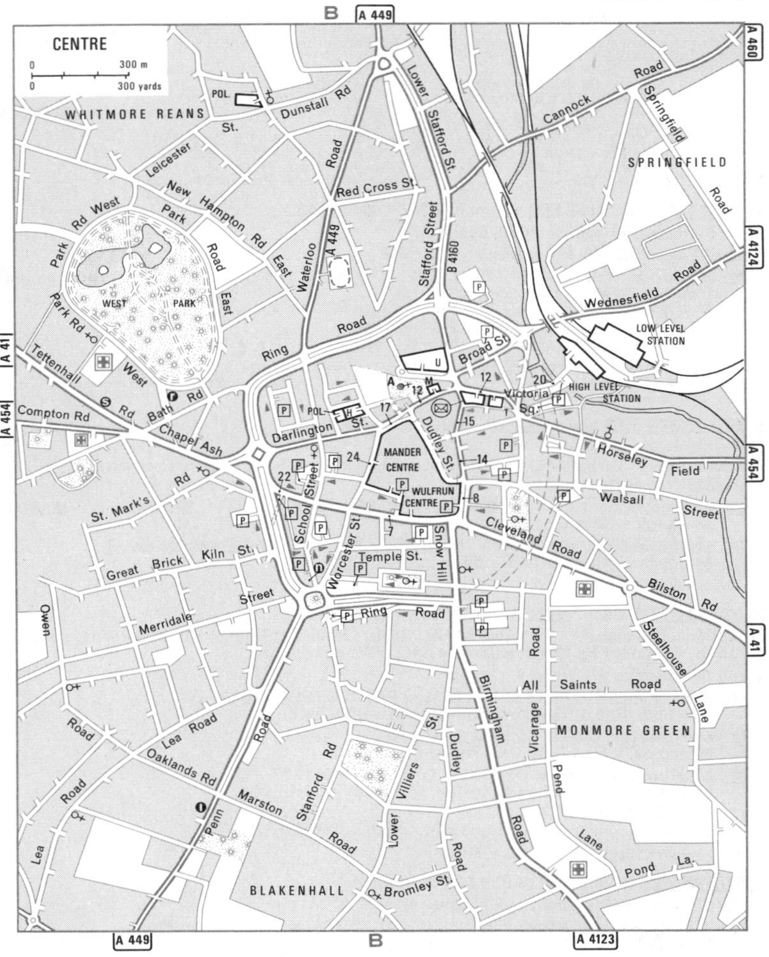

🏨 **Castlecroft** (Ansells), Castlecroft Rd, WV3 8NA, W : 3 ¼ m. off A 454 ☎ 761264, – wc wc Ⓟ — A **e**
M 3.10/4.10 **st.** 🌢 1.80 – **26 rm** 7.40/11.90 **st.**

🏨 **Goldthorn,** Penn Rd, WV3 0ER, ☎ 29216 – TV wc Ⓟ. — B **i**
M 3.00/3.50 🌢 1.35 – **55 rm** 8.20/13.90.

🏨 Fox, 118 School St., WV3 0NR, ☎ 21680 – TV wc Ⓟ — B **n**
29 rm.

🏨 Ravensholt, Summerfield Rd, WV1 4PR, ☎ 24140 – wc wc Ⓟ — B **r**
29 rm.

at Shipley (Salop) W : 7 m. on A 454 – A – ✉ 0902 Pattingham :

✕✕ **Thornescroft,** Bridgnorth Rd, WV6 7EQ, ☎ 700253 – Ⓟ
closed Sunday, Monday, Bank Holiday Tuesdays, 8-10 days at Christmas and Bank Holidays – **M** a la carte 3.85/6.35 **s.** 🌢 1.50.

MICHELIN Branch, Millfields Rd, Millfields, Wolverhampton, WV4 6JQ, ☎ 44466/7/8.

P.T.O. ⟶

ALFA-ROMEO, BMW Merridale Lane ☎ 23295
AUSTIN-JAGUAR-MG-WOLSELEY, ROLLS ROYCE Wolverhampton Rd East ☎ 090 73 (Sedgley) 3725
AUSTIN-DAIMLER-JAGUAR-MORRIS-MG-ROVER TRIUMPH Stafford St. ☎ 29122
AUSTIN-MG 372 Penn Rd, Penn ☎ 35570
AUSTIN-MORRIS-MG-ROVER-TRIUMPH-WOLSELEY Chapel Ash ☎ 26781
CHRYSLER-SIMCA Cleveland Rd ☎ 25961
CHRYSLER-SIMCA 67/71 Bilston Rd ☎ 52611
CITROEN Stafford St. ☎ 771295
FIAT, SAAB Warstones Rd ☎ 37488
FORD Bilston Rd ☎ 51515
FORD 59/73 Birmingham Rd ☎ 27651
LANCIA, MERCEDES-BENZ Penn Rd ☎ 27897
MORRIS-MG-WOLSELEY, VAUXHALL Finchfield ☎ 761171
MORRIS-MG-WOLSELEY Wolverhampton Rd, Wednesfield ☎ 731372
OPEL Dudley Rd ☎ 25821
PEUGEOT Parkfield Rd, Ettingshall, ☎ 0902 (Bilston) 41735
RENAULT Bilston Rd ☎ 53111
ROVER-TRIUMPH 1 Evans St. ☎ 20362
VAUXHALL Raglan St. ☎ 27897
VOLVO 657 Parkfield Rd ☎ 333211

WOODBRIDGE Suffolk 986 ㉜ – pop. 7,283 – ✆ 039 43.

18, 9 Bromeswell Heath, ☎ 2038, E: 2 m.

London 81 – Great Yarmouth 45 – **Ipswich 8** – **Norwich 47.**

Seckford Hall, IP13 6NU, SW: 1 ¼ m off A 12, ☎ 5678, ≤, « Tudor country house », park – wc Ⓟ.
M a la carte 4.00/5.15 1.25 – **20 rm** 7.50/21.00 **s.**

Captain's Table, 3 Quay St., ☎ 3145 – Ⓟ
closed 25 and 26 December – **M** a la carte 3.35/5.75 **t.** 1.25.

AUSTIN-MG-MORRIS-WOLSELEY Melton Rd ☎ 3456
FORD 96 Thorough Fare ☎ 3333
FORD Bawsey ☎ 039 441 (Shottisham) 368
ROVER-TRIUMPH Ipswich Rd ☎ 2282
SAAB Hollesey ☎ 039 441 (Shottisham) 687

WOODHALL SPA Lincs. 986 ㉘ – pop. 2,261 – ✆ 0526.

18 ☎ **52511.**

i Council Offices, Stanhope Av. ☎ 52461 – Jubilee Park, Stixwould Rd ☎ 52448 (summer only).

London 138 – Lincoln 18.

Petwood Moat House, Stixwould Rd, LN10 6QF, ☎ 52411, park – wc Ⓟ. – **35 rm.**

Golf (Crest), The Broadway, LN10 6SG, ☎ 52434, – wc Ⓟ.
M approx. 3.30 **s.** 1.55 – **57 m** 10.50/15.50 **s.**

SAAB Whitham Rd ☎ 52157

WOODSTOCK Oxon. 986 ㉛ – pop. **1,961** – ✆ **0993.**

See : Blenheim Palace★★★ 18C (park★★) *AC.* **Envir. :** Rousham (Manor House gardens : statues★) NE : 5 m. – Ditchley Park★ (Renaissance) *AC,* NW : 6 m.

London 65 – Gloucester 47 – **Oxford 8.**

Bear, Park St., OX7 1SZ, ☎ 811511, « Part 16C inn » – TV Ⓟ.
M 4.95/5.40 1.85 – 2.40 – **33 rm** 14.50/28.00.

Dorchester, Market St., OX7 1SX, ☎ 812291 – wc
M approx. 3.50 0.85 – **16 rm** 6.50/13.00.

Marlborough Arms, Oxford St., OX7 1TS, ☎ 811227 – Ⓟ
M a la carte 2.35/3.60 **t.** 1.40 – **14 rm** 7.00/14.00 **t.**

Luis, 19 High St., ☎ 811017
closed Monday lunch – **M** a la carte 4.80/7.30 **t.** 1.70.

MORRIS-MG-WOLSELEY 2 Oxford St. ☎ 811286

WOODY BAY Devon – ✉ ✆ 059 83 Parracombe.

London 211 – Exeter 57 – Minehead 25 – Taunton 48.

Woody Bay, Parracombe, EX31 4QY, ☎ 264, ≤ bay – wc Ⓟ
M 3.50/4.50 1.60 – **12 rm** 7.00/15.00.

WOOL Dorset – pop. 4,126 – ✉ Wareham – ✆ 0929 Bindon Abbey.

Envir. : Durdle Door★★ SW : 6 m.

London 126 – Bournemouth 19 – Dorchester 12 – Weymouth 14.

Woolbridge Manor, BH20 6HQ, off A 352 ☎ 462200, « Farm manor house », – Ⓟ
March-October – **M** *(closed lunch to non-residents)* a la carte 2.80/4.10 **s.** 1.90 – **5 rm** 9.00/15.00 **s.**

WOOLACOMBE Devon 986 ㉞㉟ – pop. 809 – ✆ 027 187.

i Hall 70, Beach Rd ☎ 553 (summer only).

London 237 – Barnstaple 15 – Exeter 55.

Woolacombe Bay, EX34 7BN, ☎ 388, heated, – Ⓟ
mid May-mid September – **M** approx. 4.25 **t.** 1.50 – **65 rm.**

Watersmeet, EX34 7EB, ☎ 333, ≤ sea and coast, heated, – wc Ⓟ
Easter-October – **M** 4.00/6.00 – **40 rm** 7.00/15.00.

Whin Bay, Bay View Rd, EX34 7DQ, ☎ 475, ≤ – Ⓟ
Easter-mid September – **M** (dinner only) approx. 4.00 **t.** 1.00 – **19 rm** 7.00/14.00 **t.**

WOOLER Northumb. **986** ⑮ – pop. **1,833** – ☎ **066 82.**
' Padgepool Place Car Park ☎ 602 (summer only).
.ondon 332 – Edinburgh 62 – Newcastle-upon-Tyne 46.

- **Tankerville Arms,** Cottage Rd, NE71 6AD, (A 697) ☎ 581, – wc **M** 3.00/4.00 **st.** 1.30 – **14 rm** 7.25/14.50 **st.**

\USTIN-MG-WOLSELEY South Rd ☎ 472
JAGUAR-MORRIS-MG-ROVER-TRIUMPH-WOLSELEY South Rd ☎ 267

WOOLTON Merseyside – see Liverpool.

WORCESTER Heref. and Worc. **986** ㉛ – pop. **73,452** – ☎ **0905.**
;ee : Cathedral** 13C-15C (crypt** 11C) **A** – The Commandery* (15C) *AC* **B.**
☎ **27171** ext **33.** – *i* Guildhall ☎ 23471.
.ondon 124 – Birmingham 26 – Bristol 61 – Cardiff 74.

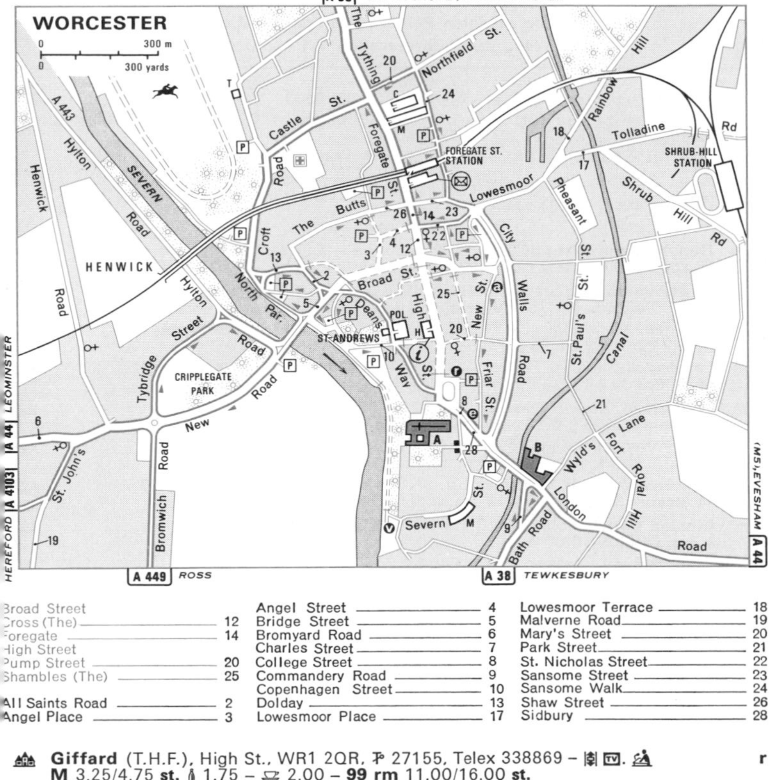

Broad Street
Cross (The) 12
Foregate 14
High Street
Pump Street 20
Shambles (The) 25

All Saints Road 2
Angel Place 3
Angel Street 4
Bridge Street 5
Bromyard Road 6
Charles Street 7
College Street 8
Commandery Road 9
Copenhagen Street 10
Dolday 13
Lowesmoor Place 17
Lowesmoor Terrace 18
Malverne Road 19
Mary's Street 20
Park Street 21
St. Nicholas Street 22
Sansome Street 23
Sansome Walk 24
Shaw Street 26
Sidbury 28

- **Giffard** (T.H.F.), High St., WR1 2QR, ☎ 27155, Telex 338869 – **M** 3.25/4.75 **st.** 1.75 – 2.00 – **99 rm** 11.00/16.00 **st.** **r**
- **Diglis,** Riverside, Severn St., WR1 2NF, ☎ 353518, – wc **M** *(closed Christmas to non-residents)* 3.60/8.00 1.80 – **15 rm** 7.50/16.00. **v**
- **Ye Olde Talbot,** College St., WR1 2NA, ☎ 23573 – **M** approx. 2.75 **st.** – **12 rm** 8.50/16.00 **st.** **e**
- XXX **King Charles II,** 29 New St., WR1 2DP, ☎ 22449, « 16C heavily timbered building » *closed Sunday and Bank Holidays* – **M** a la carte 4.70/6.50 **t.** 1.10. **a**

MICHELIN Branch, Blackpole Trading Estate, WR3 8TJ, ☎ 55626.

\USTIN-MG-MORRIS-WOLSELEY Castle St. ☎ 27100
CHRYSLER-SIMCA Farrier St. ☎ 2726
DAF, PEUGEOT Angel St. ☎ 28461
DAIMLER-MORRIS-MG-WOLSELEY Farrier St. ☎ 23338
FIAT, LANCIA Spetchley Rd ☎ 351821
PEUGEOT 21 Barbourne Rd ☎ 28461
RENAULT St. Martins Gate ☎ 21215
ROVER-TRIUMPH 26/30 Sidbury ☎ 26988
VAUXHALL Brook St. ☎ 27781
VW, AUDI-NSU Hallow Rd ☎ 640512

WORKINGTON Cumbria 986 ⑲ – pop. 28,431 – ✆ 0900.

Branthwaite Rd ✆ 3460, E: 2 m.

i Finkle St. ✆ 2122.

London 313 – Carlisle 33 – Keswick 21.

Westland, Branthwaite Rd, CA14 4SS, ✆ 4544 – wc ☎ P – **29 rm.**

DAF Annie Pitt Lane ✆ 3915
MORRIS-MG-WOLSELEY Jane St. ✆ 2227
RENAULT Clay Flatts Estate ✆ 4542
VAUXHALL Harrington Rd ✆ 2159

WORSLEY Greater Manchester 986 ⑤ – pop. 49,651 – ✆ 061 Manchester.

London 207 – Liverpool 29 – Manchester 7.

XX **Casserole,** 2 Worsley Rd, M28 4NL, junction 13 on M 63 ✆ 794 2660 – P
closed Sunday and Monday – **M** a la carte 3.80/5.70 **s.** 1.20.

CITROEN Manchester Rd ✆ 4448

WORTHING West Sussex 986 ㊱ – pop. 88,407 – ✆ 0903.

Envir.: Shoreham-by-Sea (St. Mary of Haura's Church* 12C-13C – St. Nicholas' Church: carved arches* 12C) E: 5 m. by A 259 BY.

Links Rd ✆ 60801 AY – Hill Barn Lane ✆ 37301 BY.

i Marine Par. ✆ 35934 – Amenities Department, Town Hall ✆ 204226.

London 59 – Brighton 11 – Southampton 50.

Plan opposite

Beach, Marine Par., BN11 3QJ, ✆ 34001, ← – TV P.
M approx. 4.00 **st.** 1.50 – **97 rm** 11.90/21.75 **st.** – P 12.70/16.50 **st.** AZ e

Chatsworth, The Steyne, BN11 3DU, ✆ 36103 – TV wc ☎.
M 3.50/4.50 **t.** 1.25 – **90 rm** 10.50/16.00 **t.** BZ x

Warnes, Marine Par. BN11 3PR, ✆ 35222, ← – wc ☎ P.
M a la carte 4.90/5.95 1.60 – 1.25 – **63 rm** 8.00/17.50. BZ z

Eardley, 3-7 Marine Par., BN11 3PW, ✆ 34444, ← – TV wc ☎ P
M 3.00/3.30 1.00 – **69 rm** 9.00/17.00. BZ u

Ardington, Steyne Gdns, BN11 3DZ, ✆ 30451 – wc
M approx. 2.40 0.90 – **54 rm** 6.25/14.00. BZ s

Kingsway, 117 Marine Par., BN11 3QQ, ✆ 37542 –
M 3.00/3.75 **t.** 1.35 – **35 rm** 7.00/14.00. AZ n

Beechwood Hall, Wykeham Rd, BN11 4AH, ✆ 32872, – wc P
M approx. 3.00 1.20 – **16 rm** 6.50/14.50 – P 11.50/12.50. AZ a

Ainslea Court, Abbey Rd, BN11 3RW, ✆ 30442,
8 rm 5.00/10.00 **s.** AZ r

Wansfell, 49 Chesswood Rd, BN11 2AA, ✆ 30612, – TV
11 rm 5.00/10.00 **t.** BY a

XX **Paragon,** 9-10 Brunswick Rd, BN11 3NG, ✆ 33367 AZ c
closed Sunday, Tuesday, first 3 weeks June and Bank Holidays – **M** a la carte 5.30/8.70 **t.** 1.50.

XX **Robert's Parade Wine Lodge,** 1st floor, 80-82 Marine Par., BN11 3QE, ✆ 33825
closed Monday dinner and Sunday – **M** a la carte 2.55/5.20 **t.** 1.40. BZ o

X Gianmario, 1 st floor, 42 Marine Par., ✆ 32538, Italian rest. BZ r

at Findon **N: 4 m. off A 24** – AY – ✉ **Worthing** – ✆ **090 671 Findon:**

Village House, Horsham Rd, BN14 0TE, ✆ 3350, – P
M *(closed Monday dinner to non-residents)* 2.50/5.00 **t.** 1.40 – **10 rm** 6.50/12.00 **t.**

at Sompting **NE: 2 ½ m. on B 2222 by A 27** – BY – ✉ ✆ **0903 Worthing:**

X **Smugglers,** West St., BN15 0AP, ✆ 36072 – P
closed Sunday, Monday and Bank Holidays – **M** a la carte 4.20/6.05 1.70.

ALFA-ROMEO, VOLVO 187 Findon Rd ✆ 090 671 (Findon) 3022
AUSTIN-MG-WOLSELEY Western Pl. ✆ 206901
AUSTIN-MORRIS-MG-WOLSELEY The Boulevard, Durrington ✆ 4344
BMW Lancing ✆ 2961
CHRYSLER-SIMCA Broadwater Rd ✆ 30494
CITROEN 28 Broadwater Rd ✆ 39573
DAF, PEUGEOT, SAAB 11/17 Alfred Pl. ✆ 35769
DAIMLER-JAGUAR-ROVER-TRIUMPH 30 Chapel Rd ✆ 31671
FIAT Selden Lane ✆ 204626
FORD 58 High St. ✆ 38141
LANCIA, MERCEDES-BENZ Heene Place ✆ 35655
MORRIS-MG-WOLSELEY Arundel Rd ✆ 64980
MORRIS-MG-WOLSELEY 57 Chapel Rd ✆ 31111
RENAULT 1/3 Park Rd ✆ 33790
TOYOTA South Farm Rd ✆ 32111
VAUXHALL Palatine Rd ✆ 42916
VAUXHALL ✆ 37527
VW, AUDI-NSU Ivy Arch Rd ✆ 200272

WORTHING

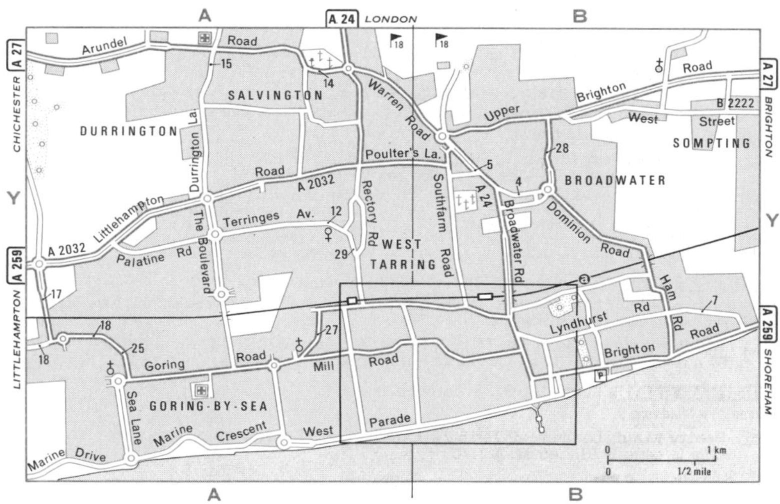

CENTRE

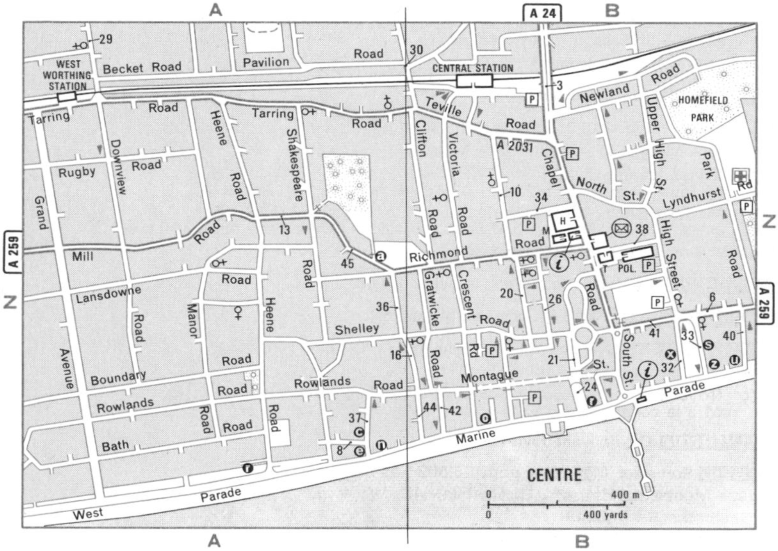

WOTTON Surrey – see Dorking.

WOTTON-UNDER-EDGE Glos. – pop. 4,318 – ☏ 045 385.
London 125 – Bristol 21 – Gloucester 18 – Swindon 34.

- **Swan,** Market St., GL12 7AE, ☏ 2329 – TV wc ☎ P
  M 5.50/7.00 **st.** – 1.75 – **22 rm** 9.50/16.50 **st.**

AUSTIN-MG-WOLSELEY Gloucester St. ☏ 2240

WRAFTON Devon – ✉ ☏ 0271 Braunton.
London 227 – Barnstaple 5 – Exeter 45 – Ilfracombe 9.

- XX **Poyers Farm,** EX33 2DN, ☏ 812149, « 16C farmhouse » – P
  closed Saturday lunch, Sunday dinner, Monday, last 3 weeks October and Bank Holiday Mondays – **M** a la carte 3.75/8.55 1.35.

WREXHAM Clwyd 986 ⑨ and ㉗ – pop. 39,052 – ☏ 0978.
See : St. Giles' Church (tower*).
18 **Holt Rd ☏ 4268 and 2189, NE: 2 m.**
i Tourist Information Centre, Guildhall Car Park, Town Centre ☏ 57845 (Easter-September).
London 192 – Chester 12 – Shrewsbury 28.

- **Wrexham Crest Motel** (Crest), 20 High St., LL13 8HP, ☏ 53431 – TV wc ☎ P.
  M 2.70/3.20 **s.** 1.55 – 1.60 – **80 rm** 10.95/15.50 **s.**

AUSTIN-JAGUAR-MORRIS-MG-ROVER-TRIUMPH Holt Rd ☏ 3514
AUSTIN-MG-WOLSELEY 15/17 Hill St. ☏ 4024
CHRYSLER-SIMCA Hightown Rd ☏ 4151
CITROEN, VAUXHALL Mold Rd ☏ 3431
DATSUN New Broughton ☏ 3173
FORD 67/73 Regent St. ☏ 51001
PEUGEOT Kingsmills Rd ☏ 4551
RENAULT Regent St. ☏ 56822
VOLVO Market St. ☏ 2159

WROTHAM Kent 986 ㊱ – pop. 1,785 – ☏ 0732 Borough Green.
Envir. : NE : Coldrum Long Barrow (prehistoric stones) site* : from Trottiscliffe 1 m. NE, plus 5 mn walk. – London 27 – Maidstone 10.

- XX **Moat** with rm, London Rd, TN15 7RP, S : ½ m. on A 20 ☏ 882263 – P
  M a la carte 4.05/6.80 **s.** – **9 rm** 8.00/18.00 **st.**

WROTHAM HEATH Kent – ☏ 0732 Borough Green.
London 29 – Maidstone 9.

- XX **Pretty Maid,** London Rd, TN15 7RU, on A 20 ☏ 882330 – P
  M a la carte 3.70/6.80 **st.** 1.70.

CHRYSLER-SIMCA ☏ 883255

WROXHAM Norfolk 986 ㉘ – pop. 1,254 – ✉ Hoveton – ☏ 060 53.
London 122 – Great Yarmouth 21 – **Norwich 7.**

- Wroxham, Broads Centre, NR12 8UR, ☏ 2061, ← – TV wc P
  M 3.65/3.95 **st.** 1.25 – **18 rm.**

MORRIS-MG-WOLSELEY Norwich Rd ☏ 2961

WROXTON Oxon. – see Banbury.

WYE Kent – pop. 2,028 – ✉ ☏ 0233 Ashford.
London 61 – Folkestone 21 – Maidstone 24 – Margate 28.

- **Kings Head,** Church St., TN25 5BN, ☏ 812418
  M (buffet lunch) 1.60/2.00 **t.** 1.10 – **8 rm** 6.00/12.00 **t.**
- XX **Wife of Bath,** 4 Upper Bridge St., TN25 5AW, ☏ 812540 – P
  closed Sunday, Monday and Bank Holidays – **M** a la carte 4.40/5.50 **t.** 1.70.

MORRIS-MG-WOLSELEY Bridge St. ☏ 812331

WYNDS POINT Heref. and Worc. – see Malvern.

YARMOUTH I.O.W. 986 ㊴ – see Wight (Isle of).

YATTENDON Berks. – pop. 240 – ✉ Newbury – ☏ 0635 Hermitage.
London 62 – Newbury 8 – Reading 12.

- X **Royal Oak** with rm, The Square, RG16 0UF, ☏ 201325 – wc P
  M a la carte 3.95/6.55 **t.** 1.50 – **5 rm** 15.50/23.40 **st.**

YELVERTON Devon – see Plymouth.

YEOVIL Somerset 986 ㉟ – pop. 25,503 – ☏ 0935.
Envir. : Montacute House* (Elizabethan) *AC*, W : 4 m.
18 Sherborne Rd ☏ 5949.
London 135 – Exeter 48 – **Southampton 71** – Taunton 26.

Manor (Crest), BA20 1TG, on A 30 ℡ 23116 – TV ⇔wc ☎ P
M 2.55/3.10 **s.** 1.55 – **24 rm** 9.50/18.10 **s.**

Mermaid, High St., BA20 1RE, ℡ 23151 – ⇔wc P
M (steak bar) a la carte 2.05/3.75 **t.** 0.70 – **15 rm** 7.50/15.50 **st.**

Pickett Witch, 100 Ilchester Rd, BA21 3BL, ℡ 4317, – ⇔wc P
closed Christmas – **17 rm** 5.50/10.50 **t.**

The Maestro, 51 Princes St., BA20 1EG, ℡ 6960, Bistro
closed Sunday lunch and Monday – **M** a la carte 2.75/5.05 **t.** 1.10.

at Montacute **W: 4 m. on A 3088 – ✉ Yeovil – ☎ 093 582 Martock:**

Milk House, 17 The Borough, TA15 6XB, ℡ 3823
closed Sunday, Monday, 2 weeks February and 2 weeks October – **M** (lunch by arrangement) a la carte 3.85/5.65 **st.** 1.35.

AUSTIN-DAIMLER-JAGUAR-MORRIS-MG-ROVER-TRIUMPH Princes St. ℡ 5242
CHRYSLER-SIMCA Reckleford ℡ 4911
FORD Westminster St. ℡ 5131
PEUGEOT Sherborne Rd ℡ 23581
RENAULT Mudford ℡ 093 585 (Marston Magna) 386
RENAULT East Coker ℡ 093 586 (West Coker) 2181
SAAB 12 Oxford Rd ℡ 6284
VAUXHALL Addlewell Lane ℡ 4842
VW, AUDI-NSU Vale Rd ℡ 22158

YORK North Yorks. 986 ㉓㉔ – pop. 104,782 – ☎ 0904.

See: Minster* 13C-15C (Chapter House***, ✳** from tower, *AC*, 275 steps)** CDY **A – National Railway Museum***** CY **M¹ – Castle Museum** *AC*** DZ **M² – Clifford's Tower* (13C) *AC*** DYZ **B – Art Gallery*** CX **M³ – Treasurer's House* (14C) *AC*** DX **E – City Walls* 14C – The Shambles*** DY.

18 Heslington Lane ℡ 55212, S: 2 m. BZ **– 18 Strensall ℡ 090 481 (Strensall) 304, NE: 6 m. by Huntington Rd** BY.

℡ 53022 ext 2067.

i De Grey Rooms, Exhibition Sq. ℡ 21756/7.

London 210 – Kingston-upon-Hull 37 – Leeds 24 – Middlesbrough 48 – Nottingham 84 – Sheffield 60.

Plan on next page

Viking (County), North St., YO1 1JF, ℡ 59822, Telex 57937, ← – TV P. — CY **n**
M approx. 4.25 **st.** 1.10 – **100 rm** 20.00/29.00 **st.** – P approx. 27.50 **st.**

Royal Station (B.T.H.), Station Rd, YO2 2AA, ℡ 53681, Telex 57912, – TV P. — CY **e**
M 5.00/5.50 **st.** 1.20 – **129 rm** 20.00/30.00 **st.**

Post House (T.H.F.), Tadcaster Rd, YO2 2QF, SW: 1 ¾ m. on A 64 ℡ 707921, Telex 57798, – TV ⇔wc ☎ P. — AZ **r**
M 2.95/4.00 **st.** 1.50 – 2.00 – **104 rm** 13.00/21.00 **st.**

Abbey Park (Myddleton), 77-79 The Mount, YO2 2BN, ℡ 25481 – ⇔wc ☎. — CZ **c**
M 4.25/5.60 **st.** 1.35 – **63 rm** 13.85/21.80 **st.**

Chase, Tadcaster Rd, YO2 2QQ, SW: 1 ½ m. on A 64 ℡ 707171, ←, – TV ⇔wc ☎ P. — AZ **e**
closed 3 days at Christmas – **M** a la carte 4.50/8.75 1.50 – 1.75 – **75 rm** 9.00/16.50.

Dean Court, Duncombe Pl., YO1 2EF, ℡ 25082 – TV ⇔wc ☎ — CY **a**
M approx. 5.00 **st.** 1.40 – **25 rm** 14.00/28.00 **st.**

Sheppard, 63 The Mount, YO2 2BD, ℡ 20500 – P – **20 rm.** — CZ **i**

Priory, 126 Fulford Rd, YO1 4BE, ℡ 25280, – P — DZ **r**
closed Christmas – **12 rm** 10.00/12.00 **st.**

Bootham Bar, 4 High Petergate, YO1 2EH, ℡ 58516 – — CX **a**
closed Christmas – **8 rm** 5.15/10.25 **t.**

Mount Royale with rm, 119 The Mount, YO2 2DA, ℡ 56261, – TV ⇔wc P — AZ **s**
closed 24 December-18 January – **M** *(closed Sunday)* (dinner only) 4.50/6.00 1.95 – **11 rm** 9.50/16.00.

Trattoria Giovanni, 55 Goodramgate, YO1 2LS, ℡ 23413, Italian rest. — DY **a**
closed Monday and 25-26 December – **M** a la carte 2.95/5.10 **t.** 1.20.

at Bishopthorpe **S: 3 ¼ m. by Bishopthorpe Rd** – BZ – **✉ ☎ 0904 York:**

L'Octogone, Ferry Field, Ferry Lane off Acaster Lane, YO2 1SB, ℡ 707878, ←, – P
closed Sunday dinner and Monday – **M** a la carte 3.75/6.10.

ALFA-ROMEO Leeman Rd ℡ 22772
AUSTIN-MG-WOLSELEY 130 Lawrence St. ℡ 21551
AUSTIN-MG-WOLSELEY Boroughbridge Rd ℡ 792651
AUSTIN-MG Gladstone St. ℡ 58781
CHRYSLER-SIMCA, MAZDA The Stonebow ℡ 55118
CITROEN Lowther St. ℡ 22064
DAF, OPEL 100 Layerthorpe ℡ 56671
DAIMLER-JAGUAR-ROVER-TRIUMPH Layerthorpe ℡ 58252
DATSUN 21/27 Layerthorpe ℡ 58809
DATSUN 45 Gillygate ℡ 25646
FIAT Front St., Haxby ℡ 768344
MERCEDES-BENZ, PEUGEOT Boroughbridge Rd ℡ 798388
MORRIS-MG-WOLSELEY, VAUXHALL Long St. ℡ 0347 (Easingwold) 294
RENAULT Clifton ℡ 58647
RENAULT Kirkbymoorside ℡ 0751 (Kirkbymoorside) 31401
SAAB 223 Malton Rd ℡ 55787
SIMCA Elvington ℡ 090 485 (Elvington) 268
TOYOTA Stockton Lane ℡ 59200
TOYOTA 172 Fulford Rd ℡ 52947
VOLVO 88/96 Walmgate ℡ 53798
VW, AUDI-NSU Clarence St. ℡ 23220

YORK

Blake Street — CY 5
Coney Street — CY 13
Davygate — CY 16
Lendal — CY 32
Parliament Street — DY 42
Shambles (The) — DY 54
Stonegate — CY 58

Bishopgate Street — CZ 3
Bishophill Senior — CZ 4
Campleshon Road — AZ 7
Church Street — DY 8
Clarence Street — CX 9
Clifford Street — DY 10
Colliergate — DY 12
Cromwell Road — CZ 15
Deangate — DY 18
Duncombe Place — CY 20
Fawcett Street — DZ 21
Fetter Lane — CY 22
Fossgate — DY 23
Goodramgate — DY 25
High Ousegate — DY 26
High Petergate — CY 28
Knavesmire Road — AZ 29
Leeman Road — AY, CY 30
Lord Mayor's Walk — DX 33
Low Petergate — DY 35
Melrosegate — BY 36
Museum Street — CY 39
Pavement — DY 43
Peasholme Green — DY 45
Penley's Grove Street — DX 46
Queen Street — CZ 49
St. Helen's Road — AZ 50
St. Leonard's Place — CY 52
St. Maurice's Road — DXY 53
Station Road — CY 55
Stonebow (The) — DY 56
Tower Street — DZ 59
University Road — BZ 60
Wetherby Road — AZ 62

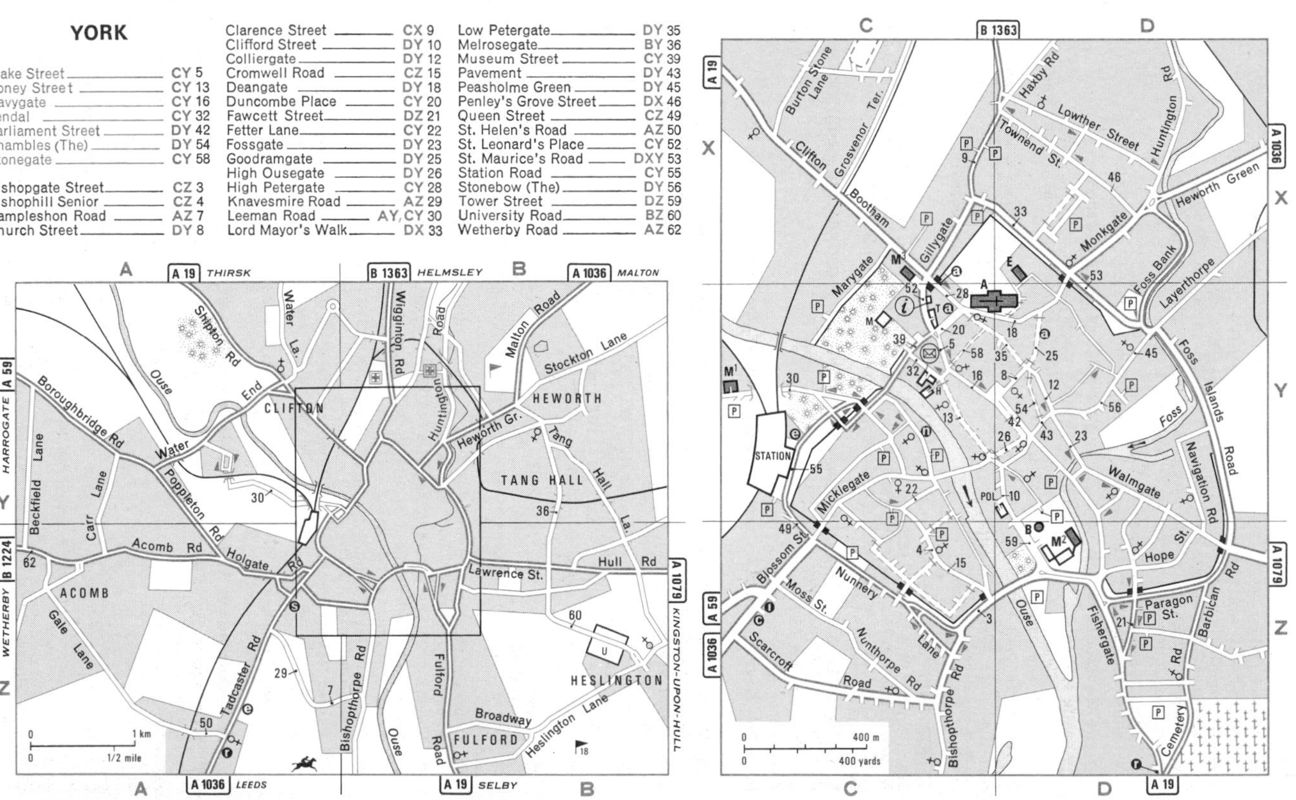

Scotland

LICENSING HOURS - WHEN DRINKING ALCOHOLIC BEVERAGES IS PERMITTED IN PUBS AND BARS AND OTHER LICENSED PREMISES (The General Rule).

HEURES PERMISES POUR LA CONSOMMATION DES BOISSONS ALCOOLISÉES (Règle Générale).

ORARI CONSENTITI PER LA CONSUMAZIONE DI BEVANDE ALCOOLICHE (Regola Generale).

AUSSCHANKZEITEN FÜR ALKOHOLISCHE GETRÄNKE (Allgemeine Regelung).

		from de dalle von	to à alle bis	from de dalle von	to à alle bis		
Weekdays Jours de semaine		**11.00**	**14.30**	**17.00**	**23.00**		Giorni della settimana Wochentags
Sundays, Dimanches,	Hotels Restaurants	**12.30**	**14.30**	**18.30**	**23.00**	Alberghi Ristoranti Hotels Restaurants	Domeniche, Sonntags,
	Pubs	Closed - Fermés - Chiusi - Geschlossen				Pubs	

Wines and beverages may be taken with meals on licensed premises until 16.00 hours in the afternoon and until 01.00 hours in the morning.

Boissons avec un repas : service dans les lieux autorisés jusqu'à 16 h (déjeuner) et 1 h du matin (dîner).

Bevande con il pasto: servite nei locali autorizzati, fino alle 16 (colazione) e fino all'una (cena).

Getränke zu den Mahlzeiten: in den lizensierten Betrieben bis 16 Uhr (Mittagessen) bzw. bis 1 Uhr morgens (Abendessen).

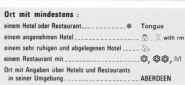

Place with at least :

- one hotel or restaurant ● Tongue
- one pleasant hotel ⌂ , ✕ with rm.
- one quiet, secluded hotel 🪑
- one restaurant with ✿, ✿✿, M
- See this town for establishments located in its vicinity ABERDEEN

La località possiede come minimo :

- una risorsa alberghiera ● Tongue
- un albergo ameno ⌂ , ✕ with rm.
- un albergo molto tranquillo, isolato 🪑
- un'ottima tavola con ✿, ✿✿, M
- La località raggruppa nel suo testo le risorse dei dintorni ABERDEEN

Localité offrant au moins :

- une ressource hôtelière ● Tongue
- un hôtel agréable ⌂ , ✕ with rm.
- un hôtel très tranquille, isolé 🪑
- une bonne table à ✿, ✿✿, M
- Localité groupant dans le texte les ressources de ses environs ABERDEEN

Ort mit mindestens :

- einem Hotel oder Restaurant ● Tongue
- einem angenehmen Hotel ⌂ , ✕ with rm
- einem sehr ruhigen und abgelegenen Hotel 🪑
- einem Restaurant mit ✿, ✿✿, M
- Ort mit Angaben über Hotels und Restaurants in seiner Umgebung ABERDEEN

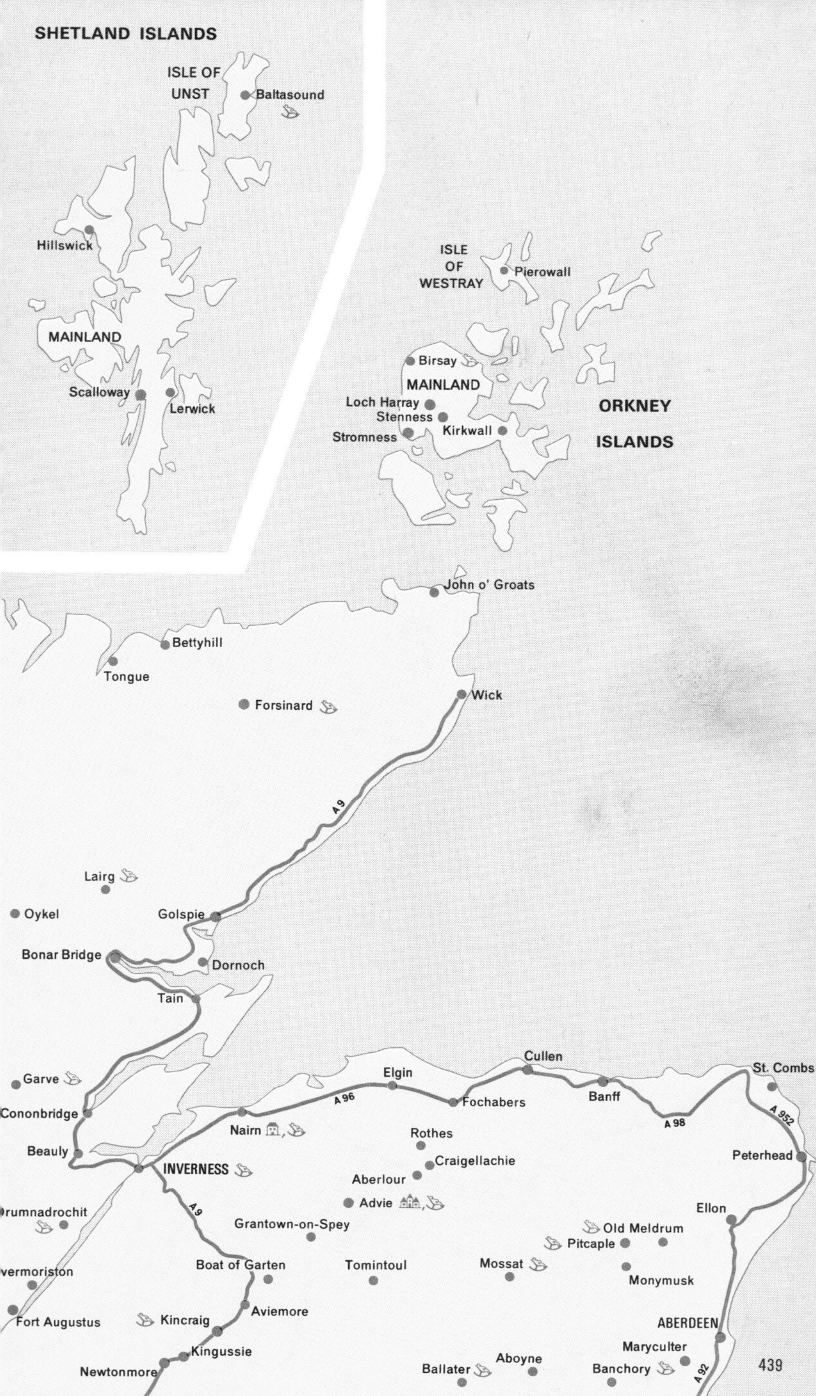
SHETLAND ISLANDS
ISLE OF
UNST
Baltasound
Hillswick
MAINLAND
Scalloway
Lerwick
ISLE
OF
WESTRAY
Pierowall
Birsay
MAINLAND
Loch Harray
Stenness
Stromness
Kirkwall
ORKNEY
ISLANDS
John o' Groats
Bettyhill
Tongue
Forsinard
Wick
A 9
Lairg
Oykel
Golspie
Bonar Bridge
Dornoch
Tain
Cullen
Elgin
St. Combs
Garve
A 96
Banff
Fochabers
Cononbridge
A 98
A 952
Nairn
Rothes
Beauly
Peterhead
Craigellachie
INVERNESS
Aberlour
Advie
rumnadrochit
A 9
Ellon
Grantown-on-Spey
Old Meldrum
Pitcaple
Boat of Garten
Tomintoul
Mossat
vermoriston
Monymusk
Aviemore
Fort Augustus
Kincraig
ABERDEEN
Kingussie
Maryculter
Aboyne
Newtonmore
Ballater
Banchory
A 92

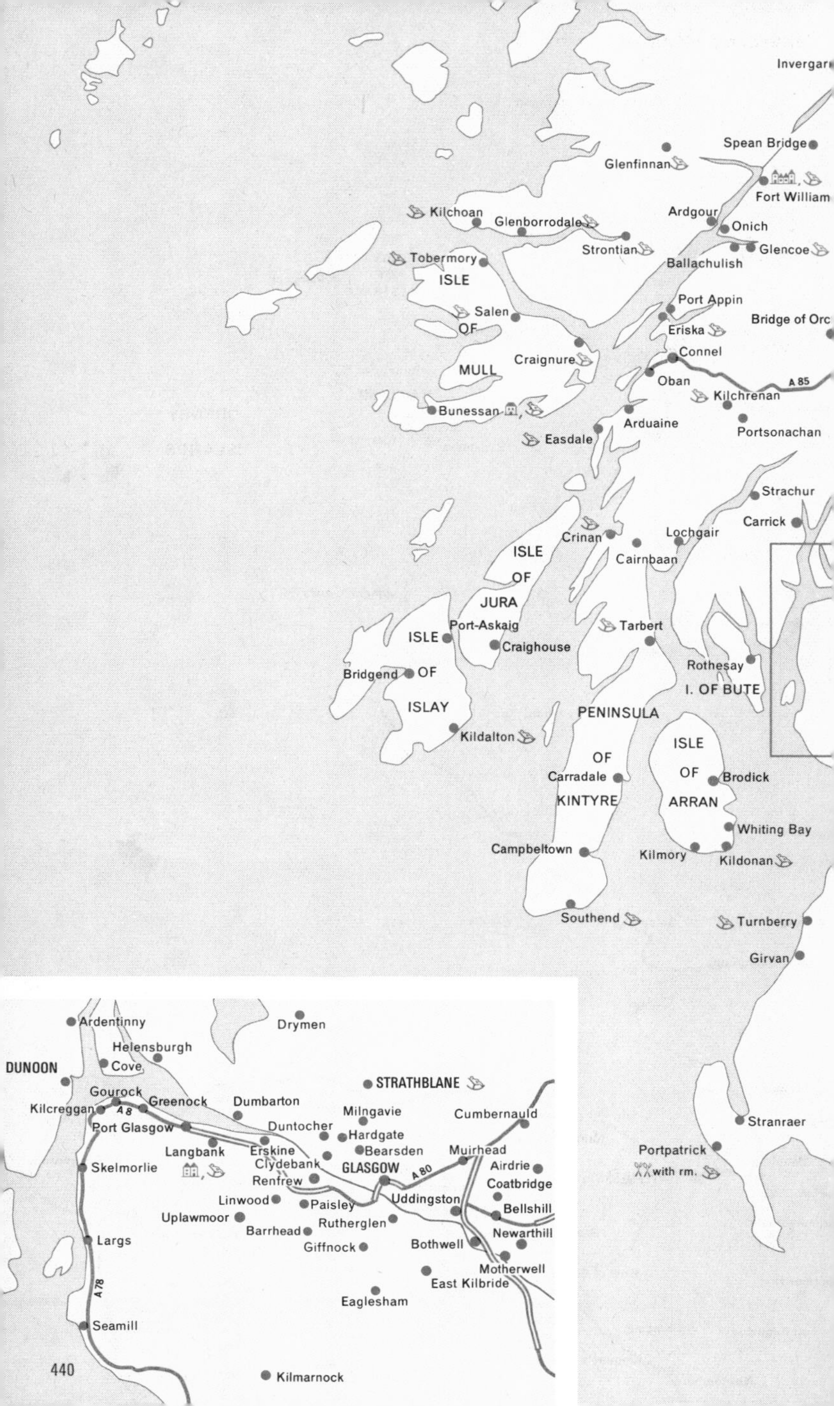

Invergar
Spean Bridge
Glenfinnan
Fort William
Kilchoan
Glenborrodale
Ardgour
Onich
Strontian
Glencoe
Ballachulish
Tobermory
ISLE
Salen
OF
MULL
Craignure
Port Appin
Eriska
Bridge of Orc
Connel
Oban
A 85
Kilchrenan
Bunessan
Arduaine
Portsonachan
Easdale
Strachur
Carrick
Crinan
Lochgair
Cairnbaan
ISLE
OF
JURA
Port-Askaig
Tarbert
ISLE
Craighouse
Bridgend
OF
ISLAY
Rothesay
I. OF BUTE
PENINSULA
Kildalton
ISLE
OF
Carradale
KINTYRE
Brodick
OF
ARRAN
Whiting Bay
Campbeltown
Kilmory
Kildonan
Southend
Turnberry
Girvan
Stranraer
Portpatrick
with rm.
Ardentinny
Drymen
Helensburgh
DUNOON
Cove
STRATHBLANE
Gourock
Kilcreggan
A 8
Greenock
Dumbarton
Milngavie
Cumbernauld
Port Glasgow
Duntocher
Hardgate
Langbank
Erskine
Bearsden
Muirhead
Skelmorlie
Clydebank
GLASGOW
Airdrie
Renfrew
A 80
Coatbridge
Linwood
Paisley
Uddingston
Uplawmoor
Bellshill
Rutherglen
Barrhead
Newarthill
Largs
Giffnock
Bothwell
Motherwell
A 78
East Kilbride
Eaglesham
Seamill
Kilmarnock

Kincraig
Kingussie
Newtonmore
ABERDEEN
Maryculter
Aboyne
Banchory
Ballater
Braemar
Stonehaven
Auchenblae
Clova
A 9
Edzell
Kirkmichael
Kinloch Rannoch
Pitlochry
MONTROSE
Bridge of Cally
ABERFELDY
Alyth
Forfar
Glamis
KENMORE
Meigle
A 92
Dunkeld
Kinclaven
Bankfoot
Carnoustie
Killin
A 85
Dundee
St. Fillans
Perth
Inchture
Wormit
Lochearnhead
Crieff
Glencarse
Comrie
A 9
A 90
Letham
ST. ANDREWS
Auchterarder
Cupar
Blackford
Falkland
Kingskettle
Callander
Crail
A 84
KINROSS
Lundin Links
Dunblane
Anstruther
Aberfoyle
Glenrothes
Leven
Elie
Bridge of Allan
M 90
Kippen
Stirling
with rm.
Kirkcaldy
Dunfermline
Halbeath
Airth
Dirleton
North Berwick
Aberdour
Falkirk
Grangemouth
Gullane
Dunbar
Aberlady
Polmont
A 90
EDINBURGH
East Linton
South Queensferry
Haddington
A 80
Longniddry
Bathgate
Uphall
M
Gifford
Pathhead
M 8
A 68
Blyth Bridge
Lauder
Lanark
PEEBLES
Quothquan
Walkerburn
Galashiels
Kelso
Innerleithen
Symington
Melrose
Dryburgh
Broughton
Abington
St. Mary's Loch
Hawick
A 74
Sanquhar
Moffat
Beattock
Thornhill
LOCKERBIE
Dalry
New Galloway
DUMFRIES
Crocketford
Annan
Castle Douglas
Rockcliffe
Kirkcudbright
Auchencairn
Whithorn (Isle of)

SCOTLAND

Towns

By the Local Government Act (Scotland) of 1973, Scotland is divided into 12 Administrative Regions or Island Areas. The relevant Region or Area in which each town lies is shown after the town and county name. (Ex. Grampian).

ABERDEEN Aberdeen. (Grampian) 986 ⑦ – pop. 182,071 – ✆ 0224.

See : Marischal College★ Y **U** – Art Gallery and Museum★ Y **M** – ←★ from the lighthouse X – St. Machar's Cathedral★ X **B** – King's College Chapel★ (Crown Tower) X **U** – Rubislaw Quarry (granite)★ X. **Envir. :** Dunnottar Castle (site★★, ruins★) *AC*, S : 14 ½ m. by A 92 X.

18 19 Golf Rd ✆ 21464 X – 18, 18 Hazlehead ✆ 35747, W : 3 m. by King's Gate X – 18 St. Fittick's Rd, Balnagask ✆ 871286 X.

✈ Aberdeen Airport ✆ 722331, NW : 5 ½ m. by A 96 X – **Terminal:** Bus Station, Guild St. (adjacent to Railway Station).

🚗 ✆ 23432.

⛴ to Orkney Islands : Kirkwall (P & O Ferries : Orkney and Shetland Services) Monday (11 h) – to Shetland Islands : Lerwick (P & O Ferries : Orkney and Shetland Services) Monday and Thursday (12 h).

i St. Nicholas House, Broad St. ✆ 23456 (Saturdays ✆ 24890/21814/21810), Telex 73366 – Information Caravan, Stonehaven Rd ✆ 873030 (mid May-mid October).

Edinburgh 124 – Dundee 64.

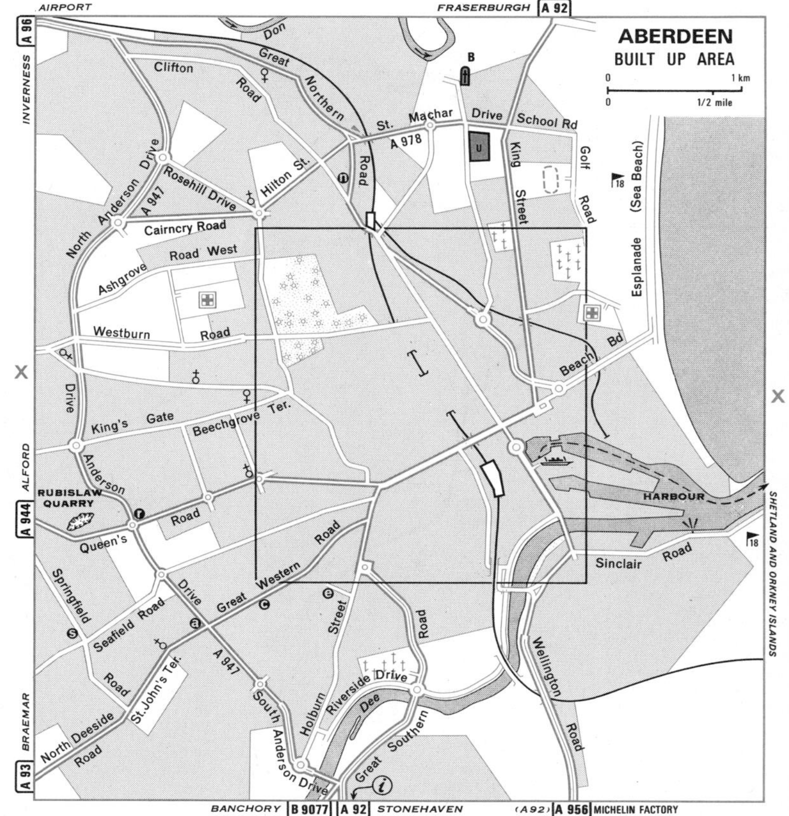

ABERDEEN

George Street .... Y
St. Nicolas Street .... Y 30
Union Street .... Z

Bridge Street .... Z 4
Broad Street .... Y 6
Castle Street .... Y 7
College Street .... Z 9
Craigie Loanings .... Y 12
Denburn Viaduct .... Y 15
East North Street .... Y 16
Great Southern Road .... Z 18
Guild Street .... Z 19
Hadden Street .... Z 20
Justice Street .... Y 21
Loch Street .... Y 22
Millburn Street .... Z 24
Rosemount Terrace .... Y 25
Rosemount Viaduct .... Y 26
St. Andrew Street .... Y 28
St. Swithin Street .... Z 31
School Hill .... YZ 32
South Mount Street .... Y 33
Springbank Terrace .... Z 34
Spring Garden .... Y 36
Stirling Street .... Z 37
Trinity Quay .... Z 39
Upperkirkgate .... Y 40
Victoria Street .... Z 42
Waverley Place .... Z 43
Wellington Place .... Z 45
Wellington Road .... Z 47
Woolmanhill .... Y 48

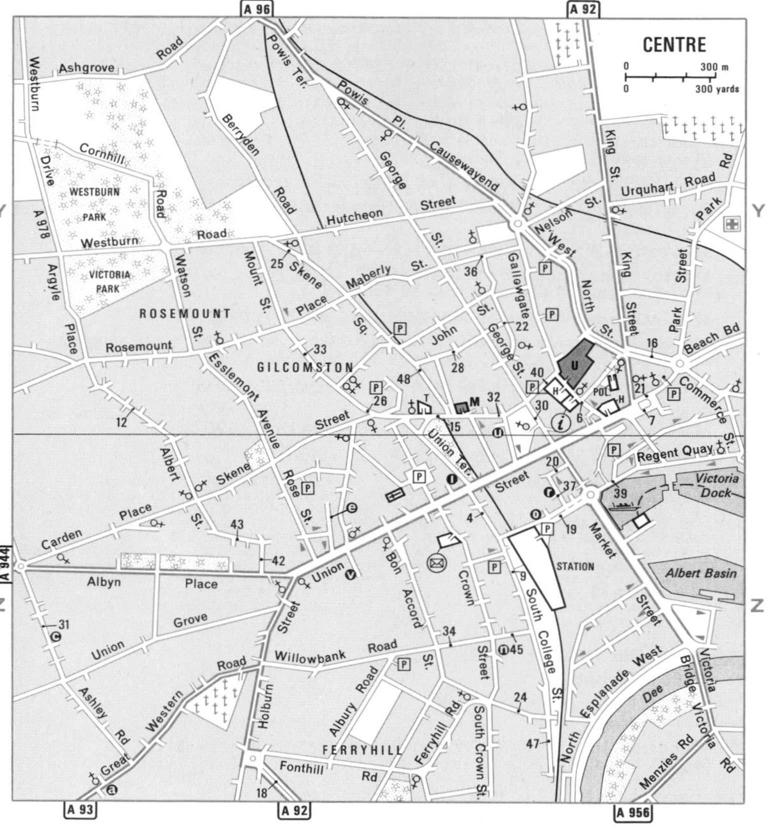

Station (B.T.H.), 78 Guild St., AB9 2DN, ☎ 27214, Telex 73161 – TV P. — Z o
M approx. 6.50 **st.** 1.35 – **57 rm.**

Tree Tops, 161 Springfield Rd, AB9 2QH, ☎ 33377, Telex 73794, – TV wc P. — X s
M 4.70/4.95 1.65 – 2.00 – **96 rm** 10.45/26.50.

Amatola, 448 Great Western Rd, AB1 6NP, ☎ 38724 – TV wc wc P. — X a
M 3.50/5.00 **st.** 1.30 – **36 rm** 10.25/22.00 **st.**

Caledonian (Thistle), Union Ter., AB9 1HE, ☎ 29233 – TV wc wc — Z i
77 rm.

Imperial (Swallow), Stirling St. ☎ 29101, Telex 73365 – TV wc wc — Z r
104 rm.

Earl's Court, 96 Queen's Rd, AB9 2PT, ☎ 321234 – TV wc wc P. – **10 rm.** — X r

Struan, 239 Great Western Rd, AB1 6PS, ☎ 574484 – TV wc P — Z a
M (bar lunch) 3.00/6.00 **st.** 1.50 – **16 rm** 11.00/17.00 **st.**

P.T.O. →

Northern (Swallow), 1 Great Northern Rd, AB9 2UL, ☎ 43342 – wc ☎ P. X n
34 rm.

George (Open House), 2-4 Bon Accord Ter., AB9 1YF, ☎ 27266 – ☎ Z v
48 rm.

Russel without rest., 50 St. Swithin St., AB1 6XJ, ☎ 323555 – ☎ P Z c
9 rm 7.50/15.00 **s.**

Broomfield, 15 Balmoral Pl., AB1 6HR, ☎ 28758 – P X e
8 rm 7.50/8.50 **s.**

Fiddler's, 1 Portland St., AB1 2LN, ☎ 52050 Z n
closed Saturday lunch, Sunday, 25-26 December and 1 to 3 January – **M** a la carte 6.00/7.70 **st.**

Gerard's, 50 Chapel St., AB1 1SN, ☎ 571782, French rest. Z e
closed Sunday and Bank Holidays – **M** a la carte 3.90/7.20 1.70.

Malacca with rm, 349 Great Western Rd ☎ 28901 – TV wc ☎ P X c
M a la carte approx. 6.05 – **6 rm** 12.00/20.00 **s.**

Poldino's, 7 Little Belmont St., AB1 1JG, ☎ 27777, Italian rest. YZ u
M a la carte 2.30/4.50 1.50.

at Cults **SW : 3 ½ m. on A 93 – X – ✉ ☎ 0224 Aberdeen :**

Royal Darroch (Stakis), North Deeside Rd, AB1 9SE, ☎ 48811 – TV wc ☎ P.
67 rm.

at Westhill **W : 6 ½ m. off A 944 – X – ✉ ☎ 0224 Aberdeen :**

Westhill Inn, Skene, AB3 6TT, ☎ 740388 – TV wc ☎ P.
M 3.25/3.55 **st.** 1.00 – **39 rm** 12.50/17.75 **st.**

at Bucksburn **NW : 4 m. on A 947 by A 96 – X – ✉ ☎ 0224 Aberdeen :**

Holiday Inn, Old Meldrum Rd, AB2 9LN, ☎ 3911, Telex 73108, – TV P.
M approx. 5.50 **t.** – 2.50 – **99 rm** 20.25/26.50 **st.**

at Dyce **NW : 6 ¼ m. on A 947 by A 96 – X – ✉ ☎ 0224 Aberdeen :**

Skean Dhu, Aberdeen Airport, AB2 0DW, ☎ 723101, Telex 73473 – TV P.
M a la carte 4.40/5.85 **st.** 0.95 – 1.50 – **154 rm** 13.90/15.90 **st.**

MICHELIN Branch, 214 Hardgate, AB1 6AA, ☎ 29461/2.

ALFA-ROMEO 542 Gt Western Rd ☎ 30181
AUSTIN-MG-WOLSELEY 16/22 Mid Stocket Rd ☎ 25981
AUSTIN-MG-WOLSELEY 19 Justice Mill Lane ☎ 52265
CHRYSLER-SIMCA 130 Gt Western Rd ☎ 52391
DATSUN 78 Powis Ter. ☎ 41313
FIAT 870 Gt Northern Rd ☎ 41373
FORD Rennies Wynd ☎ 24331
FORD Menzies Rd ☎ 52206
FORD 35 Union Glen ☎ 29022
LANCIA 3 Whitehall Rd ☎ 29349
MERCEDES-BENZ 366 King St. ☎ 24211
MORRIS-MG-WOLSELEY 92 Crown St. ☎ 50381
MORRIS-MG-WOLSELEY 8 Affleck St. ☎ 52721
PEUGEOT 519 King St. ☎ 42330
RENAULT 44/48 Rose St. ☎ 54401
ROLLS ROYCE-BENTLEY Forsbefield Rd ☎ 33286
SAAB 116/124 Stanley St. ☎ 20911
TOYOTA, VAUXHALL North Anderson Drive ☎ 692392
VAUXHALL 16 Dee St. ☎ 29216
VW, AUDI-NSU 94 Hilton Drive ☎ 43327

ABERDOUR Fife. (Fife) – pop. 1,950 – ☎ 0383.

See : ≤** from the harbour.

18 ☎ 860256.

Edinburgh 17 – Dunfermline 7.

Woodside, High St., KY3 0SW, ☎ 860328 – TV wc wc ☎ P.
M 4.10/4.35 **st.** 1.20 – **12 rm** 9.00/20.50 **st.** – P 13.75/15.75 **st.**

ABERFELDY Perth. (Tayside) 986 ⑪ – pop. 1,537 – ☎ 088 72.

Envir. : Loch Rannoch** NW : 20 m.

9 ☎ 361, Central Perthshire.

i District Tourist Association, The Square ☎ 276 (mid May-mid September).

Edinburgh 74 – Glasgow 72 – Oban 77 – Perth 32.

Cruachan, Kenmore St., PH15 2BL, ☎ 545, ≤, – P
M 3.00/3.50 1.10 – **10 rm** 6.00/14.00.

Balnearn, Crieff Rd, PH15 2BJ, ☎ 431, – P
April-October – **13 rm** 4.00/8.00.

at Weem **N : 1 m. on B 846 – ✉ ☎ 088 72 Aberfeldy :**

Ailean Chraggan with rm, PH15 2LD, ☎ 346, ≤, – P
April-October – **M** 4.50/7.00 **t.** – **4 rm** 8.50/17.00.

AUSTIN-MG-WOLSELEY 19/25 Bank St. ☎ 409
FORD ☎ 254

Prévenez immédiatement l'hôtelier si vous ne pouvez pas occuper la chambre que vous avez retenue.

ABERFOYLE Perth. (Central) 986 ⑪ – pop. 580 – ✉ Stirling – ☎ 087 72.
Envir. : Loch Ard** W: 3 ½ m. – The Trossachs** and Loch Katrine** NW: 5 ½ m. – Loch Chon** NW: 8 m. – Loch Arklet Reservoir* NW: 11 m.

i Main St. ☎ 352 (April-September).

Edinburgh 55 – Glasgow 27.

Forest Hills, Lochard Rd, Kinlochard, FK8 3SZ, W: 4 m. on B 829 ☎ 087 77 (Kinlochard) 277, ←, « Extensive gardens » – wc P
season – **37 rm.**

AUSTIN-MG-WOLSELEY Main St. ☎ 342

ABERLADY E. Lothian (Lothian) – pop. 1,071 – ☎ 087 57.
Edinburgh 16 – Haddington 5 – North Berwick 7.

Kilspindie, Main St., EH32 0RE, ☎ 319 – wc P
M approx. 3.20 1.40 – **13 rm** 6.00/12.60 – P 10.00/12.00.

ABERLOUR Banff. (Grampian) 986 ⑦ – pop. 763 – ☎ 034 05.
Edinburgh 187 – Aberdeen 63 – Inverness 54.

Dowans, AB3 9LS, SW: ¾ m. off A 95 ☎ 488, ←, – wc P
M approx. 3.30 – **13 rm** 7.70/15.40.

Aberlour, High St., AB3 9QB, ☎ 287 – wc P
M (dinner only) 3.80 **st.** 1.40 – **18 rm** 8.00/13.00 **s.**

AUSTIN-MORRIS-MG-WOLSELEY 19 High St. ☎ 248

ABINGTON Lanark. (Strathclyde) 986 ⑮ – pop. 250 – ✉ Biggar – ☎ 086 43.
9 Leadhills ☎ 328, 6 m. off A 74.

i Little Chef ☎ 636 (June-September).

Edinburgh 41 – Carlisle 57 – Dumfries 36 – Glasgow 38.

Abington, Carlisle Rd, ML12 6SD, ☎ 278 – wc P
M approx. 3.80 **t.** – **25 m** 6.50/16.20 **t.** – P 9.10 **t.**

ABOYNE Aberdeen. (Grampian) 986 ⑦ – pop. 1,012 – ☎ 0339.
Envir. : Craigievar Castle* (17C) *AC*, NE: 12 m.

18 Formaston Park ☎ 2328 E: end of Village – 9 Tarland ☎ 033 981 (Tarland) 413, NW: 5 m.

Edinburgh 137 – Aberdeen 31 – Dundee 80.

Birse Lodge, Charleston Rd, AB3 5EL, ☎ 2253, – wc P
March-October – **M** approx. 4.50 **t.** 1.40 – **17 rm** 9.00/18.00 **t.**

AUSTIN-MG-WOLSELEY Main Rd ☎ 2440

ACHILTIBUIE Ross and Cromarty (Highland) – ☎ 085 482.
Edinburgh 243 – Inverness 84 – Ullapool 25.

Summer Isles, IV26 2YQ, ☎ 282, ←, – wc P
Easter-mid October – **M** (dinner only) 5.50 1.70 – **15 rm** 8.50/25.00.

ACHNASHEEN Ross and Cromarty (Highland) 986 ⑥ – pop. 100 – ☎ 044 588.
Envir. : Glen Docherty** W: 6 m. – Glen Carron* SW: 8 m.

Edinburgh 202 – Inverness 43.

Ledgowan, IV22 2EJ, on A 890 ☎ 252, ←, – P
May-November – **M** 4.25/5.00 1.75 – **18 rm** 6.50/16.00 – P 14.00/15.00.

ADVIE Moray. (Grampian) – ✉ Grantown-on-Spey – ☎ 080 75.
Edinburgh 153 – Inverness 46.

Tulchan Lodge, PH26 3PW, on B 9102 ☎ 200, Telex 75405, ← Spey Valley, « Tasteful decor », park – P
closed February and March – **M** approx. 7.50 1.00 – **9 rm** 14.50/61.00 – P 28.50/42.00.

AIRDRIE Lanark. (Strathclyde) 986 ⑮ – pop. 37,740 – ☎ 023 66.
Edinburgh 32 – Glasgow 14 – Motherwell 6,5 – Perth 53.

Staging Post (S & N), 8-10 Anderson St., ML6 0LM, ☎ 67525
M approx. 2.20 **st.** 1.20 – **7 rm** 6.05/12.10 **st.**

AUSTIN-MG-WOLSELEY Carlisle Rd, Chapelhall ☎ 2225
FORD South Bigggar Rd ☎ 64702
HONDA, OPEL-VAUXHALL 28/48 High St. ☎ 62401

AIRTH Stirling. (Central) – ✉ Falkirk – ☎ 032 483.
Edinburgh 27 – Dunfermline 14 – Falkirk 6 – Stirling 8.

Airth Castle, FK2 9QR ☎ 411, ←, « Former castle in extensive grounds », park – TV P
M a la carte 5.90/9.65 1.50 – **19 rm** 15.00/25.00.

ALYTH Perth. (Tayside) 986 ⑪ – pop. 1,701 – ☎ 082 83.
Envir. : Reekie Linn (waterfall)* N : 5 ½ m. – Glen Clova** NE : 19 m. by Kirriemuir.
18 Pitcrocknie ☎ 268, E : 1 ½ m.
Edinburgh 63 – Aberdeen 69 – Dundee 16 – Perth 21.

Lands of Loyal, Loyal Rd, PH11 8JQ, N : ½ m. off B 954 ☎ 2481, ←, « Country house atmosphere », park – wc P
closed February and 3 days at Christmas – **M** approx. 4.50 1.30 – **14 rm** 7.50/14.00 – P 13.00/14.50.

ANNAN Dumfries. (Dumfries and Galloway) 986 ⑲ – pop. 6,051 – ☎ 046 12.
Envir.: Ruthwell Cross* 8C, W : 7 m.
Edinburgh 82 – Carlisle 19 – Dumfries 16 – Newcastle-upon-Tyne 72.

Queensberry Arms (Osprey), High St., DG12 6AD, ☎ 2024 – wc ☎ P
27 rm.

CHRYSLER-SIMCA Eastriggs ☎ 203
MORRIS-MG-WOLSELEY Scotts St. ☎ 2382
PEUGEOT 25 High St. ☎ 2772

ANSTRUTHER Fife. (Fife) 986 ⑪ – pop. 2,979 – ☎ 0333.
See : Harbour*. **Envir. :** St. Monance (church*) SW : 3 m. – Kellie Castle* (16C-17C) *AC*, W : 5 m.
i Scottish Fisheries Museum, St. Ayles ☎ 310628.
Edinburgh 46 – Dundee 23 – Dunfermline 34.

Craw's Nest, Bankwell Rd, KY10 3DA, ☎ 310691, – TV wc ☎ P.
M 4.50/6.00 1.65 – **31 rm** 9.30/16.60.

Smugglers Inn, High St., KY10 3DQ, ☎ 310506 – wc P
M a la carte 4.00/7.00 **s.** 1.20 – **9 rm** 7.20/17.00 **s.** – P 12.00/15.00 **s.**

ARBROATH Angus (Tayside) 986 ⑪ – pop. 22,586 – ☎ 0241.
See : Cliffs** (nature trail) – Abbey* *AC.*
18 Elliot ☎ 2272, S : 1 m.
i Angus District Council, 105 High St. ☎ 2609/6680.
Edinburgh 72 – Aberdeen 51 – Dundee 16.

Hotels see : Carnoustie SW : 7 m.
Montrose NE : 13 ½ m.

AUSTIN-MORRIS-MG-ROVER-TRIUMPH-WOLSELEY 1 Burnside Drive ☎ 292
BMW Montrose Rd ☎ 2919

ARDENTINNY Argyll. (Strathclyde) – pop. 150 – ☎ 036 981.
Edinburgh 107 – Dunoon 13 – **Glasgow 64 – Oban 71.**

Ardentinny, PA23 8TR, ☎ 209, ←, – P
March-October – **M** (dinner only) 3.50/4.25 **st.** 1.60 – **9 rm** 5.60/11.20 **st.**

ARDGOUR Argyll. (Highland) 986 ⑩ – pop. 200 – ✉ Fort William (Inverness.) – ☎ 085 55.
Edinburgh 123 – Inverness 74 – Kyle of Lochalsh 84 – **Oban 40.**

Ardgour, PH33 7AA, ☎ 225, ← Loch Linnhe – P
M (dinner only) 3.50 – **11 rm** 5.50/11.00.

ARDROSSAN Ayr. (Strathclyde) 986 ⑭ – pop. 10,562 – ☎ 0294.
to the Isle of Man : Douglas (Isle of Man Steam Packet Co.) 28 May-16 September 1-5 weekly (6 h) – to the Isle of Arran : Brodick (Caledonian MacBrayne) 2-7 daily; (55 mn).
Edinburgh 75 – Ayr 18 – Glasgow 32.

Hotels see : Kilmarnock SE : 11 ½ m.
Largs N : 11 ½ m.

ARDUAINE Argyll. (Strathclyde) – ✉ Oban – ☎ 085 22 Kilmelford.
Envir. : Loch Craignish (site**) S : 6 m.
Edinburgh 142 – Oban 20.

Loch Melfort, PA34 4XG, ☎ 233, ← Sound of Jura, – wc P
April-October – **M** approx. 5.00 **s.** 1.75 – 1.10 – **28 rm** 15.00/20.00 **s.**

ARMADALE Inverness. (Highland) 986 ⑥ – Shipping Services : see Skye (Isle of).

ARRAN (Isle of) Bute. (Strathclyde) 986 ⑭ – pop. 3,576.
See : Kilbrannan Sound** – Lamlash Bay** – Brodick Bay** – Sound of Bute* – Lochranza (site*) – Catacol Bay* – Whiting Bay*.
18 at Brodick ☎ 2349, ½ m. from pier – 18 at Lamlash ☎ 296, 4 m. from Brodick Pier.
from Brodick to Ardrossan (Caledonian MacBrayne) 2-7 daily (55 mn) – from Lochranza to Claonaig (Kintyre) (Caledonian Mac-Brayne) 6-8 daily (30 mn).

Brodick – ✉ ☎ 0770 Brodick.
i The Pier ☎ 2401.

Douglas, KA27 8AW, ☎ 2155 – ⇔wc ☎ P
51 rm.

Kildonan – ✉ Brodick – ☎ 077 082 Kildonan.
⛳9 ☎ 2349, ½ m. from pier.

Kildonan 🐚, KA27 8SE, ☎ 207, ≤, ✂ – P
Easter-September – **M** approx. 3.75 🍷 1.25 – **29 rm** ☐ 7.00/16.00.

Kilmory – ✉ Brodick – ☎ 077 087 Sliddery.

Lagg, KA27 8PQ, ☎ 255, 🌳 – ⇔wc P
Easter-October – **M** 4.25/5.00 **t.** 🍷 1.30 – **18 rm** ☐ 6.50/15.00 **t.** – P 13.00/14.50 **t.**

Whiting Bay – ✉ Brodick – ☎ 077 07 Whiting Bay – ⛳18.

Whiting Bay 🐚, KA27 8QJ, ☎ 247, ≤, 🌳 – P
M 3.25/3.75 **t.** 🍷 1.25 – **22 rm** ☐ 7.50/17.00 **t.**

AUCHENCAIRN Kirkcudbright. (Dumfries and Galloway) 986 ⑲ – pop. 452 – ✉ Castle Douglas – ☎ 055 664.
Edinburgh 98 – Dumfries 21 – Stranraer 62.

Balcary Bay 🐚, Balcary, DG7 1QZ, SE: 2 m. off A 711 ☎ 217, ≤ bay, hills and countryside, 🎣, 🌳 – ⇔wc ☎ P
M approx. 5.00 **st.** 🍷 1.90 – **12 rm** ☐ 10.00/22.00 **st.** – P 17.50/22.50 **st.**

Carte	In den Hotels und Restaurants, für die ein Menu zu festem Preis angegeben ist, kann man jedoch im allgemeinen auch nach der Karte essen.

AUCHTERARDER Perth. (Tayside) 986 ⑪ – pop. 2,446 – ☎ 076 46.
Envir. : Drummond Castle Gardens** *AC,* NW: **10 m.**
⛳9 Orchild Rd ☎ 2804, S: 1 m.
Edinburgh 55 – Glasgow 45 – Perth 14.

Gleneagles (B.T.H.) 🐚, PH3 1NF, SW: 1 ½ m. ☎ 2231, Telex 76105, ≤, ✂, 🏊, ⛳18, 🌳, park – 🛗 📺 ♿ 🚗 P. 🏋
mid April-October – **M** a la carte 9.20/12.10 **st.** 🍷 1.50 – **210 rm** ☐ 28.60/59.40 **st.** – P 42.00/45.60 **st.**

Ruthven Tower, Abbey Rd, PH3 1DN, ☎ 2578, 🌳 – ⇔wc P – **19 rm.**

AVIEMORE Inverness. (Highland) 986 ⑦ – pop. 1,000 – ☎ 0479 – Winter Sports.
Envir. : Cairngorm Mountains ✲*** from the summit (alt. 4084 ft) SE: 8 ½ m. and by chairlift (*AC*) 40 mn Rtn and 45 mn on foot Rtn.
i Area Tourist Officer, ☎ 810363, Telex 75127.
Edinburgh 127 – Inverness 32 – Perth 85.

Strathspey (Thistle), PH22 1PG, ☎ 810681, Telex 75213, ≤ Cairngorms – 🛗 📺 P. 🏋
90 rm.

Coylumbridge (Rank), PH22 1QN, SE: 1 ¾ m. on A 951 ☎ 810661, Telex 75272, ≤ Cairngorms, 🎣, 🌳 – 📺 ♿ P. 🏋
M approx. 5.05 **s.** 🍷 1.45 – ☐ 2.30 – **131 rm** 11.80/21.40 **s.** – P 17.50/21.00 **st.**

Post House (T.H.F.), PH22 1PJ, ☎ 810771, ≤, 🌳 – 🛗 📺 ⇔wc ☎ P. 🏋
M 3.00/4.00 **st.** 🍷 1.50 – ☐ 2.00 – **103 rm** 14.00/21.00 **st.**

Badenoch (Osprey), PH22 1PH, ☎ 810261 – 🛗 ⇔wc ☎ P
M 4.00/7.00 **st.** 🍷 1.25 – **77 rm** ☐ 7.15/17.40 **st.** – P 9.80/15.30 **st.**

High Range, Grampian Rd, PH22 1PS, ☎ 810636, ≤ – ⇔wc 🚿wc P
M (dinner only) 3.00/3.50 – **21 rm** ☐ 5.60/11.20.

Lynwilg, PH22 1QB, S: 1 ½ m. on A 9 ✉ Loch Alvie ☎ 810207 – ⇔wc P
M 3.50/5.00 **t.** – **13 rm** ☐ 10.00/20.50 **t.**

Cairngorm (Interchange), PH22 1PE, on A 9 ☎ 810233 – ⇔wc 🚿wc P
24 rm.

AYR Ayr. (Strathclyde) 986 ⑭ – pop. 47,896 – ☎ 0292.
See: Harbour* AY. **Envir.** : Culzean Castle 18C (site**, interior*) *AC,* SW: 14 ½ m. by A 719 BZ – Alloway* (Burn's Museum *AC,* Burn's birthplace *AC,* Auld brig) S: 2 ½ m. by B 7024 BZ.
⛳18, ⛳18 Belleisle ☎ 0292 (Alloway) 41258 BZ – ⛳18 Westwood Av., Whitletts ☎ 63893 BZ.
i Tourist Information Bureau, 30 Miller Rd ☎ 68077.
Edinburgh 77 – Glasgow 34.

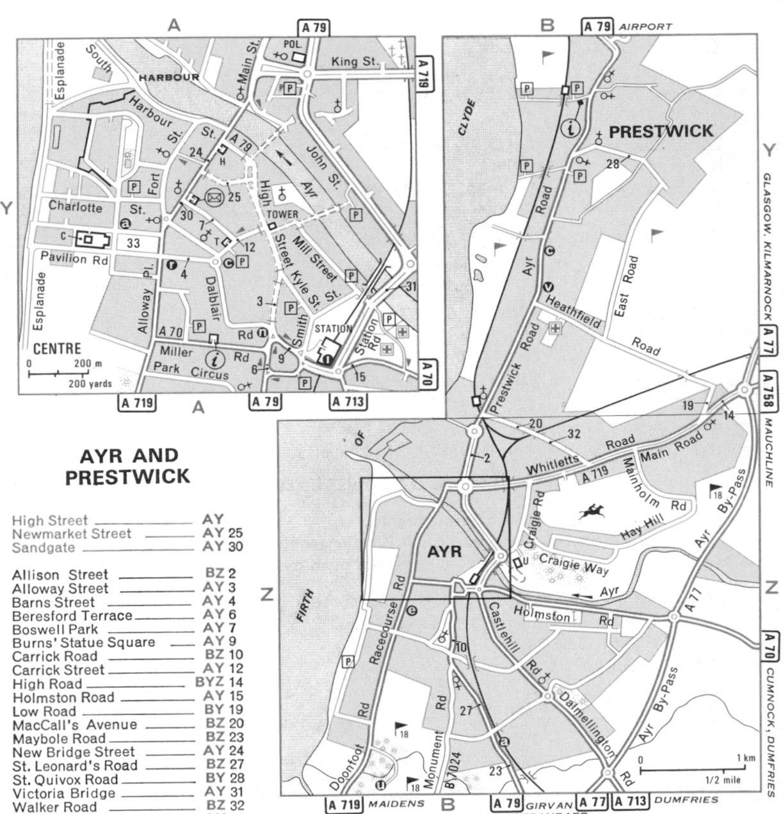

AYR AND PRESTWICK

Caledonian, Dalblair Rd, KA7 1UG, ☎ 69331 – lift TV P. – AY c
M a la carte 3.85/6.60 🍾 1.00 – **120 rm** ☕ 14.00/28.00 **st.**

Belleisle House ⛳, Belleisle Park, KA7 4DU, S : 1 ½ m. on A 719 ☎ 0292 (Alloway) 42331, ← – TV bath wc shower wc ☎ P – BZ u
M 3.50/4.00 🍾 1.10 – **17 rm** ☕ 10.00/18.50 – P 15.50/25.50.

Pickwick, 19 Racecourse Rd, KA7 2TD, ☎ 60111, garden – TV bath wc shower wc ☎ P – BZ e
M a la carte 2.65/7.75 🍾 1.85 – **13 rm** ☕ 10.00/18.00 – P 16.00/20.00.

Station (Stakis), Burns Statue Sq., KA7 3AT, ☎ 63268 – lift TV bath wc ☎ P. – AY i
M (buffet lunch) a la carte 3.85/6.40 **s.** 🍾 1.35 – **66 rm** ☕ 11.00/18.00 **s.**

Balgarth, 8 Dunure Rd, Doonfoot, KA7 4HR, S : 2 ¼ m. by A 719 ☎ 42603, garden – bath wc P – by A719 BZ
M a la carte 4.70/6.30 🍾 1.10 – **10 rm** ☕ 7.00/16.00.

Ayrshire and Galloway (Open House), 1 Killoch Pl., KA7 2EA, ☎ 62626 – bath wc P – AY n
24 rm.

County (Open House), 11-13 Wellington Sq., KA7 1EY, ☎ 63368 – P – AY a
31 rm.

Berkeley, 1 Barns St., KA7 1XB, ☎ 63658, garden – bath wc P – AY r
M 3.50/3.85 **s.** 🍾 1.65 – **11 rm** ☕ 11.25/24.00 **st.** – P 16.35/20.20 **st.**

Annfield, 49 Maybole Rd, KA7 4SF, S : 1 ½ m. by A 79 on A 77 ☎ 41986 – P – BZ a
6 rm ☕ 6.00/12.00 **st.**

at Hollybush **SE : 6 m. on A 713** – BZ – ✉ **Ayr** – ☎ **029 256 Dalrymple :**

Hollybush House, ⛳, KA6 7EA, ☎ 214, ←, garden, park – bath wc P
closed 25 to 28 December – **M** 3.95/4.95 🍾 1.30 – **11 rm** ☕ 8.00/18.50 – P 14.25/16.50.

AUSTIN-MG Maybole Rd ☎ 62991
AUSTIN-DAIMLER-JAGUAR-MG-ROVER-TRIUMPH 18 Holmston Rd ☎ 68373
CHRYSLER, VW, AUDI-NSU 80 Prestwick Rd ☎ 69522
CITROEN 216 Prestwick Rd ☎ 67282
DAF, TOYOTA 65 Peebles St. ☎ 67606
DATSUN Alloway Pl. ☎ 63140
FIAT Galloway Av. ☎ 60416
MORRIS-MG-WOLSELEY 7 Fullarton St. ☎ 66944
RENAULT 84 Prestwick Rd ☎ 81938
SAAB Cambuslea Rd ☎ 66146
VAUXHALL 196 Prestwick Rd ☎ 61631
VAUXHALL 12/28 Dalblair Rd ☎ 62215
VOLVO 16 Smith St. ☎ 60228

BALLACHULISH Argyll. (Highland) 986 ⑩ – pop. 1,089 – ☎ 085 52.

Envir. : Glen Coe** (glen and waterfall) E : 6 m.

Edinburgh 117 – Inverness 80 – Kyle of Lochalsh 90 – **Oban 38.**

Ballachulish (Interchange), PA39 4JY, NW: 2 m. on A 828 ☎ 239, ≤ Loch Linnhe and mountains, – wc P
May-October – **M** a la carte 4.60/7.70 **t.** 1.50 – **33 rm** 10.50/24.25 **st.** – P 16.80/20.50 **st.**

BALLATER Aberdeen. (Grampian) 986 ⑦ – pop. 982 – ☎ 033 82.

Envir. : Lecht Road ≤** of the Grampian Mountains NW: 16 m. – Balmoral Castle* (not open) and park* *AC*, W : 9 m.

i Station Sq. ☎ 306 (May-October).

Edinburgh 109 – Aberdeen 41 – Inverness 69 – Perth 67.

Tullich Lodge, AB3 5SB, E: 1 ½ m. on A 93 ☎ 406, ≤ Dee valley and Grampians, « Country house atmosphere », – wc P
April-December – **M** (lunch by arrangement) approx. 4.50 **st.** 1.85 – **10 rm** 13.50/23.00 **st.**

Craigendarroch, AB3 5XA, W: ¾ m. on A 93 ☎ 217, ≤ Dee valley and Grampians, – wc P
32 rm.

Darroch Learg, Braemar Rd, AB3 5UX, ☎ 443, ≤, – wc P
March-October – **M** approx. 4.00 **st.** – **25 rm** 7.50/18.00 **st.** – P 13.50/15.00 **st.**

Invercauld Arms, AB3 5QJ, ☎ 417, ≤ river Dee, – wc P
23 rm.

Craigard, Abergeldie Rd, AB3 5RR, ☎ 445, ≤ – wc P
M 4.00/5.00 **st.** 1.00 – **14 rm** 7.00/18.00 **st.**

BALMACARA Ross and Cromarty (Highland) – pop. 150 – ✉ Kyle of Lochalsh – ☎ 059 986.

i Lochalsh House, Kyle of Lochalsh ☎ 207 (Easter-mid October).

Edinburgh 197 – Kyle of Lochalsh 4.5.

Balmacara, IV40 8DH, ☎ 283, ≤ – wc P
M 3.25/5.25 **st.** 1.25 – **28 rm** 8.95/19.90 **st.**

BALNAKEIL Sutherland (Highland).

See : Balnakeil Bay**. **Envir. :** Smoo Cave* SE: 3 ½ m – SW: Dionard Valley*.

Edinburgh 294 – Durness 2 – **Inverness 135 –** Thurso 83.

BANCHORY Kincardine. (Grampian) 986 ⑦ – pop. 2,355 – ☎ 033 02.

Envir. : Crathes Castle* (16C) *AC*, E: 3 m.

18 Kinneskie ☎ 2365 – 9 Torphins ☎ 033 982 (Torphins) 493, NW: 6 m.

i Dee St. Car Park ☎ 2000 (May-October).

Edinburgh 125 – Aberdeen 17 – Dundee 66 – Inverness 92.

Raemoir House, AB3 4ED, N : 2½ m. on A 980 ☎ 2846, ≤, « 18 C mansion in extensive grounds », , park – wc P
M 5.00/8.00 **t.** 1.25 – **21 rm** 12.00/26.00.

Banchory Lodge, AB3 3HS, ☎ 2625, ≤, , – wc P
M approx. 5.40 **st.** – **18 rm** 9.70/19.45 **st.** – P 12.95/16.20 **st.**

Tor-Na-Coille, Inch Marlo Rd, AB3 4AB, ☎ 2242, , park – wc ☎ P.
28 rm 8.50/17.00.

AUSTIN-MG-WOLSELEY High St. ☎ 2293
MORRIS-MG-WOLSELEY North Deeside Rd ☎ 2255

BANFF Banff. (Grampian) 986 ⑦ – pop. 3,723 – ☎ 026 12.

See : Duffhouse*. **Envir. :** Gardenstown (site*) E : 8 m.

18 Duff House Royal 2278 – 18 Macduff ☎ 0261 (Macduff) 32548.

i Collie Lodge ☎ 2419 (June-September).

Edinburgh 170 – Aberdeen 46 – Fraserburgh 26 – **Inverness 74.**

Banff Springs, Golden Knowes Rd, AB4 2JE, W : ¾ m. on A 98 ☎ 2881, ≤ – TV wc wc ☎ P.
closed 1 and 2 January – **M** a la carte 4.10/8.00 **s.** 1.00 – **30 rm** 10.45/20.45 **s.**

AUSTIN-MG-WOLSELEY High St. ☎ 2473
FORD Bridge Rd ☎ 2673

BANKFOOT Perth. (Tayside) – pop. **1,100** – 073 887.
Edinburgh 51 – Perth 9.

Hunters Lodge, PH1 4DX, on A 9 ℡ 325, – wc ℗
M a la carte 2.95/4.90 **st.** 1.80 – 1.40 – **10 rm** 7.50/14.00 **st.** – P 12.00/15.00 **st.**

BARRA (Isle of) Inverness. (Outer Hebrides) (Western Isles) 986 ⑥ – pop. **1,147.**

Castlebay – ✉ 087 14 Castlebay.
to Oban (Caledonian MacBrayne) 3-4 weekly (5 to 8 h) – to Lochboisdale (South Uist) (Caledonian MacBrayne) 3-4 weekly (1 h 30 mn).
to Lochaline (Caledonian MacBrayne) 4 weekly summer only (2 h).
i ℡ 336 (May-September).

Isle of Barra, PA80 5XW, NW: 2 m. on A 888 ℡ 383, ≤ sea and mountains – wc ℗
April-October – **M** approx. 4.85 **st.** 1.45 – **41 rm** 13.00/21.70 **st.**

BARRHEAD Renfrew. (Strathclyde) 986 ⑮ – pop. **18,289** – ✉ 041 Glasgow.
Edinburgh 51 – Ayr 30 – Glasgow 8.

Dalmeny Park, Lochlibo Rd, G78 1LG, SW: ½ m. on A 736 ℡ 881 9211, « Attractive gardens » – TV wc ℗.
20 rm.

BATHGATE W. Lothian (Lothian) 986 ⑮ – pop. **14,224** – 0506.
Envir.: Cairnpapple Hill (burial cairn* *AC*, ≤*) N : 3 m.
18 ℡ 52232.
Edinburgh 19 – Glasgow 26.

Golden Circle (Swallow), Blackburn Rd, EH48 2EL, ℡ 53771, Telex 72606 – TV wc ℗
50 rm.

Balbairdie, Bloomfield Pl., EH48 1PB, ℡ 55448 – ℗
closed Sunday and 1 January – **M** a la carte 4.00/9.00 **s.** 1.50.

AUSTIN-MORRIS-MG-ROVER-TRIUMPH-WOLSELEY Blackburn Rd ℡ 53500
FORD Torphichen Rd ℡ 53781
VW, AUDI-NSU Blackburn Rd ℡ 52948

BEARSDEN Dunbarton. (Strathclyde) – pop. **25,013** – ✉ 041 Glasgow.
Edinburgh 49 – Glasgow 6.

Burnbrae (Stakis), Milngavie Rd, G61 3TA, NE: 1 m. on A 81 ℡ 942 5951 – TV wc ℗.
13 rm.

La Bavarde, 9 New Kirk Rd, G61 2SS, ℡ 942 2202
closed Sunday, Monday, last 3 weeks July and 1 January – **M** a la carte 4.05/6.00 **t.** 1.50.

AUSTIN-MG-WOLSELEY Rannock Drive ℡ 5824
MORRIS-MG Kirk Rd ℡ 2225

BEATTOCK Dumfries. (Dumfries and Galloway) 986 ⑮ – pop. **294** – ✉ 068 33 Moffat.
Edinburgh 58 – Carlisle 40 – Dumfries 19 – Glasgow 55.

Auchen Castle, DG10 9SH, N: 2 m. by A 74 ℡ 407, ≤, « 19C mansion in park », – TV wc wc ℗
season – **31 rm.**

Old Brig Inn with rm, DG10 9PS, ℡ 401 – ℗
closed January and February – **M** 4.40/5.50 1.40 – **8 rm** 6.50/15.00.

BEAULY Inverness. (Highland) 986 ⑦ – pop. **2,167** – 046 371.
Envir.: Channory Point ≤* NW: 16 m.
Edinburgh 171 – Inverness 12 – Wick 111.

Priory, The Square, IV4 7BX, ℡ 2309 – wc ℗
M 4.00/4.50 **s.** 1.40 – **12 rm** 6.00/13.00 **s.** – P 8.50/13.00 **s.**

CHRYSLER ℡ 266

BELLSHILL Lanark. (Strathclyde) – pop. **29,512** – 0698.
18 ℡ 745124.
Edinburgh 34 – Glasgow 11.

Hattonrigg (S & N), Hattonrigg Rd, ML4 1RW, ℡ 748488 – wc ℗
M approx. 1.90 **st.** 1.20 – **8 rm** 7.85/16.00 **st.**

AUSTIN-MG-WOLSELEY 5/27 North Rd ℡ 5216
MAZDA New Edinburgh Rd ℡ 747995
OPEL-VAUXHALL 296 Main St. ℡ 747645

BETTYHILL Sutherland. (Highland) 986 ③ – pop. 340 – ✉ Thurso – ☎ 064 12.
See : Cliffs★. **Envir.:** Strathy Point★★★ NE: 12 m. – Torrisdale Bay★★ W: 2 m. – Mellvich Bay ≤★ (cliffs) E: 13 ½ m. **Exc. :** Loch Eriboll★★★ W: 28 ½ m.
Edinburgh 299 – Inverness 140 – Thurso 32.

- Bettyhill, KW14 7SP, ☎ 352, ≤, – wc Ⓟ
24 rm.

BIRSAY Orkney (Orkney Islands) – see Orkney Islands (Mainland).

BLACKFORD Perth. (Tayside) – pop. 4,000 – ✉ Auchterarder – ☎ 076 482.
Edinburgh 51 – Glasgow 41 – Perth 18.

- **Blackford,** Moray St., PH4 1OF, ☎ 246 – Ⓟ
M a la carte 2.30/5.05 🍷 1.40 – **6 rm** 7.50/16.00.

BLYTH BRIDGE Peebles. (Borders) – pop. 1,000 – ✉ West Linton – ☎ 072 15 Drochil Castle.
Edinburgh 22 – Glasgow 44 – Peebles 8.

- **Old Mill Inn,** EH46 7DG, ☎ 220, « Converted water mill », – Ⓟ
M a la carte 3.70/6.55 🍷 0.70.

BOAT OF GARTEN Inverness. (Highland) – pop. 500 – ☎ 047 983.
18 ☎ 282.
Edinburgh 133 – Inverness 29 – Perth 91.

- **Boat,** PH24 3BH, ☎ 258, – wc Ⓟ
M approx. 4.00 **s.** 🍷 1.00 – **34 rm** 7.65/17.80 **s.** – P 13.45/14.15 **s.**

BONAR BRIDGE Sutherland (Highland) 986 ③ – pop. 600 – ☎ 086 32 Ardgay – 9.
See : Site★.
i Information Centre ☎ 333 (mid May-September).
Edinburgh 220 – Inverness 61 – Wick 75.

- Caledonian, IV24 3EB, ☎ 214, ≤ Kyle of Sutherland and Bonar Bridge, – wc Ⓟ
24 rm.
- **Bridge,** Dornoch Rd, IV24 3EB, ☎ 204 – wc Ⓟ
M (bar lunch) approx. 2.25 **t.** 🍷 1.00 – **17 rm** 9.00/20.00 **t.**

BOTHWELL Lanark. (Strathclyde) 986 ⑮ – ☎ 0698.
Edinburgh 38 – Glasgow 8.5.

- **Silvertrees,** 27 Silverwells Crescent, G71 8DP, ☎ 852311, – TV wc Ⓟ.
M 2.50/2.75 🍷 1.30 – **24 rm** 9.00/14.00.
- **Da Luciano,** 2 Silverwells Crescent ☎ 852722, Italian rest. – Ⓟ
closed Monday – **M** a la carte 4.15/7.40 **t.** 🍷 1.50.

BRAEMAR Aberdeen. (Grampian) 986 ⑦ – pop. 1.018 – ☎ 033 83.
Envir. : NW: Cairngorm Mountains ☼★★★ from the summit (alt. 4084 ft) by chairlift *AC*, 40 mn Rtn and 45 mn on foot Rtn – Glenshee ☼★★ by chairlift 15 mn *AC*, S: 19 ½ m. – Devil's Elbow★★ S: 11 m. – Linn of Dee★ W: 6 m.
18 ☎ 618, S: ½ m.
i Fife Arms Mews ☎ 600 (May-October).
Edinburgh 92 – Aberdeen 58 – Dundee 52 – Perth 50.

- **Invercauld Arms,** AB3 5YR, ☎ 605, Telex 73448, ≤, – wc Ⓟ.
March-October – **M** approx. 5.00 🍷 1.50 – **57 rm** 6.50/20.00 – P 14.00/20.00.
- Callater Lodge, 9 Glenshee Rd, AB3 5YQ, ☎ 275 – Ⓟ
9 rm.

VW, AUDI-NSU ☎ 210

BRESSAY (Isle of) Shetland (Shetland Islands) 986 ⑯ – Shipping services: see Shetland Islands.

BRIDGEND Argyll. (Strathclyde) – see Islay (Isle of).

BRIDGE OF ALLAN Stirling. (Central) 986 ⑪ – pop. 4,314 – ☎ 0786.
See : Wallace Monument ≤★.
9 Sunnylaw ☎ 2332.
Edinburgh 39 – Dundee 52 – Glasgow 30.

- **Royal,** Henderson St., FK9 4MG, ☎ 832284, – wc Ⓟ.
M 4.50/5.00 **s.** – **32 rm** 11.50/20.00 **s.** – P 15.00/18.75 **s.**

BRIDGE OF CALLY Perth. (Tayside) – ✉ Blairgowrie – ☎ 025 086.
Edinburgh 63 – Dundee 23 – Perth 21.

Bridge of Cally, PH10 7JJ, ☎ 231, ⚲, – **P**
M (bar lunch) 4.10/5.10 🍷 1.20 – **9 rm** 7.10/13.50 **st.** – P 11.00/14.00 **st.**

BRIDGE OF ORCHY Argyll. (Strathclyde) – pop. 100 – ☎ 083 84 Tyndrum.
Edinburgh 94 – Ballachullish 25 – Glasgow 63 – Oban 42.

Bridge of Orchy, PA36 4AB, ☎ 208, ⩤, – wc **P**
M 2.50/3.50 – **12 rm** 6.50/16.00.

BROADFORD Inverness. (Highland) 986 ⑥ – see Skye (Isle of).

BRODICK Bute. (Strathclyde) 986 ⑭ – see Arran (Isle of).

BROUGHTON Peebles. (Borders) – pop. 975 – ✉ Biggar (Lanark) – ☎ 089 94.
Edinburgh 30 – Moffat 24 – Peebles 12.

Greenmantle, ML12 6HQ, ☎ 302 – wc **P**
6 rm.

BUCKSBURN Aberdeen. (Grampian) – see Aberdeen.

BULLERS OF BUCHAN Inverness. (Highland) 986 ⑦.
See: Cliffs**.
Edinburgh 152 – Aberdeen 28 – Peterhead 6.

Hotels see: Ellon SW: 12 m.
Peterhead N: 6 m.

BUNESSAN Argyll. (Strathclyde) – see Mull (Isle of).

BUSBY Lanark. (Strathclyde) – see Glasgow.

BUTE (Isle of) Bute. (Strathclyde) 986 ⑭.
See: N: Kyles of Bute** – S: Sound of Bute*.
⛴ from Rothesay to Wemyss Bay (Caledonian MacBrayne) frequent services every day (30 mn) – from Rhubodach to Colintraive (Caledonian Macbrayne) frequent services every day (5 mn).

Rothesay – pop. 6,225 – ✉ ☎ 0700 Rothesay.
See: Site* – Castle* (13C) *AC.*
18 ☎ 94.
i The Pier ☎ 2151.

Glenburn, Glenburn Rd, PA20 9JP, ☎ 2500, ⩤, – wc **P**.
M approx. 4.40 **s.** 🍷 1.25 – **103 rm** 7.70/15.40 **s.** – P 13.75/15.95 **s.**

Royal (Osprey), Albert Pl. ☎ 3044
20 rm.

TRIUMPH 1 East Princess St. ☎ 2317

CAIRNBAAN Argyll. (Strathclyde) – pop. 170 – ✉ ☎ 0546 Lochgilphead.
Edinburgh 128 – Glasgow 85 – Oban 34.

Cairnbaan Motor Inn, PA31 8SH, NW: 2 ½ m. on B 841 ☎ 2488 – wc **P**
M (bar lunch) 3.00/5.00 🍷 1.20 – 0.85 – **24 rm** 7.00/17.00.

CAIRNGORM (Mountains) Inverness. (Highland) 986 ⑦.
See: *** from the summit (alt. 4084 ft) by chairlift *AC*, 40 mn Rtn and 45 mn on foot Rtn.

Hotels see: Aviemore NW
Braemar SE.

CAIRNRYAN Wigtown. (Dumfries and Galloway).
⛴ to Larne (Townsend Thoresen: Transport Ferry Service) 4-5 daily (2 to 2 h 30 mn).

Hotels and restaurant see: Stranraer S: 6 ½ m.

Ne confondez pas:

Confort des hôtels	:	...
Confort des restaurants	:	XXXXX X
Qualité de la table	:	✿✿✿, ✿✿, ✿, M

CALLANDER Perth. (Central) 986 ⑪ – pop. 1,768 – ☎ 0877.
Envir. : The Trossachs** and Loch Katrine** W : 8 ½ m – Loch Venacher* W : 4 m.
18 ☎ 30090.
i Leny Rd ☎ 30342 (April-September).
Edinburgh 51 – Glasgow 43 – Oban 70 – Perth 40.

- **Roman Camp**, Main St., FK17 8BG, ☎ 30003, « 17C hunting lodge in extensive gardens », – wc ☎ P
  Easter-October – **M** 5.50/7.75 1.50 – **14 rm** 12.50/24.00 – P 20.50/23.50.

PEUGEOT 124/126 Main St. ☎ 30022

CAMPBELTOWN Argyll. (Strathclyde) 986 ⑭ – see Kintyre (Peninsula).

CAMPSIE GLEN Stirling. (Central) – see Strathblane.

CANNA (Isle of) Inverness. (Highland) 986 ⑥ – Shipping Services : see Mallaig.

CARNOUSTIE Angus (Tayside) 986 ⑪ – pop. 6,232 – ☎ 0241.
Envir. : Arbroath (cliffs ** : nature trail) NE : 7 m.
18, 18 ☎ 53249 (Starter's Box).
i 24 High St. ☎ 52258.
Edinburgh 67 – Dundee 11.

- **Bruce,** 1 Links Par., DD7 7DJ, ☎ 52364, ←, – wc ☎ P
  M approx. 3.60 – **38 rm** 9.50/21.00.

VAUXHALL 37 High St. ☎ 52156

CARRADALE Argyll. (Strathclyde) – see Kintyre (Peninsula).

CARRICK Argyll. (Strathclyde) – pop. 60 – ✉ ☎ 030 13 Lochgoilhead.
Edinburgh 97 – Glasgow 54 – Oban 65.

- **Carrick Castle,** , PA24 8AG, ☎ 251, ← Lochgoil and hills – TV wc ☎ P
  M approx. 4.00 **t.** 1.05 – **14 rm** 8.20/15.00 – P 14.00.

CASTLEBAY Inverness. (Outer Hebrides) (Western Isles) 986 ⑥ – see Barra (Isle of).

CASTLE DOUGLAS Kirkcudbright. (Dumfries and Galloway) 986 ⑲ – pop. 3,331 – ☎ 0556.
9 ☎ 2801.
i Markethill ☎ 2611 (May-September).
Edinburgh 95 – Ayr 50 – Dumfries 18 – Stranraer 58.

- **Douglas Arms** (Interchange), King St., DG7 1DB, ☎ 2231 – wc ☎ P
  M 5.00/5.75 **t.** 1.30 – **27 rm** 12.00/27.00 **t.**
- **King's Arms,** St. Andrews St., DG7 1EL, ☎ 2097 – wc P
  M approx. 4.60 **st.** 0.90 – **17 rm** 7.50/21.00 **st.**

CHRYSLER-SIMCA 227/229 King St. ☎ 2476
MORRIS-MG-WOLSELEY Morris House ☎ 2560
VAUXHALL King St. ☎ 2038

CLAONAIG (Cap) Argyll. (Strathclyde) – Shipping Services : see Kintyre (Peninsula).

CLEISH Kinross. (Tayside) – see Kinross.

CLOVA Angus (Tayside) – ✉ Kirriemuir – ☎ 057 55.
See : Glen**.
Edinburgh 86 – Dundee 31 – Perth 44.

- **Rottal Lodge** , DD8 4QT, ☎ 224, ←, « Country house atmosphere », – wc P
  Easter-December – **M** 5.50/6.00 – **12 rm** 12.00/24.00 – P 20.00.
- Ogilvy Arms , Glen Glova ☎ 222, ←, – wc P
  M (bar lunch except Sunday in winter) (by arrangement) – **7 rm.**

CLYDEBANK Dunbarton. (Strathclyde) 986 ⑮ – pop. 48,300 – ✉ ☎ 041 Glasgow.
18 Dalmuir Park ☎ 952 6372.
Edinburgh 48 – Glasgow 5.

- Radnor (Osprey), Kilbowie Rd, G81 2AP, ☎ 952 3427 – wc ☎ P – **12 rm.**
- Boulevard (Open House), 1710 Great Western Rd, G81 2XT, N : 1 ½ m. on A 82 ☎ 0389 (Duntocher) 72381 – ☎ P
  13 rm.

CHRYSLER Napier St. ☎ 952 1325
DATSUN Kilbowie Rd, Hardgate ☎ 0389 (Duntocher) 75367
PEUGEOT Oceanfield, Great Western Rd ☎ 377 2285

COATBRIDGE Lanark. (Strathclyde) 986 ⑮ – pop. 52,145 – ☎ 0236.
Townhead Rd ☏ 28975.
Edinburgh 36 – Glasgow 9.5.

Coatbridge (Thistle), Glasgow Rd, ML5 1EL, ☏ 24392 – TV wc ☎ **P**.
22 rm.

CHRYSLER-SIMCA 200 Main St. ☏ 22612 VAUXHALL Main St. ☏ 27201

COLINTRAIVE Argyll. (Strathclyde) 986 ⑭.
to Isle of Bute: Rhubodach (Caledonian MacBrayne) frequent services every day (5 mn).
Edinburgh 121 – Glasgow 78 – Oban 80.

COLL (Isle of) Argyll. (Strathclyde) 986 ⑩.
by Caledonian MacBrayne: to Oban: Monday/Saturday 3-4 weekly (3 to 3 h 50 mn) – to Lochaline : 2 weekly summer only (2 h 30 mn) – to Isle of Mull (Tobermory) 3 weekly summer only (1 h 30 mn) – to Isle of Tiree: 4 weekly (1 h).
to Isle of Mull: Tobermory (Caledonian MacBrayne) 3 weekly (1 h 30 mn).

COLONSAY (Isle of) Argyll. (Strathclyde) 986 ⑩⑭.
to Oban (Caledonian MacBrayne) 3 weekly (2 h 30 mn).

COMRIE Perth. (Tayside) – pop. 2,200 – ☎ 076 47 – 9.
Edinburgh 58 – Glasgow 49 – Oban 70 – Perth 23.

Royal, Melville Sq., PH6 2DN, ☏ 200 – wc **P**
M a la carte 3.15/6.30 **st.** 1.50 – **16 rm** 6.00/14.00 **st.** – P 10.00/13.50 **st.**

Comrie, Drummond St., PH6 2DY, ☏ 239 – wc wc **P**
April-October – **M** 4.50/5.50 **st.** 0.90 – **12 rm** 6.90/18.00 **st.** – P 10.50/12.50 **st.**

CONNEL Argyll. (Strathclyde) 986 ⑩ – pop. 501 – ☎ 063 171.
Envir. : Loch Creran* N : 7 m.
Edinburgh 117 – Glasgow 88 – Inverness 109 – Oban 5.

Falls of Lora, PA37 1PB, on A 85 ☏ 483, ← – wc **P**
mid March-mid October – **M** (buffet lunch) approx. 4.50 **st.** 1.20 – **35 rm** 9.10/23.00 **st.** – P 15.10/17.50 **st.**

Ossians , Bonawe Rd, North Connel, PH37 1RB, ☏ 322, ← – wc **P**
April-third week October – **M** (bar lunch) approx. 3.90 1.50 – **14 rm** 8.25/16.50 **s.**

CONONBRIDGE Ross and Cromarty (Highland) – pop. 400 – ☎ 034 982.
Edinburgh 177 – Inverness 18 – Wick 105.

Conon, IV7 8HD, ☏ 206 – **P** – **14 rm.**

COVE Dunbarton. (Strathclyde) – pop. 1,343 (inc. Kilcreggan) – ✉ Helensburgh – ☎ 043 684 Kilcreggan.
Edinburgh 83 – Glasgow 40 – Helensburgh 17.

Knockderry House , G84 0NX, ☏ 2283, ←, – wc **P**
14 rm.

CRAIGELLACHIE Banff. (Grampian) 986 ⑦ – pop. 450 – ☎ 034 04.
Edinburgh 185 – Aberdeen 61 – Inverness 52.

Craigellachie, Victoria St., AB3 9SS, ☏ 204, , – wc **P**
March-September – **M** 3.00/3.50 **st.** – **31 rm** 8.50/19.00 **st.**

CRAIGHOUSE Argyll. (Strathclyde) 986 ⑭ – see Jura (Isle of).

CRAIGNURE Argyll. (Strathclyde) 986 ⑩ – see Mull (Isle of).

CRAIL Fife. (Fife) 986 ⑪ – pop. 1,083 – ☎ 033 35.
18 Balcomie Clubhouse, ☏ 278.
Edinburgh 52 – Dundee 24 – Dunfermline 39.

Marine, 52 Nethergate, KY10 3TU, ☏ 207, ←,
M (bar lunch) 3.50/4.00 1.45 – **11 rm** 5.00/10.00 – P 8.50/10.00.

CRAMOND FORESHORE Midlothian (Lothian) – see Edinburgh.

CRIEFF Perth. (Tayside) 986 ⑪ – pop. 5,603 – ✆ 0764.
nvir.: Drummond Castle Gardens** *AC*, S : 3 ½ m.
Peat Rd, Muthill, S : 3 m. on A 822.
James Sq. ☎ 2578 (March-September).
dinburgh 58 – Glasgow 48 – Oban 76 – Perth 17.

- **Murraypark** ⚘, Connaught Ter., PH7 3DJ, ☎ 3731, – wc ☎ Ⓟ
  M 4.50/5.50 1.50 – **15 rm** 6.50/16.00 – P 11.00/14.00.
- **Gwydyr,** Comrie Rd, PH7 4BP, ☎ 3277, ≤, – Ⓟ
  March-November – **M** *(closed Sunday dinner)* (bar lunch except Sunday) 2.50/3.00 **s.** 1.00 – **9 rm** 5.00/10.00 **s.**
- **Leven House,** Comrie Rd, PH7 4BA, ☎ 2529
  March-October – **13 rm** 5.50/10.00 **t.**

HRYSLER-SIMCA Ferntower Rd ☎ 2494
ORRIS-MG-ROVER-TRIUMPH Comrie Rd ☎ 2125
VAUXHALL ☎ 2147

CRINAN Argyll. (Strathclyde) – ✉ Lochgilphead – ✆ 054 683.
ee : Site** – Crinan Canal*. **Envir. :** N : Loch Craignish (site **) – Tayvallich (harbour*) SW: m. – Keills (site and ≤ *) SW : 13 m.
dinburgh 132 – Glasgow 89 – Oban 34.

- **Crinan** ⚘, PA31 8SR, ☎ 235, ≤ coast and bay, – wc Ⓟ
  M 4.75/5.50 1.50 – 1.25 – **24 rm** 10.50/17.00.

CROCKETFORD Kirkcudbright. (Dumfries and Galloway) – pop. 90 – ✉ Dumfries – ✆ 055 669.
dinburgh 86 – Dumfries 9 – Stranraer 67.

- **Galloway Arms,** DG2 8RA, ☎ 240 – Ⓟ
  closed 3 weeks mid October-mid November – **M** 3.70/4.80 **st.** 1.90 – **11 rm** 6.60/15.00 **t.** – P 14.00/18.00 **t.**

Prices — For notes on the prices quoted in this Guide, see p. 16.

CULLEN Banff. (Grampian) 986 ⑦ – pop. 1,207 – ✆ 0542.
e : Cullen Bay*, Cullen House* (16C) *AC*.
The Links ☎ 40685.
20 Seafield St. ☎ 40757 (June-September).
inburgh 184 – Aberdeen 60 – Banff 14 – Inverness 60.

- **Seafield Arms** (Interchange), Seafield St., AB5 2SG, ☎ 40791, « Tastefully furnished » – Ⓟ
  M 2.80/3.25 1.75 – **25 rm** 10.25/21.40 **st.**

CULLODEN MOOR Inverness. (Highland) 986 ⑦ – see Inverness.

CULTS Aberdeen. (Grampian) – see Aberdeen.

CUMBERNAULD Dunbarton. (Strathclyde) 986 ⑮ – pop. 31,784 – ✆ 023 67.
☎ 23230, N : 3 m.
inburgh 37 – Glasgow 13 – Stirling 12.

- Golden Eagle (Osprey), Town Centre, G67 1BX, ☎ 25631 – wc wc ☎ Ⓟ
  38 rm.

UXHALL Carbrain Ring Rd, South Carbrain ☎ 25574

CUPAR Fife. (Fife) 986 ⑪ – pop. 11,925 – ✆ 0334.
Hill Tarvitt ☎ 3549.
nburgh 45 – Dundee 14 – Perth 21.

- **Eden House,** 2 Pitscottie Rd, East Rd, KY15 4MF, ☎ 2510 – Ⓟ
  12 rm 5.00/10.00 **t.**
- ✕ Timothy's, 43 Bonnygate, KY15 4BU, ☎ 2830, Smorrebrod.

STIN-MORRIS-MG Edenplace Garage ☎ 4228
RYSLER-SIMCA Bonnygate ☎ 2048
DATSUN, MERCEDES-BENZ James Pl., Ceres Rd ☎ 3346
VAUXHALL South Rd ☎ 2481

DALRY Kirkcudbright. (Dumfries and Galloway) – pop. 752 – ✉ Castle Douglas – ✆ 064 43.
nburgh 83 – Dumfries 27 – Glasgow 65 – Stranraer 48.

- **Lochinvar,** 3 Main St., DG7 3UP, on A 713 ☎ 210 – wc Ⓟ
  M (dinner only) approx 3.00 1.00 – **18 rm** 5.00/20.00 – P 8.00.

DIRLETON E. Lothian (Lothian) – pop. 500 – ✆ 062 085.
See : Castle* (gardens*) *AC.*
Edinburgh 21 – North Berwick 3.

Castle Inn, EH39 5EP, ☎ 221, – Ⓟ
May-September – **M** 3.00/4.00 **st.** 1.10 – **9 rm** 6.00/12.00 **t.**

Open Arms (Interchange) with rm, EH39 5EG, ☎ 241, « Tastefully furnished interior »
– wc Ⓟ – **7 rm.**

DORNIE Ross and Cromarty (Highland) – pop. 250 – ✉ Kyle of Lochalsh – ✆ 059 985.
Edinburgh 191 – Inverness 74 – Kyle of Lochalsh 8.

Loch Duich, IV40 8DY, ☎ 213, ≤ Eilean Donan Castle and hills, – Ⓟ
M 3.00/3.25 **s.** 1.10 – **19 rm** 6.00/12.00 **s.**

DORNOCH Sutherland. (Highland) 986 ③ – pop. 929 – ✆ 086 281.
18, 9 ☎ 219.
i The Square, ☎ 400 (April-September), Telex 75126.
Edinburgh 220 – Inverness 61 – Wick 64.

Royal Golf (Interchange) , Grange Rd, IV25 3LG, ☎ 283, ≤, – wc wc
Ⓟ
season – **36 rm.**

Dornoch Castle, Castle St., IV25 3SD, ☎ 216, « Former bishop's palace, part 16C
– wc Ⓟ
April-October – **M** approx. 4.00 1.80 – **21 rm** 7.60/15.70 – P 15.00/17.00 **s.**

MORRIS-MG-WOLSELEY The Square ☎ 232

DRUMNADROCHIT Inverness. (Highland) 986 ⑦ – pop. 100 – ✆ 045 62.
Envir. : Loch Ness** E : 1 ½ m. – Urquhart Castle (site*) *AC,* E : 2 ½ m. – Glencannich* ar
Glen Affric* W : 12 m. by Cannich.
Edinburgh 174 – Inverness 15 – Kyle of Lochalsh 67.

Polmaily House , IV3 6XT, W : 2 m. on A 831 ✉ Milton ☎ 343, ≤, ,
wc Ⓟ
Easter-November – **M** approx. 4.60 1.50 – **10 rm** 8.50/21.50.

DRYBURGH Berwick. (Borders) 986 ⑮ – pop. 50 – ✉ ✆ 083 52 St. Boswells (Roxburgh).
See : Abbey* *AC.* **Envir. :** Jedburgh Abbey** *AC,* SE : 8 ½ m. – Scott's View* N : 2 m.
Edinburgh 38 – Hawick 22 – **Newcastle-upon-Tyne 69.**

Dryburgh Abbey , TD6 0RQ, off B 6356 ☎ 2261, ≤, , park – wc Ⓟ.
M 4.50/5.00 1.65 – **29 rm** 8.90/20.20.

DRYMEN Stirling. (Central) 986 ⑪ ⑮ – pop. 940 – ✆ 036 06.
Envir. : Loch Ard** N : 14 m. – W : Loch Lomond**.
Edinburgh 60 – Glasgow 17 – Stirling 21.

Buchanan Arms, Main St., G63 0BQ, ☎ 588, – wc Ⓟ
M 4.75/5.75 **st.** 2.30 – **20 rm** 10.30/22.80 **st.**

VOLVO Croftamie, Drymen Station ☎ 555

DUMBARTON Dunbarton. (Strathclyde) 986 ⑭ ⑮ – pop. 25,640 – ✆ 0389.
Envir. : Loch Lomond** NW : 5 m.
Edinburgh 57 – Glasgow 14.

Dumbuck (Open House), Glasgow Rd, G82 1EG, E : ¾ m. on A 814 ☎ 62148 –
wc Ⓟ. – **25 rm.**

AUSTIN-MG-WOLSELEY Cardross Rd ☎ 3678

DUMFRIES Dumfries. (Dumfries and Galloway) 986 ⑲ – pop. 29,382 – ✆ 0387.
Envir. : Caerlaverock Castle* (mediaeval) *AC,* SE : 7 ½ m. by B 725 B – New Abbey* *AC,* S : 6
by A 75 B and A 710.
18 Laurieston Av. ☎ 3582 A.
i Whitesands ☎ 3862 (May-September).
Edinburgh 77 – Ayr 59 – Carlisle 35 – Glasgow 75 – Manchester 155 – Newcastle-upon-Tyne 88.

Plan opposite

Cairndale (Interchange), 136-138 English St., DG1 2DF, ☎ 4111 – wc Ⓟ B
M 4.50/5.50 **t.** 1.25 – **44 rm** 15.50/34.00 **st.**

Station, 49 Lovers Walk, DG1 1LT, ☎ 4316 – wc wc Ⓟ B
M approx. 3.50 **t.** 0.80 – **30 rm** 7.40/13.50 **t.** – P 12.00 **t.**

County, 79 High St., DG1 2BN, ☎ 5401 – wc Ⓟ A
M 4.00/5.00 **st.** – **45 rm** 8.50/18.00 **st.**

Bruno's, 3 Balmoral Rd, DG1 3BE, ☎ 5757. B

at Kingholm Quay S : 1 ¾ m. by B 726 – B – ✉ ✆ 0387 Dumfries :

Swan at Kingholm , DG1 4SU, ☎ 3756 – Ⓟ
M 2.95/4.50 **st.** 1.50 – **12 rm** 5.50/12.50 **st.** – P 9.00/11.00 **st.**

DUMFRIES

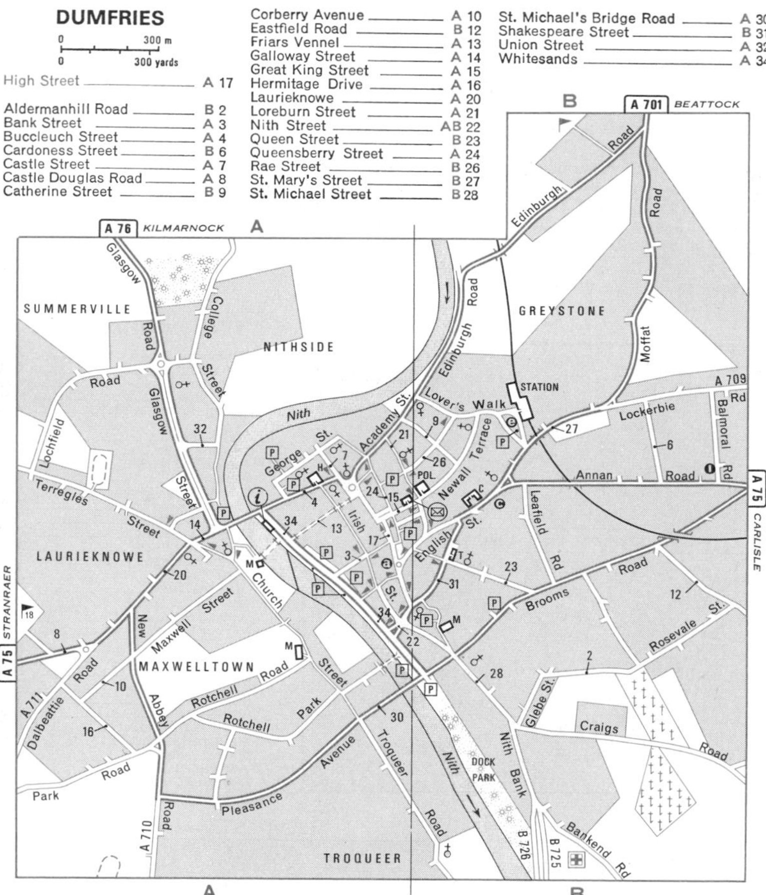

at Glencaple S : 5 m. on B 725 – B – ⊠ Dumfries – ✆ 038 777 Glencaple :

⌂ Nith, DG1 4RE, ☎ 213, ⩤ – TV ⋒wc ☏ P – **10 rm.**

AUSTIN-MG-WOLSELEY ☎ 2862
BMW, VAUXHALL Glencaple ☎ 038 777 (Glencaple) 242
CHRYSLER-SIMCA Terregles St. ☎ 61997
CITROEN, JAGUAR, VAUXHALL York Pl. ☎ 5291
DAIMLER-JAGUAR-MORRIS-MG-ROVER-TRIUMPH-WOLSELEY Charlotte St. ☎ 4301
FIAT 77 Whitesands ☎ 61378
PEUGEOT St. Mary's Industrial Estate ☎ 2203
RENAULT 33/35 Glasgow St. ☎ 3430
VW, AUDI-NSU English St. ☎ 5111

DUNAIN PARK Inverness. (Highland) – see Inverness.

DUNBAR East Lothian (Lothian) 986 ⑮ – pop. **4,611** – ✆ 0368.

See : Site*.

18 North Rd ☎ 2280 – 18 ☎ 62317, S : ½ m.

i Town House, High St. ☎ 63353.

Edinburgh 30 – Newcastle-upon-Tyne 91.

⌂ **Royal Mackintosh,** Station Rd, EH42 1JY, ☎ 63231 – ⊟wc ⋒wc P
M approx. 4.25 **st.** 1.00 – **15 rm** ☕ 5.00/15.00 **st.**

AUSTIN-MG-WOLSELEY ☎ 62255

DUNBLANE Perth. (Central) **986** ⑪ – pop. 4,497 – ☎ 0786.
See : Cathedral*.
Edinburgh 41 – Glasgow 31 – Perth 28.

- **Westlands,** Doune Rd, EK15 9HT, on A 820 ☎ 822118 – Ⓟ
  M 3.85/4.20 – **5 rm** ☕ 7.50/12.00 – P 10.00/12.50.

AUSTIN-MORRIS-MG-WOLSELEY High St. ☎ 823271

DUNDEE Angus (Tayside) **986** ⑪ – pop. 182,204 – ☎ 0382.
See : Dundee Law ≤** Z – Museum and Art Gallery* Y **M. Envir. :** Affleck Castle* (15C) NE : 11 ½ m. by B 961 Z – Leuchars (church*) SE: 8 m. by A 92 Z.
18, 9 ☎ 451147, off Kingsway Bypass at Mains Loan Z – 18 Camperdown Park ☎ 645450, NW: 2 m. by A 923 Z.
i 16 City Sq. ☎ 27723 – Nethergate ☎ 23141 ext 214/421.
Edinburgh 56 – Aberdeen 64 – Glasgow 81.

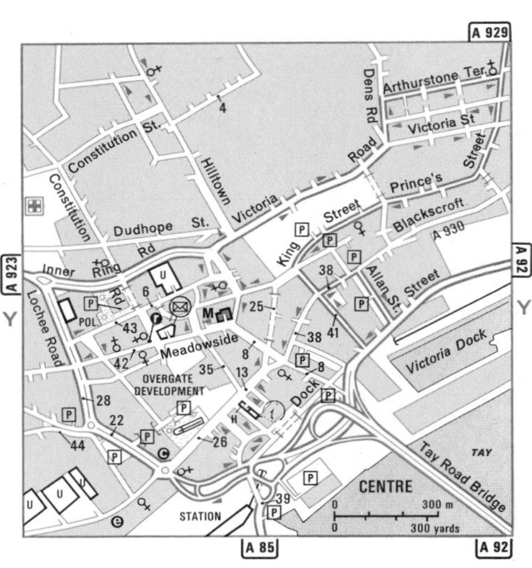

DUNDEE

Commercial Street	Y 8
High Street	Y 13
Murraygate	Y 25
Nethergate	Y 26
Reform Street	Y 35
Albert Street	Z 2
Ancrum Road	Z 3
Alexander Street	Y 4
Bell Street	Y 6
Coupar Angus Road	Z 9
Douglas Road	Z 10
Drumgeith Road	Z 12
Dudhope Terrace	Z 13
East Dock Street	Z 14
Greendykes Road	Z 15
Logie Street	Z 18
Longtown Road	Z 20
Mains Road	Z 21
Marketgait	Y 22
Moncur Crescent	Z 23
North Tay Street	Y 28
Old Craigie Road	Z 30
Old Glamis Road	Z 32
Provost Road	Z 34
Riverside Drive	Z 37
Seagate	Y 38
South Union Street	Y 39
Strathmartine Road	Z 40
Trades Lane	Y 41
Ward Road	Y 42
West Bell Street	Y 43
West Port	Y 44

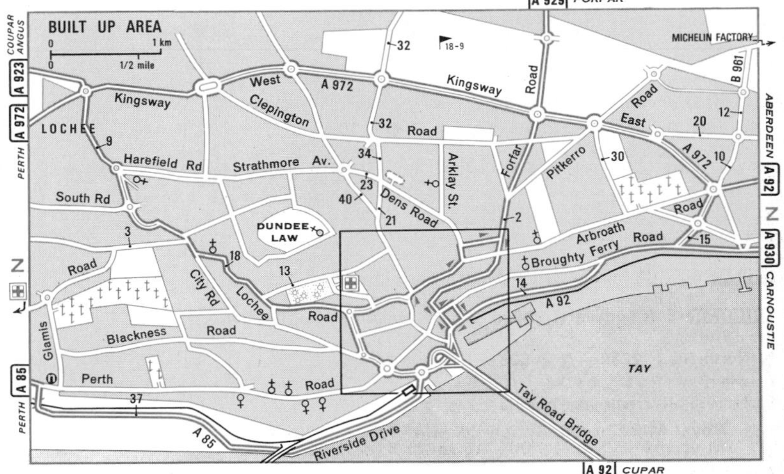

Angus (Thistle), 101 Marketgait, DD1 1QU, ☎ 26874, Telex 76456 – 🛗 TV. 🏊 — Y c
55 rm.

Invercarse (Thistle), 371 Perth Rd, DD2 1PG, W: 2 m. by A 85 ☎ 69231 – TV 🛁wc 🚿wc ☎ P — Z n
27 rm.

Queen's (T.H.F.), 160 Nethergate, DD1 4DU, ☎ 22515 – 🛗 TV 🛁wc ☎ P — Y e
M a la carte 3.95/5.20 **st.** 🍷 1.50 – **55 rm** ☕ 9.50/18.50 **st.**

Le Mirage, 2 Constitution Rd, DD1 1LP, ☎ 27072, Dancing. — Y r

Tay Park with rm, 30 Dundee Rd, West Ferry, DD5 1LX, ☎ 78924, 🌳 – TV 🛁wc ☎ P
M a la carte 4.45/6.20 **st.** 🍷 1.75 – ☕ 1.00 – **7 rm** 7.00/16.00 **st.** — by A 930 Z

ALFA-ROMEO Queen St., Broughty Ferry ☎ 77257
AUSTIN-MG-WOLSELEY 41 Trades Lane ☎ 27181
AUSTIN-MG-WOLSELEY 212 Strathmartine Rd ☎ 88344
CITROEN Roseangle ☎ 23000
DAF, VOLVO Riverside Drive ☎ 643295
DAIMLER-JAGUAR-MORRIS-MG-ROVER-TRIUMPH, ROLLS ROYCE Baird Av., Dryburg Industrial Estate ☎ 84101
FIAT 42/44 Milnbank Rd ☎ 642166
LANCIA 166 Seagate ☎ 25007
MAZDA, SAAB Mac Alpine Rd ☎ 88561
MORRIS-MG-WOLSELEY 64 Ward Rd ☎ 24013
PEUGEOT 25 Rosebank St. ☎ 25406
RENAULT Riverside Drive ☎ 644401
SAAB MacAlpine Rd ☎ 88561
TOYOTA East Kingsway ☎ 41715
VAUXHALL East Dock St. ☎ 26521
VW, AUDI-NSU 60/68 Constitution St. ☎ 25301
VW, AUDI-NSU 33/35 Gellatly St. ☎ 24251

Utilizzate la Guida dell'anno in corso.

DUNDONNELL Ross and Cromarty (Highland) – pop. 120 – ☎ 085 483.
Envir.: Little Loch Broom* NW: 7 m.
Edinburgh 218 – Inverness 59.

Dundonnel, IV23 2QS, ☎ 204 – 🛁wc P
March October – **M** (bar lunch) 4.20/5.00 **t.** 🍷 1.20 – **23 rm** ☕ 7.25/15.50 **t.**

DUNFERMLINE Fife. (Fife) 986 ⑪⑮ – pop. 49,897 – ☎ 0383.
See: Abbey* *AC.*
🏌18 Venturefair ☎ 24969 N: **1** m. – 🏌18 Queensferry Rd ☎ 22591.
ℹ Glen Bridge Car Park (Easter-September).
Edinburgh 16 – Dundee 43 – Motherwell 37.

King Malcolm (Thistle), Wester Pitcorthie, KY11 5DS, S: 1 m. ☎ 22611 – TV 🛁wc ☎ P. 🏊
48 rm.

MICHELIN Branch, Taxi Way, Hillend Industrial Estate, Hillend, KY11 5JT, ☎ 822961.

AUSTIN-MORRIS-MG-ROVER-TRIUMPH-WOLSELEY 18 Halbeath Rd ☎ 24544
CHRYSLER-SIMCA 45/47 Baldridgeburn ☎ 22279
DAF Main Rd ☎ 24078
OPEL Upper Station Rd ☎ 22565
PEUGEOT Headwell Av. ☎ 21914
TOYOTA Bruce St. ☎ 23675
VAUXHALL Nethertown Broad St. ☎ 21511

DUNKELD Perth. (Tayside) 986 ⑪ – pop. 500 – ☎ 035 02.
See: Cathedral*.
🏌9 N: **1** m. on A 923.
ℹ The Square ☎ 460 (Easter-October).
Edinburgh 57 – Aberdeen 85 – Inverness 102 – Perth 15.

Dunkeld House 🐟, PH8 0HX, off A 9 ☎ 243, ←, « Country house in extensive grounds on banks of river Tay », 🎾, 🎣, 🌳, park – TV 🛁wc P
closed November-14 January – **M** a la carte 4.50/6.00 **t.** 🍷 1.30 – **26 rm** ☕ 9.00/25.20 **t.** – P 13.80/21.95 **t.**

MORRIS-MG-WOLSELEY Birnam ☎ 223

DUNNET HEAD Caithness. (Highland) 986 ③ and ⑳.
See: ❋*** (sea birds' nests) and cliffs.
Edinburgh 303 – Wick 23.

Hotels see: John O'Groats E : 16 m.
Wick SE: 23 m.

DUNOON Argyll. (Strathclyde) 986 ⑭ – pop. 9,718 – ☎ 0369.
🏌18 Ardenstale Rd ☎ 2216, NE: boundary – 🏌9 Innellan ☎ 036 983 (Innellan) 350, S: 4 m.
⛴ to Gourock (Caledonian MacBrayne) frequent services every day (20 mn).
to Gourock: McInroys Point (Western Ferries) frequent services every day (20 mn).
ℹ Pier Esplanade, PA23 7HL, ☎ 3785, Telex 778867.
Edinburgh 69 – Glasgow 26 – Oban 79.

DUNOON

McColl's (Osprey), West Bay, ☎ 2764, ≤ – |$| ⇔wc Ⓟ – **59 rm.**

at Kirn N: **1** m. on A 815 – ✉ ☎ 0369 Dunoon:

Queen's, PA23 8HE, ☎ 4224 – Ⓟ
28 rm.

at Hunter's Quay N: **2** m. on A 815 – ✉ ☎ 0369 Dunoon:

Royal Marine, PA23 7HL, ☎ 3001 – ⋔wc Ⓟ
15 February-15 November – **M** approx. 4.25 **t.** 1.30 – **45 rm** 7.50/17.00 **t.**

AUSTIN-MORRIS-MG-ROVER-TRIUMPH East Bay Promenade ☎ 1094

DUNTOCHER Dunbarton. (Strathclyde) – pop. 7,963 – ✉ Clydebank – ☎ 0389.
Edinburgh 51 – Glasgow 8 – Dumbarton 6.

Maltings, Dumbarton Rd, G81 6DP, ☎ 75371 – ⇔wc ☎ Ⓟ
M 2.60 **s.** 1.00 – **26 rm** 8.00/16.00 **s.**

DUNVEGAN Inverness. (Highland) 986 ⑥ – see Skye (Isle of).

DYCE Aberdeen. (Grampian) 986 ⑦ – see Aberdeen.

EAGLESHAM Renfrew. (Strathclyde) – ☎ 035 53.
Edinburgh 47 – Ayr 26 – Glasgow 9.

Eglington Arms (Open House), Gilmour St., G76 0LG, ☎ 2631 – TV ⇔wc ☎ Ⓟ
12 rm.

EASDALE Argyll. (Strathclyde) – pop. 125 – ✉ Oban – ☎ 085 23 Balvicar.
Edinburgh 137 – Oban 15.

Dunmor House ⛰, PA34 4RF, E: ½ m. ☎ 203, ≤, ≤, park – ⋔ Ⓟ
May-15 October – **M** (snack lunch) 5.10/5.80 – **13 rm** 9.00/16.30 **s.**

EAST KILBRIDE Lanark. (Strathclyde) 986 ⑮ – pop. 63,502 – ☎ 035 52.
18 Strathaven Rd ☎ 48638.
Edinburgh 44 – Ayr 34 – Glasgow 8.

Bruce (Swallow), Cornwall Way, G74 1AF, ☎ 29771, Telex 778428 – |$| TV Ⓟ.
65 rm.

Stuart (Thistle), 2 Cornwall Way, G74 1JS, ☎ 21161 – |$| TV ⇔wc ⋔wc ☎.
29 rm.

Torrance (Open House), 135 Main St., G74 4LN, ☎ 25241 – ☎ Ⓟ
18 rm.

AUSTIN-MG-WOLSELEY Telford Rd ☎ 23455 MORRIS-MG-WOLSELEY The Murray Rd ☎ 20028

EAST LINTON E. Lothian (Lothian) 986 ⑮ – pop. 900 – ☎ 062 086.
Edinburgh 24 – Newcastle-upon-Tyne 96.

XX **Harvesters** (Interchange) with rm, Station Rd, EH40 3DP, ☎ 395, ≤ – ⇔wc Ⓟ
M 5.60/7.90 **st.** 2.00 – **13 rm** 14.50/28.50 **st.** – P 20.00/21.00 **st.**

EDAY (Isle of) Orkney (Orkney Islands) 986 ⑯ – Shipping Services: see Orkney Islands (Mainland: Kirkwall).

EDDLESTON Peebles. (Borders) – see Peebles.

EDINBURGH Midlothian (Lothian) 986 ⑮ – pop. 453,584 – ☎ 031.

See: Castle★ (site★, ≤★★, Regalia★, Scottish United Services Museum★, Scottish National War Memorial) *AC* DZ – National Museum of Antiquities★★ EY **M**¹ – National Gallery★★ DY **M**² – St. Giles' Cathedral★ EYZ **B** – Charlotte Square★ CY – National Portrait Gallery★ *AC* EY **M**¹ – Royal Scottish Museum★ EZ **M**³ – Old houses and closes near Lawnmarket, Grassmarket★ – Abbey of Holyrood★ *AC* BV **A** – Royal Botanic Gardens★ ABV – Princes Street ≤★★ DY – Palace of Holyrood (State apartments★, historic apartments★★) *AC* BV **A** – Calton Hill ≤★ EY – Arthur's Seat ≤★ BV – Drama and Music Festival in summer.

Envir.: Roslyn Chapel★★ (15C) *AC*, S: 6 ½ m. by A 701 BX – Forth Bridge★★ *AC*, W: 8 ½ m. by A 90 AV – Leith ≤★ of the firth of Forth, NE: 2 ½ m. BV – Craigmillar Castle★ (stronghold) 14C, *AC*, SE: 3 m. BX **D** – Crichton Castle★ (16C) *AC*, SE: 13 m. by A7 BX.

18 Kingston Grange ☎ 664 8580, SE: 3 ½ m. BX – 18 Silverknowes Parkway ☎ 336 5359, W: 4 m. AV – 18 Observatory Rd ☎ 667 2837 BX – 18 Glendevon Park ☎ 337 1096, W: 5 m.

✈ ☎ 334 2351, W: 6 m. by A 8 AV – **Terminal:** Waverley Bridge – ☎ 556 5633.

i Scottish Tourist Board, 5 Waverley Bridge, ☎ 332 2436, Telex 72272 – Tourist Information, 5 Waverley Bridge, ☎ 226 6591 and 225 5801, Telex 727143.

Glasgow 43 – Newcastle-upon-Tyne 108.

Plans on following pages

Caledonian (B.T.H.), Princes St., EH1 2AB, ☎ 225 2433, Telex 72179 – lift TV P. – CY **n**
M a la carte 7.75/14.25 **st.** 1.60 – **212 rm** 27.50/47.50 **st.**

North British (B.T.H.), Princes St., EH2 2EQ, ☎ 556 2414, Telex 72332 – lift TV. – EY **o**
M approx. 5.75 **st.** – **193 rm** 19.00/29.00 **st.**

George (County), 19-25 George St., EH2 2PB, ☎ 225 1251, Telex 72570 – lift TV P. – DY **z**
M 4.00/5.25 **st.** – **196 rm** 19.55/32.50 **s.**

Roxburghe, 38 Charlotte Sq., EH2 4HG, ☎ 225 3921 – lift. – DY **o**
M approx. 4.35 1.50 – 1.00 – **66 rm** 15.00/25.00 **s.**

Royal Scot (Swallow), 111 Glasgow Rd, EH12 8NF, W: 4 ½ m. on A 8 ☎ 334 9191, Telex 727197 – lift TV P. – by A 8 AV
138 rm.

King James (Thistle), 107 St. James Centre, EH1 3SW, ☎ 556 0111, Telex 727200 – lift TV – EY **u**
154 rm.

Edinburgh Eurocrest (Crest.), Queensferry Rd, EH4 3HL, NW: 2 m. on A 90 ☎ 332 2442, Telex 72541 – lift TV P. – AV **x**
M 3.30/3.40 **s.** 1.60 – 1.80 – **120 rm** 13.00/16.80 **s.**

Post House (T.H.F.), Corstorphine Rd, EH12 6UA, W: 3 m. on A 8 ☎ 334 8221, Telex 727103, ≤ – lift TV wc P. – AV **u**
M 2.95/4.00 **st.** 1.50 – 2.00 – **208 rm** 13.00/18.00 **st.**

Carlton (T.H.F.), North Bridge, EH1 1SD, ☎ 556 7277 – lift TV wc. – EY **e**
M a la carte 3.90/5.60 **st.** 1.50 – **92 rm** 13.50/22.50 **st.**

Barnton (Thistle), 562 Queensferry Rd, EH4 6AS, NW: 4 ¾ m. on A 90 ☎ 336 2291 – lift TV wc wc P. – AV **o**
46 rm.

Ellersly House, Ellersly Rd, EH12 6HZ, W: 2 ½ m. by A 8 ☎ 337 6888, – lift wc P – AV **v**
M 2.50/4.50 **st.** 1.75 – **58 rm** 13.50/27.00 **st.**

Howard (Interchange), 34 Gt. King St., EH3 6QH, ☎ 556 1393 – lift wc wc P – DY **s**
M (bar lunch) 4.50/5.75 **st.** 2.00 – **26 rm** 13.00/24.00 **st.** – P 20.50/26.50 **st.**

Braid Hills, 134 Braid Rd, EH10 6JD, S: 3 m. by A 702 ☎ 447 8888, – wc P – AX **i**
M 3.00/3.40 **t.** 1.00 – **51 rm** 9.00/20.00 **t.**

Mount Royal, 53 Princes St., EH2 2DG, ☎ 225 7161 – lift wc – **148 rm.** – DY **c**

Lady Nairne, Willowbrae Rd, EH8 7MG, E: 2 ½ m. on A 1 ☎ 661 3396 – lift wc P – BV **a**
M *(closed 1 January)* 2.75/4.50 1.85 – **29 rm** 9.50/17.50.

Hailes (S & N), 2 Wester Hailes Centre, Wester Hailes Rd, EH14 2SW, SW: 4 ¾ m. by A 71 on A 720 ☎ 443 8082 – wc P – AX **a**
M approx. 1.80 1.20 – **17 rm** 8.80/16.20 **st.**

Harp (Osprey), 116 St. John's Rd, EH12 8AX, W: 3 ¼ m. on A 8 ☎ 334 4750 – wc P – AV **s**
20 rm.

Murrayfield (Swallow), 18 Corstorphine Rd, EH12 6HN, W: 2½ m. on A 8 ☎ 337 2207 – wc P – **20 rm.** – AV **z**

County, 8 Abercromby Pl., EH3 6LB, ☎ 556 2333 – lift wc P – EY **c**
52 rm.

Old Waverley, 43 Princes St., EH2 2BY, ☎ 556 4648 – lift wc – EY **r**
M 5.00/6.00 **s.** 1.25 – **75 rm** 10.50/21.00 **s.**

St. Andrew, 8-10 South St., Andrew St., EH2 2AZ, ☎ 556 8774 – lift wc – EY **s**
M approx. 3.00 2.00 – **40 rm** 10.00/20.00 **st.**

Sighthill (S & N), Calder Rd, EH11 4AS, SW: 4 m. on A 71 ☎ 443 5151 – wc P – AX **z**
M a la carte 2.50/5.00 **st.** 1.20 – **10 rm** 8.15/15.05 **st.**

Albany, 39 Albany St., EH1 3QY, ☎ 556 0397 – wc – EY **v**
10 rm 8.50/18.50 **st.**

Glenisla, 12 Lygon Rd, EH16 5QB, ☎ 667 4098 – BX **a**
closed Christmas and 1 January – **9 rm** 6.00/10.50 **st.**

Dorstan Private, 7 Priestfield Rd, EH16 5HJ, ☎ 667 6721 – wc P – BX **e**
closed Christmas and 1 January – **14 rm** 4.35/9.75 **t.**

Gordon, 7-9 Royal Circus, EH3 6TL, ☎ 225 3000 – DY **s**
April-October – **25 rm** 10.00/17.00 **t.**

Southdown, 20 Graigmillar Park, EH16 5PS, ☎ 667 2410 – P – BX **n**
8 rm.

St. Margaret's, 32-34 Murrayfield Av., EH12 6AX, ☎ 337 1170 – AV **c**
16 rm 7.00/11.00 **s.**

Kildonan Lodge, 27 Graigmillar Park, EH16 5PE, ☎ 667 2793 – P – BX **r**
9 rm 5.00/10.00.

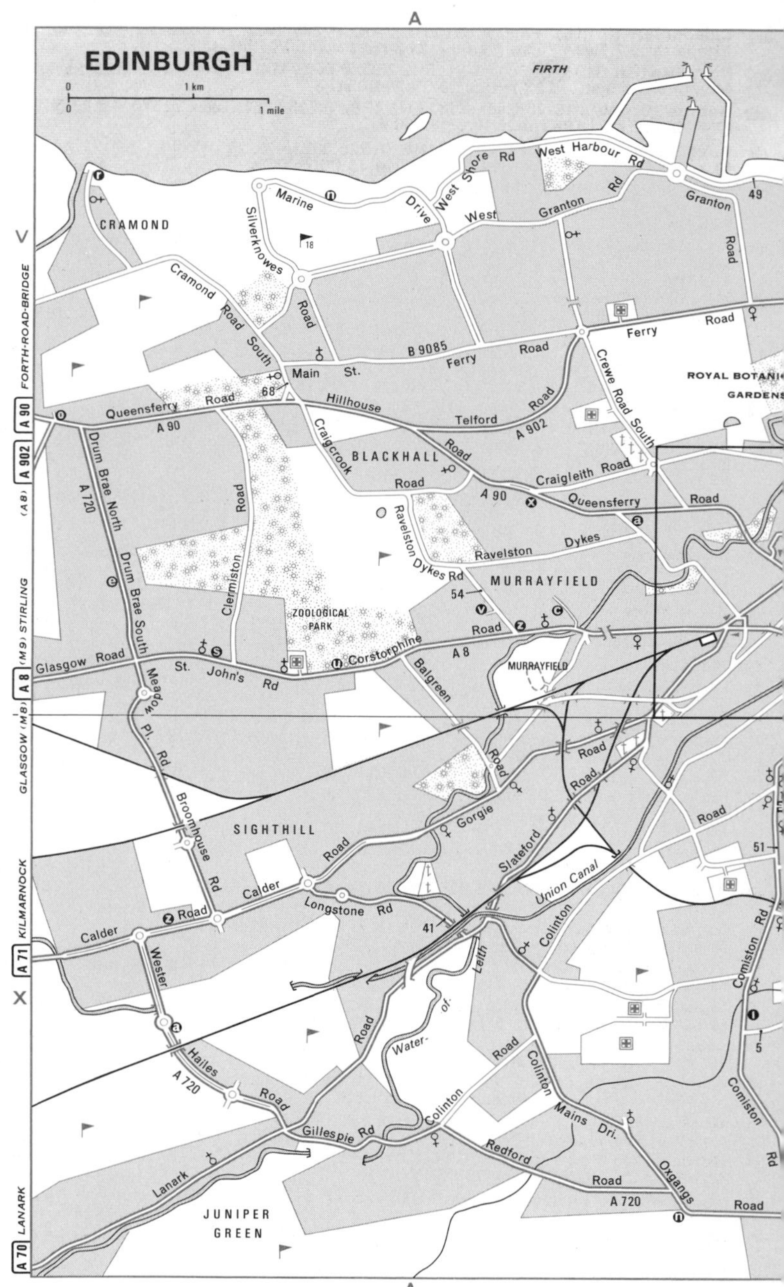
EDINBURGH
0
1 km
0
1 mile
FIRTH
A
V
X
FORTH-ROAD-BRIDGE
A 90
A 902
(A 8)
(M 9) STIRLING
A 8
GLASGOW (M 8)
KILMARNOCK
A 71
LANARK
A 70
CRAMOND
Marine Drive
Silverknowes Road
West Shore Rd
West Harbour Rd
West Granton Rd
Granton Road
49
Cramond Road South
Main St.
68
B 9085
Ferry Road
Queensferry Road
A 90
Hillhouse
Telford Road
A 902
Crewe Road South
ROYAL BOTANIC GARDENS
BLACKHALL
Craigcrook Road
Craigleith Road
Queensferry Road
Drum Brae North
A 720
Drum Brae South
Clermiston Road
Ravelston Dykes Rd
Ravelston Dykes
MURRAYFIELD
54
ZOOLOGICAL PARK
Glasgow Road
St. John's Rd
Corstorphine Road
A 8
Balgreen Road
MURRAYFIELD
Meadow Pl. Rd
Broomhouse Rd
SIGHTHILL
Gorgie Road
Slateford Road
Calder Road
Longstone Rd
Union Canal
41
51
Wester Hailes Road
A 720
Water of Leith
Colinton Road
Colinton Mains Dri.
Comiston Rd
Comiston Rd
5
Gillespie Rd
Redford Road
A 720
Oxgangs Road
Lanark Road
JUNIPER GREEN
18

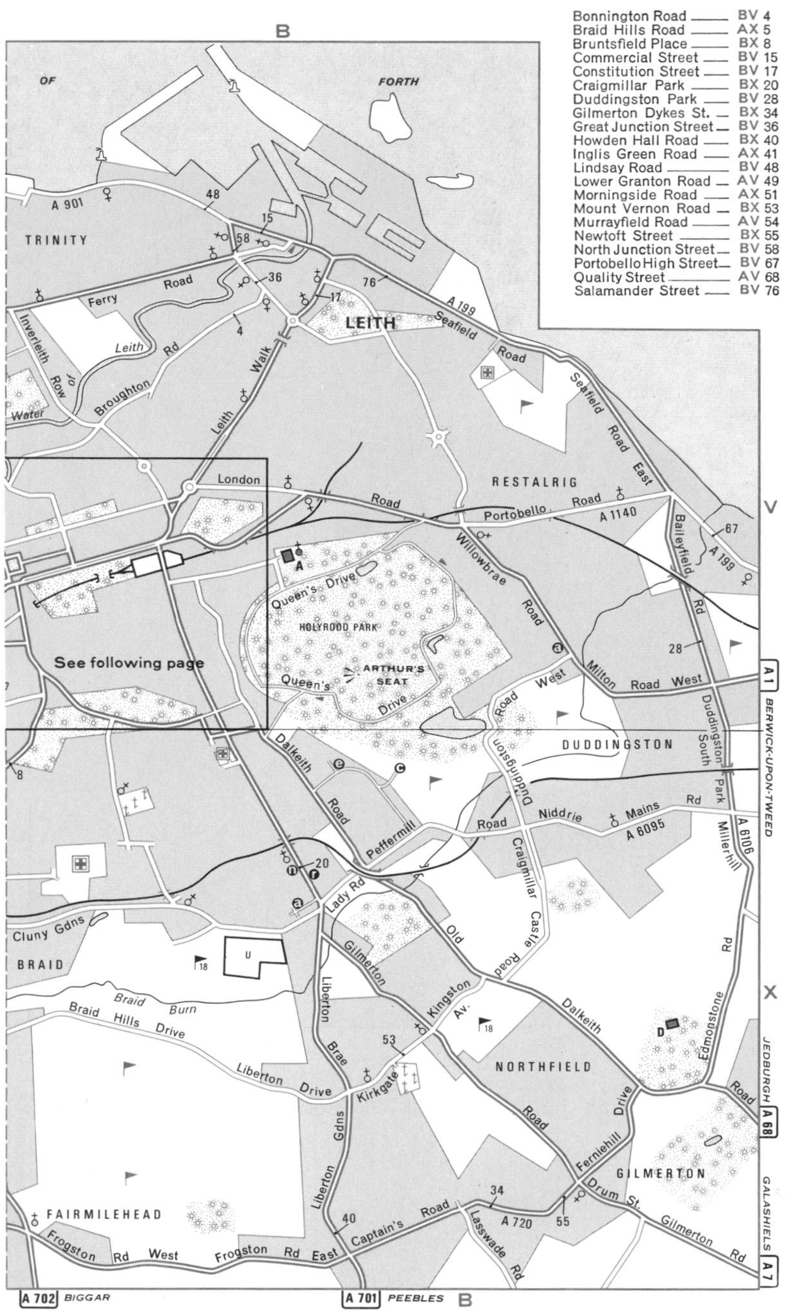
Bonnington Road BV 4
Braid Hills Road AX 5
Bruntsfield Place BX 8
Commercial Street BV 15
Constitution Street BV 17
Craigmillar Park BX 20
Duddingston Park BV 28
Gilmerton Dykes St. BX 34
Great Junction Street BV 36
Howden Hall Road BX 40
Inglis Green Road AX 41
Lindsay Road BV 48
Lower Granton Road AV 49
Morningside Road AX 51
Mount Vernon Road BX 53
Murrayfield Road AV 54
Newtoft Street BX 55
North Junction Street BV 58
Portobello High Street BV 67
Quality Street AV 68
Salamander Street BV 76
B
OF
FORTH
A 901
TRINITY
Ferry Road
LEITH
Seafield Road
A 199
Inverleith Row
Water of Leith
Broughton Rd
Leith Walk
Seafield Road East
RESTALRIG
London Road
Portobello Road
A 1140
Baileyfield Rd
Willowbrae Road
Queen's Drive
HOLYROOD PARK
ARTHUR'S SEAT
See following page
Milton Road West
A 1
BERWICK-UPON-TWEED
Duddingston South
Duddingston Park
DUDDINGSTON
Dalkeith Road
Peffermill Road
Niddrie Mains Rd
A 6095
Craigmillar Castle Road
A 6106
Millerhill Rd
Cluny Gdns
BRAID
Lady Rd
Old Dalkeith Road
Gilmerton
Braid Burn
Braid Hills Drive
Liberton Brae
Kingston Av.
NORTHFIELD
Edmonstone Road
JEDBURGH
A 68
Liberton Drive
Kirkgate
Liberton Gdns
Ferniehill Drive
GILMERTON
GALASHIELS
Drum St.
Gilmerton Rd
FAIRMILEHEAD
Captain's Road
A 720
Lasswade Rd
Frogston Rd West
Frogston Rd East
A 7
A 702 BIGGAR
A 701 PEEBLES
V
X

EDINBURGH
CENTRE

0 — 400 m
0 — 400 yards

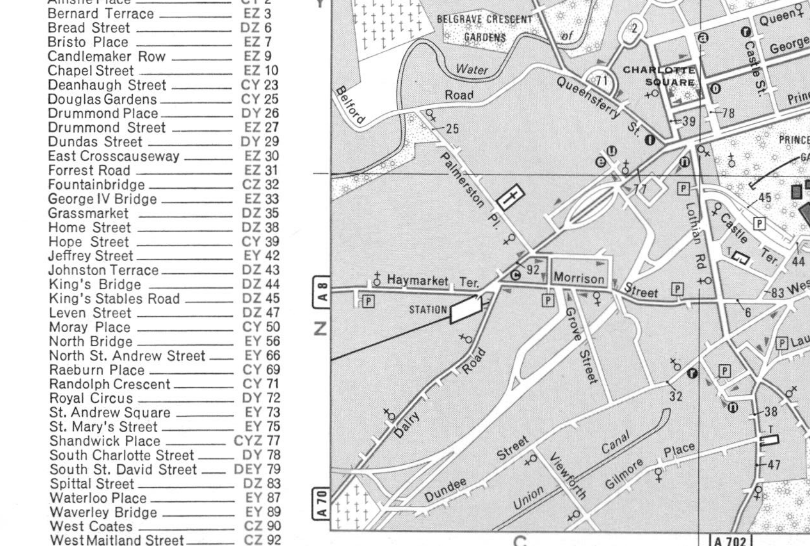

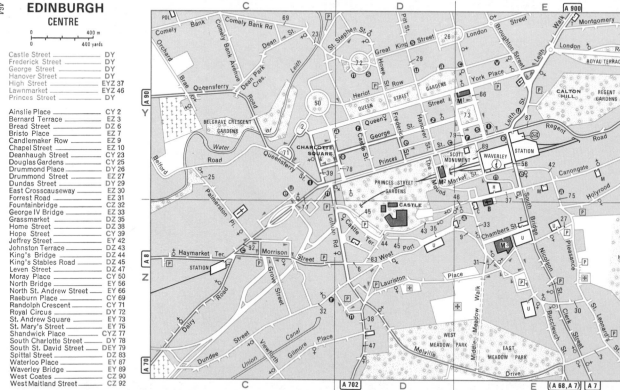

XXX **Prestonfield House** with rm, Priestfield Rd, EH16 5UT, SE : 2 ½ m. off A 68 ☎ 667 8055, Telex 727396, ≤, « Elegant 17C mansion », park – wc ☎ P
M a la carte 5.80/9.15 **t.** 1.45 – **5 rm** 14.50/25.00 **t.** BX **c**

XXX **Café Royal** (County), 17 West Register St., EH2 2AA, ☎ 556 1884 EY **i**
closed Sunday – **M** a la carte 4.80/10.55 **t.** 1.20.

XXX **Howtowdie,** 27a Stafford St., EH3 7BP, ☎ 225 6291 CY **u**
closed Sunday, Christmas and 1 January – **M** a la carte 4.80/7.35 1.35.

XX **Cavalier,** 20 Abercromby Pl., EH3 6LB, ☎ 556 2270 DY **a**
closed Sunday and 1-2 January – **M** a la carte approx. 5.70 1.40.

XX **Handsel,** 22 Stafford St., EH3 7BH, ☎ 225 5521 CY **e**
closed Sunday and Bank Holidays – **M** a la carte 4.30/6.20 **t.** 1.40.

XX **Cosmo,** 58a North Castle St., EH2 3LU, ☎ 226 6743, Italian rest. DY **r**
closed Sunday – **M** a la carte 4.35/5.75 **t.** 1.50.

XX **Vito,** 109 Fountainbridge, EH3 9QG, ☎ 229 2747, Italian rest. CZ **r**
closed Sunday – **M** (dinner only) a la carte 3.40/6.00 **t.** 1.40.

XX Oscar's, 19 Royal Circus, EH3 1TL, ☎ 225 5219. DY **n**

XX **Ristorante Milano,** 7 Victoria St. ☎ 226 5260, Italian rest. EZ **a**
closed Sunday, 25-26 December and 1 January – **M** a la carte 3.70/6.50 **t.** 1.30.

XX **Flappers,** 8 West Maitland St., EH12 5DS, ☎ 228 1001, Italian rest. CZ **c**
closed Sunday – **M** a la carte 3.65/5.30 **t.** 1.45.

XX Hunter's Tryst (Swallow), Oxgangs Rd, EH13 9NG, S : 4 ¾ m. on B 701 by A 702 ☎ 445 3132 – P. AX **n**

XX **Denzler's,** 80 Queen St, EH2 4NF, ☎ 226 5467 CDY **a**
closed Sunday, 25-26 December, 1-2 January and Bank Holidays – **M** a la carte 2.65/5.05 **t.** 1.60.

XX Rainbow (Swallow), Drum Brae South, EH12 8HG, W: 4 m. off A 8 ☎ 334 8262 – P. AV **e**

XX Dario Ristorante Italiano, 56 St. Mary's St., EH1 1SX, ☎ 556 5888, Italian rest. EY **a**

XX **Gimi's International,** 11-15 Cockburn St., EH1 1BP, ☎ 225 7469, Italian rest. EY **n**
closed Sunday, Monday, Christmas Day and 1 January – **M** a la carte 2.45/4.75 1.20.

X **Casa Siciliana,** 11 Lochrin Ter., Toll Cross, EH3 9QJ, ☎ 229 1690, Italian rest. DZ **n**
closed Sunday – **M** a la carte 3.30/5.00 1.25.

X **Concordia,** 20a Abercromby Pl., EH3 6LB, ☎ 556 2270, Italian rest. DY **a**
closed Sunday and 1-2 January – **M** a la carte approx. 2.45 1.00.

X **Le Caveau,** 13b Dundas St., EH3 6QG, ☎ 556 5707, French rest. DY **u**
closed Sunday and Bank Holidays – **M** a la carte 3.15/4.05 **t.** 1.40.

X **Casa Española,** 61-65 Rose St., EH2 2NH, ☎ 225 5979, Spanish rest. DY **e**
closed Sunday and Bank Holidays – **M** a la carte 2.50/4.50 1.00.

X **Queensway,** Queensferry Rd, EH4 3EY, ☎ 332 6492, Spanish rest. – P AV **a**
M a la carte 2.50/4.50 1.00.

X **Rendezvous,** 10a Queensferry St., EH2 4PG, ☎ 225 2023, Chinese rest. CY **i**
closed 25 and 26 December – **M** a la carte 3.40/4.00 1.50.

at Cramond Foreshore **NW: 5 ¼ m. off A 90 – ✉ 031 Edinburgh:**

Commodore (Stakis), 46 West Marine Drive, EH4 5EP, ☎ 336 1700, ≤ – wc ☎ P. AV **n**
M 3.25/3.50 **st.** 1.40 – **50 rm.**

X **Cramond Inn,** Cramond Glebe Rd, EH4 6JM, ☎ 336 2035 – P AV **r**
closed Sunday, Christmas Day, 1 January and Bank Holidays – **M** a la carte 3.00/5.35 **t.** 2.00.

ALFA-ROMEO 22 Canning St. ☎ 229 5561
AUSTIN-DAIMLER-JAGUAR-MORRIS-MG-ROVER-TRIUMPH, ROLLS ROYCE Gylemuir Rd ☎ 334 9101
AUSTIN-MG-WOLSELEY 300 Colinton Rd ☎ 441 4567
AUSTIN-MG-WOLSELEY Goldenacre Ter. ☎ 552 4695
AUSTIN-MORRIS-MG-ROVER-TRIUMPH-WOLSELEY Comely Bank ☎ 332 1344
AUSTIN-MG-WOLSELEY 107 Glasgow Rd ☎ 334 1351
AUSTIN-MG-WOLSELEY Falcon Av. ☎ 447 6161
AUSTIN-DAIMLER-JAGUAR-MORRIS-MG-ROVER-TRIUMPH-WOLSELEY Westfield Av. ☎ 337 3222
AUSTIN-MG-ROVER-TRIUMPH 70 Slateford Rd ☎ 337 1252
CHRYSLER Blackford Av. ☎ 667 5427
CHRYSLER-SIMCA Lochrin Tollcross ☎ 229 1555
CHRYSLER 82 Braid Rd ☎ 447 1707
CHRYSLER Piershill ☎ 661 2525
CHRYSLER-SIMCA 162 St. Johns Rd ☎ 334 6248
CITROEN 13 Lauriston Gardens ☎ 229 4207
DAF, SAAB Westfield Rd ☎ 337 7204
DAF, POLSKI 1/3 Newcraighall Rd ☎ 669 2602
DATSUN 63/65 London Rd ☎ 661 7966
DATSUN 2 Joppa Rd, Portobello ☎ 669 7966
DATSUN 6 Bankhead Av. ☎ 443 8761
FIAT 8 Glenogle Rd ☎ 556 6404
FORD Baileyfield Rd ☎ 669 6261
FORD Semple St. ☎ 229 3331
FORD 12 West Mayfield ☎ 667 4475
JENSEN Telford Rd ☎ 332 9002
PORSCHE 55 Belford ☎ 225 6633
MORRIS-MG-ROVER-TRIUMPH-WOLSELEY 4/40 Ratcliffe Ter. ☎ 667 3764
MORRIS-MG-WOLSELEY 77/78 Ferry Rd ☎ 554 6528
MORRIS-MG-WOLSELEY Lanark Rd ☎ 443 2936
OPEL Meadow Pl. Rd ☎ 334 4919
RENAULT 376 Gilmerton Rd ☎ 664 2900
RENAULT Belford Bridge ☎ 332 2293
RENAULT Portobello Rd ☎ 669 7481
ROVER-TRIUMPH 127 Willowbrae Rd ☎ 661 580
TOYOTA Polwarth Pl. ☎ 337 3787
VAUXHALL 39 Fountainbridge ☎ 229 2488
VAUXHALL Seafield Rd ☎ 554 9321
VOLVO 38 Seafield Rd East ☎ 669 8301
VOLVO Saughton Cres. ☎ 337 3282
VW, AUDI-NSU Belford Rd ☎ 225 4664
VW, AUDI-NSU Marionville Rd ☎ 661 7177

EDZELL Angus (Tayside) – pop. 800 – ☎ 035 64.
See: Castle* (16C) *AC* (Walled garden). **Envir.:** Brechin (Cathedral: round tower*) S: 6 ½ m. – Glen Esk* NW: 11 m.
18 ☎ 235.
Edinburgh 91 – **Aberdeen 36** – **Dundee 32.**

- **Glenesk,** High St., DD9 7TF, ☎ 319, – wc wc P
  M approx. 3.90 **t.** 1.80 – **24 rm** 7.00/16.00.

EGILSAY (Isle of) Orkney (Orkney Islands) – Shipping Services: see Orkney Islands (Mainland: Kirkwall).

EIGG (Isle of) Inverness. (Highland) 986 ⑥ ⑩ – Shipping Services: see Mallaig.

ELGIN Moray (Grampian) 986 ⑦ – pop. 17,580 – ☎ 0343.
See: Cathedral*. **Envir.:** Burghead (** from the lighthouse) NW: 10 m. – Findhorn (site*) W: 12 m.
18 Hardhillock, New Elgin ☎ 2238, S: 1 m.
i 17 High St. ☎ 3388 (May-October).
Edinburgh 191 – **Aberdeen 67** – Fraserburgh 61 – **Inverness 39.**

- **Eight Acres,** Sheriff Mill, IV30 3UN, W: 1 m. on A 96 ☎ 3077, <, – TV wc wc P.
  M a la carte 2.35/6.40 1.75 – **45 rm** 12.00/24.00 **st.**
- **Enrico's,** 15 Greyfriars St., IV30 1LF, ☎ 2849, Italian rest.
  closed Sunday, Christmas, 1 January and Bank Holidays – **M** a la carte 2.15/6.35.

AUDI-NSU, VOLVO South College St. ☎ 7561
AUSTIN-MORRIS-MG-WOLSELEY 27 Greyfriars St. ☎ 7416
CHRYSLER-SIMCA East Rd ☎ 3066
DAF, MAZDA Sheriff Mill ☎ 7121
DAIMLER-JAGUAR-ROVER-TRIUMPH Station Rd ☎ 2633
DATSUN Borough Briggs Rd ☎ 7473
FIAT School Brae ☎ 3088
FORD 266 High St. ☎ 3191
OPEL 215/219 High St. ☎ 7514
PEUGEOT Bridge Motors ☎ 2955
RENAULT Edgar Rd ☎ 7688
VW 41/3 Blackfriars Rd ☎ 2792

ELIE Fife. (Fife) 986 ⑪ – pop. 895 (inc. Earlsferry) – ☎ 0333.
See: Site and <*.
18 9 ☎ 327.
Edinburgh 42 – **Dundee 25** – Kirkcaldy 16.

- **The Elms,** 12 Park Pl., KY9 1DH, ☎ 330404,
  March-October – **8 rm** 5.00/10.40 **t.**

ELLON Aberdeen. (Grampian) 986 ⑦ – pop. 2,349 – ☎ 0358.
9 ☎ 576.
i Market St. Car Park ☎ 20730 (June-September).
Edinburgh 140 – **Aberdeen 16** – Fraserburgh 26.

- **Ellon Mercury Motor Inn,** AB4 9NP, ☎ 20666, Telex 628064 – TV wc P.
  M a la carte approx. 3.80 **st.** 1.35 – 1.50 – **36 rm** 10.00/17.00 **st.**

ERIBOLL (Loch) *** Sutherland (Highland).
Edinburgh 276 – Tongue 21.

Hotels see Tongue E: 21 m.

ERISKA (Isle of) Argyll. (Strathclyde) – ✉ Oban – ☎ 063 172 Ledaig.

- **Isle of Eriska** , PA37 1SD, ☎ 205, <, « Country house atmosphere », , park – wc P
  April-November – **M** approx. 7.00 – **21 rm** 13.00/26.00.

ERSKINE Renfrew. (Strathclyde) – pop. 3,300 – ☎ 041 Glasgow.
Edinburgh 56 – **Glasgow 13.**

- **Glasgow Eurocrest** (Crest) , PA8 6AN, on A 726 ☎ 812 0123, Telex 777713, < – TV P.
  M 3.60/4.10 **s.** 1.65 – 1.80 – **198 rm** 10.35/13.80 **s.**

FALKIRK Stirling. (Central) 986 ⑮ – pop. 37,579 – ☎ 0324.
Envir.: Linlithgow Palace* (15C-16C) *AC,* E: 7 ½ m.
Edinburgh 24 – Dumfermline 19 – **Glasgow 23** – Motherwell 26 – Perth 43.

- Cladhan, Kemper Av., FK1 1UF, ☎ 27421 – TV wc P. – **32 rm.**
- Park (Stakis), Arnothill, Camelon Rd, FK1 5RY, ☎ 28331 – TV wc P. – **54 rm.**

AUSTIN-MORRIS-MG-ROVER-TRIUMPH-WOLSELEY Main St. ☎ 22584
AUSTIN, PEUGEOT West End ☎ 23042
CHRYSLER-SIMCA 95 Glasgow Rd ☎ 22571
FIAT Callendar Rd ☎ 24204
FORD Callendar Rd ☎ 21511
POLSKI, SAAB 2 High Station Rd ☎ 22956
TOYOTA Lady'smill ☎ 22396
VAUXHALL Callendar Rd ☎ 21141
VAUXHALL 67/80 Grahams Rd ☎ 21234
VOLVO Victoria Rd ☎ 24693
VW High Station Rd ☎ 24221

FALKLAND Fife. (Fife) 986 ⑪ – pop. 896 – ☎ 033 75.
See : Palace* (16C) *AC.*
i ☎ 397 (end March - end October).
Edinburgh 36 – Dundee 23 – Perth 18.

Covenanter with rm, KY7 7BU, ☎ 224 – Ⓟ
M *(closed Monday and last 2 weeks July)* a la carte 3.25/5.05 **st.** 1.20 – **4 rm** 4.50/8.50 **st.**

FEOLIN Argyll. (Strathclyde) 986 ⑭ – Shipping Services: see Jura (Isle of).

FETLAR (Isle of) Shetland (Shetland Islands) 986 ⑯ – Shipping services : see Shetland Islands.

FIONNPHORT Argyll. (Strathclyde) 986 ⑩ – Shipping Services: see Mull (Isle of).

FISHNISH Argyll. (Strathclyde) – Shipping Services: see Mull (Isle of).

FOCHABERS Moray (Grampian) 986 ⑦ – pop. 4,230 – ☎ 0343.
Edinburgh 182 – Aberdeen 58 – Fraserburgh 52 – Inverness 48.

Gordon Arms, 89 High St., IV32 7DH, ☎ 820508, – wc Ⓟ.
M approx. 4.50 1.10 – **17 rm** 8.00/18.00 – P 16.00/18.00.

FORFAR Angus (Tayside) 986 ⑪ – pop. 10,499 – ☎ 0307.
Exc.: Glen Clova** NW: 20 ½ m.
18 Cunninghill ☎ 2120, E: 1 ½ m.
Edinburgh 72 – Aberdeen 52 – Dundee 13 – Perth 30.

Royal, 33 Castle St., DD8 3AE, ☎ 2691 – wc Ⓟ
M 3.50/4.00 1.50 – **19 rm** 6.00/13.00.

County, 7 Castle St., DD8 3AE, ☎ 2878
M 2.50/3.00 1.20 – **10 rm** 5.00/10.00.

AUSTIN-MORRIS-MG-ROVER-TRIUMPH-WOLSELEY 128 Castle St. ☎ 2542
CHRYSLER Lochside Rd ☎ 2676
DATSUN Lochside Rd ☎ 2281
VW Kirriemuir Rd ☎ 2347

FORSINARD Sutherland. (Highland) – ☎ 064 17 Halladale.
Edinburgh 283 – Inverness 124 – Thurso 29 – Wick 62.

Forsinard, KW13 6YT, ☎ 221, park – wc Ⓟ
14 rm.

FORT AUGUSTUS Inverness. (Highland) 986 ⑥ ⑦ – pop. 770 – ☎ 0320 – 9.
See : Site*, lochs and canal*.
i Car Park ☎ 367 (May-September).
Edinburgh 155 – Inverness 34 – Kyle of Lochalsh 58 – Oban 80.

Inchnacardoch Lodge, PH32 4BL, on A 82 ☎ 258, – Ⓟ
Easter-October – **M** 4.50/6.00 **st.** 2.00 – **20 rm** – P 13.50/15.50 **st.**

FORTINGALL Perth. (Tayside) – see Kenmore.

FORT WILLIAM Inverness. (Highland) 986 ⑩ – pop. 4,214 – ☎ 0397.
Envir.: NE: Loch Lochy** – SE: Glen Nevis*.
18 ☎ 4464, N: 3 m. on A 82.
i Area Tourist Officer ☎ 3581, Telex 778869.
Edinburgh 131 – Glasgow 102 – Inverness 66 – Oban 48.

Inverlochy Castle, Inverlochy, PH33 6SN, NE: 3 m. by A 82 ☎ 2177, garden, lake and mountains, « Victorian castle in extensive grounds », park – TV Ⓟ
Easter-October – **M** (dinner only) 10.50 – **12 rm** 30.00/46.00.

West End, Auchintore Rd, PH33 6ED, ☎ 2614, – wc Ⓟ
M 3.75/4.25 **s.** 1.95 – **50 rm** 9.50/19.00.

Fort William Mercury Motor Inn, Auchintore Rd, PH33 6TG, on A 82 ☎ 3117, – TV wc Ⓟ
M a la carte approx. 3.80 **st.** 1.35 – 1.50 – **60 rm** 11.00/16.80 **st.**

Alexandra, The Parade, PH33 6AZ, ☎ 2241 – wc Ⓟ
M approx. 4.20 **s.** 2.00 – **93 rm** 11.50/22.00 **s.**

Nevis Bank, Belford Rd, PH33 6BY, ☎ 2595 – wc Ⓟ
M approx. 3.50 – **20 rm** 7.00/16.00 – P 12.85/13.85.

Grand, Gordon Sq., PH33 6DX, ☎ 2928 – wc Ⓟ
M 3.75/4.50 **s.** 0.95 – **33 rm** 9.00/18.50 **s.**

AUSTIN-MORRIS-MG-ROVER-TRIUMPH Gordon Sq. ☎ 2345
CHRYSLER Fort William ☎ 3354

GAIRLOCH Ross and Cromarty (Highland) 986 ⑥ – pop. 1,783 – ☎ 0445.

Envir. : Gruinard Bay* NE : 18 m. – Glen Docherty** SE : 21 m. – Inverewe gardens* (rhododendrons) NE : 6 m. – SE : Loch Maree*.**

i Area Tourist Officer, Achtercairn, IV21 2DN, ☎ 213.

Edinburgh 230 – Inverness 71 – Kyle of Lochalsh 65.

- Gairloch, IV21 2BL, ☎ 2001, ≤ sea and bay, ✗, ⚓, 🌳 – |‡| Ⓟ
  April-mid October – **50 rm.**
- **Gairloch Sands,** IV21 2BJ, ☎ 2131, ≤ sea and bay – 🛁wc Ⓟ
  April-October (snack lunch) approx. 4.90 **st.** 🍾 1.45 – **36 rm** ☕ 13.05/21.70 **st.**

GALASHIELS Selkirk. (Borders) 986 ⑮ – pop. 12,609 – ☎ 0896.

18 Ladhope, ☎ 3724, NE : ¼ m. – 9 ☎ 2260, N : 1 m. on A 7.

i Reiver Gallery, Gala Park Rd ☎ 4208.

Edinburgh 33 – Hawick 17 – **Newcastle-upon-Tyne 73.**

- Douglas (Open House), Channel St., TD1 1BJ, ☎ 2189 – |‡| 🛁wc ☎ Ⓟ
  38 rm.
- ✗ **Redgauntlet,** 34 Market St., TD1 3AA, ☎ 2098
  closed Tuesday, 3 weeks Easter, 25-26 December, 1 January and Bank Holiday Mondays – **M** (dinner only) a la carte 3.30/5.75 **t.** 🍾 1.45.

AUSTIN-MORRIS-MG-ROVER-TRIUMPH-WOLSELEY 3 Market St. ☎ 2301
DATSUN Melrose Rd ☎ 4518
FORD, FIAT Stow ☎ 057 83 (Stow) 286
RENAULT Bridge St. ☎ 2363
VAUXHALL Galashiels ☎ 2729

GARVE Ross and Cromarty (Highland) 986 ⑥ – pop. 200 – ☎ 099 74.

Envir. : SE : Blackwater Valley (Falls of Rogie*).

Edinburgh 186 – Inverness 27 – Wick 116.

- **Strathgarve Lodge** 🐦, IV23 2PU, ☎ 204, ≤, « Former hunting lodge », ⚓, 🌳, park – 🛁wc Ⓟ
  May-7 October – **M** approx. 5.50 **t.** 🍾 1.20 – **19 rm** ☕ 11.00/24.00 **t.**
- **Inchbae Lodge** 🐦, IV23 2PH, Ullapool Rd N : 6 m. on A 835 ☎ 099 75 (Aultguish) 269, ≤, ⚓, 🌳 – 🛁wc 🚿wc Ⓟ
  May-September – **M** 5.50/6.60 **t.** 🍾 1.50 – **13 rm** ☕ 10.00/20.00 **t.** – P 17.30/18.30 **t.**

GATEHOUSE OF FLEET Kirkcudbright. (Dumfries and Galloway) 986 ⑲ – pop. 837 – ☎ 055 74 – 9.

i Car Park ☎ 212 (May-September).

Edinburgh 109 – Dumfries 32 – Stranraer 44.

- **Cally** (T.H.F.) 🐦, DG7 2DL, S : 1 m. off A 75 ☎ 341, Telex 778082, ≤, ✗, 🏊 heated, ⚓, 🌳, park – |‡| Ⓟ. 🏛
  M approx. 4.00 **st.** 🍾 1.50 – **90 rm** ☕ 12.50/28.00 **st.** – P 15.00/22.00 **st.**
- **Murray Arms** (Interchange), High St., DG7 2HY, ☎ 207, ✗, 🌳 – 🛁wc Ⓟ
  M 4.10/5.00 **st.** 🍾 0.70 – **29 rm** ☕ 11.30/24.60 **st.**
- **Anwoth,** Fleet St., DG7 2JT, ☎ 217 – 🚿wc
  M (bar lunch) approx. 4.10 **st.** 🍾 1.00 – **14 rm** ☕ 6.50/14.00 **s.**

AUSTIN ☎ 227
MORRIS-MG-WOLSELEY ☎ 214

GIFFNOCK Renfrew. (Strathclyde) – pop. 12,000 – ✉ ☎ 041 Glasgow.

Edinburgh 48 – Ayr 29 – Glasgow 5.

- MacDonald (Thistle), Eastwood Toll, G46 6RA, at intersection A 77 with A 726 ☎ 638 2225 – TV 🛁wc 🚿wc ☎ Ⓟ. 🏛
  58 rm.
- Redhurst (Stakis), 27 Eastwoodmains Rd, G46 6QE, ☎ 638 6465 – TV 🛁wc ☎ Ⓟ
  15 rm.

RENAULT 158 Fenwick Rd ☎ 638 6471

GIFFORD E. Lothian (Lothian) – pop. 500 – ✉ Haddington – ☎ 062 081 – 9.

Edinburgh 20 – Hawick 50.

- **Goblin Ha',** Main St., EH41 4QH, ☎ 244, 🌳 – Ⓟ
  M 4.00/4.75 **t.** 🍾 1.15 – **7 rm** ☕ 6.70/13.40 **st.**
- ✗✗ **Tweeddale Arms** with rm, EH41 4QU, ☎ 240, 🌳 – 🚿wc Ⓟ
  M a la carte 3.40/5.45 **st.** 🍾 1.65 – **7 rm** ☕ 7.70/16.50 **st.**

GIGHA (Isle of) Argyll. (Strathclyde) 986 ⑭.

⛴ to Kintyre Peninsula : West Loch Tarbert (Caledonian MacBrayne) 3 weekly (1 h 15 mn) – to Isle of Islay : Port Ellen (Caledonian MacBrayne) 3 weekly (1 h 15 mn).

Die Preise Einzelheiten über die in diesem Reiseführer angegebenen Preise, siehe S. 40.

GIRVAN Ayr. (Strathclyde) 986 ⑭ – pop. 7,597 – ☎ 0465.

Envir.: Culzean Castle 18C (site**, interior*) *AC*, N : 9 m.

18 ☎ 4272.

i Bridge St. ☎ 2056/7.

Edinburgh 98 – Ayr 23 – Glasgow 55 – Stranraer 30.

King's Arms (Swallow), Dalrymple St., KA26 0DU, ☎ 3322 – TV wc ☎ P
39 rm.

GLAMIS Angus (Tayside) 986 ⑪ – pop. 205 – ✉ Forfar – ☎ 030 784.

See: Castle* *AC*.

Edinburgh 66 – Dundee 12 – Forfar 5 – Perth 24.

XX **Strathmore Arms,** Main St., DD8 1RS, ☎ 248 – P
Easter-October – **M** *(closed Sunday)* 4.00/8.50 **t.** 1.50.

This Guide is not a comprehensive list of all hotels and restaurants, nor even of all good hotels and restaurants in Great Britain and Ireland.

Since our aim is to be of service to all motorists, we must show establishments in all categories and so we have made a selection of some in each.

GLASGOW Lanark. (Strathclyde) 986 ⑭⑮ – pop. 897,483 – ☎ 041.

See: St. Mungo Cathedral*** DZ **B** – Art Gallery and Museum** CY **M** – Provand's Lordship* DZ **D** – Pollock House* (Spanish paintings) AX **E**.

18 Linn Park ☎ 637 5871, S : 4 m. BX – 18 Cumbernauld Rd ☎ 770 6220 BV – 9 Lincoln Av. ☎ 959 2131, W : 4 m. AV – 9 Brassey St. ☎ 946 9728 BV.

Glasgow Airport : ☎ 887 1111, W : 8 m. by M 8 AV – **Terminal:** Stand nº 23 Anderston Cross Bus Station, Blythswood St.

see also Prestwick.

i George Sq., G2 1ES, ☎ 221 6136/7 or 221 7371/2, Telex 779504.

Edinburgh 43 – Manchester 216.

Town plans : Glasgow pp. 2-5

Albany (T.H.F.), Bothwell St., G2 7EN, ☎ 248 2656, Telex 77440 – TV P. CZ **z**
M a la carte 5.30/10.80 **t.** 1.45 – 2.00 – **243 rm** 19.50/28.50 **st.**

Central (B.T.H.), Gordon St., G1 3SF, ☎ 221 9680, Telex 777771 – TV. DZ **e**
M a la carte 3.55/10.30 **st.** (see also rest. **Malmaison**) – **221 rm** 21.50/35.00 **st.**

North British (B.T.H.), 50 George Sq., G2 1DS, ☎ 332 6711, Telex 778147 – TV P. DZ **u**
M 4.20/4.80 **st.** 1.30 – **140 rm** 16.05/26.15 **st.**

Bellahouston (Swallow), 517 Paisley Rd West, G51 1RW, ☎ 427 3146, Telex 778795 – TV wc ☎ P. AX **a**
45 rm.

Pond (Stakis), 2-4 Shelley Rd, G12 0XP, ☎ 334 8161 – TV wc ☎ P AV **i**
134 rm.

Tinto Firs (Thistle), 470 Kilmarnock Rd, G43 2BB, ☎ 637 2353 – TV wc ☎ P. AX **c**
30 rm.

Lorne (Thistle), 923 Sauchiehall St., G3 7TE, ☎ 334 4891 – TV wc ☎ P. CY **a**
84 rm.

Ingram (Stakis), 201 Ingram St., G1 1DQ, ☎ 248 4401 – TV wc ☎ DZ **c**
90 rm.

Shawlands (Open House), 30 Shawlands Sq., G41 3NR, ☎ 632 9226 – TV wc ☎ P. AX **e**
20 rm.

Beacons, 7 Park Ter., G3 6BY, ☎ 332 9438 – TV wc ☎ CY **c**
M *(closed Sunday and Bank Holidays)* a la carte 3.85/5.70 1.50 – 1.50 – **26 rm** 13.10/17.50.

Glasgow Centre (Centre), Argyle St., G2 8LL, ☎ 248 2355, Telex 779652 – TV wc ☎ CZ **x**
M (Carvery rest.) approx. 3.95 **s.** 1.25 – 1.50 – **120 rm** 10.75/14.50 **s.**

Royal Stuart, 316 Clyde St., G1 4NR, ☎ 248 4261, Telex 778833 – wc ☎. DZ **n**
M a la carte 3.95/6.75 **t.** 1.25 – **112 rm** 10.30/15.70 **st.** – P 13.60 **st.**

P.T.O. →

GLASGOW
BUILT UP AREA

0 — 1 km
0 — 1/2 mile

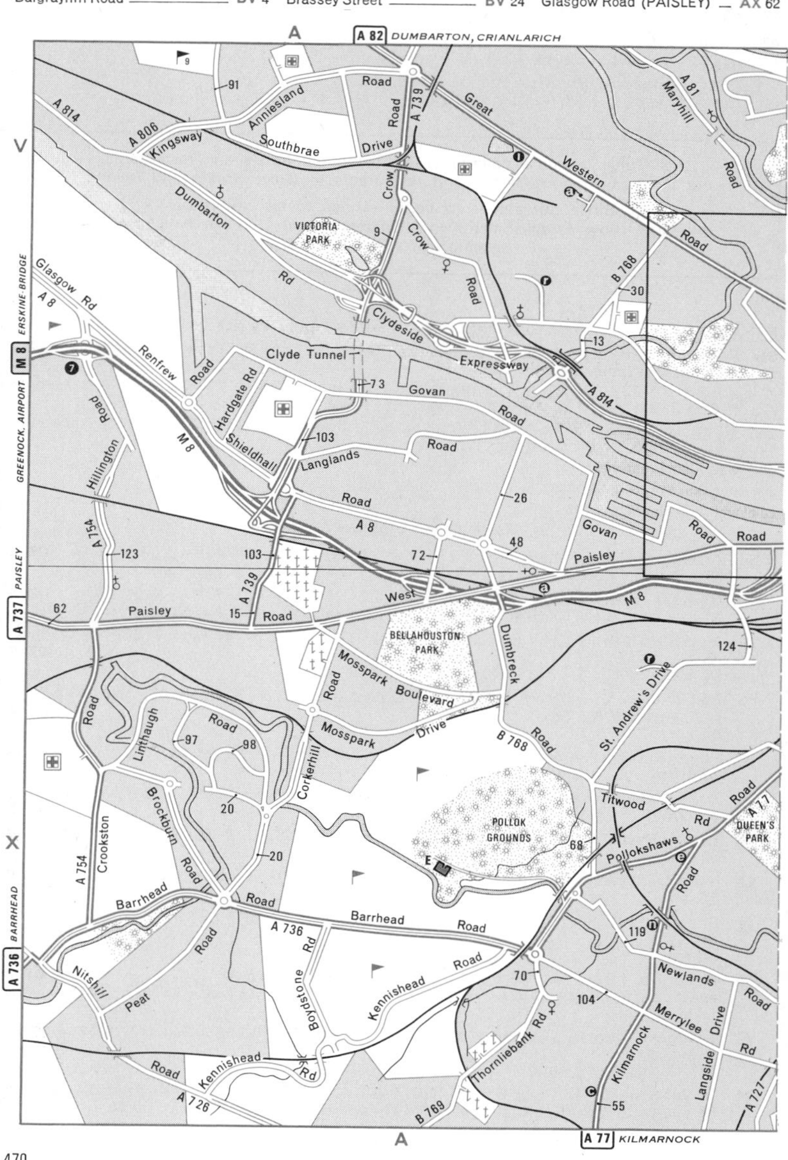

For Street Index see Glasgow p. 6

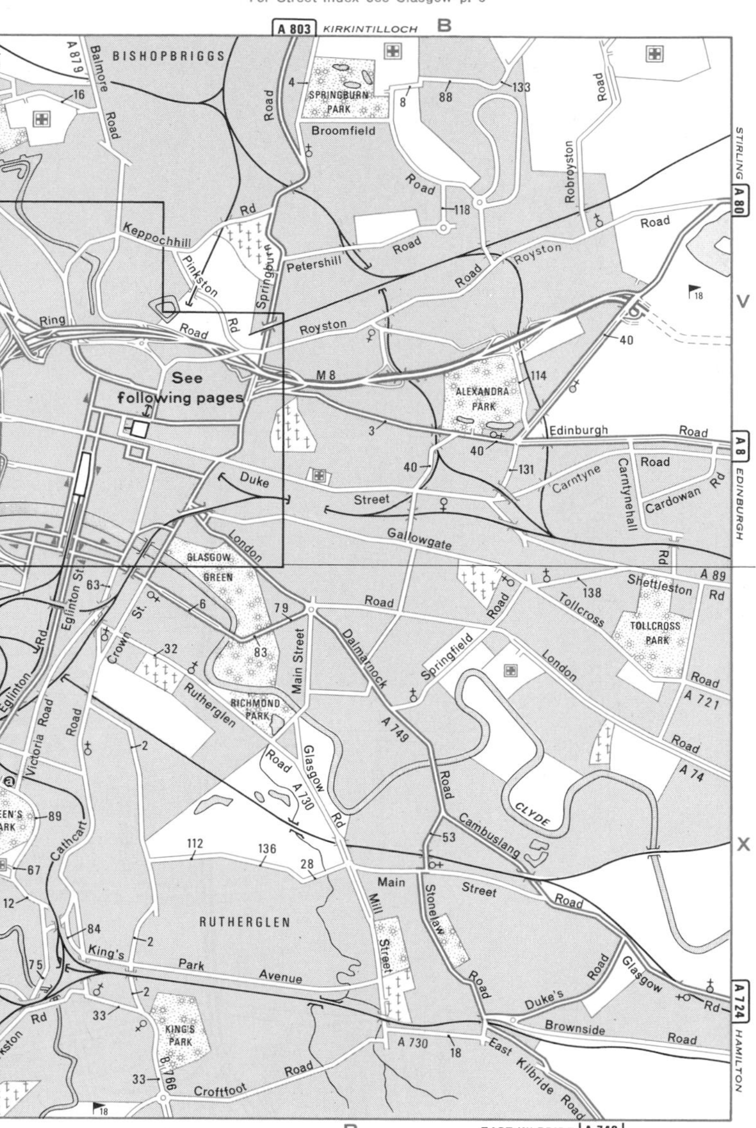

C

Y

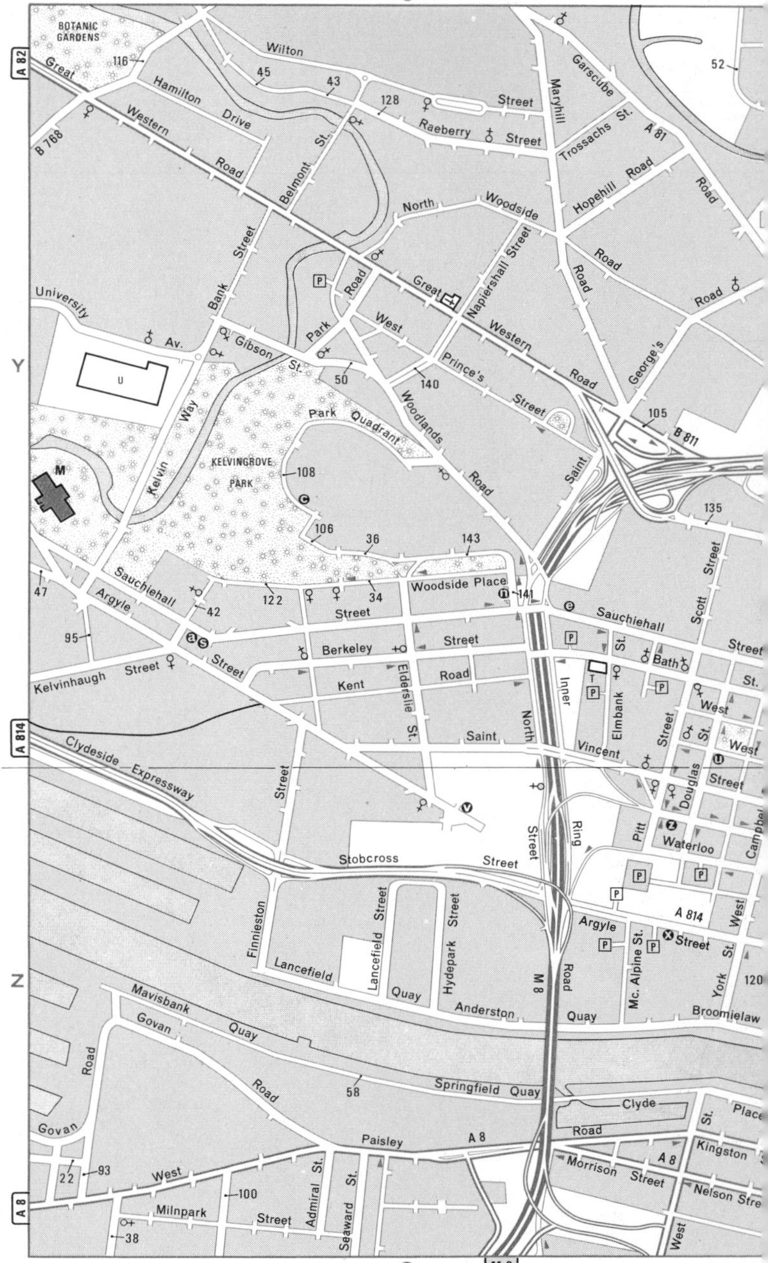

Z

BOTANIC GARDENS
Great Western Road
Hamilton Drive
Wilton
Belmont St.
Raeberry Street
Maryhill
Garscube
Trossachs St.
Hopehill Road
North Woodside Road
Napiershall Street
University Av.
Bank Street
Park Road
Gibson St.
West Prince's Street
Woodlands Road
Saint George's Road
KELVINGROVE PARK
Kelvin Way
Park Quadrant
Sauchiehall Street
Argyle Street
Woodside Place
Berkeley Street
Kent Road
Elderslie St.
Kelvinhaugh Street
Saint Vincent Street
North Street
Inner Ring Road
Elmbank St.
Bath St.
Scott Street
West Street
Douglas St.
Pitt St.
Waterloo Street
Clydeside Expressway
Finnieston Street
Stobcross Street
Lancefield Street
Lancefield Quay
Hydepark Street
Anderston Quay
Mc. Alpine St.
York St.
Broomielaw
Mavisbank Quay
Govan Road
Springfield Quay
Clyde Place
Paisley Road West
Kingston St.
Morrison Street
Nelson Street
Milnpark Street
Admiral St.
Seaward St.
A 82
A 81
A 814
A 8
B 768
B 811
M 8

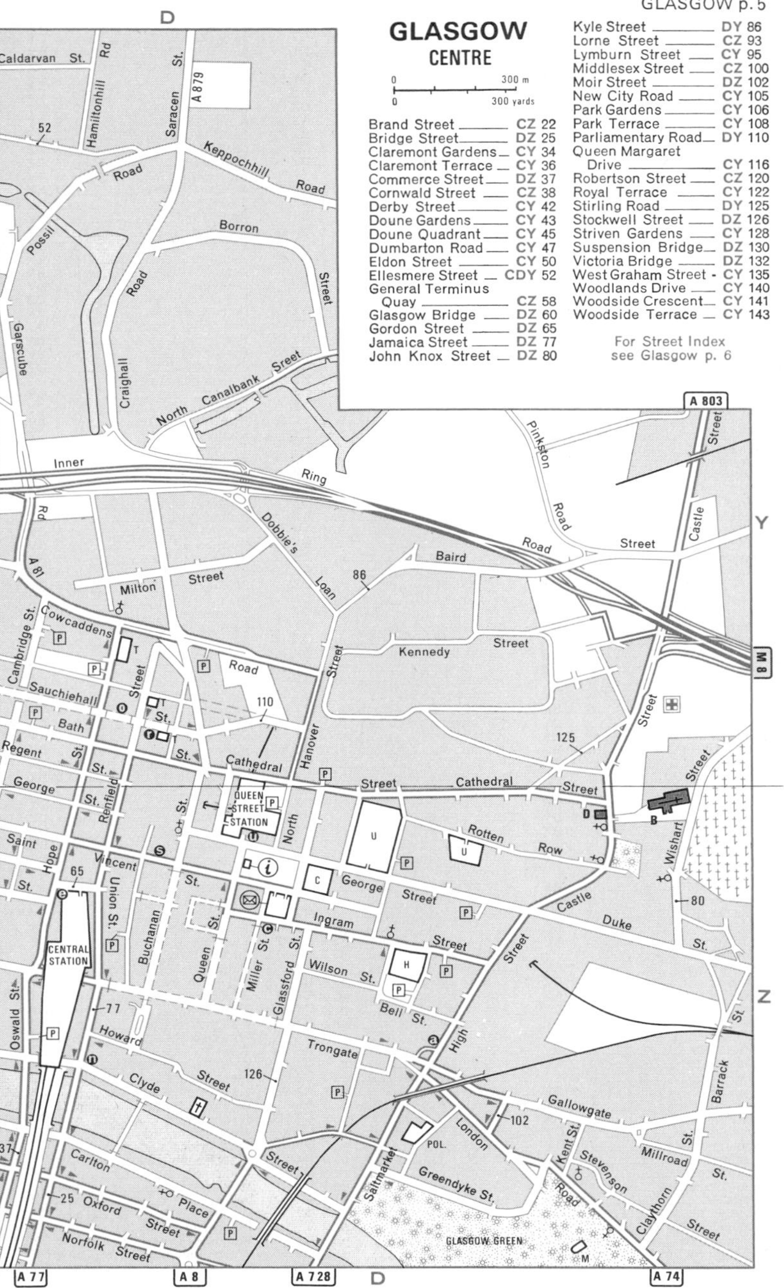
GLASGOW
CENTRE
0 300 m
0 300 yards
Brand Street CZ 22
Bridge Street DZ 25
Claremont Gardens CY 34
Claremont Terrace CY 36
Commerce Street DZ 37
Cornwald Street CZ 38
Derby Street CY 42
Doune Gardens CY 43
Doune Quadrant CY 45
Dumbarton Road CY 47
Eldon Street CY 50
Ellesmere Street CDY 52
General Terminus Quay CZ 58
Glasgow Bridge DZ 60
Gordon Street DZ 65
Jamaica Street DZ 77
John Knox Street DZ 80
Kyle Street DY 86
Lorne Street CZ 93
Lymburn Street CY 95
Middlesex Street CZ 100
Moir Street DZ 102
New City Road CY 105
Park Gardens CY 106
Park Terrace CY 108
Parliamentary Road DY 110
Queen Margaret Drive CY 116
Robertson Street CZ 120
Royal Terrace CY 122
Stirling Road DY 125
Stockwell Street DZ 126
Striven Gardens CY 128
Suspension Bridge DZ 130
Victoria Bridge DZ 132
West Graham Street CY 135
Woodlands Drive CY 140
Woodside Crescent CY 141
Woodside Terrace CY 143
For Street Index see Glasgow p. 6
D
Y
Z
D
A 879
A 803
M 8
A 81
A 77
A 8
A 728
A 74
Caldarvan St.
Hamiltonhill Rd
Saracen St.
Keppochhill Road
Possil Road
Borron Street
Garscube Rd
Craighall Road
North Canalbank Street
Inner Ring Road
Pinkston Road
Castle Street
Dobbie's Loan
Baird Street
Milton Street
Cowcaddens Road
Cambridge St.
Kennedy Street
Hanover Street
Sauchiehall St.
Bath St.
Regent St.
George St.
Renfield Street
West Nile St.
Cathedral Street
QUEEN STREET STATION
North
Rotten Row
Wishart Street
Saint Vincent St.
Hope St.
Union St.
Buchanan St.
Queen St.
Miller St.
Glassford St.
George Street
Ingram Street
Castle Street
Duke St.
Wilson St.
Bell St.
High Street
CENTRAL STATION
Oswald St.
Howard Street
Trongate
Clyde Street
Gallowgate
Barrack St.
London Road
Kent St.
Stevenson St.
Millroad St.
Claythorn Street
Saltmarket
Greendyke St.
GLASGOW GREEN
Carlton Place
Oxford Street
Norfolk Street
POL.
52
86
110
125
65
77
126
102
37
25
80

STREET INDEX TO GLASGOW TOWN PLAN

Royal (Osprey), 106 Sauchiehall St., G2 3DE, ☎ 332 3416 – DY o
46 rm.

Charing Cross (Stakis), 528 Sauchiehall St., G2 3LW, ☎ 332 7401 – wc CY e
10 rm.

Wickets, 52-54 Fortrose St., G11 5LP ☎ 334 9851 – wc AV r
M a la carte 2.55/4.50 **s.** 1.50 – **8 rm** 9.00/14.00 **s.** – P 14.00/18.00 **s.**

Newlands (S & N), 290 Kilmarnock Rd, G43 2XS, ☎ 632 9171 – wc AX n
M a la carte 2.50/5.00 **st.** 1.20 – **17 rm** 8.65/16.00 **st.**

Blythswood, 320 Argyle St., G2 8LZ, ☎ 221 4133 – CZ s
M a la carte 1.80/3.10 **st.** 1.20 – **51 rm** 7.00/12.50 **st.**

Ewington, 132 Queen's Drive, G42 8QW, ☎ 423 1152 – wc wc BX a
M 3.50/4.50 **t.** – **47 rm** 6.50/14.00.

Linwood House, 356 Albert Drive, Pollockshields, G41 5PJ, ☎ 427 1642, – AX r
16 rm 5.50/11.00 **st.**

Apsley, 903 Sauchiehall St., G3 7TD, ☎ 334 3510 CY s
17 rm 5.00/10.00 **s.**

Cavendish, 1 Devonshire Gdns, Great Western Rd, G12 0UX, ☎ 339 2001 AV a
15 rm.

XXXX **Malmaison** (B.T.H.), Hope St., G1 3SF, ☎ 221 9680, Telex 777771, French rest. DZ e
closed Saturday lunch, Sunday, August and Bank Holidays – **M** a la carte 6.50/10.30.

XXX **Fountain,** 2 Woodside Crescent, Charing Cross, G3 7UL, ☎ 332 6396 CY n
closed Saturday lunch, Sunday, Christmas Day, 1-2 January and Bank Holidays – **M** a la carte 5.50/8.85 **st.** 1.60.

XXX **Ambassador,** 19-20 Blythswood Sq., G2 4AS, ☎ 221 3530, Dancing CY u
closed Sunday and Bank Holidays – **M** a la carte 4.60/8.80 **t.** 1.85.

XX **Colonial,** 25 High St., G1 1LX, ☎ 552 1923 DZ a
closed Sunday and Bank Holidays – **M** 4.00/8.00 **t.** 1.85.

X **Ferrari,** 39 Sauchiehall St., G2 3AT, ☎ 332 8414, Italian rest. DY r
closed Saturday lunch and Sunday – **M** a la carte 3.70/5.75 1.35.

X **Danish Food Centre** (Copenhagen Room), 56-60 St. Vincent St., G2 5TS, ☎ 221 0518, Smorrebrod DZ s
closed Sunday and Bank Holidays – **M** approx. 4.50 **st.**

X The Buttery, 654 Argyle St., G3 8UF, ☎ 221 8188. CZ v

at Stepps **NE : 5 m. by M 8 and A 80** – BV – ✉ **041 Glasgow :**

Garfield (Open House), Cumbernauld Rd, G33 6HW, ☎ 779 2111 – wc .
17 rm.

at Busby **S : 5 ½ m. on A 726 by A 727** – AX – ✉ **041 Glasgow :**

Busby, 1 Field Rd, Clarkston, G76 8RX, ☎ 644 2661 – wc
M (bar lunch) a la carte 3.00/5.45 1.25 – **14 rm** 7.00/12.00 **s.**

MICHELIN Branch, Southcroft Rd, Rutherglen, Industrial Estate, G73 1U2, ☎ 647 0261.

AUSTIN-MORRIS-MG-WOLSELEY 76 James St. ☎ 554 7571
AUSTIN-MORRIS-MG-WOLSELEY, ROLLS ROYCE 65 Springbel Av. ☎ 423 3011
AUSTIN-MG-WOLSELEY 338 Maryhill Rd ☎ 332 6941
AUSTIN-MG-WOLSELEY 60 Tantallon Rd ☎ 632 2331
AUSTIN-DAIMLER-JAGUAR-MG-MORRIS-ROVER-TRIUMPH-WOLSELEY 55 Hamilton Rd ☎ 778 8383
AUSTIN-MG-WOLSELEY 215 Queensborough Gardens ☎ 357 1234
AUSTIN-MG-WOLSELEY 470 Royston Rd ☎ 552 4713
AUSTIN-MG-WOLSELEY 32 Finnieston St. ☎ 248 6101
CHRYSLER 400/420 Gallowgate ☎ 554 3868
CHRYSLER-SIMCA 268 Ayr Rd ☎ 639 2271
CHRYSLER-SIMCA 100 Minerva St. ☎ 248 2345
CITROEN 113 St. George Rd ☎ 332 2213
DAF, VOLVO 136 Merrylee Rd ☎ 633 0500
DAIMLER-JAGUAR-ROVER-TRIUMPH 47 Kirklee Rd ☎ 334 2231
DATSUN 77/81 Dumbarton Rd ☎ 334 1241
FIAT 691 Clarkson Rd ☎ 633 1020
FORD 1009 Gallowgate ☎ 554 4321
FORD 1040 Maryhill Rd ☎ 946 2177
FORD 34 Fenwick Rd ☎ 637 7161
FORD 370 Pollokshaws Rd ☎ 423 6644
MORRIS-MG-WOLSELEY St. Andrews Garage, 198 Maxwell Rd ☎ 429 4298
MORRIS-MG-WOLSELEY 459 Crow Rd ☎ 954 5041
OPEL 10 Holmbank Av. ☎ 649 9321
OPEL, VAUXHALL 712 Edinburgh Rd ☎ 774 2791
PEUGEOT 28 Old Mearns Rd, Clarkston ☎ 638 6505
RENAULT 117 Berkeley St. ☎ 248 7701
RENAULT 1900 Gt Western Rd ☎ 959 1288
ROVER-TRIUMPH 21/37 Nithsdale St. ☎ 423 5544
SAAB 162 Crow Rd ☎ 334 4661
SAAB 265 Clarkston Rd ☎ 637 2206
TOYOTA 1158 Cathcart Rd ☎ 632 9511
VAUXHALL 44/46 New City Rd ☎ 332 2940
VAUXHALL 640 Pollokshaws Rd ☎ 423 3074
VOLVO 2413/2493 London Rd ☎ 778 8501
VW, AUDI-NSU 512 Kilmarnock Rd ☎ 637 2241

Questa guida non è un repertorio di tutti gli alberghi e ristoranti,
nè comprende tutti i buoni alberghi e ristoranti di Gran Bretagna ed Irlanda.

Nell'intento di tornare utili a tutti i turisti,
siamo indotti ad indicare esercizi
di tutte le classi ed a citarne soltanto un certo numero di ognuna.

GLENBORRODALE Argyll. (Strathclyde) – 097 24.
Edinburgh 153 – Inverness 104 – Oban 70.

Glenborrodale Castle (T.H.F.), PH36 4JP, Salen 266, Loch Sunart and gardens, « Victorian castle in extensive gardens », park – wc
M 4.00/6.00 **st.** 1.50 – **27 rm** 12.50/26.00 **st.**

Clan Morrison, PH36 4JP, Acharacle 232, park – wc
March-October – **M** (dinner only) 7.00/10.00 **st.** 1.50 – **6 rm** 18.00/22.00 **st.**

GLENCAPLE Dumfries. (Dumfries and Galloway) – see Dumfries.

GLENCARSE Perth. (Tayside) – pop. 43 – Perth – 073 886.
Edinburgh 48 – Dundee 16 – Perth 6.

Newton House with rm, PH2 7LX, off A 85 250, –
April-November – **M** *(closed Monday)* (dinner only) 3.75 **st.** 1.50 – **7 rm** 7.75/14.85 **st.**

GLENCOE Argyll. (Highland) 986 ⑩ – pop. 490 – 085 56 Kingshouse.
Envir.: SE: Glen Coe** (glen and waterfall).
Claymore Filling Station 085 52 (Ballachulish) 296 (May-September).
Edinburgh 115 – Glasgow 86 – Oban 40.

King's House, PA39 4HY, SE: 12 m. off A 82 259 – wc
March-October – **M** (bar lunch) approx. 4.50 **st.** 1.10 – **22 rm** 9.00/20.00 **st.**

GLENFINNAN Inverness. (Highland) 986 ⑩ – pop. 70 – Fort William – 039 783 Kinlocheil.
See: Glenfinnan Monument *.
250 (mid April-mid October).
Edinburgh 149 – Inverness 80 – Kyle of Lochalsh 89 – Oban 66.

Glenfinnan House, PH37 4LT, 235, Loch Shiel and Ben Nevis, park –
Easter-mid October – **M** (bar lunch) 4.00/4.50 – **19 rm** 7.00/14.00.

GLENROTHES Fife. (Fife) 986 ⑪ – pop. 27,103 – 0592.
Golf Course Rd 758686.
Town Centre, 754954.
Edinburgh 31 – Dundee 23 – Stirling 35.

Balgeddie House, Leslie Rd, KY6 3ET, W: 2 m. off A 911 742511, « Country house style », – wc
closed 1-2 January – **M** a la carte 3.30/6.70 1.40 – **11 rm** 8.00/20.00.

Rothes Arms (Open House), South Parks Rd, KY6 1PB, 753701 – wc
16 rm.

Golden Acorn (Osprey), 1 North St., KY7 5NA, 752292 – wc
24 rm.

AUSTIN-MORRIS-MG-WOLSELEY North St. 2262

GOLSPIE Sutherland. (Highland) 986 ③ – pop. 1,700 – 040 83.
See: Dunrobin Castle gardens* *AC*, NE : 1 ½ m.
266.
Edinburgh 229 – Inverness 70 – Wick 53.

Sutherlands Arms, Old Bank Rd, KW10 6RS, 216, –
18 rm.

AUSTIN-MG-WOLSELEY 205

GOUROCK Renfrew. (Strathclyde) 986 ⑭ – pop. 10,922 – 0475.
Cowal View 31001, SW: 3 m.
to Dunoon (Caledonian MacBrayne) frequent services every day (20 mn) – to Dunoon: Hunters Quay (Western Ferries) frequent services every day (20 mn).
to Kilcreggan (Caledonian MacBrayne) Monday/Saturday 6-7 daily (10 mn).
Municipal Buildings, PA19 1QY, 31126.
Edinburgh 69 – Ayr 43 – Glasgow 26.

Gantock (Stakis), Cloch Rd, PA19 1AR, SW: 2 m. on A 78 34671, Firth of Clyde – wc
M 3.00/3.50 1.65 – **60 rm** 10.75/17.50.

Claremont, 34 Victoria Rd, PA19 1DF, 31687,
6 rm 4.75/9.50 **s.**

CITROEN Manor Crescent 32356

GRANGE Fife. (Fife) – see St. Andrews.

GRANGEMOUTH Stirling. (Central) 986 ⑮ – pop. 24,569 – 032 44.
0324 (Polmont) 711500.
Edinburgh 24 – Dunfermline 17 – **Glasgow 25.**

Lea Park, 130 Bo'ness Rd, F43 9BX, ℗ 6733 – TV ⌂wc ☎ **P.**
M approx. 3.00 **s.** 1.20 – **35 rm** 11.00/20.00 **st.**

GRANTOWN-ON-SPEY Moray. (Highland) 986 ⑦ – pop. 1,600 – 0479.
℗ 79, East town boundary.
The Square ℗ 2773 (May-September).
Edinburgh 142 – **Inverness 35** – Perth 100.

Grant Arms, 25-26 The Square, PH26 3HF, ℗ 2526, – ⌂wc ⌂wc ☎ **P**
M 5.00/6.00 **s.** 1.50 – **55 rm** 13.50/27.00 **s.**

Holmhill, Woodside Av., PH26 3JR, ℗ 2645, – **P**
10 rm 6.00/12.00 **st.**

AUSTIN-MORRIS-MG-WOLSELEY 69 High St. ℗ 229

GREAT CUMBRAE ISLAND Bute. (Strathclyde) – pop. 56 – 047 553 Millport.
at Millport ℗ 311.
from Millport Slip to Largs (Caledonian MacBrayne) frequent services every day (10 mn).
from Millport (Old Pier) to Largs (Caledonian MacBrayne) frequent services every day summer only (30 mn).
Garrison House at Millport ℗ 356.

GREENOCK Renfrew. (Strathclyde) 986 ⑭ – pop. 69,502 – 0475.
Beith Rd ℗ 24694.
Municipal Buildings, PA15 1NB, ℗ 24400.
Edinburgh 66 – Ayr 46 – **Glasgow 23** – **Oban 97.**

Tontine (Interchange), 6 Ardgowan Sq., PA16 8NG, ℗ 23316, – TV ⌂wc ☎ **P.**
M 4.50/5.00 **st.** 1.25 – **44 rm** 11.00/19.50 **st.**

AUSTIN-MORRIS-MG-WOLSELEY 1 Ker St. ℗ 21313
CHRYSLER-SIMCA 1 Campbell St. ℗ 24355
FIAT 152 Inverkip Rd ℗ 29123
DATSUN 26/30 Brougham St. ℗ 23254
ROVER-TRIUMPH 29 Forsyth St. ℗ 20202
VAUXHALL Pottery St. ℗ 42511
VOLVO 46 Campbell St. ℗ 21610

GRUINARD BAY *** Ross and Cromarty (Highland).

GULLANE E. Lothian (Lothian) 986 ⑮ – pop. 2,000 – 0620.
Edinburgh 19 – North Berwick 5.

Greywalls, Duncur Rd, EH31 2EG, ℗ 842144, ≤ gardens and golf course, « Edwardian country house with fine walled gardens », – ⌂wc ☎ **P**
mid April-mid October – **M** 6.50/8.50 **t.** 1.60 – **25 rm** 15.00/32.35 **t.**

Bissets (Osprey), Main St., EH31 2AA, ℗ 842230, – ☎ **P**
24 rm.

HADDINGTON E. Lothian (Lothian) 986 ⑮ – pop. 6,502 – 062 082.
Amisfield Park ℗ 3627.
Edinburgh 17 – Hawick 53 – **Newcastle-upon-Tyne 103.**

George, 91 High St., EH41 3ET, ℗ 3372 – ⌂wc ☎ **P**
M 2.90/3.80 1.00 – **11 rm** 5.00/12.00.

AUSTIN-MORRIS-MG-ROVER-TRIUMPH-WOLSELEY 6 High St. ℗ 3661
CHRYSLER Knox Pl. ℗ 3277

HALBEATH Fife. (Fife) – pop. 800 – ✉ 0383 Dunfermline.
Edinburg 17 – Dunfermline 2 – Kirkcaldy 11.

Armando's Hide-Away, Kingseat Rd, KY12 0UB, N: ½ m. off A 907 ℗ 25474 – **P**
closed Sunday – **M** 2.75/5.05 1.50.

HARDGATE Dunbarton. (Strathclyde) – pop. 7.963 – ✉ Clydebank – 0389 Duntocher.
Edinburgh 51 – Dumbarton 7 – **Glasgow 8.**

Cameron House, Glasgow Rd, G81 5PJ, ℗ 73535 – TV ⌂wc ⌂wc ☎ **P.**
M 3.50/5.00 **st.** – **16 rm** 10.50/12.50 **st.**

Dieser Führer ist kein vollständiges Hotel- und Restaurantverzeichnis.
Um den Ansprüchen aller Touristen gerecht zu werden, haben wir uns auf eine Auswahl in jeder Kategorie beschränkt.

HARRIS (Isle of) Inverness. (Outer Hebrides) (Western Isles) 986 ② – pop. 2,879.
by Caledonian MacBrayne: from Kyles Scalpay to the Isle of Scalpay: Monday/Saturd 5-8 daily (10 mn) – from Tarbert to Isle of Skye (Uig) direct Monday/Saturday 3-6 week (2 h) – from Tarbert to North Uist (Lochmaddy) 1-2 weekly (2 h.).

Tarbert – ✉ ☎ 0859 Harris.

i Information Centre ☎ 2011 (May-September).

See : Site★. **Envir. :** Loch Seaforth★ NE: 6 m. **Exc. :** Golden Road★ from Tarbert to Rode Rodel (site★) S: 21 ½ m.

Harris, PA85 3DL, ☎ 2154, ⛰, 🌳 – 🛁wc Ⓟ
M 3.30/3.60 **st.** – ☕ 1.70 – **22 rm** 5.30/10.60 **st.**

HAWICK Roxburgh. (Borders) 986 ⑮ – pop. 16,286 – ☎ 0450.
Envir. : Jedburgh Abbey★★ *AC*, NE : 10 ½ m. – Hermitage (castle★ : stronghold 14C) A S: 15 m.

⛳18 Vertish Hill ☎ 2293, S: 1 ½ m.

i Volunter Park ☎ 2547 (mid May - mid October).

Edinburgh 50 – Ayr 123 – Carlisle 43 – Dumfries 63 – Motherwell 74 – **Newcastle-upon-Tyne 62.**

Mansfield Park, Weensland Rd, TD9 9EL, NE: 1 m. on A 698, ☎ 3988, 🌳, park – 🛁wc 🚿wc ☎ Ⓟ
M (bar lunch in winter) approx. 4.95 🍷 1.95 – ☕ 1.50 – **11 rm** 9.50/16.50.

Crown (Osprey), 22 High St., TD9 9EH, ☎ 3344 – Ⓟ. 🏔
36 rm.

Kirklands 🐦 with rm, West Stewart Pl., TD9 8BH, N : off A 7 ☎ 2263 – TV 🛁wc ☎
closed January – **M** a la carte 3.30/4.55 **t.** – **6 rm** ☕ 7.00/13.00 **t.** – P 18.00/21.00

AUSTIN-MG-WOLSELEY Earl St. ☎ 3316
CHRYSLER-SIMCA 61 High St. ☎ 2287
DAIMLER-JAGUAR, ROVER-TRIUMPH Croft Rd ☎ 3881
MORRIS-MG-WOLSELEY Commercial Rd ☎ 2285
VAUXHALL, MAZDA Bridge St. ☎ 2179
VW, AUDI-NSU Weensland Rd ☎ 3211

HELENSBURGH Dunbarton. (Strathclyde) 986 ⑭ – pop. 12,870 – ☎ 0436.
Envir. : Loch Lomond★★ NE: 7 ½ m.

i Pier Head Car Park, ☎ 2642 (June-September).

Edinburgh 65 – Glasgow 22.

Queen's, 114 East Clyde St., G84 7AH, ☎ 3404, ≤, 🌳 – 🛁wc Ⓟ
24 rm.

CHRYSLER, TOYOTA 5/7 John St. ☎ 2779
JAGUAR-ROVER-TRIUMPH 15/27 East Clyde St. ☎ 2233
MORRIS-MG-WOLSELEY 135 East Clyde St. ☎ 3344
RENAULT 103 East Clyde St. ☎ 6021

HILLSWICK Shetland (Shetland Islands) 986 ⑯ – see Shetland Islands (Mainland).

HOLLYBUSH Ayr. (Strathclyde) – see Ayr.

HOY (Isle of) Orkney (Orkney Islands) 986 ⑯ – see Orkney Islands.

HUNTER'S QUAY Argyll. (Strathclyde) – see Dunoon.

INCHNADAMPH Sutherland. (Highland) 986 ② – ✉ Lairg – ☎ 057 12 Assynt.
See : ≤★.

Edinburgh 244 – Inverness 85.

Inchnadamph 🐦, IV27 4HN, ☎ 202, ≤ Loch Assynt and mountains, ⛰ – 🛁wc Ⓟ
March-October – **M** approx. 3.70 **t.** 🍷 1.35 – **30 rm** ☕ 7.50/17.25 **t.**

INCHTURE Perth. (Tayside) – ☎ 082 886.
Edinburgh 55 – Dundee 9 – Perth 13.

Maison Bonne Chère (Inchture Hotel), PH14 9RN, ☎ 203 – Ⓟ.

CHRYSLER-SIMCA ☎ 401

INNERLEITHEN Peebles. (Borders) 986 ⑮ – pop. 2,218 – ☎ 089 683 – ⛳9.
Edinburgh 30 – Hawick 26 – Peebles 65.

Tighnuilt, Tweeddale, EH44 6RD, NW: ¾ m. on A 72 ☎ 491, 🌳 – Ⓟ
6 rm ☕ 5.00/12.00 **st.**

INVERGARRY Inverness. (Highland) 986 ⑥ – ☎ 080 93.
Envir. : Loch Garry (☼★★ from the A 87) – SW: Loch Lochy★★.

Edinburgh 148 – Inverness 41 – Kyle of Lochalsh 51 – **Oban 73.**

Invergarry, PH35 4HJ, ☎ 206, ≤, ⛰, 🌳 – Ⓟ
Easter-25 October – **M** 3.55/5.50 – **14 rm** ☕ 8.00/16.00 – P 16.50.

INVERMORISTON Inverness. (Highland) 986 ⑥⑦ – pop. 280 – ☎ 0320 Glenmoriston.
Envir. : Loch Ness★★ – Loch Knockie ⋞★★ from Glendoebeg (A 862) E : 16 m.
Edinburgh 162 – Inverness 27 – Kyle of Lochalsh 55.

Glenmoriston Arms, IV3 6YB, ☎ 206, – wc – *season* – **6 rm.**

INVERNESS Inverness. (Highland) 986 ⑦ – pop. 34,839 – ☎ 0463.
See : Tomnahurich cemetery★ – ⋞★ from the Castle Terrace. **Envir.** : SW : Loch Ness★★ by A 82 – Culloden Battlefield, site of the defeat (1746) of Bonnie Prince Charlie, E: 5 m. by Culcabock Rd.
18 ☎ 33422, S : 1 m. by Culcabock Rd.
Dalcross Airport: ☎ 32471, NE: 8 m. by A 96 – ☎ 32651.
i 23 Church St. ☎ 34353, Telex 75114 – Culloden Battlefield, ☎ Culloden Moor 607 (April-mid October).
Edinburgh 159 – Aberdeen 106 – Dundee 130.

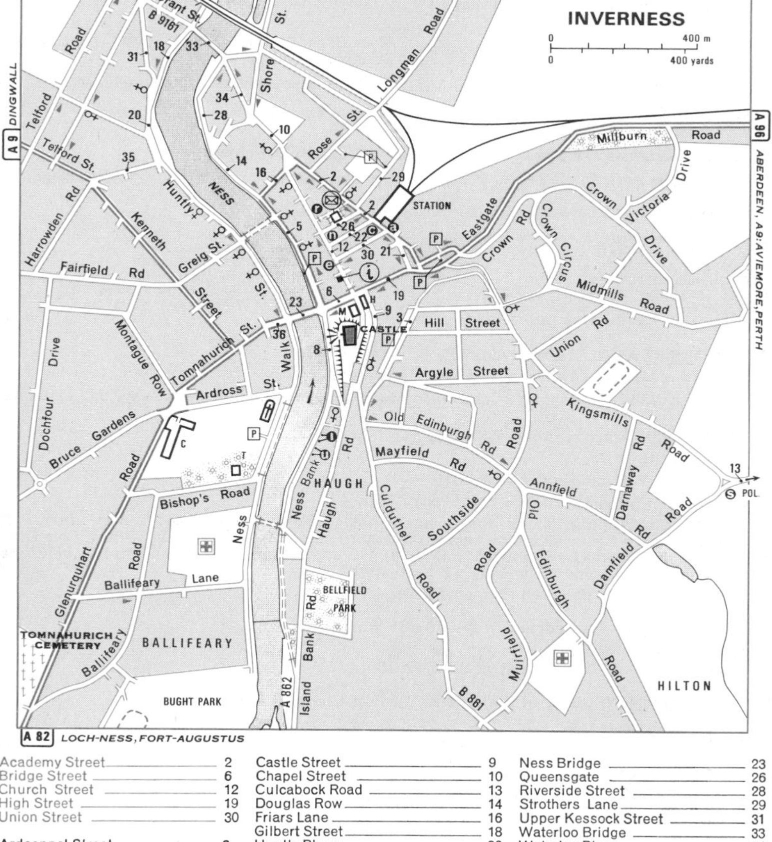

Academy Street	2	Castle Street	9	Ness Bridge	23
Bridge Street	6	Chapel Street	10	Queensgate	26
Church Street	12	Culcabock Road	13	Riverside Street	28
High Street	19	Douglas Row	14	Strothers Lane	29
Union Street	30	Friars Lane	16	Upper Kessock Street	31
		Gilbert Street	18	Waterloo Bridge	33
Ardconnel Street	3	Huntly Place	20	Waterloo Place	34
Bank Street	5	Inglis Street	21	Well Street	35
Castle Road	8	Market Arcade	22	Young Street	36

Station (B.T.H.), 18-22 Academy St., IV1 1LG, ☎ 31926, Telex 75275 – TV. *closed 24 to 27 December* – **M** 5.50/6.50 **st.** 1.05 – **63 rm** 21.00/37.50 **st.** **a**

Inverness Mercury Motor Inn, Nairn Rd, IV2 3TR, E: by A 96, junction A 9 and A 96 ☎ 39666, Telex 75377 – TV wc ☎ **P**.
M a la carte approx. 3.80 **st.** 1.35 – 1.50 – **84 rm** 14.00/21.00 **st.**

Queensgate, Queensgate, IV1 1HA, ☎ 37211, Telex 75235 – TV wc ☎ **n**
March-November – **M** approx. 4.85 **t.** 1.75 – **54 rm** 14.05/23.75 **t.**

Caledonian, Church St., IV1 1DX, ☎ 35181, Telex 76357 – lift TV bath wc ☎ P. e
M approx. 3.50 ♁ 1.75 – **120 rm** 12.00/24.00.

Royal (T.H.F.), Academy St., IV1 1JR, ☎ 30665 – lift TV bath wc ☎ c
48 rm 8.50/17.00 **st.**

Kingsmills, Damfield Rd, IV2 3LP, ☎ 37166, ≤, – TV bath wc P s
M (bar lunch) 4.50/5.25 **st.** ♁ 1.50 – **37 rm** 14.50/26.50 **st.**

Glen Mhor, 9-12 Ness Bank, IV2 4SG, ☎ 34308 – bath wc ☎ P i
closed 1 and 2 January – **M** (bar lunch) approx. 5.50 **t.** ♁ 1.25 – 2.25 – **26 rm** 8.25/25.00 **t.**

Cumming's, 70 Church St., IV1 1EW, ☎ 32531 – lift bath wc ☎ P r
M 3.25/3.75 **st.** ♁ 1.50 – **38 rm** 9.00/20.00 **st.**

Felstead, 18 Ness Bank, IV2 4SF, ☎ 31634 – P u
May-September – **7 rm** 5.00/10.00 **st.**

Larchfield and Struan House, 14-15 Ness Bank, IV2 4SF, ☎ 33874, ≤ i
15 rm 5.50/10.00 **s.**

Glenmoriston (La Fayette) with rm, 20 Ness Bank, IV2 4SF, ☎ 37418, – shower wc P u
M (dinner only) 4.50/5.00 **s.** ♁ 1.30 – **28 rm** 9.50/18.50.

at Culloden Moor **E: 3 m. off A 96 – ✉ Inverness – ☎ 046 372 Culloden Moor:**

Culloden House ⛰, IV1 2NZ, ☎ 461, ≤, , park – TV P
M 5.50/8.00 ♁ 2.00 – **21 rm** 25.00/40.00.

at Dunain Park **SW: 2 ½ m. on A 82 – ✉ ☎ 0463 Inverness:**

Dunain Park ⛰, IV3 6JN, ☎ 30512, ≤, « Country house with large gardens », park – bath wc P
March-November – **M** 6.50 ♁ 1.30 – **6 rm** 19.00/29.00.

ALFA-ROMEO VAUXHALL Academy St. ☎ 34311
AUSTIN-MORRIS-MG, ROLLS ROYCE 36 Academy St. ☎ 34422
BMW Harbour Rd ☎ 36566
CHRYSLER-SIMCA Harbour Rd ☎ 30777
DAF Anderson St. ☎ 35752
DAIMLER-JAGUAR Strothers Lane ☎ 33701
FIAT 31/48 Tomnahurich St. ☎ 35777
FORD Harbour Rd ☎ 35843
RENAULT 16 Telford St. ☎ 34367
ROVER-TRIUMPH, PEUGEOT Harbour Rd ☎ 31536
VOLVO, DATSUN Harbour Rd ☎ 30885
VW, AUDI-NSU 57 King St. ☎ 31313

IONA (Isle of) Argyll. (Strathclyde) 986 ⑩ – ☎ 068 17.

See: Site★ – MacLean's Cross★ – St. John's Cross★.

⛴ to Isle of Mull: Fionnphort (Caledonian MacBrayne) frequent services every day (10 mn).

ISLAY (Isle of) Argyll. (Strathclyde) 986 ⑭ – pop. 3,837.

See: Machir Bay★.

⛳18 Port Ellen, ☎ 0496 (Port Ellen) 2310.

✈ Port Ellen Airport: ☎ 0496 (Port Ellen) 2361.

⛴ from Port Askaig to Isle of Jura: Feolin (Western Ferries) 3-12 daily (5 mn) – from Port Askaig to Kintyre Peninsula: Kennacraig (Western Ferries) 1-2 daily (3 h) – from Port Ellen to West Loch Tarbert (Caledonian MacBrayne) 1-3 daily (2 h to 2 h 30 mn), to Isle of Gigha (Caledonian MacBrayne) 3 weekly (1 h 15 mn).

i at Bowmore ☎ 049 681 (Bowmore) 254 (April-September).

Bridgend – ✉ Bridgend – ☎ 049 681 Bowmore.

Bridgend, PA44 7PJ, ☎ 212, – P
M approx. 4.50 **s.** – **9 rm** 9.00/12.00.

Kildalton NE: 5 m. of Port Ellen – ✉ Port Ellen – ☎ 049 683 Kildalton.

Dower House ⛰, PA42 7EF, ☎ 225, ≤, – bath wc P
M 4.00/5.00 ♁ 1.50 – **7 rm** 6.20/11.80 – P 12.85.

Port Askaig – ✉ ☎ 049 684 Port Askaig.

Port Askaig, PA46 7RD, ☎ 245 – bath wc P
M approx. 3.00 **st.** ♁ 1.00 – **9 rm** 8.75/15.50 **st.** – P 13.75 **st.**

JOHN O'GROATS Caithness. (Highland) 986 ③ and ⑳ – pop. 100 – ☎ 095 581.

See: ≤★ of Orkney. **Envir.:** Dunnet Head ★★★ (sea bird's nests) NW: 16 m. – Dunnet Bay★★ W: 11 m. – Duncansby Head (cliffs: birds' nests★) E: 2 ½ m. – Skirza Head (cliffs: birds' nests★) S: 5 m.

Edinburgh 299 – Wick 17.

John O'Groats House ⛰, KW1 4YR, ☎ 203, ≤ – P
season – **15 rm.**

JOHNSTONEBRIDGE Dumfries. (Dumfries and Galloway) – see Lockerbie.

JURA (Isle of) Argyll. (Strathclyde) 986 ⑩⑭ – pop. 368.
from Feolin to Isle of Islay: Port Askaig (Western Ferries) 3-12 daily (5 mn).

Craighouse – ✉ ☎ 049 682 Jura.

Jura, PA60 7XU, ☎ 243, ≤ Small Isles Bay, – wc P
18 rm.

KELSO Roxburgh. (Borders) 986 ⑮ – pop. 4,852 – ☎ 057 32.
Envir.: Jedburgh Abbey** *AC*, SW: **11** m.
9 ☎ 2113.
Edinburgh 44 – Hawick 22 – **Newcastle-upon-Tyne 67.**

Ednam House, Bridge St., TD5 7HT, ☎ 2168, ≤, – wc ☎ P. – **32 rm.**

Woodside, Edenside Rd, TD5 7SJ, ☎ 2152, ≤, , park – TV wc wc ☎ P
M approx. 5.50 **st.** 2.20 – **10 rm** 15.00/20.00 **st.** – P 18.00/20.00 **st.**

AUSTIN-MG-WOLSELEY Crawford St. ☎ 2720
CHRYSLER-SIMCA 47/51 Horsemarket ☎ 2488
MORRIS-MG-WOLSELEY Bridge St. ☎ 2345

KENMORE Perth. (Tayside) – pop. 500 – ✉ Aberfeldy – ☎ 088 73.
See: Loch Tay*.
18 ☎ 263.
Edinburgh 80 – Dundee 60 – Oban 71 – Perth 38.

Kenmore, PH15 2NU, ☎ 205, , – wc ☎ P – **38 rm.**

at Fortingall NW: 5 m. off A 827 – ✉ Aberfeldy – ☎ 088 73 Kenmore:

Fortingall, PH15 2NQ, ☎ 367, , – P
29 March-16 October – **M** (bar lunch) 6.35 **st.** – **21 rm** 7.50/18.00 **st.** – P 12.85/17.90 **st.**

KENNACRAIG Argyll. (Stratchyde) – Shipping services: see Kintyre (Peninsula).

KILCHOAN Argyll. (Highland) – pop. 349 – ✉ Acharacle – ☎ 097 23.
Edinburgh 163 – Inverness 114 – Oban 80.

Kilchoan, PH36 4LH, ☎ 200, ≤, « Country house atmosphere », , – TV wc ☎ P
closed Christmas and 1 January – **M** (bar lunch) approx. 5.00 **st.** 1.80 – **9 rm** (dinner included) approx. 23.35 **s.**

Sonachan, PH36 4LN, ☎ 211, ≤ – P
season – **8 rm.**

KILCHRENAN Argyll. (Strathclyde) – pop. 109 – ✉ Taynuilt – ☎ 086 63.
Edinburgh 116 – Glasgow 88 – Oban 19.

Taychreggan, Lochaweside, PA35 1HQ, SE: 1 m. ☎ 211, ≤, « Extensive grounds on banks of Loch Awe », , – wc P
15 March-15 October – **M** 5.00/5.50 2.00 – **22 rm** (dinner included) 16.00/32.00.

KILCREGGAN Dunbarton. (Strathclyde) – ✉ Helensburgh – ☎ 043 684.
to Gourock (Caledonian MacBrayne) Monday/Saturday 8 daily (10 mn).
Edinburgh 80 – Glasgow 37 – Helensburgh 15.

Kilcreggan, Argyll Rd, G84 0JP, ☎ 2243, ≤, – wc wc P
M 3.85/4.50 1.50 – **8 rm** 6.20/12.40 – P 10.00/12.00.

KILDALTON Argyll. (Strathclyde) – see Islay (Isle of).

KILDONAN Bute. (Strathclyde) – see Arran (Isle of).

KILLIN Perth. (Central) 986 ⑪ – pop. 1,265 – ☎ 056 72.
See: Loch Tay*. **Envir.:** N: Glen Lyon*.
9 ☎ 312.
i Main St. ☎ 254 (May-September).
Edinburgh 72 – Dundee 65 – Perth 43 – **Oban 54.**

Bridge of Lochay, FK21 8TS, N: ½ m. on A 827 ☎ 272, – wc P
April-October – **M** approx. 3.50 1.00 – **18 rm** 5.00/12.00.

AUSTIN-MG-WOLSELEY ☎ 319

KILMARNOCK Ayr. (Strathclyde) 986 ⑭ ⑮ – pop. 16,877 – ☎ 0563.
18 Irvine Rd ☎ 21644, W: **1** m.
Edinburgh 64 – Ayr 14 – Dumfries 58 – Glasgow 21.

Howard Park (Swallow), 136 Glasgow Rd, KA3 1UT, N: 2 m. on A 77 ☎ 31211, Group Telex 53168 – TV wc ☎ P. – **50 rm.**

KILMORY Bute. (Strathclyde) – see Arran (Isle of).

KINCLAVEN Perth. (Tayside) – pop. 560 – ✉ Stanley – ☎ 025 083 Meikleour.
Edinburgh 54 – Perth 12.

Ballathie House ⛰, PH1 4QN, ☎ 268, ≤, « Country house in extensive grounds on banks of river Tay », 🎾, 🎣, 🌳, park – 📺 wc ☎ 🅿
closed December-14 January – **M** 5.00/6.00 – **31 rm** 15.00/28.50 **st.** – P 27.00 **st.**

KINCRAIG Inverness. (Highland) – pop. 214 – ✉ Kingussie – ☎ 054 04.
Edinburgh 121 – Inverness 38 – Perth 79.

Ossian, PH21 1NA, off A 9 ☎ 242, ≤, 🌳 – 🅿
closed November-15 December – **M** *(closed Monday)* (dinner only) a la carte 3.60/5.55 – **9 rm** 7.50/15.00 **st.**

Invereshie House ⛰ with rm, PH21 1NA, E: ½ m. off A 9 ☎ 332, 🎣 – 🅿
15 February-30 October – **M** *(closed Monday in winter)* a la carte 3.75/5.85 **s.** 🍷 1.20 – **6 rm** 12.00/24.00 **s.** – P 18.00 **s.**

KINGHOLM QUAY Dumfries. (Dumfries and Galloway) – see Dumfries.

KINGSKETTLE Fife. (Fife) – pop. 1,423 – ☎ 033 73 Ladybank.
Edinburgh 46 – Dundee 18 – Kirkcaldy 10.

Annfield House ⛰, KY7 7TW, ☎ 245, ≤ countryside, « Country house style », 🌳 – wc 🅿
closed last 2 weeks October and first week January – **M** *(closed Monday from November to March, Sunday dinner and 26 December)* a la carte 3.85/6.65 🍷 1.10 – **6 rm** 8.25/16.00.

KINGUSSIE Inverness. (Highland) 986 ⑦ – pop. 1,104 – ☎ 054 02.
18 ☎ 374, ½ m. from town shops off A 9.
i 26 High St. ☎ 297 (May-September).
Edinburgh 115 – Inverness 44 – Perth 73.

Duke of Gordon (Interchange), Newtonmore Rd, PH21 1HE, on A 9 ☎ 302 – 🛗 wc 🅿.
M 3.40/4.05 **st.** 🍷 1.10 – **47 rm** 9.40/20.20 **st.**

KINLOCH RANNOCH Perth. (Tayside) 986 ⑪ – pop. 300 – ☎ 088 22.
See : Loch★★.
Edinburgh 88 – Inverness 92 – Perth 46.

Dunalastair, PH16 5PW, ☎ 323, 🎣, 🌳 – wc ♿ – 🚗 🅿
M approx. 4.95 **s.** 🍷 1.45 – **23 rm** 6.95/16.90 **s.**

KINROSS Kinross. (Tayside) 986 ⑪ – pop. 2,418 – ☎ 0577.
See : Loch Leven★.
18 Beeches Park ☎ 63467.
Edinburgh 25 – Dunfermline 12 – Perth 17 – Stirling 23.

Green (Interchange), 2 The Muirs, KY13 7AS, ☎ 63467, « Attractive gardens », 🎾, 🏊, 18, 🎣 – wc 🅿.
M 4.75/7.25 **st.** 🍷 1.25 – **47 rm** 11.50/27.00 **st.**

at Cleish SW : 4 ½ m. by B 996 and B 9097 – ✉ Kinross – ☎ 057 75 Cleish Hills :

Nivingston House ⛰ with rm, KY13 7LS, ☎ 216, ≤, 🌳 – 🅿
closed Monday and 26 September to 21 October – **M** approx. 6.50 – **5 rm** 7.50/15.00.

AUSTIN-MG-WOLSELEY, FORD High St. ☎ 62424
MAZDA 10/14 High St. ☎ 62244
MORRIS-MG-ROVER-TRIUMPH South St., Milnathort ☎ 2453

KINTYRE (Peninsula) Argyll. (Strathclyde) 986 ⑭ – pop. 6,051.
⛴ from Claonaig to Isle of Arran: Lochranza (Caledonian MacBrayne) 6-8 daily (30 mn) – from Kennacraig to Isle of Islay: Port Askaig (Western Ferries) 1-2 daily (3 h) – from West Loch Tarbert to Islay: Port Ellen (Caledonian MacBrayne) 1-3 daily (2 h to 2 h 30 mn) – from West Loch Tarbert to Isle of Gigha (Caledonian MacBrayne) 3 weekly (1 h 15 mn).

Campbeltown – ✉ ☎ 0586 Campbeltown.
See : Site★. Envir. : Machrihanish Bay★ W : 6 m. – Black Bay★ NE : 5 m. – Ugadale Bay★ NE : 7 m. – Saddell Bay★ NE : 8 m.
18 Machrihanish ☎ 213, W : 5 m.
i ☎ 2056, Telex 778868.
Edinburgh 117 – Glasgow 134 – Oban 87.

Ardshiel, Kilkerran Rd, PA28 6JL, ☎ 2133, 🌳 – 🅿
closed 2 weeks October, 1-3 January and 1 week February – **M** approx. 3.50 **st.** – **11 rm** 7.00/14.00 **st.**

PEUGEOT Bolgam St. ☎ 2030
VAUXHALL County Garage ☎ 2235

Carradale – ✉ ☎ 058 33 Carradale – 9.
See : Site★, ≤★ over Kilbronnan Sound, harbour★, Carradale Bay★.
Edinburgh 164 – Glasgow 121 – Oban 74.

Carradale, PA28 6RY, W: ¾ m. ☎ 223, – wc P
M 3.00/3.75 1.40 – **22 rm** 7.00/15.60.

Southend – ✉ Campbeltown – ☎ 058 683 Southend – 18.
Edinburgh 186 – Glasgow 143 – Oban 96.

Keil, PA28 6RT, W: ¾ m. ☎ 253, ≤, – P
M 4.25/5.85 **st.** 1.10 – **25 rm** 5.50/11.00.

Tarbert – ✉ ☎ 088 02 Tarbert.
See: West Loch Tarbert★. **Envir. :** SW: Sound of Gigha★.
9 W: **1** m.
i ☎ 429 (April-September).
Edinburgh 139 – Glasgow 96 – Oban 49.

Stonefield Castle, PA29 6YJ, N: 2 m. on A 83 ☎ 207, ≤ Loch Fyne and gardens, « Extensive gardens », heated, park – P
M approx. 5.00 1.10 – 1.25 – **34 rm.**

*Do not always take your holidays in **July** or **August**; some districts are more beautiful in other months.*

KIPPEN Stirling. (Central) – pop. **1**,500 – ✉ Stirling – ☎ 078 687.
Edinburgh 45 – Glasgow 29 – Stirling 9.

Cross Keys (Vinery Rest.), FK8 3JF, ☎ 293 – P.

SAAB Main St. ☎ 287

KIRKCALDY Fife. (Fife) 986 ⑪ – pop. 50,360 – ☎ 0592.
18 Balwearie ☎ 60370 – 18 Dunnikier Way ☎ 61599, North boundary – 9 Cardenden ☎ 720575, N: 3 m.
i Esplanade (Easter-September).
Edinburgh 26 – Dundee 28 – Glasgow 52.

Royal Albert, 18 West Albert Rd, KY1 1DL, ☎ 65627, – TV wc P.
M 3.00/5.00 1.60 – **21 rm** 8.50/14.50.

Station (Osprey), 4 Bennochy Rd, KY1 1YQ, ☎ 62461 – wc.
34 rm.

AUSTIN-MORRIS-MG-ROVER-TRIUMPH-WOLSELEY 39 Rosslyn St. ☎ 51997
AUSTIN-MG-WOLSELEY Bannochy Rd ☎ 62191
AUSTIN-DAIMLER-JAGUAR-MORRIS-MG-ROVER-TRIUMPH Forth Av. ☎ 3703
DAF, SAAB 180/186 St. Clair St. ☎ 52291
DATSUN Meldrum Rd ☎ 61353
FORD Wemyssfield ☎ 62141
OPEL 9 Park Rd ☎ 51932
RENAULT 15 Esplanade ☎ 3123
VAUXHALL, CITROEN 24 Victoria Rd ☎ 4755
VOLVO Overton Rd ☎ 52048
VW, AUDI-NSU Dunnikier Way ☎ 52771

KIRKCUDBRIGHT Kirkcudbright. (Dumfries and Galloway) 986 ⑲ – pop. 2,502 – ☎ 0557.
i Harbour Sq. ☎ 30494 (May-September).
Edinburgh 105 – Dumfries 28 – Stranraer 52.

Royal, St. Cuthbert St., DG6 4DY, ☎ 30551 – wc P
M (bar lunch) 3.00/4.50 **s.** 1.10 – **16 rm** 6.00/13.00 **s.** – P 11.00/13.00 **s.**

Selkirk Arms, High St., DG6 4JG, ☎ 30402, – wc P
M (bar lunch) approx. 3.50 1.10 – **27 rm** 7.20/16.55 **st.**

DAF Tongland Rd ☎ 30696
MORRIS-MG-ROVER-TRIUMPH-WOLSELEY Mews Lane ☎ 412

KIRKMICHAEL Perth. (Tayside) – pop. 100 – ✉ Blairgowrie – ☎ 025 081 Strathardle.
Envir. : E: Glenshee (★★ by chairlift 15 mn, AC).
Edinburgh 70 – Perth 28 – Pitlochry 12.

Log Cabin, PH10 7NB, SW: 1 m. ☎ 288, ≤, heated, – TV wc P
M (bar lunch) 4.15/4.75 **st.** 1.00 – **9 rm** 9.05/18.10 **st.**

KIRKWALL Orkney (Orkney Islands) 986 ⑯ – see Orkney Islands (Mainland).

KIRN Argyll. (Strathclyde) – see Dunoon.

KYLEAKIN Inverness. (Highland) 986 ⑥ – Shipping Services: see Skye (Isle of).

KYLE OF LOCHALSH Ross and Cromarty (Highland) 986 ⑥ – pop. 700 – 0599.

See : Loch*.

to the Isle of Skye: Kyleakin (Caledonian MacBrayne) frequent services every day (5 mn).

to Mallaig (Caledonian MacBrayne) 2-3 weekly (2 h to 2 h 45 mn).

i 4276 (Easter and May-October).

Edinburgh 202 – Dundee 173 – Inverness 85 – Oban 127.

Lochalsh (B.T.H.), Ferry Rd, IV40 8AF, 4202, ← –
closed 23 to 29 December – **M** a la carte 7.70/12.60 **st.** 1.40 – **45 rm** 16.70/37.55 **st.** – P 26.65/32.95 **st.**

CHRYSLER 4328

MORRIS-MG The Garage 4210

KYLES SCALPAY Inverness. (Highland) – Shipping Services: see Harris (Isle of).

LAIRG Sutherland. (Highland) 986 ③ – pop. 1,050 – 0549.

i Information Centre 2160 (June-September).

Edinburgh 218 – Inverness 59 – Wick 71.

Sutherland Arms, IV27 4AT, 2291, ←, – wc
April-October – **M** approx. 4.90 **st.** 1.45 – **33 rm** 9.45/19.65 **st.**

Aultnagar Lodge , IV27 4EX, S: 5 m. on A 836 054 982 (Invershin) 245, ← countryside and hills, , park – wc
26 rm.

Overscaig , NW: 17 m. by A 836 on A 838 054 983 (Merkland) 203, ← Loch Shin, , park – wc
M (bar lunch) a la carte 3.50/5.60 1.00 – **15 rm** 6.00/14.00 **st.**

MORRIS-TRIUMPH 2465

LANARK Lanark. (Strathclyde) 986 ⑮ – pop. 8,700 – 0555.

Main St., Carnwath 251, E: 7 m. – Douglas Water, SW: 7 m.

Edinburgh 33 – Carlisle 76 – Glasgow 28.

Cartland Bridge , ML11 9UF, N: ¾ m. on A 73 4426, –
M approx. 2.75 **st.** 1.30 – **15 rm** 8.50/17.00 **st.**

AUSTIN-MORRIS-MG-WOLSELEY 17/19 Bloomgate 2371

AUSTIN-MG-ROVER-TRIUMPH 178 Hyndford Rd 2674

BMW 30 West Port 2581

CHRYSLER-SIMCA Ladyacre Rd 2581

FORD 144 Hyndford Rd 2465

VAUXHALL St. Leonard St. 2185

LANGBANK Renfrew. (Strathclyde) – pop. 1,000 – 047 554.

Edinburgh 59 – Glasgow 16 – Greenock 7.

Gleddoch House (Interchange) , PA14 6YE, SE: 1 m. off B 789 711, ← Clyde and countryside, , , , , park – wc
M approx. 7.00 **st.** 1.60 – **10 rm** 14.00/32.50 **st.**

LARGS Ayr. (Strathclyde) 986 ⑭ – pop. 9,771 – 0475.

See : Skelmorlie Aisle* in old churchyard.

Irvine Rd 3594 – Routenburn, 3230.

to Great Cumbrae Island: Millport Slip (Caledonian MacBrayne) frequent services every day (10 mn).

to Great Cumbrae Island: Millport Old Pier (Caledonian MacBrayne) frequent services every day summer only (30 mn).

i Esplanade 673765.

Edinburgh 72 – Ayr 30 – Glasgow 29.

Marine and Curlinghall, South Promenade, KA30 8DZ, 674551, ←, – wc
M approx. 4.05 **t.** 1.30 – **63 rm** 10.00/20.20 **st.**

Royal, The Esplanade, KA30 8LZ, 674653 – wc
M 2.75/4.25 **t.** 1.25 – **12 rm** 8.60/15.10 **t.**

Castle (Osprey), 1 Broomfield, South Promenade, KA30 9HH, 673302, – wc
40 rm.

VW, AUDI-NSU 28/34 Irvine Rd 675431

LAUDER Berwick. (Borders) 986 ⑮ – pop. 604 – 057 85 Oxton.

381, W : ½ m.

Edinburgh 27 – Hawick 31 – **Newcastle-upon-Tyne 78.**

Carfraemill (Osprey), TD2 6RA, N: 4 m. on junction A 68 and A 697 200 – wc
10 rm.

AUSTIN-MORRIS-MG-WOLSELEY Edinburgh Rd 228

LECKMELM Ross and Cromarty (Highland) – pop. 28 – ✉ Garve – ☎ 0854 Ullapool.
Edinburgh 214 – Inverness 55 – Ullapool 4.

- **Leckmelm Motel,** Loch Broom, IV23 2RL, ☎ 2471, ≤ Loch Broom – ⇔wc ☎ Ⓟ
1 week before Easter-mid October – **M** (buffet lunch) approx. 5.50 **st.** 🍷 1.30 – **20 rm** ⊡ 8.50/16.90 **st.**
- **Tir Aluinn** ⑤, Loch Broom, IV23 2RJ, ☎ 2074, ≤ Loch Broom and hills, 🌳, park - ⇔wc Ⓟ
May-September – **M** (dinner only) 3.00 🍷 2.00 – **16 rm** ⊡ 7.00/16.00.

LERWICK Shetland (Shetland Islands) 986 ⑯ – see Shetland Islands (Mainland).

LETHAM Fife. (Fife) – pop. 170 – ✉ Ladybank – ☎ 033 781.
⛳18 Annsmuir, Ladybank ☎ 033 73 (Ladybank) 320.
Edinburgh 41 – Dundee 14 – Perth 18.

- **Fernie Castle** ⑤, KY7 7RU, NE: ½ m. on A 914 ☎ 209, « Castle with 14C origins », 🌳, park – TV ⇔wc ⋒wc ☎ Ⓟ
M a la carte 5.90/7.05 **t.** 🍷 1.90 – ⊡ 1.95 – **11 rm** 10.00/20.00 **t.**

LEVEN Fife. (Fife) 986 ⑪ – pop. 9,472 – ☎ 0333 – ⛳18.
i South St. ☎ 26533.
Edinburgh 34 – Dundee 23 – Glasgow 61.

- Caledonian (Osprey), High St., KY8 4NG, ☎ 24101 – TV ⇔wc ☎ Ⓟ
37 rm.

AUSTIN-MG-WOLSELEY The Promenade ☎ 23449
FIAT Sconnie Rd ☎ 26348

LEWIS (Isle of) Ross and Cromarty (Outer Hebrides) (Western Isles) 986 ② – pop. 15,174.

Stornoway – pop. 5,282 – ✉ ☎ 0851 Stornoway.
See: Broad Bay**. **Envir.:** Tiumpan Head ≤** NE: 11 m. – Loch Erisort** SW: 12 m. – Callanish Standing Stones** W: 16 m. – East Loch Roag* W: 13 ½ m. – Tolsta (site*) NE: 13 m. **Exc.:** Dun Carloway* (stone fort) W: 21 m. – Port of Ness* NE: 25 ½ m. – Valtos* W: 32 m.

✈ ☎ 2256, E: 2 ½ m. – **Terminal:** British Airways, Cromwell St.

⛴ from Stornoway to Ullapool (Caledonian MacBrayne) Monday/Saturday 1-2 daily (3 h 15 mn).

i Area Tourist Officer, South Beach Quay ☎ 3088, Telex 75125.

- Caberfeidh, PA87 2EU, ☎ 2604 – 🛗 TV ⇔wc Ⓟ – **35 rm.**
- Caledonian, South Beach St., PA87 2XY, ☎ 2411, ≤
10 rm.
- **Royal** (S & N), Cromwell St., PA87 2DG, ☎ 2109, ≤
M 1.90/3.25 **st.** 🍷 1.20 – **16 rm** ⊡ 7.60/14.50 **st.**

AUSTIN-MG-WOLSELEY Bayhead St. ☎ 3246
DAF Sandwick Rd ☎ 2956
FORD 7 Bayhead St. ☎ 3225
RENAULT Bells Rd ☎ 2303
ROVER-TRIUMPH 4 Inaclete Rd ☎ 2346
VAUXHALL Bayhead St. ☎ 2888

LINWOOD Renfrew. (Strathclyde) – pop. 2,583 – ☎ 0505 Johnstone.
Edinburgh 54 – Glasgow 11 – Greenock 13.

- Golden Pheasant (Swallow), 1 Moss Rd, PA3 3HP, ☎ 21266 – ⇔wc ☎ Ⓟ
12 rm.

LISMORE (Isle of) Argyll. (Strathclyde).
⛴ to Oban (Caledonian MacBrayne) Monday/Saturday 2-4 daily (1 h).

Hotels see: Oban.

LOCHALINE Argyll. (Strathclyde) 986 ⑩.
⛴ by Caledonian MacBrayne: to Isle of Mull (Fishnish) frequent services every day (15 mn), (Tobermory) 2 weekly summer only (1 h 40 mn) – to Isles of Coll and Tiree: 2 weekly summer only (2 h 50 mn to 3 h 50 mn) – to Oban: 2 weekly summer only (1 h 10 mn).
⛴ by Caledonian MacBrayne: to Isle of Mull: Craignure via Fishnish Monday/Friday 1 daily (1 h 5 mn) – to Oban: 6 weekly summer only (55 mn) – to Isle of Barra (Castlebay) 4 weekly summer only (4 h) – to South Uist (Lochboisdale) 6 weekly summer only (4 to 6 h.).
Edinburgh 129 – Inverness 105 – Kyle of Lochalsh 115 – Oban 7.

Hotels see: Mull (Isle of).

LOCHBOISDALE Inverness. (Outer Hebrides) (Western Isles) 986 ⑥ – see Uist (South) (Isles of).

LOCHCARRON Ross and Cromarty (Highland) 986 ⑥ – pop. 1,144 – ☎ 052 02 – 9.
Edinburgh 223 – Inverness 64 – Kyle of Lochalsh 23.

Lochcarron, IV54 8YS, ☎ 226, ≤ – P
closed Christmas and 1 January – **M** *(closed Monday)* (bar lunch) approx. 4.50 **t.** – **7 rm** 7.00/18.00 **t.**

LOCHEARNHEAD Perth. (Central) 986 ⑪ – pop. 202 – ☎ 056 73.
i ☎ 220 (April-September).
Edinburgh 65 – Glasgow 56 – Oban 57 – Perth 36.

Lochearnhead, FK19 8HB, ☎ 237, ≤, – wc P
February-October – **M** approx. 4.25 **s.** 1.00 – **48 rm** 8.00/18.00 – P 12.00/14.00.

LOCHGAIR Argyll. (Strathclyde) – pop. 100 – ☎ 054 682.
Edinburgh 119 – Glasgow 76 – Oban 43.

Lochgair, PA31 8SA, on A 83 ☎ 233, – wc P
closed November – **M** *(closed in winter)* (dinner only) 4.00/5.00 0.80 – **18 rm** 7.50/22.00.

LOCHGILPHEAD Argyll. (Strathclyde) 986 ⑭ – pop. 1,251 – ☎ 0546.
Envir. : Loch Fyne** E: 4 m. – Crarae Lodge gardens* *AC*, NE: 12 m.
i Colchester Sq. ☎ 2344 (April-September).
Edinburgh 126 – Glasgow 83 – Oban 36.

Hotels see : Cairnbaan NW: 2 ½ m.
Crinan NW: 4 ½ m.

LOCH HARRAY Orkney (Orkney Islands) – see Orkney Islands (Mainland).

LOCHINVER Sutherland. (Highland) 986 ② – pop. 354 – ✉ Lairg – ☎ 057 14.
See : Site*. **Envir.**: E: Inver Valley*.
i Information Centre ☎ 330 (June-September).
Edinburgh 259 – Inverness 100 – Wick 118.

Culag, IV27 4LQ, ☎ 209, ≤, – wc P
May-15 October – **M** approx. 6.00 **s.** 1.80 – **51 rm** 9.50/21.00 **s.**

LOCHMADDY Inverness. (Outer Hebrides) (Western Isles) 986 ⑥ – see Uist (North) (Isles of).

LOCHRANZA Bute. (Strathclyde) 986 ⑭ – Shipping Services : see Arran (Isle of).

LOCKERBIE Dumfries. (Dumfries and Galloway) 986 ⑲ – pop. 2,999 – ☎ 057 62.
9 ☎ 2463.
Edinburgh 72 – Carlisle 26 – Dumfries 13 – Glasgow 69.

Lockerbie House , Dryfe Rd, DG11 2RD, N: 1 m. on B 723 ☎ 2610, , park – wc ☎ P
M 3.50/5.00 **t.** 1.00 – **30 rm** 8.65/14.60 **t.**

Dryfesdale House , DG11 2SF, NW: 1 m. off A 74 ☎ 2427, ≤, – TV wc ☎ P
M 4.00/5.00 **t.** 2.00 – **15 rm** 10.00/19.50 **st.**

at Johnstonebridge N: 6 m. on A 74 – ✉ Lockerbie – ☎ 057 64 Johnstonebridge:

Dinwoodie Lodge, DG11 2SL, ☎ 289, – P
M 4.00/4.50 **t.** 1.35 – **7 rm** 7.00/14.00 **t.**

ALFA-ROMEO, SAAB ☎ 2569 MORRIS-MG-WOLSELEY High St. ☎ 2648

LONGNIDDRY E. Lothian (Lothian) – ☎ 0875.
18 ☎ 52141.
Edinburgh 13 – North Berwick 10.

Longniddry Inn (Swallow), on A 198 ☎ 52402 – P.

LOSSIEMOUTH Moray (Grampian) 986 ⑦ – pop. 5,678 – ☎ 034 381.
See : Site**. **Envir.** : Burghead (** from the lighthouse) W: 8 m.
18, 9 ☎ 2018.
Edinburgh 196 – Aberdeen 72 – Fraserburgh 66 – Inverness 44.

Hotel and restaurant see : Elgin S: 5 ½ m.

LUNAN Angus (Tayside) – see Montrose.

LUNDIN LINKS Fife. (Fife) – pop. 770 – ✉ Leven – ☎ 0333.
⛳9 ☎ 320022.
Edinburg 36 – Dundee 25 – Dunfermline 23.

- **Elmwood,** 12 Links Rd, KY8 6AT, ☎ 320397, ⛰ – Ⓟ
  March-October – **12 rm** ⊐ 5.70/11.40 **st.**

MAINLAND Orkney (Orkney Islands) 986 ⑯ – see Orkney Islands.

MAINLAND Shetland (Shetland Islands) 986 ⑯ – see Shetland Islands.

MALLAIG Inverness. (Highland) 986 ⑥ – pop. 1,050 – ☎ 0687.
See: Site★ – Harbour★. **Envir.:** Sound of Sleat★★ – Sound of Arisaig★ S: 9 m.
⛴ to Isle of Skye: Armadale (Caledonian MacBrayne) Monday/Saturday 4-5 daily summer only (30 mn).
⛴ by Caledonian MacBrayne: to Isles of Eigg, Muck, Rhum, Canna, return Mallaig 3 weekly (except to Muck: 1 weekly only) (4 h 30 mn) – to Kyle of Lochaish 2-3 weekly (2 to 2 h 30 mn) – to Isle of Skye (Armadale) Monday/Saturday 1-2 daily winter only (30 mn).
i Information Centre, ☎ 2170 (May-September).
Edinburgh 181 – Inverness 111 – Oban 97.

MARYCULTER Kincardine. (Grampian) – pop. 813 – ✉ ☎ 0224 Aberdeen.
Edinburgh 118 – Aberdeen 8 – Stonehaven 9.

- ✕ **Maryculter House,** AB1 0BB, W: 1 m. on B 9077 ☎ 732124 – Ⓟ
  closed Sunday and 1 January – **M** a la carte 6.50/8.50.

MEIGLE Perth. (Tayside) 986 ⑪ – pop. 860 – ☎ 082 84.
See: Museum (Crosses)★.
Edinburgh 60 – Dundee 13 – Perth 18.

- ✕ **Kings of Kinloch** with rm, Coupar Angus Rd, PH12 8QX, W: 1 m. on A 94 ☎ 273, ≤, ⛰ – Ⓟ
  M a la carte 4.10/5.60 **t.** – **7 rm** ⊐ 7.00/16.00 **t.**

MELROSE Roxburgh. (Borders) 986 ⑮ – pop. 4,814 – ☎ 089 682.
See: Abbey★ *AC*. **Envir.:** Abbotsford House★ (Sir Walter Scott's home) *AC*, W: 2 m.
⛳9 Dingleton ☎ 2177, South boundary.
i Priorwood, near Abbey ☎ 2555 (Easter-mid December).
Edinburgh 37 – Hawick 21 – Newcastle-upon-Tyne 69.

- George and Abbotsford (Swallow), High St., TD6 9PD, ☎ 2308, Group Telex 53168, ⛰ – ⛀wc Ⓟ. ⛺
  22 rm.
- **Burts,** Market Sq., TD6 9PN, ☎ 2285, ⛰ – ⛀wc Ⓟ
  M 3.75/4.25 **t.** 🍷 1.25 – **19 rm** ⊐ 6.50/12.50 **t.**

CHRYSLER High St. ☎ 2400
MORRIS-MG-WOLSELEY Palma Pl. ☎ 2048
RENAULT Lilliesleaf ☎ 083 57 (Lilliesleaf) 231

MILLPORT Bute. (Strathclyde) 986 ⑭ – Shipping Services: see Great Cumbrae Island.

MILNGAVIE Dunbarton. (Strathclyde) 986 ⑮ – pop. 10,741 – ✉ ☎ 041 Glasgow.
Edinburgh 50 – Glasgow 7.

- Black Bull (Thistle), Main St., G62 6BH, ☎ 956 2291 – TV ⛀wc ☎ Ⓟ
  27 rm.

OPEL Glasgow Rd ☎ 956 1126
MORRIS-MG-WOLSELEY 3 Strathblane Rd ☎ 956 2373
TOYOTA, VAUXHALL Main St. ☎ 956 2255

MINGARY Argyll. (Strathclyde).
⛴ to Isle of Mull: Tobermory (Caledonian MacBrayne) Monday/Saturday 4 daily (35 mn).
Edinburgh 164 – Inverness 115 – Kilchoan 1.

Hotels see: Kilchoan W: 1 m.

MOFFAT Dumfries. (Dumfries and Galloway) 986 ⑮ – pop. 2,031 – ☎ 0683.
Envir.: E: Moffatwater Valley★ – Grey Mare's Tail Waterfall★ NE: 11 m.
Edinburgh 58 – Dumfries 21 – Carlisle 42 – Glasgow 54.

- **Moffat Mercury Motor Inn,** Church St., DG10 9EP, ☎ 20464 – TV ⛀wc ☎ Ⓟ
  M a la carte approx. 3.80 **st.** 🍷 1.35 – ⊐ 1.50 – **51 m** 10.00/16.00 **st.**
- **Annandale,** High St., DG10 9HF, ☎ 20013 – ⛀wc Ⓟ
  M 3.50/4.50 **st.** 🍷 1.60 – **24 rm** ⊐ 8.50/18.00 **st.**

MONTROSE Angus (Tayside) 986 ⑪ – pop. 10,915 – ☎ 0674 – 18.

i 212 High St. ☎ 2000.

Edinburgh 85 – Aberdeen 38 – Dundee 29.

Links, Mid-Links, DD10 8RL, ☎ 2288, – wc ☎ **P**.
M a la carte 3.40/4.60 **t.** 1.70 – **20 rm** 9.30/16.60 **t.**

Park, John St., DD10 8EQ, ☎ 3415, Telex 76367, – TV wc ☎ **P**.
M a la carte 4.20/5.60 **st.** 1.30 – **41 rm** 10.30/18.50 **st.**

at Lunan S: 4 ½ m. by A 92 – ✉ Arbroath – ☎ 024 13 Inverkeilor:

Lunan Bay, DD10 9TG, ☎ 265, ←, – wc **P**
closed 1-2 January – **M** a la carte 4.80/7.80 – **8 rm** 7.50/15.00.

AUSTIN-MG-ROVER-TRIUMPH Craigo ☎ 067 483 (Hillside) 374
CHRYSLER 99 Bridge St. ☎ 4682
DATSUN New Wynd ☎ 3606
MAZDA, PEUGEOT ☎ 024 13 (Inverkeilor) 276

MONYMUSK Aberdeen. (Grampian) – pop. 970 – ☎ 046 77.

Edinburgh 143 – Aberdeen 19 – Old Meldrum 13.

Grant Arms, The Square, AB3 7HJ, ☎ 226 – wc wc ☎ **P**
M approx. 4.25 **t.** – **15 rm** 6.50/15.80 **t.** – P 13.00/14.40 **t.**

MOSSAT Aberdeen. (Grampian) – pop. 400 – ✉ Alford – ☎ 033 65 Kildrummy.

Envir.: Kildrummy Castle gardens* *AC*, SW: 2 ½ m.

Edinburgh 137 – Aberdeen 33.

Kildrummy Castle, AB3 8RA, S: 2 ¼ m. on A 97 ☎ 288, ← gardens and Kildrummy castle, « 19C mansion in extensive park », – wc **P**
Easter-October – **M** 4.50 **t.** 2.15 – **12 rm** 6.95/17.20 **t.**

MOTHERWELL Lanark. (Strathclyde) 986 ⑮ – pop. 41,247 – ☎ 0698.

Edinburgh 35 – Carlisle 84 – Glasgow 12.

Garrion (Open House), 73 Merry St., ML1 1JN, ☎ 64561 – wc wc ☎ **P**.
54 rm.

CHRYSLER 99 Airbles Rd ☎ 65286
FIAT Cleland Rd, Cerfin ☎ 860345
FORD Airbles Rd ☎ 66621
MORRIS-MG-PRINCESS 228/232 Hamilton Rd ☎ 64162

MUCK (Isle of) Inverness. (Highland) – Shipping Services: see Mallaig.

MUIRHEAD Lanark. (Strathclyde) – ✉ ☎ 041 Glasgow.

Edinburgh 41 – Glasgow 6 – Stirling 18.

Crowwood House (S & N), Cumbernauld Rd, G69 9LX, ☎ 779 2134 – wc **P**
M a la carte 2.50/5.00 **st.** 1.20 – **10 rm** 8.00/16.00 **st.**

AUSTIN-MG-WOLSELEY Cumbernauld Rd ☎ 2413

MULL (Isle of) Argyll. (Strathclyde) 986 ⑩ – pop. 1,438.

See: Coast*.

by Caledonian MacBrayne: from Craignure to Oban: 4-7 daily except Sunday from October to May (45 mn) – from Fishnish to Lochaline frequent services every day (15 mn) – from Tobermory to Oban: 3 weekly summer only (2 to 2 h 10), to Lochaline: 2 weekly summer only (1 h), to Isles of Coll and Tiree: 3 weekly summer only (1 h 45 mn to 2 h 45 mn).

by Caledonian MacBrayne: from Fionnphort to Isle of Iona frequent services (10 mn) – from Craignure to Lochaline via Fishnish Monday/Friday 1 daily (1 h 15 mn) – from Tobermory to Mingary Monday/Saturday 4 daily (35 mn), to Oban: 3 weekly (1 h 45 mn to 2 h 15 mn), to Isles of Coll and Tiree: 3 weekly (1 h 45 mn to 2 h 45 mn).

i 48 Main St. at Tobermory ☎ 2182 (April-September).

Bunessan – ✉ Bunessan – ☎ 068 17 Fionnphort.

See: Loch Scridain*. **Envir.:** Fionnphort (site*) W: 6 m.

Ardfenaig House, PA67 6DX, W: 3 m. by A 849 ☎ 210, ←, – **P**
May-2 October – **M** (dinner only) 5.00 0.60 – **5 rm** 8.00/16.00.

Craignure – ✉ ☎ 068 02 Craignure.

Envir.: Glen More* SW: **11** m. – Loch Uisg* SW: **13** m.

Isle of Mull, PA65 6BB, ☎ 351, ← mountains, sea and Duart Castle – wc **P**
April-October – **M** approx. 4.90 **st.** 1.45 – **60 rm** 13.05/21.70 **st.**

Salen – ✉ Salen – ☎ 068 03 Aros.

See: Sound of Mull**. **Envir.:** Loch Na Keal** SW: 2 ½ m.

Glenforsa, PA72 6JN, E: 1 ¼ m. by A 849 ☎ 377, ← Sound of Mull, « Norwegian wood chalet », park – wc **P**
April-October, Christmas and 1 January – **M** (bar lunch) 3.00/3.50 0.80 – **14 rm** 9.00/16.00 – P 11.25/12.75.

Tobermory – pop. 634 – 0688 Tobermory.
See : Site★. Envir. : Calgary Bay★★ SW : 14 m. – Loch Tuath★★ SW : 17 m.

Western Isles, PA75 6PR, 2012, bay and harbour, 9, – wc
M approx. 4.50 **st.** 1.20 – **42 rm** 8.50/22.00 **s.**

NAIRN Nairn. (Highland) 986 ⑦ – pop. 8,037 – 0667.
See : ★ from the harbour. **Envir. :** Fort George★ (Museum of the Queen's Own Highlanders★) W : 8 ½ m. – Sveno's Stone★ E : 11 m. – 18, 9 **52103** – 18 **52741.**
Bus Station, King St. 2753 (mid May-mid September).
Edinburgh 175 – Aberdeen 91 – Inverness 16.

Newton, IV12 4RX, off A 96 53144, « Country house in extensive grounds », park –
M 4.25/4.75 **s.** 1.00 – **34 rm** 16.00/28.00 **s.**

Golf View, Seabank Rd, IV12 4HD, 52301, heated, –
M 4.50/4.95 1.80 – **57 rm** 14.00/28.00.

Royal Marine, Marine Rd, IV12 4EA, 53381, – wc wc
April-October – **M** approx. 4.85 **st.** 1.45 – **47 rm** 9.45/18.90 **st.**

Clifton, Viewfield St., IV12 4HV, 53119, – wc
March-November – **M** (bar lunch) approx. 5.00 **t.** 1.50 – **19 rm** 8.50/18.00 **t.**

AUSTIN-MORRIS-MG-ROVER-TRIUMPH King. St. 2304 CHRYSLER-SIMCA Inverness Rd 52335

NEWARTHILL Lanark. (Strathclyde) – pop. 6,640 – Motherwell – 0698 Holytown.
Edinburgh 31 – Glasgow 13 – Motherwell 3.

Silverburn (S & N), 2 Loanhead Rd, ML1 5BA, 732503 – wc
M approx. 2.20 **st.** 1.20 – **5 rm** 8.25/16.50 **st.**

NEW GALLOWAY Kirkcudbright. (Dumfries and Galloway) 986 ⑲ – pop. 338 – Castle Douglas – 064 42 – 9.
Edinburgh 84 – Dumfries 24 – Glasgow 68 – Stranraer 45.

Kenmure Arms, DG7 3RL, 360 –
M approx. 3.00 **s.** 1.50 – **18 rm** 4.50/9.00 – P 8.00/9.00.

NEWTONMORE Inverness. (Highland) 986 ⑦ – pop. 900 – 054 03.
18 328.
Main St. 253 (May-September).
Edinburgh 112 – Inverness 47 – Perth 70.

Glen, Main St., PH20 1DD, 203 – wc
M (bar lunch) 3.30/4.00 **st.** 1.50 – **9 rm** 5.00/13.00 **st.**

Ard-na-Coille, Kingussie Rd, 214, –
closed November and December – **13 rm** 5.25/7.25 **s.**

NEWTON STEWART Wigtown. (Dumfries and Galloway) 986 ⑱ – pop. 1,883 – 0671.
Dashwood Sq. 2431 (May-September).
Edinburgh 127 – Dumfries 50 – Glasgow 84 – Stranraer 26.

Bruce, Queen St., DG8 6JL, 2294, – wc
M (buffet lunch) approx. 4.00 **st.** 1.40 – 2.00 – **16 rm** 7.00/14.00 **st.** – P 13.40/14.40 **st.**

Kirroughtree, DG8 6SM, E : 1 ½ m. by A 75 off A 712 2141, park – wc
M approx. 3.50 – **18 rm** 7.50/17.00 – P 11.00.

Crown, Queen St., DG8 6JW, 2727 –
M approx. 3.25 **t.** 0.95 – **11 rm** 6.50/13.00 **s.**

MORRIS-MG-ROVER-TRIUMPH-WOLSELEY 100 Queen St. 2467
RENAULT Duncan Park, Wigtown 098 84 (Wigtown) 3287

NORTH BERWICK E. Lothian (Lothian) 986 ⑮ – pop. 4,414 – 0620.
See : Site★. **Envir. :** Tantallon Castle★ (ruins 14C), site★ *AC*, E : 2 ½ m.
18 East Links **2726** – 18 West Links, Beach Rd **2135.**
18 Quality St. 2197 (mid November-September).
Edinburgh 24 – Newcastle-upon-Tyne 101.

Marine (T.H.F.), Cromwell Rd, EH39 4LZ, 2406, Telex 727363, heated, –
M approx. 4.00 **st.** 1.45 – **85 rm** 11.00/17.00 **st.** – P 17.00 **st.**

Royal, Station Rd, EH39 4AU, 2401, – wc wc – **50 rm.**

Nether Abbey, 26 Dirleton Av., EH39 4BQ, 2802, – wc
Easter-October – **M** 4.00/4.50 **t.** 1.80 – **18 rm** 7.00/16.00.

AUSTIN-MG-MORRIS-ROVER-TRIUMPH-WOLSELEY 18/24 High St. 2304
CHRYSLER-SIMCA 52 Dunbar Rd 2232

NORTH RONALDSAY (Isle of) Orkney (Orkney Islands) – Shipping Services : see Orkney Islands (Mainland : Kirkwall).

OBAN Argyll. (Strathclyde) 986 ⑩ – pop. 6,897 – ✆ 0631.

See : Site★.

Glen Cruitten ✆ 2868, E : **1** m.

by Caledonian MacBrayne : to Isle of Barra (Castlebay) 3-6 weekly (5 to 8 h 45 mn) – to South Uist (Lochboisdale) 3-6 weekly (5 to 7 h) – to Isle of Mull (Craignure) 4-7 daily except Sunday from October to May (45 mn), (Tobermory) 3 weekly summer only (2 to 2 h 15 mn) – to Isle of Colonsay : 3 weekly (2 h 30 mn) – to Isles of Coll and Tiree : 3-4 weekly (3 h 15 mn to 5 h 30 mn) – to Lismore : 2-3 daily (1 h) – to Lochaline : 2 weekly summer only (1 h 05 mn).

to Lochaline (Caledonian MacBrayne) summer only 6 weekly (55 mn). – to Isle of Mull (Tobermory) 3 weekly (1 h 45 mn to 2 h 15 mn) – to Isles of Coll and Tiree : 3 weekly (3 h 45 mn to 4 h 55 mn)

i Boswell House, Argyll Sq. ✆ 3122/3551, Telex 778866.

Edinburgh 122 – Dundee 115 – Glasgow 93 – Inverness 114.

- **Alexandra,** The Esplanade, PA34 5AA, ✆ 2381, ≤ – lift wc P
  April-October – **M** approx. 4.90 **st.** 1.45 – **58 rm** 9.45/18.90 **st.**
- **Rowan Tree,** George St., PA34 5HN, ✆ 2954 – wc P
  M approx. 3.75 **s.** 1.10 – **24 rm** 7.95/17.50 **s.** – P 14.00 **s.**
- **Regent,** The Esplanade, PA34 5PZ, ✆ 2341 – lift wc
  M approx. 3.75 1.30 – **31 rm** 7.00/16.00.
- **Caledonian,** Station Sq., PA34 5RT, ✆ 3133 – lift wc ✆
  May-15 October – **M** approx. 4.20 **s.** 2.00 – **66 rm** 11.50/22.00 **s.**
- **Marine,** The Esplanade, PA34 5QA, ✆ 2211, ≤ – lift wc wc ✆ P
  May-October – **M** approx. 4.25 **s.** – **44 rm** 7.15/16.50 **s.**
- **Manor House,** Gallanach Rd, PA34 4LS, ✆ 2087, ≤ – wc wc P
  M (bar lunch) a la carte 3.45/6.15 1.25 – **10 rm** 10.00/16.50.
- **Westbay,** The Esplanade, PA34 5PW, ✆ 2067, ≤
  mid May-mid October – **M** (bar lunch) 3.00/3.50 **st.** 1.20 – **14 rm** 6.50/19.00 **st.**
- **Soroba House,** Soroba Rd (A 816), PA34 4SB, ✆ 2628, – P
  M approx. 4.50 1.40 – **13 rm** 5.80/11.60.

AUSTIN-MORRIS-MG-ROVER-TRIUMPH Airds Pl. ✆ 3173
CHRYSLER-SIMCA Dunollie Rd ✆ 3717
FORD Soroba Rd ✆ 3061
VAUXHALL Lochside St. ✆ 3463
VOLVO, VW, AUDI-NSU Breadalbane Pl. ✆ 3066

OLD MELDRUM Aberdeen. (Grampian) 986 ⑦ – pop. 1,085 – ✆ 065 12 – 9.

Envir. : Pitmedden gardens★ *AC*, E : **6** m. – Tolquhon Castle★ (16C) *AC*, E : **7 ½** m.

Edinburgh 142 – Aberdeen 18 – Fraserburgh 29 – Inverness 89.

- XX **Meldrum House** with rm, AB5 0AE, N : 1 ½ m. off A 947 ✆ 294, ≤, « Large country house, part 13C », park – wc P
  April-December – **M** approx. 6.00 1.25 – **9 rm** 10.00/24.00 – P 16.00/24.00.

ONICH Inverness. (Highland) 986 ⑩ – pop. 280 – ✆ 085 53.

Edinburgh 122 – Glasgow 93 – Inverness 75 – Oban 39.

- **Creag Dhu,** PH33 6RY, on A 82 ✆ 238, ≤, – P
  Easter-mid October – **M** (bar lunch) 4.00/5.30 **st.** 1.30 – **20 rm** 8.00/18.00 **st.**
- **Onich,** PH33 6RY, on A 82 ✆ 214, ≤ Loch Linnhe and mountains, – P
  May-15 October – **M** (bar lunch) 4.00/4.50 **st.** – **25 rm** 8.00/16.00 **st.**

ORKNEY ISLANDS Orkney (Orkney Islands) 986 ⑯.

see Mainland : Kirkwall.

see Mainland : Kirkwall and Stromness.

HOY

Old Man of Hoy

See : Rock spike★★★.

MAINLAND

Birsay – ✉ ✆ 085 672 Birsay.

See : Brough of Birsay (site and ≤★★) *AC*. **Envir. :** Kitchener Memorial ★★★ (birds'nests) S : 5 m. – Skara Brae (prehistoric village★★ *AC*) S : 7 ½ m. – Yesnaby (cliffs★★ : birds' nests) S : 11 m. – Broch of Gurness★ E : 12 m.

- Barony, KW17 2LS, ✆ 327, ≤ Loch Boardhouse and hills, – P
  12 rm.

Kirkwall – ✉ ☎ 0856 Kirkwall.

See : Site★ – St. Magnus Cathedral★★. **Envir. :** Wideford Hill Cairn (Megalithic cairn★, ≤★) W : 2 m.

Grainbank ☎ 2055, W : 1 m.

✈ ☎ 2421, S : 3 ½ m. – British Airways ☎ 2478 – Loganair ☎ 3025.

by P & O Ferries : Orkney and Shetland Services : to Aberdeen : Thursday (11 h) – to Shetland (Lerwick) Tuesday (8 h) – by Orkney Islands Shipping Co.: to Westray via Eday, Stronsay, Sanday, Papa Westray 3 weekly (2 to 6 h) – to North Ronaldsay 1 weekly (2 h 30 mn) – to Shapinsay 2 weekly (30 mn) – to Wyre via Rousay, Egilsay 1 weekly (1 to 4 h).

to Shapinsay (Orkney Islands Shipping Co.) Monday/Saturday 9-10 weekly (25 mn).

i Junction Rd ☎ 2856.

Kirkwall, Harbour St., KW15 1LF, ☎ 2232 –
M approx. 3.50 **st.** – **40 rm** 7.50/15.00 **st.**

Lynnfield, Holm Rd, S : 1 m. on A 961 ☎ 2505, ≤, – Ⓟ
7 rm.

AUSTIN-MG-WOLSELEY Junction Rd ☎ 2308
CHRYSLER-SIMCA Gt Western Rd ☎ 2805
FORD Castle St. ☎ 3212
MORRIS-MG-WOLSELEY 25 Broad St. ☎ 2490
RENAULT Gt Western Rd ☎ 2601
ROVER-TRIUMPH Junction Rd ☎ 2158
VAUXHALL Burnmouth Rd ☎ 2950

Loch Harray – ✉ Loch Harray – ☎ 085 677 Harray.

Merkister, KW17 2LF, ☎ 366, ≤, – Ⓟ
April-September – **M** 4.50/6.00 **s.** 1.90 – **19 rm** 12.00/24.00 **s.**

Stenness – ✉ ☎ 085 685 Stromness.

Envir. : Maes Howe Cairn★★ (Neolithic chambered cairn) *AC*, NE : 1 ½ m. – Ring of Brodgar (stone circle)★ NW : 2 ½ m.

Standing Stones, ☎ 449, ≤ – Ⓟ
24 rm.

Stromness – ✉ ☎ 085 685 Stromness.

See : Site★.

Ness ☎ 593.

i Ferry Terminal Building, Pierhead ☎ 716 (June-September).

to Scrabster (P & O Ferries: Orkney and Shetland Services) Summer: **1-3 daily**; Winter: Monday/Saturday **1-3 daily** (2 h).

Stromness, KW16 3AA, ☎ 298, – wc wc
M approx. 3.75 – 1.00 – **35 rm** 6.60/12.00.

WESTRAY

Pierowall – ✉ Pierowall – ☎ 085 77 Westray.

Pierowall, ☎ 208, – Ⓟ
6 rm.

OYKEL BRIDGE Sutherland. (Highland) – ✉ Lairg – ☎ 054 984 Rosehall.
Edinburgh 225 – Inverness 66 – Lochinver 31.

Oykell Bridge, ☎ 218, ≤, – wc Ⓟ
17 rm.

PAISLEY Renfrew. (Strathclyde) 986 ⑮ – pop. 95,434 – ☎ 041 Glasgow.
Barshaw Park.
Edinburgh 50 – Ayr 36 – Glasgow 7 – Greenock 16.

Excelsior (T.H.F.), Glasgow Airport, Abbotsinch, PA3 2TR, ☎ 887 1212, Telex 77733 – TV Ⓟ.
M 3.85/4.25 **st.** 1.65 – 2.00 – **305 rm** 15.50/22.00 **st.**

Watermill (Stakis), Lonend, PA1 1SR, ☎ 889 3201 – TV wc Ⓟ
M (grill rest. only) 1.50/4.00 **st.** 1.45 – **30 rm** 10.00/15.50 **s.**

Rockfield, Renfrey Rd, PA3 4EA, ☎ 889 6182 – TV wc Ⓟ
9 rm.

Silver Thread (S & N), Lonend, PA1 1TN, on A 726 ☎ 887 2196 – wc wc Ⓟ
M approx. 1.90 **st.** 1.20 – **11 rm** 8.85/16.40 **st.**

Broadstones Private, 17 High Calside, PA2 6BY, ☎ 889 4055, – Ⓟ
8 rm 6.50/12.00 **st.**

PAISLEY

ALFA-ROMEO, FIAT 255 Glasgow Rd ☏ 882 3221
AUSTIN-MG-WOLSELEY 46 New Sneddon St. ☏ 887 7882
CHRYSLER-SIMCA 7 West St. ☏ 889 6233
DATSUN Weir St. ☏ 889 6866
FIAT 4/8 Lochfield Rd ☏ 884 2281
FORD 37/41 Lonend ☏ 887 6231
JAGUAR-ROVER-TRIUMPH 92 Glasgow Rd ☏ 889 8526
MORRIS-MG-WOLSELEY 53 Love St. ☏ 889 5111
OPEL 69 Espedair St. ☏ 889 5254
ROVER, TRIUMPH New St. ☏ 889 3111
VAUXHALL 15/17 St. James St. ☏ 889 7951

PAPA WESTRAY (Isle of) Orkney (Orkney Islands) – Shipping Services : see Orkney Islands (Mainland : Kirkwall).

PATHHEAD Midlothian (Lothian) – 0875 Ford.

i Hope Cottage ☏ 320525 (April-September).

Edinburgh 12 – Haddington 11.

Stair Arms (Open House), EX37 5TX, on A 68 ☏ 320277, – **7 rm.**

PEEBLES Peebles. (Borders) 986 ⑮ – pop. 5,884 – 0721.

Envir. : Neidpath Castle (site*) W : 1 m. – Traquair House* ***AC,*** **SE : 7 ½ m.**

Kirkland St. ☏ 20197.

i High St. ☏ 20138 (mid May-September).

Edinburgh 23 – Hawick 32 – **Glasgow 52.**

Peebles Hydro, Innerleithen Rd, EH45 8LX, ☏ 20602, <, , – .
M approx. 4.50 **st.** 1.25 – **133 rm** 11.25/25.00 **st.** – P 17.25/20.00 **st.**

Tontine (T.H.F.), 39 High St., EH45 8AJ, ☏ 20892 – wc
M a la carte 4.10/5.30 **st.** 1.50 – **37 rm** 10.50/16.00 **st.** – P 14.00/16.50 **st.**

Park (Swallow), Innerleithen Rd, EH45 8BA, ☏ 20451, Group Telex 53168, < – wc wc – **23 rm.**

Cringletie House, EH45 8PL, N : 3 m. on A 703 ☏ 072 13 (Eddleston) 233, <, « Country house in extensive grounds », , , park – wc
end March-end October – **M** 5.00/5.25 **t.** – **16 rm** 8.50/18.50 **t.**

Dilkusha with rm, Chambers Ter., EH45 9DZ, ☏ 20590, –
M a la carte 4.60/6.50 **t.** 1.20 – **5 rm** 11.50/14.00 **st.**

at Eddleston **N : 4 ½ m. on A 703 – ✉ Peebles – 072 13 Eddleston :**

Horse Shoe Inn, EH45 8QP, ☏ 225 –
closed Christmas and 1 January – **M** (bar lunch) a la carte 3.60/5.80 **t.** 1.55.

AUSTIN-MORRIS-MG-WOLSELEY Innerleithen Rd ☏ 20627
AUSTIN-MG-WOLSELEY St. Andrews Rd ☏ 20886
SIMCA George St. ☏ 20545
VAUXHALL 64/66 Old Town ☏ 20711

PERTH Perth. (Tayside) 986 ⑪ – pop. 43,030 – 0738.

Envir. : Scone Palace* (furniture) ***AC,*** **N : 4 m. by A 93** Y.

Moncrieffe Island ☏ 25170 by A 90 Z – **Cherrybank ☏ 24377, West boundary, by A 9** Z.

☏ 23366.

i The Round House, Marshall Pl. PH2 8NU, ☏ 22900 and 27108.

Edinburgh 42 – Aberdeen 82 – Dundee 22 – Dunfermline 29 – **Glasgow 59 – Inverness 117 – Oban 93.**

Plan opposite

Station (B.T.H.), Leonard St., PH2 8HE, ☏ 24141, Telex 76481, – Z **n**
closed Christmas and 1 January – **M** 5.90/6.85 **st.** 1.75 – **53 rm** 17.50/28.50 **st.**

Royal George (T.H.F.), Tay St., PH1 5LD, ☏ 24455 – wc . Y **c**
M a la carte 4.10/5.80 **st.** 1.50 – **43 rm** 10.50/16.00 **st.**

City Mills (Stakis), West Mill St., PH1 5QP, ☏ 28281 – wc Y **a**
M approx. 4.00 **st.** 1.50 – **40 rm** 12.50/20.00 **st.**

Pitcullen, 17-18 Pitcullen Crescent, PH2 7HT, NE : ¾ m. on A 94 ☏ 26506 Y **r**
closed Christmas and 1 January – **10 rm** 7.50/9.00 **t.**

Huntingtower with rm, Crieff Rd, PH1 3JT, W : 3 ½ m. on A 85 ☏ 073 883 (Almond bank) 241, <, – wc on A 85 Y
M a la carte 4.65/7.40 **t.** 1.50 – **8 rm** 11.25/18.00 **st.**

Timothy's, 24 St. John St., PH1 5SP, ☏ 26641, Smorrebrod Y **e**
closed Sunday, Monday, Christmas Day and 1 January – **M** a la carte 2.35/8.35 **t.** 1.10.

AUDI-NSU Bridgend ☏ 29141
AUSTIN-DAIMLER-MG-WOLSELEY 15 King Edward St. ☏ 26101
BMW, FERRARI, PEUGEOT, ROLLS ROYCE 50/56 Leonard St. ☏ 25481
CHRYSLER-SIMCA Dunkeld Rd ☏ 25252
CITROEN 55/60 South St. ☏ 23335
DAF 16 Crieff Rd ☏ 21010
DATSUN, MERCEDES-BENZ, SAAB 2 Dunkeld Rd ☏ 28211
FORD Riggs Rd ☏ 25121
JAGUAR-MORRIS-MG-ROVER-TRIUMPH-WOLSELEY 10/16 York Pl. ☏ 20811
MAZDA 23/29 South Methven St. ☏ 23757
VAUXHALL Dunkeld Rd ☏ 26241
VOLVO Arran Rd, North Muirton ☏ 22156
VW-AUDI-NSU Perth Rd, Scone ☏ 0738 (Scone) 51276

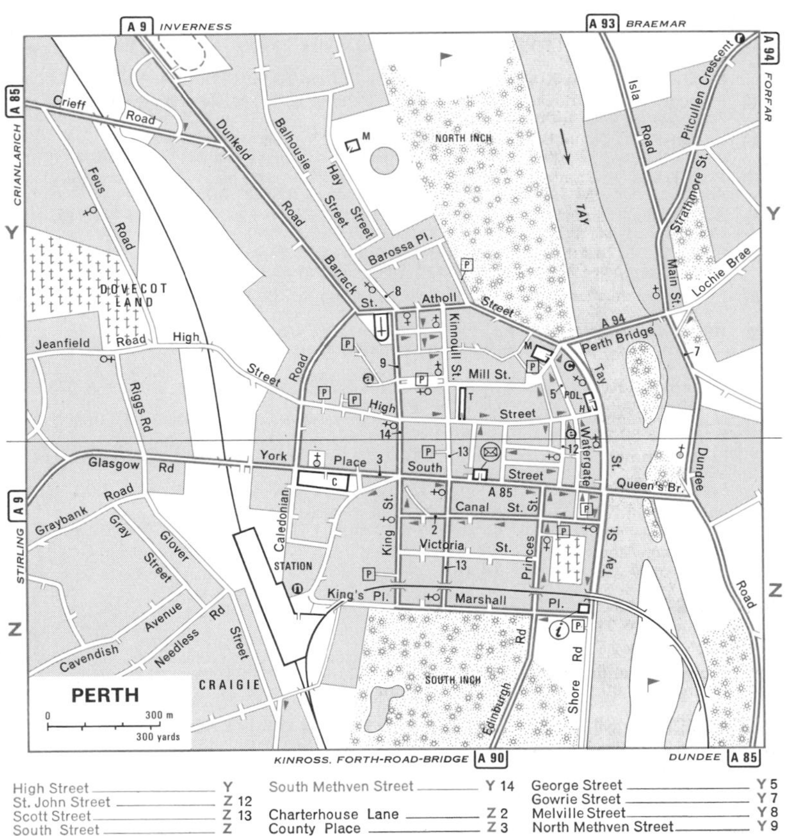

High Street	Y	South Methven Street	Y 14	George Street	Y 5
St. John Street	Z 12			Gowrie Street	Y 7
Scott Street	Z 13	Charterhouse Lane	Z 2	Melville Street	Y 8
South Street	Z	County Place	Z 3	North Methven Street	Y 9

PETERHEAD Aberdeen. (Grampian) 986 ⑦ – pop. **14,384** – [telephone] **0779.**

Envir. : Bullers of Buchan (cliffs**) S: 6 m. – Cruden Bay (site*) SW: 8 m.

18, 9 Craigewan ☎ 2149.

Edinburgh 158 – Aberdeen 34 – Fraserburgh 18.

- Palace (Swallow), Prince St., AB4 6PL, ☎ 4821 – [lift] [TV] wc ☎ Ⓟ. **59 rm.**

PIEROWALL Orkney (Orkney Islands) – see Orkney Islands (Westray).

PITCAPLE Aberdeen. (Grampian) – [telephone] **046 76.**

Edinburgh 145 – Aberdeen 21.

- **Pittodrie House** , AB5 9HS, SW: 1 ¾ m. off A 96 ☎ 202, ≤, « Country house with many antiques », , park – wc Ⓟ
M (lunch by arrangement Monday-Friday) 6.00/10.00 **t.** 1.65 – **11 rm** 15.00/22.00 **t.**

PITLOCHRY Perth. (Tayside) 986 ⑪ – pop. **2,599** – [telephone] **0796.**

Envir. : Blair Castle (interior**) *AC*, NW: 7 ½ m. – Loch Rannoch** W : 19 m. – Linn of Tummel* NW : 4 m. – Quenn's View (≤* of Loch Tummel) NW : 6 m.

18 ☎ 2792.

i 28 Atholl Rd ☎ 2215 (mid April-October).

Edinburgh 68 – Inverness 91 – Perth 26.

Atholl Palace (T.H.F.) ⚘, on A 9 ☎ 2400, Telex 76406, ≤, ✂, heated, 9, park – 🛗 TV P.
M a la carte 4.20/6.30 **st.** 1.60 – 2.00 – **117 rm** 10.50/18.00 **st.** – P 16.00/20.00 **st.**

Pitlochry Hydro, Knockard Rd, PH16 5JH, ☎ 2666, ≤, ✂, 9, – 🛗 wc P
April-September – **68 rm** 9.80/19.55 **st.**

Green Park, Clunie Bridge Rd, PH16 5JY, ☎ 2537, ≤, – wc wc P
mid March-end October – **M** approx. 5.10 **st.** 1.25 – **36 rm** 6.50/14.00 **st.**

Pine Trees ⚘, Strathview Ter., PH16 5QR, ☎ 2121, ≤, park – wc P
April-October – **M** 4.75/5.50 **st.** 2.00 – **30 rm** 8.00/21.00 **st.**

Scotlands (Interchange), Bonnethill Rd, PH16 5BT, ☎ 2292, – 🛗 wc P
M 4.30/4.80 **st.** 1.50 – **59 rm** 12.00/24.00 **st.**

Fisher's, 75-79 Atholl Rd, PH16 5BN, ☎ 2000, – 🛗 wc P
May-September – **M** approx. 4.25 **t.** 1.50 – **78 rm** 8.90/17.40.

Moulin, Kirkmichael Rd, PH16 5EW, N: 1 m. on A 924 ☎ 2196, – wc P
23 rm.

Burnside, West Moulin Rd, PH16 5EA, ☎ 2203, – wc P
early March-early November – **M** (snack lunch) approx. 3.50 **s.** 1.75 – **23 rm** 5.75/13.30 **s.**

Queen's View ⚘, Strathtunnel, PH16 5NR, NW: 6 m. by A 9 on B 8019 ☎ 079 684 (Killiecrankie) 291, ≤ Loch Tummel – wc P
closed November to February except by arrangement – **M** a la carte 3.10/6.00 1.50 – **9 rm** 8.80/16.70 **st.** – P 12.15/13.70 **st.**

Loch Tummel, Strathtummel, PH16 5RP, NW: 9 m. by A 9 on B 8019 ☎ 088 24 (Tummel-bridge) 272, ≤ Loch Tummel and hills, – wc P
Easter-end October – **M** (bar lunch) a la carte 3.10/5.90 1.90 – **9 rm** 8.00/19.00.

Acarsaid, 8 Atholl Rd, PH16 5BX, ☎ 2389 – wc wc P
April-October – **M** (dinner only) 4.50/5.50 **st.** 1.75 – **20 rm** 7.75/17.00 **st.**

Claymore, Atholl Rd, ☎ 2888, – P
season – **M** (bar lunch) – **12 rm.**

POLMONT Stirling. (Central) – pop. 2,268 – ☎ 0324.

18 Grangemouth ☎ 711500.

Edinburgh 21 – Falkirk 2.5 – Stirling 14.

Inchyra Grange, Grange Rd, FK2 0YB, ☎ 711911, – TV wc P.
M approx. 3.60 **t.** 2.00 – **33 rm** 9.50/19.50 **t.**

PORT APPIN Argyll. (Strathclyde) – ✉ pop. 100 – ☎ 063 173 Appin.

Edinburgh 136 – Ballachulish 20 – **Oban 24.**

Airds ⚘, PA38 4DF, ☎ 236, ≤ Loch Linnhe and hills of Morvern, – wc P
25 March-15 October – **M** 4.70 1.20 – **20 rm** 7.45/19.10 **s.**

PORT ASKAIG Argyll. (Strathclyde) 986 ⑭ – see Islay (Isle of).

PORT ELLEN Argyll. (Strathclyde) 986 ⑭ – Shipping Services : see Islay (Isle of).

PORT GLASGOW Renfrew. (Strathclyde) 986 ⑭ – pop. 22,482 – ☎ 0475.

Edinburgh 63 – Glasgow 20 – Greenock 3.

Clune Brae (S & N), Boglestone Roundabout, on A 761 ☎ 42626 – wc P
M approx. 2.50 **st.** 1.20 – **10 rm** 6.40/12.80 **st.**

PORTPATRICK Wigtown. (Dumfries and Galloway) 986 ⑱ – pop. 1,063 – ✉ Stranraer – ☎ 077 681.

Envir.: Logan gardens* *AC*, SE: 13 m. **Exc.:** Mull of Galloway (site and ≤**) SE: 24 ½ m. by Drummore.

18 ☎ 273.

Edinburgh 138 – Ayr 61 – Dumfries 80 – Stranraer 8.

Portpatrick (Mt. Charlotte), Heugh Rd, DG9 8TD, ☎ 333, ≤, heated, – 🛗 wc P
28 April-mid September – **M** approx. 3.25 **s.** 1.60 – **61 rm** 10.00/12.00 **s.**

Fernhill, Heugh Rd, DG9 8TD, ☎ 220, ≤, – wc P
March-end October – **M** (bar lunch) 3.50/5.00 **t.** 1.50 – **17 rm** 8.00/18.00 **t.**

XX **Knockinaam Lodge** ⚘ with rm, DG9 9AD, SE: 5 m. by A 7 ☎ 203, ≤, , park – wc P
21 March-2 January – **M** *(closed Monday)* (by arrangement) a la carte 3.75/5.60 1.10 – 1.30 – **8 rm** 10.50/21.00.

PORTREE Inverness. (Highland) 986 ⑥ – see Skye (Isle of).

PORTSONACHAN Argyll. (Strathclyde) – pop. **24** – ✉ Dalmally – ☎ 086 63 Kilchrenan.
See : Loch Awe*. **Envir. :** Inverary (site*, castle* 18C) S: **12** m.
Edinburgh **106** – Dalmally 8.5 – **Oban 34.**

- **Portsonachan**, PA33 1BL, on B 840 ☎ 224, ≤ Loch Awe and mountains, – wc Ⓟ
  closed 3 days at Christmas – **M** approx. 5.25 **st.** – **20 rm** 10.00/18.30 **st.**

PORT WILLIAM Wigtown. (Dumfries and Galloway) – pop. **528** – ☎ 098 87.
9 ☎ 358, SE: 3 m.
Edinburgh **144** – **Dumfries 67** – Stranraer 23.

- **Monreith Arms,** The Square, DG8 9SE, ☎ 232 – Ⓟ
  M a la carte 2.00/3.50 **st.** 1.10 – **13 rm** 5.50/12.00 **st.** – P 9.65 **st.**

OPEL South St. ☎ 277

PRESTWICK Ayr. (Strathclyde) 986 ⑭ – pop. **13,437** – ☎ 0292.
☎ 79822 – **Glasgow Terminal :** Stand no. 23, Anderston Cross Bus Station, Blythswood St.
see also Glasgow.
i Station Rd ☎ 77084 – Prestwick Airport ☎ 77309, Telex 778916.
Edinburgh 73 – Ayr 4 – Glasgow 30.

Plan of Built up Area : see Ayr

- Carlton (Osprey), 187 Ayr Rd, KA9 1TP, ☎ 76811 – TV wc Ⓟ – **39 rm.** BY **v**
- **Kincraig,** 39 Ayr Rd, KA9 1SY, ☎ 79480 – Ⓟ BY **c**
  7 rm 4.00/8.00 **st.**

MORRIS-MG-WOLSELEY 1 Monkton Rd ☎ 77415 OPEL 97/99 Main St. ☎ 70545

QUOTHQUAN Lanark. (Strathclyde) – pop. **73** – ✉ ☎ 0899 Biggar.
Edinburgh 30 – Carlisle 72 – Glasgow 37.

- **Shieldhill**, ML12 6NA, NE: ¾ m. ☎ 20035, ≤, – wc wc Ⓟ
  M 2.50/4.50 1.30 – **19 rm** 7.50/14.00.

RAASAY (Isle of) Inverness. (Highland).
to Isle of Skye: Sconser (Caledonian MacBrayne) Monday/Saturday 3-4 daily (15 mn).

RENFREW Renfrew. (Strathclyde) 986 ⑭⑮ – pop. **18,595** – ☎ 041 Glasgow.
Edinburgh 50 – Glasgow 7.

- Normandy (Stakis), Inchinnan Rd, PA4 9EJ, ☎ 886 4100, Telex 778897 – TV wc Ⓟ. – **142 rm.**
- **Glasgow Airport,** 91 Glasgow Rd, PA4 8YB, ☎ 886 3771, Telex 779032 – TV wc Ⓟ.
  M 3.25/4.35 **t.** 1.75 – **120 rm** 11.50/16.50 **t.**
- **Piccolo Mondo,** 63 Hairst St., PA4 8QY, ☎ 886 3055, Italian rest., Dancing
  closed Sunday – **M** a la carte 4.90/8.55 1.50.

CHRYSLER-SIMCA 14/18 Fulbar St. ☎ 886 3354 VAUXHALL Porterfield Rd ☎ 886 2777

RHUBODACH Bute. (Strathclyde) – Shipping Services: see Bute (Isle of).

RHUM (Isle of) Inverness. (Highland) 986 ⑥ – Shipping Services: see Mallaig.

ROCKCLIFFE Kirkcudbright. (Dumfries and Galloway) – pop. **170** – ✉ Dalbeattie – ☎ 055 663.
See : Site*.
Edinburgh 95 – Dumfries 18 – Stranraer 69.

- **Baron's Craig**, DG5 4QF, ☎ 225, ≤, , park – wc Ⓟ
  April-mid October – **M** approx. 5.00 **t.** 1.30 – **27 rm** 10.40/24.00 **st.** – P 17.50/21.00 **st.**

ROSLIN Midlothian (Lothian).
See: Roslyn Chapel** (15C) *AC.*
Edinburgh 7 – Peebles 16.

Hotels and restaurants see : Edinburgh N: 7 m.

ROTHES Moray. (Grampian) 986 ⑦ – pop. **1,204** – ☎ 034 03.
Edinburgh 185 – Aberdeen 61 – Fraserburgh 59 – **Inverness 49.**

- **Rothes Glen,** IV33 7AH, N: 3 m. on A 941 ☎ 254, ≤, « Country house atmosphere », , park – wc Ⓟ
  March-mid November – **M** 4.80 **t.** 1.30 – **19 rm** 9.90/21.80 **t.**

ROVER-TRIUMPH New St. ☎ 231

ROTHESAY Bute. (Strathclyde) 986 ⑭ – see Bute (Isle of).

ROUSAY (Isle of) Orkney (Orkney Islands) – Shipping Services: see Orkney Islands (Mainland: Kirkwall).

RUTHERGLEN Lanark. (Strathclyde) – pop. 24,732 – ✉ ☎ 041 Glasgow.
Edinburgh 42 – Glasgow 1.5.

Mill (Open House), Mill St., G73 2AP, ☎ 647 5491 – wc ☎ P. – **30 rm.**
Burnside (Stakis), East Kilbride Rd, G73 5EA, on A 749 ☎ 634 1276 – TV wc ☎ P
M (grill rest. only) approx. 3.00 1.45 – **16 rm** 7.00/14.50.

MICHELIN Branch, Southcroft Rd ☎ 647 0261.

ROVER-TRIUMPH 23 Hamilton Rd ☎ 1569

ST. ANDREWS Fife. (Fife) 986 ⑪ – pop. **11,630** – ☎ 033 481 (4 fig.) or 0334 (5 fig.).
See: Cathedral* (St. Rule's tower and Museum *AC*).
18 ☎ 3938, St. Andrews Links – 18 ☎ 4296, St. Andrews Links.
i South St. ☎ 2021.
Edinburgh 49 – Dundee 14 – Stirling 51.

Old Course (B.T.H.), Old Station Rd, KY16 9SP, ☎ 4371, Telex 76280, ←, 18 – TV P.
M approx. 7.00 **st.** 1.55 – **68 rm** 24.00/42.50 **st.**
Rufflets, Strathkinness Low Rd, KY16 9TX, W: 1 ½ m. on B 939 ☎ 2594, ←, « Country house in large garden » – wc P
closed mid January-mid February – **M** a la carte 3.35/6.45 **st.** 1.65 – **22 rm** 9.50/22.00 **st.**
St. Andrews, 40 The Scores ☎ 2611, ← – TV wc ☎.
M (dinner only from November to March) 2.70/4.15 **st.** 0.75 – **26 rm** 9.20/18.40 **st.**
Star, Market St. KY16 9PA, ☎ 5701 – TV wc wc ☎
M 2.70/4.15 **st.** 0.75 – **26 rm** 8.50/17.00 **st.**

at Grange S: 1 ½ m. by A 959 – ✉ St. Andrews – ☎ 033 481:

Grange Inn, KY16 8LJ, ☎ 2670, ←, « 16C Inn », – P
M a la carte 4.90/7.85 1.50.

AUSTIN-MORRIS-MG-WOLSELEY 66 Largo Rd ☎ 2101
CHRYSLER Bridge St. ☎ 2424
ROVER-TRIUMPH 106/108 South St. ☎ 2685

ST. COMBS Aberdeen. (Grampian) – ✉ Fraserburgh – ☎ 034 65 Inverallochy.
Edinburgh 166 – Aberdeen 42 – Fraserburgh 6.

Tufted Duck, AB4 5YS, ☎ 481, ← – TV wc ☎ P
M approx. 4.00 **t.** 1.25 – **11 rm** 12.50/22.00 **t.**

ST. FILLANS Perth. (Tayside) – pop. 200 – ☎ 076 485.
9 ☎ 261.
Edinburgh 65 – Glasgow 55 – Oban 64 – Perth 29.

Four Seasons, PH6 2NF, ☎ 281, ← Loch Earn and mountains – TV wc ☎ P
April-October – **M** 5.00/6.00 1.50 – **17 rm** 20.00/28.00 – P 22.00/24.00.

ST. MARY'S LOCH Selkirk (Borders) – ☎ 075 04 Cappercleuch.
See: Loch*.
Edinburgh 56 – Moffat 19 – Selkirk 17.

Rodono, TD7 5LH, ☎ 232, ← St. Mary's Loch and hills, – P
closed November – **M** approx. 3.60 1.30 – **10 rm** 6.50/14.00 – P 12.20.

SALEN Argyll. (Strathclyde) 986 ⑩ – see Mull (Isle of).

SANDAY (Isle of) Orkney (Orkney Islands) 986 ⑯ – Shipping Services: see Orkney Islands (Mainland: Kirkwall).

SANQUHAR Dumfries. (Dumfries and Galloway) 986 ⑮ – pop. 2,030 – ☎ 065 92.
9 ☎ 577, SW: ¼ m.
Edinburgh 57 – Ayr 32 – Dumfries 27 – Glasgow 51.

Mennockfoot Lodge, DG3 5LU, SE: 2 m. on A 76 ☎ 382, ←, – wc P
closed 24 to 31 December – **M** approx. 4.00 – **12 rm** 7.00/15.00 – P 13.50/14.00.

SCALLOWAY Shetland (Shetland Islands) 986 ⑯ – see Shetland Islands (Mainland).

SCALPAY (Isle of) Inverness. (Highland).
to Isle of Harris: Kyles Scalpay (Caledonian MacBrayne) 6 daily (10 mn).

SCOURIE Sutherland. (Highland) 986 ② – pop. 250 – ✉ Lairg – ☎ 0971.
See: Site★. **Envir.**: Kinlochbervie (site★) NE: 15 m.
Edinburgh 261 – Inverness 102.

Scourie, IV27 4SX, ☎ 2396, ≤, – wc P
March-21 October – **M** *(28 May-30 September) (closed Friday)* 3.60/4.00 **t.** 1.00 – **22 rm** 6.95/16.10 **t.** – P 8.90/12.00 **t.**

SCRABSTER Caithness. (Highland) 986 ③ – Shipping Services: see Thurso.

SEAMILL Ayr. (Strathclyde) – ✉ ☎ 0294 West Kilbride.
Edinburgh 73 – Ayr 22 – Glasgow 30.

Inverclyde, 31 Ardrossan Rd, KA23 9NA, ☎ 823124 – P
M a la carte approx. 7.25 **st.** 1.20 – **9 rm** 6.00/12.00 **st.**

SHAPINSAY (Isle of) Orkney (Orkney Islands) – Shipping Services: see Orkney Islands (Mainland: Kirkwall).

SHETLAND ISLANDS Shetland (Shetland Islands) 986 ⑯ ⑳.
see Mainland: Sumburgh.
by Shetland Islands Council: from Toft (Mainland) to Ulsta (Yell) May-October **14-16** daily (22 mn) – from Gutcher (Yell) to Belmont (Unst) May-October **7-14** daily (12 mn); to Oddsta (Fetlar) May-October **1-3** daily (25 mn) – from Laxo (Mainland) to Symbister (Whalsay) May-October 4-7 daily (25 mn).
, see also Mainland: Lerwick.

MAINLAND

Hillswick – ✉ ☎ 080 623 Hillswick.
See: Site★. **Envir.**: Esha Ness (St. Magnus Bay★★★) W: 8 m. – E: Sullom Voe★★.

St. Magnus Bay, ZE2 9RW, ☎ 209, ≤ St. Magnus Bay, – wc P
M 4.00/4.50 **s.** – **33 rm** 8.50/19.50 **s.**

Lerwick – pop. 5,933 – ✉ ☎ 0595 Lerwick.
See: Site★ – Harbour★ – Clickhimin Broch★. **Envir.**: W: The Deeps (cliff)★★★ – Loch of Tingwall★ NW: 5 m. – Gulberwick (wick ≤★) SW: 5 m.
18 ☎ 059 584 (Gott) 369, N: 3 ½ m.
to Aberdeen (P & O Ferries: Orkney and Shetland Services) Tuesday and Saturday (12 h.) – to Orkney: Kirkwall (P & O Ferries: Orkney and Shetland Services) Wednesday (8 h) – to Bressay (Shetland Islands Council) May-October 8-10 daily (10 mn).
to the Isles of Skerries: May-October Tuesday and Friday **1** daily (3 h.).
i Area Tourist Officer, Alexandra Wharf ☎ 3434, Telex 75119.

Lerwick (Thistle), 15 South Rd, ZE1 0RB, ☎ 2166, Telex 75128 ≤ – TV wc wc P
25 rm.

Kveldsro House, ZE1 0AQ, ☎ 2195 – TV wc P
closed Christmas – **14 rm.**

AUSTIN-MORRIS-MG-WOLSELEY Commercial Rd ☎ 1313
CHRYSLER-SIMCA 20 Commercial Rd ☎ 895
RENAULT North Rd ☎ 3315
ROVER-TRIUMPH, VAUXHALL 26 North Rd ☎ 2855

Scalloway – ✉ ☎ 059 588 Scalloway.
See: Site and ≤★★.
9 Berry Farm ☎ 219.

Scalloway, Main St, ZE1 0TR, ☎ 444, ≤ – TV wc P
M a la carte 3.45/5.00 1.50 – **15 rm** 9.50/17.00.

Sumburgh – ✉ ☎ 095 06 Sumburgh.
See: Jarlshof (prehistoric village★★, site★). **Envir.**: St. Ninian's Isle★★ NW 9 m. – Levenwick ≤★ N: 9 m.
☎ 274.

Voe – ✉ ☎ 080 68 Voe.
See: Site★. **Envir.**: Dales Voe★ N: 5 m. – Walls (site★) SW: 18 ½ m. **Exc.**: W: Voe of Snarraness★★ – Swarbacks Minn (from B 9071 ≤★★) – Sound of Papa★★ – The Rona Aith Voe (from B 9071 ≤★★).

UNST

Baltasound – ✉ ✆ 095 781 Baltasound.

Baltasound (Thistle) ⛰, ZE2 9DS, ☎ 334, ≤ – ⛾wc Ⓟ
10 rm.

SKEABOST Inverness. (Highland) – see Skye (Isle of).

SKELMORLIE Ayr. (Strathclyde) 986 ⑭ – pop. **1,233** – ✆ 0475 Wemyss Bay.
Edinburgh 73 – Ayr 36 – Glasgow 30.

Manor Park ⛰, PA17 5HE, S: 2 ¾ m. on A 78 ☎ 520832, ≤ gardens and Firth of Clyde, « Extensive well kept gardens », park – TV ⛾wc ☎ Ⓟ
closed January – **M** approx. 4.25 ₰ 1.50 – **8 rm** ⊐ 9.50/19.00.

SKERRIES (Isles of) Shetland (Shetland Islands) – Shipping services: see Shetland Islands.

SKYE (Isle of) Inverness. (Highland) 986 ⑥ – pop. **11,065**.
See : East coast scenery and Cuillin Hills★★★.

✈ ☎ 34121.

⛴ by Caledonian MacBrayne: from Kyleakin to Kyle of Lochalsh: frequent services every day (5 mn) – from Armadale to Mallaig: Monday/Saturday 4-5 daily Summer only (30 mn) – from Uig to North Uist (Lochmaddy)) Monday/Saturday 1-2 daily (2 h) – from Sconser to Isle of Raasay: Monday/Saturday 3-4 daily (15 mn) – from Uig to the Isle of Harris (Tarbert) Monday/ Saturday 1-2 daily (2 h).

⛴ from Armadale to Mallaig (Caledonian MacBrayne) Monday/Saturday **1-2** daily winter only (30 to 45 mn).

AUSTIN-MG-WOLSELEY Armadale ☎ 30343

Broadford – ✉ ✆ 047 12 Broadford.
See : Broadford Bay★★ – Red Hills★★. **Envir.** : Elgol (site★★★) SW: 13 ½ m. – Sound of Sleat★★ SE: by A 851 – Armadale (site★★) S: 16 ½ m. – Kyleakin (site★) E: 8 m.
i ☎ 361 and 463 (April-October).

Broadford, IV49 9AB, ☎ 204, ≤, ⚲ – Ⓟ
M (bar lunch) 4.35/5.40 **st.** ₰ 1.00 – **31 rm** ⊐ 9.20/20.50 **st.**

VW Broadford ☎ 210

Dunvegan – ✉ ✆ 047 022 Dunvegan.
See : Loch★★ – Dunvegan Castle★ *AC.*

Dunvegan, IV51 9SP, ☎ 202, ≤ Loch Dunvegan – ⛾wc Ⓟ
M 2.00/4.00 ₰ 1.15 – **16 rm** ⊐ 5.50/11.00.

Portree – ✉ ✆ Portree.
See : Site★ – Sound of Raasay★★★. **Envir.** : Old Man of Storr★★ N : 7 m. – Loch Bracadale★★ SW : 9 m. **Exc.** : Kilt Rocks (≤★★★), Staffin Bay and Quiraing★★★ N: 18 m.
i Meall House, ☎ 2137, Telex 75202.

Royal, Bank St., IV51 9BU, ☎ 2525 – ⛾wc 🚗 Ⓟ
M 3.25/3.50 **st.** ₰ 1.50 – **26 rm** ⊐ 9.00/20.00 **st.**

Rosedale, IV51 9DB, ☎ 2531, ≤ harbour – ⛾wc
May-mid October – **M** 3.75/4.25 **t.** ₰ 1.30 – **20 rm** ⊐ 7.50/17.00 **t.**

AUSTIN-MG Dunvegan Rd ☎ 2554 MORRIS-MG-WOLSELEY ☎ 2002

Skeabost Bridge – ✉ ✆ 047 032 Skeabost Bridge.

Skeabost House ⛰, IV51 9NR, ☎ 202, ≤ Loch Snizort Beag, « Country house in grounds bordering Loch Snizort Beag », ⚑, park – ⛾wc Ⓟ
April-October – **M** approx. 4.25 – **22 rm** ⊐ 7.50/19.90 **st.**

Sligachan – ✉ ✆ 047 852 Sligachan.
See : Site★★★ – Loch★★. **Envir.** : Loch Harport★★ W: 6 m.

Sligachan, IV47 8SW, ☎ 204, ≤ mountains and Loch Sligachan, ⚲, ⚑ – ⛾wc 🚗 Ⓟ
April-third week October – **M** 5.00/5.30 **st.** ₰ 1.60 – **23 rm** ⊐ 9.50/19.80 **st.**

Uig – ✉ ✆ 047 042 Uig.
See : Loch Snizort★★. **Envir.** : Score Bay★ N: 8 m.

Uig ⛰, IV51 9YE, ☎ 205, ≤ Uig bay and harbour, ⚑ – ⛾wc ⛾wc Ⓟ
Easter-end September – **M** 4.00/4.50 **st.** ₰ 1.75 – **24 rm** ⊐ 10.50/21.00 **st.**

Es ist empfehlenswert, in der Hauptsaison und vor allen Dingen in Urlaubsorten, Hotelzimmer im voraus zu bestellen.

SLIGACHAN Inverness. (Highland) 986 ⑥ – see Skye (Isle of).

SOUTHEND Argyll. (Strathclyde) 986 ⑭ – pop. **136** – see Kintyre (Peninsula).

SOUTH QUEENSFERRY W. Lothian (Lothian) 986 ⑮ – pop. 5,056 – ✆ 031 Edinburgh.
See : Forth Bridge ** *AC*. **Envir. :** Hopetoun House ** *AC*, W : 3 m. – Blackness Castle* (15C) *AC*, W : 8 ½ m.
Edinburgh 9 – Dunfermline 7 – **Glasgow 40.**

- **Forth Bridges Lodge** (County), EH30 9SF, junction A 90 and Forth Bridge ☎ 331 1199, ≤ Firth of Forth and Bridges, – TV wc ☎ ♿ P. **M** a la carte 5.90/7.50 **st.** 2.50 – **98 rm** 15.00/24.00 **s.**
- Hawes Inn (Swallow) with rm, Edinburgh Rd, EH30 9TA, ☎ 331 1990, Group Telex 53168, – wc ☎ P
9 rm.

SPEAN BRIDGE Inverness. (Highland) 986 ⑩ – pop. **350** – ✆ 039 781.
Envir. : N : Loch Lochy**, Loch Garry (** from the A 87) by Invergarry – Clunes Forest (waterfall)* NW : 3 ½ m.
Edinburgh 133 – **Inverness 56** – Kyle of Lochalsh 66 – **Oban 58** – Perth 91.

- **Letterfinlay Lodge,** PH34 4DZ, N : 7 m. on A 82 ☎ 039 784 (Invergloy) 222, ≤, – P
M (bar lunch) approx. 3.50 2.00 – **12 rm** 6.50/13.00.
- **Spean Bridge,** PH34 4ES, ☎ 250, – wc P
M approx. 4.00 – **28 rm** 6.90/18.00 – P 12.60/14.70.

SPITTAL OF GLENSHEE Perth. – ✉ Blairgowrie – ✆ 025 085 Glenshee – Winter Sports.
Envir. : Devil's Elbow** N : 6 m. – S : Glenshee (** by chairlift 15 mn, *AC*).
Edinburgh 76 – **Dundee 36** – Perth 34.

Hotels see : Braemar N : 19 ½ m.

STENNESS Orkney (Orkney Islands) – see Orkney Islands (Mainland).

STEPPS Lanark. (Strathclyde) – see Glasgow.

STIRLING Stirling. (Central) 986 ⑪ – pop. 29,776 – ✆ 0786.
See : Stirling Castle** *AC* B – Church of the Holy Rude* B **A** – **Envir. :** Bannockburn (battlefield) *AC*, S : 3 m. by Glasgow Rd A – Doune Castle* (stronghold 15C) *AC*, NW : 8 m. by A 84 A.
18 Queen's Rd ☎ 3801 B – 9 Tillicoultry ☎ 741, E : 9 m. by A 9 A.
☎ 3085.
i Information Centre, Dumbarton Rd ☎ 5019 – Pirnhall Interchange, Bannockburn ☎ 0786 (Bannockburn) 814026 (May-October).
Edinburgh 36 – Dunfermline 21 – Falkirk 15 – **Glasgow 25** – Greenock 48 – Motherwell 28 – **Oban 86** – Perth 33.

Plan on next page

- **Golden Lion,** 8 King St., FK8 1BD, ☎ 5351 – TV wc wc ☎ P. — B c
M 3.75/5.75 1.10 – **59 rm** 9.50/20.00.
- King Robert (Open House), Glasgow Rd, FK7 0LJ, ☎ 0786 (Bannockburn) 811666 – TV wc ☎ P — A x
20 rm.
- **Station** (Stakis), 56 Murray Pl., FK8 2BX, ☎ 2017 – TV wc wc ☎ P — B n
M (grill rest. only) approx. 3.00 **t.** – **25 rm** 10.50/18.00 **t.**
- **Royal,** 2 Queen St., FK8 1HN, ☎ 5137 – wc — B a
M approx. 4.00 **st.** 2.00 – **12 rm** 10.00/18.00 **st.**
- **Heritage** with rm, 16 Allan Park, FK8 2QG, ☎ 3660, « Tastefully furnished », , French rest. – wc P — B e
M approx. 5.00 1.50 – **4 rm** 9.00/16.00.
- **Hollybank** with rm, 54 Glasgow Rd, St. Ninians, FK7 0PH, ☎ 0786 (Bannockburn) 812311, – P — A v
closed October – **M** *(closed Sunday and Monday)* (dinner only) a la carte 4.60/5.60 1.40 – **4 rm** 10.00/12.00.

ALFA-ROMEO, TOYOTA Kerse Rd ☎ 62618
AUSTIN-DAIMLER-JAGUAR-MORRIS-MG-ROVER-TRIUMPH, ROLLS ROYCE-BENTLEY Wallace St. ☎ 62821
CHRYSLER Goosecroft Rd ☎ 4477
CITROEN, VAUXHALL 119/139 Glasgow Rd ☎ 0786 (Bannockburn) 811234
FIAT 44 Causeway Rd ☎ 62426
FORD Drip Rd ☎ 4891
OPEL Birkhill Rd, Cambusbarron ☎ 61808
PEUGEOT 124/126 Main St. ☎ 0877 (Callander) 30022
RENAULT Kildean Market ☎ 4793
VW, AUDI-NSU Drip Rd ☎ 5101

STIRLING

Dumbarton Road .... B 10
Murray Place .... B 16
Port Street .... B
Upper Craigs .... B 29

Borestone Crescent .... A 2
Burgh Muir Road .... B 3
Causewayhead Road .... A, B 4
Corn Exchange Road .... B 5
Cornton Road .... A 7
Coxithill Road .... A 8
Gladstone Place .... B 9
Goosecroft Road .... B 12
King Street .... B 13
Newhouse .... A 15
Park Place .... A 18
Queen Street .... B 20
Randolph Terrace .... A 22
Seaforth Place .... B 24
Shirra's Brae Road .... A 26
Southfield Crescent .... B 27
Union Street .... B 28
Victoria Square .... B 30
Weaver Row .... A 31

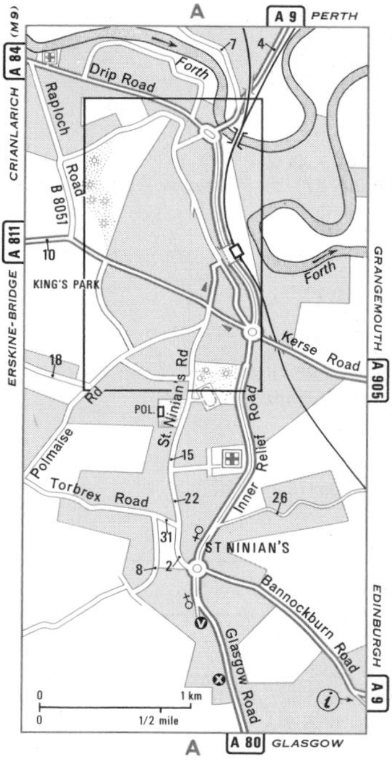

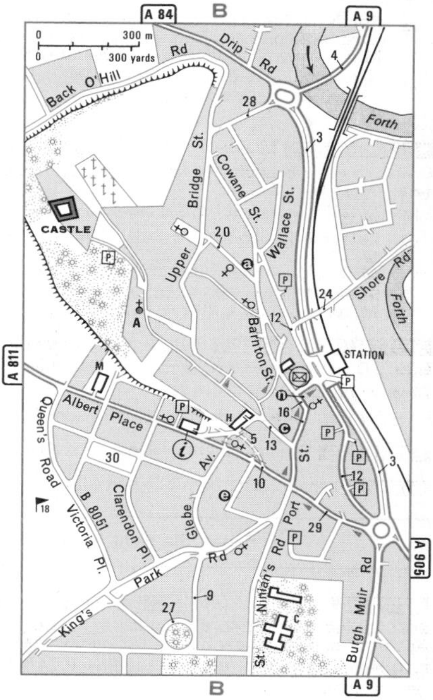

STONEHAVEN Kincardine (Grampian) 986 ⑦⑪ – pop. 4,730 – ☎ 0569.
See : Site*. **Envir. :** Dunnottar Castle (site**, ruins*) *AC*, S : 1 ½ m.
18 Cowie, ☎ 2124.
i The Square ☎ 62806 (May-October).
Edinburgh 109 – Aberdeen 15 – Dundee 50.

- **Commodore,** Cowie Park, AB3 2PZ, ☎ 62936 – TV wc ☎ P. **M** approx. 3.95 **t.** 1.30 – 1.50 – **36 rm** 13.95/16.95 **t.**
- **St. Leonard's,** 2 Bath St., AB3 2DE, ☎ 62044, – TV wc ☎ P. **M** approx. 3.50 **t.** 2.00 – **12 rm** 8.00/18.00.

AUSTIN-MORRIS-MG-ROVER-TRIUMPH-WOLSELEY 64/74 Barclay St. ☎ 2077

STORNOWAY Ross and Cromarty (Outer Hebrides) (Western Isles) 986 ② – see Lewis (Isle of).

STRACHUR Argyll. (Strathclyde) – pop. 700 – ✉ Cairndow – ☎ 036 986.
See : Loch Fyne**. **Envir. :** Glen Croe* NE: 15 m.
Edinburgh 99 – Glasgow 56 – Oban 60.

- Creggans Inn, PA27 8BX, ☎ 279, ≤ Loch Fyne Bay, – wc ♿ P **27 rm.**

STRANRAER Wigtown. (Dumfries and Galloway) 986 ⑱ – pop. 9,853 – ☎ 0776.
Envir. : Castle Kennedy gardens* *AC*, E: 3 ½ m. **Exc.**: Mull of Galloway (site and ≤**) SE: 22 m.
18 Creachmore, Leswalt ☎ 87245, SW: 2 m.
to Larne (Sealink) 1-6 daily (2 h 15 mn).
i Breastwork Car Park ☎ 2595 (mid May-September).
Edinburgh 128 – Ayr 53 – Dumfries 76.

- **North West Castle,** Royal Crescent, DG9 8EH, ☎ 2644 – wc ☎ P
  M 3.25/4.00 **st.** 2.00 – **81 rm** 7.00/16.00 **st.** – P 10.25/11.15 **st.**
- **George** (Interchange), George St., DG9 7RJ, ☎ 2487 – wc ☎
  M 3.50/4.50 **t.** 1.65 – 1.50 – **28 rm** 9.00/21.00 **st.**
- **L'Apéritif,** London Rd, DG9 8EP, ☎ 2991 – P
  closed Sunday and 10 September-17 October – **M** 3.50/5.50 **st.** 1.25.

AUSTIN-MORRIS-MG-ROVER-TRIUMPH Charlotte St. ☎ 2301
CHRYSLER Station St. ☎ 3521
DAF, MAZDA The Garage, Leswalt ☎ 077687 (Leswalt) 634
DATSUN Hanover Sq. ☎ 2833
FIAT, VAUXHALL North Strand St. ☎ 2561

STRATHBLANE Stirling. (Central) – pop. 1,584 – ✉ Glasgow – ☎ 0360 Blanefield.
Edinburgh 48 – Glasgow 11 – Stirling 25.

- **Kirkhouse Inn,** Glasgow Rd, G63 9AA, ☎ 70621 – wc ☎ P
  M approx. 2.50 **s.** – **19 rm** 9.00/16.00 **s.**

at Campsie Glen W: 3 ¼ m. on A 891 – ✉ Glasgow – ☎ 0360 Lennoxtown:

- **Campsie Glen** , G65 7AF, ☎ 310666, , park – TV wc ☎ P
  M approx. 3.00 **t.** 1.45 – **8 rm** 13.00/20.00 **t.**

STRATHY Sutherland (Highland) – ☎ 064 14.
Envir. : Strathy Point*** N: 3 ½ m.
Edinburgh 301 – Inverness 142 – Thurso 21 – Tongue 23.

Hotel see: Bettyhill SW: 12 m.

STROMNESS Orkney (Orkney Islands) 986 ⑯ – see Orkney Islands (Mainland).

STRONSAY (Isle of) Orkney (Orkney Islands) 986 ⑯ – Shipping Services: see Orkney Islands (Mainland: Kirkwall).

STRONTIAN Argyll. (Highland) – pop. 275 – ☎ 0967.
Edinburgh 137 – Inverness 88 – Kyle of Lochalsh 98 – Oban 54.

- **Kilcamb Lodge** , PH36 4HY, ☎ 2257, ≤, , park – wc P
  closed November – **M** approx. 4.00 1.00 – **11 rm** (dinner included) 10.50/13.50.

SUMBURGH Shetland (Shetland Islands) 986 ⑯ – see Shetland Islands (Mainland).

SYMINGTON Lanark. (Strathclyde) – pop. 713 – ✉ Biggar – ☎ 089 93 Tinto.
Edinburgh 31 – Dumfries 49 – Glasgow 38.

- Tinto (Open House), ML12 6LQ, on A 72 ☎ 454, Telex 77986, ≤, – P – **21 rm.**

AUSTIN-MG-WOLSELEY 61 Biggar Rd ☎ 200

TAIN Ross and Cromarty (Highland) 986 ③ and ⑦ – pop. 1,942 – ☎ 0862.
Envir. : Portmahomack ≤* E: 10 m.
18 ☎ 2314.
Edinburgh 206 – Inverness 47 – Wick 89.

- **Royal,** High St., IV19 1AB, ☎ 2013 – wc P.
  M 3.50/4.50 – **21 rm** 6.00/14.00.

AUSTIN-MORRIS-MG-ROVER-TRIUMPH-WOLSELEY Geanies St. ☎ 2375
TOYOTA Knockbreck Rd ☎ 2175

TARBERT Argyll. (Strathclyde) 986 ⑭ – see Kintyre (Peninsula).

TARBERT Inverness. (Outer Hebrides) (Western Isles) 986 ② – see Harris (Isle of).

THORNHILL Dumfries. (Dumfries and Galloway) 986 ⑮ – pop. 6,087 – ☎ 084 83.
Envir.: Drumlanrig Castle* NW: 2 ½ m.
9 ☎ 546.
Edinburgh 62 – Ayr 44 – Dumfries 15 – Glasgow 59.

- **Buccleuch and Queensberry,** Drumlanrig St., DG3 5LU, ☎ 215 – wc P
  M (bar lunch) a la carte 3.25/4.00 **t.** 1.50 – **10 rm** 7.75/15.50 **t.** – P 11.50/12.50 **t.**

THURSO Caithness. (Highland) 986 ③ – pop. 9,025 – ☎ 0847.

Envir.: Dunnet Head *** (sea birds' nests) NE: 13 m. – Dunnet Bay ** NE: 9 m. **Exc.:** Strathy Point *** W: 23 m.

18 ☎ 3807, 2 m. from railway station.

from Scrabster to the Orkney Islands : Stromness (P & O Ferries: Orkney and Shetland Services) 1-3 daily (except Sunday September-June) (2 h).

i Car Park, Riverside ☎ 2371 (May-October).

Edinburgh 290 – Inverness 131 – Wick 21.

Hotels see : John O'Groats NE: 19 m.
Wick SE: 21 m.

CITROEN Couper Sq. Riverside ☎ 2778 | RENAULT Bridgend ☎ 3161

TIGHNABRUAICH Argyll. (Strathclyde) 986 ⑭ – pop. 1,100 – ☎ 070 081 – 9.

See : Kyles of Bute**. **Envir.:** Loch Fyne** NW: 12 m.

i Information Centre ☎ 393 (April-September).

Edinburgh 122 – Glasgow 79 – Oban 83.

TIREE (Isle of) Argyll. (Strathclyde) 986 ⑩.

☎ 087 92 (Scarinish) 456/7.

by Caledonian MacBrayne: to Oban: Monday/Saturday 3-4 weekly (4 h 15 to 4 h 50 mn) – to Isle of Coll: Monday/Saturday 3-4 weekly (1 h 15 mn) – to Isle of Mull (Tobermory) 2 weekly summer only (2 h 30 mn) – to Lochaline: 2 weekly summer only (3 h 30 mn).

to Isle of Mull: Tobermory (Caledonian MacBrayne) 3 weekly (2 h 45 mn).

TOBERMORY Argyll. (Strathclyde) 986 ⑩ – see Mull (Isle of).

TOMINTOUL Banff. (Grampian) 986 ⑦ – pop. 400 – ✉ Ballindalloch – ☎ 080 74.

See : Site*. **Envir. :** SE: Lecht Road ≤** of the Grampian Mountains.

i Main St. ☎ 285 (June-September).

Edinburgh 122 – Aberdeen 63 – Inverness 47.

Richmond Arms, The Square, AB3 9ET, ☎ 209, – wc **P**
27 rm.

TONGUE Sutherland. (Highland) 986 ③ – pop. 108 – ✉ Lairg – ☎ 080 05.

Envir. : Torrisdale Bay** NE : 9 m. – Tongue Bay (≤* from Coldbackie) N: 2 ½ m. **Exc.:** Strathy Point*** NE : 22 ½ m. – Loch Eriboll*** W : 21 m. – SW : Ben Loyal and Ben Hope (≤*) : road from Tongue to Durness.

Edinburgh 255 – Inverness 96 – Thurso 44.

Tongue, IV27 4XD, ☎ 206, ≤, « Tastefully furnished in Victorian style », – wc **P**
mid April-early October – **M** (snack lunch) 4.25/5.00 **st.** 0.95 – **19 rm** 11.00/22.00 **st.**

Ben Loyal, Main St., IV27 4XE, ☎ 216, ≤, – wc **P**
M (bar lunch) 3.25/3.75 **t.** 1.20 – **19 rm** 6.75/16.00.

TROON Ayr. (Strathclyde) 986 ⑭ – pop. 11,318 – ☎ 0292.

18, 18 ☎ 312464.

i 14 Templehill ☎ 314455.

Edinburgh 72 – Ayr 7 – Glasgow 29.

Marine, Crosbie Rd, KA10 6HE, ☎ 314444, ≤, – **P**.
M approx. 4.75 **s.** 0.95 – **70 rm** 15.80/27.60 **s.**

Sun Court, 19 Crosbie Rd, KA10 6HF, ☎ 312727, ≤, – wc **P**
M approx. 4.50 **st.** 1.00 – **20 rm** 9.00/18.00 **st.**

Craiglea, 78-80 South Beach, KA10 6EG, ☎ 311366, ≤, – TV wc **P**
M 2.50/5.50 **t.** 1.20 – **21 rm** 8.00/18.00 **t.** – P 11.00/14.00 **t.**

Ardneil, 51 St. Meddans St., KA10 6NU, ☎ 311611 – TV wc **P**
M 3.00/5.00 1.50 – **9 rm** 6.50/15.00.

XX **Auberge de Provence,** (at Marine Hotel), Crosbie Rd, KA10 6HE, ☎ 314444, French rest. – **P**
M (dinner only) a la carte 5.30/7.35 **t.**

AUSTIN-MG-WOLSELEY 72 Portland St. ☎ 312312 | MORRIS-MG-WOLSELEY Dundonald Rd ☎ 314141
CHRYSLER-SIMCA Cavendish Pl. ☎ 311001 | ROVER-TRIUMPH St. Meddans St. ☎ 312099

TURNBERRY Ayr. (Strathclyde) – pop. 500 – ✉ Girvan – ☎ 065 53.

18, 18 ☎ 202.

Edinburgh 93 – Ayr 18 – Glasgow 50 – Stranraer 35.

Turnberry (B.T.H.), Maidens Rd, KA26 9LT, on A 719 ☎ 202, Telex 777779, ≤ golf course and bay, 18, – TV **P**.
M approx. 6.10 **st.** 1.95 – **122 rm** 28.60/49.20 **st.** – P 28.80/34.90 **st.**

UDDINGSTON Lanark. (Strathclyde) – pop. 5,163 – ✉ Glasgow – ☎ 0698.
Edinburgh 38 – Glasgow 7.5.

- **Redstones,** 8-10 Glasgow Rd, G71 7AS, ☎ 813774 – TV wc ☎ P
  M approx. 3.50 **st.** 2.00 – **19 rm** 7.75/16.50 **st.**

UIG Inverness. (Highland) 986 ⑥ – see Skye (Isle of).

UIST (Isles of) ★ Inverness. (Outer Hebrides) (Western Isles) 986 ⑥ – pop. 5,105.
See : Benbecula (≤★ from Peinavalla, South Nunton).
✈ ☎ 0870 (Benbecula) 2051.

Lochboisdale (South Uist) – ✉ ☎ 087 84 Lochboisdale.
Envir. : Sound of Eriskay (≤★ from Ludac) S : 9 m. by A 865 and B 888.
18 ☎ 253, N : 5 m.
by Caledonian MacBrayne : to Oban : 3-6 weekly (5 h 30 mn to 8 h 15 mn) – to Isle of Barra (Castlebay) 2-4 weekly summer only (1 h 30 mn to 1 h 45 mn).
to Lochaline (Caledonian MacBrayne) 6 weekly summer only (4 to 6 h).
i Information Centre ☎ 286 (May-September).

- Lochboisdale, ☎ 332, ≤, – P – **19 rm.**

Lochmaddy (North Uist) – ✉ ☎ 087 63 Lochmaddy.
See: Site★. **Envir.:** Sound of Berneray★★ NE : 8 m. by A 865 – Vallay Strand★ NW by A 865.
by Caledonian MacBrayne : to Isle of Skye : (Uig) Monday/Saturday 1-2 daily (2 h) – to Isle of Harris (Tarbert) 1-2 weekly (2 h).
i Information Centre ☎ 321 (May-September).

- **Lochmaddy,** PA28 5AA, ☎ 331, ≤, – P
  M 4.50 **t.** 1 10 – **16 rm** 8.50/17.00 **t.**

ULLAPOOL Ross and Cromarty (Highland) 986 ② – pop. 950 – ☎ 0854.
See : Site★. **Envir. :** Corrieshalloch Gorge★, Falls of Measach★ SE : 12 m. – Strath More (≤★ from the A 832) SE : 10 m.
to Isle of Lewis : Stornoway (Caledonian MacBrayne) Monday/Saturday 1-2 daily (3 h 15 mn).
i Information Centre ☎ 2135 (May-October).
Edinburgh 218 – Inverness 59.

- **Royal,** IV26 2SY, ☎ 2181, ≤, park – P.
  M 3.75/4.90 1.70 – **60 rm** 9.00/28.00 **t.** – P 16.00/22.00 **t.**
- **Ullapool Mercury Motor Inn,** North Rd, IV26 2TG, ☎ 2314, ≤ – wc P
  closed 12 November-4 March – **M** a la carte approx. 3.80 **st.** 1.35 – 1.50 – **60 rm** 10.00/16.00 **st.**
- **Caledonian,** Quay St., IV26 2UG, ☎ 2306, Group Telex 778215 – wc P
  April-October – **M** approx. 4.85 **st.** 1.45 – **40 rm** 9.45/18.90 **st.**
- **Ceilidh Place,** 14 West Argyle St., IV26 2TY, ☎ 2103 – wc P
  M a la carte 4.55/6.25 **st.** 1.70 – **9 rm** 8.10/19.20 **st.**
- **Ferry Boat Inn,** Shore St., IV26 2UJ, ☎ 2366, ≤
  M (bar lunch) a la carte approx. 3.00 – **9 rm** 5.00/14.00.

UNST (Isle of) Shetland (Shetland Islands) 986 ⑯ – see Shetland Islands.

UPHALL W. Lothian (Lothian) – pop. 14,180 – ☎ 0506 Broxburn.
Envir. : Hopetoun House★★ *AC,* NE : 9 m.
18 ☎ 2404.
Edinburgh 11 – Glasgow 32.

- **Houstoun House** , EH52 6JS, ☎ 853831, ≤, « Gardens », park – TV wc wc ☎ P
  closed 25 and 26 December – **M** 5.75/6.50 **st.** 1.40 – **21 rm** 16.00/24.00 **st.**

UPLAWMOOR Renfrew. (Strathclyde) – pop. 800 – ✉ Barrhead – ☎ 050 585.
Edinburgh 55 – Ayr 24 – Glasgow 12.

- **Uplawmoor,** Neilston Rd, G78 4AF, ☎ 565 – P
  M a la carte 4.00/8.65 **t.**

VOE Shetland (Shetland Islands) – see Shetland Islands (Mainland).

WALKERBURN Peebles. (Borders) – pop. 932 – ☎ 089 687.
See : Tweed Valley★.
Edinburgh 32 – Galashiels 9 – Peebles 9.

- **Tweed Valley** , Galashiels Rd, EH43 6AA, ☎ 220, , – P
  M 4.50/5.50 **st.** 1.50 – **14 rm** 8.20/13.40 **st.** – P 13.45/16.20 **st.**
  20

WEEM Perth. (Tayside) – see Aberfeldy.

WEMYSS BAY Renfrew. (Strathclyde) 986 ⑭ – ✆ 0475.
⛴ to the Isle of Bute: Rothesay (Caledonian MacBrayne) frequent services every day (30 mn).

Hotels see : Largs S: 4 ½ m.
Skelmorlie S: 1 ½ m.

WESTHILL Aberdeen. (Grampian) – see Aberdeen.

WEST LOCH TARBERT Argyll. (Strathclyde) 986 ⑭ – Shipping Services: see Kintyre (Peninsula).

WESTRAY (Isle of) Orkney (Orkney Islands) 986 ⑯ – see Orkney Islands.

WHALSAY (Isle of) Shetland (Shetland Islands) 986 ⑯ – Shipping Services: see Shetland Islands.

WHITING BAY Bute. (Strathclyde) – see Arran (Isle of).

WHITHORN (Isle of) Wigtown. (Dumfries and Galloway) – pop. 988 – ✆ 098 85.
See : Harbour*.
Edinburgh 149 – Ayr 74 – Dumfries 72 – Stranraer 32.

Queen's Arms, Main St., DG8 8QJ ☎ 369, – wc P
M approx. 3.50 **t.** – **10 rm** 6.25/14.50 **t.**

WICK Caithness. (Highland) 986 ③ – pop. 7,617 – ✆ 0955.
18 Reiss ☎ **2726, N: 3 m.**
✈ ☎ **2215, N: 1 m.**
i Whitechapel Rd off High St. ☎ 2596, Telex 75124.
Edinburgh 282 – Inverness 123.

Wick Mercury Motor Inn, Riverside, KW1 4NL, ☎ 3344 – TV wc P
M a la carte 3.50/5.25 **s.** 1.50 – 1.50 – **30 rm** 11.00/16.00.

AUSTIN-MORRIS-MG-ROVER-TRIUMPH-WOLSELEY Bridge St. ☎ 2195
CHRYSLER-SIMCA George St. ☎ 2322
DATSUN, VAUXHALL Francis St. ☎ 2240
FORD Francis St. ☎ 2103

WORMIT Fife. (Fife) – pop. 3,750 – ✉ ✆ 0382 Newport-on-Tay.
Edinburgh 53 – Dundee 4 – St. Andrews 12.

XX **Sandford Hill** with rm, DD6 8RG, S : 2 m. junction A 914 and B 946 ☎ 541802, ←, – TV wc P
M a la carte 4.75/7.75 **t.** 1.30 – **5 rm** 8.45/16.75 **t.**

WYRE (Isle of) Orkney (Orkney Islands) 986 ⑯ – Shipping Services: see Orkney Islands.

YELL (Isle of) Shetland (Shetland Islands) 986 ⑯ – Shipping Services: see Shetland Islands.

Northern Ireland

LICENSING HOURS - WHEN DRINKING ALCOHOLIC BEVERAGES IS PERMITTED IN PUBS AND BARS AND OTHER LICENSED PREMISES (The General Rule).

HEURES PERMISES POUR LA CONSOMMATION DES BOISSONS ALCOOLISÉES (Règle Générale).

ORARI CONSENTITI PER LA CONSUMAZIONE DI BEVANDE ALCOOLICHE (Regola Generale).

AUSSCHANKZEITEN FÜR ALKOHOLISCHE GETRÄNKE (Allgemeine Regelung).

	from / de / dalle / von	to / à / alle / bis	drinking up time / consommation jusqu'à / consumazione fino alle / getrunken werden darf bis	from / de / dalle / von	to / à / alle / bis	drinking up time / consommation jusqu'à / consumazione fino alle / getrunken werden darf bis	
Weekdays (other than Good Friday and Christmas Day) **Jours de semaine** (autres que Vendredi Saint et Jour de Noël)	11.30				23.00	23.30	**Giorni della Settimana** (esclusi Venerdì Santo e Natale) **Wochentags** (außer Karfreitag und Weihnachten)
Good Friday **Vendredi Saint**				17.00	23.00	23.30	**Venerdì Santo** **Karfreitag**
Hotels / Rest. — **Sundays** (except Christmas Day) **Dimanche** (sauf Jour de Noël)	12.30	14.30	15.00	19.00	22.00		**Domeniche** (escluso Natale) **Sonntags** (außer Weihnachten) — **Alberghi / Hotels / Ristoranti / Rest.**
Hotels / Rest. — **Christmas Day** **Jour de Noël**	12.30				22.00		**Natale** **Weihnachten** — **Alberghi / Hotels / Ristoranti / Rest.**
Pubs — Sundays and Christmas Day / Dimanches et jour de Noël	Closed - Fermés - Chiusi - Geschlossen						**Pubs** — Domeniche e Natale / Sonntags und Weihnachten

Hotels may serve alcoholic beverages to non-residents at any time on Christmas Day or Sundays but they have to be accompanied by a meal.
RESIDENTS: There are no drinking restrictions in licensed hotels for residents and their private friends.

Les hôtels peuvent servir des boissons alcoolisées aux non-résidents les dimanches et le jour de Noël mais seulement avec un repas.
RÉSIDENTS : Pas de restriction pour les résidents et leurs invités.

Gli alberghi possono servire bevande alcooliche ai non residenti la domenica ed a Natale ma soltanto con il pasto.
RESIDENTI: Nessuna restrizione per i residenti ed i loro amici privati nel loro albergo.

Hotels dürfen alkoholische Getränke Sonntags und an Weihnachten den Besuchern servieren, aber nur in Verbindung mit einer Mahlzeit.
FÜR HOTELGÄSTE und ihre persönlichen Freunde besteht im Hotel selbst keine Beschränkung.

Place with at least :

one hotel or restaurant ● Larne
one pleasant hotel 🏠, ✗ with rm.
one quiet, secluded hotel 🐎
one restaurant with ✿, ✿✿, M
See this town for establishments located in its vicinity BELFAST

La località possiede come minimo :

una risorsa alberghiera ● Larne
un albergo ameno 🏠, ✗ with rm.
un albergo molto tranquillo, isolato 🐎
un'ottima tavola con ✿, ✿✿, M
La località raggruppa nel suo testo le risorse dei dintorni BELFAST

Localité offrant au moins :

une ressource hôtelière ● Larne
un hôtel agréable 🏠, ✗ with rm.
un hôtel très tranquille, isolé 🐎
une bonne table à ✿, ✿✿, M
Localité groupant dans le texte les ressources de ses environs BELFAST

Ort mit mindestens :

einem Hotel oder Restaurant ● Larne
einem angenehmen Hotel 🏠, ✗ with rm.
einem sehr ruhigen und abgelegenen Hotel 🐎
einem Restaurant mit ✿, ✿✿, M
Ort mit Angaben über Hotels und Restaurants in seiner Umgebung BELFAST

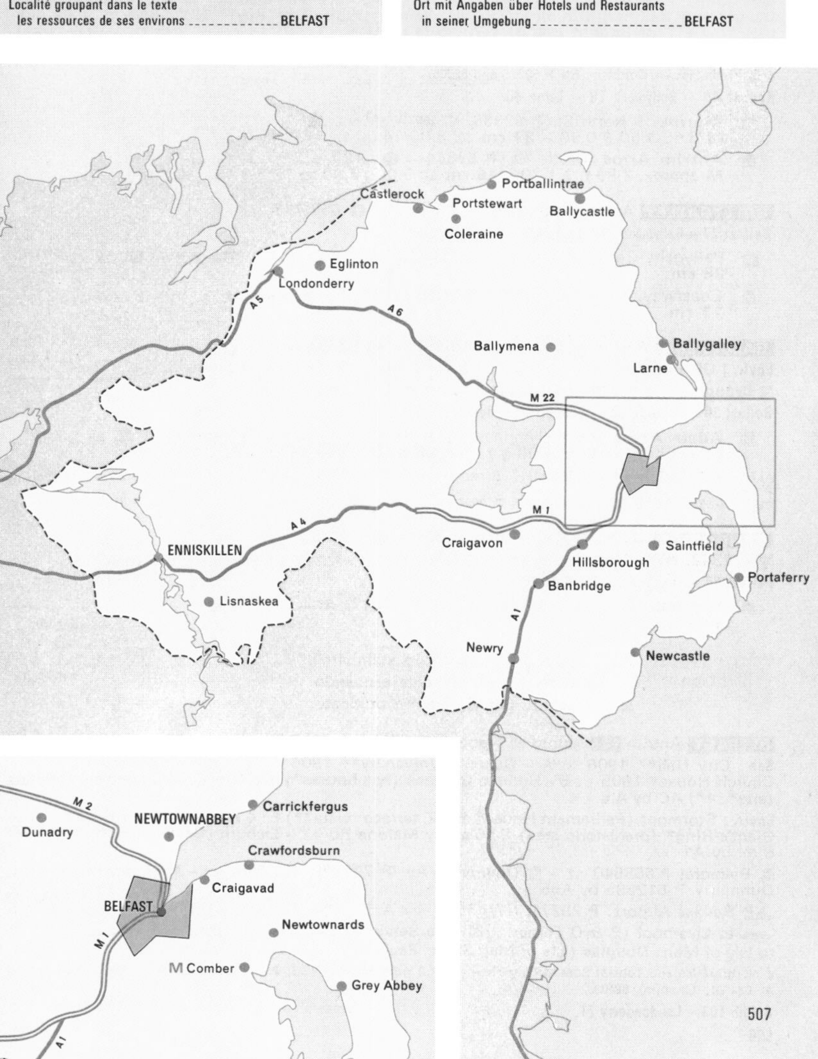

NORTHERN IRELAND

Towns

ANTRIM (Coast Road) Antrim 986 ⑭ ⑱.

i The Forum ☎ 084 941 (Antrim) 4131.

See : Road*** (A 2) from Larne to Portrush.

BALLYCASTLE Antrim 986 ⑭ – ✆ 026 57.

See : Site**. **Envir. :** Giant's Causeway*** (Chaussée des Géants) basalt formation (from the car-park *AC*, ½ h Rtn on foot) NW : **12** m. – White Park Bay** NW : 8 ½ m. – Carrick-a-Rede (≤** of Rathlin Island) NW : 5 ½ m.

18 ☎ 62536.

i Dalriada House, Coleraine Rd ☎ 62225 and 62565.

Belfast 60 – Ballymena 28 – Larne 40.

- **Marine,** 1 North St. ☎ 62336, ≤, – wc.
  M 3.50/4.50 0.90 – **37 rm** 8.00/14.00 **t.**
- **Antrim Arms,** Castle St. ☎ 62884 – P
  M approx. 2.80 **t.** 1.20 – **16 rm** 5.00/12.00 **t.**

BALLYGALLEY Antrim – pop. 487 – ✉ Larne – ✆ 057 483.

Belfast 27 – Ballymena 24 – Larne 4.

- Ballygally Castle, 274 Coast Rd, BT40 2QX, ☎ 212, ≤, – wc P.
  28 rm.
- Coastway, 352 Coast Rd, BT40 2QQ, ☎ 265, ≤ – wc P.
  13 rm.

BALLYMENA Antrim 986 ⑱ – pop. 16,487 – ✆ 0266.

Envir. : Glen of Glenariff*** – Glenariff (or Waterfoot) site* NE: 19 m.

18 Broughshane ☎ 026 686 (Broughshane) 207, E: 2 m. on A 42.

Belfast 30 – **Dundalk 82** – Larne 20 – **Londonderry 50** – **Omagh 55.**

- **Adair Arms,** 1-5 Ballymoney Rd, BT43 5BS, ☎ 3674 – TV wc P.
  M a la carte approx. 4.00 1.00 – **28 rm** 7.50/14.00.

ALFA-ROMEO, CHRYSLER, TRIUMPH Broadway Av. ☎ 2161
AUSTIN-MG-WOLSELEY Waveney Av. ☎ 3557
MORRIS-MG-WOLSELEY 34/36 George St. ☎ 6288
RENAULT 120 Antrim Rd ☎ 2650
VW, AUDI-NSU 1/5 Railway St. ☎ 2167

BANBRIDGE Down 986 ⑱ – pop. 6,864 – ✆ 082 06.

9 ☎ 2342, NW: **1** m.

Belfast 26 – Armagh 20 – **Dundalk 26.**

- Belmont, Rathfriland Rd, BT32 3LH, ☎ 22517, – wc P
  11 rm.

Red Lion — Se il nome di un albergo è stampato in carattere magro, chiedete arrivando le condizioni che vi saranno praticate.

BELFAST Antrim 986 ⑱ and ㊲ – pop. 360,150 – ✆ 0232.

See : City Hall** 1906 BZ **A** – Queen's University** 1906 AZ **U** – Ulster Museum* AZ **M** – Church House* 1905 BZ **B** – Botanic Gardens (hot houses*) AZ – Bellevue Zoological Gardens (site*, ≤*) *AC* by A 6 AY.

Envir. : Stormont (Parliament House* 1932, terrace: vista**) E: 4 m. by Belmont Rd AZ – The Giant's Ring* (prehistoric area) S: 5 m. by Malone Rd AZ – Lisburn (Castle gardens ≤*) SW: 8 m. by A1 AZ.

18 Balmoral ☎ 668540 AZ – 18 Downview Av. ☎ 771770, N : 2 m. AY – 18 Upper Malone Rd, Dunmurry ☎ 612695 by A55 AZ.

Belfast Airport: ☎ 29271, NW: 12 m. by A 52 AY – **Terminal :** Great Victoria St. Station.

to Liverpool (P & O Ferries: Irish Sea Services) 6-8 weekly (10 h).
to Isle of Man: Douglas (Isle of Man Steam Packet Co.) 1-3 weekly summer only (4 h 30 mn).

i Northern Ireland Tourist Board, River House, 48-52 High St., BT1 2DS, ☎ 31221 and 36609 – Aldergrove Airport ☎ 084 94 (Crumlin) 52103.

Dublin 103 – **Londonderry 71.**

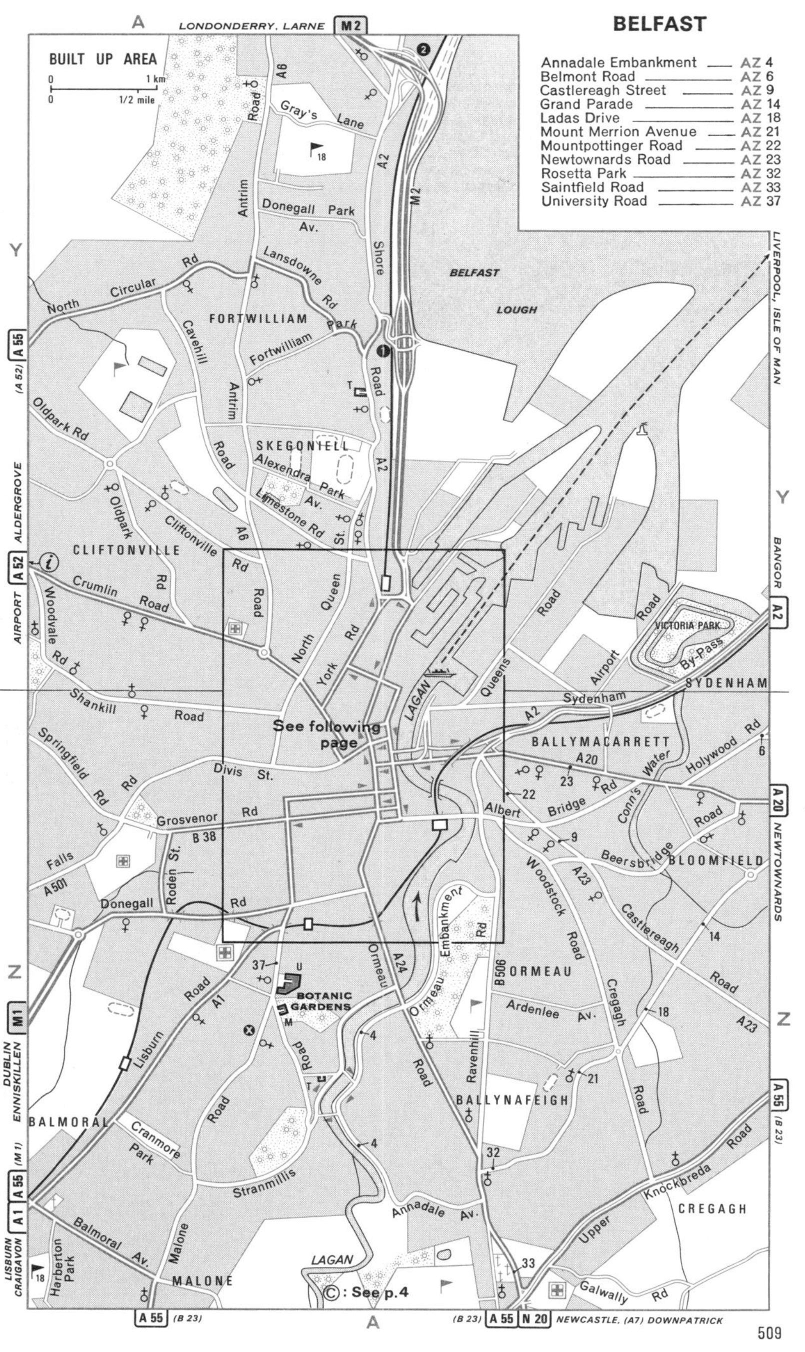
BELFAST
Annadale Embankment AZ 4
Belmont Road AZ 6
Castlereagh Street AZ 9
Grand Parade AZ 14
Ladas Drive AZ 18
Mount Merrion Avenue AZ 21
Mountpottinger Road AZ 22
Newtownards Road AZ 23
Rosetta Park AZ 32
Saintfield Road AZ 33
University Road AZ 37
BUILT UP AREA
LONDONDERRY, LARNE
M2
LIVERPOOL, ISLE OF MAN
BANGOR
A2
NEWTOWNARDS
A20
A55
(B 23)
AIRPORT
ALDERGROVE
A52
(A 52)
DUBLIN
ENNISKILLEN
M1
LISBURN
CRAIGAVON
A1
(M1)
NEWCASTLE, (A7) DOWNPATRICK
N 20
BELFAST LOUGH
FORTWILLIAM
SKEGONIELL
CLIFTONVILLE
SYDENHAM
BALLYMACARRETT
BLOOMFIELD
ORMEAU
BALLYNAFEIGH
CREGAGH
BALMORAL
MALONE
BOTANIC GARDENS
VICTORIA PARK
LAGAN
See following page
©: See p.4

BELFAST
CENTRE

0 — 400 m
0 — 400 yards

Castle Place .... BZ
Donegal Place .... BZ
Royal Avenue .... BYZ

Albert Bridge Road .... BZ 2
Albert Square .... BY 3
Ann Street .... BZ 5
Bradbury Place .... BZ 7
Bridge Street .... BZ 8
Corporation Square .... BY 10
Donegall Quay .... BYZ 12
Donegall Square .... BZ 13
Great Patrick Street .... BY 15
High Street .... BYZ 16
Howard Street .... BZ 17
Limestone Road .... BY 19
Mountpottinger Road .... BZ 22
Newtownards Road .... BZ 23
Queen Elizabeth Bridge .... BZ 25
Queen's Quay Road .... BY 26
Queen's Bridge .... BZ 27
Queen's Square .... BY 29
Rosemary Street .... BZ 30
Station Street .... BY 35
University Road .... BZ 37
Waring Street .... BY 38
Wellington Place .... BZ 39

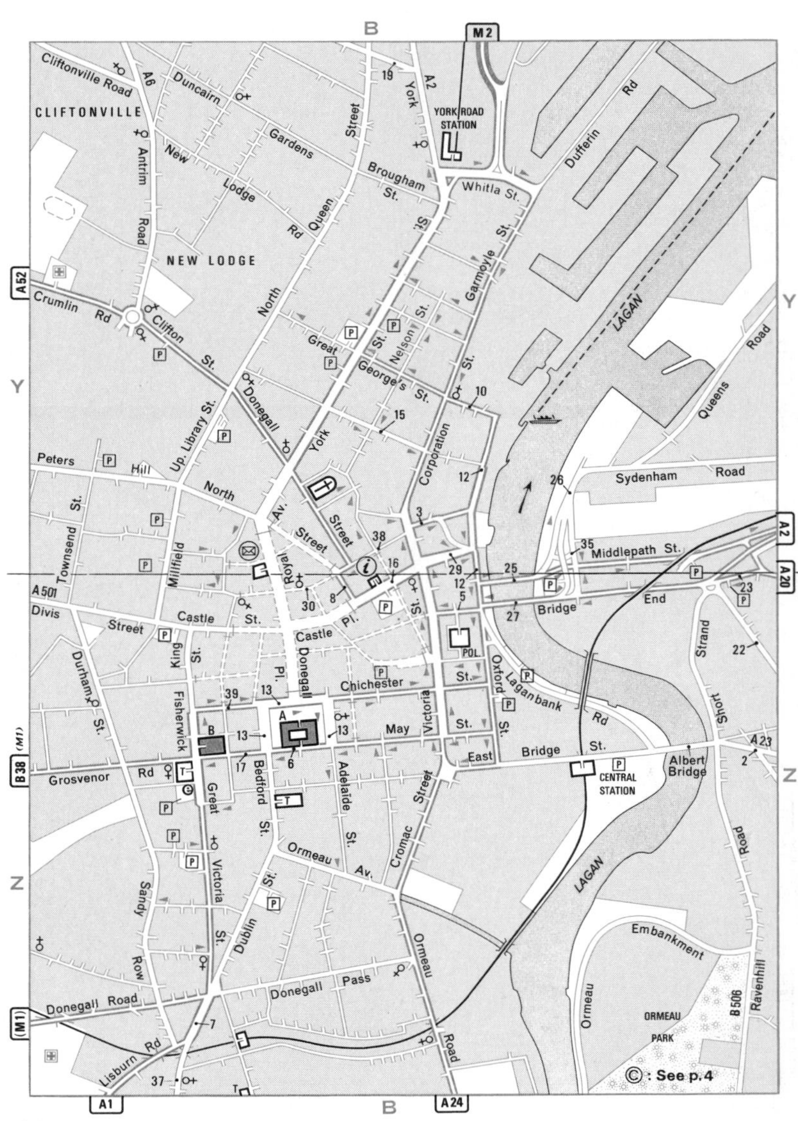

Belfast Europa (Gd. Met.), Great Victoria St., BT2 7AP, ℡ 45161, Telex 74491, ← – lift TV Ⓟ. – BZ e
M a la carte 6.20/9.90 **st.** – ☕ 2.50 – **180 rm** 13.50/22.00 **s.**

Wellington Park, 21 Malone Rd, BT9 6RY, ℡ 669421 – lift TV wc ☎ Ⓟ. – AZ x
24 rm.

Stormont, 587 Upper Newtownards Rd, BT4 3LP, E : 4 ½ m. by A 2 on A 20 ℡ 658 621 – lift TV wc ☎ Ⓟ. – on A 20 AZ
M approx. 4.50 🍷 1.30 – **51 rm** ☕ 10.50/16.00.

at Dunmurry **SW : 5 ½ m. on A 1 – AZ – ✉ ☎ 0232 Belfast:**

Conway (T.H.F.), Kingsway, BT17 9ES, ℡ 612101, heated, – lift TV Ⓟ.
M 4.00/6.00 **st.** 🍷 1.50 – ☕ 2.00 – **77 rm** 11.50/16.00 **st.**

XX Stage Coach Inn, Queensway, BT17 9HG, ℡ 617018 – Ⓟ.

MICHELIN Branch, 101/3 Limestone Rd, BT15 3AB, ℡ 748255.

AUSTIN-MG-WOLSELEY Saintfield Rd ℡ 649774
AUSTIN-MG-WOLSELEY 3 Diamond St. ℡ 42456
AUSTIN-DAIMLER-JAGUAR-MG-ROVER-TRIUMPH-WOLSELEY 10/18 Adelaide St. ℡ 30566
CHRYSLER-SIMCA Annadale Embankment ℡ 642972
CITROEN 118/124 Donegall Pass ℡ 23441
DAIMLER 25/27 Alfred St. ℡ 30566
DAF, MAZDA, POLSKI Antrim Rd ℡ 779338
DATSUN 226 York St. ℡ 747133
FIAT 47/57 Rosetta Av. ℡ 648049
FORD Lislea Drive ℡ 662231
FORD 58/72 Antrim Rd ℡ 744744
JENSEN 39/49 Adelaide St. ℡ 28225
LANCIA, ROLLS ROYCE-BENTLEY 4 Clarence St. West ℡ 41057
MORRIS-MG-WOLSELEY 90/106 Victoria St. ℡ 32361
MORRIS-MG-WOLSELEY 6 Agincourt Av. ℡ 24193
MORRIS-MG-WOLSELEY 307 Upper Newtownards Rd ℡ 654687
MORRIS-MG-WOLSELEY 203 Castlereagh Rd ℡ 51111
MORRIS-MG-WOLSELEY Upper Newtownards Rd, Dundonald ℡ 2651
PEUGEOT 133 Lisburn Rd ℡ 661911
RENAULT 48/50 Corporation St. ℡ 37101
SAAB 250/252 Donegall Rd ℡ 21019
TOYOTA 269/285 Upper Newtownards Rd ℡ 655208
VAUXHALL 46 Florenceville Av. ℡ 641350
VAUXHALL 22/28 Brougham St. ℡ 744869
VAUXHALL 29/33 Ravenhill Rd ℡ 51422
VAUXHALL Lisburn Rd, Dunmurry ℡ 614211
VOLVO 27 Pakenham St. ℡ 29390
VW 5/8a Sandown Rd ℡ 653082

CARRICKFERGUS Antrim 986 ⑱ and ㉞ – pop. 15,162 – ☎ 023 83.

See : Castle (13C) *AC* – Sea Front* – St. Nicholas' Church* 12C-18C. Envir. : Island Magee Peninsula (Port Muck*, Isle of Muck*, Power Station ←*) NE : 9 m.**

18 North Rd ℡ 62203.

i Town Hall, ℡ 63604.

Belfast 10 – Larne 14.

Coast Road, 28 Scotch Quarter, BT38 7DP, ℡ 61021 – TV wc wc ☎ – **20 rm.**

CHRYSLER-SIMCA 72 Belfast Rd ℡ 62299
POLSKI Greensland ℡ 0231 (Whiteabbey) 63465
RENAULT Larne Rd ℡ 63516
VAUXHALL Irish Quarter South ℡ 62216

CASTLEROCK Londondery – see Coleraine.

COLERAINE Londonderry 986 ⑱ – pop. 14,871 – ☎ 0265.

Envir. : Giant's Causeway* (Chaussée des Géants) basalt formation (from the car-park *AC*, ½ h Rtn on foot) NE : 9 m. – Downhill Castle (Mussenden Temple* 18C : ←*** *AC*) NW : 7 m. – Portrush (site*, ←*) N : 6 m. – Dunluce Castle (site*, ←*) NE : 8 m. – W : Benevenagh Mountain*.**

18 Castlerock ℡ 026 584 (Castlerock) 314, W : 5 m.

i Council Offices, Bannfield ℡ 52181.

Belfast 61 – Ballymena 29 – **Londonderry 30** – Omagh 62.

Bohill Auto Inn, Bushmills Rd, BT52 2BB, NE : 2 m. on B 17 ℡ 4406 – TV wc wc ☎ Ⓟ.
M (dinner only and Sunday lunch) 2.50/5.00 **t.** 🍷 2.00 – **30 rm** ☕ 8.00/18.00 **t.** – P 13.00/20.00 **t.**

Lodge, Lodge Rd, BT52 1NF, ℡ 4848 – wc ☎ Ⓟ.
M a la carte 3.90/8.15 🍷 1.80 – **14 rm** ☕ 13.00/19.00.

Gorteen, Lodge Rd, BT52 1LU, ℡ 2814 – wc Ⓟ
closed Christmas – **14 rm.**

Westbrook, 62 Railway Pl., ℡ 3145
closed 25 December to 1 January – **M** (closed Sunday dinner) a la carte 4.25/6.05 **s.** 🍷 1.50 – **16 rm** ☕ 5.00/10.00 **s.**

XX **MacDuffs,** Blackheath House, Blackhill, S : 8 m. by A 29 on Macosquin Rd ℡ 026 585 (Aghadowey) 433 – Ⓟ
closed Sunday from September to March, Monday and Tuesday – **M** (dinner only) a la carte 4.00/5.50 **t.** 🍷 1.30.

at Castlerock **NW : 6 m. by A 2 – ✉ ☎ 0265 Coleraine:**

Maritima, 43 Main St., BT51 4RA, ℡ 388, ← – wc
6 rm ☕ 5.00/10.00 **st.**

AUSTIN-MORRIS-MG-WOLSELEY Kingsgate St. ℡ 2718
CHRYSLER-SIMCA Ballycastle Rd ℡ 2909
FORD Church St. ℡ 2361
JAGUAR-ROVER-TRIUMPH-VAUXHALL Hanover Pl. ℡ 2386
PEUGEOT 1/3 Railway Pl. ℡ 2513

COMBER Down 986 ⑱ and ㊳ – pop. 5,575 – ✆ 0247.
Belfast 9 – Bangor 9.

XX **Blades,** 39-41 High St., BT23 5HJ, ☎ 872229 – Ⓟ
closed Sunday, Monday and Christmas Day – M (dinner only) a la carte 3.75/5.75 **t.** 🍷 1.50.

XX **Old Crow,** Glen Rd, BT23 5EL, ☎ 872255 – Ⓟ
M a la carte 3.65/6.30 **s.**

CRAIGAVAD Down 986 ㊳ – pop. 679 – ✉ ✆ 023 17 Holywood.
See : Ulster Folk and Transport Museum* (Cultra Manor) *AC*.
18 at Hollywood, Nuns Walk, Demesne Rd ☎ 2138, SW : 3 m.
Belfast 8 – Bangor 5.

Culloden , Holywood, BT18 0EY, on A 2 ☎ 5223, ≤, , park – Ⓟ.
M a la carte 5.30/7.30 **s.** 🍷 1.60 – **32 rm** 15.00/20.00 **s.**

XX Clanbrassil House, Cultra Av., Seafront Rd, BT18 0BB, ☎ 2494, ≤, – Ⓟ.

CRAIGAVON Armagh – pop. 12,594 – ✆ 0762.
Envir. : Ardress House* 17C (site*, drawing-room plasterwork**) *AC*, W : 11 m. – Rich Hill (site*, church : scenery*) SW : 9 ½ m. – Armagh (St. Patrick's Protestant Cathedral* 18 C, ≤*, St. Patrick's Catholic Cathedral : interior*) SW : 14 m.
i Oxford Island ☎ 076 22 (Lurgan) 2205.
Belfast 28 – Armagh 13.

Country Club, Silverwood Rd, BT66 6NA, near M1 junction 10 ✉ ☎ 076 22 (Lurgan) 2332 – wc ☎ Ⓟ.
M 3.75/8.00 **s.** – **28 rm** 10.75/15.00 **s.**

Seagoe, Old Lurgan Rd ☎ 0762 (Portadown) 33076, – wc ☎ Ⓟ. – **47 rm.**

XX **Green Garter,** Magowan Building, West St., Portadown ✉ ☎ 0762 (Portadown) 35164
closed Sunday and Monday – **M** a la carte 6.15/8.05 **s.** 🍷 1.40.

CRAWFORDSBURN Down 986 ㊳ – pop. 487 – ✆ 024 783 Helen's Bay.
18 Carnalea ☎ 0247 (Bangor) 5004 – 18, 9 Conlig ☎ 0247 (Bangor) 60596.
Belfast 10 – Bangor 3.

Old Inn, 15 Main St., BT19 1JH, ☎ 3255, « Part 17C inn », – TV wc ☎ Ⓟ
M approx. 4.75 **st.** – 1.65 – **24 rm** 6.45/21.00 **st.** – P 14.95/23.45 **st.**

DUNADRY Antrim 986 ㉝ – ✆ 084 94 Templepatrick.
Envir. : Antrim (round tower* 10C) NW : 5 m. – Shane's Castle* (16 C ruins) *AC*, NW : 5 ½ m. (access by miniature railway).
Belfast 15 – Larne 18 – **Londonderry 56.**

Dunadry Inn, 2 Islandreagh Drive, BT41 2HB, ☎ 32474, Telex 747245, – TV Ⓟ.
M a la carte 4.45/9.20 **st.** 🍷 1.35 – **57 rm** 14.00/24.25 **st.**

DUNMURRY Antrim 986 ㊲ – see Belfast.

EGLINTON Londonderry 986 ⑱ – ✆ 050 481.
Belfast 79 – Coleraine 25 – **Londonderry 8.**

Glen House, Main St., BT47 3AH, ☎ 527, – wc ☎ Ⓟ.
closed 1 to 14 August and 25-26 December – **M** 3.80/8.00 **t.** 🍷 1.40 – **16 rm** 6.00/12.00 **t.** – P 12.85/17.35 **t.**

ENNISKILLEN Fermanagh 986 ⑱ – pop. 6,558 – ✆ 0365.
See : Lough Erne*** (Upper and Lower) – On Lower Lough Erne, by boat *AC* : Devenish Island (site**, monastic ruins : scenery*) and White Island*. **Envir. :** Castle Coole* 18C (site*) E : 1 m. – Florence Court (site*, park*) *AC*, SW : 8 m.
9 Castlecoole ☎ 2900.
i 37 Town Hall St. ☎ 3110 (Easter-mid October) – Council Offices, Ardhowen, Dublin Rd ☎ 4361 (October-March).
Belfast 87 – **Londonderry 59.**

Killyhevlin, Dublin Rd, BT74 6DX, SE : 1 ¾ m. on A 4 ☎ 3481, ≤, , park – TV wc ☎ Ⓟ.
M 4.50/5.50 **s.** 🍷 1.40 – **25 rm** 7.50/18.50 **st.**

Willoughby, 24 Willoughby Pl., ☎ 22882
closed Christmas week – **11 rm** 4.00/8.00.

at Killedeas N : 7 m. on B 82 – ✉ Enniskillen – ✆ 036 562 Irvinestown :

Manor House , BT74 7LF, ☎ 561, ≤, , park – wc ☎ Ⓟ
M 3.75/5.75 **s.** 🍷 1.60 – **15 rm** 6.00/16.50 **s.**

AUSTIN-MG-ROVER-TRIUMPH-WOLSELEY Dublin Rd ☎ 3475
CHRYSLER Quay Lane ☎ 2187
PEUGEOT Dublin Rd ☎ 22323
RENAULT Queen Elizabeth Rd ☎ 2731
VAUXHALL Tempo Rd ☎ 4366
VW, AUDI-NSU 74 Forthill St. ☎ 2974

GIANT'S CAUSEWAY Antrim 986 ⑭.

See : Giant's Causeway*** (Chaussée des Géants) basalt formation (from the car-park *AC*, ½ h Rtn on foot).

ℹ National Trust Information Centre, ☎ 026 57 (Bushmills) 582 (Easter-mid October).

Belfast 72 – Ballycastle 13 – **Londonderry 41.**

Hotel see : Portballintrae SW : 4 m.

GLENGORMLEY Antrim – see Newtonabbey.

GLENARIFF (Glen of)* Antrim.

GREY ABBEY Down 986 ⑱ – ✆ 024 774.

See : Abbey* (Cistercian ruins 12C) *AC*. **Envir.** : Mount Stewart Gardens* *AC*, Temple of the Winds ≤* *AC*, NW : 1 ½ m.

Belfast 18 – Bangor 13.

✕ **White Satin Inn,** 23-25 Main St., BT22 2NF, ☎ 330, Chinese rest.
closed Christmas Day and Chinese New Year's Day – **M** (dinner only) a la carte 2.25/4.40.

HILLSBOROUGH Down – pop. 780 – ✆ 0846.

See : Government House* 18C – the Fort* 17C.

Belfast 13.

🏨 **White Gables,** Dromore Rd, BT26 6HU, ☎ 682755 – wc ☎ Ⓟ.
closed Christmas Day – **M** a la carte 3.75/6.40 🍷 1.80 – **24 rm** ☕ 9.00/12.50.

✕✕✕ **Number 10,** 10 Ballynahinch St., BT26 6AW, ☎ 682866, French rest. – Ⓟ
closed Saturday lunch and Sunday – **M** a la carte 5.55/7.65 **st.** 🍷 1.75.

CHRYSLER Dromore Rd ☎ 357

KESH Fermanagh 986 ⑱ – pop. 311 – ✆ 036 563.

Envir. : Lough Erne*** (Upper and Lower) – On Lower Lough Erne, by boat *AC* : Devenish Island (site**, monastic ruins : scenery*) and White Island*.

Belfast 89 – Enniskillen 15 – **Londonderry 52.**

Hotels see : Enniskillen SE : 15 m.

KILLEDEAS Fermanagh – see Enniskillen.

LARNE Antrim 986 ⑱ – pop. 18,242 – ✆ 0574.

Exc. : Antrim Coast Road*** (A 2) from Larne to Portrush.

⛴ to Stranraer (Sealink) 1-6 daily (2 h 15 mn) – to Cairnryan (Townsend Thoresen : Transport Ferry Service) 4-5 daily (2 h to 2 h 30 mn).

⛳18 192 Coast Rd ☎ 057 483 (Ballygally) 248, N : 4 m.

ℹ Larne Harbour ☎ 2270 (Easter and June-September) – Council Offices, Victoria Rd ☎ 2313.

Belfast 23 – Ballymena 20.

🏨 **King's Arms,** Broadway, BT40 2LP, ☎ 3322 – wc ☎ Ⓟ.
M a la carte 3.55/6.50 **st.** – **48 rm** ☕ 9.00/12.00 **st.**

AUSTIN-MG-WOLSELEY 98 Glenarm Rd ☎ 2137
AUSTIN-MG-WOLSELEY Point St. ☎ 2091
FORD Glynn Rd ☎ 3311

LISNASKEA Fermanagh 986 ⑱ – pop. 15,990 – ✆ 036 572.

ℹ Public Library ☎ 222.

Belfast 83 – Dundalk 53 – Omagh 39 – Sligo 53.

🏨 **Ortine,** Main St. ☎ 206 – wc Ⓟ.
M 2.60/5.00 **st.** 🍷 0.70 – **17 rm** ☕ 7.50/14.00 **s.** – P 12.00 **s.**

LONDONDERRY Derry 986 ⑱ – pop. 31,437 – ☎ 0504.

See : City Walls 17C – Guildhall* 1908 – Memorial Hall*. Envir. Grianan of Aileach* (Republic of Ireland) (stone fort) ☀*** NW : 5 m. – Dungiven (priory : site*) SE : 18 m.**

18 Prehen ☎ 2610.

i Council Offices, Limavady Rd ☎ 61504.

Belfast 71 – Dublin 145.

Everglades, Prehen Rd, BT47 2PA, S : 1 ½ m. on A 5, ☎ 46722, Telex 747645, – TV P.
38 rm.

AUSTIN-MG-WOLSELEY 18 John St. ☎ 2748
AUSTIN-MG-ROVER-TRIUMPH-WOLSELEY 78 Strand Rd ☎ 4181
CHRYSLER-SIMCA 76 Strand Rd ☎ 4377
FORD 173 Stroud Rd ☎ 4441
MORRIS-MG-WOLSELEY 52 Strand Rd ☎ 2338
PEUGEOT Campsie ☎ 860588
RENAULT Strand Rd ☎ 68648
VAUXHALL Maydown ☎ 4706
VW, AUDI-NSU Bunorana Rd ☎ 65985

NEWCASTLE Down 986 ㉒ – pop. 4,621 – ☎ 039 67.

Envir. : Tollymore Forest Park* AC, NW : 2 m. by B 180 – Dundrum (castle* 13C ruins : top ☀, 70 steps) NE : 3 m. – Loughinisland (the 3 churches* : 1000 - 1547 - 1636) NE : 8 m. Exc. : SW : Mourne Mountains** (Slieve Donard*, Silent Valley*, Lough Shannagh* : reservoir 1948).**

i Council Offices, The Promenade ☎ 2222.

Belfast 30 – Londonderry 101.

Slieve Donard, Downs Rd, BT33 0AH, ☎ 23681, <, , , park – P.
M approx. 4.00 2.00 – **112 rm** 7.50/12.00 – P 14.00.

Enniskeen, 98 Bryansford Rd, BT33 0LF, NW : ¾ m. ☎ 22392, <, , park – wc P
March - 4 November – **M** 3.50/4.00 1.60 – **14 rm** 5.00/13.70 – P 9.50/10.50.

NEWRY Down 986 ㉒ – pop. 11,393 – ☎ 0693.

Envir. : Slieve Gullion, Ring of Gullion : Ballitemple viewpoint**, Bernish Rock viewpoint**, Cam Lough* SW : 5 m. – Derrymore House (site*) AC, NW : 2 ½ m. – Rostrevor (Fairy Glen*) SE : 8 ¾ m.**

i Council Offices, Monaghan Rd ☎ 4424.

Belfast 39 – Armagh 20 – Dundalk 13.

Ardmore, Belfast Rd, BT34 1QH, ☎ 3161, – wc P.
M a la carte 2.95/4.75 **st.** 1.50 – **25 rm** 7.75/14.25 **st.**

AUSTIN-MORRIS-MG-WOLSELEY Railway Av. ☎ 2201
PEUGEOT 18 Edward St. ☎ 2877
RENAULT 52/53 Merchants Quay ☎ 3626

NEWTOWNABBEY Antrim 986 ㊲ – pop. 57,908 – ✉ ☎ 0231 Whiteabbey.

Belfast 6 – Larne 18.

Glenavna House, 590 Shore Rd, Whiteabbey ☎ 4461, <, , park – TV wc wc P.
17 rm.

at Glengormley W : 7 m. on A 6 by A 2, M 2 – ✉ Newtownabbey – ☎ 023 13 Glengormley :

Chimney Corner Motor, 630 Antrim Rd, BT36 8RH, NW : 2 ¼ m. on A 6 ☎ 44925, – TV wc P.
M approx. 4.00 1.25 – **48 rm** 10.50/16.00 – P 17.25/21.00.

SAAB Glengormley ☎ 2742

NEWTOWNARDS Down 986 ⑱ and ㊳ – pop. 15,387 – ☎ 0247.

Envir. : Scrabo Tower (site*) SW : 1 m.

18 ☎ 2355.

Belfast 10 – Bangor 5.

Strangford Arms, Church St. ☎ 814141 – TV wc P. – **18 rm.**

FORD Regent St. ☎ 2626
MORRIS Old Cross Garage ☎ 3279
TRIUMPH Belfast Rd ☎ 2446
VAUXHALL Portaferry Rd ☎ 3376

OMAGH Tyrone 986 ⑱ – pop. 27,998.

Envir. : St. Gortin Forest Park*, Gortin Gap* (on B 48) NE : 9 m. – Glenelly Valley* NE : 17 m. by Plumbridge.

9 Dublin Rd ☎ 3160.

i 10 Holmview Ter. ☎ 3666.

Belfast 69 – Dublin 113 – Dundalk 64 – Londonderry 32 – Sligo 68.

AUDI-NSU Derry Rd, Mountjoy ☎ 2443
AUSTIN-MORRIS-MG-WOLSELEY Dublin Rd ☎ 3116
FIAT 60 Dublin Rd ☎ 2021
FORD Derry Rd ☎ 2788
RENAULT Cookstown Rd ☎ 3451
VAUXHALL Derry Rd ☎ 2782

PORTAFERRY Down 986 ⑱ – pop. 1,592 – ☎ 024 772.

See: Strangford (site*, Audley's Castle: top ※**, 44 steps). **Envir.**: Castle Ward 1765 (great hall*) SW: 2 m. – Saul (St. Patrick's Memorial Church: site*, ≤*) SW: 5 m.

Belfast 29 – Bangor 24.

- **Portaferry,** 9 The Strand, ☎ 231 – ⇔wc
  M a la carte 3.50/5.70 🍷 1.50 – **8 rm** ☕ 5.00/11.00.
- ✗ **Scotsman,** 156-158 Shore Rd, BT22 1LA, ☎ 326
  M a la carte 4.45/6.30 **t.**

PORTBALLINTRAE Antrim 986 ⑭ – pop. 496 – ✉ ☎ 026 57 Bushmills.

⛳9 ☎ 026 57 (Bushmills) 31317.

i Information Office (July-August).

Belfast 71 – Larne 54 – **Londonderry 40.**

- **Beach,** Beach Rd, BT57 8RT, ☎ 31214, ≤ – ⇔wc ☎
  M 4.00/5.25 🍷 1.30 – **28 rm** ☕ 6.50/16.00 – P 14.00/16.00.

PORTSTEWART Londonderry 986 ⑭ – pop. 4,975 – ☎ 026 583.

⛳18, ⛳18 Strand Rd ☎ 2015, West boundary.

i Town Hall, The Crescent ☎ 2286.

Belfast 67 – Coleraine 6.

- **Edgewater,** 88 Strand Rd, BT55 7LZ, ☎ 2224, ≤ – ⇔wc ⌂wc Ⓟ. 🏨
  M 3.25/4.95 🍷 1.50 – **17 rm** ☕ 7.50/19.00.

SAINTFIELD Down – pop. 1,500 – ✉ Ballynahinch – ☎ 0238.

⛳9 at Ballynahinch ☎ 2365, SW: 5 m.

Belfast 11.

- ✗ **Barn,** 120 Monlough Rd, BT24 7EU, N: 1 ¾ m. ☎ 510396 – Ⓟ
  closed Sunday, Monday, Tuesday, Thursday and 25-26 December – **M** (dinner only) approx. 6.00 🍷 1.50.

Channel Islands

LICENSING HOURS - WHEN DRINKING ALCOHOLIC BEVERAGES IS PERMITTED IN PUBS AND BARS AND OTHER LICENSED PREMISES (The General Rule).

HEURES PERMISES POUR LA CONSOMMATION DES BOISSONS ALCOOLISÉES (Règle Générale).

ORARI CONSENTITI PER LA CONSUMAZIONE DI BEVANDE ALCOOLICHE (Regola Generale).

AUSSCHANKZEITEN FÜR ALKOHOLISCHE GETRÄNKE (Allgemeine Regelung).

ALDERNEY

		from de dalle von	to à alle bis	from de dalle von	to à alle bis		
Monday to Friday (other than Good Friday and Christmas Day)	Pubs Hotels	10.00			24.00 * (01.00 in summer)	Pubs Alberghi Hotels	Da Lunedì a Venerdì (esclusi Venerdì Santo e Natale)
Lundi au Vendredi (autres que Vendredi Saint et Jour de Noël)	Rest.	11.00	15.00	19.00	24.00	Ristoranti Rest.	Montag-Freitag (außer Karfreitag und Weihnachten)
Saturday (other than Christmas Day)	Pubs Hotels	10.00			24.00	Pubs Alberghi Hotels	Sabato (escluso Natale)
Samedi (autre que Jour de Noël)	Rest.	11.00	15.00	19.00	24.00	Ristoranti Rest.	Samstag (außer Weihnachten)
Sunday, Good Friday and Christmas Day	Pubs Hotels	12.00	14.00	20.00	24.00	Pubs Alberghi Hotels	Domenica, Venerdì Santo e Natale
Dimanche, Vendredi Saint et Jour de Noël	Rest.	11.00	15.00	19.00	24.00	Ristoranti Rest.	Sonntag, Karfreitag und Weihnachten

* Summer applies from 1st April to 30th September.
* *Période d'été applicable du 1er avril au 30 septembre.*
* Stagione estiva applicabile dal 1° aprile al 30 settembre.
* *Sommerzeit vom 1. April bis 30. September.*

GUERNSEY

		from / de	to / à	from / de	to / à		
Weekdays (other than Good Friday, and Christmas Day) / **Jours de semaine** (autres que Vendredi Saint et Jour de Noël)	Pubs	**10.30**			**23.00**	Pubs	**Giorni della settimana** (esclusi Venerdì Santo, e Natale) / **Wochentags** (außer Karfreitag und Weihnachten)
	Rest.	**12.00**			**23.00**	Ristoranti Rest.	
Sundays / **Dimanches**	Pubs	Closed - Fermés - Chiusi - Geschlossen				Pubs	**Domeniche** / **Sonntags**
	Rest.	**12.00**	**14.30**	**19.30**	**22.30**	Ristoranti Rest.	
Good Friday Christmas Day (if not a Sunday) / **Vendredi Saint et Jour de Noël** (si non un dimanche)	Pubs	**11.00**	**12.30**	**19.00**	**21.30**	Pubs	**Venerdì Santo e Natale** (se non è domenica) / **Karfreitag und Weihnachten** (falls nicht Sonntag)
	Rest.	**12.00**	**14.30**	**19.00**	**21.30**	Ristoranti Rest.	
		dalle / von	alle / bis	dalle / von	alle / bis		

JERSEY

		from / de	to / à	from / de	to / à		
Weekdays (other than Good Friday and Christmas Day) / **Jours de semaine** (autres que Vendredi Saint et Jour de Noël)	Pubs	**9.00**			**23.00**	Pubs	**Giorni della settimana** (esclusi Venerdì Santo e Natale) / **Wochentags** (außer Karfreitag und Weihnachten)
	Rest.	**9.00**			**1.00**	Rist. Rest.	
Sundays, Good Friday and Christmas Day / **Dimanches, Vendredi Saint et Jour de Noël**	Pubs	**11.00**	**13.00**	**16.30**	**23.00**	Pubs	**Domeniche, Venerdì Santo e Natale** / **Sonntags, Karfreitag und Weihnachten**
	Rest.	**11.00**			**1.00**	Rist. Rest.	
		dalle / von	alle / bis	dalle / von	alle / bis		

Residents: no restrictions on licensed premises.
Hotels with a pub or restaurants attached are obliged to keep official licensing hours.

Résidents: pas de restriction dans les lieux ayant une licence.
Hôtels: s'ils possèdent un pub ou un restaurant, ils doivent respecter les horaires légaux.

Per i residenti: nessuna restrizione nei locali con licenza.
Alberghi: possono possedere un pub od un ristorante. Devono rispettare gli orari legali.

Für Hotelgäste: keine Beschränkung in den lizensierten Hotels.
Die Hotels können ein « Pub » oder ein Restaurant besitzen, müssen aber die jeweils geltenden Vorschriften beachten.

Place with at least :

one hotel or restaurant ● Catel
one pleasant hotel 🏨, ✕ with rm.
one quiet, secluded hotel 🐦
one restaurant with ✿, ✿✿, M
See this town for establishments located in its vicinity

La località possiede come minimo :

una risorsa alberghiera ● Catel
un albergo ameno 🏨, ✕ with rm.
un albergo molto tranquillo, isolato 🐦
un'ottima tavola con ✿, ✿✿, M
La località raggruppa nel suo testo le risorse dei dintorni

Localité offrant au moins :

une ressource hôtelière ● Catel
un hôtel agréable 🏨, ✕ with rm.
un hôtel très tranquille, isolé 🐦
une bonne table à ✿, ✿✿, M
Localité groupant dans le texte les ressources de ses environs

Ort mit mindestens :

einem Hotel oder Restaurant ● Catel
einem angenehmen Hotel 🏨, ✕ with rm.
einem sehr ruhigen und abgelegenen Hotel 🐦
einem Restaurant mit ✿, ✿✿, M
Ort mit Angaben über Hotels und Restaurants in seiner Umgebung

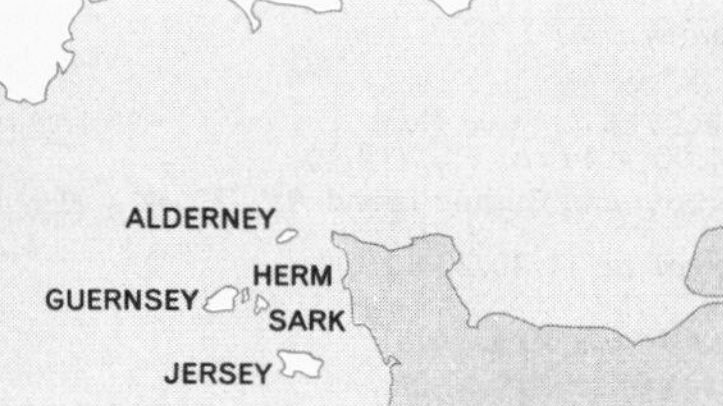

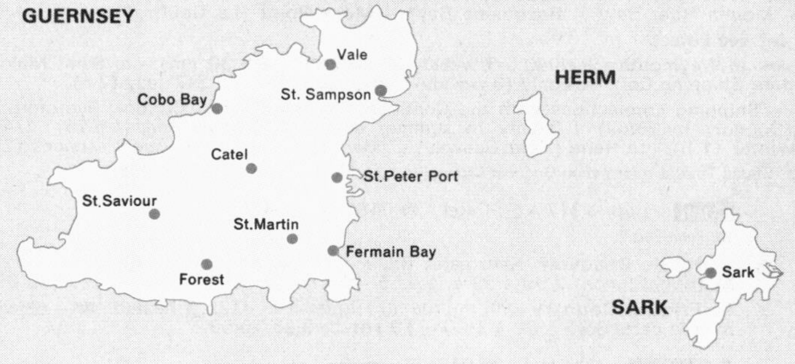

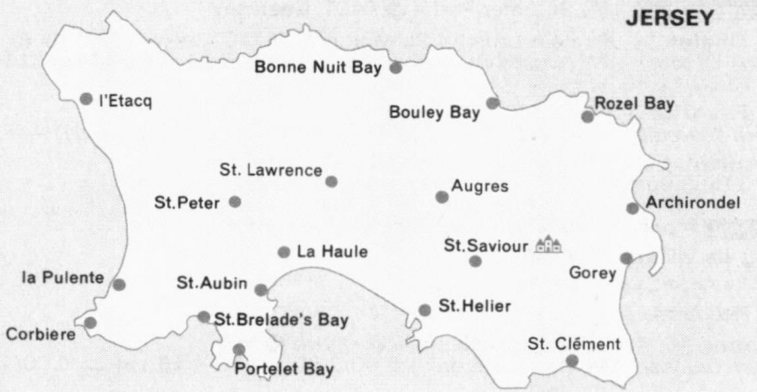

CHANNEL ISLANDS

Towns

ALDERNEY 59 ③ and 230 ⑨ – pop. 1,686 – ✆ 048 182.
See : Telegraph Bay★ (cliffs★) – Clonque Bay★ – Braye Bay★.
✈ ✆ 2886 – Booking Office : Aurigny Air Services.
Shipping connections with the Continent : to Saint-Malo (Condor : hydrofoil) – to Guernsey, Sark, Jersey 2 weekly summer only.
i States Offices, New St. ✆ 2811.

St. Anne – ✉ St. Anne – ✆ 048 182 Alderney.
⛳9 ✆ 2835, E : 1 m.

Royal Connaught, Royal Connaught Sq. ✆ 2756 – wc wc
Easter October – **M** 3.50/5.50 0.90 – 1.00 – **17 rm** 7.50/19.40.

Grand Island, The Butes ✆ 2848, ≤ harbour and Burhou Island, , , – wc wc P
May-October – **M** 4.35/4.90 1.10 – **32 rm** 11.30/22.60.

Town House, 10 High St. ✆ 2330
closed Christmas to 1 January – **12 rm** 4.75/9.50 **s.**

Chez André with rm, Victoria St. ✆ 2777 – wc
Easter-November – **M** a la carte 3.85/5.55 1.20 – **14 rm** 8.25/19.00 – P 12.50/14.00.

GUERNSEY 59 ④ and 230 ⑨ ⑩ – pop. 51,458 – ✆ 0481.
See : Icart Point ≤★★★ – Cobo Bay★★ – Fort Pézéries ≤★★ – Fort Doyle ≤★ – Fort Saumarez ≤★ – Moulin Huet Bay★ – Rocquaine Bay★ – Moye Point (Le Gouffre★).
✈ see Forest.
to Weymouth (Sealink) 3-7 weekly (4 h 45 mn to 6 h 30 mn) – to Saint-Malo (Commodore Shipping Co.) cars only (3 weekly) – to Jersey (Sealink) 3-7 daily (2 h).
Shipping connections with the Continent : to Saint-Malo (Condor : hydrofoil) – to Jersey (Condor : hydrofoil) 1-3 daily in summer direct (1 h) or via Sark (1 h 15) ; 1-4 weekly in winter (1 h) – to Herm (Herm Seaway) (Trident Charter Co.) frequent services (25 mn).
i States Tourist Information Bureau, Crown Pier, St. Peter Port ✆ 23552, Telex 41612.

Catel – pop. 6,317 – ✉ Catel – ✆ 0481 Guernsey.
St. Peter Port 2.

Hotel de Beauvoir, Sausmarez Rd, ✆ 54750 – wc wc P
M (buffet lunch) 2.00/4.50 **s.** 0.55 – **29 rm** 7.50/15.00 – P 9.50/10.00.

Le Friquet Country with rm, rue du Friquet ✆ 56422, heated, – wc wc P
M a la carte 3.30/5.00 1.30 – **13 rm** 8.25/16.50.

Cobo Bay – ✉ Catel – ✆ 0481 Guernsey.

Cobo Bay, ✆ 57102 – wc P
closed December – **M** 2.50/3.50 1.20 – **40 rm** 6.00/12.00 – P 10.50/11.00.

Fermain Bay – ✉ St. Peter Port – ✆ 0481 Guernsey.

Le Chalet, Fermain Lane ✉ St. Martin ✆ 35716 – wc wc ✆ P
April-October – **M** *(closed Sunday dinner)* 2.75/3.75 1.00 – **48 rm** 10.00/16.00 **s.** – P 10.50/12.50 **s.**

La Favorita, ✆ 35666, – wc P
April-November – **M** 3.00/3.40 **s.** 1.25 – **30 rm** (full board only) – P 10.50/12.90 **s.**

Fermain, Fort Rd ✆ 37763, heated, – wc P
M 3.00/3.50 **s.** 0.75 – **32 rm** 9.00/21.00 **s.**

Forest – pop. 1,460 – ✉ Forest – ✆ 0481 Guernsey.
✈ La Villiaze ✆ 37766.
i The Airport, La Villiaze ✆ 63422.
St. Peter Port 4.

Manor, Petit Bôt ✆ 37788, – wc P
April-October – **M** (residents only) 2.40/2.80 0.80 – **56 rm** 6.00/14.00.

St. Martin – pop. 6,161 – ✉ St. Martin – ☎ 0481 Guernsey.

See : Church★ 11C. – St. Peter Port 2.

St. Margaret's Lodge, Forest Rd ☎ 35757, Group Telex 41305, heated, – TV Ⓟ
M 3.00/3.75 **s.** 0.90 (see also rest. **Anniversary Room**) – **42 rm** 18.00/30.00 **s.** – P 19.00 **s.**

Bella Luce, La Fosse ☎ 38764, heated, – TV wc wc Ⓟ
M 3.50/3.95 0.80 – **22 rm** 12.00/23.00 – P 14.45/16.95.

Green Acres, Les Hubits ☎ 38668, heated, – wc Ⓟ
48 rm.

Idlerocks , Jerbourg Point ☎ 37711, ≤ islands, heated – wc wc Ⓟ
M 2.95/3.95 0.95 – **22 rm** 4.50/7.50 – P 9.00/13.00.

Captain's, La Fosse ☎ 38990 – Ⓟ
May-September – **M** (residents only) 2.00/3.00 0.95 – **11 rm** 8.00/16.00 **s.**

Anniversary Room (at St. Margaret's Lodge Hotel), Forest Rd ☎ 35757 – Ⓟ
M a la carte 2.50/5.20 0.90.

AUSTIN-MORRIS-MG-WOLSELEY ☎ 37661 FERRARI, FIAT Forest Rd ☎ 35753

St. Peter Port – pop. 16,303 – ✉ St. Peter Port – ☎ 0481 Guernsey.

See : St. Peter's Church★ 14C Z **A** – Castle Cornet★ (✻★) *AC* Z – Hauteville House (Victor Hugo Museum★: 5 pearl-embroidered tapestries★★) *AC* Z **M** – Victoria Tower : top ✻★★, 100 steps Y. **Envir. :** Les Vauxbelets (Little Chapel★) SW : 2 ½ m. by Mount Durand Z – Saumarez Park★ W : 2 ½ m. by Grange Rd Z.

i Crown Pier ☎ 23552, Telex 41612.

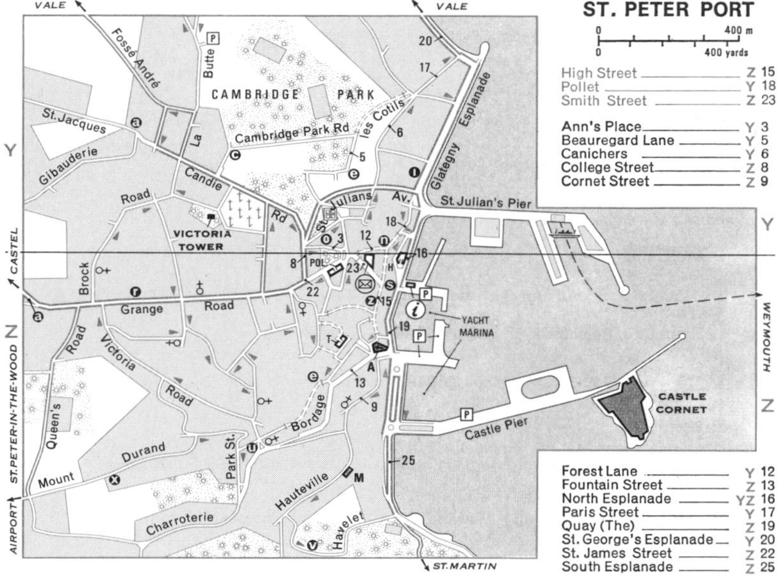

Old Government House, Ann's Pl. ☎ 24921, Group Telex 41305, ≤ harbour and sea, heated, – TV Ⓟ. Y **o**
M a la carte 3.10/6.40 **s.** 1.05 – **74 rm** 17.50/35.00 **s.** – P 19.80/22.20 **s.**

Duke of Richmond, Cambridge Park ☎ 26221, Telex 41462, heated – TV Y **c**
M 3.75/4.25 **s.** 1.25 – **61 rm** 16.00/30.00 **s.** – P 18.00/24.00 **s.**

Royal, Glategny Esplanade ☎ 23921, ≤, heated, – TV Ⓟ. Y **i**
M 3.50/6.00 0.60 (see also rest. **Royal Grill Room**) – **79 rm** 10.20/20.40 **s.** – P 18.00/19.00 **s.**

De Havelet, Havelet ☎ 22199, – wc Ⓟ Z **v**
M 2.75/3.75 1.00 – **37 rm** 8.50/17.00 **s.**

La Collinette, St. Jacques ☎ 22585, heated – wc Ⓟ Y **a**
M 2.50/3.00 0.70 – **29 rm** 8.00/16.00 – P 9.00/13.75.

P.T.O. →

Summerland House, Mount Durand ☎ 24196, – wc P Z x
M (residents only) 3.25/4.50 1.00 – **14 rm** 10.00/17.00 – P 16.00/18.00.

Moore's, Pollet ☎ 24452 – wc Y n
M 2.75/3.75 1.00 – **41 rm** 8.80/16.00 **s.**

Dunchoille, Guelles Rd ☎ 22912, – wc P N : by la Butte Y
Easter-October – **M** (residents only) 2.50/3.50 1.30 – **24 rm** 7.20/15.40 – P 10.00/12.00.

Grange Lodge, The Grange ☎ 25161, heated, – wc P Z r
14 March-24 October – **M** (dinner and residents only) approx. 2.50 **s.** 0.75 – **35 rm** (dinner included) 8.50/17.00 **s.**

Baltimore House, Les Gravées ☎ 23641, Z a
closed 1 to 23 November – **13 rm** 4.40/6.00 **s.**

La Frégate with rm, Les Côtils Lane ☎ 24624, ← town and harbour, « Country house atmosphere », – wc P Y e
M a la carte 3.25/7.85 1.00 – 2.00 – **13 rm** 10.50/19.00.

Le Nautique, Quay Steps ☎ 21714, ← Z s
M a la carte 3.90/5.50 1.00.

Le Français, Le Marchand House, Market St. ☎ 20963, French rest. Z e
closed Saturday lunch, Sunday, February and Bank Holidays – **M** a la carte 4.55/5.40 2.00.

Royal Grill Room (at Royal Hotel), Glategny Esplanade ☎ 23921 – P Y i
closed Sunday – **M** a la carte 3.90/9.00 0.60.

Chez L'Artisan, Trinity Sq. (Craft Centre) ☎ 25085. Z u

Nino's Italian, Lefebvre St. ☎ 23052, Bistro Z z
M a la carte 4.20/5.20 1.05.

BMW, MERCEDES-BENZ, VW 16 Glategny Esplanade ☎ 23916
CHRYSLER-SIMCA, LANCIA Doyle Rd ☎ 24025
DAIMLER-JAGUAR-ROVER-TRIUMPH, ASTON MARTIN, ROLLS ROYCE Rue du Pré ☎ 24261
DAF La Plaque Lane ☎ 64104
FORD Les Banques ☎ 24774
PEUGEOT Lower Colbourne Rd ☎ 20115
RENAULT Upland Rd ☎ 26846

St. Sampson's – pop. 6,534 – ✉ St. Sampson's – ☎ 0481 Guernsey.

St. Peter-Port 3.5.

Pinetops, rue des Pointues Rocques, ☎ 44020, – wc P
March-October – **M** approx. 3.00 0.80 – **15 rm** 8.00/14.00 **s.**

Mayfield, Vale Rd, ☎ 44891 – P
closed Christmas – **17 rm** 4.50/9.00 **s.**

St. Saviour – pop. 2,116 – ✉ St. Peter in the Wood – ☎ 0481 Guernsey.

St. Peter Port 4.

La Hougue Fouque Farm, Route-des-Bas-Courtil ☎ 63800, – wc wc P
19 rm.

L'Atlantique, Perelle Bay ☎ 64056, heated – wc P
14 rm.

Vale – pop. 7,558 – ✉ Vale – ☎ 0481 Guernsey.

See : Castle ←*.

St. Peter-Port 4.5.

Marina, Yacht Marina, Beaucette ☎ 47066 – P
closed mid December-mid January – **M** a la carte 4.30/8.45 0.80.

HERM ISLAND 59 ⑤ and 230.

to Guernsey (Herm Seaway) (Travel Trident) frequent services (25 mn).

i Herm Office ☎ 5.

JERSEY 59 ⑤⑥ and 230 ⑪ – pop. 72,629 – ☎ 0534.

See : Devil's Hole* (site**) *AC* private access, ¾ h Rtn on foot by a steep road – Grosnez Castle ←* – La Hougue Bie Tumulus* (prehistoric tomb) *AC* – St. Catherine's Bay* – Fliquet Bay (St. Catherine's Breakwater ←**) – Sorel Point ←* – Noirmont Point ←* – Jersey zoo (site*) *AC*.

see St. Peter.

Shipping connections with the Continent: to Saint-Malo (Commodore Shipping Co.) cars only (3 weekly) – to Weymouth (Sealink) Summer 2 daily; Winter 3-6 weekly (6 h 30 mn to 9 h) – to Guernsey (Sealink) 3-7 daily (2 h).

Shipping connections with the Continent: to Saint-Malo (Condor: hydrofoil) March-December 1-6 daily (1 h 15 mn) – to Granville (Navifrance: Vedettes Armoricaines) – to Carteret (Service Maritime).
to Guernsey (Condor: hydrofoil) in summer 1-3 daily (1 h); in winter 1-4 weekly (1 h) – to Sark summer Monday/Saturday 1-3 daily (45 mn) – to Alderney summer 2 weekly (2 h).

i States of Jersey Tourism Committee, Weighbridge ☎ 21281 and 24779, Telex 41623.

Archirondel – ✉ Gorey – ☎ 0534 Jersey.
St. Helier 5.

Les Arches, ☎ 53839, ←, heated, – wc wc ☎ P.
M 4.00/5.00 **s.** 1.20 – **51 rm** 8.75/26.00 **s.** – P 11.50/17.50 **s.**

Augres – ✉ Trinity – ☎ 0534 Jersey.
St. Helier 4.

Oaklands Lodge, Trinity Hill ☎ 61735 – TV wc ☎ P
Easter-November – **M** *(closed Tuesday)* (dinner only and Sunday lunch) 3.00/5.00 **s.** 1.00 – **10 rm** 9.00/14.00 **s.**

Bonne Nuit Bay – ✉ St. John – ☎ 0534 Jersey.
St. Helier 6.

Bonne Nuit, ☎ 61644, ←, – wc ☎ P
season – **34 rm.**

Cheval Roc, ☎ 62865, ← Bonne Nuit Bay, heated – wc wc P
mid May-September – **M** approx. 3.00 **s.** 2.00 – **45 rm** 9.50/22.50 **s.** – P 26.00/29.00 **s.**

Bouley Bay – ✉ Trinity – ☎ 0534 Jersey.
St. Helier 5.

Water's Edge, ☎ 62777, ← Bouley Bay, « Tasteful decor », heated, – TV P
57 rm.

Corbiere – ✉ St. Brelade – ☎ 0534 Jersey.
St. Helier 8.

Le Chalet, ☎ 41216, ←, – wc wc P
M 3.00/5.00 0.90 – **31 rm** 5.50/11.50 **s.** – P 9.50/17.00 **s.**

Sea Crest with rm, Petit Port ☎ 42687, ←, , – TV wc ☎ P
M a la carte 3.50/6.40 1.00 – **7 rm** 18.00/22.00 **s.**

L'Etacq – ✉ St. Ouens – ☎ 0534 Jersey.
St. Helier 7.5.

Lobster Pot, Mont du Vallet ☎ 82888 – P
closed Sunday dinner and January – **M** a la carte 6.50/9.50 1.10.

Gorey – ✉ St. Martin – ☎ 0534 Jersey.
See: Mont Orgueil Castle* (←**, tableaux*) *AC.*
St. Helier 4.

Old Court House, Gorey Village ☎ 54444, heated, – TV wc ☎ P
M a la carte 6.45/8.95 1.00 – **24 rm** 10.00/28.00 – P 15.75/17.00.

Trafalgar Bay, Gorey Village ☎ 53216, – wc P
May-October – **M** (residents only) approx. 3.00 1.20 – **40 rm** 6.50/14.00 – P 9.25/10.70.

at Gorey Pier – ✉ St. Martin – ☎ 0534 Jersey:

Dolphin, ☎ 53370, Telex 41385 – wc ☎
M approx. 3.20 **s.** 1.20 – **17 rm** 11.00/24.00 **s.** – P 14.00/16.00 **s.**

Moorings with rm, ☎ 53633 – wc ☎
closed 25 and 26 December – **M** a la carte 4.00/11.00 **s.** 2.35 – **10 rm** 9.30/18.60 **s.** – P 14.40/16.80 **s.**

Seascale with rm, ☎ 54395 – wc wc
closed January and February – **M** *(closed Monday lunch except Bank Holidays)* a la carte 4.50/9.50 1.10 – **10 rm** 8.25/17.90 **s.**

La Haule – ✉ St. Brelade – ☎ 0534 Jersey.

La Place, Route du Coin ☎ 44261, heated – P – **42 rm.**

Portelet Bay – ✉ St. Brelade – ☎ 0534 Jersey.
St. Helier 5.

Portelet, ☎ 41204, ←, , heated – wc P
22 March-16 October – **M** 4.00/4.50 1.25 – **85 rm** 14.10/29.00 **s.** – P 17.60/18.00 **s.**

La Pulente – ✉ St. Brelade – ☎ 0534 Jersey.
St. Helier 7.

Atlantic, ☎ 44101, ←, , heated, – TV P.
last 2 weeks January – **M** a la carte 4.55/6.95 – **42 rm** 9.90/19.80 – P approx. 14.30.

Rozel Bay – ✉ St. Martin – ☎ 0534 Jersey.
St. Helier 6.

- **Le Couperon de Rozel,** ☎ 62190, heated – wc P
mid April-October – **M** *(closed Wednesday and February-mid April)* 3.50/8.00 1.10 – **23 rm** 15.00/35.00.
- **Le Bistro Frère de Borsalino,** Gorselands ☎ 61000, < – P
M a la carte 4.50/6.50 1.15.

St. Aubin – ✉ St. Brelade – ☎ 0534 Jersey.
St. Helier 4.

- **Old Court House Inn** with rm, St. Aubin's Harbour, ☎ 41156 – wc
M a la carte 4.30/9.95 1.20 – **9 rm** 6.00/12.00 **s.**

St. Brelade's Bay – pop. 8,224 – ✉ St. Brelade – ☎ 0534 Jersey.
See : Site★. – St. Helier 6.

- **L'Horizon,** ☎ 43101, Telex 41281, < – TV P.
M a la carte 3.90/7.05 (see also rest. Star Grill) – **94 rm** 18.70/22.10.
- **Chateau Valeuse,** ☎ 43476, heated – P
closed February – **M** *(closed Monday in winter)* 3.80/4.50 2.80 – **26 rm** 7.50/16.00 **s.** – P 13.50/15.75 **s.**
- St. Brelade's Bay, ☎ 43281, <, heated – wc P
83 rm.
- **Star Grill** (at l'Horizon Hotel), ☎ 43101, < – P
M a la carte 3.90/7.05 1.00.

FORD Airport Rd ☎ 43222 — SAAB Route de Noirmont ☎ 41911

St. Clement – pop. 5,329 – ✉ St. Clement – ☎ 0534 Jersey.
St. Helier 2.

- **Shakespeare,** Coast Rd, ☎ 51915 – wc wc P
M approx. 2.80 – **23 rm** 13.50/27.00 **s.**

St. Helier – pop. 28,135 – ✉ St. Helier – ☎ 0534 Jersey.
See : Fort Regent ※★★★ (Militia Museum) *AC* – Elizabeth Castle ※★ *AC* Z – Rocher des Proscrits (au Havre des Pas) Z.

Plan opposite

- **Beaufort,** Green St. ☎ 32471, Telex 41160 – TV P — Z r
M 3.50/4.00 **s.** – **50 rm** (full board only in season) 11.00/22.00 – P 15.00.
- **De la Plage,** Havre des Pas ☎ 23474, Group Telex 41356, < – TV P — Z s
M 3.85/4.75 1.45 – **97 rm** 12.80/36.60 – P 15.30/20.80 **s.**
- **Apollo,** 9 St. Saviour's Rd ☎ 25441 – TV wc P — Z e
M 4.00/5.00 **s.** 1.25 – **43 rm** 9.50/19.00 **s.** – P 11.00/14.50 **s.**
- **Royal Yacht,** Weighbridge ☎ 20511 – wc wc — Z c
M approx. 4.25 **s.** 1.35 – **43 rm** 11.50/23.00 **s.** – P 14.50/16.00 **s.**
- **Savoy,** Rouge Bouillon ☎ 30012, heated – wc P — Y i
March-October – **M** *(open all year except Sunday in winter)* approx. 3.50 **s.** 1.30 – **66 rm** 8.00/18.00 **s.** – P 12.00/13.00 **s.**
- **Mont Millais,** Mont Millais ☎ 30281, – wc P — Z v
M 3.00/3.50 **s.** 1.00 – **50 rm** 8.50/19.00.
- **Mountview,** 49 New St., John's Rd ☎ 30080 – wc wc P — Y e
29 April-14 October – **M** approx. 3.00 **s.** 0.75 – **35 rm** 9.50/21.00 **s.** – P 10.50/11.50 **s.**
- **Uplands,** St. John's Rd, ☎ 30151, – wc P — Y a
March-October – **M** (dinner only) approx. 3.00 1.00 – **28 rm** (dinner included) 9.80/19.60.
- **Merton,** 48 Roseville St. ☎ 20044, – wc — Z x
closed mid November-February – 1.00 – **25 rm** 5.50/11.00 **s.**
- **La Capannina,** 65-67 Halkett Pl. ☎ 34602, Italian rest. — Z n
closed Sunday and 25 December-1 February – **M** a la carte 3.05/4.85 1.20.
- **Mauro's,** 37 La Motte St. ☎ 20147 — Z a
M a la carte 3.55/8.05 1.15.
- **Le Coq au Vin,** 6 Cheapside ☎ 33705, Italian rest. — Y o
closed Monday, 25 December-23 January and Bank Holidays – **M** a la carte 3.40/5.25 1.50.
- **Bistro Borsalino,** 12 Cattle St. ☎ 35299, Bistro — Z u
closed Sunday – **M** a la carte 4.40/6.70 1.25.

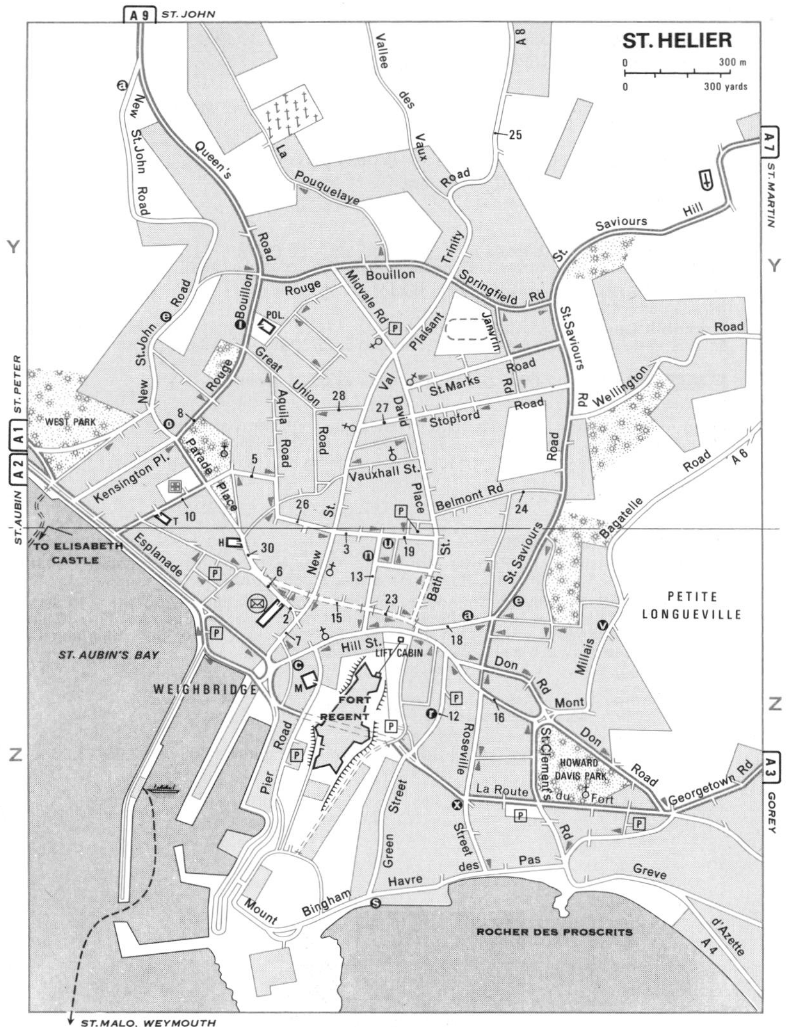

Halkett Place	Z 13	Charing Cross	Z 6	Minden Place	Z 19
King Street	Z 15	Conway Street	Z 7	Simon Place	Y 24
Queen Street	Z 23	Elizabeth Place	Y 8	Trinity Hill	Y 25
		Gloucester Street	Y 10	Union Street	Y 26
Broad Street	Z 2	Green Street	Z 12	Victoria Street	Y 27
Burrard Street	Z 3	La Colomberie	Z 16	Windsor Road	Y 28
Cannon Street	Y 5	La Motte Street	Z 18	York Street	Z 30

AUDI-NSU, OPEL Parade Garage ☎ 23272
AUSTIN-MORRIS-MG-WOLSELEY Havre des Pas ☎ 33233
CHRYSLER-SIMCA, LANCIA 1/2 Victoria St. ☎ 37357
CITROEN, VAUXHALL 27 New St. ☎ 24541
FORD ☎ 31361
JAGUAR-DAIMLER-ROVER-TRIUMPH, ASTON-MARTIN, ROLLS ROYCE-BENTLEY 87 Bath St. ☎ 31341
PEUGEOT 17 Esplanade ☎ 33623

Do not use yesterday's maps for today's journey.

St. Lawrence – **pop. 3,535** – ✉ **St. Lawrence** – ☎ **0534 Jersey.**
See : German Military Underground Hospital* *AC.*
St. Helier 3.

Little Grove, rue de Haut ☎ 25321, heated, – wc
18 rm.

St. Peter – **pop. 4,000** – ✉ **St. Peter** – ☎ **0534 Jersey.**
Envir. : St. Ouen Manor* *AC*, NW : 2 m.
☎ **Central 41272/3-4.**
St. Helier 5.

Mermaid, ☎ 41255, Telex 41649, heated, – TV.
M 3.50/4.00 **s.** (see also rest. **Mermaid Grill**) – **68 rm** 15.50/18.50.

XX **Mermaid Grill** (at Mermaid Hotel), ☎ 41255 –
M a la carte 4.30/5.80.

XX **Greenhill Country** with rm, Coin Varin ☎ 81042, heated – wc wc
M a la carte 3.80/6.20 1.75 – **17 rm** 15.00/30.00 – P 18.00/22.00.

St. Saviour – **pop. 11,064** – ✉ **St. Saviour** – ☎ **0534 Jersey.**
St. Helier 1.

Longueville Manor, ☎ 25501, Telex 41306, heated, park – TV
M approx. 6.00 **s.** – **35 rm** 18.75/35.50 **s.** – P 20.75/25.25 **s.**

Talana Private, Bagot Rd ☎ 30317, – wc
36 rm.

RENAULT Bagot Rd ☎ 32571

SARK **59** ④⑤ and **230** ⑩ – **pop. 590.**
See : La Coupée* (isthmus) – Port du Moulin** – Creux Harbour* – Happy Valley* – Little Sark* – La Seigneurie* (manor 18C, Residence of the Seigneur of Sark).**
Shipping connections with the Continent : to Saint-Malo (Condor : hydrofoil) – to Jersey (Condor : hydrofoil) in summer Monday/Saturday : direct (45 mn) or via Guernsey (1 h 30 mn) ; in winter Monday/Saturday : direct (1 h 15 mn) – to Guernsey (Isle of Sark Shipping Co.) summer Monday/Saturday 2-6 daily ; winter 3 weekly (35 mn).
i Sark Publicity Officer ☎ 135.

Petit Champ, ☎ 46, ≤ countryside and sea, heated, – wc
April-October – **M** 3.75/5.50 0.90 – **18 rm** 6.50/17.50 **st.**

Aval du Creux, Harbour Hill ☎ 36,
April-October – **M** approx. 3.60 0.85 – **10 rm** (full board only) – P 12.60/13.60 **s.**

Isle of Man

LICENSING HOURS-WHEN DRINKING ALCOHOLIC BEVERAGES IS PERMITTED IN PUBS AND BARS (The General Rule).

HEURES PERMISES POUR LA CONSOMMATION DES BOISSONS ALCOOLISÉES (Règle Générale).

ORARI CONSENTITI PER LA CONSUMAZIONE DI BEVANDE ALCOOLICHE (Regola Generale).

AUSSCHANKZEITEN FÜR ALKOHOLISCHE GETRÄNKE (Allgemeine Regelung).

		from de dalle von	to à alle bis	from de dalle von	to à alle bis		
WEEKDAYS JOURS DE SEMAINE	SUMMER ÉTÉ	10.30			22.45	ESTATE SOMMER	GIORNI DELLA SETTIMANA WOCHENTAGS
	WINTER - HIVER Monday to Thursday Lundi au Jeudi	12.00			22.00	INVERNO-WINTER Da lunedì a giovedì Montag - Donnerstag	
	Friday and Saturday Vendredi et Samedi	12.00			22.45	Venerdì e sabato Freitag und Samstag	
SUNDAYS DIMANCHES	SUMMER ÉTÉ	12.00	13.30	20.00	22.00	ESTATE SOMMER	DOMENICHE SONNTAGS
	WINTER HIVER	Closed - Fermés - Chiusi - Geschlossen				INVERNO WINTER	

RESIDENTS (hotels): no restrictions in licensed hotels even on Sundays.

SUMMER: from Maundy Thursday (the Thursday before Good Friday) to 30 September.

RÉSIDENTS (hôtels) : aucune restriction dans les lieux autorisés recevant le résident, même les dimanches.

ÉTÉ: du Jeudi Saint au 30 septembre.

RESIDENTI (alberghi): nessuna restrizione nei locali autorizzati che ospitano il residente, anche la domenica.

ESTATE: dal giovedi precedente il Venerdi Santo al 30 settembre.

FÜR HOTELGÄSTE keine Beschränkung (auch nicht an Sonntagen) in den lizensierten Hotels

SOMMER: Von Gründonnerstag bis 30. September.

Place with at least :

one hotel or restaurant ● Ramsey
one pleasant hotel 🏠, ✗ with rm.
one quiet, secluded hotel 🐦
one restaurant with ✿, ✿✿, M
See this town for establishments located in its vicinity DOUGLAS

Localité offrant au moins :

une ressource hôtelière ● Ramsey
un hôtel agréable 🏠, ✗ with rm.
un hôtel très tranquille, isolé 🐦
une bonne table à ✿, ✿✿, M
Localité groupant dans le texte les ressources de ses environs DOUGLAS

La località possiede come minimo :

una risorsa alberghiera ● Ramsey
un albergo ameno 🏠, ✗ with rm.
un albergo molto tranquillo, isolato 🐦
un'ottima tavola con ✿, ✿✿, M
La località raggruppa nel suo testo le risorse dei dintorni DOUGLAS

Ort mit mindestens :

einem Hotel oder Restaurant ● Ramsey
einem angenehmen Hotel 🏠, ✗ with rm.
einem sehr ruhigen und abgelegenen Hotel 🐦
einem Restaurant mit ✿, ✿✿, M
Ort mit Angaben über Hotels und Restaurants in seiner Umgebung DOUGLAS

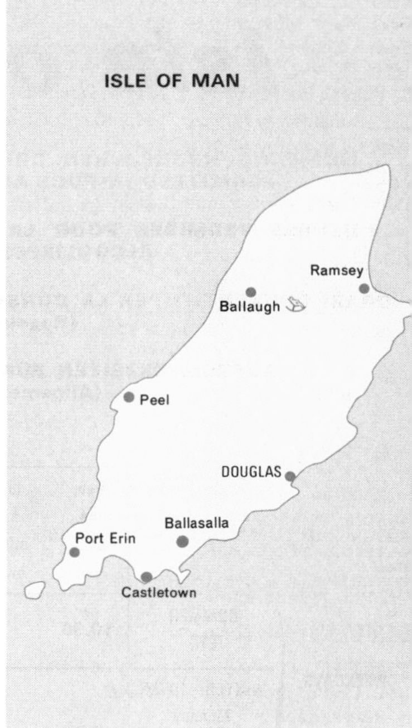

ISLE OF MAN

Towns

BALLASALLA – ☎ 062 482 Castletown.
Douglas 8.5.

✗✗✗ **Coach House,** Silverburn Bridge ☎ 2343 – Ⓟ
M a la carte 4.10/8.20 🍾 1.50.

MERCEDES-BENZ, VW, AUDI-NSU Douglas Rd ☎ 2224

BALLAUGH – pop. 524 – ✉ Kirkmichael – ☎ 062 489 Sulby.
Envir. : Curragh Wildlife Park★ *AC.* NE : 1 ½ m.
Douglas 18.

Ravensdale Castle 🐦, Ballaugh Glen ☎ 330, ⛱, park – wc Ⓟ
M (bar lunch) 4.00/4.50 🍾 1.50 – **11 rm** 8.00/17.00.

SAAB, SKODA Main Rd ☎ 229

CASTLETOWN 986 ㉒ – pop. 2,820 – ☎ 062 482.
See : Rushen Castle★★ (13C) *AC :* keep ✻★.
⛳18 Fort Island ☎ 2201, E : 2 m.
ℹ Town Hall, ☎ 823518.
Douglas 10.

Castletown Golf Links 🐦, Fort Island E : 2 m. ☎ 2201, Telex 627636, ≤ sea and golf links, 🎾, ⛱, ⛳18, – Ⓟ
Easter-mid October – **M** approx. 4.50 **t.** 🍾 0.90 – **80 rm** 11.00/22.00 **t.** – P 15.00/16.00 **t.**

DOUGLAS 986 ㉒㉓ – pop. 21,100 – ☎ 0624.

See: Manx Museum** – The Promenades* – A 18 Road** from Douglas to Ramsey.

Envir.: Snaefell ☼*** (by electric railway from Laxey) *AC*, NE: 7 m. – Laxey (waterwheel*: Lady Isabella) NE: 6 m. – St. John's (Tynwald Hill) NW : 8 m.

Pulrose Park ☎ 5952, 1 m. from Douglas Pier – at Onchan, N: 1 m.

Ronaldsway Airport, ☎ 062 482 (Castletown) 3311, SW: 7 m. – **Terminal:** Lord St., Douglas.

by Isle of Man Steam Packet Co. to Ardrossan: 28 May-16 September 1-5 weekly (6 h) – to Belfast: 27 May-18 September 1-3 weekly (4 h 30 mn) – to Dublin: summer only 1-3 weekly (4 h 30 mn) – to Fleetwood: May-September 2-5 weekly (4 h) – to Liverpool: Summer 1-7 daily; Winter Monday/Saturday 1 daily (4 h 15 mn).

to Llandudno (Isle of Man Steam Packet Co.) summer only 2-4 weekly (3 h).

i 13 Victoria St. ☎ 4323 – 79 Main Rd at Onchan ☎ 22311/5564.

Palace, Central Prom. ☎ 4521, Telex 627742, ←, – TV wc ☎ P
M 2.95/3.40 **t.** 1.35 – **100 rm** 12.70/20.70 **t.** – P 14.10/16.70 **t.**

Villiers, Loch Prom. ☎ 5465, Telex 628105, ← – wc wc
M 2.75 1.30 – **122 rm** 6.50/17.00.

Castle Mona, Central Prom. ☎ 4356, ← – wc ☎ P
season – **104 rm.**

at Onchan NE: 1 ½ m. – ✉ ☎ 0624 Douglas:

Douglas Bay, ☎ 3863 – wc wc P
May-October – **M** approx. 2.50 0.75 – **80 rm** (full board only) – P 8.00/10.00.

Howstrake, Harbour Rd ☎ 6225 – P.

AUSTIN-MG-WOLSELEY Victoria Rd ☎ 3141
AUSTIN-DAIMLER-JAGUAR-MG-ROVER-TRIUMPH-WOLSELEY, ROLLS ROYCE Westmoreland Rd ☎ 23481
CHRYSLER-SIMCA Demesne Rd ☎ 21952
DATSUN Peel Rd ☎ 6515
FORD Douglas ☎ 3211
MORRIS-MG-WOLSELEY Hill St. ☎ 4428
OPEL-VAUXHALL 43/45 Bucks Rd ☎ 3781
PEUGEOT 2 Derby Sq. ☎ 5373
RENAULT Peel Rd ☎ 3342
VOLVO Alexander Drive ☎ 21830

ONCHAN – see Douglas.

PEEL 986 ㉒ – pop. 3,081 – ☎ 062 484.

See: Castle* (ruins 13C-16C) *AC*.

Rheast Lane ☎ 2227.

i Town Hall, Derby Rd ☎ 842341.

Douglas 11.

Lively Lobster, The Quay ☎ 2789
March-September – **M** a la carte 4.35/6.35 **t.** 1.00.

PORT ERIN 986 ㉒ – pop. 1,714 – ☎ 0624.

See: Site*.

i Town Commissioners, Station Rd ☎ 832298.

Douglas 14.

The Restaurant, Station Rd ☎ 833566 – P
March-October – **M** *(closed Sunday dinner and Monday)* a la carte 3.60/5.60 **t.** 1.75.

RAMSEY 986 ⑲㉓ – pop. 5,048 – ☎ 0624.

See: Mooragh Park* – A 18 Road** from Ramsey to Douglas.

Brookfield ☎ 812244, West boundary.

i Town Hall, Parliament Sq. ☎ 812228.

Douglas 18.

Grand Island, ☎ 812455, ← sea, – wc wc P
season – **61 rm.**

AUSTIN-MG-WOLSELEY Lezayre Rd ☎ 2494
PEUGEOT, VW Albert Rd ☎ 813060

Republic of Ireland

LICENSING HOURS - WHEN DRINKING ALCOHOLIC BEVERAGES IS PERMITTED IN PUBS AND BARS AND OTHER LICENSED PREMISES (The General Rule).

HEURES PERMISES POUR LA CONSOMMATION DES BOISSONS ALCOOLISÉES (Règle Générale).

ORARI CONSENTITI PER LA CONSUMAZIONE DI BEVANDE ALCOOLICHE (Regola Generale).

AUSSCHANKZEITEN FÜR ALKOHOLISCHE GETRÄNKE (Allgemeine Regelung).

		from de dalle von	to à alle bis	from de dalle von	to à alle bis		
Weekdays Jours de semaine	APRIL to OCTOBER AVRIL à OCTOBRE	10.30			23.30	da APRILE a OTTOBRE APRIL - OKTOBER	Giorni della settimana Wochentags
	NOVEMBER to MARCH NOVEMBRE à MARS	10.30			23.00	da NOVEMBRE a MARZO NOVEMBER - MÄRZ	
Sundays and St. Patrick's Day (17 March) Dimanches et Jour de la St-Patrick (17 mars)		12.30	14.00	16.00	22.00	Domeniche e giorno di St. Patrick (17 Marzo) Sonntags und am St. Patricks Tag (17. März)	
Good Friday and Christmas Day Vendredi Saint et Jour de Noël		Closed - Fermés - Chiusi - Geschlossen				Venerdì Santo e Natale Karfreitag und Weihnachten	

DUBLIN AND CORK : Pubs close on weekdays from 14.30 - 15.30 hours.

RESIDENTS : there are no time restrictions in licensed hotels apart from Good Friday when alcoholic beverages may only be served with meals.

RESTAURANTS : not attached to a hotel or other establishment with a full licence may only sell wine (i.e. no spirits or beer).

DUBLIN AND CORK : Pubs fermés entre 14 h 30 et 15 h 30 les jours de semaine.

RESIDENTS : aucune restriction, sauf le Vendredi Saint où les boissons alcoolisées ne sont servies qu'à l'occasion des repas.

RESTAURANTS : si non installés dans un hôtel ou autre établissement ayant une licence complète, ne peuvent vendre que du vin, à l'exclusion de toute autre boisson alcoolisée.

DUBLIN E CORK : Pubs chiusi dalle 14.30 alle 15.30 i giorni della settimana.

RESIDENTI : nessuna restrizione, escluso il Venerdì Santo in cui le bevande alcooliche sono servite soltanto in occasione dei pasti.

RISTORANTI : se non si trovano in un albergo o in un altro esercizio munito di licenza completa, possono vendere soltanto del vino, con esclusione di tutte le altre bevande alcooliche.

DUBLIN UND CORK : Pubs sind wochentags von 14.30 bis 15.30 Uhr geschlossen.

FÜR HOTELGÄSTE : keine Beschränkung außer für Karfreitag, an dem alkoholische Getränke nur zu den Mahlzeiten serviert werden.

IN RESTAURANTS dürfen, außer Wein, keine alkoholischen Getränke ausgegeben werden. Ausnahmen sind hier Hotelrestaurants oder Restaurants anderer lizensierter Betriebe.

Rosapenna
Port-na-Blagh
Buncrana
Gortahork
Rathmullan
Dunglow
Letterkenny
Raphoe
Lifford
Ballybofey
N 15
Killybegs
Donegal
Rossnowlagh
Bundoran
SLIGO
N 59
N 16
Ballina
ACHILL ISLAND
Pontoon
Newport
Castlebar
Boyle
Carrick-on-Shannon
Kiltimagh
Westport
Lough Gowna
Castlerea
Strokestown
Longford
Renvyle
Leenane
T 40
Moyard
Letterfrack
Cong
N 4
Clifden
Clonbur
Cashel Bay
Oughterard
Mullingar
Carraroe
ROSSCAHILL
Athlone
Spiddal
GALWAY
Moate
Bearna
Ballinasloe
Banagher
Ballyvaughan
Portumna
Birr
Emo
Liscannor
N 18
Roscrea
Scarriff
Ennis
Nenagh
Quin
Abbeyleix
N 7
Newmarket-on-Fergus
Killaloe
Durrow
Shannon Airport
Bunratty
Limerick
Thurles
Ballybunion
Adare
N 21
Kilkenny
N 24
Listowel
CASHEL
Abbeyfeale
Templeglantine
Tipperary
Glen of Aherlow
Castlegregory
Charleville
(Rath Luirc)
Cahir
Clonmel
Tralee
Ballyferriter
Dingle
Inch
Kanturk
Ballyduff
WATERFORD
Caragh Lake
Glenbeigh
Killarney
Lismore
VALENTIA ISLAND
Mallow
Tramore
Glencar
Caherciveen
Dunmore
N 22
Waterville
Sneem
Kenmare
Macroom
Blarney
Youghal
N 25
Ardmore
Ballinskelligs
Parknasilla
Caherdaniel
Garryvoe Strand
Shanagarry
Castletownbere
Crookhaven

Place with at least :

one hotel or restaurant ● Longford
one pleasant hotel ⌂, ✗ with rm.
one quiet, secluded hotel
one restaurant with ✿, ✿✿, M
See this town for establishments located in its vicinity SLIGO

Localité offrant au moins :

une ressource hôtelière ● Longford
un hôtel agréable ⌂, ✗ with rm.
un hôtel très tranquille, isolé
une bonne table à ✿, ✿✿, M
Localité groupant dans le texte les ressources de ses environs SLIGO

La località possiede come minimo :

una risorsa alberghiera ● Longford
un albergo ameno ⌂, ✗ with rm.
un albergo molto tranquillo, isolato
un'ottima tavola con ✿, ✿✿, M
La località raggruppa nel suo testo le risorse dei dintorni SLIGO

Ort mit mindestens :

einem Hotel oder Restaurant ● Longford
einem angenehmen Hotel ⌂, ✗ with rm.
einem sehr ruhigen und abgelegenen Hotel
einem Restaurant mit ✿, ✿✿, M
Ort mit Angaben über Hotels und Restaurants in seiner Umgebung SLIGO

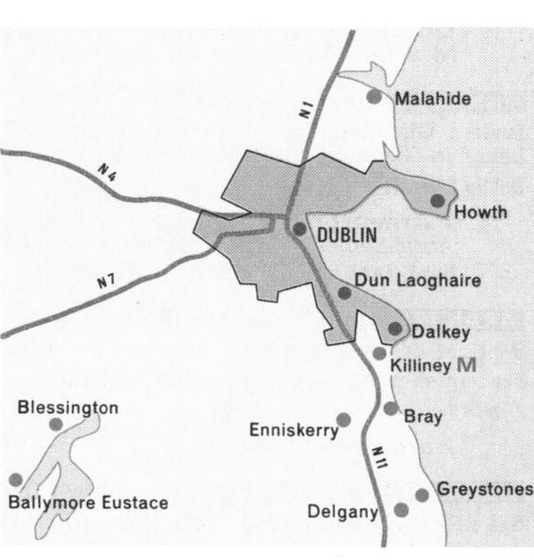

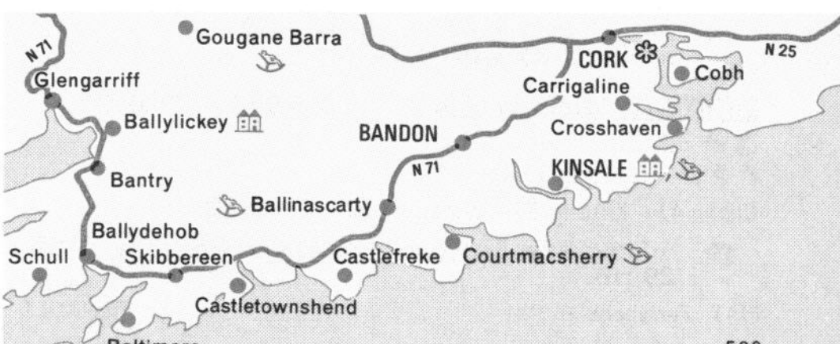

REPUBLIC OF IRELAND

Towns

ABBEYFEALE Limerick 986 ㉕.
Dublin 160 – Killarney 30 – Limerick 39.

Leen's Main St. ☎ 31121 – wc
M a la carte 2.80/5.00 **t.** – **14 rm** 4.50/9.50 **t.** – P 10.00 **t.**

ABBEYLEIX Laois 986 ㉖ – pop. 1,919 – 0502 Port Laoise – 9.
Envir.: Dunamase Rock (castle** 13C-16C ruins), site**, ** NE: 13 ½ m.
Dublin 64 – Kilkenny 21 – **Limerick 65** – **Tullamore 30.**

Hibernian, ☎ 31252 – P
10 rm.

FORD Market Sq. ☎ 31125

ACHILL ISLAND Mayo 986 ㉑ – pop 1,163.
See: Achill Sound* – The Atlantic Drive*** SW: Coast Rd from Cloghmore to Dooega – Keel (the strand*) – Lough Keel*.
9 Achill Sound, Westport, in Keel.
i ☎ Achill Sound 51 (June-August).

at Achill Sound – ✉ Achill Sound:

Achill Sound, ☎ 6 – wc P
April-September – **M** (dinner only) 3.50/4.00 **t.** 1.50 – **25 rm** 7.50/12.00 **st.**

ADARE Limerick 986 ㉕ – pop. 2,604 – 061 Limerick.
See: <* from the bridge of the River Maigue.
9 ☎ 94204.
i ☎ 94255 (July-August).
Dublin 131 – Killarney 59 – Limerick 10.

Dunraven Arms, Main St., ☎ 94209, « Gardens » – wc P
M approx.6.25 **t.** 2.50 – 2.50 – **22 rm** 10.70/20.00 **t.**

ANNAMOE Wicklow – ✉ 0404 Wicklow.
Envir.: Glendalough (ancient monastic city** : site***, St. Kervin's Church*) and Upper Lake* in Glendalough Valley*** SW: 5 m. – Lough Tay** NW: 8 m.
Dublin 29 – Wexford 72.

XX ❀ **Armstrong's Barn,** on T 61 ☎ 5194, – P
April-September – **M** *(closed Sunday and Monday)* (dinner only) 7.95/8.95 **t.** 1.35
Spec. Lamb's kidneys, Roast loin of lamb (March-September), Fresh poached salmon (June-September).

ARAN ISLANDS ** Galway 986 ⑰.
By boat or aeroplane from Galway City or by boat from Kilkieran, or Fisherstreet (Clare).
See: Inishmore Island (Kilronan harbour*).
i ☎ Kilronan 29 (July - August).

Hotels see: Galway.

ARDMORE Waterford 986 ㉙ – pop. 1,076 – 024.
See: Site*, round tower* 10C, cathedral ruins* 12C, <*.
Dublin 138 – Cork 33 – Waterford 44.

Cliff House, ☎ 4106, <, – P
season – **21 rm.**

ARKLOW Wicklow 986 ㉖ – pop. 6,948 – 0402.
18 ☎ 2492.
i ☎ 2484 (June-August).
Dublin 47 – Kilkenny 68 – **Waterford 66** – Wexford 49.

Arklow Bay, Ferrybank, Brittas Bay Rd N: ½ m. off L 29 ☎ 2289, – wc P.
29 rm.

FIAT Ferrybank ☎ 2481 RENAULT Wexford Rd ☎ 2716

ASHBOURNE Meath – ✆ 01 Dublin.
Dublin 13 – Drogheda 24 – **Dundalk 42.**

✕ Ashbourne House, with rm, on T 2 ☎ 250167 – Ⓟ
10 rm.

ASHFORD Wicklow – pop. 341 – ✆ 0404 Wicklow.
See : Mount Usher or Walpole's Gardens* *AC.*
Dublin 29 – Waterford 84 – Wexford 67.

✕ River Room (Marty O'Gara's Pub), ☎ 4321 – Ⓟ.

ATHLONE Westmeath 986 ㉑ – pop. 9,825 – ✆ 0902.
Envir. : Clonmacnois** (mediaeval ruins) SW : 8 m. – N : Lough Ree*.
ℹ 17 Church St. ☎ 2866.
Dublin 75 – Galway 57 – Limerick 75 – Roscommon 20 – **Tullamore 24.**

Prince of Wales, Church St. ☎ 2626 – wc ☎ Ⓟ.
50 rm.

Royal Hoey, Mardyke St. ☎ 2924 – wc Ⓟ.
closed Christmas Holidays – **M** approx. 4.00 **st.** 1.20 – **47 rm** 6.00/14.50 **st.**

✕ **Kilcleagh Park** with rm, Castledaly SE : 7 m. off N 6 ☎ 31221, park – Ⓟ
M *(closed Christmas Day)* 3.75/4.50 **t.** 1.80 – **10 rm** 6.00/12.00 **t.** – P 10.00/12.00 **t.**

CHRYSLER-SIMCA Dublin Rd ☎ 4009
CITROEN, PEUGEOT, VAUXHALL Magazine Rd ☎ 2619
CITROEN Dublin Rd ☎ 4095
FIAT Ballydangan ☎ 37105
FORD Magazine Rd ☎ 2007
OPEL Dublin Rd ☎ 2726
VW, AUDI-NSU, MERCEDES-BENZ, TOYOTA Lakeview ☎ 2734

Für die , , geben wir keine Einzelheiten
über die Einrichtung an,
da diese Hotels im allgemeinen jeden Komfort besitzen.

wc wc ☎

ATHY Kildare 986 ㉖ – pop. 4,270 – ✆ 0507.
Dublin 42 – Kilkenny 33 – **Tullamore 35** – Wexford 58.

Leinster Arms, Leinster St. ☎ 21307
22 rm.

DATSUN Leinster St. ☎ 21662
FIAT Timolin, Moone ☎ 24104
FORD Kildare Rd ☎ 21607
RENAULT Leinster St. ☎ 21169
VW, AUDI-NSU 50 Duke St. ☎ 21373

AVOCA Wicklow 986 ㉖ – pop. 2,266 – ✆ 0402 Arklow.
See: Vale of Avoca* from Arklow to Rathdrum on T 7.
9 ☎ 5202.
Dublin 47 – Waterford 72 – Wexford 55.

Vale View, N : 1 ¾ m. on T 7 ☎ 5236, ← – Ⓟ
M 4.25/6.00 **t.** 1.45 – **10 rm** 10.00/20.00 **t.**

BALLINA Mayo 986 ㉑ – pop. 4,616.
Envir. : Rosserk Abbey* (Franciscan Friary 15 C) N : 4 m. – Ballycastle (cliffs* NW : 3 m. near L 133) NW : 15 m. – Downpatrick Head* NW : 18 m.
9 ☎ 88, E : 1 m.
ℹ ☎ 464 (June - August).
Dublin 147 – Galway 73 – Roscommon 63 – **Sligo 37.**

Downhill , Sligo Rd ☎ 7, , – wc wc ☎ Ⓟ
closed 19 to 27 December – **M** 4.85/5.50 **t.** 1.30 – **54 rm** 6.75/18.00 **t.**

Mount Falcon Castle , S : 4 m. on Foxford-Ballina Rd ☎ 21172, « Country house atmosphere », , , park – wc Ⓟ
M (by arrangement only for non-residents) – **11 rm.**

DATSUN Bachelor Walk ☎ 53
FIAT Ballina ☎ 358
FORD Pearse St. ☎ 13
OPEL Killala Rd ☎ 63
PEUGEOT, VAUXHALL Sligo Rd ☎ 430
RENAULT Lord Edward St. ☎ 260
VW, AUDI-NSU Pearse St. ☎ 91

BALLINASCARTY Cork – ✉ Clonakilty – ✆ 023 Bandon.
Dublin 188 – Cork 27.

Ardnavaha House , SE : 2 m. by L 63 ☎ 49135, ←, , heated, , , park – wc ☎ Ⓟ
May-15 October – **M** 6.00/8.00 **t.** 2.20 – **24 rm** 10.50/18.00 **t.** – P 18.50 **t.**

23

BALLINASLOE Galway 986 ㉑ – pop. 5,969 – ✪ 0905.
🏌 9 ☎ 2126.
i ☎ 2332 (May-September).
Dublin 91 – Galway 41 – Limerick 66 – Roscommon 36 – Tullamore 34.

Hayden's, Dunlo St. ☎ 2347, – lift wc ☎ Ⓟ
closed 2 days at Christmas – **M** a la carte 3.65/5.45 **t.** 1.50 – 1.50 – **55 rm** 7.05/15.80 **t.**

FORD ☎ 2204
PEUGEOT, VW, AUDI-NSU Dunlo St. ☎ 2290
RENAULT Brackernagh ☎ 2420

BALLINSKELLIGS Kerry 986 ㉙ – pop. 355.
See : Augustinian Monastery ≤*.
Dublin 238 – Killarney 48.

Reenroe, NE: 2 ¾ m. on Waterville Rd ☎ 23, ≤ coast and mountains, park – Ⓟ.
season – **45 rm.**

BALLYBOFEY Donegal – pop. 2,214 – ✉ Lifford.
🏌 9 ☎ 93.
Dublin 148 – Londonderry 30 – Sligo 58.

Jackson's, Glenfinn St. ☎ 21 – wc ☎ Ⓟ
closed Christmas week – **M** 3.40/4.20 **t.** 0.80 – **42 rm** 5.00/12.00 **t.** – P 13.00/14.00 **t.**

RENAULT ☎ 122

BALLYBUNION Kerry 986 ㉕.
🏌 18 ☎ 20.
i ☎ 75 (June-September).
Dublin 174 – Killarney 40 – Limerick 53.

Marine, Sandhill Rd ☎ 17
M 4.00/5.00 **t.** 1.20 – **22 rm** 5.50/11.00 **t.**

Eagle Lodge, ☎ 27224 – wc Ⓟ
May-September – **11 rm** 4.50/9.00 **t.**

BALLYDEHOB Cork.
Dublin 220 – Cork 59 – Killarney 58.

Basil Bush, Main St. ☎ 59
season.

BALLYDUFF Waterford.
Dublin 150 – Cork 30 – Waterford 51.

Blackwater Lodge, SW: 1 ½ m. ☎ 35, ≤, – wc Ⓟ
30 January-September – **M** (bar lunch) 4.00/6.00 **t.** 1.50 – **10 rm** 6.00/12.00 **t.** – P 9.00/12.00 **t.**

BALLYFERRITER Kerry.
Envir.: Kilmalkedar (church* 12C) NE: 4 ½ m. – Gallarus Oratory* 8C, NE: 2 m.
Dublin 224 – Killarney 59 – Limerick 103.

Dun an Oir, NW: 2 m. ☎ 33, ≤, heated, 🏌 9 – wc Ⓟ
season – **20 rm.**

BALLYLICKEY Cork – pop. 350 – ✉ ✪ Bantry.
Envir. : Glengarriff (site***) NW: 8 m. – SW: Bantry Bay**.
Dublin 216 – Cork 55 – Killarney 45.

Ballylickey House, ☎ 71, ≤, heated, , park – wc ☎ Ⓟ
February-November – **M** approx. 6.75 **t.** 1.75 – 1.85 – **25 rm** 11.50/22.50 **t.**

Green Acre Lodge, ☎ 182, – Ⓟ
Easter-October – **M** (snack lunch) 4.00/5.00 **t.** 1.70 – **10 rm** 4.50/9.00 **t.**

Seaview, ☎ 73, ≤, – Ⓟ
season – **12 rm.**

BALLYMORE EUSTACE Kildare – pop. 433 – ✪ 045 Naas.
Dublin 23.

Ardenode, SW: 1 ¼ m. off L 25 ☎ 64198, , park – wc Ⓟ
June-September – **M** 3.50/5.50 **t.** 1.00 – **10 rm** 4.75/12.50 **t.** – P 10.00/12.50 **t.**

P 9.00/9.50

I prezzi di pensione che figurano
nella guida sono indicativi.
Per un soggiorno, consultate sempre l'albergatore.

BALLYVAUGHAN Clare – pop. 200 – ✉ Galway (Galway).

Envir.: SW : Coast road L 54 from Ailladie to Fanore : Burren District (Burren limestone terraces**) – Corcomroe Abbey* (or Abbey of St. Maria de Petra Fertilis: 12C Cistercian ruins) NE : 6 m.

Dublin 149 – Ennis 34 – Galway 29.

- **Gregans Castle**, SW: 3 ¼ m. on T 69 ☎ 5, ← – wc Ⓟ
  M 5.00/6.50 **t.** 1.50 – **16 rm** 9.50/18.00 **t.**

BALRATH Meath – ✉ Navan – ⊙ 041 Drogheda.

Dublin 22 – Drogheda 15 – Dundalk 33.

- XX Mullaghfin, NE: 1 ½ m. off T 2 ☎ 25137, – Ⓟ.

BALTIMORE Cork – pop. 200.

Dublin 221 – Cork 60 – Killarney 75.

- **Baltimore House**, ☎ 27, ← Baltimore Bay and islands, , park – wc Ⓟ
  Easter-October – **M** (dinner only) approx. 4.50 **t.** 1.25 – **19 rm** 5.15/12.00 **t.**
- Corner House, ☎ 43
  season – **9 rm.**

BANAGHER Offaly – pop. 1,052.

See : ←* from the bridge of Shannon. **Envir.:** Clonfert (St. Brendan's Cathedral : west door* 12C, east windows* 13C) NW: 4 ½ m.

Dublin 83 – Galway 54 – Limerick 56 – Tullamore 24.

- Brosna Lodge, Main St. ☎ 50, – wc Ⓟ
  M (buffet lunch) – **15 rm.**

BANDON Cork 986 ㉙ – pop. 2,257 – ⊙ 023.

9 ☎ 41111.

Dublin 180 – Cork 19 – Killarney 51.

- **Munster Arms,** Oliver Plunkett St. ☎ 41562 – wc wc Ⓟ.
  M 3.50/6.50 **t.** – **35 rm** 9.50/19.50 **t.**

at Innishannon NE: 4 ½ m. on T 65 – ✉ Innishannon – ⊙ 021 Cork:

- X **Innishannon** with rm, S: ¾ m. on L 41 ☎ 75121, , – wc Ⓟ
  closed Christmas Day – **M** 4.00/4.70 **t.** – **5 rm** 7.00/17.00 **t.** – P 13.00 **t.**

CHRYSLER ☎ 41264
DATSUN Convent Rd, Clonakilty ☎ 43374
FIAT, LANCIA ☎ 41514
FORD 72 Main St. ☎ 41522
RENAULT ☎ 41617

BANTRY Cork 986 ㉙ – pop. 2,579.

See : Bantry House (interior**, ←*) *AC*. **Envir.:** Glengarriff (site***) NW : 8 m. – W: Bantry Bay** – NE : Shehy Mountains**.

i ☎ 229 (June-September).

Dublin 218 – Cork 57 – Killarney 48.

- **Westlodge,** SW: 1 ½ m. on T 65 ☎ 360, – wc Ⓟ.
  M 4.85/5.75 **t.** 1.50 – **60 rm** 9.50/14.50 **t.** – P 9.70/11.40 **t.**
- **Bantry Motor Inn** without rest., N: 1 m. on T 65 ☎ 249, ← Bantry Bay – wc Ⓟ
  1.50 – **10 rm** 7.00/11.00.
- **Bantry Bay,** The Square ☎ 62
  M approx. 3.50 **t.** 1.20 – **18 rm** 4.50/9.00 **t.** – P 8.50 **t.**

CHRYSLER The Square ☎ 23
RENAULT Barrack St. ☎ 92

BEARNA PIER Galway.

Dublin 135 – Galway 3.

- XX **Ty Ar Mor,** Sea Point ☎ 65031, ← Bearna Harbour and Galway Bay, Seafood – Ⓟ
  closed January – **M** (dinner only) a la carte 5.10/9.20 **st.** 1.50.

BETTYSTOWN Meath – ✉ ⊙ 041 Drogheda.

18 ☎ 7134.

Envir.: Monasterboice (3 tall crosses** 10C) NW: 11 m. – Mellifont Abbey** (Cistercian ruins 1142) NW: 10 m.

Dublin 28 – Drogheda 6.

- **Village,** NW: ¾ m. on L125 ☎ 27136, – wc Ⓟ
  M a la carte 5.80/8.15 **t.** 1.50 – **10 rm** 6.70/15.90 **t.** – P 16.50/20.50 **t.**
- X **Coastguard Inn,** ☎ 27115, ← – Ⓟ
  closed 25 December-31 January – **M** *(closed Sunday and Monday)* (dinner only) a la carte 6.60/8.10 **t.** 1.95.

BIRR Offaly 986 ㉕ – pop. 3319.
See : Birr Castle Demesne (arboretum*, gardens*, telescope of Lord Rosse) *AC.*
18 The Glenns, ☎ 82, N : 2 m.
ℹ ☎ 206 (May-September).
Dublin 81 – Galway 56 – Kilkenny 48 **– Limerick 48 – Tullamore 22.**

Dooly's, ☎ 32
20 rm.

FORD Railway Rd ☎ 10

BLACKROCK Cork – see Cork.

BLARNEY Cork 986 ㉙ – pop. 1,128 – ✉ ☎ 021 Cork.
See : Castle* 15C (top ※*, 112 steps) *AC.*
Dublin 167 – Cork 6.

Blarney, ☎ 85281, – wc wc ☎ P
76 rm.

BLESSINGTON Wicklow – pop. 637 – ☎ 045 Naas.
Envir.: Lackan ≤* SE : 4 ½ m. – SE: Poulaphuca Lake* (reservoir).
Dublin 20.

Downshire House, Main St. ☎ 65199, – wc ☎ **P**.
closed mid December-mid January – **M** 4.50/5.50 **t.** 1.20 – 2.50 – **25 rm** 9.00/14.00 **t.** – P 17.00/22.00 **t.**

BOYLE Roscommon 986 ㉑ – pop. 1,727.
See : Cistercian Abbey* 12C. **Envir. :** NE : Lough Key*.
9 Knockadoo, Roscommon Rd.
ℹ ☎ 145 (May-September).
Dublin 107 – Ballina 40 **– Galway 74 –** Roscommon 26 **– Sligo 24.**

Forest Park, Carrick Rd E: ½ m. on T 3 ☎ 229, – wc ☎ P
12 rm.

FORD Elphin St. ☎ 22

BRAY Wicklow 986 ㉖ – pop. 15,550 – ☎ 01 Dublin.
9 ☎ 862484.
ℹ ☎ 867128 (June-August).
Dublin 13 – Wicklow 20.

XX **Lacy's** with rm, Strand Rd, Sea Front ☎ 862127
closed Sunday dinner and 1 week after Christmas – **M** a la carte 5.45/6.35 **st.** 1.50 – **10 rm** 6.00/10.50.

XX Old Court, Velvay Rd ☎ 860789.

BUNCRANA Donegal 986 ⑭ – pop. 5,458.
Envir. : Lough Naminn* NE: 7 m. – Carndonagh (Donagh Cross*) NE: 15 m.
9 ☎ 1.
ℹ ☎ 158 (June-August).
Dublin 161 – Donegal 64 **– Londonderry 16.**

White Strand Motor Inn, Railway Rd ☎ 253, ≤ – wc P – **9 rm.**

BUNDORAN Donegal 986 ⑰ – pop. 1,337 – ☎ 072.
Envir. : S: Lough Gill*** (Innisfree*), Park's Castle (site**).
18 Great Northern Hotel ☎ 41302.
ℹ ☎ 41350 (May-September).
Dublin 145 – Sligo 21.

Maghery House, Brighton Ter. ☎ 41234 – wc P
32 rm.

VW, AUDI-NSU ☎ 41300

BUNRATTY Clare 986 ㉕ – ✉ ☎ 061 Limerick.
See : Castle (great hall*) *AC* – Folk Park* *AC.*
Dublin 129 – Ennis 15 **– Limerick 8.**

Fitzpatrick's Shannon Shamrock Inn, ☎ 61177, Telex 6214, – wc ☎ P
M approx. 6.25 **t.** – 2.50 – **82 rm** 14.00/21.00 **t.**

CAHERDANIEL Kerry – pop. 357.
Envir. : Sheehan's Point ≤ *** W : 5 m. – Staigue Fort* (prehistoric stone fort : site*, ≤ *) *AC*, NE : 5 m.
Dublin 238 – Killarney 48.

Derrynane, SE : 1 m. on T 66 ☎ 36, ≤ Kenmare river Bay, heated – wc ☎ P
21 March-2 October – **M** approx. 6.00 **t.** 1.60 – **62 rm** 10.90/15.80 **t.** – P 16.45/19.45 **t.**

CAHERSIVEEN (CAHIRCIVEEN) Kerry 986 ㉙ – pop. 1,547.
Envir. : Remains of Carhan House (birthplace of Daniel O'Connell) NE : 1 m.
i ☎ 113 (June-September)
Dublin 228 – Killarney 38 – Limerick 105.

O'Connell, O'Connell St. ☎ 10 – wc – **15 rm.**

Ringside Rest, Valentia Rd. ☎ 89 – wc P
M *(closed Christmas)* 4.00/5.00 **t.** – **14 rm** 4.00/9.00 **t.** – P 10.00/12.00 **t.**

FIAT ☎ 77
RENAULT ☎ 91

CAHIR Tipperary 986 ㉙ – pop. 1,747.
See : Castle* (12C-15C) the most extensive mediaeval castle in Ireland.
9 ☎ 474, S : 1 m.
i ☎ 453 (June-August).
Dublin 112 – Cork 49 – Kilkenny 41 – Limerick 38 – Waterford 39.

Kilcoran Lodge, SW : 5 m. on T 6 ☎ 261, ≤, park – wc P.
23 rm.

Earl of Glengall, The Square ☎ 205
closed Sunday and Bank Holidays – **M** 6.75/7.50 **t.** 1.30.

FORD Dublin Rd ☎ 316
SAAB ☎ 432

CARAGH LAKE Kerry 986 ㉙.
See : Lough Caragh*.
Dublin 212 – Killarney 22 – Tralee 25.

Caragh Lodge, ☎ 15, ≤, « Fine gardens and lakeside setting », park – wc P
May-15 September – **M** (dinner only) 5.00/5.50 **t.** 1.50 – **8 rm** 5.00/15.00 **t.**

CARLOW Carlow 986 ㉖ – pop. 9,588 – ☎ 0503.
18 Oak Park ☎ 41695.
i ☎ 41554 (July-August).
Dublin 52 – Kilkenny 25 – Tullamore 44 – Wexford 46.

Royal, Dublin St. ☎ 41621 – wc P.
M a la carte 3.50/5.70 **t.** 1.10 – **40 rm** 6.75/14.50 **t.**

Carlow Lodge, S : 2 m. on N 9/T 51 ☎ 42002 – wc ☎ P
10 rm.

ALFA-ROMEO, SAAB Dublin Rd ☎ 41704
AUSTIN-ROVER-TRIUMPH The Haymarket ☎ 41706
BMW, TOYOTA Dublin Rd ☎ 41572
CHRYSLER, PEUGEOT Tullow Rd ☎ 41391
FIAT, LANCIA Tullow Rd ☎ 41955
FORD Court Place ☎ 41665
MORRIS Dublin Rd ☎ 41938
OPEL Tullow Rd ☎ 41303
VAUXHALL 55 Tullow St. ☎ 41141
VW, AUDI-NSU, CITROEN, MERCEDES-BENZ Green Lane ☎ 41047

CARRAROE Galway – ☎ 091 Galway.
Dublin 159 – Galway 27

Carraroe, ☎ 72105, ≤ – wc ☎ P
M approx. 5.20 **t.** 2.00 – **24 rm** 7.90/15.80 **t.** – P 16.00 **t.**

CARRICK-ON-SHANNON Leitrim 986 ㉑ – pop. 6,429.
9 ☎ 157.
i ☎ 170 (May-September).
Dublin 97 – Ballina 50 – Roscommon 26 – Sligo 34.

Bush, Main St. ☎ 14, Telex 4394, – wc wc ☎ P
closed 20 to 30 December – **M** 4.50/6.00 **st.** 1.25 – **28 rm** 8.25/18.60 **st.** – P 16.40 **st.**

County, Bridge St. ☎ 42 – wc.
closed 25 to 27 December – **M** 4.00/5.00 **t.** 1.50 – **22 rm** 7.50/16.00 **t.** – P 10.00/12.00 **t.**

Cartown House, Leitrim Rd N : 1 ½ m. on T 54 ☎ 103, – ☎ P
11 rm.

BRITISH LEYLAND Cartober ☎ 206

CARRIGALINE Cork – pop. 951 – ☎ 021 Cork.
Dublin 168 – Cork 7.

XX Chez Rivero, ☎ 882327 – Ⓟ.

TOYOTA ☎ 882309

CASHEL Tipperary 986 ㉕ – pop. 2,692 – ☎ 062.
See : St. Patrick's Rock*** (or Rock of Cashel) : site and ecclesiastical ruins 12C-15C (✻**) *AC* – Hore Abbey* ruins 13C – St. Dominick's Abbey* ruins 13C. **Envir. :** Holycross Abbey** (12C) *AC*, N : 9 m.

i Town Hall ☎ 61333.

Dublin 101 – Cork 60 – Kilkenny 34 – **Limerick 36 – Waterford 44.**

Cashel Palace, Main St. ☎ 131, ←, « Interesting art collection », – Ⓟ
19 rm.

Cashel Kings, Dublin Rd, Ballypadeen NE : 1 m. on N 8 ☎ 61477, ← Cashel Rock and mountains – wc ☎ Ⓟ
M 4.50/6.00 **t.** 1.50 – 1.80 – **40 rm** 9.00/18.00 **t.** – P 15.50/17.00.

XX **Chez Hans,** Rockside ☎ 61177, « Converted 19C church » – Ⓟ
closed Sunday, Monday and January – **M** approx. 6.50 **t.** 2.50.

at Goolds Cross NW : 6 m. off L 185 – ✉ ☎ Goolds Cross :

Longfield House, SE : 1 m. off L 185 ☎ 63, ←, « Georgian manor house », park – wc ☎ Ⓟ
April-September – **M** approx. 6.50 **t.** 1.75 – **10 rm** 10.00/18.50 **t.**

BMW, OPEL Cahir Rd ☎ 310
CHRYSLER ☎ 61155

CASHEL BAY Galway.
Envir. : N : Connemara** – SE : Kilkieran Peninsula**.
Dublin 173 – Galway 41.

Cashel House, ☎ 9, « Country house set in attractive gardens », – wc Ⓟ
March-October – **M** a la carte 3.30/5.65 **t.** 1.50 – **19 rm** 9.00/16.00 **t.** – P 15.40/17.15 **t.**

Zetland, ☎ 8, ←, – wc Ⓟ
Easter and May-October – **M** approx. 5.75 **t.** 1.00 – **18 rm** 7.50/25.80 **t.**

CASTLEBAR Mayo 986 ㉑ – pop. 5,979 – ☎ 094.
Envir. : Ballintuber Abbey* (13C-15C) S : 7 m.
9 ☎ 111.
i ☎ 201 (June-September).

Dublin 152 – Ballina 25 – **Galway 48 – Sligo 54.**

Breaffy House, SE : 2 ¾ m. on T 39 ☎ 22033, park – wc ☎ Ⓟ
closed 20 to 27 December – **M** 5.00/6.00 **t.** 1.20 – **43 rm** 12.00/20.00 **t.** – P 15.50/18.50 **t.**

CITROEN, DATSUN Breaffy Rd ☎ 140
FIAT Turlough Rd ☎ 712
FORD 3 Ellison St. ☎ 276
RENAULT Spencer St. ☎ 255
VW, AUDI-NSU, MERCEDES-BENZ Spencer Park ☎ 238

CASTLEDERMOT Kildare 986 ㉖ – pop. 583 – ☎ 0503 Carlow.
Envir.: Baltinglass (abbey ruins : scenery *) NE : 7 m.
Dublin 44 – Kilkenny 33 – Wexford 54.

Kilkea Castle, Kilkea NW : 3 ½ m. ☎ 45156, Telex 5388, ←, « 12C castle », park – Ⓟ.
50 rm.

PEUGEOT ☎ 44114

CASTLEFREKE Cork – ✉ Clonakilty – ☎ 023 Bandon.
Dublin 199 – Cork 38.

Castlefreke, Strand SE : 1 m. ☎ 48106, ←, – wc Ⓟ
29 rm.

CASTLEGREGORY Kerry – pop. 804 – ☎ 066 Tralee.
Dublin 201 – Killarney 36 – Limerick 80.

X **Tralee Bay** with rm, SE : 2 ¾ m. ☎ 39138, ← – wc Ⓟ
closed November – **M** (snack lunch) 4.50/8.50 **st.** 2.00 – **14 rm** 7.20/16.00 **st.**

CASTLEKNOCK Dublin – see Dublin.

CASTLEREA Roscommon 986 ㉑ – pop. 1,752.
Clonalis, ☎ 68.
Dublin 110 – Galway 49 – Roscommon 17 – Sligo 42.

- Tully's, Main St. ☎ 163 – wc wc – **19 rm.**

CASTLETOWNBERE Cork 986 ㉙ – pop. 812.
Berehaven ☎ 24.
i ☎ 85 (June - September).
Dublin 247 – Cork 86 – Killarney 68.

- Beara Bay, Main St. ☎ 130 – wc wc Ⓟ – **18 rm.**
- **Cametringane House**, ☎ 27, ←, – wc Ⓟ
  M *(closed Christmas Day)* 4.00/4.50 **t.** 1.20 – **18 rm** 4.50/10.00 **t.**

CASTLETOWNSHEND Cork – pop. 170.
Dublin 220 – Cork 59.

- Mary Ann's Bar, ☎ 15.

CHARLEVILLE (RATH LUIRC) Cork 986 ㉙ – pop. 2,232 – 063.
Envir. : Kilmallock (Dominican Friary ruins 13C, SS. Peter and Paul church 14C : scenery*) NE : 6 m. – Kilfinnane (site*) E : 11 m.
18 ☎ 257.
Dublin 138 – Cork 38 – Killarney 57 – Limerick 24.

- Deerpark, Limerick Rd N : ½ m. on T 11 ☎ 581 – wc Ⓟ. – **10 rm.**

FORD Limerick Rd ☎ 561

CLIFDEN Galway 986 ㉑ – pop. 790.
Envir. : E : Connemara** : Ballynahinch Lake*, The Twelve Pins* (mountains), Lough Inagh*, Kylemore Lake*, Kylemore Abbey (site**), Streamstown Bay* NW : 2 m. – Cleggan (site**) NW : 6 m.
18 Aillebrack, Ballyconneely ☎ Ballyconneely 5.
i ☎ 103 (May-September).
Dublin 181 – Ballina 77 – Galway 49.

- **Alcock and Brown,** The Square ☎ 134 – wc Ⓟ
  Easter-October – **M** approx. 4.35 **t.** 1.25 – 1.70 – **20 rm** 6.50/12.60 **t.** – P 12.75 **t.**
- **Abbeyglen House**, Sky Rd W : ½ m. ☎ 33, ←, heated, , park – wc Ⓟ
  Easter-mid October – **M** 6.00/7.00 **t.** 1.50 – **17 rm** 8.00/16.00 **t.**
- **Clifden Bay,** Main St. ☎ 128, , , – wc
  23 May-15 October – **M** (dinner only) 4.00/5.00 **t.** 2.00 – 2.50 – **44 rm** 5.50/13.00 **t.**
- **Rock Glen Country House**, S : 1 ½ m. on Roundstone Rd ☎ 16 – wc Ⓟ
  March-October – **M** (dinner only) 5.00 **t.** 1.75 – **20 rm** 5.50/12.00 **t.**
- **Celtic,** Main St. ☎ 115, – wc
  March-October – **M** (dinner only) 4.00/5.00 **t.** 1.50 – 1.75 – **20 rm** 5.00/10.00 **t.**

CLONBUR Galway.
Dublin 161 – Galway 29 – Wesport 32.

- **Fairhill,** ☎ 6 – Ⓟ
  Easter-October – **9 rm** 4.00/8.00 **t.**

CLONDALKIN Dublin 986 ㉖ and ㊲ – see Dublin.

CLONMEL Tipperary 986 ㉙ – pop. 11,622 – 052.
See : The Main Guard* 1674. **Envir.** : Ahenny (2 high crosses*) NE : 16 m. – S : Nire Valley* (←**).
9 Lyranearla, ☎ 310.
i ☎ 22960 (July-August).
Dublin 108 – Cork 59 – Kilkenny 31 – Limerick 48 – Waterford 29.

- Clonmel Arms, Sarsfield St. ☎ 21233 – wc wc Ⓟ. – **41 rm.**
- Minella , Caville Rd SE : 1 m. on L 27 ☎ 22388, , park – wc Ⓟ.
  34 rm.
- **Inislounaght House** , Marlfield W : 1 ½ m. off N 24/T 6 ☎ 22847, ←, « Country house atmosphere », , – wc Ⓟ
  15 March-15 October – **M** (dinner and residents only) 5.00 **st.** 1.25 – **6 rm** 6.00/13.50 **st.**

CHRYSLER Cashel Rd ☎ 22387
CITROEN, VOLVO Thomas St. ☎ 22430
DATSUN Anglesea St. ☎ 21238
FIAT, OPEL Main St. ☎ 22972
FORD Davis Rd ☎ 21199
RENAULT Dungarvon Rd ☎ 22399
TOYOTA Chasel Rd ☎ 21652
VW, AUDI-NSU Upper Irishtown ☎ 22199

COBH Cork 986 ㉙ – pop. 6,076 – ✆ 021 Cork.
Dublin 170 – Cork 15 – Waterford 76.

Commodore, Westbourne Pl. ℗ 811277, ≤, – wc.
M *(closed 24 to 26 December)* 5.00/7.00 **t.** – **50 rm** 9.00/17.00 **t.** – P 16.00 **t.**

CONG Mayo – ✆ 094 Castlebar.
See : Lough Corrib*** – Ashford Castle (site*). **Envir. :** Ross Abbey**, Franciscan Friary (tower *, 80 steps) SE : 9 m.
Dublin 160 – Ballina 49 – Galway 28.

Ashford Castle , ℗ 22644, Telex 4749, ≤ Lough Corrib and countryside, « Tastefully converted castle », , 9, , , park – P
closed March – **M** a la carte 5.35/10.80 **t.** 1.60 – **79 rm** 18.00/34.30 **t.** – P 30.90 **t.**

COOTEHILL Cavan 986 ㉒ – pop. 3,273.
Envir. : Bellamont Forest* N : 1 ½ m.
Dublin 68 – Dundalk 33.

White Horse, Market St. ℗ 24 – P
M approx. 3.85 **t.** 1.25 – **32 rm** 7.00/15.00 **t.** – P 13.35 **t.**

CORK Cork 986 ㉙ – pop. 128,645 – ✆ 021.
See : St. Patrick's Street* YZ – St. Ann's Shandon Church* 18C (steeple * *AC*, 134 steps) Y **A** – University College* 1845 X **U** – The Marina ≤* X.
18 Little Island ℗ 821263 E : 5 m. by N 25 X.
℗ 25341, S : 4 m. by L 42 X – **Terminal:** Bus Station, Parnell Pl.
to Swansea (B. & I. Line) 4-6 weekly (10 h).
i Cork City, 42 Grand Parade ℗ 23251 – Cork Airport, ℗ 22923 (June-September).
Dublin 161.

Plan opposite

Jury's, Western Rd ℗ 26651, Telex 6073, – TV P — Z **v**
M 6.00/7.00 **t.** – 2.50 – **96 rm** 14.90/22.50 **t.**

Silver Springs, E : 2 ½ m. on T 6 ℗ 51231, Telex 6111, – TV P. — X **c**
72 rm.

Imperial, South Mall ℗ 23304 – P. — Z **n**
closed Christmas Day – **M** *(closed Sunday and Monday)* 4.50/7.00 **t.** 1.25 – **84 rm** 13.00/19.00 **t.**

Metropole, MacCurtain St. ℗ 51301 – wc . — Y **r**
closed Christmas – **M** 4.75/5.60 **t.** – 2.00 – **120 rm** 12.60/17.60 **t.**

Arbutus Lodge, Middle Glanmire Rd, Montenotte ℗ 51237, – wc wc P
closed 5 days at Christmas – **M** *(closed Sunday dinner to non-residents)* a la carte 5.90/7.90 **t.** 1.55 – 2.00 – **20 rm** 12.50/18.50 **t.** — Y **a**
Spec. Cassolette of fresh prawns, Carré d'agneau aux herbes, Home made ice creams.

Airport Motel, Kinsale Rd S : 3 ½ m. on L 42 ℗ 961616 – TV wc P by L42 X
M (dinner and residents only) 4.00/5.00 **t.** – **20 rm** 14.50/19.50 **t.**

Glengarriffe, Orchard Rd, Victoria Cross ℗ 417851, , , – wc P — X **x**
closed 20 December-20 January – **M** 4.00/6.00 **t.** 3.00 – **20 rm** 8.25/21.00 **t.**

Moore's, Morrisons Island ℗ 227361 – wc — Z **a**
39 rm.

St. Anthony's, Victoria Cross ℗ 413451 — X **a**
9 rm 4.00/7.00 **st.**

at Glounthaune E : 7 m. on N 25 – X – ✉ ✆ 021 Cork :

Ashbourne House , ℗ 821230, « Extensive gardens », heated, park – wc wc P
M approx. 5.00 **t.** – 1.80 – **26 rm** 10.00/17.50 **t.** – P 16.00 **t.**

at Blackrock E : 3 ¼ m. South of River – ✉ ✆ 021 Cork :

Blackrock Castle, E : ½ m. ℗ 33737, « 17C Fort on River » – P. — X **u**

Pier Head Inn, ℗ 31616 — X **e**
closed Sunday and Monday – **M** (dinner only) 4.50/5.50 **t.** 0.80.

at Douglas SE : 2 m. on L 66 – X – ✉ ✆ 021 Cork :

Briar Rose, Douglas Rd ℗ 34794 – P.

at Rochestown SE : 3 ¾ m. on L 67 by L 66 – X – ✉ ✆ 021 Cork :

Norwood Court, without rest., ℗ 32961, ≤ – wc P
12 rm.

at Killeens NW : 3 ¾ m. on L 69 – X – ✉ ✆ 021 Cork :

Sunset Ridge Motel, Blarney Rd ℗ 85271 – TV wc P
10 rm.

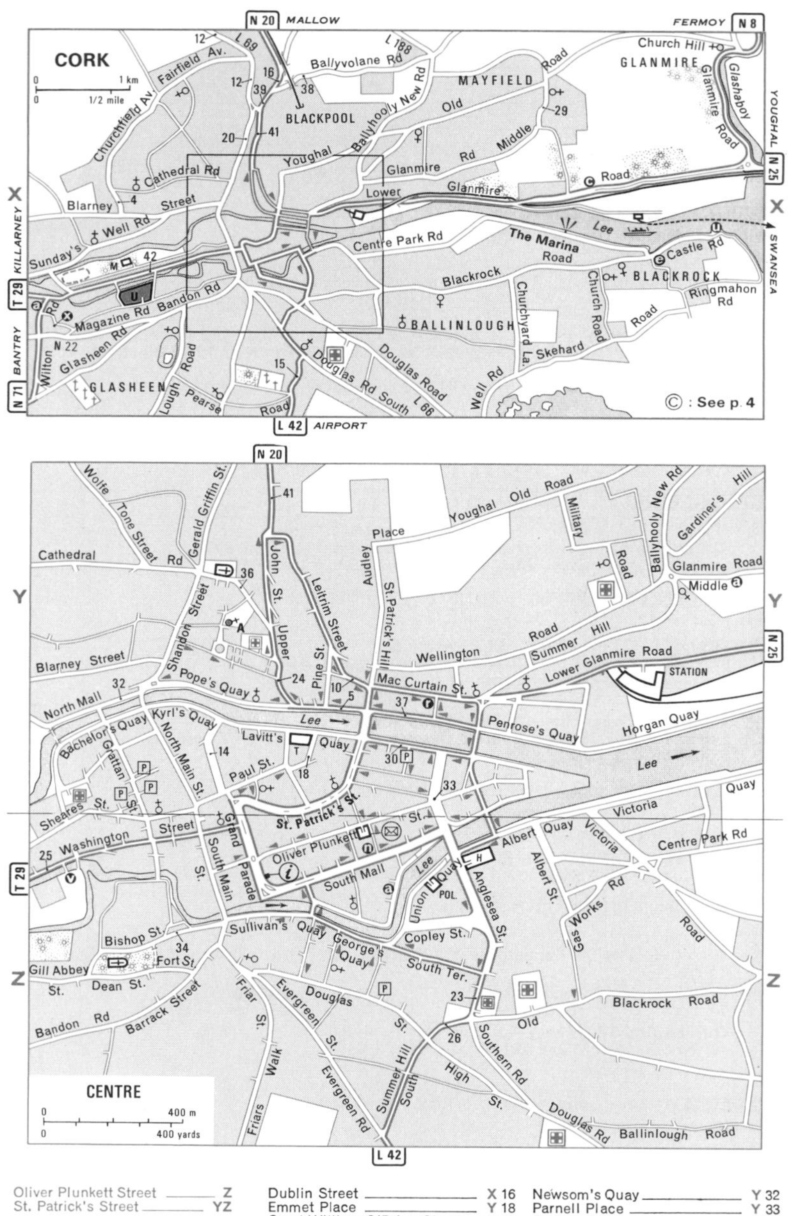

Oliver Plunkett Street Z
St. Patrick's Street YZ

Baker's Road X 4
Camden Place Y 5
Coburg Street Y 10
Commons Road X 12
Corn Market Street Y 14
Curragh Road X 15
Dublin Street X 16
Emmet Place Y 18
Great William O'Brien Street X 20
Infirmary Road Z 23
John Redmond Street Y 24
Lancaster Quay Z 25
Langford Row Z 26
Lower Mayfield Road X 29
Merchant's Quay Y 30
Newsom's Quay Y 32
Parnell Place Y 33
Proby's Quay Z 34
Roman Street Y 36
St. Patrick's Quay Y 37
Spring Lane X 38
Thomas Davis Street X 39
Watercourse Road X 41
Western Road X 42

AUSTIN-ROVER-TRIUMPH Ivy Lawn, Douglas Rd ☏ 54055
BMW, CITROEN, VW, AUDI-NSU, MERCEDES-BENZ Douglas Rd ☏ 34805
BRITISH LEYLAND Victoria Cross ☏ 41851
BRITISH LEYLAND 26 St. Patricks Quay ☏ 26657
CHRYSLER Mallow Rd ☏ 53271
CHRYSLER Mallow Rd ☏ 51094
DATSUN, VOLVO 20-24 Lavitts Quay ☏ 25008
FIAT 24 Watercourse Rd ☏ 53228
FIAT 11 South Terrace ☏ 20528
FORD Dennehys Cross ☏ 42846
FORD Monaghan Rd ☏ 53381
OPEL Blackrock Rd ☏ 32888
PEUGEOT, TOYOTA Emmett Pl. ☏ 23296
RENAULT Douglas Rd ☏ 31861
RENAULT Tivoli ☏ 53397
RENAULT Mill St. ☏ Millstreet 42
SAAB St. Patricks Quay ☏ 51291
VAUXHALL Douglas Rd ☏ 32861
VW, AUDI-NSU Kinsale Rd ☏ 21713

COURTMACSHERRY Cork – pop. 210 – ✉ ☎ 023 Bandon.

Envir. : Timoleague (Franciscan Abbey* 16C) W : 1 ½ m.

Dublin 190 – Cork 29.

Courtmacsherry ⑤, ☏ 46198, ←, « Extensive gardens », park – ⇔wc Ⓟ
March-mid October – **M** *(closed Saturday dinner and Sunday lunch)* 4.50/5.00 **t.** – **17 rm** ⊡ 6.00/13.50 **t.** – P 11.00/11.75 **t.**

Lislee House ⑤, S : 2 m. ☏ 40126, ←, « Country house atmosphere », ⚘ – Ⓟ
M (dinner only) (residents only) 6.00 **st.** ♁ 1.00 – **7 rm** ⊡ 10.00/18.00 **st.**

COURTOWN Wexford 986 ㉖ – pop. 291 – ☎ 055 Gorey.

18 Gorey ☏ 21566.

Dublin 62 – Waterford 59 – Wexford 42.

Courtown, Courtown Harbour ☏ 25108, ▣ – ⇔wc ⋒wc Ⓟ
Easter-October – **M** 3.90/4.50 **t.** ♁ 1.00 – **26 rm** ⊡ 6.20/13.70 **t.** – P 12.30 **t.**

CROOKHAVEN Cork – pop. 76 – ☎ Goleen.

Dublin 240 – Cork 79 – Killarney 78.

Crookhaven Inn with rm, Main St. ☏ 51, ← Crookhaven Bay
closed Christmas Day – **M** a la carte 3.55/5.85 **t.** ♁ 1.60 – **10 rm** ⊡ 7.50/12.00 **t.**

CROSSHAVEN Cork 986 ㉙ – pop. 1,222 – ✉ ☎ 021 Cork.

Dublin 173 – Cork 12.

Grand, ☏ 831444, ←, ▣ – TV ⇔wc ☎ Ⓟ
M 5.00/7.00 **t.** ♁ 1.50 – ⊡ 1.50 – **25 rm** 10.00/19.00 **t.**

Whispering Pines, ☏ 831448, ←, ⚓ – ⋒wc Ⓟ
9 rm ⊡ 6.00/11.00 **st.**

Cobbles, Church Bay Rd ☏ 831 525 – Ⓟ
closed Tuesday, Wednesday from October to May and 25-26 December – **M** a la carte 3.30/4.85 **t.** ♁ 1.70.

CURRAGH Kildare – ✉ Kildare – ☎ 045 Naas.

18 ☏ 41238.

Dublin 31 – Kilkenny 54 – Tullamore 33.

Jockey Hall, ☏ 41416 – Ⓟ
M (dinner only) a la carte 4.55/6.75 **t.** ♁ 1.30.

DALKEY Dublin 986 ㊲ – ☎ 01 Dublin.

Dublin 11.

Dalkey Heights ⑤, Sorrento Rd ☏ 805261, ←, ⚘ – ⇔wc ⋒wc ☎ Ⓟ
11 rm.

Dalkey Island, Coliemore Rd ☏ 800223 – ⇔wc ⋒wc ☎ Ⓟ
17 rm.

Guinea Pig, 17 Railway Rd ☏ 807432
closed Sunday – **M** a la carte 4.50/7.05 **t.** ♁ 1.10.

FIAT Convent Rd ☏ 802046

DELGANY Wicklow – pop. 4,517 – ✉ Bray – ☎ 01 Dublin.

Dublin 19.

Glenview ⑤, Glen of the Downs NW : 2 ¼ m. on T 7 by L 164 ☏ 862896, ←, ⚘ – Ⓟ.
closed 24 to 26 December – **M** 6.00/7.50 **t.** ♁ 1.40 – **23 rm** ⊡ 12.00/22.00 **t.** – P 17.00/20.00 **t.**

Delgany Inn, ☏ 875701, ⚘ – ⇔wc ☎
M 4.95/6.00 **t.** ♁ 1.95 – **10 rm** ⊡ 6.00/10.50.

DINGLE Kerry 986 ㉙ – pop. 1,401.

See : Dingle Bay*. **Envir. :** NE: Conair Pass ☼* – Fahan : Belvedere (coast road) ≤* SW: 7 ½ m.

i ☎ 88 (June-September).

Dublin 216 – Killarney 51 – Limerick 95.

- **Sceilig** ⌂, ☎ 104, Telex 6900, ≤, ⚲, ⛱ heated – Ⓟ
  15 March-October – **M** (dinner only from 15 March to 24 June) 6.00/8.00 **t.** 1.60 – ▭ 1.50 – **79 rm** 7.60/18.00 **t.**
- **Alpine,** Mail Rd ☎ 15 – ⌂wc Ⓟ
  March-31 October – **15 rm** ▭ 5.00/8.50 **t.**
- **Doyle's Seafood Bar,** John St. ☎ 144, Seafood
  mid March-mid October – **M** *(closed Sunday and Good Friday)* a la carte 3.40/5.50 **t.** 1.30.

DONEGAL Donegal 986 ⑰ – pop. 1,725.

See : Franciscan Priory (site*, ≤*). **Exc.:** Glen Bay** – Glencolumbkille (site**, folk village) NW: 30 m.

18 Murvagh ☎ Ballintra 54, S: 8 m.

i ☎ 148 (May-September).

Dublin 164 – Londonderry 48 – Sligo 40.

- **Hyland Central,** The Diamond ☎ 27, Telex 4404, ⚲ – ⌂ ⌂wc ☎
  M 4.50/5.50 **t.** – **44 rm** ▭ 8.00/16.00 **t.**
- Abbey, The Diamond ☎ 14 – ⌂wc ☎
  19 rm.
- National, Main St. ☎ 35, ⚲
  16 rm.

BMW, CHRYSLER, PEUGEOT, VAUXHALL, VOLVO Milford ☎ 7
DATSUN Dunkineely ☎ 14
DATSUN Kerrykell ☎ 3
FORD The Glebe ☎ 17
RENAULT ☎ 117
ROVER-TRIUMPH Quay St. ☎ 39

DOUGLAS Cork – see Cork.

DROGHEDA Louth 986 ㉒ – pop. 19,762 – ☎ 041.

See : St. Lawrence's Gate* 13C. **Envir. :** Mellifont Abbey** (Cistercian ruins 1142) NW: 4 ½ m.– Monasterboice (3 tall crosses** 10C) NW: 5 ½ m. – Dowth Tumulus ☼* W: 4 m. – Duleek (priory* 12C ruins) SW: 5 m. – Newgrange Tumulus* (prehistoric tomb) *AC,* SW: 7 m. – Bective Abbey* (12C ruins) SW: 20 m.

18 Baltray ☎ 8860, E: 3 m.

i ☎ 7070 (June-August).

Dublin 29 – Dundalk 22 – Tullamore 67.

- Rosnaree, SE: 2 m. on T 1 ☎ 7673 – ⌂wc ☎ Ⓟ – **20 rm.**
- **Boyne Valley,** SE: 1 ½ m. on T 1 ☎ 7737, ⚲, park – ⌂wc ☎ Ⓟ
  M 3.80/4.50 **t.** 1.50 – ▭ 1.30 – **18 rm** 6.00/12.00 **t.**

AUSTIN-ROVER-TRIUMPH, DATSUN Dublin Rd ☎ 8511
FIAT, LANCIA North Rd ☎ 7920
FORD North Rd ☎ 8951
PEUGEOT Palace St. ☎ 7304
RENAULT Mary St. ☎ 6246
TOYOTA North Rd ☎ 8566

DROICHEAD NUA Kildare 986 ㉖ – see Newbridge.

DUBLIN Dublin 986 ㉒ ㉖ and ㊲ – pop. 567,866 – ☎ 01.

See : National Gallery*** BY M^1 – Castle (State apartments*** *AC*) BY – Christ Church Cathedral** 12C BY **A** – National Museum (Irish antiquities, Art and Industrial)** BY M^2 – Trinity College* (Library**) BY – National Museum (Zoological Collection)* BY M^1 – Municipal Art Gallery* BX M^3 – O'Connell Street* (and the General Post Office) BXY – St. Stephen's Green* BZ – St. Patrick's Cathedral (interior*) BZ **B** – Phoenix Park (Zoological Gardens*) AY.

Envir.: Howth (Howth Summit ≤**, Cliff Walk ≤**, harbour*, St. Mary's Abbey* ruins 13C-15C and site*, Howth Gardens: rhododendrons*, site*, ≤* *AC*) NE: 9 m. by L 86 AY – St. Doulagh's Church* 13C (open Saturday and Sunday, afternoon only) NE: 7 m. by L 87 AY – Castletown House* 18C (Georgian mansion) *AC,* W: 11 m. by N 4 AY – Maynooth: St. Patrick's College: museum Ecce Homo* 12 C, leaf of ivory diptych Northern French* 14C – College Chapel: interior wainscots*) W: 15 m. by N 4 AY.

18 Dun Laoghaire, Eglinton Park ☎ 801055 SE: 7 m. by T 44 AZ – 18 Nutley House, Donnybrook ☎ 693438, S: 3 m. AZ – 18 Lower Churchtown Rd ☎ 977060 S : by T 43 AZ.

✈ ☎ 379900, N: 5 ½ m. by N 1 AY – **Terminal:** Busaras (Central Bus Station) Store St.

⛴ to Liverpool (B & I Line) 6-8 weekly (7 h to 8 h 45 mn) – to the Isle of Man: Douglas (Isle of Man Steam Packet Co.) 1-3 weekly Summer only (4 h 30 mn).

i 51 Dawson St. ☎ 747733 – Dublin Airport ☎ 376387 and 375533 – Upper O'Connell St. ☎ 747733.

Belfast 103 – Cork 161 – Londonderry 145.

DUBLIN

Street	Grid	No.
Anne Street South	BY	2
Dawson Street	BY	
Duke Street	BY	27
Grafton Street	BY	
Henry Street	BY	
O'Connell Street	BXY	
Bath Avenue	AZ	3
Benburb Street	AY	4
Blessington Street	BX	5
Botanic Road	AY	6
Brunswick Street North	BY	8
Bull Alley	BY	9
Camden Row	BZ	12
Chancery Street	BY	13
Charlotte Street	BZ	15
College Street	BY	19
Denmark Street	BX	23
D'Olier Street	BY	24
Donnybrook Road	AZ	25
Earlsfort Terrace	BZ	28
Eglinton Road	AZ	29
Essex Quay	BY	30
Fitzgibbon Street	BX	31
Fitzwilliam Place	BZ	32
Frederick Street North	BX	33
Gardiner Place	BX	35
George's Quay	BY	36
Golden Lane	BY	39
Grantham Street	BZ	41
Harrington Street	BZ	44
Infirmary Road	AY	46
Kevin Street Upper	BZ	47
King Street South	BY	48
Marlborough Street	BY	53
Merchants Quay	BY	56
Mobhi Road	AY	57
Montague Street	BZ	59
Morehampton Road	AZ	60
Mountjoy Street	BX	62
Nicholas Street	BY	64
Parnell Square East	BX	67
Parnell Square North	BX	68
Parnell Square West	BX	69
Rathgar Road	AZ	72
Rathmines Road Upper	AZ	73
Ringsend Road	AZ	75
Sandford Road	AZ	77
Stephen Street	BY	80
Tara Street	BY	81
Terenure Road East	AZ	83
Terenure Road North	AZ	84
Townsend Street	BY	89
Wellington Quay	BY	95
Westland Row	BY	96
Westmoreland Street	BY	97
Wexford Street	BZ	99
Winetavern Street	BY	100
Wolfe Tone Quay	AYZ	102
Wood Quay	BY	103

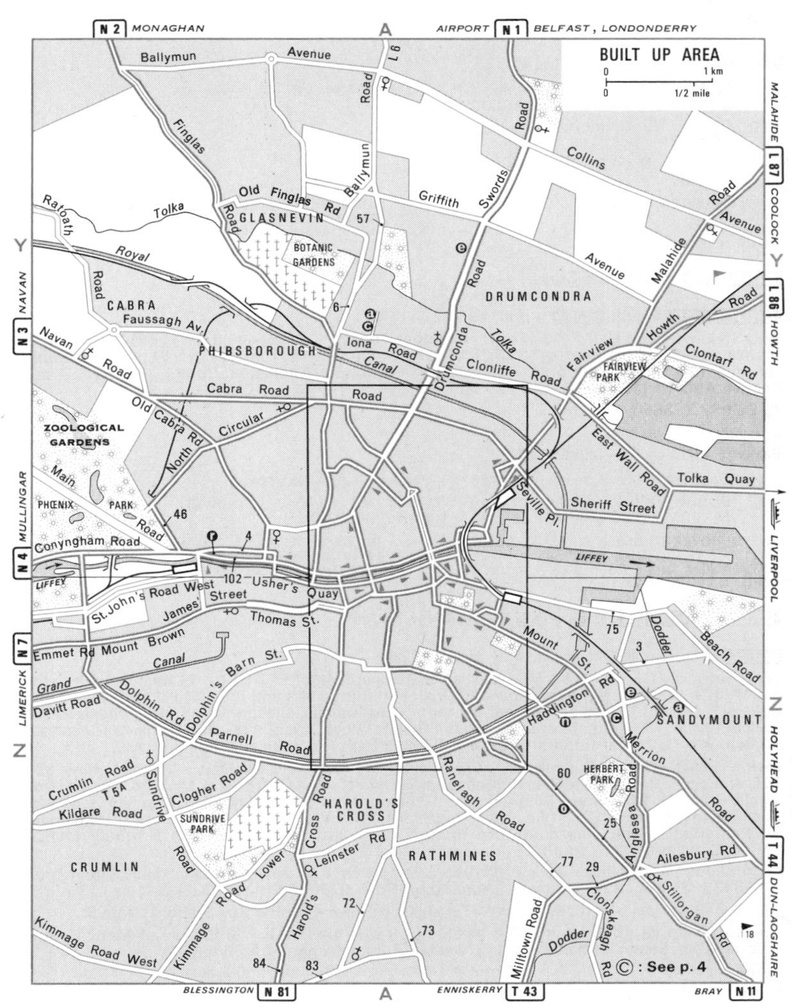

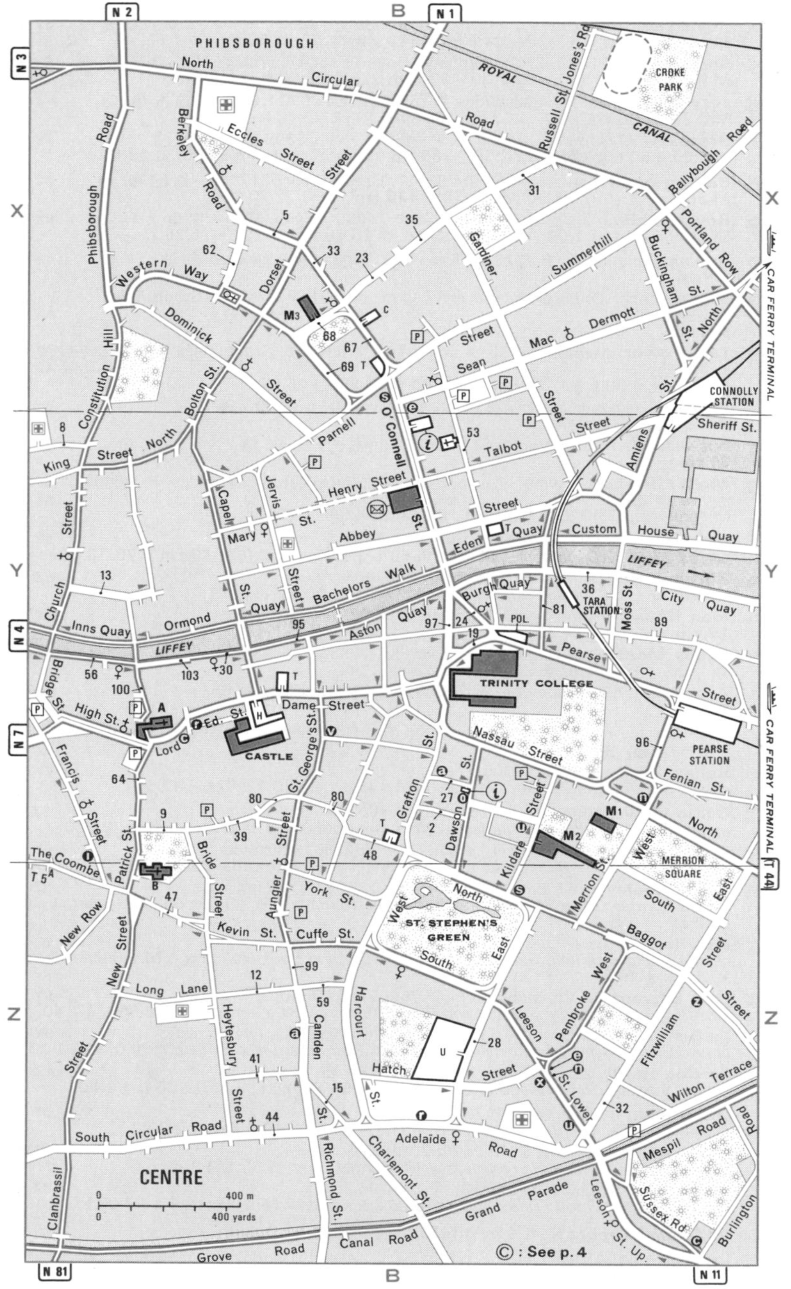
PHIBSBOROUGH
North Circular Road
ROYAL CANAL
CROKE PARK
Eccles Street
Berkeley Road
Phibsborough Road
Western Way
Dominick Street
Dorset Street
Gardiner Street
Summerhill
Ballybough Road
Portland Row
Buckingham St.
North St.
Sean Mac Dermott Street
Russell St.
Jones's Rd
CAR FERRY TERMINAL
CONNOLLY STATION
Sheriff St.
Constitution Hill
Bolton St.
Parnell Street
O' Connell St.
Talbot Street
Amiens St.
King Street North
Church Street
Henry Street
Jervis Street
Capel St.
Mary St.
Abbey Street
Eden Quay
Custom House Quay
LIFFEY
Bachelors Walk
Burgh Quay
City Quay
TARA STATION
Moss St.
Ormond Quay
Inns Quay
Aston Quay
POL.
Pearse Street
TRINITY COLLEGE
Bridge St.
High St.
Dame Street
Lord Ed. St.
CASTLE
St. George's St.
Nassau Street
PEARSE STATION
Francis Street
Grafton St.
Dawson St.
Kildare Street
Fenian St.
Merrion St.
MERRION SQUARE
The Coombe
Patrick St.
Bride Street
Aungier Street
York St.
ST. STEPHEN'S GREEN
New Row
Kevin St.
Cuffe St.
New Street
Baggot Street
Long Lane
Heytesbury Street
Camden St.
Harcourt St.
Leeson Street
Pembroke West
Fitzwilliam Street
Hatch Street
Wilton Terrace
South Circular Road
Adelaïde Road
Richmond St.
Charlemont St.
Mespil Road
Sussex Rd
Burlington Road
CENTRE
Clanbrassil Street
Grand Parade
Canal Road
Grove Road
Leeson St. Up.
© : See p. 4
0 400 m
0 400 yards
N 1
N 2
N 3
N 4
N 7
N 11
N 81
T 44
T 5A
X
Y
Z
B

Royal Hibernian (T.H.F.), 46-48 Dawson St. ℗ 772991, Telex 5220 – lift. — BY **o**
M approx. 6.00 **t.** 1.75 – 2.50 – **110 rm** 14.00/29.50 **t.**

Shelbourne (T.H.F.), 27 St. Stephen's Green ℗ 766471, Telex 5184 – lift TV P. — BZ **s**
M 5.00/7.00 **t.** 1.15 – 2.30 – **176 rm** 22.00/33.50 **t.**

Jury's, Pembroke Rd, Ballsbridge ℗ 767511, Telex 5304, – lift TV P. — AZ **c**
M 6.25/10.00 **t.** 1.50 – 2.50 – **314 rm** 19.90/28.90 **t.**

Gresham, 20 Upper O'Connell St. ℗ 746881, Telex 5308 – lift TV P. — BX **e**
M 5.95/8.50 **t.** 2.50 – 2.50 – **180 rm** 18.00/27.00 **t.** – P 26.00/30.00 **t.**

Burlington, Upper Leeson St. ℗ 785711, Group Telex 5517, – lift TV P. — BZ **c**
M approx. 5.75 **t.** 1.50 – 2.10 – **420 rm** 16.70/22.70 **t.**

Royal Dublin, 42 Upper O'Connell St. ℗ 749351, Telex 4288 – lift P — BX **s**
M 4.75/6.00 **t.** 1.00 – **100 rm** 16.25/25.80 **t.** – P 19.65/26.25 **t.**

Ashling, Parkgate St. ℗ 772324, Telex 5891 – TV wc wc P — AY **r**
42 rm.

Skylon, Upper Drumcondra Rd N: 2 ½ m. on N 1 ℗ 379121, Group Telex 5517 – lift TV wc P — AY **e**
88 rm.

Tara Tower, Merrion Rd SE: 4 m. on T 44 ℗ 694666, Group Telex 5517 – lift TV wc P. — on T 44 AZ
M approx. 4.00 **t.** 1.20 – 1.80 – **83 rm** 9.85/14.25 **t.**

Central, Exchequer St. ℗ 778341 – lift wc wc P. — BY **v**
86 rm.

Buswells, 25-26 Molesworth St. ℗ 764013 – lift wc . — BY **u**
60 rm.

Mount Herbert (wine license only), 7 Herbert Rd, Ballsbridge ℗ 684321, – wc P — AZ **a**
M (grill rest.) 3.40/5.25 **t.** 1.60 – **84 rm** 4.95/11.90 **t.**

Mont Clare, 13-14 Clare St. ℗ 762896 – — BY **n**
closed 23 to 27 December – **M** 5.00/6.60 **t.** 1.25 – 2.00 – **29 rm** 6.70/13.00 **t.**

Kilronan House, 70 Adelaide Rd ℗ 755266 – wc — BZ **r**
closed 23 to 30 December – **12 rm** 7.50/11.00 **t.**

Iona House, 5 Iona Park, Glasnevin ℗ 306217 – wc — AY **c**
15 rm 10.50/14.30 **st.**

Egans Montrosa, 7 Iona Park, Glasnevin ℗ 303611 – wc — AY **a**
1.50 – **14 rm** 5.75/9.95 **st.**

Ariel House, 52 Lansdowne Rd ℗ 685512 – wc wc P — AZ **e**
16 rm.

XXX Sach's, with rm, 19-29 Morehampton Rd, Donnybrook ℗ 680995, French rest. – lift wc P. . — AZ **o**

XXX **Bailey,** 2-3 Duke St. ℗ 773055 — BY **a**
closed Sunday and 25-26 December – **M** a la carte 6.30/12.75 **t.** 1.55.

XX **Celtic Mews,** 109a Lower Baggot St. ℗ 760796 — BZ **z**
closed Sunday and Bank Holidays – **M** (dinner only) a la carte 6.25/8.35 **t.** 1.30.

XX **Tandoori Rooms,** 27 Lower Leeson St. ℗ 762286, Indian rest. — BZ **x**
closed Sunday and Bank Holidays – **M** (dinner only) a la carte 5.95/8.50 **t.**

XX **Buck Whaley's,** 67 Lower Leeson St. ℗ 785097, Dancing — BZ **n**
closed Sunday, 24 to 26 December and Bank Holidays – **M** (dinner only) a la carte 6.50/8.20 **t.**

XX **Snaffles,** 47 Lower Leeson St. ℗ 760790 — BZ **u**
closed Monday dinner, Saturday lunch, Sunday and Bank Holidays – **M** a la carte 4.65/10.65 **t.** 1.25.

XX **Lord Edward,** 23 Christchurch Pl. ℗ 752557, Seafood — BY **c**
closed Saturday lunch, Sunday and Bank Holidays – **M** a la carte 4.55/8.95 **t.** 1.40.

XX **Le Bistro** (Castle Inn), 5-7 Lord Edward St. ℗ 780663, French rest. — BY **r**
closed Good Friday and Christmas Day – **M** (bar lunch) a la carte 2.75/9.00 **t.** 1.00.

XX **Le Coq Hardi,** 29 Pembroke Rd ℗ 689070 – P — AZ **n**
closed Sunday, January and Bank Holidays – **M** a la carte 6.25/12.00 **t.** 1.50.

X **Old Dublin,** 91 Francis St. ℗ 751173 — BY **i**
closed Sunday, Monday and Bank Holidays – **M** 6.00/10.00 **st.** 2.00.

X **Bay Leaf,** 41 Pleasants St. ℗ 753257, Bistro — BZ **a**
closed Sunday and Bank Holidays – **M** (dinner only) 5.50 **t.** 1.40.

X **Olde Hob,** 68 Lower Leeson St. ℗ 764745 — BZ **e**
closed Sunday, Good Friday and 24 to 26 December – **M** a la carte 5.10/7.00 **t.**

at Dublin Airport **N: 6 ½ m. off N 1** – AY – ✉ **01 Dublin:**

International Airport (T.H.F.), ℗ 379211, Telex 4612 – TV wc P.
M 4.00/5.00 **t.** 1.30 – 2.00 – **150 rm** 10.50/15.00 **t.**

at Sutton NE: 9 m. by L 86 – AY – ✉ ☎ 01 Dublin:

Marine, Sutton Cross, Dublin Rd ☎ 322613, Group Telex 4858, ≤, ⛱, 🌳 – TV ⛀wc ☎ P
closed Christmas – **M** approx. 5.50 **t.** 🍾 1.25 – ☕ 2.00 – **21 rm** 10.00/18.00 **t.**

at Stillorgan SE: 6 m. on N 11 – AZ – ✉ ☎ 01 Dublin:

Montrose, Stillorgan Rd, Donnybrook NW: 1 ½ m. on N 11 ☎ 693311, Group Telex 5517 – lift TV ⛀wc ☎ P. 🏋
177 rm.

Beaufield Mews, Woodlands Av. ☎ 880375, « Antiques », 🌳 – P
closed Sunday, Monday, 1 week Easter and 1 week Christmas – **M** (dinner only) 4.50/5.00 **t.** 🍾 1.75.

at Clondalkin SW: 7 m. on N 7 – AZ – ✉ ☎ 01 Dublin:

Green Isle, Naas Rd ☎ 593406, Group Telex 5517 – TV ⛀wc ☎ P. 🏋
M approx. 4.00 **t.** 🍾 1.20 – ☕ 1.80 – **58 rm** 9.85/14.25 **t.**

at Castleknock NW: 4 m. by N 3 – AY – on L 92 – ✉ ☎ 01 Dublin:

Weigh Inn, Phoenix Park Racecourse ☎ 300042 – P
closed Sunday, Monday dinner and Bank Holidays – **M** a la carte 4.20/7.00 **t.** 🍾 1.25.

MICHELIN Branch 4 Spilmak Pl., Bluebell Industrial Estate, Naas Rd, Dublin 12, ☎ 509096.

ALFA-ROMEO 457 North Circular Rd ☎ 749588
ALFA-ROMEO 52/55 Lower Camden St. ☎ 783377
BMW, PEUGEOT, ROLLS ROYCE-BENTLEY, VOLVO Lad Lane ☎ 763921
BMW, VOLVO Ballygall Rd ☎ 342577
BMW, PEUGEOT, TOYOTA Rathgar Av. ☎ 979456
BRITISH LEYLAND, CITROEN Donnybrook ☎ 693055
BRITISH LEYLAND Temple Rd ☎ 885085
BRITISH LEYLAND, DATSUN, FORD, SAAB 5/7 New St. ☎ 780033
BRITISH LEYLAND Northbrook Rd ☎ 970811
BRITISH LEYLAND Richmond Rd ☎ 379132
BRITISH LEYLAND Donnybrook ☎ 694359
CHRYSLER North Rd ☎ 343033
CHRYSLER, PEUGEOT Dorset St. ☎ 301400
CHRYSLER-SIMCA South Circular Rd ☎ 780800
CITROEN Bluebell Av. ☎ 507887
CITROEN Waterford St. ☎ 745821
CITROEN, PEUGEOT, TOYOTA 54 Glasnevin Hill ☎ 373771
DATSUN, VOLVO Howth Rd ☎ 314066
DATSUN, VOLVO North Rd ☎ 343970
FIAT Milltown Rd ☎ 971098
FIAT Stillorgan Rd ☎ 886977
FIAT, LANCIA Dublin Rd, Bray ☎ 867671
FIAT, LANCIA Sandyford Rd ☎ 982389
FIAT, LANCIA 56 Howth Rd ☎ 332301
FIAT Church Pl. ☎ 973999
FIAT North Rd ☎ 342977
FIAT, LANCIA 84 Prussia St. ☎ 721622
FIAT Taney Rd ☎ 987166
FIAT Herberton Rd ☎ 754216
FIAT, PEUGEOT, TOYOTA Smithfield Market ☎ 721222
FORD 151 South Circular Rd ☎ 764131
FORD 172/175 Parnell St. ☎ 747831
FORD Nass Rd ☎ 505721
FORD 40/51 Benburb St. ☎ 771521
OPEL, PEUGEOT Beach Rd ☎ 686011
OPEL 146 Cabra Rd ☎ 301222
OPEL Emmet Rd, Inchiore ☎ 755535
OPEL New Rd ☎ 592438
OPEL Lower Rathmines Rd ☎ 976661
PEUGEOT, VOLVO Maxwell Rd ☎ 973338
PEUGEOT Stillorgan Rd ☎ 885179
PEUGEOT, TOYOTA Kilbarrack Rd ☎ 322701
PEUGEOT 23 Parkgate St. ☎ 771277
PEUGEOT, RENAULT 232 Nth Circular Rd, Grangegorm ☎ 300799
PEUGEOT, VOLVO Maxwell Rd ☎ 973338
RENAULT 19 Conyham Rd ☎ 775677
RENAULT 27 Upper Drumcondra Rd ☎ 373706
RENAULT Newlands Cross ☎ 593751
RENAULT Merrion Rd ☎ 693911
RENAULT Crumlin Rd ☎ 752297
SAAB Upper Rathmines Rd ☎ 971227
SAAB North Circular Rd ☎ 306925
VAUXHALL 46 Manor St. ☎ 723490
VAUXHALL Capel St. ☎ 745294
VAUXHALL Longmile Rd ☎ 508227
VAUXHALL Swords Rd ☎ 379933
VW, AUDI-NSU, MERCEDES-BENZ 218/224 North Circular Rd ☎ 722011
VW, AUDI-NSU, MERCEDES-BENZ Deans Grange ☎ 893611
VW, AUDI-NSU, MERCEDES-BENZ Ballybough Rd ☎ 749991
VW, AUDI-NSU, MERCEDES-BENZ Harolds Cross Rd ☎ 975757

DUNDALK Louth 986 ㉒ – pop. 21,672 – ☎ 042.

Envir.: N: Slieve Gullion (Northern Ireland), Ring of Gullion: Cam Lough*, Ballintemple viewpoint**, Killevy Churches (site*), Bernish Rock viewpoint** – Carlingford Lough* NE: 10 m.**

⛳18 Blackrock, ☎ 35379, S: 3 m.

i Dromad Lay-By, ☎ 71221 (June-August).

Dublin 51 – Belfast 52 – Londonderry 96.

Imperial, Park St. ☎ 32241 – lift ⛀wc ☎ P. 🏋
50 rm.

Ballymascanlon House, NE: 3 ½ m. by T 1 on T 62 ☎ 71124, Telex 33860, 🎾, 🌳, park – ⛀wc 🚿wc ☎ P. 🏋
M 4.25/4.75 **t.** 🍾 1.20 – **43 rm** ☕ 9.00/18.00 **t.**

Derryhale, Carrick Rd, W: 1 m. on T 24 ☎ 35471 – 🚿wc ☎ P
23 rm.

at Rockmarshall E: 7 m. by T 1 on T 62 – ✉ ☎ 042 Dundalk:

Angela's, Jenkinstown ☎ 76193 – P
closed Sunday, October and 1 week before Easter – **M** (dinner only) 5.50/8.00 **t.** 🍾 1.50.

ALFA-ROMEO Quay St. ☎ 32279
BRITISH LEYLAND The Ramparts ☎ 35514
CHRYSLER-SIMCA Dublin Rd ☎ 35422
FIAT Park St. ☎ 34820
FORD Dublin St. ☎ 34655
OPEL Newry Rd ☎ 34297
PEUGEOT, VAUXHALL Newry Rd ☎ 35053
RENAULT Newry Rd ☎ 34604
TOYOTA Dublin Rd ☎ 34083

DUNGLOW Donegal 986 ⑰ – pop. 2,956 – ✉ Lifford.

i ☎ Dunglow 72 (June-September).

Dublin 210 – Donegal 46 – **Londonderry 61.**

- **Ostan na Rosann,** ☎ 91, ⋲, ▣ – ⌂wc ☎ Ⓟ. ⛹
  M 3.50/4.00 **st.** 🌡 1.20 – **48 rm** ☕ 8.50/14.00 **t.** – P 13.50 **t.**

DUN LAOGHAIRE Dublin 986 ㉖ and ㊲ – pop. 53,171 – ✪ 01 Dublin.

See : Windsor Terrace ⋲★ over Dublin Bay. **Envir. :** Killiney Bay★★ SE: 2 m. by T 44.

⛳18 Eglinton Park ☎ 801055.

⛴ to Holyhead (Sealink) 1-4 daily (3 h 30 mn).

i ☎ 806984 and 807048.

Dublin 9.

DUN LAOGHAIRE

0 — 500 m
0 — 500 yards

Georges Street
Mulgrave Street
Patrick Street

Cumberland Street	2
Dunleary Hill	4
Longford Place	5
Marine Road	7
Monkstown Avenue	8
Monkstown Crescent	9
Mount Town Upper	10
Pakenham Road	13

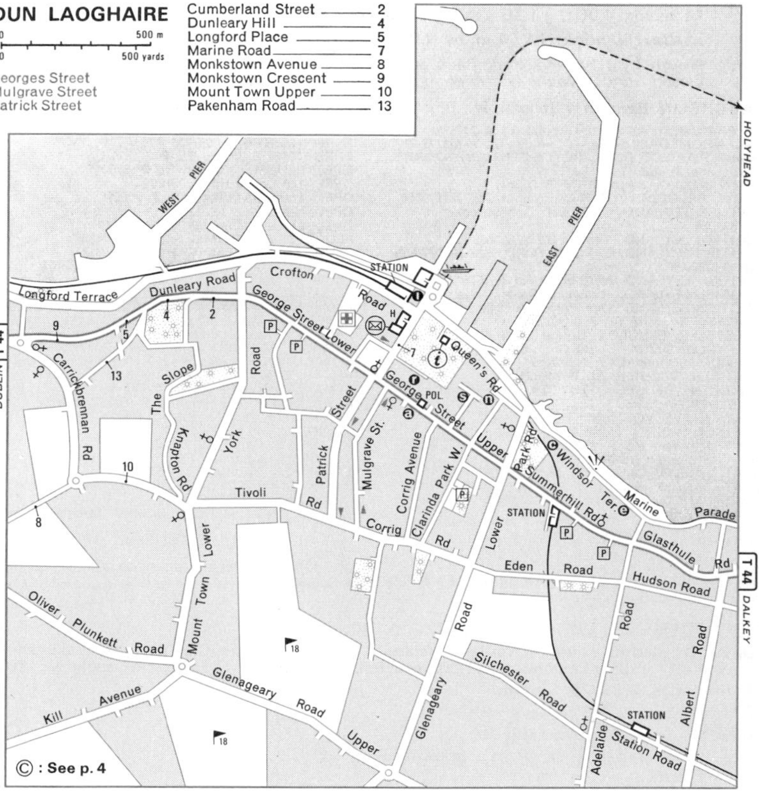

Ⓒ : See p. 4

- **Royal Marine,** Marine Rd ☎ 801911, ⋲, 🌳 – 🛗 Ⓟ. ⛹ **r**
  M 6.00/7.00 **t.** 🌡 1.00 – **115 rm** ☕ 12.00/22.00 **t.**
- Avenue, Northumberland Av. ☎ 808541 – Ⓟ **a**
  20 rm.
- Pierre, Seafront ☎ 800291 – ⌂wc ☎ Ⓟ **n**
  40 rm.
- XXX **Mirabeau,** Marine Parade, Sandy Cove ☎ 809873 **e**
  closed Sunday and Bank Holidays – **M** (dinner only) a la carte 7.50/11.50 **t.** 🌡 2.25.
- XXX **Na Mara,** Mallin Station ☎ 806767, Seafood **i**
  closed Sunday, Monday, Easter week and Bank Holidays – **M** a la carte 7.25/13.50 **t.**

✗ **Salty Dog,** 3a Haddington Terrace off Adelaide St. ☎ 808015 **s**
closed Sunday, Monday and Bank Holidays – **M** (dinner only) a la carte 4.70/7.55 **t.** 1.20.

✗ **Hatters,** 5 Windsor Ter. ☎ 804600, ≤ **c**
closed Sunday, 3 weeks October, 1 week December and Bank Holidays – **M** (dinner only) a la carte 7.20/9.15 **t.** 1.75.

CHRYSLER-SIMCA Crofton Pl. ☎ 800341
FORD 127 Lower Georges St. ☎ 800372
PEUGEOT Glenageary Rd ☎ 852405
RENAULT Rochestown Av. ☎ 852555
RENAULT Marine Rd ☎ 808431
TOYOTA, VOLVO Glasthule Rd ☎ 802991

DUNMORE EAST Waterford 986 ㉚ – pop. 656 – ✉ ✪ 051 Waterford.
Dublin 109 – Waterford 10.

Ocean, Dock Rd ☎ 83136 – wc Ⓟ
16 rm.

Haven, ☎ 83150, ≤, park – wc wc Ⓟ
Easter-October – **M** approx. 5.00 **t.** 1.00 – **20 rm** (dinner included) 7.50/19.00 **t.**

DURROW Laois – pop. 1,122.
Dublin 70 – Kilkenny 16 – **Limerick 63 – Tullamore 36.**

Castle Arms, The Square ☎ 36117 – wc
17 rm.

EMO Laois – pop. 200 – ✉ ✪ 052 Port Laoise.
Dublin 49 – Limerick 74 – Tullamore 20.

Montague Motel, E: 1 ¾ m. on T 5 ☎ 26154, ✗ – wc ☎ Ⓟ.
M 3.50/4.50 **t.** 1.75 – **20 rm** 7.50/13.00 **t.**

ENNIS Clare 986 ㉕ – pop. 5,972 – ✪ 065.
See : Franciscan Friary★ (13C ruins). **Envir. :** Tulla (site★, ancient church ☼★★) E: 10 m. – Killone Abbey (site★) S: 4 m. – Dysert O'Dea (site★) NW: 6 ½ m. – Kilmacduagh monastic ruins★ (site★) NE: 16 ½ m.
18 ☎ 21070.
i Bank Pl. ☎ 21366.
Dublin 144 – Galway 41 – Limerick 23 – Roscommon 85 – **Tullamore 93.**

Old Ground (T.H.F.), O'Connell St. ☎ 21127, Telex 8103, – Ⓟ.
M a la carte 7.00/8.60 **t.** 1.40 – **63 rm** 14.50/21.00 **t.**

FORD Lifford ☎ 21035
RENAULT Tulla Rd ☎ 22758
TOYOTA Gort Rd ☎ 21904
VW, AUDI-NSU, MAZDA Mill Rd ☎ 21505

ENNISCORTHY Wexford 986 ㉖ – pop. 10,845 – ✪ 054.
9 ☎ 2191.
i Castle Hill ☎ 2341 (July-August).
Dublin 77 – Kilkenny 36 – **Waterford 36** – Wexford 14.

Murphy Floods, 27 Main St., Market Sq. ☎ 2592 – wc
M *(closed Good Friday and Christmas Day)* a la carte 2.45/3.00 **st.** 1.25 – **22 rm** 6.00/14.00 **t.** – P 10.50/12.00 **t.**

CHRYSLER Templeshannon Quay ☎ 2575
FORD Dublin Rd ☎ 2337

ENNISKERRY Wicklow 986 ㉖ – pop. 772 – ✪ 01 Dublin.
See : Site★ – Powerscourt Demesne (gardens★★★, Araucaria Walk★) *AC*. **Envir. :** Powerscourt Waterfall★ *AC*, S: 4 m. – Lough Tay★★ SW by T 43, T 61, L 161.
18 Woodbrook ☎ 01 (Bray) 862073, NE: 3 m. – 9 Bray ☎ 01 (Bray) 862484.
Dublin 17.

Summerhill, Cookstown Rd ☎ 863508, ≤, – ☎ Ⓟ
14 rm.

ENNISTYMON Clare 986 ㉕ – pop. 1,013.
Envir. : Cliffs of Moher★★★ (O'Brien's Tower ☼★★ N: 1 h Rtn on foot) NW: 9 m. – NW: Coast Road L 54 from Ailladie to Fanore : Burren District (Burren limestone terraces★★)
Dublin 160 – Ennis 16 – **Galway 47 – Limerick 39.**

Hotel see : Ennis SE: 16 m.

FAHAN Donegal – pop. 332 – ✉ Lifford.
18 Lisfannon, ☎ Buncrana 12.
Dublin 156 – Londonderry 11 – Sligo 95.

✗✗ Roneragh House, with rm. ☎ 14, ≤ Lough Swilly, – wc ☎ Ⓟ
10 rm.

GALWAY Galway 986 ㉑ – pop. 27,726 – ☎ 091.

See: Lynch's Castle* 16C – **Envir.:** NW: Lough Corrib*** – Ross Abbey**, Franciscan Friary (tower ※*, 80 steps) NW: 16 ½ m. – Claregalway (Franciscan Friary* 13C) NE: 7 m. – Abbeyknockmoy (Cistercian Monastery* 12C ruins) NE: 18 m. – Tuam (St. Mary's Cathedral: chancel arch* 12C) NE: 20 m.

18 Salthill ☎ 62422, W: 3 m.

i ☎ 63081.

Dublin 132 – Limerick 57 – Sligo 88.

- Great Southern, Eyre Sq. ☎ 64041, Telex 8364, – P.
  M a la carte 6.00/7.70 **t.** 1.50 – 3.00 – **123 rm.**
- Corrib Great Southern, Dublin Rd E : 2 m. on T 4 ☎ 65281, ←, – P
  117 rm.
- **Ardilaun House**, Taylor's Hill ☎ 65452, – wc P
  M 4.75/5.25 **t.** 1.35 – **56 rm** 10.50/17.00 **t.** – P 12.00/16.00 **t.**
- Galway Ryan, Dublin Rd E: ½ m. on T 4 ☎ 63181, Telex 8349, – wc P
  96 rm.
- Imperial, Eyre Sq. ☎ 63033, Group Telex 4858 – wc
  65 rm.
- **Odeon,** Eyre Sq. ☎ 62041 – wc P
  M 4.00/5.00 **t.** 1.00 – **60 rm** 9.00/16.00 **t.** – P 14.00/16.00 **t.**
- Adare House, Father Griffin Pl., Lower Salthill ☎ 62638
  10 rm.

at Salthill **SW: 2 m. – ✉ Salthill – ☎ 091 Galway :**

- **Banba,** ☎ 63075 – P
  closed Christmas – **M** *(closed for lunch from October to Easter)* approx. 4.50 **t.** – **31 rm** 6.50/14.00 **t.**

BMW, CITROEN, OPEL, VOLVO Tuam Rd ☎ 65451
BRITISH LEYLAND ☎ 62364
CHRYSLER-SIMCA Headford Rd ☎ 65296
DATSUN Dominick St. ☎ 64037
FIAT, LANCIA Tuam Rd ☎ 63037
FORD Headford Rd ☎ 67691
PEUGEOT, TOYOTA Bohermore ☎ 63664
RENAULT Tuam Rd ☎ 64066
SAAB Spanish Par. ☎ 62167
VAUXHALL College Rd ☎ 62044
VOLVO Salthill ☎ 62833
VW, AUDI-NSU, MERCEDES-BENZ Lower Salthill ☎ 62583

GARRETTSTOWN STRAND Cork – see Kinsale.

GARRYVOE STRAND Cork – pop. 50 – ✉ Castlemartyr – ☎ 021 Cork.

Dublin 161 – Cork 23 – Waterford 62.

- **Garryvoe,** ☎ 62718 – wc wc P
  closed Christmas Day – **M** 3.75/6.50 **t.** 0.85 – 1.80 – **20 rm** 4.00/9.50 **t.**

GLENBEIGH Kerry 986 ㉙ – pop. 266.

18 Dooks ☎ 5, N: 3 m.

Dublin 211 – Killarney 21.

- Glenbeigh, NE: ½ m. on T 66 ☎ 4, – wc P
  21 rm.
- **Falcon Inn,** SW: 1 m. on T 66 ☎ 56, ← – P
  M 4.00/7.50 **t.** 2.50 – **15 rm** 7.50/12.50 **t.** – P 11.50/15.00 **t.**
- **Towers** with rm, ☎ 12, Ballad Singing, Seafood – wc P
  closed mid October-mid November – **M** a la carte 5.25/8.25 **t.** 2.50 – **21 rm** 9.00/22.00 **t.**

GLENCAR Kerry.

Dublin 215 – Cork 80 – Killarney 25.

- **Glencar** , ☎ 102, ←, park – wc P
  February-September – **M** (dinner only) 5.00 **t.** 2.00 – **30 rm** 7.00/17.00 **t.**

GLENDALOUGH Wicklow 986 ㉖ - pop. 184 – ☎ 0404 Wicklow.

See : Ancient monastic city** (site***, St. Kervin's Church*) and Upper Lake* in Glendalough Valley***.

Dublin 34 – Wexford 71.

- **Royal** , ☎ 5135, – wc P
  Easter-mid October – **M** approx. 6.25 **st.** – **34 rm** 8.35/20.25 **st.** – P 17.20 **st.**

at Laragh **E: 1 ½ m. on T 61 – ✉ Glendalough – ☎ Wicklow:**

- **Laragh Inn,** ☎ 5141 – P
  April-September, Good Friday and Christmas Day – **M** *(closed Wednesday)* (buffet lunch) 5.05/5.75 **t.** 0.90.

GLENGARRIFF Cork 986 ㉙ – pop. 244.
See : Site★★★. **Envir. :** N : Kenmare River Valley★★ – S: Garinish Island (20 mn by boat *AC*): Italian gardens★ – Martello Tower ☼★★ *AC* – SE : Bantry Bay★★.
⛳9 ☏ 29, E : 1 m.
i ☏ 84 (June-September).
Dublin 224 – Cork 63 – Killarney 37.

Casey's, ☏ 10, – wc Ⓟ
20 rm.

GLEN OF AHERLOW Tipperary – ✉ ☏ 062 Tipperary.
See : Glen of Aherlow★ (statue of Christ the King★★).
Dublin 118 – Cahir 6 – Tipperary 9.

Aherlow House, ☏ 56153, ≤ countryside and Galtee mountains, park – wc wc ☏ Ⓟ.
M *(closed Christmas Day)* 4.45/5.00 **t.** 2.50 – **11 rm** 9.00/16.00 **t.**

Glen, ☏ 56146 – wc ☏ Ⓟ
12 rm.

GLOUNTHAUNE Cork – see Cork.

GOOLDS CROSS Tipperary – see Cashel.

GORTAHORK Donegal – pop. 3,000 – ☏ Falcarragh.
Envir.: W: Bloody Foreland Head★.
Dublin 182 – Londonderry 53 – Sligo 113.

McFaddens, ☏ 17 – wc Ⓟ
Easter-1 October and Christmas – **M** 5.00/5.75 **t.** 1.25 – **35 rm** 6.70/14.90 **t.** – P 11.00/12.70 **t.**

GOUGANE BARRA Cork – ✉ Macroom – ☏ Ballingeary.
See : Lake (site★). **Envir. :** SE: Shehy Mountains★★.
Dublin 206 – Cork 45.

Gougane Barra, ☏ 31, ≤ lough and mountains, – wc Ⓟ
M approx. 4.00 **t.** – **33 rm** 6.00/12.50 **t.** – P 9.00 **t.**

GREYSTONES Wicklow 986 ㉖ – pop. 4,517 – ☏ 01 Dublin.
⛳18 ☏ 874614.
Dublin 18.

Woodlands, S: ¾ m. off L 29 ☏ 874423, – wc ☏ Ⓟ
18 rm.

BRITISH LEYLAND, VOLVO ☏ 974494 DATSUN, SAAB ☏ 874510

HOWTH Dublin 986 ㉒㉖ and ㊲ – pop. 6,990 – ✉ ☏ 01 Dublin.
See : Howth Summit ≤★★ – Cliff Walk ≤★★ – Harbour★ – St. Mary's Abbey★ (ruins 13C, 15C), site★ – Howth Gardens (rhododendrons★, site★, ≤★) *AC*.
⛳9 Hill of Howth ☏ 322624, NE: 8 m.
Dublin 10.

St. Lawrence, Harbour Rd ☏ 322643, ≤, – wc ☏ Ⓟ.
21 rm.

XX **King Sitric,** East Pier ☏ 325235, Seafood
closed Saturday lunch, Sunday, 10 days at Christmas and Bank Holidays – **M** a la carte 5.05/8.20 **t.** 1.30.

X Abbey Tavern, Abbey St. ☏ 322006, Ballad singing, Seafood.

INCH Kerry – ✉ Annascaul.
Dublin 210 – Dingle 16 – Killarney 30 – Tralee 25.

Inch Heights, W: ¼ m. off L 103 ☏ 12, ≤ Dingle Bay and McGillycuddy's Reeks – Ⓟ
Easter-October – **10 rm** 3.85/7.70 **st.**

INNISHANNON Cork – see Bandon.

KANTURK Cork 986 ㉙.
Dublin 161 – Cork 33 – Killarney 31 – Limerick 44.

Assolas Country House, E: 3 ¼ m. by L 38 and L 186 ☏ 15, ≤, « Country house atmosphere », , , park – wc Ⓟ
15 April-15 October – **M** (dinner only) 5.50 **st.** – **7 rm** 8.80/20.90 **st.** – P 16.25 **st.**

MERCEDES-BENZ, TOYOTA, VW, AUDI-NSU ☏ 35

KELLS Kilkenny – pop. 423.

See : Augustinian Priory** 14C.

Dublin 86 – Kilkenny 9 – **Waterford 23.**

Hotel see : Kilkenny N : 9 m.

KENMARE Kerry 986 ㉙ – pop. 903 – ⊙ 064 Killarney – 9.

Envir. : Kenmare River Valley** E : by L 62.

i T 41233 (June-September).

Dublin 210 – Cork 58 – Killarney 20.

- **Kenmare Bay,** W : ½ m. by T 65 on T 66 T 41300, <, – wc ☎ P.
  January-15 March – **M** approx. 5.50 **t.** 1.40 – 2.00 – **50 rm** 10.50/18.00 **t.**
- **Riversdale House,** S : ¾ m. on T 65 T 41299, <, , park – wc ☎ P
  M 4.95/7.50 **t.** 1.60 – 2.20 – **40 rm** 10.00/14.50 **t.** – P 16.00/19.00 **t.**
- **Purple Heather Bistro,** Henry St. T 41016
  Easter-September – **M** *(closed Sunday)* a la carte 5.70/7.00 **t.** 1.50.

BRITISH LEYLAND Shelbourne St. T 41355
FORD Henry St. T 17

KILKENNY Kilkenny 986 ㉖ – pop. 9,838 – ⊙ 056.

See : St. Canice's Cathedral 13C – Grace's Castle (Courthouse)* – Castle (park*, <*). Envir. : Jerpoint Abbey**(ruins 12C-15C) SE : 12 m. – Kilree's Church (site*, round tower*) S : 10½ m. – Callan (St. Mary's Church* 13C-15C) SW : 13 m.**

18 Glendine T 22125, N : 1 m.

i The Parade T 21755.

Dublin 77 – Cork 90 – Killarney 118 – Limerick 68 – Tullamore 51 – Waterford 30.

- Newpark, Castlecomer Rd N : ¾ m. on T 6 T 22122, , , park – P.
  45 rm.

CHRYSLER-SIMCA Green St. T 21304
DATSUN Castlecomer T 41358
FIAT Waterford Rd T 22195
FORD Patrick St. T 21016
PEUGEOT Waterford Rd T 21782
RENAULT Irishtown T 21494
VAUXHALL Upper John St. T 21140

KILKIERAN (Peninsula) ** Galway 986 ㉑.

KILLALOE Clare 986 ㉕ – pop. 875 – ⊙ 061 Limerick.

See : Site*. **Envir. :** N : Lough Derg Coast Road** (L12) to Tuamgraney, Lough Derg***.

i T 76155 (July-August).

Dublin 109 – Ennis 32 – **Limerick 13 – Tullamore 58.**

- **Lakeside** , T 76122, <, heated, – wc wc ☎ P
  M 5.50/8.50 **t.** 2.00 – **28 rm** 8.50/17.00 **t.** – P 16.25/17.25 **t.**
- **Ballyvalley** , T 76187, <, , park – wc ☎ P
  M (dinner only) 3.75/6.00 **t.** 1.90 – 1.65 – **15 rm** 6.25/11.50 **t.** – P 14.65 **t.**

KILLARNEY Kerry 986 ㉙ – pop. 7,184 – ⊙ 064.

Envir. : SW : Killarney District, Ring of Kerry : Lough Leane***, Muckross House (gardens***), Muckross Abbey* (ruins 13C), Tork Waterfall (Belvedere : <**, 251 steps), Lady's View Belvedere** – Gap of Dunloe**.

18, 18 Mahoney's Point T 31034, W : 3 m.

i Town Hall, T 31633.

Dublin 190 – Cork 55 – Limerick 69 – Waterford 116.

- Dunloe Castle , Beaufort W : 6 ½ m. off T 67 T 32118, <, , , , , park – P.
  season – **140 rm.**
- **Europe** , Fossa, W : 3 ½ m. on T 67 T 31900, Telex 8213, < lake and mountains, , , , park – P.
  closed mid January-February – **M** a la carte 8.40/12.30 **st.** 2.40 – **170 rm** 20.00/37.00 **st.**
- **Great Southern,** T 31262, Group Telex 6998, , , , park – P.
  M a la carte 4.50/8.50 **t.** 2.00 – 2.35 – **180 rm** 14.00/28.80 **t.**
- **Aghadoe Heights** , NW : 3 ½ m. by T 67 T 31766, Telex 6942, < countryside, lake and mountains, – P.
  closed 21 December-13 January – **M** 4.90/6.00 **t.** 1.75 – 2.00 – **46 rm** 11.50/17.00 **t.** – P 16.10 **t.**
- **Castlerosse** , W : 2 m. on T 67 T 31144, Telex 4404, <, , , – wc ☎ P
  closed 3 days at Christmas – **M** (dinner only) 4.75/6.00 **t.** 1.80 – **40 rm** 12.55/21.15 **t.**
- **Cahernane** , Kenmare Rd T 31895, <, , , – wc ☎ P
  Easter-October – **M** 5.00/5.50 **t.** 1.50 – **38 rm** 9.25/17.50 **t.**

International, Kenmare Pl. ☎ 31816 – wc ☎
M a la carte 3.00/5.50 **t.** 1.20 – 2.00 – **122 rm** 6.50/11.00 **t.** – P 12.50/14.00 **t.**

Three Lakes, Kenmare Pl. ☎ 31479 – wc ☎ P
M 4.50/6.00 **t.** 2.00 – 1.85 – **70 rm** 9.00/14.00 **t.** – P 18.10 **t.**

Scott's, College St. ☎ 31060 – wc P
March-November – **M** 2.75/3.50 **t.** 1.50 – **27 rm** 5.00/11.00 **t.** – P 8.00/10.00 **t.**

Dromhall, Muckross Rd S : ½ m. on T 65 ☎ 31431 – wc P
Easter-November – **M** 3.50/4.50 **t.** 2.00 – **63 rm** 5.00/12.00 **t.**

Castle Heights, Cork Rd E : 1 ¼ m. on T 29 ☎ 31158 – wc P
season – **27 rm.**

Whitegates, Muckross Rd S : ¾ m. on T 65 ☎ 31164, – wc P
M 3.50/5.50 **t.** – **16 rm** 6.65/13.80 **t.**

Linden House, New Rd ☎ 31379 – wc
closed mid December-mid January – **M** *(open February-October - closed Wednesday and Friday to non-residents)* (dinner only) 3.00/4.50 **t.** 1.20 – **12 rm** 3.00/6.00 **t.**

Carriglea House , Muckross Rd S : 1 ½ m. on T 65/N 71 ☎ 31116, ←, – wc wc P
Easter-20 October – **10 rm** 3.60/8.70 **t.**

Marian House, Woodlawn Rd off Muckross Rd ☎ 31275 – P
8 rm 3.75/7.00 **st.**

Castle Lodge, Muckross Rd ☎ 31545 – P
season – **12 rm.**

Cooldruma, Muckross Rd ☎ 31553 – P – **15 rm.**

Gardens , Countess Rd off Muckross Rd ☎ 31147, – P
March-October – **16 rm** 3.75/7.00 **t.**

BRITISH LEYLAND Muckross Rd ☎ 31237
CHRYSLER-SIMCA Park Rd ☎ 31355
FIAT New St. ☎ 31416
FORD New Rd ☎ 31087
VW, AUDI-NSU, MERCEDES-BENZ 94 New St. ☎ 31190

KILLEENS Cork – see Cork.

KILLINEY Dublin 986 ㊲ – 01 Dublin.
See : Killiney Bay★★.
☎ 851983.
Dublin 12.

Fitzpatrick's Castle, Killiney Hill Rd off Dalkey Av. ☎ 851533, Telex 30353, , , – P.
M 5.00/6.00 **t.** 1.40 – 2.50 – **48 rm** 16.50/24.75 **t.**

The Court, Station Rd, Killiney Bay ☎ 851622, ←, – wc ☎ P.
10 rm.

Rolland, Killiney Hill Rd ☎ 851329, French rest. – P
closed Sunday, Monday and Bank Holidays – **M** (dinner only) a la carte 5.05/8.25 **t.**

KILLYBEGS Donegal 986 ⑰ – pop. 1,094.
See : Fishing harbour★ – Carpet factory. **Envir. :** NW : Glen Bay★★ – Glencolumbkille (site★★, folk village) NW : 14 m. – Portnoo (site★) N : 16 ½ m.
Dublin 181 – Londonderry 65 – Sligo 57.

Killybegs, ☎ 120, ← – wc ☎ P
11 June-August – **M** a la carte 4.35/5.55 **t.** 1.30 – **30 rm** 8.85/17.05 **t.**

KILTIMAGH Mayo 986 ㉑ – pop. 1,396.
Dublin 136 – Ballina 23 – Galway 48 – Roscommon 42 – Sligo 43.

Westway, George's St. ☎ 63 – wc P – **23 rm.**

CHRYSLER-SIMCA ☎ 38
OPEL Claremorris Rd ☎ 88

KINGSCOURT Cavan 986 ㉒ – pop. 1,016.
Dublin 50 – Dundalk 31 – Tullamore 64.

Cabra Castle , NE : 2 m. on L 14 ☎ 60, ←, « Converted 17 C castle », , , park – wc P
M 4.50/5.50 1.50 – **25 rm** 8.50/15.60 – P 13.00/15.00.

CHRYSLER ☎ 26
RENAULT Corrygarry ☎ 83

KINSALE Cork 986 ㉙ – pop. 1,622 – 021 Cork.
See : St. Multose's Church★ 12C.
Ringenane ☎ 72197.
i ☎ 72234 (June - September).
Dublin 178 – Cork 17.

Acton's (T.H.F.), The Pier ☎ 72135, ≤, heated, – **P**
M 2.95/4.70 **t.** 1.35 – **59 rm** 6.50/13.00 **t.** – P 16.50/19.20 **t.**

Monastery, Blindgate ☎ 72624, ≤, « Country house atmosphere », – wc wc **P**
M a la carte 5.10/6.70 **t.** – 1.80 – **10 rm** 14.00/19.50 **t.**

Blue Haven, Pearse St. ☎ 72209,
closed 2 January-16 March – **M** a la carte 5.00/7.25 **t.** 1.25 – **11 rm** 7.25/14.50 **t.** – P 12.25/13.75 **t.**

Gino's, Market Sq. ☎ 72374
April-November – **M** *(closed Sunday and Monday)* (dinner only) a la carte 4.50/6.75 **t.** 1.50.

The Bistro, Guardwell ☎ 72470
closed Monday and 15 December-15 February – **M** (dinner only) a la carte 3.65/7.30 **t.**

Bacchus, 13 Pearse St. ☎ 72659.

The Man Friday, Village of Scilly ☎ 72260
closed Sunday and November – **M** (dinner only) a la carte 4.60/6.35 **t.** 1.25.

at Garrettstown Strand **SW: 8 ¾ m. by L 42 – ✉ Kinsale – 021 Cork:**

Coakley's Atlantic, ☎ 73215, ≤ – wc **P**
40 rm.

KNOCKFERRY **Galway – see Roscahill.**

LAHINCH **Clare 986 ㉕ – pop. 455.**
Envir.: Cliffs of Moher* (O'Brien's Tower ☼** N: 1 h Rtn of foot) NW: 5 ½ m.**
18, 18, ☎ Lahinch 3.
☎ 48 (June - August).
Dublin 162 – Galway 49 – Limerick 41.

LARAGH **Wicklow – see Glendalough.**

LEENANE **Galway 986 ㉑.**
See: ≤* on Killary Harbour*. Exc.: SE: Joyces Country: by road L 100 from Leenane to Clonbur: Lough Nafooey*, ☼* from the bridge on Lough Mask.**
Dublin 173 – Ballina 56 – Galway 41.

Leenane, ☎ 8, ≤, – wc **P**
38 rm.

LETTERFRACK **Galway – Moyard.**
Envir.: Kylemore Abbey (site), Kylemore Lake* NE: 3 m.**
Dublin 189 – Ballina 69 – Galway 57.

Rosleague Manor, W: 1 ¼ m. on T 71 ☎ 7, ≤, « Country house furnished with antiques », – wc **P**
Easter-15 October – **M** a la carte 3.50/5.75 **t.** 1.25 – **16 rm** 9.50/15.00 **t.** – P 18.50/20.00 **t.**

LETTERKENNY **Donegal 986 ⑱ – pop. 4,930.**
See: St. Eunan's Cathedral ≤*. Envir.: Grianan of Aileach* (stone fort) ☼* NE: 18 m. – Gartan Lake* NW: 8 ½ m.**
18 ☎ 144, NE: 1 m.
Derry Rd ☎ 348.
Dublin 150 – Londonderry 21 – Sligo 72.

Ballyraine, Port Rd NE: 1 ½ m. on T 72 by T 59 ☎ 411, Telex 33406, – wc **P**.
M 4.50/5.50 **st.** 1.75 – **56 rm** 9.00/17.00 **t.**

Gallagher's, 100 Main St. ☎ 8 – wc **P**
19 rm.

ALFA-ROMEO, OPEL, RENAULT Ballymacool ☎ 256
BRITISH LEYLAND Port Rd ☎ 60
CHRYSLER Ramelton Rd ☎ 22
FIAT, LANCIA Railway Rd ☎ 791
TOYOTA ☎ 671

LIFFORD **Donegal 986 ⑱ – pop. 1,121.**
☎ 151 (May-September).
Dublin 133 – Donegal 34 – Londonderry 14 – Omagh 20.

Inter County, Coneyburrow Rd ☎ 153 – wc **P**.
M 3.00/3.50 **st.** 1.20 – **36 rm** 4.40/8.00 **t.** – P 8.50/9.50 **t.**

LIMERICK Limerick 986 ㉕ – pop. 57,161 – ☎ 061.

Envir. : Monasteranenagh Abbey* (ruins 12C) S : **14** m. by **T 11** Z.

Ballyclough ☎ 44083, S : 3 m. by **T 11** Z.

Shannon Airport : ☎ 061 (Shannon) **61222**, W : **16** m. by **T 11** Y – **Terminal :** Limerick Railway Station.

i 62 O'Connell St. ☎ 47522.

Dublin 121 – Cork 62.

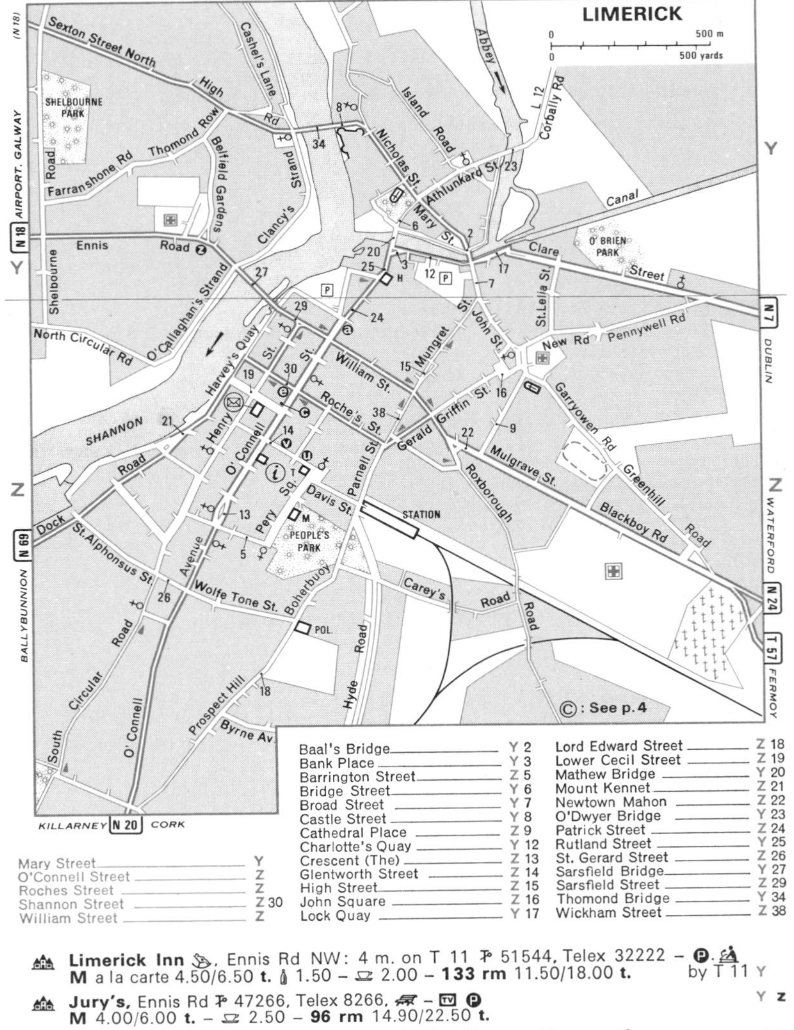

Baal's Bridge Y 2
Bank Place Y 3
Barrington Street Z 5
Bridge Street Y 6
Broad Street Y 7
Castle Street Y 8
Cathedral Place Z 9
Charlotte's Quay Y 12
Crescent (The) Z 13
Glentworth Street Z 14
High Street Z 15
John Square Z 16
Lock Quay Y 17

Lord Edward Street Z 18
Lower Cecil Street Z 19
Mathew Bridge Y 20
Mount Kennet Z 21
Newtown Mahon Z 22
O'Dwyer Bridge Y 23
Patrick Street Z 24
Rutland Street Y 25
St. Gerard Street Z 26
Sarsfield Bridge Y 27
Sarsfield Street Z 29
Thomond Bridge Y 34
Wickham Street Z 38

Mary Street Y
O'Connell Street Z
Roches Street Z
Shannon Street Z 30
William Street Z

Limerick Inn, Ennis Rd NW : 4 m. on T 11 ☎ 51544, Telex 32222 – Ⓟ. by T 11 Y
M a la carte 4.50/6.50 **t.** 1.50 – 2.00 – **133 rm** 11.50/18.00 **t.**

Jury's, Ennis Rd ☎ 47266, Telex 8266, – TV Ⓟ Y z
M 4.00/6.00 **t.** – 2.50 – **96 rm** 14.90/22.50 **t.**

Cruise's Royal, 4-6 O'Connell St. ☎ 44977 – wc wc . Z a
closed Christmas Day – **M** 3.75/4.25 **t.** – **80 rm** 8.00/16.00 **t.**

Royal George, O'Connell St. ☎ 44566 – wc . Z c
60 rm.

P.T.O. →

Limerick Ryan, Ennis Rd NW: 1 ¼ m. on T 11 ☎ 53922, Telex 6920 – lift wc ☎ P – 184 rm. — on T 11 Y

Two Mile Motor Inn, Ennis Rd NW: 3 ¾ m. on T 11 ☎ 53122 – wc wc ☎ P. – 47 rm. — on T 11 Y

Park Way Motor Inn, Dublin Rd, E: 1 ½ m. on T 5 ☎ 47599 – wc wc ☎ P. — on T 5 Z
M 4.00/6.00 **t.** 1.75 – 2.00 – **103 rm** 7.75/13.70 **t.**

Glentworth, Glentworth St. ☎ 43822 – lift wc ☎. – **58 rm.** — Z u

Hanratty's, 4 Glentworth St. ☎ 43466 – wc wc ☎ – **43 rm.** — Z v

Green Hills, Ennis Rd NW: 2 ¼ m. on T 11 ☎ 53033 – wc ☎ P. — on T 11 Y
M a la carte 4.00/4.70 **t.** 3.50 – 2.50 – **25 rm** 11.50/20.00 **t.**

Woodfield House, Ennis Rd NW: 1 ¼ m. on T 11 ☎ 53022 – wc wc ☎ P — on T 11 Y
M *(closed Sunday and November-February)* (dinner only) 3.95/4.95 **t.** 1.25 – 1.95 – **25 rm** 8.40/12.00 **t.**

XX Merryman, 5 Glentworth St. ☎ 43466. — Z v

XX Ted's, 112 O'Connell St. ☎ 47412. — Z e

AUSTIN-ROVER-TRIUMPH Lower Cecil St. ☎ 46255
BMW, CITROEN 2a Georges Quay ☎ 43133
BRITISH LEYLAND Coonagh Cross ☎ 51577
CHRYSLER Dublin Rd ☎ 49455
DATSUN Ennis Rd ☎ 45523
FIAT, LANCIA Punch's Cross ☎ 45566
FORD Mulgrave St. ☎ 45844
FORD Lansdowne ☎ 52244
RENAULT City Park ☎ 47463
TOYOTA Ennis Rd ☎ 51611
VAUXHALL, VOLVO Henry St. ☎ 45577
VW, AUDI-NSU Mulgrave St. ☎ 44224

LISCANNOR Clare – pop. 319 – ✆ Lahinch.

Envir.: Cliffs of Moher* (O'Brien's Tower ✻** N: 1 h. Rtn on foot) NW: 3 m.**

Dublin 165 – Galway 52 – Limerick 44.

Liscannor, ☎ 96, ← – wc ☎ P – **36 rm.**

LISMORE Waterford 986 ㉙ – pop. 884 – ✆ 058 – 9.

See: Castle (site*). **Envir.:** SE: Blackwater Valley** (from Lismore to the mouth, by a scenic road along the right bank of the River Blackwater).

Dublin 143 – Cork 37 – Killarney 74 – Waterford 44.

Ballyrafter House , ☎ 54002, , park – wc P
Easter-September – **M** (bar lunch) approx. 4.60 **t.** – **14 rm** 5.75/12.25 **t.** – P 11.75/13.00 **t.**

TOYOTA Lismore ☎ 24

LISTOWEL Kerry 986 ㉕ – pop. 3,021 – ✆ 068.

Envir.: Carrigafoyle Castle* 15C-16C (top ✻*, 106 steps) N: 9 m.

Dublin 168 – Killarney 37 – Limerick 47.

Listowel Arms, The Square ☎ 14 – lift wc ☎ – **34 rm.**

North County, 67 Church St. ☎ 21238 – **8 rm** 3.50/7.00 **st.**

FORD Market St. ☎ 6

LONGFORD Longford 986 ㉑㉒ – pop. 3,876 – ✆ 043.

18 **Glack, ☎ 6310.**

i ☎ 6566 (May - September).

Dublin 74 – Roscommon 19 – Sligo 57 – Tullamore 47.

Longford Arms, Main St. ☎ 6296 – wc ☎ P.
closed Christmas Day – **M** 4.00/5.50 **t.** 1.20 – **40 rm** 8.00/17.00 **t.**

Annaly, Main St. ☎ 6253 – ☎ P – **49 rm.**

X Weavers Loft, Ballymahon St. ☎ 6184.

BRITISH LEYLAND Richmond St. ☎ 6217
CHRYSLER Dublin Rd ☎ 6221
DATSUN Drumlish ☎ 24104
FORD Dublin Rd ☎ 6421
PEUGEOT Dublin Rd ☎ 6496
PEUGEOT, VW, AUDI-NSU Dublin Rd ☎ 6321
RENAULT Athlone Rd ☎ 6615
TOYOTA Lanesboro ☎ 21159

LOUGH GOWNA Cavan – pop. 125.

Dublin 81 – Tullamore 54.

Robin Hill , ☎ 21, – P
M *(closed Monday)* (dinner only for non-residents) approx. 4.00 **st.** – **5 rm** 4.00/8.00 **st.** – P 10.00 **st.**

MACROOM Cork 986 ㉙ – pop. 2,256.
🏌 ☎ 27.
Dublin 186 – Cork 25 – Killarney 30.

- Castle, Main St. ☎ 74, – wc
31 rm.
- Castleville House, South Sq ☎ 283, – wc
season – **11 rm.**

FORD Main St. ☎ 29
TOYOTA Emmet Pl. ☎ 23296

MALAHIDE Dublin 986 ㉒ and ㉝ – pop. 3,834 – ✆ 01.
Envir.: Swords (St. Columba's Church: towers*) W: 2 ½ m. – Lusk (church: round towers*) NW: 8 m.
🏌 ☎ 350248.
Dublin 9 – Drogheda 24.

- **Johnny's,** 9 James Ter. ☎ 450314
closed Sunday, Monday, Easter week, mid September-mid October and Christmas week –
M (dinner only) a la carte 6.65/7.80 **t.**

MALIN Donegal – pop. 2,723 – ✉ Lifford.
Dublin 176 – Londonderry 31.

- Malin, ☎ 6 – wc P
17 rm.

MALLARANY (MULRANY) Mayo 986 ㉑ – pop. 97.
Envir.: NW : Achill Island (Achil Sound*, The Atlantic Drive*** : coast road from Cloghmore to Dooega, Kell: the strand*, Lough Keel*).
🏌 G.S.R. Hotel ☎ Mulrany 3.
Dublin 175 – Ballina 48 – **Galway 71.**

MALLOW Cork 986 ㉙ – pop. 5,901 – ✆ 022.
🏌18 ☎ 21145, SE: 1 ½ m. of Mallow Bridge.
Dublin 149 – Cork 21 – Killarney 40 – Limerick 41.

- **Longueville House** , W: 3½ m. by T 30 ☎ 27156, ≤, « Country house atmosphere », , , park – wc P
Easter-mid October – **M** *(closed Sunday dinner and Monday dinner) (open Friday dinner from mid October to Easter)* approx. 6.50 **t.** – **18 rm** 7.00/16.00 **t.**

FIAT Shortcastle ☎ 21711
OPEL Castlecor ☎ 28137
RENAULT Ballydaheen ☎ 21107

MOATE Westmeath 986 ㉑㉒ – pop. 1,378 – ✆ 0902.
Envir.: Clonmacnoise** (medieval ruins) SW: 15 m.
🏌 ☎ 31271, N: 1 m.
Dublin 65 – Galway 67 – Roscommon 30 – **Tullamore 14.**

- **Grand,** Main St. ☎ 31104 – wc P.
M a la carte 3.40/8.10 **t.** 2.25 – **10 rm** 5.50/11.00 **t.** – P 9.50/10.50 **t.**

RENAULT ☎ 31170

MONAGHAN Monaghan 986 ⑱ – pop. 5,256 – ✆ 047.
See: St. Macartan's Cathedral* 19C.
🏌 ☎ 135, 3 m. Cotehill Rd.
i ☎ 81122 (May-September).
Dublin 80 – Dundalk 31.

- Hillgrove, Old Armagh Rd E: ¾ m. off T 2 ☎ 81288, – wc wc P
28 rm.
- Four Seasons, N: 1 m. on T 2 ☎ 81888 – wc P
25 rm.
- **Westenra Arms,** The Diamond ☎ 82298 – wc P
M 2.50/3.00 1.20 – **25 rm** 5.15/10.25 **t.** – P 9.45/10.50 **t.**

BRITISH LEYLAND Old Cross Sq. ☎ 82011
CHRYSLER Glaslough St. ☎ 81504
FORD Dawson St. ☎ 81399
VAUXHALL 15 Farney St. ☎ 61637
TOYOTA, VW, AUDI-NSU, MERCEDES-BENZ North Rd ☎ 81044

MONASTEREVIN Kildare 986 ㉖ – pop. 1,897 – ✆ 045 Naas.
Dublin 41 – Kilkenny 44 – **Limerick 80 – Tullamore 23.**

- Hazel, SW: ¼m. on T 5 ☎ 25373 – wc wc P
10 rm.

FIAT Monasterevin ☎ 25331

MOYARD Galway – pop. 382.

Dublin 187 – Galway 55.

Crocnaraw ⑤, ☎ 9, ←, « Country house atmosphere », ⑤, ⑥, park – ⌂wc Ⓟ
Easter-October – **M** *(closed Sunday and Monday)* 5.00/6.00 **t.** 🍷 1.35 – **10 rm** ☕ 7.00/15.00 **t.** – P 14.50/16.50 **t.**

MULLINGAR Westmeath 986 ㉒ – pop. 6,790 – ☎ 044.

Envir.: N: Lough Derravaragh★ – Lough Owel★ – Multyfarman (Franciscan College park: Stations of the Cross★) – NE: Lough Lene★ – Fore (St. Feichin's Church and ruined Priory★) 13C – S: Lough Ennel★.

🏌18 Belvedere ☎ 8366, S: 3 m.

ℹ Clonard House, Dublin Rd ☎ 8650 and 8761.

Dublin 48 – Dundalk 58 – Tullamore 21.

Greville Arms, Pearse St. ☎ 8563 – ⌂wc ⋒wc ☎
28 rm.

BRITISH LEYLAND Harbour St. ☎ 8508
DATSUN Dublin Rd ☎ 8508
FIAT Dublin Rd ☎ 8806
FORD Castle St. ☎ 8347
RENAULT Lynn Rd ☎ 8977
TOYOTA Lynn Rd ☎ 22133
VAUXHALL Patrick St. ☎ 8365
VW, AUDI-NSU Millmount Rd ☎ 8437

NAVAN Meath 986 ㉒ – pop. 10,099 – ☎ 046.

🏌18 Bellinter Park ☎ 25244.

Dublin 30 – Drogheda 16 – **Dundalk 34.**

Ardboyne, Dublin Rd SE: 1 m. on T 35 ☎ 23119 – ⌂wc ☎ Ⓟ
26 rm.

CHRYSLER Dublin Rd ☎ 21212
FORD Academy St. ☎ 21129
PEUGEOT Dublin Rd ☎ 21929
TOYOTA Kells Rd ☎ 21336

NENAGH Tipperary 986 ㉕ – pop. 5,085 – ☎ 067.

See: Butler Castle (keep★ 13C). **Envir.**: NW: Lough Derg★★★ (Holy Island: site★★).

🏌18 Beechwood, ☎ 476, NE: 3 m.

ℹ Kickham St. ☎ 31610.

Dublin 96 – Limerick 25 – Tullamore 45.

Ormond, 51 Kenyon St. ☎ 31404 – ⌂wc ⋒wc ☎ Ⓟ
M 5.00/6.75 **t.** 🍷 1.50 – **20 rm** ☕ 6.50/14.50 **st.**

DATSUN Templederry ☎ 12
FIAT Tyone ☎ 298
PEUGEOT Puckane ☎ 551
RENAULT Limerick Rd ☎ 321

NEWBRIDGE **(DROICHEAD NUA)** Kildare 986 ㉖ – pop. 5,053 – ☎ 045 Naas.

Envir.: Kildare (St. Brigid's Cathedral★ 13C-19C and round tower★ 9C-10C) SW: 5 m – Tully (National Stud★, Japanese gardens★ *AC*) SW: 6 m. via Kildare – Old Kilcullen (site★, ☀★) S: 7 ½ m.

Dublin 28 – Kilkenny 57 – **Tullamore 36.**

Keadeen, Ballymany SW: 1 m. on T 5 ☎ 31666, Telex 4326, ⑥, park – TV ⌂wc ⋒wc ☎ Ⓟ.
M *(closed Christmas Day)* 6.00/9.00 **st.** 🍷 0.80 – **22 rm.**

✕✕ **Red House,** NE: 3 m. on T 5 ☎ 31516, ⑥ – Ⓟ
closed Sunday, Monday, 2 weeks February and 2 weeks August – **M** (dinner only) 4.40/5.50 **t.**

FIAT ☎ 31725
PEUGEOT, SAAB, VAUXHALL Ballymany ☎ 31281

NEWMARKET-ON-FERGUS Clare 986 ㉕ – pop. 1,054 – ☎ 061 Limerick.

Dublin 136 – Ennis 8 – **Limerick 15.**

Dromoland Castle ⑤, NW: 1 ½ m. on T 11 ☎ 71144, Group Telex 6854, ←, « Tastefully converted castle », ✕, 🏌9, ⑤, ⑥, park – Ⓟ
April-October – **M** approx. 9.00 **t.** – ☕ 3.75 – **67 rm** 27.00/60.00 **t.**

Clare Inn ⑤, Ennis Rd NW: 2 ¼ m. off T 11 ☎ 71161, Group Telex 6854, ←, 🏌9, ⑤, park – ♿ Ⓟ
M 6.50/7.00 **t.** – ☕ 3.20 – **121 rm** 19.40/26.60 **t.**

NEWPORT Mayo 986 ㉑ – pop. 1,387.

See: St. Patrick's Church★, modern Irish-Romanesque style (site★). **Envir.**: Burrishoole Abbey (site★) NW: 2 m.

Dublin 164 – Ballina 37 – **Galway 60.**

Newport House ⑤, ☎ 12, 🏌9, ⑥, park – ⌂wc ⋒wc Ⓟ
April-September – **M** 4.50/5.50 **t.** 🍷 1.00 – **24 rm** ☕ 11.00/20.00 **t.** – P 18.00/20.00 **t.**

BRITISH LEYLAND Castlebar St. ☎ 3
TOYOTA, VOLVO ☎ 57

NEW ROSS Wexford 986 ⑳ – pop. 4,775 – ☎ 051 Waterford.
Envir. : Jerpoint Abbey** (ruins 12C-15C) NW : 15 m. – St. Mullins Monastery (site*) N : 9 m. – John F. Kennedy Memorial Park* 1968 (arboretum, ≤*) S : 7 ½ m. – SW : River Barrow Valley*.

Tinneranny ☎ 21433.

i ☎ 21857 (July-August) – J.F. Kennedy Park ☎ 88156 (July-August).

Dublin 88 – Kilkenny 27 – **Waterford 15** – Wexford 23.

- **Five Counties,** Wexford Rd S : 1 m. on T 12 ☎ 21703, – wc ☎ **P**.
  M 5.00/6.00 **t.** 2.00 – 1.85 – **36 rm** 7.40/13.35 **t.** – P 17.25/18.50 **t.**
- **Inishross,** 96 St. Mary St. ☎ 21335
  7 rm 4.00/6.50 **st.**
- **New Ross Galley,** Bridge Quay ☎ 21723, « Scenic boat trip »
  Sailings : 12 a. m and 7 p. m – *April-September* – **M** *(closed Monday in winter and Sunday dinner)* approx. 7.50 **st.** 1.00.

BRITISH LEYLAND South St. ☎ 21205
FORD The Quay ☎ 21235
FORD Waterford Rd ☎ 21403
RENAULT The Quay ☎ 21415

OUGHTERARD Galway 986 ㉑ – pop. 628 – ☎ 091 Galway.
See: The northern scenic road (cul-de-sac) ≤** on Lough Corrib***. **Envir.:** Aughnanure Castle* (16C) SE: 3 m. – Leckavrea Mountain* NW: 13 m. – Gortmore (≤** S: on Kilkieran Bay, ≤* NW: on the Twelve Pins) SW: 16 m.

☎ 82131.

i ☎ 82142 (June - August).

Dublin 149 – **Galway 17.**

- **Sweeney's Oughterard House**, W: ½ m. on T 71 ☎ 82207, « Country house set in attractive gardens », park – wc ☎ **P**
  M approx. 6.50 **t.** 2.00 – 2.00 – **33 rm** 10.00/26.00 **t.**
- **Connemara Gateway Motor Inn** (T.H.F.), SE: 1 m. on T 71 ☎ 82328, ≤, heated – wc **P**
  M approx. 4.75 **t.** 1.50 – 2.00 – **48 rm** 7.50/11.50 **t.** – P 15.25/17.15 **t.**
- Corrib, ☎ 82329 – wc wc ☎ **P** – **17 rm.**
- **Egan's Lake,** Main St. ☎ 82205, – wc ☎ **P**
  M 4.50/6.50 **t.** 1.50 – **18 rm** 6.50/13.00 **t.**
- **Currarevagh House**, NW: 4 m. ☎ 82313, « Country house atmosphere », park – wc **P**
  Easter-5 October – **M** (residents only) approx. 5.10 **t.** 1.45 – **15 rm** 8.50/18.70 **t.** – P 14.40 **t.**

PARKNASILLA Kerry – pop. 250 – ☎ Sneem.

Parknasilla, ☎ 3.

Dublin 224 – **Cork 72** – **Killarney 34.**

- **Great Southern**, ☎ 3, Group Telex 5695, ≤, park – **P**
  M 6.50/10.00 **t.** 2.00 – 2.25 – **60 rm** 16.00/28.00 **t.** – P 20.25/28.25 **t.**

PONTOON Mayo – ✉ ☎ Foxford.
See : ✻* – moraines*. **Envir.** : Glen Nephin ≤* W: 6 m.

Dublin 141 – Ballina 11 – **Galway 59.**

- **Pontoon Bridge**, NE: 1 m. on L 22 ☎ 20, ≤, – wc ☎ **P**
  May-15 October – **M** approx. 5.00 **t.** 1.00 – **24 rm** 7.00/16.00 **t.** – P 14.00/16.00 **t.**

PORT NA BLAGH Donegal 986 ⑬⑭ – pop. 400 – ✉ Letterkenny – ☎ Dunfanaghy.
Envir. : Doe Castle* 16C ruins (site*, ≤*) SE: 6 m.

Dublin 170 – **Londonderry 41** – **Sligo 105.**

- **Shandon**, Marble Hill Strand, NE : 2 ½ m. ☎ 15, ≤ bay and hills, – wc ☎ **P**
  Easter week and June-mid September – **M** 4.80/5.40 **t.** – **59 rm** 7.00/17.00 **t.** – P 10.50/12.00 **t.**
- **Port-Na-Blagh,** ☎ 11, ≤ Sheephaven Bay and harbour, – wc **P**
  Easter-September – **M** approx. 5.00 **t.** 1.05 – **58 rm** 6.80/13.60 **t.** – P 9.00/10.50 **t.**

PORTUMNA Galway 986 ㉕ – pop. 1,669.
Envir.: S: Lough Derg*** (Holy Island : site**).

☎ 59.

i ☎ 54 (July - August).

Dublin 96 – **Galway 41** – Kilkenny 63 – **Limerick 45** – **Tullamore 37.**

- Westpark, ☎ 112 – wc wc ☎ **P** – **27 rm.**

FORD Clonfert Av. ☎ 9

QUIN Clare – pop. 300 – ☎ 065 Ennis.
Envir.: Tulla (site*, ancient church ☼**) NE: 6 m.
Dublin 139 – Ennis 6 – **Limerick 18.**

- **Ballykilty Manor** ⛰, SW: 1 m. ☎ 25627, ↝, park – ⇔wc Ⓟ
  M 4.50/7.00 **t.** 🍷 2.00 – **11 rm** ☕ 11.50/13.50 **t.**

RAPHOE Donegal – pop. **1,257.**
Envir.: Beltany Stone Circle (site*) from the road 10 mn on foot, S: 2 m.
Dublin 139 – Donegal 29 – **Londonderry 20** – **Sligo 69.**

- **Central,** The Diamond ☎ 8
  closed 24 to 30 December – **M** (snack lunch only on Saturday and Sunday) 2.50/2.95 **t.** – **10 rm** ☕ 3.60/7.00 **t.**

RATHDRUM Wicklow 986 ㉖ – pop. 2,304 – ☎ 0404 Wicklow.
Dublin 39 – Kilkenny 65 – **Wicklow 11.**

- **Avonbrae House,** ☎ 6198, ≤, ✂, ◪, ⚘ – ⋒wc Ⓟ
  15 March-November – **8 rm** ☕ 5.75/12.75 **st.**

RATH LUIRC Cork 986 ㉙ – see Charleville.

RATHMULLAN Donegal 986 ⑭⑱ – pop. 486 – ✉ Letterkenny – ⛳9.
Envir.: Mulroy Bay** NW: 8 m. – Fanad Head ≤* N: 20 m.
Dublin 165 – **Londonderry 36** – **Sligo 87.**

- **Rathmullan House** ⛰, N: ½ m. on L 77, ☎ 4, ≤ Lough Swilly and hills, « Country house atmosphere », ✂, ⚘, park – ⇔wc ⋒wc Ⓟ
  Easter-end September – **M** a la carte 3.60/6.05 **st.** – ☕ 0.70 – **21 rm** 7.50/24.00 **st.**
- **Fort Royal** ⛰, N: 1 m. off L 77 ☎ 11, ≤, ✂, ⛳9, ⚘, park – ⇔wc Ⓟ
  Easter-October – **M** approx. 3.75 **t.** 🍷 1.50 – **27 rm** ☕ 8.00/20.00 **t.** – P 12.00/15.00 **t.**

Avvertite immediatamente l'albergatore se non potete più occupare la camera prenotata.

RATHNEW Wicklow 986 ㉖ – pop. 954 – ✉ ☎ 0404 Wicklow.
Dublin 31 – **Waterford 82** – Wexford 65.

- **Hunter's** ⛰, N: ¾ m. on L 29 ☎ 4106, « Garden », ✂, ↝ – ⇔wc Ⓟ
  M 5.40/6.20 **t.** 🍷 1.50 – **17 rm** ☕ 7.00/15.50 **t.**

REDCASTLE Donegal – pop. 467 – ✉ Moville.
Dublin 162 – **Londonderry 17.**

- **Redcastle** ⛰, ☎ 73, ≤, ↝, park – ⇔wc Ⓟ. ⛺
  M a la carte 3.30/5.60 **st.** 🍷 1.10 – **20 rm** ☕ 4.50/9.50 **t.** – P 9.00/9.50 **t.**

RENVYLE Galway.
See: Castle ≤*.
Dublin 194 – Ballina 74 – **Galway 62.**

- **Renvyle House,** ☎ 3, ≤, ✂, ⛳9, ↝, ⚘, park – ⇔wc ☎ Ⓟ
  Easter-October, Christmas and 1 January – **M** 4.50/5.50 **t.** 🍷 1.25 – **70 rm** ☕ 10.50/21.00 **t.**

ROCHESTOWN Cork – see Cork.

ROCKMARSHALL Louth – see Dundalk.

ROSAPENNA Donegal – ✉ Letterkenny – ☎ Downings.
Envir.: SE: Mulroy Bay**.
Dublin 175 – **Londonderry 46** – **Sligo 97.**

- **Rosapenna Golf** ⛰, ☎ 4, ≤, ✂, ⛳18, park – ⇔wc ☎ Ⓟ
  Easter-November – **M** 4.50/6.00 **t.** – **40 rm** ☕ 12.00/20.00 **t.** – P 13.00/17.00 **t.**

ROSCREA Tipperary 986 ㉕ – pop. 3,855.
⛳9 ☎ 311, 2 m. on Dublin Rd.
Dublin 78 – Kilkenny 36 – **Limerick 43** – **Tullamore 28.**

- **Pathé,** Castle St. ☎ 241 – ⇔wc Ⓟ
  closed Christmas Day – **M** 3.50/5.00 **st.** 🍷 1.50 – **23 rm** ☕ 8.00/16.00 **st.**

CITROEN Grove St. ☎ 351
PEUGEOT, RENAULT Abbey Garage ☎ 38
TOYOTA Birr Rd ☎ 401
VAUXHALL Limerick Rd ☎ 403
VW, AUDI-NSU, MERCEDES-BENZ ☎ 76

ROSSCAHILL Galway – ☎ 091 Galway.
Dublin 144 – Galway 12.

Ross Lake ⛱, W: 1 ½ m. off T 71, ☎ 80109, %, park – ⓟ
Easter-11 October – **M** 4.50/5.50 **t.** 2.00 – 0.50 – **12 rm** 5.50/12.00 **t.**

at Knockferry (on Lough Corrib) NE: 5 m. off T 71 – ✉ Rosscahill – ☎ 091 Galway:

Knockferry Lodge ⛱, ☎ 80122, ←, – wc ⓟ
April-October – **M** (by arrangement only) 4.00/5.50 **st.** – **10 rm** 6.75/11.50 **st.** – P 9.50 **st.**

ROSSES POINT Sligo 986 ⑰ – see Sligo.

ROSSLARE Wexford 986 ㉚ – pop. 588 – ☎ 053 Wexford.
18 ☎ 32113.
Shipping connections with the Continent : to Le Havre (Irish Continental Line) – to Fishguard (Sealink) 1-2 daily except Sundays mid September-June (3 h 15 mn).
Dublin 104 – Waterford 50 – Wexford 12.

Strand, Main Rd ☎ 32114, %, – ⓟ
closed 15 December-15 February – **M** 3.50/5.00 **t.** 1.30 – **95 rm** 6.40/12.80 **t.** – P 14.00/16.00 **t.**

Golf, Strand Rd ☎ 32179, %, – wc ⓟ
M approx. 5.10 **t.** 2.25 – **25 rm** 7.15/16.45 **t.** – P 10.55/14.70 **t.**

ROSSLARE HARBOUR Wexford 986 ㉚ – pop. 725 – ☎ 053 Wexford.
i ☎ 33232 (June - August).
Dublin 105 – Waterford 51 – Wexford 13.

Great Southern, ☎ 33233, Telex 8788, %, – ⓟ
March-December – **M** 4.20/6.70 **t.** 1.40 – 2.25 – **100 rm** 11.50/18.00 **t.**

ROSSNOWLAGH Donegal – ☎ 072 Bundoran.
Dublin 157 – Donegal 9 – Sligo 33.

Sand House ⛱, ☎ 65343, ←, 9 – wc ⓟ
Easter-September – **M** 4.50/5.50 **t.** 1.20 – **40 rm** 9.50/19.00 **t.** – P 12.00/14.50 **t.**

SALTHILL Galway 986 ㉕ – see Galway.

SCARRIFF Clare 986 ㉕ – pop. 619.
Envir.: E: Lough Derg*** (Holy Island: site**) – SE: Lough Derg Coast Road** (L 12) to Tuamgraney.
Dublin 119 – Ennis 21 – Limerick 20.

Clare Lakelands, ☎ 18, – wc
M *(closed Christmas week)* 3.00/5.00 **t.** 1.50 – **24 rm** 8.50/16.00 **t.** – P 12.00/14.00 **t.**

SCHULL (SKULL) Cork 986 ㉙ – pop. 457.
Dublin 226 – Cork 65 – Killarney 64.

East End, Main St. ☎ 14, – ⓟ
Easter-September – **M** (dinner only) 4.20/6.00 **st.** – **17 rm** 7.00/14.00 **st.**

O'Keeffe's, Main St. ☎ 93.

SHANAGARRY Cork – ✉ ☎ 021 Cork.
Dublin 163 – Cork 25 – Waterford 64.

✕✕ ✿ **Ballymaloe House** ⛱ with rm, NW: 1 ¾ m. on L 35 A ☎ 62531, ←, « Farmhouse atmosphere », %, , 9, , park – wc wc ⓟ
M (buffet lunch) 6.50/7.20 **t.** 1.50 – 2.00 – **21 rm** 6.50/20.00 **t.** – P 16.60/19.90 **t.**
Spec. Hot buttered oysters, Irish stew, Carrigeen with Irish coffee sauce.

SHANNON AIRPORT Clare 986 ㉕ – pop. 3,657 – ☎ 061 Limerick.
18 ☎ Shannon 61020.
✈ ☎ 61666 – Terminal: Limerick Railway Station.
i ☎ 61664.
Dublin 136 – Ennis 16 – Limerick 15.

Shannon International without rest., ☎ 61122 – ⓟ
2.50 – **126 rm** 16.00/23.00 **t.**

Red Lion — Wenn der Name eines Hotels dünn gedruckt ist, dann hat uns der Hotelier Preise und Öffnungszeiten nicht angegeben.

SHEEHAN'S POINT Kerry.
See: ≤***.

Hotels see: Caherdaniel E: 5 m.
Waterville N: 6 m.

SKIBBEREEN Cork 986 ㉙ – pop. 2,104.
Envir: Roaringwater Bay* W: 5 m.
9 ℱ 82.
i Main St. ℱ 189.
Dublin 213 – Cork 52 – Killarney 67.

Eldon, Bridge St. ℱ 12 – wc ☎ P
26 rm.

FIAT Ilen St. ℱ 103
FORD 14 North St. ℱ 38
RENAULT Townsend St. ℱ 22
VW, AUDI-NSU Skibbereen ℱ 111

SLANE Meath – pop. 483 – ☎ 041 Drogheda.
See: Hill of Slane (site*, ≤ *).
Dublin 42 – Drogheda 8 – Dundalk 26.

XX **Slane Castle,** W: 1 m. on T 26 ℱ 24207, Dancing – P
M (dinner only) a la carte 6.50/9.45 **t.** 1.50.

SLIEVERUE Waterford – see Waterford.

SLIGO Sligo 986 ⑰ – pop. 14,080 – ☎ 071.
See: Sligo Abbey* (13C ruins) – Court House*. **Envir.:** E: Lough Gill*** (Innisfree*), Park's Castle (site**), Lough Colgagh**, Drumcliff (High Cross) ≤* on Belbulbin Mountain N: 4 m. – Glencar Lough* NE: 6 m. – Carrowmore (Megalithic cemetery*) SW: 2 m.
i Stephen St. ℱ 2436.
Dublin 131 – Belfast 128 – Dundalk 106 – Londonderry 88.

Sligo Park, Pearse Rd S: 1 ½ m. on T 3 ℱ 3291, Telex 4397 – P.
M 3.95/4.65 **t.** 1.20 – **60 rm** 11.50/16.00 **t.** – P 9.95/11.45 **t.**

Innisfree, Lord Edward St. ℱ 2101, – wc ☎ P.
58 rm.

Ballincar House, Rosses Point Rd NW: 2 ½ m. on L 16 ℱ 5361, ≤, – wc wc ☎ P
M 4.50/5.50 **t.** 1.50 – **17 rm** 8.50/16.00 **t.** – P 14.50/16.50 **t.**

Silver Swan, Hyde Bridge ℱ 3231 – wc wc ☎ P.
closed Christmas Day – **M** 4.75/5.25 **t.** 2.00 – 1.75 – **24 rm** 5.50/10.70 **t.** – P 14.00/17.00 **t.**

at Rosses Point NW: 5 m. on **L 16** – ✉ ☎ 071 Sligo:

Yeats Country Ryan, ℱ 77211, Telex 6403, ≤, – wc P.
closed January-mid February – **79 rm.**

AUDI-NSU Ballisodare ℱ 71291
BMW Carton Hill ℱ 2193
BRITISH LEYLAND Teeling St. ℱ 2248
CHRYSLER-SIMCA Finisklin ℱ 3267
DATSUN J.-F. Kennedy Par. ℱ 2539
FIAT, LANCIA Ballinode ℱ 2188
FORD Wine St. ℱ 2610
RENAULT Bridge St. ℱ 2091

SNEEM Kerry 986 ㉙ – pop. 285.
Dublin 226 – Killarney 36.

Cantharella Country Motel, ℱ 47, – wc wc P
May-September – **M** (snack lunch) 3.50/4.00 **t.** – 1.50 – **16 rm** 5.00/8.00 **t.**

SPIDDAL Galway 986 ㉑ – pop. 819 – ☎ 091 Galway.
Dublin 143 – Galway 11.

Bridge House, Main St. ℱ 83118 – P
M *(Easter-October)* 4.00/5.00 **st.** 2.50 – **14 rm** 5.50/13.00 **st.** – P 12.50/14.00 **st.**

STILLORGAN Dublin 986 ㊲ – see Dublin.

STRAFFAN Kildare – ✉ Celbridge – ☎ 01 Dublin.
Dublin 16 – Limerick 108.

Barberstown Castle, N: ¾ m. on L 2 ℱ 288206, ≤ – wc P
M (lunch by arrangement) a la carte 5.30/8.00 **t.** 1.40 – **10 rm** 8.00/20.00 **st.**

STROKESTOWN Roscommon – pop. 563.
Dublin 88 – Roscommon 12 – Sligo 46.

Percy French, Bridge St. ℱ 46 – wc P
M 3.50/4.25 **t.** 1.50 – **22 rm** 4.50/8.75 **t.** – P 10.50/15.00 **t.**

CHRYSLER-SIMCA ℱ 29

SUTTON Dublin – see Dublin.

TEMPLEGLANTINE Limerick – pop. 855.
Dublin 154 – Killarney 36 – Limerick 33.

Devon, ☎ 7 – wc P
M 4.00/5.00 **t.** 1.50 – **10 rm** 6.50/11.00 **t.**

THURLES Tipperary 986 ㉕ – pop. 6,840 – ☎ 0504.
See : Catholic Cathedral (interior*). **Envir. :** Holycross Abbey** (12C) *AC*, SW : 4 ½ m.
18 ☎ 87.
i ☎ 332 (July - August).
Dublin 93 – Cork 73 – Kilkenny 29 – Limerick 39.

Anner, Dublin Rd E : ½ m. on T 19 ☎ 449, – wc P.
15 rm.

BRITISH LEYLAND Kicham St. ☎ 21288
FIAT Thurles ☎ 226
FORD The Mall ☎ 83
TOYOTA Stradavoher ☎ 255
VW, AUDI-NSU Racecourse Rd ☎ 695

TIPPERARY Tipperary 986 ㉕ – pop. 16,874 – ☎ 062.
Envir. : S : Glen of Aherlow* (statue of Christ the King ≤ **).
9 Rathanny ☎ **51119**, S : 2 m.
i ☎ 51457 (July-August).
Dublin 113 – Cork 57 – Limerick 24 – Waterford 53.

Ach-na-sheen House, Waterford Rd ☎ 51298 – wc P
10 rm 4.50/9.50 **st.**

TOMHAGGARD Wexford – ✉ ☎ 053 Wexford.
Dublin 101 – Waterford 47 – Wexford 9.

Bargy Castle, NE : ½ m. ☎ 35203, « 12C castle with country house atmosphere », park – wc P
season – **20 rm.**

TRALEE Kerry 986 ㉙ – pop. 12,287 – ☎ 066.
9 Mount Hawke ☎ 21150.
i The Mall ☎ 21288.
Dublin 185 – Killarney 20 – Limerick 64.

Ballyseede Castle, SE : 2 ¾ m. by T 28 ☎ 21585, ≤, « Part 15C and 17C castle », park – wc P.
13 rm.

Earl of Desmond, SE : 2 ¾ m. on T 28 ☎ 21299, – wc P.
M 5.00/6.00 **t.** 1.50 – **52 rm** 10.00/15.00 **t.** – P 17.50/19.50 **t.**

Benner's, 1-2 Castle St. ☎ 21422 – wc P.
50 rm.

Ballyroe Country Club, NW : 2 ¾ m. on L 105 ☎ 22796 – wc P
12 rm.

BRITISH LEYLAND 100 Rock St. ☎ 21113
CHRYSLER-SIMCA Rathass ☎ 22411
CITROEN Rock St. ☎ 21877
FIAT Ashe St. ☎ 21124
FORD Edward St. ☎ 21555
OPEL ☎ 22675
PEUGEOT, TOYOTA Denny St. ☎ 21688
VW, AUDI-NSU The Market and Rock St. ☎ 21193

TRAMORE Waterford 986 ㉚ – pop. 3,792 – ✉ ☎ 051 Waterford.
18 ☎ 81247.
i ☎ 81572 (June - August).
Dublin 107 – Cork 72 – Waterford 8.

Majestic, ☎ 81761, ≤, – .
closed January – **M** 4.30/5.75 **t.** 1.15 – **90 rm** 8.65/20.00 **t.**

Grand, Market Sq. ☎ 81414, ≤ – wc wc P.
M 4.00/4.75 **t.** 1.30 – 2.00 – **48 rm** 7.50/14.00 **t.** – P 12.50 **t.**

Shalloe's Cliff, Strand St. ☎ 81723 – P
21 rm.

VALENTIA ISLAND Kerry 986 ㉙.
Dublin 242 – Killarney 52 – Limerick 119.

Royal, Knightstown ☎ 44, ≤, – wc P
47 rm.

Valentia Heights, ☎ 38, ≤ Valentia harbour and islands – wc P
April-September – **M** approx. 4.25 **t.** 1.40 – **10 rm** 4.25/10.95 **t.** – P 11.25/12.50 **t.**

VIRGINIA Cavan 986 ㉒ – pop. 1,651.

Envir.: Kells (St. Columba's House* 9C – St. Columba's Church : old tower* 1783 – Churchyard high crosses*) SE : **11** m. – 9 ℗ 35.

Dublin 52 – Dundalk 39 – Roscommon 56 **– Tullamore 59.**

Park, ℗ 35, ≤, « Country house atmosphere », park – wc wc ℗.
closed mid December-mid January – **M** 4.50/5.00 **st.** 1.00 – **30 rm** 10.50/20.00 **t.**

WATERFORD Waterford 986 ㉚ – pop. 31,968 – 051.

See : Franciscan ruins of the French Church* 13C-16C (Grey Friars Street).

18 Newrath ℗ 41821.

i 41 The Quay ℗ 75788.

Dublin 99 – Cork 77 – Limerick 77.

Tower, The Mall ℗ 75801, Telex 8699 – ℗.
M 3.25/4.50 **t.** 1.30 – 1.85 – **100 rm** 8.60/13.20 **t.**

Ardree, Ferrybank ℗ 3491, Telex 8684, ≤ Waterford and estuary, – ℗.
M 4.20/5.60 **t.** 1.25 – 1.80 – **100 rm** 10.50/17.50 **t.**

Dooley's, The Quay ℗ 3531 – wc
closed Christmas – **M** a la carte 2.65/5.70 **t.** – **28 rm** 7.00/15.10 **t.**

at Slieverue N : 2 m. on T 7 – 051 Waterford :

Diamond Hill, ℗ 75543, – ℗
8 rm 4.50/9.00 **st.**

BRITISH LEYLAND Arundel Sq. ℗ 5339
CHRYSLER Railway Sq. ℗ 5930
DATSUN Slieverue ℗ 3676
FIAT Catherine St. ℗ 4988
FIAT, LANCIA Wellington St. ℗ 5879
FORD The Mall and Cork Rd ℗ 32891
PEUGEOT, OPEL Morgan St. ℗ 4232
RENAULT 16 The Quay ℗ 4047
TOYOTA William St. ℗ 4037
VAUXHALL Cork Rd ℗ 5844
VW, AUDI-NSU, MERCEDES-BENZ 22/24 The Quay ℗ 4919

WATERVILLE Kerry 986 ㉙ – pop. 547.

Envir. : Sheehan's Point ≤*** S : **6** m.

i ℗ 60 (June-September).

Dublin 238 – Killarney 48.

Waterville Lake, ℗ 7, Telex 8246, ≤ lake and mountains, 18, – ℗
April-October – **M** approx. 6.00 **t.** 2.00 – **100 rm** 15.25/25.20 **t.** – P 22.50 **t.**

Butler Arms, ℗ 5, ≤, – wc wc ℗
March-12 October – **M** 5.00/5.50 **t.** 1.50 – **40 rm** 6.85/15.70 **t.** – P 14.50 **t.**

Villa Maria, ℗ 83 – wc – *season* – **13 rm.**

WESTPORT Mayo 986 ㉑ – pop. 3,023.

See : Westport House* *AC*. **Envir. :** Croagh Patrick Mountain* (statue of St. Patrick ≤*, pilgrimage) SW : 6 m. – Roonah Quay ≤* on Clare Island W : 15 m. – S : Joyces Country (* from the bridge on Lough Mask**, Lough Nafooey*).

9 Carrowholy ℗ 547.

i The Mall ℗ 269.

Dublin 163 – Galway 50 – Sligo 65.

Westport Wood's, Quay Rd W : ½ m. on T 39 ℗ 333, Telex 4757 – wc ℗ – **50 rm.**

Westport, The Demesne ℗ 351, Telex 6397 – wc ℗
M (snack lunch) 4.50/5.25 **t.** 1.30 – 2.00 – **49 rm** 12.00/20.00 **t.**

FIAT, Fairgreen ℗ 15
OPEL Belclare ℗ 284
VW, AUDI-NSU Mill St. ℗ 106

WEXFORD Wexford 986 ㉚ – pop. 11,849 – 053.

Envir. : Johnstown Castle (the park-arboretum*) SW : 4 m.

9 Mulgannon ℗ 22238, SE : **1** m.

i Crescent Quay ℗ 23111.

Dublin 92 – Kilkenny 50 **– Waterford 38.**

Talbot, Trinity St. ℗ 22566, Telex 8658, – ℗.
M a la carte 5.50/6.50 **t.** 2.50 – 2.50 – **116 rm** 10.00/18.00 **t.** – P 9.50/13.00 **t.**

White's, Abbey St. ℗ 22311, Telex 8630 – ℗.
M 5.85/6.50 **t.** 2.75 – 2.00 – **97 rm** 7.40/15.70 **t.** – P 17.00/19.00 **t.**

Ferrycarrig Castle, Ferrycarrig Bridge NW : 2 ¾ m. on T 8 ℗ 22999, ≤ – wc ℗
Easter-October – **M** (dinner only) 4.50/5.50 **t.** 1.35 – 1.75 – **40 rm** 8.75/12.50 **s.**

BMW, OPEL Ferrybank ℗ 22107
BRITISH LEYLAND Ballycanew, Gorey ℗ 21282
CHRYSLER-SIMCA Redmond Rd ℗ 23133
DATSUN Enniscorthy ℗ 8554
FORD Ferrybank ℗ 23329
PEUGEOT, RENAULT The Faythe ℗ 22998
TOYOTA, VAUXHALL Custom House Quay ℗ 22165
VW, AUDI-NSU, MERCEDES-BENZ Westgate ℗ 22011

WICKLOW Wicklow 986 ㉖ – pop. 3,786 – ☎ 0404.

Dublin 33 – Waterford 84 – Wexford 67.

- **Grand,** Abbey St. ☎ 2337 – wc P
  M 2.85/5.50 **t.** 1.15 – **18 rm** 5.35/10.25 **t.** – P 12.50/14.50 **t.**
- **Knockrobin House** with rm, NW: 1 ½ m. on Dublin Rd ☎ 2344, – wc P
  M approx. 6.00 **st.** 1.50 – **5 rm** 8.00/16.00 **st.**

FIAT Bollarney ☎ 2212
FORD Whitegates ☎ 2331
VW, AUDI-NSU The Glebe ☎ 2126

WOODENBRIDGE Wicklow – ✉ ☎ 0402 Arklow.

9 Avoca, Arklow ☎ 5202.

Dublin 48 – Waterford 71 – Wexford 54.

- **Woodenbridge,** ☎ 5146, – P
  closed Good Friday and Christmas Day – **M** 5.00/5.75 **t.** 1.25 – **12 rm** 7.50/13.50 **t.** – P 14.25/17.50 **t.**

YOUGHAL Cork 986 ㉙ – pop. 5,445 – ☎ 024.

See : St. Mary's Collegiate Church* 13C. **Envir. :** Ardmore (site*, round tower* 10C, cathedral ruins* 12C, ≤*) E: 5 ½ m. – N: Blackwater Valley** (from Lismore to the mouth, by a scenic road along the right bank of the River Blackwater).

18 Knockaverry ☎ 2447.

i ☎ 2390 (June-September).

Dublin 146 – Cork 30 – Waterford 47.

- **Aherne's Seafood Bar,** 163 North Main St. ☎ 2424 – P
  closed Sunday lunch and Monday dinner – **M** a la carte 3.05/5.05 **s.** 0.90.

FIAT North Main St. ☎ 2470
RENAULT North Abbey ☎ 2354

MAJOR HOTEL GROUPS

Abbreviations used in the Guide and central reservation telephone numbers

PRINCIPALES CHAÎNES HÔTELIÈRES

Abréviations utilisées dans nos textes et centraux téléphoniques de réservation

PRINCIPALI CATENE ALBERGHIERE

Abbreviazioni utilizzate nei nostri testi e centrali telefoniche di prenotazione

DIE WICHTIGSTEN HOTELKETTEN

Im Führer benutzte Abkürzungen der Hotelketten und ihre Zentralen für telefonische Reservierung

ANCHOR HOTELS & TAVERNS LTD.	ANCHOR	01 (London) 402 6069
ANSELLS BREWERY LTD.	ANSELLS	—
BRITISH TRANSPORT HOTELS	B.T.H.	01 (London) 278 4211
CENTRE HOTELS (CRANSTON) LTD.	CENTRE	01 (London) 637 1661
CREST HOTELS LTD.	CREST	01 (London) 903 6422
DE VERE HOTELS LTD.	DE VERE	01 (London) 493 2114
EMBASSY HOTELS	EMBASSY	01 (London) 584 8224
GRAND METROPOLITAN COUNTY HOTELS	COUNTY	01 (London) 629 6611
GRAND METROPOLITAN HOTELS	GD. MET.	01 (London) 629 6611
INTERCHANGE HOTELS LTD.	INTERCHANGE	01 (London) 278 2007
MOUNT CHARLOTTE	MT. CHARLOTTE	01 (London) 568 1955
MYDDLETON HOTELS LTD.	MYDDLETON	0323 (Eastbourne) 21858
NORFOLK CAPITAL HOTELS LTD.	NORFOLK CAP.	01 (London) 589 7000
OPEN HOUSE INNS	OPEN HOUSE	0632 (Newcastle) 21133
OSPREY HOTELS	OSPREY	041 (Glasgow) 332 2281
RANK HOTELS LTD.	RANK	01 (London) 262 2893
REO STAKIS HOTELS	STAKIS	041 (Glasgow) 221 4343
E.M.I. ROYAL LONDON HOTELS LTD.	ROYAL LONDON	01 (London) 734 0197
SCOTTISH & NEWCASTLE BREWERIES LTD.	S & N	0632 (Newcastle) 21073
SWALLOW HOTELS	SWALLOW	0783 (Sunderland) 77424
THISTLE HOTELS LTD.	THISTLE	0632 (Newcastle) 21073
TRUST HOUSES FORTE LTD.	T.H.F.	01 (London) 567 3444

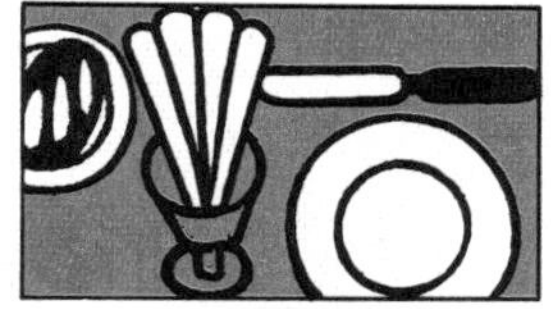

TRAFFIC SIGNS
A few important signs

SIGNALISATION ROUTIÈRE
Quelques signaux routiers importants

SEGNALETICA STRADALE
Alcuni segnali importanti

VERKEHRSZEICHEN
Die wichtigsten Straßenverkehrszeichen

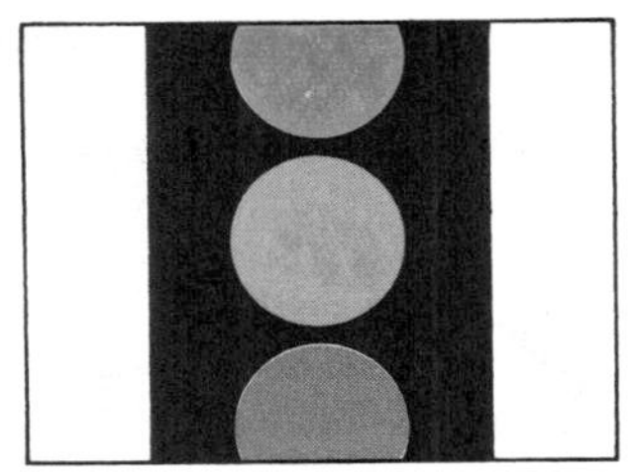

Please note: The maximum speed allowed on any road in Great Britain is 70 mph. In the Republic of Ireland 60 mph.

N.B. La vitesse maximale autorisée sur toutes les routes de Grande-Bretagne est limitée à 70 mph (env. 110 km/h). En République d'Irlande elle est limitée à 60 mph (env. 95 km/h).

N.B. In Gran Bretagna la velocità massima su tutte le strade è limitata a 70 miglia orarie (circa 110 km all'ora); nella Repubblica d'Irlanda a 60 miglia orarie (circa 95 km all'ora).

Bitte beachten Sie, daß in Großbritannien die zulässige Höchstgeschwindigkeit auf allen Straßen 70 mph (ca. 110 km/h) und in der Republik Irland 60 mph (ca. 95 km/h) beträgt.

Warning signs — Signaux d'avertissement
Segnali di avvertimento — Warnzeichen

T junction
Jonction avec autre route
Confluenza con altra strada
Straßeneinmündung

Roundabout
Sens giratoire
Senso rotatorio
Kreisverkehr

Dual carriageway ends
Fin de chaussée à deux voies
Fine di doppia carreggiata
Ende der zweispurigen Fahrbahn

Change to opposite carriageway
Déviation sur chaussée opposée
Deviazione sulla carreggiata opposta
Überleitung auf Gegenfahrbahn

Distance to give way sign ahead
Cédez le passage à 50 yards
Dare la precedenza a 50 iarde
Vorfahrt gewähren in 50 yards Entfernung

Ralentir maintenant
Rallentare subito
Geschwindigkeit verringern

Right-hand lane closed
Voie de droite barrée
Corsia di destra sbarrata
Rechte Fahrbahn gesperrt

Quayside or river bank
Débouché sur un quai ou une berge
Banchina o argine senza sponda
Ufer

Two-way traffic crosses one-way road
Voie à deux sens croisant voie à sens unique
Strada a due sensi che incrocia una strada a senso unico
Straße mit Gegenverkehr kreuzt Einbahnstraße

Level crossing with automatic half barriers ahead
Passage à niveau automatique
Passaggio a livello automatico con semi-barriere
Bahnübergang mit automatischen Halbschranken

Height limit
Hauteur limitée (en pieds et pouces)
Altezza limitata (piedi e pollici)
Maximale Höhe (in Fuß und Zoll)

Opening or swing bridge
Pont mobile
Ponte mobile
Bewegliche Brücke

Signs giving orders
Signaux de prescriptions absolues
Segnali di prescrizione (di divieto o d'obbligo)
Gebots- und Verbotszeichen

End of speed limit
Fin de limitation de vitesse
Fine di limitazione di velocità
Ende der Geschwindigkeitsbeschränkung

No stopping (« clearway »)

Arrêt interdit

Fermata vietata

Haltverbot

Give priority to vehicles from opposite direction
Priorité aux véhicules venant de face
Dare la precedenza ai veicoli che provengono dal senso opposto
Dem Gegenverkehr Vorrang gewähren

Width limit
Largeur limitée (en pieds et pouces)
Larghezza limitata (piedi e pollici)
Breite begrenzt (in Fuß und Zoll)

School crossing patrol
Sortie d'école
Uscita di scolari
Achtung Schule

All vehicles prohibited (plate gives details)
Circulation interdite à tous véhicules (plaque donnant détails)
Divieto di transito a tutti i veicoli (la placca sottostante fornisce dei dettagli)
Verkehrsverbot für Fahrzeuge aller Art (näherer Hinweis auf Zusatzschild)

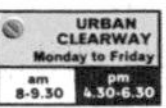

Voie à stationnement réglementé

Sosta regolamentata

Fahrbahn mit zeitlich begrenzter Parkerlaubnis

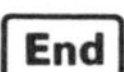

Plate below sign at end of prohibition
Fin d'interdiction
Fine del divieto posta sotto il segnale
Ende einer Beschränkung

Information signs
Signaux de simple indication
Segnali di indicazione
Hinweiszeichen

One-way street
Rue à sens unique
Via a senso unico
Einbahnstraße

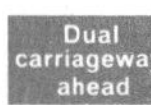

Accès à une chaussée à deux voies

Accesso ad una carreggiata a due corsie

Zufahrt zu einer zweispurigen Fahrbahn

No through road
Voie sans issue
Strada senza uscita
Sackgasse

Ring road
Voie de contournement
Strada di circonvallazione
Ringstraße

Warning signs on rural motorways
Signaux d'avertissement sur autoroutes
Segnali di avvertimento su autostrade
Warnzeichen auf Autobahnen

Maximum advised speed
Vitesse maximum conseillée
Velocità massima consigliata
Empfohlene Höchstgeschwindigkeit

1 Lane closed
1 voie barrée
1 Corsia sbarrata
1 Fahrstreifen gesperrt

Count-down markers at exit from motorway or primary route
Balises situées sur autoroute ou route principale et annonçant une sortie
Segnali su autostrada annuncianti un'uscita
Hinweise auf Abfahrten an Autobahnen und Hauptverkehrsstraßen

---

Road clear

Route libre

Strada libera

Straße frei

Direction to service area, with fuel, parking, cafeteria and restaurant facilities.

Indication d'aire de service avec carburant, parc à voitures, cafeteria et restaurant.

Indicazione di area di servizio con carburante, parcheggio, bar e ristorante

Hinweis auf Tankstelle, Parkplatz, Cafeteria und Restaurant

Warning signs on urban motorways
Signaux d'avertissement sur autoroutes urbaines
Segnali di avvertimento su autostrade urbane
Warnzeichen auf Stadtautobahnen

_1_

_2_

_3_

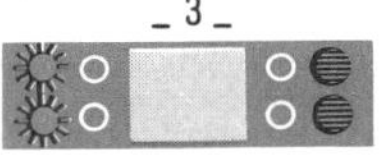

The insets show (flashing amber lights) (1) advised maximum speed, (2) lane to be used; (3) (flashing red lights), you must stop.

L'ensemble de ces panneaux indique : (1) la vitesse maximale conseillée, (2) la voie à utiliser (signaux lumineux jaunes) ; (3) l'arrêt obligatoire (signaux lumineux rouges).

L'insieme di questi segnali indica: (1) la velocità massima consigliata, (2) la corsia da imboccare (segnali luminosi gialli) ; (3) la fermata obbligatoria (segnali luminosi rossi).

Diese Schilder (mit blinkenden Ampeln) weisen hin auf : 1. die empfohlene Höchstgeschwindigkeit, 2. die zu befahrende Fahrbahn (gelbes Licht) und 3. Halt (rotes Licht).

In town — En ville
In città — in der Stadt

SIGNALISATION SHOWN ON OR ALONG KERBS
SIGNALISATION MATÉRIALISÉE SUR OU AU LONG DES TROTTOIRS
SEGNALI TRACCIATI SOPRA O LUNGO I MARCIAPIEDI
ZEICHEN AUF ODER AN GEHWEGEN

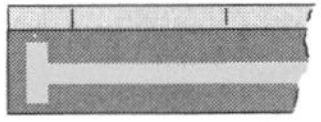

No waiting during every working day
Stationnement interdit tous les jours ouvrables
Sosta vietata nei giorni feriali con indicazioni complementari
Parkverbot an Werktagen

OTHER ROAD SIGNS

AUTRES PANNEAUX

ALTRI CARTELLI INDICATORI

ZUSÄTZLICHE VERKEHRSZEICHEN

Stationnement interdit de 8 h 30 à 18 h 30 du lundi au samedi
Sosta vietata da lunedì a sabato dalle 8,30 alle 18,30
Parkverbot Montag bis Samstag von 8.30 bis 18.30 Uhr

No loading or unloading during every working day

Livraisons interdites tous les jours ouvrables

Carico e scarico vietato nei giorni feriali con indicazioni complementari

Be- und Entladen verboten an allen Werktagen

No loading
Mon-Sat
8.30 am-6.30 pm

Livraisons interdites de 8 h 30 à 18 h 30 du lundi au samedi
Carico e scarico vietato da lunedì a sabato dalle 8,30 alle 18,30
Be- und Entladen verboten von Montag bis Samstag von 8.30 bis 18.30 Uhr

---

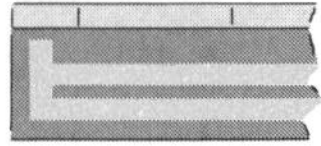

No waiting during every working day and additional times
Stationnement interdit tous les jours ouvrables plus autres périodes indiquées sur panneaux
Divieto di sosta tutti i giorni feriali e negli altri periodi indicati sul cartello
Parkverbot an Werktagen und den auf Zusatzschildern angegebenen Zeiten

Stationnement interdit en permanence

Divieto permanente di sosta

Parkverbot zu jeder Zeit

No loading or unloading during every working day and additional times
Livraisons interdites tous les jours ouvrables plus autres périodes indiquées sur panneaux
Divieto di carico e scarico tutti i giorni feriali e negli altri periodi indicati sul cartello
Be- und Entladen verboten an Werktagen und den auf Zusatzschildern angegebenen Zeiten

No loading
at any time

Livraisons interdites en permanence

Divieto permanente di carico e scarico

Be- und Entladeverbot zu jeder Zeit

No waiting during any other periods
Stationnement interdit à toute autre période
Sosta vietata in determinate ore
Parkverbot zu bestimmten Zeiten

Waiting
Limited
8 am-6 pm
20 minutes
in any hour

Stationnement limité à 20 mn de 8 h à 18 h
Sosta limitata a 20 mn dalle 8 alle 18
Höchstparkdauer 20 min. in der Zeit von 8.00 bis 18.00 Uhr

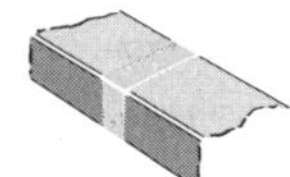

No loading or unloading during any other periods

Livraisons interdites à toute autre période

Divieto di carico e scarico in determinate ore

Be- und Entladeverbot zu bestimmten Zeiten

No loading
Mon-Fri
8.00-9.30 am
4.30-6.30 pm

Livraisons interdites du lundi au vendredi de 8 h à 9 h 30 et de 16 h 30 à 18 h 30
Carico e scarico vietato da lunedì a venerdì dalle 8 alle 9,30 e dalle 16,30 alle 18,30
Be- und Entladeverbot Montag bis Freitag von 8.00 bis 9.30 und von 16.30 bis 18.30 Uhr

***Remember :** speed limit in Great Britain 70 mph and in Eire 60 mph.*

ADDRESSES OF SHIPPING COMPANIES AND THEIR PRINCIPAL AGENTS

ADRESSES DES COMPAGNIES DE NAVIGATION ET DE LEURS PRINCIPALES AGENCES

INDIRIZZI DELLE COMPAGNIE DI NAVIGAZIONE E DELLE LORO PRINCIPALI AGENZIE

ADRESSEN DER SCHIFFAHRTSGESELLSCHAFTEN UND IHRER WICHTIGSTEN AGENTUREN

BALTIC SHIPPING CO.

C.T.C. Lines (UK), 1-3 Regent St., London, SW1Y 4NN, ℡ (01) 930 5833, Telex 917193.

Oy Saimaa Lines, P. Makasiinikatu, 7a, P.O. Box 008 SF-00131, Helsinki 13, Finland, Telex 121671.

Baltic Shipping Co, 35 Herzen St., Leningrad, U.S.S.R. ℡ 211 77 76, Telex 551.

B & I LINE

British & Irish Steam Packet Co., Ltd, 155 Regent St., London, W1R 7FD, ℡ (01) 734 4681, Telex 23523.

6-8 Temple Row, Birmingham, B2 5HG, ℡ (021) 236 5552.

16 Westmoreland St., Dublin 2, Eire, ℡ (01) 778271, Telex 5651.

8 Bridge St., Cork, Eire, ℡ (021) 54100, Telex 6137.

Reliance House, Water St., Liverpool, L2 8TP, ℡ (051) 227 5331, Telex 627839.

28 Cross St., Manchester, M2 3NH, ℡ (061) 832 5981.

BRITISH RAIL see SEALINK and SOLENT SEASPEED

BRITTANY FERRIES

Millbay Docks, Plymouth, PL1 3EF, Devon, ℡ (0752) 21321.

Norman House, Albert Johnson Quay, Portsmouth, PO2 7AE, Hampshire, ℡ (0705) 27701.

Nouvelle Gare Maritime, 35400 St-Malo, France, ℡ (99) 56.42.29.

Gare Maritime, Roscoff, Port du Bloscon 29211, France, ℡ (98) 69-07-20.

CALEDONIAN MACBRAYNE LTD.

The Pier, Gourock, PA19 1QP, Renfrewshire, Scotland, ℡ (0475) 33755, Telex 779318.

COMMODORE SHIPPING CO. AND CONDOR LTD.

Commodore House, Bulwer Av., St. Sampsons, Guernsey, Channel Islands, ℡ (0481) 46841, Telex 41289.

Commodore Shipping Services Ltd., 28 Conway St., St. Helier, Jersey, Channel Islands, ℡ (0534) 36331, Telex 41479.

Condor Ltd, 4 North Quay, P.O. Box 33, St. Peter Port, Guernsey ℡ (0481) 26121, Telex 41275.

Morvan Fils, 4, rue des Cordiers et Gare Maritime, 35400 St-Malo, France, ℡ (99) 56.42.29, Telex 950486.

DFDS SEAWAYS

DFDS (UK) Ltd., Mariner House, Pepys St., London, EC3N 4BX, ℡ (01) 481 3211.

DFDS (UK) Ltd., Tyne Commission Quay, North Shields, NE29 6EE, Tyne and Wear, ℡ (089 45) 77110, Telex 537285.

DFDS Ekspedition Englandskajen, DK-6700 Esbjerg, Denmark, ℡ (05) 12.17.00.

DFDS (UK) Ltd., Parkeston Quay, Harwich, CO12 4SY, Essex, ℡ (025 55) 4411, Telex 98582.

FRED. OLSEN-BERGEN LINE

Fred. Olsen-Bergen Line, 229 Regent St., London, W1R 8AP, ☎ (01) 437 9888.
Fred. Olsen-Bergen, Reisebyra, Prinsensgt. 2B, Oslo, Norway, ☎ 41.50.70.
Fred. Olsen-Bergen Line, P.O. Box 82, 4601 Kristiansand, Norway, ☎ 26500.
Fred. Olsen-Bergen Line, P.O. Box 4121, 5015 Dreggen, Bergen, Norway, ☎ 21.40.97.

HOVERLLOYD LTD.

49 Charles St., London W1X 8AE, ☎ (01) 493 5525.
International Hoverport, Pegwell Bay, Ramsgate, CT12 5HS, Kent, ☎ 0843 (Thanet) 54761.
International Hoverport, 62100 Calais, France, ☎ 34-67-10.
Hoverlloyd Ltd., 24 rue de St-Quentin, 75010 Paris, France, ☎ 723.73.05.

HOVERTRAVEL LTD.

Quay Road, Ryde, Isle of Wight, ☎ (0983) 65241.
Clarence Pier, Southsea, Portsmouth, PO5 3AD, Hampshire, ☎ (0705) 29988.

IRISH CONTINENTAL LINE LTD.

19/21 Aston Quay, Dublin 2, Eire, ☎ (01) 774331, Telex 30355.
Agent: P & O Ferries (Normandy Ferries), Gare Maritime, Route du Mole Central, 76600 Le Havre, France, ☎ (35) 48.32.81, Telex 190736.
Transport et Voyages, 8, rue Auber, 75009 Paris, ☎ 742.31.49, Telex 660400.

ISLE OF MAN STEAM PACKET CO. LTD.

P.O. Box 5, Douglas, Isle of Man, ☎ (0624) 3824, Telex 629414.
McBride's Shipping Agencies Ltd., 93 Hope St., Glasgow C2, Scotland, ☎ (041) 248 5161, Telex 77181.
W.E. Williames & Co. Ltd., 82-84 High St., Belfast, Northern Ireland, ☎ (0232) 29281, Telex 74619.
British & Irish Steam Packet Co. Ltd., 16 Westmoreland St., Dublin, Eire ☎ (01) 778271.
India Buildings, 40 Brunswick St., Liverpool 2, ☎ (051) 236 3214, Telex 629415.

ISLE OF SARK SHIPPING CO. LTD.

White Rock, St. Peter Port, Guernsey, Channel Islands, ☎ (0481) 24059, Telex 41549.
The Knowl, Rue Lucas, Sark, Channel Islands, ☎ 10.

ISLES OF SCILLY STEAMSHIP CO. LTD.

St. Mary's, Isles of Scilly, ☎ 072 04 (Scillonia) 357/8.
16 Quay St., TR18 4BD, Penzance, Cornwall, ☎ (0736) 2009/4013.

NORFOLK LINE

Atlas House, Southgates Rd, Great Yarmouth, Norfolk, ☎ (0493) 56133, Telex 97449.
Kranenburgweg 211, Scheveningen, Netherlands, ☎ (070) 514601, Telex 31515.

NORTH SEA FERRIES LTD.

King George Dock, Hedon Rd, Hull, HU9 5QA, North Humberside, ☎ (0482) 795141, Telex 52349.
Noordzee Veerdiensten B.V., Beneluxhaven, Netherlands, Europoort, P.O. Box 1123 Rozenburg 3208, ☎ (01819) 62077, Telex 26571.
Prins Fillipsdok, Lanceloot Blondeellaan, 8380 Zeebrugge, Belgium, ☎ (050) 545601, Telex 81469.

OLAU-LINE LTD.

Sherness Docks, Sheerness, ME12 1SN, Kent, ☎ (079 56) 4981, Telex 965605.
Olau-Line (Nederland) B.V., Buitenhaven, Postbus 231, Vlissingen (Flushing), Netherlands, ☎ (01184) 65400, Telex 55317.
Olau-Line Terminal, Port Ouest, B.P. 282, 59140 Dunkerque, France, ☎ (20) 684333, Telex 160150.

ORKNEY ISLANDS SHIPPING CO. LTD.

4 Ayre Road, Kirkwall, Orkney Islands, Scotland, ☎ (0856) 2044.

P & O FERRIES IRISH SEA SERVICES (BELFAST STEAMSHIP CO.)

94 High St., Belfast BT1 2DH, Northern Ireland, ☎ (0232) 23636 and 34534.
Seaway House, St. Nicholas Pl., Liverpool, L3 0AA, ☎ (051) 236 5464.

P & O NORMANDY FERRIES

Arundel Towers, Portland Terrace, Southampton, SO9 4AE, Hampshire, ☎ (0703) 34141, Telex 47485.

Easter Docks, Dover, ☎ (0304) 206909, Telex 965726.

9 Place de la Madeleine, 75009 Paris, France, ☎ 266.40.17.

Route du Mole Central, BP. 1031, 76061 Le Havre, France, ☎ (35) 48.32.81.

Gare Maritime, Quai de Chanzy, 62200 Boulogne Sur-Mer, France, ☎ (21) 31.78.00.

P & O FERRIES, ORKNEY & SHETLAND SERVICES

P.O. Box 5, Ferry Terminal, Jamiesons Quay, Aberdeen, AB9 8DL, Scotland, ☎ (0224) 29111.

Scrabster Ferry Terminal, Caithness, Scotland, ☎ (0847) 2052.

Harbour Street, Kirkwall, Orkney Islands, Scotland, ☎ (0856) 3330.

Holmsgarth Terminal, Lerwick, Shetland Islands, Scotland, ☎ (0595) 4848.

Ferry Terminal, Stromness, Orkney Islands, Scotland, ☎ (085 685) 655.

PRINS FERRIES

Prins Ferries (Lion Ferry AB, Halmstad, Sweden), 13-14 Queen St., London, W1X 8BA, ☎ (01) 629 7961 and 491 7641, Telex 264311.

Hadag Seetouristik und Fahrdienst AG, Johannisbollwerk 6-8,2000 Hamburg 11, Germany, ☎ (040) 31.24.21, Telex 02 13846.

Karl Geuther & Co, Martinistrasse 58, 2800 Bremen 1, Germany ☎ (0421) 31 49 70, Telex 02 45502.

RED FUNNEL SERVICES

12 Bugle St., Southampton, SO9 4LJ, Hampshire, ☎ (0703) 26211.

Fountain Pier, West Cowes, Isle of Wight, ☎ (098 382) 2101.

SEALINK (British Rail)

Sealink Car Ferry Centre, P.O. Box 303, 52 Grosvenor Gardens, London, SW1W 0AG, ☎ (01) 730 3440.

12 boulevard de la Madeleine, 75009 Paris, France, ☎ 073.56.70.

Gare Maritime, B.P. 327/1, 62200 Boulogne-sur-Mer, France, ☎ (21) 30-25-11.

Gare Maritime, 62100 Calais, France, ☎ (21) 34.64.12 (passengers) 34.48.40 (cars).

Jean-Claude Tellier, Agent Maritime, Quai de l'Ancien Arsenal, 50100 Cherbourg, France, ☎ 010.33-53-24-27.

c/o Chef de Gare Principal (SNCF), Dieppe Maritime, 76200 Dieppe BP 85, France, ☎ (35) 84.24.89 (cars) 84.24.68/69 (passengers)

A.L.A. Steamship Co., Gare Maritime, 59140 Dunkerque, France, ☎ (20) 66.80.01.

Régie des Transports Maritimes, 5 Natienkaai, Oostende, Belgium, Telex 81033.

Harwich Ferry Agency, Hoek Van Holland, Netherlands, ☎ 01747-2681.

The Agent, British Rail, Rosslare Harbour, Co. Wexford, Eire, ☎ (053) 33115.

British Rail, North Wall, Dublin 1, Eire, ☎ (01) 742931.

British Rail, 24 Donegall Place, Belfast, BT1 5BH, Northern Ireland, ☎ (0232) 27525.

Sealink Car Ferry Office, Holyhead, Gwynedd, ☎ (0407) 2304.

Sealink (Scotland) Ltd. Stranraer Harbour, DG9 8EJ, Strathclyde, ☎ (0776) 3531.

Central Reservations Office, Isle of Wight Car Ferry Services, Portsmouth Harbour Station, Portsmouth, PO1 3EU, ☎ (0705) 812 011 and Car Ferry Terminal, Fishbourne Lane, Fishbourne, Isle of Wight, ☎ (0983) 882432.

Sealink, Lymington Pier, Lymington, SO4 8OE, Hampshire, ☎ (059 07) 3301.

Shipping Manager, British Rail, Weymouth Quay, Weymouth, Dorset, ☎ (030 57) 6363.

Sealink, The Jetty, St. Peter Port, Guernsey, ☎ (0481) 24742, Telex 41249.

Sealink, 9 Bond St. St. Helier, Jersey, ☎ (0534) 23412, Telex 41262.

SEASPEED HOVERCRAFT

Reservations Office: 7 Cambridge Terrace, Dover, CT16 1JT, Kent, ☎ (0304) 202266.

Gare Maritime, 62106 Calais, France, ☎ (21) 34.62.12 (passengers) and 34.48.40 (cars).

Also the Sealink Offices above.

SERVICE MARITIME

Service Maritime, 50270 Carteret, France, ☎ (33) 54.87.21 et 54.80.72 Barneville, Telex 170477.

SOLENT SEASPEED

Crosshouse Rd, Southampton, SO1 9GZ, Hampshire, ☎ (0703) 21249.

Medina Rd, Cowes, PO31 7BV, Isle of Wight, ☎ (098 382) 2337.

TOR LINE LTD.

P.O. Box 40, DN40 2PH Grimsby, South Humberside, ☎ 0469 (Immingham) 73131, Telex 527101.

34 Panton St., London, SW1Y 4DY, ☎ (01) 930 0881, Telex 25882.

Tor Line Travel Services, Hotelplatsen 2, 41106 Gothenburg, Sweden, ☎ 17.20.50.

Passenger Terminal, No 2 Gate, IP11 8HD, Felixstowe ☎ (039 42) 78777, Telex 987861.

TOWNSEND THORESEN CAR FERRIES LTD.

127 Regent Street, London, W1R 8LB, ☎ (01) 734 4431 and 437 7800, Telex 23802.

Car Ferry Centre, 1 Camden Crescent, Dover, CT16 1LD, Kent, ☎ (0304) 202822, Telex 96200.

Car Ferry House, Canute Road, Southampton, SO9 5GP, Hampshire, ☎ (0703) 34444, Telex 47637.

Continental Ferry Port, Mile End, Portsmouth, ☎ (0705) 815231.

The Ferry Centre, The Docks, Felixstowe, IP11 8TA, Suffolk, ☎ (039 42) 79461, Telex 98232.

Car Ferry Terminal, Doverlaan 7, B-8380 - Zeebrugge, Belgium, ☎ (050) 54-48-73.

41 place d'Armes, 62226 Calais Cedex, France, ☎ (21) 34.41.90, Telex 810750.

41 boulevard des Capucines 75002 Paris, France, ☎ 261.51.75.

Gare Maritime, 50101 Cherbourg, France, ☎ (33) 53.29.98, Telex 170765.

Quai de Southampton, 76600 Le Havre, France, ☎ (35) 21.36.50, Telex 190757.

Doverlaan 7, B-8380 Zeebrugge ☎ (050) 54 48 73, Telex 81306.

TRANSPORT FERRY SERVICE

P.O. Box 7, The Ferry Centre, The Docks, Felixstowe, Suffolk, IP11 8TA, ☎ (039 42) 78711, Telex 98232.

The Harbour, Larne, Co. Antrim, Northern Ireland, ☎ (0574) 4321.

Lighterage Wharf, Cairnryan, near Stranraer, Scotland, ☎ (058 12) 276.

Beneluxhaven, Europoort, Netherlands, ☎ West Rozenburg 2366, Telex 22640.

VEDETTES ARMORICAINES S.A.

1er Bassin, Port de Commerce, P.O. Box 88, 29268 Brest Cedex, France, ☎ (98) 44.44.04 et 44.42.47, Telex 940210 F.

12 rue Georges-Clemenceau, P.O. Box 24, 50400 Granville, France, ☎ (33) 50.09.87.

WESTERN FERRIES LTD.

Kennacraig, Tarbert (Loch Fyne) Argyll Scotland, ☎ (088 073) 271/2.

NOTES

MANUFACTURE FRANÇAISE DES PNEUMATIQUES MICHELIN

Société en commandite par actions au capital de 700 millions de francs
R.C. Clermont-Fd B 855 200 507 (55-B-50) - Siège Social Clermont-Fd (France)
ISBN 2 06 006 588 – 7

Danel - S.C.I.A. — La Chapelle d'Armentières 10669 — Printed in France 2.78.51 — Dépôt légal, 1er trimestre 1978
578

The inseparables :
Michelin maps and guides

inséparables :
les cartes et guides Michelin

inseparabili :
le carte e le guide Michelin

unzertrennlich : die Straßenkarten
und Reiseführer von Michelin

GREAT BRITAIN and IRELAND
GRANDE-BRETAGNE et IRLANDE
GRAN BRETAGNA e IRLANDA
GROẞBRITANNIEN und IRLAND

main road map

carte des grandes routes

carta delle grandi strade

Karte der Hauptverkehrsstraßen

986 14 miles: 1 inch

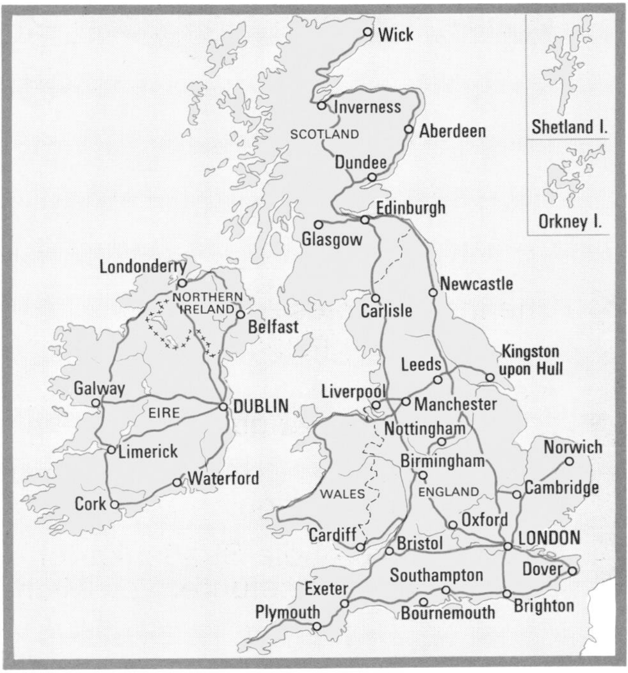

Wick
Inverness
SCOTLAND
Aberdeen
Shetland I.
Dundee
Orkney I.
Edinburgh
Glasgow
Londonderry
Newcastle
NORTHERN IRELAND
Carlisle
Belfast
Kingston upon Hull
Leeds
Galway
Liverpool
EIRE
DUBLIN
Manchester
Nottingham
Limerick
Norwich
Birmingham
Waterford
Cambridge
WALES
ENGLAND
Cork
Oxford
Cardiff
Bristol
LONDON
Dover
Southampton
Exeter
Plymouth
Bournemouth
Brighton